"BANK ON BARRON'S" $100,000 Sweepstakes

GRAND PRIZES
THREE $10,000 COLLEGE SCHOLARSHIPS
PLUS OVER 1,600 OTHER PRIZES

5 FIRST PRIZES
APPLE IIc STARTER SYSTEM

25 SECOND PRIZES
SMITH CORONA TYPEWRITER

1,000 THIRD PRIZES
PANASONIC SOLAR POCKET CALCULATOR

NO PURCHASE NECESSARY

EARLY BIRD BONUS:

Enter by October 31 and you may win your choice of one of 600 Computer Study Programs for SAT or ACT

Entries limited to high school juniors and seniors. Entry Forms must be received by Dec. 31, 1986.

(continued on next page...)

Barron's shows you exactly how to pinpoint your trouble spots and correct your weaknesses:

First, a diagnostic test shows you what an actual SAT is like. It presents you with questions similar to those you'll encounter, both in the model SATs contained later in this book and also on the actual SAT that you'll take for your record. Both the diagnostic test and the model SATs are followed by fully explained answers to all test questions, plus a Self-Evaluation section to help you focus on areas where you need further study. As you progress from one test to the next, you'll find your scores getting better and better!

Barron's offers you not just one — but *three* distinct study plans:

We understand that no two students have the same needs. You might have weeks to prepare for your SAT, or you might only have days. You might be strong in most of your study areas, or you might have many weaknesses to correct. Barron's lets you choose among three sensible study plans: *Crash, Concentrated,* and *Comprehensive*. One of them will be exactly right for you.

Barron's gives you the facts you'll need before applying to the college of your choice:

Taking the SAT is only your first step toward getting into college. This book will take you one important step further. Look at the section entitled ORGANIZE YOUR ADMISSIONS GAME PLAN. You'll find *up-to-date and accurate information* on how to choose the college that's best for you, and how to go about filling out college applications. This section also gives you valuable tips on how to meet the high costs of a college education.

Barron's SAT Guide has been prepared by the most highly qualified authors in the field:

Our authors are three highly distinguished educators: Samuel C. Brownstein, Mitchel Weiner, and Sharon Weiner Green. Samuel Brownstein and Mitchel Weiner specialized in test preparation for many years, and conducted a school devoted to preparing students like you for the SAT. In addition, Samuel Brownstein was Chairman of the Science Department at George W. Wingate High School in Brooklyn, New York, and Mitchel Weiner taught for many years in the English Department at James Madison High School, Brooklyn, New York. This all-new 13th edition of Barron's SAT Guide introduces a new co-author, Sharon Weiner Green, who is an instructor of English at Merritt College, Oakland, California. She is also a specialist in reading, and is well versed in the special requirements of guidance for SAT testing. Here is a team of authors highly qualified to coach you to success!

BARRON'S SAT GUIDE SETS THE STANDARD FOR EXCELLENCE!

HOW TO PREPARE FOR THE SCHOLASTIC APTITUDE TEST

SAT*

THIRTEENTH EDITION

SAMUEL C. BROWNSTEIN
Formerly Chairman Science Department
George W. Wingate High School, Brooklyn, N.Y.

MITCHEL WEINER
Formerly Member, Department of English
James Madison High School, Brooklyn, N.Y.

SHARON WEINER GREEN
Instructor in English
Merritt College, Oakland, California

BARRON'S

BARRON'S EDUCATIONAL SERIES, INC.

Formerly Published as Barron's How to prepare for college entrance examinations.

All inquiries should be addressed to:
Barron's Educational Series, Inc.
113 Crossways Park Drive
Woodbury, New York 11797

Library of Congress Catalog Card No. 86-14055

Cloth International Standard Book No. 0-8120-5763-5
Paper International Standard Book No. 0-8120-3723-5

Library of Congress Cataloging-in-Publication Data

Brownstein, Samuel C.
How to prepare for the scholastic aptitude test.

Rev. ed. of: How to prepare for the scholastic aptitude test/Mitchel Weiner, Samuel C. Brownstein. 12th ed. c1984. . Universities and colleges—United States—Entrance examinations—Study guides. I. Weiner, Mitchel II. Green, Sharon. III. Title.

LB2353.2.B765 1986 378'.1664 86-14055

ISBN 0-8120-3723-5

PRINTED IN THE UNITED STATES OF AMERICA

6789 100 98765432

Contents

MATHEMATICS

TSWE

PART FOUR—TEST YOURSELF

PART FIVE—ORGANIZE YOUR ADMISSIONS GAME PLAN

Preface

More than thirty years ago the appearance of the First Edition of this book marked the opening of a long-term campaign to give *all* students — not just those able to afford the fees of private preparatory schools — a better chance to gain admission to the nation's most prestigious universities. Based on the authors' experience as founders of New York's College Entrance Tutoring Service, this book provided a wealth of comprehensive review materials and updated study techniques for all those who sought that better chance.

Millions of teachers and students have found this book their most valuable tool for success in preparing for the SAT. It can be your most valuable tool today.

Today's Thirteenth Edition contains the best features of that ground-breaking First Edition and much, much more.

It offers you a full-length Diagnostic Test geared to today's SAT, an examination that will enable you to pinpoint your areas of weakness right away and concentrate your review on subjects where you need most work.

It offers you 6 complete Model SAT Tests, all with Diagnostic Guides, that in format, difficulty, and content echo today's SAT.

It offers you dozens of new, highlighted Testing Tactics that will help you to attack every question type you will find on the SAT.

It offers you Barron's newly revised and expanded 3,500-word Basic Word List, your best chance to acquaint yourself with the college-level vocabulary you will face on the SAT.

It offers you the *brand-new*, exclusive 101-word High-Frequency Word List, 101 words that have been shown by computer analysis to occur and reoccur on actual published SATs.

It offers you not one, but 3 personalized Study Plans, plans that will help you maximize your score whether you have 2 days to study or 10 weeks or more.

This Thirteenth Edition is a sign of Barron's ongoing commitment to make this publication America's outstanding SAT study guide.

The appearance of this Thirteenth Edition is a time for us of recommitment and of pride. It is a major revision and the authors wish to thank Ruth Pecan and Judy Makover of the editorial staff of Barron's Educational Series for their dedicated labors that helped to make this edition possible.

This edition is dedicated to the memory of Mitchel Weiner, educator.

TIMETABLE FOR THE SAT*

Total Time: 3 Hours

9:00 to **9:30**	Section 1	**Verbal**	15 Antonym Questions 10 Analogy Questions	10 Sentence Completion Questions 10 Reading Comprehension Questions
9:30 to **10:00**	Section 2	**Mathematics**	25 Standard Multiple-Choice Questions	
10:00 to **10:05**			Break	
10:05 to **10:35**	Section 3	**Test of Standard Written English**	35 Usage Questions 15 Sentence Correction Questions	
10:35 to **11:05**	Section 4	**Verbal**	10 Antonym Questions 10 Analogy Questions	5 Sentence Completion Questions 15 Reading Comprehension Questions
11:05 to **11:10**			Break	
11:10 to **11:40**	Section 5	**Mathematics**	15 Standard Multiple-Choice Questions 20 Quantitative Comparison Questions	
11:40 to **12:10**	Section 6	**Verbal** (40 or 45 Questions) or **Mathematics** (25 or 35 Questions) or **Test of Standard Written English** (50 Questions)		

*Actual times will vary in accordance with the time the proctor takes to complete the preliminary work and begin the actual test. Format and timing are subject to change.

SAT TEST DATES

Test Dates		**Registration Deadlines**	
National	**New York State**	**Regular**	**Late**
*October 11, 1986		September 19, 1986	
November 1, 1986	November 1, 1986	September 26, 1986	October 8, 1986
December 6, 1986		October 31, 1986	November 12, 1986
January 24, 1987	January 24, 1987	December 19, 1986	December 31, 1986
April 4, 1987	April 4, 1987	February 27, 1987	March 11, 1987
May 2, 1987	May 2, 1987	March 27, 1987	April 8, 1987
June 6, 1987	June 6, 1987	May 1, 1987	May 13, 1987

*Only given in California, Florida, Georgia, Illinois, North Carolina, South Carolina, and Texas.

WHAT YOU NEED TO KNOW ABOUT THE SAT

1

- **The College Entrance Examinations**
  - **The SAT**
  - **Achievement Tests**
- **Ten Commonly Asked Questions About the SAT**

THE COLLEGE ENTRANCE EXAMINATIONS

What Are College Entrance Examinations?

These are standardized tests required for admission to most colleges. About 850 colleges and 300 scholarship sponsors require applicants to take the Scholastic Aptitude Tests (SAT) and often, in addition, the Achievement Tests of the College Entrance Examination Board.

These objective tests are designed to predict how well a student will perform in college. Admissions officers of colleges rely on standardized test scores, because they can use these scores to compare candidates from all sorts of secondary schools. High school records alone are inadequate; the admissions officers know as well as you do that work that gets an A in one school in another may get only a B.

The Scholastic Aptitude Test (SAT)

The SAT is a three-hour test of multiple-choice questions designed to measure your ability to do college work. Part of the test deals with verbal skills, including the ability to read with understanding and to use words correctly. The verbal parts of the SAT measure the extent of your vocabulary, your ability to interpret and relate ideas, and your ability to reason logically and draw conclusions correctly. The mathematics sections measure your ability to use and reason with numbers or mathematical concepts. These sections test your ability to handle general number concepts rather than specific achievement in mathematics. You get no extra points for having carefully memorized formulas. You get points for being able to apply fundamental mathematical knowledge to new situations. A Test of Standard Written English is given as part of the test, but is not included in the SAT score.

College Board Achievement Tests (CBATs)

The College Board Achievement Tests (CBATs) are one-hour tests designed to measure your level of achievement in a particular subject. Tests are offered in English composition, literature, American history and social studies, European history and world cultures, mathematics level I and level II, French, Hebrew, German, Latin, Spanish, biology, chemistry, and physics.

These tests serve many functions. Some colleges use such tests to confirm or verify the secondary school record of the applicant. Since the marking systems of schools differ, such standardized tests are sometimes used by colleges to choose applicants. More often these tests are used for placement purposes. For example, in a foreign language, your performance on the achievement test may help decide whether you will be registered in the elementary, intermediate, or advanced course of that language. In some cases, a college may even excuse you from taking a foreign language in college on the basis of your score on the achievement test.

Applying for College Entrance Examinations

If a registration form is not available at your school, request one by mail. You can obtain a form from the College Entrance Examination Board, Box 6200, Princeton, New Jersey 08541 or Box 1025 Berkeley, California 94701.

TEN COMMONLY ASKED QUESTIONS ABOUT THE SAT

1. How Does the SAT Differ from Other School Tests?

Most tests secondary school students take are achievement tests. They attempt to find out how much the student learned and how well he or she can apply that information. Without emphasis on memorized information, the SAT measures ability with questions on verbal aptitude and quantitative thinking.

2. What Are the Various Parts of the SAT?

There are six sections. Thirty minutes is allowed for each of these parts. Two sections test verbal ability with questions on antonyms, analogies, sentence completion, and reading comprehension. Two sections test quantitative thinking with mathematics questions. One section, known as the Test of Standard Written English (TSWE), has questions on grammar, usage, and sentence structure. (The result of the TSWE does not affect your SAT score. The main purpose of this section is to help the college determine which freshman English class will be right for you.) Finally, one part of the SAT is an experimental part with questions that the examiners are trying out for possible use in future tests. Your performance on this part will not affect your SAT score.

3. How Can I Determine Which Is the Experimental Part?

Don't waste time in the examination room trying to identify this section. Do your best on all sections. Some claim that most often the last section is the experimental part. Others claim that the section with unusual questions is the one that does not count. If you do encounter a series of questions that seem strange, do your best. Either these won't count, in which case you have no reason to worry about them, or they will count, in which case they probably will seem just as strange and troublesome to everyone taking the test with you. Again, remember that no one is expected to answer all the questions correctly.

4. Is It Wise to Leave Troublesome Questions Unanswered?

Some tests give credit for correct answers and do not penalize guesses. The SAT gives one point for each correct answer and deducts a fraction of a point for each wrong answer. No deduction is made for answers left blank. The resulting raw score is then converted to a scale of 200 to 800. Since wrong answers count against you, you can penalize yourself by guessing wildly.

5. Can I Make an Educated Guess?

Sure, if you're a good guesser. At times you may have a strong feeling that a certain choice is correct, but you have difficulty proving or explaining your choice. On a test where a penalty is imposed for wrong answers, you may hesitate to answer the question. The best advice is for you to find out whether you are a good guesser. Use the practice exercises and model tests in this book as a chance to analyze your guessing skills. The next chapter will show you how.

6. Is It Advisable to Begin by Doing All the Easy Questions First?

Yes, but don't get hung up on a question just because you think it should be an easy one for you. Usually, the earlier questions in each section, except for reading comprehension questions, are easier. Most tests begin with "warm-up" questions. That is fair for all. But what is easy for one person may be hard for another, so it is good advice not to get bogged down with any one question. Remember, all questions carry the same point value. After a reasonable length of time, give up. Leave it blank. Just make sure the answer sheet correctly reflects your omission, and check to make certain that the subsequent answers are placed in the proper spot. Again, almost no one gets all the answers correct. Don't aim for a "perfect" score; aim for your personal best.

7. How Important Is Scrap Work on the SAT?

Your scrap work, including your doodling, is done directly in the question booklet and is strictly to help you. Don't hesitate to underline key words or phrases in the verbal sections. Do any necessary mathematics calculations on or near the problem. Since scrap work is not subject to inspection, keep it down to a minimum to save time. Be careful not to do any scrap work or leave any stray markings on your answer sheet. The machine that scores the test may mistake a stray mark for a second answer and give you no credit for a question.

8. How Much High School Mathematics Is Required for the SAT?

The purpose of the SAT is not to find out how much mathematics you know. The test attempts to discover your ability to understand and to reason with mathematical symbols, to solve problems, and to interpret data. No advanced mathematics is required. The subject matter covered includes the mathematics studied by most college-bound students. It includes basic arithmetic, elementary algebra, and plane geometry. Since these questions are designed to test thinking power rather than recall of complicated formulas, you should expect to solve most problems by close inspection, insight, and reasoning rather than by complicated computational work.

9. How Are SAT Scores Reported?

The raw score, the number of correct answers minus a fraction of a point for each wrong answer, is converted to a score on a scale of 200 to 800. With no correct answers at all, a student would still have a score of 200, and a student could have a score of 800 even with unanswered or incorrectly answered questions. Separate scores (from 200 to 800) are given for the verbal and the mathematical sections. The score given in the TSWE (from 20 to 60) does not affect the other two.

10. How Important Are SAT Scores?

Most colleges will hesitate to officially announce any cut-off points for SAT scores. They feel that announcing such scores would discourage otherwise potential candidates for admission. Most schools consider far more than these scores when making their admissions decisions. You should bear in mind, however, that a poor score on the examination, even if accompanied by a fairly good high school record, may make a college think twice about accepting you. On the other hand, a good college entrance examination score with an accompanying mediocre high school record is not uncommon. Since the scores are a sign you have good potential, admissions officers may spend some time going over the reasons your grades were only so-so.

The results of college entrance examinations are important because they are a scientific way of comparing all candidates in regard to their abilities to do college work. A high school record alone cannot be a yardstick of academic promise. Marking standards differ among high schools. Class standing in a small high school is not as significant as it is in a large city school. The standing in a specialized school is of little significance except for those at the very top. Entrance examinations afford equal opportunity to every one of you.

PART ONE

ORGANIZE YOUR STUDY PLAN

MAXIMIZE YOUR TEST SCORE

2

- Strategies for Handling the SAT
- Format of the SAT
- Sample SAT Questions
- Three Sensible Study Programs

STRATEGIES FOR HANDLING THE SAT

Like most of its sister multiple-choice exams, the SAT is based on a limited number of standardized question types. What this means is that you can improve your chances for a top SAT score by getting acquainted with these basic question types before you take the exam. Once you've learned how the questons are structured, and how to go about answering them, half the battle is won.

The easiest way to answer a question correctly is to know the answer. If you know what all the words mean in an antonym question, you won't have any trouble choosing the right answer. If you know exactly how to solve a mathematics question and don't make any mistakes in arithmetic, you won't have any trouble choosing the right answer. However, some sensible strategies will help you maximize your score.

Guessing

Since wrong answers count against you on the SAT, you may think that you should never guess if you aren't sure of the right answer to a question. But even if you guessed wrong four times for every time you guessed right, you would still come out even. A wrong answer costs you only 1/4 of a point (1/3 on the quantitative comparison questions). The most usual advice is to guess if you can eliminate one or two of the answers. You have a better chance of hitting the right answer when you make this sort of "educated guess." To find out whether this advice works for you, test yourself. Use the chart at the end of this section to see how guessing would affect your score.

First, take part of any test that you have not taken before. You don't have to take an entire test section, but you should take at least 25 questions. Answer only those questions to which you definitely know the answer. See what your score is.

Next, retake the same test section. Do not change any of your original answers, but whenever you can make an educated guess on one of the questions you originally passed, do so. See what your score is now. Finally, take the same test section one last time, this time guessing blindly to answer all the remaining questions. Don't forget to subtract 1/4 point for wrong answers (1/3 point on quantitative comparison questions).

Compare your scores from the three different approaches to the test. For most people, the second score will be the best one. But you may be different. Maybe you are such a poor guesser that you should never guess at all. Or maybe you are such a good guesser that you should try every question you hit.

SHOULD YOU GUESS?

	Number Right	Number Wrong	Total
No guesses			
Educated guesses			
Blind guesses			

Timing

You have only a limited amount of time in which to complete each section of the test, and you don't want to waste any of it. So here are three suggestions.

1. By the time you get to the actual SAT, you should have a fair idea of how much time to spend on each question. If a question is taking too long, leave it and go on to the next question. This is no time to try to show the world

that you can stick to a job no matter how long it takes. All the machine that grades the test will notice is that you didn't have any correct answers.

2. On the other hand, don't rush. Since your score will depend on how many *correct* answers you give *within a definite period* of time, speed and accuracy are both important. You will be better off answering 75 percent of the questions carefully and accurately than answering 100 percent of the questions hastily and inaccurately. Make sure you are answering *the question asked* and not one it may have reminded you of or the one you thought was going to be asked. Underline key words like "not" and "except" to make sure that you do not end up trying to answer the exact opposite of the question asked.

3. The questions in each segment of the test get harder as you go along (except the reading comprehension questions). But each new segment starts with easy questions. So don't get bogged down on a difficult antonym question when only three questions away the easy sentence completion questions begin. *First* answer all the easy questions; *then* tackle the hard ones if you have time. (Circle any questions that you're not sure of. Then if you have time at the end of the test, you will be able to locate them quickly.)

4. Memorize the directions for each type of question. These don't change. The test time you would spend reading the directions can be better spent answering the questions.

The Exam As A Whole

1. The best way to prepare for any test you ever take is to get a good night's sleep before the test so you are well rested and alert.

2. Allow plenty of time for getting to the test site. Taking a test is pressure enough. You don't need the extra tension that comes from worrying about whether you will get there on time.

3. Remember that you are allowed to write in the test book. You can write anything you want in the test book. You can and should do your mathematics computations in the booklet. There is absolutely no need to try to do them in your head. And if it helps you to doodle while you think, then doodle away. What is written in the test booklet does not matter to anyone.

4. What is written on the answer sheet does matter. Be very careful not to make any stray marks on it. This test is graded by a machine, and a machine cannot tell the difference between an accidental mark and a filled-in answer. When the machine sees two marks, it calls the answer wrong.

5. Check frequently to make sure you are answering the questions in the right spots. No machine is going to notice that you made a mistake early in the test, answered question 4 in the space for question 5, and all your following answers are the right answers, but in the wrong place.

6. Know what to expect. By the time you have finished with this preparation program, you will be familiar with all the kinds of questions that are going to appear on the SAT. You should also remember how long it is going to take. There are six sections on the test. Each one is a half-an-hour long, and there is supposed to be a five-minute break between sections. If you are scheduled to start the SAT at 9 a.m., do not make a dentist appointment for noon. You can't possibly get there on time, and you'll just spend the last two sections of the test worrying about it.

7. The College Board tells you to bring two sharpened number 2 pencils to the test. Bring four. They don't weigh much, and this might be the one day in the decade when two pencil points decide to break. And bring full-size pencils, not little stubs. They are easier to write with, and you might as well be comfortable.

8. Speaking of being comfortable, wear comfortable clothes. This is a test, not a fashion show. And bring a sweater. The test room may be hot, or it may be cold. You can't change the room, but you can put on a sweater.

9. Bring an accurate watch. The room in which you take the test may not have a clock, and some proctors are not very good about posting the time on the blackboard. Each time you begin a test section, write down in your booklet the time by your watch. That way you will always know how much time you have left.

10. Eliminate as many wrong answers as you can. Decid ing between two choices is easier than deciding among five. Even if you have to guess, every answer you eliminate improves your chances of guessing correctly.

11. Change answers if you have a reason for doing so. However, it's usually best not to change based on a hunch or a whim.

12. Remember that you don't have to answer every question to do well. According to the College Board, "many students who receive average or slightly above-average scores answer only 40–60 percent of the questions correctly."

FORMAT OF THE SCHOLASTIC APTITUDE TEST

There are six sections, with thirty minutes allowed for each section. The sections listed below always appear on the SAT, but the order varies. Do not assume that the Experimental Section will always be the one given at the end of the test.

Section 1. Verbal Ability. This has 45 questions consisting of:
15 antonym questions
10 analogy questions
10 sentence completion questions
10 reading comprehension questions

Section 2. Mathematical Ability. This consists of:
25 standard multiple-choice questions

Section 3. Test of Standard Written English. This has 50 questions consisting of:
35 usage questions
15 sentence correction questions

Section 4. Mathematical Ability. This has 35 questions consisting of:
15 standard multiple-choice questions
20 quantitative comparison questions

Section 5. Verbal Ability. This has 40 questions consisting of:
10 antonym questions
10 analogy questions
5 sentence completion questions
15 reading comprehension questions

Section 6. The Experimental Section. This section may be similar to any one of the 5 sections described above. The Experimental Section tests the questions more than it tests you. Your performance here does not affect your score. However, you must answer the quesions in all the sections of the test. Trying to guess which is the experimental section is too risky. Try to do your best on each part of the test.

SAMPLE SAT QUESTIONS*

The purpose of this section is to familiarize you with the kinds of questions that appear on the SAT by reprinting questions from recent SATs with the permission of Educational Testing Service. Knowing what to expect when you take the examination is an important step in preparing for the test and succeeding in it.

The Verbal Sections

The two verbal sections have a total of 85 questions: 25 antonyms, 20 analogies, 15 sentence completions, and 25 reading comprehension questions. Your college success will be closely bound up with your verbal abilities—especially your ability to understand what you read. This often means your ability to understand the words you read: your vocabulary. The SAT tests these verbal skills of yours in several different ways, but throughout the test the emphasis is on the formal written language, rather than on the casual English you might speak.

Antonyms

These are the most straightforward vocabulary questions on the test. You are given a word and must choose, from the five choices that follow it, the best antonym. The vocabulary in this section includes words that you have probably seen in your reading, although you may never have used or even heard them in everyday conversations.

Here are the directions for the antonym questions and 5 sample questions from a recent SAT.

> Each question below consists of a word in capital letters, followed by five lettered words or phrases. Choose the word or phrase that is most nearly opposite in meaning to the word in capital letters. Since some of the questions require you to distinguish fine shades of meaning, consider all the choices before deciding which is best.
> Example:
> GOOD: (A) sour (B) bad (C) red (D) hot (E) ugly
> Ⓐ ● Ⓒ Ⓓ Ⓔ

1. HEFTY: (A) wise (B) slight (C) cheerful (D) cooperative (E) indecisive
2. ABBREVIATE: (A) foretell (B) protract (C) perfect (D) proceed (E) arrange
3. DIMINUTION: (A) classification (B) escalation (C) brightness (D) separation (E) consciousness
4. CENSURE: (A) excite (B) repay (C) increase (D) expedite (E) praise
5. PENURY: (A) haste (B) silence (C) enmity (D) apathy (E) opulence

*SAT questions selected from *5 SATs*, 1985 Edition, and from *Taking the SAT*, 1985, College Entrance Examination Board. Reprinted by permission of Educational Testing Service, the copyright owner of the sample questions.

Sentence Completion

The sentence completion questions ask you to choose the best way to complete a sentence from which one or two words have been omitted. These questions test a combination of reading comprehension skills and vocabulary. You must be able to recognize the logic, style, and tone of the sentence, so that you will be able to choose the answer that makes sense in this context. You must also be able to recognize the way words are normally used. At some time in your schooling, you have probably had a vocabulary assignment in which you were asked to define a word and use it in a sentence. In this part of the SAT, you have to use the words in sentences. Once you understand the implications of the sentence, you should be able to choose the answer that will make the sentence clear, logical, and stylistically consistent. The sentences cover a wide variety of topics of the sort you have probably encountered in your general reading. However, this is not a test of your general knowledge. You may feel more comfortable if you are familiar with the topic the sentence is discussing, but you should be able to handle any of the sentences using your understanding of the English language.

Here are the directions for the sentence completion questions and 5 sample questions from a recent SAT.

> Each sentence below has one or two blanks, each blank indicating that something has been omitted. Beneath the sentence are five lettered words or sets of words. Choose the word or set of words that best fits the meaning of the sentence as a whole.
>
> Example:
>
> Although its publicity has been ----, the film itself is intelligent, well-acted, handsomely produced, and altogether ----.
>
> (A) tasteless..respectable (B) extensive..moderate (C) sophisticated..amateur (D) risqué..crude (E) perfect..spectacular
>
> ● Ⓑ Ⓒ Ⓓ Ⓔ

6. Metabolic by-products of oxygen are so ---- that breathing organisms have developed elaborate defense systems against them.
   (A) insignificant (B) useful (C) toxic (D) unpredictable (E) necessary

7. Recent legislative action will ---- the Pine Barrens from random and harmful growth while conversely ensuring that orderly and sound commercial development will not be ----.
   (A) protect. . halted
   (B) remove. . slowed
   (C) defend. . continued
   (D) isolate. . undertaken
   (E) preserve. . allowed

8. As a young man, Jean Toomer spoke of his desire to integrate the seemingly ---- elements of his racial heritage so that they might ----, rather than oppose, each other.
   (A) archaic. . reprove
   (B) contrary. . complement
   (C) dissimilar. . dispel
   (D) baffling. . exceed
   (E) inverted. . induce

9. Mary Cassatt, an Impressionist painter, was the epitome of the ---- American: a native of Philadelphia who lived most of her life in Paris.
   (A) conservative (B) provincial (C) benevolent (D) prophetic (E) expatriate

10. Long after science has recognized that appearances are relative, many people nevertheless continue to consider them ----.
   (A) illusive (B) uncertain (C) absolute (D) dependent (E) exceptional

Analogies

These are the questions that people seem to think of most often when they think about the SAT. Analogies may well be the most difficult kind of question on the test, but they aren't impossible, and at least some of them will be fairly easy. Questions of this kind test your understanding of the relationships among words and ideas. You are given one pair and must choose another pair that is related in the same way. Many relationships are possible. The two terms in the pair can be synonyms; one term can be a cause, the other the effect; one can be a tool, the other the user. Consider the first pair in each question carefully, and try to make a brief sentence using the two terms. Then look at the other pairs. It should be possible to substitute the correct answer (and only the correct answer) into your sentence and still have the sentence make sense.

Here are the directions for the analogy questions and 5 sample questions from recent SATs.

> Each question below consists of a related pair of words or phrases, followed by five lettered pairs of words or phrases. Select the lettered pair that best expresses a relationship similar to that expressed in the original pair.
>
> Example:
>
> YAWN : BOREDOM :: (A) dream : sleep (B) anger : madness (C) smile : amusement (D) face : expression (E) impatience : rebellion
>
> Ⓐ Ⓑ ● Ⓓ Ⓔ

11. SIEVE : DRAINING :: (A) paper : writing (B) oven : cleaning (C) faucet : washing (D) film : developing (E) filter : separating

12. MARBLE : SCULPTURE ::
(A) canvas : portrait
(B) slivers : kaleidoscope
(C) upholstery : sofa
(D) glass : goblet
(E) glue : collage

13. COVEN : WITCHES ::
(A) tavern : bartenders
(B) altar : clergy
(C) amulet : vampires
(D) castle : royalty
(E) choir : singers

14. PURITANICAL : FRIVOLITY ::
(A) secretive : ascendancy
(B) neurotic : phobia
(C) intrepid : courage
(D) religious : doctrine
(E) lazy : exertion

15. UPROARIOUS : FUNNY ::
(A) mysterious : alarming
(B) outrageous : improper
(C) anxious : serene
(D) thunderous : rainy
(E) ponderous : tired

Reading Comprehension

These questions take more time than any other questions on the test because you have to read a passage before you can answer them. They test your ability to understand and interpret what you read. This is probably the most important ability you will need in college and afterward. It's the ability you are using right now, when you are reading about the SAT.

There will be several reading passages on the SAT, of varying length. The shorter passages may have only three questions, and the longer passages may have five or six questions. The passages are usually nonfiction, although fiction sometimes appears. The passages may be about any subject matter. However, you do not need to know anything about the subject discussed in the passage. The purpose of these questions is to test your reading ability, not your knowledge of history or science. Some of the questions will be factual, asking you about specific details in the passage. Others will ask you to interpret the passage, to make judgments about it.

Here are the directions for the reading comprehension questions and a reading passage with 5 questions that appeared on a recent SAT.

> Each passage below is followed by questions based on its content. Answer all questions following a passage on the basis of what is stated or implied in that passage.

The tremendous explosion, known as the Tunguska blast, that flattened hundreds of square miles of Siberian pine forest in 1908 was probably equal in power to that of a modern thermonuclear bomb. The blasted region of the forest had an irregular shape similar to that of a butterfly. Decades later, specialists noticed an accelerated growth of trees in the region immediately surrounding the blast. Any theory describing the cause of the Tunguska blast must account for these puzzling factors.

For many years scientists just assumed that the blast had been caused by the impact of a large meteor, although no crater was ever found. After the bombings of Hiroshima and Nagasaki in 1945, suggestions were made that the otherwise enigmatic Tunguska blast had actually been an atomic explosion that had been set off by an alien vehicle from another world. The spaceship hypothesis claims that an interstellar vehicle was attempting to make a landing on Earth when its nuclear power plant accidentally detonated. The hull of the ship acted like a Claymore mine, shaping the charge into the irregular pattern. As at Hiroshima and Nagasaki, radiation caused the accelerated growth of trees around the bomb site.

The generally accepted hypothesis, however, is that the Tunguska blast was caused by the impact of a cometary nucleus with Earth. The explosion of the comet, which occurred at an altitude of several miles above the ground, was caused when the tremendous kinetic energy of the onrushing comet was converted into heat by its passage through Earth's atmosphere.

Proponents of the comet hypothesis also suggest that the forest fire ignited by the thermal pulse of the blast caused the accelerated growth of trees around the blast site by clearing the undergrowth and fertilizing the soil. In fact, a Soviet survey team discovered that the accelerated growth did indeed follow the outline of the burned areas quite well—even though some unburned areas were quite close to ground zero, and some burned areas were quite distant.

Comet hypothesis advocates also contend that a combination of sonic boom and detonation were quite sufficient to account for the seemingly odd shape of the flattened area. Dynamics specialists in Moscow attempted to recreate the shock waves of the original event, assuming that the passage of the object through the air produced a supersonic shock wave, and that at the end of this trail a detonation wave resulted from the sudden disintegration of the comet. The specialists strung explosives along a string suspended above a "forest" of miniature match sticks. When the explosives were set off, the match sticks were smashed down in a beautiful butterfly pattern.

16. The main purpose of the passage is to discuss the
(A) explosive power of comets
(B) puzzling cause of the Tunguska blast
(C) role of atomic energy in explosions
(D) major features of the Tunguska blast
(E) attempts to recreate the Tunguska blast

17. The passage suggests that which of the following would indicate that the Tunguska blast was caused by a meteor, rather than a spaceship exploding above the Earth?
    I. The presence of a crater in the area
    II. Evidence of accelerated tree growth in the area surrounding the blast
    III. A circular pattern of destruction in the area surrounding the blast
    (A) I only (B) III only (C) I and II only (D) II and III only (E) I, II, and III

18. According to the comet hypothesis, the Tunguska blast occurred when the
    (A) forest fire produced by the heat of the comet ignited the comet nucleus
    (B) impact of the comet's nucleus against the Earth's surface caused the comet to explode
    (C) extremely high temperature of the comet heated up the atmospheric gases surrounding it to the point that they exploded
    (D) tremendous speed of the comet through the Earth's atmosphere created so much heat that the comet nucleus suddenly disintegrated
    (E) supersonic shock wave produced by the comet's flight through the atmosphere caused the explosive material in the comet to detonate

19. Which of the following best describes the author's tone in the discussion of the comet hypothesis?
    (A) Amused (B) Defensive (C) Impartial (D) Sarcastic (E) Overstated

20. If the experiment described in the last paragraph helps support the comet hypothesis, all of the following assumptions must be made EXCEPT:
    (A) A series of small explosions will produce an effect similar to that of a supersonic shock wave.
    (B) A supersonic shock wave will cause the object that created it to disintegrate.
    (C) A "forest" of matchsticks will behave in much the same way as trees in an ordinary forest.
    (D) The disintegration of a comet could create a detonation blast.
    (E) A falling comet can travel through the Earth's atmosphere at a speed sufficient to cause a supersonic shock wave.

Test of Standard Written English

This test is not really part of the SAT. It is graded separately and is intended to help colleges place students in composition courses. There is only one half-hour section to this test. It includes 50 questions. Of these, 35 are usage questions and 15 are sentence correction questions. You do not have to write anything yourself on this test, but you are expected to recognize the grammatical forms and usage that are considered acceptable in formal written English.

Usage

In the usage questions, four words or groups of words will be underlined in each sentence. You do not have to correct the sentence. All you need to do is find the error, if there is one.

Here are the directions for the usage questions and 3 sample questions from a recent SAT.

<u>Directions:</u> The following sentences contain problems in grammar, usage, diction (choice of words), and idiom.

Some sentences are correct.

No sentence contains more than one error.

You will find that the error, if there is one, is underlined and lettered. Assume that elements of the sentence that are not underlined are correct and cannot be changed. In choosing answers, follow the requirements of standard written English.

If there is an error, select the <u>one underlined part</u> that must be changed to make the sentence correct and blacken the corresponding space on your answer sheet.

If there is no error, blacken answer space Ⓔ.

EXAMPLE:

The region has a climate <u>so severe that</u> (A) plants <u>growing there</u> (B) rarely <u>had been</u> (C) more than twelve inches <u>high</u> (D). <u>No error</u> (E)

SAMPLE ANSWER

Ⓐ Ⓑ ● Ⓓ Ⓔ

1. Whenever we hear of a natural disaster, even in a
A B
distant part of the world, you feel sympathy for the
C D
people affected. No error
E

2. The leading roles in the widely acclaimed play, a
A
modern version of an Irish folktale, were performed
B C
by Jessica and he. No error
D E

3. The energy question, along with several other issues,
A
are going to be discussed at the next meeting of the
B C D
state legislature. No error
E

Sentence Correction

In this section you have to do more than just spot the error. You have to find the correction as well. These questions give you sentences in which one section is underlined. The answer choices repeat the underlined section and give you four other versions of the same section. You must decide which version is best. Since these questions can deal with large sections of a sentence, many of them cover errors in the structure or logic of a sentence.

Here are the directions for these questions and 3 sample questions from a recent SAT.

Directions: In each of the following sentences, some part or all of the sentence is underlined. Below each sentence you will find five ways of phrasing the underlined part. Select the answer that produces the most effective sentence, one that is clear and exact, without awkwardness or ambiguity, and blacken the corresponding space on your answer sheet. In choosing answers, follow the requirements of standard written English. Choose the answer that best expresses the meaning of the original sentence.

Answer (A) is always the same as the underlined part. Choose answer (A) if you think the original sentence needs no revision.

EXAMPLE:

Laura Ingalls Wilder published her first book and she was sixty-five years old then.

(A) and she was sixty-five years old then
(B) when she was sixty-five years old
(C) at age sixty-five years old
(D) upon reaching sixty-five years
(E) at the time when she was sixty-five

SAMPLE ANSWER

Ⓐ ● Ⓒ Ⓓ Ⓔ

4. Many memos were issued by the director of the agency that had an insulting tone, according to the staff members.
(A) Many memos were issued by the director of the agency that
(B) Many memos were issued by the director of the agency who
(C) The issuance of many memos by the director of the agency which
(D) The director of the agency issued many memos that
(E) The director of the agency, who issued many memos that

5. Consumers are beginning to take notice of electric cars because they are quiet, cause no air pollution, and gasoline is not used.
(A) cause no air pollution, and gasoline is not used
(B) air pollution is not caused, and gasoline is not used
(C) cause no air pollution, and use no gasoline
(D) causing no air pollution and using no gasoline
(E) air pollution is not caused, and no gasoline is used

6. Light reaching earth from the most distant stars originated billions of years ago.
(A) reaching earth from the most distant stars
(B) which reaching earth from the most distant stars
(C) from the most distant stars reaching earth
(D) that is from the most distant stars and reaches earth
(E) reaching earth which is from stars that are most distant

The Mathematics Sections

The two mathematics sections have a total of 60 questions, including 20 quantitative comparison questions. These questions assume that you have had, and remember, arithmetic, elementary algebra, and geometry. You do not need to know any more advanced mathematics. You will be asked to use graphic, spatial, numerical, and symbolic techniques in a variety of problems. Many will be similar to the kinds of problems you had in your textbooks; others will not. The questions are intended to show how well you understand elementary mathematics, how well you can apply your knowledge to solve problems, and how good your mathematical instincts are—how well you can use nonroutine ways of thinking. What do we mean by "mathematical instincts" or "nonroutine ways of thinking"? In one sense, you need some insight to spot the right approach for solving any mathematical question. More important, on the SAT, is the ability to see which answer must be correct, or at least which answers are impossible, without actually solving the problem. This is basically the ability to apply mathematical rules and principles that you already know. For example, imagine that you are asked to multiply 27,654 × 3,042. You should see right away that the answer will have to end in 8. When the multiplicand ends in a 4 and the multiplier ends in a 2, then the product must end with an 8. This is a typical illustration of saving time with insight rather than doing lengthy, time-consuming computation, which, incidentally, may lead to computational errors. So not only is it a time-saver, it may also be an error-saver.

Standard Multiple-Choice Questions

These questions have 5 answer choices. The questions cover a wide range of content and difficulty.

Here are the test directions and 10 sample questions from a recent SAT. As you will see, the directions include many mathematical formulas and definitions. These are the actual directions that will be on the test when you take it, so the formulas and definitions will be in your test booklet. You may refer to them during the test, if necessary, but it makes sense to learn them now so that you don't waste valuable test time looking them up.

In this section, solve each problem, using any available space on the page for scratchwork. Then decide which is the best of the choices given and blacken the corresponding space on the answer sheet.

The following information is for your reference in solving some of the problems.

Circle of radius r: Area $= \pi r^2$; Circumference $= 2\pi r$

The number of degrees of arc in a circle is 360.

The measure in degrees of a straight angle is 180.

Definitions of symbols:

$=$ is equal to	$\leq$ is less than or equal to
$\neq$ is unequal to	$\geq$ is greater than or equal to
$<$ is less than	$\parallel$ is parallel to
$>$ is greater than	$\perp$ is perpendicular to

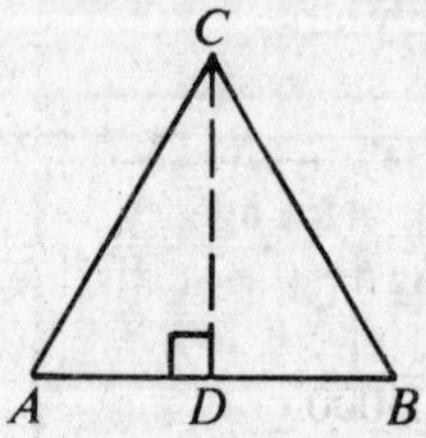

Triangle: The sum of the measures in degrees of the angles of a triangle is 180.

If $\angle CDA$ is a right angle, then

(1) area of $\triangle ABC = \frac{AB \times CD}{2}$

(2) $AC^2 = AD^2 + DC^2$

Note: Figures that accompany problems in this test are intended to provide information useful in solving the problems. They are drawn as accurately as possible EXCEPT when it is stated in a specific problem that its figure is not drawn to scale. All figures lie in a plane unless otherwise indicated. All numbers used are real numbers.

1. The following are coordinates of points in the XY-plane. Which of these points is nearest the origin?

(A) $(0, -1)$

(B) $\left(0, \frac{1}{2}\right)$

(C) $\left(\frac{1}{2}, -\frac{1}{2}\right)$

(D) $\left(\frac{1}{2}, \frac{1}{2}\right)$

(E) $(-1, -1)$

$A = \{3, 6, 9\}$
$B = \{5, 7, 9\}$
$C = \{7, 8, 9\}$

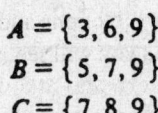

2. If three *different* numbers are selected, one from each of the sets shown above, what is the greatest sum that these three numbers could have?

(A) 22 (B) 23 (C) 24 (D) 25 (E) 27

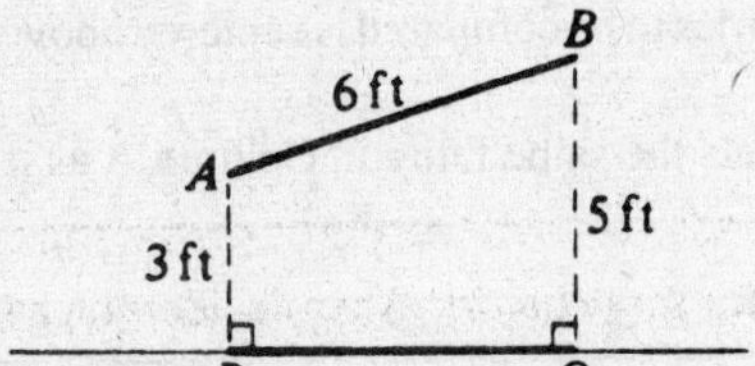

3. In the figure above, a straight stick AB casts a shadow PQ on a flat table. What is the length, in feet, of PQ?

(A) 4 (B) 4.5 (C) 5

(D) $3\sqrt{3}$ (E) $4\sqrt{2}$

4. Of the following, the least number is

(A) $-\frac{1}{10}$ (B) $-\frac{1}{100}$ (C) $-\frac{11}{1,000}$

(D) $-\frac{1}{9}$ (E) $\frac{1}{1,000}$

5. What is the total value, in cents, of x coins worth 5 cents each and $x + 7$ coins worth 10 cents each?

(A) $15x + 70$ (B) $15x + 7$ (C) $10x + 75$
(D) $6x + 7$ (E) $2x + 7$

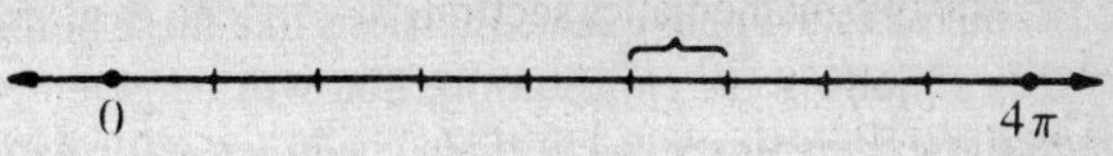

6. On the number line shown, the segment from 0 to 4π is divided into 9 intervals of equal length. Which of the following numbers would be in the sixth interval indicated above?

(A) $\frac{4\pi}{3}$ (B) $\frac{13\pi}{7}$ (C) 2π (D) $\frac{12\pi}{5}$ (E) 3π

7. If a plane intersects a cube, which of the following can be the shape of the intersection?

I. A rectangle
II. A quadrilateral with exactly two parallel sides
III. A triangle

(A) None (B) I only (C) III only
(D) I and II only (E) I, II, and III

8. If $(5.5 \times 10^2) \times (8.0 \times 10^3) = 4.4 \times 10^y$, then $y =$

(A) 2
(B) 3
(C) 4
(D) 5
(E) 6

9. If 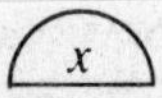 represents the area of a semicircle with diameter x, then 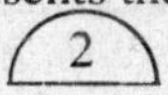 + 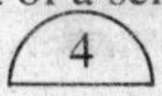 =

(A) 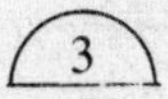

(B) 

(C) 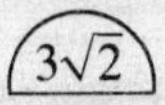

(D) 

(E) 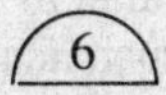

10. Two partners divide a profit of \$3,000 so that the difference between the two amounts is $\frac{1}{3}$ of their average (arithmetic mean). What is the ratio of the larger to the smaller amount?

(A) 7:5 (B) 5:1 (C) 4:3
(D) 3:2 (E) 3:1

Quantitative Comparisons

You may never have seen questions like these before, so they require some explanation. You will be given two quantities. Sometimes you will also be given information about one or both of them. Then you must decide whether one of the quantities is greater than the other, or whether they are equal. Sometimes there will not be enough information for you to be able to make a decision.

These questions reflect the contemporary emphasis on inequalities in school mathematics courses. In general, these questions require less time than the other mathematics questions, since they require less reading and, usually, less computation. These are the only questions on the SAT that have only four answer choices.

Here are the directions for the quantitative comparison questions and 10 sample questions from a recent SAT.

Questions 11–20 each consist of two quantities, one in Column A and one in Column B. You are to compare the two quantities and on the answer sheet blacken space

A if the quantity in Column A is greater;
B if the quantity in Column B is greater;
C if the two quantities are equal;
D If the relationship cannot be determined from the information given.

AN E RESPONSE WILL NOT BE SCORED.

EXAMPLES

	Column A	Column B	Answers
E1.	2×6	$2 + 6$	● Ⓑ Ⓒ Ⓓ Ⓔ
	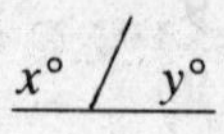		
E2.	$180 - x$	y	Ⓐ Ⓑ ● Ⓓ Ⓔ
E3.	$p - q$	$q - p$	Ⓐ Ⓑ Ⓒ ● Ⓔ

Notes:
1. In certain questions, information concerning one or both of the quantities to be compared is centered above the two columns.
2. In a given question, a symbol that appears in both columns represents the same thing in Column A as it does in Column B.
3. Letters such as *x*, *n*, and *k* stand for real numbers.

	Column A	Column B
11.	$2^2 + 3^2$	5^2

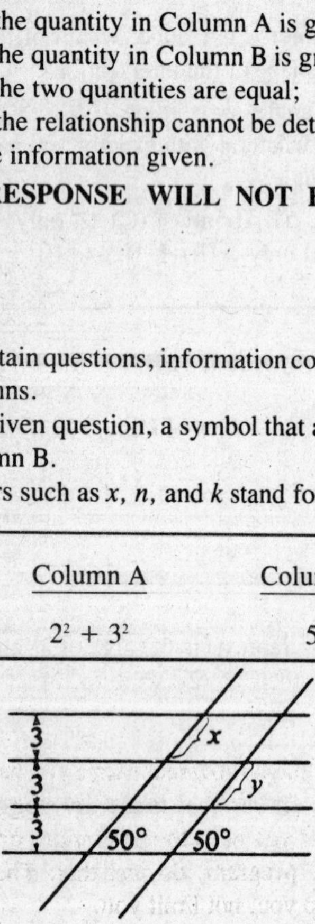

Four parallel lines are intersected by two other lines.

	Column A	Column B
12.	$\frac{y}{x}$	$\frac{x}{y}$

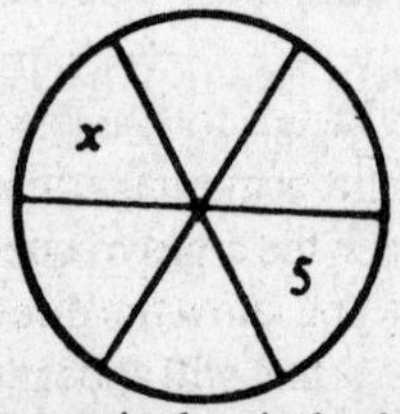

Each of the six sectors in the circle above is assigned a number such that the sum of the numbers in any two sectors adjacent to each other is 9.

	Column A	Column B
13.	x	5

The ratio of men to women in a room is $\frac{4}{5}$.

	Column A	Column B
14.	The total number of men and women in the room	9

Let the operation ϕ have the property that $x \phi y = y \phi x$.

$1 \phi 2 = 6$

	Column A	Column B
15.	$2 \phi 1$	7

Rose has more money than Juanita, Juanita has less money than Sam, and Sam has less money than Rose.

	Column A	Column B
16.	Amount of money Rose has	The combined total of the amounts that Sam and Juanita have

In a bag containing exactly 200 marbles, 30 are white, 60 are black, and the remainder are red.

	Column A	Column B
17.	The percent of marbles in the bag that are red	60%

Column A	Column B

The perimeter of equilateral triangle T is equal to the perimeter of square S.

	Column A	Column B
18.	Length of a side of T	Length of a side of S

A box contains a number of discs each marked with a number less than 10. A disc is chosen without looking.

	Column A	Column B
19.	The probability of choosing a disc numbered 4 from the box	The probability of choosing a disc numbered 5 from the box

Column A	Column B

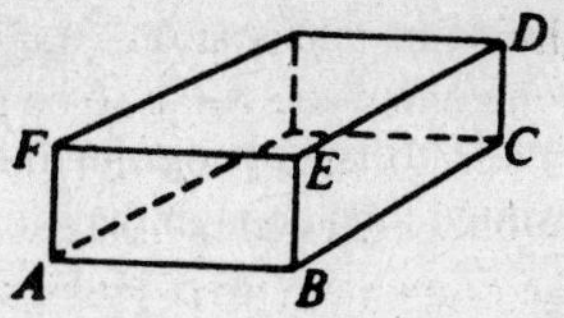

Note: Figure not drawn to scale.

The area of face *ABEF* of the rectangular solid is 12 and the area of face *BCDE* is 8.

	Column A	Column B
20.	The volume of the rectangular solid	24

ANSWERS TO THE SAMPLE QUESTIONS

Verbal Questions

1.	**B**	6.	**C**	11.	**E**	16.	**B**
2.	**B**	7.	**A**	12.	**D**	17.	**A**
3.	**B**	8.	**B**	13.	**E**	18.	**D**
4.	**E**	9.	**E**	14.	**E**	19.	**C**
5.	**E**	10.	**C**	15.	**B**	20.	**B**

Standard Written English Questions

1.	**C**	4.	**D**
2.	**D**	5.	**C**
3.	**B**	6.	**A**

Mathematics Questions

1.	**B**	6.	**D**	11.	**B**	16.	**D**
2.	**C**	7.	**E**	12.	**C**	17.	**B**
3.	**E**	8.	**E**	13.	**B**	18.	**A**
4.	**D**	9.	**D**	14.	**D**	19.	**D**
5.	**A**	10.	**A**	15.	**B**	20.	**D**

THREE SENSIBLE STUDY PROGRAMS

No matter how little time you have to prepare for the SAT, it can be put to good use if you use it efficiently. To help you organize your SAT preparation, we offer three plans for different amounts of time—two days, two weeks, and ten or more weeks. Choose the one that's best for you, depending on how much time you have available. But please remember that these are suggestions, not requirements. If you need to spend more or less time on any part of the program, do just that. The program is intended to help you, not limit you.

THE TWO-DAY CRASH PROGRAM

It's Wednesday and you are taking the SAT on Saturday, and you are starting to panic. You just became acquainted with this "bible" for preparing for the SAT. Follow this crash program. It's not the ideal way to prepare, but intensive preparation with this book is better than walking in cold.

Day 1: Do the Sample Questions (pages 9-17). Make sure you know how to do each type. Take the Diagnostic Test (pages 27-51). Score your test. Study the analysis of answers for all questions you missed or omitted, so you understand where you went wrong.

Day 2: Study the Tactics for handling verbal and mathematics questions at the beginning of chapters 4–10, paying particular attention to the types of questions that gave you trouble. Make sure you know the directions for the different types of questions that will appear on the SAT. Review the test-taking strategies in this chapter. Spend as much time as you can reviewing the High Frequency Word List on pages 126–128 and Mathematics Facts and Formulas on pages 269–271.

THE TWO-WEEK CONCENTRATED PROGRAM

This is the program to follow when you haven't waited until the *very* last minute, but you've waited long enough that time is getting tight.

Session	Topic	Activity
1.	The SAT	Study the Strategies and Test Format, and do the Sample Questions in this chapter. Check your answers.
2.	The Trial Run	Under simulated test conditions, take the Diagnostic SAT.
3.	Self-Evaluation	Score and evaluate the results of your diagnostic test. Make a list of your weak areas to use later in doing practice exercises. Carefully study the analyses of correct answers for the questions you missed.
4.	Vocabulary Building	Study the Basic Word Parts, High-Frequency Word List, and Tactics in Chapter 8. Study the Tactics and do the exercises in Chapters 4 and 5. Compare your answers with the correct ones.
5.	Reviewing Arithmetic and Algebra	Study the Tactics in Chapter 9 and the review material in Chapter 11. Do the exercises. Concentrate on areas of weakness discovered in the Diagnostic SAT.
6.	Vocabulary Building	Continue studying the Basic Word Parts and the High-Frequency Word List. Study the Tactics for handling sentence completion questions in Chapter 6. Do the exercises, and compare your answers with the correct ones.
7.	Plane Geometry	Review geometric facts (Chapter 11). Do the geometry exercises, and study the correct answers.
8.	Reading Comprehension	Study the Tactics in Chapter 7. Do the first half of the reading comprehension exercises. Compare your answers with the correct ones. Go over the questions you missed.
9.	Solving Verbal Problems	Do the verbal problems in Chapter 11: Fractions (page 326), Percent (page 332), Average (page 335), Motion (page 337), Ratio and Proportion (page 340), Mixtures (page 346), and Work (page 349).
10.	Reading Comprehension	Finish the exercises in Chapter 7. Compare your answers with the correct ones. Go over the questions you missed.

Session	Topic	Activity
11.	Quantitative Comparison	Study the Tactics in Chapter 10. Do the exercises.
12.	Getting Ready	Establish test conditions and take Model SAT Test 1. Score your results. Study the answer explanations for questions you missed.
13–14.	Final Dress Rehearsal	Complete as many Model SAT Tests as you can in the time you have left. Score your results. Study the answer explanations for questions you missed.

NOTE: Sessions 4 through 11 need not be followed in this sequence.

Concentrate on the areas that give you trouble. Don't spend your time reviewing material you already know well. Do as many of the exercises as you can in your problem areas.

THE COMPREHENSIVE STUDY PROGRAM

This is the plan to use when you have ten weeks or more to study for the SAT. It allows you to work slowly and steadily, building on what you have already learned, which is the best way to prepare for this or any other test.

The study program includes 15 math sessions and 15 verbal/TSWE sessions. Together, the 30 sessions total approximately 30 hours of work. The sessions are keyed to specific review material and practice exercises in the verbal, mathematical, and standard written English parts of this book.

The verbal section covers antonym, sentence completion, analogy, and reading comprehension questions, as well as the usage and sentence correction questions on the TSWE section of the SAT. Each session will require 30 to 45 minutes of your time, though this will vary according to individual needs.

The math section of this study program covers the material expected of a high school senior. Each session will require approximately 90 minutes of your time, though, again, this will vary. You may find that you can complete several sessions in that time, and you may find sessions on which you need to spend more time.

Take the Diagnostic SAT before you begin this study program. Use the Self-Evaluation section to discover which topics and/or types of questions are troublesome for you. Adjust the study program, if necessary, so that you concentrate on the areas that give you trouble.

Work out a suitable time schedule and carefully follow it until you have completed the study program. In planning your schedule, find time to work on vocabulary in addition to working with the topics covered in the study program given here (see the separate plans for vocabulary study on page 149). After you finish your review, take the six model SATs in Chapter 13. Each test will provide you with valuable test-taking experience. Though you may decide to work on these tests section-by-section rather than as a complete test, you should make time to take at least one or two of the three-hour tests in one sitting, under test conditions.

VERBAL AND TSWE

Session	Topic	Activity
1.	Antonyms	Study the Tactics in Chapter 4. Take Antonym Test A and check your answers.
2.	Sentence Completion	Study the Tactics in Chapter 6. Do questions 1-25 in Test A. Check your answers.
3.	Analogies	Study the Tactics in Chapter 5. Do questions 1-25 in Test A. Check your answers.
4.	Reading Comprehension	Study the Tactics in Chapter 7.
5.	Reading Comprehension	Do the first exercise in Chapter 7. Compare your answers with the correct ones. Go over the questions you missed.
6.	Antonyms	Take Test B in Chapter 4. Check your answers.
7.	Sentence Completion	Do questions 26-50 in Test A (Chapter 6). Check your answers.
8.	Analogies	Do questions 26-50 in Test A (Chapter 5). Check your answers.
9.	Reading Comprehension	Do exercise B in Chapter 7. Compare your answers with the correct ones. Go over the questions you missed.
10.	Reading Comprehension	Do exercise C in Chapter 7. Compare your answers with the correct ones. Go over the questions you missed.
11.	Antonyms	Take Tests C and D in Chapter 4. Check your answers.
12.	Sentence Completion	Take Test B in Chapter 6. Check your answers.
13.	Analogies	Take Test B in Chapter 5. Check your answers.
14.	Reading Comprehension and the TSWE	Do exercise D in Chapter 7. Take Tests A and B in Chapter 12, and study the correct answers.
15.	Reading Comprehension and the TSWE	Do exercise E in Chapter 7. Take Tests C and D in Chapter 12, and study the correct answers.

Note: Answers to all exercises appear at the end of each chapter.

MATHEMATICS

Session	Topic	Activity
1.	Reviewing Algebra	Study the Tactics in Chapter 9. Study real (signed) numbers, the language of algebra, and algebraic operations on pages 300-305, and do questions 1-66. Do the Practice Exercises on pages 312-313.
2.	Reviewing Algebra	Study factoring, roots, and solving equations on pages 305-308, and do questions 67-97. Do the Practice Exercises on page 313.
3.	Using Algebra	Study solving problems by equations on pages 308-309, and do questions 98-102. Do the Practice Exercises on pages 314-315.
4.	Reviewing Inequalities and the Number Line	Study pages 309-311, and do questions 103-123. Do the Practice Exercises on pages 315-316.
5.	Reviewing Fractions	Study the definitions and basic operations on pages 316-320, and do questions 124-165. Do the Practice Exercises on pages 321-323.
6.	Reviewing Fractions	Study the sections on solving fractional equations and problems involving fractions (pages 320-321), and do questions 166-179. Do the Practice Exercises on pages 325-329.
7.	Reviewing Fractions	Practice using principles involving fractions by doing the Practice Exercises on pages 324-325.
8.	Reviewing Decimals and Percentages	Study the sections on decimals and percents on pages 329-332, and do questions 180-202. Do the Practice Exercises on page 330 and pages 332-334.
9.	Reviewing Averages and Motion	Study the definitions, formulas, and verbal problems on pages 335-337, and do questions 203-211. Do the Practice Exercises on pages 335-336 and pages 337-340.
10.	Reviewing Ratio and Proportion	Study the definitions, principles, and verbal problems on pages 340-342, and do questions 212-222. Do the Practice Exercises on pages 342-346.
11.	Reviewing Mixtures and Solutions, and Work Problems	Study the section on mixtures and solutions on pages 346-347 and the section on work problems on page 349. Do questions 223-228 and the Practice Exercises on pages 347-348 and pages 349-352.

Continued on next page.

MATHEMATICS

Session	Topic	Activity
12.	Reviewing Coordinate Geometry	Study the principles, formulas, and applications of coordinate geometry on page 352. Do questions 229-233 and the Practice Exercises on pages 353-355.
13.	Reviewing Geometry	Study the definitions and formulas, and the applications of definitions and formulas on pages 355-362. Do the Practice Exercises on pages 362-368.
14.	Reviewing Data Interpretation of Graphs, Number Sequences.	Study the definitions and applications on pages 369 and 377, and do the Practice Exercises on pages 369-376 and page 397.
15.	Reviewing Quantitative Comparisons	Study the Tactics in Chapter 10, and do the exercises.

PART TWO

PINPOINT YOUR TROUBLE SPOTS

ANSWER SHEET
DIAGNOSTIC SAT TEST

Remove answer sheet by cutting on dotted line

SECTION 1

1. Ⓐ Ⓑ Ⓒ Ⓓ Ⓔ	11. Ⓐ Ⓑ Ⓒ Ⓓ Ⓔ	21. Ⓐ Ⓑ Ⓒ Ⓓ Ⓔ	31. Ⓐ Ⓑ Ⓒ Ⓓ Ⓔ	41. Ⓐ Ⓑ Ⓒ Ⓓ Ⓔ
2. Ⓐ Ⓑ Ⓒ Ⓓ Ⓔ	12. Ⓐ Ⓑ Ⓒ Ⓓ Ⓔ	22. Ⓐ Ⓑ Ⓒ Ⓓ Ⓔ	32. Ⓐ Ⓑ Ⓒ Ⓓ Ⓔ	42. Ⓐ Ⓑ Ⓒ Ⓓ Ⓔ
3. Ⓐ Ⓑ Ⓒ Ⓓ Ⓔ	13. Ⓐ Ⓑ Ⓒ Ⓓ Ⓔ	23. Ⓐ Ⓑ Ⓒ Ⓓ Ⓔ	33. Ⓐ Ⓑ Ⓒ Ⓓ Ⓔ	43. Ⓐ Ⓑ Ⓒ Ⓓ Ⓔ
4. Ⓐ Ⓑ Ⓒ Ⓓ Ⓔ	14. Ⓐ Ⓑ Ⓒ Ⓓ Ⓔ	24. Ⓐ Ⓑ Ⓒ Ⓓ Ⓔ	34. Ⓐ Ⓑ Ⓒ Ⓓ Ⓔ	44. Ⓐ Ⓑ Ⓒ Ⓓ Ⓔ
5. Ⓐ Ⓑ Ⓒ Ⓓ Ⓔ	15. Ⓐ Ⓑ Ⓒ Ⓓ Ⓔ	25. Ⓐ Ⓑ Ⓒ Ⓓ Ⓔ	35. Ⓐ Ⓑ Ⓒ Ⓓ Ⓔ	45. Ⓐ Ⓑ Ⓒ Ⓓ Ⓔ
6. Ⓐ Ⓑ Ⓒ Ⓓ Ⓔ	16. Ⓐ Ⓑ Ⓒ Ⓓ Ⓔ	26. Ⓐ Ⓑ Ⓒ Ⓓ Ⓔ	36. Ⓐ Ⓑ Ⓒ Ⓓ Ⓔ	46. Ⓐ Ⓑ Ⓒ Ⓓ Ⓔ
7. Ⓐ Ⓑ Ⓒ Ⓓ Ⓔ	17. Ⓐ Ⓑ Ⓒ Ⓓ Ⓔ	27. Ⓐ Ⓑ Ⓒ Ⓓ Ⓔ	37. Ⓐ Ⓑ Ⓒ Ⓓ Ⓔ	47. Ⓐ Ⓑ Ⓒ Ⓓ Ⓔ
8. Ⓐ Ⓑ Ⓒ Ⓓ Ⓔ	18. Ⓐ Ⓑ Ⓒ Ⓓ Ⓔ	28. Ⓐ Ⓑ Ⓒ Ⓓ Ⓔ	38. Ⓐ Ⓑ Ⓒ Ⓓ Ⓔ	48. Ⓐ Ⓑ Ⓒ Ⓓ Ⓔ
9. Ⓐ Ⓑ Ⓒ Ⓓ Ⓔ	19. Ⓐ Ⓑ Ⓒ Ⓓ Ⓔ	29. Ⓐ Ⓑ Ⓒ Ⓓ Ⓔ	39. Ⓐ Ⓑ Ⓒ Ⓓ Ⓔ	49. Ⓐ Ⓑ Ⓒ Ⓓ Ⓔ
10. Ⓐ Ⓑ Ⓒ Ⓓ Ⓔ	20. Ⓐ Ⓑ Ⓒ Ⓓ Ⓔ	30. Ⓐ Ⓑ Ⓒ Ⓓ Ⓔ	40. Ⓐ Ⓑ Ⓒ Ⓓ Ⓔ	50. Ⓐ Ⓑ Ⓒ Ⓓ Ⓔ

SECTION 2

1. Ⓐ Ⓑ Ⓒ Ⓓ Ⓔ	11. Ⓐ Ⓑ Ⓒ Ⓓ Ⓔ	21. Ⓐ Ⓑ Ⓒ Ⓓ Ⓔ	31. Ⓐ Ⓑ Ⓒ Ⓓ Ⓔ	41. Ⓐ Ⓑ Ⓒ Ⓓ Ⓔ
2. Ⓐ Ⓑ Ⓒ Ⓓ Ⓔ	12. Ⓐ Ⓑ Ⓒ Ⓓ Ⓔ	22. Ⓐ Ⓑ Ⓒ Ⓓ Ⓔ	32. Ⓐ Ⓑ Ⓒ Ⓓ Ⓔ	42. Ⓐ Ⓑ Ⓒ Ⓓ Ⓔ
3. Ⓐ Ⓑ Ⓒ Ⓓ Ⓔ	13. Ⓐ Ⓑ Ⓒ Ⓓ Ⓔ	23. Ⓐ Ⓑ Ⓒ Ⓓ Ⓔ	33. Ⓐ Ⓑ Ⓒ Ⓓ Ⓔ	43. Ⓐ Ⓑ Ⓒ Ⓓ Ⓔ
4. Ⓐ Ⓑ Ⓒ Ⓓ Ⓔ	14. Ⓐ Ⓑ Ⓒ Ⓓ Ⓔ	24. Ⓐ Ⓑ Ⓒ Ⓓ Ⓔ	34. Ⓐ Ⓑ Ⓒ Ⓓ Ⓔ	44. Ⓐ Ⓑ Ⓒ Ⓓ Ⓔ
5. Ⓐ Ⓑ Ⓒ Ⓓ Ⓔ	15. Ⓐ Ⓑ Ⓒ Ⓓ Ⓔ	25. Ⓐ Ⓑ Ⓒ Ⓓ Ⓔ	35. Ⓐ Ⓑ Ⓒ Ⓓ Ⓔ	45. Ⓐ Ⓑ Ⓒ Ⓓ Ⓔ
6. Ⓐ Ⓑ Ⓒ Ⓓ Ⓔ	16. Ⓐ Ⓑ Ⓒ Ⓓ Ⓔ	26. Ⓐ Ⓑ Ⓒ Ⓓ Ⓔ	36. Ⓐ Ⓑ Ⓒ Ⓓ Ⓔ	46. Ⓐ Ⓑ Ⓒ Ⓓ Ⓔ
7. Ⓐ Ⓑ Ⓒ Ⓓ Ⓔ	17. Ⓐ Ⓑ Ⓒ Ⓓ Ⓔ	27. Ⓐ Ⓑ Ⓒ Ⓓ Ⓔ	37. Ⓐ Ⓑ Ⓒ Ⓓ Ⓔ	47. Ⓐ Ⓑ Ⓒ Ⓓ Ⓔ
8. Ⓐ Ⓑ Ⓒ Ⓓ Ⓔ	18. Ⓐ Ⓑ Ⓒ Ⓓ Ⓔ	28. Ⓐ Ⓑ Ⓒ Ⓓ Ⓔ	38. Ⓐ Ⓑ Ⓒ Ⓓ Ⓔ	48. Ⓐ Ⓑ Ⓒ Ⓓ Ⓔ
9. Ⓐ Ⓑ Ⓒ Ⓓ Ⓔ	19. Ⓐ Ⓑ Ⓒ Ⓓ Ⓔ	29. Ⓐ Ⓑ Ⓒ Ⓓ Ⓔ	39. Ⓐ Ⓑ Ⓒ Ⓓ Ⓔ	49. Ⓐ Ⓑ Ⓒ Ⓓ Ⓔ
10. Ⓐ Ⓑ Ⓒ Ⓓ Ⓔ	20. Ⓐ Ⓑ Ⓒ Ⓓ Ⓔ	30. Ⓐ Ⓑ Ⓒ Ⓓ Ⓔ	40. Ⓐ Ⓑ Ⓒ Ⓓ Ⓔ	50. Ⓐ Ⓑ Ⓒ Ⓓ Ⓔ

SECTION 3

1. Ⓐ Ⓑ Ⓒ Ⓓ Ⓔ	11. Ⓐ Ⓑ Ⓒ Ⓓ Ⓔ	21. Ⓐ Ⓑ Ⓒ Ⓓ Ⓔ	31. Ⓐ Ⓑ Ⓒ Ⓓ Ⓔ	41. Ⓐ Ⓑ Ⓒ Ⓓ Ⓔ
2. Ⓐ Ⓑ Ⓒ Ⓓ Ⓔ	12. Ⓐ Ⓑ Ⓒ Ⓓ Ⓔ	22. Ⓐ Ⓑ Ⓒ Ⓓ Ⓔ	32. Ⓐ Ⓑ Ⓒ Ⓓ Ⓔ	42. Ⓐ Ⓑ Ⓒ Ⓓ Ⓔ
3. Ⓐ Ⓑ Ⓒ Ⓓ Ⓔ	13. Ⓐ Ⓑ Ⓒ Ⓓ Ⓔ	23. Ⓐ Ⓑ Ⓒ Ⓓ Ⓔ	33. Ⓐ Ⓑ Ⓒ Ⓓ Ⓔ	43. Ⓐ Ⓑ Ⓒ Ⓓ Ⓔ
4. Ⓐ Ⓑ Ⓒ Ⓓ Ⓔ	14. Ⓐ Ⓑ Ⓒ Ⓓ Ⓔ	24. Ⓐ Ⓑ Ⓒ Ⓓ Ⓔ	34. Ⓐ Ⓑ Ⓒ Ⓓ Ⓔ	44. Ⓐ Ⓑ Ⓒ Ⓓ Ⓔ
5. Ⓐ Ⓑ Ⓒ Ⓓ Ⓔ	15. Ⓐ Ⓑ Ⓒ Ⓓ Ⓔ	25. Ⓐ Ⓑ Ⓒ Ⓓ Ⓔ	35. Ⓐ Ⓑ Ⓒ Ⓓ Ⓔ	45. Ⓐ Ⓑ Ⓒ Ⓓ Ⓔ
6. Ⓐ Ⓑ Ⓒ Ⓓ Ⓔ	16. Ⓐ Ⓑ Ⓒ Ⓓ Ⓔ	26. Ⓐ Ⓑ Ⓒ Ⓓ Ⓔ	36. Ⓐ Ⓑ Ⓒ Ⓓ Ⓔ	46. Ⓐ Ⓑ Ⓒ Ⓓ Ⓔ
7. Ⓐ Ⓑ Ⓒ Ⓓ Ⓔ	17. Ⓐ Ⓑ Ⓒ Ⓓ Ⓔ	27. Ⓐ Ⓑ Ⓒ Ⓓ Ⓔ	37. Ⓐ Ⓑ Ⓒ Ⓓ Ⓔ	47. Ⓐ Ⓑ Ⓒ Ⓓ Ⓔ
8. Ⓐ Ⓑ Ⓒ Ⓓ Ⓔ	18. Ⓐ Ⓑ Ⓒ Ⓓ Ⓔ	28. Ⓐ Ⓑ Ⓒ Ⓓ Ⓔ	38. Ⓐ Ⓑ Ⓒ Ⓓ Ⓔ	48. Ⓐ Ⓑ Ⓒ Ⓓ Ⓔ
9. Ⓐ Ⓑ Ⓒ Ⓓ Ⓔ	19. Ⓐ Ⓑ Ⓒ Ⓓ Ⓔ	29. Ⓐ Ⓑ Ⓒ Ⓓ Ⓔ	39. Ⓐ Ⓑ Ⓒ Ⓓ Ⓔ	49. Ⓐ Ⓑ Ⓒ Ⓓ Ⓔ
10. Ⓐ Ⓑ Ⓒ Ⓓ Ⓔ	20. Ⓐ Ⓑ Ⓒ Ⓓ Ⓔ	30. Ⓐ Ⓑ Ⓒ Ⓓ Ⓔ	40. Ⓐ Ⓑ Ⓒ Ⓓ Ⓔ	50. Ⓐ Ⓑ Ⓒ Ⓓ Ⓔ

SECTION 4

1. Ⓐ Ⓑ Ⓒ Ⓓ Ⓔ	11. Ⓐ Ⓑ Ⓒ Ⓓ Ⓔ	21. Ⓐ Ⓑ Ⓒ Ⓓ Ⓔ	31. Ⓐ Ⓑ Ⓒ Ⓓ Ⓔ	41. Ⓐ Ⓑ Ⓒ Ⓓ Ⓔ
2. Ⓐ Ⓑ Ⓒ Ⓓ Ⓔ	12. Ⓐ Ⓑ Ⓒ Ⓓ Ⓔ	22. Ⓐ Ⓑ Ⓒ Ⓓ Ⓔ	32. Ⓐ Ⓑ Ⓒ Ⓓ Ⓔ	42. Ⓐ Ⓑ Ⓒ Ⓓ Ⓔ
3. Ⓐ Ⓑ Ⓒ Ⓓ Ⓔ	13. Ⓐ Ⓑ Ⓒ Ⓓ Ⓔ	23. Ⓐ Ⓑ Ⓒ Ⓓ Ⓔ	33. Ⓐ Ⓑ Ⓒ Ⓓ Ⓔ	43. Ⓐ Ⓑ Ⓒ Ⓓ Ⓔ
4. Ⓐ Ⓑ Ⓒ Ⓓ Ⓔ	14. Ⓐ Ⓑ Ⓒ Ⓓ Ⓔ	24. Ⓐ Ⓑ Ⓒ Ⓓ Ⓔ	34. Ⓐ Ⓑ Ⓒ Ⓓ Ⓔ	44. Ⓐ Ⓑ Ⓒ Ⓓ Ⓔ
5. Ⓐ Ⓑ Ⓒ Ⓓ Ⓔ	15. Ⓐ Ⓑ Ⓒ Ⓓ Ⓔ	25. Ⓐ Ⓑ Ⓒ Ⓓ Ⓔ	35. Ⓐ Ⓑ Ⓒ Ⓓ Ⓔ	45. Ⓐ Ⓑ Ⓒ Ⓓ Ⓔ
6. Ⓐ Ⓑ Ⓒ Ⓓ Ⓔ	16. Ⓐ Ⓑ Ⓒ Ⓓ Ⓔ	26. Ⓐ Ⓑ Ⓒ Ⓓ Ⓔ	36. Ⓐ Ⓑ Ⓒ Ⓓ Ⓔ	46. Ⓐ Ⓑ Ⓒ Ⓓ Ⓔ
7. Ⓐ Ⓑ Ⓒ Ⓓ Ⓔ	17. Ⓐ Ⓑ Ⓒ Ⓓ Ⓔ	27. Ⓐ Ⓑ Ⓒ Ⓓ Ⓔ	37. Ⓐ Ⓑ Ⓒ Ⓓ Ⓔ	47. Ⓐ Ⓑ Ⓒ Ⓓ Ⓔ
8. Ⓐ Ⓑ Ⓒ Ⓓ Ⓔ	18. Ⓐ Ⓑ Ⓒ Ⓓ Ⓔ	28. Ⓐ Ⓑ Ⓒ Ⓓ Ⓔ	38. Ⓐ Ⓑ Ⓒ Ⓓ Ⓔ	48. Ⓐ Ⓑ Ⓒ Ⓓ Ⓔ
9. Ⓐ Ⓑ Ⓒ Ⓓ Ⓔ	19. Ⓐ Ⓑ Ⓒ Ⓓ Ⓔ	29. Ⓐ Ⓑ Ⓒ Ⓓ Ⓔ	39. Ⓐ Ⓑ Ⓒ Ⓓ Ⓔ	49. Ⓐ Ⓑ Ⓒ Ⓓ Ⓔ
10. Ⓐ Ⓑ Ⓒ Ⓓ Ⓔ	20. Ⓐ Ⓑ Ⓒ Ⓓ Ⓔ	30. Ⓐ Ⓑ Ⓒ Ⓓ Ⓔ	40. Ⓐ Ⓑ Ⓒ Ⓓ Ⓔ	50. Ⓐ Ⓑ Ⓒ Ⓓ Ⓔ

SECTION 5

1. Ⓐ Ⓑ Ⓒ Ⓓ Ⓔ	11. Ⓐ Ⓑ Ⓒ Ⓓ Ⓔ	21. Ⓐ Ⓑ Ⓒ Ⓓ Ⓔ	31. Ⓐ Ⓑ Ⓒ Ⓓ Ⓔ	41. Ⓐ Ⓑ Ⓒ Ⓓ Ⓔ
2. Ⓐ Ⓑ Ⓒ Ⓓ Ⓔ	12. Ⓐ Ⓑ Ⓒ Ⓓ Ⓔ	22. Ⓐ Ⓑ Ⓒ Ⓓ Ⓔ	32. Ⓐ Ⓑ Ⓒ Ⓓ Ⓔ	42. Ⓐ Ⓑ Ⓒ Ⓓ Ⓔ
3. Ⓐ Ⓑ Ⓒ Ⓓ Ⓔ	13. Ⓐ Ⓑ Ⓒ Ⓓ Ⓔ	23. Ⓐ Ⓑ Ⓒ Ⓓ Ⓔ	33. Ⓐ Ⓑ Ⓒ Ⓓ Ⓔ	43. Ⓐ Ⓑ Ⓒ Ⓓ Ⓔ
4. Ⓐ Ⓑ Ⓒ Ⓓ Ⓔ	14. Ⓐ Ⓑ Ⓒ Ⓓ Ⓔ	24. Ⓐ Ⓑ Ⓒ Ⓓ Ⓔ	34. Ⓐ Ⓑ Ⓒ Ⓓ Ⓔ	44. Ⓐ Ⓑ Ⓒ Ⓓ Ⓔ
5. Ⓐ Ⓑ Ⓒ Ⓓ Ⓔ	15. Ⓐ Ⓑ Ⓒ Ⓓ Ⓔ	25. Ⓐ Ⓑ Ⓒ Ⓓ Ⓔ	35. Ⓐ Ⓑ Ⓒ Ⓓ Ⓔ	45. Ⓐ Ⓑ Ⓒ Ⓓ Ⓔ
6. Ⓐ Ⓑ Ⓒ Ⓓ Ⓔ	16. Ⓐ Ⓑ Ⓒ Ⓓ Ⓔ	26. Ⓐ Ⓑ Ⓒ Ⓓ Ⓔ	36. Ⓐ Ⓑ Ⓒ Ⓓ Ⓔ	46. Ⓐ Ⓑ Ⓒ Ⓓ Ⓔ
7. Ⓐ Ⓑ Ⓒ Ⓓ Ⓔ	17. Ⓐ Ⓑ Ⓒ Ⓓ Ⓔ	27. Ⓐ Ⓑ Ⓒ Ⓓ Ⓔ	37. Ⓐ Ⓑ Ⓒ Ⓓ Ⓔ	47. Ⓐ Ⓑ Ⓒ Ⓓ Ⓔ
8. Ⓐ Ⓑ Ⓒ Ⓓ Ⓔ	18. Ⓐ Ⓑ Ⓒ Ⓓ Ⓔ	28. Ⓐ Ⓑ Ⓒ Ⓓ Ⓔ	38. Ⓐ Ⓑ Ⓒ Ⓓ Ⓔ	48. Ⓐ Ⓑ Ⓒ Ⓓ Ⓔ
9. Ⓐ Ⓑ Ⓒ Ⓓ Ⓔ	19. Ⓐ Ⓑ Ⓒ Ⓓ Ⓔ	29. Ⓐ Ⓑ Ⓒ Ⓓ Ⓔ	39. Ⓐ Ⓑ Ⓒ Ⓓ Ⓔ	49. Ⓐ Ⓑ Ⓒ Ⓓ Ⓔ
10. Ⓐ Ⓑ Ⓒ Ⓓ Ⓔ	20. Ⓐ Ⓑ Ⓒ Ⓓ Ⓔ	30. Ⓐ Ⓑ Ⓒ Ⓓ Ⓔ	40. Ⓐ Ⓑ Ⓒ Ⓓ Ⓔ	50. Ⓐ Ⓑ Ⓒ Ⓓ Ⓔ

SECTION 6

1. Ⓐ Ⓑ Ⓒ Ⓓ Ⓔ	11. Ⓐ Ⓑ Ⓒ Ⓓ Ⓔ	21. Ⓐ Ⓑ Ⓒ Ⓓ Ⓔ	31. Ⓐ Ⓑ Ⓒ Ⓓ Ⓔ	41. Ⓐ Ⓑ Ⓒ Ⓓ Ⓔ
2. Ⓐ Ⓑ Ⓒ Ⓓ Ⓔ	12. Ⓐ Ⓑ Ⓒ Ⓓ Ⓔ	22. Ⓐ Ⓑ Ⓒ Ⓓ Ⓔ	32. Ⓐ Ⓑ Ⓒ Ⓓ Ⓔ	42. Ⓐ Ⓑ Ⓒ Ⓓ Ⓔ
3. Ⓐ Ⓑ Ⓒ Ⓓ Ⓔ	13. Ⓐ Ⓑ Ⓒ Ⓓ Ⓔ	23. Ⓐ Ⓑ Ⓒ Ⓓ Ⓔ	33. Ⓐ Ⓑ Ⓒ Ⓓ Ⓔ	43. Ⓐ Ⓑ Ⓒ Ⓓ Ⓔ
4. Ⓐ Ⓑ Ⓒ Ⓓ Ⓔ	14. Ⓐ Ⓑ Ⓒ Ⓓ Ⓔ	24. Ⓐ Ⓑ Ⓒ Ⓓ Ⓔ	34. Ⓐ Ⓑ Ⓒ Ⓓ Ⓔ	44. Ⓐ Ⓑ Ⓒ Ⓓ Ⓔ
5. Ⓐ Ⓑ Ⓒ Ⓓ Ⓔ	15. Ⓐ Ⓑ Ⓒ Ⓓ Ⓔ	25. Ⓐ Ⓑ Ⓒ Ⓓ Ⓔ	35. Ⓐ Ⓑ Ⓒ Ⓓ Ⓔ	45. Ⓐ Ⓑ Ⓒ Ⓓ Ⓔ
6. Ⓐ Ⓑ Ⓒ Ⓓ Ⓔ	16. Ⓐ Ⓑ Ⓒ Ⓓ Ⓔ	26. Ⓐ Ⓑ Ⓒ Ⓓ Ⓔ	36. Ⓐ Ⓑ Ⓒ Ⓓ Ⓔ	46. Ⓐ Ⓑ Ⓒ Ⓓ Ⓔ
7. Ⓐ Ⓑ Ⓒ Ⓓ Ⓔ	17. Ⓐ Ⓑ Ⓒ Ⓓ Ⓔ	27. Ⓐ Ⓑ Ⓒ Ⓓ Ⓔ	37. Ⓐ Ⓑ Ⓒ Ⓓ Ⓔ	47. Ⓐ Ⓑ Ⓒ Ⓓ Ⓔ
8. Ⓐ Ⓑ Ⓒ Ⓓ Ⓔ	18. Ⓐ Ⓑ Ⓒ Ⓓ Ⓔ	28. Ⓐ Ⓑ Ⓒ Ⓓ Ⓔ	38. Ⓐ Ⓑ Ⓒ Ⓓ Ⓔ	48. Ⓐ Ⓑ Ⓒ Ⓓ Ⓔ
9. Ⓐ Ⓑ Ⓒ Ⓓ Ⓔ	19. Ⓐ Ⓑ Ⓒ Ⓓ Ⓔ	29. Ⓐ Ⓑ Ⓒ Ⓓ Ⓔ	39. Ⓐ Ⓑ Ⓒ Ⓓ Ⓔ	49. Ⓐ Ⓑ Ⓒ Ⓓ Ⓔ
10. Ⓐ Ⓑ Ⓒ Ⓓ Ⓔ	20. Ⓐ Ⓑ Ⓒ Ⓓ Ⓔ	30. Ⓐ Ⓑ Ⓒ Ⓓ Ⓔ	40. Ⓐ Ⓑ Ⓒ Ⓓ Ⓔ	50. Ⓐ Ⓑ Ⓒ Ⓓ Ⓔ

Remove answer sheet by cutting on dotted line

A DIAGNOSTIC SAT

3

- **Diagnostic Test**
- **Answer Key**
- **Answer Explanations**
- **Self-Evaluation**

This chapter provides a diagnostic test that can serve several purposes. First, it is a tool to identify problem areas. Take the test, evaluate your results as suggested and you will discover your strengths and weaknesses. In setting up your study program, use one of the study plans in the preceding chapter and make a realistic, practical schedule to meet your particular needs. You may find that certain areas or topics need more of your attention. Provide this extra time and when you are ready to take those "dress rehearsals" with the model SAT tests in Chapter 13, you should find improvement in these areas.

Another purpose of this test is to give you experience with the format and level of difficulty of the SAT questions. You will also gain experience with "traps" set by the test makers and "shortcuts" provided by the authors in their analyses of the answers. Finally, you can develop the technique of profiting from your mistakes. Study the carefully worded explanations for the questions you missed. Don't repeat your errors!

Students who have used this book wisely have scored high on the SAT.

SECTION 1 VERBAL ABILITY

45 QUESTIONS - 30 MINUTES

For each question in this section, choose the best answer and blacken the corresponding space on the answer sheet.

Each question below consists of a word in capital letters, followed by five lettered words or phrases. Choose the word or phrase that is most nearly <u>opposite</u> in meaning to the word in capital letters. Since some of the questions require you to distinguish fine shades of meaning, consider all the choices before deciding which is best.

Example:

GOOD: (A) sour (B) bad (C) red (D) hot (E) ugly

Ⓐ ● Ⓒ Ⓓ Ⓔ

1. PULCHRITUDE:
   (A) magnificence
   (B) ignorance
   (C) ugliness
   (D) lassitude
   (E) punctuality

2. WARY:
   (A) plump
   (B) promiscuous
   (C) inept
   (D) careless
   (E) naked

3. DEFUNCT:
   (A) extant
   (B) bankrupt
   (C) qualified
   (D) notable
   (E) wayward

4. SUCCINCT:
   (A) sweet
   (B) vapid
   (C) illustrious
   (D) brassy
   (E) verbose

5. INNOCUOUS:
(A) fetid
(B) blasphemous
(C) blatant
(D) hallowed
(E) harmful

6. RESOLUTE:
(A) jaundiced
(B) vacillating
(C) variegated
(D) parliamentary
(E) placid

7. SALLOW:
(A) fish
(B) deep
(C) ruddy
(D) fragrant
(E) vapid

8. AUTHENTIC:
(A) gracious
(B) intellectual
(C) incomprehensible
(D) spurious
(E) internal

9. INTREPID:
(A) pusillanimous
(B) punctilious
(C) propitious
(D) portentous
(E) putative

10. CHANGEABLE:
(A) impervious
(B) natural
(C) intractable
(D) immutable
(E) immortal

11. REDOLENT:
(A) appropriate
(B) noisome
(C) rotten
(D) industrious
(E) felicitous

12. PLACATE:
(A) anticipate
(B) exaggerate
(C) berate
(D) delude
(E) exasperate

13. AGGRAVATE:
(A) mitigate
(B) reduce
(C) mystify
(D) scatter
(E) inter

14. HACKNEYED:
(A) driven
(B) fresh
(C) started
(D) dominant
(E) rational

15. LAUD:
(A) quiet
(B) silent
(C) affect
(D) contain
(E) chide

Each sentence below has one or two blanks, each blank indicating that something has been omitted. Beneath the sentence are five lettered words or sets of words. Choose the word or set of words that best fits the meaning of the sentence as a whole.

Example:

Although its publicity has been ----, the film itself is intelligent, well-acted, handsomely produced, and altogether ----.

(A) tasteless..respectable (B) extensive..moderate (C) sophisticated..amateur (D) risqué..crude (E) perfect..spectacular

● Ⓑ Ⓒ Ⓓ Ⓔ

16. American society is based on an economy of _______ consumption and _______ displays of wealth.
(A) unavoidable . . . purposeful
(B) utopian . . . valid
(C) sound . . . vaunted
(D) conspicuous . . . ostentatious
(E) surreptitious . . . vain

17. The officers of the corporation pledged there would be no _______ ; nothing would be held against the strikers.
(A) truce
(B) retaliations
(C) reservations
(D) scabs
(E) favoritism

18. A man who cannot win honor in his own _______ will have a very small chance of winning it from posterity.
(A) right
(B) field
(C) country
(D) way
(E) age

19. Such a ______ expenditure of public funds must be ______.
(A) rapid . . . hastened
(B) proper . . . vindicated
(C) lavish . . . justified
(D) judicious . . . condemned
(E) judicious . . . justified

20. A(n) ______ writer, he has published fifteen books in the past thirteen years.
(A) poor
(B) active
(C) enterprising
(D) prolific
(E) indigenous

Each passage below is followed by questions based on its content. Answer all questions following a passage on the basis of what is stated or implied in that passage.

Rumor is the most primitive way of spreading stories — by passing them on from mouth to mouth. But civilized countries in normal times have better sources of news than rumor. They have radio, television, and newspapers. In times of stress and confusion, however, rumor emerges and becomes rife. At such times the different kinds of news are in competition: the press, television, and radio versus the grapevine.

Especially do rumors spread when war requires censorship on many important matters. The customary news sources no longer give out enough information. Since the people cannot learn through legitimate channels all that they are anxious to learn, they pick up "news" wherever they can and when this happens, rumor thrives.

Rumors are often repeated even by those who do not believe the tales. There is a fascination about them. The reason is that the cleverly designed rumor gives expression to something deep in the hearts of the victims — the fears, suspicions, forbidden hopes, or daydreams which they hesitate to voice directly. Pessimistic rumors about defeat and disasters show that the people who repeat them are worried and anxious. Optimistic rumors about record production or peace soon coming point to complacency or confidence — and often to overconfidence.

21. The phrase that best expresses the ideas of this passage is
(A) The nature of rumor
(B) The fascination of rumors
(C) Rumor, primitive man's newspaper
(D) Breeding places of rumors
(E) A case against rumor

22. The author suggests that rumors usually
(A) alarm their hearers
(B) are hardy in their growth
(C) are disheartening
(D) can be suppressed by censorship
(E) reflect a lack of confidence in government

23. According to the passage, people who repeat a rumor as truth want to do so because they
(A) are impressed with antiquity of this method of spreading news
(B) are naturally gullible
(C) are pessimistic by nature
(D) find that the rumor reflects their own unexpressed beliefs
(E) fear the truth

24. The author states that during wartime the regular sources of news present only
(A) optimistic reports
(B) pessimistic reports
(C) limited information
(D) government propaganda
(E) distorted and biased viewpoints

25. The author suggests that, in times of stress, man frequently
(A) supports radical movements
(B) becomes more close-mouthed
(C) stops regular news services
(D) distrusts his fellow man
(E) reverts to primitive techniques

Next to his towering masterpiece, *Moby Dick*, *Billy Budd* is Melville's greatest work. It has the tone of a last testament, and the manuscript was neatly tied up by his wife, Elizabeth, and kept in a trunk for some thirty years. It was not until 1924 that it was first published. Slowly it has become recognized as the remarkable work it is. *Billy Budd* has been dramatized for Broadway, done on T.V., made into an opera, and reached a highly satisfying form in Ustinov's movie.

Scholars disagree, somewhat violently, about what Melville was trying to say. He did make it pretty clear that he was recounting a duel between Good and Evil.

Several times he remarked that Billy Budd is as innocent and ignorant as Adam before the fall. His enemy is like Satan in Milton's *Paradise Lost*.

When Billy Budd destroys the letter and is sentenced to be hanged according to the letter of the law, controversy exists as to whether the Captain is simply a mortal man preserving order or a Jehovah-like figure, dispensing cruel justice.

Melville, it is claimed, cleverly took pains to hide his heretical feelings. *Billy Budd* is written as if told by a pious, God-loving man.

Ironically, Melville's iconoclasm has largely misfired, for the story today is accepted as either one of simple suspense or a reverent parable of God, Satan, and Adam. Meanwhile the scholars are still arguing, and *Billy Budd* remains like a porcupine, thorny, with interesting ambiguities.

26. Regarding *Billy Budd*, critics seem to disagree about the book's
(A) plot
(B) theme
(C) mood
(D) setting
(E) introduction

27. The passage suggests that the character Billy Budd was
(A) Satanic
(B) ambiguous
(C) naive
(D) brutal
(E) vain

28. The author's purpose in writing this passage seems to be to
(A) point out aspects of *Billy Budd*
(B) show that *Billy Budd* is well written
(C) defend Melville against his critics
(D) defend Melville's iconoclasm
(E) describe Melville's growth as a literary artist

29. The passage indicates that the Captain
(A) disobeyed the law
(B) treated his crew very badly
(C) disliked Billy intensely
(D) was incapable of action
(E) was responsible for discipline

30. Certain lines in this passage suggest that Melville was
(A) Jehovah-like
(B) childishly naive
(C) very scholarly
(D) rather shrewd
(E) immune to pain

Select the word or set of words that best completes each of the following sentences.

31. Because of the _______ failure of his plans, he seemed more _______ than was usual.
(A) violent . . . exhilarated
(B) monetary . . . extravagant
(C) ultimate . . . pleasant
(D) unexpected . . . morose
(E) thorough . . . benevolent

32. Because his time was limited, John decided to read the _______ novel *War and Peace* in a (an) _______ edition.
(A) Russian . . . English
(B) lengthy . . . abridged
(C) famous . . . modern
(D) Russian . . . autographed
(E) lengthy . . . complete

33. Although he had spent many hours in the laboratory trying to solve the problem, he was the first to admit that the final solution was _______ and not the _______ of his labor.
(A) trivial . . . cause
(B) incomplete . . . intent
(C) adequate . . . result
(D) worthwhile . . . fault
(E) fortuitous . . . result

34. The voters never thought that the candidate would resort to _______ to win; he seemed to be a (an) _______ man.
(A) charm . . . amazing
(B) bombast . . . devious
(C) innuendo . . . devious
(D) subterfuge . . . honest
(E) bombast . . . honest

35. He remained _______ and in full command of the situation in spite of the hysteria and panic all around him.
(A) impervious
(B) imperturbable
(C) imperious
(D) frenetic
(E) lackadaisical

Each question below consists of a related pair of words or phrases, followed by five lettered pairs of words or phrases. Select the lettered pair that best expresses a relationship similar to that expressed in the original pair.

Example:

YAWN : BOREDOM :: (A) dream : sleep (B) anger : madness (C) smile : amusement (D) face : expression (E) impatience : rebellion

Ⓐ Ⓑ ● Ⓓ Ⓔ

36. QUARRY : MARBLE ::
(A) metal : silver
(B) ore : gold
(C) oysters : pearls
(D) prey : rabbit
(E) necklace : diamonds

37. CONSTITUTION : PREAMBLE ::
(A) play : overture
(B) legislation : introduction
(C) opera : intermezzo
(D) book : preface
(E) play : epilogue

38. DESERT : OASIS ::
(A) work : rest
(B) sparse : lavish
(C) arid : mirage
(D) highway : motel
(E) weak : powerful

39. NOISOME : FETID ::
(A) propitious : plentiful
(B) sanguine : sanguinary
(C) erudite : ignorant
(D) blatant : loud
(E) arrogant : sycophantic

40. CHAIRMAN : GAVEL ::
(A) conductor : baton
(B) violinist : bow
(C) orator : dais
(D) teacher : blackboard
(E) pianist : keys

41. EMACIATED : GAUNT ::
(A) liberated : gigantic
(B) dwarfed : tall
(C) overweight : haggard
(D) eaten : distinguished
(E) obese : corpulent

42. BLIND : SIGHT ::
(A) diabetic : sugar
(B) indigent : tact
(C) amnesiac : memory
(D) benevolent : charity
(E) misanthropic : hate

43. JOY : ECSTASY ::
(A) rain : drought
(B) breeze : hurricane
(C) river : creek
(D) deluge : downpour
(E) jazz : opera

44. GAMBIT : CHESS ::
(A) pass : bridge
(B) jump : checkers
(C) fumble : football
(D) queen : pawn
(E) finesse : bridge

45. COD : SCROD ::
(A) gosling : goose
(B) tiger : cat
(C) hen : pullet
(D) puppy : dog
(E) shad : roe

S T O P

IF YOU FINISH BEFORE TIME IS CALLED, YOU MAY CHECK YOUR WORK ON THIS SECTION ONLY. DO NOT WORK ON ANY OTHER SECTION IN THE TEST.

SECTION 2 MATHEMATICAL ABILITY

25 QUESTIONS - 30 MINUTES

In this section, solve each problem, using any available space on the page for scratchwork. Then decide which is the best of the choices given and blacken the corresponding space on the answer sheet.

The following information is for your reference in solving some of the problems.

Circle of radius r: Area = πr^2; Circumference = $2\pi r$
The number of degrees of arc in a circle is 360.
The measure in degrees of a straight angle is 180.

Definitions of symbols:

= is equal to	≤ is less than or equal to
≠ is unequal to	≥ is greater than or equal to
< is less than	∥ is parallel to
> is greater than	⊥ is perpendicular to

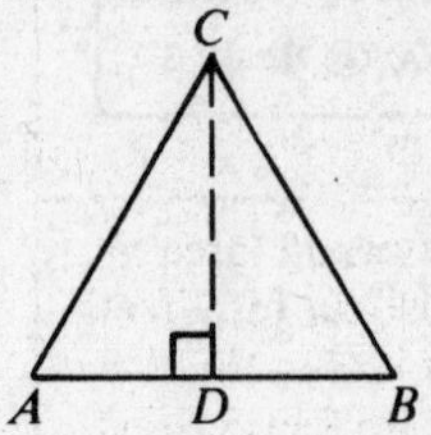

Triangle: The sum of the measures in degrees of the angles of a triangle is 180.
If $\angle CDA$ is a right angle, then

(1) area of $\triangle ABC = \frac{AB \times CD}{2}$

(2) $AC^2 = AD^2 + DC^2$

Note: Figures that accompany problems in this test are intended to provide information useful in solving the problems. They are drawn as accurately as possible EXCEPT when it is stated in a specific problem that its figure is not drawn to scale. All figures lie in a plane unless otherwise indicated. All numbers used are real numbers.

1. If 87955936 is divided by 284, the quotient is equal to exactly
(A) 390701
(B) 309702
(C) 309703
(D) 309704
(E) 309705

2. If $a = -6$, then $(a + 3)(a - 3)$ equals
(A) -27
(B) 12
(C) 27
(D) 45
(E) 81

3. If $x = 3$, and $y = \frac{1}{6}$ then the value of x in terms of y is
(A) $\frac{1}{2}y$
(B) $2y$
(C) $3\frac{1}{6}y$
(D) $6\frac{1}{3}y$
(E) $18y$

4. What is the value of $x - 2$, when $3x - 6 = 1$?
(A) $\frac{1}{3}$
(B) $\frac{2}{3}$
(C) $\frac{5}{3}$
(D) 4
(E) 5

5. B and C are points on straight line AD, on which $AB = BC = CD$. What percent of AC is AD?
(A) 1.5%
(B) 50%
(C) $66\frac{2}{3}$%
(D) $133\frac{1}{3}$%
(E) 150%

6. A mixture of 17 parts of A, 3 parts of B and 4 parts of C weighs 72 ounces. How many ounces of substance B are in this mixture?
(A) 3.4
(B) 9
(C) 12
(D) 17
(E) 51

Questions 7–8 refer to the following.

A ship covered the following distances (in nautical miles) on a recent Caribbean cruise.

New York — Curacao	1,770
Curacao — St. Maarten	630
St. Maarten — St. Thomas	100
St. Thomas — New York	1,500

7. What percent of the total distance covered on this cruise was covered from New York to Curacao?
(A) 17.7%
(B) 22%
(C) $33\frac{1}{3}$%
(D) $44\frac{1}{4}$%
(E) 50%

8. The distance from St. Maarten to St. Thomas may be expressed as 160 kilometers. Approximately how many nautical miles equal 1 kilometer?
(A) 0.625
(B) 0.89
(C) 0.9
(D) 1.14
(E) 1.25

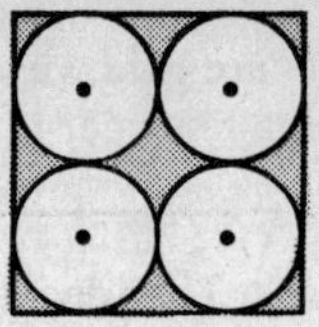

9. In the figure above, the area of each circle is 9π. What is the area of the shaded part?
(A) $36 - 9\pi$
(B) $36 - 36\pi$
(C) $36\pi - 144$
(D) $144 - 9\pi$
(E) $144 - 36\pi$

10. After purchasing a square sheet of plywood (area = 169 square feet), I found that I must cut off 2 feet from one of its edges in order to fit it onto the side of a wall. What is the area (in square feet) of this wall?
(A) 117
(B) 121
(C) 143
(D) 165
(E) 167

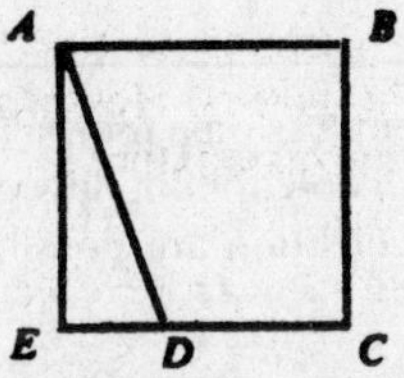

11. In the figure above, the area of square $ABCE = x^2$ and $DC = y$. What is the area of triangle AED?
(A) $\frac{x^2 - xy}{2}$
(B) $\frac{y(x - y)}{2}$
(C) $x^2 - xy$
(D) $y^2 - xy$
(E) $xy - x^2$

12. If n and p are both odd numbers, which of the following numbers *must* be an even number?
(A) $n + p$
(B) np
(C) $np + 2$
(D) $n + p + 1$
(E) $2n + p$

13. For the State Football Championship game, of the 30,000 tickets ¼ were sold at \$3.00, ⅓ were sold at \$2.50, and the rest were sold at \$1.25. How many were sold at \$1.25?
(A) 5,000
(B) 7,500
(C) 10,000
(D) 12,500
(E) 25,000

14. The average weight of 3 boys is 53 pounds. No one of these boys weighs less than 51 pounds. What is the maximum weight of any one boy? (in pounds)
(A) 53
(B) 55
(C) 57
(D) 59
(E) 61

15. If $a < b$ and $c < d$, then
(A) $c + a < d + b$
(B) $c + a > d + b$
(C) $c = b$
(D) $a = b$
(E) $ac = bd$

16. Mark can row downstream on the Saco River for five miles in two hours. It takes him 4 hours to return to his original destination. What is Mark's average rate of speed (in miles per hour) for the round trip?
(A) ⅚
(B) 1⅔
(C) 1⅞
(D) 3
(E) 3¾

17. Michael takes 20 minutes to cover a newspaper delivery route which Philip does on bicycle in ¼ of an hour. The average time (expressed in hours) to do this task is
(A) 1/7
(B) 2/7
(C) 7/24
(D) 1/12
(E) 7/12

18. Point $A(1,0)$ is drawn to $B(5,0)$ and is joined to $C(3,4)$. Which of the following is true?
(A) $CA = CB$
(B) $AB = BC$
(C) $AC = AB$
(D) $AC > BC$
(E) $AC < BC$

Questions 19–22 refer to the following table.

Payroll of the ABC Manufacturing Company

Rank	Number of Employees	Wages Paid (in thousands)
Office Managers	5	$ 110
Factory Supervisors	25	$ 350
Assembly Workers	500	$ 600
TOTALS	530	$1060

19. The wages paid to managers make up what percent (to the nearest percent) of the total payroll?
(A) 5
(B) 9
(C) 10
(D) 11
(E) 42

20. The average wage for all employees is
(A) $1,200
(B) $2,000
(C) $18,000
(D) $20,000
(E) $22,000

21. The ratio of the average salary of a manager to the average salary of an assembly worker is
(A) 3 to 55
(B) 11 to 60
(C) 11 to 6
(D) 60 to 11
(E) 55 to 3

22. If 4 of the managers are paid wages of x dollars each, then the remaining manager is paid
(A) $22,000
(B) $(110,000 − x)
(C) $(110,000 − x)/4
(D) $(110,000 − 4$x$)
(E) $(22,000 − x)

23. The base of an isosceles triangle is 16 units and each side is 10 units. What is the area of this triangle in square units?
(A) 24
(B) 36
(C) 48
(D) 50
(E) 100

24. If the area of rectangle *R* with altitude 4 feet is equal to the area of square *S*, which has a perimeter of 24 feet, then the perimeter of rectangle *R* equals
(A) 9 feet
(B) 16 feet
(C) 24 feet
(D) 26 feet
(E) 36 feet

25. There are 20 members on a football squad. In electing a captain and a co-captain, how many different outcomes of the election are possible?
(A) 20
(B) 39
(C) 190
(D) 380
(E) 760

S T O P

IF YOU FINISH BEFORE TIME IS CALLED, YOU MAY CHECK YOUR WORK ON THIS SECTION ONLY. DO NOT WORK ON ANY OTHER SECTION IN THE TEST.

SECTION 3 TEST OF STANDARD WRITTEN ENGLISH

50 QUESTIONS - 30 MINUTES

The questions in this section measure skills that are important to writing well. In particular, they test your ability to recognize and use language that is clear, effective, and correct according to the requirements of standard written English, the kind of English found in most college textbooks.

Directions: The following sentences contain problems in grammar, usage, diction (choice of words), and idiom.
Some sentences are correct.
No sentence contains more than one error.

You will find that the error, if there is one, is underlined and lettered. Assume that elements of the sentence that are not underlined are correct and cannot be changed. In choosing answers, follow the requirements of standard written English.

If there is an error, select the one underlined part that must be changed to make the sentence correct and blacken the corresponding space on your answer sheet.

If there is no error, blacken answer space Ⓔ.

EXAMPLE:

The region has a climate so severe that plants
A
growing there rarely had been more than twelve
B C
inches high. No error
D E

SAMPLE ANSWER

Ⓐ Ⓑ ● Ⓓ Ⓔ

1. His salary is lower than a caretaker. No error
A B C D E

2. Not one of the children has ever sang in public
A B C
before. No error
D E

3. The book must be old, for it's cover is torn.
A B C D
No error
E

4. Neither the players nor the trainer were in the locker
A B C
room when the thief broke in. No error
D E

5. We have come to the conclusion that we can end hos-
A
tilities in that area of the world by providing food
B
to both sides, bringing the opposing forces to the
negotiation table, and to guarantee financial aid to
C D
both sides once peace is established. No error
E

6. I should like you and him to attend my birthday party
A B C
on Saturday afternoon. No error
D E

7. Neither you nor I can realize the affect his
A B
behavior will have on his chances for promotion.
C D
No error
E

8. In order to conserve valuable gasoline, motorists
A
had ought to check their speedometers while driv-
B C
ing along the highways; it is very easy to exceed
D
55 miles per hour while driving on open roads.
No error
E

9. He awaited final instructions about giving the reward
A B
to whoever had found the lost dog. No error
C D E

10. The ancient concept where the sun revolves around
A B C
the earth was contradicted by Copernicus.
D
No error
E

11. Reggie Jackson's (A) three home runs in the final game of the 1977 World Series proved (B) that few (C) players in the game deserved more respect than him. (D) No error (E)

12. The apparently (A) obvious (B) solution to the problem was overlooked (C) by many (D) of the contestants. No error (E)

13. The Senate Committee investigating (A) the Watergate affair was (B) surprised (C) to hear that conversations in the Oval Office is (D) being recorded on tape by order of President Nixon. No error (E)

14. Without a (A) moment (B) delay, the computer began (C) to print out the answer (D) to the problem. No error (E)

15. I cannot (A) hardly believe your story; it (B) seems (C) so (D) incredible. No error (E)

16. Writing a beautiful sonnet (A) is as much (B) an achievement as to finish (C) a 400-page (D) novel. No error (E)

17. Today's (A) program on public television, consisting of (B) a play and a telecast (C) of a live performance from (D) the stage of the Metropolitan Opera House. No error (E)

18. Of (A) the two candidates for this government position, John is the most (B) qualified (C) because of (D) his experience in the field. No error (E)

19. Diligence and honesty, as well as (A) being intelligent, (B) are (C) qualities which I look for when (D) I interview applicants. No error (E)

20. Dashing (A) across (B) the campus, John tried to (C) overtake the instructor who had forgotten (D) his briefcase. No error (E)

21. Jane, Mary, and Richard (A) play musical instruments, but (B) only (C) the latter (D) has real talent. No error (E)

22. Rebecca Jones is (A) one of the nurses' (B) aides who have (C) been so (D) helpful to the staff. No error (E)

23. After (A) he had drank (B) the warm milk, he began to feel (C) sleepy and decided (D) to go to bed. No error (E)

24. The colorful (A) dressed (B) natives and the strange architecture made (C) the traveler realize (D) he was now in a new world. No error (E)

25. After conferring (A) with John Brown and Mary Smith, I have decided that she (B) is better (C) qualified than him (D) to edit the school newspaper. No error (E)

Directions: In each of the following sentences, some part or all of the sentence is underlined. Below each sentence you will find five ways of phrasing the underlined part. Select the answer that produces the most effective sentence, one that is clear and exact, without awkwardness or ambiguity, and blacken the corresponding space on your answer sheet. In choosing answers, follow the requirements of standard written English. Choose the answer that best expresses the meaning of the original sentence.

Answer (A) is always the same as the underlined part. Choose answer (A) if you think the original sentence needs no revision.

EXAMPLE:

Laura Ingalls Wilder published her first book and she was sixty-five years old then.

(A) and she was sixty-five years old then
(B) when she was sixty-five years old
(C) at age sixty-five years old
(D) upon reaching sixty-five years
(E) at the time when she was sixty-five

SAMPLE ANSWER

Ⓐ ● Ⓒ Ⓓ Ⓔ

26. If he was to decide to go to college, I, for one, would recommend that he plan to go to Yale.
(A) If he was to decide to go to college,
(B) If he were to decide to go to college,
(C) Had he decided to go to college,
(D) In the event that he decides to go to college,
(E) Supposing he was to decide to go to college,

27. Except for you and I, everyone brought a present to the party.
(A) Except for you and I, everyone brought
(B) With the exception of you and I, everyone brought
(C) Except for you and I, everyone had brought
(D) Except for you and me, everyone brought
(E) Except for you and me, everyone had brought

28. When one reads the poetry of the 17th-century, you find a striking contrast between the philosophy of the Cavalier poets such as Suckling and the attitude of the Metaphysical poets such as Donne.
(A) When one reads the poetry of the 17th-century, you find
(B) When you read the poetry of the 17th-century, one finds
(C) When one reads the poetry of the 17th-century, he finds
(D) If one reads the poetry of the 17th-century, you find
(E) As you read the poetry of the 17th-century, one finds

29. Because of his broken hip, John Jones has not and possibly never will be able to run the mile again.
(A) has not and possibly never will be able to run
(B) has not and possibly will never be able to run
(C) has not been and possibly never would be able to run
(D) has not and possibly never would be able to run
(E) has not been able to run and possibly never will be able to run

30. Had I realized how close I was to failing, I would not have gone to the party.
(A) Had I realized how close
(B) If I would have realized how close
(C) Had I had realized how close
(D) When I realized how close
(E) If I realized how close

31. Having finished the marathon in record-breaking time, the city awarded him its Citizen's Outstanding Performance Medal.
(A) the city awarded him its Citizen's Outstanding Performance Medal.
(B) the city awarded the Citizen's Outstanding Performance Medal to him.
(C) he was awarded the Citizen's Outstanding Performance Medal by the city.
(D) the Citizen's Outstanding Performance Medal was awarded to him.
(E) he was awarded by the city with the Citizen's Outstanding Performance Medal.

32. The football team's winning it's first game of the season excited the student body.
(A) The football team's winning it's first game of the season
(B) The football team having won it's first game of the season
(C) The football team's having won it's first game of the season
(D) The football team's winning its first game of the season
(E) The football team winning it's first game of the season

33. Anyone interested in the use of computers can learn much if you have access to a Radio Shack TRS-80 or a Pet Microcomputer.
(A) if you have access to
(B) if he has access to
(C) if access is available to
(D) by access to
(E) from access to

34. No student had ought to be put into a situation where he has to choose between his loyalty to his friends and his duty to the class.
(A) No student had ought to be put into a situation where
(B) No student had ought to be put into a situation in which
(C) No student should be put into a situation where
(D) No student ought to be put into a situation in which
(E) No student ought to be put into a situation where

35. Being a realist, I could not accept his statement that supernatural beings had caused the disturbance.
(A) Being a realist,
(B) Since I am a realist,
(C) Being that I am a realist,
(D) Being as I am a realist,
(E) Realist that I am,

36. The reason I came late to class today is because the bus broke down.
(A) I came late to class today is because
(B) why I came late to class today is because
(C) I was late to school today is because
(D) that I was late to school today is because
(E) I came late to class today is that

37. I have to make dinner, wash the dishes, do my homework, and then relaxing.
(A) to make dinner, wash the dishes, do my homework and then relaxing.
(B) to make dinner, washing the dishes, do my homework, and then relax.
(C) to make dinner, wash the dishes, doing my homework and then relaxing.
(D) to prepare dinner, wash the dishes, do my homework, and then relaxing.
(E) to make dinner, wash the dishes, do my homework and then relax.

38. The climax occurs when he asks who's in the closet.
(A) occurs when he asks who's
(B) is when he asks whose
(C) occurs when he asks whose
(D) is when he asks who'se
(E) occurs when he asked who's

39. The grocer hadn't hardly any of those kind of canned goods.
(A) hadn't hardly any of those kind
(B) hadn't hardly any of those kinds
(C) had hardly any of those kind
(D) had hardly any of those kinds
(E) had scarcely any of those kind

40. Having stole the money, the police searched the thief.
(A) Having stole the money, the police searched the thief.
(B) Having stolen the money, the thief was searched by the police.
(C) Having stolen the money, the police searched the thief.
(D) Having stole the money, the thief was searched by the police.
(E) Being that he stole the money, the police searched the thief.

Note: The remaining questions are like those at the beginning of the section.

Directions: For each sentence in which you find an error, select the one underlined part that must be changed to make the sentence correct and blacken the corresonding space on your answer sheet.

If there is no error, blacken answer space Ⓔ.

EXAMPLE:

The region has a climate so severe that (A) plants growing there (B) rarely had been (C) more than twelve inches high (D). No error (E)

SAMPLE ANSWER

Ⓐ Ⓑ ● Ⓓ Ⓔ

41. Either (A) of the two boys who sing (B) in the chorus are (C) capable of taking the job of understudy (D) to the star. No error (E)

42. By the time (A) I reached (B) the bank, the doors were closed; (C) I could not cash (D) my check. No error (E)

43. If (A) anyone calls (B) while we are (C) in conference, tell them (D) I will return the call after the meeting. No error (E)

44. The principal (A) of equal justice for all (B) is one (C) of the cornerstones of our democratic (D) way of life. No error (E)

45. Except (A) for you (B) and me (C), no one else knows (D) about this plan. No error (E)

46. Neither the earthquake or (A) the subsequent (B) fire was (C) able (D) to destroy the spirit of the city dwellers. No error (E)

47. My plane was grounded (A) for thirty minutes, which (B) made me miss (C) my (D) connecting flight at Atlanta. No error (E)

48. I might of passed (A) if I had done (B) my homework, but (C) I had to go (D) to work. No error (E)

49. The customer (A) had scarcely (B) enough (C) money to pay the clerk at (D) the checkout counter. No error (E)

50. I have lived (A) in this house for three years, but I now live (B) in a different (C) neighborhood (D). No error (E)

S T O P

IF YOU FINISH BEFORE TIME IS CALLED, YOU MAY CHECK YOUR WORK ON THIS SECTION ONLY. DO NOT WORK ON ANY OTHER SECTION IN THE TEST.

SECTION 4 VERBAL ABILITY

40 QUESTIONS - 30 MINUTES

For each question in this section, choose the best answer and blacken the corresponding space on the answer sheet.

Each question below consists of a word in capital letters, followed by five lettered words or phrases. Choose the word or phrase that is most nearly opposite in meaning to the word in capital letters. Since some of the questions require you to distinguish fine shades of meaning, consider all the choices before deciding which is best.

Example:

GOOD: (A) sour (B) bad (C) red (D) hot (E) ugly

Ⓐ ● Ⓒ Ⓓ Ⓔ

1. SATED:
   (A) famished
   (B) finished
   (C) finicky
   (D) fitting
   (E) fortunate

2. SELFISHNESS:
   (A) antipathy
   (B) chauvinism
   (C) altruism
   (D) algorism
   (E) empathy

3. ASTUTE:
   (A) emaciated
   (B) fatuous
   (C) enigmatic
   (D) elaborate
   (E) propitious

4. INTENTIONAL:
   (A) final
   (B) unwitting
   (C) suggestive
   (D) aggressive
   (E) stoical

5. PROPER:
   (A) unseemly
   (B) insecure
   (C) exact
   (D) out of focus
   (E) unstable

6. GLOOMY:
   (A) late
   (B) basic
   (C) avid
   (D) lively
   (E) jocund

7. NAIVE:
   (A) devoted
   (B) urbane
   (C) ingenious
   (D) hostile
   (E) foreign

8. TRITE:
   (A) sad
   (B) redundant
   (C) benign
   (D) original
   (E) resilient

9. ATROPHY:
   (A) prize
   (B) incite
   (C) flourish
   (D) refuse
   (E) maintain

10. COMPLAISANT:
    (A) distasteful
    (B) egotistical
    (C) alone
    (D) ugly
    (E) recalcitrant

Each sentence below has one or two blanks, each blank indicating that something has been omitted. Beneath the sentence are five lettered words or sets of words. Choose the word or set of words that best fits the meaning of the sentence as a whole.

Example:

Although its publicity has been ----, the film itself is intelligent, well-acted, handsomely produced, and altogether ----.

(A) tasteless..respectable (B) extensive..moderate (C) sophisticated..amateur (D) risqué..crude (E) perfect..spectacular

● Ⓑ Ⓒ Ⓓ Ⓔ

11. The rebels sought to overcome the _______ of strength of the government forces by engaging in guerilla tactics.
    (A) accumulation
    (B) lack
    (C) predilection
    (D) preponderance
    (E) majority

12. Even though your argument is ______. I still would like to have more ______.
(A) specious . . . analysis
(B) fallacious . . . evidence
(C) plausible . . . proof
(D) dubious . . . example
(E) cogent . . . time

13. Much of the clown's success may be attributed to the ______ mien he presents in the midst of the general ______ of the circus.
(A) giddy . . . sobriety
(B) lugubrious . . . hilarity
(C) gaudy . . . clamor
(D) joyful . . . hysteria
(E) frenetic . . . excitement

14. Many members avoided the company of the ______ old gentleman because his constant chatter about ______ matters bored them.
(A) erudite . . . important
(B) senile . . . obscure
(C) venerable . . . historical
(D) garrulous . . . trivial
(E) gregarious . . . insignificant

15. For such a ______ crime, no punishment can be too ______.
(A) viscous . . . painful
(B) ingenuous . . . surprising
(C) cross . . . severe
(D) vindicable . . . excessive
(E) reprehensible . . . severe

Each question below consists of a related pair of words or phrases, followed by five lettered pairs of words or phrases. Select the lettered pair that best expresses a relationship similar to that expressed in the original pair.
Example:
YAWN : BOREDOM :: (A) dream : sleep
(B) anger : madness (C) smile : amusement
(D) face : expression (E) impatience : rebellion
Ⓐ Ⓑ ● Ⓓ Ⓔ

16. GEOLOGY : SCIENCE ::
(A) stimulus : goad
(B) rocks : data
(C) fashion : style
(D) fir : tree
(E) practical : theoretical

17. FUNDS : EMBEZZLED ::
(A) loot : safe
(B) writings: plagiarized
(C) ransom : kidnapping
(D) money : deposited
(E) truth : exaggerated

18. PIPE LINE : REFINERY ::
(A) oil : gas
(B) knife : cutlery
(C) artery : blood
(D) tube : rubber
(E) vein : heart

19. TACITURNITY : LACONIC ::
(A) improvisation : unrehearsed
(B) verbosity : pithy
(C) silence : golden
(D) ballet : chaotic
(E) vacation : leisurely

20. EMACIATED : OBESITY ::
(A) penurious : wealth
(B) calorific : heat
(C) affluent : wealth
(D) honest : truth
(E) penurious : knowledge

21. PLAY : ACTS ::
(A) opera : arias
(B) novel : chapters
(C) poem : verses
(D) essay : paragraphs
(E) link : chains

22. ELEVATOR : SHAFT ::
(A) electricity : outlet
(B) water : conduit
(C) shell : rifle
(D) shell : cannon
(E) soda : bottle

23. UNCOUTH : GRACELESSNESS ::
(A) petulant : agreement
(B) avaricious : greed
(C) indifference : concern
(D) meretricious : honest
(E) reticent : brazenness

24. TOURNIQUET : BLEEDING ::
(A) resuscitation : drowning
(B) fatigue : sunshine
(C) red light : traffic
(D) panacea : coughing
(E) microbe : disease

25. PARSIMONY : FRUGALITY ::
(A) agony : pain
(B) steam : water
(C) anger : wrath
(D) warmth : flame
(E) pleasure : gloom

Each passage below is followed by questions based on its content. Answer all questions following a passage on the basis of what is stated or implied in that passage.

There was a stumbling rush for the cover of fortification proper; and there the last possible line of defense was established instinctively and in a moment. Officers and men dropped on their knees behind the low bank of earth and continued an irregular deliberate fire, each discharging his piece as fast as he could load and aim. The garrison was not sufficient to form a continuous rank along even this single front, and on such portions of the works as were protected by the ditch, the soldiers were scattered almost as sparsely as sentinels. Nothing saved the place from being carried by an assault except the fact that the assailants were unprovided with scaling ladders. The adventurous fellows who had flanked the palisade rushed to the gate, and gave entrance to a torrent of tall, lank men in butternut or dirty gray clothing, their bronzed faces flushed with the excitement of supposed victory, and their yells of exultation drowning for a minute the sharp outcries of the wounded, and the rattle of the musketry. But the human billow was met by such a fatal discharge that it could not come over the rampart. The foremost dead fell across it, and the mass reeled backward. Unfortunately for the attack, the exterior slope was full of small knolls and gullies, besides being cumbered with rude shanties, of four or five feet in height made of bits of board, and shelter tents, which had served as the quarters of the garrison. Behind these covers, scores if not hundreds sought refuge and could not be induced to leave them for a second charge.

26. Which statement is true of the final defense line?
- (A) It was organized by the officers.
- (B) It was abandoned by the cowardly.
- (C) It was guarded by sentinels.
- (D) It was discharged by the officers.
- (E) It was arranged without command.

27. The reader can infer from this passage that
- (A) there are many guards in the garrison
- (B) sentinels fight alongside regular soldiers
- (C) sentinels are placed widely apart
- (D) sentinels are usually officers
- (E) guards and sentinels form a continuous rank

28. Which statement is most probably true of the men who flanked the palisade?
- (A) They were warmly dressed.
- (B) They followed up an initial advantage.
- (C) They were supported by the sentinels.
- (D) They were scattered widely in the attack.
- (E) They drowned in the ditches.

29. The attackers were most hindered in their attack by
- (A) the terrain
- (B) their wounded
- (C) lack of ammunition
- (D) their presupposed victory
- (E) their cowardly leaders

30. Many of the attackers
- (A) surrendered to the garrison
- (B) were hampered by inferior training
- (C) refused to make another assault
- (D) were overwhelmed by superior numbers
- (E) were scattered sparsely around the fortification

When I arrived at a few minutes before seven, I found the platoon assembled and ready to go. It was cold, and in the ranks the men were shivering and dancing up and down to keep warm. I was only the second-in-command of the platoon at that time, under instruction from a senior lieutenant, who was the platoon commander. Punctually at seven I said to Broadhurst, "March off, Sergeant. To the aerodrome, at the double."

Broadhurst asked doubtfully whether we hadn't better wait for the platoon commander, who had not turned up. Unversed in the ways of the army, I said, "No, march off. The men are cold." We doubled off.

Three or four minutes later the platoon commander, who had about fourteen years of service, appeared. He was in a towering rage. He rushed straight up to Broadhurst and asked him furiously what he meant by marching off without permission.

Broadhurst said, "I'm sorry, sir."

My feet wouldn't move. My mouth wouldn't open. I made a gigantic effort and said, "Sir —" But the lieutenant had given Broadhurst a final blast and taken command. I looked at Broadhurst, but he was busy. After parade I apologized to him, but I never explained to the lieutenant. Broadhurst told me the incident wasn't worth worrying about.

Does this seem a small crime to remember all one's life? I don't think so. It was the worst thing that I ever did in the army, because in it I showed cowardice and disloyalty. The only excuses I could find for myself were that it happened quickly and that I was very young. It had a result, though. I had been frightened of the lieutenant, frightened of being reprimanded, frightened of failure even in the smallest endeavor. I discovered now that being ashamed of yourself is worse than any fear. Duty, orders, loyalty, obedience — all things boiled down to one simple idea: whatever the consequences, a man must act so that he can live with himself.

31. From the passage the reader can most safely conclude that the narrator never explained the truth to the platoon commander because
- (A) army custom forbade his doing so
- (B) he felt that the incident was unimportant
- (C) he hoped that Broadhurst would do it for him
- (D) he feared the reaction of the platoon commander
- (E) the episode had happened too quickly

32. Which statement can most safely be made about the platoon commander?
(A) He refused to give the narrator any instructions.
(B) He gave command of the troops to Broadhurst.
(C) He lacked experience as a soldier.
(D) He expected his subordinates to execute orders on their own.
(E) He observed army customs to the letter.

33. From the passage the reader can most safely conclude that Broadhurst was
(A) familiar with army routine
(B) proud of the platoon
(C) friendly with the platoon commander
(D) higher in rank than the platoon commander
(E) inconsiderate of the narrator

34. In looking back on the episode which he describes in the first five paragraphs, the narrator concludes that the episode
(A) proved that he had been improperly trained in army discipline
(B) caused him to "lose face" with the troops
(C) helped him to gain self-understanding
(D) showed his greater power over the troops
(E) encouraged him to obey orders without question

35. It is most probable that *before* this episode took place
(A) plans had been made for the troops to march
(B) the narrator had not been told the time of departure
(C) plans had been made for Broadhurst to stay behind
(D) the narrator had given several other incorrect orders
(E) the platoon commander had relied greatly upon the narrator

One potential hideaway that until now has been completely ignored is De Witt Isle, off the coast of Tasmania.* Its assets are 4,000 acres of jagged rocks, tangled undergrowth and trees twisted and bent by battering winds. Settlers have avoided it like the plague, but bandicoots (ratlike marsupials native to Australia), wallabies, eagles, and penguins think De Witt is just fine.

So does Jane Cooper, 18, a pert Melbourne high school graduate, who emigrated there with three goats, several chickens and a number of cats brought along to stand guard against the bandicoots. Why De Witt? "I was frightened at the way life is lived today in our cities," says Jane. "I wanted to be alone, to have some time to think and find out about myself."

*a large island southeast of Australia

She has been left alone to write poems and start work on a book, play the flute and dive for crayfish and abalone to supplement her diet of cereal, canned goods and home-grown vegetables.

Her solitary life isn't easy. "Dear God," she wrote in her diary on her first day ashore, "how I love this island . . . but I don't know if I'm strong enough to stay. I found myself walking along the rocks crying." Then her mood began to change: "I'm going to conquer this island. I won't let it beat me . . . I had been feeling so sorry for myself that I was unaware of the beauty that surrounded me." Recently she sent a letter home via the local fishermen. She wrote: "I feel very old and very young. I'm more determined than ever to stay here." She has made a friend — a penguin named Mickey Mouse — and she is beginning to feel that "this is my world and my life . . . it is so beautiful here I can't imagine Melbourne any longer." To millions of city-bound Australians, Jane has become something of a heroine.

36. Which phrase best expresses the main ideas of this passage?
(A) life in Melbourne
(B) planning a wildlife station
(C) the pesky bandicoots
(D) true grit
(E) the island menagerie

37. Which statement can best be made on the basis of the passage?
(A) Jane never doubted her ability to survive.
(B) The Isle's weather proved quite an obstacle.
(C) The local fishermen trust Jane.
(D) Jane is basically rather unemotional.
(E) Jane's days on the Isle are very full ones.

38. From this passage we can most safely conclude that Jane is
(A) a religious fanatic
(B) a fancy cook
(C) a careless camper
(D) a strong swimmer
(E) a compulsive gambler

39. By the end of the passage we realize that Jane
(A) is still rather lonesome
(B) has apparently won the battle
(C) will probably go home
(D) is deceiving herself
(E) greatly needs encouragement

40. In the *first* paragraph, which word is used in an ironic sense?
(A) "hideaway"
(B) "coast"
(C) "assets"
(D) "winds"
(E) "bandicoots"

S T O P

IF YOU FINISH BEFORE TIME IS CALLED, YOU MAY CHECK YOUR WORK ON THIS SECTION ONLY. DO NOT WORK ON ANY OTHER SECTION IN THE TEST.

SECTION 5 MATH ABILITY

35 QUESTIONS - 30 MINUTES

In this section, solve each problem, using any available space on the page for scratchwork. Then decide which is the best of the choices given and blacken the corresponding space on the answer sheet.

The following information is for your reference in solving some of the problems.

Circle of radius r: Area $= \pi r^2$; Circumference $= 2\pi r$
The number of degrees of arc in a circle is 360.
The measure in degrees of a straight angle is 180.

Definitions of symbols:

$=$ is equal to
$\neq$ is unequal to
$<$ is less than
$>$ is greater than
$\leqq$ is less than or equal to
$\geqq$ is greater than or equal to
$\|$ is parallel to
$\perp$ is perpendicular to

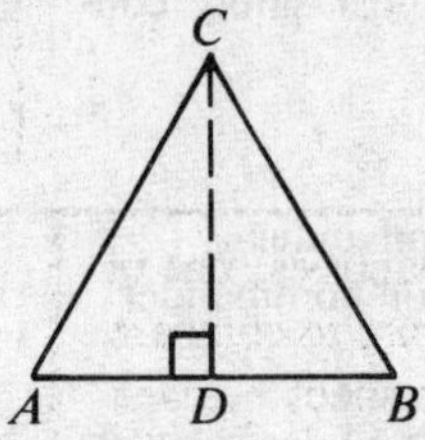

Triangle: The sum of the measures in degrees of the angles of a triangle is 180.

If $\angle CDA$ is a right angle, then

(1) area of $\triangle ABC = \frac{AB \times CD}{2}$

(2) $AC^2 = AD^2 + DC^2$

Note: Figures that accompany problems in this test are intended to provide information useful in solving the problems. They are drawn as accurately as possible EXCEPT when it is stated in a specific problem that its figure is not drawn to scale. All figures lie in a plane unless otherwise indicated. All numbers used are real numbers.

1. Out of a group of 80 applicants for a civil service examination, 20 persons failed to appear for the first part of this test. What percent of the total applicants did appear for this part of the test?
(A) 4
(B) 16
(C) 25
(D) 60
(E) 75

2. A class has b number of boys and g number of girls. The ratio of girls to boys is
(A) bg
(B) $\frac{b}{g}$
(C) $\frac{b}{b+g}$
(D) $\frac{g}{b}$
(E) $\frac{g}{b+g}$

3. What is the value of $\sqrt{\frac{1}{16} + \frac{1}{9}}$?
(A) $\frac{1}{7}$
(B) $\frac{2}{7}$
(C) $\frac{25}{144}$
(D) $\frac{5}{12}$
(E) $\frac{7}{12}$

4. The fraction $\frac{a+b}{b}$ equals
(A) a
(B) $\frac{a}{b} + b$
(C) $\frac{a}{b} + 1$
(D) $a^2 + 1$
(E) $\frac{a+b}{a}$

5. How many kilometers are there in 12 miles? (1 kilometer = $\frac{5}{8}$ of a mile)
(A) 7.2
(B) 7.5
(C) 19.2
(D) 19.5
(E) 22.3

6. Having installed a new gas tank in my car, it took the attendant $1\frac{3}{4}$ minutes to completely fill my gas tank. What part of the tank would be filled if he had stopped after a full minute?
(A) $\frac{2}{7}$
(B) $\frac{3}{7}$
(C) $\frac{4}{7}$
(D) $\frac{3}{4}$
(E) $\frac{5}{7}$

7. If I can purchase 2 items for c ¢, at the same rate, how many items will I receive for x ¢?

(A) $\frac{c}{2x}$

(B) $\frac{2c}{x}$

(C) $\frac{cx}{2}$

(D) $2cx$

(E) $\frac{2x}{c}$

<u>Questions 8–27</u> each consist of two quantities, one in Column A and one in Column B. You are to compare the two quantities and on the answer sheet blacken space

A if the quantity in Column A is greater;
B if the quantity in Column B is greater;
C if the two quantities are equal;
D If the relationship cannot be determined from the information given.

AN E RESPONSE WILL NOT BE SCORED.

EXAMPLES

	Column A	Column B	Answers
E1.	2×6	$2 + 6$	● Ⓑ Ⓒ Ⓓ Ⓔ
E2.	$180 - x$	y	Ⓐ Ⓑ ● Ⓓ Ⓔ
E3.	$p - q$	$q - p$	Ⓐ Ⓑ Ⓒ ● Ⓔ

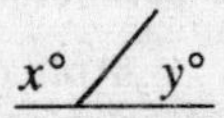

Notes:
1. In certain questions, information concerning one or both of the quantities to be compared is centered above the two columns.
2. In a given question, a symbol that appears in both columns represents the same thing in Column A as it does in Column B.
3. Letters such as x, n, and k stand for real numbers.

	Column A		Column B
		$(a)(b) = 0$	
8.	a		b
		$xy = 5$, $x^2 + y^2 = 7$	
9.	$(x + y)^2$		17
10.	$\sqrt{0.3}$		0.49
11.	one-half of one percent		0.05
		$x = 2,\ y = 3,\ z = 7$	
12.	$x(y + z)$		$xz + y$

Column A | Column B

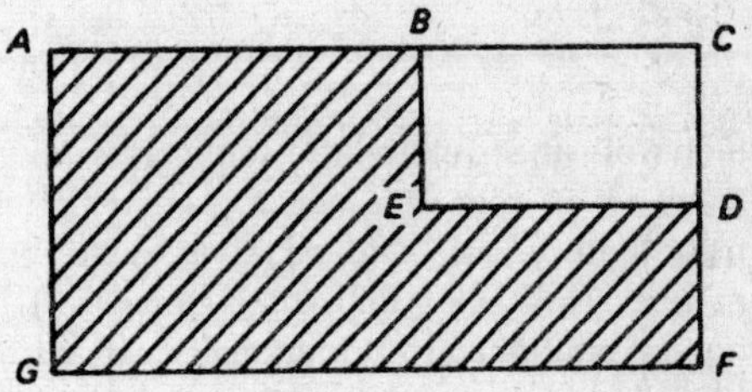

AGFC and *BEDC* are rectangles

	Column A	Column B
13.	Perimeter of *AGFC*	Perimeter of shaded region

	Column A		Column B
		$x > 0$	
14.	$2x^2$		$(2x)^2$

Basketball Player	Points Scored in Game
A	20
B	8
C	22
D	14
E	2

15. Average score of all players | Points scored by player *D*

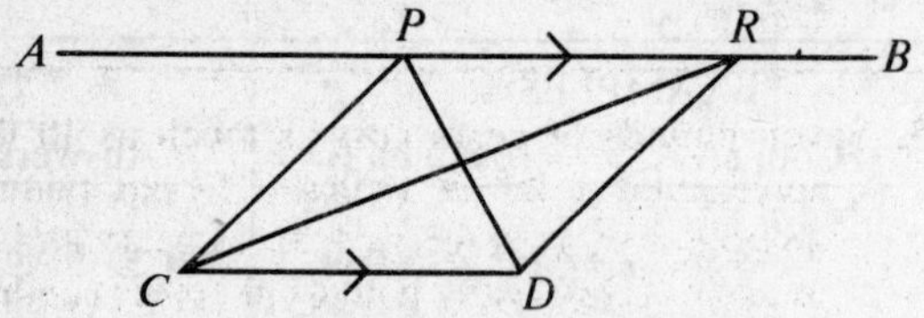

16. *AB* and *CD* are parallel lines

Area of triangle *PCD* | Area of triangle *RCD*

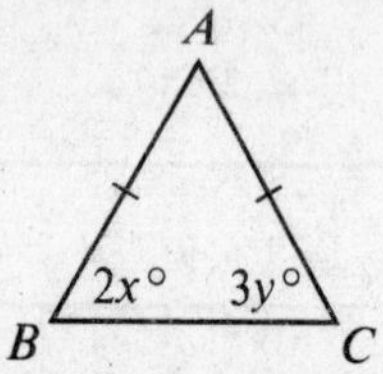

17. x | y

$5x = 729$

$3y = 729$

18. x | y

	Column A		Column B
		In 19 years from now Mark will be three times as old as Philip is now. Michael is 3 years younger than Mark.	
19.	Michael's age now		Philip's age now
		$1 < a < 5$ $1 < b < 5$	
20.	$b - a$		$a - b$
21.	$3\frac{1}{2}\%$		$^{35}/_{1000}$
		$\frac{1}{A} = \frac{1}{x} + \frac{1}{y}$	
22.	A		$\frac{xy}{x + y}$
		$x < -1$	
23.	x		$\frac{1}{x}$
		$a > 1$ and $b > 1$	
24.	$\frac{a^2 - b^2}{(a - b)^2}$		$\frac{a + b}{a - b}$
25.	120		$\sqrt{1440}$
26.	3 feet, 5 inches		1.5 yards
		$\frac{x}{y} = 1$	
27.	x^2		y^2

Solve each of the remaining problems in this section using any available space for scratchwork. Then decide which is the best of the choices given and blacken the corresponding space on the answer sheet.

28. Which of the following statements is always true? I. A root of a negative number may be a real number. II. The positive square root of a number is smaller than the number. III. A binomial multiplied by a binomial yields a trinomial.

(A) only I
(B) only II
(C) only III
(D) II and III
(E) all are true

29. The radius of the pool in Shelter Rock Park is twice the radius of the pool in Martin's backyard. The area of the pool in the park is how many times the area of Martin's pool?

(A) ¼
(B) ½
(C) 2
(D) 4
(E) 8

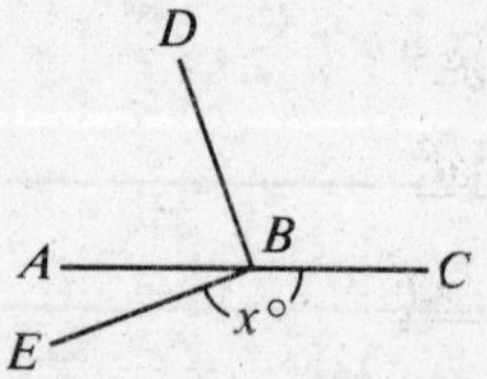

30. In the figure above, $BD \perp BE$ and $\angle DBA = 70$. What is the value of x?

(A) 20
(B) 110
(C) 120
(D) 160
(E) 290

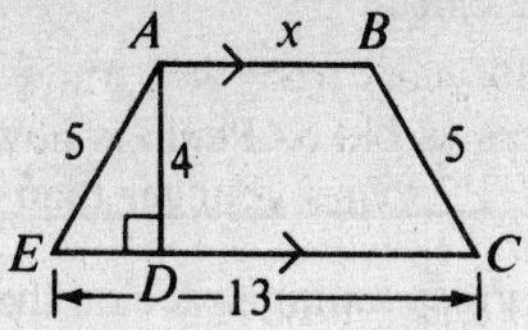

31. In the figure above, what is the value of x?
(A) 5
(B) 6
(C) 7
(D) 8
(E) 9

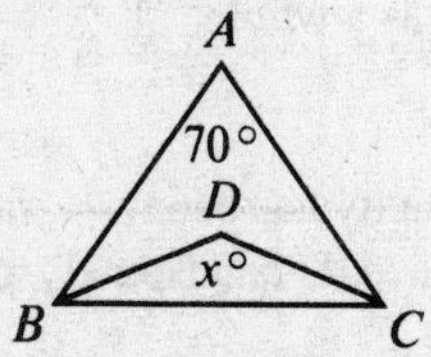

32. In isosceles triangle ABC above, BD and CD are the bisectors of the base angles. The vertex angle has a measure of 70°. Find the value of x.
(A) 35
(B) 70
(C) 100
(D) 125
(E) 155

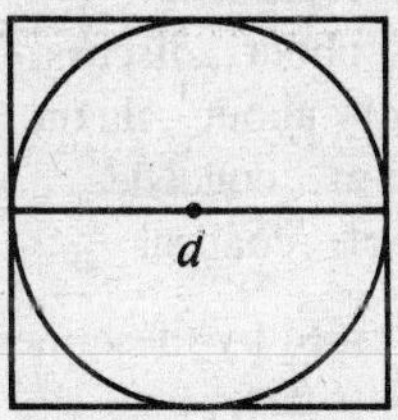

33. In the figure above, how much paper (in terms of π) is wasted if the largest possible circle with a diameter of d is cut out of the square?
(A) $d - \pi d^2$
(B) $\frac{d^2\pi}{4}$
(C) $\frac{\pi d^2}{4} - d^2$
(D) $\frac{4d^2 - \pi d^2}{4}$
(E) $\frac{16d^2 - \pi d^2}{4}$

34. Using formulas
Circumference $= 2\pi r$
Area $= \pi r^2$
where r = radius, find the area of a circle whose circumference is x.
(A) $\frac{x^2}{4\pi^2}$
(B) $\frac{x^2}{4\pi}$
(C) $\frac{x^2}{4}$
(D) πx^2
(E) πx

35. Seven pounds of pears cost as much as 10 lbs. of apples and 1 lb. of oranges. Seven pounds of oranges cost as much as 1 lb. of pears and 2 lbs. of apples. How many pounds of apples can be purchased for the amount of money required to purchase 12 lbs. of pears?
(A) 8
(B) 14
(C) 16
(D) 18
(E) 24

S T O P

IF YOU FINISH BEFORE TIME IS CALLED, YOU MAY CHECK YOUR WORK ON THIS SECTION ONLY. DO NOT WORK ON ANY OTHER SECTION IN THE TEST.

SECTION 6 VERBAL ABILITY

45 QUESTIONS - 30 MINUTES

For each question in this section, choose the best answer and blacken the corresponding space on the answer sheet.

Each question below consists of a word in capital letters, followed by five lettered words or phrases. Choose the word or phrase that is most nearly opposite in meaning to the word in capital letters. Since some of the questions require you to distinguish fine shades of meaning, consider all the choices before deciding which is best.

Example:

GOOD: (A) sour (B) bad (C) red (D) hot (E) ugly

Ⓐ ● Ⓒ Ⓓ Ⓔ

1. FLOURISH: (A) darken (B) decay (C) beckon (D) endure (E) invest
2. PROFUSION: (A) rejection (B) hobby (C) order (D) scarcity (E) separation
3. ENHANCE: (A) retreat (B) hate (C) detract (D) pursue (E) put to sleep
4. DIN: (A) hunger (B) stillness (C) holy place (D) caress (E) pleasure
5. HEFTY: (A) slight (B) liquid (C) feminine (D) pointed (E) undisturbed
6. SAGACIOUS: (A) upright (B) foolish (C) cheerful (D) deliberate (E) concerned
7. PURIFICATION: (A) resolution (B) desire (C) pollution (D) discrimination (E) agitation
8. ENACT: (A) improvise (B) defy (C) repeal (D) suffer (E) externalize
9. DISMANTLE: (A) kindle (B) reassure (C) equip (D) impede (E) suppose
10. SURREPTITIOUS: (A) sugary (B) monotonous (C) rash (D) aboveboard (E) healthy
11. MITIGATE: (A) disarm (B) worsen (C) predict (D) open (E) take back
12. CLEMENCY: (A) stupidity (B) filth (C) lack of money (D) lack of mercy (E) slowness
13. CORPULENT: (A) alive (B) spiritual (C) young (D) untidy (E) slender
14. VIRULENT: (A) effeminate (B) peaceful (C) colorless (D) malodorous (E) innocuous
15. METICULOUS: (A) careless (B) shapeless (C) transient (D) intrepid (E) dogmatic

Each sentence below has one or two blanks, each blank indicating that something has been omitted. Beneath the sentence are five lettered words or sets of words. Choose the word or set of words that best fits the meaning of the sentence as a whole.

Example:

Although its publicity has been ----, the film itself is intelligent, well-acted, handsomely produced, and altogether ----.

(A) tasteless..respectable (B) extensive..moderate (C) sophisticated..amateur (D) risqué..crude (E) perfect..spectacular

● Ⓑ Ⓒ Ⓓ Ⓔ

16. She was ---- her accomplishments and unwilling to ---- them before her friends.
(A) excited by..parade
(B) immodest about..discuss
(C) deprecatory about..flaunt
(D) uncertain of..concede
(E) unaware of..conceal

17. We were distressed by these inexplicable ---- from his generally ---- taste.
(A) departures..execrable
(B) lapses..flawless
(C) divergences..questionable
(D) results..efficacious
(E) variations..unusual

18. Because they did not accept his basic ----, they were ---- by his argument.
(A) assumption..convinced
(B) motivation..confused
(C) bias..impressed
(D) premise..unconvinced
(E) supposition..justified

19. Despite their ---- of Twain's *Huckleberry Finn* for its stereotyped portrait of the slave Jim, even the novel's ---- agreed it was a masterpiece of American prose.
(A) admiration..critics
(B) denunciation..supporters
(C) criticism..detractors
(D) defense..censors
(E) praise..advocates

20. Pain is the body's early warning system: loss of ---- in the extremities leaves a person ---- injuring himself unwittingly.
(A) agony. . incapable of
(B) sensation . . vulnerable to
(C) consciousness . . desirous of
(D) feeling . . habituated to
(E) movement . . prone to

Each passage below is followed by questions based on its content. Answer all questions following a passage on the basis of what is stated or implied in that passage.

Studies serve for delight, for ornament, and for ability. Their chief use for delight is in privateness and retiring; for ornament, is in discourse; and for ability, is in the judgment and disposition of business. For expert men can execute, and perhaps judge of particulars, one by one; but the general counsels, and the plots and marshaling of affairs, come best from those that are learned. To spend too much time in studies is sloth; to use them too much for ornament is affectation; to make judgment wholly by their rules, is the humor of a scholar. They perfect nature, and are perfected by experience; for natural abilities are like natural plants, that need pruning by study; and studies themselves do give forth directions too much at large, except they be bounded by experience. Crafty men contemn studies, simple men admire them, and wise men use them; for they teach not their own use; but that is a wisdom without them, and above them, won by observation. Read not to contradict and confute; nor to believe and take for granted; nor to find talk and discourse; but to weigh and consider. Some books are to be tasted, others to be swallowed, and some few to be chewed and digested; that is, some books are to be read only in parts; others to be read, but not curiously; and some few to be read wholly, and with diligence and attention. Some books also may be read by deputy, and extracts made of them by others; but that would be only in the less important arguments, and the meaner sort of books; else distilled books are like common distilled waters, flashy things.

21. By "Studies," the author means
(A) homework (B) reading (C) experience
(D) experiment (E) natural observation

22. Reading for pleasure is best done
(A) aloud (B) by tasting (C) alone
(D) by chewing and digesting (E) by deputy

23. "Sloth" in line 8 means
(A) an animal (B) laziness (C) showing off
(D) wisdom (E) diligence

24. Which of the following books may we infer should be "chewed and digested"?
(A) *Poetry of the 19th Century*
(B) *The Case of the Missing Corpse*
(C) *Medical Practice and Jurisprudence*
(D) *The Small Family Cook Book*
(E) *Baseball Stars of the Seventies*

25. We can infer from the passage that the author would be likely to disapprove of
I. abridged books
II. plot summaries
III. scholarly monographs
(A) I only
(B) II only
(C) III only
(D) I and II
(E) II and III

There are exceptions to the rule of male insects being smaller than the females, and some of these exceptions are intelligible. Size and strength would be an advantage to the males which fight for the possession of the females, and in these cases, as with the stag-beetle (Lucanus), the males are larger than the females. There are, however, other beetles which are not known to fight together, of which the males exceed the females in size, and the meaning of this fact is not known, but in some of these cases, as with the huge Dynastes and Megasoma, we can at least see that there would be no necessity for the males to be smaller than the females, in order to be matured before them, for these beetles are not short-lived, and there would be ample time for the pairing of the sexes.

26. According to the author,
(A) male insects are always smaller than females
(B) in a given species nature provides differences between sexes to insure successful reproduction
(C) size and strength protect females from other females
(D) longevity is characteristic of the Dynastes and Megasoma
(E) in the stag-beetle females are larger than the males

27. Where male beetles are smaller than female beetles, it is because
(A) they have to fight for their mates
(B) they are more intelligent
(C) they are ephemeral creatures
(D) there is ample time for mating
(E) they do not have to fight for their mates

28. The paragraph preceding this one probably
(A) discusses a generalization about the size of insects
(B) develops the idea that male insects do not live long after maturity
(C) discusses male and female beetles
(D) emphasizes that beetles are belligerent animals
(E) discusses insect behavior

29. The male Lucanus is particularly
(A) adaptable
(B) strong
(C) large
(D) belligerent
(E) stagnant

30. We may infer from the name "stag-beetles" that in all probability
(A) stag-beetles are mammals
(B) stag-beetles are combative
(C) stag-beetles have appendages that resemble horns
(D) stag-beetles are herbivorous by nature
(E) all stag-beetles are males

Select the word or set of words that best completes each of the following sentences.

31. Because he saw no point to the task assigned him, he worked at it in a very ---- way.
(A) systematic (B) dutiful (C) diligent (D) rigid (E) perfunctory

32. The herb Chinese parsley or cilantro is an ---- taste; Westerners who originally dislike it eventually come to ---- its flavor in Oriental foods.
(A) offensive . . enjoy (B) acquired . . welcome (C) idiosyncratic . . dislike (D) omnipresent . . accept (E) evident . . savor

33. Despite the ---- of the materials with which he worked, many of Tiffany's glass masterpieces have survived for over seventy years.
(A) beauty (B) translucence (C) abundance (D) majesty (E) fragility

34. Although similar to mice, voles may be ---- mice by the shortness of their tails.
(A) distinguished from (B) classified with (C) reminiscent of (D) categorized as (E) enumerated with

35. Although the doctor's words were ----, the patient's family still hoped for a ---- of his disease.
(A) discouraging . . resurgence
(B) disheartening . . remission
(C) inaudible . . report
(D) reassuring . . medication
(E) authoritative . . diagnosis

Each question below consists of a related pair of words or phrases, followed by five lettered pairs of words or phrases. Select the lettered pair that best expresses a relationship similar to that expressed in the original pair.

Example:

YAWN : BOREDOM :: (A) dream : sleep
(B) anger : madness (C) smile : amusement
(D) face : expression (E) impatience : rebellion

Ⓐ Ⓑ ● Ⓓ Ⓔ

36. BREEZE : TORNADO ::
(A) ice : floe
(B) trickle : gusher
(C) conflagration : flame
(D) river : stream
(E) eruption : volcano

37. MAID : CRONE ::
(A) prince : sceptre
(B) butler : apron
(C) youth : graybeard
(D) mother : infant
(E) nurse : midwife

38. ARCHIVES : RECORDS ::
(A) catalog : drawers
(B) aviary : birds
(C) thread : spindle
(D) photographs : albums
(E) pedestal : statue

39. ENVELOP : SURROUND ::
(A) efface : confront
(B) house : dislodge
(C) loiter : linger
(D) distend : struggle
(E) ascend : acquiesce

40. INDIFFERENT : CONCERN ::
(A) intrepid : bravery
(B) arrogant : modesty
(C) unbigoted : tolerance
(D) unusual : emotion
(E) variable : change

41. DILETTANTE : DABBLE ::
(A) coquette : flirt
(B) gymnast : exercise
(C) soldier : drill
(D) embezzler : steal
(E) benefactor : donate

42. BARREN : FECUND ::
(A) dry : parched
(B) naked : sinful
(C) hackneyed : original
(D) incessant : continuous
(E) impetuous : rash

43. SLANDER : DEFAMATORY ::
(A) fraud : notorious
(B) tenet : devotional
(C) panegyric : laudatory
(D) edict : temporary
(E) exhortation : cautionary

44. SLOUGH : SKIN ::
(A) shed : hair
(B) polish : teeth
(C) shade : eyes
(D) tear : ligaments
(E) remove : tonsils

45. HYPERBOLIC : EXAGGERATED ::
(A) metabolic : restrained
(B) choleric : fitful
(C) capricious : whimsical
(D) idiomatic : impersonal
(E) melancholy : bemused

S T O P

IF YOU FINISH BEFORE TIME IS CALLED, YOU MAY CHECK YOUR WORK ON THIS SECTION ONLY. DO NOT WORK ON ANY OTHER SECTION IN THE TEST.

ANSWER KEY

Note: The answers to the math sections are keyed to the corresponding review areas in Chapter 11. The numbers in parentheses after each answer refer to topics as listed below. (Note that to review for number 16, Quantitative Comparison, study Chapter 10.)

1. Fundamental Operations
2. Algebraic Operations
3. Using Algebra
4. Roots and Radicals
5. Inequalities
6. Fractions
7. Decimals
8. Percent
9. Averages
10. Motion
11. Ratio and Proportion
12. Mixtures and Solutions
13. Work
14. Coordinate Geometry
15. Geometry
16. Quantitative Comparison
17. Data Interpretation

SECTION 1 VERBAL ABILITY

1. **C**	10. **D**	19. **C**	28. **A**	37. **D**
2. **D**	11. **B**	20. **D**	29. **E**	38. **B**
3. **A**	12. **E**	21. **A**	30. **D**	39. **D**
4. **E**	13. **A**	22. **B**	31. **D**	40. **A**
5. **E**	14. **B**	23. **D**	32. **B**	41. **E**
6. **B**	15. **E**	24. **C**	33. **E**	42. **C**
7. **C**	16. **D**	25. **E**	34. **D**	43. **B**
8. **D**	17. **B**	26. **B**	35. **B**	44. **E**
9. **A**	18. **E**	27. **C**	36. **C**	45. **C**

SECTION 2 MATH ABILITY

1. **D (1)**	6. **B (6)**	11. **A (15)**	16. **B (10)**	21. **E (11) (17)**
2. **C (2)**	7. **D (8) (17)**	12. **A (1) (3)**	17. **C (13)**	22. **D (3) (17)**
3. **E (2)**	8. **A (11) (17)**	13. **D (6)**	18. **A (14)**	23. **C (15)**
4. **A (2)**	9. **E (15)**	14. **C (9)**	19. **C (8) (17)**	24. **D (15)**
5. **E (8)**	10. **C (15)**	15. **A (5)**	20. **B (9) (17)**	25. **D (1)**

SECTION 3 TEST OF STANDARD WRITTEN ENGLISH

1. **D**	11. **D**	21. **D**	31. **C**	41. **C**
2. **C**	12. **E**	22. **E**	32. **D**	42. **C**
3. **C**	13. **D**	23. **B**	33. **B**	43. **D**
4. **C**	14. **B**	24. **A**	34. **D**	44. **A**
5. **D**	15. **A**	25. **D**	35. **A**	45. **E**
6. **E**	16. **C**	26. **B**	36. **E**	46. **A**
7. **B**	17. **B**	27. **D**	37. **E**	47. **B**
8. **B**	18. **B**	28. **C**	38. **A**	48. **A**
9. **E**	19. **B**	29. **E**	39. **D**	49. **E**
10. **B**	20. **E**	30. **A**	40. **B**	50. **A**

SECTION 4 VERBAL ABILITY

1. **A**	9. **C**	17. **B**	25. **A**	33. **A**
2. **C**	10. **E**	18. **E**	26. **E**	34. **C**
3. **B**	11. **D**	19. **A**	27. **C**	35. **A**
4. **B**	12. **C**	20. **A**	28. **B**	36. **D**
5. **A**	13. **B**	21. **B**	29. **A**	37. **E**
6. **E**	14. **D**	22. **B**	30. **C**	38. **D**
7. **B**	15. **E**	23. **B**	31. **D**	39. **B**
8. **D**	16. **D**	24. **C**	32. **E**	40. **C**

SECTION 5 MATH ABILITY

1. **E** (8)	8. **D** (2) (16)	15. **B** (9) (16)	22. **C** (2) (16)	29. **D** (15)
2. **D** (11)	9. **C** (2) (16)	16. **C** (15) (16)	23. **B** (6) (16)	30. **D** (15)
3. **D** (4)	10. **A** (4) (7) (16)	17. **A** (15) (16)	24. **C** (2) (16)	31. **C** (15)
4. **C** (2) (6)	11. **B** (7) (8) (16)	18. **B** (2) (16)	25. **A** (4) (16)	32. **D** (15)
5. **C** (11)	12. **A** (2) (16)	19. **D** (3) (16)	26. **B** (1) (16)	33. **D** (15)
6. **C** (6) (11)	13. **C** (15) (16)	20. **D** (2) (16)	27. **C** (4) (16)	34. **B** (2)
7. **E** (3) (11)	14. **B** (4) (16)	21. **C** (6) (8) (16)	28. **A** (2) (4)	35. **D** (3)

SECTION 6 VERBAL ABILITY

1. **B**	10. **D**	19. **C**	28. **A**	37. **C**
2. **D**	11. **B**	20. **B**	29. **D**	38. **B**
3. **C**	12. **D**	21. **B**	30. **C**	39. **C**
4. **B**	13. **E**	22. **C**	31. **E**	40. **B**
5. **A**	14. **E**	23. **B**	32. **B**	41. **A**
6. **B**	15. **A**	24. **C**	33. **E**	42. **C**
7. **C**	16. **C**	25. **D**	34. **A**	43. **C**
8. **C**	17. **B**	26. **D**	35. **B**	44. **A**
9. **C**	18. **D**	27. **C**	36. **B**	45. **C**

SELF-EVALUATION

Now that you have completed the Diagnostic Test, evaluate your performance. Identify your strengths and weaknesses, and then plan a practical study program based on what you have discovered. Follow these steps to evaluate your work on the Diagnostic Test. (Note: You'll find the charts referred to in steps 1–5 on the next three pages.)

STEP 1 Use the Answer Key to check your answers for each section.

STEP 2 For each section, count the number of correct and incorrect answers (remember that you don't count omitted answers), and enter the numbers on the appropriate lines of the chart "Obtaining Your Raw Score." Then do the indicated calculations to get your Raw Verbal Score, your Raw TSWE Score, and your Raw Math Score.

STEP 3 Consult the chart "Evaluate Your Performance" to see how well you did.

STEP 4 To pinpoint the specific areas in which you need to improve, circle the numbers of the questions that you either left blank or got wrong on the "Identify Your Weaknesses" charts. This will tell you where to concentrate your efforts to get the most out of your study time. The chart for the math sections gives you page references for review and practice by skill areas. The charts for the verbal and TSWE sections refer you to the appropriate chapters to study for each question type.

STEP 5 Do the review and practice indicated on the charts wherever you had a concentration of circles.

Remember that in addition to evaluating your scores, you should read all of the answer explanations for questions you answered incorrectly, questions you omitted, and questions you answered correctly but found difficult. Reviewing the answer explanations will help you understand concepts and strategies, and may point out shortcuts.

OBTAINING YOUR RAW SCORE

Verbal

Section 1 ______ − 1/4 (______) = ______ (A)
number correct — number incorrect

Section 4 ______ − 1/4 (______) = ______ (B)
number correct — number incorrect

Section 6 ______ − 1/4 (______) = ______ (C)
number correct — number incorrect

Raw Verbal Score = (A) + (B) + (C) = ______

TSWE

Section 3 ______ − 1/4 (______) = Raw TSWE Score = ______
number correct — number incorrect

Math

Section 2 ______ − 1/4 (______) = ______ (D)
number correct — number incorrect

Section 5 (1-7, 28-35) ______ − 1/4 (______) = ______ (E)
number correct — number incorrect

Section 5 (8-27) ______ − 1/3 (______) = ______ (F)
number correct — number incorrect

Raw Math Score = (D) + (E) + (F) = ______

EVALUATE YOUR PERFORMANCE

	Verbal	TSWE	Math
Excellent	111-130	45-50	52-60
Very Good	91-110	39-44	45-51
Good	81-90	34-38	36-44
Average	61-80	25-33	30-35
Below Average	40-60	15-24	25-29
Unsatisfactory	below 40	below 15	below 25

IDENTIFY YOUR WEAKNESSES
Verbal

Question Type	Question Numbers			Chapter to Study
	Section 1	Section 4	Section 6	
Antonym	1, 2, 3, 4, 5, 6, 7, 8, 9, 10, 11, 12, 13, 14, 15	1, 2, 3, 4, 5, 6, 7, 8, 9, 10	1, 2, 3, 4, 5, 6, 7, 8, 9, 10, 11, 12, 13, 14, 15	Chapter 4
Analogy	36, 37, 38, 39, 40, 41, 42, 43, 44, 45	16, 17, 18, 19, 20, 21, 22, 23, 24, 25	36, 37, 38, 39, 40, 41, 42, 43, 44, 45	Chapter 5
Sentence Completion	16, 17, 18, 19, 20, 31, 32, 33, 34, 35	11, 12, 13, 14, 15	16, 17, 18, 19, 20, 31, 32, 33, 34, 35	Chapter 6
Reading Comprehension	21, 22, 23, 24, 25, 26, 27, 28, 29, 30	26, 27, 28, 29, 30, 31, 32, 33, 34, 35, 36, 37, 38, 39, 40	21, 22, 23, 24, 25, 26, 27, 28, 29, 30	Chapter 7

TSWE

Question Type	Question Numbers	Chapter to Study
Usage	1, 2, 3, 4, 5, 6, 7, 8, 9, 10, 11, 12, 13, 14, 15, 16, 17, 18, 19, 20, 21, 22, 23, 24, 25, 41, 42, 43, 44, 45, 46, 47, 48, 49, 50	Chapter 12
Sentence Correction	26, 27, 28, 29, 30, 31, 32, 33, 34, 35, 36, 37, 38, 39, 40	Chapter 12

Math

Skill Area	Question Numbers		Pages to Study
	Section 2	Section 5	
Fundamental Operations	1, 12, 25	26	300–302
Algebraic Operations	2, 3, 4	4, 8, 9, 12, 14, 18, 20, 22, 24, 28, 34	302–308
Using Algebra	12, 22	7, 19, 35	308–316
Fractions	6, 13	4, 6, 21, 23	316–329
Decimals and Percents	5, 7, 19	1, 10, 11, 21	329–334
Verbal Problems	14, 16, 17, 20	15	335–352
Ratio and Proportion	8, 21	2, 5, 6, 7	340–346
Geometry	9, 10, 11, 23, 24	13, 16, 17, 29, 30, 31, 32, 33	355–368
Coordinate Geometry	18		352–355
Inequalities	15		309–311; 315–316
Quantitative Comparison		8, 9, 10, 11, 12, 13, 14, 15, 16, 17, 18, 19, 20, 21, 22, 23, 24, 25, 26, 27	279–299
Roots and Radicals		3, 10, 14, 25, 27, 28	306–307; 312–313

ANSWER EXPLANATIONS

SECTION 1 VERBAL ABILITY

1. *Pulchritude* (beauty) is the opposite of (C) *ugliness*.

2. The opposite of *wary* (cautious) is (D) *careless*.

3. The opposite of *defunct* (no longer existing) is (A) *extant* (existing).

4. *Succinct* (brief) is the opposite of (E) *verbose* (excessively wordy).

5. *Innocuous* (harmless) is the opposite of (E) *harmful*.

6. *Resolute* (determined, steadfast) is the opposite of (B) *vacillating* (wavering, showing indecision).

7. *Sallow* (having a pale, yellowish color) is the opposite of (C) *Ruddy* (having a healthy, reddish color).

8. *Authentic* (genuine) is the opposite of (D) *spurious* (false, sham).

9. *Intrepid* (fearless) is the opposite of (A) *pusillanimous* (lacking courage).

10. *Changeable* is the opposite of (D) *immutable* (not changeable).

11. *Redolent* (having a pleasant odor) is the opposite of (B) *noisome* (having an offensive odor).

12. *Placate* (appease) is the opposite of (E) *exasperate* (irritate).

13. *Aggravate* (worsen) is the opposite of (A) *mitigate* (make less severe).

14. *Hackneyed* (trite, banal) is the opposite of (B) *fresh*.

15. *Laud* (praise) is the opposite of (E) *chide* (scold).

16. (D) One criticism of American life is that we like to show off our wealth so that all may recognize the situation.

17. (B) Strikers would want assurances that no *retaliation* (reprisal) would be taken by management.

18. (E) The use of the word *posterity* (future generations) justifies our use of *age* as a comparison.

19. (C) Any expenditure of public funds must be *justified; lavish* or extravagant ones, definitely should be.

20. (D) Any author who has produced so much can be described as *prolific*.

21. (A) While all the choices are mentioned in the passage, Choice (A) is best because the nature of rumor is treated throughout the three paragraphs.

22. (B) Since rumor has persisted since primitive times even though we have better sources of information at hand, we may say that "rumor is hardy in its growth."

23. (D) The third sentence of the third paragraph supports Choice (D).

24. (C) The second sentence of the second paragraph supports Choice (C).

25. (E) In times of stress, when news is limited, man resorts to rumor for information. He reverts to a primitive form of newscasting.

26. (B) The last paragraph of the passage indicates that at least two interpretations of the book are currently in favor. The second paragraph indicates that there is doubt about Melville's message.

27. (C) *Naive* means innocent. The third paragraph supports the choice of (C).

28. (A) Throughout the passage, the author is pointing out different aspects of *Billy Budd*. The author does not state that it is "well-written" (B) nor does it defend Melville against his critics. Similarly, support for choices (D) and (E) cannot be found in the passage.

29. (E) The phrase "preserving order" in the fourth paragraph indicates that the Captain was responsible for discipline.

30. (D) The statement that Melville "cleverly took pains" (fifth paragraph) supports choice (D).

31. (D) Any failure will make an individual *morose* or bitter. An *unexpected* failure will be even harder to accept.

32. (B) A person with limited time would tend to read an *abridged* (shortened, condensed) version of a *lengthy* novel.

33. (E) The clause beginning with *although* indicates that the *result* was accidental or *fortuitous*.

34. (D) *Subterfuge* means trickery or evasion. An *honest* person would not have to resort to such devices.

35. (B) *Imperturbable* means calm, incapable of being agitated.

36. *Marble* is dug out of a *quarry*; (C) *pearls* are extracted from *oysters*.

37. A *constitution* is introduced by a *preamble*; (D) a *book*, by a *preface*.

38. Vegetation in a *desert* is (B) *sparse* or nonexistent; in an *oasis*, the vegetation is more lush and *lavish*.

39. *Fetid* (decaying) things are *noisome* (foul-smelling); (D) obtrusively *loud* noises are *blatant*.

40. The *chairman* controls the conduct of the meeting by using a *gavel*; (A) a *conductor* uses a *baton* to control his orchestra.

41. *Emaciated* people are lean, haggard, and *gaunt*; (E) *obese* people are *corpulent* (fat).

42. The *blind* have a loss of *sight*; (C) an *amnesiac* suffers a loss of *memory*.

43. *Ecstasy* is extreme *joy*; (B) a *hurricane* is an extremely strong wind or *breeze*.

44. A *gambit* is a move in *chess*; (E) a *finesse* is a maneuver in the game of *bridge*.

45. A *scrod* is a young *cod*; (C) a *pullet* is a young *hen*.

SECTION 2 MATH ABILITY

1. (D) Time does not permit actually doing the long division. Also, bear in mind this is not an arithmetic test. Observe that the dividend ends with a 6 and the divisor ends with a 4. Only one choice ends in a 4.

2. (C) $(a + 3)(a - 3) = a^2 - 9$

Substitute value of a: $(-6)(-6) - 9$

$+36 - 9 = 27.$

The time-consuming method is to substitute the values given and multiply. $(-6 + 3)(-6 - 3)$ which equals $(-3)(-9)$ or $+27$. In incorrect choice (B) algebraic addition is done incorrectly and multiplication is not done. In (C) one fails to observe the signed number properties $(+)(+) = +$ and $(-)(-) = +$ and $(-)(+) = -$ (D) and (E) fail to add algebraically.

3. (E)

$y = \frac{1}{6}$

$6y = 1$

$18y = 3$

Since $x = 3$ (given)

then $x = 18y$ (things equal to the same thing are equal).

4. (A) $3x - 6 = 1$

Then $x - 2 = \frac{1}{3}$ (dividing by 3).

5. (E) $\frac{AD}{AC} = \frac{\text{3 of the equal units}}{\text{2 of the equal units}} = 1\frac{1}{2}$ or 150%.

6. (B) Substance B makes up $\frac{3}{24}$ or $\frac{1}{8}$ of the total mix- $\frac{1}{8}$ of 72 ounces equals 9 ounces.

7. (D) The total distance covered during the cruise was 4,000 nautical miles. The part covered from New York to Curaçao was

$$\frac{1770}{4000} = \frac{44.25}{100} = 44.25\%$$

8. (A) Let x = number of nautical miles in 1 kilometer. Set up a proportion:

$$\frac{\text{nautical mile}}{\text{kilometer}} = \frac{100}{160} = \frac{x}{1} = \frac{5}{8} = 0.625.$$

9. (E) Since the area of each circle $= 9\pi$, then the radii of each circle = 3 and the diameter of each circle = 6. Each side of the square = two diameters or 12. The area of the square = 144. The shaded area constitutes the area of the square minus the area of the 4 circles (4 times 9π).

10. (C)

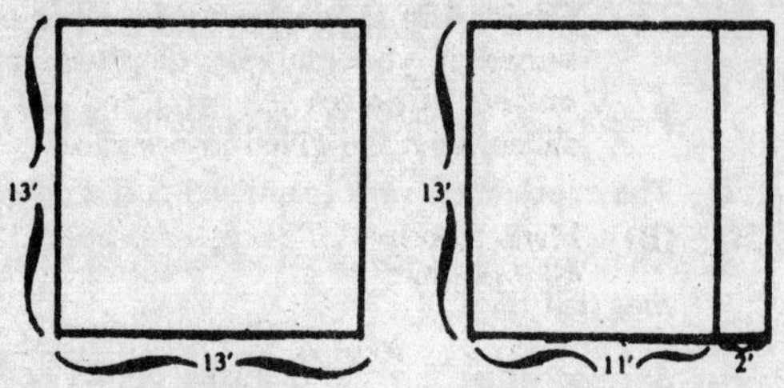

Original size of plywood

Shaded part shows part cut to fit wall.

Area of wall = (13')(11') or 143 square feet.

11. (A) Since the area of the square $= x^2$ each side $= x$. ED, the base of triangle AED $= x - y$ since $EC = x$ and $DC = y$. Area of triangle AED $= \frac{1}{2}(AE)(ED)$ or $\frac{1}{2}(x)(x - y)$ or $\frac{x^2 - xy}{2}$.

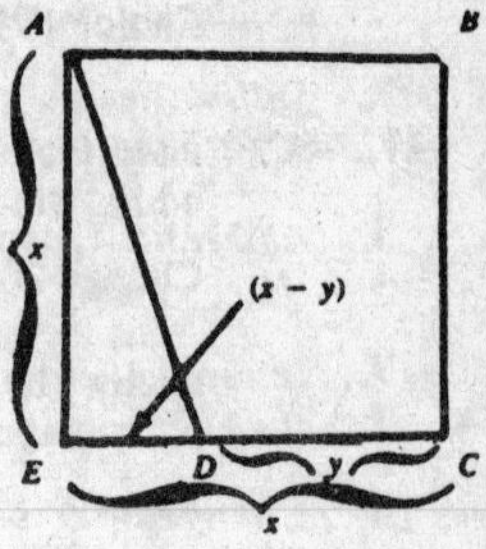

12. (A) Odd numbers are of the form $2x + 1$ where x is an integer. Thus if $n = 2x + 1$ and $p = 2k + 1$, then $n + p = 2x + 1 + 2k + 1 = 2x + 2k + 2$ which is even. Using $n = 3$ and $p = 5$, all the other choices give an odd number. In general, if a problem involves odd or even numbers, try using the fact that odd numbers are of the form $2x + 1$ and even numbers of the form $2y$ where x and y are integers.

13. (D) The time-consuming method would calculate the number sold at \$3 ($^1/_4$ of 30,000) and add the number sold at \$2.50 ($^1/_3$ of 30,000) and subtract that from 30,000. The suggested method first alerts you to the fact that you may disregard the prices in your computation for the problem could have referred to color of tickets. $^1/_4 + {}^1/_3$ or $^7/_{12}$ of the tickets in the upper price ranges were sold, so that the rest or $^5/_{12}$ of 30,000 or 12,500 were sold at \$1.25.

14. (C) Since the average of the 3 persons is 53, the total weight of the 3 is 159. Since we are looking for the maximum weight for one boy, we should assume the minimum weight for the other 2. (A) and (B) fail to do so. Assume two of them each weigh 51 pounds for a total of 102, leaving 57 pounds for the third boy. Choice (D) leaves 100 pounds to be divided between the other 2 which is impossible since each must have a minimum weight of 51 pounds. (E) is incorrect for the same line of reasoning.

15. (A) Recall the basic principles of inequalities. Choice (A) is correct since, if two inequalities are of the same type (both greater or both less), adding the respective sides gives the same type of inequality. Choice (B) is incorrect since inequalities are reversed if you multiply or divide by a negative number. Choices (C), (D) and (E) are not consistent with the given information.

16. (B) Mark traveled 10 miles in 6 hours. Substitute in the formula:

$$\text{Rate} = \frac{\text{Distance (in miles)}}{\text{Time (in hours)}}$$

Choice (C) is incorrect. The rate going may not be averaged with the rate returning since the time spent returning was twice as much as the time spent with the faster rate going downstream. Choice (D) gives the sum of the rates.

17. (C) Note that Michael's time is expressed in minutes while the answer is to be expressed in hours. Change 20 minutes to $\frac{1}{3}$ of an hour. The incorrect choice (E) is the sum of $\frac{1}{3}$ and $\frac{1}{4}\left(\frac{7}{12}\right)$.

$$\text{Average} = \frac{\text{Sum}}{\text{Number of Cases}} \text{ or } \frac{7}{12} \div 2 \text{ or } \frac{7}{24}.$$

Choice (A) adds the denominators and choice (B) adds numerators and denominators. Recall that in adding fractions, numerators are added with common denominators.

18. (A) Observe that an isosceles triangle is formed.

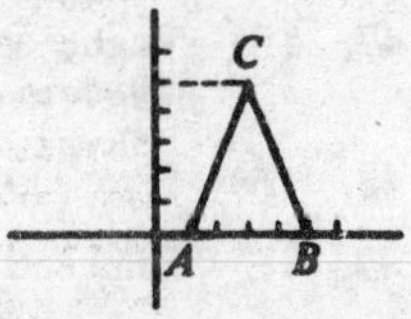

19. (C) The total payroll is \$1,060,000, and the wages paid to managers = \$110,000. Since 110,000/1,060,000 = 11/106 = .10 (rounding to the nearest hundredth) or 10%.

20. (B) The average wage is \$1,060,000 divided by 530 or \$2,000.

21. (E) The average salary of a manager is \$110,000/5 or \$22,000. The average salary of an assembly worker is \$600,000 divided by 500 or \$1,200. So the ratio is 220 to 12 or 55 to 3.

22. (D) All 5 managers together earn \$110,000. Since each one of the four makes x dollars, the remaining manager is paid \$(110,000 − $4x$).

23. (C) Draw altitude AH which bisects BC. Therefore BH equals 8. In right triangle ABH, since AB equals 10 and BH equals 8, then AH equals 6. The area of ABC equals 1/2(base)(altitude) or 1/2(16)(6) or 48 units.

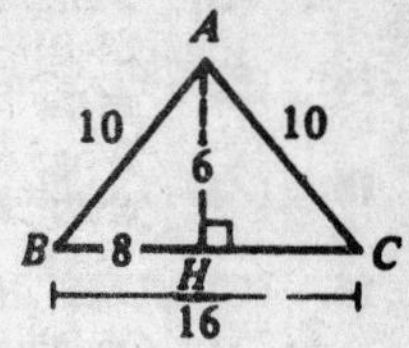

In choice (A) area of triangle ABH is given. In (D) and (E) the formula for area of right triangles was applied. Recall that in right triangles one leg may be regarded as the base and the other leg may be regarded as the altitude. In (E) an additional error was committed by failing to multiply by 1/2.

24. (D) Since the perimeter of the square is 24, each side is 6 and its area is 36. Since the area of R is also 36 and its altitude is 4, its base is 9 (note this is incorrect choice A). The perimeter of R is (2)(4) + (2)(9) or 26 feet. Choice (E) gives the area of R. Choice (B) fails to consider R a rectangle. Choice (C) assumes that the base of R equals the side of the square.

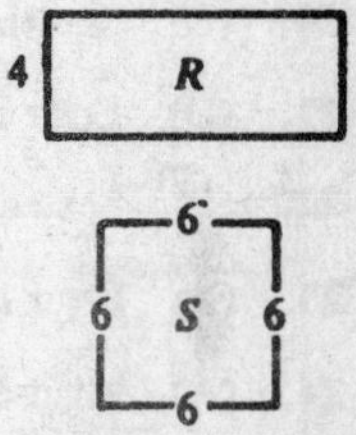

25. (D) Since there are 20 members on the squad any one of these may be elected captain. Since the elected captain may not also be co-captain that leaves any one of the remaining 19 squad members as a possible co-captain. Therefore there are (20)(19) or 380 different outcomes of this election. Choice (A) fails to account for the fact that one election can occur in 20 different ways and is followed by a second election that can occur in 20 − 1 or 19 different ways.

SECTION 3 TEST OF STANDARD WRITTEN ENGLISH

1. (D) Lack of parallel structure. Change *lower than a caretaker* to *lower than that of a caretaker*.

2. (C) Error in tense. Change *has sang* to *has sung*.

3. (C) Error in punctuation. Change *it's* to *its*.

4. (C) Error in agreement. Change *were* to *was*.

5. (D) Lack of parallel structure. Change *to guarantee* to *guaranteeing*.

6. (E) Sentence is correct.

7. (B) Error in diction. Change *affect* to *effect*.

8. (B) Error in diction. Change *had ought* to *ought*.

9. (E) Sentence is correct.

10. (B) Misuse of an adverbial clause when an adjective clause is needed. Change *where* to *that*.

11. (D) Error in case. Change *him* to *he*.

12. (E) Sentence is correct.

13. (D) Errors in tense and agreement. Change *is* to *were*.

14. (B) Error in case. Change *moment* to *moment's*.

15. (A) Double negative. Change *cannot* to *can*.

16. (C) Lack of parallel structure. Change *to finish* to *finishing*.

17. (B) Incomplete sentence. Change *, consisting* to *consists*.

18. (B) Incorrect use of the superlative. Change *most* to *more*.

19. (B) Lack of parallel structure. Change *being intelligent* to *intelligence*.

20. (E) Sentence is correct.

21. (D) Error in diction. Change *latter* to *last*.

22. (E) Sentence is correct.

23. (B) Error in verb. Change *had drank* to *had drunk*.

24. (A) Misuse in adjective instead of adverb. Change *colorful* to *colorfully*.

25. (D) Error in case. Change *him* to *he*.

26. (B) This corrects the misuse of the subjunctive.

27. (D) This corrects the error in the case of the pronoun. Choice E corrects the error in case but introduces an error in tense.

28. (C) The improper use of the pronouns *one* and *you* is corrected in Choice C.

29. (E) The omission of the past participle *been* is corrected in Choice E.

30. (A) The clause is correct..

31. (C) This corrects the dangling participle.

32. (D) Misuse of word. The pronoun is *its*.

33. (B) This corrects the unnecessary switch in the pronouns, *anyone – you*.

34. (D) This corrects the error in tense and in the use of adjective and adverbial clauses.

35. (A) Sentence is correct.

36. (E) *The reason is that* is preferable to *The reason is because*.

37. (E) This corrects the error in parallel structure.

38. (A) Sentence is correct.

39. (D) This corrects the double negative (hadn't hardly) and the misuse of *those* with *kind*.

40. (B) This corrects the dangling participle and the misuse of *stole* for *stolen*.

41. (C) Error in agreement. Change *are* to *is*.

42. (C) Error in sequence of tenses. Change *were closed* to *had been closed*.

43. (D) Error in agreement. Change *them* to *him*.

44. (A) Error in diction. Change *principal* to *principle*.

45. (E) Sentence is correct.

46. (A) Error in diction. Change *or* to *nor*.

47. (B) Vague antecedent of pronoun. Change *minutes, which* to *minutes. This delay*.

48. (A) Error in diction. Change *might of* to *might have*.

49. (E) Sentence is correct.

50. (A) Error in tense. Change *have lived* to *lived*.

SECTION 4 VERBAL ABILITY

1. *Sated* (glutted, surfeited) is the opposite of (A) *famished* (suffering extreme hunger).
2. *Selfishness* (concern only for one's interests or person) is the opposite of (C) *altruism* (unselfish concern for others).
3. *Astute* (keenly perceptive) is the opposite of (B) *fatuous* (silly).
4. *Intentional* (having a purpose) is the opposite of (B) *unwitting* (unintentional).
5. *Proper* (appropriate) is the opposite of (A) *unseemly* (unsuitable for the occasion).
6. *Gloomy* (melancholic) is the opposite of (E) *jocund* (merry).
7. *Naive* (unsophisticated, ingenuous) is the opposite of (B) *urbane* (sophisticated).
8. *Trite* (hackneyed, overworked) is the opposite of (D) *original* (new).
9. The opposite of *atrophy* (waste away) is (C) *flourish*.
10. *Complaisant* (aiming to please) is the opposite of (E) *recalcitrant* (hard to deal with or manage).
11. (D) *Preponderance* means superiority of power or force.
12. (C) A *plausible* argument has an appearance of truth; however, *proof* will remove any questions or doubt.
13. (B) A *lugubrious* (gloomy, mournful to the point of exaggeration) appearance may create laughter because it is so inappropriate in the *hilarity* (gaiety, merriment) of the circus atmosphere.
14. (D) A *garrulous* person is given to excessive chatter. Such wordiness about *trivial* matters would bore his listeners.

15. (E) A *reprehensible* crime is blameworthy: it calls for *severe* punishment.

16. (D) *Geology* is a science: a *fir* is a tree.

17. (B) When *funds* are *embezzled*, they are appropriated fraudulently. Similarly, when *writings* are *plagiarized* (stolen from another) they are appropriated fraudulently.

18. (E) A *pipe line* carries oil to a *refinery:* a *vein* carries blood to the *heart*.

19. (A) *Taciturnity* (the state of not speaking much) is the mark of *laconic* (brief, curt) speakers. *Improvisation* (composing and performing without previous preparation) is resorted to by the *unrehearsed*.

20. (A) *Emaciated* (very thin as a result of malnutrition or disease) is not characteristic of people who suffer from *obesity* (extreme fatness). *Penurious* (extremely poor) people do not have *wealth*.

21. (B) A *play* is divided into *acts;* a *novel*, into *chapters*.

22. (B) An *elevator* moves through a *shaft; water*, through a *conduit* (a pipe or channel for fluids).

23. (B) *Uncouth* (not polished or graceful) individuals display *gracelessness* (lack of beauty or elegance). An *avaricious* person displays *greed*.

24. (C) A *tourniquet* stops *bleeding;* a *red light* stops *traffic*.

25. (A) The relationship is one of degree of intensity. *Parsimony* (stinginess) is extreme thrift. *Frugality* implies a lesser degree of thriftiness. *Agony* and *pain*,similarly, convey the idea of extreme suffering and a lesser degree of suffering.

26. Choice (E) is supported by the statement in the first sentence that the line of defense was established "instinctively."

27. (C) The statement in sentence 3 that "the soldiers were scattered almost as sparsely as sentinels" implies that sentinels are usually spread apart.

28. (B) The fifth sentence supports choice (B).

29. (A) The reference to knolls and gullies in the next to last sentence describes the terrain (a tract of land considered with reference to its physical attributes).

30. (C) The last sentence supports choice (C).

31. (D) In the last paragraph of the passage we are told that the speaker "had been frightened of the lieutenant, frightened of being reprimanded."

32. (E) Choices (A), (B), (C), and (D) are not supported by the passage. The outburst of the platoon commander at Broadhurst indicates that he expected his subordinates not to act "without permission."

33. (A) Broadhurst's questioning of the narrator's order to march indicates that he was familiar with army routine.

34. (C) The last two sentences of the passage support choice (C).

35. (A) The opening sentence supports choice (A).

36. (D) Jane's struggle to exist on the barren island and her determination to live alone are illustrations of "true grit."

37. (E) The third paragraph gives us a picture of a busy program.

38. (D) Since she dives for crayfish and abalone, Jane must be a good swimmer.

39. (B) Jane's love for the island has won over her loneliness. She has apparently "won the battle."

40. (C) Irony may be defined as a figure of speech in which words express a meaning that is the opposite of the intended meaning. Thus, to call jagged rocks, tangled undergrowth and twisted trees "assets" is an ironical description.

SECTION 5 MATH ABILITY

1. (E) 60 out of 80 applicants did appear.

$$\frac{60}{80} = \frac{3}{4} = 75\%$$

Choice (C) does not answer the question. It gives the percent of the total applicants that failed to appear. Choices (A) and (D) result from guessing by dividing or subtracting the numerals given. Choice (B) evidently tries multiplication and then rounds off zeros to change to percent. This simple problem illustrates the danger of wild guessing.

2. (D) Ratio is a comparison of two quantities by division in correct order. Unlike the correct choice (D), in (B) the ratio of boys to girls is given. Choice (C) gives the part of the number of boys in the entire class and (E) gives the part of the number of girls in the entire class. This question does not ask for that information.

3. (D) $\sqrt{\frac{1}{16} + \frac{1}{9}} = \sqrt{\frac{25}{144}}$ or $\frac{5}{12}$

Choice (E) incorrectly answers the question

$$\sqrt{\frac{1}{16}} + \sqrt{\frac{1}{9}}$$

which is $\frac{1}{4} + \frac{1}{3}$ or $\frac{7}{12}$. Choices (A) and (B) incorrectly add $\frac{1}{4} + \frac{1}{3}$. Choice (C) fails to extract the square root.

4. (C) The fraction $\frac{a+b}{b}$ may be written as $\frac{a}{b} + \frac{b}{b}$.

Since $\frac{b}{b} = 1$, the correct choice is (C). Choice (A) subtracts b from numerator and denominator. Recall that in multiplying (or dividing) an equal quantity by the numerator and denominator of a fraction we are actually multiplying (or dividing) by 1.

5. (C) Conversion problems involve ratio and proportion. Kilometers bear a direct ratio to miles, since 1 kilometer = $\frac{5}{8}$ of a mile. Let x = the number of kilometers in 12 miles.

$$\frac{\text{kilometers}}{\text{miles}} = \frac{1}{5/8} = \frac{x}{12}$$

$$\frac{5}{8}x = 12$$

$$\left(\frac{8}{5}\right)\frac{5}{8}x = 12\left(\frac{8}{5}\right)$$

$$x = \frac{96}{5} = 19\frac{1}{5} \text{ or}$$

19.2 kilometers

Note that the incorrect choices (A) and (B) fail to keep the correct order of kilometers:miles. Those who choose (D) evidently perform the operations and when the numeral 5 appears as a remainder of the division of 96 by 5 they carelessly choose 19.5 as their answer.

6. (C) Since the tank was completely filled in $1\frac{3}{4}$ minutes, it would be proportionately less full in one minute.

$$\frac{\text{time (in minutes)}}{\text{part filled}} = \frac{1\frac{3}{4}}{1} = \frac{1}{x}$$

$$\frac{7}{4}x = 1$$

$$x = \frac{4}{7}$$

Choice (B) gives the part not filled in the one minute. Choice (D) gives the time not used to completely fill the tank.

7. (E) The time-consuming method is to find the cost of one item $\left(\frac{c}{2}\right)$¢ and divide the amount of money available (x¢) by the cost of one item. Choice (C) multiplies. The quick method sets up a proportion:

$$\frac{\text{number of items purchased}}{\text{cost (in cents)}} = \frac{2}{c} = \frac{?}{x}$$

$$(c)(?) = 2x \text{ and } ? = \frac{2x}{c}$$

8. (D) Both a and b, or either a or b may be equal to zero.

9. (C) $(x + y)^2 = x^2 + 2xy + y^2$
Substitute $xy = 5$ and $x^2 + y^2 = 7$
$2xy = 10$ and $x^2 + y^2 = 7$
$x^2 + 2xy + y^2 = 17.$

10. (A) $\sqrt{0.3} = 0.5+$; $0.5+ > 0.49$.

11. (B) 1% = 0.01 and ½% = 0.005; 0.05 > 0.005.

12. (A) Substitute values given: $x(y + z) = 2(3 + 7)$ or 20
$xz + y = (2)(7) + 3$ or 17.

13. (C) Perimeter of $AGFC = AG + GF + FC + AC$
Perimeter of shaded part $= AG + GF + FD + ED + BE + AB$
Since both figures are rectangles, $ED = BC$ and $BE = CD$.
$AC = AB + BC$ and $FC = CD + DF$.

14. (B) Since x is positive, $2x^2 = (2)(x)(x)$ and $(2x)^2 = 4x^2$ or $(4)(x)(x)$.

15. (B) The team scored a total of 66 points in this game. The average for all players is therefore 66 ÷ 5 or 13 ⅕ points. Player D scored 14 points, which is better than the average for the entire team.

16. (C) Both triangles have a common base (CD). Both triangles have equal altitudes since perpendiculars between parallel lines are equal.

17. (A) $2x = 3y$
$x = \frac{3}{2}y$ or $x = 1\frac{1}{2}$ times y

18. (B) Things equal to the same thing are equal to each other. Therefore $5x = 3y$ and $x = \frac{3}{5}y$.

19. (D) Let x = Mark's age now
Let y = Philip's age now
Let z = Michael's age now
From the first sentence we may write the equation: $x + 9 = 3y$ and from the second sentence the equation: $x = z + 3$. With three unknowns we must have 3 different equations in order to solve the unknowns.

20. (D) You may assume that a and b have values in the range of 2 to 4. The substitution of any of these values in $b - a$ and $a - b$ may produce many possibilities.

21. (C) $3\frac{1}{2}\% = 3.5\% = \frac{3.5}{100}$ or $\frac{35}{1000}$

22. (C) $\frac{1}{A} = \frac{1}{x} + \frac{1}{y}$

$$\frac{1}{A} = \frac{x + y}{xy}$$

$$A = \frac{xy}{x + y} \text{ (reciprocals of equals are equal)}$$

23. (B) Since x has a value less than -1, let $x = -5$.

$$\frac{1}{-5} = 1 \div -5 \text{ or } -0.2$$

$$-0.2 > -5.0$$

24. (C) $\frac{a^2 - b^2}{(a - b)^2} = \frac{(a + b)(a - b)}{(a - b)(a - b)} = \frac{a + b}{a - b}$

25. (A) $\sqrt{1440}$ is a two-digit number (37+)
Note: for this test you are required only to estimate square roots.

26. (B) 1 yard = 3 feet
(.5) or ½ yard = 1 foot, 6 inches
(1.5) or 1½ yards = 4 feet, 6 inches

27. (C) $x = y$
Therefore $x^2 = y^2$

28. (A) I is true, e.g., $\sqrt[3]{-8} = -2$
II is false: $\sqrt{\frac{1}{4}}$ is not smaller than $\frac{1}{4}$
$\sqrt{\frac{1}{4}} = \frac{1}{2}$; $\frac{1}{2}$ is larger than $\frac{1}{4}$
III is false: $(A - B)(A + B) = A^2 - B^2$

29. (D) This problem tests your ability to apply the formula used to find areas of circles. Since the area of a circle is πR^2, any change in R will affect the area by that quantity squared. Since we are concerned with area, we are evidently concerned with the area of the empty pool or its floor. Since the radius is doubled, the area will be 4 times as much. Some of the incorrect choices are caused by confusion between the effect on the circumference by changes in radius. Since the formula for circumference is $C = \pi D$ or $2\pi r$, any change in radius or diameter will affect the circumference in the same numerical way.

30. (D) Since angle DBE is a right angle, angle ABE is the complement of angle DBA and has a measure of 90° − 70° or 20°. Choice (A) does not complete the question. Since ABC is a straight line, $x = 180° - 20°$ or 160°.

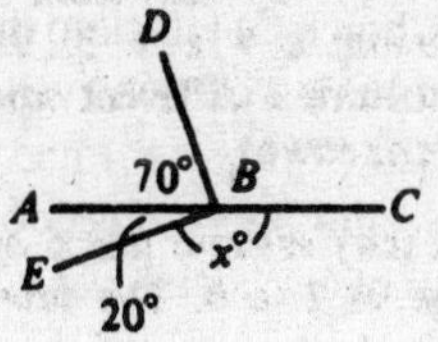

31. (C) Draw $BF \perp EC$
$BF = AD = 4$
$ED = 3$ and $FC = 3$
$DF = 13 - 6$ or 7
$AB = DF = 7$

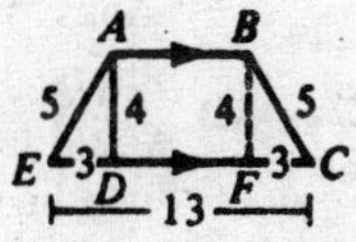

32. (D) Since $\angle A \doteq 70$, then $\angle ABC + \angle ACB \doteq 110$ or each $\doteq 55$, and each bisected angle (DBC and DCB) has a measure of $\frac{55}{2}$ degrees. In triangle DBC, the measure of $\angle BDC + \angle DCB + \angle DBC$ is 180 degrees. Since $\angle DBC + \angle DCB \doteq 55$, $x = 180 - 55$ or 125.

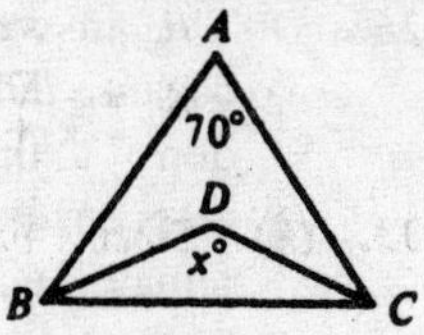

33. (D) The paper wasted is the difference between the area of the square and the area of the circle. Note choice (C) gives the difference of the circle from the square. Since we are cutting the largest possible circle, the diameter must equal the side of the square. The area of the square is d^2 and the radius of the circle is $\frac{d}{2}$ and the area of the circle is $\pi\left(\frac{d}{2}\right)^2$ or $\frac{\pi d^2}{4}$. Note that choice (B) gives the area of the circle only. The correct solution is

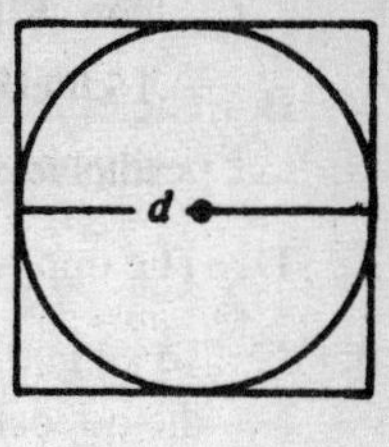

$$d^2 - \left(\frac{d}{2}\right)^2 \pi$$
$$\frac{d^2}{1} - \frac{\pi d^2}{4}$$
$$\frac{4d^2}{4} - \frac{\pi d^2}{4}$$
$$\frac{4d^2 - \pi d^2}{4}$$

34. (B) $x = 2\pi r$
Solve for r: $r = \frac{x}{2\pi}$
Area $= \pi r^2 = \pi \left(\frac{x}{2\pi}\right)^2$ or $\frac{\pi x^2}{4\pi^2} = \frac{x^2}{4\pi}$

35. (D) Let A = cost of one lb. of apples
P = cost of one lb. of pears
R = cost of one lb. of oranges
Then $7P = 10A + R$ (1)
$7R = P + 2A$ (2)
$R = 7P - 10A$ (3) from (1)

$R = \frac{P + 2A}{7}$ (4) from (2)

$\frac{7P - 10A}{1} = \frac{P + 2A}{7}$ (5) $R = R$

$49P - 70A = P + 2A$ (6) Product of means equals product of extremes

$48P = 72A$ (7)
$12P = 18A$ (8)

SECTION 6 VERBAL ABILITY

1. B. The opposite of *flourish* (flower; increase in prosperity) is *decay*.

2. D. The opposite of *profusion* (abundance) is *scarcity*.

3. C. To *enhance* something is to advance or increase it; the opposite is to *detract* from it.

4. B. The opposite of *din* (noise) is *stillness*.

5. A. The opposite of *hefty* (big; burly) is *slight* (small; delicate).

6. B. The opposite of *sagacious* (perceptive; shrewd) is *foolish*.

7. C. The opposite of *purification* (cleansing) is *pollution* (dirtying; defiling).

8. C. The opposite of *enact* (make into law) is *repeal*.

9. C. The opposite of *dismantle* (remove coverings or equipment) is *equip*.

10. D. The opposite of *surreptitious* (secret; done by stealth) is *aboveboard*.

11. B. To *mitigate* is to soften or make less severe; the opposite is to *worsen*.

12. D. The opposite of *clemency* (mercy) is a *lack of mercy*.

13. E. The opposite of *corpulent* (fat) is *slender*.

14. E. The opposite of *virulent* (malignant; deadly) is *innocuous* (harmless).

15. A. The opposite of *meticulous* (painstaking; very careful) is *careless*.

16. C. If she *deprecated* her accomplishments (diminished them or saw nothing praiseworthy in them), she wouldn't want to boast about them.

17. B. For us to be distressed, his usual taste must be good or even *flawless* so that the *lapses* or deviations would be bad.

18. D. An argument is *unconvincing* if you don't agree to all its *premises*.

19. C. *Despite* in the first clause implies a contrast, and *even* in the second clause implies that the subjects reluctantly agree that the novel was a masterpiece. That is, the subjects are *detractors* of the novel because of their *criticism* of it as stereotyped.

20. B. Pain is a *sensation*. Losing the ability to feel pain would leave the body *vulnerable*, defenseless, lacking its usual warnings against impending bodily harm.

21. B. The entire passage refers to reading, to the enjoyment and appreciation of books.

22. C. In line 2 of the passage, we learn that their chief use for the delight is in privateness. That is our clue to the correct answer, Choice C.

23. B. Let us assume that we do not know the meaning of the word in question. By examining the sentence in which *sloth* appears and the sentences preceding and following, we can get a general impression of the author's meaning. The author is talking about three different ways of using or *misusing* books. To use books just as an ornament, a way of prettying up your language with fancy quotations, is affectation. *Affectation* here means "*showing off*." If affectation means showing off, *sloth* means something else. We can eliminate Choice C. The author apparently disapproves of all three ways of dealing with books. Therefore, we can eliminate Choices D and E. *Sloth* has two meanings, "laziness" and "an animal that hangs from trees." The general sense of the sentence makes it unlikely that the author is indulging in animal lore. Hence, the correct answer is Choice B.

24. C. Only serious books, ones that have to be mastered, should be "chewed and digested." The medical text (Choice C) falls into this category. Cook books and volumes of poetry may be read in bits and snatches ("in parts") and in any order. Detective stories and sports anecdotes require no thought: they may be "swallowed" whole.

25. D. We may infer that both *plot summaries* ("distilled books") and *abridged books* ("extracts made…by others") are among the meaner sort of books, and would most likely be disliked by the author. However, he would probably agree that *scholarly monographs* must be weighed and considered. The correct answer is Choice D.

26. D. The answer is D. We can eliminate Choice A because in line 1 we are told that "there are exceptions" to the rule. Lines 8 and 11 contain additional references to male insects that are larger than female. Incidentally, this illustrates one area where you should exercise caution. Whenever an answer is in the superlative—best, worst, etc.—or is all-inclusive—always, all—or all-exclusive—none—, be sure to reread the paragraph to make certain that the author actually makes the statement. Choice B may be correct biologically and logically but the author has not stated it in the paragraph. You are adding your own interpretation to the paragraph if you select this choice. Choice C is not stated in the paragraph. Choice D is found in line 13. Longevity means long life. Choice E is wrong. In lines 5–6, the author states that males are larger.

27. C. You can support Choice C by analyzing lines 10-14. While the author is discussing large male beetles in these lines, you learn why other male beetles are smaller than female beetles. Male beetles are smaller (1) because they mature earlier and (2) because they are short-lived. The word *ephemeral* means short-lived. Choice A is incorrect. In lines 3–4, we find that male beetles are larger if they have to fight for their mates. Choice B is not stated in the paragraph. Choice D is incorrect. Beetles grow *large* when there is ample time for mating. Choice E is likewise incorrect. Size is important when males have to fight for their mates and therefore would explain the largeness of male beetles rather than the smallness.

28. A. This question calls for inferences. The clue lies in the first sentence. It is fair to assume that, if the author discusses exceptions to a rule, he has explained the rule in the preceding paragraph. There is no evidence in the paragraph that any of the other ideas were discussed previously. The correct answer is Choice A.

29. D. The answer is D. The second sentence of this paragraph (lines 3 through 6) develops the idea that the male Lucanus is larger and stronger than the female beetle. However, we cannot accept either B or C as the answer because *strong* and *large* are relative terms. We are told in the same sentence that the males fight for the females. The word *belligerent* fits this situation. Answers A and E are not found in the paragraph.

30. C. Just as tiger-lilies take their name fron their tiger-like stripes, so too stag-beetles take their name from their stag-like appearance. Just as a tiger's most obvious attribute is its stripes, so a stag's most obvious attribute is its horns.

31. E. Feeling that a job was pointless might well lead you to perform it in a *perfunctory* (indifferent or mechanical) manner.

32. B. If you originally dislike a taste, you must *acquire* that taste before you can genuinely *welcome* it.

33. E. *Despite* signals you that Tiffany's glass works were unlikely candidates to survive for several decades. That is the case because they are *fragile* (easily breakable), not because they are majestic or beautiful.

34. A. *Although* here sets up a contrast. Voles are similar to mice; they are also different from them, and may be *distinguished from* them.

35. B. Again, *Although* sets up a contrast. The doctor's *disheartening* (discouraging) words should cause the family to lose hope. Instead, they cling to the hope of a *remission* (lessening of the symptoms of a disease).

36. B. Just as a *breeze* is less intense than a *tornado* (violent windstorm), a *trickle* is a less intense outpouring of liquid than a *gusher*.

37. C. A *maid* may in time wither into a *crone* (old woman); a *youth*, into a *graybeard* (old man).

38. B. *Records* are kept in *archives*, *birds* in an *aviary*.

39. C. *Envelop* and *surround* are synonyms; *loiter* and *linger* are synonyms also.

40. B. Someone *indifferent* is lacking in *concern;* someone *arrogant,* lacking in *modesty.*

41. A. A *dilettante* is not serious about his art; he merely *dabbles*. A *coquette* is not serious about her affairs of the heart; she merely *flirts*.

42. C. *Barren* and *fecund* (fertile) are antonyms, as are *hackneyed* (trite) and *original*.

43. C. *Slander* is by its nature *defamatory* (injurious to one's reputation); a *panegyric* (formal praise) is by its nature *laudatory.*

44. A. A snake *sloughs* or casts off its dead *skin*; people and animals *shed* their unneeded *hair*.

45. C. *Hyperbolic* and *exaggerated* are synonyms, as are *capricious* and *whimsical*.

PART THREE

MASTER THE TESTING GAME: TACTICS, STRATEGIES, PRACTICE

THE ANTONYM QUESTION 4

- **Testing Tactics**
- **Long-Range Strategies**
- **Practice Exercises**
- **Answer Key**

TESTING TACTICS

The antonym questions on the SAT primarily test the extent of your vocabulary. These are the most straightforward vocabulary questions on the test. You are given a word and must choose, from the five choices that follow it, the best antonym (opposite). The vocabulary in this section includes words that you have probably seen in your reading, although you may never have used or even heard them in everyday conversations.

The directions for the antonym questions are simple and easy to follow. They are:

> Each question below consists of a word in capital letters, followed by five lettered words or phrases. Choose the word or phrase that is most nearly <u>opposite</u> in meaning to the word in capital letters. Since some of the questions require you to distinguish fine shades of meaning, consider all the choices before deciding which is best.
>
> Example:
>
> GOOD: (A) sour (B) bad (C) red (D) hot (E) ugly
>
> Ⓐ ● Ⓒ Ⓓ Ⓔ

TACTIC 1: THINK OF A CONTEXT FOR THE CAPITALIZED WORD

Take a quick look at the word in capital letters. If you don't recollect its meaning right away, try to think of a phrase or sentence in which you have heard it used. The context may help you come up with the word's meaning. For example:

> MAGNIFY: (A) forgive (B) comprehend (C) extract (D) diminish (E) electrify

The term "magnifying glass" should immediately come to mind. A magnifying glass enlarges things. The opposite of enlarging something is to make it smaller or *diminish* it. The answer is D.

Similarly, take the word *confiscate.*

> CONFISCATE: (A) correct (B) distribute (C) hasten (D) organize (E) shatter

Think of the sentence "The police confiscated the gang's weapons." From the context you realize that to confiscate weapons is to seize or commandeer them. Once you feel sure of the capitalized word's meaning, you are on firmer ground when you look for its antonym. The opposite of seizing weapons is giving them out or *distributing* them. *Distribute* (B) is correct.

TACTIC 2: BEFORE YOU LOOK AT THE CHOICES, THINK OF ANTONYMS FOR THE CAPITALIZED WORD

Suppose your word is *industrious*, hard-working. What opposites come to your mind? You might come up with *lazy, idle, slothful, inactive*—all words that mean lacking industry and energy.

Now look at the choices.

EXAMPLE 1:

> INDUSTRIOUS: (A) stupid (B) harsh
> (C) indolent (D) complex (E) inexpensive

Lazy, idle, and *slothful* all are synonyms for *indolent*. Your correct answer is Choice C.

This tactic will help you even when you have to deal with unfamiliar words among your answer choices. Suppose you do not know the meaning of the word *indolent*. You know that one antonym for your key word *industrious* is *lazy*. Therefore, you know that you are looking for a word that means the same as *lazy*. At this point you can go through the answer choices eliminating answers that don't work. Does *stupid* mean the same as *lazy*? No, smart people can be lazy, too. Does *harsh* mean the same as *lazy*? No, *harsh* means cruel or rough. Does *indolent* mean the same as *lazy*? You don't know; you should check the other choices and then come back. Does *complex* mean the same as *lazy*? No, *complex* means complicated or intricate. Does *inexpensive* mean the same as *lazy*? No. So what is left? *Indolent*. Once again, your correct answer is Choice C.

EXAMPLE 2:

> DEBASE: (A) recall (B) import (C) found
> (D) participate in (E) enhance

To *debase* something is to lower or lessen it in value. In thinking of possible antonyms for *debase*, you may have come up with words like *elevate, augment*, or *exalt*, words signifying raising something or increasing it in value. *Elevate, augment*, and *exalt* are all synonyms for *enhance*. The correct answer is E.

TACTIC 3: READ ALL THE CHOICES BEFORE YOU DECIDE WHICH IS BEST

On the SAT you are working under time pressure. You may be tempted to mark down the first answer that feels right and ignore the other choices given. Don't do it. Consider each answer. Only in this way can you be sure to distinguish between two possible answers and come up with the best answer for the question.

EXAMPLE:

> ANTECEDENT: (A) precedent (B) final
> (C) temporary (D) causal (E) subsequent

Antecedent means "existing or occurring before in time or order." At first glance, you might find *final* a good choice because it refers to an end to come while *antecedent* refers to an earlier beginning. *Final*, however, is absolute. *Antecedent* and *subsequent* are both relative: they place something in sequence within an order. The best answer is Choice E.

TACTIC 4: CHOOSE AN ANSWER AS <u>EXTREME</u> AS THE CAPITALIZED WORD

Words have shades of meaning. In matching a word with its opposite, you must pay attention to these shades of meaning. Check to see whether the capitalized word and your answer have the same degree of intensity.

EXAMPLE 1:

> MINUTE: (A) large (B) unpatriotic
> (C) gigantic (D) whole (E) average

If you are in a hurry, you may choose *large* (A) as your answer. After all, the adjective *minute* (pronounced mī-'n(y)üt) means small, right? And the opposite of small is large.

Wrong. *Minute* is an adjective meaning *extremely* small. *Gigantic* (C) is a better answer because it means exceedingly large and therefore is a better opposite of a word meaning extremely small.

EXAMPLE 2:

OBESE: (A) disobedient (B) slim (C) sturdy
(D) emaciated (E) young

Obese means fat. Therefore, you might rapidly decide on (B), *slim*, as the best choice. However, an *obese* person is not simply plump. He or she is excessively fat, dangerously, unhealthily so. A good antonym for *obese* should convey this sense of extremism and of potential danger. *Emaciated* means thin and wasted away, enfeebled as if by illness or starvation. Thus, it is a better antonym for *obese* than is *slim*. The correct answer is D.

TACTIC 5: LOOK AT THE ANSWER CHOICES TO DETERMINE THE MAIN WORD'S PART OF SPEECH

Look at the capitalized word. What part of speech is it? Words often exist in several forms. You may think of *run* as a verb, for example, but in the phrases "a run in her stocking" and "hit a home run" *run* is a noun.

The SAT plays on this confusion in testing your verbal ability. When you look at a particular capitalized word, you may not know whether you are dealing with a noun, a verb, or an adjective. *Harbor*, for example, is a very common noun; in "to harbor a fugitive; to give refuge to a runaway," it is a much less common verb.

If you suspect that a capitalized word may have more than one part of speech, don't worry. Just look at the answer choices and see what part of speech they are. That part of speech will be the capitalized word's part of speech.

In SAT Antonym Questions, all the answer choices belong to the same part of speech.

EXAMPLE 1:

CONTRACT: (A) weaken (B) resist
(C) dilate (D) specify (E) resemble

Are you dealing with *contract* ('kon-ˌtrakt) the noun or *contract* (kun-'trakt) the verb?

A quick look at the answers assures you that they are all verbs. (The *-en* and *-ify* word endings are common verb endings.) *Contract* means "to shrink or lessen." Its opposite is "to expand or *dilate*." The correct answer is Choice C.

EXAMPLE 2:

IMPORT: (A) definition (B) insignificance
(C) cost (D) lack of direction (E) product

Are you dealing with *import* the verb or *import* the noun?

A look at the answer choices reveals that they are all nouns. (The *-tion* and *-ance* word endings are common noun endings.) One definition of the noun *import* is significance, or meaning. Its opposite is *insignificance*, Choice B.

TACTIC 6: CONSIDER SECONDARY MEANINGS OF THE CAPITALIZED WORD AS WELL AS ITS PRIMARY MEANING

If none of the answer choices seems right to you, take another look at the capitalized word. It may have more than one meaning. The SAT often constructs questions that make use of secondary, less well-known meanings of deceptively familiar words.

EXAMPLE 1:

RESERVED: (A) alone (B) communicative
(C) proud (D) elegant (E) dilapidated

Here, *reserved* does not mean "set apart" or "kept back," like reserved books at the library or reserved seats at a concert. Instead *reserved* means "restrained, lacking in openness or candor." Its antonyms are *open, candid, unrestrained*—in other words, *communicative*. Choice B is the best answer.

EXAMPLE 2:

GRAVITY: (A) frivolity (B) planet
(C) depth (D) altitude (E) tranquillity

If you think the only opposite of *gravity* is weightlessness, you're wrong. Here, *gravity* means seriousness or solemnity. Its antonyms are *levity, lightness, giddiness*—in other words, *frivolity*. Choice A is the best answer.

EXAMPLE 3:

CONVICTION: (A) crime (B) veto
(C) dearth (D) argument (E) uncertainty

The most familiar context for the word *conviction* is a legal one. The district attorney is out to get a *conviction*, to prove someone guilty of a crime. However, a *conviction* is also a strong persuasion or belief. Its antonyms are *doubt, lack of belief*—in other words, *uncertainty.* Choice E is the best answer.

TACTIC 7: BREAK DOWN UNFAMILIAR WORDS INTO RECOGNIZABLE PARTS

When you come upon a totally unfamiliar word, don't give up. Break it down and see if you recognize any of its parts. Pay particular attention to prefixes—word parts added to the beginning of a word—and to roots, the building blocks of the language.

More than half of the words in the English language derive from Latin and Greek. Students who attend prep schools and study Latin or Greek have a built-in advantage when they take standard vocabulary tests. Knowing Latin and Greek word parts helps them figure out the meanings of new words they come across.

Without spending three or four years studying Latin in high school, you still can profit from the word-parts approach. See how it works.

EXAMPLE 1:

CIRCUMSPECT: (A) disregarded (B) rash
(C) unclear (D) idle (E) roundabout

You may not have seen *circumspect* before, but you've seen other words beginning with *circum-*: *circumstance, circumference,* even *circumcise.* Take *circumference*. What is a circumference? The distance around a circle. *Circum-* means *around.* To circumnavigate the globe, you sail around it.

What about the other part, *-spect*? Think of spectacles or spectator. *-Spect* means *look*. And when you look around before you cross the street, you're being cautious or careful—in other words, *circumspect.*

At this point, you know the meaning of the capitalized word. What answer is most nearly opposite to it in meaning? Choice B, *rash* or careless.

EXAMPLE 2:

BENEFACTOR: (A) lawyer (B) rebel
(C) evildoer (D) child (E) intruder

You may not know the word *benefactor*, but you know the word *benefit*. Benefit concerts to aid people starving in Ethiopia, bake sales and car washes to benefit the baseball team—these are attempts to do good. *Bene* basically means good. A *benefactor* is someone who does good works to benefit others. So the antonym of *benefactor* is *evildoer*. Your answer is Choice C.

EXAMPLE 3:

CURSE: (A) harangue (B) benediction
(C) pathology (D) anathema (E) aphorism

In this example you have an opportunity to use your knowledge of word parts to select the correct answer from a group of five unfamiliar words. A *curse* is a wish that something evil or *bad* happen to someone. You are, therefore, looking for an opposite of *bad*. In working through the previous example, you have seen that the prefix *bene* means well or *good*. This knowledge can justify your hazarding an "intelligent guess" and choosing *benediction*, Choice B, as your answer. Guessing is usually advisable if you can eliminate two or more of the choices, often by using your knowledge of prefixes, suffixes, and roots.

The opposite of *curse* is *benediction* or blessing. To help you remember this word, picture a chaplain, hands raised in *benediction*, blessing a group of men and women before they go off on a dangerous mission.

LONG-RANGE STRATEGIES

"Build Your Vocabulary," Chapter 8, contains a thorough description of strategies you can use to increase your word power, as well as a program to help you work your way through our entire Basic Word List. In addition, it contains an expanded Word Parts List—prefixes, suffixes, and roots—invaluable for both short-term and long-term SAT study programs.

One special feature in Chapter 8 is our new High-Frequency SAT Word List, 101 words which computer analysis has shown turn up again and again on actual SAT tests. Master these words: no matter what words turn up on your particular SAT test, these words *will* turn up in your college textbooks and your general reading. They are words every educated reader should know.

Work with the Word List

Flash Cards

Use our word lists as a guide in making flash cards. Scan a list looking for words you don't quite know—not words you are totally unfamiliar with, but words you are on the brink of knowing. Look for words you have heard or seen before but can't use in a sentence or define. Effort you put into mastering such "borderline" words will pay off—soon!

Be brief—but include all the information you need. On one side write the word. On the other side write *concise* definitions—two or three words at most—for each major meaning of the word you want to learn. Include an antonym, too: the synonym-antonym associations can help you remember both words. To fix the word in your mind, use it in a short phrase. Then write that phrase down.

Sample Flash Card

Front	Back
conviction	1. judgement of guilt 2. strong belief "speak with conviction" ant. doubt

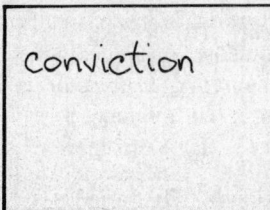

Carry a few of your flash cards with you every day. Look them over whenever you have a spare moment or two. Work in short bursts. Try going through five flash cards at a time, shuffling through them rapidly so that you can build up your rapid sight recognition of the words for the test. You want these words and their antonyms to spring to your mind instantaneously, so that you can speed through the antonym section of the SAT.

Test your memory: don't look at the back of the card unless you must. Go through your five cards several times a day. Then, when you have mastered two or three of the cards and have them down pat, set those cards aside and add a couple of new ones to your working pile. That way you will always be working with a limited group, but you won't be wasting time reviewing words you already recognize on sight.

Never try to master a whole stack of flash cards in one long cram session. It won't work.

Dictionary Drill

Use the Basic Word List as you would a specialized dictionary. You will find in it thousands of college-level words and their meanings, plus illustrative sentences to give you a sense of just how these words are used. Often the Word List does *not* include a word's most common definition; instead, it contains unusual definitions of familiar words, definitions that are not commonly known but that you need to know.

Consider, for example, the word *intimate*. As an adjective it is familiar: an intimate friend, a close personal friend. As a verb, however, its meaning is less familiar: "Jim *intimated* he had something more to say to her after her little brother left." Here *intimate* means to hint or suggest. This is the meaning you will find in the Word List.

Beyond the Word List

Learn to consult an unabridged dictionary when you need to find out just how a word is used (and how it differs in usage from other similar words). At the end of the entry for *obese*, for example, you will find this direction:

syn see FAT

If you then turn to the entry for *fat*, glancing down the lengthy entry you will eventually come to:

syn FLESHY, STOUT, CORPULENT, OBESE, CHUBBY, ROTUND, PORTLY, PLUMP...

By reading the usage note that follows, you will learn the exact shades of meaning conveyed by each of these similar, but very different words.

A word of warning. Some unabridged dictionaries arrange their definitions chronologically, giving the oldest definition of a word first. Others give a word's commonest definition first. The way a word was used in Shakespeare's time is often *not* the way it is most commonly used today. Look at your dictionary's introduction to see which approach it takes.

PRACTICE EXERCISES

The four tests that follow will give you practice in handling antonym questions. The time for each test of 50 questions is 25 minutes. Scores may be interpreted as follows:

45 to **50—EXCELLENT**
38 to **44—SUPERIOR**
32 to **37—SATISFACTORY**
25 to **31—AVERAGE**
19 to **24—BELOW AVERAGE**
0 to **18—UNSATISFACTORY**

ANTONYM TEST A

Each question below consists of a word in capital letters, followed by five lettered words or phrases. Choose the word or phrase that is most nearly opposite in meaning to the word in capital letters. Since some of the questions require you to distinguish fine shades of meaning, consider all the choices before deciding which is best.

Example:

GOOD: (A) sour (B) bad (C) red (D) hot (E) ugly

Ⓐ ● Ⓒ Ⓓ Ⓔ

1. ABOMINATE: (A) love (B) despair (C) abate (D) deplore (E) attach
2. RAVENOUS: (A) fortunate (B) nibbling (C) sated (D) stable (E) unsatisfied
3. PITHY: (A) central (B) federal (C) homogeneous (D) autological (E) gregarious
4. ADAMANT: (A) yielding (B) primitive (C) elementary (D) primeval (E) inefficient
5. EPHEMERAL: (A) evergreen (B) deciduous (C) biennial (D) everlasting (E) tactile
6. SYNTHETIC: (A) cosmetic (B) affable (C) plastic (D) viscous (E) natural
7. VIVACIOUS: (A) affable (B) dramatic (C) versatile (D) phlegmatic (E) vigilant
8. AUDACITY: (A) quivering (B) cowardice (C) conciseness (D) patricide (E) pugnacity
9. IRASCIBLE: (A) pictorial (B) piscatorial (C) benign (D) crafty (E) good-natured
10. BUCOLIC: (A) citified (B) rusty (C) intoxicated (D) sick (E) healthy
11. INFINITESIMAL: (A) everlasting (B) colossal (C) picayune (D) major (E) telescopic
12. GELID: (A) lurid (B) torpid (C) torrid (D) piebald (E) vapid
13. CIRCUITOUS: (A) diagrammed (B) direct (C) round (D) labyrinthine (E) radial
14. PROVINCIAL: (A) urbane (B) governmental (C) logical (D) pastoral (E) native
15. CLANDESTINE: (A) open (B) daylight (C) miasmic (D) pugnacious (E) banal
16. ABHOR: (A) deter (B) absolve (C) accuse (D) bedizen (E) adore
17. FLAMBOYANT: (A) decorative (B) apparent (C) plain (D) female (E) terse
18. REDUNDANT: (A) taut (B) risky (C) curt (D) voluminous (E) opulent
19. IMPOVERISHED: (A) pecuniary (B) affluent (C) rococo (D) iniquitous (E) pendent
20. OBSEQUIOUS: (A) obsolete (B) salty (C) supercilious (D) improper (E) first
21. DISCRETE: (A) wise (B) foolish (C) unkempt (D) organized (E) continuous
22. FATUOUS: (A) indignant (B) thin (C) witty (D) planned (E) stout
23. AMENABLE: (A) responsive (B) intractable (C) indifferent (D) affable (E) correct
24. FALLACIOUS: (A) urgent (B) foolish (C) accurate (D) afraid (E) plucky
25. ALTRUISM: (A) honesty (B) tolerance (C) bigotry (D) thievery (E) selfishness
26. INDIFFERENT: (A) curious (B) varied (C) uniform (D) alike (E) covert
27. COHESIVE: (A) attracted (B) detached (C) associated (D) affiliated (E) sticky
28. INSIPID: (A) tasty (B) silly (C) angry (D) active (E) emaciated
29. DISCORD: (A) noise (B) amity (C) irritation (D) scrap (E) use
30. PRIORITY: (A) anxiety (B) irregular (C) subsequence (D) pious (E) impious
31. CRABBED: (A) fished (B) saccharine (C) warped (D) viscous (E) violent
32. CORROBORATION: (A) polish (B) arrest (C) invalidation (D) alibi (E) alias
33. DECORUM: (A) ribaldry (B) balladry (C) high collar (D) solo (E) freedom
34. VIGILANT: (A) surgical (B) unwary (C) girlish (D) inert (E) boyish
35. INGENUOUS: (A) clever (B) stupid (C) naive (D) valid (E) certain
36. ALLEVIATE: (A) allow (B) aggravate (C) instigate (D) belittle (E) refuse
37. OBSOLETE: (A) acute (B) fancy (C) free (D) renovated (E) old
38. BLASÉ: (A) different (B) awed (C) afraid (D) cultured (E) worldly

39. SANGUINE: (A) bland (B) gloomy (C) happy (D) thin (E) red-faced

40. LANGUID: (A) pusillanimous (B) sick (C) sad (D) vigorous (E) motley

41. RESPITE: (A) reason (B) interment (C) exertion (D) friendly (E) angry

42. OBLOQUY: (A) shape (B) fame (C) name (D) coloquy (E) inquiry

43. PLACATE: (A) nettle (B) label (C) saturate (D) reply (E) retaliate

44. COMPLACENT: (A) staged (B) avid (C) nasty (D) querulous (E) asking

45. ASSENT: (A) save (B) inquire (C) resent (D) introduce (E) disavow

46. HUSBANDRY: (A) munificence (B) wife (C) malignancy (D) matrimony (E) widower

47. NOISOME: (A) quiet (B) salubrious (C) eager (D) foolish (E) deodorant

48. PERMANENT: (A) indifferent (B) tardy (C) mutable (D) improper (E) disheveled

49. COVETOUS: (A) unfinished (B) uncovered (C) undesirous (D) birdlike (E) plying

50. CORPOREAL: (A) internal (B) private (C) caustic (D) spiritual (E) balanced

ANTONYM TEST B

Each question below consists of a word in capital letters, followed by five lettered words or phrases. Choose the word or phrase that is most nearly <u>opposite</u> in meaning to the word in capital letters. Since some of the questions require you to distinguish fine shades of meaning, consider all the choices before deciding which is best.

Example:

GOOD: (A) sour (B) bad (C) red (D) hot (E) ugly

Ⓐ ● Ⓒ Ⓓ Ⓔ

1. ZEALOT: (A) heretic (B) hypocrite (C) person who is careless (D) person who is rich (E) person who is indifferent

2. ABSTEMIOUS: (A) fastidious (B) punctilious (C) pusillanimous (D) dissipated (E) prodigal

3. SATIETY: (A) starvation (B) dissatisfaction (C) pretense (D) lowest class (E) grandeur

4. DECIDUOUS: (A) undecided (B) hesitant (C) evergreen (D) annual (E) perennial

5. INNOCUOUS: (A) large (B) toxic (C) spotless (D) impeccable (E) sober

6. GERMANE: (A) Teutonic (B) healthful (C) irrelevant (D) massive (E) puny

7. EGREGIOUS: (A) nostalgic (B) splendid (C) abortive (D) maturing (E) birdlike

8. NEPOTISM: (A) midnight (B) partiality (C) impartiality (D) dawn (E) noon

9. AUTONOMOUS: (A) magnanimous (B) ambiguous (C) exiguous (D) dependent (E) operated by hand

10. EXCULPATE: (A) parole (B) destroy (C) create (D) convict (E) admonish

11. EARTHY: (A) pithy (B) salty (C) watery (D) refined (E) moldy

12. CONTENTIOUS: (A) pacific (B) masterful (C) satisfied (D) dissatisfied (E) hungry

13. GAINSAY: (A) denigrate (B) lose money (C) audit (D) applaud (E) affirm

14. AMELIORATE: (A) harden (B) coarsen (C) aggravate (D) improvise (E) scrape

15. IGNOMINIOUS: (A) disdainful (B) erudite (C) scholarly (D) incognito (E) laudatory

16. EVANESCENT: (A) permanent (B) incandescent (C) lusty (D) putrid (E) perfunctory

17. CORPULENT: (A) sallow (B) partnership (C) emaciated (D) entrepreneur (E) red-blooded

18. JOCUND: (A) round (B) flat (C) judicial (D) jugular (E) melancholy

19. HIBERNAL: (A) Irish (B) estival (C) English (D) festival (E) awake

20. EBULLIENT: (A) intoxicated (B) placid (C) effervescent (D) gregarious (E) jovial

21. ASSUAGE: (A) meet (B) abate (C) separate (D) irritate (E) demonstrate

22. INDIGENOUS: (A) alien (B) digestible (C) comestible (D) pleased (E) irate

23. DEARTH: (A) birth (B) brevity (C) abundance (D) brightness (E) morning

24. DELETERIOUS: (A) sane (B) intoxicated (C) sober (D) wholesome (E) adding

25. FELL: (A) downed (B) risen (C) propitious (D) cruel (E) officious

26. EXEMPLARY: (A) deplorable (B) imitative (C) good (D) condoning (E) additional

27. CHOLERIC: (A) red (B) serene (C) severe (D) stern (E) irritating

28. BAROQUE: (A) common (B) boorish (C) rancid (D) simple (E) stupid

29. DILETTANTE: (A) amateur (B) professional (C) late arrival (D) superior (E) advancement

30. AMORPHOUS: (A) diaphanous (B) translucent (C) organic (D) opaque (E) having a definite form

31. CAPRICIOUS: (A) whimsical (B) consistent (C) goatlike (D) honest (E) hypocritical

32. SALUBRIOUS: (A) healthy (B) plagued (C) rustic (D) fashioned (E) miasmic

33. DISPARITY: (A) similarity (B) aspersion (C) allusion (D) equanimity (E) suture

34. APOTHEGM: (A) right angle (B) pithy statement (C) prolix statement (D) false (E) letter

35. CHARY: (A) lavish (B) malevolent (C) insinuating (D) cautious (E) irritable

36. CANDOR: (A) hypocrisy (B) ingenuousness (C) sweetmeat (D) pleasure (E) velocity

37. EQUIVOCATE: (A) cavil (B) whisper (C) balance (D) tell the truth (E) be unequal

38. ESTRANGED: (A) reconciled (B) smug (C) foreign (D) traded (E) embarrassed

39. PRETENTIOUS: (A) real (B) excusing (C) modest (D) unpardonable (E) typical

40. SUB ROSA: (A) under the rose (B) fragrant (C) fashionable (D) open (E) simple

41. SUBSERVIENT: (A) complacent (B) omnipresent (C) opaque (D) haughty (E) miserly

42. UNTENABLE: (A) rented (B) maintainable (C) occupied (D) permanent (E) picayune

43. HERBIVOROUS: (A) ravenous (B) starving (C) carnivorous (D) voracious (E) veracious

44. OPULENCE: (A) glamor (B) sobriety (C) badinage (D) penury (E) petulance

45. THRENODY: (A) stanza (B) lyric (C) ballade (D) paean (E) epic

46. VAUNTED: (A) crept (B) belittled (C) crossed (D) worried (E) wicked

47. CEDE: (A) exhume (B) harvest (C) annex (D) examine (E) mimic

48. OBFUSCATE: (A) clarify (B) magnify (C) intensify (D) belittle (E) resist

49. CONCAVE: (A) hollow (B) solid (C) convex (D) complex (E) broken

50. PRECIPITATE: (A) wary (B) arid (C) audacious (D) masterly (E) conquered

ANTONYM TEST C

Each question below consists of a word in capital letters, followed by five lettered words or phrases. Choose the word or phrase that is most nearly opposite in meaning to the word in capital letters. Since some of the questions require you to distinguish fine shades of meaning, consider all the choices before deciding which is best.

Example:

GOOD: (A) sour (B) bad (C) red (D) hot (E) ugly Ⓐ ● Ⓒ Ⓓ Ⓔ

1. HALCYON: (A) revered (B) belligerent (C) futile (D) outrageous (E) expeditious

2. PAEAN: (A) slave (B) inactivity (C) chatter (D) denunciation (E) sadness

3. CELIBATE: (A) married (B) bald (C) hypocritical (D) mendacious (E) powerful

4. CHASTISE: (A) reward (B) pursue (C) abuse (D) stop (E) prolong

5. MERETRICIOUS: (A) expensive (B) blonde (C) torpid (D) unworthy (E) angry

6. REBUKE: (A) assign (B) mature (C) matriculate (D) commend (E) falsify

7. PLACID: (A) effervescent (B) energetic (C) copious (D) derelict (E) irate

8. MAUDLIN: (A) outrageous (B) modish (C) unemotional (D) unimaginative (E) exaggerated

9. HOMOGENEOUS: (A) female (B) triangular (C) milky (D) stirred (E) motley

10. WANE: (A) enlarge (B) endorse (C) minimize (D) enforce (E) anger

11. DOLOROUS: (A) certain (B) arbitrary (C) jocund (D) factual (E) rational

12. VARIEGATED: (A) baroque (B) plain (C) renewed (D) organized (E) futile

13. FECUND: (A) altruistic (B) malevolent (C) primary (D) barren (E) stolid

14. INFINITE: (A) wise (B) enduring (C) limited (D) gracious (E) placid

15. DEMISE: (A) repetition (B) residence (C) act (D) arrival (E) birth

16. FRUGALITY: (A) extravagance (B) ripening (C) timeliness (D) anxiety (E) ire

17. EQUALED: (A) outstanding (B) praised (C) unique (D) certain (E) abnormal

18. GARRULOUS: (A) laconic (B) strangling (C) ecstatic (D) frozen (E) tiny

19. ADVERSITY: (A) partner (B) ease (C) opening (D) agency (E) agreement

20. FASTIDIOUS: (A) slow (B) careless (C) squeamish (D) stuffed (E) expeditious

21. DILATORY: (A) pretending (B) confusing (C) closing (D) prompt (E) friendly

22. MUNIFICENT: (A) palatial (B) stingy (C) parochial (D) fetid (E) eloquent

23. VAPID: (A) oral (B) impatient (C) indecisive (D) unwilling (E) spirited

24. PERFUNCTORY: (A) thorough (B) individual (C) anxious (D) irate (E) sinister

25. INDIGENCE: (A) nativity (B) tolerance (C) gossip (D) wealth (E) altruism

26. VENAL: (A) ambitious (B) gracious (C) incorruptible (D) brazen (E) sane

27. PERIPHERAL: (A) central (B) lasting (C) mandatory (D) glorious (E) picturesque

28. LOQUACIOUS: (A) situated (B) gregarious (C) tactical (D) antisocial (E) taciturn

29. PHLEGMATIC: (A) emotional (B) respiratory (C) inanimate (D) pneumatic (E) dire

30. SATURNINE: (A) planetary (B) cheerful (C) delinquent (D) futility (E) hostility

31. PALLIATIVE: (A) temporary setback (B) permanent cure (C) large pill (D) small tip (E) eternal evil

32. COGENT: (A) docile (B) major (C) illiterate (D) irrelevant (E) aromatic

33. PENURY: (A) custom (B) power (C) numismatics (D) affluence (E) crime

34. EFFUSIVE: (A) vapid (B) assumed (C) desirous (D) reserved (E) eroded

35. VINDICTIVE: (A) forgiving (B) triumphant (C) strategic (D) demonstrative (E) bigoted

36. FURTIVE: (A) sated (B) facile (C) overt (D) nostalgic (E) lethargic

37. PUNCTILIOUS: (A) lax (B) varied (C) ready (D) tardy (E) vicarious

38. HAGGARD: (A) robust (B) irascible (C) wise (D) sluggish (E) witty

39. STAID: (A) weary (B) remaining (C) flighty (D) afraid (E) unkempt

40. PESSIMISTIC: (A) doubtful (B) elastic (C) futile (D) sanguine (E) salubrious

41. DECOROUS: (A) unadorned (B) ugly (C) insane (D) improper (E) childish

42. ONEROUS: (A) possessive (B) humble (C) droll (D) light (E) sly

43. SUCCULENT: (A) asking help (B) wicked (C) anxious (D) concise (E) dry

44. EXPEDIENT: (A) precise (B) expert (C) expendable (D) inadvisable (E) erratic

45. NEBULOUS: (A) distinct (B) factual (C) fictional (D) determined (E) notable

46. PROPENSITY: (A) disinclination (B) dishonesty (C) probity (D) intelligence (E) fascination

47. TRACTABLE: (A) varied (B) placid (C) weary (D) forward (E) recalcitrant

48. IMMUTABLE: (A) forgetful (B) victorious (C) changeable (D) showy (E) unprejudiced

49. TORTUOUS: (A) straight (B) sadistic (C) tempting (D) reminiscent (E) carefree

50. MOLLIFY: (A) loosen (B) irritate (C) applaud (D) worry (E) discourage

ANTONYM TEST D

Each question below consists of a word in capital letters, followed by five lettered words or phrases. Choose the word or phrase that is most nearly opposite in meaning to the word in capital letters. Since some of the questions require you to distinguish fine shades of meaning, consider all the choices before deciding which is best.

Example:

GOOD: (A) sour (B) bad (C) red (D) hot (E) ugly Ⓐ ● Ⓒ Ⓓ Ⓔ

1. RECONDITE: (A) renewed (B) pacific (C) commonplace (D) fashionable (E) ambitious
2. TACIT: (A) explicit (B) quick (C) frigid (D) indifferent (E) gloomy
3. PERFIDIOUS: (A) blessed (B) hirsute (C) fantastic (D) mercenary (E) loyal
4. RELINQUISH: (A) afford (B) follow (C) scorn (D) claim (E) qualify
5. IMPECCABLE: (A) impervious (B) faulty (C) turgid (D) naive (E) irate
6. ABETTOR: (A) gambler (B) savior (C) hinderer (D) factor (E) copier
7. DEBILITATE: (A) argue (B) engage (C) correct (D) soothe (E) strengthen
8. MUNDANE: (A) outrageous (B) modish (C) uncommon (D) unimaginative (E) exaggerated
9. HUMBLE: (A) pompous (B) complimentary (C) silent (D) placid (E) meddling
10. ERUDITE: (A) rough (B) ignorant (C) ornate (D) entire (E) fierce
11. ADROIT: (A) bungling (B) antique (C) jovial (D) affirmative (E) entire
12. INANE: (A) lifeless (B) clever (C) hopeful (D) faithless (E) futile
13. CULPABLE: (A) free (B) guileless (C) vindicable (D) wholesome (E) authentic
14. SOPHISTICATED: (A) naive (B) clever (C) original (D) plastic (E) crusty
15. FEALTY: (A) kingdom (B) treachery (C) anger (D) anxiety (E) personality
16. COMMODIOUS: (A) equipped (B) formidable (C) unequal (D) cramped (E) rhetorical
17. EXPUNGE: (A) interdict (B) predict (C) unite (D) insert (E) assign
18. CONCILIATORY: (A) disputatious (B) hairy (C) violent (D) gelid (E) puny
19. INDIGENT: (A) wealthy (B) bilious (C) foreign (D) scholarly (E) frank
20. FORTUITOUS: (A) unlucky (B) premeditated (C) poor (D) artificial (E) concerted
21. ANIMOSITY: (A) unanimity (B) intensity (C) failure (D) alacrity (E) amity
22. DUPLICITY: (A) canoe (B) miserliness (C) calm (D) candor (E) original
23. CRYPTIC: (A) exhumed (B) written (C) imitated (D) active (E) clear
24. ILLICIT: (A) literate (B) private (C) weary (D) angry (E) lawful
25. DORMANT: (A) open (B) active (C) vigilant (D) basic (E) factual
26. ASPERITY: (A) smoothness (B) hope (C) goal (D) drug (E) futility
27. ALTERCATION: (A) adjustment (B) repair (C) amity (D) reaction (E) reply
28. CAPTIOUS: (A) prominent (B) approving (C) caustic (D) epigrammatic (E) alone
29. ACCOLADE: (A) balcony (B) outer garment (C) drink (D) opprobrium (E) fruition
30. DEPRECATE: (A) discourage (B) approve (C) increase (D) immigrate (E) exile
31. BOMBASTIC: (A) exaggerated (B) revengeful (C) simple (D) colorful (E) pacific
32. INTER: (A) carry (B) suggest (C) exhume (D) meddle (E) illustrate
33. ACUMEN: (A) lack of strength (B) poverty (C) paucity (D) lack of perception (E) excellence
34. BUMPTIOUS: (A) smooth (B) resisting (C) shy (D) devilish (E) exact
35. CANARD: (A) fowl (B) bugle call (C) playground (D) true report (E) exaggeration

36. SUMPTUOUS: (A) swampy (B) irritable (C) meager (D) fanciful (E) eloquent

37. AVARICIOUS: (A) altruistic (B) mandatory (C) wicked (D) renowned (E) eager

38. QUERULOUS: (A) violent (B) arrogant (C) condoning (D) willing (E) curious

39. MOROSE: (A) cheerful (B) mortal (C) benevolent (D) questioning (E) fortuitous

40. SURMISE: (A) be uneasy (B) have qualms (C) make ready (D) be certain (E) rest

41. UBIQUITOUS: (A) bellicose (B) localized (C) aping (D) affable (E) inquisitive

42. ATTRITION: (A) grief (B) sustenance (C) tears (D) fright (E) addition

43. RETICENCE: (A) brazenness (B) mansion (C) retention (D) taciturnity (E) magnitude

44. CHAGRIN: (A) grimace (B) intuition (C) affectation (D) sympathy (E) elation

45. PLAUDIT: (A) denunciation (B) debacle (C) demonstration (D) deficiency (E) determination

46. VIVA VOCE: (A) singing (B) crying (C) written (D) available (E) operatic

47. MALFEASANCE: (A) seasickness (B) criticism (C) cure (D) good conduct (E) poor performance

48. HAMLET: (A) thinker (B) benefactor (C) large rodent (D) metropolis (E) extrovert

49. PUERILE: (A) feminine (B) mature (C) valiant (D) bedridden (E) potent

50. TEPID: (A) embarrassed (B) equatorial (C) cool (D) enraged (E) intrepid

ANSWER KEY

Antonym Test A

1.	**A**	11.	**B**	21.	**E**	31.	**B**	41.	**C**
2.	**C**	12.	**C**	22.	**C**	32.	**C**	42.	**B**
3.	**D**	13.	**B**	23.	**B**	33.	**A**	43.	**A**
4.	**A**	14.	**A**	24.	**C**	34.	**B**	44.	**D**
5.	**D**	15.	**A**	25.	**E**	35.	**A**	45.	**E**
6.	**E**	16.	**E**	26.	**A**	36.	**B**	46.	**A**
7.	**D**	17.	**C**	27.	**B**	37.	**D**	47.	**B**
8.	**B**	18.	**C**	28.	**A**	38.	**B**	48.	**C**
9.	**E**	19.	**B**	29.	**B**	39.	**B**	49.	**C**
10.	**A**	20.	**C**	30.	**C**	40.	**D**	50.	**D**

Antonym Test B

1.	**E**	11.	**D**	21.	**D**	31.	**B**	41.	**D**
2.	**D**	12.	**A**	22.	**A**	32.	**E**	42.	**B**
3.	**A**	13.	**E**	23.	**C**	33.	**A**	43.	**C**
4.	**C**	14.	**C**	24.	**D**	34.	**C**	44.	**D**
5.	**B**	15.	**E**	25.	**C**	35.	**A**	45.	**D**
6.	**C**	16.	**A**	26.	**A**	36.	**A**	46.	**B**
7.	**B**	17.	**C**	27.	**B**	37.	**D**	47.	**C**
8.	**C**	18.	**E**	28.	**D**	38.	**A**	48.	**A**
9.	**D**	19.	**B**	29.	**B**	39.	**C**	49.	**C**
10.	**D**	20.	**B**	30.	**E**	40.	**D**	50.	**A**

Antonym Test C

1.	**B**	11.	**C**	21.	**D**	31.	**B**	41.	**D**
2.	**D**	12.	**B**	22.	**B**	32.	**D**	42.	**D**
3.	**A**	13.	**D**	23.	**E**	33.	**D**	43.	**E**
4.	**A**	14.	**C**	24.	**A**	34.	**D**	44.	**D**
5.	**A**	15.	**E**	25.	**D**	35.	**A**	45.	**A**
6.	**D**	16.	**A**	26.	**C**	36.	**C**	46.	**A**
7.	**E**	17.	**C**	27.	**A**	37.	**A**	47.	**E**
8.	**C**	18.	**A**	28.	**E**	38.	**A**	48.	**C**
9.	**E**	19.	**B**	29.	**A**	39.	**C**	49.	**A**
10.	**A**	20.	**B**	30.	**B**	40.	**D**	50.	**B**

Antonym Test D

1. C	11. A	21. E	31. C	41. B
2. A	12. B	22. D	32. C	42. E
3. E	13. C	23. E	33. D	43. A
4. D	14. A	24. E	34. C	44. E
5. B	15. B	25. B	35. D	45. A
6. C	16. D	26. A	36. C	46. C
7. E	17. D	27. C	37. A	47. D
8. C	18. A	28. B	38. D	48. D
9. A	19. A	29. D	39. A	49. B
10. B	20. B	30. B	40. D	50. C

THE ANALOGY QUESTION

5

- **Testing Tactics**
- **Long-Range Strategies**
- **Practice Exercises**
- **Answer Key**

TESTING TACTICS

The directions for the analogy question on the SAT are straightforward. They are:

> Each question below consists of a related pair of words or phrases, followed by five lettered pairs of words or phrases. Select the lettered pair that best expresses a relationship similar to that expressed in the original pair.
>
> Example:
>
> YAWN : BOREDOM :: (A) dream : sleep
> (B) anger : madness (C) smile : amusement
> (D) face : expression (E) impatience : rebellion
>
> Ⓐ Ⓑ ● Ⓓ Ⓔ

Just as a *yawn* is a physical sign of *boredom*, a *smile* is a physical sign of *amusement*. A face may show expression, but a face is not a physical sign of expression. Analogies can be tricky.

Analogy questions challenge your ability to analyze relationships which may be similar or parallel. In some questions you are asked to carry an analogy from a concrete example to a more abstract or less tangible one. For example:

> SURGEON : SCALPEL :: satirist : words

A *surgeon* literally uses a *scalpel* to make an incision, to cut. A *satirist* uses *words* to cut and ridicule the pride and folly of his subjects. As you can see, answering such questions correctly involves more than knowing single meanings of words.

At first analogy questions may be a stumbling block to you, but once you master our techniques for solving them, you may even find them fun.

TACTIC 1: BEFORE YOU LOOK AT THE CHOICES, TRY TO STATE THE RELATIONSHIP BETWEEN THE CAPITALIZED WORDS IN A GOOD SENTENCE

In answering an analogy question, your first problem is to determine the exact nature of the relationship that exists between the two capitalized words. Before you look at the answer pairs, make up a sentence that shows how these capitalized words are related. Then test the possible answers by seeing how well they fit in your sentence.

EXAMPLE 1:

> CONSTELLATION : STARS :: (A) prison : bars
> (B) assembly : speaker (C) troupe : actors
> (D) mountain : peak (E) flock : shepherds

A *constellation* is made up of *stars*. A *troupe* (not *troop* but *troupe*) is made up of *actors* (and actresses, of course). Choice C is correct.

Don't let Choice E fool you: a *flock* is made up of *sheep*, not of *shepherds*.

EXAMPLE 2:

> COMPOSER : SYMPHONY :: (A) porter : terminal
> (B) writer : plagiarism (C) coach : team
> (D) painter : mural (E) doctor : stethoscope

A *composer* creates a *symphony*. You therefore are looking for a relationship between a worker and a work he or she has created. You can easily eliminate choices A and E: a porter works at a terminal; a doctor works with a stethoscope. You can also eliminate Choice C: no coach literally creates a team in the same way that a composer creates a symphony.

Writers and painters, however, both create works of art. Which answer is better, B or D?

If you do not know the meaning of *plagiarism* and *mural*, think of a context for them. Someone is "accused of plagiarism." From this you can infer that plagiarism is a crime (passing off someone else's work as your own), not a created work. A mural is a picture painted on a wall. The correct answer is Choice D.

TACTIC 2: FAMILIARIZE YOURSELF WITH COMMON ANALOGY TYPES

Synonyms
MAGNIFICENT : GRANDIOSE
Magnificent and *grandiose* have the same meaning.

Antonyms
WAX : WANE
Wax, to grow larger, and *wane*, to dwindle, are opposites.

Worker and article created
POET : SONNET
A *poet* creates a *sonnet*.

Worker and tool used
PAINTER : BRUSH
A *painter* uses a *brush*.

Tool and material it acts upon
KNIFE : BREAD
A *knife* cuts *bread*.

Tool and its action
SAW : CUT
A *saw* is a tool used to *cut* wood.

Time sequence
FIRST : LAST
First and *last* mark the beginning and end of a sequence.

Cause and effect
VIRUS : INFLUENZA
A *virus* is the cause of *influenza*.

Degree of intensity
LUKEWARM : BOILING
Lukewarm is less intense than *boiling*.

Class and member
MAMMAL : WHALE
The class known as *mammal* has as one of its members the *whale*.

Member and class
SOFA : FURNITURE
The *sofa* is a member of the class known as *furniture*.

Type and characteristic
TIGER : CARNIVOROUS
A *tiger* can be described as *carnivorous* (meat-eating).

Part
ARCHIPELAGO : ISLAND
An *archipelago* is made up of many *islands*.

Person and thing he or she seeks
PROSPECTOR : GOLD
A *prospector* seeks *gold*.

Person and thing he or she learns to avoid
PILOT : SANDBAR
A ship's *pilot* tries to avoid hazards such as *sandbars*.

Sex
DOE : STAG
A *doe* is a female deer; a *stag*, a male deer.

Age
FOAL : STALLION
A *foal* (newborn horse) is younger than a *stallion*.

Symbol and what it represents
DOVE : PEACE
A *dove* is the symbol of *peace*.

TACTIC 3: IF MORE THAN ONE ANSWER FITS THE RELATIONSHIP IN YOUR SENTENCE, LOOK FOR A NARROWER APPROACH

When you try to express the relationship between the two capitalized words in sentence form, make sure you include enough details to particularize your analogy. Otherwise, more than one answer may fit the relationship, and you will have to go back to the original pair and analyze it again.

EXAMPLE 1:

SKYCAP : AIRPORT :: (A) stenographer : office
(B) cashier : box office (C) waitress : restaurant
(D) actress : theater (E) typist : paper

If you word your sentence "A skycap works at an airport," you will find that Choices A, B, C, and D all are good analogies. At this point, take a second look at the original relationship. A skycap works at an airport, true. What else do you know about a skycap's work? For one, he carries things for people. What's more, when he works at the airport, he relies on tips.

Refine your original sentence to include these additional facts. "A skycap carries bags for travellers at the airport in the hope of earning tips." Now test the answers. Only one answer fits: "A waitress carries food for patrons at a restaurant in the hope of earning tips." Choice C is the correct answer.

Your sentence should reflect the relationship between the two capitalized words *exactly*. If it doesn't, try, try again.

EXAMPLE 2:

ELEVATOR : SHAFT :: (A) magnet : electricity
(B) soda : bottle (C) bridge : tunnel
(D) water : conduit (E) rifle : shell

Suppose you phrase your sentence as follows: "You find an elevator in a shaft." You can immediately eliminate Choices A, C, and E. However, you still have to choose between Choices B and D.

Rephrase your sentence. "An elevator moves up and down through a shaft." *Water* flows through a *conduit* (a pipe or channel). Choice D is correct.

TACTIC 4: WATCH OUT FOR ERRORS STEMMING FROM REVERSALS

In an analogy you have two capitalized words in a set order. In the analogy CARELESSNESS : ACCIDENT, Word A, carelessness, is a cause; Word B, accident, is an effect. "*Carelessness* can cause an *accident*." Your answer pair must follow this same set order: Word C must be a cause; Word D, an effect.

Word A		Word B		Word C		Word D
CARELESSNESS	:	ACCIDENT	::	OVEREATING	:	INDIGESTION
cause		**effect**		**cause**		**effect**

EXAMPLE 1:

BIRD : SPARROW :: (A) boy : human being
(B) fish : gill (C) amphibian : species
(D) raven : dove (E) mammal : human being

If you read through this analogy quickly, you may easily make the error of choosing Choice A. After all, a sparrow is a type of bird, and a boy is a type of human being. What could be more straightforward than that?

Unfortunately, your original pair is not SPARROW: BIRD. It is BIRD: SPARROW. That translates into "One type of *bird* is a *sparrow*." Follow that same pattern with Choice A and you wind up with "One type of *boy* is a *human being*," a ridiculous statement. All boys are human beings by definition.

Go through the answer choices looking for a class of creature paired with a member of that class. Only one answer works, Choice E. "One type of *mammal* is a *human being*."

EXAMPLE 2:

> SUCCESS : ASSIDUITY :: (A) irritation : perseverance
> (B) incompetence : diligence (C) stupidity : failure
> (D) sweetness : light (E) proficiency : practice

In this analogy you are dealing with a cause and effect relationship in reverse. The effect (*success*) is presented before the cause (*assiduity*, or hard work). A good model sentence is "*Success* comes from *assiduity*." In the same way, *proficiency* comes from *practice*. Choice E is correct.

TACTIC 5: BE GUIDED BY THE PARTS OF SPEECH

Check that the relationship between the parts of speech of the capitalized words and the parts of speech of your answer choice is consistent. If your capitalized words are a noun and a verb, you need a noun and a verb (in that order) in your answer pair. If they are an adjective and a verb, you need an adjective and a verb.

EXAMPLE 1:

> LOQUACIOUS:TALK :: (A) vicious : criminal
> (B) pitiless : forgive (C) miserly : spend
> (D) chatter : prattle (E) gluttonous : eat

"Someone *loquacious* tends to *talk*." To fit this pattern, you need an adjective and a verb. You can immediately eliminate Choice A (two adjectives) and Choice D (two verbs). A person described as loquacious (talkative) is characterized by talking. A *pitiless* person would not tend to *forgive*, nor would a *miserly* person tend to *spend*. However, someone *gluttonous*, greedy for food, does tend to *eat*. The correct answer is Choice E.

EXAMPLE 2:

> PRICK : STAB :: (A) sword : thrust
> (B) sip : gulp (C) cure : wound
> (D) needle : thread (E) push : shove

In this analogy, the relationship is one of degree of intensity. "To *prick* someone (with a needle, for example) is not as extreme as to *stab* him." As used in this pattern sentence, *prick* and *stab* are both verbs. Only in choices B and E are both words verbs. However, *push* and *shove*, the words in Choice E, do not differ in degree: neither is more extreme than the other. Therefore, the best answer is Choice B. "To *sip* something is not as extreme as to *gulp* it."

LONG-RANGE STRATEGIES

The vocabulary in the analogy section differs slightly from the vocabulary tested in the antonym section. Somewhat fewer words come from Latin. Fewer words are abstract; more are concrete.

You need to know the names of everyday objects and parts of objects, names which the testmakers assume are in your everyday vocabulary but which nonetheless may be unfamiliar to you. You need to know that hawks have talons and trout have gills, that a group of islands is called an archipelago and a group of lions is called a pride. You need to know that calipers measure and that augers bore, that painters paint murals and that poets write odes.

How can you build up the sort of wide-ranging, concrete vocabulary you need to see the variety of relationships possible between words? The words are there; they're yours for the taking.

Words for the Taking

To meet new words, branch out in your reading. Try magazines in fields you haven't pursued before. Geology, geography, natural history, astronomy, art—terms from these disciplines appear again and again. Branch out in your viewing as well. You can watch *National Geographic* specials and other documentaries on television and build your vocabulary by attaching the names of objects to the things themselves: people need pictures as well as words.

Unabridged dictionaries often provide pictures of everyday objects: color plates of insects and flowers, birds and fish; line drawings of tools and machines. Picture dictionaries also exist. There is even a splendid visual glossary entitled *What's What*, consisting of hundreds of illustrations of everyday objects—from paper clips to passenger ships—carefully labeled to identify every part.

Learn by Doing

As you expand your vocabulary, try constructing some analogies using your new words. Go through the list of analogy types, modeling your analogies on the samples given. You should have no difficulty constructing innumerable synonyms and antonyms. Challenge yourself. Try to construct analogies where the relationship is one of cause and effect or one of a part to the whole. The better able you are to create good analogies of your own, the better able you will be to analyze the analogies of others.

PRACTICE EXERCISES

The two tests that follow will give you practice in handling analogy questions. The time for each test is thirty minutes. You may interpret your scores as follows:

42 to 50—EXCELLENT
34 to 41—SUPERIOR
26 to 33—SATISFACTORY
21 to 25—AVERAGE
0 to 20—UNSATISFACTORY

ANALOGY TEST A

Each question below consists of a related pair of words or phrases, followed by five lettered pairs of words or phrases. Select the lettered pair that best expresses a relationship similar to that expressed in the original pair.

Example:

YAWN : BOREDOM :: (A) dream : sleep (B) anger : madness (C) smile : amusement (D) face : expression (E) impatience : rebellion

Ⓐ Ⓑ ● Ⓓ Ⓔ

1. FISH : BIRD :: (A) rifle : tank (B) master : eagle (C) submarine : airplane (D) aquarium : tree (E) Audubon : Newton

2. LION : CARNIVOROUS ::
(A) jackal : herbivorous
(B) invalid : omnipotent
(C) human : mortal
(D) man : omnivorous
(E) tiger : striped

3. DOCTOR : DISEASE ::
(A) moron : imbecility
(B) pediatrician : senility
(C) psychiatrist : maladjustment
(D) poor man : poverty
(E) charlatan : truth

4. CLOCK : SECOND :: (A) calendar : year (B) calendar : month (C) calendar : day (D) watch : hour (E) program : date

5. SCISSORS : SEVER :: (A) scales : average (B) barrel : rolls (C) stapler : cuts (D) millstone : grinds (E) honesty : rewards

6. FRUGAL : PARSIMONIOUS ::
(A) kindly : benevolent
(B) magnanimous : philanthropic
(C) generous : prodigal
(D) stingy : miserly
(E) placid : active

7. TEACHER : IGNORANCE ::
(A) light : darkness (B) wattage : bulb
(C) lightning : electricity (D) stream : current
(E) interest : usury

8. DUSK : DAWN ::
(A) senility : childhood
(B) adolescence : infancy
(C) loquaciousness : garrulity
(D) necromancy : magic
(E) corpulence : obesity

9. STETHOSCOPE : PHYSICIAN ::
(A) canvas : sculptor (B) pestle : pharmacist
(C) scalpel : teacher (D) editor : author
(E) water : tank

10. PLAGIARISM : EMBEZZLEMENT ::
(A) writing : banking (B) brushes : painting
(C) blue print : etching (D) stillness : motion
(E) fact : fiction

11. CAT : FELINE :: (A) man : masculine
(B) dog : canine (C) sheep : bovine
(D) poetry : doggerel (E) tiger : carnivorous

12. OCEAN : BAY ::
(A) archipelago : atoll
(B) island : peninsula
(C) headland : promontory
(D) continent : peninsula
(E) salt water : sweet water

13. FISH : SCALES :: (A) planes : wings
(B) birds : feathers (C) cat : claws
(D) birds : beak (E) song : notes

14. INTREPID : COURAGEOUS ::
(A) noisome : fetid (B) malodorous : fragrant
(C) silent : boisterous (D) raucous : quiet
(E) original : banal

15. LEOPARD : CARNIVOROUS ::
(A) tiger : striped (B) cat : feline
(C) cow : herbivorous (D) seal : trained
(E) quadruped : four-legged

16. VACCINE : ANTIDOTE ::
(A) preventive : cure
(B) infantile paralysis : measles
(C) smallpox : poison
(D) horse : cow
(E) infection : elixir

17. ANARCHY : GOVERNMENT ::
(A) penury : wealth
(B) chaos : disorder
(C) monarch : president
(D) verbosity : words
(E) too little : too much

18. CIRCUITOUS : DIRECT ::
(A) cautious : straight (B) reckless : winding
(C) faulty : improper (D) tortuous : straight
(E) sanctimonious : pious

19. IMPECUNIOUS : MONEY ::
(A) hypocrite : integrity
(B) mendacious : falsehoods
(C) dishonest : integrity
(D) bankrupt : industry
(E) thieving : victim

20. DELUGE : SHOWER ::
(A) ecstatic : joyful
(B) sophisticated : unsophisticated
(C) conductor : director
(D) umbrella : boots
(E) brief : interminable

21. ROBIN : NEST :: (A) animal : cave
(B) dog : kennel (C) alligator : swamp
(D) clam : shell (E) fox : lair

22. SILO : CORN :: (A) memory : thoughts
(B) vault : valuables (C) hay : barn
(D) alone : grain (E) museum : art

23. TIRADE : ABUSIVE :: (A) diatribe : laudatory
(B) satire : pungent (C) panegyric : laudatory
(D) eulogy : lament (E) elegy : religious

24. INDUSTRY : BEAVER :: (A) ferocity : lion
(B) stripes : tiger (C) indolence : wolf
(D) speed : horse (E) stupidity : cow

25. CHARITY : VIRTUE :: (A) greed : evil
(B) avaricious : vicious (C) penury : crime
(D) avarice : vice (E) frugality : economy

26. VINDICATE : CONDEMN ::
(A) charge : accuse (B) indict : convict
(C) judge : jury (D) defendant : plaintiff
(E) dismiss : indict

27. INDUSTRIOUS : ASSIDUOUS ::
(A) affluent : impoverished
(B) mendacious : beggarly
(C) fortuitous : fortunate
(D) impecunious : poor
(E) qualitative : quantitative

28. TERPSICHOREAN : DANCE STUDIO ::
(A) forensic : theater (B) culinary : kitchen
(C) histrionic : court (D) judicial : law office
(E) residential : rumpus room

29. VERBOSE : GARRULOUS :: (A) novel : essay
(B) poem : short story (C) taciturn : loquacious
(D) laconic : wordy (E) laconic : taciturn

30. SILK : NYLON :: (A) Japan : America
(B) natural : synthetic (C) synthetic : natural
(D) dress : stockings (E) formal : informal

31. STUBBORN : MULISH ::
(A) coy : kittenish (B) fierce : doglike
(C) obtuse : wily (D) meek : temperate
(E) contrite : lionhearted

32. HELMET : HEAD :: (A) escutcheon : knee
(B) amulet : shoulder (C) sceptre : hand
(D) gauntlet : hand (E) crown : jewels

33. KANGAROO : MARSUPIAL ::
(A) rose : hybrid (B) antelope : gazelle
(C) mushroom : cloud (D) bear : bovine
(E) mushroom : fungus

34. ANATHEMA : BLESSING ::
(A) superstition : religion (B) song : benediction
(C) national song : paean
(D) curse : benediction (E) curse : charm

35. GUSTATORY : TASTE :: (A) olfactory : touch
(B) crossed : eyes (C) dulled : hearing
(D) myopic : taste (E) olfactory : smell

36. VENISON : PORK :: (A) sow : cow
(B) sheep : pig (C) deer : sheep (D) deer : pig
(E) pig : sheep

37. STERN : PROW :: (A) caboose : locomotive
(B) starboard : port (C) rudder : helm
(D) intermission : prologue (E) climax : inception

38. SOPHISTICATED : URBANE ::
(A) suave : naive (B) ingenuous : clever
(C) callow : rustic (D) naive : ingenuous
(E) wise : witty

39. DEBATER : LARYNGITIS ::
(A) actor : stage fright
(B) pedestrian : lameness
(C) doctor : diagnosis
(D) writer : paper
(E) swimmer : fatigue

40. SOLDIER : REGIMENT ::
(A) colonel : martinet (B) dancer : balletomane
(G) singer : chorus (D) trooper : rifle
(E) student : teacher

41. PORTER : TERMINAL :: (A) clerk : store
(B) cashier : restaurant (C) lawyer : court
(D) carpenter : construction site
(E) waitress : restaurant

42. AVARICE : ALTRUISM :: (A) anemic : sick
(B) sporadic : frequent (C) haggard : gaunt
(D) noisy : raucous (E) seldom : infrequent

43. DECIBEL : LIGHT YEAR ::
(A) distance : time (B) sound : time
(C) sound : distance (D) volume : length
(E) intensity : brightness

44. CYLINDER : CIRCLE :: (A) cone : triangle
(B) prism : spectrum (C) cone : circle
(D) prism : triangle (E) square : rectangle

45. LARIAT : CHAPS :: (A) gaucho : cowboy
(B) ranch : range (C) rope : leather
(D) ranch : rodeo (E) noose : fetter

46. TEAM : ATHLETES :: (A) game : series
(B) alliance : nations (C) delegated : convention
(D) squad : group (E) association : alliance

47. WEEK : MONTH :: (A) pint : gallon
(B) quart : pint (C) inch : foot (D) dime : dollar
(E) minute : second

48. ENTREPRENEUR : LABORER ::
(A) profits : wages
(B) arbitrator : capitalist
(C) mediator : conflict
(D) moonlighting : worker
(E) capitalism : communism

49. DECREPIT : NEW ::
(A) rehabilitated : renovated (B) worn out : fresh
(C) stale : fresh (D) sick : healthy
(E) ancient : modern

50. DETRITUS : GLACIERS :: (A) ice : iceberg
(B) thaw : cold (C) silt : rivers
(D) sediment : bottom (E) dregs : society

ANALOGY TEST B

Each question below consists of a related pair of words or phrases, followed by five lettered pairs of words or phrases. Select the lettered pair that best expresses a relationship similar to that expressed in the original pair.

Example:

YAWN : BOREDOM :: (A) dream : sleep
(B) anger : madness (C) smile : amusement
(D) face : expression (E) impatience : rebellion

Ⓐ Ⓑ ● Ⓓ Ⓔ

1. SPOKE : WHEEL ::
(A) square : circle
(B) balance : lever
(C) door : latch
(D) book : shelf
(E) rung : ladder

2. VESSEL : FLEET ::
(A) wolf : pack
(B) forest : tree
(C) vehicle : truck
(D) carriage : horse
(E) squadron : plane

3. TORY : WHIG ::
(A) Republican : Democrat
(B) Democrat : Republican
(C) traitor : patriot
(D) Conservative : Liberal
(E) Republican : Socialist

4. PICADOR : BULL :: (A) heckler : speaker
(B) mote : eye (C) executioner : victim
(D) singer : song (E) matador : cow

5. MUTTON : SHEEP :: (A) lamb : sheep
(B) pork : pig (C) veal : beef
(D) steer : beef (E) old : young

6. CORPULENCE : STOUT ::
(A) baldness : hirsute
(B) erudition : learned
(C) gauntness : beautiful
(D) steadfastness : mercurial
(E) intelligent : wit

7. GOLD : ORE :: (A) dear : cheap
(B) iron : steel (C) pearls : oysters
(D) steel : iron (E) intelligence : astuteness

8. MAESTRO : CONCERTMASTER ::
(A) orchestra : band (B) boss : foreman
(C) symphony : concerto
(D) Italian : English (E) general : private

9. CINEMA : SCENARIO :: (A) play : thing
(B) play : plot (C) movies : theme
(D) theater : plan (E) auditorium : screen

10. TITLE : COGNOMEN :: (A) king : queen
(B) king : duke (C) book : man
(D) book : cover (E) man : animal

11. TEAM : COACH :: (A) corporal : squad
(B) army : general (C) team : member
(D) club : advisor (E) club : president

12. INTRINSIC : EXTRINSIC ::
(A) intentional : unintentional
(B) vivid : dull
(C) real : simulated
(D) intentional : accidental
(E) real : extraneous

13. LARIAT : COWBOY ::
(A) medicine : patient
(B) scalpel : surgeon
(C) manuscript : author
(D) lawyer : client
(E) spice : gourmet

14. CALLOW : MATURITY ::
(A) incipient : fruition
(B) spoiled : purity
(C) young : old
(D) eager : anxiety
(E) young : senility

15. AWL : AUGER :: (A) wood : leather
(B) leather : shoe (C) cobbler : carpenter
(D) uppers : lowers (E) knife : prophet

16. CARELESSNESS : ACCIDENT ::
(A) assiduity : success
(B) indifference : fruition
(C) care : avoidance
(D) writer : blot
(E) thoughtlessness : oversight

17. MAY : MONTH :: (A) year : decade
(B) Thursday : day (C) second : minute
(D) day : hour (E) Friday : week

18. SALUTATORIAN : VALEDICTORIAN ::
(A) crisis : climax
(B) beginning : climax
(C) incipient : terminal
(D) runner-up : best
(E) prologue : play

19. HYPOCHONDRIAC : HEALTH ::
(A) addict : drugs (B) miser : money
(C) glutton : food (D) narcotic : sickness
(E) weakness : strength

20. BRAKE : AUTOMOBILE ::
(A) choke : carburetor
(B) conscience : man
(C) detergent : society
(D) stop : horse
(E) thinker : doer

21. MASON : WALL :: (A) doctor : cure
(B) magician : magic (C) stranger : friendship
(D) painter : mural (E) bricklayer : trowel

22. KENNEL : BOXER :: (A) nest : bird
(B) cage : bird (C) net : fish
(D) cage : parakeet (E) ring : pugilist

23. AREA : VOLUME :: (A) plane : circle
(B) circle : triangle (C) sphere : box
(D) box : sphere (E) circle : sphere

24. AMULET : SUPERSTITION ::
(A) talisman : charm
(B) savage : ritual
(C) antitoxin : experiment
(D) barbaric : savage
(E) peaceful : belief

25. HALCYON : MARTIAL ::
(A) moon : Mars
(B) military song : warlike
(C) peaceful : warlike
(D) soothed : worried
(E) belligerent : fighting

26. CHAFF : WHEAT :: (A) dregs : humanity
(B) gold : lead (C) dregs : wine
(D) ore : dross (E) cunning : wisdom

27. ENIGMA : RIDDLE :: (A) labyrinth : maze (B) dilemma : alternatives (C) Sphinx : Egyptian (D) bull : matador (E) labyrinth : string

28. PASSED : ELATION :: (A) failed : dejected (B) failed : dejection (C) rejected : angry (D) success : emotion (E) approved : disapproval

29. EAR : CORN :: (A) eye : storm (B) neck : bottle (C) stalk : wheat (D) stem : carrot (E) nose : bouquet

30. SOLDIER : CARBINE :: (A) author : book (B) chemist : test tube (C) sailor : pirate (D) sailor : marine (E) knight : spear

31. SURREY : HORSE :: (A) Buick : donkey (B) chariot : Shetland (C) rickshaw : coolie (D) prodigy : pedagogue

32. ARCHIPELAGO : ISLAND ::
(A) peninsula : strait
(B) Oceania : Alaska
(C) multitude : individual
(D) nucleus : cerebrum
(E) cell : nucleus

33. EXUBERANT : DOWNCAST ::
(A) exultant : lavish
(B) parsimonious : abundant
(C) congregation : dispersal
(D) eager : beaverlike
(E) effusive : melancholy

34. MINISTER : SERMON ::
(A) politician : promises
(B) heckler : interruptions
(C) doctor : cure
(D) teacher : lecture
(E) curator : cure

35. GOURMET : CAVIAR ::
(A) plebeian : patrician (B) clairvoyant : seance
(C) connoisseur : masterpiece (D) critic : edition
(E) million : caviar

36. GAUCHE : GRACEFUL ::
(A) clandestine : secretive
(B) inadvertent : thoughtless
(C) lugubrious : melancholy
(D) sad : poised
(E) indigent : wealthy

37. ABSTEMIOUS : SPARING ::
(A) irascible : militant
(B) gregarious : latent
(C) truculent : dogmatic
(D) lethargic : comatose
(E) absent : pusillanimous

38. DISCONSOLATE : GRIEF ::
(A) fatuous : weight (B) incurable : disease (C) explicit : statement (D) credulous : worry (E) sad : philosophy

39. CATCALL : DERISION :: (A) encore : approval (B) prodigality : generosity (C) wave : indifference (D) smile : contempt (E) horselaugh : bray

40. TOLERANCE : BIGOTRY ::
(A) prodigality : ribaldry
(B) avocation : profession
(C) magnanimity : parsimony
(D) exigency : urgency
(E) emulation : rivalry

41. GELID : ARCTIC ::
(A) halcyon : disturbed
(B) exhilarating : invigorating
(C) torrid : torpid
(D) sticky : cold
(E) luxuriant : tropical

42. ABHOR : DISLIKE :: (A) rebuke : ridicule (B) torture : distress (C) calcify : petrify (D) like : love (E) magnify : enlarge

43. GEOLOGIST : GNEISS ::
(A) archaeologist : tombstone (B) botanist : zinnia (C) architect : monolith (D) patriarch : progenitor (E) theologian : sky

44. FELON : PENITENTIARY ::
(A) perjurer : perjury
(B) conniver : constabulary
(C) juvenile delinquent : reformatory
(D) hedonist : confessional
(E) malefactor : sanctuary

45. GRATUITY : WAITER ::
(A) tip : porter
(B) wages : chauffeur
(C) recompense : proprietor
(D) employee : raise
(E) advice : friend

46. CONVICTION : THOUGHT ::
(A) persuasion : emotion (B) argument : style (C) arrest : fine (D) scene : action (E) sentence : vocabulary

47. EPHEMERAL : EVERLASTING ::
(A) rented : owned (B) temporary : permanent (C) earthly : heavenly (D) useless : permanent (E) latest : lasting

48. IMPROMPTU : MEMORIZED ::
(A) spontaneous : calculated
(B) read : recited
(C) glib : forced
(D) unrehearsed : extemporaneous
(E) tacit : verbose

49. TRAVELER : ITINERARY ::
(A) tourist : vacation (B) lecturer : outline
(C) pedestrian : routine (D) explorer : safari
(E) soldier : furlough

50. ASP : COBRA :: (A) hawk : eagle
(B) viper : reptile (C) fang : rattlesnake
(D) lair : wolf (E) mammal : whale

ANSWER KEY

Analogy Test A

1. **C**	11. **B**	21. **E**	31. **A**	41. **E**
2. **D**	12. **D**	22. **B**	32. **D**	42. **B**
3. **C**	13. **B**	23. **C**	33. **E**	43. **C**
4. **C**	14. **A**	24. **E**	34. **D**	44. **D**
5. **D**	15. **C**	25. **D**	35. **E**	45. **C**
6. **C**	16. **C**	26. **E**	36. **D**	46. **B**
7. **A**	17. **A**	27. **D**	37. **A**	47. **C**
8. **A**	18. **D**	28. **B**	38. **D**	48. **A**
9. **B**	19. **C**	29. **E**	39. **B**	49. **B**
10. **A**	20. **A**	30. **B**	40. **C**	50. **C**

Analogy Test B

1. **E**	11. **D**	21. **D**	31. **C**	41. **E**
2. **A**	12. **E**	22. **D**	32. **C**	42. **B**
3. **D**	13. **B**	23. **E**	33. **E**	43. **B**
4. **A**	14. **A**	24. **C**	34. **D**	44. **C**
5. **B**	15. **C**	25. **C**	35. **C**	45. **A**
6. **B**	16. **A**	26. **C**	36. **E**	46. **A**
7. **C**	17. **B**	27. **A**	37. **D**	47. **B**
8. **B**	18. **D**	28. **B**	38. **B**	48. **A**
9. **B**	19. **B**	29. **C**	39. **A**	49. **B**
10. **C**	20. **B**	30. **E**	40. **C**	50. **A**

THE SENTENCE COMPLETION QUESTION

6

- **Testing Tactics**
- **Long-Range Strategies**
- **Practice Exercises**
- **Answer Key**

TESTING TACTICS

These questions ask you to choose the word or words that will fill in the blanks in a given sentence. Here are the directions.

> Each sentence below has one or two blanks, each blank indicating that something has been omitted. Beneath the sentence are five lettered words or sets of words. Choose the word or set of words that best fits the meaning of the sentence as a whole.
>
> Example:
>
> Although its publicity has been ----, the film itself is intelligent, well-acted, handsomely produced, and altogether ----.
>
> (A) tasteless..respectable (B) extensive..moderate (C) sophisticated..amateur (D) risqué..crude (E) perfect..spectacular
>
> ● Ⓑ Ⓒ Ⓓ Ⓔ

The word *although* is a signal word: it suggests that the film's publicity contrasts with the film itself. The main clause describes the film in positive, even glowing terms: "intelligent, well-acted, handsomely produced." The film is well-done. Therefore, the film's publicity must be poorly done.

You are looking for two words more or less opposite in meaning. The first, describing the publicity, must be negative; the second, summing up the film as intelligent, well-acted, must be positive.

A quick glance at the first words in each of the answer choices reveals two negative terms: (A) *tasteless*, and (D) *risqué*. Since *crude*, the second half of Choice D, is not positive, it is an unlikely word to describe this "intelligent, well-acted . . . " film. Eliminate Choice D; Choice A is correct.

The type of question treated in this chapter tests your ability to use your vocabulary and recognize logical consistency among the elements in a sentence. To merely know a synonym of a word does not assure success, for these questions put words to use.

Sentence completion questions actually measure a phase of reading comprehension. If you can recognize the implications of a sentence, you will have no difficulty in choosing the answer that best fulfills the meaning of the sentence or which provides a clear, logical statement of fact.

TACTIC 1: BEFORE YOU LOOK AT THE CHOICES, READ THE SENTENCE AND THINK OF A WORD THAT MAKES SENSE

Your problem here is to find the word that best completes the sentence's thought. Before you look at the answer choices, see if you can come up with a word that makes logical sense in this context. Then look at all five choices supplied by the examiner. If the word you thought of is one of your five choices, select it as your answer. If the word you thought of is *not* one of your five choices, look for a synonym of that word. Select the synonym as your answer.

EXAMPLE:

> It was ---- to everyone in the courtroom that the witness was not telling the truth.

What words come to your mind? *Obvious*, perhaps, or *clear*. Either of these words can complete the thought of the sentence.

Here are the five choices provided by the examiner:

> (A) oblivious (B) enigmatic (C) evident (D) vindictive (E) imperative

The only word that can be a synonym of *obvious* is Choice C, *evident*. The correct answer is Choice C.

TACTIC 2: LOOK AT ALL THE POSSIBLE ANSWERS BEFORE YOU MAKE YOUR FINAL CHOICE

You are looking for the word that *best* fits the meaning of the sentence as a whole. To be sure you have not been hasty in making your decision, substitute all the answer choices for the missing word. That way you can satisfy yourself that you have indeed come up with the answer that best fits.

EXAMPLE 1:

> Because the enemy had a reputation for engaging in sneak attacks, we were ---- on the alert.
> (A) frequently (B) furtively (C) evidently (D) constantly (E) occasionally

A hasty reader might be content with Choice A, *frequently*, but *frequently* is not the best fit. The best answer is Choice D, *constantly*. Even *frequent* periods of alertness would not be enough to provide the necessary protection against sneak attacks that could occur at any time. *Constant* vigilance is called for. The troops would have to be always on the alert.

EXAMPLE 2:

> As a bachelor teaching in a girls' school, he was ---- paying compliments to his more attractive pupils, fearing the gossip that would inevitably arise.
> (A) fond of (B) aware of (C) prone to (D) reckless about (E) chary of

No bachelor teacher who feared gossip would be *reckless about* paying compliments to his pupils, nor would he be *prone to* or *fond of* paying them. At first glance, Choice B, *aware of*, may seem possible. However, he is more than merely aware of paying compliments; he is nervous about complimenting the girls, wary even. Your answer is Choice E, *chary*.

Note that the key phrase *fearing... gossip* comes near the end of the sentence, while the blank comes near its beginning. In single-blank sentences, the part of the sentence that does not have the blank often has the clues to tell you what the word in the blank should be. Read the whole sentence closely.

TACTIC 3: IN DOUBLE-BLANK SENTENCES GO THROUGH THE ANSWERS, TESTING THE FIRST WORD IN EACH CHOICE (AND ELIMINATING THOSE THAT DON'T FIT)

In a sentence completion question with two blanks, read through the entire sentence. Then insert the first word of each answer pair in the sentence's first blank. Ask yourself whether this particular word makes sense in this blank. If the initial word of an answer pair makes no sense in the sentence, you can eliminate that answer pair.

EXAMPLE:

> Her true feelings ---- themselves in her sarcastic asides; only then was her ---- revealed.
> (A) concealed..sweetness (B) manifested..bitterness (C) hid..sarcasm (D) developed..anxiety (E) grieved..charm

If you test the first word in each choice, you can eliminate several choices. *Concealed* (Choice A) and *hid* (Choice C) conflict with the statement that something is *revealed*. You may also feel, without being able to say why, that *grieved* (Choice E) does not work in its suggested context. Trust your instincts in this case. *Grieve* belongs to a small class of English verbs which *must* have a person as their subject or object. You can say "She *grieved* (mourned) over her father's death." You can also say "His behavior *grieved* her (caused her to grieve)." Feelings are things, not people. Therefore, feelings cannot grieve themselves.

Having eliminated choices E, A, and C, turn to the second blank. What feelings are revealed in sarcastic asides? Feelings of *bitterness* or feelings of *anxiety*? The word *sarcastic* describes something that is *bitter* or cutting, something intended to wound. The correct answer, therefore, is Choice B.

Remember, in double-blank sentences, the right answer must correctly fill both blanks. A wrong answer choice often includes one possibly correct and one definitely incorrect answer. ALWAYS test the second word.

TACTIC 4: USE YOUR KNOWLEDGE OF WORD PARTS AND CONTEXT CLUES TO GET AT THE MEANINGS OF UNFAMILIAR WORDS

If a word used by the author is unfamiliar, or if an answer choice is unknown to you, look at its context in the sentence to see whether the context provides a clue to the meaning of the word. Often authors will use an unfamiliar word and then immediately define it within the same sentence.

EXAMPLE 1:

> His phlegmatic nature, invariably stolid and composed, ---- him to ignore her tantrums and get on with the job.
>
> (A) predisposed (B) excited (C) prevented
> (D) contradicted (E) disinclined

Suppose you don't know the meaning of the word *phlegmatic* in the opening phrase, "His phlegmatic nature." You may feel unequipped to try to tackle the sentence at all. However, the phrase that immediately follows ("invariably stolid and composed") is there to explain and identify that opening phrase. The two groups of words are juxtaposed—set beside one another—to make their relationship clear. *Phlegmatic* means "stolid, lacking emotion, dull."

Once you know what *phlegmatic* means, the sentence is easy to complete. You can eliminate Choice B at once: a phlegmatic nature is unexcitable. Choice C doesn't work grammatically (one prevents someone *from doing* something). Choices D and E don't make logical sense. Choice A is correct.

Word parts also can reveal the meanings of unfamiliar words.

EXAMPLE 2:

> After a tragedy, many people claim to have had a ---- of disaster.
>
> (A) taste (B) dislike (C) presentiment
> (D) context (E) verdict

Take the unfamiliar word *presentiment*. Break it down into parts. A *sentiment* is a feeling (the root *sens* means feel). *Pre-* means before. A *presentiment* is something you feel before it happens, a foreboding. Your best answer is Choice C.

TACTIC 5: WATCH FOR SIGNAL WORDS THAT LINK ONE PART OF THE SENTENCE TO ANOTHER

Writers use transitions to link their ideas logically. These transitions or signal words are clues that can help you figure out what the sentence actually means.

Contrast Signals

Look for words or phrases that indicate a **contrast** between one idea and another. In such cases an antonym or near-antonym for another word in the sentence should provide the correct answer.

Signal	Words
although	instead of
but	nevertheless
despite	on the contrary
even though	on the other hand
however	rather than
in contrast	still
in spite of	yet

EXAMPLE 1:

> We expected him to be jubilant over his victory, but he was ---- instead.
>
> (A) triumphant (B) adult (C) morose (D) talkative (E) culpable

But suggests that the winner's expected reaction contrasts with his actual one. Instead of being *jubilant* (extremely joyful), he is sad. The correct answer is Choice C, *morose*.

Support Signals

Look for words or phrases that indicate that the omitted portion of the sentence **supports** or **continues a thought** developed elsewhere in the sentence. In such cases, a synonym or near-synonym for another word in the sentence should provide the correct answer.

Signal Words	
additionally	furthermore
also	in addition
and	likewise
besides	moreover

EXAMPLE 2:

> The simplest animals are those whose bodies are simplest in structure and which do the things done by all animals, such as eating, breathing, moving, and feeling, in the most ---- way.
>
> (A) haphazard (B) bizarre (C) advantageous (D) primitive (E) unique

The transition *and* signals you that the writer intends to develop the concept of simplicity introduced in the sentence. You should know from your knowledge of biology that *primitive* life forms were simple in structure and that the more complex forms evolved later. Choice C may seem possible. However, to secure the most *advantageous* way of conducting the activities of life, the animal would have to become specialized and complex. Thus, Choice D (*primitive*) is best, because it is the only choice which develops the idea of simplicity.

Cause Signals

Look for words or phrases which indicate that one thing **causes** another.

Signal Words	
accordingly	in order to
because	so
consequently	therefore
for	thus
hence	when . . . then

EXAMPLE 3:

> Because his delivery was ----, his speech had no effect on the voters.
>
> (A) halting (B) plausible (C) moving (D) respectable (E) audible

What sort of delivery would cause a speech to have no effect? Obviously, you would not expect a moving or eloquent delivery to have such a sorry result. A *halting* or stumbling speech, however, would normally have little or no effect. Thus, Choice A is best.

LONG-RANGE STRATEGIES

Although you certainly will wish to consult "Build Your Vocabulary," Chapter 8, and work on the vocabulary-development methods there, answering sentence completion questions involves more than recognizing individual words. You need to know idiomatic expressions—groups of words always used together—particularly those involving prepositions, and those used so frequently in formal prose that they seem clichés. Similarly, you need to know the typical patterns that writers follow in developing their thoughts.

Idiomatic Expressions and Clichés

In their general tips for answering sentence completion questions, the SAT makers say, "Don't select an answer simply because it is a popular cliché or 'sounds good.'" The key word here is *simply.* If an answer is a popular cliché, it may well be right. *Don't* disregard an answer just because it's a cliché.

If you look at the answers to the sentence completion questions in *10 SATs* and *5 SATs*, the College Board's own publications, you will swiftly discover that a high proportion of the correct answers are, in fact, clichés—set phrases an experienced reader will find extremely familiar. Consider, for example, phrases such as *avert disaster, cavalier treatment, render unnecessary, overt acts*. The more formal prose you read, the more you will encounter set phrases such as these.

Sometimes the presence of a preposition in the body of a sentence can give you a clue to the missing word. The list below indicates which preposition is idiomatically correct after the following words:

accede to	dissent from
accuse of	distaste for
addicted to	enamored of
adhere to	enveloped in
(an) advocate of	expert in
agreeable to	hallowed by
agreed on (something)	hint at
agreed with (someone)	implicit in
amazement at	indulge in
amenable to	negligent of
appetite for	oblivious to
appreciation of	observant of
aside from	partial to
associate with	peculiar to
blame for	preview of
capable of	prior to
characterized by	prone to
chary of	revel in
compatible with	separate from
conversant with	suspaect of
desire for	tamper with
desirous of	threatened with
desist from	try to
different from	void of
disagree with	weary of
disdain for	willing to

Sentence Patterns

Definitions

In a definition, the author restates a word or phrase to clarify its meaning. The author commonly will set the definition beside the word being defined, juxtaposing them. Commas, hyphens, and parentheses are used to signal definitions.

1. The *rebec*, a medieval stringed instrument played with a bow, has only three strings.
2. *Paleontologists*—students of fossil remains—explore the earth's history.
3. Most mammals are *quadrupeds* (four-footed animals).

Definitions also follow forms of the verb "to be" and other connecting verbs.

1. A *stoic* is a person who is indifferent to pleasure or pain.
2. A three-pronged spear is called a *trident*.

Often an unfamiliar word in one clause of a sentence will be defined in the sentence's other clause.

1. That Barbie doll is a *lethal* weapon; your daughter nearly killed me with it!
2. The early morning dew had frozen, and everything was covered with a thin coat of *rime*.

Examples

By presenting specific, concrete examples, an author makes a general, abstract word come to life.

1. Crates of coins, paintings by Rubens and Renoir, diamond tiaras and rings of rubies and gold—I never realized the extent of President Marcos' *affluence* until I read the accounts of what he brought with him from the Philippines.
2. Cowards, we use *euphemisms* when we cannot bear the truth, calling our dead "the dear departed," as if they have just left the room.
3. I'm impressed by Trudy's business *acumen*: she buys sound but aging houses, renovates them relatively inexpensively, and then rents them out for fabulous sums.

Comparisons

Just as concrete examples make abstract words come to life, in the same way the use of a familiar object in a comparison can bring home the meaning of an unfamiliar word or phrase.

1. Some *circumstantial evidence* is very strong, as when you find a trout in the milk. —Thoreau
2. Our impact on this world is as *evanescent* as a skywriter's impact on the sky.

Contrasts

You can learn a great deal about what something *is* if you come to terms with what it *is not*. Notice the signal words in the sentences that follow.

1. Although America's total Vietnamese population is *minuscule*, the number of Vietnamese students attending major American universities is surprisingly high.
2. Marriage has many pains, but *celibacy* has no pleasures. —Johnson
3. In place of *complacency*, I give you unrest; in place of sameness I give you variety.

Often a writer contrasts two ideas without using a signal word. The contrast is implicit in the juxtaposition of the two clauses.

1. The *optimist* proclaims that we live in the best of all possible worlds; the *pessimist* fears this is true. —Cabell.
2. Lord, make me an instrument of Your peace.
   Where there is hatred, let me sow love;
   Where there is injury, pardon;
   Where there is doubt, faith;
   Where there is despair, hope;
   Where there is darkness, light; and
   Where there is sadness, joy. —St. Francis

Arguments

Sentences which present arguments often follow the pattern of cause and effect. You must try to follow the author's reasoning as you work towards his or her conclusion.

1. When *tillage* begins, other arts follow. The farmers, therefore, are the founders of human civilization. —Webster

2. A man ought to read just as *inclination* leads him; for what he reads as a task will do him little good. —Johnson

PRACTICE EXERCISES

The two tests that follow will give you an indication of your ability to handle these sentence completion questions. The time for each test is thirty minutes. Scoring may be interpreted as follows:

43 TO 50—EXCELLENT
35 TO 42—SUPERIOR
27 TO 34—SATISFACTORY
21 TO 26—AVERAGE
0 TO 20—UNSATISFACTORY

SENTENCE COMPLETION TEST A

Each sentence below has one or two blanks, each blank indicating that something has been omitted. Beneath the sentence are five lettered words or sets of words. Choose the word or set of words that best fits the meaning of the sentence as a whole.

Example:

Although its publicity has been ----, the film itself is intelligent, well-acted, handsomely produced, and altogether ----.

(A) tasteless..respectable (B) extensive..moderate
(C) sophisticated..amateur (D) risqué..crude
(E) perfect..spectacular

● Ⓑ Ⓒ Ⓓ Ⓔ

1. Now that we have succeeded in isolating this drug and discovering its nature, our next problem is to plan its ---- in the laboratory.
(A) amalgamation (B) synthesis
(C) introduction (D) qualities (E) nature

2. The teacher suspected cheating as soon as he noticed the pupil's ---- glances at his classmate's paper.
(A) overt (B) sporadic (C) furtive
(D) futile (E) inconsequential

3. The ---- was noted for his ----.
(A) hypocrite..honesty (B) braggart..modesty
(C) craven..integrity (D) philanthropist..altruism
(E) mercenary..benevolence

4. If you listen carefully, you can hear this simple ---- throughout the entire score.
(A) cadence (B) paean (C) banality
(D) motif (E) trilogy

5. I am amazed to see such fine work done by a mere ----.
(A) amateur (B) entrepreneur (C) tyro
(D) despot (E) libertine

6. The sociologist maintained that the ---- and filth contributed to the delinquency in the ---- area.
(A) crime..entire (B) squalor..redolent
(C) terror..beseiged (D) litter..renovated
(E) penury..slum

7. Your ---- remarks spoil the effect of your speech; try not to stray from your subject.
(A) digressive (B) demoniac (C) discerning
(D) disingenuous (E) disputatious

8. We need both ornament and implement in our society; we need the artist and the ----.
(A) beautician (B) writer (C) artistic
(D) artisan (E) engineer

9. When such ---- remarks are circulated, we can only blame and despise those who produce them.
(A) adulatory (B) avid (C) rhetorical
(D) redundant (E) reprehensible

10. We need more men of culture and enlightenment in our society; we have too many ---- among us.
(A) pedants (B) philistines (C) moralists
(D) ascetics (E) paragons

11. To be ---- is to be ----.

(A) petulant . . eager (B) avid . . thirsty (C) parsimonious . . niggardly (D) vacillating . . resolute (E) phlegmatic . . ardent

12. ---- his many hours of hard work at his bench, he realized that his progress was tenuous.

(A) Despite (B) Because of (C) Through (D) Besides (E) By

13. It is difficult to enforce these rules because they are too ----.

(A) subservient (B) truculent (C) pellucid (D) stringent (E) decrepit

14. A sanguine personality is the sign of the ----.

(A) pessimist (B) optimist (C) philanthropist (D) profiteer (E) rationalist

15. Many educators argued that a ---- grouping of students would improve instruction as the range of student abilities would be limited.

(A) heterogeneous (B) intensive (C) homogeneous (D) systematic (E) varied

16. As news of his indictment spread through the town, the citizens began to ---- him and to avoid meeting him.

(A) ostracize (B) capitulate (C) desecrate (D) minimize (E) harass

17. These sporadic raids seem to indicate that the enemy is waging a war of ---- rather than attacking us directly.

(A) fragments (B) attrition (C) intensity (D) barbarism (E) words

18. There are too many ---- and not enough serious workers.

(A) sycophants (B) kleptomaniacs (C) tyros (D) recreants (E) dilettantes

19. As the debate continued, the speakers became more vehement and their remarks more ----.

(A) pertinent (B) prolix (C) prolonged (D) acrimonious (E) ravenous

20. Many elderly people are capable of working, but they are kept from gainful employment by a ---- on the part of employers which leads them to believe that young people alone can give them adequate service.

(A) philosophy (B) conviction (C) device (D) tendency (E) short-sightedness

21. The fire marshals spent many hours seeking the cause of the ---- in which so many lives were lost and so many others hospitalized with major burns.

(A) disaster (B) maelstrom (C) catastrophe (D) holocaust (E) debacle

22. To ---- a person is to ---- him.

(A) abjure . . admire (B) venerate . . revere (C) intimidate . . encourage (D) mulct . . despise (E) revile . . canonize

23. If you come to the conference table with such an ---- attitude, we can not expect to reach any harmonious agreement.

(A) ancillary (B) effervescent (C) indolent (D) obdurate (E) unwonted

24. I can vouch for his honesty; I have always found him ----.

(A) venal (B) venial (C) voracious (D) veracious (E) volatile

25. If Shakespeare needs any excuse for the ---- of language (the high key in which he pitched most of his dramatic dialogue) it should be remembered that he was doing on the plastic stage of his own day what on the pictorial stage of our day is not so much required.

(A) paucity (B) verbosity (C) placidity (D) prolixity (E) exuberance

26. Micawber was always ---- because he spent more than he earned.

(A) imprisoned (B) indigent (C) tired (D) intoxicated (E) friendly

27. She felt that Jack's ---- in the face of the evidence which she had presented was an example of his ---- mind.

(A) incredulity . . unbiased (B) skepticism . . open (C) incredulity . . closed (D) acquiescence . . open (E) agreement . . impartial

28. ---- his broker told him the stock was a ---- investment, he insisted on buying 100 shares.

(A) Because . . speculative
(B) Although . . precarious
(C) Since . . good
(D) Although . . bona fide
(E) When . . benign

29. An excessively high rate of interest is called ----.

(A) askance (B) exorbitant (C) outlandish (D) usury (E) unusual

30. It is foolish to combat the ----; it is wiser to accept it.

(A) impossible (B) inevitable (C) conquerors (D) gamblers (E) inconsequential

31. He sought ---- from the enemy in the church.

(A) salvation (B) relief (C) hiding (D) sanctuary (E) speciousness

32. A ---- is a contradictory statement.

(A) paragon (B) paramount (C) paradox (D) partition (E) parsimony

33. We cannot pardon such and ----act of violence.
(A) acute (B) ominous (C) unusual (D) insipid (E) egregious

34. I do not understand how you can ignore such ---- signs of an ominous future.
(A) prominent (B) portentous (C) pretentious (D) fortuitous (E) flagrant

35. I like to go north for my vacation because warm weather always ---- me.
(A) bores (B) stimulates (C) entices (D) enervates (E) energizes

36. At the present time, we are suffering from a ---- of articles about the war; try writing about another subject.
(A) plague (B) series (C) plethora (D) dearth (E) calumny

37. Because he was a ----, he shunned human society.
(A) misanthrope (B) oligarch (C) anomaly (D) corsair (E) myrmidon

38. In that terrific ----, many people lost their lives and countless others were burned.
(A) sirocco (B) typhoon (C) maelstrom (D) holocaust (E) accident

39. The police feel that the ---- shown by the judges to first offenders ---- many youngsters to embark on a career of crime.
(A) understanding. . deters
(B) clemency. . encourages
(C) penalties. . encourages
(D) indifference. . enhances
(E) tolerance. . induces

40. At this time of the year, this stream is so ---- that it is unwise to try to travel by canoe.
(A) turbid (B) turgid (C) torpid (D) tortuous (E) tranquil

41. He has the ---- distinction of being the only one in the class to fail the examination.
(A) outstanding (B) dubious (C) impressive (D) remarkable (E) extrinsic

42. As the conductor mounted the ----, the audience burst into applause.
(A) stage (B) dais (C) podium (D) platform (E) ladder

43. It is wise to treat a disease while it is still in its ---- stage.
(A) introductory (B) quiet (C) dangerous (D) contagious (E) incipient

44. I move we ---- the remarks from the record.
(A) edit (B) emboss (C) exculpate (D) evidence (E) expunge

45. We must discover and develop each student's ---- talents.
(A) unrecognized (B) unacknowledged (C) intrinsic (D) dormant (E) specious

46. I believe that play is the most fatuous and ---- production of the season.
(A) gripping (B) inane (C) resplendent (D) prophetic (E) glamorous

47. His olfactory sense was so highly developed that he was often called in to judge ----.
(A) colors (B) textures (C) seasonings (D) perfumes (E) music

48. This stream is so ---- that it is impossible to see the bottom even where it is shallow.
(A) turbid (B) turgid (C) torpid (D) turbulent (E) tortuous

49. Although I have always been confused by our ---- system, I ---- traveling on the subways occasionally.
(A) mercantile. . remember
(B) monetary. . dislike
(C) social. . evaluate
(D) transit. . enjoy
(E) revolutionary. . explore

50. The word "bowdlerize" recalls the time when Mr. Bowdler tried to ---- certain passages in Shakespeare's works which he felt were offensive.
(A) rewrite (B) extirpate (C) expurgate (D) expound (E) evoke

SENTENCE COMPLETION TEST B

Each sentence below has one or two blanks, each blank indicating that something has been omitted. Beneath the sentence are five lettered words or sets of words. Choose the word or set of words that best fits the meaning of the sentence as a whole.

Example:

Although its publicity has been ----, the film itself is intelligent, well-acted, handsomely produced, and altogether ----.

(A) tasteless..respectable (B) extensive..moderate (C) sophisticated..amateur (D) risqué..crude (E) perfect..spectacular

● Ⓑ Ⓒ Ⓓ Ⓔ

1. Because he is so ----, we cannot predict what course he will follow at any moment.

(A) incoherent (B) whimsical (C) capricious (D) deleterious (E) inebriated

2. The old-fashioned orator spoke in a ---- and pompous manner.

(A) orotund (B) brazen (C) burnished (D) bombastic (E) flaccid

3. The students gathered in the ---- for their evening meal.

(A) solarium (B) refectory (C) buttery (D) nave (E) galley

4. The bank teller's ---- of the funds was not discovered until the auditors examined the accounts.

(A) burglary (B) pilfering (C) theft (D) lifting (E) embezzlement

5. Because of the ---- outcome of the game, the spectators were ----; many suspected collusion with the gamblers.

(A) violent..dismayed
(B) surprising..elated
(C) unexpected..shocked
(D) fortuitous..overjoyed
(E) exciting..horrified

6. He was so convinced that people were driven by ---- motives that he could not believe that anyone could be unselfish.

(A) different (B) personal (C) altruistic (D) ulterior (E) intrinsic

7. Because he was an ----, he preferred reading a book in his own study to attending a night club.

(A) extrovert (B) exhibitionist (C) egoist (D) introvert (E) epicurean

8. It is more difficult to write about the ---- than the strange and ----.

(A) people..foreign (B) commonplace.. laity (C) commonplace..exotic (D) simple.. routine (E) ludicrous..dejected

9. The plot of this story is so ---- that I can predict the outcome.

(A) clever (B) inveterate (C) involved (D) trite (E) insipid

10. When the infant displayed signs of illness, the anxious parents called in a ----.

(A) podiotrist (B) pediatrician (C) practitioner (D) pedagogue (E) plagiarist

11. Because this liquid is highly ----, it should be kept in a tightly stoppered bottle.

(A) voluble (B) volatile (C) voluptuous (D) expensive (E) explosive

12. These regulations are so ---- that we feel we have lost all our privileges.

(A) stringent (B) redundant (C) specious (D) meretricious (E) tawdry

13. He was pleased by the encomiums heaped upon him because, like everyone else, he liked being ----.

(A) rewarded (B) praised (C) elected (D) remunerated (E) abhorred

14. The old man's garrulity was so well know that all of us avoided his ----.

(A) stories (B) food (C) loans (D) kindnesses (E) imbecilities

15. The younger members of the company resented the domineering and ---- manner of the office manager.

(A) paternal (B) fatherly (C) sycophantic (D) impossible (E) imperious

16. His ---- attitude offends many because they feel he is suffering from ----.

(A) bellicose..hesitancy
(B) truculent..ennui
(C) supercilious..arrogance
(D) paternalistic..benevolence
(E) conciliatory..uncertainty

17. In ---- days, primitive man first began to use simple tools.

(A) past (B) antiquated (C) antecedent (D) antediluvian (E) abysmal

18. In view of the fact that there are mitigating circumstances, we must consider this a ---- offense.

(A) heinous (B) venal (C) propitious (D) venial (E) vendible

19. Industrial leaders are worried lest new inventions make their plants unprofitable to operate; they, therefore, wish to protect themselves against possible ----.

(A) depreciation (B) despoliation (C) obsolescence (D) casualties (E) bankruptcies

20. A musical piece for soloist with orchestral accompaniment is a ----.

(A) symphony (B) tone poem (C) concert piece (D) concertina (E) concerto

21. He was ---- in his colorful dress uniform.

(A) attired (B) bedecked (C) outfitted (D) resplendent (E) redolent

22. Upon realizing that his position was ----, the general ---- his men to retreat to a neighboring hill.

(A) valuable . . remonstrated
(B) untenable . . ordered
(C) evident . . urged
(D) exposed . . neglected
(E) salubrious . . commended

23. We were certain that disaster was ----.

(A) impeccable (B) inherent (C) immutable (D) invidious (E) imminent

24. Only the fear of immediate ---- prevents that country from launching an attack.

(A) revenge (B) bombing (C) reprisal (D) retort (E) destruction

25. The seriousness of the drought could only be understood by those who had seen the ---- crops in the fields.

(A) copious (B) wilted (C) meager (D) verdant (E) crippled

26. You should ---- this paragraph in order to make your essay more ----.

(A) delete . . succint (B) enlarge . . poignant (C) excise . . expansive (D) revise . . abstruse (E) expunge . . witty

27. Because of his ---- appetite, he found most foods ----.

(A) sated..filling (B) jaded..cloying (C) keen..cloying (D) jaded..appealing (E) voracious..vitiating

28. The members of the Better Government League vowed to ---- all traces of ---- between criminals and politicians.

(A) eradicate..controversy
(B) investigate..contact
(C) abhor..contact
(D) impound..ties
(E) extirpate..collusion

29. He asked the druggist for a bottle of ---- of iodine.

(A) solution (B) tincture (C) mixture (D) medley (E) melange

30. Our only hope is to prove that the witness was ---- and guilty of perjury.

(A) prejudiced (B) improper (C) mendacious (D) meretricious (E) meddlesome

31. At the height of the storm, the savages tried to ---- the angry gods by offering sacrifices.

(A) appall (B) bribe (C) dissuade (D) cajole (E) propitiate

32. Criticism which tears down without suggesting areas of improvement is not ---- and should be avoided if possible.

(A) reprehensible (B) constructive (C) mandatory (D) conciliatory (E) sagacious

33. Such an ---- act of hostility can only lead to war.

(A) overt (B) opportunistic (C) occasional (D) oscillating (E) unequaled

34. The judge stated that although he could not ---- the prisoner's criminal act, he could understand what had prompted the culprit's ---- behavior.

(A) overlook..nocturnal
(B) condone..nefarious
(C) acknowledge..notorious
(D) accept..illegal
(E) disregard..exemplary

35. I feel that my client's offense is ---- and that you will be merciful.

(A) heinous (B) migratory (C) vindicable (D) migraine (E) vindictive

36. The advocates of anarchy are ignoring the ---- such a form of government will bring with it.

(A) dictatorship (B) chaos (C) autocracy (D) republicanism (E) internationalism

37. The ---- reasoning used by the demagogue is certain to fool many people.

(A) plausible (B) involved (C) syllogistic (D) specious (E) splenetic

38. I cannot forgive such a ---- crime.

(A) reprobate (B) recidivist (C) reprehensible (D) regurgitate (E) repudiated

39. The old man in his walk and talk, his recollections of childhood days, his lapses of memory, indicated that he was----.

(A) feeble (B) an octogenarian (C) forgetful (D) sentimental (E) senile

40. Fear of enclosed places is called----.

(A) kleptomania (B) agoraphobia (C) hypochondria (D) insanity (E) claustrophobia

41. Her----remarks proved that she was really naive and unsophisticated.

(A) churlish (B) uninhibited (C) ingenuous (D) worldly (E) unmitigated

42. A(n) ----is not----.

(A) pessimist..gloomy
(B) optimist..cheerful
(C) pessimist..sanguine
(D) pessimist..sanguinary
(E) optimist..exuberant

43. When the news of his----with the enemy became known, he was hanged in effigy.

(A) involvement (B) conversations (C) bickering (D) collusion (E) complacency

44. The physicians were worried about the possibility of finding a----growth in the patient.

(A) benign (B) tumorous (C) malicious (D) benignant (E) malignant

45. The dispute became so----that we were afraid that the arguers would come to blows.

(A) ascetic (B) acetic (C) bellicose (D) acrimonious (E) bilious

46. John was a----and had an inexplicable desire to ----.

(A) paranoiac..escape (B) kleptomaniac..steal (C) madman..reform (D) reactionary..hate (E) litigant..depart

47. A----glance pays----attention to details.

(A) furtive..sly (B) cautious..careful (C) cursory..little (D) bleak..cold (E) cryptic..cautious

48. I regret that my remarks seemed----; I never intended to belittle you.

(A) derogatory (B) defamatory (C) depreciating (D) delinquent (E) deprecatory

49. He----devoted himself to the completion of the book.

(A) deliberately (B) assiduously (C) ingenuously (D) deliriously (E) devotedly

50. Shakespeare's reference to clocks in "Julius Caesar" is an example of----.

(A) poetic license (B) antiquarianism (C) anachronism (D) ignorance (E) free verse

ANSWER KEY

Sentence Completion Test A

1.	**B**	11.	**C**	21.	**D**	31.	**D**	41.	**B**
2.	**C**	12.	**A**	22.	**B**	32.	**C**	42.	**C**
3.	**D**	13.	**D**	23.	**D**	33.	**E**	43.	**E**
4.	**D**	14.	**B**	24.	**D**	34.	**B**	44.	**E**
5.	**C**	15.	**C**	25.	**E**	35.	**D**	45.	**D**
6.	**E**	16.	**A**	26.	**B**	36.	**C**	46.	**B**
7.	**A**	17.	**B**	27.	**C**	37.	**A**	47.	**D**
8.	**D**	18.	**E**	28.	**B**	38.	**D**	48.	**A**
9.	**E**	19.	**D**	29.	**D**	39.	**B**	49.	**D**
10.	**B**	20.	**E**	30.	**B**	40.	**B**	50.	**C**

Sentence Completion Test B

1.	**C**	11.	**B**	21.	**D**	31.	**E**	41.	**C**
2.	**D**	12.	**A**	22.	**B**	32.	**B**	42.	**C**
3.	**B**	13.	**B**	23.	**E**	33.	**A**	43.	**D**
4.	**E**	14.	**A**	24.	**C**	34.	**B**	44.	**E**
5.	**C**	15.	**E**	25.	**B**	35.	**C**	45.	**D**
6.	**D**	16.	**C**	26.	**A**	36.	**B**	46.	**B**
7.	**D**	17.	**D**	27.	**B**	37.	**D**	47.	**C**
8.	**C**	18.	**D**	28.	**E**	38.	**C**	48.	**E**
9.	**D**	19.	**C**	29.	**B**	39.	**E**	49.	**B**
10.	**B**	20.	**E**	30.	**C**	40.	**E**	50.	**C**

THE READING COMPREHENSION QUESTION

7

- Testing Tactics
- Long-Range Strategies
- Practice Exercises
- Answer Key

TESTING TACTICS

The reading comprehension questions test your ability to understand what you read. Each verbal section of the SAT will include two or more passages of different length, followed by several questions based on their content. The passages may be from a novel, a short story, a biography, or an essay; they may deal with science (including medicine, botany, zoology, chemistry, physics, astronomy), the humanities (including art, literature, music, philosophy, folklore), or social studies (including history, economics, sociology, government). Some passages are what the College Board calls "argumentative"; these present a definite point of view on a subject.

You will have to answer several types of questions here that may be asked about the passages. Some of the questions will be factual, asking you about specific details in the passage. Others will ask you to interpret the passage, to make judgments about it. (Tactics 4–10 below will give you hints about how to answer each type of question.)

The directions for the reading comprehension section on the SAT are minimal. They are:

> Each passage below is followed by questions based on its content. Answer all questions following a passage on the basis of what is <u>stated</u> or <u>implied</u> in that passage.

TACTIC 1: SAVE THE READING COMPREHENSION QUESTIONS FOR LAST

To answer an antonym question takes you seconds; to answer a reading comprehension question, you have to spend minutes going over the passage before you ever get to the questions at all.

On the SAT, you get the same points for answering a "quick and easy" question correctly as you do for answering a time-consuming one. Each correct answer on the Verbal Section is worth roughly 10 points to you. The more questions you answer correctly, the higher your score will be. Therefore, it makes sense for you to tackle the quick-to-answer questions—the antonyms, the analogies, the sentence completions—*first*. Get as many of them right as you can, and then settle down to answering the reading questions, knowing you've done everything possible to maximize your score.

One word of caution: In a 45-question Verbal Section, the reading questions typically occur in the *middle* of the section. If you plan to skip them and come back to them later, *be very careful in marking your answer sheet*. Check the numbering of your answer sheet often.

TACTIC 2: TACKLE PASSAGES WITH FAMILIAR SUBJECTS BEFORE PASSAGES WITH UNFAMILIAR ONES

Just as it is common sense for you to tackle quick-to-answer questions before you tackle time-consuming ones, it is also common sense for you to tackle reading passages with familiar subjects before you tackle reading passages with unfamiliar ones. If you know very little about botany or are uninterested in it, you are all too likely to run into trouble reading a passage about plant life.

It is hard to concentrate when you read about something wholly unfamiliar to you. Give yourself a break. Concentrate on the reading passages that interest you or that deal with topics you are well-grounded in. There is nothing wrong in skipping questions. Just remember to check the numbering of your answer sheet.

TACTIC 3: FIRST READ THE PASSAGE; THEN READ THE QUESTIONS

Students often ask whether it is better to read the passage first or the questions first. Those who want to read the questions before reading the passage think it will save time. Ninety-nine times out of a hundred they are wrong.

Reading the questions before you read the passage will not save you time. It will cost you time. If you read the questions first, when you turn to the passage you will have a number of question words and phrases dancing around in your head. These phrases won't focus you; they'll distract you. You will be so involved in trying to spot the places they occur in the passage that you'll be unable to concentrate on comprehending the passage as a whole. Why increase your anxiety and decrease your capacity to think? First read the passage, using the following technique:

1. Read as rapidly as you can with understanding, but do not force yourself. Do not worry about the time element. If you worry about not finishing the test, you will begin to take short cuts and miss the correct answer in your haste. Remember, if you have followed Tactic 1 and answered the quick questions first, you've maximized your score and made the best use of your time.

2. As you read the opening sentences, try to anticipate what the passage will be about. Who or what is the author talking about?

3. As you continue reading, try to remember in what part of the passage the author makes major points. In that way, when you start looking for the phrase or sentence which will justify your choice of answer, you will be able to save time by going to that section of the passage immediately rather than having to reread the entire selection. (This is particularly important when the passages become longer than 250 words.)

4. Your first reading of the passage should give you a general impression of the theme of the passage and the location of its major subdivisions. In order to answer each question properly, *you must go back to the passage* to verify your choice of answer. Do not rely on memory, and, above all, do not rely on knowledge gained outside of the paragraph.

5. Underline sparingly, if at all. Underlining is great when you're reading a textbook chapter that you want to review at a later time. On the SAT, underlining is not so great. It slows you down. It also can confuse you. If you underline everything in sight, it will be harder for you to spot an important word or phrase. A * or ✓ in the margin is all the underlining you could possible need.

If you have any serious reservations about this tactic, feel free to try alternate approaches doing some of the practice exercises at the end of this chapter. Compare the scores you get using each different approach. Reading is a highly individual skill. See what approach works best for you. The important thing is to know yourself and to feel comfortable with what you do.

TACTIC 4: LEARN TO SPOT THE MAJOR READING QUESTION TYPES

Just as it will help you to know the directions for the antonym, analogy, and sentence completion questions on the SAT, it will also help you to familiarize yourself with the major types of reading questions on the test.

If you can recognize just what a given question is asking for, you'll be better able to tell which particular reading tactic to apply.

Here are five categories of reading questions you are sure to face:

1. **Main Idea.** Questions that test your ability to find the central thought of a passage or to judge its significance often take the following form:
   a. The main point of the passage is to...
   b. The passage is primarily concerned with...
   c. The author's primary purpose in this passage is to...
   d. The chief theme of the passage can best be described as...
   e. Which of the following titles best describes the content of the passage?

2. **Finding Specific Details.** Questions that test your ability to understand what the author states *explicitly* are often worded:
   a. The author states...
   b. The author states all of the following EXCEPT...
   c. According to the passage, which of the following is true of the...
   d. According to the passage, the chief characteristic of the subject is...
   e. Which of the following statements is (are) best supported by the passage?

3. **Drawing Inferences.** Questions that test your ability to go beyond the author's explicit statements and see what these statements imply may be worded:
   a. It can be inferred from the passage that...
   b. The passage suggests that the author would support which of the following views?
   c. The author apparently feels that...
   d. According to the passage, it is likely that...
   e. The passage is most likely directed toward an audience of...

4. **Tone/Attitude.** Questions that test your ability to sense an author's or character's emotional state often take the form:
   a. The author's attitude to the problem can best be described as...
   b. Which of the following best describes the author's tone in the passage?
   c. The author's tone in the passage is that of a person attempting to...
   d. The author's presentation is marked by a tone of...
   e. The passage indicates that the author experiences a feeling of...

5. **Determining the Meaning of Strange Words.** Questions that test your ability to work out the meaning of unfamiliar words from their context often are worded:
   a. As it is used in the passage, the term... can best be described as...
   b. The phrase... is used in the passage to mean that...
   c. In the passage, the word... means...

TACTIC 5: WHEN ASKED TO FIND THE MAIN IDEA, BE SURE TO CHECK THE OPENING AND SUMMARY SENTENCES OF EACH PARAGRAPH

The opening and closing sentences of a paragraph are key sentences for you to read. They can serve as guideposts for you, pointing out the author's main idea.

Whenever you are asked to determine a passage's main idea, *always* check the opening and summary sentences of each paragraph. Authors typically provide readers with a sentence which expresses a paragraph's main idea succinctly. Although such *topic sentences* may appear anywhere in the paragraph, readers customarily look for them in the opening or closing sentences.

Notice the impact of words like *again, also, as well as, furthermore, moreover,* and *significantly* in the passage. These signal words may call your attention to the main idea.

EXAMPLE:

Your mind, like your body, is a thing whereof the powers are developed by effort. That is a principal use, as I see it, of hard work in studies. Unless you train your body you cannot be an athlete, and unless you train your mind you cannot be much of a scholar. The four miles an oarsman covers at top speed is in itself nothing to the good, but the physical capacity to hold out over the course is thought to be of some worth. So a good part of what you learn by hard study may not be permanently retained, and may not seem to be of much final value, but your mind is a better and more powerful instrument because you have learned it. "Knowledge is power," but still more the faculty of acquiring and using knowledge is power. If you have a trained and powerful mind, you are bound to have stored it with something, but its value is more in what it can do, what it can grasp and use, than in what it contains; and if it were possible, as it is not, to come out of college with a trained and disciplined mind and nothing useful in it, you would still be ahead, and still, in a manner, educated.

The main idea of this passage may be best expressed in the phrase

(A) "Knowledge Is Power"
(B) How to Retain and Use Facts
(C) Why Acquire Knowledge
(D) Physical and Mental Effort
(E) The Trained Mind

Look at the opening and summary sentences of the paragraph: "Your *mind*, like your body, is a thing whereof the powers are developed by effort... if it were possible, as it is not, to come out of college with *a trained and disciplined mind* and nothing useful in it, you would still be ahead, and still, in a manner, educated." Note the italicized phrases.

In this passage, the author stresses the need for hard work in studies. He compares the training the athlete gets to the training the scholar needs. He concedes that you may forget much that you learn, but he stresses the value of knowing how to get and use knowledge. This comes from training. It is not the knowledge that you get from college that is valuable, but the training of your mind.

Now go through the choices. You may eliminate Choice A ("Knowledge Is Power"): the author states that the faculty of acquiring knowledge is more important than the knowledge itself. You may eliminate Choice B (How to Retain and Use Facts): the passage is not a "how-to" guide. Choice C (Why Acquire Knowledge) may be supported by the quotation that "Knowlege Is Power," but you can see that the author is undercutting this statement in the sentence in which he quotes it. You may argue in favor of Choice D (Physical and Mental Effort) because you recognize that the author is making an analogy between the training of the athlete and the training of the scholar. However, Choice D is not as good as Choice E (The Trained Mind) because *throughout the passage* the author is stressing that the trained mind is something that must be developed and that is in itself a valuable and important faculty.

Note: In readings that occur on the SAT, topic sentences are sometimes implied rather than stated directly. If you cannot find a topic sentence, ask yourself these questions.

1. Who or what is this passage about?
2. What aspect of this subject is the author talking about?
3. What is the author trying to get across about this aspect of the subject?

TACTIC 6: WHEN ASKED TO CHOOSE A TITLE, WATCH OUT FOR CHOICES THAT ARE TOO SPECIFIC OR TOO BROAD

A paragraph has been defined as a group of sentences revolving around a central theme. An appropriate title for a paragraph, therefore, must include this central theme that each of the sentences in the paragraph is developing. it should be neither too broad nor too narrow in its scope; it should be specific and yet comprehensive enough to include all the essential ideas presented by the sentences. A good title for a passage of two or more paragraphs should include the thoughts of ALL the paragraphs.

EXAMPLE:

But there is more to the Library of Congress for the American dream than merely the wise appropriation of public money. The Library of Congress could not have become what it is today, with all the generous aid of Congress, without such a citizen as Dr. Herbert Putnam at the directing head of it. He and his staff have devoted their lives to making the four million and more books and pamphlets serve the public to a degree that cannot be approached by any similar great institution in the Old World. Then there is the public that uses these facilities. As one looks down on the general reading room, which alone contains ten thousand volumes that may be read without even the asking, one sees the seats filled with silent readers, old and young, rich and poor, black and white, the executive and the laborer, the general and the private, the noted scholar and the schoolboy, all reading at their own library provided by their own democracy.

The title that best expresses the ideas of the passage is
(A) Wise Use of Public Funds
(B) An Institution of Democracy
(C) Dr. Herbert Putnam, Director
(D) Intelligent Use of Books
(E) The Old World and the New

When you are trying to select the best title for a passage, watch out for words or phrases that come straight out of the passage. They may not always be your best choice. A more careful reading will reveal shortcomings in most of them. Consider Choice A. In the first sentence, the author talks of the "wise appropriation of public money." This is not the same as "wise use." Likewise, although the passage mentions Dr. Herbert Putnam, Choice C (Dr. Herbert Putnam, Director) is too narrow in scope to be a good title for this text.

Choices D and E also have flaws. While the passage describes the public's use of books, it does not describe the use of books in general; instead, it describes the public's use of books at one particular institution. Thus Choice D is poor. Again, while the passage refers to libraries in the Old World, it does so only to contrast them with our own Library of Congress. This contrast is too limited to justify the very broad implications of Choice E.

The best of the titles is Choice B (An Institution of Democracy). This choice of title is supported by the author's emphasis on the varied and contrasting groups using the facilities of the library provided (through *democratic* processes) for the use of all.

TACTIC 7: WHEN ASKED ABOUT SPECIFIC DETAILS, SPOT THE KEY WORDS IN THE QUESTION AND SCAN THE PASSAGE TO FIND THEM

In developing the main idea of a passage, a writer will make statements to support his or her point. To answer questions about such supporting details, you *must* find a word or group of words in the passage which supports your choice of answer. The words "according to the passage" or "according to the author" should focus your attention on what the passage explicitly states. Do not be misled into choosing an answer (even one that makes good sense) if you can not find it supported in the text.

Often detail questions ask about a particular phrase or line. In such instances, use the following technique:

1. Look for key words (nouns or verbs) in the answer choices.

2. Run your eye down the passage, looking for those key words or their synonyms. (This is called *scanning*. It is what you do when you look up someone's number in the phone book.)

3. When you find a key word or its synonym, reread the sentence to make sure the test-writer hasn't used the original wording to mislead you.

EXAMPLE:

Good American English is simple good English, English that differs a little in pronunciation, vocabulary, and occasionally in idiom from good English as spoken in London or South Africa, but differs no more than our physical surroundings, our political and social institutions, and the other circumstances reflected in language differ from those of other English-speaking areas. It rests upon the same basis as that which the standard speech of England rests upon—the usage of reputable speakers and writers throughout the country. No American student of language is so provincial as to hope, or wish, that the American standard may some day be adopted in England. Nor does he share the views of such in England as think that we would do well to take our standard readymade from them. He will be content with the opinion of Henry Bradley that "the wiser sort among us will not dispute that Americans have acquired the right to frame their own standards of correct English on the usage of their best writers and speakers."

According to the author, correctness in language is determined by

(A) the majority of those who speak it
(B) the dominant social and political institutions
(C) geographical conditions
(D) good speakers and writers
(E) those who wish to standardize the language

The justification for Choice D as the best answer to the question can be found in two sentences in the passage. Mr. Bradley's quotation mentions the usage of the "best writers and speakers." Likewise, the same thought is found in the second sentence ("the usage of reputable speakers and writers throughout the country").

Always verify your answers by finding support for them in the text.

TACTIC 8: WHEN ASKED TO MAKE INFERENCES, BASE YOUR ANSWERS ON WHAT THE PASSAGE IMPLIES, NOT WHAT IT STATES DIRECTLY

In *Language in Thought and Action*, S. I. Hayakawa defines an inference as "a statement about the unknown made on the basis of the known."

Inference questions require you to use your own judgment. You must not take anything directly stated by the author as an inference. Instead, you must look for clues in the passage that you can use in coming up with your own conclusion. You should choose as your answer a statement which is a logical development of the information the author has provided.

EXAMPLE:

Most people do not think of fishes and other marine animals as having voices, and of those who are aware of the fact that many of them can "speak," few understand that these "conversations" have significance. Actually, their talk may be as meaningful as much of our own. For example, some sea animals use their "voices" to locate their food in the ocean expanses; others, to let their fellows know of their whereabouts; and still others, as a means of obtaining mates. Sometimes, "speaking" may even mean the difference between life and death to a marine animal. It appears in some cases that when a predator approaches, the prey depends on no more than the sounds it makes to escape.

Fish sounds are important to man, also. By listening to them he can learn a great deal about the habits of the creatures that make them, the size of the schools they form, the patterns of their migrations, and the nature of the environments in which they live. He can also apply this information to the more effective utilization of the listening posts he has set up to detect enemy submarines. A knowledge of fish sounds can avoid confusion and unneeded effort when a "new" sound is picked up and the sound sentry must decide whether or not to call an alert.

Which of the following statements can *best* be inferred from the information given?
(A) Fish noises cannot be transmitted through air.
(B) Hearing in fishes is more acute than in people.
(C) The chief use of "fish voices" is to enable one fish to communicate with another fish.
(D) The significance of some fish noises has been studied.
(E) Fish are noisier than people.

Go through the answer choices one by one. Remember that in answering inference questions you must go beyond the obvious, go beyond what the author explicitly states, to look for logical implications of what the author says.

Choice A is incorrect *as an inference*. It may or may not be true as a statement of fact. The passage never mentions anything about air transmission of fish noises; you have no basis in the paragraph for coming to this conclusion.

Similarly, Choices B and E are incorrect inferences. Don't answer inference questions on the basis of your personal opinions. Answer them on the basis of what the passage implies. Hearing in fishes may or may not be more acute than hearing in people. Fish may or may not be noisier than people. From the passage you have no way to tell.

Choices A, B and E are assumptions, not inferences. Choice C is an inference, but an unwarranted one. Nothing in the passage justifies the statement that the "chief" use of fish voices is for communication. From the passage, you can't tell.

The best answer is Choice D: the opening sentences of the second paragraph which discuss listening to fish sounds and learning from them obviously imply that people have been studying them.

TACTIC 9: WHEN ASKED TO DETERMINE THE AUTHOR'S MOOD, LOOK FOR WORDS WHICH CONVEY EMOTION OR WHICH PAINT PICTURES

In determining an author's mood, examine the author's language. Is the author using adjectives to describe the subject? If so, are they words like *fragrant*, *tranquil*, *magnanimous*—words with positive connotations? Or are they words like *fetid*, *ruffled*, *stingy*—words with negative connotations?

When we speak, our tone of voice conveys our mood frustrated, cheerful, critical, gloomy, angry. When we write, our images and descriptive phrases get our feelings across.

EXAMPLE:

It takes no calendar to tell root and stem that the calm days of mid-summer are here. Last spring's sprouted seed comes to fruit. None of these things depends on a calendar of the days and months. They are their own calendar, marks on a span of time that reaches far back into the shadows of time. The mark is there for all to see, in every field and meadow and treetop, as it was last year and ten years ago and when the centuries were young.

The time is here. This is that point in the great continuity when these things happen, and will continue to happen year after year. Any summer arrives at this point, only to lead on to the next and the next, and so to summer again. These things we can count on; these things will happen again and again, so long as the earth turns.

The passage indicates that the author experiences a feeling of
(A) frustration
(B) fear of the forces of nature
(C) pessimism
(D) regret at the rapid passage of time
(E) serene confidence

Note the descriptive adjective the author chooses: *calm*. Note also the pictures and images: seed coming to fruit, shadows of time. The author sees in Nature a great continuity of events. Things have happened in the past and will continue "so long as the earth turns." This is a statement that is serenely confident (Choice E).

TACTIC 10: WHEN ASKED TO GIVE THE MEANING OF AN UNFAMILIAR WORD, LOOK FOR CONTEXT CLUES

Every student who has ever looked into a dictionary is aware that many words have more than one meaning. A common question that appears on the SAT tests your ability to determine the correct meaning of a word from its context. Sometimes the word is a common one, and you must determine its exact meaning as used by the author. At other times, the word is uncommon. You can determine its meaning by a careful examination of the text.

As always, use your knowledge of context clues and word parts (Chapter 6) to help you discover the meanings of unfamiliar words.

EXAMPLE:

All museum adepts are familiar with examples of *ostrakoi*, the oystershells used in balloting. As a matter of fact, these "oystershells" are usually shards of pottery, conveniently glazed to enable the voter to express his wishes in writing. In the Agora a great number of these have come to light, bearing the thrilling name, Themistocles. Into rival jars were dropped the ballots for or against his banishment. On account of the huge vote taken on the memorable day, it was to be expected that many ostrakoi would be found, but the interest of this collection is that a number of these ballots are inscribed in an *identical* handwriting. There is nothing mysterious about it! The Boss was on the job, then as now. He prepared these ballots and voters cast them—no doubt for the consideration of an obol or two. *The ballot box was stuffed*.

How is the glory of the American boss diminished! A vile imitation, he. His methods as old as Time!

An obol, as used in the passage, is evidently

(A) an oyster shell
(B) a Greek coin
(C) a promise of bread
(D) a complimentary remark
(E) an appointive public office

What's an *obol*? It's certainly not an everyday word. You may never have encountered the term before you read this passage. But you can figure it out. How, after all, do political bosses tempt voters to cast their ballots the way the party wants? They use bribes of some kind, preferably money. Therefore, you can logically assume that an obol is a Greek coin.

LONG-RANGE STRATEGIES

Are you a good reader? Do you read twenty-five or more books a year in addition to those books assigned in school? When you read light fiction, do you cover a page per minute? Do you read only light fiction, or have you begun to read "heavy" books—books on science, political theory, literary criticism, art? Do you browse regularly through magazines and newspapers?

Faced with the above questions, students frequently panic. Used to gathering information from television and radio rather than from books, they don't know how to get back on the track. But getting back on the track is easier than they think.

Read, Read, Read!

Just do it.

There is no substitute for extensive reading as a preparation for the SAT and for college work. The only way to obtain proficiency in reading is by reading books of all kinds. As you read, you will develop speed, stamina, and the ability to comprehend the printed page. But if you want to turn yourself into the kind of reader the colleges are looking for, you must develop the habit of reading—every day.

25 Books a Year

Suppose you're an average reader; you read an ordinary book at about 300 words a minute. In 20 minutes, how many words can you read? Six thousand, right?

In a week of reading 20 minutes per day, how many words can you read? Seven days, 42,000 words.

Now get out your calculator. In 52 weeks of reading 20 minutes per day, how many words can you read? That's 52 times 42,000, a grand total of 2,184,000 words!

Now here comes the hard part. Full-length books usually contain 60,000 to 100,000 words. Say the average book runs about 75,000 words. If reading 20 minutes a day you can read 2,184,000 words in a year, how many average, 75,000-word books can you read in a year?

The answer is a little over 29. Twenty-nine books in a year. So don't panic at the thought of reading 25 books a year. Anybody can find 20 minutes a day, and if you can do that, you can read *over* 25 books a year. The trick is always to have your book on hand, so that you don't have to waste time hunting around for it if you suddenly find yourself with some free time.

Schedule a set time for non-school reading. Make the 20-minute-a-day plan part of your life.

Upgrade What You Read

Challenge yourself. Don't limit your reading to light fiction and biography as so many high school students do. Branch out a bit. Go beyond *People* magazine. Try to develop an interest in as many fields as you can. Sample some of the quality magazines: *The New Yorker, Smithsonian, Scientific American, National Geographic, Newsweek, Time*. In these magazines you'll find articles on literature, music, science, philosophy, history, the arts—the whole range of fields touched on by the SAT. If you take time to acquaint yourself with the contents of these magazines, you won't find the subject matter of the reading passages on the examination so strange.

Speed Up Your Reading

If you have trouble getting through a typical verbal section in 30 minutes, you may want to work on ways to build up your reading speed.

One thing you should be aware of is that to build speed you have to practice with easy materials. Most slow readers are used to reading everything—technical material, sports columns, comics—at one slow, careful speed. To build up speed, you have to get your eyes and brain accustomed to moving rapidly, and that means working with passages that are easy for you. Given sufficiently easy material, there are all sorts of techniques that you can try: you can draw a line down the middle of a newspaper column, for example, and then, focusing your eyes on the line, try to get the meanings of the words on each side as you read straight down the column. It's a great exercise for your peripheral vision.

One major cause of slow reading is that sometimes you don't focus. Your eyes keep moving down the page, but your mind is out to lunch. Then bang! You wake up from your daydream and say, "Hey! What was I reading?" And your eyes jump back to an earlier spot on the page and you wind up rereading the whole thing.

Obviously regressing, going back and rereading words or whole passages you've already supposedly read, slows you down. Regressing is a habit, but like any other habit, you can break it.

One way to reduce regressions is to preview a passage before you read. A quick look at the introductory sentences of paragraphs, at titles and section headings, at words in italics and other key words, will give you an idea of what you're about to read. At that point, you have a sense of the material and you come to read the passage with some questions in mind—you read actively, not passively.

A second way to reduce regressions is to make it impossible to look back. Take a 3 x 5 card and use it like a shutter to cover what you've already read. That way you force yourself to keep going. You have to concentrate: you have no choice.

One last speed-reading technique you should be aware of is called clustering or phrase-reading. Have you ever watched somebody's eyes when he's busy reading? Do it sometime. You'll see his eyes move, then come to a stop, then dart back for a second, stop, then sweep forward again, stop, and so on. The stops last only a fraction of a second, but they're important: it's only when the eyes stop that you actually read. In that fraction-of-a-second stop, or fixation, your eyes *fix* on a word. If you're skilled at clustering, however, in that one stop your eyes fix on not one, but a group of words. Clustering, phrase-reading, prevents word-by-word reading. it speeds you up where word-by-word reading slows you down.

Here's how to practice clustering. First, find something easy to read. Don't start out with SAT tests. Divide up the passage into 3 or 4 word phrases. Next read it trying to see those 3 or 4 words in a single fixation. Then reread it at your normal speed to catch anything you've missed.

One final, crucial point: These pointers on how to build up your reading speed are long-range strategies. They are not specific tactics for how to go about dealing with the SAT test you're going to face next Saturday morning. The SAT is no time for you to try out new techniques you've heard of but have yet to master.

PRACTICE EXERCISES

On the following pages you will find two groups of reading exercises. Allow about an hour at first for each group. The correct answers are given at the end of the chapter. If you find you have made an error, do not justify your answer. You will probably be able to find a good reason for the choice you made, since, in many of these exercises, there are several good answers but only one BEST one. Try to discover what makes the answer given on the answer page BEST. You will, thus, discover the nature of the trap that you are falling into and will learn how to recognize it.

Practice the testing tactics you have learned as you work. Your reading score will improve.

READING EXERCISE A

In the long run a government will always encroach upon freedom to the extent to which it has the power to do so; this is almost a natural law of politics, since, whatever the intentions of the men who exercise political power, the sheer momentum of government leads to a constant pressure upon the liberties of the citizen. But in many countries society has responded by throwing up its own defenses in the shape of social classes or organized corporations which, enjoying economic power and popular support, have been able to set limits to the scope of action of the executive. Such, for example, in England was the origin of all our liberties—won from government by the stand first of the feudal nobility, then of churches and political parties, and latterly of trade unions, commercial organizations, and the societies for promoting various causes. Even in European lands which were arbitrarily ruled, the powers of the monarchy, though absolute in theory, were in their exercise checked in a similar fashion. Indeed the fascist dictatorships of today are the first truly tyrannical governments which western Europe has known for centuries and they have been rendered possible only because on coming to power they destroyed all forms of social organization which were in any way rivals to the state.

1. The main idea of this paragraph is best expressed by which of the following?
   (A) Limited powers of monarchies
   (B) The ideal of liberal government
   (C) Functions of trade unions
   (D) Ruthless ways of dictators
   (E) Safeguards of individual liberty

2. The writer maintains that there is a natural tendency for governments to
   (A) become more democratic
   (B) become fascist
   (C) suppress trade unions and social societies
   (D) increase individual liberties
   (E) assume more power

3. According to the passage, monarchy was first checked in England by the
   (A) trade unions
   (B) church
   (C) people
   (D) nobles
   (E) political parties

Geometry is a very old science. We are told by Herodotus, a Greek historian, that geometry had its origin in Egypt along the banks of the river Nile. The first record we have of its study is found in a manuscript written by Ahmes, an Egyptian scholar, about 1550 B.C. This manuscript is believed to be a copy of a treatise which dated back probably more than a thousand years, and describes the use of geometry at that time in a very crude form of surveying or measurement. In fact, geometry, which means "earth measurement," received its name in this manner. This re-measuring of the land was necessary due to the annual overflow of the river Nile and the consequent destroying of the boundaries of farm lands. This early geometry was very largely a list of rules or formulas for finding the areas of plane figures. Many of these rules were inaccurate, but, in the main, they were fairly satisfactory.

4. The title below that best expresses the ideas of this passage is
   (A) Floods of the River Nile
   (B) Beginnings of Geometry
   (C) Manuscript of Ahmes
   (D) Surveying in Egypt
   (E) Importance of the Study of Geometry

5. According to the passage, in developing geometry the early Egyptians were primarily concerned with
   (A) discovering why formulas used in measuring were true
   (B) determining property boundaries
   (C) measuring the overflow of the Nile
   (D) generalizing formulas
   (E) constructing a logical system of geometry

6. It can be inferred that one of the most important factors in the development of geometry as a science was
   (A) Ahmes' treatise
   (B) the inaccuracy of the early rules and formulas
   (C) the annual flooding of the Nile Valley
   (D) the destruction of farm crops by the Nile
   (E) an ancient manuscript copied by Ahmes

The change in the treatment of his characters is a significant index to Shakespeare's growth as a dramatist. In the earlier plays, his men and women are more engaged with external forces than with internal struggles. In as excellent an early tragedy as *Romeo and Juliet,* the hero fights more with outside obstacles than with himself. In the great later tragedies, the internal conflict is more emphasized, as in the cases of *Hamlet* and *Macbeth.* He grew to care less for mere incident, for plots based on mistaken identity, as in the *Comedy of Errors;* he became more and more interested in the delineation of character, in showing the effect of evil on Macbeth and his wife, of jealousy on Othello, of indecision on Hamlet, as well as in exploring the ineffectual attempts of many of his characters to escape the consequences of their acts.

7. Which of the following titles best expresses the main idea of this passage?
(A) Comedies and Tragedies of Shakespeare
(B) Shakespeare's Best Plays
(C) Shakespeare's Development as a Dramatist
(D) The Moral Aspects of Shakespeare's Later Plays
(E) Shakespeare's Interest in Good and Evil

8. In the passage the author indicates that in his later plays Shakespeare became interested in
(A) plots based on mistaken identity
(B) great characters from history
(C) the history of his country
(D) the study of human nature
(E) the struggle of the hero with external forces

9. According to the author, the development of Shakespeare as a dramatist is most clearly revealed in his
(A) improved treatment of complications
(B) increased use of involved plots
(C) handling of emotional conflicts
(D) increased variety of plots
(E) decreased dependency on historical characters

Solitude is a great chastener when once you accept it. It quietly eliminates all sorts of traits that were a part of you—among others, the desire to pose, to keep your best foot forever in evidence, to impress people as being something you would like to have them think you are even when you aren't. Some men I know are able to pose even in solitude; had they valets they no doubt would be heroes to them. But I find it the hardest kind of work myself, and as I am lazy I have stopped trying. To act without an audience is so tiresome and profitless that you gradually give it up and at last forget how to act at all. For you become more interested in making the acquaintance of yourself as you really are, which is a meeting that, in the haunts of men, rarely takes place. It is gratifying, for example, to discover that you prefer to be clean rather than dirty even when there is no one but God to care which you are; just as it is amusing to note, however, that for scrupulous cleanliness you are not inclined to make superhuman sacrifices, although you used to believe you were. Clothes, you learn, with something of a shock, have for you no interest whatsoever.... You learn to regard dress merely as covering, a precaution. For its color and its cut you care nothing.

10. The title that best expresses the ideas of this paragraph is
(A) Carelessness in Clothes
(B) Acting Without an Audience
(C) Discoveries through Solitude
(D) Showing Off to Best Advantage
(E) Being a Hero to Yourself

11. According to the author, a desire to appear at your best is a trait that
(A) goes with laziness
(B) may disappear when you are alone
(C) depends primarily on clothes
(D) is inhuman
(E) is evil

12. According to the passage, in solitude, clothes
(A) constitute one item that pleases the valet
(B) make one careless
(C) are part of acting
(D) are valued for their utility alone
(E) are tiresome

13. In describing his self-discoveries, the author's tone can best be described as
(A) boastful
(B) petulant
(C) detached
(D) merry
(E) abashed

14. The author points out that the activities of everyday life seldom give us the chance to
(A) learn our own peculiarities
(B) keep our best foot forward
(C) impress people
(D) dress as we would like
(E) be immaculately clean

In width of scope, Yeats far exceeds any of his contemporaries. He is the only poet since the 18th century who has been a public man in his own country and the only poet since Milton who has been a public man at a time when his country was involved in a struggle for political liberty. This may not seem an important matter, but it is a question whether the kind of life lived by poets for the last two hundred years or so has not been one great reason for the drift of poetry away from the life of the community as a whole, and the loss of touch with tradition. Once the life of contemplation has been divorced from the life of action, or from real knowledge of men of action, something is lost which it is difficult to define, but which leaves poetry enfeebled and incomplete. Yeats responded with all his heart as a young man to the reality and the romance of Ireland's struggle but he lived to be completely disillusioned about the value of the Irish rebellion. He saw his dreams of liberty blotted out in horror by "the innumerable clanging wings that have put out the moon." It brought him to the final conclusion of the futility of all discipline that is not of the whole being, and of "how base at moments of excitement are minds without culture"; but he remained a man to whom the life of action always meant something very real.

15. The title below that best expresses the ideas of this paragraph is
(A) Basis of True Poetry
(B) The Necessity of Culture
(C) Action versus Contemplation
(D) Yeats as a Poet and Patriot
(E) Yeats' Part in the Irish Rebellion

16. According to the passage, Yeats was primarily a
(A) soldier
(B) man of action
(C) dreamer
(D) rigid disciplinarian
(E) politician

17. The writer implies that, as compared with older poetry, present-day poetry is more
(A) complete
(B) romantic
(C) alive
(D) ineffectual
(E) comprehensive

18. According to the author, great poetry is most often produced by poets who
(A) are involved in the problems of life around them
(B) spend their time in contemplation
(C) drift away from the community
(D) break away from tradition
(E) take part in war

There are few books which go with midnight, solitude and a candle. It is much easier to say what does not please us than what is exactly right. The book must be, anyhow, something benedictory by a sinning fellow man. Cleverness would be repellent at such an hour. Cleverness, anyhow, is the level of mediocrity today; we are all too infernally clever. The first witty and perverse paradox blows out the candle. Only the sick mind craves cleverness, as a morbid body turns to drink. The late candle throws its beams a great distance; and its rays make transparent much that seemed massy and important. The mind at rest beside that light, when the house is asleep, and the consequential affairs of the urgent world have diminished to their right proportions because we see them distantly from another and a more tranquil place in the heavens, where duty, honor, witty arguments, controversial logic on great questions, appear such as will hardly leave a trace of fossil in the indurated mud which will cover them—the mind then smiles at cleverness. For though at that hour the body may be dog-tired, the mind is white and lucid, like that of a man from whom a fever has abated. It is bare of illusions. It has a sharp focus, small and starlike, as a clear and lonely flame left burning by the altar of a shrine from which all have gone but one. A book which approaches that light in the privacy of that place must come, as it were, with open and honest pages.

19. Which of the following titles best expresses the ideas of this passage?
(A) Reading by Candlelight
(B) Books for Convalescents
(C) Not a Time to Read
(D) Books for Tired Minds
(E) Books for Midnight Reading

20. According to the passage, to make good reading at bedtime, a book must be
(A) light
(B) witty
(C) controversial
(D) historical
(E) straightforward

21. The author considers the average book of today
(A) inane
(B) sinful
(C) benedictory
(D) restful
(E) open and honest

22. The author contends that at midnight in the solitude of one's room, the mind is
(A) tired
(B) keen
(C) sick
(D) troubled
(E) clever

As we know the short story today it is largely a product of the nineteenth and twentieth centuries and its development parallels the rapid development of industrialism in America. We have been a busy people, busy principally in evolving a production system supremely efficient. Railroads and factories have blossomed almost overnight; mines and oil fields have been discovered and exploited; mechanical inventions by the thousands have been made and perfected. Speed has been an essential element in our endeavors, and it has affected our lives, our very natures. Leisurely reading has been, for most Americans, impossible. As with our meals, we have grabbed bits of reading standing up, cafeteria style, and gulped down cups of sentiment on the run. We have had to read while hanging on to a strap in a swaying trolley car or in a rushing subway or while tending to a clamoring telephone switchboard. Our popular magazine has been our literary automat and its stories have often been no more substantial than sandwiches.

23. The title below that best expresses the ideas of this paragraph is
(A) "Quick-lunch" Literature
(B) Life in the Machine Age
(C) Culture in Modern Life
(D) Reading while Traveling
(E) The Development of Industrialism

24. According to the passage, the short story today owes its popularity to its
(A) settings
(B) plots
(C) style
(D) length
(E) characters

25. The author implies that the short story has developed because of Americans'
(A) reactions against the classics
(B) need for reassurance
(C) lack of culture
(D) lack of education
(E) taste for speed

26. From this selection we may infer that the author's attitude toward short stories is one of
(A) approval
(B) indifference
(C) contempt
(D) impartiality
(E) regret

Nationalism is not a harmonious natural growth, qualitatively identical with the love for family and home. It is frequently assumed that man loves in widening circles—his family, his village, his tribe or clan, the nation, and finally humanity and the supreme good. But love of home and family is a concrete feeling, accessible to everyone in daily experience, while nationalism, and in an even higher degree cosmopolitanism, is a highly complex and originally an abstract feeling. Nationalism—our identification with the life and aspirations of uncounted millions whom we shall never know, with a territory which we shall never visit in its entirety—is qualitatively different from love of family or of home surroundings. It is qualitatively akin to the love of humanity or of the whole earth.

27. Which of the following titles best expresses the ideas of this passage?
(A) A Distinction Without a Difference
(B) Love of One's Fellow Beings
(C) The Nature of Nationalism
(D) An Abstract Affection
(E) Our Complex Emotions

28. The author states that compared with love of family and home, nationalism is more
(A) natural
(B) clannish
(C) accessible
(D) concrete
(E) inclusive

29. According to the passage, a common assumption regarding nationalism is that it is
(A) an outgrowth of love of home and family
(B) more nearly related to humanity than to the home
(C) highly abstract and complex
(D) identified with the lives of millions whom we do not know
(E) stimulated by travel within one's own country

A tradesman behind his counter must have no flesh and blood about him, no passions, no resentment; he must never be angry—no, not so much as seem to be so, if a customer troubles him five hundred pounds' worth of goods, and scarce bids money for anything; nay, though they really come to his shop with no intent to buy, as many do, only to see what is to be sold, and though he knows they cannot be better pleased than they are at some other shop where they intend to buy, 'tis all one; the tradesman must take it, he must place it to the account of his calling that 'tis his business to be ill used and resent nothing; and so must answer as obligingly to those who give him an hour or two's trouble and buy nothing as he does to those who, in half the time, lay out ten or twenty pounds. The case is plain; and if some do give him trouble, and do not buy, others make amends, and do buy; and as for the trouble; 'tis the business of the shop.

30. According to the passage, a retailer must
(A) account for his callers
(B) make amends
(C) look for large purchases to make up for people who enter his shop but do not make purchases
(D) treat all customers alike
(E) be anemic

31. From this paragraph we may infer that
(A) customers take a pound of blood for every pound of meat they purchase
(B) the customer is always right
(C) customers making large purchases take less time marketing than do customers making small purchases
(D) all customers impose upon shopkeepers
(E) customers resent tradesmen

32. According to the passage, tradesmen are generally
    (A) ill used
    (B) troubled
    (C) passionless
    (D) obliging
    (E) undersold

When a new movement in Art attains a certain vogue, it is advisable to find out what its advocates are aiming at, for however farfetched and unreasonable their tenets may seem today, it is possible that in years to come they may be regarded as normal. With regard to Futurist poetry, however, the case is rather different; for whatever Futurist poetry may be—even admitting that the theory on which it is based may be right—it can hardly be classed as Literature.

This, in brief, is what the Futurist says: for a century past conditions of life have been continually speeding up, till now we live in a world of noise and violence and speed. Consequently, our feelings, thoughts and emotions have undergone a corresponding change. This speeding up of life, says the Futurist, requires a new form of expression. We must speed up our literature too, if we want to interpret modern stress. We must pour out a cataract of essential words, unhampered by stops, or qualifying adjectives, or finite verbs. Instead of describing sounds we must make up words that imitate them; we must use many sizes of type and different colored inks on the same page, and shorten or lengthen words at will.

Certainly their descriptions of battles are vividly chaotic. But it is a little disconcerting to read in the explanatory notes that a certain line describes a fight between a Turkish and a Bulgarian officer on a bridge over which they both fall into the river—and then to find that the line consists of the noise of their falling and the weights of the officers: "Pluff! Pluff! a hundred and eighty-five kilograms."

This, though it fulfils the laws and requirements of Futurist poetry, can hardly be classed as Literature. All the same, no thinking man can refuse to accept their first proposition: that a great change in our emotional life calls for a change of expression. The whole question is really this: have we essentially changed?

33. The main idea of this selection is best expressed as
    (A) The Past versus the Future
    (B) Changes in modern life
    (C) Merits of the Futurist movement
    (D) What constitutes literature
    (E) An evaluation of Futurist poetry

34. When novel ideas appear, it is desirable, according to the writer, to
    (A) discover the aims of their adherents
    (B) ignore them
    (C) follow the fashion
    (D) regard them as normal
    (E) adopt them slowly

35. The writer considers that Futurist poetry is
    (A) too emotional
    (B) too new in type to be acceptable
    (C) not worth literary recognition
    (D) significant of a basic change in the nature of mankind
    (E) theoretically unsound

36. According to the passage, the Futurist poet uses all of the following devices EXCEPT
    (A) imitative words
    (B) qualifying adjectives
    (C) different colored inks
    (D) stream of essential words
    (E) lengthened words

The single business of Henry Thoreau, during forty-odd years of eager activity, was to discover an economy calculated to provide a satisfying life. His one concern, that gave to his ramblings in Concord fields a value of high adventure, was to explore the true meaning of wealth. As he understood the problem of economics, there were three possible solutions open to him: to exploit himself, to exploit his fellows, or to reduce the problem to its lowest denominator. The first was quite impossible—to imprison oneself in a treadmill when the morning called to great adventure. To exploit one's fellows seemed to Thoreau's sensitive social conscience an even greater infidelity. Freedom with abstinence seemed to him better than serfdom with material well-being, and he was content to move to Walden Pond and so set about the high business of living, "to front only the essential facts of life and to see what it had to teach." He did not advocate that other men should build cabins and live isolated. He had no wish to dogmatize concerning the best mode of living—each must settle that for himself. But that a satisfying life should be lived, he was vitally concerned. The story of his emancipation from the lower economics is the one romance of his life, and *Walden* is his great book. It is a book in praise of life rather than of Nature, a record of calculating economies that studied saving in order to spend more largely. But it is a book of social criticism as well, in spite of its explicit denial of such a purpose. In considering the true nature of economy he concluded, with Ruskin, that the cost of a thing is the amount of life which is required in exchange for it, immediately or in the long run. In *Walden* Thoreau elaborated the text: "The only wealth is life."

37. The main idea of this paragraph is best expressed as
(A) Problems of economics
(B) Thoreau's philosophy of life
(C) *Walden*, Thoreau's greatest book
(D) How Thoreau saved money
(E) Life at Walden Pond

38. According to the passage, Thoreau's chief aim in life was to
(A) discover a satisfactory economy
(B) do as little work as possible
(C) convert others to his way of life
(D) write about Nature
(E) life in isolation

39. The author's tone in speaking of Thoreau is
(A) ironic
(B) critical
(C) indifferent
(D) admiring
(E) effusive

40. We learn from the passage that Thoreau's solution to the problem of living was to
(A) study nature
(B) make other men work for him
(C) work in a mill
(D) live in a simple way
(E) write for a living

41. According to the passage, Thoreau believed that the wealth of an individual is measured by
(A) the money he makes
(B) the experience he gains
(C) the amount he saves
(D) the books he writes
(E) his social standing

Music and literature, the two temporal arts, contrive their pattern of sounds in time; or, in other words of sounds and pauses. Communication may be made in broken words, the business of life be carried on with substantives alone; but that is not what we call literature; and the true business of the literary artist is to plait or weave his meaning, involving it around itself; so that each sentence, by successive phrases, shall first come into a kind of knot, and then, after a moment of suspended meaning, solve and clear itself. In every properly constructed sentence there should be observed this knot or hitch; so that (however delicately) we are led to foresee, to expect, and then to welcome the successive phrases. The pleasure may be heightened by an element of surprise, as, very grossly, in the common figure of the antithesis, or, with much greater subtlety, where an antithesis is first suggested and then deftly evaded. Each phrase, besides, is to be comely in itself; and between the implication and the evolution of the sentence there should be a satisfying equipoise of sound; for nothing more often disappoints the ear than a sentence solemnly and sonorously prepared, and hastily and weakly finished. Nor should the balance be too striking and exact, for the one rule is to be infinitely various; to interest, to disappoint, to surprise, and yet still to gratify; to be ever changing, as it were, the stitch, and yet still to give the effect of an ingenious neatness.

42. According to the author, great literature depends on its
(A) meaning
(B) sound
(C) ideas
(D) balance
(E) antithesis

43. The author calls music and literature "the two temporal arts" because
(A) they are not lasting
(B) they are both used in the temples
(C) they are both based on antithesis
(D) they depend on time patterns
(E) they both depend on balance

44. According to the author, the function of the writer is to
(A) communicate with the reader
(B) carry on the business of life
(C) provide a knot and stitch
(D) present his ideas attractively
(E) capture balance and antithesis

45. Antithesis is a means of securing
(A) surprise
(B) subtlety
(C) comeliness
(D) balance
(E) equipoise

46. The author believes that the enjoyment of literature comes from
(A) shock
(B) an anticipation of phrase
(C) the attractiveness of the sentences
(D) balance
(E) ingeniousness

During the first year that Mr. Wordsworth and I were neighbours, our conversations turned frequently on the two cardinal points of poetry, the power of exciting the sympathy of the reader by a faithful adherence to the truth of nature, and the power of giving the interest of novelty by the modifying colours of imagination. The sudden charm, which accidents of light and shade, which moonlight or sunset diffused over a known and familiar landscape, appeared to represent the practicability of combining both. These are the poetry of nature. The thought suggested itself—(to which of us I do not recollect)—that a series of poems might be composed of two sorts. In the one, the incidents and agents were to be, in part at least, supernatural; and the excellence aimed at was to consist in the interesting of the affections by the dramatic truth of such emotions, as would naturally accompany such situations, supposing them real. And real in this sense they have been to every human being who, from whatever source of delusion, has at any time believed himself under supernatural agency. For the second class, subjects were to be chosen from ordinary life; the characters and incidents were to be such as will be found in every village and its vicinity, where there is a meditative and feeling mind to seek after them, or to notice them, when they present themselves.

In this idea originated the plan of the LYRICAL BALLADS; in which it was agreed, that my endeavours should be directed to persons and characters supernatural, or at least romantic; yet so as to transfer from our inward nature a human interest and a semblance of truth sufficient to procure for these shadows of imagination that willing suspension of disbelief for the moment, which constitutes poetic faith. Mr. Wordsworth, on the other hand, was to propose to himself as his object, to give the charm of novelty to things of every day, and to excite a feeling analogous to the supernatural, by awakening the mind's attention to the lethargy of custom, and directing it to the loveliness and the wonders of the world before us; an inexhaustible treasure, but for which, in consequence of the film of familiarity and selfish solicitude, we have eyes, yet see not, ears that hear not, and hearts that neither feel nor understand.

47. Mr. Coleridge, the author of this passage, felt that one characteristic of his poetry was its emphasis on
(A) ordinary life
(B) nature
(C) the supernatural
(D) the lethargy of custom
(E) the sudden charm of the familiar

48. Familiarity often
(A) breeds contempt
(B) is an inexhaustible treasure
(C) has novel elements
(D) hides the beauty of the surroundings
(E) is a shadow of the imagination

49. Mr. Coleridge wrote
(A) none of the poems in *Lyrical Ballads*
(B) some of the poems in *Lyrical Ballads*
(C) half of the poems in *Lyrical Ballads*
(D) most of the poems in *Lyrical Ballads*
(E) all of the poems in *Lyrical Ballads*

50. The best title for this passage is
(A) Suspension of Belief
(B) A Great Collaboration
(C) Adherence to Nature
(D) Two Great Minds
(E) Wordsworth and Coleridge

READING EXERCISE B

If you already feel inside you the urge of self-expression, then the first thing that you have to do is to study the means of expressing yourself. You will have to study very carefully the English language and especially its grammar. Although most people do not understand the art of good writing, they unconsciously assimilate more easily ideas which are expressed in correct English. It should be pointed out also that good English is not necessarily flowery English, and the simple phrase—which looks so easy to write—is often the most difficult to construct. I can not stress too strongly the desirability of writing your sentences word by word and not phrase by phrase. Many writers fail to get their ideas across to the public solely because they use expressions whose meaning has been killed by repetition.

1. The title that best expresses the idea of this passage is
(A) The Art of Writing
(B) Dependence of English upon Grammar
(C) Self-expression an Essential to Writing
(D) The Curse of Triteness
(E) Flowery English: Its Value

2. According to the author, writing phrase by phrase is
(A) important
(B) indispensable
(C) economical
(D) easily assimilated
(E) undesirable

3. According to the author, correct English
   (A) assists understanding of ideas
   (B) is easily written
   (C) is best secured through repetition
   (D) is secured through use of trite phrases
   (E) stresses use of flowery language

A need for beauty, lightness, corrosion resistance, or other specific properties must be present before plastics can even be considered as competitors of brick, window glass, cement, cast iron, or steel, since volumetric prices are so low for the last substance and for wood. It is not particularly unfortunate that plastics do not appear economical for every use. There is no reason why industry should want to replace wood, brick, concrete, and metals when the latter are adequate and inexpensive. Too much has been written about the coming "Plastics and Light Metal Age," which is prophesized as the successor to the Stone Age, the Bronze Age, and the Iron Age. In the historical sequence of these earlier periods, there is logic in the quantitative sense; one age gave way to another when the use of a new material exceeded in quantity that of its predecessor. For the plastics and light metals, however, a different picture presents itself; less than 3,000,000 tons of all these materials are being produced annually, while steel production exceeded 90,000,000 tons last year and will probably not recede to less than 60,000,000 tons for many years. This is still the Iron Age—or rather the Steel Age.

4. The title that best expresses the ideas of this passage is
   (A) New Uses for Plastics
   (B) How One Age Succeeds Another
   (C) Advantages of Plastics
   (D) Limitations on the Use of Plastics
   (E) New Demands in a Post-war World

5. The writer considers that the Bronze Age succeeded the Stone Age because
   (A) there was a scarcity of wood and other building materials
   (B) bronze was less expensive than stone
   (C) stone was no longer available
   (D) more bronze than stone came into use
   (E) the use of bronze was a step toward the Steel Age

6. The writer regards the change to a "Plastic and Light Metal Age" in the near future as
   (A) necessary
   (B) desirable
   (C) improbable
   (D) economical
   (E) logical

The whole atmosphere of the world in which we live is tinged by science, as is shown most immediately and strikingly by our modern conveniences and material resources. A little deeper thinking shows that the influence of science goes much farther and colors the entire mental outlook of modern civilized man on the world about him. Perhaps one of the most telling evidences of this is his growing freedom from superstition. Freedom from superstition is the result of the conviction that the world is not governed by caprice, but that it is a world of order and can be understood by man if he will only try hard enough and be clever enough. This conviction that the world is understandable is, doubtless, the most important single gift of science to civilization. The widespread acceptance of this view can be dated to the discovery by Newton of the universal sway of the law of gravitation; and for this reason Newton may be justly regarded as the most important single contributor to modern life.

7. The title that best expresses the ideas of this passage is
   (A) Science Produces Modern Conveniences
   (B) Important Scientific Principles
   (C) Freedom from Superstition through Science
   (D) Science and the World of Moral Order
   (E) Discovery of Scientific Laws

8. According to the author, the greatest benefit of science has been
   (A) the encouragement of deep thinking
   (B) an understanding of a world of order
   (C) the development of material resources
   (D) the work of reconstruction
   (E) the rapid growth of everyday conveniences

It has been said that I am chasing after my youth. This is true. And not only after my own. Even more than beauty, youth attracts me, and with an irresistible appeal. I believe the truth lies in youth; I believe it is always right against us. I believe that, far from trying to teach it, it is in youth that we, the elders, must seek out lessons. I am well aware that youth is capable of errors; I know that our role is to forewarn youth as best we can; but I believe that often, in trying to protect youth, we impede it. I believe that each new generation arrives bearing a message that it must deliver; our role is to help that delivery. I believe that what is called experience is often but an avowed fatigue, resignation, blighted hope.

9. The title that best expresses the ideas of this passage is
   (A) The Lessons Youth Offers
   (B) The Needs of Youth
   (C) The Nature of Experience
   (D) Advice to Youth
   (E) A New Generation

10. The writer's attitude toward the progress of each new generation is
(A) skeptical
(B) questioning
(C) bitter
(D) optimistic
(E) indifferent

As the market for hay declined, other farmers looked west and saw that in the flat lands of the prairie country the farmers were growing rich by raising corn and hogs; and they said, without thought or wisdom or knowledge, "If they can do it, we can." And so they plowed the grass and meadowlands and even the pastures of that rolling, hilly country and planted corn. They planted the corn in rows, running more often than not up and down slopes and hills. Every time it rained, each furrow between the standing corn became a miniature gully carrying off the precious rainfall and bearing with it the good topsoil that remained and the fertilizer the farmer had bought out of his hard-earned income.

11. The title that best expresses the ideas of this passage is
(A) Waste of the Soil
(B) Rotating Crops
(C) Rainfall and the Corn Crop
(D) Why Farmers Become Discouraged
(E) The Reward of Courage

12. The author implies that corn was a less satisfactory crop in the more easterly section because the land in this section was less
(A) fertile
(B) moist
(C) flat
(D) thoroughly fertilized
(E) arid

13. We may infer from the passage that the farmers would have been wiser to
(A) use flat land
(B) raise hogs
(C) plow furrows across the slope
(D) use more fertilizer
(E) fill the gullies

To stop science would create more problems than solutions. Aside from military considerations, it would be disastrous to freeze culture at its present high point. The highly technical civilization of the 20th century is like an airplane in flight, supported by its forward motion. It can not stop without falling. If all the world's inhabitants, for instance, learn to use natural resources as fast as Americans do now, many necessary substances will be exhausted. Scientists confidently count on improvements, including atomic energy, to provide ample substitutes. Present techniques won't do it.

Where will man's curve of scientific progress take him ultimately? The surprises since 1900 have made scientists humble. They know that as science grows, it only penetrates deeper into mystery. Human knowledge may be visualized as an expanding sphere whose volume grows larger as its diameter increases. But the area of the sphere's surface, its frontier with the unknown, increases as the square of the diameter. Beyond that frontier—nobody can know, until the frontier advances.

14. The title that best expresses the ideas of this passage is
(A) The Future of Science
(B) New Frontiers
(C) Progress Unlimited
(D) The 20th Century
(E) Our Technical Civilization

15. Scientists feel that improvements which can provide substitutes are required to
(A) prevent useless loss of life
(B) keep culture advancing
(C) advance scientific knowledge
(D) prevent exhaustion of basic materials
(E) improve techniques of aviation

16. The author's attitude toward the expansion of scientific knowledge is one of
(A) enthusiasm
(B) despair
(C) humility
(D) pride
(E) disgust

Many observers have commented on what seems to be the fact that fear plays a much smaller part than we should think it must in the life of an animal which lives dangerously. Terror he can know, and perhaps he knows it frequently. But it seems to last only a little longer than the immediate danger it helps him to avoid, instead of lingering, as in the human being it does, until it becomes a burden and a threat. The frightened bird resumes his song as soon as danger has passed and so does the frightened rabbit his games. It is almost as if they knew that "cowards die many times before their deaths; the valiant never taste of death but once."

17. The title that best expresses the ideas of this passage is
(A) A Comparison of Fear and Terror
(B) A Comparison of Man and the Lower Animals
(C) Animal Traits
(D) Fear in Animals
(E) The Nature of Courage

18. The writer believes that
    (A) terror is a permanent form of fear
    (B) fear is almost unknown in animals
    (C) fear has a permanent effect on animals
    (D) animals live less dangerously than men
    (E) animals remember fear only a short time

19. "Cowards die many times before their deaths" means
    (A) many times the coward is almost caught in his misdeeds
    (B) the coward is frequently seriously ill
    (C) the coward's frequent fears are often as bad as death
    (D) cowards many times wish they were dead
    (E) the coward has several lives

The English are a heterogeneous and contradictory race with conservative tendencies. While progress is the aim of every Englishman, he nevertheless distrusts and resents change. When he goes to bed, he insists that his mattress shall be supported by a symphony of springs that is the newest word in comfort, but when he wakes up in the morning he requires that the view from his bedroom window shall be the same as it was yesterday and for centuries of yesterdays before that. Thus it is that Great Britain is a land in which the past is always becoming the present, in which history is inescapably part of the picture of today, and thus it is that Great Britain has become a storehouse of treasures that are both the work of nature and the work of man.

20. The title that best expresses the ideas of this passage is
    (A) History and the British
    (B) The Losing Battle of the Past
    (C) The Contradictory British
    (D) Great Britain, Noblest Work of Nature and of Men
    (E) No Escape from Tradition

21. The passage implies that Englishmen
    (A) oppose progress
    (B) are careless of their ancient natural beauties
    (C) are favorable to changes
    (D) are a race of few and unvaried characteristics
    (E) enjoy luxuries

For the sad state of criticism the writers must hold themselves much to blame. The literary artist, concerned solely in the creation of a book or story as close to perfection as his powers will permit, is generally a quiet individual, contemplative, retiring. On occasion he can be influenced to anger by some grievous social wrong which calls for desperate remedy. But mostly he is prone to sit in his tower reflecting on the absurdities of a foolish world, asking only to be left alone with his labor. Never aggressive in his own interest, seeking only peace, he lays himself open to aggression. Thus he does not see the enemy who has stolen into the shadows at the rear of his retreat and is slowly scaling the walls. Such has been the course of events. While the artists have slept, the critical dwarfs have appeared. They have evolved a new language, written out a new set of definitions. Black is white, and white is black. The ugly and the nauseous are the beautiful; the beautiful is nightmare.

22. The title below that best expresses the ideas of this passage is
    (A) Writers as Champions of Social Wrongs
    (B) Cooperation Between Writer and Critic
    (C) Domination by the Critic
    (D) Progressive Standards of Criticism
    (E) Development of the Writing Profession

23. In speaking of critics, the author's tone can best be described as
    (A) grief-stricken
    (B) desperate
    (C) contemplative
    (D) scornful
    (E) whimsical

24. The author contends that the literary artist is inclined to
    (A) be unconcerned with what is happening around him
    (B) be continually aroused by wrongs
    (C) slight the work of writing
    (D) welcome aggression
    (E) accept criticism gladly

Although vocal cords are lacking in cetaceans, phonation is undoubtedly centered in the larynx.

The toothed whales or odontocetes (sperm whale and porpoises) are much more vociferous than the whalebone whales, or mysticetes. In this country observers have recorded only occasional sounds from two species of mysticetes (the humpback and right whale). A Russian cetologist reports hearing sounds from at least five species of whalebone whales but gives no details of the circumstances or descriptions of the sounds themselves. Although comparison of the sound-producing apparatus in the two whale groups cannot yet be made, it is interesting to note that the auditory centers of the brain are much more highly developed in the odontocetes than in the mysticetes, in fact, to a degree unsurpassed by any other mammalian group.

25. According to the passage, the noises produced by whales
   (A) are produced in the upper part of the windpipe
   (B) are louder than those of other sea animals
   (C) are used to locate their mates
   (D) can be heard only by other whales
   (E) travel along their vocal cords

26. In which of the following is the auditory center of the brain *most* highly developed?
   (A) humpback whale
   (B) right whale
   (C) sperm whale
   (D) whalebone whale
   (E) mysticete

Let us consider how voice training may contribute to personality development and an improved social adjustment. In the first place, it has been fairly well established that individuals tend to become what they believe other people think them to be. When people react more favorably toward us because our voices convey the impression that we are friendly, competent, and interesting, there is a strong tendency for us to develop those qualities in our personality. If we are treated with respect by others, we soon come to have more respect for ourselves. Then, too, one's own consciousness of having a pleasant, effective voice of which he does not need to be ashamed contributes materially to a feeling of poise, self-confidence, and a just pride in himself. A good voice, like good clothes, can do much for an ego that otherwise might be inclined to droop.

27. The title that best expresses the ideas of this passage is
   (A) Our Ego
   (B) The Reflection of Our Personality
   (C) How to Acquire a Pleasant Voice
   (D) Voice Training in Personality Development
   (E) Social Adjustment and Self-respect

28. According to the passage, a good voice
   (A) contributes greatly to a feeling of poise
   (B) conveys the impression that we are friendly
   (C) is less important than good clothes
   (D) is more important than good clothes
   (E) makes others unconscious of our faults

One of the most urgent problems in teaching handwriting is presented by the left-handed child. The traditional policy has been to attempt to induce all children to write with their right hands. Parents and teachers alike have an antipathy to the child's using his left hand. On the other hand, psychologists have shown beyond a doubt that some persons are naturally left-handed and that it is much more difficult for them to do any skillful act with the right hand than with the left hand. Some believe, furthermore, that to compel a left-handed child to write with his right hand may make him nervous and may cause stammering. There seems to be some cases in which this is true, although in the vast majority of children who change over, no ill effects are noticed. In addition to these difficulties, left-handedness sometimes seems to cause mirror writing—writing from right to left—and reversals in reading, as reading "was" for "saw."

29. The title below that best expresses the ideas of this passage is
   (A) Nervous Aspects Connected with Handwriting
   (B) Teaching Handwriting
   (C) The Problems of the Left-handed Child
   (D) A Special Problem in Teaching Handwriting
   (E) Stammering, Mirror Writing and Reversals

30. The author implies that
   (A) parents should break children of left-handedness
   (B) left-handed children need special consideration
   (C) left-handed persons are inclined to stutter
   (D) left-handed persons are not more brilliant than right-handed ones
   (E) left-handed persons are less skillful than right-handed ones

31. According to the passage, the traditional policy in teaching handwriting has
   (A) dismayed the experts
   (B) resulted in failure to learn to write
   (C) aimed at mirror writing
   (D) made many children skillful with both hands
   (E) resulted in unsolved problems

TOKYO—I wish that everyone worried about foreign imports could visit Japan. They would quickly realize that imports do not, on balance, "cost" American workmen their jobs. Quite the contrary. The very prosperity of Japanese industry—a prosperity which depends entirely on exports—is in fact *creating* jobs for Americans. Coal, mined by West Virginia miners, fuels a large part of Japan's industry. Its cars, trucks, buses and machinery run to a large extent on oil produced in U.S. refineries. Japan's airlines fly U.S. planes and are kept in the air by U.S. parts. U.S.-made machinery and office equipment is commonplace here. And virtually the whole of Japan's giant cotton textile industry runs on U.S. raw materials.

The trade balance figures tell the story. Last year we sold Japan $1,325 million worth of merchandise. Total Japanese sales here came to just $1,126 million. In short, Japan actually bought $200 million worth more of goods from the U.S. than they sold us. From this it is certainly clear that U.S. workers and U.S. businessmen are by no means net losers as a result of the increasing quantities of food, textiles, toys and cameras that Japan ships to the U.S.

This being so, Americans can rejoice in the great and growing prosperity of Japan. They can do so out of the sheerest self-interest. For with every upward thrust of Japan's GNP, the docks of Yokohama and Kobe become even busier unloading goods produced by U.S. workers. The dollars we spend for Japanese goods have a way of making a fast return trip to U.S. shores.

In an economic sense Japan has become one of our closest partners. It is our third best customer. Its economy is more closely tied to the U.S. economy than are those of Western Europe (whereas Western Europe markets about 10% of its exports in the U.S., Japan markets 27% of hers).

In this context, thinking Americans ought to share the Ikeda government's hopes for doubling Japan's gross national product over the next decade. The experts I talked with regard this goal as attainable, but they do not minimize the difficulties. Such expansion will require a tremendous increase in Japanese exports; lacking raw materials, Japan must sell steadily increasing amounts of manufactured goods to pay for the raw materials its growing industry is gulping. To double the GNP, experts estimate Japan will also have to double its exports and the U.S. will have to swallow its share of them.

The U.S., of course, cannot take them all. There is naturally, a point beyond which we cannot permit domestic industry to be hurt. Nor is our market limitless. As for Western Europe, it remains basically cool to trade with Japan. Hence the U.S. is pressing Japan to open new markets in Asia and other under-developed areas through the use of long-term credits.

32. The author maintains that Japan's exports to the United States
   (A) cannot be absorbed by this country
   (B) should go to Western Europe
   (C) actually provide jobs for Americans
   (D) exceed its imports from this country
   (E) constitute its GNP

33. According to the passage, Japan is largely dependent upon the United States for
   (A) toys
   (B) food
   (C) doubling its exports
   (D) $200 million a year
   (E) oil

34. The author contends that one of the advantages of trading with Japan is that
   (A) we get cheap cameras, textiles and toys
   (B) the money we spend in Japan returns quickly to the United States
   (C) Japan will double her economy
   (D) Japan will give credit to her Asiatic neighbors
   (E) Japan is our partner

35. According to the passage, Japan ships to the United States
   (A) 10% of its exports
   (B) about one fourth of its exports
   (C) half of its exports
   (D) 75% of its exports
   (E) all of its exports

36. According to the passage, in order to develop its industries further, Japan will have to
   (A) extend long term credit to poorer nations
   (B) buy less from the United States
   (C) sell its increased products to the United States
   (D) break away from the U.S. economy
   (E) find markets in Western Europe

The great question that this paper will, but feebly, attempt to answer is: What is the creative process?

Though much theory has accumulated, little is really known about the power that lies at the bottom of poetic creation. It is true that great poets and artists produce beauty by employing all the powers of personality and by fusing emotions, reason and intuitions. But, what is the magical synthesis that joins and arranges these complex parts into poetic unity?

John L. Lowes, in his justly famous *The Road to Xanadu*, developed one of the earliest and still generally acceptable answers to this tantalizing question. Imaginative creation, he concludes, is a complex process in which the conscious and unconscious minds "jointly operate." "There is . . . the deep well with its chaos of fortuitously blending images; but there is likewise the Vision which sees shining in and through the chaos, the potential lines of Form, and with the Vision the controlling Will, which gives to that potential beauty actuality."

The Deep Well is the unconscious mind that is peopled with the facts, ideas, feelings of conscious activity. The imaginative vision, an unconscious activity, shines through this land of chaos, of lights and shadows, silently seeking pattern and form. Finally, the conscious mind again, through Will, captures and embodies the idea in the final work of art. In this way is unity born out of chaos.

Though there can be no absolute certainty, there is general agreement that the periods in the development of a creative work parallel, to some extent, Lowes' theory of Well, Vision, Form and Will. There are at least three stages in the creative process: *preparation, inspiration, work.*

In a sense, the period of preparation is all of the writer's life. It is the Deep Well. It is especially a period of concentration which gives the unconscious mind an opportunity to communicate with the conscious mind. When remembrance of things past reach the conscious level of the writer's mind, he is ready to go on with the process. Part of this preparation involves learning a medium—learning a language, learning how to write, learning literary forms. It is important to note here that form cannot be imposed upon the idea. Evidence, though sparse, shows that the idea gives birth to the form that can best convey it. It is the Vision, according to Lowes, "which sees shining in and through the chaos the potential lines of Form..."

37. According to the author, when remembrance of things past reach the conscious level, the poet has reached the stage called
    (A) Well
    (B) Vision
    (C) Form
    (D) Will
    (E) Magical synthesis

38. Which of the following statements is true?
    (A) The form determines the subject matter
    (B) The idea determines the form
    (C) Vision makes beauty an actuality
    (D) A writer's period of preparation is spent at school
    (E) A writer is unconscious when he prepares his work

39. In the third paragraph "fortuitously" means
    (A) accidentally
    (B) luckily
    (C) thoroughly
    (D) unconsciously
    (E) potentially

In 1896 Henri Becquerel found that uranium salts emitted penetrating radiations similar to those which Roentgen had produced only a year earlier with a gas discharge tube. The tremendous importance of this discovery was not apparent until a few years later when Pierre and Marie Curie announced the isolation from a uranium mineral, pitchblende, of two substances many times more radioactive than uranium itself. These two substances were subsequently shown to be two new elements, polonium and radium. Elements which are naturally radioactive spontaneously emit radiations without the addition of any energy to them. Later we shall see that artificial radioactivity can be produced by adding energy to originally stable nuclei.

Rutherford and Soddy, investigating the phenomenon discovered by Becquerel, found that the empirical facts of radioactivity could be explained by assuming that radioactive atoms were not stable but disintegrated at characteristic rates to form new atoms of other elements. As soon as the radioactive emissions were experimentally identified and it was proved that alpha "rays" are actually helium ions, it became clear that the assumptions made by Rutherford and Soddy were correct. It was soon found that the disintegration product of radium is also naturally radioactive and investigations of decay products led to the identification of other radioelements ranging in atomic number from 92 (uranium) to 81 (thallium). These radioelements are now known to be intimately related to each other in the *radioactive series.*

During the early years of the Curie investigations uranium had only a limited industrial use, chiefly in the glass industry, and most of the material came from the Joachimstal mines in Czechoslovakia. As industrial uses for radioactive elements developed, uranium ore was found widely scattered throughout the world with extensive deposits in the Belgian Congo and in the Great Bear Lake region in Canada. The element is principally mined in the form of pitchblende, which may contain a high percentage of U_3O_8. The ore presents a brown-black appearance somewhat resembling pitch in luster. In the United States, deposits of another uranium ore, known as carnotite, are found in several Rocky Mountain states.

40. According to the passage, uranium
    (A) was discovered in 1896
    (B) is used in the glass industry
    (C) is found in pure form in the United States
    (D) is more radioactive than polonium
    (E) contains helium atoms

41. According to the passage naturally radioactive elements
    (A) disintegrate
    (B) have energy added to the nuclei
    (C) were discovered by Rutherford
    (D) were discovered by Roentgen
    (E) are mined in the Congo

When we take the most distant prospect of life, what does it present to us but a chaos of unhappiness, a confused and tumultuous scene of labor and contest, disappointment and defeat? If we view past ages in the reflection of history, what do they offer to our meditation but crimes and calamities? One year is distinguished by a famine, another by an earthquake: kingdoms are made desolate, sometimes by war and sometimes by pestilence; the peace of the world is interrupted at one time by the caprices of a tyrant, at another by the rage of the conqueror. The memory is stored only with vicissitudes of evil; and the happiness, such as it is, of one part of mankind, is found to arise commonly from sanguinary success, from victories which confer upon them the power not so much of improving life by any new enjoyment as of inflicting misery on others and gratifying their own pride by comparative greatness.

42. The best title for this paragraph is
(A) Reflections on History
(B) Suffering Humanity
(C) A Distant View of Life
(D) Failure and Success
(E) The Price of Victory

43. The author maintains that man's happiness often comes from
(A) enjoyment
(B) ultimate success
(C) desolation of kingdoms
(D) vicissitudes of evil
(E) the sufferings of others

44. The author's view of the human condition is
(A) utopian
(B) philosophical
(C) pessimistic
(D) sanguinary
(E) confused

Our theory and practice in the area of sentencing have undergone a gradual but dramatic metamorphosis through the years. Primitive man believed that a crime created an imbalance which could be rectified only by punishing the wrongdoer. Thus, sentencing was initially vengeance-oriented. Gradually, emphasis began to be placed on the deterrent value of a sentence upon future wrongdoing.

Though deterrence is still an important consideration, increased emphasis on the possibility of reforming the offender—of returning him to the community a useful citizen—bars the harsh penalties once imposed and brings into play a new set of sentencing criteria. Today, each offender is viewed as a unique individual, and the sentencing judge seeks to know why he has committed the crime and what are the chances of a repetition of the offense. The judge's prime objective is not to punish but to treat.

This emphasis on treatment of the individual has created a host of new problems. In seeking to arrive at the best treatment for individual prisoners, judges must weigh an imposing array of factors. I believe that the primary aim of every sentence is the prevention of future crime. Little can be done to correct past damage, and a sentence will achieve its objective to the extent that it upholds general respect for the law, discourages those tempted to commit similar crimes, and leads to the rehabilitation of the offender, so that he will not run afoul of the law again. Where the offender is so hardened that rehabilitation is plainly impossible, the sentence may be designed to segregate the offender from society so that he will be unable to do any future harm. The balancing of these interacting, and often mutually antagonistic, factors requires more than a good heart and a sense of fair play on the judge's part, although these are certainly prerequisites. It requires the judge to know as much as he can about the prisoner before him. He should know the probable effects of sentences upon those who might commit similar crimes and how the prisoner is likely to react to imprisonment or probation. Because evaluation of these various factors may differ from judge to judge, the same offense will be treated differently by different judges.

The task of improving our sentencing techniques is so important to the nation's moral health that it deserves far more careful attention than it now receives from the bar and the general public. Some of those at the bar and many civic-minded individuals who usually lead even the judges in the fight for legal reform approach this subject with apathy or with erroneous preconceptions. For example, I have observed the sentiment shared by many that, after a judge has sentenced several hundred defendants, the whole process becomes one of callous routine. I have heard this feeling expressed even by attorneys who should know better.

45. According to the passage, in determining what sentence to impose, a judge today
(A) tries to punish the offender
(B) is callous
(C) is inconsistent
(D) tries to prevent future crimes
(E) is a therapist

46. Ancient sentences were motivated by
(A) a desire to reform
(B) imbalance
(C) a desire for revenge
(D) a desire to deter future wrongdoing
(E) apathy and erroneous preconceptions

47. Which of the following statement is incorrect?
(A) A judge should treat each offender as an individual
(B) A judge should try to correct past damage
(C) The problem of sentencing deserves study
(D) A judge refrains from imposing harsh penalties
(E) A judge has to be a student of human nature

48. "Metamorphosis" (first sentence) means
(A) evolution
(B) interpretation
(C) lethargy
(D) change
(E) revolution

Both plants and animals of many sorts show remarkable changes in form, structure, growth habits, and even mode of reproduction in becoming adapted to different climatic environment, types of food supply, or mode of living. This divergence in response to evolution is commonly expressed by altering the form and function of some part or parts of the organism, the original identity of which is clearly discernible. For example, the creeping foot of the snail is seen in related marine pteropods to be modified into a flapping organ useful for swimming, and is changed into prehensile arms that bear suctorial disks in the squids and other cephalopods. The limbs of various mammals are modified according to several different modes of life—for swift running (cursorial) as in the horse and antelope, for swinging in trees (arboreal) as in the monkeys, for digging (fossorial) as in the moles and gophers, for flying (volant) as in the bats, for swimming (aquatic) as in the seals, whales and dolphins, and for other adaptations. The structures or organs that show main change in connection with this adaptive divergence are commonly identified readily as homologous, in spite of great alterations. Thus, the finger and wristbones of a bat and whale, for instance, have virtually nothing in common excpet that they are definitely equivalent elements of the mammalian limb.

49. The best title for this passage is
 (A) Adaptive Divergence
 (B) Evolution
 (C) Homologous Structures
 (D) Changes in Organs
 (E) Our Changing Times

50. According to the passage, plants and animals change in form
 (A) as they evolve
 (B) to adjust to environment
 (C) because of their structure
 (D) because of their mode of reproduction
 (E) in swimming

ANSWER KEY

Reading Exercise A

1. **C**	11. **B**	21. **A**	31. **B**	41. **B**
2. **E**	12. **D**	22. **B**	32. **D**	42. **B**
3. **D**	13. **C**	23. **A**	33. **E**	43. **D**
4. **B**	14. **A**	24. **D**	34. **A**	44. **D**
5. **B**	15. **D**	25. **E**	35. **C**	45. **A**
6. **C**	16. **B**	26. **E**	36. **B**	46. **B**
7. **C**	17. **D**	27. **C**	37. **B**	47. **C**
8. **D**	18. **A**	28. **E**	38. **A**	48. **D**
9. **C**	19. **E**	29. **A**	39. **A**	49. **B**
10. **C**	20. **E**	30. **D**	40. **D**	50. **B**

Reading Exercise B

1. **A**	11. **A**	21. **E**	31. **E**	41. **A**
2. **E**	12. **C**	22. **C**	32. **C**	42. **B**
3. **A**	13. **C**	23. **B**	33. **E**	43. **E**
4. **D**	14. **A**	24. **A**	34. **B**	44. **C**
5. **D**	15. **D**	25. **A**	35. **B**	45. **D**
6. **C**	16. **C**	26. **C**	36. **A**	46. **C**
7. **C**	17. **D**	27. **D**	37. **D**	47. **B**
8. **B**	18. **E**	28. **A**	38. **B**	48. **D**
9. **A**	19. **C**	29. **D**	39. **A**	49. **A**
10. **D**	20. **C**	30. **B**	40. **B**	50. **A**

BUILD YOUR VOCABULARY 8

- **Short-Term Tactics**
  SAT High-Frequency Word List
  Basic Word Parts
- **Long-Range Strategies**
  3500 Basic Word List
- **Answer Key**

SHORT-TERM TACTICS

No matter how little time you have before you take the SAT, you can familiarize yourself with the sort of vocabulary you will be facing on the test. First, review the testing tactics sections at the beginning of each of the previous chapters. Look particularly at the examples used to illustrate each tactic: these examples often involve words that occur on actual SAT tests. Next, look over the 101 words you will find on our SAT High-Frequency Word List. Each of these 101 words, ranging from everyday words such as *abbreviate* and *humid* to less-commonly known ones such as *amorphous* and *virtuoso*, has appeared (as answer choices or as question words) at least two or three times in SAT tests published in the 1980's.

How will looking over the High-Frequency Word List help you? First, it will reassure you: if you recognize these words, you *will* know some of the words on the SAT test you take. Attending lectures, listening to radio programs, watching TV, you have been exposed to thousands and thousands of words. You may be unable to define them with precision, you may feel insecure about using them, but you have a handle on them.

Not only will looking over the High-Frequency Word List reassure you, but also it may well help you on the actual day of the test. These words have turned up on recent tests—some of them may turn up on the test you take. Look over these words. Review any of them that are unfamiliar to you. Try using them on your parents and friends. Then, if they do turn up on your test, feel confident: your knowledge of them will help you come up with the correct answer or eliminate an incorrect answer choice.

SAT HIGH-FREQUENCY WORD LIST *101 Words You Should Know*

abbreviate V. shorten. Because we were running out of time, the lecturer had to *abbreviate* her speech.

abstemious ADJ. sparing in eating or drinking; temperate. The drunkards mocked him because of his *abstemious* habits.

amass V. collect. The miser's aim is to *amass* and hoard as much gold as possible.

ambiguous ADJ. unclear or doubtful in meaning. His *ambiguous* instructions misled us; we did not know which road to take. **ambiguity,** N.

ambivalence N. the state of having contradictory or conflicting emotional attitudes. Torn between loving her parents one minute and hating them the next, she was confused by the *ambivalence* of her feelings. **ambivalent,** ADJ.

amorphous ADJ. shapeless. She was frightened by the *amorphous* mass which had floated in from the sea.

anarchy N. absence of governing body; state of disorder. The assassination of the leaders led to a period of *anarchy.*

angular ADJ. sharp-cornered; stiff in manner. His features, though *angular,* were curiously attractive.

apathetic ADJ. indifferent. He felt apathetic about the conditions he had observed and did not care to fight against them. **apathy,** N.

apprehensive ADJ. fearful; discerning. His *apprehensive* glances at the people who were walking in the street revealed his nervousness.

arrogance N. pride; haughtiness. The *arrogance* of the nobility was resented by the middle class.

ascetic ADJ. practicing self-denial; austere. The cavalier could not understand the *ascetic* life led by the monks. also N.

assiduous ADJ. diligent. His employer praised him for his *assiduous* work. **assiduity,** N.

assuage V. ease; lessen (pain). Your messages of cheer should *assuage* her suffering. **assuagement,** N.

atrophy N. wasting away. Polio victims need physiotherapy to prevent the *atrophy* of affected limbs. also V.

augment V. increase. How can we hope to *augment* our forces when our allies are deserting us?

authoritative ADJ. having the weight of authority; dictatorial. We accepted her analysis of the situation as *authoritative.*

benevolent ADJ. generous; charitable. His *benevolent* nature prevented him from refusing any beggar who accosted him.

bizarre ADJ. fantastic; odd; violently contrasting. The plot of the novel was too *bizarre* to be believed.

candor N. frankness. The *candor* and simplicity of his speech impressed all. **candid,** ADJ.

censor N. overseer of morals; person who reads to eliminate inappropriate remarks. Soldiers dislike having their mail read by a *censor* but understand the need for this precaution. also V.

censure V. blame; criticize. He was *censured* for his inappropriate behavior. also N.

chaotic ADJ. in utter disorder. He tried to bring order into the *chaotic* state of affairs. **chaos,** N.

circumspect ADJ. prudent; cautious. Investigating before acting, she tried always to be *circumspect.*

coerce V. force; repress. Do not *coerce* me into doing this; I hate force. **coercion,** N.

collaborate V. work together. Two writers *collaborated* in preparing this book.

combustible ADJ. easily burned. After the recent outbreak of fires in private homes, the fire commissioner ordered that all *combustible* materials be kept in safe containers. also N.

commensurate ADJ. equal in extent or size; proportionate. Your reward will be *commensurate* with your effort.

conflagration N. fire. In the *conflagration* that followed the 1906 earthquake, much of San Francisco was destroyed.

conspiracy N. treacherous plot. Brutus and Cassius joined in the *conspiracy* to murder Julius Caesar.

contaminate V. pollute. The sewage system of the city so *contaminated* the water that swimming was forbidden.

conviction N. strongly held belief. Nothing could shake his *conviction* that she was innocent.

dawdle V. loiter; waste time. Inasmuch as we must meet a deadline, do not *dawdle* over this work.

dearth N. scarcity. The *dearth* of skilled labor compelled the employers to open trade schools.

debilitate V. weaken; enfeeble. Overindulgence *debilitates* character as well as physical stamina.

deference N. courteous regard for another's wish. In *deference* to his desires, the employers granted him a holiday. **deferential,** ADJ.

deleterious ADJ. harmful. Workers in nuclear research must avoid the *deleterious* effects of radioactive substances.

despotism N. tyranny. The people rebelled against the *despotism* of the king.

digression N. act of wandering away from the subject. His book was marred by his many *digressions.* **digress,** V.

dilapidated ADJ. ruined because of neglect. The *dilapidated* building needed several coats of paint. **dilapidation,** N.

dilute V. make less concentrated; reduce in strength. She preferred her coffee *diluted* with milk.

diminution N. lessening; reduction in size. The blockaders hoped to achieve victory as soon as the *diminution* of the enemy's supplies became serious.

disparity N. difference; condition of inequality. The *disparity* in their ages made no difference at all.

dissuade V. advise against. He could not dissuade his friend from joining the conspirators. **dissuasion,** N.

domineer V. rule over tyrannically. Students prefer teachers who guide, not ones who *domineer.*

eccentricity N. oddity; idiosyncrasy. Some of his friends tried to account for his rudeness to strangers as the *eccentricity* of genius. **eccentric,** ADJ.

emaciated ADJ. thin and wasted. His long period of starvation had left him *emaciated.*

embellish V. adorn. His handwriting was *embellished* with flourishes.

embezzlement N. stealing. The bank teller confessed his *embezzlement* of the funds.

erratic ADJ. odd; unpredictable. Investors become anxious when the stock market appears *erratic.*

expedite V. hasten. We hope you will be able to *expedite* the delivery of our order.

explicit ADJ. clear; direct. In seeing her boy friend secretly, she was defying her father's *explicit* orders.

expunge V. cancel; remove. If you behave, I will *expunge* this notation from your record.

extricate V. free; disentangle. He found that he could not *extricate* himself from the trap.

fallacious ADJ. misleading. Your reasoning must be *fallacious* because it leads to a ridiculous answer. **fallacy,** N.

fallow ADJ. plowed but not sowed; uncultivated. Farmers have learned that it is advisable for land to lie *fallow* every few years.

fastidious ADJ. difficult to please; squeamish. The waitresses disliked serving him dinner because of his very *fastidious* taste.

flagrant ADJ. conspicuously wicked. We cannot condone such *flagrant* violations of the rules.

frivolity N. lack of seriousness. We were distressed by his frivolity during the recent crisis.

furtive ADJ. stealthy. The boy took a *furtive* glance at his classmate's test paper.

gluttonous ADJ. greedy for food. The *gluttonous* boy ate all the cookies. **gluttony,** N.

gullible ADJ. easily deceived. He preyed upon *gullible* people, who believed his stories of easy wealth.

humid ADJ. damp. He could not stand the *humid* climate and moved to a drier area.

implication N. that which is hinted at or suggested. If I understand the *implications* of your remark, you do not trust our captain. **implicate,** V.

indefatigable ADJ. tireless. He was *indefatigable* in his constant efforts to raise funds for the Red Cross.

indifferent ADJ. unmoved; lacking concern. Because she felt no desire to marry, she was *indifferent* to his constant proposals.

inevitable ADJ. unavoidable. Death and taxes are both *inevitable.*

inflated ADJ. exaggerated; pompous; enlarged (with air or gas). His claims about the new product were *inflated;* it did not work as well as he had promised.

innocuous ADJ. harmless. Let him drink it; it is *innocuous.*

inopportune ADJ. untimely; poorly chosen. A rock concert is an *inopportune* setting for quiet conversation.

insipid ADJ. tasteless; dull. I am bored by your *insipid* talk.

insolvency N. bankruptcy; lack of ability to repay debts. When rumors of his *insolvency* reached his creditors, they began to press him for the money due them. **insolvent,** ADJ.

intractable ADJ. stubborn; hard to manage. How do you deal with such an *intractable* child?

labyrinth N. maze. Tom and Becky were lost in the *labyrinth* of secret caves.

languid ADJ. weary; sluggish; listless. Her illness left her *languid* and pale.

leniency N. mildness; permissiveness. Considering the gravity of the offense, we were surprised by the *leniency* of the sentence. **lenient,** ADJ.

levity N. lightness; unseemly frivolity. Such *levity* is improper on this serious occasion.

marred ADJ. damaged. She had to refinish the *marred* surface of the table.

miserly ADJ. stingy; mean. The *miserly* man hoarded his coins not out of prudence but out of greed.

monotony N. sameness leading to boredom. He took a clerical job, but soon grew to hate the *monotony* of his daily routine.

opaque ADJ. dark; not transparent. The *opaque* shade in the window kept the sunlight out of the room.

prattle V. babble. The children prattled endlessly about their new toys. also N.

precocious ADJ. advanced in development. By her rather adult manner of discussing serious topics, the child demonstrated that she was *precocious.*

prodigal ADJ. wasteful; reckless with money. The *prodigal* son squandered his inheritance. also N.

prodigious ADJ. marvelous; enormous. She marveled at his *prodigious* appetite.

profusion N. lavish expenditure; overabundant condition. Seldom have I seen food and drink served in such *profusion.* **profuse,** ADJ.

prolific ADJ. abundantly fruitful. She was a *prolific* writer and wrote as many as three books a year.

recalcitrant ADJ. obstinately stubborn. Donkeys are reputed to be the most *recalcitrant* of animals.

rescind V. cancel. Because of public resentment, the king had to *rescind* his order.

respite N. delay in punishment; interval of relief; rest. The judge granted the condemned man a *respite* to enable his attorneys to file an appeal.

restraint N. controlling force. She dreamt of living an independent life, free of all *restraints.*

revere V. respect; honor. In Asian societies, people *revere* their elders.

sequester V. retire from public life; segregate; seclude. Although he had hoped for a long time to *sequester* himself in a small community, he never was able to drop his busy round of activities in the city.

servile ADJ. slavish; cringing. Uriah Heep was a very *servile* individual.

squalid ADJ. dirty; neglected; poor. It is easy to see how crime can breed in such a *squalid* neighborhood. **squalor,** N.

squander V. waste. The prodigal son *squandered* the family estate.

superficial ADJ. trivial; shallow. Since your report gave only a *superficial* analysis of the problem, I cannot give you more than a passing grade.

taciturn ADJ. habitually silent; talking little. New Englanders are reputedly *taciturn* people.

venerate V. revere. In China, the people *venerate* their ancestors.

vilify V. slander. Why is she always trying to *vilify* my reputation? **vilification,** N.

virtuoso N. highly skilled artist. Heifetz is a violin *virtuoso.*

BASIC WORD PARTS

In addition to reviewing the High-Frequency Word List, what other quick vocabulary-building tactics can you follow when you face an SAT deadline?

One good approach is to learn how to build up (and tear apart) words. You know that words are made up of other words: the *room* in which you *store* things is the *storeroom*; the person whose job is to *keep* the *books* is the *bookkeeper*.

Just as words are made up of other words, words are also made up of word parts: prefixes, suffixes, and roots. A knowledge of these word parts and their meanings can help you determine the meanings of unfamiliar words.

Most modern English words are derived from Anglo-Saxon (Old English), Latin, and Greek. Because few students nowadays study Latin and Greek (and even fewer study Anglo-Saxon!), the majority of high school juniors and seniors lack a vital tool for unlocking the meaning of unfamiliar words.

Build your vocabulary by mastering basic word parts. Learning thirty key word parts can help you unlock the meaning of over 10,000 words. Learning fifty key word parts can help you unlock the meaning of over 100,000!

COMMON PREFIXES

Prefixes are syllables that precede the root or stem and change or refine its meaning.

Prefix	Meaning	Illustration
ab, abs	from, away from	*abduct* lead away, kidnap *abjure* renounce *abject* degraded
ad, ac, af, ag, an, ap, ar, as, at	to, forward	*adit* entrance *adjure* request earnestly *admit* allow entrance *accord* agreement, harmony *affliction* distress *aggregation* collection *annexation* add to *apparition* ghost *arraignment* indictment *assumption* arrogance, the taking for granted *attendance* presence, the persons present
ambi	both	*ambidextrous* skilled with both hands *ambiguous* of double meaning *ambivalent* having two conflicting emotions
an, a	without	*anarchy* lack of government *anemia* lack of blood *amoral* without moral sense
ante	before	*antecedent* preceding event or word *antediluvian* ancient (before the flood) *ante-nuptial* before the wedding
anti	against, opposite	*antipathy* hatred *antiseptic* against infection *antithetical* exactly opposite
arch	chief, first	*archetype* original *archbishop* chief bishop *archeology* study of first or ancient times
be	over, thoroughly	*bedaub* smear over *befuddle* confuse thoroughly *beguile* deceive, charm thoroughly
bi	two	*bicameral* composed of two houses (Congress) *biennial* every two years *bicycle* two-wheeled vehicle

Prefix	Meaning	Illustration
cata	down	*catastrophe* disaster *cataract* waterfall *catapult* hurl (throw down)
circum	around	*circumnavigate* sail around (the globe) *circumspect* cautious (looking around) *circumscribe* limit (place a circle around)
com, co, col, con, cor	with, together	*combine* merge with *commerce* trade with *communicate* correspond with *coeditor* joint editor *collateral* subordinate, connected *conference* meeting *corroborate* confirm
contra, contro	against	*contravene* conflict with *controversy* dispute
de	down, away	*debase* lower in value *decadence* deterioration *decant* pour off
demi	partly, half	*demigod* partly divine being
di	two	*dichotomy* division into two parts *dilemma* choice between two bad alternatives
dia	across	*diagonal* across a figure *diameter* distance across a circle *diagram* outline drawing
dis, dif	not, apart	*discord* lack of harmony *differ* disagree (carry apart) *disparity* condition of inequality; difference
dys	faulty, bad	*dyslexia* faulty ability to read *dyspepsia* indigestion
ex, e	out	*expel* drive out *extirpate* root out *eject* throw out
extra, extro	beyond, outside	*extracurricular* beyond the curriculum *extraterritorial* beyond a nation's bounds *extrovert* person interested chiefly in external objects and actions
hyper	above; excessively	*hyperbole* exaggeration *hyperventilate* breathe at an excessive rate

Prefix	Meaning	Illustration
hypo	beneath; lower	*hypoglycemia* low blood sugar
in, il, im, ir	not	*inefficient* not efficient *inarticulate* not clear or distinct *illegible* not readable *impeccable* not capable of sinning; flawless *irrevocable* not able to be called back
in, il, im, ir	in, on, upon	*invite* call in *illustration* something that makes clear *impression* effect upon mind or feelings *irradiate* shine upon
inter	between, among	*intervene* come between *international* between nations *interjection* a statement thrown in
intra, intro	within	*intramural* within a school *introvert* person who turns within himself
macro	large, long	*macrobiotic* tending to prolong life *macrocosm* the great world (the entire universe)
mega	great, million	*megalomania* delusions of grandeur *megaton* explosive force of a million tons of TNT
meta	involving change	*metamorphosis* change of form
micro	small	*microcosm* miniature universe *microbe* minute organism *microscopic* extremely small
mis	bad, improper	*misdemeanor* minor crime; bad conduct *mischance* unfortunate accident *misnomer* wrong name
mis	hatred	*misanthrope* person who hates mankind *misogynist* woman-hater
mono	one	*monarchy* government by one ruler *monotheism* belief in one god
multi	many	*multifarious* having many parts *multitudinous* numerous
neo	new	*neologism* newly coined word *neophyte* beginner; novice
non	not	*noncommittal* undecided *nonentity* person of no importance

Prefix	**Meaning**	**Illustration**
ob, oc, of, op	against	*obloquy* infamy; disgrace *obtrude* push into prominence *occlude* close; block out *offend* insult *opponent* someone who struggles against; foe
olig	few	*oligarchy* government by a few
pan	all, every	*panacea* cure-all *panorama* unobstructed view in all directions
para	beyond, related	*parallel* similar *paraphrase* restate; translate
per	through, completely	*permeable* allowing passage through *pervade* spread throughout
peri	around, near	*perimeter* outer boundary *periphery* edge *periphrastic* stated in a roundabout way
poly	many	*polygamist* person with several spouses *polyglot* speaking several languages
post	after	*postpone* delay *posterity* generations that follow *posthumous* after death
pre	before	*preamble* introductory statement *prefix* word part placed before a root/stem *premonition* forewarning
prim	first	*primordial* existing at the dawn of time *primogeniture* state of being the first born
pro	forward, in favor of	*propulsive* driving forward *proponent* supporter
proto	first	*prototype* first of its kind
pseudo	false	*pseudonym* pen name
re	again, back	*reiterate* repeat *reimburse* pay back
retro	backward	*retrospect* looking back *retroactive* effective as of a past date
se	away, aside	*secede* withdraw *seclude* shut away *seduce* lead astray

Prefix	Meaning	Illustration
semi	half, partly	*semiannual* every six months *semiconscious* partly conscious
sub, suc, suf, sug, sup, sus	under, less	*subway* underground road *subjugate* bring under control *succumb* yield; cease to resist *suffuse* spread through *suggest* hint *suppress* put down by force *suspend* delay
super, sur	over, above	*supernatural* above natural things *supervise* oversee *surtax* additional tax
syn, sym, syl, sys	with, together	*synchronize* time together *synthesize* combine together *sympathize* pity; identify with *syllogism* explanation of how ideas relate *system* network
tele	far	*telemetry* measurement from a distance *telegraphic* communicated over a distance
trans	across	*transport* carry across *transpose* reverse, move across
ultra	beyond, excessive	*ultramodern* excessively modern *ultracritical* exceedingly critical
un	not	*unfeigned* not pretended; real *unkempt* not combed; disheveled *unwitting* not knowing; unintentional
under	below	*undergird* strengthen underneath *underling* someone inferior
uni	one	*unison* oneness of pitch; complete accord *unicycle* one-wheeled vehicle
vice	in place of	*vicarious* acting as a substitute *viceroy* governor acting in place of a king
with	away, against	*withhold* hold back; keep *withstand* stand up against; resist

COMMON ROOTS AND STEMS

Roots are basic words which have been carried over into English. *Stems* are variations of roots brought about by changes in declension or conjugation.

Root or Stem	Meaning	Illustration
ac, acr	sharp	*acrimonious* bitter; caustic *acerbity* bitterness of temper *acidulate* to make somewhat acid or sour
aev, ev	age, era	*primeval* of the first age *coeval* of the same age or era *medieval* or *mediaeval* of the middle ages
ag, act	do	*act* deed *agent* doer
agog	leader	*demagogue* false leader of people *pedagogue* teacher (leader of children)
agri, agrari	field	*agrarian* one who works in the field *agriculture* cultivation of fields *peregrination* wandering (through fields)
ali	another	*alias* assumed (another) name *alienate* estrange (turn away from another)
alt	high	*altitude* height *altimeter* instrument for measuring height
alter	other	*altruistic* unselfish, considering others *alter ego* a second self
am	love	*amorous* loving, especially sexually *amity* friendship *amicable* friendly
anim	mind, soul	*animadvert* cast criticism upon *unanimous* of one mind *magnanimity* greatness of mind or spirit
ann, enn	year	*annuity* yearly remittance *biennial* every two years *perennial* present all year; persisting for several years
anthrop	man	*anthropology* study of man *misanthrope* hater of mankind *philanthropy* love of mankind; charity

Root or Stem	Meaning	Illustration
apt	fit	*aptitude* skill *adapt* make suitable or fit
aqua	water	*aqueduct* passageway for conducting water *aquatic* living in water *aqua fortis* nitric acid (strong water)
arch	ruler, first	*archaeology* study of antiquities (study of first things) *monarch* sole ruler *anarchy* lack of government
aster	star	*astronomy* study of the stars *asterisk* star-like type character (*) *disaster* catastrophe (contrary star)
aud, audit	hear	*audible* able to be heard *auditorium* place where people may be heard *audience* hearers
auto	self	*autocracy* rule by one person (self) *automobile* vehicle that moves by itself *autobiography* story of one's own life
belli	war	*bellicose* inclined to fight *belligerent* inclined to wage war *rebellious* resisting authority
ben, bon	good	*benefactor* one who does good deeds *benevolence* charity (wishing good) *bonus* something extra above regular pay
biblio	book	*bibliography* list of books *bibliophile* lover of books *Bible* The Book
bio	life	*biography* writing about a person's life *biology* study of living things *biochemist* student of the chemistry of living things
breve	short	*brevity* briefness *abbreviate* shorten *breviloquent* marked by brevity of speech
cad, cas	to fall	*decadent* deteriorating *cadence* intonation, musical movement *cascade* waterfall
cap, capt, cept, cip	to take	*capture* seize *participate* take part *precept* wise saying (originally a command)

Root or Stem	Meaning	Illustration
capit, capt	head	*decapitate* remove (cut off) someone's head *captain* chief
carn	flesh	*carnivorous* flesh-eating *carnage* destruction of life *carnal* fleshly
ced, cess	to yield, to go	*recede* go back, withdraw *antecedent* that which goes before *process* go forward
celer	swift	*celerity* swiftness *decelerate* reduce swiftness *accelerate* increase swiftness
cent	one hundred	*century* one hundred years *centennial* hundredth anniversary *centipede* many-footed, wingless animal
chron	time	*chronology* timetable of events *anachronism* a thing out of time sequence *chronicle* register events in order of time
cid, cis	to cut, to kill	*incision* a cut (surgical) *homicide* killing of a man *fratricide* killing of a brother
cit, citat	to call, to start	*incite* stir up, start up *excite* stir up *recitation* a recalling (or repeating) aloud
civi	citizen	*civilization* society of citizens, culture *civilian* member of community *civil* courteous
clam, clamat	to cry out	*clamorous* loud *declamation* speech *acclamation* shouted approval
claud, claus, clos, clud	to close	*claustrophobia* fear of close places *enclose* close in *conclude* finish
cognosc, cognit	to learn	*agnostic* lacking knowledge, skeptical *incognito* traveling under assumed name *cognition* knowledge
compl	to fill	*complete* filled out *complement* that which completes something *comply* fulfill

Root or Stem	Meaning	Illustration
cord	heart	*accord* agreement (from the heart) *cordial* friendly *discord* lack of harmony
corpor	body	*incorporate* organize into a body *corporeal* pertaining to the body, fleshly *corpse* dead body
cred, credit	to believe	*incredulous* not believing, skeptical *credulity* gullibility *credence* belief
cur	to care	*curator* person who has the care of something *sinecure* position without responsibility *secure* safe
curr, curs	to run	*excursion* journey *cursory* brief *precursor* forerunner
da, dat	to give	*data* facts, statistics *mandate* command *date* given time
deb, debit	to owe	*debt* something owed *indebtedness* debt *debenture* bond
dem	people	*democracy* rule of the people *demagogue* (false) leader of the people *epidemic* widespread (among the people)
derm	skin	*epidermis* skin *pachyderm* thick-skinned quadruped *dermatology* study of skin and its disorders
di, diurn	day	*diary* a daily record of activities, feelings, etc. *diurnal* pertaining to daytime
dic, dict	to say	*abdicate* renounce *diction* speech *verdict* statement of jury
doc, doct	to teach	*docile* obedient; easily taught *document* something that provides evidence *doctor* learned person (originally, teacher)
domin	to rule	*dominate* have power over *domain* land under rule *dominant* prevailing

Root or Stem	Meaning	Illustration
duc, duct	to lead	*viaduct* arched roadway *aqueduct* artificial waterway
dynam	power, strength	*dynamic* powerful *dynamite* powerful explosive *dynamo* engine making electrical power
ego	I	*egoist* person who is self-interested *egotist* selfish person *egocentric* revolving about self
erg, urg	work	*energy* power *ergatocracy* rule of the workers *metallurgy* science and technology of metals
err	to wander	*error* mistake *erratic* not reliable, wandering *knight-errant* wandering knight
eu	good, well, beautiful	*eupeptic* having good digestion *eulogize* praise *euphemism* substitution of pleasant way of saying something blunt
fac, fic, fec, fect	to make, to do	*factory* place where things are made *fiction* manufactured story *affect* cause to change
fall, fals	to deceive	*fallacious* misleading *infallible* not prone to error, perfect *falsify* lie
fer, lat	to bring, to bear	*transfer* bring from one place to another *translate* bring from one language to another *conifer* bearing cones, as pine trees
fid	belief, faith	*infidel* nonbeliever, heathen *confidence* assurance, belief
fin	end, limit	*confine* keep within limits *finite* having definite limits
flect, flex	bend	*flexible* able to bend *deflect* bend away, turn aside
fort	luck, chance	*fortuitous* accidental, occurring by chance *fortunate* lucky

Root or Stem	Meaning	Illustration
fort	strong	*fortitude* strength, firmness of mind *fortification* strengthening *fortress* stronghold
frag, fract	break	*fragile* easily broken *infraction* breaking of a rule *fractious* unruly, tending to break rules
fug	flee	*fugitive* someone who flees *refuge* shelter, home for someone fleeing
fus	pour	*effusive* gushing, pouring out *diffuse* widespread (poured in many directions)
gam	marriage	*monogamy* marriage to one person *bigamy* marriage to two people at the same time *polygamy* having many wives or husbands at the same time
gen, gener	class, race	*genus* group of animals with similar traits *generic* characteristic of a class *gender* class organized by sex
grad, gress	go, step	*digress* go astray (from the main point) *regress* go backwards *gradual* step by step, by degrees
graph, gram	writing	*epigram* pithy statement *telegram* instantaneous message over great distance *stenography* shorthand (writing narrowly)
greg	flock, herd	*gregarious* tending to group together as in a herd *aggregate* group, total *egregious* conspicuously bad; shocking
helio	sun	*heliotrope* flower that faces the sun *heliograph* instrument that uses the sun's rays to send signals
it, itiner	journey, road	*exit* way out *itinerary* plan of journey
jac, jact, jec	to throw	*projectile* missile; something thrown forward *trajectory* path taken by thrown object *ejaculatory* casting or throwing out
jur, jurat	to swear	*perjure* testify falsely *jury* group of men and women sworn to seek the truth *adjuration* solemn urging

Root or Stem	Meaning	Illustration
labor, laborat	to work	*laboratory* place where work is done *collaborate* work together with others *laborious* difficult
leg, lect, lig	to choose, to read	*election* choice *legible* able to be read *eligible* able to be selected
leg	law	*legislature* law-making body *legitimate* lawful *legal* lawful
liber, libr	book	*library* collection of books *libretto* the "book" of a musical play *libel* slander (originally found in a little book)
liber	free	*liberation* the act of setting free *liberal* generous (giving freely); tolerant
log	word, study	*entomology* study of insects *etymology* study of word parts and derivations *monologue* speech by one person
loqu, locut	to talk	*soliloquy* speech by one individual *loquacious* talkative *elocution* speech
luc	light	*elucidate* enlighten *lucid* clear *translucent* allowing some light to pass through
magn	great	*magnify* enlarge *magnanimity* generosity, greatness of soul *magnitude* greatness, extent
mal	bad	*malevolent* wishing evil *malediction* curse *malefactor* evil-doer
man	hand	*manufacture* create (make by hand) *manuscript* written by hand *emancipate* free (let go from the hand)
mar	sea	*maritime* connected with seafaring *submarine* undersea craft *mariner* seaman
mater, matr	mother	*maternal* pertaining to motherhood *matriarch* female ruler of a family, group, or state *matrilineal* descended on the mother's side

Root or Stem	Meaning	Illustration
mit, miss	to send	*missile* projectile *dismiss* send away *transmit* send across
mob, mot, mov	move	*mobilize* cause to move *motility* ability to move *immovable* not able to be moved
mon, monit	to warn	*admonish* warn *premonition* foreboding *monitor* watcher (warner)
mori, mort	to die	*mortuary* funeral parlor *moribund* dying *immortal* not dying
morph	shape, form	*amorphous* formless, lacking shape *metamorphosis* change of shape *anthropomorphic* in the shape of man
mut	change	*immutable* not able to be changed *mutate* undergo a great change *mutability* changeableness, inconstancy
nat	born	*innate* from birth *prenatal* before birth *nativity* birth
nav	ship	*navigate* sail a ship *circumnavigate* sail around the world *naval* pertaining to ships
neg	deny	*negation* denial *renege* deny, go back on one's word *renegade* turncoat, traitor
nomen	name	*nomenclature* act of naming, terminology *nominal* in name only (as opposed to actual) *cognomen* surname, distinguishing nickname
nov	new	*novice* beginner *renovate* make new again *novelty* newness
omni	all	*omniscient* all knowing *omnipotent* all powerful *omnivorous* eating everything

Root or Stem	Meaning	Illustration
oper	to work	*operate* work *cooperation* working together
pac	peace	*pacify* make peaceful *pacific* peaceful *pacifist* person opposed to war
pass	feel	*dispassionate* free of emotion *impassioned* emotion-filled *impassive* showing no feeling
pater, patr	father	*patriotism* love of one's country (fatherland) *patriarch* male ruler of a family, group, or state *paternity* fatherhood
path	disease, feeling	*pathology* study of diseased tissue *apathetic* lacking feeling; indifferent *antipathy* hostile feeling
ped, pod	foot	*impediment* stumbling-block; hindrance *tripod* three-footed stand *quadruped* four-footed animal
ped	child	*pedagogue* teacher of children *pediatrician* children's doctor
pel, puls	to drive	*compulsion* a forcing to do *repel* drive back *expel* drive out, banish
pet, petit	to seek	*petition* request *appetite* craving, desire *compete* vie with others
phil	love	*philanthropist* benefactor, lover of humanity *Anglophile* lover of everything English *philanderer* one involved in brief love affairs
pon, posit	to place	*postpone* place after *positive* definite, unquestioned (definitely placed)
port, portat	to carry	*portable* able to be carried *transport* carry across *export* carry out (of country)
poten	able, powerful	*omnipotent* all-powerful *potentate* powerful person *impotent* powerless

Root or Stem	Meaning	Illustration
psych	mind	*psychology* study of the mind *psychosis* mental disorder *psychopath* mentally ill person
put, putat	to trim, to calculate	*putative* supposed (calculated) *computation* calculation *amputate* cut off
quer, ques, quir, quis	to ask	*inquiry* investigation *inquisitive* questioning *query* question
reg, rect	rule	*regicide* murder of a ruler *regent* ruler *insurrection* rebellion; overthrow of a ruler
rid, ris	to laugh	*derision* scorn *risibility* inclination to laughter *ridiculous* deserving to be laughed at
rog, rogat	to ask	*interrogate* question *prerogative* privilege
rupt	to break	*interrupt* break into *bankrupt* insolvent *rupture* a break
sacr	holy	*sacred* holy *sacrilegious* impious, violating something holy *sacrament* religious act
sci	to know	*science* knowledge *omniscient* knowing all *conscious* aware
scop	watch, see	*periscope* device for seeing around corners *microscope* device for seeing small objects
scrib, script	to write	*transcribe* make a written copy *script* written text *circumscribe* write around, limit
sect	cut	*dissect* cut apart *bisect* cut into two pieces
sed, sess	to sit	*sedentary* inactive (sitting) *session* meeting
sent, sens	to think, to feel	*consent* agree *resent* show indignation *sensitive* showing feeling

Root or Stem	Meaning	Illustration
sequi, secut, seque	to follow	*consecutive* following in order *sequence* arrangement *sequel* that which follows *non sequitur* something that does not follow logically
solv, solut	to loosen	*absolve* free from blame *dissolute* morally lax *absolute* complete (not loosened)
somn	sleep	*insomnia* inability to sleep *somnolent* sleepy *somnambulist* sleepwalker
soph	wisdom	*philosopher* lover of wisdom *sophisticated* worldly wise
spec, spect	to look at	*spectator* observer *aspect* appearance *circumspect* cautious (looking around)
spir	breathe	*respiratory* pertaining to breathing *spirited* full of life (breath)
string, strict	bind	*stringent* strict *constrict* become tight *stricture* limit, something that restrains
stru, struct	build	*constructive* helping to build *construe* analyze (how something is built)
tang, tact, ting	to touch	*tangent* touching *contact* touching with, meeting *contingent* depending upon
tempor	time	*contemporary* at same time *extemporaneous* impromptu *temporize* delay
ten, tent	to hold	*tenable* able to be held *tenure* holding of office *retentive* holding; having a good memory
term	end	*interminable* endless *terminate* end
terr	land	*terrestrial* pertaining to earth *subterranean* underground
therm	heat	*thermostat* instrument that regulates heat *diathermy* sending heat through body tissues

Root or Stem	Meaning	Illustration
tors, tort	twist	*distort* twist out of true shape or meaning *torsion* act of twisting *tortuous* twisting
tract	drag, pull	*distract* pull (one's attention) away *intractable* stubborn, unable to be dragged *attraction* pull, drawing quality
trud, trus	push, shove	*intrude* push one's way in *protrusion* something sticking out
urb	city	*urban* pertaining to a city *urbane* polished, sophisticated (pertaining to a city dweller) *suburban* outside of a city
vac	empty	*vacuous* lacking content, empty-headed *evacuate* compel to empty an area
vad, vas	go	*invade* enter in a hostile fashion *evasive* not frank; eluding
veni, vent, ven	to come	*intervene* come between *prevent* stop *convention* meeting
ver	true	*veracious* truthful *verify* check the truth *verisimilitude* appearance of truth
verb	word	*verbose* wordy *verbiage* excessive use of words *verbatim* word for word
vers, vert	turn	*vertigo* turning dizzy *revert* turn back (to an earlier state) *diversion* something causing one to turn aside
via	way	*deviation* departure from the way *viaduct* roadway (arched) *trivial* trifling (small talk at crossroads)
vid, vis	to see	*vision* sight *evidence* things seen *vista* view
vinc, vict, vanq	to conquer	*invincible* unconquerable *victory* winning *vanquish* defeat

Root or Stem	Meaning	Illustration
viv, vit	alive	*vivisection* operating on living animals *vivacious* full of life *vitality* liveliness
voc, vocat	to call	*avocation* calling, minor occupation *provocation* calling or rousing the anger of *invocation* calling in prayer
vol	wish	*malevolent* wishing someone ill *voluntary* of one's own will
volv, volut	to roll	*revolve* roll around *evolve* roll out, develop *convolution* coiled state

COMMON SUFFIXES

Suffixes are syllables which are added to a word. Occasionally, they change the meaning of the word; more frequently, they serve to change the grammatical form of the word (noun to adjective, adjective to noun, noun to verb).

Suffix	Meaning	Illustration
able, ible	capable of (adjective suffix)	*portable* able to be carried *interminable* not able to be limited *legible* able to be read
ac, ic	like, pertaining to (adjective suffix)	*cardiac* pertaining to the heart *aquatic* pertaining to the water *dramatic* pertaining to the drama
acious, icious	full of (adjective suffix)	*audacious* full of daring *perspicacious* full of mental perception *avaricious* full of greed
al	pertaining to (adjective or noun suffix)	*maniacal* insane *final* pertaining to the end *logical* pertaining to logic
ant, ent	full of (adjective or noun suffix)	*eloquent* pertaining to fluid, effective speech *suppliant* pleader *verdant* green
ary	like, connected with (adjective or noun suffix)	*dictionary* book connected with words *honorary* with honor *luminary* celestial body
ate	to make (verb suffix)	*consecrate* to make holy *enervate* to make weary *mitigate* to make less severe
ation	that which is (noun suffix)	*exasperation* irritation *irritation* annoyance
cy	state of being (noun suffix)	*democracy* government ruled by the people *obstinacy* stubbornness *accuracy* correctness
eer, er, or	person who (noun suffix)	*mutineer* person who rebels *lecher* person who lusts *censor* person who deletes improper remarks
escent	becoming (adjective suffix)	*evanescent* tending to vanish *pubescent* arriving at puberty

Suffix	Meaning	Illustration
fic	making, doing (adjective suffix)	*terrific* arousing great fear *soporific* causing sleep
fy	to make (verb suffix)	*magnify* enlarge *petrify* torn to stone *beautify* make beautiful
iferous	producing, bearing (adjective suffix)	*pestiferous* carrying disease *vociferous* bearing a loud voice
il, ile	pertaining to, capable of (adjective suffix)	*puerile* pertaining to a boy or child *ductile* capable of being hammered or drawn *civil* polite
ism	doctrine, belief (noun suffix)	*monotheism* belief in one god *fanaticism* excessive zeal; extreme belief
ist	dealer, doer (noun suffix)	*fascist* one who believes in a fascist state *realist* one who is realistic *artist* one who deals with art
ity	state of being (noun suffix)	*annuity* yearly grant *credulity* state of being unduly willing to believe *sagacity* wisdom
ive	like (adjective suffix)	*expensive* costly *quantitative* concerned with quantity *effusive* gushing
ize, ise	make (verb suffix)	*victimize* make a victim of *rationalize* make rational *harmonize* make harmonious *enfranchise* make free or set free
oid	resembling, like (adjective suffix)	*ovoid* like an egg *anthropoid* resembling man *spheroid* resembling a sphere
ose	full of (adjective suffix)	*verbose* full of words *lachrymose* full of tears
osis	condition (noun suffix)	*psychosis* diseased mental condition *neurosis* nervous condition *hypnosis* condition of induced sleep
ous	full of (adjective suffix)	*nauseous* full of nausea *ludicrous* foolish
tude	state of (noun suffix)	*fortitude* state of strength *beatitude* state of blessedness *certitude* state of sureness

LONG-RANGE STRATEGIES

There is only one effective long-range strategy for vocabulary building: **READ.**

Read widely, read deeply, read daily. If you do, your vocabulary will grow. If you don't, it won't.

Reading widely, however, will not always help you remember the words you read. You may have the words in your passive vocabulary and be able to recognize them when you see them in a context and yet be unable to define them clearly or think of antonyms for them.

Remembering words takes work. It also takes wit. You can spend hours memorizing dictionary definitions and get no place. You can also capitalize on your native intelligence to think up mnemonic devices—memory tricks—to help you remember new words.

Memory Tricks

Consider the word *hovel.* A *hovel* is a dirty, mean house. How can you remember that? *Hovel* rhymes with *shovel*. You need to shovel out the hovel to live in it. Rhymes can help you remember what words mean.

Now consider the word *hover*. To *hover* is to hang fluttering in the air or to wait around. Can rhyme help you here? *Hover* rhymes with *cover*. That doesn't seem to work. However, take another look at *hover*. Cut off the letter *h* and you're left with the word *over*. If a helicopter hovers over an accident, it hangs in the air; if a mother hovers over a sick child, she waits around. Hidden little words can help you remember bigger words.

Try the hidden work trick with a less familiar word than *hover*. Take the word *credulous*. *Credulous* means "gullible or easily fooled." A credulous person will give money to someone who wants to sell him the Brooklyn Bridge. Now look closely at *credulous*. What little word is hidden within it? The hidden word is *red*. What happens when a person finds out he's been taken for a fool? Often, the poor fool turns red. Credulous, red in the face. There's your memory trick.

SAT Word List Study

Just as reading widely may not help you remember the new words you encounter, reading widely also will not acquaint you most efficiently with the sorts of words you must know to do well on the SAT. To get an idea of the level of vocabulary you must master, look over the Basic Word List that follows. *Do not let this list overwhelm you*. You do not need to memorize every word.

The more than 3,500 words in this list have been compiled from various sources. They have been taken from the standard literature read by high school students throughout the country and from the many tests taken by high school and college students. Ever since this book first appeared in 1954, countless students have reported that working with this list has helped them immensely in taking all kinds of college entrance and scholarship tests. It has been used with profit by people preparing for civil service examinations, placement tests, and promotional examinations in many industrial fields. Above all, it has been used with profit by people studying for the SAT.

Even before the College Board began publishing its own SAT sample examinations, the Basic Word List was unique in its ability to reflect, and often predict, actual vocabulary items appearing on the SAT. Today, thanks to our ongoing research and computer analysis of published SAT materials, we believe our 3,500 Basic Word List is the best in the field.

For those of you who wish to work your way through the word list and feel the need for a plan, we recommend that you follow the procedure described below in order to use the lists and the exercises most profitably.

1. Allot a definite time each day to study a list.
2. Devote at least one hour to each list.
3. First go through the list looking at the short, simple-looking words (6 letters at most). Mark those you don't know. In studying, pay particular attention to them.
4. Go through the list again looking at the longer words. Pay particular attention to words with more than one meaning and familiar-looking words which have unusual definitions that come as a surprise to you. Many tests make use of these secondary definitions.
5. List unusual words on index cards which you can shuffle and review from time to time. (Use the flash card technique described in Chapter 4.)
6. Use the illustrative sentences in the list as models and make up new sentences of your own.
7. Take the test that follows each list at least one day after studying the words. In this way, you will check your ability to remember what you have studied.
8. If you can answer correctly 12 of the 15 questions in the test, proceed to the next list; if you cannot answer them, restudy the list.
9. Keep a record of your guesses and of your success as a guesser. (Use the chart in Chapter 2.)

For each word, the following is provided:

1. The word (printed in heavy type).
2. Its part of speech (abbreviated).
3. A brief definition.
4. A sentence illustrating the word's use.
5. Whenever appropriate, related words are provided, together with their parts of speech.

The word lists are arranged in strict alphabetical order.

3500 BASIC WORD LIST

WORD LIST 1 abase - adroit

abase V. lower; humiliate. His refusal to *abase* himself in the eyes of his followers irritated the king, who wanted to humiliate the proud leader.

abash V. embarrass. He was not at all *abashed* by her open admiration.

abbreviate V. shorten. Because we were running out of time, the lecturer had to *abbreviate* her speech.

abdicate V. renounce; give up. When Edward VIII *abdicated* the British throne, he surprised the entire world.

aberration N. wandering or staying away; in optics, failure of rays to focus. In designing a good lens for a camera, the problem of correcting chromatic and rectilinear *aberration* was a serious one. aberrant, ADJ. and N.

abettor N. encourager. She was accused of being an aider and *abettor* of the criminal. abet, V.

abeyance N. suspended action. The deal was held in *abeyance* until her arrival.

abhor V. detest; hate. She *abhorred* all forms of bigotry. abhorrence, N.

abjure V. renounce upon oath. He *abjured* his allegiance to the king. abjuration, N.

ablution N. washing. His daily *ablutions* were accompanied by loud noises which he humorously labeled "Opera in the Bath."

abnegation N. repudiation; self-sacrifice. No act of *abnegation* was more pronounced than his refusal of any rewards for his discovery.

abolish V. cancel; put an end to. The president of the college refused to *abolish* the physical education requirement.

abominate V. loathe; hate. Moses scolded the idol worshippers in the tribe because he *abominated* the custom.

aboriginal ADJ., N. being the first of its kind in a region; primitive; native. Her studies of the primitive art forms of the *aboriginal* Indians were widely reported in the scientific journals. aborigines, N.

abortive ADJ. unsuccessful; fruitless. We had to abandon our *abortive* attempts.

abrade V. wear away by friction; erode. The skin of her leg was *abraded* by the sharp rocks. abrasion, N.

abrogate V. abolish. He intended to *abrogate* the decree issued by his predecessor.

abscond V. depart secretly and hide. The teller *absconded* with the bonds and was not found.

absolve V. pardon (an offense). The father confessor *absolved* him of his sins. absolution, N.

abstemious ADJ. sparing in eating and drinking; temperate. The drunkards mocked him because of his *abstemious* habits.

abstinence N. restraint from eating or drinking. The doctor recommended total *abstinence* from salted foods. abstain, V.

abstruse ADJ. obscure; profound; difficult to understand. She read *abstruse* works in philosophy.

abusive ADJ. coarsely insulting; physically harmful. An *abusive* parent damages a child both mentally and physically.

abut V. border upon; adjoin. Where our estates *abut*, we must build a fence.

abysmal ADJ. bottomless. His arrogance is exceeded only by his *abysmal* ignorance.

accede V. agree. If I *accede* to this demand for blackmail, I am afraid that I will be the victim of future demands.

accelerate V. move faster. In our science class, we learn how falling bodies *accelerate*.

accessible ADJ. easy to approach; obtainable. We asked our guide whether the ruins were *accessible* on foot.

accessory N. additional object; useful but not essential thing. The *accessories* she bought cost more than the dress. also ADJ.

acclimate V. adjust to climate. One of the difficulties of our present air age is the need of travelers to *acclimate* themselves to their new and often strange environments.

acclivity N. sharp upslope of a hill. The car could not go up the *acclivity* in high gear.

accolade N. award of merit. In Hollywood, an "Oscar" is the highest *accolade*.

accomplice N. partner in crime. Because he had provided the criminal with the lethal weapon, he was arrested as an *accomplice* in the murder.

accord N. agreement. She was in complete *accord* with the verdict.

accost V. approach and speak first to a person. When the two young men *accosted* me, I was frightened because I thought they were going to attack me.

accoutre V. equip. The fisherman was *accoutred* with the best that the sporting goods store could supply. accoutrements, N.

accretion N. growth; increase. The *accretion* of wealth marked the family's rise in power.

accrue V. come about by addition. You must pay the interest which has *accrued* on your debt as well as the principal sum. accrual, N.

acephalous ADJ. headless. Because the country was in a state of anarchy and lacked a leader, it was described as an *acephalous* monstrosity.

acerbity N. bitterness of speech and temper. The meeting of the United Nations Assembly was marked with such *acerbity* that little hope of reaching any useful settlement of the problem could be held.

acetic ADJ. vinegary. The salad had an exceedingly *acetic* flavor.

acidulous ADJ. slightly sour; sharp, caustic. James was unpopular because of his sarcastic and *acidulous* remarks.

acknowledge V. recognize; admit. When pressed for an answer, she *acknowledged* the existence of another motive for the crime.

acme N. top; pinnacle. His success in this role marked his *acme* as an actor.

acoustics N. science of sound; quality that makes a room easy or hard to hear in. Carnegie Hall is liked by music lovers because of its fine *acoustics.*

acquiescence N. submission; compliance. It is impossible to obtain their *acquiescence* to the proposal because it is abhorrent to their philosophy.

acquiescent ADJ. accepting passively. His *acquiescent* manner did indicate the extent of his reluctance to join the group. acquiesce, V.

acquittal N. deliverance from a charge. His *acquittal* by the jury surprised those who had thought him guilty. acquit, V.

acrid ADJ. sharp; bitterly pungent. The *acrid* odor of burnt gunpowder filled the room after the pistol had been fired.

acrimonious ADJ. stinging; caustic. His tendency to utter *acrimonious* remarks alienated his audience. acrimony, N.

actuarial ADJ. calculating; pertaining to insurance statistics. According to recent *actuarial* tables, life expectancy is greater today than it was a century ago.

actuate V. motivate. I fail to understand what *actuated* you to reply to this letter so nastily.

acuity N. sharpness. In time his youthful *acuity* of vision failed him, and he came to need glasses.

acumen N. mental keenness. His business *acumen* helped him to succeed where others had failed.

adage N. wise saying; proverb. There is much truth in the old *adage* about fools and their money.

adamant ADJ. hard; inflexible. He was *adamant* in his determination to punish the wrongdoer. adamantine, ADJ.

adapt V. alter; modify. Some species of animals have become extinct because they could not *adapt* to a changing environment.

addiction N. compulsive, habitual need. His *addiction* to drugs caused his friends much grief.

addle ADJ. rotten; muddled; crazy. This *addle*-headed plan is so preposterous that it does not deserve any consideration. also V.

adduce V. present as evidence. When you *adduce* evidence of this nature, you must be sure of your sources.

adept ADJ. expert at. She was *adept* at the fine art of irritating people. also N.

adhere V. stick fast to. I will *adhere* to this opinion until proof that I am wrong is presented. adhesion, N.

adipose ADJ. fatty. Excess *adipose* tissue should be avoided by middle-aged people.

adjunct N. something attached to but holding an inferior position. I will entertain this concept as an *adjunct* to the main proposal.

adjuration N. solemn urging. Her *adjuration* to tell the truth did not change the witnesses' testimony.

adjure V. request solemnly. I must *adjure* you to consider this matter carefully as it is of utmost importance to all of us.

admonish V. warn; reprove. He *admonished* his listeners to change their wicked ways. admonition, N.

admonition N. warning. After repeated rejections of its *admonitions,* the country was forced to issue an ultimatum.

adorn V. decorate. Wall paintings and carved statues *adorned* the temple. adornment, N.

adroit ADJ. skillful. His *adroit* handling of the delicate situation pleased his employers.

TEST—WORD LIST 1—*Synonyms*

Each of the questions below consists of a word in capital letters, followed by five lettered words or phrases. Choose the lettered word or phrase that is most nearly similar in meaning to the word in capital letters and write the letter of your choice on your answer paper.

1. ABASE (A) incur (B) tax (C) ground floor (D) humility (E) humiliate

2. ABERRATION (A) deviation (B) abhorrence (C) dislike (D) absence (E) anecdote

3. ABETTOR (A) conception (B) one who wagers (C) encourager (D) evidence (E) protection
4. ABEYANCE (A) obedience (B) discussion (C) excitement (D) suspended action (E) editorial
5. ABJURE (A) discuss (B) renounce (C) run off secretly (D) perjure (E) project
6. ABLUTION (A) censure (B) forgiveness (C) mutiny (D) survival (E) washing
7. ABNEGATION (A) blackness (B) self-denial (C) selfishness (D) cause (E) effect
8. ABORIGINES (A) first designs (B) absolutions (C) finales (D) concepts (E) primitive inhabitants
9. ABORTIVE (A) unsuccessful (B) consuming (C) financing (D) familiar (E) fruitful
10. ABSTINENCE (A) restrained eating or drinking (B) vulgar display (C) deportment (D) reluctance (E) population
11. ABSTRUSE (A) profound (B) irrespective (C) suspended (D) protesting (E) not thorough
12. ABUT (A) stimulate (B) grasp (C) oppose (D) widen (E) adjoin
13. ABYSMAL (A) bottomless (B) eternal (C) meteoric (D) diabolic (E) internal
14. ACCEDE (A) fail (B) compromise (C) correct (D) consent (E) mollify
15. ACCLIVITY (A) index (B) report (C) upslope of a hill (D) character (E) negotiator

WORD LIST 2 adulation - amend

adulation N. flattery; admiration. He thrived on the *adulation* of his henchmen.

adulterate V. make impure by mixing with baser substances. It is a crime to *adulterate* foods without informing the buyer.

adulterated ADJ. made impure or spoiled by the addition of inferior materials. The health authorities ordered the sale of the meat stopped because they found it *adulterated.*

adumbration N. foreshadowing; outlining. The *adumbration* of the future in science fiction is often extremely fantastic.

advent N. arrival. Most Americans were unaware of the *advent* of the Nuclear Age until the news of Hiroshima reached them.

adventitious ADJ. accidental; casual. He found this *adventitious* meeting with his friend extremely fortunate.

adverse ADJ. unfavorable; hostile. *Adverse* circumstances compelled him to close his business.

adversity N. poverty; misfortune. We must learn to meet *adversity* gracefully.

advert V. refer to. Since you *advert* to this matter so frequently, you must regard it as important.

advocate V. urge; plead for. The abolitionists *advocated* freedom for the slaves. also N.

aegis N. shield; defense. Under the *aegis* of the Bill of Rights, we enjoy our most treasured freedoms.

aeon N. long period of time; an age. It has taken *aeons* for our civilization to develop.

aesthetic ADJ. artistic; dealing with or capable of appreciation of the beautiful. Because of his *aesthetic* nature, he was emotionally disturbed by ugly things. aesthete, N.

affable ADJ. courteous. Although he held a position of responsibility, he was an *affable* individual and could be reached by anyone with a complaint.

affected ADJ. artificial; pretended. His *affected* mannerisms irritated many of us who had known him before his promotion. affectation, N.

afferent ADJ. carrying toward the center. The nerves that carry stimuli to the brain are called *afferent;* those that convey messages from the brain, efferent.

affidavit N. written statement made under oath. The court refused to accept his statement unless he presented it in the form of an *affidavit.*

affiliation N. joining; associating with. His *affiliation* with the political party was of short duration for he soon disagreed with his colleagues.

affinity N. kinship. He felt an *affinity* with all who suffered; their pains were his pains.

affirmation N. solemn pledge by one who refuses to take an oath. The Constitution of this country provides for oath or *affirmation* by officeholders.

afflatus N. inspiration. The poet boasted of his divine *afflatus* as the source of his greatness.

affluence N. abundance; wealth. Foreigners are amazed by the *affluence* and luxury of the American way of life.

affray N. public brawl. He was badly mauled by the fighters in the *affray.*

agape ADJ. openmouthed. She stared, *agape,* at the many strange animals in the zoo.

agenda N. items of business at a meeting. We had so much difficulty agreeing upon an *agenda* that there was very little time for the meeting.

agglomeration N. collection; heap. It took weeks to assort the *agglomeration* of miscellaneous items she had collected on her trip.

aggrandize V. increase or intensify. The history of the past quarter century illustrates how a President may *aggrandize* his power to act aggressively in international affairs without considering the wishes of Congress.

aggregate ADJ. sum; total. The *aggregate* wealth of this country is staggering to the imagination. also V.

aghast ADJ. horrified. He was *aghast* at the nerve of the speaker who had insulted his host.

agility N. nimbleness. The *agility* of the acrobat amazed and thrilled the audience.

agitate V. stir up; disturb. Her fiery remarks *agitated* the already angry mob.

agitation N. strong feeling; excitement. We felt that he was responsible for the *agitation* of the mob because of the inflammatory report he had issued.

agnostic N. one who is skeptical of the existence or knowability of a god or any ultimate reality. The *agnostic* demanded proof before she would accept the statement of the minister. also ADJ.

agrarian ADJ. pertaining to land or its cultivation. The country is gradually losing its *agrarian* occupation and turning more and more to an industrial point of view.

agronomist N. scientist engaged in the management of land. Because the country failed to heed the warnings of its *agronomists,* it was faced with serious famine.

alacrity N. cheerful promptness. He demonstrated his eagerness to serve by his *alacrity* in executing the orders of his master.

albeit CONJ. although. *Albeit* fair, she was not sought after.

alchemy N. medieval chemistry. The changing of baser metals into gold was the goal of the students of *alchemy.* alchemist, N.

alias N. an assumed name. John Smith's *alias* was Bob Jones. also ADV.

alienate V. make hostile; separate. Her attempts to *alienate* the two friends failed because they had complete faith.

alimentary ADJ. supplying nourishment. The *alimentary* canal in our bodies is so named because digestion of foods occurs there.

alimony N. payment by a husband to his divorced wife. Mrs. Jones was awarded $200 monthly *alimony* by the court when she was divorced from her husband.

allay V. calm; pacify. The crew tried to *allay* the fears of the passengers by announcing that the fire had been controlled.

allege V. state without proof. It is *alleged* that she had worked for the enemy. allegation, N.

allegory N. story in which characters are used as symbols; fable. *Pilgrim's Progress* is an *allegory* of the temptations and victories of man's soul. allegorical, ADJ.

alleviate V. relieve. This should *alleviate* the pain; if it does not, we shall have to use stronger drugs.

alliteration N. repetition of beginning sound in poetry. "The furrow followed free" is an example of *alliteration.*

allocate V. assign. Even though the Red Cross had *allocated* a large sum for the relief of the sufferers of the disaster, many people perished.

alloy N. a mixture as of metals. *Alloys* of gold are used more frequently than the pure metal.

allude V. refer indirectly. Try not to *allude* to this matter in his presence because it annoys him to hear of it.

allure V. entice; attract. *Allured* by the song of the sirens, the helmsman steered the ship toward the reef. also N.

allusion N. indirect reference. The *allusions* to mythological characters in Milton's poems bewilder the reader who has not studied Latin.

alluvial ADJ. pertaining to soil deposits left by rivers, etc. The farmers found the *alluvial* deposits at the mouth of the river very fertile.

aloof ADJ. apart; reserved. He remained *aloof* while all the rest conversed.

aloft ADV. upward. The sailor climbed *aloft* into the rigging.

altercation N. wordy quarrel. Throughout the entire *altercation,* not one sensible word was uttered.

altruism N. unselfish aid to others; generosity. The philanthropist was noted for his *altruism.* altruistic, ADJ.

amalgamate V. combine; unite in one body. The unions will attempt to *amalgamate* their groups into one national body.

amass V. collect. The miser's aim is to *amass* and hoard as much gold as possible.

amazon N. female warrior. Ever since the days of Greek mythology we refer to strong and aggressive women as *amazons.*

ambidextrous ADJ. capable of using either hand with equal ease. A switch-hitter in baseball should be naturally *ambidextrous*.

ambience N. environment; atmosphere. She went to the restaurant not for the food but for the *ambience.*

ambiguous ADJ. unclear or doubtful in meaning. His *ambiguous* instructions misled us; we did not know which road to take. ambiguity, N.

amble N. moving at an easy pace. When she first mounted the horse, she was afraid to urge the animal to go faster than a gentle *amble.* also V.

ambivalence N. the state of having contradictory or conflicting emotional attitudes. Torn between loving her parents one minute and hating them the next, she was confused by the *ambivalence* of her feelings. ambivalent, ADJ.

ambrosia N. food of the gods. *Ambrosia* was supposed to give immortality to any human who ate it.

ambulatory ADJ. able to walk. He was described as an *ambulatory* patient because he was not confined to his bed.

ameliorate V. improve. Many social workers have attempted to *ameliorate* the conditions of people living in the slums.

amenable ADJ. readily managed; willing to be led. He was *amenable* to any suggestions which came from those he looked up to; he resented advice from his inferiors.

amend V. correct; change, generally for the better. Hoping to *amend* his condition, he left Vietnam for the United States.

TEST—WORD LIST 2—*Antonyms*

Each of the questions below consists of a word in capital letters, followed by five lettered words or phrases. Choose the lettered word or phrase that is most nearly opposite in meaning to the word in capital letters and write the letter of your choice on your answer paper.

16. ADULATION (A) youth (B) purity (C) brightness (D) defense (E) criticism
17. ADVOCATE (A) define (B) oppose (C) remove (D) inspect (E) discern
18. AFFABLE (A) rude (B) ruddy (C) needy (D) useless (E) conscious
19. AFFECTED (A) weary (B) unfriendly (C) divine (D) unfeigned (E) slow
20. AFFLUENCE (A) poverty (B) fear (C) persuasion (D) consideration (E) neglect
21. AGILITY (A) awkwardness (B) solidity (C) temper (D) harmony (E) warmth
22. ALACRITY (A) slowness (B) plenty (C) filth (D) courtesy (E) despair
23. ALLEVIATE (A) endure (B) worsen (C) enlighten (D) maneuver (E) humiliate
24. ALLURE (A) hinder (B) repel (C) ignore (D) leave (E) wallow
25. ALOOF (A) triangular (B) gregarious (C) comparable (D) honorable (E) savory
26. AMALGAMATE (A) equip (B) separate (C) generate (D) materialize (E) repress
27. AMBIGUOUS (A) salvageable (B) corresponding (C) responsible (D) clear (E) auxiliary
28. AMBLE (A) befriend (B) hasten (C) steal (D) browse (E) prattle
29. AMBULATORY (A) convalescent (B) conservatory (C) bedridden (D) emergency (E) congenital
30. AMELIORATE (A) make slow (B) make sure (C) make young (D) make worse (E) make able

---

WORD LIST 3 amenities - apothecary

amenities N. agreeable manners; courtesies. She observed the social *amenities.*

amiable ADJ. agreeable; lovable. His *amiable* disposition pleased all who had dealings with him.

amicable ADJ. friendly. The dispute was settled in an *amicable* manner with no harsh words.

amiss ADJ. wrong; faulty. Seeing her frown, he wondered if anything were *amiss.* also ADV.

amity N. friendship. Student exchange programs such as the Experiment in International Living were established to promote international *amity.*

amnesia N. loss of memory. Because she was suffering from *amnesia,* the police could not get the young girl to identify herself.

amnesty N. pardon. When his first child was born, the king granted *amnesty* to all in prison.

amoral ADJ. nonmoral. The *amoral* individual lacks a code of ethics; he should not be classified as immoral.

amorous ADJ. moved by sexual love; loving. Don Juan was known for his amorous adventures.

amorphous ADJ. shapeless. She was frightened by the *amorphous* mass which had floated in from the sea.

amortization N. act of reducing a debt through partial payments. Your monthly payments to the bank include provisions for taxes, interest on the principal, and *amortization* of the mortgage.

amphibian ADJ. able to live both on land and in water. Frogs are classified as *amphibian.* also N.

amphitheater N. oval building with tiers of seats. The spectators in the *amphitheater* cheered the gladiators.

ample ADJ. abundant. He had *ample* opportunity to dispose of his loot before the police caught up with him.

amplify V. enlarge. His attempts to *amplify* his remarks were drowned out by the jeers of the audience.

amputate V. cut off part of body; prune. When the doctors decided to *amputate* his leg to prevent the spread of gangrene, he cried that he preferred death to incapacity.

amuck ADV. in a state of rage. The police had to be called in to restrain him after he ran *amuck* in the department store.

amulet N. charm; talisman. Around his neck he wore the *amulet* which the witch doctor had given him.

anachronism N. an error involving time in a story. The reference to clocks in *Julius Caesar* is an *anachronism.*

analgesic ADJ. causing insensitivity to pain. The *analgesic* qualities of this lotion will provide temporary relief.

analogous ADJ. comparable. She called our attention to the things that had been done in an *analogous* situation and recommended that we do the same.

analogy N. similarity; parallelism. Your *analogy* is not a good one because the two situations are not similar.

anarchy N. absence of governing body; state of disorder. The assassination of the leaders led to a period of *anarchy.*

anathema N. solemn curse. He heaped *anathema* upon his foe.

anathematize V. curse. The high priest *anathematized* the heretic.

ancillary ADJ. serving as an aid or accessory; auxiliary. In an *ancillary* capacity he was helpful; however, he could not be entrusted with leadership. also N.

andirons N. metal supports in a fireplace for cooking utensils or logs. She spent many hours in the department stores looking for a pair of ornamental *andirons* for her fireplace.

anemia N. condition in which blood lacks red corpuscles. The doctor ascribes her tiredness to *anemia.* anemic, ADJ.

anesthetic N. substance that removes sensation with or without loss of consciousness. His monotonous voice acted like an *anesthetic;* his audience was soon asleep. anesthesia, N.

angular ADJ. sharp-cornered; stiff in manner. His features, though *angular*, were curiously attractive.

animadversion N. critical remark. He resented the *animadversions* of his critics, particularly because he realized they were true.

animated ADJ. lively. Her *animated* expression indicated a keenness of intellect.

animosity N. active enmity. He incurred the *animosity* of the ruling class because he advocated limitations of their power.

animus N. hostile feeling or intent. The *animus* of the speaker became obvious to all when he began to indulge in sarcastic and insulting remarks.

annals N. records; history. In the *annals* of this period, we find no mention of democratic movements.

anneal V. reduce brittleness and improve toughness by heating and cooling. After the glass is *annealed,* it will be less subject to chipping and cracking.

annihilate V. destroy. The enemy in its revenge tried to *annihilate* the entire population.

annotate V. comment; make explanatory notes. In the appendix to the novel, the critic sought to *annotate* many of the more esoteric references.

annuity N. yearly allowance. The *annuity* he set up with the insurance company supplements his social security benefits so that he can live very comfortably without working.

annul V. make void. The parents of the eloped couple tried to *annul* the marriage.

anodyne N. drug that relieves pain; opiate. His pain was so great that he felt no *anodyne* could relieve it.

anoint V. consecrate. The prophet Samuel *anointed* David with oil, crowning him king of Israel.

anomalous ADJ. abnormal; irregular. He was placed in the *anomalous* position of seeming to approve procedures which he despised.

anomaly N. irregularity. A bird that cannot fly is an *anomaly.*

anonymous ADJ. having no name. She tried to ascertain the identity of the writer of the *anonymous* letter.

antagonism N. active resistance. We shall have to overcome the *antagonism* of the natives before our plans for settling this area can succeed.

antecede V. precede. The invention of the radiotelegraph *anteceded* the development of television by a quarter of a century.

antediluvian ADJ. antiquated; ancient. The *antediluvian* customs had apparently not changed for thousands of years. also N.

anthropoid ADJ. manlike. The gorilla is the strongest of the *anthropoid* animals. also N.

anthropologist N. a student of the history and science of mankind. *Anthropologists* have discovered several relics of prehistoric man in this area.

anthropomorphic ADJ. having human form or characteristics. Primitive religions often have deities with *anthropomorphic* characteristics.

anticlimax N. letdown in thought or emotion. After the fine performance in the first act, the rest of the play was an *anticlimax*. anticlimactic, ADJ.

antipathy N. aversion; dislike. His extreme *antipathy* to dispute caused him to avoid argumentative discussions with his friends.

antiseptic N. substance that prevents infection. It is advisable to apply an *antiseptic* to any wound, no matter how slight or insignificant. also ADJ.

antithesis N. contrast; direct opposite of or to. This tyranny was the *antithesis* of all that he had hoped for, and he fought it with all his strength.

apathetic ADJ. indifferent. He felt *apathetic* about the conditions he had observed and did not care to fight against them. apathy, N.

ape V. imitate or mimic. He was suspended for a week because he had *aped* the principal in front of the whole school.

aperture N. opening; hole. She discovered a small *aperture* in the wall, through which the insects had entered the room.

apex N. tip; summit; climax. He was at the *apex* of his career.

aphasia N. loss of speech due to injury. After the automobile accident, the victim had periods of *aphasia* when he could not speak at all or could only mumble incoherently.

aphorism N. pithy maxim. An *aphorism* differs from an adage in that it is more philosophical or scientific. aphoristic, ADJ.

apiary N. a place where bees are kept. Although he spent many hours daily in the *apiary*, he was very seldom stung by a bee.

aplomb N. poise. His nonchalance and *aplomb* in times of trouble always encouraged his followers.

apocalyptic ADJ. prophetic; pertaining to revelations. His *apocalyptic* remarks were dismissed by his audience as wild surmises.

apocryphal ADJ. not genuine; sham. Her *apocryphal* tears misled no one.

apogee N. highest point. When the moon in its orbit is furthest away from the earth, it is at its *apogee*.

apologue N. moral fable. Aesop's *Fables* are classic examples of the *apologue*.

apoplexy N. stroke; loss of consciousness followed by paralysis. He was crippled by an attack of *apoplexy*.

apostate N. one who abandons his religious faith or political beliefs. Because he switched from one party to another, his former friends shunned him as an *apostate*.

apothecary N. druggist. In the *apothecaries'* weight, twelve ounces equal one pound.

TEST—WORD LIST 3—*Antonyms*

Each of the questions below consists of a word in capital letters, followed by five lettered words or phrases. Choose the lettered word or phrase that is most nearly opposite in meaning to the word in capital letters and write the letter of your choice on your answer paper.

31. AMICABLE (A) penetrating (B) compensating (C) unfriendly (D) zig-zag (E) inescapable
32. AMORAL (A) unusual (B) unfriendly (C) ethical (D) suave (E) firm
33. AMORPHOUS (A) nauseous (B) obscene (C) providential (D) definite (E) happy
34. AMPLIFY (A) distract (B) infer (C) publicize (D) decrease (E) pioneer
35. ANALAGOUS (A) not comparable (B) not capable (C) not culpable (D) not corporeal (E) not congenial
36. ANATHEMATIZE (A) locate (B) deceive (C) regulate (D) radiate (E) bless
37. ANEMIC (A) pallid (B) cruel (C) red-blooded (D) ventilating (E) hazardous
38. ANIMATED (A) worthy (B) dull (C) humorous (D) lengthy (E) realistic
39. ANIMUS (A) pterodactyl (B) bastion (C) giraffe (D) grimace (E) favor
40. ANOMALY (A) desperation (B) requisition (C) registry (D) regularity (E) radiation
41. ANONYMOUS (A) desperate (B) signed (C) defined (D) expert (E) written
42. ANTEDILUVIAN (A) transported (B) subtle (C) isolated (D) celebrated (E) modern
43. ANTIPATHY (A) profundity (B) objection (C) willingness (D) abstention (E) fondness
44. ANTITHESIS (A) velocity (B) maxim (C) similarity (D) acceleration (E) reaction
45. APHASIA (A) volubility (B) necessity (C) pain (D) crack (E) prayer

---

WORD LIST 4 apothegm - astigmatism

apothegm N. pithy, compact saying. Proverbs are *apothegms* that have become familiar sayings.

apotheosis N. deification; glorification. The *apotheosis* of a Roman emperor was designed to insure his eternal greatness.

appall V. dismay; shock. We were *appalled* by the horrifying conditions in the city's jails.

apparition N. ghost; phantom. Hamlet was uncertain about the identity of the *apparition* that had appeared and spoken to him.

appease V. pacify; soothe. We have discovered that, when we try to *appease* our enemies, we encourage them to make additional demands.

appellation N. name; title. He was amazed when the witches hailed him with his correct *appellation.*

append V. attach. I shall *append* this chart to my report.

apposite ADJ. appropriate; fitting. He was always able to find the *apposite* phrase, the correct expression for every occasion.

appraise V. estimate value of. It is difficult to *appraise* the value of old paintings; it is easier to call them priceless. appraisal, N.

apprehend V. arrest (a criminal); dread; perceive. The police will *apprehend* the culprit and convict him before long.

apprehensive ADJ. fearful; discerning. His *apprehensive* glances at the people who were walking in the street revealed his nervousness.

apprise V. inform. When he was *apprised* of the dangerous weather conditions, he decided to postpone his trip.

approbation N. approval. She looked for some sign of *approbation* from her parents.

appropriate V. acquire; take possession of for one's own use. The ranch owners *appropriated* the lands that had originally been set aside for the Indians' use.

appurtenances N. subordinate possessions. He bought the estate and all its *appurtenances.*

apropos PREP. with reference to; properly. I find your remarks *apropos* of the present situation timely and pertinent. also ADJ. and ADV.

aptitude N. fitness; talent. The counselor gave him an *aptitude* test before advising him about the career he should follow.

aquiline ADJ. curved, hooked. He can be recognized by his *aquiline* nose, curved like the beak of the eagle.

arable ADJ. fit for plowing. The land was no longer *arable;* erosion had removed the valuable topsoil.

arbiter N. a person with power to decide a dispute; judge. As an *arbiter* in labor disputes, she has won the confidence of the workers and the employers.

arbitrary ADJ. fixed or decided; despotic. Any *arbitrary* action on your part will be resented by the members of the board whom you do not consult.

arcade N. a covered passageway, usually lined with shops. The *arcade* was popular with shoppers because it gave them protection from the summer sun and the winter rain.

arcane ADJ. secret; mysterious. What was *arcane* to us was clear to the psychologist.

archaeology N. study of artifacts and relics of early mankind. The professor of *archaeology* headed an expedition to the Gobi Desert in search of ancient ruins.

archaic ADJ. antiquated. "Methinks," "thee," and "thou" are *archaic* words which are no longer part of our normal vocabulary.

archetype N. prototype; primitive pattern. The Brooklyn Bridge was the *archetype* of the many spans that now connect Manhattan with Long Island and New Jersey.

archipelago N. group of closely located islands. When he looked at the map and saw the *archipelagoes* in the South Seas, he longed to visit them.

archives N. public records; place where public records are kept. These documents should be part of the *archives* so that historians may be able to evaluate them in the future.

ardor N. heat; passion; zeal. His *ardor* was contagious; soon everyone was eagerly working.

arduous ADJ. hard; strenuous. His *arduous* efforts had sapped his energy.

argot N. slang. In the *argot* of the underworld, she "was taken for a ride."

aria N. operatic solo. At her Metropolitan Opera audition, Marian Anderson sang an *aria* from *Norma.*

arid ADJ. dry; barren. The cactus has adapted to survive in an *arid* environment.

aromatic ADJ. fragrant. Medieval sailing vessels brought *aromatic* herbs from China to Europe.

arraign V. charge in court; indict. After his indictment by the Grand Jury, the accused man was *arraigned* in the County Criminal Court.

arrant ADJ. thorough; complete; unmitigated. "*Arrant* knave," an epithet found in books dealing with the age of chivalry, is a term of condemnation.

array V. marshall; draw up in order. His actions were bound to *array* public sentiment against him. also N.

array V. clothe; adorn. She liked to watch her mother *array* herself in her finest clothes before going out for the evening. also N.

arrears N. being in debt. He was in *arrears* with his payments on the car.

arrogance N. pride; haughtiness. The *arrogance* of the nobility was resented by the middle class.

arrogate V. claim without reasonable grounds. I am afraid that the manner in which he *arrogates* power to himself indicates that he is willing to ignore Constitutional limitations.

arroyo N. gully. Until the heavy rains of the past spring, this *arroyo* had been a dry bed.

articulate ADJ. effective; distinct. Her *articulate* presentation of the advertising campaign impressed her employers. also V.

artifacts N. products of primitive culture. Archaeologists debated the significance of the *artifacts* discovered in the ruins of Asia Minor and came to no conclusion.

artifice N. deception; trickery. The Trojan War proved to the Greeks that cunning and *artifice* were often more effective than military might.

artisan N. a manually skilled worker. Artists and *artisans* alike are necessary to the development of a culture.

ascendancy N. controlling influence. President Marcos failed to maintain his *ascendancy* over the Philippines.

ascertain V. find out for certain. Please *ascertain* her present address.

ascetic ADJ. practicing self-denial; austere. The cavalier could not understand the *ascetic* life led by the monks. also N.

asceticism N. doctrine of self-denial. We find *asceticism* carried on in many parts of the world.

ascribe V. refer; attribute; assign. I can *ascribe* no motive for her acts.

aseptic ADJ. preventing putrefaction or blood poisoning by killing bacteria. Hospitals succeeded in lowering the mortality rate as soon as they introduced *aseptic* conditions.

ashen ADJ. ash-colored. Her face was *ashen* with fear.

asinine ADJ. stupid. Your *asinine* remarks prove that you have not given this problem any serious consideration.

askance ADV. with a sideways or indirect look. Looking *askance* at her questioner, she displayed her scorn.

askew ADV. crookedly; slanted; at an angle. When he placed his hat *askew* upon his head, his observers laughed.

asperity N. sharpness (of temper). These remarks, spoken with *asperity,* stung the boys to whom they had been directed.

aspersion N. slanderous remark. Do not cast *aspersions* on her character.

aspirant N. seeker after position or status. Although I am an *aspirant* for public office, I am not willing to accept the dictates of the party bosses. also ADJ.

aspiration N. noble ambition. Man's *aspirations* should be as lofty as the stars.

assail V. assault. He was *assailed* with questions after his lecture.

assay V. analyze; evaluate. When they *assayed* the ore, they found that they had discovered a very rich vein. also N.

assent V. agree; accept. It gives me great pleasure to *assent* to your request.

assessment N. estimation. I would like to have your *assessment* of the situation in South Africa.

asseverate V. make a positive statement or solemn declaration. I will *asseverate* my conviction that she is guilty.

assiduous ADJ. diligent. He worked *assiduously* at this task for weeks before he felt satisfied with his results. assiduity, N.

assimilate V. absorb; cause to become homogeneous. The manner in which the United States was able to *assimilate* the hordes of immigrants during the nineteenth and the early part of the twentieth centuries will always be a source of pride.

assuage V. ease; lessen (pain). Your messages of cheer should *assuage* her suffering. assuagement, N.

asteroid N. small planet. *Asteroids* have become commonplace to the readers of interstellar travel stories in science fiction magazines.

astigmatism N. eye defect which prevents proper focus. As soon as his parents discovered that the boy suffered from *astigmatism,* they took him to the optometrist for corrective glasses.

TEST—WORD LIST 4—*Synonyms and Antonyms*

Each of the following questions consists of a word in capital letters, followed by five lettered words or phrases. Choose the lettered word or phrase which is most nearly similar or the opposite of the word in capital letters and write the letter of your choice on your answer paper.

46. APPEASE (A) agitate (B) qualify (C) display (D) predestine (E) interrupt
47. APPOSITE (A) inappropriate (B) diagonal (C) exponential (D) unobtrusive (E) discouraging
48. APPREHEND (A) obviate (B) set free (C) shiver (D) understand (E) contrast
49. APTITUDE (A) sarcasm (B) inversion (C) adulation (D) lack of talent (E) gluttony
50. AQUILINE (A) watery (B) hooked (C) refined (D) antique (E) rodentlike

51. ARCHAIC (A) youthful (B) cautious (C) antiquated (D) placated (E) buttressed
52. ARDOR (A) zeal (B) paint (C) proof (D) group (E) excitement
53. ARROGATE (A) swindle (B) balance (C) claim (D) perjure (E) effect
54. ARROYO (A) crevice (B) gully (C) value (D) food (E) fabric
55. ARTIFICE (A) spite (B) exception (C) anger (D) candor (E) loyalty
56. ARTISAN (A) educator (B) decider (C) sculptor (D) discourser (E) unskilled laborer
57. ASCERTAIN (A) amplify (B) master (C) discover (D) retain (E) explode
58. ASPERITY (A) anguish (B) absence (C) innuendo (D) good temper (E) snake
59. ASSUAGE (A) stuff (B) describe (C) wince (D) worsen (E) introduce
60. ASTEROID (A) Milky Way (B) radiance (C) large planet (D) rising moon (E) setting moon

---

WORD LIST 5 astral - barb

astral ADJ. relating to the stars. She was amazed at the number of *astral* bodies the new telescope revealed.

astringent ADJ. binding; causing contraction. The *astringent* quality of the unsweetened lemon juice made swallowing difficult. also N.

astronomical ADJ. enormously large or extensive. The government seems willing to spend *astronomical* sums on weapons development.

astute ADJ. wise; shrewd. That was a very *astute* observation. I shall heed it.

asunder ADV. into parts; apart. Their points of view are poles *asunder.*

atavism N. resemblance to remote ancestors rather than to parents; deformity returning after passage of two or more generations. The doctors ascribed the child's deformity to an *atavism.*

atelier N. workshop; studio. Stories of Bohemian life in Paris are full of tales of artists' starving or freezing in their *ateliers.*

atheistic ADJ. denying the existence of God. His *atheistic* remarks shocked the religious worshippers.

athwart PREP. across; in opposition. His tendency toward violence was *athwart* the philosophy of the peace movement. also ADV.

atone V. make amends for; pay for. He knew no way in which he could *atone* for his brutal crime.

atrocity N. brutal deed. In time of war, many *atrocities* are committed by invading armies.

atrophy N. wasting away. Polio victims need physiotherapy to prevent the *atrophy* of affected limbs. also V.

attenuate V. make thin; weaken. By withdrawing their forces, the generals hoped to *attenuate* the enemy lines.

attest V. testify, bear witness. Having served as a member of the Grand Jury, I can *attest* that our system of indicting individuals is in need of improvement.

attribute N. essential quality. His outstanding *attribute* was his kindness.

attribute V. ascribe; explain. I *attribute* her success in science to the encouragement she received from her parents.

attrition N. gradual wearing down. They decided to wage a war of *attrition* rather than to rely on an all-out attack.

atypical ADJ. not normal. You have taken an *atypical* case. It does not prove anything.

audacity N. boldness. Her *audacity* in this critical moment encouraged us.

audit N. examination of accounts. When the bank examiners arrived to hold their annual *audit,* they discovered the embezzlements of the chief cashier. also V.

augment V. increase. How can we hope to *augment* our forces when our allies are deserting us?

augury N. omen; prophecy. He interpreted the departure of the birds as an *augury* of evil. augur, V.

august ADJ. impressive; majestic. Visiting the palace at Versailles, she was impressed by the *august* surroundings in which she found herself.

aureole N. sun's corona; halo. Many medieval paintings depict saintly characters with *aureoles* around their heads.

auroral ADJ. pertaining to the aurora borealis. The *auroral* display was particularly spectacular that evening.

auscultation N. act of listening to the heart or lungs to discover abnormalities. The science of *auscultation* was enhanced with the development of the stethoscope.

auspicious ADJ. favoring success. With favorable weather conditions, it was an *auspicious* moment to set sail.

austere ADJ. strict, stern. His *austere* demeanor prevented us from engaging in our usual frivolous activities.

austerity N. sternness; severity. The *austerity* and dignity of the court were maintained by the new justices.

authenticate V. prove genuine. An expert was needed to *authenticate* the original Van Gogh painting from its imitation.

authoritative ADJ. having the weight of authority; dictatorial. We accepted her analysis of the situation as *authoritative.*

autocrat N. monarch with supreme power. The nobles tried to limit the powers of the *autocrat* without success. autocracy, N.

automaton N. mechanism which imitates actions of humans. Long before science fiction readers became aware of robots, writers were presenting stories of *automatons* who could outperform men.

autonomous ADJ. self-governing. This island is a colony; however, in most matters, it is *autonomous* and receives no orders from the mother country. autonomy, N.

autopsy N. examination of a dead body; post-mortem. The medical examiner ordered an *autopsy* to determine the cause of death. also V.

auxiliary ADJ. helper, additional or subsidiary. To prepare for the emergency, they built an *auxiliary* power station. also N.

avarice N. greediness for wealth. King Midas's *avarice* has been famous for centuries. avaricious, ADJ.

avatar N. incarnation. In Hindu mythology, the *avatar* of Vishnu is thoroughly detailed.

aver V. state confidently. I wish to *aver* that I am certain of success.

averse ADJ. reluctant. He was *averse* to revealing the sources of his information.

aversion N. firm dislike. Their mutual *aversion* was so great that they refused to speak to one another.

avert V. prevent; turn away. She *averted* her eyes from the dead cat on the highway.

aviary N. enclosure for birds. The *aviary* at the zoo held nearly 300 birds.

avid ADJ. greedy; eager for. He was *avid* for learning and read everything he could get. avidity, N.

avocation N. secondary or minor occupation. His hobby proved to be so fascinating and profitable that gradually he abandoned his regular occupation and concentrated on his *avocation.*

avouch V. affirm; proclaim. I am willing to employ your friend if you will *avouch* his integrity.

avow V. declare openly. I must *avow* that I am innocent.

avuncular ADJ. like an uncle. *Avuncular* pride did not prevent him from noticing his nephew's shortcomings.

awe N. solemn wonder. The tourists gazed with *awe* at the tremendous expanse of the Grand Canyon.

awry ADV. distorted; crooked. He held his head *awry,* giving the impression that he had caught cold in his neck during the night. also ADJ.

axiom N. self-evident truth requiring no proof. Before a student can begin to think along the lines of Euclidean geometry, he must accept certain principles or *axioms.*

azure ADJ. sky blue. *Azure* skies are indicative of good weather.

babble V. chatter idly. The little girl *babbled* about her doll. also N.

bacchanalian ADJ. drunken. Emperor Nero attended the *bacchanalian* orgy.

badger V. pester; annoy. She was forced to change her telephone number because she was *badgered* by obscene phone calls.

badinage N. teasing conversation. Her friends at work greeted the news of her engagement with cheerful *badinage.*

baffle V. frustrate; perplex. The new code *baffled* the enemy agents.

bagatelle N. trifle. Trying to reassure Roxanne about his wound, Cyrano claimed it was a mere *bagatelle.*

baleful ADJ. deadly; destructive. The drought was a *baleful* omen.

bait V. harass; tease. The soldiers *baited* the prisoners, terrorizing them.

balk V. foil. When the warden learned that several inmates were planning to escape, he took steps to *balk* their attempt.

balm N. something that relieves pain. Friendship is the finest *balm* for the pangs of disappointed love.

balmy ADJ. mild; fragrant. A *balmy* breeze refreshed us after the sultry blast.

banal ADJ. hackneyed; commonplace; trite. His frequent use of clichés made his essay seem *banal.* banality, N.

bandanna N. large, bright-colored handkerchief. She could be identified by the gaudy *bandanna* she wore as a head covering.

bandy V. discuss lightly; exchange blows or words. The President refused to *bandy* words with the reporters at the press conference.

bane N. cause of ruin. Lack of public transportation is the *bane* of urban life.

baneful ADJ. ruinous; poisonous. His *baneful* influence was feared by all.

bantering ADJ. good-natured ridiculing. They resented his *bantering* remarks because they thought he was being sarcastic.

barb N. sharp projection from fishhook, etc. The *barb* from the fishhook caught in his finger as he grabbed the fish. barbed, ADJ.

TEST—WORD LIST 5—*Synonyms*

Each of the questions below consists of a word in capital letters, followed by five lettered words or phrases. Choose the lettered word or phrase that is most nearly similar in meaning to the word in capital letters and write the letter of your choice on your answer paper.

61. ASTUTE (A) sheer (B) noisy (C) astral (D) unusual (E) clever
62. ATROCITY (A) endurance (B) fortitude (C) session (D) heinous act (E) hatred
63. ATROPHY (A) capture (B) wasteaway (C) govern (D) award prize (E) defeat
64. ATTENUATE (A) appear (B) be absent (C) weaken (D) testify (E) soothe
65. ATYPICAL (A) superfluous (B) fortitude (C) unusual (D) clashing (E) lovely
66. AUDACITY (A) boldness (B) asperity (C) strength (D) stature (E) anchorage
67. AUGMENT (A) make noble (B) anoint (C) increase (D) harvest (E) reach
68. AUXILIARY (A) righteous (B) prospective (C) assistant (D) archaic (E) mandatory
69. AVARICE (A) easiness (B) greed (C) statement (D) invoice (E) power
70. AVATAR (A) hedge (B) hypnosis (C) incarnation (D) perfume (E) disaster
71. AWRY (A) recommended (B) commiserating (C) startled (D) crooked (E) psychological
72. BALEFUL (A) doubtful (B) virtual (C) deadly (D) conventional (E) virtuous
73. BALMY (A) venturesome (B) dedicated (C) mild (D) fanatic (E) memorable
74. BANAL (A) philosophical (B) trite (C) dramatic (D) heedless (E) discussed
75. BANEFUL (A) intellectual (B) thankful (C) decisive (D) poisonous (E) remorseful

---

WORD LIST 6 **bard - bludgeon**

bard N. poet. The ancient *bard* Homer sang of the fall of Troy.

baroque ADJ. highly ornate. They found the *baroque* architecture amusing.

barrage N. barrier laid down by artillery fire. The company was forced to retreat through the *barrage* of heavy cannons.

barrister N. counselor-at-law. Galsworthy started as a *barrister*, but, when he found the practice of law boring, turned to writing.

barterer N. trader. The *barterer* exchanged trinkets for the natives' furs.

bask V. luxuriate; take pleasure in warmth. *Basking* on the beach, she relaxed so completely that she fell asleep.

bassoon N. reed instrument of the woodwind family. In the orchestra, the *bassoon* is related to the oboe and the clarinet.

bastion N. fortress; defense. Once a *bastion* of democracy, under its new government the island became a dictatorship.

bate V. let down; restrain. Until it was time to open the presents, the children had to *bate* their curiosity. bated, ADJ.

batten V. grow fat; thrive upon others. We cannot accept a system where a favored few can *batten* in extreme comfort while others toil.

bauble N. trinket; trifle. The child was delighted with the *bauble* she had won in the grab bag.

bawdy ADJ. indecent; obscene. She took offense at his *bawdy* remarks.

beatific ADJ. giving bliss; blissful. The *beatific* smile on the child's face made us very happy.

beatitude N. blessedness; state of bliss. Growing closer to God each day, the mystic achieved a state of indescribable *beatitude*.

bedizen V. dress with vulgar finery. The witch doctors were *bedizened* in all their gaudiest costumes.

bedraggle V. wet thoroughly. We were so *bedraggled* by the severe storm that we had to change into dry clothing. bedraggled, ADJ.

befuddle V. confuse thoroughly. His attempts to clarify the situation succeeded only in *befuddling* her further.

begrudge V. resent. I *begrudge* every minute I have to spend attending meetings.

beguile V. delude; cheat; amuse. He *beguiled* himself during the long hours by playing solitaire.

behemoth N. huge creature; monstrous animal. Sportscasters nicknamed the linebacker "The *Behemoth.*"

beholden ADJ. obligated; indebted. Since I do not wish to be *beholden* to anyone, I cannot accept this favor.

behoove V. suited to; incumbent upon. In this time of crisis, it *behooves* all of us to remain calm and await the instructions of our superiors.

belabor V. beat soundly; assail verbally. He was *belaboring* his opponent.

belated ADJ. delayed. He apologized for his *belated* note of condolence to the widow of his friend and explained that he had just learned of her husband's untimely death.

beleaguer V. besiege. As soon as the city was *beleaguered,* life became more subdued as the citizens began their long wait for outside assistance. beleaguered, ADJ.

belittle V. disparage; depreciate. Although I do not wish to *belittle* your contribution, I feel we must place it in its proper perspective.

bellicose ADJ. warlike. His *bellicose* disposition alienated his friends.

belligerent ADJ. quarrelsome. Whenever he had too much to drink, he became *belligerent* and tried to pick fights with strangers.

benediction N. blessing. The appearance of the sun after the many rainy days was like a *benediction.*

benefactor N. gift giver; patron. Scrooge later became Tiny Tim's *benefactor.*

beneficiary N. person entitled to benefits or proceeds of an insurance policy or will. You may change your *beneficiary* as often as you wish.

benevolent ADJ. generous; charitable. His *benevolent* nature prevented him from refusing any beggar who accosted him.

benighted ADJ. overcome by darkness. In the *benighted* Middle Ages, intellectual curiosity was discouraged by the authorities.

benign ADJ. kindly; favorable; not malignant. The old man was well liked because of his *benign* attitude toward friend and stranger alike.

benignity N. state of being kind, benign, gracious. We have endowed our Creator with a *benignity* which permits forgiveness of our sins and transgressions.

benison N. blessing. Let us pray that the *benison* of peace once more shall prevail among the nations of the world.

berate V. scold strongly. He feared she would *berate* him for his forgetfulness.

bereavement N. state of being deprived of something valuable or beloved. His friends gathered to console him upon his sudden *bereavement.*

bereft ADJ. deprived of; lacking. The foolish gambler soon found himself *bereft* of funds.

berserk ADV. frenzied. Angered, he went *berserk* and began to wreck the room.

beset V. harrass; trouble. Many problems *beset* the American public school system.

besmirch V. soil, defile. The scandalous remarks in the newspaper *besmirch* the reputations of every member of the society.

bestial ADJ. beastlike; brutal. We must suppress our *bestial* desires and work for peaceful and civilized ends.

bestow V. confer. He wished to *bestow* great honors upon the hero.

bête noire N. aversion; person or thing strongly disliked or avoided. Going to the opera was his personal *bête noire* because high-pitched sounds irritated him.

betroth V. become engaged to marry. The announcement that they had become *betrothed* surprised their friends who had not suspected any romance. betrothal, N.

bevy N. large group. The movie actor was surrounded by a *bevy* of starlets.

bicameral ADJ. two-chambered, as a legislative body. The United States Congress is a *bicameral* body.

bibulous ADJ. inclined to drink; affected by alcohol. We could not help laughing at his *bibulous* farewells.

bicker V. quarrel. The children *bickered* morning, noon, and night.

biennial ADJ. every two years. The plant bore *biennial* flowers. also N.

bifurcated ADJ. divided into two branches; forked. With a *bifurcated* branch and a piece of elastic rubber, he made a crude but effective slingshot.

bigotry N. stubborn intolerance. Brought up in a democratic atmosphere, the student was shocked by the *bigotry* and narrowness expressed by several of his classmates.

bilious ADJ. suffering from indigestion; irritable. His *bilious* temperament was apparent to all who heard him rant about his difficulties.

bilk V. swindle; cheat. The con man specialized in *bilking* insurance companies.

billingsgate N. vituperation; abusive language. His attempts at pacifying the mob were met by angry hoots and *billingsgate.*

bivouac N. temporary encampment. While in *bivouac,* we spent the night in our sleeping bags under the stars. also V.

bizarre ADJ. fantastic; violently contrasting. The plot of the novel was too *bizarre* to be believed.

blanch V. bleach; whiten. Although age had *blanched* his hair, he was still vigorous and energetic.

bland ADJ. soothing; mild. She used a *bland* ointment for her sunburn.

blandishment N. flattery. Despite the salesperson's *blandishments,* the customer did not buy the outfit.

blasé ADJ. bored with pleasure or dissipation. Your *blasé* attitude gives your students an erroneous impression of the joys of scholarship.

blasphemous ADJ. profane; impious. The people in the room were shocked by his *blasphemous* language.

blatant ADJ. loudly offensive. I regard your remarks as *blatant* and ill-mannered. blatancy, N.

blazon V. decorate with an heraldic coat of arms. *Blazoned* on his shield were the two lambs and the lion, the traditional coat of arms of his family. also N.

bleak ADJ. cold; cheerless. The Aleutian Islands are *bleak* military outposts.

blighted ADJ. suffering from a disease; destroyed. The extent of the *blighted* areas could be seen only when viewed from the air.

blithe ADJ. gay; joyous. Shelley called the skylark a "*blithe* spirit" because of its happy song.

bloated ADJ. swollen or puffed as with water or air. The *bloated* corpse was taken from the river.

bludgeon N. club; heavy-headed weapon. His walking stick served him as a *bludgeon* on many occasions. also V.

TEST—WORD LIST 6—*Antonyms*

Each of the questions below consists of a word in capital letters, followed by five lettered words or phrases. Choose the lettered word or phrase that is most nearly opposite in meaning to the word in capital letters and write the letter of your choice on your answer paper.

76. BAROQUE (A) polished (B) constant (C) transformed (D) simple (E) aglow
77. BEATIFIC (A) glorious (B) dreadful (C) theatrical (D) crooked (E) handsome
78. BELITTLE (A) disobey (B) forget (C) magnify (D) extol (E) envy
79. BELLICOSE (A) peaceful (B) navel (C) amusing (D) piecemeal (E) errant
80. BENIGN (A) tenfold (B) peaceful (C) blessed (D) wavering (E) malignant
81. BENISON (A) curse (B) bachelor (C) wedding (D) orgy (E) tragedy
82. BERATE (A) grant (B) praise (C) refer (D) purchase (E) deny
83. BESTIAL (A) animated (B) noble (C) zoological (D) clear (E) dusky
84. BIGOTRY (A) arrogance (B) approval (C) mourning (D) promptness (E) tolerance
85. BILLINGSGATE (A) disguise (B) debt (C) fiction (D) settlement (E) acclaim
86. BLANCH (A) bleach (B) scatter (C) darken (D) analyze (E) subdivide
87. BLAND (A) caustic (B) meager (C) soft (D) uncooked (E) helpless
88. BLASÉ (A) fiery (B) clever (C) intriguing (D) slim (E) ardent
89. BLEAK (A) pale (B) sudden (C) dry (D) narrow (E) cheerful
90. BLITHE (A) spiritual (B) profuse (C) cheerless (D) hybrid (E) comfortable

---

WORD LIST 7 **blunder - canter**

blunder N. error. The criminal's fatal *blunder* led to his capture. also V.

blurt V. utter impulsively. Before she could stop him, he *blurted* out the news.

bode V. foreshadow; portend. The gloomy skies and the sulphurous odors from the mineral springs seemed to *bode* evil to those who settled in the area.

bogus ADJ. counterfeit; not authentic. The police quickly found the distributors of the *bogus* twenty-dollar bills.

boisterous ADJ. violent; rough; noisy. The unruly crowd became even more *boisterous* when he tried to quiet them.

bolster V. support; prop up. I do not intend to *bolster* your hopes with false reports of outside assistance; the truth is that we must face the enemy alone. also N.

bombastic ADJ. pompous; using inflated language. The orator spoke in a *bombastic* manner. bombast, N.

boorish ADJ. rude; clownish. Your *boorish* remarks to the driver of the other car were not warranted by the situation and served merely to enrage him.

bootless ADJ. useless. I "trouble deaf heaven with my *bootless* cries."

bouillon N. clear beef soup. The cup of *bouillon* served by the stewards was welcomed by those who had been chilled by the cold ocean breezes.

bountiful ADJ. generous; showing bounty. She distributed gifts in a *bountiful* and gracious manner.

bourgeois N. middle class. The French Revolution was inspired by the *bourgeois.* also ADJ.

bowdlerize V. expurgate. After the film editors had *bowdlerized* the language in the script, the motion picture's rating was changed from "R" to "PG."

brackish ADJ. somewhat saline. He found the only wells in the area were *brackish;* drinking the water made him nauseated.

braggadocio N. boasting. He was disliked because his manner was always full of *braggadocio.*

bravado N. swagger; assumed air of defiance. The *bravado* of the young criminal disappeared when he was confronted by the victims of his brutal attack.

brazen ADJ. insolent. Her *brazen* contempt for authority angered the officials.

brazier N. open pan in which live coals are burned. On chilly nights, the room was warmed by coals burning in *braziers* set in the corners of the room.

breach N. breaking of contract or duty; fissure; gap. They found a *breach* in the enemy's fortifications and penetrated their lines. also V.

breadth N. width; extent. We were impressed by the *breadth* of her knowledge.

breviary N. book containing the daily prayers. The religious sect demanded daily recitals of the *breviary* as well as formal Sabbath services.

brevity N. conciseness. *Brevity* is essential when you send a telegram or cablegram; you are charged for every word.

brindled ADJ. tawny or grayish with streaks or spots. He was disappointed in the litter because the puppies were *brindled;* he had hoped for animals of a uniform color.

bristling ADJ. rising like bristles; showing irritation. The dog stood there, *bristling* with anger.

brittle ADJ. easily broken; difficult. My employer's *brittle* personality made it difficult for me to get along with her.

broach V. open up. He did not even try to *broach* the subject of poetry.

brocade N. rich, figured fabric. The sofa was covered with expensive *brocade.*

brochure N. pamphlet. This *brochure* on farming was issued by the Department of Agriculture.

brooch N. ornamental clasp. She treasured the *brooch* because it was an heirloom.

brusque ADJ. blunt; abrupt. She was offended by his *brusque* reply.

bucolic ADJ. rustic; pastoral. The meadow was the scene of *bucolic* gaiety.

buffoonery N. clowning. Jimmy Durante's *buffoonery* was hilarious.

bugaboo N. bugbear; object of baseless terror. If we become frightened by such *bugaboos,* we are no wiser than the birds who fear scarecrows.

bullion N. gold and silver in the form of bars. Much *bullion* is stored in the vaults at Fort Knox.

bulwark N. earthwork or other strong defense; person who defends. The navy is our principal *bulwark* against invasion.

bumptious ADJ. self-assertive. His classmates called him a show-off because of his *bumptious* airs.

bungle V. spoil by clumsy behavior. I was afraid you would *bungle* this assignment but I had no one else to send.

bureaucracy N. government by bureaus. Many people fear that the constant introduction of federal agencies will create a government by *bureaucracy.*

burgeon V. grow forth; send out buds. In the spring, the plants that burgeon are a promise of the beauty that is to come.

burlesque V. give an imitation that ridicules. In his caricature, he *burlesqued* the mannerisms of his adversary. also N.

burly ADJ. husky; muscular. The *burly* mover lifted the packing crate with ease.

burnish V. make shiny by rubbing; polish. The *burnished* metal reflected the lamplight.

buskin N. thick-soled half boot worn by actors of Greek tragedy. Wearing the *buskin* gave the Athenian tragic actor a larger-than-life appearance and enhanced the intensity of the play.

buttress N. support or prop. The huge cathedral walls were supported by flying *buttresses.* also V.

buxom ADJ. plump; vigorous; jolly. The soldiers remembered the *buxom* nurse who had always been so pleasant to them.

cabal N. small group of persons secretly united to promote their own interests. The *cabal* was defeated when their scheme was discovered.

cache N. hiding place. The detectives followed the suspect until he led them to the *cache* where he had stored his loot. also V.

cacophony N. discord. Some people seem to enjoy the *cacophony* of an orchestra that is tuning up.

cadaver N. corpse. In some states, it is illegal to dissect *cadavers.*

cadaverous ADJ. like a corpse; pale. By his *cadaverous* appearance, we could see how the disease had ravaged him.

cajole V. coax; wheedle. I will not be *cajoled* into granting you your wish.

calamity N. disaster; misery. As news of the *calamity* spread, offers of relief poured in to the stricken community.

caliber N. ability; capacity. A man of such *caliber* should not be assigned such menial tasks.

calligraphy N. beautiful writing; excellent penmanship. As we examine ancient manuscripts, we become impressed with the *calligraphy* of the scribes.

callous ADJ. hardened; unfeeling. He had worked in the hospital for so many years that he was *callous* to the suffering in the wards. callus, N.

callow ADJ. youthful; immature. In that youthful movement, the leaders were only a little less *callow* than their immature followers.

calorific ADJ. heat-producing. Coal is much more *calorific* than green wood.

calumniate V. slander. Shakespeare wrote that love and friendship were subject to envious and *calumniating* time.

calumny N. malicious misrepresentation; slander. He could endure his financial failure, but he could not bear the *calumny* that his foes heaped upon him.

camaraderie N. good-fellowship. What he loved best about his job was the sense of *camaraderie* he and his co-workers shared.

cameo N. shell or jewel carved in relief. Tourists are advised not to purchase *cameos* from the street peddlers of Rome who sell poor specimens of the carver's art.

canard N. unfounded rumor; exaggerated report. It is almost impossible to protect oneself from such a base *canard.*

candor N. frankness. The *candor* and simplicity of his speech impressed all. candid, ADJ.

canine ADJ. related to dogs; dog-like. Some days the *canine* population of Berkeley seems almost to outnumber the human population.

canker N. any ulcerous sore; any evil. Poverty is a *canker* in the body politic; it must be cured.

canny ADJ. shrewd; thrifty. The *canny* Scotsman was more than a match for the swindlers.

cant N. jargon of thieves; pious phraseology. Many listeners were fooled by the *cant* and hypocrisy of his speech.

cantankerous ADJ. ill humored; irritable. Constantly complaining about his treatment and refusing to cooperate with the hospital staff, he was a *cantankerous* patient.

cantata N. story set to music, to be sung by a chorus. The choral society sang the new *cantata* composed by its leader.

canter N. slow gallop. Because the racehorse had outdistanced its competition so easily, the reporter wrote that the race was won in a *canter.* also V.

TEST—WORD LIST 7—*Synonyms*

Each of the questions below consists of a word in capital letters, followed by five lettered words or phrases. Choose the lettered word or phrase that is most nearly similar in meaning to the word in capital letters and write the letter of your choice on your answer paper.

91. BOISTEROUS (A) conflicting (B) noisy (C) testimonial (D) grateful (E) adolescent
92. BOMBASTIC (A) sensitive (B) pompous (C) rapid (D) sufficient (E) expensive
93. BOORISH (A) brave (B) oafish (C) romantic (D) speedy (E) dry
94. BOUILLON (A) insight (B) chowder (C) gold (D) clear soup (E) stew
95. BRACKISH (A) careful (B) salty (C) chosen (D) tough (E) wet
96. BRAGGADOCIO (A) weaponry (B) boasting (C) skirmish (D) encounter (E) position
97. BRAZEN (A) shameless (B) quick (C) modest (D) pleasant (E) melodramatic
98. BRINDLED (A) equine (B) pathetic (C) hasty (D) spotted (E) mild tasting
99. BROCHURE (A) opening (B) pamphlet (C) censor (D) bureau (E) pin
100. BUCOLIC (A) diseased (B) repulsive (C) rustic (D) twinkling (E) cold
101. BUXOM (A) voluminous (B) indecisive (C) convincing (D) plump (E) bookish
102. CACHE (A) lock (B) hiding place (C) tide (D) automobile (E) grappling hook
103. CACOPHONY (A) discord (B) dance (C) applause (D) type of telephone (E) rooster
104. CALLOW (A) youthful (B) holy (C) mild (D) colored (E) seated
105. CANDID (A) vague (B) outspoken (C) experienced (D) anxious (E) sallow

WORD LIST 8 **canto - champ**

canto N. division of a long poem. In *The Man without a Country,* Philip Nolan is upset when he reads one of Sir Walter Scott's *cantos.*

canvass V. determine votes, etc. After *canvassing* the sentiments of his constituents, the congressman was confident that he represented the majority opinion of his district. also N.

capacious ADJ. spacious. In the *capacious* areas of the railroad terminal, thousands of travelers lingered while waiting for their train.

caparison N, V. showy harness or ornamentation for a horse; put showy ornamentation on a horse. The audience admired the *caparison* of the horses as they made their entrance into the circus ring.

capillary ADJ. having a very fine bore. The changes in surface tension of liquids in *capillary* vessels is of special interest to physicists. also N.

capitulate V. surrender. The enemy was warned to *capitulate* or face annihilation.

caprice N. whim. Do not act on *caprice.* Study your problem.

capricious ADJ. fickle; incalculable. The storm was *capricious* and changed course constantly.

caption N. title; chapter heading; text under illustration. I find the *captions* which accompany these cartoons very clever and humorous. also V.

captious ADJ. faultfinding. His criticisms were always *captious* and frivolous, never offering constructive suggestions.

carafe N. glass water bottle; decanter. With each dinner, the patron receives a *carafe* of red or white wine.

carat N. unit of weight for precious stones; measure of fineness of gold. He gave her a three-*carat* diamond mounted in an eighteen-*carat* gold band.

carcinogenic ADJ. causing cancer. Many supposedly harmless substances have been revealed to be *carcinogenic.*

cardinal ADJ. chief. If you want to increase your word power, the *cardinal* rule of vocabulary-building is to read.

careen V. lurch; sway from side to side. The taxicab *careened* wildly as it rounded the corner.

caricature N. distortion; burlesque. The *caricatures* he drew always emphasized a personal weakness of the people he burlesqued. also V.

carillon N. a set of bells capable of being played. The *carillon* in the bell tower of the Coca Cola pavilion at the New York World's Fair provided musical entertainment every hour.

carmine N. rich red. *Carmine* in her lipstick made her lips appear black in the photographs.

carnage N. destruction of life. The *carnage* that can be caused by atomic warfare adds to the responsibilities of our statesmen.

carnal ADJ. fleshly. The public was more interested in *carnal* pleasures than in spiritual matters.

carnivorous ADJ. meat-eating. The lion is a *carnivorous* animal. carnivore, N.

carousal N. drunken revel. The party degenerated into an ugly *carousal.*

carping ADJ. finding fault. A *carping* critic disturbs sensitive people.

carrion N. rotting flesh of a dead body. Buzzards are nature's scavengers; they eat the *carrion* left behind by other predators.

carte blanche N. unlimited authority or freedom. Use your own discretion in this matter; I give you *carte blanche.*

cartographer N. map-maker. Though not a professional *cartographer*, Tolkien was able to construct a map of his fictional world.

caryatid N. sculptured column of a female figure. The *caryatids* supporting the entablature reminded the onlooker of the columns he had seen in the Acropolis at Athens.

cascade N. small waterfall. We could not appreciate the beauty of the many *cascades* as we were forced to make detours around each of them. also V.

caste N. one of the hereditary classes in Hindu society. The differences created by *caste* in India must be wiped out if true democracy is to prevail in that country.

castigate V. punish. He decided to *castigate* the culprit personally.

casualty N. serious or fatal accident. The number of *casualties* on this holiday weekend was high.

casuistry N. subtle or sophisticated reasoning resulting in minute distinctions. You are using *casuistry* to justify your obvious violation of decent behavior.

cataclysm N. deluge; upheaval. A *cataclysm* such as the French Revolution affects all countries. cataclysmic, ADJ.

catalyst N. agent which brings about a chemical change while it remains unaffected and unchanged. Many chemical reactions cannot take place without the presence of a *catalyst.*

catapult N. slingshot; a hurling machine. Airplanes are sometimes launched from battleships by *catapults.* also V.

cataract N. great waterfall; eye abnormality. She gazed with awe at the mighty *cataract* known as Niagara Falls.

catastrophe N. calamity. The Johnstown flood was a *catastrophe.*

catechism N. book for religious instruction; instruction by question and answer. He taught by engaging his pupils in a *catechism* until they gave him the correct answer.

catharsis N. purging or cleansing of any passage of the body. Aristotle maintained that tragedy created a *catharsis* by purging the soul of base concepts.

cathartic N. purgative. Some drugs act as laxatives when taken in small doses but act as *cathartics* when taken in much larger doses.

catholic ADJ. broadly sympathetic; liberal. He was extremely *catholic* in his reading tastes.

caucus N. private meeting of members of a party to select officers or determine policy. At the opening of Congress, the members of the Democratic Party held a *caucus* to elect the Majority Leader of the House and the Party Whip.

caustic ADJ. burning; sarcastically biting. The critic's *caustic* remarks angered the hapless actors who were the subjects of his sarcasm.

cauterize V. burn with hot iron or caustic. In order to prevent infection, the doctor *cauterized* the wound.

cavalcade N. procession; parade. As described by Chaucer, the *cavalcade* of Canterbury pilgrims was a motley group.

cavil V. make frivolous objections. I respect your sensible criticisms, but I dislike the way you *cavil* about unimportant details. also N.

cede V. transfer; yield title to. I intend to *cede* this property to the city.

celerity N. speed; rapidity. Hamlet resented his mother's *celerity* in remarrying within a month after his father's death.

celestial ADJ. heavenly. He wrote about the music of "*celestial* spheres."

celibate ADJ. unmarried; abstaining from sexual intercourse. He vowed to remain *celibate.* celibacy, N.

censor N. overseer of morals; person who reads to eliminate inappropriate remarks. Soldiers dislike having their mail read by a *censor* but understand the need for this precaution. also V.

censorious ADJ. critical. *Censorious* people delight in casting blame.

censure V. blame; criticize. He was *censured* for his inappropriate behavior. also N.

centaur N. mythical figure, half man and half horse. I was particularly impressed by the statue of the *centaur* in the Roman Hall of the museum.

centigrade ADJ. measure of temperature used widely in Europe. On the *centigrade* thermometer, the freezing point of water is zero degrees.

centrifugal ADJ. radiating; departing from the center. Many automatic drying machines remove excess moisture from clothing by *centrifugal* force.

centripetal ADJ. tending toward the center. Does *centripetal* force or the force of gravity bring orbiting bodies to the earth's surface?

centurion N. Roman army officer. Because he was in command of a company of one hundred soldiers, he was called a *centurion.*

cerebral ADJ. pertaining to the brain or intellect. The content of philosophical works is *cerebral* in nature and requires much thought.

cerebration N. thought. Mathematics problems sometimes require much *cerebration.*

ceremonious ADJ. marked by formality. Ordinary dress would be inappropriate at so *ceremonious* an affair.

cessation N. stopping. The workers threatened a *cessation* of all activities if their demands were not met. cease, V.

cession N. yielding to another; ceding. The *cession* of Alaska to the United States is discussed in this chapter.

chafe V. warm by rubbing; make sore by rubbing. The collar *chafed* his neck. also N.

chaff N. worthless products of an endeavor. When you separate the wheat from the chaff, be sure you throw out the *chaff.*

chaffing ADJ. bantering; joking. Sometimes his flippant and *chaffing* remarks annoy us.

chagrin N. vexation; disappointment. His refusal to go with us filled us with *chagrin.*

chalice N. goblet; consecrated cup. In a small room adjoining the cathedral, many ornately decorated *chalices* made by the most famous European goldsmiths were on display.

chameleon N. lizard that changes color in different situations. Like the *chameleon,* he assumed the political thinking of every group he met.

champ V. chew noisily. His dining companions were amused by the way he *champed* his food.

TEST—WORD LIST 8—*Antonyms*

Each of the questions below consists of a word in capital letters, followed by five lettered words or phrases. Choose the lettered word or phrase that is most nearly opposite in meaning to the word in capital letters and write the letter of your choice on your answer paper.

106. CAPACIOUS (A) warlike (B) cordial (C) curious (D) not spacious (E) not capable
107. CAPRICIOUS (A) satisfied (B) insured (C) photographic (D) scattered (E) steadfast
108. CAPTIOUS (A) tolerant (B) capable (C) frivolous (D) winning (E) recollected
109. CARNAL (A) impressive (B) minute (C) spiritual (D) actual (E) private
110. CARNIVOROUS (A) gloomy (B) tangential (C) productive (D) weak (E) vegetarian
111. CAROUSAL (A) awakening (B) sobriety (C) acceleration (D) direction (E) production

112. CARPING (A) acquiescent (B) mean (C) limited (D) farming (E) racing
113. CARTE BLANCHE (A) capitalistic (B) investment (C) importance (D) restriction (E) current
114. CATHOLIC (A) religious (B) pacific (C) narrow (D) weighty (E) funny
115. CELERITY (A) assurance (B) state (C) acerbity (D) delay (E) infamy
116. CELIBATE (A) investing (B) married (C) retired (D) commodious (E) dubious
117. CENSURE (A) process (B) enclose (C) interest (D) praise (E) penetrate
118. CENTRIFUGAL (A) centripetal (B) ephemeral (C) lasting (D) barometric (E) algebraic
119. CESSATION (A) premium (B) gravity (C) beginning (D) composition (E) stoppage
120. CHAFFING (A) achieving (B) serious (C) capitalistic (D) sneezing (E) expensive

---

WORD LIST 9 **champion - colander**

champion V. support militantly. Martin Luther King, Jr., won the Nobel Peace Prize because he *championed* the oppressed in their struggle for equality.

chaotic ADJ. in utter disorder. He tried to bring order into the *chaotic* state of affairs. chaos, N.

charisma N. divine gift; great popular charm or appeal of a political leader. Political commentators have deplored the importance of a candidate's *charisma* in these days of television campaigning.

charlatan N. quack; pretender to knowledge. Because he was unable to substantiate his claim that he had found a cure for the dread disease, he was called a *charlatan* by his colleagues.

chary ADJ. cautiously watchful. She was *chary* of her favors.

chasm N. abyss. They could not see the bottom of the *chasm.*

chassis N. framework and working parts of an automobile. Examining the car after the accident, the owner discovered that the body had been ruined but that the *chassis* was unharmed.

chaste ADJ. pure. Her *chaste* and decorous garb was appropriately selected for the solemnity of the occasion. chastity, N.

chasten V. discipline; punish in order to correct. Whom God loves, God *chastens.*

chastise V. punish. I must *chastise* you for this offense.

chattel N. personal property. When he bought his furniture on the installment plan, he signed a *chattel* mortgage.

chauvinist N. blindly devoted patriot. A *chauvinist* cannot recognize any faults in his country, no matter how flagrant they may be.

checkered ADJ. marked by changes in fortune. During his *checkered* career he had lived in palatial mansions and in dreary boardinghouses.

cherubic ADJ. angelic; innocent-looking. With her cheerful smile and rosy cheeks, she was a particularly *cherubic* child.

chicanery N. trickery. Your deceitful tactics in this case are indications of *chicanery.*

chide V. scold. Grandma began to *chide* Steven for his lying.

chimerical ADJ. fantastic; highly imaginative. Poe's *chimerical* stories are sometimes too morbid for reading in bed. chimera, N.

chiromancy N. art of telling fortunes by reading the hand; palmistry. The charlatans along the Midway claimed the ability to analyze character and predict the future by such means as handwriting analysis, phrenology and *chiromancy.*

chiropodist N. one who treats disorders of the feet. The *chiropodist* treated the ingrown nail on the boy's foot.

chivalrous ADJ. courteous; faithful; brave. *Chivalrous* behavior involves not merely words but deeds.

choleric ADJ. hot-tempered. His flushed, angry face indicated a *choleric* nature.

choreography N. art of dancing. Martha Graham introduced a form of *choreography* which seemed awkward and alien to those who had been brought up on classic ballet.

chronic ADJ. long established as a disease. The doctors were able finally to attribute his *chronic* headaches and nausea to traces of formaldehyde gas in his apartment.

churlish ADJ. boorish; rude. Dismayed by his *churlish* manners at the party, the girls vowed never to invite him again.

ciliated ADJ. having minute hairs. The paramecium is a *ciliated,* one-celled animal.

cipher N. nonentity; worthless person or thing. She claimed her ex-husband was a total *cipher* and wondered why she had ever married him.

circlet N. small ring; band. This tiny *circlet* is very costly because it is set with precious stones.

circuitous ADJ. roundabout. Because of the traffic congestion on the main highways, she took a *circuitous* route. circuit, N.

circumlocution N. indirect or roundabout expression. He was afraid to call a spade a spade and resorted to *circumlocutions* to avoid direct reference to his subject.

circumscribe V. limit; confine. Although I do not wish to *circumscribe* your activities, I must insist that you complete this assignment before you start anything else.

circumspect ADJ. prudent; cautious. Investigating before acting, she tried always to be *circumspect.*

circumvent V. outwit; baffle. In order to *circumvent* the enemy, we will make two preliminary attacks in other sections before starting our major campaign.

citadel N. fortress. The *citadel* overlooked the city like a protecting angel.

cite V. quote; commend. She could *cite* passages in the Bible from memory. citation, N.

clairvoyant ADJ., N. having foresight; fortuneteller. Cassandra's *clairvoyant* warning was not heeded by the Trojans. clairvoyance, N.

clamber V. climb by crawling. She *clambered* over the wall.

clamor N. noise. The *clamor* of the children at play outside made it impossible for her to take a nap. also V.

clandestine ADJ. secret. After avoiding their chaperon, the lovers had a *clandestine* meeting.

clangor N. loud, resounding noise. The blacksmith was accustomed to the *clangor* of hammers on steel.

clarion ADJ. shrill trumpetlike sound. We woke to the *clarion* call of the bugle.

claustrophobia N. fear of being locked in. His fellow classmates laughed at his *claustrophobia* and often threatened to lock him in his room.

clavicle N. collarbone. Even though he wore shoulder pads, the football player broke his *clavicle* during a practice scrimmage.

cleave V. split asunder. The lightning *cleaves* the tree in two. cleavage, N.

cleft N. split. There was a *cleft* in the huge boulder. also ADJ.

clemency N. disposition to be lenient; mildness, as of the weather. The lawyer was pleased when the case was sent to Judge Smith's chambers because Smith was noted for her *clemency* toward first offenders.

cliché N. phrase dulled in meaning by repetition. High school compositions are often marred by such *clichés* as "strong as an ox."

clientele N. body of customers. The rock club attracted a young, stylish *clientele.*

climactic ADJ. relating to the highest point. When he reached the *climactic* portions of the book, he could not stop reading. climax, N.

clime N. region; climate. His doctor advised him to move to a milder *clime.*

clique N. small exclusive group. She charged that a *clique* had assumed control of school affairs.

cloister N. monastery or convent. The nuns lived in the *cloister.*

cloven ADJ. split. Popular legends maintain that the devil has *cloven* hooves.

coadjutor N. assistant; colleague. He was assigned as *coadjutor* of the bishop.

coalesce V. combine; fuse. The brooks *coalesce* into one large river.

cockade N. decoration worn on hat. Members of that brigade can be recognized by the green and white *cockade* in their helmets.

codicil N. supplement to the body of a will. This *codicil* was drawn up five years after the writing of the original will.

coerce V. force; repress. Do not *coerce* me into doing this; I hate force.

coddle V. to treat gently. Don't *coddle* the children so much; they need a taste of discipline.

coeval ADJ. living at the same time as; contemporary. *Coeval* with the dinosaur, the pterodactyl flourished during the Mesozoic era.

cog N. tooth projecting from a wheel. On steep slopes, *cog* railways are frequently used to prevent slipping.

cogent ADJ. convincing. She presented *cogent* arguments to the jury.

cogitate V. think over. *Cogitate* on this problem; the solution will come.

cognate ADJ. allied by blood; of the same or kindred nature. In the phrase "die a thousand deaths," the word "death" is a *cognate* object.

cognizance N. knowledge. During the election campaign, the two candidates were kept in full *cognizance* of the international situation.

cognomen N. family name. He asked the court to change his *cognomen* to a more American-sounding name.

cohere V. stick together. Solids have a greater tendency to *cohere* than liquids.

cohesion N. force which keeps parts together. In order to preserve our *cohesion,* we must not let minor differences interfere with our major purposes.

cohorts N. armed band. Caesar and his Roman *cohorts* conquered almost all of the known world.

coincident ADJ. occurring at the same time. Some people find the *coincident* events in Hardy's novels annoying.

colander N. utensil with perforated bottom used for straining. Before serving the spaghetti, place it in a *colander* to drain it.

TEST—WORD LIST 9—*Synonyms*

Each of the questions below consists of a word in capital letters, followed by five lettered words or phrases. Choose the lettered word or phrase that is most nearly similar in meaning to the word in capital letters and write the letter of your choice on your answer paper.

121. CHASTE (A) loyal (B) timid (C) curt (D) pure (E) outspoken
122. CHIDE (A) unite (B) fear (C) record (D) skid (E) scold
123. CHIMERICAL (A) developing (B) brief (C) distant (D) economical (E) fantastic
124. CHOLERIC (A) musical (B) episodic (C) hotheaded (D) global (E) seasonal
125. CHURLISH (A) marine (B) economical (C) impolite (D) compact (E) young
126. CILIATED (A) foolish (B) swift (C) early (D) constructed (E) hairy
127. CIRCUITOUS (A) indirect (B) complete (C) obvious (D) aware (E) tortured
128. CITE (A) galvanize (B) visualize (C) locate (D) quote (E) signal
129. CLANDESTINE (A) abortive (B) secret (C) tangible (D) doomed (E) approved
130. CLAUSTROPHOBIA (A) lack of confidence (B) fear of spiders (C) love of books (D) fear of grammar (E) fear of closed places
131. CLEFT (A) split (B) waterfall (C) assembly (D) parfait (E) surplus
132. CLICHÉ (A) increase (B) vehicle (C) morale (D) platitude (E) pique
133. COERCE (A) recover (B) total (C) force (D) license (E) ignore
134. COGNIZANCE (A) policy (B) knowledge (C) advance (D) omission (E) examination
135. COGNOMEN (A) family name (B) dwarf (C) suspicion (D) kind of railway (E) pseudopod

---

WORD LIST 10 collaborate - congenital

collaborate V. work together. Two writers *collaborated* in preparing this book.

collage N. work of art put together from fragments. Scraps of cloth, paper doilies, and old photographs all went into her *collage.*

collate V. examine in order to verify authenticity; arrange in order. They *collated* the newly found manuscripts to determine their age.

collateral N. security given for loan. The sum you wish to borrow is so large that it must be secured by *collateral.*

collation N. a light meal. Tea sandwiches and cookies were offered at the *collation.*

collier N. worker in coal mine; ship carrying coal. The extended cold spell has prevented the *colliers* from delivering the coal to the docks as scheduled.

colloquial ADJ. pertaining to conversational or common speech. Your use of *colloquial* expressions in a formal essay such as the one you have presented spoils the effect you hope to achieve.

colloquy N. informal discussion. I enjoy our *colloquies,* but I sometimes wish that they could be made more formal and more searching.

collusion N. conspiring in a fraudulent scheme. The swindlers were found guilty of *collusion.*

colossal ADJ. huge. Radio City Music Hall has a *colossal* stage.

comatose ADJ. in a coma; extremely sleepy. The long-winded orator soon had his audience in a *comatose* state.

combustible ADJ. easily burned. After the recent outbreak of fires in private homes, the fire commissioner ordered that all *combustible* materials be kept in safe containers. also N.

comely ADJ. attractive; agreeable. I would rather have a *comely* wife than a rich one.

comestible N. something fit to be eaten. The roast turkey and other *comestibles,* the wines, and the excellent service made this Thanksgiving dinner particularly memorable.

comeuppance N. rebuke; deserts. After his earlier rudeness, we were delighted to see him get his *comeuppance.*

comity N. courtesy; civility. A spirit of *comity* should exist among nations.

commandeer V. to draft for military purposes; to take for public use. The policeman *commandeered* the first car that approached and ordered the driver to go to the nearest hospital.

commemorative ADJ. remembering; honoring. The new *commemorative* stamp honors the late Martin Luther King, Jr.

commensurate ADJ. equal in extent. Your reward will be *commensurate* with your effort.

commiserate V. feel or express pity or sympathy for. Her friends *commiserated* with the widow.

commodious ADJ. spacious and comfortable. After sleeping in small roadside cabins, they found their hotel suite *commodious.*

communal ADJ. help in common; of a group of people. When they were divorced, they had trouble dividing their *communal* property.

compact N. agreement; contract. The signers of the Mayflower *Compact* were establishing a form of government.

compact ADJ. tightly packed; firm; brief. His short, *compact* body was better suited to wrestling than to basketball.

compatible ADJ. harmonious; in harmony with. They were *compatible* neighbors, never quarreling over unimportant matters.

compendium N. brief comprehensive summary. This text can serve as a *compendium* of the tremendous amount of new material being developed in this field.

compensatory ADJ. making up for; repaying. Can a *compensatory* education program make up for the inadequate schooling he received in earlier years?

compilation N. listing of statistical information in tabular or book form. The *compilation* of available scholarships serves a very valuable purpose.

complacent ADJ. self-satisfied. There was a *complacent* look on his face as he examined his paintings. complacency, N.

complaisant ADJ. trying to please; obliging. The courtier obeyed the king's orders in a *complaisant* manner.

complement N. that which completes. A predicate *complement* completes the meaning of the subject. also V.

compliant ADJ. yielding. He was *compliant* and ready to conform to the pattern set by his friends.

complicity N. participation; involvement. You cannot keep your *complicity* in this affair secret very long; you would be wise to admit your involvement immediately.

component N. element; ingredient. I wish all the *components* of my stereo system were working at the same time.

comport V. bear one's self; behave. He *comported* himself with great dignity.

composure N. mental calmness. Even the latest work crisis failed to shake her *composure.*

compress V. close; squeeze; contract. She *compressed* the package under her arm.

compromise V. adjust; endanger the interests or reputation of. Your presence at the scene of the dispute *compromises* our claim to neutrality in this matter. also N.

compunction N. remorse. The judge was especially severe in his sentencing because he felt that the criminal had shown no *compunction* for his heinous crime.

compute V. reckon; calculate. He failed to *compute* the interest.

concatenate V. link as in a chain. It is difficult to understand how these events could *concatenate* as they did without outside assistance.

concave ADJ. hollow. The back-packers found partial shelter from the storm by huddling against the *concave* wall of the cliff.

conceit N. whimsical idea; extravagant metaphor. He was an entertaining companion, always expressing himself in amusing *conceits* and witty turns of phrase.

concentric ADJ. having a common center. The target was made of *concentric* circles.

conception N. beginning; forming of an idea. At the first *conception* of the work, he was consulted. conceive, V.

concession N. an act of yielding. Before they could reach an agreement, both sides had to make certain *concessions.*

conch N. large seashell. In this painting we see a Triton blowing on his *conch.*

conciliate V. pacify; win over. She tried to *conciliate* me with a gift. conciliatory, ADJ.

concise ADJ. brief and compact. The essay was *concise* and explicit.

conclave N. private meeting. He was present at all their *conclaves* as a sort of unofficial observer.

concoct V. prepare by combining; make up in concert. How did you ever *concoct* such a strange dish? concoction, N.

concomitant N. that which accompanies. Culture is not always a *concomitant* of wealth. also ADJ.

concordat N. agreement, usually between the papal authority and the secular. One of the most famous of the agreements between a Pope and an emperor was the *Concordat* of Worms in 1122.

concur V. agree. Did you *concur* with the decision of the court?

concurrent ADJ. happening at the same time. In America, the colonists were resisting the demands of the mother country; at the *concurrent* moment in France, the middle class was sowing the seeds of rebellion.

condescend V. bestow courtesies with a superior air. The king *condescended* to grant an audience to the friends of the condemned man. condescension, N.

condign ADJ. adequate; deservedly severe. The public approved the *condign* punishment.

condiments N. seasonings; spices. Spanish food is full of *condiments.*

condole V. express sympathetic sorrow. His friends

gathered to *condole* with him over his loss. condolence, N.

condone V. overlook; forgive. We cannot *condone* your recent criminal cooperation with the gamblers.

conduit N. aqueduct; passageway for fluids. Water was brought to the army in the desert by an improvised *conduit* from the adjoining mountain.

confidant N. trusted friend. He had no *confidants* with whom he could discuss his problems at home.

confiscate V. seize; commandeer. The army *confiscated* all available supplies of uranium.

conflagration N. great fire. In the *conflagration* that followed the 1906 earthquake, much of San Francisco was destroyed.

confluence N. flowing together; crowd. They built the city at the *confluence* of two rivers.

conformity N. harmony; agreement. In *conformity* with our rules and regulations, I am calling a meeting of our organization.

confound V. confuse; puzzle. No mystery could *confound* Sherlock Holmes for long.

congeal V. freeze; coagulate. His blood *congealed* in his veins as he saw the dread monster rush toward him.

congenial ADJ. pleasant; friendly. My father loved to go out for a meal with *congenial* companions.

congenital ADJ. existing at birth. His *congenital* deformity disturbed his parents.

TEST—WORD LIST 10—*Synonyms and Antonyms*

Each of the following questions consists of a word in capital letters, followed by five lettered words or phrases. Choose the lettered word or phrase which is most nearly similar or the opposite of the word in capital letters and write the letter of your choice on your answer paper.

136. COLLATION (A) furor (B) emphasis (C) distillery (D) spree (E) lunch
137. COLLOQUIAL (A) burnt (B) polished (C) political (D) gifted (E) problematic
138. COLLOQUY (A) dialect (B) diversion (C) announcement (D) discussion (E) expansion
139. COMATOSE (A) cozy (B) restrained (C) alert (D) dumb (E) grim
140. COMBUSTIBLE (A) flammable (B) industrious (C) waterproof (D) specific (E) plastic
141. COMESTIBLE (A) vigorous (B) fit to be eaten (C) liquid (D) beautiful (E) circumvented
142. COMMISERATE (A) communicate (B) expand (C) repay (D) diminish (E) sympathize
143. COMMODIOUS (A) numerous (B) yielding (C) leisurely (D) limited (E) expensive
144. COMPLIANT (A) numerous (B) veracious (C) soft (D) adamant (E) livid
145. CONCILIATE (A) defend (B) activate (C) integrate (D) quarrel (E) react
146. CONCOCT (A) thrive (B) wonder (C) intrude (D) drink (E) invent
147. CONDONE (A) build (B) evaluate (C) pierce (D) infuriate (E) overlook
148. CONFISCATE (A) discuss (B) discover (C) seize (D) exist (E) convey
149. CONFORMITY (A) agreement (B) ambition (C) confinement (D) pride (E) restraint
150. CONGENITAL (A) slight (B) obscure (C) thorough (D) existing at birth (E) classified

WORD LIST 11 conglomeration -countermand

conglomeration N. mass of material sticking together. In such a *conglomeration* of miscellaneous statistics, it was impossible to find a single area of analysis.

congruence N. correspondence of parts; harmonious relationship. The student demonstrated the *congruence* of the two triangles by using the hypotenuse-arm theorem.

conifer N. pine tree; cone-bearing tree. According to geologists, the *conifers* were the first plants to bear flowers.

conjecture N. surmise; guess. I will end all your *conjectures;* I admit I am guilty as charged. also V.

conjugal ADJ. pertaining to marriage. Their dreams of *conjugal* bliss were shattered as soon as their temperaments clashed.

conjure V. summon a devil; practice magic; imagine; invent. He *conjured* up an image of a reformed city and had the voters completely under his spell.

connivance N. pretense of ignorance of something wrong; assistance; permission to offend. With the *connivance* of his friends, he plotted to embarrass the teacher. connive, V.

connoisseur N. person competent to act as a judge of art, etc.; a lover of an art. He had developed into a *connoisseur* of fine china.

connotation N. suggested or implied meaning of an

expression. Foreigners frequently are unaware of the *connotations* of the words they use.

connubial ADJ. pertaining to marriage or the matrimonial state. In his telegram, he wished the newlyweds a lifetime of *connubial* bliss.

consanguinity N. kinship. The lawsuit developed into a test of the *consanguinity* of the claimant to the estate.

consecrate V. dedicate; sanctify. We shall *consecrate* our lives to this noble purpose.

consensus N. general agreement. The *consensus* indicates that we are opposed to entering into this pact.

consequential ADJ. pompous; self-important. Convinced of his own importance, the actor strutted about the dressing room with a *consequential* air.

consonance N. harmony; agreement. Her agitation seemed out of *consonance* with her usual calm.

consort V. associate with. We frequently judge people by the company with whom they *consort.*

consort N. husband or wife. The search for a *consort* for the young Queen Victoria ended happily.

conspiracy N. treacherous plot. Brutus and Cassius joined in the *conspiracy* to kill Julius Caesar.

constituent N. supporter. The congressman received hundreds of letters from angry *constituents* after the Equal Rights Amendment failed to pass.

constraint N. compulsion; repression of feelings. There was a feeling of *constraint* in the room because no one dared to criticize the speaker. constrain, V.

construe V. explain; interpret. If I *construe* your remarks correctly, you disagree with the theory already advanced.

consummate ADJ. complete. I have never seen anyone who makes as many stupid errors as you do; you must be a *consummate* idiot. also V.

contagion N. infection. Fearing *contagion,* they took great steps to prevent the spread of the disease.

contaminate V. pollute. The sewage system of the city so *contaminated* the water that swimming was forbidden.

contemn V. regard with contempt; disregard. I will not tolerate those who *contemn* the sincere efforts of this group.

contentious ADJ. quarrelsome. We heard loud and *contentious* noises in the next room.

contest V. dispute. The defeated candidate attempted to *contest* the election results.

context N. writings preceding and following the passage quoted. Because these lines are taken out of *context,* they do not convey the message the author intended.

contiguous ADJ. adjacent to; touching upon. The two countries are *contiguous* for a few miles; then they are separated by the gulf.

continence N. self-restraint; sexual chastity. She vowed to lead a life of *continence.* continent, ADJ.

contingent ADJ. conditional. The continuation of this contract is *contingent* on the quality of your first output. contingency, N.

contortions N. twistings; distortions. As the effects of the opiate wore away, the *contortions* of the patient became more violent and demonstrated how much pain she was enduring.

contraband N, ADJ. illegal trade; smuggling. The Coast Guard tries to prevent traffic in *contraband* goods.

contravene V. contradict; infringe on. I will not attempt to *contravene* your argument for it does not affect the situation.

contrite ADJ. penitent. Her *contrite* tears did not influence the judge when he imposed sentence. contrition, N.

controvert V. oppose with arguments; contradict. To *controvert* your theory will require much time but it is essential that we disprove it.

contumacious ADJ. disobedient; resisting authority. The *contumacious* mob shouted defiantly at the police. contumacy, N.

contumely N. scornful insolence; insult. The "proud man's *contumely*" is distasteful to Hamlet.

contusion N. bruise. She was treated for *contusions* and abrasions.

conundrum N. riddle. During the long car ride, she invented *conundrums* to entertain the children.

convene V. assemble. Because much needed legislation had to be enacted, the governor ordered the legislature to *convene* in special session by January 15.

conventional ADJ. ordinary; typical. His *conventional* upbringing left him wholly unprepared for his wife's eccentric family.

converge V. come together. Marchers *converged* on Washington for the great Peace March.

conversant ADJ. familiar with. The lawyer is *conversant* with all the evidence.

converse N. opposite. The inevitable *converse* of peace is not war but annihilation.

convex ADJ. curving outward. He polished the *convex* lens of his telescope.

conveyance N. vehicle; transfer. During the transit strike, commuters used various kinds of *conveyances.*

conviction N. strongly held belief. Nothing could shake his *conviction* that she was innocent.

convivial ADJ. festive; gay; characterized by joviality. The *convivial* celebrators of the victory sang their college songs.

convoke V. call together. Congress was *convoked* at the outbreak of the emergency. convocation, N.

convoluted ADJ. coiled around; involved; intricate. His argument was so *convoluted* that few of us could follow it intelligently.

copious ADJ. plentiful. She had *copious* reasons for rejecting the proposal.

coquette N. flirt. Because she refused to give him any answer to his proposal of marriage, he called her a *coquette.* also V.

cordon N. extended line of men or fortifications to prevent access or egress. The police *cordon* was so tight that the criminals could not leave the area. also V.

cormorant N. greedy, rapacious bird. The *cormorants* spend their time eating the fish which they catch by diving. also ADJ.

cornice N. projecting molding on building (usually above columns). Because the *cornice* stones had been loosened by the storms, the police closed the building until repairs could be made.

corollary N. consequence; accompaniment. Brotherly love is a complex emotion, with sibling rivalry its natural *corollary.*

corporeal ADJ. bodily; material. He was not a churchgoer; he was interested only in *corporeal* matters.

corpulent ADJ. very fat. The *corpulent* man resolved to reduce. corpulence, N.

correlation N. mutual relationship. He sought to determine the *correlation* that existed between ability in algebra and ability to interpret reading exercises.

corroborate V. confirm. Unless we find a witness to *corroborate* your evidence, it will not stand up in court.

corrosive ADJ. eating away by chemicals or disease. Stainless steel is able to withstand the effects of *corrosive* chemicals.

corrugated ADJ. wrinkled; ridged. She wished she could smoothe away the wrinkles from his *corrugated* brow.

corsair N. pirate; pirate ship. The *corsairs,* preying on shipping in the Mediterranean, were often inspired by racial and religious hatreds as well as by the desire for money and booty.

cortege N. procession. The funeral *cortege* proceeded slowly down the avenue.

coruscate V. glitter; scintillate. His wit is the kind that *coruscates* and startles all his listeners.

cosmic ADJ. pertaining to the universe; vast. *Cosmic* rays derive their name from the fact that they bombard the earth's atmosphere from outer space. cosmos, N.

coterie N. group that meets socially; select circle. After his book had been published, he was invited to join the literary *coterie* that lunched daily at the hotel.

countenance V. approve; tolerate. He refused to *countenance* such rude behavior on their part.

countermand V. cancel; revoke. The general *countermanded* the orders issued in his absence.

TEST—WORD LIST 11—*Synonyms*

Each of the questions below consists of a word in capital letters, followed by five lettered words or phrases. Choose the lettered word or phrase that is most nearly similar in meaning to the word in capital letters and write the letter of your choice on your answer paper.

151. CONJECTURE (A) magic (B) guess (C) position (D) form (E) place
152. CONNOISSEUR (A) gourmand (B) lover of art (C) humidor (D) delinquent (E) interpreter
153. CONSANGUINITY (A) kinship (B) friendship (C) bloodletting (D) relief (E) understanding
154. CONSENSUS (A) general agreement (B) project (C) insignificance (D) sheaf (E) crevice
155. CONSTRUE (A) explain (B) promote (C) reserve (D) erect (E) block
156. CONTAMINATE (A) arrest (B) prepare (C) pollute (D) beam (E) inform
157. CONTENTIOUS (A) squealing (B) surprising (C) quarrelsome (D) smug (E) creative
158. CONTINENCE (A) humanity (B) research (C) embryology (D) bodies of land (E) self-restraint
159. CONTRABAND (A) purpose (B) rogue (C) rascality (D) difficulty (E) smuggling
160. CONTRITE (A) smart (B) penitent (C) restful (D) recognized (E) perspiring
161. CONTROVERT (A) turn over (B) contradict (C) mind (D) explain (E) swing
162. CONTUMELY (A) sensation (B) noise (C) silence (D) insult (E) classic
163. CONVERSANT (A) ignorant (B) speaking (C) incorporated (D) familiar (E) pedantic
164. COPIOUS (A) plentiful (B) cheating (C) dishonorable (D) adventurous (E) inspired
165. CORPULENT (A) regenerate (B) obese (C) different (D) hungry (E) bloody

WORD LIST 12 counterpart - decelerate

counterpart N. a thing that completes another; things very much alike. Night and day are *counterparts.*

coup N. highly successful action or sudden attack. As the news of his *coup* spread throughout Wall Street, his fellow brokers dropped by to congratulate him.

couple V. join; unite. The Flying Karamazovs *couple* expert juggling and amateur joking in their nightclub act.

courier N. messenger. The publisher sent a special *courier* to pick up the manuscript.

covenant N. agreement. We must comply with the terms of the *covenant.*

covert ADJ. secret; hidden; implied. She could understand the *covert* threat in the letter.

covetous ADJ. avaricious; eagerly desirous of. The child was *covetous* by nature and wanted to take the toys belonging to his classmates. covet, V.

cower V. shrink quivering, as from fear. The frightened child *cowered* in the corner of the room.

coy ADJ. shy; modest; coquettish. She was *coy* in her answers to his offer.

cozen V. cheat; hoodwink; swindle. He was the kind of individual who would *cozen* his friends in a cheap card game but remain eminently ethical in all his business dealings.

crabbed ADJ. sour; peevish. The *crabbed* old man was avoided by the children because he scolded them when they made noise.

crass ADJ. very unrefined; grossly insensible. The philosophers deplored the *crass* commercialism.

craven ADJ. cowardly. Her *craven* behavior in this critical period was criticized.

credence N. belief. Do not place any *credence* in his promises.

credo N. creed. I believe we may best describe his *credo* by saying that it approximates the Golden Rule.

credulity N. belief on slight evidence. The witch doctor took advantage of the *credulity* of the superstitious natives. credulous, ADJ.

creed N. system of religious or ethical belief. In any loyal American's *creed,* love of democracy must be emphasized.

crepuscular ADJ. pertaining to twilight. Bats are *crepuscular* creatures since they begin their flights as soon as the sun begins to sink below the horizon.

crescendo N. increase in the volume of sound in a musical passage. The overture suddenly changed from a quiet pastoral theme to a *crescendo* featured by blaring trumpets and clashing cymbals.

crestfallen ADJ. dejected; dispirited. We were surprised at his reaction to the failure of his project; instead of being *crestfallen,* he was busily engaged in planning new activities.

crevice N. crack; fissure. The mountain climbers found footholds in the tiny *crevices* in the mountainside.

criterion N. standard used in judging. What *criterion* did you use when you selected this essay as the prizewinner? criteria, PL.

crone N. hag. The toothless *crone* frightened us when she smiled.

crotchety ADJ. eccentric; whimsical. Although he was reputed to be a *crotchety* old gentleman, I found his ideas substantially sound and sensible.

cruet N. small glass bottle for vinegar, oil, etc. The waiter preparing the salad poured oil and vinegar from two *cruets* into the bowl.

crux N. crucial point. This is the *crux* of the entire problem.

crypt N. secret recess or vault, usually used for burial. Until recently, only bodies of rulers and leading statesmen were interred in this *crypt.*

cryptic ADJ. mysterious; hidden; secret. His *cryptic* remarks could not be interpreted.

cubicle N. small chamber used for sleeping. After his many hours of intensive study in the library, he retired to his *cubicle.*

cuisine N. style of cooking. French *cuisine* is noted for its use of sauces and wines.

cul-de-sac N. blind alley; trap. The soldiers were unaware that they were marching into a *cul-de-sac* when they entered the canyon.

culinary ADJ. relating to cooking. Many chefs attribute their *culinary* skill to the wise use of spices.

cull V. pick out; reject. Every month the farmer *culls* the nonlaying hens from his flock and sells them to the local butcher. also N.

culmination N. attainment of highest point. His inauguration as President of the United States marked the *culmination* of his political career.

culpable ADJ. deserving blame. Corrupt politicians who condone the activities of the gamblers are equally *culpable.*

culvert N. artificial channel for water. If we build a *culvert* under the road at this point, we will reduce the possibility of the road's being flooded during the rainy season.

cumbersome ADJ. heavy; hard to manage. He was burdened down with *cumbersome* parcels.

cupidity N. greed. The defeated people could not satisfy the *cupidity* of the conquerors, who demanded excessive tribute.

curator N. superintendent; manager. The members of the board of trustees of the museum expected the new *curator* to plan events and exhibitions which would make the museum more popular.

curmudgeon N. churlish, miserly individual. Although he was regarded by many as a *curmudgeon,* a few of us were aware of the many kindnesses and acts of charity which he secretly performed.

curry V. dress; treat leather; seek favor. The courtier *curried* favors of the king.

cursive ADJ. flowing, running. In normal writing we run our letters together in *cursive* form; in printing, we separate the letters.

cursory ADJ. casual; hastily done. A *cursory* examination of the ruins indicates the possibility of arson; a more extensive study should be undertaken.

curtail V. shorten; reduce. During the coal shortage, we must *curtail* our use of this vital commodity.

cynic N. one who is skeptical or distrustful of human motives. A *cynic* at all times, he was suspicious of all altruistic actions of others. cynical, ADJ.

cynosure N. the object of general attention. As soon as the movie star entered the room, she became the *cynosure* of all eyes.

dais N. raised platform for guests of honor. When he approached the *dais,* he was greeted by cheers from the people who had come to honor him.

dally V. trifle with; procrastinate. Laertes told Ophelia that Hamlet could only *dally* with her affections.

dank ADJ. damp. The walls of the dungeon were *dank* and slimy.

dappled ADJ. spotted. She fed a carrot to the *dappled* foal.

dastard N. coward. This sneak attack is the work of a *dastard.* dastardly, ADJ.

daub V. smear (as with paint). From the way he *daubed* his paint on the canvas, I could tell he knew nothing of oils. also N.

daunt V. intimidate. Your threats cannot *daunt* me.

dauntless ADJ. bold. Despite the dangerous nature of the undertaking, the *dauntless* soldier volunteered for the assignment.

dawdle V. loiter; waste time. Inasmuch as we must meet a deadline, do not *dawdle* over this work.

deadlock N. standstill; stalemate. The negotiations had reached a *deadlock.* also V.

deadpan ADJ. wooden; impersonal. We wanted to see how long he could maintain his *deadpan* expression.

dearth N. scarcity. The *dearth* of skilled labor compelled the employers to open trade schools.

debacle N. breaking up; downfall. This *debacle* in the government can only result in anarchy.

debase V. reduce to lower state. Do not *debase* yourself by becoming maudlin.

debauch V. corrupt; make intemperate. A vicious newspaper can *debauch* public ideals. debauchery, N.

debenture N. bond issued to secure a loan. The manager of the company urged that the company try to raise money by issuing *debentures* rather than to try to sell stock.

debilitate V. weaken; enfeeble. Overindulgence *debilitates* character as well as physical stamina.

debonair ADJ. friendly; aiming to please. The *debonair* youth was liked by all who met him, because of his cheerful and obliging manner.

debris N. rubble. A full year after the earthquake in Mexico City, they were still carting away the *debris.*

debutante N. young woman making formal entrance into society. As a *debutante,* she was often mentioned in the society columns of the newspapers.

decadence N. decay. The moral *decadence* of the people was reflected in the lewd literature of the period.

decant V. pour off gently. Be sure to *decant* this wine before serving it.

decapitate V. behead. They did not hang Lady Jane Grey; they *decapitated* her.

decelerate V. slow down. Seeing the emergency blinkers in the road ahead, he *decelerated* quickly.

TEST—WORD LIST 12—*Antonyms*

Each of the questions below consists of a word in capital letters, followed by five lettered words or phrases. Choose the lettered word or phrase that is most nearly opposite in meaning to the word in capital letters and write the letter of your choice on your answer paper.

166. COY (A) weak (B) airy (C) brazen (D) old (E) tiresome
167. COZEN (A) cheat (B) treat honestly (C) prate (D) shackle (E) vilify
168. CRAVEN (A) desirous (B) direct (C) bold (D) civilized (E) controlled
169. CRUX (A) acne (B) spark (C) events (D) trivial point (E) belief

170. CRYPTIC (A) tomblike (B) secret (C) famous (D) candid (E) coded
171. CUPIDITY (A) anxiety (B) tragedy (C) generosity (D) entertainment (E) love
172. CURTAIL (A) mutter (B) lengthen (C) express (D) burden (E) shore
173. CYNICAL (A) trusting (B) effortless (C) conclusive (D) gallant (E) vertical
174. DANK (A) dry (B) guiltless (C) warm (D) babbling (E) reserved
175. DASTARD (A) illegitimacy (B) hero (C) presence (D) warmth (E) idol
176. DAUNTLESS (A) stolid (B) cowardly (C) irrelevant (D) peculiar (E) particular
177. DEARTH (A) life (B) abundance (C) brightness (D) terror (E) width
178. DEBACLE (A) progress (B) refusal (C) masque (D) cowardice (E) traffic
179. DEBILITATE (A) bedevil (B) repress (C) strengthen (D) animate (E) deaden
180. DEBONAIR (A) awkward (B) windy (C) balmy (D) strong (E) stormy

---

WORD LIST 13 deciduous - dermatologist

deciduous ADJ. falling off as of leaves. The oak is a *deciduous* tree.

decimate V. kill, usually one out of ten. We do more to *decimate* our population in automobile accidents than we do in war.

decipher V. decode. I could not *decipher* the doctor's handwriting.

declivity N. downward slope. The children loved to ski down the *declivity.*

decolleté ADJ. having a low-necked dress. Current fashion decrees that evening gowns be *decolleté* this season; bare shoulders are again the vogue.

decomposition N. decay. Despite the body's advanced state of *decomposition,* the police were able to identify the murdered man.

decorous ADJ. proper. Her *decorous* behavior was praised by her teachers. decorum, N.

decoy N. lure or bait. The wild ducks were not fooled by the *decoy.* also V.

decrepit ADJ. worn out by age. The *decrepit* car blocked traffic on the highway.

decrepitude N. state of collapse caused by illness or old age. I was unprepared for the state of *decrepitude* in which I had found my old friend; he seemed to have aged twenty years in six months.

decry V. disparage. Do not attempt to increase your stature by *decrying* the efforts of your opponents.

deducible ADJ. derived by reasoning. If we accept your premise, your conclusions are easily *deducible.*

defalcate V. misuse money held in trust. Legislation was passed to punish brokers who *defalcated* their clients' funds.

defamation N. harming a person's reputation. Such *defamation* of character may result in a slander suit.

default N. failure to do. As a result of her husband's failure to appear in court, she was granted a divorce by *default.* also V.

defeatist ADJ. attitude of one who is ready to accept defeat as a natural outcome. If you maintain your *defeatist* attitude, you will never succeed. also N.

defection N. desertion. The children, who had made him an idol, were hurt most by his *defection* from our cause.

deference N. courteous regard for another's wish. In *deference* to his desires, the employers granted him a holiday.

defile V. pollute; profane. The hoodlums *defiled* the church with their scurrilous writing.

definitive ADJ. final; complete. Carl Sandburg's *Abraham Lincoln* may be regarded as the *definitive* work on the life of the Great Emancipator.

deflect V. turn aside. His life was saved when his cigarette case *deflected* the bullet.

defray V. pay the costs of. Her employer offered to *defray* the costs of her postgraduate education.

deft ADJ neat; skillful. The *deft* waiter uncorked the champagne without spilling a drop.

defunct ADJ. dead; no longer in use or existence. The lawyers sought to examine the books of the *defunct* corporation.

degraded ADJ. lowered in rank; debased. The *degraded* wretch spoke only of his past glories and honors.

deify V. turn into a god; idolize. Admire Elvis Presley all you want; just don't *deify* him.

deign V. condescend. He felt that he would debase himself if he *deigned* to answer his critics.

delete V. erase; strike out. If you *delete* this paragraph, the composition will have more appeal.

deleterious ADJ. harmful. Workers in nuclear research must avoid the *deleterious* effects of radioactive substances.

deliberate V. consider; ponder. Offered the new job, she asked for time to *deliberate* before she told them her decision.

delineation N. portrayal. He is a powerful storyteller, but he is weakest in his *delineation* of character.

deliquescent ADJ. capable of absorbing moisture from the air and becoming liquid. Since this powder is extremely *deliquescent,* it must be kept in a hermetically sealed container until it is used.

delirium N. mental disorder marked by confusion. The drunkard in his *delirium* saw strange animals.

delude V. deceive. Do not *delude* yourself into believing that he will relent.

deluge N. flood; rush. When we advertised the position, we received a *deluge* of applications.

delusion N. false belief; hallucination. This scheme is a snare and a *delusion.*

delusive ADJ. deceptive; raising vain hopes. Do not raise your hopes on the basis of his *delusive* promises.

delve V. dig; investigate. *Delving* into old books and manuscripts is part of a researcher's job.

demagogue N. person who appeals to people's prejudice; false leader of people. He was accused of being a *demagogue* because he made promises which aroused futile hopes in his listeners.

demean V. degrade; humiliate. He felt that he would *demean* himself if he replied to the scurrilous letter.

demeanor N. behavior; bearing. His sober *demeanor* quieted the noisy revelers.

demented ADJ. insane. He became increasingly more *demented* and had to be hospitalized.

demesne N. domain; land over which a person has full sovereignty. Keats is referring to epic poetry when he mentions Homer's "proud *demesne.*"

demise N. death. Upon the *demise* of the dictator, a bitter dispute about succession to power developed.

demolition N. destruction. One of the major aims of the air force was the complete *demolition* of all means of transportation by bombing of rail lines and terminals.

demoniac ADJ. fiendish. The Spanish Inquisition devised many *demoniac* means of torture. demon, N.

demotic ADJ. pertaining to the people. He lamented the passing of aristocratic society and maintained that a *demotic* society would lower the nation's standards.

demur V. delay; object. To *demur* at this time will only worsen the already serious situation; now is the time for action.

demure ADJ. grave; serious; coy. She was *demure* and reserved.

denigrate V. blacken. All attempts to *denigrate* the character of our late President have failed; the people still love him and cherish his memory.

denizen N. inhabitant of. Ghosts are *denizens* of the land of the dead who return to earth.

denotation N. meaning; distinguishing by name. A dictionary will always give us the *denotation* of a word; frequently, it will also give us its connotation.

denouement N. outcome; final development of the plot of a play. The play was childishly written; the *denouement* was obvious to sophisticated theatergoers as early as the middle of the first act.

depict V. portray. In this book, the author *depicts* the slave owners as kind and benevolent masters.

depilate V. remove hair. Many women *depilate* their legs.

deplete V. reduce; exhaust. We must wait until we *deplete* our present inventory before we order replacements.

deplore V. regret. Although I *deplore* the vulgarity of your language, I defend your right to express yourself freely.

deploy V. move troops so that the battle line is extended at the expense of depth. The general ordered the battalion to *deploy* in order to meet the offensive of the enemy.

depose V. dethrone; remove from office. The army attempted to *depose* the king and set up a military government.

deposition N. testimony under oath. He made his *deposition* in the judge's chamber.

depravity N. corruption; wickedness. The *depravity* of his behavior shocked all.

deprecate V. disapprove regretfully. I must *deprecate* your attitude and hope that you will change your mind.

deprecatory ADJ. disapproving. Your *deprecatory* criticism has offended the author.

depreciate V. lessen in value. If you neglect this property, it will *depreciate.*

depredation N. plundering. After the *depredations* of the invaders, the people were penniless.

deranged ADJ. insane. He was mentally *deranged.*

derelict ADJ. abandoned. The *derelict* craft was a menace to navigation. also N.

deride V. scoff at. The people *derided* his grandiose schemes.

derision N. ridicule. They greeted his proposal with *derision* and refused to consider it seriously.

dermatologist N. one who studies the skin and its diseases. I advise you to consult a *dermatologist* about your acne.

TEST—WORD LIST 13—*Synonyms*

Each of the questions below consists of a word in capital letters, followed by five lettered words or phrases. Choose the lettered word or phrase that is most nearly similar in meaning to the word in capital letters and write the letter of your choice on your answer paper.

181. DECIMATE (A) kill (B) disgrace (C) search (D) collide (E) deride
182. DECLIVITY (A) trap (B) quadrangle (C) quarter (D) activity (E) downward slope
183. DECOLLETÉ (A) flavored (B) demure (C) flowery (D) low-necked (E) sweet
184. DECREPIT (A) momentary (B) emotional (C) suppressed (D) worn out (E) unexpected
185. DECREPITUDE (A) feebleness (B) disease (C) coolness (D) melee (E) crowd
186. DEFALCATE (A) abscond (B) elope (C) observe (D) panic (E) invest
187. DEFECTION (A) determination (B) desertion (C) invitation (D) affection (E) reservation
188. DEFILE (A) manicure (B) ride (C) pollute (D) assemble (E) order
189. DEGRADED (A) surprised (B) lowered (C) ascended (D) learned (E) prejudged
190. DELETERIOUS (A) delaying (B) experimental (C) harmful (D) graduating (E) glorious
191. DELUGE (A) confusion (B) deception (C) flood (D) mountain (E) weapon
192. DENIGRATE (A) refuse (B) blacken (C) terrify (D) admit (E) review
193. DENOUEMENT (A) action (B) scenery (C) resort (D) character (E) solution
194. DEPRAVITY (A) wickedness (B) sadness (C) heaviness (D) tidiness (E) seriousness
195. DERANGED (A) insane (B) announced (C) neighborly (D) alphabetical (E) surrounded

---

WORD LIST 14 derogatory - disgruntle

derogatory ADJ. expressing a low opinion. I resent your *derogatory* remarks.

descant V. discuss fully. He was willing to *descant* upon any topic of conversation, even when he knew very little about the subject under discussion. also N.

descry V. catch sight of. In the distance, we could barely *descry* the enemy vessels.

desecrate V. profane; violate the sanctity of. The soldiers *desecrated* the temple.

desiccate V. dry up. A tour of this smokehouse will give you an idea of how the pioneers used to *desiccate* food in order to preserve it.

desideratum N. that which is desired. Our first *desideratum* must be the establishment of peace; we can then attempt to remove the causes of the present conflict.

desolate V. rob of joy; lay waste to; forsake. The bandits *desolated* the countryside, burning farms and carrying off the harvest.

despicable ADJ. contemptible. Your *despicable* remarks call for no reply.

despise V. scorn. I *despise* your attempts at a reconciliation at this time.

despoil V. plunder. If you do not yield, I am afraid the enemy will *despoil* the buildings.

despondency N. depression; gloom. His increasing *despondency* worried his parents.

despotism N. tyranny. The people rebelled against the *despotism* of the king.

destitute ADJ. extremely poor. The illness left the family *destitute.*

desuetude N. disused condition. The machinery in the idle factory was in a state of *desuetude.*

desultory ADJ. aimless; jumping around. The animals' *desultory* behavior indicated that they had no awareness of their predicament.

detergent N. cleansing agent. Many new *detergents* have replaced soap.

determinate ADJ. having a fixed order of procedure; invariable. At the royal wedding, the procession of the nobles followed a *determinate* order of precedence.

deterrent N. something that discourages; hindrance. Does the threat of capital punishment serve as a *deterrent* to potential killers?

detonation N. explosion. The *detonation* could be heard miles away.

detraction N. slandering; aspersion. He is offended by your frequent *detractions* of his ability as a leader.

detriment N. harm; damage. Your acceptance of her support will ultimately prove to be a *detriment* rather than an aid to your cause.

deviate V. turn away from. Do not *deviate* from the truth.

devious ADJ. going astray; erratic. Your *devious* behavior in this matter puzzles me since you are usually direct and straightforward.

devoid ADJ. lacking. He was *devoid* of any personal desire for gain in his endeavor to secure improvement in the community.

devolve V. deputize; pass to others. It *devolved* upon us, the survivors, to arrange peace terms with the enemy.

devotee N. enthusiastic follower. A *devotee* of the opera, he bought season tickets every year.

devout ADJ. pious. The *devout* man prayed daily.

dexterous ADJ. skillful. The magician was so *dexterous* that we could not follow him as he performed his tricks.

diabolical ADJ. devilish. This scheme is so *diabolical* that I must reject it.

diadem N. crown. The king's *diadem* was on display at the museum.

dialectic N. art of debate. I am not skilled in *dialectic* and, therefore, cannot answer your arguments as forcefully as I wish.

diaphanous ADJ. sheer; transparent. They admired her *diaphanous* and colorful dress.

diatribe N. bitter scolding; invective. During the lengthy *diatribe* delivered by his opponent he remained calm and self-controlled.

dichotomy N. branching into two parts. The *dichotomy* of our legislative system provides us with many safeguards.

dictum N. authoritative and weighty statement. She repeated the statement as though it were the *dictum* of the most expert worker in the group.

didactic ADJ. teaching; instructional. The *didactic* qualities of his poetry overshadow its literary qualities; the lesson he teaches is more memorable than the lines.

diffidence N. shyness. You must overcome your *diffidence* if you intend to become a salesperson.

diffusion N. wordiness; spreading in all directions like a gas. Your composition suffers from a *diffusion* of ideas; try to be more compact. diffuse, ADJ. and V.

digression N. wandering away from the subject. His book was marred by his many *digressions.* digress, V.

dilapidated ADJ. ruined because of neglect. We felt that the *dilapidated* building needed several coats of paint. dilapidation, N.

dilate V. expand. In the dark, the pupils of your eyes *dilate.*

dilatory ADJ. delaying. Your *dilatory* tactics may compel me to cancel the contract.

dilemma N. problem; choice of two unsatisfactory alternatives. In this *dilemma,* he knew no one to whom he could turn for advice.

dilettante N. aimless follower of the arts; amateur; dabbler. He was not serious in his painting; he was rather a *dilettante.*

dilute V. make less concentrated; reduce in strength. She preferred her coffee *diluted* with milk.

diminution N. lessening; reduction in size. The blockaders hoped to achieve victory as soon as the *diminution* of the enemy's supplies became serious.

dint N. means; effort. By *dint* of much hard work, the volunteers were able to place the raging forest fire under control.

dipsomaniac N. one who has a strong craving for intoxicating liquor. The picture *The Lost Weekend* was an excellent portrayal of the struggles of the *dipsomaniac.*

dire ADJ. disastrous. People ignored her *dire* predictions of an approaching depression.

dirge N. lament with music. The funeral *dirge* stirred us to tears.

disabuse V. correct a false impression; undeceive. I will attempt to *disabuse* you of your impression of my client's guilt; I know he is innocent.

disapprobation N. disapproval; condemnation. The conservative father viewed his daughter's radical boyfriend with *disapprobation.*

disarray N. a disorderly or untidy state. After the New Year's party, the once orderly house was in total *disarray.*

disavowal N. denial; disclaiming. His *disavowal* of his part in the conspiracy was not believed by the jury.

disburse V. pay out. When you *disburse* money on the company's behalf, be sure to get a receipt.

discernible ADJ. distinguishable; perceivable. The ships in the harbor were not *discernible* in the fog.

discerning ADJ. mentally quick and observant; having insight. Because he was considered the most *discerning* member of the firm, he was assigned the most difficult cases.

disclaim V. disown; renounce claim to. If I grant you this privilege, will you *disclaim* all other rights?

discomfit V. put to rout; defeat; disconcert. This ruse will *discomfit* the enemy. discomfiture, N.

disconcert V: confuse; upset; embarrass. The lawyer was *disconcerted* by the evidence produced by her adversary.

disconsolate ADJ. sad. The death of his wife left him *disconsolate.*

discordant ADJ. inharmonious; conflicting. She tried to unite the *discordant* factions.

discount V. disregard. Be prepared to *discount* what he has to say about his ex-wife.

discrepancy N. lack of consistency; difference. The

police noticed some *discrepancies* in his description of the crime.

discrete ADJ. separate; unconnected. The universe is composed of *discrete* bodies.

discretion N. prudence; ability to adjust actions to circumstances. Use your *discretion* in this matter.

discrimination N. ability to see differences; prejudice. They feared he lacked sufficient *discrimination* to judge complex works of modern art.

discursive ADJ. digressing; rambling. They were annoyed and bored by her *discursive* remarks.

disdain V. treat with scorn or contempt. You make enemies of all you *disdain.* also N.

disgruntle V. make discontented. The passengers were *disgruntled* by the numerous delays.

TEST—WORD LIST 14—*Antonyms*

Each of the questions below consists of a word in capital letters, followed by five lettered words or phrases. Choose the lettered word or phrase that is most nearly opposite in meaning to the word in capital letters and write the letter of your choice on your answer paper.

196. DEROGATORY (A) roguish (B) immediate (C) opinionated (D) praising (E) conferred
197. DESECRATE (A) desist (B) integrate (C) confuse (D) intensify (E) consecrate
198. DESPICABLE (A) steering (B) worthy of esteem (C) inevitable (D) featureless (E) incapable
199. DESTITUTE (A) affluent (B) dazzling (C) stationary (D) characteristic (E) explanatory
200. DEVOID (A) latent (B) eschewed (C) full of (D) suspecting (E) evident
201. DEVOUT (A) quiet (B) dual (C) impious (D) straightforward (E) wrong
202. DIABOLICAL (A) mischievous (B) lavish (C) seraphic (D) azure (E) red
203. DIATRIBE (A) mass (B) range (C) eulogy (D) elegy (E) starvation
204. DIFFIDENCE (A) sharpness (B) boldness (C) malcontent (D) dialogue (E) catalog
205. DILATE (A) procrastinate (B) contract (C) conclude (D) participate (E) divert
206. DILATORY (A) narrowing (B) prompt (C) enlarging (D) portentous (E) sour
207. DIMINUTION (A) expectation (B) context (C) validity (D) appreciation (E) difficulty
208. DIPSOMANIAC (A) realist (B) thief (C) teetotaller (D) pyromaniac (E) swimmer
209. DISABUSE (A) crash (B) violate (C) renege (D) control (E) deceive
210. DISCONSOLATE (A) examining (B) thankful (C) theatrical (D) joyous (E) prominent

---

WORD LIST 15 dishabille - duplicity

dishabille N. in a state of undress. Because he was certain that he would have no visitors, he lounged around the house in a state of *dishabille,* wearing only his pajamas and a pair of old bedroom slippers.

disheartened ADJ. lacking courage and hope. His failure to pass the bar exam *disheartened* him.

disheveled ADJ. untidy. Your *disheveled* appearance will hurt your chances in this interview.

disingenuous ADJ. not naive; sophisticated. Although he was young, his remarks indicated that he was *disingenuous.*

disinter V. dig up; unearth. They *disinterred* the body and held an autopsy.

disinterested ADJ. unprejudiced. The only *disinterested* person in the room was the judge.

disjointed ADJ. disconnected. His remarks were so *disjointed* that we could not follow his reasoning.

dismantle V. take apart. When the show closed, they *dismantled* the scenery before storing it.

dismember V. cut into small parts. When the Austrian Empire was *dismembered,* several new countries were established.

disparage V. belittle. Do not *disparage* anyone's contribution; these little gifts add up to large sums.

disparate ADJ. basically different; unrelated. It is difficult, if not impossible, to organize these *disparate* elements into a coherent whole.

disparity N. difference; condition of inequality. The *disparity* in their ages made no difference at all.

dispassionate ADJ. calm; impartial. In a *dispassionate* analysis of the problem, he carefully examined the causes of the conflict and proceeded to suggest suitable remedies.

dispersion N. scattering. The *dispersion* of this group throughout the world may be explained by their expulsion from their homeland.

dispirited ADJ. lacking in spirit. The coach used all the tricks at his command to buoy up the enthusiasm of his team, which had become *dispirited* at the loss of the star player.

disport V. amuse. The popularity of Florida as a winter resort is constantly increasing; each year, thousands more *disport* themselves at Miami and Palm Beach.

disputatious ADJ. argumentative; fond of argument. People avoided discussing contemporary problems with him because of his *disputatious* manner.

disquisition N. a formal systematic inquiry; an explanation of the results of a formal inquiry. In his *disquisition,* he outlined the steps he had taken in reaching his conclusions.

dissection N. analysis; cutting apart in order to examine. The *dissection* of frogs in the laboratory is particularly unpleasant to some students.

dissemble V. disguise; pretend. Even though you are trying to *dissemble* your motive in joining this group, we can see through your pretense.

disseminate V. scatter (like seeds). The invention of the radio has helped propagandists to *disseminate* their favorite doctrines very easily.

dissertation N. formal essay. In order to earn a graduate degree from many of our universities, a candidate is frequently required to prepare a *dissertation* on some scholarly subject.

dissimulate V. pretend; conceal by feigning. She tried to *dissimulate* her grief by her gay attitude.

dissipate V. squander. The young man quickly *dissipated* his inheritance.

dissolute ADJ. loose in morals. The *dissolute* life led by these people is indeed shocking.

dissonance N. discord. Some contemporary musicians deliberately use *dissonance* to achieve certain effects.

dissuade V. advise against. He could not *dissuade* his friend from joining the conspirators.

dissuasion N. advice against. All his powers of *dissuasion* were useless.

distaff ADJ. female. His ancestors on the *distaff* side were equally as famous as his father's progenitors; his mother's father and grandfather were both famous judges.

distend V. expand; swell out. I can tell when he is under stress by the way the veins *distend* on his forehead.

distortion N. twisting out of shape. It is difficult to believe the newspaper accounts of this event because of the *distortions* and exaggerations written by the reporters.

distrait ADJ. absentminded. Because of his concentration on the problem, the professor often appeared *distrait* and unconcerned about routine.

distraught ADJ. upset; distracted by anxiety. The *distraught* parents searched the ravine for their lost child.

diurnal ADJ. daily. A farmer cannot neglect his *diurnal* tasks at any time; cows, for example, must be milked regularly.

diva N. operatic singer; prima donna. Although world famous as a *diva,* she did not indulge in fits of temperament.

diverge V. vary; go in different directions from the same point. The spokes of the wheel *diverge* from the hub.

divers ADJ. several; differing. We could hear *divers* opinions of his ability.

diverse ADJ. differing in some characteristics; various. There are *diverse* ways of approaching this problem.

diversity N. variety; dissimilitude. The *diversity* of colleges in this country indicates that many levels of ability are being cared for.

divest V. strip; deprive. He was *divested* of his power to act.

divination N. foreseeing the future with aid of magic. I base my opinions not on any special gift of *divination* but on the laws of probability.

divulge V. reveal. I will not tell you this news because I am sure you will *divulge* it prematurely.

docile ADJ. obedient; easily managed. As *docile* as he seems today, that old lion was once a ferocious, snarling beast.

docket N. program as for trial; book where such entries are made. The case of Smith vs. Jones was entered in the *docket* for July 15. also V.

doddering ADJ. shaky; infirm from old age. Although he is not as yet a *doddering* and senile old man, his ideas and opinions no longer can merit the respect we gave them years ago.

doff V. take off. He *doffed* his hat to the lady.

doggerel N. poor verse. Although we find occasional snatches of genuine poetry in her work, most of her writing is mere *doggerel.*

dogmatic ADJ. positive; arbitrary. Do not be so *dogmatic* about that statement; it can be easily refuted.

doldrums N. blues; listlessness; slack period. Once the excitement of meeting her deadline was over, she found herself in the *doldrums.*

dolorous ADJ. sorrowful. He found the *dolorous* lamentations of the bereaved family emotionally disturbing and he left as quickly as he could.

dolt N. stupid person. I thought I was talking to a mature audience; instead, I find myself addressing a pack of *dolts* and idiots.

domicile N. home. Although his legal *domicile* was in New York City, his work kept him away from his residence for many years. also V.

domineer V. rule over tyrannically. Students prefer teachers who guide, not ones who *domineer.*

dormant ADJ. sleeping; lethargic; torpid. Sometimes *dormant* talents in our friends surprise those of us who never realized how gifted our acquaintances really are. dormancy, N.

dorsal ADJ. relating to the back of an animal. A shark may be identified by its *dorsal* fin, which projects above the surface of the ocean.

dotage N. senility. In his *dotage,* the old man bored us with long tales of events in his childhood.

doughty ADJ. courageous. Many folk tales have sprung up about this *doughty* pioneer who opened up the New World for his followers.

dour ADJ. sullen; stubborn. The man was *dour* and taciturn.

douse V. plunge into water; drench; extinguish. They *doused* each other with hoses and water balloons.

dowdy ADJ. slovenly; untidy. She tried to change her *dowdy* image by buying a new fashionable wardrobe.

dregs N. sediment; worthless residue. The *dregs* of society may be observed in this slum area of the city.

droll ADJ. queer and amusing. He was a popular guest because his *droll* anecdotes were always amusing.

dross N. waste matter; worthless impurities. Many methods have been devised to separate the valuable metal from the *dross.*

drone N. idle person; male bee. Content to let his wife support him, the would-be writer was in reality nothing but a *drone.*

drone V. talk dully; buzz or murmur like a bee. On a gorgeous day, who wants to be stuck in a classroom listening to the teacher *drone.*

drudgery N. menial work. Cinderella's fairy godmother rescued her from a life of *drudgery.*

dubious ADJ. doubtful. He has the *dubious* distinction of being the lowest man in his class.

duenna N. attendant of young female; chaperone. Their romance could not flourish because of the presence of her *duenna.*

dulcet ADJ. sweet sounding. The *dulcet* sounds of the birds at dawn were soon drowned out by the roar of traffic passing our motel.

duplicity N. double-dealing; hypocrisy. People were shocked and dismayed when they learned of his *duplicity* in this affair for he had always seemed honest and straightforward.

TEST—WORD LIST 15—*Synonyms and Antonyms*

Each of the following questions consists of a word in capital letters, followed by five lettered words or phrases. Choose the lettered word or phrase which is most nearly similar or the opposite of the word in capital letters and write the letter of your choice on your answer paper.

211. DISINGENUOUS (A) uncomfortable (B) eventual (C) naive (D) complex (E) enthusiastic
212. DISINTERESTED (A) prejudiced (B) horrendous (C) affected (D) arbitrary (E) bored
213. DISJOINTED (A) satisfied (B) carved (C) understood (D) connected (E) evicted
214. DISPARITY (A) resonance (B) elocution (C) relief (D) difference (E) symbolism
215. DISPASSIONATE (A) sensual (B) immoral (C) inhibited (D) impartial (E) scientific
216. DISPIRITED (A) current (B) dented (C) drooping (D) removed (E) dallying
217. DISSIPATE (A) economize (B) clean (C) accept (D) anticipate (E) withdraw
218. DISTEND (A) bloat (B) adjust (C) exist (D) materialize (E) finish
219. DISTRAIT (A) clever (B) industrial (C) absentminded (D) narrow (E) crooked
220. DIVULGE (A) look (B) refuse (C) deride (D) reveal (E) harm
221. DOFF (A) withdraw (B) take off (C) remain (D) control (E) start
222. DOGMATIC (A) benign (B) canine (C) impatient (D) petulant (E) arbitrary
223. DOTAGE (A) senility (B) silence (C) sensitivity (D) interest (E) generosity
224. DOUR (A) sullen (B) ornamental (C) grizzled (D) lacking speech (E) international
225. DROLL (A) rotund (B) amusing (C) fearsome (D) tiny (E) strange

WORD LIST 16 **durance - encroachment**

durance N. restraint; imprisonment. The lecturer spoke of a "*durance* vile" to describe his years in the prison camp.

duress N. forcible restraint, especially unlawfully. The hostages were held under *duress* until the prisoners' demands were met.

dwindle V. shrink; reduce. The food in the life boat gradually *dwindled* away to nothing; in the end, they ate the ship's cook.

dynamic ADJ. active; efficient. A *dynamic* government is necessary to meet the demands of a changing society.

dyspeptic ADJ. suffering from indigestion. All the talk about women's liberation made him feel *dyspeptic.* dyspepsia, N.

earthy ADJ. unrefined; coarse. His *earthy* remarks often embarrassed the women in his audience.

ebb V. recede; lessen. Mrs. Dalloway sat on the beach and watched the tide *ebb.* also N.

ebullient ADJ. showing excitement; overflowing with enthusiasm. His *ebullient* nature could not be repressed; he was always laughing and gay. ebullience, N.

eccentricity N. oddity; idiosyncrasy. Some of his friends tried to account for his rudeness to strangers as the *eccentricity* of genius. eccentric, ADJ.

ecclesiastic ADJ. pertaining to the church. The minister donned his *ecclesiastic* garb and walked to the pulpit. also N.

eclat N. brilliance; glory. To the delight of his audience, he completed his task with *eclat* and consummate ease.

eclecticism N. selection of elements from various sets of opinions or systems. The *eclecticism* of the group was demonstrated by their adoption of principles and practices of many forms of government.

eclipse V. darken; extinguish; surpass. The new stock market high *eclipsed* the previous record set in 1985.

ecologist N. a person concerned with the interrelationship between living organisms and their environment. The *ecologist* was concerned that the new dam would upset the natural balance of the creatures living in Glen Canyon.

ecstasy N. rapture; joy; any overpowering emotion. The announcement that the war had ended brought on an *ecstasy* of joy that resulted in many uncontrolled celebrations.

edify V. instruct; correct morally. Although his purpose was to *edify* and not to entertain his audience, many of his listeners were amused and not enlightened.

educe V. draw forth; elicit. She could not *educe* a principle that would encompass all the data.

eerie ADJ. weird. In that *eerie* setting, it was easy to believe in ghosts and other supernatural beings.

efface V. rub out. The coin had been handled so many times that its date had been *effaced.*

effectual ADJ. efficient. If we are to succeed in this endeavor, we must seek *effectual* means of securing our goals.

effeminate ADJ. having womanly traits. His voice was high-pitched and *effeminate.*

effervesce V. bubble over; show excitement. Some of us cannot stand the way she *effervesces* over trifles.

effete ADJ. worn out; exhausted; barren. The literature of the age reflected the *effete* condition of the writers; no new ideas were forthcoming.

efficacy N. power to produce desired effect. The *efficacy* of this drug depends on the regularity of the dosage.

effigy N. dummy. The mob showed its irritation by hanging the judge in *effigy.*

efflorescent ADJ. flowering. Greenhouse gardeners are concerned with the coinciding of the plants' *efflorescent* period with certain holidays.

effluvium N. noxious smell. Air pollution has become a serious problem in our major cities; the *effluvium* and the poisons in the air are hazards to life.

effrontery N. shameless boldness. She had the *effrontery* to insult the guest.

effulgent ADJ. brilliantly radiant. The *effulgent* rays of the rising sun lit the sky.

effusion N. pouring forth. The critics objected to her literary *effusion* because it was too flowery.

effusive ADJ. pouring forth; gushing. Her *effusive* manner of greeting her friends finally began to irritate them.

egoism N. excessive interest in one's self; belief that one should be interested in one's self rather than in others. His *egoism* prevented him from seeing the needs of his colleagues.

egotism N. conceit; vanity. We found her *egotism* unwarranted and irritating.

egregious ADJ. gross; shocking. She was an *egregious* liar.

egress N. exit. Barnum's sign "To the *Egress*" fooled many people who thought they were going to see an animal and instead found themselves in the street.

ejaculation N. exclamation. He could not repress an *ejaculation* of surprise when he heard the news.

elation N. a rise in spirits; exaltation. She felt no *elation* at finding the purse.

elegiacal ADJ. like an elegy; mournful. The essay on the lost crew was *elegiacal* in mood. elegy, N.

elicit V. draw out by discussion. The detectives tried to *elicit* where he had hidden his loot.

elixir N. cure-all; something invigorating. The news of her chance to go abroad acted on her like an *elixir.*

eloquence N. expressiveness; persuasive speech. The

crowds were stirred by Martin Luther King's *eloquence.*

elucidate V. explain; enlighten. He was called upon to *elucidate* the disputed points in his article.

elusive ADJ. evasive; baffling; hard to grasp. His *elusive* dreams of wealth were costly to those of his friends who supported him financially. elude, V.

elusory ADJ. tending to deceive expectations; elusive. He argued that the project was an *elusory* one and would bring disappointment to all.

elysian ADJ. relating to paradise; blissful. An afternoon sail on the bay was for her an *elysian* journey.

emaciated ADJ. thin and wasted. His long period of starvation had left him *emaciated.*

emanate V. issue forth. A strong odor of sulphur *emanated* from the spring.

emancipate V. set free. At first, the attempts of the Abolitionists to *emancipate* the slaves were unpopular in New England as well as in the South.

embellish V. adorn. His handwriting was *embellished* with flourishes.

embezzlement N. stealing. The bank teller confessed his *embezzlement* of the funds.

emblazon V. deck in brilliant colors. *Emblazoned* on his shield was his family coat of arms.

embroil V. throw into confusion; involve in strife; entangle. He became *embroiled* in the heated discussion when he tried to arbitrate the dispute.

embryonic ADJ. undeveloped; rudimentary. The evil of class and race hatred must be eliminated while it is still in an *embryonic* state; otherwise, it may grow to dangerous proportions.

emend V. correct; correct by a critic. The critic *emended* the book by selecting the passages which he thought most appropriate to the text.

emendation N. correction of errors; improvement. Please initial all the *emendations* you have made in this contract.

emeritus ADJ. retired but retained in an honorary capacity. As professor *emeritus,* he retained all his honors without having to meet the obligations of daily assignments.

emetic N. substance causing vomiting. The use of an *emetic* like mustard is useful in cases of poisoning.

eminent ADJ. high; lofty. After his appointment to this *eminent* position, he seldom had time for his former friends.

emollient N. soothing or softening remedy. He applied an *emollient* to the inflamed area. Also ADJ.

emolument N. salary; compensation. In addition to the *emolument* this position offers, you must consider the social prestige it carries with it.

empirical ADJ. based on experience. He distrusted hunches and intuitive flashes; he placed his reliance entirely on *empirical* data.

empyreal ADJ. celestial; fiery. The scientific advances of the twentieth century have enabled man to invade the *empyreal* realm of the eagle.

emulate V. rival; imitate. As long as our political leaders *emulate* the virtues of the great leaders of this country, we shall flourish.

enamored ADJ. in love. Narcissus became *enamored* of his own beauty.

embed V. enclose; place in something. Tales of actual historical figures like King Alfred have become *embedded* in legends.

enclave N. territory enclosed within an alien land. The Vatican is an independent *enclave* in Italy.

encomiastic ADJ. praising; eulogistic. Some critics believe that his *encomiastic* statements about Napoleon were inspired by his desire for material advancement rather than by an honest belief in the Emperor's genius. encomium, N.

encomium N. praise; eulogy. He was sickened by the *encomiums* and panegyrics expressed by speakers who had previously been among the first to vilify the man they were now honoring.

encompass V. surround. Although we were *encompassed* by enemy forces, we were cheerful for we were well stocked and could withstand a siege until our allies joined us.

encroachment N. gradual intrusion. The *encroachment* of the factories upon the neighborhood lowered the value of the real estate.

TEST—WORD LIST 16—*Synonyms*

Each of the questions below consists of a word in capital letters, followed by five lettered words or phrases. Choose the lettered word or phrase that is most nearly similar in meaning to the word in capital letters and write the letter of your choice on your answer paper.

226. DWINDLE (A) blow (B) inhabit (C) spin (D) lessen (E) combine
227. ECSTASY (A) joy (B) speed (C) treasure (D) warmth (E) lack
228. EDIFY (A) mystify (B) suffice (C) improve (D) erect (E) entertain
229. EFFACE (A) countenance (B) encourage (C) recognize (D) blackball (E) rub out
230. EFFIGY (A) requisition (B) organ (C) charge (D) accordion (E) dummy

231. EGREGIOUS (A) pious (B) shocking (C) anxious (D) sociable (E) gloomy
232. EGRESS (A) entrance (B) bird (C) exit (D) double (E) progress
233. ELATED (A) debased (B) respectful (C) drooping (D) gay (E) charitable
234. ELUSIVE (A) deadly (B) eloping (C) evasive (D) simple (E) petrified
235. EMACIATED (A) garrulous (B) primeval (C) vigorous (D) disparate (E) thin
236. EMBELLISH (A) doff (B) don (C) balance (D) adorn (E) equalize
237. EMEND (A) cherish (B) repose (C) correct (D) assure (E) worry
238. EMENDATION (A) correction (B) interpretation (C) exhumation (D) inquiry (E) fault
239. EMINENT (A) purposeful (B) high (C) delectable (D) curious (E) urgent
240. EMANCIPATE (A) set free (B) take back (C) make worse (D) embolden (E) run away

---

WORD LIST 17 encumber - eulogistic

encumber V. burden. Some people *encumber* themselves with too much luggage when they take short trips.

endearment N. fond statement. Your gifts and *endearments* cannot make me forget your earlier insolence.

endemic ADJ. prevailing among a specific group of people or in a specific area or country. This disease is *endemic* in this part of the world; more than 80 percent of the population are at one time or another affected by it.

endive N. species of leafy plant used in salads. The salad contained *endive* in addition to the ingredients she usually used.

endue V. provide with some quality; endow. He was *endued* with a lion's courage.

energize V. invigorate; make forceful and active. We shall have to re-*energize* our activities by getting new members to carry on.

enervate V. weaken. The hot days of August are *enervating.*

engender V. cause; produce. This editorial will *engender* racial intolerance unless it is denounced.

engross V. occupy fully. John was so *engrossed* in his studies that he did not hear his mother call.

enhance V. advance; improve. Your chances for promotion in this department will be *enhanced* if you take some more courses in evening school.

enigma N. puzzle. Despite all attempts to decipher the code, it remained an *enigma.* enigmatic, ADJ.

enigmatic ADJ. obscure; puzzling. Many have sought to fathom the *enigmatic* smile of the *Mona Lisa.*

enjoin V. command; order; forbid. The owners of the company asked the court to *enjoin* the union from picketing the plant.

ennui N. boredom. The monotonous routine of hospital life induced a feeling of *ennui* which made him moody and irritable.

enormity N. hugeness (in a bad sense). He did not realize the *enormity* of his crime until he saw what suffering he had caused.

enrapture V. please intensely. The audience was *enraptured* by the freshness of the voices and the excellent orchestration.

ensconce V. settle comfortably. The parents thought that their children were *ensconced* safely in the private school and decided to leave for Europe.

ensue V. follow. The evils that *ensued* were the direct result of the miscalculations of the leaders.

enthrall V. capture; enslave. From the moment he saw her picture, he was *enthralled* by her beauty.

entice V. lure; attract; tempt. She always tried to *entice* her baby brother into mischief.

entity N. real being. As soon as the Charter was adopted, the United Nations became an *entity* and had to be considered as a factor in world diplomacy.

entomology N. study of insects. I found *entomology* the least interesting part of my course in biology; studying insects bored me.

entrance V. put under a spell; carry away with emotion. Shafts of sunlight on a wall could *entrance* her and leave her spellbound.

entreat V. plead; ask earnestly. She *entreated* her father to let her stay out till midnight.

entree N. entrance; a way in. Because of his wealth and social position, he had *entree* into the most exclusive circles.

entrepreneur N. businessman; contractor. Opponents of our present tax program argue that it discourages *entrepreneurs* from trying new fields of business activity.

enunciate V. speak distinctly. How will people understand you if you do not *enunciate?*

environ V. enclose; surround. In medieval days, Paris was *environed* by a wall. environs, N.

ephemeral ADJ. short-lived; fleeting. The mayfly is an *ephemeral* creature.

epicure N. connoisseur of food and drink. *Epicures* frequent this restaurant because it features exotic wines and dishes.

epicurean N. person who devotes himself to pleasures

of the senses, especially to food. This restaurant is famous for its menu, which can cater to the most exotic whim of the *epicurean.* also ADJ.

epigram N. witty thought or saying, usually short. Poor Richard's *epigrams* made Benjamin Franklin famous.

epilogue N. short speech at conclusion of dramatic work. The audience was so disappointed in the play that many did not remain to hear the *epilogue.*

epitaph N. inscription in memory of a dead person. In his will, he dictated the *epitaph* he wanted placed on his tombstone.

epithet N. descriptive word or phrase. Homer's writings were featured by the use of such *epithets* as "rosy-fingered dawn."

epitome N. summary; concise abstract. This final book is the *epitome* of all his previous books. epitomize, V.

epoch N. period of time. The glacial *epoch* lasted for thousands of years.

equable ADJ. tranquil; steady; uniform. After the hot summers and cold winters of New England, he found the climate of the West Indies *equable* and pleasant.

equanimity N. calmness of temperament. In his later years, he could look upon the foolishness of the world with *equanimity* and humor.

equestrian N. rider on horseback. These paths in the park are reserved for *equestrians* and their steeds. also ADJ.

equilibrium N. balance. After the divorce, he needed some time to regain his *equilibrium.*

equine ADJ. resembling a horse. His long, bony face had an *equine* look to it.

equinox N. period of equal days and nights; the beginning of Spring and Autumn. The vernal *equinox* is usually marked by heavy rainstorms.

equipage N. horse-drawn carriage. The *equipage* drew up before the inn.

equipoise N. balance; balancing force; equilibrium. The high wire acrobat used his pole as an *equipoise* to overcome the swaying caused by the wind.

equitable ADJ. fair; impartial. I am seeking an *equitable* solution to this dispute, one which will be fair and acceptable to both sides.

equity N. fairness; justice. Our courts guarantee *equity* to all.

equivocal ADJ. doubtful; ambiguous. Macbeth was misled by the *equivocal* statements of the witches.

equivocate V. lie; mislead; attempt to conceal the truth. The audience saw through his attempts to *equivocate* on the subject under discussion and ridiculed his remarks.

erode V. eat away. The limestone was *eroded* by the dripping water.

erotic ADJ. pertaining to passionate love. The *erotic* passages in this novel should be removed as they are merely pornographic.

errant ADJ. wandering. Many a charming tale has been written about the knights-*errant* who helped the weak and punished the guilty during the Age of Chivalry.

erratic ADJ. odd; unpredictable. Investors become anxious when the stock market appears *erratic.*

erroneous ADJ. mistaken; wrong. I thought my answer was correct, but it was *erroneous.*

erudite ADJ. learned; scholarly. His *erudite* writing was difficult to read because of the many allusions which were unfamiliar to most readers. erudition, N.

erudition N. high degree of knowledge and learning. Although they respected his *erudition,* the populace refused to listen to his words of caution and turned to less learned leaders.

escapade N. prank; flighty conduct. The headmaster could not regard this latest *escapade* as a boyish joke and expelled the young man.

eschew V. avoid. He tried to *eschew* all display of temper.

escutcheon N. shield-shaped surface on which coat of arms is placed. His traitorous acts placed a shameful blot on the family *escutcheon*.

esoteric ADJ. known only to the chosen few. Those students who had access to his *esoteric* discussions were impressed by the scope of his thinking.

espionage N. spying. In order to maintain its power, the government developed a system of *espionage* which penetrated every household.

espouse V. adopt; support. She was always ready to *espouse* a worthy cause.

esprit de corps N. comradeship; spirit. West Point cadets are proud of their *esprit de corps.*

estranged ADJ. separated. The *estranged* wife sought a divorce.

ethereal ADJ. light; heavenly; fine. Visitors were impressed by her *ethereal* beauty, her delicate charm.

ethnic ADJ. relating to races. Intolerance between *ethnic* groups is deplorable and usually is based on lack of information.

ethnology N. study of man. Sociology is one aspect of the science of *ethnology.*

etymology N. study of word parts. A knowledge of *etymology* can help you on many tests.

eugenic ADJ. pertaining to the improvement of race. It is easier to apply *eugenic* principles to the raising of race-horses or prize cattle than to the development of human beings.

eulogistic ADJ. praising. To everyone's surprise, the speech was *eulogistic* rather than critical in tone.

TEST—WORD LIST 17—*Antonyms*

Each of the questions below consists of a word in capital letters, followed by five lettered words or phrases. Choose the lettered word or phrase that is most nearly opposite in meaning to the word in capital letters and write the letter of your choice on your answer paper.

241. ENERVATE (A) strengthen (B) sputter (C) arrange (D) scrutinize (E) agree
242. ENHANCE (A) degrade (B) doubt (C) scuff (D) gasp (E) agree
243. ENNUI (A) hate (B) excitement (C) seriousness (D) humility (E) kindness
244. ENUNCIATE (A) pray (B) request (C) deliver (D) wait (E) mumble
245. EPHEMERAL (A) sensuous (B) passing (C) popular (D) distasteful (E) eternal
246. EQUABLE (A) flat (B) decisive (C) stormy (D) rough (E) scanty
247. EQUANIMITY (A) agitation (B) stirring (C) volume (D) identity (E) luster
248. EQUILIBRIUM (A) imbalance (B) peace (C) inequity (D) directness (E) urgency
249. EQUITABLE (A) able to leave (B) able to learn (C) unfair (D) preferable (E) rough
250. EQUIVOCAL (A) mistaken (B) quaint (C) azure (D) clear (E) universal
251. ERRATIC (A) unromantic (B) free (C) popular (D) steady (E) unknown
252. ERRONEOUS (A) accurate (B) dignified (C) curious (D) abrupt (E) round
253. ERUDITE (A) professorial (B) stately (C) short (D) unknown (E) ignorant
254. ETHEREAL (A) long-lasting (B) earthy (C) ill (D) critical (E) false
255. EULOGISTIC (A) pretty (B) critical (C) brief (D) stern (E) free

---

WORD LIST 18 **eulogy - faculty**

eulogy N. praise. All the *eulogies* of his friends could not remove the sting of the calumny heaped upon him by his enemies.

euphemism N. mild expression in place of an unpleasant one. The expression "He passed away" is a *euphemism* for "He died."

euphonious ADJ. pleasing in sound. Italian and Spanish are *euphonious* languages and therefore easily sung.

euthanasia N. mercy-killing. Many people support *euthanasia* for terminally-ill patients who wish to die.

evanescent ADJ. fleeting; vanishing. For a brief moment, the entire skyline was bathed in an orange-red hue in the *evanescent* rays of the sunset.

evasive ADJ. not frank; eluding. Your *evasive* answers convinced the judge that you were withholding important evidence. evade, V.

evince V. show clearly. When he tried to answer the questions, he *evinced* his ignorance of the subject matter.

eviscerate V. disembowel; remove entrails. The medicine man *eviscerated* the animal and offered the entrails to the angry gods.

evoke V. call forth. He *evoked* much criticism by his hostile manner.

ewer N. water pitcher. The primitive conditions of the period were symbolized by the porcelain *ewer* and basin in the bedroom.

exacerbate V. worsen; embitter. This latest arrest will *exacerbate* the already existing discontent of the people and enrage them.

exaction N. exorbitant demand; extortion. The colonies rebelled against the *exactions* of the mother country.

exasperate V. vex. Johnny often *exasperates* his mother with his pranks.

exchequer N. treasury. He had been Chancellor of the *Exchequer* before his promotion to the high office he now holds.

excision N. act of cutting away. With the *excision* of the dead and dying limbs of this tree, you have not only improved its appearance but you have enhanced its chances of bearing fruit.

excoriate V. flay; abrade. These shoes are so ill-fitting that they will *excoriate* the feet and create blisters.

exculpate V. clear from blame. He was *exculpated* of the crime when the real criminal confessed.

execrable ADJ. very bad. The anecdote was in *execrable* taste.

execrate V. curse; express abhorrence for. The world *execrates* the memory of Hitler and hopes that genocide will never again be the policy of any nation.

exegesis N. explanation, especially of Biblical passages. I can follow your *exegesis* of this passage to a limited degree; some of your reasoning eludes me.

exemplary ADJ. serving as a model; outstanding. Her *exemplary* behavior was praised at Commencement.

exertion N. effort; expenditure of much physical work. The *exertion* spent in unscrewing the rusty bolt left her exhausted.

exhort V. urge. The evangelist will *exhort* all sinners in his audience to reform.

exhume V. dig out of the ground; remove from a grave. Because of the rumor that he had been poisoned, his body was *exhumed* in order that an autopsy might be performed.

exigency N. urgent situation. In this *exigency,* we must look for aid from our allies.

exiguous ADJ. small; minute. Grass grew there, an *exiguous* outcropping among the rocks.

exodus N. departure. The *exodus* from the hot and stuffy city was particularly noticeable on Friday evenings.

ex officio ADJ. by virtue of one's office. The Mayor was *ex officio* chairman of the committee that decided the annual tax rate. also ADV.

exonerate V. acquit; exculpate. I am sure this letter will *exonerate* you.

exorbitant ADJ. excessive. The people grumbled at his *exorbitant* prices but paid them because he had a monopoly.

exorcise V. drive out evil spirits. By incantation and prayer, the medicine man sought to *exorcise* the evil spirits which had taken possession of the young warrior.

exotic ADJ. not native; strange. Because of his *exotic* headdress, he was followed in the streets by small children who laughed at his strange appearance.

expatiate V. talk at length. At this time, please give us a brief resumé of your work; we shall permit you to *expatiate* later.

expatriate N. exile; someone who has withdrawn from his native land. Henry James was an American *expatriate* who settled in England.

expediency N. that which is advisable or practical. He was guided by *expediency* rather than by ethical considerations.

expedite V. hasten. We hope you will be able to *expedite* the delivery of our order.

expeditiously ADV. rapidly and efficiently. Please adjust this matter as *expeditiously* as possible as it is delaying important work.

expiate V. make amends for (a sin). He tried to *expiate* his crimes by a full confession to the authorities.

expletive N. interjection; profane oath. The sergeant's remarks were filled with *expletives* which reflected on the intelligence and character of the new recruits.

explicit ADJ. definite; open. Your remarks are *explicit;* no one can misinterpret them.

expostulation N. remonstrance. Despite the teacher's scoldings and *expostulations,* the class remained unruly.

expunge V. cancel; remove. If you behave, I will *expunge* this notation from your record.

expurgate V. clean; remove offensive parts of a book. The editors felt that certain passages in the book had to be *expurgated* before it could be used in the classroom.

extant ADJ. still in existence. Although the authorities suppressed the book, many copies are *extant* and may be purchased at exorbitant prices.

extemporaneous ADJ. not planned; impromptu. Because his *extemporaneous* remarks were misinterpreted, he decided to write all his speeches in advance.

extenuate V. weaken; mitigate. It is easier for us to *extenuate* our own shortcomings than those of others.

extirpate V. root up. We must *extirpate* and destroy this monstrous philosophy.

extol V. praise; glorify. The astronauts were *extolled* as the pioneers of the Space Age.

extort V. wring from; get money by threats, etc. The blackmailer *extorted* money from his victim.

extradition N. surrender of prisoner by one state to another. The lawyers opposed the *extradition* of their client on the grounds that for more than five years he had been a model citizen.

extraneous ADJ. not essential; external. Do not pad your paper with *extraneous* matters; stick to essential items only.

extricate V. free; disentangle. He found that he could not *extricate* himself from the trap.

extrinsic ADJ. external; not inherent; foreign. Do not be fooled by *extrinsic* causes. We must look for the intrinsic reason.

extrovert N. person interested mostly in external objects and actions. A good salesman is usually an *extrovert,* who likes to mingle with people.

extrude V. force or push out. Much pressure is required to *extrude* these plastics.

exuberant ADJ. abundant; effusive; lavish. His speeches were famous for his *exuberant* language and vivid imagery.

exude V. discharge; give forth. The maple syrup is obtained from the sap that *exudes* from the trees in early spring. exudation, N.

exult V. rejoice. We *exulted* when our team won the victory.

fabricate V. build; lie. If we pre*fabricate* the buildings in this project, we can reduce the cost considerably.

facade N. front of the building. The *facade* of the church had often been photographed by tourists.

facet N. small plane surface (of a gem); a side. The stonecutter decided to improve the rough diamond by providing it with several *facets.*

facetious ADJ. humorous; jocular. Your *facetious* remarks are not appropriate at this serious moment.

facile ADJ. easy; expert. Because he was a *facile* speaker, he never refused a request to address an organization.

facilitate V. make less difficult. He tried to *facilitate* matters at home by getting a part-time job.

facsimile N. copy. Many museums sell *facsimiles* of the works of art on display.

faction N. party; clique; dissension. The quarrels and bickering of the two small *factions* within the club disturbed the majority of the members.

factious ADJ. inclined to form factions; causing dissension. Your statement is *factious* and will upset the harmony that now exists.

factitious ADJ. artificial; sham. Hollywood actresses often create *factitious* tears by using glycerine.

factotum N. handyman; person who does all kinds of work. Although we had hired him as a messenger, we soon began to use him as a general *factotum* around the office.

faculty N. mental or bodily powers; teaching staff. As he grew old, he feared he might lose his *faculties.*

TEST—WORD LIST 18—*Antonyms*

Each of the questions below consists of a word in capital letters, followed by five lettered words or phrases. Choose the lettered word or phrase that is most nearly opposite in meaning to the word in capital letters and write the letter of your choice on your answer paper.

256. EUPHONIOUS (A) strident (B) lethargic (C) literary (D) significant (E) merry
257. EVASIVE (A) frank (B) correct (C) empty (D) fertile (E) watchful
258. EXASPERATE (A) confide (B) formalize (C) placate (D) betray (E) bargain
259. EXCORIATE (A) scandalize (B) encourage (C) avoid (D) praise (E) vanquish
260. EXCULPATE (A) blame (B) prevail (C) aquire (D) ravish (E) accumulate
261. EXECRABLE (A) innumerable (B) philosophic (C) physical (D) excellent (E) meditative
262. EXECRATE (A) disobey (B) enact (C) perform (D) acclaim (E) fidget
263. EXHUME (A) decipher (B) sadden (C) integrate (D) admit (E) inter
264. EXODUS (A) neglect (B) consent (C) entry (D) gain (E) rebuke
265. EXONERATE (A) forge (B) accuse (C) record (D) doctor (E) reimburse
266. EXORBITANT (A) moderate (B) partisan (C) military (D) barbaric (E) counterfeit
267. EXTEMPORANEOUS (A) rehearsed (B) hybrid (C) humiliating (D) statesmanlike (E) picturesque
268. EXTRANEOUS (A) modern (B) decisive (C) essential (D) effective (E) expressive
269. EXTRINSIC (A) reputable (B) inherent (C) swift (D) ambitious (E) cursory
270. EXTROVERT (A) clown (B) hero (C) ectomorph (D) neurotic (E) introvert

WORD LIST 19 **fain - flinch**

fain ADV. gladly. The knight said, "I would *fain* be your protector."

fallacious ADJ. misleading. Your reasoning must be *fallacious* because it leads to a ridiculous answer.

fallible ADJ. liable to err. I know I am *fallible,* but I feel confident that I am right this time.

fallow ADJ. plowed but not sowed; uncultivated. Farmers have learned that it is advisable to permit land to lie *fallow* every few years.

falter V. hesitate. When told to dive off the high board, she did not *falter.*

fanaticism N. excessive zeal. The leader of the group was held responsible even though he could not control the *fanaticism* of his followers.

fancied ADJ. imagined; unreal. You are resenting *fancied* insults. No one has ever said such things about you.

fancier N. breeder or dealer of animals. The dog *fancier* exhibited her prize collie at the annual Kennel Club show.

fanciful ADJ. whimsical; visionary. This is a *fanciful* scheme because it does not consider the facts.

fanfare N. call by bugles or trumpets. The exposition was opened with a *fanfare* of trumpets and the firing of cannon.

fantastic ADJ. unreal; grotesque; whimsical. Your fears are *fantastic* because no such animal as you have described exists.

farce N. broad comedy; mockery. Nothing went right; the entire interview degenerated into a *farce.* farcical, ADJ.

fastidious ADJ. difficult to please; squeamish. The waitresses disliked serving him dinner because of his very *fastidious* taste.

fatalism N. belief that events are determined by forces beyond one's control. With fatalism, he accepted the hardships which beset him. fatalistic, ADJ.

fathom V. comprehend; investigate. I find his motives impossible to *fathom.*

fatuous ADJ. foolish; inane. He is far too intelligent to utter such *fatuous* remarks.

fauna N. animals of a period or region. The scientist could visualize the *fauna* of the period by examining the skeletal remains and the fossils.

faux pas N. an error or slip (in manners or behavior). Your tactless remarks during dinner were a *faux pas.*

fawning ADJ. courting favor by cringing and flattering. She was constantly surrounded by a group of *fawning* admirers who hoped to win some favor.

fealty N. loyalty; faithfulness. The feudal lord demanded *fealty* of his vassals.

feasible ADJ. practical. This is an entirely *feasible* proposal. I suggest we adopt it.

febrile ADJ. feverish. In his *febrile* condition, he was subject to nightmares and hallucinations.

fecundity N. fertility; fruitfulness. The *fecundity* of his mind is illustrated by the many vivid images in his poems.

feign V. pretend. Lady Macbeth *feigned* illness in the courtyard.

feint N. trick; shift; sham blow. The boxer was fooled by his opponent's *feint* and dropped his guard. also V.

felicitous ADJ. apt; suitably expressed; well chosen. He was famous for his *felicitous* remarks and was called upon to serve as master-of-ceremonies at many a banquet.

fell ADJ. cruel; deadly. Henley writes of the "*fell* clutch of circumstance" in his poem "Invictus."

felon N. person convicted of a grave crime. A convicted felon loses the right to vote.

ferment N. agitation; commotion. The entire country was in a state of *ferment.*

ferret V. drive or hunt out of hiding. She *ferreted* out their secret.

fervent ADJ. ardent; hot. She felt that the *fervent* praise was excessive and somewhat undeserved.

fervid ADJ. ardent. Her *fervid* enthusiasm inspired all of us to undertake the dangerous mission.

fervor N. glowing ardor. Their kiss was full of the *fervor* of first love.

fester V. generate pus. When her finger began to *fester,* the doctor lanced it and removed the splinter which had caused the pus to form.

festive ADJ. joyous; celebratory. Their wedding in the park was a *festive* occasion.

fete V. honor at a festival. The returning hero was *feted* at a community supper and dance. also N.

fetid ADJ. malodorous. The neglected wound became *fetid.*

fetish N. object supposed to possess magical powers; an object of special devotion. The native wore a *fetish* around his neck toward off evil spirits.

fetter V. shackle. The prisoner was *fettered* to the wall.

fiasco N. total failure. Our ambitious venture ended in a *fiasco.*

fiat N. command. I cannot accept government by *fiat;* I feel that I must be consulted.

fickle ADJ. changeable; faithless. He discovered she was *fickle.*

fictitious ADJ. imaginary. Although this book purports to be a biography of George Washington, many of the incidents are *fictitious.*

fidelity N. loyalty. A dog's *fidelity* to its owner is one of the reasons why that animal is a favorite household pet.

fiduciary ADJ. pertaining to a position of trust. In his will, he stipulated that the bank act in a *fiduciary* capacity and manage his estate until his children became of age. also N.

figment N. invention; imaginary thing. That incident is a *figment* of your imagination.

filch V. steal. The boys *filched* apples from the fruit stand.

filial ADJ. pertaining to a son or daughter. Many children forget their *filial* obligations and disregard the wishes of their parents.

finale N. conclusion. It is not until we reach the *finale* of this play that we can understand the author's message.

finesse N. delicate skill. The *finesse* and adroitness of the surgeon impressed the observers in the operating room.

finicky ADJ. too particular; fussy. The old lady was *finicky* about her food.

finite ADJ. limited. It is difficult for humanity with its *finite* existence to grasp the infinite.

firebrand N. hothead; troublemaker. The police tried to keep track of all the local *firebrands* when the President came to town.

fissure N. crevice. The mountain climbers secured footholds in tiny *fissures* in the rock.

fitful ADJ. spasmodic; intermittent. After several *fitful* attempts, he decided to postpone the start of the project until he felt more energetic.

flaccid ADJ. flabby. His sedentary life had left him with *flaccid* muscles.

flagellate V. flog; whip. The Romans used to *flagellate* criminals with a whip that had three knotted strands.

flagging ADJ. weak; drooping. The encouraging cheers of the crowd lifted the team's *flagging* spirits.

flagrant ADJ. conspicuously wicked. We cannot condone such *flagrant* violations of the rules.

flail V. thresh grain by hand; strike or slap. In medieval times, warriors *flailed* their foe with a metal ball attached to a handle.

flair N. talent. She has an uncanny *flair* for discovering new artists before the public has become aware of their existence.

flamboyant ADJ. ornate. Modern architecture has discarded the *flamboyant* trimming on buildings and emphasizes simplicity of line.

flaunt V. display ostentatiously. She is not one of those actresses who *flaunt* their physical charms; she can act.

flay V. strip off skin; plunder. The criminal was condemned to be *flayed* alive.

fleck V. spot. Her cheeks, *flecked* with tears, were testimony to the hours of weeping.

fledgling ADJ. inexperienced. While it is necessary to provide these *fledgling* poets with an opportunity to present their work, it is not essential that we admire everything they write. also N.

fleece N. wool coat of a sheep. They shear sheep of their *fleece,* which they then comb into separate strands of wool.

fleece V. rob; plunder. The tricksters *fleeced* him of his inheritance.

flick N. light stroke as with a whip. The horse needed no encouragement; only one *flick* of the whip was all the jockey had to apply to get the animal to run at top speed.

flinch V. hesitate; shrink. He did not *flinch* in the face of danger but fought back bravely.

TEST—WORD LIST 19—*Synonyms and Antonyms*

Each of the following questions consists of a word in capital letters, followed by five lettered words or phrases. Choose the lettered word or phrase which is most nearly similar or the opposite of the word in capital letters and write the letter of your choice on your answer paper.

271. FANCIFUL (A) imaginative (B) knowing (C) elaborate (D) quick (E) lusty
272. FATUOUS (A) fatal (B) natal (C) terrible (D) sensible (E) tolerable
273. FEASIBLE (A) theoretical (B) impatient (C) constant (D) present (E) impractical
274. FECUNDITY (A) prophecy (B) futility (C) fruitfulness (D) need (E) dormancy
275. FEIGN (A) deserve (B) condemn (C) condone (D) attend (E) pretend
276. FELL (A) propitious (B) illiterate (C) catastrophic (D) futile (E) inherent
277. FERMENT (A) stir up (B) fill (C) ferret (D) mutilate (E) banish
278. FIASCO (A) cameo (B) mansion (C) pollution (D) success (E) gamble
279. FICKLE (A) fallacious (B) tolerant (C) loyal (D) hungry (E) stupid
280. FILCH (A) milk (B) purloin (C) itch (D) cancel (E) resent
281. FINITE (A) bounded (B) established (C) affirmative (D) massive (E) finicky
282. FLAIL (A) succeed (B) harvest (C) knife (D) strike (E) resent
283. FLAIR (A) conflagration (B) inspiration (C) bent (D) egregiousness (E) magnitude
284. FLAMBOYANT (A) old-fashioned (B) restrained (C) impulsive (D) cognizant (E) eloquent
285. FLEDGLING (A) weaving (B) bobbing (C) beginning (D) studying (E) flaying

---

WORD LIST 20 flippancy - gaff

flippancy N. trifling gaiety. Your *flippancy* at this serious moment is offensive.

floe N. mass of floating ice. The ship made slow progress as it battered its way through the ice *floes.*

flora N. plants of a region or era. Because she was a botanist, she spent most of her time studying the *flora* of the desert.

florid ADJ. flowery; ruddy. His complexion was even more *florid* than usual because of his anger.

flotilla N. small fleet. It is always an exciting and interesting moment when the fishing *flotilla* returns to port.

flotsam N. drifting wreckage. Beachcombers eke out a living by salvaging the *flotsam* and jetsam of the sea.

flourish V. grow well; prosper; decorate with ornaments. The orange trees *flourished* in the sun.

flout V. reject; mock. The headstrong youth *flouted* all authority; he refused to be curbed.

fluctuation N. wavering. Meteorologists watch the *fluctuations* of the barometer in order to predict the weather.

fluency N. smoothness of speech. He spoke French with *fluency* and ease.

fluster V. confuse. The teacher's sudden question *flustered* him and he stammered his reply.

fluted ADJ. having vertical parallel grooves (as in a pillar). All that remained of the ancient building were the *fluted* columns.

flux N. flowing; series of changes. While conditions are in such a state of *flux,* I do not wish to commit myself too deeply in this affair.

foible N. weakness; slight fault. We can overlook the *foibles* of our friends.

foil N. contrast. In "Star Wars," dark, evil Darth Vader is a perfect *foil* for fair-haired, naive Luke Skywalker.

foil V. defeat; frustrate. In the end, Skywalker is able to *foil* Vader's diabolical schemes.

foist V. insert improperly; palm off. I will not permit you to *foist* such ridiculous ideas upon the membership of this group.

foment V. stir up; instigate. This report will *foment* dissension in the club.

foolhardy ADJ. rash. Don't be *foolhardy.* Get the advice of experienced people before undertaking this venture.

foppish ADJ. vain about dress and appearance. He tried to imitate the *foppish* manner of the young men of the court.

foray N. raid. The company staged a midnight *foray* against the enemy outpost.

forbearance N. patience. We must use *forbearance* in dealing with him because he is still weak from his illness.

foreboding N. premonition of evil. Caesar ridiculed his wife's *forebodings* about the Ides of March.

forensic ADJ. suitable to debate or courts of law. In her best *forensic* manner, the lawyer addressed the jury.

formality N. adherence to established rules or procedures. Signing this position is a mere *formality*; it does not obligate you in any way.

formidable ADJ. menacing; threatening. We must not treat the battle lightly for we are facing a *formidable* foe.

forte N. strong point or special talent. I am not eager to play this rather serious role, for my *forte* is comedy.

fortitude N. bravery; courage. He was awarded the medal for his *fortitude* in the battle.

fortuitous ADJ. accidental; by chance. There is no connection between these two events; their timing is extremely *fortuitous.*

foster V. rear; encourage. According to the legend, Romulus and Remus were *fostered* by a she-wolf. also ADJ.

fracas N. brawl, melee. The military police stopped the *fracas* in the bar and arrested the belligerents.

fractious ADJ. unruly. The *fractious* horse unseated its rider.

frailty N. weakness. Hamlet says, "*Frailty,* thy name is woman."

franchise N. right granted by authority. The city issued a *franchise* to the company to operate surface transit lines on the streets for ninety-nine years. also V.

frantic ADJ. wild. At the time of the collision, many people became *frantic* with fear.

fraudulent ADJ. cheating; deceitful. The government seeks to prevent *fraudulent* and misleading advertising.

fraught ADJ. filled. Since this enterprise is *fraught* with danger, I will ask for volunteers who are willing to assume the risks.

fray N. brawl. The three musketeers were in the thick of the *fray.*

freebooter N. buccaneer. This town is a rather dangerous place to visit as it is frequented by pirates, *freebooters,* and other plunderers.

frenetic ADJ. frenzied; frantic. His *frenetic* activities convinced us that he had no organized plan of operation.

frenzied ADJ. madly excited. As soon as they smelled smoke, the *frenzied* animals milled about in their cages.

fresco N. painting on plaster (usually fresh). The cathedral is visited by many tourists who wish to admire the *frescoes* by Giotto.

freshet N. sudden flood. Motorists were warned that spring *freshets* had washed away several small bridges and that long detours would be necessary.

fret V. to be annoyed or vexed. To *fret* over your poor grades is foolish; instead, decide to work harder in the future.

friction N. clash in opinion; rubbing against. At this time when harmony is essential, we cannot afford to have any *friction* in our group.

frieze N. ornamental band on a wall. The *frieze* of the church was adorned with sculpture.

frigid ADJ. intensely cold. Alaska is in the *frigid* zone.

fritter V. waste. He could not apply himself to any task and *frittered* away his time in idle conversation.

frivolity N. lack of seriousness. We were distressed by his *frivolity* during the recent grave crisis. frivolous, ADJ.

frolicsome ADJ. prankish; gay. The *frolicsome* puppy tried to lick the face of its master.

frond N. fern leaf; palm or banana leaf. After the storm the beach was littered with the *fronds* of palm trees.

froward ADJ. disobedient; perverse; stubborn. Your *froward* behavior has alienated many of us who might have been your supporters.

frowzy ADJ. slovenly; unkempt; dirty. Her *frowzy* appearance and her cheap decorations made her appear ludicrous in this group.

fructify V. bear fruit. This tree should *fructify* in three years.

frugality N. thrift. In these difficult days, we must live with *frugality.*

fruition N. bearing of fruit; fulfillment; realization. This building marks the *fruition* of all our aspirations and years of hard work.

frustrate V. thwart; defeat. We must *frustrate* this dictator's plan to seize control of the government.

fulcrum N. support on which a lever rests. If we use this stone as a *fulcrum* and the crowbar as a lever, we may be able to move this boulder.

fulgent ADJ. beaming; radiant. In the *fulgent* glow of the early sunrise everything seemed bright and gleaming.

fulminate V. thunder; explode. The people against whom she *fulminated* were innocent of any wrongdoing.

fulsome ADJ. disgustingly excessive. His *fulsome* praise of the dictator annoyed his listeners.

functionary N. official. As his case was transferred from one *functionary* to another, he began to despair of ever reaching a settlement.

funereal ADJ. sad; solemn. I fail to understand why there is such a *funereal* atmosphere; we have lost a battle, not a war.

furor N. frenzy; great excitement. The story of her embezzlement of the funds created a *furor* on the Stock Exchange.

furtive ADJ. stealthy. The boy gave a *furtive* look at his classmate's test paper.

fusion N. union; coalition. The opponents of the political party in power organized a *fusion* of disgruntled groups and became an important element in the election.

fustian ADJ. pompous; bombastic. Several in the audience were deceived by her *fustian* style; they mistook pomposity for erudition.

futile ADJ. ineffective; fruitless. Why waste your time on *futile* pursuits?

gadfly N. animal-biting fly; an irritating person. Like a *gadfly,* he irritated all the guests at the hotel; within forty-eight hours, everyone regarded him as an annoying busybody.

gaff N. hook; barbed fishing spear. When he attempted to land the sailfish, he was so nervous that he dropped the *gaff* into the sea. also V.

TEST—WORD LIST 20—*Synonyms*

Each of the questions below consists of a word in capital letters, followed by five lettered words or phrases. Choose the lettered word or phrase that is most nearly similar in meaning to the word in capital letters and write the letter of your choice on your answer paper.

286. FLORID (A) ruddy (B) rusty (C) ruined (D) patient (E) poetic
287. FOIL (A) bury (B) frustrate (C) shield (D) desire (E) gain
288. FOMENT (A) spoil (B) instigate (C) interrogate (D) spray (E) maintain
289. FOOLHARDY (A) strong (B) unwise (C) brave (D) futile (E) erudite
290. FOPPISH (A) scanty (B) radical (C) orthodox (D) dandyish (E) magnificent
291. FORAY (A) excursion (B) contest (C) ranger (D) intuition (E) fish
292. FORMIDABLE (A) dangerous (B) outlandish (C) grandiloquent (D) impenetrable (E) venerable
293. FOSTER (A) speed (B) fondle (C) become infected (D) raise (E) roll
294. FRANCHISE (A) subway (B) kiosk (C) license (D) reason (E) fashion
295. FRITTER (A) sour (B) chafe (C) dissipate (D) cancel (E) abuse
296. FRUGALITY (A) foolishness (B) extremity (C) indifference (D) enthusiasm (E) economy

297. FULGENT (A) dizzy (B) empty (C) diverse (D) shining (E) dreamy
298. FUROR (A) excitement (B) worry (C) flux (D) anteroom (E) lover
299. FURTIVE (A) underhanded (B) coy (C) brilliant (D) quick (E) abortive
300. GADFLY (A) humorist (B) nuisance (C) scholar (D) bum (E) thief

---

WORD LIST 21 gainsay - gossamer

gainsay V. deny. She could not *gainsay* the truth of the report.

gait N. manner of walking or running; speed. The lame man walked with an uneven *gait.*

galaxy N. the Milky Way; any collection of brilliant personalities. The deaths of such famous actors as Clark Gable, Gary Cooper and Spencer Tracy demonstrate that the *galaxy* of Hollywood superstars is rapidly disappearing.

gall N. bitterness; nerve. The knowledge of his failure filled him with *gall.*

gall V. annoy; chafe. Their taunts *galled* him.

galleon N. large sailing ship. The Spaniards pinned their hopes on the *galleon,* the large warship; the British, on the smaller and faster pinnace.

galvanize V. stimulate by shock; stir up. The entire nation was *galvanized* into strong military activity by the news of the attack on Pearl Harbor.

gambit N. opening in chess in which a piece is sacrificed. The player was afraid to accept his opponent's *gambit* because he feared a trap which as yet he could not see.

gambol V. skip; leap playfully. Watching children *gamboling* in the park is a pleasant experience. also N.

gamely ADV. Because he had fought *gamely* against a much superior boxer, the crowd gave him a standing ovation when he left the arena.

gamester N. gambler. An inveterate *gamester,* she was willing to wager on the outcome of any event, even one which involved the behavior of insects.

gamut N. entire range. In this performance, the leading lady was able to demonstrate the complete *gamut* of her acting ability.

gape V. open widely. The huge pit *gaped* before him; if he stumbled, he would fall in.

garbled ADJ. mixed up; based on false or unfair selection. The *garbled* report confused many readers who were not familiar with the facts. garble, V.

gargantuan ADJ. huge; enormous. The *gargantuan* wrestler was terrified of mice.

gargoyle N. waterspout carved in grotesque figures on building. The *gargoyles* adorning the Cathedral of Notre Dame in Paris are amusing in their grotesqueness.

garish ADJ. gaudy. She wore a *garish* rhinestone necklace.

garner V. gather; store up. She hoped to *garner* the world's literature in one library.

garnish V. decorate. Parsley was used to *garnish* the boiled potato. also N.

garrulity N. talkativeness. The man who married a dumb wife asked the doctor to make him deaf because of his wife's *garrulity* after her cure. garrulous, ADJ.

garrulous ADJ. loquacious; wordy. Many members avoided the company of the *garrulous* old gentleman because his constant chatter on trivial matters bored them.

gasconade N. bluster; boastfulness. Behind his front of *gasconade* and pompous talk, he tried to hide his inherent uncertainty and nervousness. also V.

gastronomy N. science of preparing and serving good food. One of the by-products of his trip to Europe was his interest in *gastronomy;* he enjoyed preparing and serving foreign dishes to his friends.

gauche ADJ. clumsy; boorish. Such remarks are *gauche* and out of place; you should apologize for making them.

gaudy ADJ. flashy; showy. Her *gaudy* taste in clothes appalled us.

gaunt ADJ. lean and angular; barren. His once round face looked surprisingly *gaunt* after he had lost weight.

gauntlet N. leather glove. Now that we have been challenged, we must take up the *gauntlet* and meet our adversary fearlessly.

gazette N. official periodical publication. He read the *gazettes* regularly for the announcement of his promotion.

genealogy N. record of descent; lineage. He was proud of his *genealogy* and constantly referred to the achievements of his ancestors.

generality N. vague statement. This report is filled with *generalities;* you must be more specific in your statements.

generic ADJ. characteristic of a class or species. You have made the mistake of thinking that his behavior is *generic;* actually, very few of his group behave the way he does.

genesis N. beginning; origin. Tracing the *genesis* of a poem is fascinating work.

geniality N. cheerfulness; kindliness; sympathy. This restaurant is famous and popular because of the *geniality* of the proprietor who tries to make everyone happy.

genre N. style of art illustrating scenes of common life. His painting of fisher folk at their daily tasks is an excellent illustration of *genre* art.

genteel ADJ. well-bred; elegant. We are looking for a man with a *genteel* appearance who can inspire confidence by his cultivated manner.

gentility N. those of gentle birth; refinement. Her family was proud of its *gentility.*

gentry N. people of standing; class of people just below nobility. The local *gentry* did not welcome the visits of the summer tourists and tried to ignore their presence in the community.

genuflect V. bend the knee as in worship. A proud democrat, he refused to *genuflect* to any man.

germane ADJ. pertinent; bearing upon the case at hand. The lawyer objected that the testimony being offered was not *germane* to the case at hand.

germinal ADJ. pertaining to a germ; creative. Such an idea is *germinal;* I am certain that it will influence thinkers and philosophers for many generations.

germinate V. cause to sprout; sprout. After the seeds *germinate* and develop their permanent leaves, the plants may be removed from the cold frames and transplanted to the garden.

gerrymander V. change voting district lines in order to favor a political party. The illogical pattern of the map of this congressional district is proof that the State Legislature *gerrymandered* this area in order to favor the majority party. also N.

gestate V. evolve, as in prenatal growth. While this scheme was being *gestated* by the conspirators, they maintained complete silence about their intentions.

gesticulation N. motion; gesture. Operatic performers are trained to make exaggerated *gesticulations* because of the large auditoriums in which they appear.

ghastly ADJ. horrible. The murdered man was a *ghastly* sight.

gibber V. speak foolishly. The demented man *gibbered* incoherently.

gibbet N. gallows. The bodies of the highwaymen were left dangling from the *gibbet* as a warning to other would-be transgressors.

gibe V. mock. As you *gibe* at their superstitious beliefs, do you realize that you, too, are guilty of similarly foolish thoughts?

giddy ADJ. light-hearted; dizzy. He felt his *giddy* youth was past.

gig N. two-wheeled carriage. As they drove down the street in their new *gig,* drawn by the dappled mare, they were cheered by the people who recognized them.

gingerly ADV. very carefully. To separate egg whites, first crack the egg *gingerly.*

gist N. essence. She was asked to give the *gist* of the essay in two sentences.

glaze V. cover with a thin and shiny surface. The freezing rain *glazed* the streets and made driving hazardous. also N.

glean V. gather leavings. After the crops had been harvested by the machines, the peasants were permitted to *glean* the wheat left in the fields.

glib ADJ. fluent. He is a *glib* speaker.

gloaming N. twilight. The snow began to fall in the *gloaming* and continued all through the night.

gloat V. express evil satisfaction; view malevolently. As you *gloat* over your ill-gotten wealth, do you think of the many victims you have defrauded?

glossary N. brief explanation of words used in the text. I have found the *glossary* in this book very useful; it has eliminated many trips to the dictionary.

glossy ADJ. smooth and shining. I want this photograph printed on *glossy* paper.

glower V. scowl. The angry boy *glowered* at his father.

glut V. overstock; fill to excess. The many manufacturers *glutted* the market and could not find purchasers for the many articles they had produced. also N.

glutinous ADJ. sticky; viscous. Molasses is a *glutinous* substance.

glutton N. someone who eats too much. You can be a gourmet without being a *glutton.*

gluttonous ADJ. greedy for food. The *gluttonous* boy ate all the cookies.

gnarled ADJ. twisted. The *gnarled* oak tree had been a landmark for years and was mentioned in several deeds.

gnome N. dwarf; underground spirit. In medieval mythology, *gnomes* were the special guardians and inhabitants of subterranean mines.

goad V. urge on. He was *goaded* by his friends until he yielded to their wishes. also N.

gorge V. stuff oneself. The gluttonous guest *gorged* himself with food as though he had not eaten for days.

gory ADJ. bloody. The audience shuddered as they listened to the details of the *gory* massacre.

gossamer ADJ. sheer; like cobwebs. Nylon can be woven into *gossamer* or thick fabrics. also N.

TEST—WORD LIST 21—*Synonyms*

Each of the questions below consists of a word in capital letters, followed by five lettered words or phrases. Choose the lettered word or phrase that is most nearly similar in meaning to the word in capital letters and write the letter of your choice on your answer paper.

301. GALLEON (A) liquid measure (B) ship (C) armada (D) company (E) printer's proof
302. GARISH (A) sordid (B) flashy (C) prominent (D) lusty (E) thoughtful
303. GARNER (A) prevent (B) assist (C) collect (D) compute (E) consult
304. GARNISH (A) paint (B) garner (C) adorn (D) abuse (E) banish
305. GARRULITY (A) credulity (B) senility (C) loquaciousness (D) speciousness (E) artistry
306. GARRULOUS (A) arid (B) hasty (C) sociable (D) quaint (E) talkative
307. GASCONADE (A) transparency (B) cleanliness (C) bluster (D) imposture (E) seizure
308. GAUCHE (A) rigid (B) awkward (C) swift (D) tacit (E) needy
309. GAUNT (A) victorious (B) tiny (C) stylish (D) haggard (E) nervous
310. GENUFLECT (A) falsify (B) trick (C) project (D) bend the knee (E) pronounce correctly
311. GERMANE (A) bacteriological (B) middle European (C) prominent (D) warlike (E) relevant
312. GERMINAL (A) creative (B) excused (C) sterilized (D) primitive (E) strategic
313. GIST (A) chaff (B) summary (C) expostulation (D) expiation (E) chore
314. GLIB (A) slippery (B) fashionable (C) antiquated (D) articulate (E) anticlimactic
315. GNOME (A) fury (B) giant (C) dwarf (D) native (E) alien

WORD LIST 22 **gouge - hiatus**

gouge V. tear out. In that fight, all the rules were forgotten; the adversaries bit, kicked, and tried to *gouge* each other's eyes out.

gourmand N. epicure; person who takes excessive pleasure in food and drink. The *gourmand* liked the French cuisine.

gourmet N. connoisseur of food and drink. The *gourmet* stated that this was the best onion soup she had ever tasted.

granary N. storehouse for grain. We have reason to be thankful, for our crops were good and our *granaries* are full.

grandiloquent ADJ. pompous; bombastic; using high-sounding language. The politician could never speak simply; she was always *grandiloquent.*

grandiose ADJ. imposing; impressive. His *grandiose* manner impressed those who met him for the first time.

granulate V. form into grains. Sugar that has been *granulated* dissolves more readily than lump sugar. granule, N.

graphic ADJ. pertaining to the art of delineating; vividly described. I was particularly impressed by the *graphic* presentation of the storm.

grapple V. wrestle; come to grips with. He *grappled* with the burglar.

gratify V. please. Her parents were *gratified* by her success.

gratis ADJ. free. The company offered to give one package *gratis* to every purchaser of one of their products. also ADJ.

gratuitous ADJ. given freely; unwarranted. I resent your *gratuitous* remarks because no one asked for them. gratuity, N.

gratuity N. tip. Many service employees rely more on *gratuities* than on salaries for their livelihood.

gregarious ADJ. sociable. She was not *gregarious* and preferred to be alone most of the time.

grimace N. a facial distortion to show feeling such as pain, disgust, etc. Even though he remained silent, his *grimace* indicated his displeasure. also V.

grisly ADJ. ghastly. She shuddered at the *grisly* sight.

grotesque ADJ. fantastic; comically hideous. On Halloween people enjoy wearing *grotesque* costumes.

grotto N. small cavern. The Blue *Grotto* in Capri can be entered only by small boats rowed by natives through a natural opening in the rocks.

grovel V. crawl or creep on ground; remain prostrate. Even though we have been defeated, we do not have to *grovel* before our conquerors.

gruel N. liquid food made by boiling oatmeal, etc., in milk or water. Our daily allotment of *gruel* made the meal not only monotonous but also unpalatable.

grueling ADJ. exhausting. The marathon is a *grueling* race.

gruesome ADJ. grisly. People screamed when her *gruesome* appearance was flashed on the screen.

gruff ADJ. rough-mannered. Although he was blunt and *gruff* with most people, he was always gentle with children.

guffaw N. boisterous laughter. The loud *guffaws* that came from the closed room indicated that the members of the committee had not yet settled down to serious business. also V.

guile N. deceit; duplicity. She achieved his high position by *guile* and treachery.

guileless ADJ. without deceit. He is naive, simple, and *guileless;* he cannot be guilty of fraud.

guise N. appearance; costume. In the *guise* of a plumber, the detective investigated the murder case.

gullible ADJ. easily deceived. He preyed upon *gullible* people, who believed his stories of easy wealth.

gustatory ADJ. affecting the sense of taste. This food is particularly *gustatory* because of the spices it contains.

gusto N. enjoyment; enthusiasm. He accepted the assignment with such *gusto* that I feel he would have been satisfied with a smaller salary.

gusty ADJ. windy. The *gusty* weather made sailing precarious.

guttural ADJ. pertaining to the throat. *Guttural* sounds are produced in the throat or in the back of the tongue and palate.

habiliments N. garb; clothing. Although not a minister, David Belasco used to wear clerical *habiliments.*

hackles N. hairs on back and neck of a dog. The dog's *hackles* rose and he began to growl as the sound of footsteps grew louder.

hackneyed ADJ. commonplace; trite. The English teacher criticized her story because of its *hackneyed* plot.

haggard ADJ. wasted away; gaunt. After his long illness, he was pale and *haggard.*

haggle V. argue about prices. I prefer to shop in a store that has a one-price policy because, whenever I *haggle* with a shopkeeper, I am never certain that I paid a fair price for the articles I purchased.

halcyon ADJ. calm; peaceful. In those *halcyon* days, people were not worried about sneak attacks and bombings.

hale ADJ. healthy. After a brief illness, he was soon *hale.*

hallowed ADJ. blessed; consecrated. She was laid to rest in *hallowed* ground.

hallucination N. delusion. I think you were frightened by a *hallucination* which you created in your own mind.

hamper V. obstruct. The minority party agreed not to *hamper* the efforts of the leaders to secure a lasting peace.

hap N. chance; luck. In his poem *Hap,* Thomas Hardy objects to the part chance plays in our lives.

haphazard ADJ. random; by chance. His *haphazard* reading left him unacquainted with authors of the books.

hapless ADJ. unfortunate. This *hapless* creature had never known a moment's pleasure.

harangue N. noisy speech. In her lengthy *harangue,* the principal berated the offenders. also V.

harbor V. provide a refuge for; hide. The church *harbored* illegal aliens who were political refugees.

harass V. to annoy by repeated attacks. When he could not pay his bills as quickly as he had promised, he was *harassed* by his creditors.

harbinger N. forerunner. The crocus is an early *harbinger* of spring.

harping N. tiresome dwelling on a subject. After he had reminded me several times about what he had done for me, I told him to stop *harping* on my indebtedness to him. harp, V.

harridan N. shrewish hag. Most people avoided the *harridan* because they feared her abusive and vicious language.

harrow V. break up ground after plowing; torture. I don't want to *harrow* you at this time by asking you to recall the details of your unpleasant experience.

harry V. raid. The guerrilla band *harried* the enemy nightly.

haughtiness N. pride; arrogance. I resent his *haughtiness* because he is no better than we are.

hauteur N. haughtiness. His snobbishness is obvious to all who witness his *hauteur* when he talks to those whom he considers his social inferiors.

hawser N. large rope. The ship was tied to the pier by a *hawser.*

hazardous ADJ. dangerous. Your occupation is too *hazardous* for insurance companies to consider your application.

hazy ADJ. slightly obscure. In *hazy* weather, you cannot see the top of this mountain.

hedonism N. belief that pleasure is the sole aim in life. *Hedonism* and asceticism are opposing philosophies of human behavior.

heedless ADJ. not noticing; disregarding. He drove on, *heedless* of the warnings placed at the side of the road that it was dangerous.

hegira flight, especially Mohammed's flight from Mecca to Medina. Mohammed began his *hegira* when he was 53 years old.

heinous ADJ. atrocious; hatefully bad. Hitler's *heinous* crimes will never be forgotten.

herbivorous ADJ. grain-eating. Some *herbivorous* animals have two stomachs for digesting their food.

heresy N. opinion contrary to popular belief; opinion contrary to accepted religion. He was threatened with excommunication because his remarks were considered to be pure *heresy.*

heretic N. person who maintains opinions contrary to the doctrines of the church. She was punished by the Spanish Inquisition because she was a *heretic.*

hermetically ADV. sealed by fusion so as to be airtight. After these bandages are sterilized, they are placed in *hermetically* sealed containers.

hermitage N. home of a hermit. Even in his remote *hermitage* he could not escape completely from the world.

heterogeneous ADJ. dissimilar. In *heterogeneous* groupings, we have an unassorted grouping, while in homogeneous groupings we have people or things which have common traits.

hew V. cut to pieces with ax or sword. The cavalry rushed into the melee and *hewed* the enemy with their swords.

hiatus N. gap; pause. There was a *hiatus* of twenty years in the life of Rip van Winkle.

TEST—WORD LIST 22—*Antonyms*

Each of the questions below consists of a word in capital letters, followed by five lettered words or phrases. Choose the lettered word or phrase that is most nearly opposite in meaning to the word in capital letters and write the letter of your choice on your answer paper.

316. GRANDIOSE (A) false (B) ideal (C) proud (D) simple (E) functional
317. GRATUITOUS (A) warranted (B) frank (C) ingenuous (D) frugal (E) pithy
318. GREGARIOUS (A) antisocial (B) anticipatory (C) glorious (D) horrendous (E) similar
319. GRISLY (A) suggestive (B) doubtful (C) untidy (D) pleasant (E) bearish
320. GULLIBLE (A) incredulous (B) fickle (C) tantamount (D) easy (E) stylish
321. GUSTO (A) noise (B) panic (C) atmosphere (D) gloom (E) distaste
322. GUSTY (A) calm (B) noisy (C) fragrant (D) routine (E) gloomy
323. HACKNEYED (A) carried (B) original (C) banned (D) timely (E) oratorical
324. HAGGARD (A) shrewish (B) inspired (C) plump (D) maidenly (E) vast
325. HALCYON (A) wasteful (B) prior (C) subsequent (D) puerile (E) martial
326. HAPHAZARD (A) safe (B) indifferent (C) deliberate (D) tense (E) conspiring
327. HAPLESS (A) cheerful (B) consistent (C) fortunate (D) considerate (E) shapely
328. HEGIRA (A) return (B) harem (C) oasis (D) panic (E) calm
329. HERETIC (A) sophist (B) believer (C) interpreter (D) pacifist (E) owner
330. HETEROGENEOUS (A) orthodox (B) pagan (C) unlike (D) similar (E) banished

---

WORD LIST 23 hibernal - imbue

hibernal ADJ. wintry. Bears prepare for their long *hibernal* sleep by overeating.

hibernate V. sleep throughout the winter. Bears are one of the many species of animals that *hibernate.*

hierarchy N. body divided into ranks. It was difficult to step out of one's place in this *hierarchy.*

hieroglyphic N. picture writing. The discovery of the Rosetta Stone enabled scholars to read the ancient Egyptian *hieroglyphics.*

hilarity N. boisterous mirth. This *hilarity* is improper on this solemn day of mourning.

hindmost ADJ. furthest behind. The coward could always be found in the *hindmost* lines whenever a battle was being waged.

hireling N. one who serves for hire [usually contemptuously]. In a matter of such importance, I do not wish to deal with *hirelings;* I must meet with the chief.

hirsute ADJ. hairy. He was a *hirsute* individual with a heavy black beard.

histrionic ADJ. theatrical. He was proud of his *histrionic* ability and wanted to play the role of Hamlet. histrionics, N.

hoary ADJ. white with age. The man was *hoary* and wrinkled.

hoax N. trick; practical joke. Embarrassed by the *hoax,* he reddened and left the room. also V.

hogshead N. large barrel. On the trip to England, the ship carried munitions; on its return trip, *hogsheads* filled with French wines and Scotch liquors.

holocaust N. destruction by fire. Citizens of San Francisco remember that the destruction of the city was caused not by the earthquake but by the *holocaust* that followed.

holster N. pistol case. Even when he was not in uniform, he carried a *holster* and pistol under his arm.

homage N. honor; tribute. In her speech she tried to pay *homage* to a great man.

homespun ADJ. domestic; made at home. *Homespun* wit like *homespun* cloth was often coarse and plain.

homily N. sermon; serious warning. His speeches were always *homilies,* advising his listeners to repent and reform.

homogeneous ADJ. of the same kind. Educators try to put pupils of similar abilities into classes because they believe that this *homogeneous* grouping is advisable. homogeneity, N.

hone V. sharpen. He *honed* his razor with great care.

hoodwink V. deceive; delude. Having been *hoodwinked* once by the fast-talking salesman, he was extremely cautious when he went to purchase a used car.

horde N. crowd. Just before Christmas the stores are filled with *hordes* of shoppers.

hortatory ADJ. encouraging; exhortive. The crowd listened to his *hortatory* statements with ever growing excitement; finally they rushed from the hall to carry out his suggestions.

horticultural ADJ. pertaining to cultivation of gardens. When he bought his house, he began to look for flowers and decorative shrubs, and began to read books dealing with *horticultural* matters.

hostelry N. inn. Travelers interested in economy should stay at *hostelries* and pensions rather than fashionable hotels.

hovel N. shack; small, wretched house. He wondered how people could stand living in such a *hovel.*

hover V. hang about; wait nearby. The police helicopter *hovered* above the accident.

hoyden N. boisterous girl. Although she is now a *hoyden,* I am sure she will outgrow her tomboyish ways and quiet down.

hubbub N. confused uproar. The marketplace was a scene of *hubbub* and excitement; in all the noise, we could not distinguish particular voices.

hubris N. arrogance; excessive self-conceit. Filled with *hubris,* Lear refused to heed his friends' warnings.

hue N. color; aspect. The aviary contained birds of every possible *hue.*

hue and cry N. outcry. When her purse was snatched, she raised such a *hue and cry* that the thief was captured.

humane ADJ. kind. His *humane* and considerate treatment of the unfortunate endeared him to all.

humdrum ADJ. dull; monotonous. After his years of adventure, he could not settle down to a *humdrum* existence.

humid ADJ. damp. He could not stand the *humid* climate and moved to a drier area.

humility N. humbleness of spirit. He spoke with a *humility* and lack of pride which impressed his listeners.

hummock N. small hill. The ascent of the *hummock* is not difficult and the view from the hilltop is ample reward for the effort.

humus N. substance formed by decaying vegetable matter. In order to improve his garden, he spread *humus* over his lawn and flower beds.

hurtle V. crash; rush. The runaway train *hurtled* towards disaster.

husbandry N. frugality; thrift; agriculture. He accumulated his small fortune by diligence and *husbandry.*

hustings N. meetings particularly to choose candidates. Congress adjourned so that the members could attend to their political *hustings.*

hybrid N. mongrel; mixed breed. Mendel's formula explains the appearance of *hybrids* and pure species in breeding. also ADJ.

hydrophobia N. rabies; fear of water. A dog that bites a human being must be observed for symptoms of *hydrophobia.*

hyperbole N. exaggeration; overstatement. This salesman is guilty of *hyperbole* in describing his product; it is wise to discount his claims.

hyperborean ADJ. situated in extreme north; arctic; cold. The *hyperborean* blasts brought snow and ice to the countryside.

hypercritical ADJ. excessively exacting. You are *hypercritical* in your demands for perfection; we all make mistakes.

hypochondriac N. person unduly worried about his health; worrier without cause about illness. The doctor prescribed chocolate pills for his patient who was a *hypochondriac.*

hypocritical ADJ. pretending to be virtuous; deceiving. I resent his *hypocritical* posing as a friend for I know he is interested only in his own advancement.

hypothecate V. mortgage; pledge as security. I have no authority to *hypothecate* this property as security for the loan.

hypothetical ADJ. based on assumptions or hypotheses. Why do we have to consider *hypothetical* cases when we have actual case histories which we may examine? hypothesis, N.

ichthyology N. study of fish. Jacques Cousteau's programs about sea life have advanced the cause of *ichthyology.*

icon N. religious image; idol. The *icons* on the walls of the church were painted in the 13th century.

iconoclastic ADJ. attacking cherished traditions. George Bernard Shaw's *iconoclastic* plays often startled people.

ideology N. ideas of a group of people. That *ideology* is dangerous to this country because it embraces undemocratic philosophies.

idiom N. special usage in language. I could not understand their *idiom* because literal translation made no sense.

idiosyncrasy N. peculiarity; eccentricity. One of his personal *idiosyncrasies* was his habit of rinsing all cutlery given him in a restaurant.

idiosyncratic ADJ. private; peculiar to an individual. Such behavior is *idiosyncratic;* it is as easily identifiable as a signature.

idolatry N. worship of idols; excessive admiration. Such *idolatry* of singers of popular ballads is typical of the excessive enthusiasm of youth.

idyllic ADJ. charmingly carefree; simple. Far from the city, she led an *idyllic* existence in her rural retreat.

igneous ADJ. produced by fire; volcanic. Lava, pumice, and other *igneous* rocks are found in great abundance around Mount Vesuvius near Naples.

ignoble ADJ. of lowly origin; unworthy. This plan is inspired by *ignoble* motives and I must, therefore, oppose it.

ignominious ADJ. disgraceful. The country smarted under the *ignominious* defeat and dreamed of the day when it would be victorious. ignominy, N.

ilk N. sort; type. He hated pinkos, commies, liberals, and all others of that *ilk.*

illimitable ADJ. infinite. Man, having explored the far corners of the earth, is now reaching out into *illimitable* space.

illusion N. misleading vision. It is easy to create an optical *illusion* in which lines of equal length appear different. illusory, ADJ.

illusive ADJ. deceiving. This mirage is an illusion; let us not be fooled by its *illusive* effect.

imbecility N. weakness of mind. I am amazed at the *imbecility* of the readers of these trashy magazines.

imbibe V. drink in. The dry soil *imbibed* the rain quickly.

imbroglio N. a complicated situation; perplexity; entanglement. He was called in to settle the *imbroglio* but failed to bring harmony into the situation.

imbrue V. drench, stain, especially with blood. As the instigator of this heinous murder, he is as much *imbrued* in blood as the actual assassin.

imbue V. saturate, fill. His visits to the famous Gothic cathedrals *imbued* him with feelings of awe and reverence.

TEST—WORD LIST 23—*Antonyms*

Each of the questions below consists of a word in capital letters, followed by five lettered words or phrases. Choose the lettered word or phrase that is most nearly opposite in meaning to the word in capital letters and write the letter of your choice on your answer paper.

331. HIBERNAL (A) musical (B) summerlike (C) local (D) seasonal (E) springlike
332. HILARITY (A) gloom (B) heartiness (C) weakness (D) casualty (E) paucity
333. HIRSUTE (A) scaly (B) bald (C) erudite (D) quiet (E) long
334. HORTATORY (A) inquiring (B) denying (C) killing (D) frantic (E) dissuading
335. HOYDEN (A) burden (B) light (C) demure girl (D) game (E) traffic
336. HUBBUB (A) calm (B) fury (C) capital (D) axle (E) wax
337. HUMMOCK (A) unmusical (B) scorn (C) wakefulness (D) vale (E) vestment
338. HUSBANDRY (A) sportsmanship (B) dishonesty (C) wastefulness (D) friction (E) cowardice
339. HYBRID (A) productive (B) special (C) purebred (D) oafish (E) genius
340. HYPERBOLE (A) velocity (B) climax (C) curve (D) understatement (E) expansion
341. HYPERBOREAN (A) sultry (B) pacific (C) noteworthy (D) western (E) wooded
342. HYPERCRITICAL (A) tolerant (B) false (C) extreme (D) inarticulate (E) cautious
343. HYPOTHETICAL (A) rational (B) fantastic (C) wizened (D) opposed (E) axiomatic
344. IGNOBLE (A) produced by fire (B) worthy (C) given to questioning (D) huge (E) known
345. ILLUSIVE (A) not deceptive (B) not certain (C) not obvious (D) not coherent (E) not brilliant

WORD LIST 24 immaculate - incessant

immaculate ADJ. pure; spotless. The West Point cadets were *immaculate* as they lined up for inspection.

imminent ADJ. impending; near at hand. The *imminent* battle will determine our success or failure in this conflict.

immobility N. state of being immovable. Modern armies cannot afford the luxury of *immobility,* as they are vulnerable to attack while standing still.

immolate V. offer as a sacrifice. The tribal king offered to *immolate* his daughter to quiet the angry gods.

immune ADJ. exempt. He was fortunately *immune* from the disease and could take care of the sick.

immure V. imprison; shut up in confinement. For the two weeks before the examination, the student *immured* himself in his room and concentrated upon his studies.

immutable ADJ. unchangeable. Scientists are constantly seeking to discover the *immutable* laws of nature.

impair V. worsen; diminish in value. This arrest will *impair* his reputation in the community.

impale V. pierce. He was *impaled* by the spear hurled by his adversary.

impalpable ADJ. imperceptible; intangible. The ash is so fine that it is *impalpable* to the touch but it can be seen as a fine layer covering the window ledge.

impasse N. predicament from which there is no escape. In this *impasse,* all turned to prayer as their last hope.

impassive ADJ. without feeling; not affected by pain. The American Indian has been incorrectly depicted as an *impassive* individual, undemonstrative and stoical.

impeach V. charge with crime in office; indict. The angry congressman wanted to *impeach* the President.

impeccable ADJ. faultless. He was proud of his *impeccable* manners.

impecunious ADJ. without money. Now that he was wealthy, he gladly contributed to funds to assist the *impecunious* and the disabled.

impediment N. hindrance; stumbling-block. He had a speech *impediment* which prevented his speaking clearly.

impending ADJ. nearing; approaching. The entire country was saddened by the news of his *impending* death.

impenitent ADJ. not repentant. We could see by his brazen attitude that he was *impenitent.*

imperious ADJ. domineering. His *imperious* manner indicated that he had long been accustomed to assuming command.

impermeable ADJ. impervious; not permitting passage through its substance. This new material is *impermeable* to liquids.

impertinent ADJ. insolent. I regard your remarks as *impertinent* and resent them.

imperturbability N. calmness. We are impressed by his *imperturbability* in this critical moment and are calmed by it.

imperturbable ADJ. calm; placid. He remained *imperturbable* and in full command of the situation in spite of the hysteria and panic all around him.

impervious ADJ. not penetrable; not permitting passage through. You cannot change their habits for their minds are *impervious* to reasoning.

impetuous ADJ. violent; hasty; rash. We tried to curb his *impetuous* behavior because we felt that in his haste he might offend some people.

impetus N. moving force. It is a miracle that there were any survivors since the two automobiles that collided were traveling with great *impetus.*

impiety N. irreverence; wickedness. We must regard your blasphemy as an act of *impiety.*

impinge V. infringe; touch; collide with. How could they be married without *impinging* on one another's freedom?

impious ADJ. irreverent. The congregation was offended by his *impious* remarks.

implacable ADJ. incapable of being pacified. Madame Defarge was the *implacable* enemy of the Evremonde family.

implausible ADJ. unlikely; unbelievable. Though his alibi seemed *implausible,* it in fact turned out to be true.

implement V. supply what is needed; furnish with tools. I am unwilling to *implement* this plan until I have assurances that it has the full approval of your officials. also N.

implication N. that which is hinted at or suggested. If I understand the *implications* of your remark, you do not trust our captain.

implicit ADJ. understood but not stated. It is *implicit* that you will come to our aid if we are attacked.

imply V. suggest a meaning not expressed; signify.

Even though your statement does not declare that you are at war with that country, your actions *imply* that that is the actual situation.

impolitic ADJ. not wise. I think it is *impolitic* to raise this issue at the present time because the public is too angry.

imponderable ADJ. weightless. I can evaluate the data gathered in this study; the *imponderable* items are not so easily analyzed.

import N. significance. I feel that you have not grasped the full *import* of the message sent to us by the enemy.

importunate ADJ. urging; demanding. He tried to hide from his *importunate* creditors until his allowance arrived.

importune V. beg earnestly. I must *importune* you to work for peace at this time. importunate, ADJ.

imposture N. assuming a false identity; masquerade. He was imprisoned for his *imposture* of a doctor.

impotent ADJ. weak; ineffective. Although he wished to break the nicotine habit, he found himself *impotent* in resisting the craving for a cigarette.

imprecate V. curse; pray that evil will befall. To *imprecate* Hitler's atrocities is not enough; we must insure against any future practice of genocide.

impregnable ADJ. invulnerable. Until the development of the airplane as a military weapon, the fort was considered *impregnable.*

imprimatur N. permission to print or publish a book. The publication of the book was delayed until the *imprimatur* of the State Education Committee was granted.

impromptu ADJ. without previous preparation. His listeners were amazed that such a thorough presentation could be made in an *impromptu* speech.

impropriety N. state of being inappropriate. Because of the *impropriety* of his costume, he was denied entrance into the dining room.

improvident ADJ. thriftless. He was constantly being warned to mend his *improvident* ways and begin to "save for a rainy day."

improvise V. compose on the spur of the moment. He would sit at the piano and *improvise* for hours on themes from Bach and Handel.

impugn V. doubt; challenge; gainsay. I cannot *impugn* your honesty without evidence.

impunity N. freedom from punishment. The bully mistreated everyone in the class with *impunity* for he felt that no one would dare retaliate.

imputation N. charge; reproach. You cannot ignore the *imputations* in his speech that you are the guilty party.

impute V. attribute; ascribe. If I wished to *impute* blame to the officers in charge of this program, I would come out and state it definitely and without hesitation.

inadvertence N. oversight; carelessness. By *inadvertence,* he omitted two questions on the examination.

inalienable ADJ. not to be taken away; nontransferable. The Declaration of Independence mentions the *inalienable* rights that all of us possess.

inane ADJ. silly; senseless. Such comments are *inane* because they do not help us solve our problem. inanity, N.

inanimate ADJ. lifeless. She was asked to identify the still and *inanimate* body.

inarticulate ADJ. speechless; producing indistinct speech. He became *inarticulate* with rage and uttered sounds without meaning.

incandescent ADJ. strikingly bright; shining with intense heat. If you leave on an *incandescent* light bulb, it quickly grows too hot to touch.

incantation N. singing or chanting of magic spells; magical formula. Uttering *incantations* to make the brew more potent, the witch doctor stirred the liquid in the caldron.

incapacitate V. disable. During the winter, many people were *incapacitated* by respiratory ailments.

incarcerate V. imprison. The warden will *incarcerate* the felon.

incarnadine V. stain crimson or blood-color. After killing Duncan, Macbeth cries that his hands are so bloodstained that they would "the multitudinous seas *incarnadine.*"

incarnate ADJ. endowed with flesh; personified. Your attitude is so fiendish that you must be a devil *incarnate.*

incarnation N. act of assuming a human body and human nature. The *incarnation* of Jesus Christ is a basic tenet of Christian theology.

incendiary N. arsonist. The fire spread in such an unusual manner that the fire department chiefs were certain that it had been set by an *incendiary.* also ADJ.

incense V. enrage; infuriate. Unkindness to children *incensed* her.

incentive N. spur; motive. Students who dislike school must be given an *incentive* to learn.

inception N. start; beginning. She was involved with the project from its *inception.*

incessant ADJ. uninterrupted. The crickets kept up an *incessant* chirping which disturbed our attempts to fall asleep.

TEST—WORD LIST 24—*Synonyms and Antonyms*

Each of the following questions consists of a word in capital letters, followed by five lettered words or phrases. Choose the lettered word or phrase which is most nearly similar or the opposite of the word in capital letters and write the letter of your choice on your answer paper.

346. IMMOLATE (A) debate (B) scour (C) sacrifice (D) sanctify (E) ratify
347. IMMUTABLE (A) silent (B) changeable (C) articulate (D) loyal (E) varied
348. IMPAIR (A) separate (B) make amends (C) make worse (D) falsify (E) cancel
349. IMPALPABLE (A) obvious (B) combined (C) high (D) connecting (E) lost
350. IMPASSIVE (A) active (B) demonstrative (C) perfect (D) anxious (E) irritated
351. IMPECCABLE (A) unmentionable (B) quotable (C) blinding (D) faulty (E) hampering
352. IMPECUNIOUS (A) affluent (B) afflicted (C) affectionate (D) affable (E) afraid
353. IMPERVIOUS (A) impenetrable (B) vulnerable (C) chaotic (D) cool (E) perfect
354. IMPETUOUS (A) rash (B) inane (C) just (D) flagrant (E) redolent
355. IMPOLITIC (A) campaigning (B) advisable (C) appropriate (D) legal (E) fortunate
356. IMPORTUNE (A) export (B) plead (C) exhibit (D) account (E) visit
357. IMPROMPTU (A) prompted (B) appropriate (C) rehearsed (D) foolish (E) vast
358. INALIENABLE (A) inherent (B) repugnant (C) closed to immigration (D) full (E) accountable
359. INANE (A) passive (B) wise (C) intoxicated (D) mellow (E) silent
360. INCARCERATE (A) inhibit (B) acquit (C) account (D) imprison (E) force

---

WORD LIST 25 inchoate - ingenious

inchoate ADJ. recently begun; rudimentary; elementary. Before the Creation, the world was an *inchoate* mass.

incidence N. falling on a body; a casual occurrence. We must determine the angle of *incidence* of the rays of light.

incipient ADJ. beginning; in an early stage. I will go to sleep early for I want to break an *incipient* cold.

incisive ADJ. cutting; sharp. His *incisive* remarks made us see the fallacy in our plans.

incite V. arouse to action. The demagogue *incited* the mob to take action into its own hands.

inclement ADJ. stormy; unkind. I like to read a good book in *inclement* weather.

inclusive ADJ. tending to include all. This meeting will run from January 10 to February 15 *inclusive.*

incognito ADV. with identity concealed; using an assumed name. The monarch enjoyed traveling through the town *incognito* and mingling with the populace. also ADJ.

incoherence N. lack of relevance; lack of intelligibility. The bereaved father sobbed and stammered, caught up in the *incoherence* of his grief.

incommodious ADJ. not spacious. In their *incommodious* quarters, they had to improvise for closet space.

incompatible ADJ. inharmonious. The married couple argued incessantly and finally decided to separate because they were *incompatible.*

incongruity N. lack of harmony; absurdity. The *incongruity* of his wearing sneakers with formal attire amused the observers.

incongruous ADJ. not fitting; absurd. These remarks do not have any relationship to the problem at hand; they are *incongruous* and should be stricken from the record.

inconsequential ADJ. of trifling significance. Your objections are *inconsequential* and may be disregarded.

incontinent ADJ. lacking self-restraint; licentious. His *incontinent* behavior off stage shocked many people and they refused to attend the plays and movies in which he appeared.

incontrovertible ADJ. indisputable. We must yield to the *incontrovertible* evidence which you have presented and free your client.

incorporeal ADJ. immaterial; without a material body. We must devote time to the needs of our *incorporeal* mind as well as our corporeal body.

incorrigible ADJ. uncorrectable. Because he was an *incorrigible* criminal, he was sentenced to life imprisonment.

incredulity N. a tendency to disbelief. Your *incredulity* in the face of all the evidence is hard to understand.

incredulous ADJ. withholding belief; skeptical. The *incredulous* judge refused to accept the statement of the defendant.

increment N. increase. The new contract calls for a 10

percent *increment* in salary for each employee for the next two years.

incriminate V. accuse. The evidence gathered against the racketeers *incriminates* some high public officials as well.

incubate V. hatch; scheme. Inasmuch as our supply of electricity is cut off, we shall have to rely on the hens to *incubate* these eggs.

incubus N. burden; mental care; nightmare. The *incubus* of financial worry helped bring on his nervous breakdown.

inculcate V. teach. In an effort to *inculcate* religious devotion, the officials ordered that the school day begin with the singing of a hymn.

incumbent N. officeholder. The newly elected public official received valuable advice from the present *incumbent.* also ADJ.

incur V. bring upon oneself. His parents refused to pay any future debts he might *incur.*

incursion N. temporary invasion. The nightly *incursions* and hit-and-run raids of our neighbors across the border tried the patience of the country to the point where we decided to retaliate in force.

indefatigable ADJ. tireless. He was *indefatigable* in his constant efforts to raise funds for the Red Cross.

indemnify V. make secure against loss; compensate for loss. The city will *indemnify* all home owners whose property is spoiled by this project.

indenture V. bind as servant or apprentice to master. Many immigrants could come to America only after they had *indentured* themselves for several years. also N.

indicative ADJ. suggestive; implying. A lack of appetite may be *indicative* of a major mental or physical disorder.

indict V. charge. If the grand jury *indicts* the suspect, he will go to trial.

indifferent ADJ. unmoved; lacking concern. Because she felt no desire to marry, she was *indifferent* to his constant proposals.

indigenous ADJ. native. Tobacco is one of the *indigenous* plants which the early explorers found in this country.

indigent ADJ. poor. Because he was *indigent,* he was sent to the welfare office.

indignation N. anger at an injustice. He felt *indignation* at the ill-treatment of helpless animals.

indignity N. offensive or insulting treatment. Although he seemed to accept cheerfully the *indignities* heaped upon him, he was inwardly very angry.

indiscriminate ADJ. choosing at random; confused. She disaproved of her son's *indiscriminate* television viewing and decided to restrict him to educational programs.

indisputable ADJ. too certain to be disputed. In the face of these *indisputable* statements, I withdraw my complaint.

indissoluble ADJ. permanent. The *indissoluble* bonds of marriage are all too often being dissolved.

indite V. write; compose. Cyrano *indited* many letters for Christian.

indolence N. laziness. The sultry weather in the tropics encourages a life of *indolence.*

indomitable ADJ. unconquerable. The founders of our country had *indomitable* willpower.

indubitably ADV. beyond a doubt. Because her argument was *indubitably* valid, the judge accepted it.

induce V. persuade; bring about. Because the baby was overdue, they tried to induce *labor.*

inductive ADJ. pertaining to induction or proceeding from the specific to the general. The discovery of the planet Pluto is an excellent example of the results that can be obtained from *inductive* reasoning.

indulgent ADJ. humoring; yielding; lenient. An *indulgent* parent may spoil a child by creating an artificial atmosphere of leniency.

inebriety N. habitual intoxication. Because of his *inebriety,* he was discharged from his position as family chauffeur.

ineffable ADJ. unutterable; cannot be expressed in speech. Such *ineffable* joy must be experienced; it cannot be described.

ineluctable ADJ. irresistible; not to be escaped. He felt that his fate was *ineluctable* and refused to make any attempt to improve his lot.

inept ADJ. unsuited; absurd; incompetent. The constant turmoil in the office proved that she was an *inept* administrator.

inert ADJ. inactive; lacking power to move. Faced with the growing corruption scandal, the bureaucracy was *inert.*

inertia N. state of being inert or indisposed to move. Our *inertia* in this matter may prove disastrous; we must move to aid our allies immediately.

inevitable ADJ. unavoidable. Death and taxes are both *inevitable.*

inexorable ADJ. relentless; unyielding; implacable. After listening to the pleas for clemency, the judge was *inexorable* and gave the convicted man the maximum punishment allowed by law.

infallible ADJ. unerring. We must remember that none of us is *infallible.*

infamous ADJ. notoriously bad. Jesse James was an *infamous* outlaw.

infantile ADJ. childish; infantile. When will he outgrow such *infantile* behavior?

infer V. deduce; conclude. We must be particularly cautious when we *infer* that a person is guilty on the basis of circumstantial evidence.

inference N. conclusion drawn from data. I want you to check this *inference* because it may have been based on insufficient information.

infernal ADJ. pertaining to hell; devilish. They could think of no way to hinder his *infernal* scheme.

infidel N. unbeliever. The Saracens made war against the *infidels.*

infinitesimal ADJ. very small. In the twentieth century, physicists have made their greatest discoveries about the characteristics of *infinitesimal* objects like the atom and its parts.

infirmity N. weakness. Her greatest *infirmity* was lack of willpower.

inflated ADJ. exaggerated; pompous; enlarged (with air or gas). His claims about the new product were inflated; it did not work as well as he had promised.

influx N. flowing into. The *influx* of refugees into the country has taxed the relief agencies severely.

infraction N. violation. Because of his many *infractions* of school regulations, he was suspended by the dean.

infringe V. violate; encroach. I think your machine *infringes* on my patent.

ingenious ADJ. clever. He came up with an *ingenious* use for styrofoam packing balls.

TEST—WORD LIST 25—*Synonyms*

Each of the questions below consists of a word in capital letters, followed by five lettered words or phrases. Choose the lettered word or phrase that is most nearly similar in meaning to the word in capital letters and write the letter of your choice on your answer paper.

361. INCLEMENT (A) unfavorable (B) abandoned (C) kindly (D) selfish (E) active
362. INCOMPATIBLE (A) capable (B) reasonable (C) faulty (D) indifferent (E) alienated
363. INCONSEQUENTIAL (A) disorderly (B) insignificant (C) subsequent (D) insufficient (E) preceding
364. INCONTINENT (A) insular (B) complaisant (C) crass (D) wanton (E) false
365. INCORRIGIBLE (A) narrow (B) straight (C) inconceivable (D) unreliable (E) unreformable
366. INCRIMINATE (A) exacerbate (B) involve (C) intimidate (D) lacerate (E) prevaricate
367. INCULCATE (A) exculpate (B) educate (C) exonerate (D) prepare (E) embarrass
368. INDIGENT (A) lazy (B) pusillanimous (C) penurious (D) affluent (E) contrary
369. INDIGNITY (A) pomposity (B) bombast (C) obeisance (D) insult (E) message
370. INDOLENCE (A) sloth (B) poverty (C) latitude (D) aptitude (E) anger
371. INDUBITABLY (A) flagrantly (B) doubtfully (C) carefully (D) carelessly (E) certainly
372. INEBRIETY (A) revelation (B) drunkenness (C) felony (D) starvation (E) gluttony
373. INEPT (A) outward (B) spiritual (C) foolish (D) clumsy (E) abundant
374. INFALLIBLE (A) final (B) unbelievable (C) perfect (D) inaccurate (E) inquisitive
375. INFIRMITY (A) disability (B) age (C) inoculation (D) hospital (E) unity

---

WORD LIST 26 ingenue - invidious

ingenue N. an artless girl; an actress who plays such parts. Although she was forty, she still insisted that she be cast as an *ingenue* and refused to play more mature roles.

ingenuous ADJ. naive; young; unsophisticated. These remarks indicate that you are *ingenuous* and unaware of life's harsher realities.

ingrate N. ungrateful person. You are an *ingrate* since you have treated my gifts with scorn.

ingratiate V. become popular with. He tried to *ingratiate* himself into her parents' good graces.

inherent ADJ. firmly established by nature or habit. His *inherent* love of justice compelled him to come to their aid.

inhibit V. prohibit; restrain. The child was not *inhibited* in her responses. inhibition, N.

inimical ADJ. unfriendly; hostile. She felt that they were *inimical* and were hoping for her downfall.

inimitable ADJ. matchless; not able to be imitated. We admire Auden for his *inimitable* use of language.

iniquitous ADJ. unjust; wicked. I cannot approve of the *iniquitous* methods you used to gain your present position. iniquity, N.

inkling N. hint. This came as a complete surprise to me as I did not have the slightest *inkling* of your plans.

innate ADJ. inborn. His *innate* talent for music was soon recognized by his parents.

innocuous ADJ. harmless. Let him drink it; it is *innocuous.*

innovation N. change; introduction of something new. She loved *innovations* just because they were new.

innuendo N. hint; insinuation. I resent the *innuendos* in your statement more than the statement itself.

inopportune ADJ. untimely; poorly chosen. A rock concert is an *inopportune* setting for a quiet conversation.

inordinate ADJ. unrestrained; excessive. She had an *inordinate* fondness for candy.

insatiable ADJ. not easily satisfied; greedy. His thirst for knowledge was *insatiable;* he was always in the library.

inscrutable ADJ. incomprehensible; not to be discovered. I fail to understand the reasons for your outlandish behavior; your motives are *inscrutable.*

insensate ADJ. without feeling. She lay there as *insensate* as a log.

insidious ADJ. treacherous; stealthy; sly. The fifth column is *insidious* because it works secretly within our territory for our defeat.

insinuate V. hint; imply. What are you trying to *insinuate* by that remark?

insipid ADJ. tasteless; dull. I am bored by your *insipid* talk.

insolent ADJ. haughty and contemptuous. I resent your *insolent* manner.

insolvency N. bankruptcy; lack of ability to repay debts. When rumors of his *insolvency* reached his creditors, they began to press him for payment of the money due them.

insomnia N. wakefulness; inability to sleep. He refused to join us in a midnight cup of coffee because he claimed it gave him *insomnia.*

insouciant ADJ. indifferent; without concern or care. Your *insouciant* attitude at such a critical moment indicates that you do not understand the gravity of the situation.

instigate V. urge; start; provoke. I am afraid that this statement will *instigate* a revolt.

insubordinate ADJ. disobedient. The *insubordinate* private was confined to the barracks.

insular ADJ. like an island; narrow-minded. In an age of such rapid means of communication, we cannot afford to be hemmed in by such *insular* ideas.

insuperable ADJ. insurmountable; invincible. In the face of *insuperable* difficulties they maintained their courage and will to resist.

insurgent ADJ. rebellious. We will not discuss reforms until the *insurgent* troops have returned to their homes. also N.

insurrection N. rebellion; uprising. Given the current state of things in South Africa, an *insurrection* seems unavoidable.

integrate V. make whole; combine; make into one unit. She tried to *integrate* all their activities into one program.

integrity N. wholeness; purity; uprightness. He was a man of great *integrity.*

integument N. outer covering or skin. The turtle takes advantage of its hard *integument* and hides within its shell when threatened.

intellect N. higher mental powers. He thought college would develop his *intellect.*

intelligentsia N. the intelligent and educated classes [often used derogatorily]. She preferred discussions about sports and politics to the literary conversations of the *intelligentsia.*

inter V. bury. They are going to *inter* the body tomorrow.

interdict V. prohibit; forbid. Civilized nations must *interdict* the use of nuclear weapons if we expect our society to live.

interim N. meantime. The company will not consider our proposal until next week; in the *interim,* let us proceed as we have in the past.

interlocutory ADJ. conversational; intermediate, not final. This *interlocutory* decree is only a temporary setback; the case has not been settled.

interloper N. intruder. The merchant thought of his competitors as *interlopers* who were stealing away his trade.

interment N. burial. *Interment* will take place in the church cemetery at 2 P.M. Wednesday.

interminable ADJ. endless. Although his speech lasted for only twenty minutes, it seemed *interminable* to his bored audience.

intermittent ADJ. periodic; on and off. Our picnic was marred by *intermittent* rains.

internecine ADJ. mutually destructive. The rising death toll on both sides indicates the *internecine* nature of this conflict.

interpolate V. insert between. She talked so much that I could not *interpolate* a single remark.

interstices N. chinks; crevices. The mountain climber sought to obtain a foothold in the *interstices* of the cliff.

intervene V. come between. She *intervened* in the argument between her two sons.

intimate V. hint. She *intimated* rather than stated her preferences.

intimidation N. fear. A ruler who maintains his power by *intimidation* is bound to develop clandestine resistance.

intractable ADJ. unruly; refractory. The horse was *intractable* and refused to enter the starting gate.

intransigence N. state of stubborn unwillingness to compromise. The *intransigence* of both parties in the dispute makes an early settlement almost impossible to obtain.

intransigent ADJ. refusing any compromise. The strike settlement has collapsed because both sides are *intransigent.*

intrepid ADJ. fearless. For his *intrepid* conduct in battle, he was promoted.

intrinsic ADJ. belonging to a thing in itself; inherent. Although the *intrinsic* value of this award is small, I shall always cherish it.

introspective ADJ. looking within oneself. We all have our *introspective* moments during which we examine our souls.

introvert N. one who is introspective; inclined to think more about oneself. In his poetry, he reveals that he is an *introvert* by his intense interest in his own problems. also V.

intrude V. trespass; enter as an uninvited person. She hesitated to *intrude* on their conversation.

intuition N. power of knowing without reasoning. She claimed to know the truth by *intuition.* intuitive, ADJ.

inundate V. overflow; flood. The tremendous waves *inundated* the town.

inured ADJ. accustomed; hardened. She became *inured* to the Alaskan cold.

invalidate V. weaken; destroy. The relatives who received little or nothing sought to *invalidate* the will by claiming that the deceased had not been in his right mind when he had signed the document.

invective N. abuse. He had expected criticism but not the *invective* which greeted his proposal.

inveigh V. denounce; utter censure or invective. He *inveighed* against the demagoguery of the previous speaker and urged that the audience reject his philosophy as dangerous.

inveigle V. lead astray; wheedle. She was *inveigled* into joining the club.

inverse ADJ. opposite. There is an *inverse* ratio between the strength of light and its distance.

invert V. turn upside down or inside out. When he *inverted* his body in a hand stand, he felt the blood rush to his head.

inveterate ADJ. deep-rooted; habitual. She is an *inveterate* smoker.

invidious ADJ. designed to create ill will or envy. We disregarded her *invidious* remarks because we realized how jealous she was.

TEST—WORD LIST 26—*Synonyms*

Each of the questions below consists of a word in capital letters, followed by five lettered words or phrases. Choose the lettered word or phrase that is most nearly similar in meaning to the word in capital letters and write the letter of your choice on your answer paper.

376. INGENUOUS (A) clever (B) stimulating (C) naive (D) worried (E) cautious
377. INIMICAL (A) antagonistic (B) anonymous (C) fanciful (D) accurate (E) seldom
378. INNOCUOUS (A) not capable (B) not dangerous (C) not eager (D) not frank (E) not peaceful
379. INSINUATE (A) resist (B) suggest (C) report (D) rectify (E) lecture
380. INSIPID (A) witty (B) flat (C) wily (D) talkative (E) lucid
381. INTEGRATE (A) tolerate (B) unite (C) flow (D) copy (E) assume
382. INTER (A) bury (B) amuse (C) relate (D) frequent (E) abandon
383. INTERDICT (A) acclaim (B) dispute (C) prohibit (D) decide (E) fret
384. INTERMITTENT (A) heavy (B) fleet (C) occasional (D) fearless (E) responding
385. INTRACTABLE (A) culpable (B) flexible (C) unruly (D) efficient (E) base
386. INTRANSIGENCE (A) lack of training (B) stubbornness (C) novelty (D) timidity (E) cupidity
387. INTREPID (A) cold (B) hot (C) understood (D) callow (E) courageous
388. INTRINSIC (A) extrinsic (B) abnormal (C) above (D) abandoned (E) basic
389. INUNDATE (A) abuse (B) deny (C) swallow (D) treat (E) flood
390. INVEIGH (A) speak violently (B) orate (C) disturb (D) apply (E) whisper

WORD LIST 27 **invincible - laity**

invincible ADJ. unconquerable. Superman is *invincible.*

inviolability N. security from being destroyed, corrupted or profaned. They respected the *inviolability* of her faith and did not try to change her manner of living.

invoke V. call upon; ask for. She *invoked* her advisor's aid in filling out her financial aid forms.

invulnerable ADJ. incapable of injury. Achilles was *invulnerable* except in his heel.

iota N. very small quantity. She hadn't an *iota* of common sense.

irascible ADJ. irritable; easily angered. Her *irascible* temper frightened me.

iridescent ADJ. exhibiting rainbowlike colors. She admired the *iridescent* hues of the oil that floated on the surface of the water.

irksome ADJ. repetitious; tedious. He found working on the assembly line *irksome* because of the monotony of the operation he had to perform.

ironical ADJ. resulting in an unexpected and contrary manner. It is *ironical* that his success came when he least wanted it. irony, N.

irony N. hidden sarcasm or satire; use of words that convey a meaning opposite to the literal meaning. Gradually his listeners began to realize that the excessive praise he was lavishing was merely *irony;* he was actually denouncing his opponent.

irreconcilable ADJ. incompatible; not able to be resolved. Because the separated couple were *irreconcilable,* the marriage counselor recommended a divorce.

irrefragable ADJ. not to be disproved; indisputable. The testimonies of the witnesses provide *irrefragable* proof that my client is innocent; I demand that he be released at once.

irrelevant ADJ. not applicable; unrelated. This statement is *irrelevant* and should be disregarded by the jury.

irremediable ADJ. incurable; uncorrectable. The error she made was *irremediable.*

irreparable ADJ. not able to be corrected or repaired. Your apology cannot atone for the *irreparable* damage you have done to her reputation.

irrepressible ADJ. unable to be restrained or held back. Her high spirits were *irrepressible.*

irreverent ADJ. lacking proper respect. The worshippers resented her *irreverent* remarks about their faith.

irrevocable ADJ. unalterable. Let us not brood over past mistakes since they are *irrevocable.*

isotope N. varying form of an element. The study of the *isotopes* of uranium led to the development of the nuclear bomb.

iterate V. utter a second time; repeat. I will *iterate* the warning I have previously given to you.

itinerant ADJ. wandering; traveling. He was an *itinerant* peddler and traveled through Pennsylvania and Virginia selling his wares. also N.

itinerary N. plan of a trip. Before leaving for his first visit to France and England, he discussed his *itinerary* with people who had been there and with his travel agent.

jaded ADJ. fatigued; surfeited. He looked for exotic foods to stimulate his *jaded* appetite.

jargon N. language used by special group; gibberish. We tried to understand the *jargon* of the peddlers in the marketplace but could not find any basis for comprehension.

jaundiced ADJ. yellowed; prejudiced; envious. She gazed at the painting with *jaundiced* eyes.

jaunt N. trip; short journey. He took a quick *jaunt* to Atlantic City.

jaunty ADJ. stylish; perky; carefree. She wore her beret at a *jaunty* angle.

jejune ADJ. lacking interest; barren; meager. The plot of the play is *jejune* and fails to capture the interest of the audience.

jeopardy N. exposure to death or danger. She cannot be placed in double *jeopardy.*

jeremiad N. lament; complaint. His account of the event was a lengthy *jeremiad,* unrelieved by any light moments.

jettison V. throw overboard. In order to enable the ship to ride safely through the storm, the captain had to *jettison* much of his cargo.

jingoism N. extremely aggressive and militant patriotism. We must be careful to prevent a spirit of *jingoism* from spreading at this time; the danger of a disastrous war is too great.

jocose ADJ. giving to joking. The salesman was so *jocose* that many of his customers suggested that he become a "stand-up" comic.

jocular ADJ. said or done in jest. Do not take my *jocular* remarks seriously.

jocund ADJ. merry. Santa Claus is always vivacious and *jocund.*

jollity N. gaiety; cheerfulness. The festive Christmas dinner was a merry one, and old and young alike joined in the general *jollity.*

jostle V. shove; bumped. In the subway he was *jostled* by the crowds.

jovial ADJ. good-natured; merry. A frown seemed out of place on his invariably *jovial* face.

juggernaut N. irresistible crushing force. Nothing could survive in the path of the *juggernaut.*

jubilation N. rejoicing. There was great *jubilation* when the armistice was announced.

judicious ADJ. wise; determined by sound judgment. I believe that this plan is not *judicious;* it is too risky.

juncture N. crisis; joining point. At this critical *juncture,* let us think carefully before determining the course we shall follow.

junket N. a merry feast or picnic. The opposition claimed that her trip to Europe was merely a political *junket.*

junta N. group of men joined in political intrigue; cabal. As soon as he learned of its existence, the dictator ordered the execution of all of the members of the *junta.*

jurisprudence N. science of law. He was more a student of *jurisprudence* than a practitioner of the law.

juxtapose V. place side by side. Comparison will be easier if you *juxtapose* the two objects.

kaleidoscope N. tube in which patterns made by the reflection in mirrors of colored pieces of glass, etc., produce interesting symmetrical effects. People found a new source of entertainment while peering through Sir David Brewster's invention, the *kaleidoscope;* they found the ever-changing patterns fascinating.

ken N. range of knowledge. I cannot answer your question since this matter is beyond my *ken.*

kindle V. start a fire; inspire. Her teacher's praise *kindled* a spark of hope inside her.

kindred ADJ. related; belonging to the same family. Tom Sawyer and Huck Finn were two *kindred* spirits. also N.

kiosk N. summer house; open pavilion. She waited at the subway *kiosk.*

kinetic ADJ. producing motion. Designers of the electric automobile find that their greatest obstacle lies in the development of light and efficient storage batteries, the source of the *kinetic* energy needed to propel the vehicle.

kismet N. fate. *Kismet* is the Arabic word for "fate."

kith N. familiar friends. He always helped both his *kith* and kin.

kleptomaniac N. person who has a compulsive desire to steal. They discovered that the wealthy customer was a *kleptomaniac* when they caught her stealing some cheap trinkets.

knavery N. rascality. We cannot condone such *knavery* in public officials.

knead V. mix; work dough. Her hands grew strong from *kneading* bread.

knell N. tolling of a bell at a funeral; sound of the funeral bell. "The curfew tolls the *knell* of parting day."

knoll N. little round hill. Robert Louis Stevenson's grave is on a *knoll* in Samoa.

labyrinth N. maze. Tom and Betty were lost in the *labyrinth* of secret caves.

lacerate V. mangle; tear. Her body was *lacerated* in the automobile crash.

lachrymose ADJ. producing tears. His voice has a *lachrymose* quality which is more appropriate at a funeral than a class reunion.

lackadaisical ADJ. affectedly languid. He was *lackadaisical* and indifferent about his part in the affair.

lackey N. footman; toady. The duke was followed by his *lackeys.*

lackluster ADJ. dull. We were disappointed by the *lackluster* performance.

laconic ADJ. brief and to the point. Will Rogers' *laconic* comments on the news made him world famous.

laggard ADJ. slow; sluggish. The sailor had been taught not to be *laggard* in carrying out orders.

lagniappe N. trifling present given to a customer. The butcher threw in some bones for the dog as a *lagniappe.*

lagoon N. shallow body of water near a sea; lake. They enjoyed their swim in the calm *lagoon.*

laity N. laymen; persons not connected with the clergy. The *laity* does not always understand the clergy's problems.

TEST—WORD LIST 27—*Antonyms*

Each of the questions below consists of a word in capital letters, followed by five lettered words or phrases. Choose the lettered word or phrase that is most nearly opposite in meaning to the word in capital letters and write the letter of your choice on your answer paper.

391. IRKSOME (A) interesting (B) lazy (C) tireless (D) few (E) too many
392. IRRELEVANT (A) lacking piety (B) fragile (C) congruent (D) pertinent (E) varied
393. IRREPARABLE (A) legible (B) correctable (C) proverbial (D) concise (E) legal
394. IRREVERENT (A) related (B) mischievous (C) respecting (D) pious (E) violent
395. JADED (A) upright (B) stimulated (C) aspiring (D) applied (E) void
396. JAUNDICED (A) whitened (B) inflamed (C) quickened (D) aged (E) unbiased

397. JEJUNE (A) youthful (B) ancient (C) strong (D) fictional (E) interesting
398. JEREMIAD (A) prophecy (B) proposition (C) praise (D) overture (E) explanation
399. JETTISON (A) salvage (B) submerge (C) descend (D) decelerate (E) repent
400. JOCULAR (A) arterial (B) bloodless (C) verbose (D) serious (E) blind
401. JUDICIOUS (A) punitive (B) unwise (C) criminal (D) licit (E) temporary
402. KITH (A) outfit (B) strangers (C) brothers (D) ceramics tool (E) quality
403. LACHRYMOSE (A) cheering (B) smooth (C) passionate (D) curt (E) tense
404. LACKADAISICAL (A) monthly (B) possessing time (C) ambitious (D) pusillanimous (E) intelligent
405. LACONIC (A) milky (B) verbose (C) wicked (D) flagrant (E) derelict

WORD LIST 28 lambent - lout

lambent ADJ. flickering; softly radiant. They sat quietly before the *lambent* glow of the fireplace.

laminated ADJ. made of thin plates or scales. Banded gneiss is a *laminated* rock.

lampoon V. ridicule. This article *lampoons* the pretensions of some movie moguls. also N.

languid ADJ. weary; sluggish; listless. Her siege of illness left her *languid* and pallid.

languish V. lose animation; lose strength. In stories, lovelorn damsels used to *languish* and pine away.

languor N. lassitude; depression. His friends tried to overcome the *languor* into which he had fallen by taking him to parties and to the theater.

lank ADJ. long and thin. *Lank,* gaunt, Abraham Lincoln was a striking figure.

lapidary N. worker in precious stones. She employed a *lapidary* to cut the large diamond.

larceny N. theft. Because of the prisoner's record, the district attorney refused to reduce the charge from grand *larceny* to petit larceny.

largess N. generous gift. Lady Bountiful distributed *largess* to the poor.

lascivious ADJ. lustful. The *lascivious* books were confiscated and destroyed.

lassitude N. languor; weariness. The hot, tropical weather created a feeling of *lassitude* and encouraged drowsiness.

latent ADJ. dormant; hidden. Her *latent* talent was discovered by accident.

lateral ADJ. coming from the side. In order to get good plant growth, the gardener must pinch off all *lateral* shoots.

latitude N. freedom from narrow limitations. I think you have permitted your son too much *latitude* in this matter.

laudable ADJ. praiseworthy; commendable. His *laudable* deeds will be remembered by all whom he aided.

laudatory ADJ. expressing praise. The critics' *laudatory* comments helped to make her a star.

lave V. wash. The running water will *lave* away all stains.

lavish ADJ. liberal; wasteful. The actor's *lavish* gifts pleased her. also V.

lax ADJ. careless. We dislike restaurants where the service is *lax.*

lecherous ADJ. impure in thought and act; lustful; unchaste. He is a *lecherous* and wicked old man.

lechery N. gross lewdness; lustfulness. In his youth he led a life of *lechery* and debauchery; he did not mend his ways until middle age.

lectern N. reading desk. The chaplain delivered his sermon from a hastily improvised *lectern.*

leeway N. room to move; margin. When you set a deadline, allow a little *leeway.*

legerdemain N. sleight of hand. The magician demonstrated his renowned *legerdemain.*

leniency N. mildness; permissiveness. Considering the gravity of the offense, we were surprised by the *leniency* of the sentence.

leonine N. like a lion. He was *leonine* in his rage.

lesion N. unhealthy change in structure; injury. Many *lesions* are the result of disease.

lethal ADJ. deadly. It is unwise to leave *lethal* weapons where children may find them.

lethargic ADJ. drowsy; dull. The stuffy room made her *lethargic.*

levity N. lightness. Such *levity* is improper on this serious occasion.

lewd ADJ. lustful. They found his *lewd* stories objectionable.

lexicographer N. compiler of a dictionary. The new dictionary is the work of many *lexicographers* who spent years compiling and editing the work.

lexicon N. dictionary. I cannot find this word in any *lexicon* in the library. lexicographer, N.

liaison N. officer who acts as go-between for two armies. As the *liaison,* he had to avoid offending the leaders of the two armies. also ADJ.

libation N. drink. He offered a *libation* to the gods.

libelous ADJ. defamatory; injurious to the good name of a person. He sued the newspaper because of its *libelous* story.

libertine N. debauched person, roué. Although she was aware of his reputation as a *libertine,* she felt she could reform him and help him break his dissolute way of life.

libidinous ADJ. lustful. They objected to his *libidinous* behavior.

libido N. emotional urges behind human activity. The psychiatrist maintained that suppression of the *libido* often resulted in maladjustment and neuroses.

libretto N. text of an opera. The composer of an opera's music is remembered more frequently than the author of its *libretto.*

licentious ADJ. wanton; lewd; dissolute. The *licentious* monarch helped bring about his country's downfall.

lieu N. instead of. They accepted his check in *lieu* of cash.

lilliputian ADJ. extremely small. The model was built on a *lilliputian* scale. also N.

limber ADJ. flexible. Hours of ballet classes kept him *limber.*

limbo N. region near heaven or hell where certain souls are kept; a prison (slang). Among the divisions of Hell are Purgatory and *Limbo.*

limn V. portray; describe vividly. He was never satisfied with his attempts to *limn* her beauty on canvas.

limpid ADJ. clear. A *limpid* stream ran through his property.

lineage N. descent; ancestry. He traced his *lineage* back to Mayflower days.

lineaments N. features of the face. She quickly sketched the *lineaments* of his face.

linguistic ADJ. pertaining to language. The modern tourist will encounter very little *linguistic* difficulty as English has become an almost universal language.

lionize V. treat as a celebrity. She enjoyed being *lionized* by the public.

liquidate V. settle accounts; clearup. He was able to *liquidate* all his debts in a short period of time.

lissom ADJ. agile; lithe. As a young boy, he was *lissom* and graceful; he gave promise of developing into a fine athlete.

listless ADJ. lacking in spirit or energy. We had expected him to be full of enthusiasm and were surprised by his *listless* attitude.

litany N. supplicatory prayer. On this solemn day, the congregation responded to the prayers of the priest during the *litany* with fervor and intensity.

lithe ADJ. flexible; supple. Her figure was *lithe* and willowy.

litigation N. lawsuit. Try to settle this amicably; I do not want to start *litigation.*

litotes N. understatement for emphasis. To say,"He little realizes," when we mean that he does not realize at all, is an example of the kind of understatement we call *litotes.*

livid ADJ. lead-colored; black and blue; enraged. His face was so *livid* with rage that we were afraid that he might have an attack of apoplexy.

loath ADJ. averse; reluctant. They were both *loath* for him to go.

loathe V. detest. We *loathed* the wicked villain.

lode N. metal-bearing vein. If this *lode* which we have discovered extends for any distance, we have found a fortune.

lofty ADJ. very high. They used to tease him about his *lofty* ambitions.

loiter V. hang around; linger. The policeman told him not to *loiter* in the alley.

loll V. lounge about. They *lolled* around in their chairs watching television.

longevity N. long life. The old man was proud of his *longevity.*

lope V. gallop slowly. As the horses *loped* along, we had an opportunity to admire the ever-changing scenery.

loquacious ADJ. talkative. She is very *loquacious* and can speak on the telephone for hours.

lout N. clumsy person. The delivery boy is an awkward *lout.*

TEST—WORD LIST 28—*Antonyms*

Each of the questions below consists of a word in capital letters, followed by five lettered words or phrases. Choose the lettered word or phrase that is most nearly opposite in meaning to the word in capital letters and write the letter of your choice on your answer paper.

406. LAMPOON (A) darken (B) praise (C) abandon (D) sail (E) fly
407. LANGUOR (A) vitality (B) length (C) embarrassment (D) wine (E) avarice
408. LATENT (A) trim (B) forbidding (C) execrable (D) early (E) obvious
409. LAVISH (A) hostile (B) unwashed (C) timely (D) decent (E) frugal

410. LAUDATORY (A) dirtying (B) disclaiming (C) defamatory (D) inflammatory (E) debased
411. LAX (A) salty (B) strict (C) shrill (D) boring (E) cowardly
412. LECHERY (A) trust (B) compulsion (C) zeal (D) addiction (E) purity
413. LETHARGIC (A) convalescent (B) beautiful (C) enervating (D) invigorating (E) interrogating
414. LEVITY (A) bridge (B) dam (C) praise (D) blame (E) solemnity
415. LILLIPUTIAN (A) destructive (B) proper (C) gigantic (D) elegant (E) barren
416. LIMPID (A) erect (B) turbid (C) tangential (D) timid (E) weary
417. LITHE (A) stiff (B) limpid (C) facetious (D) insipid (E) vast
418. LIVID (A) alive (B) mundane (C) positive (D) undiscolored (E) vast
419. LOATH (A) loose (B) evident (C) deliberate (D) eager (E) tiny
420. LOQUACIOUS (A) taciturn (B) sentimental (C) soporific (D) soothing (E) sedate

WORD LIST 29 lubricity - maunder

lubricity N. slipperiness; evasiveness. He exasperated the reporters by his *lubricity;* they could not pin him down to a definite answer.

lucent ADJ. shining. The moon's *lucent* rays silvered the river.

lucid ADJ. bright; easily understood. His explanation was *lucid* and to the point.

lucrative ADJ. profitable. He turned his hobby into a *lucrative* profession.

lucre N. money. Preferring *lucre* to fame, he wrote stories of popular appeal.

ludicrous ADJ. laughable; trifling. Let us be serious; this is not a *ludicrous* issue.

lugubrious ADJ. mournful. The *lugubrious* howling of the dogs added to our sadness.

lull N. moment of calm. Not wanting to get wet, they waited under the awning for a *lull* in the rain.

luminous ADJ. shining; issuing light. The sun is a *luminous* body.

lunar ADJ. pertaining to the moon. *Lunar* craters can be plainly seen with the aid of a small telescope.

lupine ADJ. like a wolf. She was terrified of his fierce, *lupine* smile.

lurid ADJ. wild; sensational. The *lurid* stories he told shocked his listeners.

luscious ADJ. pleasing to taste or smell. The ripe peach was *luscious.*

luster N. shine; gloss. The soft *luster* of the silk in the dim light was pleasing.

lustrous ADJ. shining. Her large and *lustrous* eyes gave a touch of beauty to an otherwise drab face.

luxuriant ADJ. fertile; abundant; ornate. Farming was easy in this *luxuriant* soil.

macabre ADJ. gruesome; grisly. The city morgue is a *macabre* spot for the uninitiated.

macerate V. waste away. Cancer *macerated* his body.

Machiavellian ADJ. crafty; double-dealing. I do not think he will be a good ambassador because he is not accustomed to the *Machiavellian* maneuverings of foreign diplomats.

machinations N. schemes. I can see through your wily *machinations.*

madrigal N. pastoral song. His program of folk songs included several *madrigals* which he sang to the accompaniment of a lute.

maelstrom N. whirlpool. The canoe was tossed about in the *maelstrom.*

magnanimous ADJ. generous. The philanthropist was most *magnanimous.*

magnate N. person of prominence or influence. The steel *magnate* decided to devote more time to city politics.

magniloquent ADJ. boastful, pompous. In their stories of the trial, the reporters ridiculed the *magniloquent* speeches of the defense attorney.

magnitude N. greatness; extent. It is difficult to comprehend the *magnitude* of his crime.

maim V. mutilate; injure. The hospital could not take care of all who had been wounded or *maimed* in the railroad accident.

maladroit ADJ. clumsy; bungling. In his usual *maladroit* way, he managed to upset the cart and spill the food.

malaise N. uneasiness; distress. She felt a sudden vague *malaise.*

malapropism N. comic misuse of a word. Mrs. Warren's funniest *malapropism* occurs when she accuses Skitterby of being "a snare and an Andalusian."

malcontent N. person dissatisfied with existing state of affairs. He was one of the few *malcontents* in Congress; he constantly voiced his objections to the Presidential program. also ADJ.

malediction N. curse. The witch uttered *maledictions* against her captors.

malefactor N. criminal. We must try to bring these *malefactors* to justice.

malevolent ADJ. wishing evil. We must thwart his *malevolent* schemes.

malicious ADJ. dictated by hatred or spite. The *malicious* neighbor spread the gossip.

malign V. speak evil of; defame. Because of her hatred of the family, she *maligns* all who are friendly to them.

malignant ADJ. having an evil influence; virulent. This is a *malignant* disease; we may have to use drastic measures to stop its spread.

malingerer N. one who feigns illness to escape duty. The captain ordered the sergeant to punish all *malingerers.*

mall N. public walk. The *Mall* in Central Park has always been a favorite spot for Sunday strollers.

malleable ADJ. capable of being shaped by pounding. Gold is a *malleable* metal.

malodorous ADJ. foul-smelling. The compost heap was most *malodorous* in summer.

mammal N. a vertebrate animal whose female suckles its young. Many people regard the whale as a fish and do not realize that it is a *mammal.*

mammoth ADJ. gigantic. The *mammoth* corporations of the twentieth century are a mixed blessing.

manacle V. restrain; handcuff. The police immediately *manacled* the prisoner. also N.

mandate N. order; charge. In his inaugural address, the President stated that he had a *mandate* from the people to seek an end to social evils such as poverty, poor housing, etc. also V.

mandatory ADJ. obligatory. These instructions are *mandatory;* any violation will be severely punished.

mangy ADJ. shabby; wretched. We finally threw out the *mangy* rug.

maniacal ADJ. raving mad. His *maniacal* laughter frightened us.

manifest ADJ. understandable; clear. His evil intentions were *manifest* and yet we could not stop him. also V.

manifesto N. declaration; statement of policy. This statement may be regarded as the *manifesto* of the party's policy.

manifold ADJ. numerous; varied. I cannot begin to tell you how much I appreciate your *manifold* kindnesses.

manipulate V. operate with the hands. How do you *manipulate* these puppets?

manumit V. emancipate; free from bondage. Enlightened slave owners were willing to *manumit* their slaves and thus put an end to the evil of slavery in the country.

marauder N. raider; intruder. The sounding of the alarm frightened the *marauders.*

marital ADJ. pertaining to marriage. After the publication of his book on *marital* affairs, he was often consulted by married people on the verge of divorce.

maritime ADJ. bordering on the sea; nautical. The *Maritime* Provinces depend on the sea for their wealth.

marred ADJ. damaged; disfigured. She had to refinish the *marred* surface of the table.

marrow N. soft tissue filling the bones. The frigid cold chilled the traveler to the *marrow.*

marsupial N. one of a family of mammals that nurse their offspring in a pouch. The most common *marsupial* in North America is the opossum.

martial ADJ. warlike. The sound of *martial* music is always inspiring.

martinet N. strict disciplinarian. The commanding officer was a *martinet* who observed each regulation to the letter.

masochist N. person who enjoys his own pain. The *masochist* begs, "Hit me." The sadist smiles and says, "I won't."

masticate V. chew. We must *masticate* our food carefully and slowly in order to avoid stomach disorders.

maternal ADJ. motherly. Many animals display *maternal* instincts only while their offspring are young and helpless.

matriarch N. woman who rules a family or larger social group. The *matriarch* ruled her gypsy tribe with a firm hand.

matricide N. murder of a mother by a child. A crime such as *matricide* is inconceivable.

matrix N. mold or die. The cast around the *matrix* was cracked.

maudlin ADJ. effusively sentimental. I do not like such *maudlin* pictures. I call them tearjerkers.

maul V. handle roughly. The rock star was *mauled* by his over-excited fans.

maunder V. talk incoherently; utter drivel. You do not make sense; you *maunder* and garble your words.

TEST—WORD LIST 29—*Synonyms and Antonyms*

Each of the following questions consists of a word in capital letters, followed by five lettered words or phrases. Choose the lettered word or phrase which is most nearly similar or the opposite of the word in capital letters and write the letter of your choice on your answer paper.

421. LUGUBRIOUS (A) frantic (B) cheerful (C) burdensome (D) oily (E) militant
422. LURID (A) dull (B) duplicate (C) heavy (D) grotesque (E) intelligent
423. MACABRE (A) musical (B) frightening (C) chewed (D) wicked (E) exceptional
424. MAGNILOQUENT (A) loquacious (B) bombastic (C) rudimentary (D) qualitative (E) minimizing
425. MAGNITUDE (A) realization (B) fascination (C) enormity (D) gratitude (E) interference
426. MALADROIT (A) malicious (B) starving (C) thirsty (D) tactless (E) artistic
427. MALEDICTION (A) misfortune (B) hap (C) fruition (D) correct pronunciation (E) benediction
428. MALEFACTOR (A) quail (B) lawbreaker (C) beneficiary (D) banker (E) female agent
429. MALEVOLENT (A) kindly (B) vacuous (C) ambivalent (D) volatile (E) primitive
430. MALIGN (A) intersperse (B) vary (C) emphasize (D) frighten (E) eulogize
431. MALLEABLE (A) brittle (B) blatant (C) brilliant (D) brownish (E) basking
432. MANIACAL (A) demoniac (B) saturated (C) sane (D) sanitary (E) handcuffed
433. MANIFEST (A) limited (B) obscure (C) faulty (D) varied (E) vital
434. MANUMIT (A) print (B) impress (C) enslave (D) endeavor (E) fail
435. MARTIAL (A) bellicose (B) celibate (C) divorced (D) quiescent (E) planetary

---

WORD LIST 30 **mausoleum - misnomer**

mausoleum N. monumental tomb. His body was placed in the family *mausoleum.*

mauve ADJ. pale purple. The *mauve* tint in the lilac bush was another indication that Spring had finally arrived.

maverick N. rebel. How can you keep such a *maverick* in line?

mawkish ADJ. sickening; insipid. Your *mawkish* sighs fill me with disgust.

maxim N. proverb; a truth pithily stated. Aesop's fables illustrate moral *maxims.*

mayhem N. injury to body. The riot was marked not only by *mayhem* with its attendant loss of life and limb but also by arson and pillage.

meander V. to wind or turn in its course. It is difficult to sail up this stream because of the way it *meanders* through the countryside.

meddlesome ADJ. interfering. He felt his marriage was suffering because of his *meddlesome* mother-in-law.

mediate V. settle a dispute through the services of an outsider. Let us *mediate* our differences rather than engage in a costly strike.

mediocre ADJ. ordinary; commonplace. We were disappointed because he gave a rather *mediocre* performance in this role.

meditation N. reflection; thought. She reached her decision only after much *meditation.*

medley N. mixture. The band played a *medley* of Gershwin tunes.

megalomania N. mania for doing grandiose things. Developers who spend millions trying to build the world's tallest skyscraper suffer from *megalomania.*

mélange N. medley; miscellany. This anthology provides a *mélange* of the author's output in the fields of satire, criticism and political analysis.

melee N. fight. The captain tried to ascertain the cause of the *melee* which had broken out among the crew members.

mellifluous ADJ. flowing smoothly; smooth. Italian is a *mellifluous* language.

memento N. token; reminder. Take this book as a *memento* of your visit.

memorialize V. commemorate. Let us *memorialize* his great contribution by dedicating this library in his honor.

mendacious ADJ. lying; false. He was a pathological liar, and his friends learned to discount his *mendacious* stories.

mendicant N. beggar. From the moment we left the ship, we were surrounded by *mendicants* and peddlers.

menial ADJ. suitable for servants; low. I cannot understand why a person of your ability and talent should engage in such *menial* activities. also N.

mentor N. teacher. During this very trying period, he could not have had a better *mentor,* for the teacher was sympathetic and understanding.

mercantile ADJ. concerning trade. I am more interested in the opportunities available in the *mercantile* field than I am in those in the legal profession.

mercenary ADJ. interested in money or gain. I am certain that your action was prompted by *mercenary* motives. also N.

mercurial ADJ. fickle; changing. He was of a *mercurial* temperament and therefore unpredictable.

meretricious ADJ. flashy; tawdry. Her jewels were inexpensive but not *meretricious.*

meringue N. a pastry decoration made of whites of eggs. The lemon *meringue* pie is one of our specialties.

mesa N. high, flat-topped hill. The *mesa,* rising above the surrounding countryside, was the most conspicuous feature of the area.

mesmerize V. hypnotize. The incessant drone seemed to *mesmerize* him and place him in a hypnotic trance.

metallurgical ADJ. pertaining to the art of removing metals from ores. During the course of his *metallurgical* research, the scientist developed a steel alloy of tremendous strength.

metamorphosis N. change of form. The *metamorphosis* of caterpillar to butterfly is typical of many such changes in animal life.

metaphor N. implied comparison. "He soared like an eagle" is an example of a simile; "He is an eagle in flight," a *metaphor.*

metaphysical ADJ. pertaining to speculative philosophy. The modern poets have gone back to the fanciful poems of the *metaphysical* poets of the seventeenth century for many of their images. metaphysics, N.

mete V. measure; distribute. He tried to be impartial in his efforts to *mete* out justice.

meteoric ADJ. swift; momentarily brilliant. We all wondered at his *meteoric* rise to fame.

meticulous ADJ. excessively careful. He was *meticulous* in checking his accounts.

metropolis N. large city. Every evening this terminal is filled with the thousands of commuters who are going from this *metropolis* to their homes in the suburbs.

mettle N. courage; spirit. When challenged by the other horses in the race, the thoroughbred proved its *mettle* by its determination to hold the lead.

mews N. group of stables built around a courtyard. Let us visit the *mews* to inspect the newly purchased horse.

miasma N. swamp gas; odor of decaying matter. I suspect that this area is infested with malaria as I can readily smell the *miasma.*

microcosm N. small world. In the *microcosm* of our small village, we find illustrations of all the evils that beset the universe.

mien N. demeanor; bearing. She had the gracious *mien* of a queen.

migrant ADJ. changing its habitat; wandering. These *migrant* birds return every spring. also N.

migratory ADJ. wandering. The return of the *migratory* birds to the northern sections of this country is a harbinger of spring.

milieu N. environment; means of expression. His *milieu* is watercolor although he has produced excellent oil paintings and lithographs.

militant ADJ. combative; bellicose. Although at this time he was advocating a policy of neutrality, one could usually find him adopting a more *militant* attitude. also N.

militate V. work against. Your record of lateness and absence will *militate* against your chances of promotion.

millennium N. thousand-year period; period of happiness and prosperity. I do not expect the *millennium* to come during my lifetime.

mimicry N. imitation. Her gift for *mimicry* was so great that her friends said that she should be in the theater.

minaret N. slender tower attached to a mosque. From the balcony of the *minaret* we obtained an excellent view of the town and the neighboring countryside.

minatory ADJ. threatening. All abusive and *minatory* letters received by the mayor and other public officials were examined by the police.

mincing ADJ. affectedly dainty. Yum-Yum walked across the stage with *mincing* steps.

minion N. a servile dependent. He was always accompanied by several of his *minions* because he enjoyed their subservience and flattery.

minuscule ADJ. extremely small. Why should I involve myself with a project with so *minuscule* a chance for success?

minutiae N. petty details. She would have liked to ignore the *minutiae* of daily living.

mirage N. unreal reflection; optical illusion. The lost prospector was fooled by a *mirage* in the desert.

mire V. entangle; stick in swampy ground. Their rear wheels became *mired* in mud. also N.

mirth N. merriment; laughter. Sober Malvolio found Sir Toby's *mirth* improper.

misadventure N. mischance; ill luck. The young explorer met death by *misadventure.*

misanthrope N. one who hates mankind. We thought the hermit was a *misanthrope* because he shunned our society.

misapprehension N. error; misunderstanding. To avoid *misapprehension,* I am going to ask all of you to repeat the instructions I have given.

miscegenation N. intermarriage between races. Some states passed laws against *miscegenation.*

miscellany N. mixture of writings on various subjects. This is an interesting *miscellany* of nineteenth-century prose.

mischance N. ill luck. By *mischance,* he lost his week's salary.

miscreant N. wretch; villain. His kindness to the *miscreant* amazed all of us who had expected to hear severe punishment pronounced.

misdemeanor N. minor crime. The culprit pleaded guilty to a *misdemeanor* rather than face trial for a felony.

miserly ADJ. stingy; mean. The *miserly* old man hoarded his coins not out of prudence but out of greed.

misgivings N. doubts. Hamlet described his *misgivings* to Horatio but decided to fence with Laertes despite his foreboding of evil.

mishap N. accident. With a little care you could have avoided this *mishap.*

misnomer N. wrong name; incorrect designation. His tyrannical conduct proved to all that his nickname, King Eric the Just, was a *misnomer.*

TEST—WORD LIST 30—*Synonyms*

Each of the questions below consists of a word in capital letters, followed by five lettered words or phrases. Choose the lettered word or phrase that is most nearly similar in meaning to the word in capital letters and write the letter of your choice on your answer paper.

436. MAWKISH (A) sentimental (B) true (C) certain (D) devious (E) carefree
437. MEDIOCRE (A) average (B) bitter (C) medieval (D) industrial (E) agricultural
438. MELEE (A) heat (B) brawl (C) attempt (D) weapon (E) choice
439. MELLIFLUOUS (A) porous (B) honeycombed (C) strong (D) smooth (E) viscous
440. MENIAL (A) intellectual (B) clairvoyant (C) servile (D) arrogant (E) laudatory
441. MENTOR (A) guide (B) genius (C) talker (D) philosopher (E) stylist
442. MESMERIZE (A) remember (B) hypnotize (C) delay (D) bore (E) analyze
443. METICULOUS (A) steadfast (B) recent (C) quaint (D) painstaking (E) overt
444. MIASMA (A) dream (B) noxious fumes (C) scenario (D) quantity (E) total
445. MILITANT (A) combative (B) dramatic (C) religious (D) quaint (E) paternal
446. MINION (A) monster (B) quorum (C) majority (D) host (E) dependent
447. MIRAGE (A) dessert (B) illusion (C) water (D) mirror (E) statement
448. MISANTHROPE (A) benefactor (B) philanderer (C) hermit (D) aesthete (E) epicure
449. MISCHANCE (A) gamble (B) ordinance (C) aperture (D) anecdote (E) adversity
450. MISDEMEANOR (A) felony (B) peccadillo (C) indignity (D) fiat (E) illiteracy

WORD LIST 31 **misogamy - natal**

misogamy N. hatred of marriage. He remained a bachelor not because of *misogamy* but because of ill fate: his fiancee died before the wedding.

misogynist N. hater of women. She accused him of being a *misogynist* because he had been a bachelor all his life.

missile N. object to be thrown or projected. Scientists are experimenting with guided *missiles.*

missive N. letter. The ambassador received a *missive* from the Secretary of State.

mite N. very small object or creature; small coin. The criminal was so heartless that he even stole the widow's *mite.*

mitigate V. appease. Nothing he did could *mitigate* her wrath; she was unforgiving.

mnemonic ADJ. pertaining to memory. He used *mnemonic* tricks to master new words.

mobile ADJ. movable; not fixed. The *mobile* blood bank operated by the Red Cross visited our neighborhood today. mobility, N.

mode N. prevailing style. She was not used to their lavish *mode* of living.

modicum N. limited quantity. Although his story is based on a *modicum* of truth, most of the events he describes are fictitious.

modish ADJ. fashionable. She always discarded all garments which were no longer *modish.*

modulation N. toning down; changing from one key to another. When she spoke, it was with quiet *modulation* of voice.

mogul N. powerful person. The oil *moguls* made great profits when the price of gasoline rose.

moiety N. half; part. There is a slight *moiety* of the savage in her personality which is not easily perceived by those who do not know her well.

molecule N. the smallest part of a homogeneous substance. In chemistry, we study how atoms and *molecules* react to form new substances.

mollify V. soothe. We tried to *mollify* the hysterical child by promising her many gifts.

molt V. shed or cast off hair or feathers. The male robin *molted* in the spring.

molten ADJ. melted. The city of Pompeii was destroyed by volcanic ash rather than by *molten* lava flowing from Mount Vesuvius.

momentous ADJ. very important. On this *momentous* occasion, we must be very solemn.

momentum N. quantity of motion of a moving body; impetus. The car lost *momentum* as it tried to ascend the steep hill.

monarchy N. government under a single ruler. England today remains a *monarchy.*

monastic ADJ. related to monks. Wanting to live a religious life, he took his *monastic* vows.

monetary ADJ. pertaining to money. She was in complete charge of all *monetary* matters affecting the household.

monolithic ADJ. solidly uniform; unyielding. They sought to present a *monolithic* front.

monotheism N. belief in one God. Abraham was the first to proclaim his belief in *monotheism.*

monotony N. sameness leading to boredom. He took a clerical job, but soon grew to hate the *monotony* of his daily routine.

monumental ADJ. massive. Writing a dictionary is a *monumental* task.

moodiness N. fits of depression or gloom. We could not discover the cause of his recurrent *moodiness.*

moor N. marshy wasteland. These *moors* can only be used for hunting; they are too barren for agriculture.

moot ADJ. debatable. Our tariff policy is a *moot* subject.

moratorium N. legal delay of payment. If we declare a *moratorium* and delay collection of debts for six months, I am sure the farmers will be able to meet their bills.

morbid ADJ. given to unwholesome thought; gloomy. These *morbid* speculations are dangerous; we must lighten our thinking by emphasis on more pleasant matters.

mordant ADJ. biting; sarcastic; stinging. Actors feared the critic's *mordant* pen.

mores N. customs. The *mores* of Mexico are those of Spain with some modifications.

morganatic ADJ. describing a marriage between a member of a royal family and a commoner in which it is agreed that any children will not inherit title, etc. Refusing the suggestion of a *morganatic* marriage, the king abdicated from the throne when he could not marry the woman he loved.

moribund ADJ. at the point of death. The doctors called the family to the bedside of the *moribund* patient.

morose ADJ. ill-humored; sullen. When we first meet Hamlet, we find him *morose* and depressed.

mortician N. undertaker. The *mortician* prepared the corpse for burial.

mortify V. humiliate; punish the flesh. She was so *mortified* by her blunder that she ran to her room in tears.

mote N. small speck. The tiniest *mote* in the eye is very painful.

motif N. theme. This simple *motif* runs throughout the entire score.

motley ADJ. parti-colored; mixed. The captain had gathered a *motley* crew to sail the vessel.

mottled ADJ. spotted. When he blushed, his face took on a *mottled* hue.

mountebank N. charlatan; boastful pretender. The patent medicine man was a *mountebank.*

muddle V. confuse; mix up. His thoughts were *muddled* and chaotic. also N.

muggy ADJ. warm and damp. August in New York City is often *muggy.*

mugwump N. defector from a party. When he refused to support his party's nominees, he was called a *mugwump* and deprived of his seniority privileges in Congress.

mulct V. defraud a person of something. The lawyer was accused of trying to *mulct* the boy of his legacy.

multifarious ADJ. varied; greatly diversified. A career woman and mother, she was constantly busy with the *multifarious* activities of her daily life.

multiform ADJ. having many forms. Snowflakes are *multiform* but always hexagonal.

multilingual ADJ. having many languages. Because they are bordered by so many countries, the Swiss people are *multilingual.*

multiplicity N. state of being numerous. He was appalled by the *multiplicity* of details he had to complete before setting out on his mission.

mundane ADJ. worldly as opposed to spiritual. He was concerned only with *mundane* matters, especially the daily stock market quotations.

munificent ADJ. very generous. The *munificent* gift was presented to the bride.

murkiness N. darkness; gloom. The *murkiness* and fog of the waterfront that evening depressed me.

murrain N. plague; cattle disease. "A *murrain* on you" was a common malediction in that period.

muse V. ponder. For a moment he *mused* about the beauty of the scene, but his thoughts soon changed as he recalled his own personal problems. also N.

musky ADJ. having the odor of musk. She left a trace of *musky* perfume behind her.

muster V. gather; assemble. Washington *mustered* his forces at Trenton.

musty ADJ. stale; spoiled by age. The attic was dark and *musty.*

mutable ADJ. changing in form; fickle. His opinions were *mutable* and easily influenced by anyone who had any powers of persuasion.

mutilate V. maim. The torturer threatened to *mutilate* his victim.

mutinous ADJ. unruly; rebellious. The captain had to use force to quiet his *mutinous* crew.

myopic ADJ. nearsighted. In thinking only of your present needs and ignoring the future, you are being rather *myopic.*

myriad N. very large number. *Myriads* of mosquitoes from the swamps invaded our village every twilight. also ADJ.

nadir N. lowest point. Although few people realized it, the Dow-Jones averages had reached their *nadir* and would soon begin an upward surge.

naiveté N. quality of being unsophisticated. I cannot believe that such *naiveté* is unassumed in a person of her age and experience.

narcissist N. conceited person. A *narcissist* is his own best friend.

nascent ADJ. incipient; coming into being. If we could identify these revolutionary movements in their *nascent* state, we would be able to eliminate serious trouble in later years.

natal ADJ. pertaining to birth. He refused to celebrate his *natal* day because it reminded him of the few years he could look forward to.

TEST—WORD LIST 31—*Synonyms*

Each of the questions below consists of a word in capital letters, followed by five lettered words or phrases. Choose the lettered word or phrase that is most nearly similar in meaning to the word in capital letters and write the letter of your choice on your answer paper.

451. MODISH (A) sentimental (B) stylish (C) vacillating (D) contrary (E) adorned
452. MOLLIFY (A) avenge (B) attenuate (C) attribute (D) mortify (E) appease
453. MONETARY (A) boring (B) fascinating (C) fiscal (D) stationary (E) stationery
454. MOOT (A) visual (B) invisible (C) controversial (D) anticipatory (E) obsequious
455. MORDANT (A) dying (B) trenchant (C) fabricating (D) controlling (E) avenging
456. MORIBUND (A) dying (B) appropriate (C) leather bound (D) answering (E) undertaking
457. MOTLEY (A) active (B) disguised (C) variegated (D) somber (E) sick
458. MUGGY (A) attacking (B) fascinating (C) humid (D) characteristic (E) gelid
459. MULCT (A) swindle (B) hold (C) record (D) print (E) fertilize
460. MULTILINGUAL (A) variegated (B) polyglot (C) multilateral (D) polyandrous (E) multiplied
461. MUNDANE (A) global (B) futile (C) spatial (D) heretic (E) worldly
462. MUNIFICENT (A) grandiose (B) puny (C) philanthropic (D) poor (E) gracious
463. MUSTY (A) flat (B) necessary (C) indifferent (D) nonchalant (E) vivid
464. MYOPIC (A) visionary (B) nearsighted (C) moral (D) glassy (E) blind
465. NASCENT (A) incipient (B) ignorant (C) loyal (D) treacherous (E) unnamed

WORD LIST 32 natation - obsidian

natation N. swimming. The Red Cross emphasizes the need for courses in *natation.*

nauseate V. cause to become sick; fill with disgust. The foul smells began to *nauseate* him.

nautical ADJ. pertaining to ships or navigation. The Maritime Museum contains many models of clipper ships, log-books, anchors and many other items of a *nautical* nature.

nave N. main body of a church. The *nave* of the cathedral was empty at this hour.

neap ADJ. lowest. We shall have to navigate very cautiously over the reefs as we have a *neap* tide this time of the month.

nebulous ADJ. vague; hazy; cloudy. She had only a *nebulous* memory of her grandmother's face.

necrology N. obituary notice; list of the dead. The *necrology* of those buried in this cemetery is available in the office.

necromancy N. black magic; dealings with the dead.

Because he was able to perform feats of *necromancy,* the natives thought he was in league with the devil.

nefarious ADJ. very wicked. He was universally feared because of his many *nefarious* deeds.

negation N. denial. I must accept his argument since you have been unable to present any *negation* of his evidence.

negligence N. carelessness. *Negligence* can prove costly.

nemesis N. revenging agent. Captain Bligh vowed to be Christian's *nemesis.*

neologism N. new or newly coined word or phrase. As we invent new techniques and professions, we must also invent *neologisms* such as "microcomputer" and "astronaut" to describe them.

neophyte N. recent convert; beginner. This mountain slope contains slides that will challenge experts as well as *neophytes.*

nepotism N. favoritism (to a relative). John left his position with the company because he felt that advancement was based on *nepotism* rather than ability.

nether ADJ. lower. Tradition locates hell in the *nether* regions.

nettle V. annoy; vex. Do not let him *nettle* you with his sarcastic remarks.

nexus N. connection. I fail to see the *nexus* which binds these two widely separated events.

nib N. beak; pen point. The *nibs* of fountain pens often became clotted and corroded.

nicety N. precision; minute distinction. I cannot distinguish between such *niceties* of reasoning.

niggle V. spend too much time on minor points; carp. Let's not *niggle* over details. niggling, ADJ.

niggardly ADJ. meanly stingy; parsimonious. The *niggardly* pittance the widow receives from the government cannot keep her from poverty.

nihilism N. denial of traditional values; total skepticism. *Nihilism* holds that existence has no meaning.

nirvana N. in Buddhist teachings, the ideal state in which the individual loses himself in the attainment of an impersonal beatitude. He tried to explain the concept of *nirvana* to his skeptical students.

nocturnal ADJ. done at night. Mr. Jones obtained a watchdog to prevent the *nocturnal* raids on his chicken coops.

noisome ADJ. foul smelling; unwholesome. I never could stand the *noisome* atmosphere surrounding the slaughter houses.

nomadic ADJ. wandering. Several *nomadic* tribes of Indians would hunt in this area each year.

nomenclature N. terminology; system of names. He struggled to master scientific *nomenclature.*

nominal ADJ. in name only; trifling. He offered to drive her to the airport for only a *nominal* fee.

nonage N. immaturity. She was embarrassed by the *nonage* of her contemporaries.

nonchalance N. indifference; lack of interest. Few people could understand how he could listen to the news of the tragedy with such *nonchalance;* the majority regarded him as callous and unsympathetic.

noncommittal ADJ. neutral; unpledged; undecided. We were annoyed by his *noncommittal* reply for we had been led to expect definite assurances of his approval.

nonentity N. nonexistence; person of no importance. Of course you are a *nonentity;* you will continue to be one until you prove your value to the community.

non sequitur N. a conclusion that does not follow from the facts stated. Your term paper is full of *non sequiturs;* I cannot see how you reached the conclusions you state.

nonplus V. bring to a halt by confusion. In my efforts to correct this situation I felt *nonplussed* by the stupidity of my assistants.

nosegay N. fragrant bouquet. These spring flowers will make an attractive *nosegay.*

nostalgia N. homesickness; longing for the past. The first settlers found so much work to do that they had little time for *nostalgia.*

nostrum N. questionable medicine. No quack selling *nostrums* is going to cheat me.

notorious ADJ. outstandingly bad; unfavorably known. Captain Kidd was a *notorious* pirate.

novice N. beginner. Even a *novice* can do good work if he follows these simple directions.

noxious ADJ. harmful. We must trace the source of these *noxious* gases before they asphyxiate us.

nuance N. shade of difference in meaning or color. The unskilled eye of the layman has difficulty in discerning the *nuances* of color in the paintings.

nubile ADJ. marriageable. Mrs. Bennet, in *Pride and Prejudice* by Jane Austen, was worried about finding suitable husbands for her five *nubile* daughters.

nugatory ADJ. futile; worthless. This agreement is *nugatory* for no court will enforce it.

nullify V. to make invalid. Once the contract was *nullified,* it no longer had any legal force.

numismatist N. person who collects coins. The *numismatist* had a splendid collection of antique coins.

nuptial ADJ. related to marriage. Their *nuptial* ceremony was performed in Golden Gate Park.

nurture V. bring up; feed; educate. We must *nurture* the young so that they will develop into good citizens.

nutrient ADJ. providing nourishment. During the convalescent period, the patient must be provided with *nutrient* foods. also N.

oaf N. stupid, awkward person. He called the unfortunate waiter a clumsy *oaf.*

obdurate ADJ. stubborn. He was *obdurate* in his refusal to listen to our complaints.

obeisance N. bow. She made an *obeisance* as the king and queen entered the room.

obelisk N. tall column tapering and ending in a pyramid. Cleopatra's Needle is an *obelisk* in Central Park, New York City.

obese ADJ. fat. It is advisable that *obese* people try to lose weight.

obfuscate V. confuse; muddle. Do not *obfuscate* the issues by dragging in irrelevant arguments.

obituary ADJ. death notice. I first learned of her death when I read the *obituary* column in the newspaper. also N.

objurgate V. scold; rebuke severely. I am afraid she will *objurgate* us publicly for this offense.

objurgation N. severe rebuke; scolding. *Objurgations* and even threats of punishment did not deter the young hoodlums.

oblation N. the Eucharist; pious donation. The wealthy man offered *oblations* so that the Church might be able to provide for the needy.

obligatory ADJ. binding; required. It is *obligatory* that books borrowed from the library be returned within two weeks.

oblique ADJ. slanting; deviating from the perpendicular or from a straight line. The sergeant ordered the men to march "*Oblique* Right."

obliquity N. departure from right principles; perversity. His moral decadence was marked by his *obliquity* from the ways of integrity and honesty.

obliterate V. destroy completely. The tidal wave *obliterated* several island villages.

oblivion N. forgetfulness. Her works had fallen into a state of *oblivion;* no one bothered to read them.

obloquy N. slander; disgrace; infamy. I resent the *obloquy* that you are casting upon my reputation.

obnoxious ADJ. offensive. I find your behavior *obnoxious;* please amend your ways.

obsequious ADJ. slavishly attentive; servile; sycophantic. Nothing is more disgusting to me than the *obsequious* demeanor of the people who wait upon you.

obsequy N. funeral ceremony. Hundreds paid their last respects at his *obsequies.*

obsession N. fixed idea; continued brooding. This *obsession* with the supernatural has made him unpopular with his neighbors.

obsidian N. black volcanic rock. The deposits of *obsidian* on the mountain slopes were an indication that the volcano had erupted in ancient times.

TEST—WORD LIST 32—*Antonyms*

Each of the questions below consists of a word in capital letters, followed by five lettered words or phrases. Choose the lettered word or phrase that is most nearly opposite in meaning to the word in capital letters and write the letter of your choice on your answer paper.

466. NEBULOUS (A) starry (B) clear (C) cold (D) fundamental (E) porous
467. NEFARIOUS (A) various (B) lacking (C) benign (D) pompous (E) futile
468. NEGATION (A) postulation (B) hypothecation (C) affirmation (D) violation (E) anticipation
469. NEOPHYTE (A) veteran (B) satellite (C) desperado (D) handwriting (E) violence
470. NIGGARDLY (A) protected (B) biased (C) prodigal (D) bankrupt (E) placated
471. NOCTURNAL (A) harsh (B) marauding (C) patrolling (D) daily (E) fallow
472. NOISOME (A) quiet (B) dismayed (C) fragrant (D) sleepy (E) inquisitive
473. NOTORIOUS (A) fashionable (B) renowned (C) inactive (D) intrepid (E) invincible
474. OBDURATE (A) yielding (B) fleeting (C) finite (D) fascinating (E) permanent
475. OBESE (A) skillful (B) cadaverous (C) clever (D) unpredictable (E) lucid
476. OBJURGATION (A) elegy (B) oath (C) model (D) praise (E) approval
477. OBLIGATORY (A) demanding (B) optional (C) facile (D) friendly (E) divorced
478. OBLOQUY (A) praise (B) rectangle (C) circle (D) dialogue (E) cure
479. OBSEQUIOUS (A) successful (B) democratic (C) supercilious (D) ambitious (E) lamentable
480. OBSESSION (A) whim (B) loss (C) phobia (D) delusion (E) feud

WORD LIST 33 obsolete - pacifist

obsolete ADJ. outmoded. That word is *obsolete;* do not use it.

obstetrician N. physician specializing in delivery of babies. In modern times, the delivery of children has passed from the midwife to the more scientifically trained *obstetrician.*

obstreperous ADJ. boisterous; noisy. The crowd became *obstreperous* and shouted their disapproval of the proposals made by the speaker.

obtrude V. push into prominence. The other members of the group object to the manner in which you *obtrude* your opinions into matters of no concern to you.

obtrusive ADJ. pushing forward. I found her a very *obtrusive* person, constantly seeking the center of the stage.

obtuse ADJ. blunt; stupid. Because he was so *obtuse,* he could not follow the teacher's reasoning and asked foolish questions.

obviate V. make unnecessary; get rid of. I hope this contribution will *obviate* any need for further collections of funds.

Occident N. the West. It will take time for the *Occident* to understand the ways and customs of the Orient.

occlude V. shut; close. A blood clot *occluded* an artery to the heart.

occult ADJ. mysterious; secret; supernatural. The *occult* rites of the organization were revealed only to members. also N.

oculist N. physician who specializes in treatment of the eyes. In many states, an *oculist* is the only one who may apply medicinal drops to the eyes for the purpose of examining them.

odious ADJ. hateful. I find the task of punishing you most *odious.* odium, N.

odium N. repugnance; dislike. I cannot express the *odium* I feel at your heinous actions.

odoriferous ADJ. giving off an odor. The *odoriferous* spices stimulated her jaded appetite.

odorous ADJ. having an odor. This variety of hybrid tea rose is more *odorous* than the one you have in your garden.

odyssey N. long, eventful journey. The refugee's journey from Cambodia was a terrifying *odyssey.*

offal N. waste; garbage. In America, we discard as *offal* that which could feed families in less fortunate parts of the world.

offertory N. collection of money at religious ceremony; part of the Mass during which offerings are made. The donations collected during the *offertory* will be assigned to our mission work abroad.

officious ADJ. meddlesome; excessively trying to please. Browning informs us that the Duke resented the bough of cherries some *officious* fool brought to please the Duchess.

ogle V. glance coquettishly at; make eyes at. Sitting for hours at the sidewalk cafe, the old gentleman would *ogle* the young girls and recall his youthful romances.

olfactory ADJ. concerning the sense of smell. The *olfactory* organ is the nose.

oligarchy N. government by a few. The feudal *oligarchy* was supplanted by an autocracy.

ominous ADJ. threatening. These clouds are *ominous;* they portend a severe storm.

omnipotent ADJ. all-powerful. The monarch regarded himself as *omnipotent* and responsible to no one for his acts.

omnipresent ADJ. universally present; ubiquitous. On Christmas Eve, Santa Claus is *omnipresent.*

omniscient ADJ. all-knowing. I do not pretend to be *omniscient,* but I am positive about this item.

omnivorous ADJ. eating both plant and animal food; devouring everything. Some animals, including man, are *omnivorous* and eat both meat and vegetables; others are either carnivorous or herbivorous.

onerous ADJ. burdensome. He asked for an assistant because his work load was too *onerous.*

onomatopoeia N. words formed in imitation of natural sounds. Words like "rustle" and "gargle" are illustrations of *onomatopoeia.*

onslaught N. vicious assault. We suffered many casualties during the unexpected *onslaught* of the enemy troops.

onus N. burden; responsibility. The emperor was spared the *onus* of signing the surrender papers; instead, he relegated the assignment to his generals.

opalescent ADJ. iridescent. The Ancient Mariner admired the *opalescent* sheen on the water.

opaque ADJ. dark; not transparent. The *opaque* window kept the sunlight out of the room.

opiate N. sleep producer; deadener of pain. By such *opiates,* she made the people forget their difficulties and accept their unpleasant circumstances.

opportune ADJ. timely; well chosen. You have come at an *opportune* moment for I need a new secretary.

opportunist N. individual who sacrifices principles for expediency by taking advantage of circumstances. I do not know how he will vote on this question as he is an *opportunist.*

opprobrious ADJ. disgraceful. I find your conduct so *opprobrious* that I must exclude you from classes.

opprobrium N. infamy; vilification. He refused to defend himself against the slander and *opprobrium* hurled against him by the newspapers; he preferred to rely on his record.

optician N. maker and seller of eyeglasses. The patient took the prescription given him by his oculist to the *optician.*

optimist N. person who looks on the good side. The pessimist says the glass is half-empty; the *optimist* says it is half-full.

optimum ADJ. most favorable. If you wait for the *optimum* moment to act, you may never begin your project. also N.

optometrist N. one who fits glasses to remedy visual defects. Although an *optometrist* is qualified to treat many eye disorders, she may not use medicines or surgery in her examinations.

opulence N. wealth. Visitors from Europe are amazed at the *opulence* of this country.

oratorio N. dramatic poem set to music. The Glee Club decided to present an *oratorio* during their recital.

opus N. work. Although many critics hailed his Fifth Symphony as his major work, he did not regard it as his major *opus.*

oracular ADJ. foretelling; mysterious. Oedipus could not understand the *oracular* warning he received.

ordain V. command; arrange; consecrate. The king *ordained* that no foreigner should be allowed to enter the city.

ordinance N. decree. Passing a red light is a violation of a city *ordinance.*

orient V. get one's bearings; adjust. Philip spent his first day in Denver *orienting* himself to the city.

orientation N. act of finding oneself in society. Freshman *orientation* provides the incoming students with an opportunity to learn about their new environment and their place in it.

orifice N. mouthlike opening; small opening. The Howe Caverns were discovered when someone observed that a cold wind was issuing from an *orifice* in the hillside.

orison N. prayer. Hamlet greets Ophelia with the request, "Nymph, in thy *orisons,* be all my sins remembered."

ornate ADJ. excessively decorated; highly decorated. Furniture of the Baroque period can be recognized by its *ornate* carvings.

ornithologist N. scientific student of birds. Audubon's drawings of American bird life have been of interest not only to the *ornithologists* but also to the general public.

ornithology N. study of birds. Audubon's studies of American birds greatly influenced the course of *ornithology* in this country.

orotund ADJ. having a round, resonant quality; inflated speech. The politician found that his *orotund* voice was an asset when he spoke to his constituents.

orthodox ADJ. traditional; conservative in belief. Faced with a problem, he preferred to take an *orthodox* approach.

orthography N. correct spelling. Many of us find English *orthography* difficult to master because so many of our words are not written phonetically.

oscillate V. vibrate pendulumlike; waver. It is interesting to note how public opinion *oscillates* between the extremes of optimism and pessimism.

ossify V. change or harden into bone. When he called his opponent a "bonehead," he implied that his adversary's brain had *ossified* and that he was not capable of clear thinking.

ostensible ADJ. apparent; professed; pretended. Although the *ostensible* purpose of this expedition is to discover new lands, we are really interested in finding new markets for our products.

ostentatious ADJ. showy; pretentious. The real hero is never *ostentatious.*

ostracize V. exclude from public favor; ban. As soon as the newspapers carried the story of his connection with the criminals, his friends began to *ostracize* him. ostracism, N.

oust V. expel; drive out. The world wondered if Aquino would be able to *oust* Marcos from office.

overt ADJ. open to view. According to the United States Constitution, a person must commit an *overt* act before he may be tried for treason.

overweening ADJ. presumptuous; arrogant. His *overweening* pride in his accomplishments was not justified.

ovine ADJ. like a sheep. How *ovine* these true-believers were, following their shepherds thoughtlessly.

ovoid ADJ. egg-shaped. At Easter she had to cut out hundred of brightly colored *ovoid* shapes.

pachyderm N. thick-skinned animal. The elephant is probably the best-known *pachyderm.*

pacifist N. one opposed to force; antimilitarist. The *pacifists* urged that we reduce our military budget and recall our troops stationed overseas.

TEST—WORD LIST 33—*Antonyms*

Each of the questions below consists of a word in capital letters, followed by five lettered words or phrases. Choose the lettered word or phrase that is most nearly opposite in meaning to the word in capital letters and write the letter of your choice on your answer paper.

481. OBSOLETE (A) heated (B) desolate (C) renovated (D) frightful (E) automatic
482. OBSTREPEROUS (A) turbid (B) quiet (C) remote (D) lucid (E) active
483. OBTUSE (A) sheer (B) transparent (C) tranquil (D) timid (E) shrewd
484. ODIOUS (A) fragrant (B) redolent (C) fetid (D) delightful (E) puny
485. ODIUM (A) noise (B) liking (C) dominant (D) hasty (E) atrium
486. OMNIPOTENT (A) weak (B) democratic (C) despotic (D) passionate (E) late
487. OMNISCIENT (A) sophisticated (B) ignorant (C) essential (D) trivial (E) isolated
488. OPIATE (A) distress (B) sleep (C) stimulant (D) laziness (E) despair
489. OPPORTUNE (A) occasional (B) fragrant (C) fragile (D) awkward (E) neglected
490. OPPORTUNIST (A) man of destiny (B) man of principle (C) changeling (D) adversary (E) colleague
491. OPPROBRIUM (A) delineation (B) aptitude (C) majesty (D) freedom (E) praise
492. OPTIMUM (A) pessimistic (B) knowledgeable (C) worst (D) minimum (E) chosen
493. OPULENCE (A) pessimism (B) patriotism (C) potency (D) passion (E) poverty
494. OROTUND (A) not reddish (B) not resonant (C) loud (D) pompous (E) not eager
495. OVERWEENING (A) humble (B) impotent (C) avid (D) acrimonious (E) exaggerated

---

WORD LIST 34 **paddock - peccadillo**

paddock N. saddling enclosure at race track; lot for exercising horses. The *paddock* is located directly in front of the grandstand so that all may see the horses being saddled and the jockeys mounted.

paean N. song of praise or joy. They sang *paeans* of praise.

palatable ADJ. agreeable; pleasing to the taste. Paying taxes can never be made *palatable.*

palatial ADJ. magnificent. He proudly showed us through his *palatial* home.

palaver N. discussion; misleading speech; chatter. In spite of all the *palaver* before the meeting, the delegates were able to conduct serious negotiations when they sat down at the conference table. also V.

paleontology N. study of prehistoric life. The *paleontology* instructor had a superb collection of fossils.

palette N. board on which painter mixes pigments. At the present time, art supply stores are selling a paper *palette* which may be discarded after use.

palimpsest N. parchment used for second time after original writing has been erased. Using chemical reagents, scientists have been able to restore the original writings on many *palimpsests.*

pall V. grow tiresome. The study of word lists can eventually *pall.*

pallet N. small, poor bed. The weary traveler went to sleep on his straw *pallet.*

palliate V. ease pain; make less guilty or offensive. Doctors must *palliate* that which they cannot cure.

palliation N. act of making less severe or violent. If we cannot find a cure for this disease at the present time, we can, at least, endeavor to seek its *palliation.*

pallid ADJ. pale; wan. Because his occupation required that he work at night and sleep during the day, he had an exceptionally *pallid* complexion.

palpable ADJ. tangible; easily perceptible. I cannot understand how you could overlook such a *palpable* blunder.

palpitate V. throb; flutter. As he became excited, his heart began to *palpitate* more and more erratically.

paltry ADJ. insignificant; petty. This is a *paltry* sum to pay for such a masterpiece.

panacea N. cure-all; remedy for all diseases. There is no easy *panacea* that will solve our complicated international situation.

panache N. flair; flamboyance. Many performers imitate Noel Coward, but few have his *panache.*

pandemic ADJ. widespread; affecting the majority of people. They feared the AIDS epidemic would soon reach *pandemic* proportions.

pandemonium N. wild tumult. When the ships collided in the harbor, *pandemonium* broke out among the passengers.

pander V. cater to the low desires of others. Books which *pander* to man's lowest instincts should be banned.

panegyric N. formal praise. The modest hero blushed

as he listened to the *panegyrics* uttered by the speakers about his valorous act.

panoply N. full set of armor. The medieval knight in full *panoply* found his movements limited by the weight of his armor.

panorama N. comprehensive view; unobstructed view in all directions. Tourists never forget the impact of their first *panorama* of the Grand Canyon.

pantomime N. acting without dialogue. Because he worked in *pantomime,* the clown could be understood wherever he appeared. also V.

papyrus N. ancient paper made from stem of papyrus plant. The ancient Egyptians were among the first to write on *papyrus.*

parable N. short, simple story teaching a moral. Let us apply to our own conduct the lesson that this *parable* teaches.

paradox N. statement that looks false but is actually correct; a contradictory statement. Wordsworth's "The child is father to the man" is an example of *paradox.*

paragon N. model of perfection. The class disliked him because the teacher was always pointing to him as a *paragon* of virtue.

parallelism N. state of being parallel; similarity. There is a striking *parallelism* between the two ages.

parameter N. limits; independent variable. We need to define the *parameters* of the problem.

paramour N. illicit lover. She sought a divorce on the grounds that her husband had a *paramour* in another town.

paranoia N. chronic form of insanity marked by delusions of grandeur or persecution. The psychiatrists analyzed his ailment as *paranoia.*

paranoiac N. mentally unsound person suffering from delusions. Although he is obviously suffering from delusions, I hesitate to call him a *paranoiac.*

parapet N. low wall at edge of roof or balcony. The best way to attack the soldiers fighting behind the *parapets* on the roof is by bombardment from the air.

paraphernalia N. equipment; odds and ends. His desk was cluttered with paper, pen, ink, dictionary and other *paraphernalia* of the writing craft.

paraphrase V. restate a passage in one's own words while retaining thought of author. In 250 words or less, *paraphrase* this article. also N.

parasite N. animal or plant living on another; toady; sycophant. The tapeworm is an example of the kind of *parasite* that may infest the human body.

parched ADJ. extremely dry; very thirsty. The *parched* desert landscape seemed hostile to life.

paregoric N. medicine that eases pain. The doctor prescribed a *paregoric* to alleviate his suffering.

pariah N. social outcast. I am not a *pariah* to be shunned and ostracized.

parlance N. language; idiom. All this legal *parlance* confuses me; I need an interpreter.

parity N. equality; close resemblance. I find your analogy inaccurate because I do not see the *parity* between the two illustrations.

parley N. conference. The peace *parley* has not produced the anticipated truce. also V.

parlous ADJ. dangerous; perilous. In these *parlous* times, we must overcome the work of saboteurs and propagandists.

parody N. humorous imitation; travesty. We enjoyed the clever *parodies* of popular songs which the chorus sang.

paroxysm N. fit or attack of pain, laughter, rage. When he heard of his son's misdeeds, he was seized by a *paroxysm* of rage.

parricide N. person who murders his own father; murder of a father. The jury was shocked by the details of this vicious *parricide* and found the man who had killed his father guilty of murder in the first degree.

parry V. ward off a blow. He was content to wage a defensive battle and tried to *parry* his opponent's thrusts.

parsimonious ADJ. stingy; excessively frugal. His *parsimonious* nature did not permit him to enjoy any luxuries.

partiality N. inclination; bias. As a judge, not only must I be unbiased, but I must also avoid any evidence of *partiality* when I award the prize.

partisan ADJ. one-sided; prejudiced; committed to a party. On certain issues of conscience, she refused to take a *partisan* stand. also N.

parturition N. delivery; childbirth. The difficulties anticipated by the obstetricians at *parturition* did not materialize; it was a normal delivery.

parvenu N. upstart; newly rich person. Although extremely wealthy, he was regarded as a *parvenu* by the aristocratic members of society.

passé ADJ. old-fashioned; past the prime. Her style is *passé* and reminiscent of the Victorian era.

passive ADJ. not active; acted upon. Mahatma Gandhi urged his followers to pursue a program of *passive* resistance as he felt that it was more effective than violence and acts of terrorism.

pastiche N. imitation of another's style in musical composition or in writing. We cannot even say that her music is a *pastiche* of this composer or that; it is, rather, reminiscent of many musicians.

pastoral ADJ. rural. In these stories of *pastoral* life, we find an understanding of the daily tasks of country folk.

patent ADJ. open for the public to read; obvious. It was *patent* to everyone that the witness spoke the truth. also N.

pathetic ADJ. causing sadness, compassion, pity; touching. Everyone in the auditorium was weeping by the time he finished his *pathetic* tale about the orphaned boy.

pathological ADJ. pertaining to disease. As we study the *pathological* aspects of this disease, we must not overlook the psychological elements.

pathos N. tender sorrow; pity; quality in art or literature that produces these feelings. The quiet tone of *pathos* that ran through the novel never degenerated into the maudlin or the overly sentimental.

patina N. green crust on old bronze works; tone slowly taken by varnished painting. Judging by the *patina* on this bronze statue,we can conclude that this is the work of a medieval artist.

patois N. local or provincial dialect. His years of study of the language at the university did not enable him to understand the *patois* of the natives.

patriarch N. father and ruler of a family or tribe. In many primitive tribes, the leader and lawmaker was the *patriarch.*

patrician ADJ. noble; aristocratic. We greatly admired her well-bred, *patrician* elegance. also N.

patricide N. person who murders his father; murder of a father. The words parricide and *patricide* have exactly the same meaning.

patrimony N. inheritance from father. As predicted by his critics, he spent his *patrimony* within two years of his father's death.

paucity N. scarcity. The poor test papers indicate that the members of this class have a *paucity* of intelligence.

peccadillo N. slight offense. If we examine these escapades carefully, we will realize that they are mere *peccadilloes* rather than major crimes.

TEST—WORD LIST 34—*Synonyms and Antonyms*

Each of the following questions consists of a word in capital letters, followed by five lettered words or phrases. Choose the lettered word or phrase which is most nearly similar or the opposite of the word in capital letters and write the letter of your choice on your answer paper.

496. PAEAN (A) serf (B) pealing (C) lien (D) lament (E) folly
497. PALLET (A) bed (B) pigment board (C) bench (D) spectrum (E) quality
498. PALLIATE (A) smoke (B) quicken (C) substitute (D) alleviate (E) sadden
499. PANDEMONIUM (A) calm (B) frustration (C) efficiency (D) impishness (E) sophistication
500. PANEGYRIC (A) medication (B) panacea (C) rotation (D) vacillation (E) praise
501. PARABLE (A) equality (B) allegory (C) frenzy (D) folly (E) cuticle
502. PARADOX (A) exaggeration (B) contradiction (C) hyperbole (D) invective (E) poetic device
503. PARAMOUR (A) illicit lover (B) majority (C) importance (D) hatred (E) clandestine affair
504. PARANOIA (A) fracture (B) statement (C) quantity (D) benefaction (E) sanity
505. PARIAH (A) village (B) suburb (C) outcast (D) disease (E) benefactor
506. PARITY (A) duplicate (B) miniature (C) golf tee (D) similarity (E) event
507. PARSIMONIOUS (A) grammatical (B) syntactical (C) effective (D) extravagant (E) esoteric
508. PARTIALITY (A) completion (B) equality (C) bias (D) divorce (E) reflection
509. PASSÉ (A) scornful (B) rural (C) out-of-date (D) silly (E) barbaric
510. PASTICHE (A) imitation (B) glue (C) present (D) greeting (E) family

WORD LIST 35 peculate - philander

peculate V. steal; embezzle. His crime of *peculating* public funds entrusted to his care is especially damnable.

peculation N. embezzlement; theft. Her *peculations* were not discovered until the auditors found discrepancies in the financial statements.

pecuniary ADJ. pertaining to money. I never expected a *pecuniary* reward for my work in this activity.

pedagogue N. teacher; dull and formal teacher. He could never be a stuffy *pedagogue;* his classes were always lively and filled with humor.

pedant N. scholar who overemphasizes book learning or technicalities. Her insistence that the book be memorized marked the teacher as a *pedant* rather than a scholar.

pedantic ADJ. showing off learning; bookish. What

you say is *pedantic* and reveals an unfamiliarity with the realities of life.

pedestrian ADJ. ordinary; unimaginative. He wrote page after page of *pedestrian* prose.

pediatrician N. expert in children's diseases. The family doctor advised the parents to consult a *pediatrician* about their child's ailment.

pediment N. triangular part above columns in Greek buildings. The *pediment* of the building was filled with sculptures and adorned with elaborate scrollwork.

pejorative ADJ. having a deteriorating or depreciating effect on the meaning of a word. His use of *pejorative* language indicated his contempt for his audience.

pelf N. stolen property; money or wealth [in a contemptuous sense]. Your possessions are only *pelf;* they will give you no lasting pleasure.

pell-mell ADV. in confusion; disorderly. The excited students dashed *pell-mell* into the stadium to celebrate the victory.

pellucid ADJ. transparent; limpid; easy to understand. After reading these stodgy philosophers, I find his *pellucid* style very enjoyable.

penance N. self-imposed punishment for sin. The Ancient Mariner said, "I have *penance* done and *penance* more will do," to atone for the sin of killing the albatross.

penchant N. strong inclination; liking. He had a strong *penchant* for sculpture.

pendant ADJ. hanging down from something. Her *pendant* earrings glistened in the light.

pendent ADJ. suspended; jutting; pending. The *pendent* rock hid the entrance to the cave.

penitent ADJ. repentant. When he realized the enormity of his crime, he became remorseful and *penitent.* also N.

pendulous ADJ. hanging; suspended. The *pendulous* chandeliers swayed in the breeze and gave the impression that they were about to fall from the ceiling.

pennate ADJ. having wings or feathers. The *pennate* leaves of the sumac remind us of feathers.

pensive ADJ. dreamily thoughtful; thoughtful with a hint of sadness. The *pensive* youth gazed at the painting for a long time and then sighed.

penumbra N. partial shadow (in an eclipse). During an eclipse, we can see an area of total darkness and a lighter area which is the *penumbra.*

penurious ADJ. stingy; parsimonious. He was a *penurious* man, averse to spending money even for the necessities of life.

penury N. extreme poverty. We find much *penury* and suffering in this slum area.

peon N. unskilled laborer; drudge. He was doomed to be a *peon,* to live a lowly life of drudgery and toil.

percussion ADJ. striking one object against another sharply. The drum is a *percussion* instrument.

perdition N. damnation; complete ruin. He was damned to eternal *perdition.*

peregrination N. journey. His *peregrinations* in foreign lands did not bring understanding; he mingled only with fellow tourists and did not attempt to communicate with the native population.

peremptory ADJ. demanding and leaving no choice. I resent your *peremptory* attitude.

perennial N. lasting. These plants are hardy *perennials* and will bloom for many years. also ADJ.

perfidious ADJ. basely false. Your *perfidious* gossip is malicious and dangerous.

perfidy N. violation of a trust. When we learned of his *perfidy,* we were shocked and dismayed.

perforce ADV. of necessity. I must *perforce* leave, as my train is about to start.

perfunctory ADJ. superficial; listless; not thorough. He overlooked many weaknesses when he inspected the factory in his *perfunctory* manner.

perigee N. point of moon's orbit when it is nearest the earth. The rocket which was designed to take photographs of the moon was launched as the moon approached its *perigee.*

perimeter N. outer boundary. To find the *perimeter* of any quadrilateral, we add the four sides.

peripatetic ADJ. walking about; moving. The *peripatetic* school of philosophy derives its name from the fact that Aristotle walked with his pupils while discussing philosophy with them.

periphery N. edge, especially of a round surface. He sensed that there was something just beyond the *periphery* of his vision.

peristyle N. series of columns surrounding a building or yard. The cloister was surrounded by a *peristyle* reminiscent of the Parthenon.

perjury N. false testimony while under oath. When several witnesses appeared to challenge his story, he was indicted for *perjury.*

permeable ADJ. porous; allowing passage through. Glass is *permeable* to light.

permeate V. pass through; spread. The odor of frying onions *permeated* the air.

pernicious ADJ. very destructive. He argued that these books had a *pernicious* effect on young and susceptible minds.

perpetrate V. commit an offense. Only an insane person could *perpetrate* such a horrible crime.

perpetual ADJ. everlasting. Ponce de Leon hoped to find *perpetual* youth.

peroration N. conclusion of an oration. The *peroration* was largely hortatory and brought the audience to its feet clamoring for action at its close.

perquisite N. any gain above stipulated salary. The *perquisites* attached to this job make it even more attractive than the salary indicates.

persiflage N. flippant conversation; banter. This *persiflage* is not appropriate when we have such serious problems to discuss.

personable ADJ. attractive. The man I am seeking to fill this position must be *personable* since he will be representing us before the public.

perspicacious ADJ. having insight; penetrating; astute. We admired his *perspicacious* wisdom and sagacity.

perspicuity N. clearness of expression; freedom from ambiguity. One of the outstanding features of this book is the *perspicuity* of its author; her meaning is always clear.

perspicuous ADJ. plainly expressed. Her *perspicuous* comments eliminated all possibility of misinterpretation.

pert ADJ. impertinent; forward. I think your *pert* and impudent remarks call for an apology.

pertinacious ADJ. stubborn; persistent. He is bound to succeed because his *pertinacious* nature will not permit him to quit.

pertinent ADJ. suitable; to the point. The lawyer wanted to know all the *pertinent* details.

perturb V. disturb greatly. I am afraid this news will *perturb* him.

perturbation N. agitation. I fail to understand why such an innocent remark should create such *perturbation.*

perusal N. reading. I am certain that you have missed important details in your rapid *perusal* of this document. peruse, V.

pervade V. spread throughout. As the news of the defeat *pervaded* the country, a feeling of anger directed at the rulers who had been the cause of the disaster grew.

perverse ADJ. stubborn; intractable. Because of your *perverse* attitude, I must rate you as deficient in cooperation.

perversion N. corruption; turning from right to wrong. Inasmuch as he had no motive for his crimes, we could not understand his *perversion.*

perversity N. stubborn maintenance of a wrong cause. I cannot forgive your *perversity* in repeating such an impossible story.

pervious ADJ. penetrable. He has a *pervious* mind and readily accepts new ideas.

pessimism N. belief that life is basically bad or evil; gloominess. The good news we have been receiving lately indicates that there is little reason for your *pessimism.*

pestilential ADJ. causing plague; baneful. People were afraid to explore the *pestilential* swamp. pestilence, N.

petrify V. turn to stone. His sudden and unexpected appearance seemed to *petrify* her.

petulant ADJ. touchy; peevish. The feverish patient was *petulant* and restless.

pharisaical ADJ. pertaining to the Pharisees, who paid scrupulous attention to tradition; self-righteous; hypocritical. Walter Lippman has pointed out that moralists who do not attempt to explain the moral code they advocate are often regarded as *pharisaical* and ignored.

phial N. small bottle. Even though it is small, this *phial* of perfume is expensive.

philander V. make love lightly; flirt. Do not *philander* with my affections because love is too serious.

TEST—WORD LIST 35—*Antonyms*

Each of the questions below consists of a word in capital letters, followed by five lettered words or phrases. Choose the lettered word or phrase that is most nearly opposite in meaning to the word in capital letters and write the letter of your choice on your answer paper.

511. PEJORATIVE (A) positive (B) legal (C) determining (D) delighting (E) declaiming
512. PELLUCID (A) logistical (B) philandering (C) incomprehensible (D) vagrant (E) warranted
513. PENCHANT (A) distance (B) imminence (C) dislike (D) attitude (E) void
514. PENURIOUS (A) imprisoned (B) captivated (C) generous (D) vacant (E) abolished
515. PERFUNCTORY (A) official (B) thorough (C) insipid (D) vicarious (E) distinctive
516. PERIGEE (A) eclipse (B) planet (C) apogee (D) refugee (E) danger
517. PERIPATETIC (A) worldly (B) stationary (C) disarming (D) seeking (E) inherent
518. PERMEABLE (A) perishable (B) effective (C) plodding (D) impenetrable (E) lasting
519. PERNICIOUS (A) practical (B) comparative (C) harmless (D) tangible (E) detailed
520. PERPETUAL (A) momentary (B) standard (C) serious (D) industrial (E) interpretive
521. PERSPICUITY (A) grace (B) feature (C) review (D) difficulty (E) vagueness
522. PERT (A) polite (B) perishable (C) moral (D) deliberate (E) stubborn
523. PERTINACIOUS (A) vengeful (B) consumptive (C) superficial (D) skilled (E) advertised
524. PERTINENT (A) understood (B) living (C) discontented (D) puzzling (E) irrelevant
525. PETULANT (A) angry (B) moral (C) declining (D) underhanded (E) uncomplaining

WORD LIST 36 philanthropist - precedent

philanthropist N. lover of mankind; doer of good. As he grew older, he became famous as a *philanthropist* and benefactor of the needy.

philistine N. narrow-minded person, uncultured and exclusively interested in material gain. We need more men of culture and enlightenment; we have too many *philistines* among us.

philology N. study of language. The professor of *philology* advocated the use of Esperanto as an international language.

phlegmatic ADJ. calm; not easily disturbed. The nurse was a cheerful but *phlegmatic* person.

phobia N. morbid fear. Her fear of flying was more than mere nervousness; it was a real *phobia.*

physiognomy N. face. He prided himself on his ability to analyze a person's character by studying his *physiognomy.*

physiological ADJ. pertaining to the science of the function of living organisms. To understand this disease fully, we must examine not only its *physiological* aspects but also its psychological elements.

picaresque ADJ. pertaining to rogues in literature. *Tom Jones* has been hailed as one of the best *picaresque* novels in the English language.

piebald ADJ. mottled; spotted. You should be able to identify this horse easily as it is the only *piebald* horse in the race.

pied ADJ. variegated; multicolored. The *Pied* Piper of Hamelin got his name from the multicolored clothing he wore.

pillage V. plunder. The enemy *pillaged* the quiet village and left it in ruins.

pillory V. punish by placing in a wooden frame and subjecting to ridicule. Even though he was mocked and *pilloried,* he maintained that he was correct in his beliefs. also N.

pinion V. restrain. They *pinioned* his arms against his body but left his legs free so that he could move about. also N.

pinnacle N. peak. We could see the morning sunlight illuminate the *pinnacle* while the rest of the mountain lay in shadow.

pious ADJ. devout. The *pious* parents gave their children a religious upbringing.

piquant ADJ. pleasantly tart-tasting; stimulating. The *piquant* sauce added to our enjoyment of the meal. piquancy, N.

pique N. irritation; resentment. She showed her *pique* by her refusal to appear with the other contestants at the end of the contest.

piscatorial ADJ. pertaining to fishing. He spent many happy hours in his *piscatorial* activities.

pithy ADJ. concise; meaty. I enjoy reading his essays because they are always compact and *pithy.*

pittance N. a small allowance or wage. He could not live on the *pittance* he received as a pension and had to look for an additional source of revenue.

placate V. pacify; conciliate. The teacher tried to *placate* the angry mother.

placid ADJ. peaceful; calm. After his vacation in this *placid* section, he felt soothed and rested.

plagiarism N. theft of another's ideas or writings passed off as original. The editor recognized the *plagiarism* and rebuked the culprit who had presented the manuscript as original.

plaintive ADJ. mournful. The dove has a *plaintive* and melancholy call.

plangent ADJ. plaintive; resounding sadly. Although we could not understand the words of the song, we got the impression from the *plangent* tones of the singers that it was a lament of some kind.

platitude N. trite remark; commonplace statement. The *platitudes* in his speech were applauded by the vast majority in his audience; only a few people perceived how trite his remarks were.

platonic ADJ. purely spiritual; theoretical; without sensual desire. Although a member of the political group, she took only a *platonic* interest in its ideals and goals.

plauditory ADJ. approving; applauding. The theatrical company reprinted the *plauditory* comments of the critics in its advertisement.

plausible ADJ. having a show of truth but open to doubt; specious. Even though your argument is *plausible,* I still would like to have more proof.

plebeian ADJ. common; pertaining to the common people. His speeches were aimed at the *plebeian* minds and emotions; they disgusted the more refined.

plebiscite N. expression of the will of a people by direct election. I think this matter is so important that it should be decided not by a handful of legislators but by a *plebiscite* of the entire nation.

plenary ADJ. complete; full. The union leader was given *plenary* power to negotiate a new contract with the employers.

plenipotentiary ADJ. fully empowered. Since he was not given *plenipotentiary* powers by his government, he could not commit his country without consulting his superiors. also N.

plenitude N. abundance; completeness. Looking in the pantry, we admired the *plenitude* of fruits and pickles we had preserved during the summer.

plethora N. excess; overabundance. She offered a *plethora* of reasons for her shortcomings.

plumb ADJ. checking perpendicularity; vertical. Before hanging wallpaper it is advisable to drop a *plumb* line from the ceiling as a guide. also N. and V.

podiatrist N. doctor who treats ailments of the feet. He consulted a *podiatrist* about his fallen arches.

podium N. pedestal; raised platform. The audience applauded as the conductor made his way to the *podium.*

poignant ADJ. keen; piercing; severe. Her *poignant* grief left her pale and weak.

polemic N. controversy; argument in support of point of view. Her essays were, for the main part, *polemics* in support of the party's policy.

politic ADJ. expedient; prudent; well devised. Even though he was disappointed, he did not think it *politic* to refuse this offer.

polity N. form of government of nation or state. Our *polity* should be devoted to the concept that the government should strive for the good of all citizens.

poltroon N. coward. Only a *poltroon* would so betray his comrades at such a dangerous time.

polygamist N. one who has more than one spouse at a time. He was arrested as a *polygamist* when his two wives filed complaints about him.

polyglot ADJ. speaking several languages. New York City is a *polyglot* community because of the thousands of immigrants who settle there.

ponderous ADJ. weighty; unwieldy. His humor lacked the light touch; his jokes were always *ponderous.*

porphyry N. igneous rock containing feldspar or quartz crystals. The *porphyry* used by the Egyptians in their buildings was purplish in color.

portend V. foretell; presage. The king did not know what these omens might *portend* and asked his soothsayers to interpret them.

portent N. sign; omen; forewarning. He regarded the black cloud as a *portent* of evil.

portentous ADJ. ominous; serious. I regard our present difficulties and dissatisfactions as *portentous* omens of future disaster.

portly ADJ. stately; stout. The overweight gentleman was shown a size 44 *portly* suit.

posterity N. descendants; future generations. We hope to leave a better world to *posterity.*

posthumous ADJ. after death (as of child born after father's death or book published after author's death). The critics ignored his works during his lifetime; it was only after the *posthumous* publication of his last novel that they recognized his great talent.

postprandial ADJ. after dinner. The most objectionable feature of these formal banquets is the *postprandial* speech.

postulate N. self-evident truth. We must accept these statements as *postulates* before pursuing our discussions any further. also V.

potable ADJ. suitable for drinking. The recent drought in the Middle Atlantic States has emphasized the need for extensive research in ways of making sea water *potable.* also N.

potentate N. monarch; sovereign. The *potentate* spent more time at Monte Carlo than he did at home with his people.

potential ADJ. expressing possibility; latent. This juvenile delinquent is a *potential* murderer. also N.

potion N. dose (of liquid). Tristan and Isolde drink a love *potion* in the first act of the opera.

potpourri N. heterogeneous mixture; medley. He offered a *potpourri* of folk songs from many lands.

poultice N. soothing application applied to sore and inflamed portions of the body. He was advised to apply a flaxseed *poultice* to the inflammation.

practicable ADJ. feasible. The board of directors decided that the plan was *practicable* and agreed to undertake the project.

practical ADJ. based on experience; useful. He was a *practical* man, opposed to theory.

pragmatic ADJ. practical; concerned with practical values. This test should provide us with a *pragmatic* analysis of the value of this course.

prate V. speak foolishly; boast idly. Let us not *prate* about our qualities; rather, let our virtues speak for themselves.

prattle V. babble. The children *prattled* endlessly about their new toys. also N.

preamble N. introductory statement. In the *Preamble* to the Constitution, the purpose of the document is set forth.

precarious ADJ. uncertain; risky. I think this stock is a *precarious* investment and advise against its purchase.

precedent N. something preceding in time which may be used as an authority or guide for future action. This decision sets a *precedent* for future cases of a similar nature.

precedent ADJ. preceding in time, rank, etc. Our discussions, *precedent* to this event, certainly did not give you any reason to believe that we would adopt your proposal.

TEST—WORD LIST 36—*Synonyms*

Each of the questions below consists of a word in capital letters, followed by five lettered words or phrases. Choose the lettered word or phrase that is most nearly similar in meaning to the word in capital letters and write the letter of your choice on your answer paper.

526. PHLEGMATIC (A) calm (B) cryptic (C) practical (D) salivary (E) dishonest
527. PHYSIOGNOMY (A) posture (B) head (C) physique (D) face (E) size
528. PIEBALD (A) motley (B) coltish (C) hairless (D) thoroughbred (E) delicious
529. PILLAGE (A) hoard (B) plunder (C) versify (D) denigrate (E) confide
530. PINION (A) express (B) report (C) reveal (D) submit (E) restrain
531. PINNACLE (A) foothills (B) card game (C) pass (D) taunt (E) peak
532. PIOUS (A) historic (B) devout (C) multiple (D) fortunate (E) authoritative
533. PIQUE (A) pyramid (B) revolt (C) resentment (D) struggle (E) inventory
534. PLACATE (A) determine (B) transmit (C) pacify (D) allow (E) define
535. PLAINTIVE (A) mournful (B) senseless (C) persistent (D) rural (E) evasive
536. PLAGIARISM (A) theft of funds (B) theft of ideas (C) belief in God (D) arson (E) ethical theory
537. PLATITUDE (A) fatness (B) bravery (C) dimension (D) trite remark (E) strong belief
538. POLEMIC (A) black (B) lighting (C) magnetism (D) controversy (E) grimace
539. POLTROON (A) bird (B) tavern (C) soldier (D) coward (E) politician
540. POSTPRANDIAL (A) after dark (B) on awakening (C) in summer (D) after dinner (E) in winter

---

WORD LIST 37 precept - propititate

precept N. practical rule guiding conduct. "Love thy neighbor as thyself" is a worthwhile *precept.*

preciosity N. overrefinement in art or speech. Roxane, in the play *Cyrano de Bergerac,* illustrates the extent to which *preciosity* was carried in French society.

precipice N. cliff; dangerous position. Suddenly Indiana Jones found himself dangling from the edge of a *precipice.*

precipitate ADJ. headlong; rash. Do not be *precipitate* in this matter; investigate further.

precipitate V. throw headlong; hasten. We must be patient as we cannot *precipitate* these results.

precipitous ADJ. steep. This hill is difficult to climb because it is so *precipitous.*

precise ADJ. exact. If you don't give me *precise* directions and a map, I'll never find your place.

preclude V. make impossible; eliminate. This contract does not *preclude* my being employed by others at the same time that I am working for you.

precocious ADJ. advanced in development. By her rather adult manner of discussing serious topics, the child demonstrated that she was *precocious.*

precursor N. forerunner. Gray and Burns were *precursors* of the Romantic Movement in English literature.

predatory ADJ. plundering. The hawk is a *predatory* bird.

predilection N. partiality; preference. Although the artist used various media from time to time, she had a *predilection* for watercolor.

preeminent ADJ. outstanding; superior. The king traveled to Boston because he wanted the *preeminent* surgeon in the field to perform the operation.

preempt V. appropriate beforehand. Your attempt to *preempt* this land before it is offered to the public must be resisted.

prefatory ADJ. introductory. The chairman made a few *prefatory* remarks before he called on the first speaker.

prehensile ADJ. capable of grasping or holding. Monkeys use not only their arms and legs but also their *prehensile* tails in traveling through the trees.

prelude N. introduction; forerunner. I am afraid that this border raid is the *prelude* to more serious attacks.

premeditate V. plan in advance. She had *premeditated* the murder for months, reading about common poisons and buying weed killer that contained arsenic.

premonition N. forewarning. We ignored these *premonitions* of disaster because they appeared to be based on childish fears.

premonitory ADJ. serving to warn. You should have visited a doctor as soon as you felt these *premonitory* chest pains.

preponderance N. superiority of power, quantity, etc. The rebels sought to overcome the *preponderance* of strength of the government forces by engaging in guerrilla tactics.

preponderate V. be superior in power; outweigh. I feel confident that the forces of justice will *preponderate* eventually in this dispute.

preposterous ADJ. absurd; ridiculous. The excuse he gave for his lateness was so *preposterous* that everyone laughed.

prerogative N. privilege; unquestionable right. The President cannot levy taxes; that is the *prerogative* of the legislative branch of government.

presage V. foretell. The vultures flying overhead *presaged* the discovery of the corpse in the desert.

presentiment N. premonition; foreboding. Hamlet felt a *presentiment* about his meeting with Laertes.

prestige N. impression produced by achievements or reputation. The wealthy man sought to obtain social *prestige* by contributing to popular charities.

presumption N. arrogance; effrontery. She had the *presumption* to disregard our advice.

pretentious ADJ. ostentatious; ambitious. I do not feel that your limited resources will permit you to carry out such a *pretentious* program.

preternatural ADJ. beyond that which is normal in nature. John's mother's total ability to tell when he was lying struck him as almost *preternatural.*

pretext N. excuse. He looked for a good *pretext* to get out of paying a visit to his aunt.

prevail V. induce; triumph over. He tried to *prevail* on her to type his essay for him.

prevaricate V. lie. Some people believe that to *prevaricate* in a good cause is justifiable and regard the statement as a "white lie."

prim ADJ. very precise and formal; exceedingly proper. Many people commented on the contrast between the *prim* attire of the young lady and the inappropriate clothing worn by her escort.

primogeniture N. seniority by birth. By virtue of *primogeniture,* the first-born child has many privileges denied his brothers and sisters.

primordial ADJ. existing at the beginning (of time); rudimentary. The Neanderthal Man is one of our *primordial* ancestors.

primp V. dress up. She *primps* for hours before a dance.

pristine ADJ. characteristic of earlier times; primitive; unspoiled. This area has been preserved in all its *pristine* wildness.

privation N. hardship; want. In his youth, he knew hunger and *privation.*

privy ADJ. secret; hidden; not public. We do not care for *privy* chamber government.

probe V. explore with tools. The surgeon *probed* the wound for foreign matter before suturing it. also N.

probity N. uprightness; incorruptibility. Everyone took his *probity* for granted; his defalcations, therefore, shocked us all.

proboscis N. long snout; nose. The elephant uses his *proboscis* to handle things and carry them from place to place.

proclivity N. inclination; natural tendency. She has a *proclivity* to grumble.

procrastinate V. postpone; delay. It is wise not to *procrastinate;* otherwise, we find ourselves bogged down in a mass of work which should have been finished long ago.

prod V. poke; stir up; urge. If you *prod* him hard enough, he'll eventually clean his room.

prodigal ADJ. wasteful; reckless with money. The *prodigal* son squandered his inheritance. also N.

prodigious ADJ. marvelous; enormous. He marveled at her *prodigious* appetite.

profane V. violate; desecrate. Tourists are urged not to *profane* the sanctity of holy places by wearing improper garb. also ADJ.

profligate ADJ. dissipated; wasteful; licentious. In this *profligate* company, she lost all sense of decency. also N.

profusion N. lavish expenditure; overabundant condition. Seldom have I seen food and drink served in such *profusion.*

progenitor N. ancestor. We must not forget the teachings of our *progenitors* in our desire to appear modern.

progeny N. children; offspring. He was proud of his *progeny* but regarded George as the most promising of all his children.

prognathous ADJ. having projecting jaws. His *prognathous* face made him seem more determined than he actually was.

prognosis N. forecasted course of a disease; prediction. If the doctor's *prognosis* is correct, the patient will be in a coma for at least twenty-four hours.

prognosticate V. predict. I *prognosticate* disaster unless we change our wasteful ways.

projectile N. missile. Man has always hurled *projectiles* at his enemy whether in the form of stones or of highly explosive shells.

proletarian N. member of the working class. The aristocrats feared mob rule and gave the right to vote only to the wealthy, thus depriving the *proletarians* of a voice in government. also ADJ.

prolific ADJ. abundantly fruitful. She was a *prolific* writer and wrote as many as three books a year.

prolix ADJ. verbose; drawn out. Her *prolix* arguments irritated the jury. prolixity, N.

promiscuous ADJ. mixed indiscriminately; haphazard; irregular. In the opera *La Boheme,* we get a picture of the *promiscuous* life led by the young artists of Paris.

promontory N. headland. They erected a lighthouse on the *promontory* to warn approaching ships of their nearness to the shore.

promulgate V. make known by official proclamation or publication. As soon as the Civil Service Commission *promulgates* the names of the successful candidates, we shall begin to hire members of our staff.

prone ADJ. inclined to; prostrate. She was *prone* to sudden fits of anger.

propagate V. multiply; spread. I am sure disease must *propagate* in such unsanitary and crowded areas.

propellants N. substances which propel or drive forward. The development of our missile program has forced our scientists to seek more powerful *propellants.*

propensity N. natural inclination. I dislike your *propensity* to belittle every contribution she makes to our organization.

prophylactic ADJ. used to prevent disease. Despite all *prophylactic* measures introduced by the authorities, the epidemic raged until cool weather set in. also N.

propinquity N. nearness; kinship. Their relationship could not be explained as being based on mere *propinquity:* they were more than relatives; they were true friends.

propitiate V. appease. The natives offered sacrifices to *propitiate* the gods.

TEST—WORD LIST 37—*Antonyms*

Each of the questions below consists of a word in capital letters, followed by five lettered words or phrases. Choose the lettered word or phrase that is most nearly opposite in meaning to the word in capital letters and write the letter of your choice on your answer paper.

541. PRECIPITATE (A) dull (B) anticipatory (C) cautious (D) considerate (E) welcome
542. PREFATORY (A) outstanding (B) magnificent (C) conclusive (D) intelligent (E) predatory
543. PRELUDE (A) intermezzo (B) diva (C) aria (D) aftermath (E) duplication
544. PRESUMPTION (A) assertion (B) activation (C) motivation (D) proposition (E) humility
545. PRETENTIOUS (A) ominous (B) calm (C) unassuming (D) futile (E) volatile
546. PRIM (A) informal (B) prior (C) exterior (D) private (E) cautious
547. PRISTINE (A) cultivated (B) condemned (C) irreligious (D) cautious (E) critical
548. PROBITY (A) regret (B) assumption (C) corruptibility (D) extent (E) upswing
549. PRODIGAL (A) large (B) thrifty (C) consistent (D) compatible (E) remote
550. PRODIGIOUS (A) infinitesimal (B) indignant (C) indifferent (D) indisposed (E) insufficient
551. PROFANE (A) sanctify (B) desecrate (C) define (D) manifest (E) urge
552. PROGNATHOUS (A) chewing (B) maxillary (C) receding (D) belligerent (E) impacted
553. PROLIX (A) stupid (B) indifferent (C) redundant (D) livid (E) pithy
554. PROPHYLACTIC (A) causing growth (B) causing disease (C) antagonistic (D) brushing (E) favorable
555. PROPINQUITY (A) remoteness (B) uniqueness (C) health (D) virtue (E) simplicity

---

WORD LIST 38 **propitious - quarry**

propitious ADJ. favorable; kindly. I think it is advisable that we wait for a more *propitious* occasion to announce our plans.

propound V. put forth for analysis. In your discussion, you have *propounded* several questions; let us consider each one separately.

propriety N. fitness; correct conduct. I want you to behave at this dinner with *propriety;* don't embarrass me.

propulsive ADJ. driving forward. The jet plane has a greater *propulsive* power than the engine-driven plane.

prorogue V. dismiss parliament; end officially. It was agreed that the king could not *prorogue* parliament until it had been in session for at least fifty days.

prosaic ADJ. commonplace; dull. I do not like this author because he is so unimaginative and *prosaic.*

proscenium N. part of stage in front of curtain. In the theater-in-the-round there can be no *proscenium* or *proscenium* arch.

proscribe V. ostracize; banish; outlaw. Antony, Octavius, and Lepidus *proscribed* all those who had conspired against Julius Caesar.

proselytize V. convert to a religion or belief. In these interfaith meetings, there must be no attempt to *proselytize;* we must respect all points of view.

prosody N. the art of versification. This book on *prosody* contains a rhyming dictionary as well as samples of the various verse forms.

prostrate V. stretch out full on ground. He *prostrated* himself before the idol. also ADJ.

protean ADJ. versatile; able to take on many shapes. A remarkably *protean* actor, Alec Guinness could take on any role.

protégé N. person under the protection and support of a patron. Cyrano de Bergerac refused to be a *protégé* of Cardinal Richelieu.

protocol N. diplomatic etiquette. We must run this state dinner according to *protocol* if we are to avoid offending any of our guests.

prototype N. original work used as a model by others. The crude typewriter on display in this museum is the *prototype* of the elaborate machines in use today.

protract V. prolong. Do not *protract* this phone conversation as I expect an important business call within the next few minutes.

protrude V. stick out. His fingers *protruded* from the holes in his gloves.

provenance N. origin or source of something. I am not interested in its *provenance;* I am more concerned with its usefulness than with its source.

provender N. dry food; fodder. I am not afraid of a severe winter because I have stored a large quantity of *provender* for the cattle.

provident ADJ. displaying foresight; thrifty; preparing for emergencies. In his usual *provident* manner, he had insured himself against this type of loss.

provincial ADJ. pertaining to a province; limited. We have to overcome their *provincial* attitude and get them to become more cognizant of world problems.

proviso N. stipulation. I am ready to accept your proposal with the *proviso* that you meet your obligations within the next two weeks.

provocation N. cause for anger or retaliation. In order to prevent a sudden outbreak of hostilities, we must give our foe no *provocation.*

proximity N. nearness. The deer sensed the hunter's *proximity* and bounded away.

proxy N. authorized agent. Please act as my *proxy* and vote for this slate of candidates.

prude N. excessively modest person. The X-rated film was definitely not for *prudes.*

prudence N. caution; carefulness. A miser hoards his money not out of *prudence* but out of greed.

prune V. cut away; trim. With the help of her editor, she was able to *prune* her manuscript into publishable form.

prurient ADJ. based on lascivious thoughts. The police attempted to close the theater where the *prurient* film was being presented.

pseudonym N. pen name. Samuel Clemens' *pseudonym* was Mark Twain.

psyche N. soul; mind. It is difficult to delve into the *psyche* of a human being.

psychiatrist N. a doctor who treats mental diseases. A *psychiatrist* often needs long conferences with his patient before a diagnosis can be made.

psychopathic ADJ. pertaining to mental derangement. The *psychopathic* patient suffers more frequently from a disorder of the nervous system than from a diseased brain.

psychosis N. mental disorder. We must endeavor to find an outlet for the patient's repressed desires if we hope to combat this *psychosis.*

pterodactyl N. extinct flying reptile. The remains of *pterodactyls* indicate that these flying reptiles had a wingspan of as much as twenty feet.

puerile ADJ. childish. His *puerile* pranks sometimes offended his serious-minded friends.

pugilist N. boxer. The famous *pugilist* Cassius Clay changed his name to Muhammed Ali.

pugnacious ADJ. combative; disposed to fight. As a child he was *pugnacious* and fought with everyone.

puissant ADJ. powerful; strong; potent. We must keep his friendship for he will make a *puissant* ally.

pulchritude N. beauty; comeliness. I do not envy the judges who have to select this year's Miss America from this collection of female *pulchitrude.*

pulmonary ADJ. pertaining to the lungs. In his researches on *pulmonary* diseases, he discovered many facts about the lungs of animals and human beings.

pulsate V. throb. We could see the blood vessels in his temple *pulsate* as he became more angry.

pummel V. beat. The severity with which he was *pummeled* was indicated by the bruises he displayed on his head and face.

punctilious ADJ. laying stress on niceties of conduct, form; precise. We must be *punctilious* in our planning of this affair, for any error may be regarded as a personal affront.

pundit N. learned Hindu; any learned man; authority on a subject. Even though he discourses on the matter like a *pundit,* he is actually rather ignorant about this topic.

pungent ADJ. stinging; caustic. The *pungent* aroma of the smoke made me cough.

punitive ADJ. punishing. He asked for *punitive* measures against the offender.

puny ADJ. insignificant; tiny; weak. Our *puny* efforts to stop the flood were futile.

purblind ADJ. dim-sighted; obtuse. In his *purblind* condition, he could not identify the people he saw.

purgatory N. place of spiritual expiation. In this *purgatory,* he could expect no help from his comrades.

purge V. clean by removing impurities; to clear of charges. If you are to be *purged* of the charge of contempt of Congress, you must be willing to answer the questions previously asked. also N.

purloin V. steal. In the story, "The *Purloined* Letter," Poe points out that the best hiding place is often the most obvious place.

purport N. intention; meaning. If the *purport* of your speech was to arouse the rabble, you succeeded admirably. also V.

purveyor N. furnisher of foodstuffs; caterer. As *purveyor* of rare wines and viands, he traveled through France and Italy every year in search of new products to sell.

purview N. scope. The sociological implications of these inventions are beyond the *purview* of this book.

pusillanimous ADJ. cowardly; fainthearted. You should be ashamed of your *pusillanimous* conduct during this dispute.

putative ADJ. supposed; reputed. Although there are some doubts, the *putative* author of this work is Massinger.

putrid ADJ. foul; rotten; decayed. The gangrenous condition of the wound was indicated by the *putrid* smell when the bandages were removed. putrescence, N.

pyromaniac N. person with an insane desire to set things on fire. The detectives searched the area for the *pyromaniac* who had set these costly fires.

quack N. charlatan; impostor. Do not be misled by the exorbitant claims of this *quack.*

quadruped N. four-footed animal. Most mammals are *quadrupeds.*

quaff V. drink with relish. As we *quaffed* our ale, we listened to the gay songs of the students in the tavern.

quagmire N. bog; marsh. Our soldiers who served in Vietnam will never forget the drudgery of marching through the *quagmires* of the delta country.

quail V. cower; lose heart. He was afraid that he would *quail* in the face of danger.

quaint ADJ. odd; old-fashioned; picturesque. Her *quaint* clothes and old-fashioned language marked her as an eccentric.

qualms N. misgivings. His *qualms* of conscience had become so great that he decided to abandon his plans.

quandary N. dilemma. When the two colleges to which he had applied accepted him, he was in a *quandary* as to which one he should attend.

quarantine N. isolation of person or ship to prevent spread of infection. We will have to place this house under *quarantine* until we determine the exact nature of the disease. also V.

quarry N. victim; object of a hunt. The police closed in on their *quarry.*

quarry V. dig into. They *quarried* blocks of marble out of the hillside.

TEST—WORD LIST 38—*Antonyms*

Each of the questions below consists of a word in capital letters, followed by five lettered words or phrases. Choose the lettered word or phrase that is most nearly opposite in meaning to the word in capital letters and write the letter of your choice on your answer paper.

556. PROPITIOUS (A) rich (B) induced (C) promoted (D) indicative (E) unfavorable
557. PROSAIC (A) pacified (B) reprieved (C) pensive (D) imaginative (E) rhetorical
558. PROTEAN (A) amateur (B) catholic (C) unchanging (D) rapid (E) unfavorable
559. PROTRACT (A) make circular (B) shorten (C) further (D) retrace (E) involve
560. PROVIDENT (A) unholy (B) rash (C) miserable (D) disabled (E) remote
561. PROVINCIAL (A) wealthy (B) crass (C) literary (D) aural (E) sophisticated
562. PSYCHOTIC (A) dangerous (B) clairvoyant (C) criminal (D) soulful (E) sane
563. PUERILE (A) fragrant (B) adult (C) lonely (D) feminine (E) masterly
564. PUGNACIOUS (A) pacific (B) feline (C) mature (D) angular (E) inactive
565. PUISSANT (A) pouring (B) fashionable (C) articulate (D) healthy (E) weak
566. PULCHRITUDE (A) ugliness (B) notoriety (C) bestiality (D) masculinity (E) servitude
567. PUNCTILIOUS (A) happy (B) active (C) vivid (D) careless (E) futile
568. PUNITIVE (A) large (B) humorous (C) rewarding (D) restive (E) languishing
569. PUSILLANIMOUS (A) poverty-stricken (B) chained (C) posthumous (D) courageous (E) strident
570. PUTATIVE (A) colonial (B) quarrelsome (C) undisputed (D) powerful (E) unremarkable

WORD LIST 39 quay - recusant

quay N. dock; landing place. Because of the captain's carelessness, the ship crashed into the *quay.*

queasy ADJ. easily nauseated; squeamish. As the ship left the harbor, he became *queasy* and thought that he was going to suffer from seasickness.

quell V. put down; quiet. The police used fire hoses and tear gas to *quell* the rioters.

querulous ADJ. fretful; whining. His classmates were repelled by his *querulous* and complaining statements.

quibble V. equivocate; play on words. Do not *quibble;* I want a straightforward and definite answer. also N.

queue N. line. They stood patiently in the *queue* outside the movie theatre.

quiescent ADJ. at rest; dormant. After this geyser erupts, it will remain *quiescent* for twenty-four hours.

quietude N. tranquillity. He was impressed by the air of *quietude* and peace that pervaded the valley.

quintessence N. purest and highest embodiment. These books display the *quintessence* of wit.

quip N. taunt. You are unpopular because you are too free with your *quips* and sarcastic comments. also V.

quirk N. startling twist; caprice. By a *quirk* of fate, he found himself working for the man whom he had discharged years before.

qui vive N. wide awake; expectant. Let us be on the *qui vive.*

quixotic ADJ. idealistic but impractical. He is constantly presenting these *quixotic* schemes.

quizzical ADJ. bantering; comical; humorously serious. Will Rogers' *quizzical* remarks endeared him to his audiences.

quorum N. number of members necessary to conduct a meeting. The senator asked for a roll call to determine whether a *quorum* was present.

rabid ADJ. like a fanatic; furious. He was a *rabid* follower of the Dodgers and watched them play whenever he could go to the ball park.

raconteur N. story-teller. My father was a gifted *raconteur* with an unlimited supply of anecdotes.

ragamuffin N. person wearing tattered clothes. He felt sorry for the *ragamuffin* who was begging for food and gave him money to buy a meal.

rail V. scold; rant. You may *rail* at him all you want; you will never change him.

raiment N. clothing. "How can I go to the ball?" asked Cinderella. "I have no *raiment* fit to wear."

rakish ADJ. stylish; sporty. He wore his hat at a *rakish* angle.

ramification N. branching out; subdivision. We must examine all the *ramifications* of this problem.

ramify V. divide into branches or subdivisions. When the plant begins to *ramify,* it is advisable to nip off most of the new branches.

ramp N. slope; inclined plane. The house was built with *ramps* instead of stairs in order to enable the man in the wheelchair to move easily from room to room and floor to floor.

rampant ADJ. rearing up on hind legs; unrestrained. The *rampant* weeds in the garden killed all the flowers which had been planted in the spring.

rampart N. defensive mound of earth. "From the *ramparts* we watched" as the fighting continued.

ramshackle ADJ. rickety; falling apart. The boys propped up the *ramshackle* clubhouse with a couple of boards.

rancid ADJ. having the odor of stale fat. A *rancid* odor filled the ship's galley.

rancor N. bitterness; hatred. Let us forget our *rancor* and cooperate in this new endeavor.

rankle V. irritate; fester. The memory of having been jilted *rankled* him for years.

rant V. rave; speak bombastically. As we heard him *rant* on the platform, we could not understand his strange popularity with many people.

rapacious ADJ. excessively grasping; plundering. Hawks and other *rapacious* birds may be killed at any time.

rapprochement N. reconciliation. Both sides were eager to effect a *rapprochement* but did not know how to undertake a program designed to bring about harmony.

rarefied ADJ. made less dense [of a gas]. The mountain climbers had difficulty breathing in the *rarefied* atmosphere.

raspy ADJ. grating; harsh. The sergeant's *raspy* voice grated on the recruits' ears.

ratiocination N. reasoning; act of drawing conclusions from premises. Poe's "The Gold Bug" is a splendid example of the author's use of *ratiocination.*

rationalization N. bringing into conformity with reason. All attempts at *rationalization* at this time are doomed to failure; tempers and emotions run too high for intelligent thought to prevail.

rationalize V. reason; justify an improper act. Do not try to *rationalize* your behavior by blaming your companions.

raucous ADJ. harsh and shrill. His *raucous* laughter irritated me.

ravage V. plunder; despoil. The marauding army *ravaged* the countryside.

ravening ADJ. rapacious; seeking prey. We kept our fires burning all night to frighten the *ravening* wolves.

ravenous ADJ. extremely hungry. The *ravenous* dog upset several garbage pails in its search for food.

raze V. destroy completely. The owners intend to *raze* the hotel and erect an office building on the site.

reactionary ADJ. recoiling from progress; retrograde. His program was *reactionary* since it sought to abolish many of the social reforms instituted by the previous administration. also N.

realm N. kingdom; sphere. The *realm* of possibilities for the new invention was endless.

rebate N. discount. We offer a *rebate* of ten percent to those who pay cash.

rebuff V. snub; beat back. She *rebuffed* his invitation so smoothly that he did not realize he had been snubbed.

recalcitrant ADJ. obstinately stubborn. Donkeys are reputed to be the most *recalcitrant* of animals.

recant V. repudiate; withdraw previous statement. Unless you *recant* your confession, you will be punished severely.

recapitulate V. summarize. Let us *recapitulate* what has been said thus far before going ahead.

recession N. withdrawal; retreat. The *recession* of the troops from the combat area was completed in an orderly manner.

recherché ADJ. choice, sought after; rare. His language was peculiarly literary; he avoided common expressions and used *recherché* terminology as often as possible.

recidivism N. habitual return to crime. Prison reformers in the United States are disturbed by the high rate of *recidivism;* the number of men serving second and third terms in prison indicates the failure of the prisons to rehabilitate the inmates.

recipient N. receiver. Although he had been the *recipient* of many favors, he was not grateful to his benefactor.

reciprocal ADJ. mutual; exchangeable; interacting. The two nations signed a *reciprocal* trade agreement.

reciprocate V. repay in kind. If they attack us, we shall be compelled to *reciprocate* and bomb their territory.

recluse N. hermit. The *recluse* lived in a hut in the forest.

reconcile V. make friendly after quarrel; correct inconsistencies. Each month we *reconcile* our checkbook with the bank statement.

recondite ADJ. abstruse; profound; secret. He read many *recondite* books in order to obtain the material for his scholarly thesis.

reconnaissance N. survey of enemy by soldiers; reconnoitering. If you encounter any enemy soldiers during your *reconnaissance,* capture them for questioning.

recourse N. resorting to help when in trouble. The boy's only *recourse* was to appeal to his father for aid.

recreant N. coward; betrayer of faith. The religious people ostracized the *recreant* who had abandoned their faith.

recrimination N. countercharges. Loud and angry *recriminations* were her answer to his accusations.

recrudescence N. reopening of a wound or sore. Keep this wound bandaged until it has completely healed to prevent its *recrudescence.*

rectify V. correct. I want to *rectify* my error before it is too late.

rectitude N. uprightness. He was renowned for his *rectitude* and integrity.

recumbent ADJ. reclining; lying down completely or in part. The command "AT EASE" does not permit you to take a *recumbent* position.

recuperate V. recover. The doctors were worried because the patient did not *recuperate* as rapidly as they had expected.

recurrent ADJ. occurring again and again. These *recurrent* attacks disturbed us and we consulted a physician.

recusant N. person who refuses to comply; applied specifically to those who refused to attend Anglican services. In that religious community, the *recusant* was shunned as a pariah.

TEST—WORD LIST 39—*Synonyms and Antonyms*

Each of the following questions consists of a word in capital letters, followed by five lettered words or phrases. Choose the lettered word or phrase which is most nearly similar or the opposite of the word in capital letters and write the letter of your choice on your answer paper.

571. QUEASY (A) toxic (B) easily upset (C) chronic (D) choleric (E) false

572. QUELL (A) boast (B) incite (C) reverse (D) wet (E) answer

573. QUIXOTIC (A) rapid (B) exotic (C) longing (D) timid (E) idealistic
574. RAGAMUFFIN (A) dandy (B) biscuit (C) exotic dance (D) light snack (E) baker
575. RAUCOUS (A) mellifluous (B) uncooked (C) realistic (D) veracious (E) anticipating
576. RAVAGE (A) rank (B) revive (C) plunder (D) pillory (E) age
577. RAZE (A) shave (B) heckle (C) finish (D) tear down (E) write
578. REACTIONARY (A) conservative (B) retrograde (C) dramatist (D) militant (E) chemical
579. REBATE (A) relinquish (B) settle (C) discount (D) cancel (E) elicit
580. RECALCITRANT (A) grievous (B) secretive (C) cowardly (D) thoughtful (E) cooperative
581. RECHERCHÉ (A) learned (B) tiresome (C) usual (D) studied (E) outrageous
582. RECREANT (A) vacationing (B) faithful (C) indifferent (D) obliged (E) reviving
583. RECTIFY (A) remedy (B) avenge (C) create (D) assemble (E) attribute
584. RECUPERATE (A) reenact (B) engage (C) recapitulate (D) recover (E) encounter
585. RECUSANT (A) nonconformer (B) deliberator (C) abstainer (D) qualifier (E) patient

---

WORD LIST 40 **redolent - rescind**

redolent ADJ. fragrant; odorous; suggestive of an odor. Even though it is February, the air is *redolent* of spring.

redoubtable ADJ. formidable; causing fear. The neighboring countries tried not to offend the Russians because they could be *redoubtable* foes.

redress N. remedy; compensation. Do you mean to tell me that I can get no *redress* for my injuries? also V.

redundant ADJ. superfluous; excessively wordy; repetitious. Your composition is *redundant;* you can easily reduce its length.

reek V. emit (odor). The room *reeked* with stale tobacco smoke. also N.

refection N. slight refreshment. In our anxiety to reach our destination as rapidly as possible, we stopped on the road for only a quick *refection.*

refectory N. dining hall. In this huge *refectory,* we can feed the entire student body at one sitting.

refraction N. bending of a ray of light. When you look at a stick inserted in water, it looks bent because of the *refraction* of the light by the water.

refractory ADJ. stubborn; unmanageable. The *refractory* horse was eliminated from the race.

refulgent ADJ. radiant. We admired the *refulgent* moon and watched it for a while.

refurbish V. renovate; make bright by polishing. The flood left a deposit of mud on everything; it was necessary to *refurbish* our belongings.

refutation N. disproof of opponents' arguments. I will wait until I hear the *refutation* before deciding whom to favor.

regal ADJ. royal. He has a *regal* manner.

regale V. entertain. John *regaled* us with tales of his adventures in Africa.

regatta N. boat or yacht race. Many boating enthusiasts followed the *regatta* in their own yachts.

regeneration N. spiritual rebirth. Modern penologists strive for the *regeneration* of the prisoners.

regicide N. murder of a king or queen. The death of Mary Queen of Scots was an act of *regicide.*

regime N. method or system of government. When a Frenchman mentions the Old *Regime,* he refers to the government existing before the revolution.

regimen N. prescribed diet and habits. I doubt whether the results warrant our living under such a strict and inflexible *regimen.*

rehabilitate V. restore to proper condition. We must *rehabilitate* those whom we send to prison.

reimburse V. repay. Let me know what you have spent and I will *reimburse* you.

reiterate V. repeat. I shall *reiterate* this message until all have understood it.

rejuvenate V. make young again. The charlatan claimed that his elixir would *rejuvenate* the aged and weary.

relegate V. banish; consign to inferior position. If we *relegate* these experienced people to positions of unimportance because of their political persuasions, we shall lose the services of valuably trained personnel.

relevancy N. pertinence; reference to the case in hand. I was impressed by the *relevancy* of your remarks. relevant, ADJ.

relinquish V. abandon. I will *relinquish* my claims to this property if you promise to retain my employees.

relish V. savor; enjoy. I *relish* a good joke as much as anyone else. also N.

remediable ADJ. reparable. Let us be grateful that the damage is *remediable.*

remedial ADJ. curative; corrective. Because he was a slow reader, he decided to take a course in *remedial* reading.

reminiscence N. recollection. Her *reminiscences* of her experiences are so fascinating that she ought to write a book.

remiss ADJ. negligent. He was accused of being *remiss* in his duty.

remnant N. remainder. I suggest that you wait until the store places the *remnants* of these goods on sale.

remonstrate V. protest. I must *remonstrate* about the lack of police protection in this area.

remorse N. guilt; self-reproach. The murderer felt no *remorse* for his crime.

remunerative ADJ. compensating; rewarding. I find my new work so *remunerative* that I may not return to my previous employment. remuneration, N.

rend V. split; tear apart. In his grief, he tried to *rend* his garments.

render V. deliver; provide; represent. He *rendered* aid to the needy and indigent.

rendezvous N. meeting place. The two fleets met at the *rendezvous* at the appointed time. also V.

rendition N. translation; artistic interpretation of a song, etc. The audience cheered enthusiastically as she completed her *rendition* of the aria.

renegade N. deserter; apostate. Because he refused to support his fellow members in their drive, he was shunned as a *renegade.*

renege V. deny; go back on. He *reneged* on paying off his debt.

renounce V. abandon; discontinue; disown; repudiate. Joan of Arc refused to *renounce* her statements even though she knew she would be burned at the stake as a witch.

renovate V. restore to good condition; renew. They claim that they can *renovate* worn shoes so that they look like new ones.

renunciation N. giving up; renouncing. Do not sign this *renunciation* of your right to sue until you have consulted a lawyer.

reparable ADJ. capable of being repaired. Fortunately, the damages we suffered in the accident were *reparable.*

reparation N. amends; compensation. At the peace conference, the defeated country promised to pay *reparations* to the victors.

repartee N. clever reply. He was famous for his witty *repartee* and his sarcasm.

repellent ADJ. driving away; unattractive. Mosquitoes find the odor so *repellent* that they leave any spot where this liquid has been sprayed. also N.

repercussion N. rebound; reverberation; reaction. I am afraid that this event will have serious *repercussions.*

repertoire N. list of works of music, drama, etc., a performer is prepared to present. The opera company decided to include *Madame Butterfly* in its *repertoire* for the following season.

repine V. fret; complain. There is no sense *repining* over the work you have left undone.

replenish V. fill up again. The end of rationing enabled us to *replenish* our supply of canned food.

replete ADJ. filled to capacity; abundantly supplied. This book is *replete* with humorous situations.

replica N. copy. Are you going to hang this *replica* of the Declaration of Independence in the classroom or in the auditorium?

repository N. storehouse. Libraries are *repositories* of the world's best thoughts.

reprehensible ADJ. deserving blame. Your vicious conduct in this situation is *reprehensible.*

reprieve N. temporary stay. During the twenty-four-hour *reprieve,* the lawyers sought to make the stay of execution permanent. also V.

reprimand V. reprove severely. I am afraid that my parents will *reprimand* me when I show them my report card. also N.

reprisal N. retaliation. I am confident that we are ready for any *reprisals* the enemy may undertake.

reproach N. blame; censure. I want my work to be above *reproach*. also V.

reprobate N. person hardened in sin, devoid of a sense of decency. I cannot understand why he has so many admirers if he is the *reprobate* you say he is.

reprobation N. severe disapproval. The students showed their *reprobation* of his act by refusing to talk with him.

reprove V. censure; rebuke. The principal *reproved* the students when they became unruly in the auditorium.

repudiate V. disown; disavow. He announced that he would *repudiate* all debts incurred by his wife.

repugnance N. loathing. She looked at the snake with *repugnance.*

reputed ADJ. supposed. He is the *reputed* father of the child. also V.

requiem N. mass for the dead; dirge. They played Mozart's *Requiem* at the funeral.

requisite N. necessary requirement. Many colleges state that a student must offer three years of a language as a *requisite* for admission.

requite V. repay; revenge. The wretch *requited* his benefactors by betraying them.

rescind V. cancel. Because of public resentment, the king had to *rescind* his order.

TEST—WORD LIST 40—*Synonyms*

Each of the questions below consists of a word in capital letters, followed by five lettered words or phrases. Choose the lettered word or phrase that is most nearly similar in meaning to the word in capital letters and write the letter of your choice on your answer paper.

586. REFRACTORY (A) articulate (B) sinkable (C) vaunted (D) useless (E) unmanageable
587. REGAL (A) opressive (B) royal (C) major (D) basic (E) entertaining
588. REITERATE (A) gainsay (B) revive (C) revenge (D) repeat (E) return
589. RELISH (A) desire (B) nibble (C) savor (D) vindicate (E) avail
590. REMISS (A) lax (B) lost (C) foolish (D) violating (E) ambitious
591. REMONSTRATE (A) display (B) restate (C) protest (D) resign (E) reiterate
592. REPARTEE (A) witty retort (B) willful departure (C) spectator (D) monologue (E) sacrifice
593. REPELLENT (A) propulsive (B) unattractive (C) porous (D) stiff (E) elastic
594. REPERCUSSION (A) reaction (B) restitution (C) resistance (D) magnificence (E) acceptance
595. REPLENISH (A) polish (B) repeat (C) reinstate (D) refill (E) refuse
596. REPLICA (A) museum piece (B) famous site (C) battle emblem (D) facsimile (E) replacement
597. REPRISAL (A) reevaluation (B) assessment (C) loss (D) retaliation (E) nonsense
598. REPROVE (A) prevail (B) rebuke (C) ascertain (D) prove false (E) scarify
599. REPUDIATE (A) besmirch (B) appropriate (C) annoy (D) reject (E) avow
600. REPUGNANCE (A) belligerence (B) tenacity (C) renewal (D) pity (E) loathing

---

WORD LIST 41 rescission - sacrosanct

rescission N. abrogation; annulment. The *rescission* of the unpopular law was urged by all political parties.

reserved ADJ. self-controlled; careful in expressing oneself. She was outspoken and uninhibited; he was cautious and *reserved.*

residue N. remainder; balance. In his will, he requested that after payment of debts, taxes, and funeral expenses, the *residue* be given to his wife.

resilient ADJ. elastic; having the power of springing back. Steel is highly *resilient* and therefore is used in the manufacture of springs.

resonant ADJ. echoing; resounding; possessing resonance. His *resonant* voice was particularly pleasing.

respite N. delay in punishment; interval of relief; rest. The judge granted the condemned man a *respite* to enable his attorneys to file an appeal.

resplendent ADJ. brilliant; lustrous. The toreador wore a *resplendent* costume.

responsiveness N. state of reacting readily to appeals, orders, etc. The audience cheered and applauded, delighting the performers by its *responsiveness.*

restitution N. reparation; indemnification. He offered to make *restitution* for the window broken by his son.

restive ADJ. unmanageable; fretting under control. We must quiet the *restive* animals.

restraint N. controlling force. She dreamt of living an independent life, free of all *restraints.*

resurgent ADJ. rising again after defeat, etc. The *resurgent* nation surprised everyone by its quick recovery after total defeat.

resuscitate V. revive. The lifeguard tried to *resuscitate* the drowned child by applying artificial respiration.

retaliate V. repay in kind (usually for bad treatment). Fear that we will *retaliate* immediately deters our foe from attacking us.

retentive ADJ. holding; having a good memory. The pupil did not need to spend much time in study as he had a *retentive* mind.

reticence N. reserve; uncommunicativeness; inclination to be silent. Because of the *reticence* of the key witness, the case against the defendant collapsed.

reticulated ADJ. covered with a network; having the appearance of a mesh. She wore the *reticulated* stockings so popular with teenagers at that time.

retinue N. following; attendants. The queen's *retinue* followed her down the aisle.

retort N. quick sharp reply. Even when it was advisable for her to keep her mouth shut, she was always ready with a quick *retort.* also V.

retraction N. withdrawal. He dropped his libel suit after the newspaper published a *retraction* of its statement.

retrench V. cut down; economize. If they were to be able to send their children to college, they would have to *retrench.*

retribution N. vengeance; compensation; punishment

for offenses. The evangelist maintained that an angry Deity would exact *retribution* from the sinners.

retrieve V. recover; find and bring in. The dog was intelligent and quickly learned to *retrieve* the game killed by the hunter.

retroactive ADJ. of a law which dates back to a period before its enactment. Because the law was *retroactive* to the first of the year, we found he was eligible for the pension.

retrograde V. going backwards; degenerating. Instead of advancing, our civilization seems to have *retrograded* in ethics and culture.

retrospective ADJ. looking back on the past. It is only when we become *retrospective* that we can appreciate the tremendous advances made during this century.

revelry N. boisterous merrymaking. New Year's Eve is a night of *revelry.*

reverberate V. echo; resound. The entire valley *reverberated* with the sound of the church bells.

revere V. respect; honor. In Asian societies, people *revere* their elders.

reverie N. daydream; musing. He was awakened from his *reverie* by the teacher's question.

revile V. slander; vilify. He was avoided by all who feared that he would *revile* and abuse them if they displeased him.

revulsion N. sudden violent change of feeling; reaction. Many people in this country who admired dictatorships underwent a *revulsion* when they realized what Hitler and Mussolini were trying to do.

rhapsodize V. to speak or write in an exaggeratedly enthusiastic manner. She greatly enjoyed her Hawaiian vacation and *rhapsodized* about it for weeks.

rhetoric N. art of effective communication; insincere language. All writers, by necessity, must be skilled in *rhetoric.* rhetorical, ADJ.

rheumy ADJ. pertaining to a discharge from nose and eyes. His *rheumy* eyes warned us that he was coming down with a cold.

ribald ADJ. wanton; profane. He sang a *ribald* song which offended many of us.

rife ADJ. abundant; current. In the face of the many rumors of scandal,which are *rife* at the moment, it is best to remain silent.

rift N. opening; break. The plane was lost in the stormy sky until the pilot saw the city through a *rift* in the clouds.

rigor N. severity. Many settlers could not stand the *rigors* of the New England winters.

rime N. white frost. The early morning dew had frozen and everything was covered with a thin coat of *rime.*

risible ADJ. inclined to laugh; ludicrous. His remarks were so *risible* that the audience howled with laughter. risibility, N.

risqué ADJ. verging upon the improper; offcolor. Please do not tell your *risqué* anecdotes at this party.

roan ADJ. brown mixed with gray or white. You can distinguish this horse in a race because it is *roan* while all the others are bay or chestnut.

robust ADJ. vigorous; strong. The candidate for the football team had a *robust* physique.

rococo ADJ. ornate; highly decorated. The *rococo* style in furniture and architecture, marked by scrollwork and excessive decoration, flourished during the middle of the eighteenth century.

roil V. to make liquids murky by stirring up sediment. Be careful when you pour not to *roil* the wine; if you stir up the sediment you'll destroy the flavor.

rood N. crucifix. "By the *rood*" used to be a strong oath.

roseate ADJ. rosy; optimistic. I am afraid you will have to alter your *roseate* views in the light of the distressing news that has just arrived.

roster N. list. They print the *roster* of players in the season's program.

rostrum N. platform for speech-making; pulpit. The crowd murmured angrily and indicated that they did not care to listen to the speaker who was approaching the *rostrum.*

rote N. repetition. He recited the passage by *rote* and gave no indication he understood what he was saying.

rotunda N. circular building or hall covered with a dome. His body lay in state in the *rotunda* of the Capitol.

rotundity N. roundness; sonorousness of speech. Washington Irving emphasized the *rotundity* of the governor by describing his height and circumference.

rout V. stampede; drive out. The reinforcements were able to *rout* the enemy. also N.

rubble N. fragments. Ten years after World War II, some of the *rubble* left by enemy bombings could still be seen.

rubicund ADJ. having a healthy reddish color; ruddy; florid. His *rubicund* complexion was the result of an active outdoor life.

ruddy ADJ. reddish; healthy-looking. His *ruddy* features indicated that he had spent much time in the open.

rudimentary ADJ. not developed; elementary. His dancing was limited to a few *rudimentary* steps.

rueful ADJ. regretful; sorrowful; dejected. The artist has captured the sadness of childhood in his portrait of the boy with the *rueful* countenance.

ruffian N. bully; scoundrel. The *ruffians* threw stones at the police.

ruminate V. chew the cud; ponder. We cannot afford to wait while you *ruminate* upon these plans.

rummage V. ransack; thoroughly search. When we *rummaged* through the trunks in the attic, we found many souvenirs of our childhood days. also N.

ruse N. trick; stratagem. You will not be able to fool your friends with such an obvious *ruse.*

rustic ADJ. pertaining to country people; uncouth. The backwoodsman looked out of place in his *rustic* attire.

rusticate V. banish to the country; dwell in the country. I like city life so much that I can never understand how people can *rusticate* in the suburbs.

ruthless ADJ. pitiless. The escaped convict was a dangerous and *ruthless* murderer.

saccharine ADJ. cloyingly sweet. She tried to ingratiate herself, speaking sweetly and smiling a *saccharine* smile.

sacerdotal ADJ. priestly. The priest decided to abandon his *sacerdotal* duties and enter the field of politics.

sacrilegious ADJ. desecrating; profane. His stealing of the altar cloth was a very *sacrilegious* act.

sacrosanct ADJ. most sacred; inviolable. The brash insurance salesman invaded the *sacrosanct* privacy of the office of the president of the company.

TEST—WORD LIST 41—*Antonyms*

Each of the questions below consists of a word in capital letters, followed by five lettered words or phrases. Choose the lettered word or phrase that is most nearly opposite in meaning to the word in capital letters and write the letter of your choice on your answer paper.

601. RESILIENT (A) pungent (B) foolish (C) worthy (D) insolent (E) unyielding
602. RESTIVE (A) buoyant (B) placid (C) remorseful (D) resistant (E) retiring
603. RETENTIVE (A) forgetful (B) accepting (C) repetitive (D) avoiding (E) fascinating
604. RETICENCE (A) fatigue (B) fashion (C) treachery (D) loquàciousness (E) magnanimity
605. RETROGRADE (A) progressing (B) inclining (C) evaluating (D) concentrating (E) directing
606. REVERE (A) advance (B) dishonor (C) age (D) precede (E) wake
607. RIFE (A) direct (B) scant (C) peaceful (D) grim (E) mature
608. ROBUST (A) weak (B) violent (C) vicious (D) villainous (E) hungry
609. ROTUNDITY (A) promenade (B) nave (C) grotesqueness (D) slimness (E) impropriety
610. RUBICUND (A) dangerous (B) pallid (C) remote (D) indicative (E) nonsensical
611. RUDDY (A) robust (B) witty (C) wan (D) exotic (E) creative
612. RUDIMENTARY (A) pale (B) fundamental (C) asinine (D) developed (E) quiescent
613. RUEFUL (A) sad (B) content (C) capable (D) capital (E) zealous
614. RUSTIC (A) urban (B) slow (C) corroded (D) mercenary (E) civilian
615. RUTHLESS (A) merciful (B) majestic (C) mighty (D) militant (E) maximum

---

WORD LIST 42 sadistic - sepulcher

sadistic ADJ. inclined to cruelty. If we are to improve conditions in this prison, we must first get rid of the *sadistic* warden.

saffron ADJ. orange-colored; colored like the autumn crocus. The Halloween cake was decorated with *saffron*-colored icing.

saga N. Scandinavian myth; any legend. This is a *saga* of the sea and the men who risk their lives on it.

sagacious ADJ. keen; shrewd; having insight. He is much too *sagacious* to be fooled by a trick like that.

salient ADJ. prominent. One of the *salient* features of that newspaper is its excellent editorial page.

saline ADJ. salty. The slighty *saline* taste of this mineral water is pleasant.

sallow ADJ. yellowish; sickly in color. We were disturbed by his *sallow* complexion.

saltatory ADJ. relating to leaping. The male members of the ballet company were renowned for their *saltatory* exploits.

salubrious ADJ. healthful. Many people with hay fever move to more *salubrious* sections of the country during the months of August and September.

salutary ADJ. tending to improve; beneficial; wholesome. The punishment had a *salutary* effect on the boy, as he became a model student.

salvage V. rescue from loss. All attempts to *salvage* the wrecked ship failed. also N.

salver N. tray. The food was brought in on silver *salvers* by the waiters.

sanctimonious ADJ. displaying ostentatious or hypocritical devoutness. You do not have to be so *sanctimonious* to prove that you are devout.

sangfroid N. coolness in a trying situation. The captain's *sangfroid* helped to allay the fears of the passengers.

sanguinary ADJ. bloody. The battle of Iwo Jima was unexpectedly *sanguinary.*

sanguine ADJ. cheerful; hopeful. Let us not be too *sanguine* about the outcome.

sapid ADJ. savory; tasty; relishable. This chef has the knack of making most foods more *sapid* and appealing.

sapient ADJ. wise; shrewd. The students enjoyed the professor's *sapient* digressions more than his formal lectures.

sarcophagus N. stone coffin, often highly decorated. The display of the *sarcophagus* in the art museum impresses me as a morbid exhibition.

sardonic ADJ. disdainful; sarcastic; cynical. The *sardonic* humor of nightclub comedians who satirize or ridicule patrons in the audience strikes some people as amusing and others as rude.

sartorial ADJ. pertaining to tailors. He was as famous for the *sartorial* splendor of his attire as he was for his acting.

sate V. satisfy to the full; cloy. Its hunger *sated,* the lion dozed.

satellite N. small body revolving around a larger one. During the first few years of the Space Age, hundreds of *satellites* were launched by Russia and the United States.

satiate V. surfeit; satisfy fully. The guests, having eaten until they were *satiated,* now listened inattentively to the speakers.

satiety N. condition of being crammed full; glutted state; repletion. The *satiety* of the guests at the sumptuous feast became apparent when they refused the delicious dessert.

satire N. form of literature in which irony, sarcasm, and ridicule are employed to attack vice and folly. *Gulliver's Travels,* which is regarded by many as a tale for children, is actually a bitter *satire* attacking man's folly.

satrap N. petty ruler working for a superior despot. The monarch and his *satraps* oppressed the citizens of the country.

saturate V. soak. Their clothes were *saturated* by the rain.

saturnine ADJ. gloomy. Do not be misled by his *saturnine* countenance; he is not as gloomy as he looks.

satyr N. half-human, half-bestial being in the court of Dionysos, portrayed as wanton and cunning. He was like a *satyr* in his lustful conduct.

saunter V. stroll slowly. As we *sauntered* through the park, we stopped frequently to admire the spring flowers.

savant N. scholar. Our faculty includes many world-famous *savants.*

savoir faire N. tact; poise; sophistication. I envy his *savoir faire;* he always knows exactly what to do and say.

savor V. have a distinctive flavor, smell, or quality. I think your choice of a successor *savors* of favoritism.

scanty ADJ. meager; insufficient. Thinking his helping of food was *scanty,* Oliver Twist asked for more.

scapegoat N. someone who bears the blame for others. After the Challenger disaster, NASA searched for *scapegoats* on whom they could cast the blame.

scarify V. make slight incisions in; scratch. He was not severely cut; the flying glass had merely *scarified* him.

scavenger N. collector and disposer of refuse; animal that devours refuse and carrion. The Oakland *Scavenger* Company is responsible for the collection and disposal of the community's garbage.

schism N. division; split. Let us not widen the *schism* by further bickering.

scintilla N. shred; least bit. You have not produced a *scintilla* of evidence to support your argument.

scintillate V. sparkle; flash. I enjoy her dinner parties because the food is excellent and the conversation *scintillates.*

sciolism N. quackery; superficial information. His superficial scientific treatises were filled with *sciolisms* and outmoded data.

scion N. offspring. The farm boy felt out of place in the school attended by the *scions* of the wealthy and noble families.

scoff V. mock; ridicule. He *scoffed* at dentists until he had his first toothache.

scourge N. lash; whip; severe punishment. They feared the plague and regarded it as a deadly *scourge.* also V.

screed N. long, tiresome harangue. His letters were no more than *screeds* in which he listed his complaints.

scrupulous ADJ. conscientious; extremely thorough. I can recommend him for a position of responsibility for I have found him a very *scrupulous* young man.

scullion N. menial kitchen worker. Lynette was angry because she thought she had been given a *scullion* to act as her defender.

scurrilous ADJ. obscene; indecent. Your *scurrilous* remarks are especially offensive because they are untrue.

scurry V. move briskly. The White Rabbit had to *scurry* to get to his appointment on time.

scuttle V. sink. The sailors decided to *scuttle* their vessel rather than surrender it to the enemy.

sebaceous ADJ. oily; fatty. The *sebaceous* glands secrete oil to the hair follicles.

secession N. withdrawal. The *secession* of the Southern states provided Lincoln with his first major problem after his inauguration.

seclusion N. isolation; solitude. One moment she loved crowds; the next, she sought *seclusion.*

secular ADJ. worldly; not pertaining to church matters; temporal. The church leaders decided not to interfere in *secular* matters.

sedate ADJ. composed; grave. The parents were worried because they felt their son was too quiet and *sedate.*

sedentary ADJ. requiring sitting. Because he had a *sedentary* occupation, he decided to visit a gymnasium weekly.

sedition N. resistance to authority; insubordination. His words, though not treasonous in themselves, were calculated to arouse thoughts of *sedition.*

sedulous ADJ. diligent. Stevenson said that he played the "*sedulous* ape" and diligently imitated the great writers of the past.

seethe V. be disturbed; boil. The nation was *seething* with discontent as the noblemen continued their arrogant ways.

seine N. net for catching fish. When the shad run during the spring, you may see fishermen with *seines* along the banks of our coastal rivers.

seismic ADJ. pertaining to earthquakes. The instrument was able to measure the slightest *seismic* disturbance.

semblance N. outward appearance; guise. Although this book has a *semblance* of wisdom and scholarship, a careful examination will reveal many errors and omissions.

senescence N. state of growing old. He did not show any signs of *senescence* until he was well past seventy.

senility N. old age; feeble mindedness of old age. Most of the decisions are being made by the junior members of the company because of the *senility* of the president.

sensual ADJ. devoted to the pleasures of the senses; carnal; voluptuous. I cannot understand what caused him to drop his *sensual* way of life and become so ascetic.

sententious ADJ. terse; concise; aphoristic. After reading so many redundant speeches, I find his *sententious* style particularly pleasing.

sensuous ADJ. pertaining to the physical senses; operating through the senses. He was stimulated by the sights, sounds and smells about him; he was enjoying his *sensuous* experience.

septic ADJ. putrid; producing putrefaction. The hospital was in such a filthy state that we were afraid that many of the patients would suffer from *septic* poisoning.

sepulcher N. tomb. Annabel Lee was buried in the *sepulcher* by the sea.

TEST—WORD LIST 42—*Antonyms*

Each of the questions below consists of a word in capital letters, followed by five lettered words or phrases. Choose the lettered word or phrase that is most nearly opposite in meaning to the word in capital letters and write the letter of your choice on your answer paper.

616. SADISTIC (A) happy (B) quaint (C) kindhearted (D) vacant (E) fortunate
617. SAGACIOUS (A) foolish (B) bitter (C) voracious (D) veracious (E) fallacious
618. SALLOW (A) salacious (B) ruddy (C) colorless (D) permitted (E) minimum
619. SALUBRIOUS (A) salty (B) bloody (C) miasmic (D) maudlin (E) wanted
620. SALVAGE (A) remove (B) outfit (C) burn (D) lose (E) confuse
621. SANCTIMONIOUS (A) hypothetical (B) paltry (C) mercenary (D) pious (E) grateful
622. SANGUINE (A) choleric (B) sickening (C) warranted (D) irritated (E) pessimistic
623. SATIETY (A) emptiness (B) warmth (C) erectness (D) ignorance (E) straight
624. SCANTY (A) collected (B) remote (C) invisible (D) plentiful (E) straight
625. SCURRILOUS (A) savage (B) scabby (C) decent (D) volatile (E) major
626. SECULAR (A) vivid (B) clerical (C) punitive (D) positive (E) varying
627. SEDENTARY (A) vicarious (B) loyal (C) accidental (D) active (E) afraid
628. SENESCENCE (A) youth (B) romance (C) doldrums (D) quintessence (E) friendship
629. SENILITY (A) virility (B) loquaciousness (C) forgetfulness (D) youth (E) majority
630. SENTENTIOUS (A) paragraphed (B) positive (C) posthumous (D) pacific (E) wordy

WORD LIST 43 sequacious - somatic

sequacious ADJ. eager to follow; ductile. The *sequacious* members of Parliament were only too willing to do the bidding of their leader.

sequester V. retire from public life; segregate; seclude. Although he had hoped for a long time to *sequester* himself in a small community, he never was able to drop his busy round of activities in the city.

seraph N. high-ranking, six-winged angel. In "Annabel Lee" Poe maintains that the "winged *seraphs* of Heaven" envied their great love.

serendipity N. gift for finding valuable things not searched for. Many scientific discoveries are a matter of *serendipity.*

serenity N. calmness; placidity. The *serenity* of the sleepy town was shattered by a tremendous explosion.

serpentine ADJ. winding; twisting. The car swerved at every curve in the *serpentine* road.

serrated ADJ. having a sawtoothed edge. The beech tree is one of many plants that have *serrated* leaves.

serried ADJ. standing shoulder to shoulder; crowded. In these days of automatic weapons, it is suicidal for troops to charge in *serried* ranks against the foe.

servile ADJ. slavish; cringing. Uriah Heep was a very *servile* individual.

severance N. division; partition; separation. The *severance* of church and state is a basic principle of our government.

shackle V. chain; fetter. The criminal's ankles were *shackled* to prevent his escape. also N.

sham V. pretend. He *shammed* sickness to get out of going to school. also N.

shambles N. slaughterhouse; scene of carnage. By the time the police arrived, the room was a *shambles.*

sheaf N. bundle of stalks of grain; any bundle of things tied together. The lawyer picked up a *sheaf* of papers as he rose to question the witness.

sheathe V. place into a case. As soon as he recognized the approaching men, he *sheathed* his dagger and hailed them as friends.

sherbet N. flavored dessert ice. I prefer raspberry *sherbet* to ice cream since it is less fattening.

shibboleth N. watchword; slogan. We are often misled by *shibboleths.*

shimmer V. glimmer intermittently. The moonlight *shimmered* on the water as the moon broke through the clouds for a moment. also N.

shoal N. shallow place. The ship was stranded on a *shoal* and had to be pulled off by tugs.

shoddy ADJ. sham; not genuine; inferior. You will never get the public to buy such *shoddy* material.

shrew N. scolding woman. No one wanted to marry Kate because she was a *shrew.*

sibling N. brother or sister. We may not enjoy being *siblings,* but we cannot forget that we still belong to the same family.

sibylline ADJ. prophetic; oracular. Until their destruction by fire in 83 B.C., the *sibylline* books were often consulted by the Romans.

sidereal ADJ. relating to the stars. The study of *sidereal* bodies has been greatly advanced by the new telescope.

silt N. sediment deposited by running water. The harbor channel must be dredged annually to remove the *silt.*

simian ADJ. monkeylike. Lemurs are nocturnal mammals and have many *simian* characteristics, although they are less intelligent than monkeys.

simile N. comparison of one thing with another, using the word *like* or *as.* We are constantly using *similes* and metaphors to convey our thoughts to others.

similitude N. similarity; using comparisons such as similes, etc. Although the critics deplored his use of mixed metaphors, he continued to write in *similitudes.*

simpering ADJ. smirking. I can overlook his *simpering* manner, but I cannot ignore his stupidity.

simulate V. feign. He *simulated* insanity in order to avoid punishment for his crime.

sinecure N. well-paid position with little responsibility. My job is no *sinecure;* I work long hours and have much responsibility.

sinewy ADJ. tough; strong and firm. The steak was too *sinewy* to chew.

sinister ADJ. evil. We must defeat the *sinister* forces that seek our downfall.

sinuous ADJ. winding; bending in and out; not morally honest. The snake moved in a *sinuous* manner.

sirocco N. warm, sultry wind blown from Africa to southern Europe. We can understand the popularity of the siesta in southern Spain; when the *sirocco* blows, the afternoon heat is unbearable.

skeptic N. doubter; person who suspends judgment until he has examined the evidence supporting a point of view. In this matter, I am a *skeptic;* I want proof.

skimp V. provide scantily; live very economically. They were forced to *skimp* on necessities in order to make their limited supplies last the winter.

skinflint N. miser. The old *skinflint* refused to give her a raise.

skittish ADJ. lively; frisky. She is as *skittish* as a kitten playing with a piece of string.

skulduggery N. dishonest behavior. The investigation into municipal corruption turned up new instances of *skulduggery* daily.

skulk V. move furtively and secretly. He *skulked* through the less fashionable sections of the city in order to avoid meeting any of his former friends.

slacken V. slow up; loosen. As they passed the finish line, the runners *slackened* their pace.

slake V. quench; sate. When we reached the oasis, we were able to *slake* our thirst.

slander N. defamation; utterance of false and malicious statements. Unless you can prove your allegations, your remarks constitute *slander.* also V.

slattern N. untidy or slovenly person. If you persist in wearing such sloppy clothes, people will call you a *slattern.*

sleazy ADJ. flimsy; unsubstantial. This is a *sleazy* material; it will not wear well.

sleeper N. something originally of little value or importance which in time becomes very valuable. Unnoticed by the critics at its publication, the eventual Pulitzer Prize winner was a classic *sleeper.*

sleight N. dexterity. The magician amazed the audience with his *sleight* of hand.

slither V. slip or slide. During the recent ice storm, many people *slithered* down this hill as they walked to the station.

sloth N. laziness. Such *sloth* in a young person is deplorable.

slough V. cast off. Each spring, the snake *sloughs* off its skin.

slovenly ADJ. untidy; careless in work habits. Such *slovenly* work habits will never produce good products.

sluggard N. lazy person. "You are a *sluggard,* a drone, a parasite," the angry father shouted at his lazy son.

sluice N. artificial channel for directing or controlling the flow of water. This *sluice* gate is opened only in times of drought to provide water for irrigation.

smattering N. slight knowledge. I don't know whether it is better to be ignorant of a subject or to have a mere *smattering* of information about it.

smirk N. conceited smile. Wipe that *smirk* off your face! also V.

smolder V. burn without flame; be liable to break out at any moment. The rags *smoldered* for hours before they burst into flame.

snicker N. half-stifled laugh. The boy could not suppress a *snicker* when the teacher sat on the tack. also V.

snivel V. run at the nose; snuffle; whine. Don't you come *sniveling* to me complaining about your big brother.

sobriety N. soberness. The solemnity of the occasion filled us with *sobriety.*

sobriquet N. nickname. Despite all his protests, his classmates continued to call him by that unflattering *sobriquet.*

sodden ADJ. soaked; dull, as if from drink. He set his *sodden* overcoat near the radiator to dry.

sojourn N. temporary stay. After his *sojourn* in Florida, he began to long for the colder climate of his native New England home.

solace N. comfort in trouble. I hope you will find *solace* in the thought that all of us share your loss.

solecism N. construction that is flagrantly incorrect grammatically. I must give this paper a failing mark because it contains many *solecisms.*

solicitous ADJ. worried; concerned. The employer was very *solicitous* about the health of her employees as replacements were difficult to get.

soliloquy N. talking to oneself. The *soliloquy* is a device used by the dramatist to reveal a character's innermost thoughts and emotions.

solstice N. point at which the sun is farthest from the equator. The winter *solstice* usually occurs on December 21.

solvent ADJ. able to pay all debts. By dint of very frugal living, he was finally able to become *solvent* and avoid bankruptcy proceedings.

somatic ADJ. pertaining to the body; physical. Why do you ignore the spiritual aspects and emphasize only the corporeal and the *somatic?*

TEST—WORD LIST 43—*Synonyms and Antonyms*

Each of the following questions consists of a word in capital letters, followed by five lettered words or phrases. Choose the lettered word or phrase which is most nearly similar or the opposite of the word in capital letters and write the letter of your choice on your answer paper.

631. SERAPH (A) messenger (B) harbinger (C) demon (D) official (E) potentate
632. SERRIED (A) worried (B) embittered (C) in close order (D) fallen (E) infantile
633. SERVILE (A) moral (B) puerile (C) futile (D) foul (E) haughty
634. SHODDY (A) superior (B) barefoot (C) sunlit (D) querulous (E) garrulous
635. SIMILITUDE (A) gratitude (B) magnitude (C) likeness (D) aptitude (E) kindness
636. SINISTER (A) unwed (B) ministerial (C) good (D) returned (E) splintered
637. SKITTISH (A) tractable (B) inquiring (C) dramatic (D) vain (E) frisky
638. SLEAZY (A) fanciful (B) creeping (C) substantial (D) uneasy (E) warranted
639. SLOTH (A) penitence (B) filth (C) futility (D) poverty (E) industry
640. SLOUGH (A) toughen (B) trap (C) violate (D) cast off (E) depart
641. SLOVENLY (A) half-baked (B) loved (C) inappropriate (D) tidy (E) rapidly
642. SOBRIETY (A) inebriety (B) aptitude (C) scholasticism (D) monotony (E) aversion
643. SOBRIQUET (A) ingenue (B) livelihood (C) bar (D) epitaph (E) nickname
644. SOLSTICE (A) equinox (B) sunrise (C) pigsty (D) interstices (E) iniquity
645. SOLVENT (A) enigmatic (B) bankrupt (C) fiducial (D) puzzling (E) gilded

---

WORD LIST 44 somber - sublime

somber ADJ. gloomy; depressing. From the doctor's expression, I could tell he had *somber* news.

somnambulist N. sleepwalker. The most famous *somnambulist* in literature is Lady Macbeth; her monologue in the sleepwalking scene is one of the highlights of Shakespeare's play.

somnolent ADJ. half asleep. The heavy meal and the overheated room made us all *somnolent* and indifferent to the speaker.

sonorous ADJ. resonant. His *sonorous* voice resounded through the hall.

sophist N. teacher of philosophy; quibbler; employer of fallacious reasoning. You are using all the devices of a *sophist* in trying to prove your case; your argument is specious.

sophistication N. artificiality; unnaturalness; act of employing sophistry in reasoning. *Sophistication* is an acquired characteristic, found more frequently among city dwellers than among residents of rural areas.

sophomoric ADJ. immature; shallow. Your *sophomoric* remarks indicate that you have not given much thought to the problem.

soporific N. sleep producer. I do not need a *soporific* when I listen to one of his speeches. also ADJ.

sordid ADJ. filthy; base; vile. The social worker was angered by the *sordid* housing provided for the homeless.

soupçon N. suggestion; hint; taste. A *soupçon* of garlic will improve this dish.

spangle N. small metallic piece sewn to clothing for ornamentation. The thousands of *spangles* on her dress sparkled in the glare of the stage lights.

spasmodic ADJ. fitful; periodic. The *spasmodic* coughing in the auditorium annoyed the performers.

spate N. sudden flood. I am worried about the possibility of a *spate* if the rains do not diminish soon.

spatial ADJ. relating to space. It is difficult to visualize the *spatial* extent of our universe.

spatula N. broad-bladed instrument used for spreading or mixing. The manufacturers of this frying pan recommend the use of a rubber *spatula* to avoid scratching the specially treated surface.

spawn V. lay eggs. Fish ladders had to be built in the dams to assist the salmon returning to *spawn* in their native streams. also N.

specious ADJ. seemingly reasonable but incorrect. Let us not be misled by such *specious* arguments.

spectral ADJ. ghostly. We were frightened by the *spectral* glow that filled the room.

spectrum N. colored band produced when beam of light passes through a prism. The visible portion of the *spectrum* includes red at one end and violet at the other.

sphinx-like ADJ. enigmatic; mysterious. The Mona Lisa's *sphinx-like* expression has puzzled art lovers for centuries.

splenetic ADJ. spiteful; irritable; peevish. People shunned him because of his *splenetic* temper. spleen, N.

spoliation N. pillaging; depredation. We regard this unwarranted attack on a neutral nation as an act of *spoliation* and we demand that it cease at once and that proper restitution be made.

spoonerism N. accidental transposition of sounds in successive words. When the radio announcer introduced the President as Hoobert Herver, he was guilty of a *spoonerism*.

sporadic ADJ. occurring irregularly. Although there

are *sporadic* outbursts of shooting, we may report that the major rebellion has been defeated.

sportive ADJ. playful. Such a *sportive* attitude is surprising in a person as serious as you usually are.

spry ADJ. vigorously active; nimble. She was eighty years old, yet still *spry* and alert.

spume N. froth; foam. The *spume* at the base of the waterfall extended for a quarter of a mile downriver.

spurious ADJ. false; counterfeit. She tried to pay the check with a *spurious* ten-dollar bill.

spurn V. reject; scorn. The heroine *spurned* the villain's advances.

squalid ADJ. dirty; neglected; poor. It is easy to see how crime can breed in such a *squalid* neighborhood.

squander V. waste. The prodigal son *squandered* the family estate.

staccato ADJ. played in an abrupt manner; marked by abrupt sharp sound. His *staccato* speech reminded one of the sound of a machine gun.

stagnant ADJ. motionless; stale; dull. The *stagnant* water was a breeding ground for disease. stagnate, V.

staid ADJ. sober; sedate. Her conduct during the funeral ceremony was *staid* and solemn.

stalemate N. deadlock. Negotiations between the union and the employers have reached a *stalemate;* neither side is willing to budge from previously stated positions.

stalwart ADJ. strong, brawny; steadfast. His consistent support of the party has proved that he is a *stalwart* and loyal member. also N.

stamina N. strength; staying power. I doubt that she has the *stamina* to run the full distance of the marathon race.

stanch V. check flow of blood. It is imperative that we *stanch* the gushing wound before we attend to the other injuries.

statute N. law. We have many *statutes* in our law books which should be repealed.

statutory ADJ. created by statute or legislative action. This is a *statutory* crime.

stein N. beer mug. She thought of college as a place where one drank beer from *steins* and sang songs of lost lambs.

stellar ADJ. pertaining to the stars. He was the *stellar* attraction of the entire performance.

stentorian ADJ. extremely loud. The town crier had a *stentorian* voice.

stereotyped ADJ. fixed and unvarying representation. My chief objection to the book is that the characters are *stereotyped.*

stertorous ADJ. having a snoring sound. He could not sleep because of the *stertorous* breathing of his roommates.

stilted ADJ. bombastic; inflated. His *stilted* rhetoric did not impress the college audience; they were immune to bombastic utterances.

stigma N. token of disgrace; brand. I do not attach any *stigma* to the fact that you were accused of this crime; the fact that you were acquitted clears you completely.

stigmatize V. brand; mark as wicked. I do not want to *stigmatize* this young offender for life by sending her to prison.

stint N. supply; allotted amount; assigned portion of work. He performed his daily *stint* cheerfully and willingly. also, V.

stipend N. pay for services. There is a nominal *stipend* attached to this position.

stoic N. person who is indifferent to pleasure or pain. The doctor called her patient a *stoic* because he had borne the pain of the examination without whimpering. also ADJ.

stoke V. to feed plentifully. They swiftly *stoked* themselves, knowing they would not have another meal until they reached camp.

stolid ADJ. dull; impassive. I am afraid that this imaginative poetry will not appeal to such a *stolid* person.

stratagem N. deceptive scheme. We saw through his clever *stratagem.*

stratum N. layer of earth's surface; layer of society. Unless we alleviate conditions in the lowest *stratum* of our society, we may expect grumbling and revolt.

striated ADJ. marked with parallel bands. The glacier left many *striated* rocks.

stricture N. critical comments; severe and adverse criticism. His *strictures* on the author's style are prejudiced and unwarranted.

strident ADJ. loud and harsh. She scolded him in a *strident* voice.

stringent ADJ. binding; rigid. I think these regulations are too *stringent.*

stultify V. cause to appear foolish or inconsistent. By changing your opinion at this time, you will *stultify* yourself.

stupor N. state of apathy; daze; lack of awareness. In his *stupor,* the addict was unaware of the events taking place around him.

stygian ADJ. gloomy; hellish; deathly. They descended into the *stygian* sub-basement.

stymie V. present an obstacle; stump. The detective was *stymied* by the contradictory evidence in the robbery investigation. also N.

suave ADJ. smooth; bland. He is the kind of individual who is more easily impressed by a *suave* approach than by threats or bluster.

suavity N. urbanity; polish. He is particularly good in roles that require *suavity* and sophistication.

subaltern N. subordinate. The captain treated his *subalterns* as though they were children rather than commissioned officers.

subjective ADJ. occurring or taking place within the subject; unreal. Your analysis is highly *subjective;* you have permitted your emotions and your opinions to color your thinking.

subjugate V. conquer; bring under control. It is not our aim to *subjugate* our foe; we are interested only in establishing peaceful relations.

sublimate V. refine; purify. We must strive to *sublimate* these desires and emotions into worthwhile activities.

sublime ADJ. exalted; noble; uplifting. We must learn to recognize *sublime* truths.

TEST—WORD LIST 44—*Synonyms and Antonyms*

Each of the following questions consists of a word in capital letters, followed by five lettered words or phrases. Choose the lettered word or phrase which is most nearly similar or the opposite of the word in capital letters and write the letter of your choice on your answer paper.

646. SONOROUS (A) resonant (B) reassuring (C) repetitive (D) resinous (E) sisterly
647. SOPHOMORIC (A) unprecedented (B) mature (C) insipid (D) intellectual (E) illusionary
648. SOPORIFIC (A) dining (B) caustic (C) memorial (D) awakening (E) springing
649. SPASMODIC (A) intermittent (B) fit (C) inaccurate (D) violent (E) physical
650. SPORADIC (A) seedy (B) latent (C) vivid (D) inconsequential (E) often
651. SPORTIVE (A) competing (B) playful (C) indignant (D) foppish (E) fundamental
652. SPURIOUS (A) genuine (B) angry (C) mitigated (D) interrogated (E) glorious
653. SQUANDER (A) fortify (B) depart (C) roam (D) preserve (E) forfeit
654. STACCATO (A) musical (B) long (C) legato (D) sneezing (E) pounded
655. STAMINA (A) patience (B) pistils (C) weakness (D) fascination (E) patina
656. STEREOTYPED (A) original (B) antique (C) modeled (D) repetitious (E) continued
657. STILTED (A) candid (B) pompous (C) modish (D) acute (E) inarticulate
658. STRINGENT (A) binding (B) reserved (C) utilized (D) lambent (E) indigent
659. SUAVITY (A) ingeniousness (B) indifference (C) urbanity (D) constancy (E) paucity
660. SUBLIME (A) unconscious (B) respected (C) exalted (D) sneaky (E) replaced

---

WORD LIST 45 subliminal - tantamount

subliminal ADJ. below the threshold. We may not be aware of the *subliminal* influences which affect our thinking.

sub rosa ADV. in strict confidence; privately. I heard of this *sub rosa* and I cannot tell you about it.

subsequent ADJ. following; later. In *subsequent* lessons, we shall take up more difficult problems.

subservient ADJ. behaving like a slave; servile; obsequious. He was proud and dignified; he refused to be *subservient* to anyone.

subsidiary ADJ. subordinate; secondary. This information may be used as *subsidiary* evidence but is not sufficient by itself to prove your argument. also N.

subsidy N. direct financial aid by government, etc. Without this *subsidy,* American ship operators would not be able to compete in world markets.

subsistence N. existence; means of support; livelihood. In these days of inflated prices, my salary provides a mere *subsistence.*

substantiate V. verify; support. I intend to *substantiate* my statement by producing witnesses.

substantive ADJ. essential; pertaining to the substance. Although the delegates were aware of the importance of the problem, they could not agree on the *substantive* issues.

subterfuge N. pretense; evasion. As soon as we realized that you had won our support by a *subterfuge,* we withdrew our endorsement of your candidacy.

subtlety N. nicety; cunning; guile; delicacy. The *subtlety* of his remarks was unnoticed by most of his audience.

subversive ADJ. tending to overthrow or ruin. We must destroy such *subversive* publications.

succinct ADJ. brief; terse; compact. His remarks are always *succinct* and pointed.

succor N. aid; assistance; relief. We shall be ever grateful for the *succor* your country gave us when we were in need. also V.

succulent ADJ. juicy; full of richness. The citrus foods from Florida are more *succulent* to some people than those from California. also N.

succumb V. yield; give in; die. I *succumb* to temptation whenever it comes my way.

sudorific ADJ. pertaining to perspiration. Manufacturers of deodorants have made the public conscious of the need to avoid offending people with *sudorific* odors.

suffuse V. spread over. A blush *suffused* her cheeks when we teased her about her love affair.

sully V. tarnish; soil. He felt that it was beneath his dignity to *sully* his hands in such menial labor.

sultry ADJ. sweltering. He could not adjust himself to the *sultry* climate of the tropics.

summation N. act of finding the total; summary. In his *summation,* the lawyer emphasized the testimony given by the two witnesses.

sumptuary ADJ. limiting or regulating expenditures. While no *sumptuary* law has been enacted, the public will never tolerate the expenditure of so large a sum.

sumptuous ADJ. lavish; rich. I cannot recall when I have had such a *sumptuous* feast.

sunder V. separate; part. Northern and southern Ireland are politically and religiously *sundered.*

sundry ADJ. various; several. My suspicions were aroused when I read *sundry* items in the newspapers about your behavior.

superannuated ADJ. retired on pension because of age. The *superannuated* man was indignant because he felt that he could still perform a good day's work.

supercilious ADJ. contemptuous; haughty. I resent your *supercilious* and arrogant attitude.

superficial ADJ. trivial; shallow. Since your report gave only a *superficial* analysis of the problem, I cannot give you more than a passing grade.

superfluity N. excess; overabundance. We have a definite lack of sincere workers and a *superfluity* of leaders.

superimpose V. place over something else. Your attempt to *superimpose* another agency in this field will merely increase the bureaucratic nature of our government.

supernal ADJ. heavenly; celestial. His tale of *supernal* beings was skeptically received.

supernumerary N. person or thing in excess of what is necessary; extra. His first appearance on the stage was as a *supernumerary* in a Shakespearean tragedy.

supersede V. cause to be set aside; replace. This regulation will *supersede* all previous rules.

supine ADJ. lying on back. The defeated pugilist lay *supine* on the canvas.

supplant V. replace; usurp. Ferdinand Marcos was *supplanted* by Corazon Aquino as president of the Philippines.

supple ADJ. flexible; pliant. The angler found a *supple* limb and used it as a fishing rod.

suppliant ADJ. entreating; beseeching. He could not resist the dog's *suppliant* whimpering, and he gave it some food. also N.

supplicate V. petition humbly; pray to grant a favor. We *supplicate* your majesty to grant him amnesty.

supposititious ADJ. assumed; counterfeit; hypothetical. I find no similarity between your *supposititious* illustration and the problem we are facing.

suppurate V. create pus. The surgeon refused to lance the abscess until it *suppurated.*

surcease N. cessation. He begged the doctors to grant him *surcease* from his suffering.

surfeit V. cloy; overfeed. I am *surfeited* with the sentimentality of the average motion picture film.

surly ADJ. rude; cross. Because of his *surly* attitude, many people avoided his company.

surmise V. guess. I *surmise* that he will be late for this meeting. also N.

surmount V. overcome. He had to *surmount* many obstacles in order to succeed.

surpass V. exceed. Her SAT scores *surpassed* our expectations.

surreptitious ADJ. secret. News of their *surreptitious* meeting gradually leaked out.

surrogate N. substitute. For a fatherless child, a male teacher may become a father *surrogate.*

surveillance N. watching; guarding. The FBI kept the house under constant *surveillance* in the hope of capturing all the criminals at one time.

sustenance N. means of support, food, nourishment. In the tropics, the natives find *sustenance* easy to obtain.

suture N. stitches sewn to hold the cut edges of a wound or incision; material used in sewing. We will remove the *sutures* as soon as the wound heals. also V.

swarthy ADJ. dark; dusky. Despite the stereotypes, not all Italians are *swarthy:* many are fair and blond.

swathe V. wrap around; bandage. When I visited him in the hospital, I found him *swathed* in bandages.

swelter V. be oppressed by heat. I am going to buy an air conditioning unit for my apartment as I do not intend to *swelter* through another hot and humid summer.

sybarite N. lover of luxury. Rich people are not always *sybarites;* some of them have little taste for a life of luxury.

sycophantic ADJ. servilely flattering. The king enjoyed the *sycophantic* attentions of his followers.

syllogism N. logical formula utilizing a major premise, a minor premise and a conclusion. There must be a fallacy in this *syllogism;* I cannot accept the conclusion.

sylvan ADJ. pertaining to the woods; rustic. His paintings of nymphs in *sylvan* backgrounds were criticized as overly sentimental.

symmetry N. arrangement of parts so that balance is obtained; congruity. The addition of a second tower will give this edifice the *symmetry* which it now lacks.

synchronous ADJ. similarly timed; simultaneous with. We have many examples of scientists in different parts of the world who have made *synchronous* discoveries.

synthesis N. combining parts into a whole. Now that we have succeeded in isolating this drug, our next problem is to plan its *synthesis* in the laboratory.

synthetic ADJ. artificial; resulting from synthesis. During the twentieth century, many *synthetic* products have replaced the natural products. also N.

tacit ADJ. understood; not put into words. We have a *tacit* agreement.

taciturn ADJ. habitually silent; talking little. New Englanders are reputedly *taciturn* people.

tactile ADJ. pertaining to the organs or sense of touch. His callused hands had lost their *tactile* sensitivity.

tainted ADJ. contaminated; corrupt. Health authorities are always trying to prevent the sale and use of *tainted* food.

talisman N. charm. She wore the *talisman* to ward off evil.

talon N. claw of bird. The falconer wore a leather gauntlet to avoid being clawed by the hawk's *talons.*

tantalize V. tease; torture with disappointment. Tom loved to *tantalize* his younger brother.

tantamount ADJ. equal. Your ignoring their pathetic condition is *tantamount* to murder.

TEST—WORD LIST 45—*Synonyms and Antonyms*

Each of the following questions consists of a word in capital letters, followed by five lettered words or phrases. Choose the lettered word or phrase which is most nearly similar or the opposite of the word in capital letters and write the letter of your choice on your answer paper.

661. SUBLIMINAL (A) radiant (B) unknown (C) obvious (D) domestic (E) horizontal
662. SUPERANNUATED (A) senile (B) experienced (C) retired (D) attenuated (E) accepted
663. SUPERCILIOUS (A) haughty (B) highbrow (C) angry (D) subservient (E) philosophic
664. SUPERFICIAL (A) abnormal (B) portentous (C) shallow (D) angry (E) tiny
665. SUPERNUMERARY (A) star (B) extra (C) associate (D) astronomer (E) inferiority
666. SUPPLIANT (A) intolerant (B) swallowing (C) beseeching (D) finishing (E) flexible
667. SURFEIT (A) belittle (B) cloy (C) drop (D) estimate (E) claim
668. SURREPTITIOUS (A) secret (B) snakelike (C) nightly (D) abstract (E) furnished
669. SUTURE (A) stitch (B) reflection (C) knitting (D) tailor (E) past
670. SWATHED (A) wrapped around (B) waved (C) gambled (D) rapt (E) mystified
671. SYCOPHANTIC (A) quiet (B) recording (C) servilely flattering (D) frolicsome (E) eagerly awaiting
672. SYNTHETIC (A) simplified (B) doubled (C) tuneful (D) artificial (E) fiscal
673. TACIT (A) spoken (B) allowed (C) neural (D) misunderstood (E) unwanted
674. TALISMAN (A) chief (B) juror (C) medicine man (D) amulet (E) gift
675. TANTALIZE (A) tease (B) wax (C) warrant (D) authorize (E) total

---

WORD LIST 46 **tantrum - tome**

tantrum N. fit of petulance; caprice. The child learned that he could have almost anything if he went into *tantrums.*

taper N. candle. He lit the *taper* on the windowsill.

tarantula N. venomous spider. We need an antitoxin to counteract the bite of the *tarantula.*

tarn N. small mountain lake. This mountainous area is famous for its picturesque *tarns* and larger lakes.

tarry V. delay; dawdle. We can't *tarry* if we want to get to the airport on time.

tatterdemalion N. ragged fellow. Do you expect an army of *tatterdemalions* and beggars to put up a real fight?

taurine ADJ. like a bull. The bull charged into the ring, a mighty specimen of *taurine* power.

taut ADJ. tight; ready. The captain maintained that he ran a *taut* ship.

tautological ADJ. needlessly repetitious. In the sentence "It was visible to the eye," the phrase "to the eye" is *tautological.*

tautology N. unnecessary repetition; pleonasm. "Joyful happiness" is an illustration of *tautology.*

tawdry ADJ. cheap and gaudy. He won a few *tawdry* trinkets in Coney Island.

tedium N. boredom; weariness. We hope this radio will help overcome the *tedium* of your stay in the hospital.

teleology N. belief that a final purpose or design exists for the presence of individual beings or of the universe itself. The questions propounded by *teleology* have long been debated in religious and scientific circles.

temerarious ADJ. rash. Mountain climbing at this time of year is *temerarious* and foolhardy.

temerity N. boldness; rashness. Do you have the *temerity* to argue with me?

temper V. restrain; blend; toughen. His hard times in high school only served to *temper* his strength.

temperate ADJ. restrained; self-controlled. Noted for his *temperate* appetite, he seldom gained weight.

tempo N. speed of music. I find the conductor's *tempo* too slow for such a brilliant piece of music.

temporal ADJ. not lasting forever; limited by time; secular. At one time in our history, *temporal* rulers assumed that they had been given their thrones by divine right.

temporize V. avoid committing oneself; gain time. I cannot permit you to *temporize* any longer; I must have a definite answer today.

tenacious ADJ. holding fast. I had to struggle to break his *tenacious* hold on my arm. tenacity, N.

tenacity N. firmness; persistency; adhesiveness. It is extremely difficult to overcome the *tenacity* of a habit such as smoking.

tendentious ADJ. having an aim; designed to further a cause. The editorials in this periodical are *tendentious* rather than truth-seeking.

tenebrous ADJ. dark; gloomy. We were frightened as we entered the *tenebrous* passageways of the cave.

tenet N. doctrine; dogma. I cannot accept the *tenets* of your faith.

tensile ADJ. capable of being stretched. Mountain climbers must know the *tensile* strength of their ropes.

tentative ADJ. provisional; experimental. Your *tentative* plans sound plausible.

tenuous ADJ. thin; rare; slim. The allegiance of our allies is held by rather *tenuous* ties.

tenure N. holding of an office; time during which such an office is held. He has permanent *tenure* in this position.

tepid ADJ. lukewarm. During the summer, I like to take a *tepid* bath.

tergiversation N. evasion; fickleness. I cannot understand your *tergiversation;* I was certain that you were devoted to our cause.

termagant N. shrew; scolding, brawling woman. *The Taming of the Shrew* is one of many stories of the methods used in changing a *termagant* into a demure lady.

terminate V. to bring to an end. When his contract was *terminated* unexpectedly, he desperately needed a new job.

terminology N. terms used in a science or art. The special *terminology* developed by some authorities in the field has done more to confuse the layman than to enlighten him.

terminus N. last stop of railroad. After we reached the railroad *terminus,* we continued our journey into the wilderness on saddle horses.

terrapin N. American marsh tortoise. The flesh of the diamondback *terrapin* is considered by many epicures to be a delicacy.

terrestrial ADJ. on the earth. We have been able to explore the *terrestrial* regions much more thoroughly than the aquatic or celestial regions.

terse ADJ. concise; abrupt; pithy. I admire his *terse* style of writing.

tertiary ADJ. third. He is so thorough that he analyzes *tertiary* causes where other writers are content with primary and secondary reasons.

tesselated ADJ. inlaid; mosaic. I recall seeing a table with a *tesselated* top of bits of stone and glass in a very interesting pattern.

testator N. maker of a will. The attorney called in his secretary and his partner to witness the signature of the *testator.*

testy ADJ. irritable; short-tempered. My advice is to avoid discussing this problem with him today as he is rather *testy.*

tether V. tie with a rope. Before we went to sleep, we

tethered the horses to prevent their wandering off during the night.

thaumaturgist N. miracle worker; magician. I would have to be a *thaumaturgist* and not a mere doctor to find a remedy for this disease.

theocracy N. government of a community by religious leaders. Some Pilgrims favored the establishment of a *theocracy* in New England.

theosophy N. wisdom in divine things. *Theosophy* seeks to embrace the essential truth in all religions.

therapeutic ADJ. curative. These springs are famous for their *therapeutic* qualities.

thermal ADJ. pertaining to heat. The natives discovered that the hot springs gave excellent *thermal* baths and began to develop their community as a health resort. also N.

thespian ADJ. pertaining to drama. Her success in the school play convinced her she was destined for a *thespian* career. also N.

thrall N. slave; bondage. The captured soldier was held in *thrall* by the conquering army.

threnody N. song of lamentation; dirge. When he died, many poets wrote *threnodies* about his passing.

throes N. violent anguish. The *throes* of despair can be as devastating as the spasms accompanying physical pain.

throng N. crowd. *Throngs* of shoppers jammed the aisles. also V.

throttle V. strangle. The criminal tried to *throttle* the old man.

thwart V. baffle; frustrate. He felt that everyone was trying to *thwart* his plans.

thyme N. aromatic plant used for seasoning. The addition of a little *thyme* will enhance the flavor of the clam chowder.

timbre N. quality of a musical tone produced by a musical instrument. We identify the instrument producing a musical sound by its *timbre.*

timidity N. lack of self-confidence or courage. If you are to succeed as a salesman, you must first lose your *timidity.*

timorous ADJ. fearful; demonstrating fear. His *timorous* manner betrayed the fear he felt at the moment.

tipple V. drink (alcoholic beverages) frequently. He found that his most enjoyable evenings occurred when he *tippled* with his friends at the local pub.

tirade N. extended scolding; denunciation. Long before he had finished his *tirade,* we were sufficiently aware of the seriousness of our misconduct.

titanic ADJ. gigantic. *Titanic* waves beat against the shore during the hurricane.

tithe N. tax of one-tenth. Because he was an agnostic, he refused to pay his *tithes* to the clergy. also V.

titillate V. tickle. I am here not to *titillate* my audience but to enlighten it.

titter N. nervous laugh. Her aunt's constant *titter* nearly drove her mad. also V.

titular ADJ. nominal holding of title without obligations. Although he was the *titular* head of the company, the real decisions were made by his general manager.

toady V. flatter for favors. I hope you see through those who are *toadying* you for special favors. also N.

tocsin N. alarm bell. Awakened by the sound of the *tocsin,* we rushed to our positions to await the attack.

toga N. Roman outer robe. Marc Antony pointed to the slashes in Caesar's *toga.*

tome N. large volume. He spent much time in the libraries poring over ancient *tomes.*

TEST—WORD LIST 46—*Synonyms*

Each of the questions below consists of a word in capital letters, followed by five lettered words or phrases. Choose the lettered word or phrase that is most nearly similar in meaning to the word in capital letters and write the letter of your choice on your answer paper.

676. TATTERDEMALION (A) confetti (B) crudity (C) stubborn individual (D) ragged fellow (E) artist
677. TAUTOLOGY (A) memory (B) repetition (C) tension (D) simile (E) lack of logic
678. TAWDRY (A) orderly (B) meretricious (C) reclaimed (D) filtered (E) proper
679. TEMERITY (A) timidity (B) resourcefulness (C) boldness (D) tremulousness (E) caution
680. TEMPORAL (A) priestly (B) scholarly (C) secular (D) sleepy (E) sporadic
681. TENACIOUS (A) fast running (B) intentional (C) obnoxious (D) holding fast (E) collecting
682. TENACITY (A) splendor (B) perseverance (C) tendency (D) ingratitude (E) decimation
683. TENDENTIOUS (A) biased (B) likely (C) absurd (D) festive (E) literary
684. TENTATIVE (A) prevalent (B) portable (C) mocking (D) wry (E) experimental
685. TENUOUS (A) vital (B) thin (C) careful (D) dangerous (E) necessary
686. TEPID (A) boiling (B) lukewarm (C) freezing (D) gaseous (E) cold

687. TERGIVERSATION (A) fickleness (B) conversation (C) altercation (D) swollen state (E) acquiescence
688. TESSELATED (A) striped (B) made of mosaics (C) piebald (D) uniform (E) trimmed
689. THAUMATURGIST (A) producer (B) dreamer (C) philosopher (D) thief (E) miracle worker
690. TITILLATE (A) hasten (B) fasten (C) stimulate (D) incorporate (E) enlarge

WORD LIST 47 tonsure - ukase

tonsure N. shaving of the head, especially by person entering religious orders. His *tonsure,* even more than his monastic garb, indicated that he was a member of the religious order.

topography N. physical features of a region. Before the generals gave the order to attack, they ordered a complete study of the *topography* of the region.

torpid ADJ. dormant; dull; lethargic. The *torpid* bear had just come out of his cave after his long hibernation.

torso N. trunk of statue with head and limbs missing; human trunk. This *torso,* found in the ruins of Pompeii, is now on exhibition in the museum in Naples.

tortilla N. flat cake made of cornmeal, etc. As we traveled through Mexico, we became more and more accustomed to the use of *tortillas* instead of bread.

tortuous ADJ. winding; full of curves. Because this road is so *tortuous,* it is unwise to go faster than twenty miles an hour on it.

touchstone N. stone used to test the fineness of gold alloys; criterion. What *touchstone* can be used to measure the character of a person?

touchy ADJ. sensitive; irascible. Do not discuss this phase of the problem as he is very *touchy* about it.

toxic ADJ. poisonous. We must seek an antidote for whatever *toxic* substance he has eaten.

tract N. pamphlet; a region of indefinite size. The King granted William Penn a *tract* of land in the New World.

tractable ADJ. docile. You will find the children in this school very *tractable* and willing to learn.

traduce V. expose to slander. His opponents tried to *traduce* the candidate's reputation by spreading rumors about his past.

trajectory N. path taken by a projectile. The police tried to locate the spot from which the assassin had fired the fatal shot by tracing the *trajectory* of the bullet.

tranquillity N. calmness; peace. After the commotion and excitement of the city, I appreciate the *tranquillity* of these fields and forests.

transcend V. exceed; surpass. This accomplishment *transcends* all our previous efforts. transcendental, ADJ.

transcribe V. copy. When you *transcribe* your notes, please send a copy to Mr. Smith and keep the original for our files. transcription, N.

transgression N. violation of a law; sin. Forgive us our *transgressions.*

transient ADJ. fleeting; quickly passing away; staying for a short time. This hotel caters to a *transient* trade.

transition N. going from one state of action to another. During the period of *transition* from oil heat to gas heat, the furnace will have to be shut off.

translucent ADJ. partly transparent. We could not recognize the people in the next room because of the *translucent* curtains which separated us.

transmute V. change; convert to something different. He was unable to *transmute* his dreams into actualities.

transparent ADJ. permitting light to pass through freely; easily detected. Your scheme is so *transparent* that it will fool no one.

transpire V. exhale; become known; happen. In spite of all our efforts to keep the meeting a secret, news of our conclusions *transpired.*

trappings N. outward decorations; ornaments. He loved the *trappings* of success: the limousines, the stock options, the company jet.

traumatic ADJ. pertaining to an injury caused by violence. In his nightmares, he kept on recalling the *traumatic* experience of being wounded in battle.

travail N. painful labor. How long do you think a man can endure such *travail* and degradation without rebelling?

traverse V. go through or across. When you *traverse* this field, be careful of the bull.

travesty N. comical parody; treatment aimed at making something appear ridiculous. The decision the jury has arrived at is a *travesty* of justice.

treacle N. syrup obtained in refining sugar. *Treacle* is more highly refined than molasses.

treatise N. article treating a subject systematically and thoroughly. He is preparing a *treatise* on the Elizabethan playwrights for his graduate degree.

trek V. travel; migrate. The tribe *trekked* further north that summer in search of available game. also N.

tremor N. trembling; slight quiver. She had a nervous *tremor* in her right hand.

tremulous ADJ. trembling; wavering. She was *tremulous* more from excitement than from fear.

trenchant ADJ. cutting; keen. I am afraid of his *trenchant* wit for it is so often sarcastic.

trencherman N. good eater. He is not finicky about his food; he is a *trencherman.*

trepidation N. fear; trembling agitation. We must face the enemy without *trepidation* if we are to win this battle.

tribulation N. distress; suffering. After all the trials and *tribulations* we have gone through, we need this rest.

tribunal N. court of justice. The decision of the *tribunal* was final.

tribute N. tax levied by a ruler; mark of respect. The colonists refused to pay *tribute* to a foreign despot.

trident N. three-pronged spear. Neptune is usually depicted as rising from the sea, carrying his *trident* on his shoulder.

trilogy N. group of three works. Romain Rolland's novel *Jean Christophe* was first published as a *trilogy.*

triolet N. eight-line stanza with rhyme scheme *a b aaa b a b.* The *triolet* is a difficult verse pattern because it utilizes only two rhymes in its eight lines.

trite ADJ. hackneyed; commonplace. The *trite* and predictable situations in many television programs alienate many viewers.

trivia N. trifles; unimportant matters. Too many magazines ignore newsworthy subjects and feature *trivia.*

troglodyte N. cave dweller. We know that the first men in this area were *troglodytes* by the artifacts we have discovered in the caves.

trope N. figure of speech. The poem abounds in *tropes* and alliterative expressions.

troth N. pledge of good faith especially in betrothal. He gave her his *troth* and vowed he would cherish her always.

truckle V. curry favor; act in an obsequious way. If you *truckle* to the lord, you will be regarded as a sycophant; if you do not, you will be considered arrogant.

truculent ADJ. aggressive; savage. They are a *truculent* race, ready to fight at any moment.

truism N. self-evident truth. Many a *truism* is well expressed in a proverb.

trumpery N. objects that are showy, valueless, deceptive. All this finery is mere *trumpery.*

truncate V. cut the top off. The top of a cone which has been *truncated* in a plane parallel to its base is a circle.

tryst N. meeting. The lovers kept their *tryst* even though they realized their danger.

tumbrel N. a farm tipcart. The *tumbrels* became the vehicles which transported the condemned people from the prisons to the guillotine.

tumid ADJ. swollen; pompous; bombastic. I especially dislike his *tumid* style; I prefer writing which is less swollen and bombastic.

tumult N. commotion; riot; noise. She could not make herself heard over the *tumult* of the mob.

tundra N. rolling, treeless plain in Siberia and arctic North America. Despite the cold, many geologists are trying to discover valuable mineral deposits in the *tundra.*

turbid ADJ. muddy; having the sediment disturbed. The water was *turbid* after the children had waded through it.

turbulence N. state of violent agitation. We were frightened by the *turbulence* of the ocean during the storm.

tureen N. deep table dish for holding soup. The waiters brought the soup to the tables in silver *tureens.*

turgid ADJ. swollen; distended. The *turgid* river threatened to overflow the levees and flood the countryside.

turmoil N. confusion; strife. Conscious he had sinned, he was in a state of spiritual *turmoil.*

turnkey N. jailer. By bribing the *turnkey,* the prisoner arranged to have better food brought to him in his cell.

turpitude N. depravity. A visitor may be denied admittance to this country if she has been guilty of moral *turpitude.*

tutelage N. guardianship; training. Under the *tutelage* of such masters of the instrument, she made rapid progress as a virtuoso.

tutelary ADJ. protective; pertaining to a guardianship. I am acting in my *tutelary* capacity when I refuse to grant you permission to leave the campus.

tycoon N. wealthy leader. John D. Rockefeller was a prominent *tycoon.*

tyro N. beginner; novice. For a mere *tyro,* you have produced some marvelous results.

ubiquitous ADJ. being everywhere; omnipresent. You must be *ubiquitous* for I meet you wherever I go.

ukase N. official decree, usually Russian. It was easy to flaunt the *ukases* issued from St. Petersburg; there was no one to enforce them.

TEST—WORD LIST 47—*Antonyms*

Each of the questions below consists of a word in capital letters, followed by five lettered words or phrases. Choose the lettered word or phrase that is most nearly opposite in meaning to the word in capital letters and write the letter of your choice on your answer paper.

691. TRACTABLE (A) unmanageable (B) irreligious (C) mortal (D) incapable (E) unreal
692. TRADUCE (A) exhume (B) increase (C) purchase (D) extol (E) donate
693. TRANQUILITY (A) lack of sleep (B) lack of calm (C) emptiness (D) renewal (E) closeness
694. TRANSIENT (A) carried (B) close (C) permanent (D) removed (E) certain
695. TREMULOUS (A) steady (B) obese (C) young (D) healthy (E) unkempt
696. TRENCHERMAN (A) finicky eater (B) infantryman (C) angler (D) imbiber (E) pacifist
697. TREPIDATION (A) slowness (B) amputation (C) fearlessness (D) adroitness (E) death
698. TRITE (A) correct (B) original (C) distinguished (D) premature (E) certain
699. TRUCULENT (A) juicy (B) overflowing (C) peaceful (D) determined (E) false
700. TRUMPERY (A) silence (B) defeat (C) percussion (D) murder (E) valuables
701. TURBID (A) clear (B) improbable (C) invariable (D) honest (E) turgid
702. TURBULENCE (A) reaction (B) approach (C) impropriety (D) calm (E) hostility
703. TURGID (A) rancid (B) shrunken (C) cool (D) explosive (E) painful
704. TURPITUDE (A) amplitude (B) heat (C) wealth (D) virtue (E) quiet
705. TYRO (A) infant (B) rubber (C) personnel (D) idiot (E) expert

WORD LIST 48 ulterior - vehement

ulterior ADJ. situated beyond; unstated. You must have an *ulterior* motive for your behavior.

ultimate ADJ. final; not susceptible to further analysis. Scientists are searching for the *ultimate* truths.

ultimatum N. last demand; warning. Since they have ignored our *ultimatum,* our only recourse is to declare war.

umbrage N. resentment; anger; sense of injury or insult. She took *umbrage* at his remarks.

unanimity N. complete agreement. We were surprised by the *unanimity* with which our proposals were accepted by the different groups.

unassuaged ADJ. unsatisfied; not soothed. Her anger is *unassuaged* by your apology.

unassuming ADJ. modest. He is so *unassuming* that some people fail to realize how great a man he really is.

unbridled ADJ. violent. She had a sudden fit of *unbridled* rage.

uncanny ADJ. strange; mysterious. You have the *uncanny* knack of reading my innermost thoughts.

unconscionable ADJ. unscrupulous; excessive. She found the loan shark's demands *unconscionable* and impossible to meet.

uncouth ADJ. outlandish; clumsy; boorish. Most biographers portray Lincoln as an *uncouth* and ungainly young man.

unction N. the act of anointing with oil. The anointing with oil of a person near death is called extreme *unction.*

unctuous ADJ. oily; bland; insincerely suave. Uriah Heep disguised his nefarious actions by *unctuous* protestations of his " 'umility."

undulate V. move with a wavelike motion. The waters *undulated* in the breeze.

unearth V. dig up. When they *unearthed* the city, the archeologists found many relics of an ancient civilization.

unearthly ADJ. not earthly; weird. There is an *unearthly* atmosphere in her work which amazes the casual observer.

unequivocal ADJ. plain; obvious. My answer to your proposal is an *unequivocal* and absolute "No."

unerringly ADV. infallibly My teacher *unerringly* pounced on the one typographical error in my essay.

unfaltering ADJ. steadfast. She approached the guillotine with *unfaltering* steps.

unfeigned ADJ. genuine; real. I am sure her surprise was *unfeigned.*

unfledged ADJ. immature. It is hard for an *unfledged* writer to find a sympathetic publisher.

ungainly ADJ. awkward. He is an *ungainly* young man.

unguent N. ointment. Apply this *unguent* to the sore muscles before retiring.

unilateral ADJ. one-sided. This legislation is *unilateral* since it binds only one party in the controversy.

unimpeachable ADJ. blameless and exemplary. Her conduct in office was *unimpeachable.*

uninhibited ADJ. unrepressed. The congregation was shocked by her *uninhibited* laughter during the sermon.

unique ADJ. without an equal; single in kind. You have the *unique* distinction of being the first student whom I have had to fail in this course.

unison N. unity of pitch; complete accord. The choir sang in *unison.*

unkempt ADJ. disheveled; with uncared-for appearance. The beggar was dirty and *unkempt.*

unmitigated ADJ. harsh; severe; not lightened. I sympathize with you in your *unmitigated* sorrow.

unruly ADJ. disobedient; lawless. The only way to curb this *unruly* mob is to use tear gas.

unsavory ADJ. distasteful; morally offensive. People with *unsavory* reputations should not be allowed to work with young children.

unscathed ADJ. unharmed. They prayed he would come back from the war *unscathed.*

unseemly ADJ. unbecoming; indecent. Your levity is *unseemly* at this time.

unsullied ADJ. untarnished. I am happy that my reputation is *unsullied.*

untenable ADJ. unsupportable. I find your theory *untenable* and must reject it.

untoward ADJ. unfortunate; annoying. *Untoward* circumstances prevent me from being with you on this festive occasion.

unwitting ADJ. unintentional; not knowing. She was the *unwitting* tool of the swindlers.

unwonted ADJ. unaccustomed. He hesitated to assume the *unwonted* role of master of ceremonies at the dinner.

upbraid V. scold; reproach. I must *upbraid* him for his misbehavior.

upshot N. outcome. The *upshot* of the rematch was that the former champion proved that he still possessed all the skills of his youth.

urbane ADJ. suave; refined; elegant. The courtier was *urbane* and sophisticated. urbanity, N.

urchin N. mischievous child (usually a boy). Get out! This store is no place for grubby *urchins!*

ursine ADJ. bearlike; pertaining to a bear. Because of its *ursine* appearance, the great panda has been identified with the bears; actually, it is closely related to the raccoon.

usufruct N. right of enjoying things belonging to another. By contract, the tenant has the *usufruct* of all the livestock and machinery on the farm.

usurpation N. act of seizing power and rank of another. The revolution ended with the *usurpation* of the throne by the victorious rebel leader.

usury N. lending money at illegal rates of interest. The loan shark was found guilty of *usury.*

utopia N. imaginary land with perfect social and political system. Shangri-la was the name of James Hilton's Tibetan *utopia.*

uxorious ADJ. excessively devoted to one's wife. His friends laughed at him because he was so *uxorious* and submissive to his wife's desires.

vacillation N. fluctuation; wavering. His *vacillation* when confronted with a problem annoyed all of us who had to wait until he made his decision.

vacuous ADJ. empty; inane. The *vacuous* remarks of the politician annoyed the audience, who had hoped to hear more than empty platitudes.

vagabond N. wanderer; tramp. In summer college students wander the roads of Europe like carefree *vagabonds.* also ADJ.

vagary N. caprice; whim. She followed every *vagary* of fashion.

vagrant ADJ. stray; random. He tried to study, but could not collect his *vagrant* thoughts. also N.

vainglorious ADJ. boastful; excessively conceited. She was a *vainglorious* and arrogant individual.

valance N. short drapery hanging above window frame. The windows were curtainless; only the tops were covered with *valances.*

valedictory ADJ. pertaining to farewell. I found the *valedictory* address too long; leave-taking should be brief.

valetudinarian N. invalid. He enjoyed the attentions showered upon him while he was a *valetudinarian* and insisted that they be continued long after his recovery from his illness. also ADJ.

validate V. confirm; ratify. I will not publish my findings until I *validate* my results.

valor N. bravery. He received the Medal of Honor for his *valor* in battle.

vampire N. ghostly being that sucks the blood of the living. Children were afraid to go to sleep at night because of the many legends of *vampires.*

vanguard N. forerunners; advance forces. We are the *vanguard* of a tremendous army that is following us.

vantage N. position giving an advantage. They fired upon the enemy from behind trees, walls and any other point of *vantage* they could find.

vapid ADJ. insipid; inane. She delivered an uninspired and *vapid* address.

variegated ADJ. many-colored. He will not like this blue necktie as he is addicted to *variegated* clothing.

vassal N. in feudalism, one who held land of a superior lord. The lord demanded that his *vassals* contribute more to his military campaign.

vaunted ADJ. boasted; bragged; highly publicized. This much *vaunted* project proved a disappointment when it collapsed.

veer V. change in direction. After what seemed an eternity, the wind *veered* to the east and the storm abated.

vegetate V. live in a monotonous way. I do not understand how you can *vegetate* in this quiet village after the adventurous life you have led.

vehement ADJ. impetuous; with marked vigor. He spoke with *vehement* eloquence in defense of his client.

TEST—WORD LIST 48—*Antonyms*

Each of the questions below consists of a word in capital letters, followed by five lettered words or phrases. Choose the lettered word or phrase that is most nearly opposite in meaning to the word in capital letters and write the letter of your choice on your answer paper.

706. UNEARTH (A) conceal (B) gnaw (C) clean (D) fling (E) react
707. UNFEIGNED (A) pretended (B) fashionable (C) wary (D) switched (E) colonial
708. UNGAINLY (A) ignorant (B) graceful (C) detailed (D) dancing (E) pedantic
709. UNIMPEACHABLE (A) fruitful (B) rampaging (C) faulty (D) pensive (E) thorough
710. UNKEMPT (A) bombed (B) washed (C) neat (D) showy (E) tawdry
711. UNRULY (A) chatting (B) obedient (C) definite (D) lined (E) curious
712. UNSEEMLY (A) effortless (B) proper (C) conducive (D) pointed (E) informative
713. UNSULLIED (A) tarnished (B) countless (C) soggy (D) papered (E) homicidal
714. UNTENABLE (A) supportable (B) tender (C) sheepish (D) tremulous (E) adequate
715. UNWITTING (A) clever (B) intense (C) sensitive (D) freezing (E) intentional
716. VACILLATION (A) remorse (B) relief (C) respect (D) steadfastness (E) inoculation
717. VALEDICTORY (A) sad (B) collegiate (C) derivative (D) salutatory (E) promising
718. VALETUDINARIAN (A) senile person (B) farewell speaker (C) healthy person (D) servant (E) agent
719. VANGUARD (A) regiment (B) rear (C) echelon (D) protection (E) loyalty
720. VAUNTED (A) unvanquished (B) fell (C) belittled (D) exacting (E) believed

---

WORD LIST 49 vellum - vogue

vellum N. parchment. Bound in *vellum* and embossed in gold, this book is a beautiful example of the binder's craft.

velocity N. speed. The train went by at considerable *velocity.*

vendetta N. blood feud. The rival mobs engaged in a bitter *vendetta.*

vendor N. seller. The fruit *vendor* sold her wares from a stall on the sidewalk.

venal ADJ. capable of being bribed. The *venal* policeman accepted the bribe offered him by the speeding motorist whom he had stopped.

veneer N. thin layer; cover. Casual acquaintances were deceived by his *veneer* of sophistication and failed to recognize his fundamental shallowness.

venerable ADJ. deserving high respect. We do not mean to be disrespectful when we refuse to follow the advice of our *venerable* leader.

venerate V. revere. In China, the people *venerate* their ancestors.

venial ADJ. forgivable; trivial. We may regard a hungry man's stealing as a *venial* crime.

venison N. the meat of a deer. The hunters dined on *venison.*

vent N. a small opening; outlet. The wine did not flow because the air *vent* in the barrel was clogged.

vent V. express; utter. He *vented* his wrath on his class.

ventral V. abdominal. We shall now examine the *ventral* plates of this serpent.

ventriloquist N. someone who can make his or her voice seem to come from another person or thing. This *ventriloquist* does an act in which she has a conversation with a wooden dummy.

venturous ADJ. daring. The five *venturous* young men decided to look for a new approach to the mountain top.

venturesome ADJ. bold. A group of *venturesome* women were the first to scale Mt. Annapurna.

venue N. location. The attorney asked for a change of *venue;* he thought his client would do better if the trial were held in a less conservative county.

veracious ADJ. truthful. I can recommend him for this position because I have always found him *veracious* and reliable.

verbalize V. to put into words. I know you don't like to talk about these things, but please try to *verbalize* your feelings.

verbatim ADV. word for word. He repeated the message *verbatim.* also ADJ.

verbiage N. pompous array of words. After we had waded through all the *verbiage,* we discovered that the writer had said very little.

verbose ADJ. wordy. This article is too *verbose;* we must edit it.

verdant ADJ. green; fresh. The *verdant* meadows in the spring are always an inspiring sight.

verge N. border; edge. Madame Curie knew she was on the *verge* of discovering the secrets of radioactive elements. also V.

verdigris N. a green coating on copper which has been exposed to the weather. Despite all attempts to protect the statue from the elements, it became coated with *verdigris.*

verisimilitude N. appearance of truth; likelihood. Critics praised her for the *verisimilitude* of her performance as Lady Macbeth.

verity N. truth; reality. The four *verities* were revealed to Buddha during his long meditation.

vermicular ADJ. pertaining to a worm. The *vermicular* burrowing in the soil helps to aerate it.

vernal ADJ. pertaining to spring. We may expect *vernal* showers all during the month of April.

vernacular N. living language; natural style. Cut out those old-fashioned thee's and thou's and write in the *vernacular.* also ADJ.

versatile ADJ. having many talents; capable of working in many fields. He was a *versatile* athlete; at college he had earned varsity letters in baseball, football, and track.

vertex N. summit. Let us drop a perpendicular line from the *vertex* of the triangle to the base.

vertiginous ADJ. giddy; causing dizziness. I do not like the rides in the amusement park because they have a *vertiginous* effect on me.

vertigo N. dizziness. We test potential plane pilots for susceptibility to spells of *vertigo.*

verve N. enthusiasm; liveliness. She approached her studies with such *verve* that it was impossible for her to do poorly.

vestige N. trace; remains. We discovered *vestiges* of early Indian life in the cave.

vex N. annoy; distress. Please try not to *vex* your mother; she is doing the best she can.

viable ADJ. capable of maintaining life. The infant, though prematurely born, is *viable* and has a good chance to survive.

viand N. food. There was a variety of *viands* at the feast.

vicarious ADJ. acting as a substitute; done by a deputy. Many people get a *vicarious* thrill at the movies by imagining they are the characters on the screen.

vicissitude N. change of fortune. I am accustomed to life's *vicissitudes,* having experienced poverty and wealth, sickness and health, and failure and success.

victuals N. food. I am very happy to be able to provide you with these *victuals.*

vie V. contend; compete. When we *vie* with each other for his approval, we are merely weakening ourselves and strengthening him.

vigilance N. watchfulness. Eternal *vigilance* is the price of liberty.

vignette N. picture; short literary sketch. *The New Yorker* published her latest *vignette.*

vilify V. slander. Why is she always trying to *vilify* my reputation?

vindicate V. clear of charges. I hope to *vindicate* my client and return him to society as a free man.

vindictive ADJ. revengeful. She was very *vindictive* and never forgave an injury.

viper N. poisonous snake. The habitat of the horned *viper,* a particularly venomous snake, is in sandy regions like the Sahara or the Sinai peninsula.

virago N. shrew. Rip Van Winkle's wife was a veritable *virago.*

virile ADJ. manly. I do not accept the premise that a man is *virile* only when he is belligerent.

virtual ADJ. in essence; for practical purposes. She is a *virtual* financial wizard when it comes to money matters.

virtuoso N. highly skilled artist. Heifetz is a violin *virtuoso.*

virulent ADJ. extremely poisonous. The virus is highly *virulent* and has made many of us ill for days.

virus N. disease communicator. The doctors are looking for a specific medicine to control this *virus.*

visage N. face; appearance. The stern *visage* of the judge indicated that she had decided to impose a severe penalty.

visceral ADJ. felt in one's inner organs. She disliked

the *visceral* sensations she had whenever she rode the roller coaster.

viscid ADJ. sticky; adhesive. This is a *viscid* liquid.

viscous ADJ. sticky; gluey. Melted tar is a *viscous* substance.

visionary ADJ. produced by imagination; fanciful; mystical. She was given to *visionary* schemes which never materialized. also N.

vitiate V. spoil the effect of; make inoperative. Fraud will *vitiate* the contract.

vitreous ADJ. pertaining to or resembling glass. Although this plastic has many *vitreous* qualities such as transparency, it is unbreakable.

vitriolic ADJ. corrosive; sarcastic. Such *vitriolic* criticism is uncalled for.

vituperative ADJ. abusive; scolding. He became more *vituperative* as he realized that we were not going to grant him his wish.

vivacious ADJ. animated; gay. She had always been *vivacious* and sparkling.

vivisection N. act of dissecting living animals. The Society for the Prevention of Cruelty to Animals opposed *vivisection* and deplored the practice of using animals in scientific experiments.

vixen N. female fox; ill-tempered woman. Aware that she was right once again, he lost his temper and called her a shrew and a *vixen*.

vizier N. powerful Muslim government official. The *vizier* decreed that all persons in the city were to be summoned to the ceremony.

vociferous ADJ. clamorous; noisy. The crowd grew *vociferous* in its anger and threatened to take the law into its own hands.

vogue N. popular fashion. Slacks became the *vogue* on many college campuses.

TEST—WORD LIST 49—*Synonyms and Antonyms*

Each of the following questions consists of a word in capital letters, followed by five lettered words or phrases. Choose the lettered word or phrase which is most nearly similar or the opposite of the word in capital letters and write the letter of your choice on your answer paper.

721. VENAL (A) springlike (B) honest (C) angry (D) indifferent (E) going
722. VENERATE (A) revere (B) age (C) reject (D) reverberate (E) degenerate
723. VENIAL (A) unforgivable (B) unforgettable (C) unmistaken (D) fearful (E) fragrant
724. VERACIOUS (A) worried (B) slight (C) alert (D) truthful (E) instrumental
725. VERDANT (A) poetic (B) green (C) red (D) autumnal (E) frequent
726. VERITY (A) sanctity (B) reverence (C) falsehood (D) rarity (E) household
727. VESTIGE (A) trek (B) trail (C) trace (D) trial (E) tract
728. VIABLE (A) moribund (B) salable (C) useful (D) foolish (E) inadequate
729. VIAND (A) wand (B) gown (C) food (D) orchestra (E) frock
730. VICARIOUS (A) substitutional (B) aggressive (C) sporadic (D) reverent (E) internal
731. VIGILANCE (A) bivouac (B) guide (C) watchfulness (D) mob rule (E) posse
732. VILIFY (A) erect (B) eulogize (C) better (D) magnify (E) horrify
733. VINDICTIVE (A) revengeful (B) fearful (C) divided (D) literal (E) convincing
734. VIRULENT (A) sensuous (B) malignant (C) masculine (D) conforming (E) approaching
735. VISAGE (A) doubt (B) personality (C) hermitage (D) face (E) armor

---

WORD LIST 50 **volatile - zephyr**

volatile ADJ. evaporating rapidly; lighthearted; mercurial. Ethyl chloride is a very *volatile* liquid.

volition N. act of making a conscious choice. She selected this dress of her own *volition*.

voluble ADJ. fluent; glib. She was a *voluble* speaker, always ready to talk.

voluminous ADJ. bulky; large. Despite her family burdens, she kept up a *voluminous* correspondence with her friends.

voluptuous ADJ. gratifying the senses. The nobility during the Renaissance led *voluptuous* lives.

voracious ADJ. ravenous. The wolf is a *voracious* animal.

votary N. follower of a cult. She was a *votary* of every new movement in literature and art.

vouchsafe V. grant condescendingly; guarantee. I can safely *vouchsafe* you a fair return on your investment.

vulnerable ADJ. susceptible to wounds. Achilles was *vulnerable* only in his heel.

vulpine ADJ. like a fox; crafty. She disliked him, but granted him a certain *vulpine* intelligence.

vying V. contending. Why are we *vying* with each other for her favors? vie, V.

waft V. moved gently by wind or waves. Daydreaming, he gazed at the leaves which *wafted* past his window.

waggish ADJ. mischievous; humorous; tricky. He was a prankster who, unfortunately, often overlooked the damage he could cause with his *waggish* tricks.

waif N. homeless child or animal. Although he already had eight cats, he could not resist adopting yet another feline *waif.*

waive V. give up temporarily; yield. I will *waive* my rights in this matter in order to expedite our reaching a proper decision.

wallow V. roll in; indulge in; become helpless. The hippopotamus *wallowed* in the mud.

wan ADJ. having a pale or sickly color; pallid. Suckling asked, "Why so pale and *wan,* fond lover?"

wane V. grow gradually smaller. From now until December 21, the winter equinox, the hours of daylight will *wane.*

wangle V. wiggle out; fake. She tried to *wangle* an invitation to the party.

wanton ADJ. unruly; unchaste; excessive. His *wanton* pride cost him many friends.

warble V. sing; babble. Every morning the birds *warbled* outside her window. also N.

warrant V. justify; authorize. Before the judge issues the injunction, you must convince her this action is *warranted.*

warranty N. guarantee; assurance by seller. The purchaser of this automobile is protected by the manufacturer's *warranty* that he will replace any defective part for five years or 50,000 miles.

warren N. tunnels in which rabbits live; crowded conditions in which people live. The tenement was a veritable *warren,* packed with people too poor to live elsewhere.

wary ADJ. very cautious. The spies grew *wary* as they approached the sentry.

wastrel N. profligate. He was denounced as a *wastrel* who had dissipated his inheritance.

wax V. increase; grow. With proper care the frail child *waxed* and grew tall.

waylay V. ambush; lie in wait. They agreed to *waylay* their victim as he passed through the dark alley going home.

wean V. accustom a baby not to nurse; give up a cherished activity. He decided he would *wean* himself away from eating junk food and stick to fruits and vegetables.

weather V. endure the effects of weather or other forces. He *weathered* the changes in his personal life with difficulty, as he had no one in whom to confide.

welkin N. sky. They made the *welkin* ring with their shouts.

well-nigh ADV. almost, very nearly. This is *well-nigh* the worst trouble you've ever gotten us into!

welt N. mark from a beating or whipping. The evidence of child abuse was very clear; Jennifer's small body was covered with *welts* and bruises.

welter V. wallow. At the height of the battle, the casualties were so numerous that the victims *weltered* in their blood while waiting for medical attention.

wheedle V. cajole; coax; deceive by flattery. She knows she can *wheedle* almost anything she wants from her father.

whelp N. young wolf, dog, tiger, etc. This collie *whelp* won't do for breeding, but he'd make a fine pet.

whet V. sharpen; stimulate. The odors from the kitchen are *whetting* my appetite; I will be ravenous by the time the meal is served.

whimsical ADJ. capricious; fanciful; quaint. *Peter Pan* is a *whimsical* play.

whinny V. neigh like a horse. When he laughed through his nose, it sounded as if he *whinnied.*

whit N. smallest speck. There is not a *whit* of intelligence or understanding in your observations.

whorl N. ring of leaves around stem; ring. Identification by fingerprints is based on the difference in shape and number of the *whorls* on the fingers.

wily ADJ. cunning; artful. She is as *wily* as a fox in avoiding trouble.

wince V. shrink back; flinch. The screech of the chalk on the blackboard made her *wince.*

windfall N. fallen fruit; unexpected lucky event. This huge tax refund is quite a *windfall.*

winnow V. sift; separate good parts from bad. This test will *winnow* out the students who study from those who don't bother.

winsome ADJ. agreeable; gracious; engaging. By her *winsome* manner, she made herself liked by everyone who met her.

witless ADJ. foolish; idiotic. Such *witless* and fatuous statements will create the impression that you are an ignorant individual.

witticism N. witty saying; facetious remark. What you regard as *witticisms* are often offensive to sensitive people.

wizardry N. sorcery; magic. Merlin amazed the knights with his *wizardry.*

wizened ADJ. withered; shriveled. The *wizened* old man in the home for the aged was still active and energetic.

wont N. custom; habitual procedure. As was his *wont,* he jogged two miles every morning before going to work.

worldly ADJ. engrossed in matters of this earth; not spiritual. You must leave your *worldly* goods behind you when you go to meet your Maker.

wraith N. ghost; phantom of a living person. It must be a horrible experience to see a ghost; it is even more horrible to see the *wraith* of a person we know to be alive.

wrangle V. quarrel; obtain through arguing; herd cattle. They *wrangled* over their inheritance.

wrath N. anger; fury. She turned to him, full of *wrath,* and said, "What makes you think I'll accept lower pay for this job than you get?"

wreak V. inflict. I am afraid he will *wreak* his vengeance on the innocent as well as the guilty.

wrench V. pull; strain; twist. She *wrenched* free of her attacker and landed a powerful kick to his kneecap.

wrest V. pull away; take by violence. With only ten seconds left to play, our team *wrested* victory from their grasp.

writhe V. squirm, twist. He was *writhing* in pain, desperate for the drug his body required.

wry ADJ. twisted; with a humorous twist. We enjoy Dorothy Parker's verse for its *wry* wit.

xenophobia N. fear or hatred of foreigners. When the refugee arrived in America, he was unprepared for the *xenophobia* he found there.

yen N. longing; urge. She had a *yen* to get away and live on her own for a while.

yeoman N. man owning small estate; middle-class farmer. It was not the aristocrat but the *yeoman* who determined the nation's policies.

yoke N. join together, unite. I don't wish to be *yoked* to him in marriage, as if we were cattle pulling a plow.

yokel N. country bumpkin. At school, his classmates regarded him as a *yokel* and laughed at his rustic mannerisms.

yore N. time past. He dreamed of the elegant homes of *yore,* but gave no thought to their inelegant plumbing.

zany ADJ. crazy; comic. I can watch the Marx brothers' *zany* antics for hours.

zealot N. fanatic; person who shows excessive zeal. It is good to have a few *zealots* in our group for their enthusiasm is contagious.

zenith N. point directly overhead in the sky; summit. When the sun was at its *zenith,* the glare was not as strong as at sunrise and sunset.

zephyr N. gentle breeze; west wind. When these *zephyrs* blow, it is good to be in an open boat under a full sail.

TEST—WORD LIST 50—*Synonyms*

Each of the questions below consists of a word in capital letters, followed by five lettered words or phrases. Choose the lettered word or phrase that is most nearly similar in meaning to the word in capital letters and write the letter of your choice on your answer paper.

736. VOLUBLE (A) worthwhile (B) serious (C) terminal (D) loquacious (E) circular
737. VORACIOUS (A) ravenous (B) spacious (C) truthful (D) pacific (E) tenacious
738. VOUCHSAFE (A) borrow (B) grant (C) punish (D) desire (E) qualify
739. WAIF (A) soldier (B) urchin (C) surrender (D) breeze (E) spouse
740. WANTON (A) needy (B) passive (C) rumored (D) oriental (E) unchaste
741. WARRANTY (A) threat (B) guarantee (C) order for arrest (D) issue (E) fund
742. WASTREL (A) refuse (B) spendthrift (C) mortal (D) tolerance (E) song
743. WAYLAY (A) ambush (B) journey (C) rest (D) roadmap (E) song
744. WELKIN (A) bell (B) greeting (C) cloudy (D) pressure (E) sky
745. WHINNY (A) complain (B) hurry (C) request (D) neigh (E) gallop
746. WINDFALL (A) unexpected gain (B) widespread destruction (C) calm (D) autumn (E) wait
747. WINSOME (A) victorious (B) gracious (C) married (D) permanent (E) pained
748. WIZENED (A) magical (B) clever (C) shriveled (D) swift (E) active
749. YEOMAN (A) masses (B) middle-class farmer (C) proletarian (D) indigent person (E) man of rank
750. ZEALOT (A) beginner (B) patron (C) fanatic (D) murderer (E) leper

ANSWER KEY

TEST—WORD LIST 1

1. **E** 6. **E** 11. **A**
2. **A** 7. **B** 12. **E**
3. **C** 8. **E** 13. **A**
4. **D** 9. **A** 14. **D**
5. **B** 10. **A** 15. **C**

TEST—WORD LIST 2

16. **E** 21. **A** 26. **B**
17. **B** 22. **A** 27. **D**
18. **A** 23. **B** 28. **B**
19. **D** 24. **B** 29. **C**
20. **A** 25. **B** 30. **D**

TEST—WORD LIST 3

31. **C** 36. **E** 41. **B**
32. **C** 37. **C** 42. **E**
33. **D** 38. **B** 43. **E**
34. **D** 39. **E** 44. **C**
35. **A** 40. **D** 45. **A**

TEST—WORD LIST 4

46. **A** 51. **C** 56. **E**
47. **A** 52. **A** 57. **C**
48. **B** 53. **C** 58. **D**
49. **D** 54. **B** 59. **D**
50. **B** 55. **D** 60. **C**

TEST—WORD LIST 5

61. **E** 66. **A** 71. **D**
62. **D** 67. **C** 72. **C**
63. **B** 68. **C** 73. **C**
64. **C** 69. **B** 74. **B**
65. **C** 70. **C** 75. **D**

TEST—WORD LIST 6

76. **D** 81. **A** 86. **C**
77. **B** 82. **B** 87. **A**
78. **D** 83. **B** 88. **E**
79. **A** 84. **E** 89. **E**
80. **E** 85. **E** 90. **C**

TEST—WORD LIST 7

91. **B** 96. **B** 101. **D**
92. **B** 97. **A** 102. **B**
93. **B** 98. **D** 103. **A**
94. **D** 99. **B** 104. **A**
95. **B** 100. **C** 105. **B**

TEST—WORD LIST 8

106. **D** 111. **B** 116. **B**
107. **E** 112. **A** 117. **D**
108. **A** 113. **D** 118. **A**
109. **C** 114. **C** 119. **C**
110. **E** 115. **D** 120. **B**

TEST—WORD LIST 9

121. **D** 126. **E** 131. **A**
122. **E** 127. **A** 132. **D**
123. **E** 128. **D** 133. **C**
124. **C** 129. **B** 134. **B**
125. **C** 130. **E** 135. **A**

TEST—WORD LIST 10

136. **E** 141. **B** 146. **E**
137. **B** 142. **E** 147. **E**
138. **D** 143. **D** 148. **C**
139. **C** 144. **D** 149. **A**
140. **A** 145. **D** 150. **D**

TEST—WORD LIST 11

151. **B** 156. **C** 161. **B**
152. **B** 157. **C** 162. **D**
153. **A** 158. **E** 163. **D**
154. **A** 159. **E** 164. **A**
155. **A** 160. **B** 165. **B**

TEST—WORD LIST 12

166. **C** 171. **C** 176. **B**
167. **B** 172. **B** 177. **B**
168. **C** 173. **A** 178. **A**
169. **D** 174. **A** 179. **C**
170. **D** 175. **B** 180. **A**

TEST—WORD LIST 13

181. **A** 186. **A** 191. **C**
182. **E** 187. **B** 192. **B**
183. **D** 188. **C** 193. **E**
184. **D** 189. **B** 194. **A**
185. **A** 190. **C** 195. **A**

TEST—WORD LIST 14

196. **D** 201. **C** 206. **B**
197. **E** 202. **C** 207. **D**
198. **B** 203. **C** 208. **C**
199. **A** 204. **B** 209. **E**
200. **C** 205. **B** 210. **D**

TEST—WORD LIST 15

211. **C** 216. **C** 221. **B**
212. **A** 217. **A** 222. **E**
213. **D** 218. **A** 223. **A**
214. **A** 219. **C** 224. **A**
215. **D** 220. **D** 225. **B**

TEST—WORD LIST 16

226. **D** 231. **B** 236. **D**
227. **A** 232. **C** 237. **C**
228. **C** 233. **D** 238. **A**
229. **E** 234. **C** 239. **B**
230. **E** 235. **E** 240. **A**

TEST—WORD LIST 17

241. **A** 246. **C** 251. **D**
242. **A** 247. **A** 252. **A**
243. **B** 248. **A** 253. **E**
244. **E** 249. **C** 254. **B**
245. **E** 250. **D** 255. **B**

TEST—WORD LIST 18

256. **A** 261. **D** 266. **A**
257. **A** 262. **D** 267. **A**
258. **C** 263. **E** 268. **C**
259. **D** 264. **C** 269. **B**
260. **A** 265. **B** 270. **E**

TEST—WORD LIST 19

271. **A** 276. **A** 281. **A**
272. **D** 277. **A** 282. **D**
273. **E** 278. **D** 283. **C**
274. **C** 279. **C** 284. **B**
275. **E** 280. **B** 285. **C**

TEST—WORD LIST 20

286. **A** 291. **A** 296. **E**
287. **B** 292. **A** 297. **D**
288. **B** 293. **D** 298. **A**
289. **B** 294. **C** 299. **A**
290. **D** 295. **C** 300. **B**

TEST—WORD LIST 21

301. **B** 306. **E** 311. **E**
302. **B** 307. **C** 312. **A**
303. **C** 308. **B** 313. **B**
304. **C** 309. **D** 314. **D**
305. **C** 310. **D** 315. **C**

TEST—WORD LIST 22

316. **D** 321. **E** 326. **C**
317. **A** 322. **A** 327. **C**
318. **A** 323. **B** 328. **A**
319. **D** 324. **C** 329. **B**
320. **A** 325. **E** 330. **D**

TEST—WORD LIST 23

331. **B** 336. **A** 341. **A**
332. **A** 337. **D** 342. **A**
333. **B** 338. **C** 343. **E**
334. **E** 339. **C** 344. **B**
335. **C** 340. **D** 345. **A**

TEST—WORD LIST 24

346. **C** 351. **D** 356. **B**
347. **B** 352. **A** 357. **C**
348. **C** 353. **A** 358. **A**
349. **A** 354. **A** 359. **B**
350. **B** 355. **B** 360. **D**

TEST—WORD LIST 25

361. **A**	366. **B**	371. **E**
362. **E**	367. **B**	372. **B**
363. **B**	368. **C**	373. **D**
364. **D**	369. **D**	374. **C**
365. **E**	370. **A**	375. **A**

TEST—WORD LIST 26

376. **C**	381. **B**	386. **B**
377. **A**	382. **A**	387. **E**
378. **B**	383. **C**	388. **E**
379. **B**	384. **C**	389. **E**
380. **B**	385. **C**	390. **A**

TEST—WORD LIST 27

391. **A**	396. **E**	401. **B**
392. **D**	397. **E**	402. **B**
393. **B**	398. **C**	403. **A**
394. **D**	399. **A**	404. **C**
395. **B**	400. **D**	405. **B**

TEST—WORD LIST 28

406. **B**	411. **B**	416. **B**
407. **A**	412. **E**	417. **A**
408. **E**	413. **D**	418. **D**
409. **E**	414. **E**	419. **D**
410. **C**	415. **C**	420. **A**

TEST—WORD LIST 29

421. **B**	426. **D**	431. **A**
422. **A**	427. **E**	432. **C**
423. **B**	428. **B**	433. **B**
424. **B**	429. **A**	434. **C**
425. **C**	430. **E**	435. **A**

TEST—WORD LIST 30

436. **A**	441. **A**	446. **E**
437. **A**	442. **B**	447. **B**
438. **B**	443. **D**	448. **C**
439. **D**	444. **B**	449. **E**
440. **C**	445. **A**	450. **B**

TEST—WORD LIST 31

451. **B**	456. **A**	461. **E**
452. **E**	457. **C**	462. **C**
453. **C**	458. **C**	463. **A**
454. **C**	459. **A**	464. **B**
455. **B**	460. **B**	465. **A**

TEST—WORD LIST 32

466. **B**	471. **D**	476. **D**
467. **C**	472. **C**	477. **B**
468. **C**	473. **B**	478. **A**
469. **A**	474. **A**	479. **C**
470. **C**	475. **B**	480. **A**

TEST—WORD LIST 33

481. **C**	486. **A**	491. **E**
482. **B**	487. **B**	492. **C**
483. **E**	488. **C**	493. **E**
484. **D**	489. **D**	494. **B**
485. **B**	490. **B**	495. **A**

TEST—WORD LIST 34

496. **D**	501. **B**	506. **D**
497. **A**	502. **B**	507. **D**
498. **D**	503. **A**	508. **C**
499. **A**	504. **E**	509. **C**
500. **E**	505. **C**	510. **A**

TEST—WORD LIST 35

511. **A**	516. **C**	521. **E**
512. **C**	517. **B**	522. **A**
513. **C**	518. **D**	523. **C**
514. **C**	519. **C**	524. **E**
515. **B**	520. **A**	525. **E**

TEST—WORD LIST 36

526. **A**	531. **E**	536. **B**
527. **D**	532. **B**	537. **D**
528. **A**	533. **C**	538. **D**
529. **B**	534. **C**	539. **D**
530. **E**	535. **A**	540. **D**

TEST—WORD LIST 37

541. **C**	546. **A**	551. **A**
542. **C**	547. **A**	552. **C**
543. **D**	548. **C**	553. **E**
544. **E**	549. **B**	554. **B**
545. **C**	550. **A**	555. **A**

TEST—WORD LIST 38

556. **E**	561. **E**	566. **A**
557. **D**	562. **E**	567. **D**
558. **C**	563. **B**	568. **C**
559. **B**	564. **A**	569. **D**
560. **B**	565. **E**	570. **C**

TEST—WORD LIST 39

571. **B**	576. **C**	581. **C**
572. **B**	577. **D**	582. **B**
573. **E**	578. **A**	583. **A**
574. **A**	579. **C**	584. **D**
575. **A**	580. **E**	585. **A**

TEST—WORD LIST 40

586. **E**	591. **C**	596. **D**
587. **B**	592. **A**	597. **D**
588. **D**	593. **B**	598. **B**
589. **C**	594. **A**	599. **D**
590. **A**	595. **D**	600. **E**

TEST—WORD LIST 41

601. **E**	606. **B**	611. **C**
602. **B**	607. **B**	612. **D**
603. **A**	608. **A**	613. **B**
604. **D**	609. **D**	614. **A**
605. **A**	610. **B**	615. **A**

TEST—WORD LIST 42

616. **C**	621. **D**	626. **B**
617. **A**	622. **E**	627. **D**
618. **B**	623. **A**	628. **A**
619. **C**	624. **D**	629. **D**
620. **D**	625. **C**	630. **E**

TEST—WORD LIST 43

631. **C**	636. **C**	641. **D**
632. **C**	637. **E**	642. **A**
633. **E**	638. **C**	643. **E**
634. **A**	639. **E**	644. **A**
635. **C**	640. **D**	645. **B**

TEST—WORD LIST 44

646. **A**	651. **B**	656. **A**
647. **B**	652. **A**	657. **B**
648. **D**	653. **D**	658. **A**
649. **A**	654. **C**	659. **C**
650. **E**	655. **C**	660. **C**

TEST—WORD LIST 45

661. **C**	666. **C**	671. **C**
662. **C**	667. **B**	672. **D**
663. **A**	668. **A**	673. **A**
664. **C**	669. **A**	674. **D**
665. **B**	670. **A**	675. **A**

TEST—WORD LIST 46

676. **D**	681. **D**	686. **B**
677. **B**	682. **B**	687. **A**
678. **B**	683. **A**	688. **B**
679. **C**	684. **E**	689. **E**
680. **C**	685. **B**	690. **C**

TEST—WORD LIST 47

691. **A**	696. **A**	701. **A**
692. **D**	697. **C**	702. **D**
693. **B**	698. **B**	703. **B**
694. **C**	699. **C**	704. **D**
695. **A**	700. **E**	705. **E**

TEST—WORD LIST 48

706. **A**	711. **B**	716. **D**
707. **A**	712. **B**	717. **D**
708. **B**	713. **A**	718. **C**
709. **C**	714. **A**	719. **B**
710. **C**	715. **E**	720. **C**

TEST—WORD LIST 49

721. **B**	726. **C**	731. **C**
722. **A**	727. **C**	732. **B**
723. **A**	728. **A**	733. **A**
724. **D**	729. **C**	734. **B**
725. **B**	730. **A**	735. **D**

TEST—WORD LIST 50

736. **D**	741. **B**	746. **A**
737. **A**	742. **B**	747. **B**
738. **B**	743. **A**	748. **C**
739. **B**	744. **E**	749. **B**
740. **E**	745. **D**	750. **C**

THE STANDARD MULTIPLE-CHOICE MATHEMATICS QUESTION

9

- **Testing Tactics**
- **Long-Range Strategies**
- **Important Facts and Formulas**
- **Practice Exercises**
- **Answer Key**

TESTING TACTICS

The SAT assumes that you are familiar with arithmetic, elementary algebra, and plane geometry. The questions on the test are about equally divided among those three areas. You do not need to know any more advanced mathematics to do well on this part of the SAT. If you are afraid you may have forgotten some of the math that you had in 9th or 10th grade, use the review in Chapter 11 of this book. It is divided into topics, so you can concentrate on specific areas that seem unfamiliar.

There are two types of questions in the mathematics test. Quantitative comparison questions, which make up about one third of the test, are discussed specifically in the next chapter. Two thirds of the test consists of standard multiple-choice questions. The directions for these are:

The following information is for your reference in solving some of the problems.

Circle of radius r: Area $= \pi r^2$; Circumference $= 2\pi r$

The number of degrees of arc in a circle is 360.

The measure in degrees of a straight angle is 180.

Definitions of symbols:

$=$ is equal to	$\leq$ is less than or equal to
$\neq$ is unequal to	$\geq$ is greater than or equal to
$<$ is less than	$\parallel$ is parallel to
$>$ is greater than	$\perp$ is perpendicular to

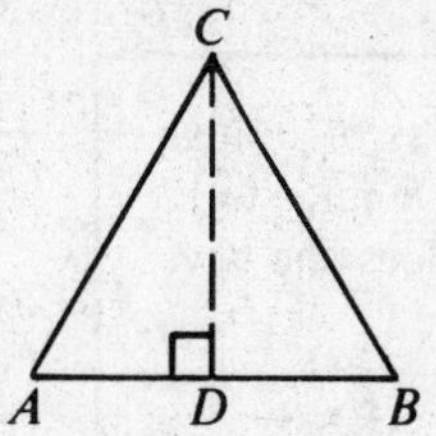

Triangle: The sum of the measures in degrees of the angles of a triangle is 180.

If $\angle CDA$ is a right angle, then

(1) area of $\triangle ABC = \dfrac{AB \times CD}{2}$

(2) $AC^2 = AD^2 + DC^2$

Note: Figures that accompany problems in this test are intended to provide information useful in solving the problems. They are drawn as accurately as possible EXCEPT when it is stated in a specific problem that its figure is not drawn to scale. All figures lie in a plane unless otherwise indicated. All numbers used are real numbers.

TACTIC 1: LOOK FOR SHORTCUTS

Many of the problems will have shortcuts built into them. In fact, if you are about to start on a long, complicated series of computations to solve a problem, look again. Either you have missed a shortcut, or you have misread the problem.

Whenever possible, estimate before you begin to solve a problem. If you have at least a rough idea of what the answer should be, you may see that there is only one possible answer among the choices offered. At the very least, you will be able to keep a mistake in arithmetic from leading you astray. Consider the following problem.

> One side of a rectangle is 22 feet. Which of the following could be the perimeter of the rectangle?
>
> (A) 11 feet (B) 28 feet (C) 33 feet
> (D) 44 feet (E) 54 feet

Before you begin setting up equations, or worrying about how to find a perimeter when you only know one side, stop to think. A rectangle has four sides, and the opposite sides are equal. If one side is 22 feet, two sides are 44 feet. Since you are being asked about a rectangle, there have to be two more sides, so your answer has to be more than 44. Choice E is therefore the only possibility.

Roundoff whenever possible to simplify your calculations. For example, $3{,}978 \times 289$ can be rounded off to $4{,}000 \times 300$. Then, if only one of the answer choices is slightly less than 1,200,000 you have your answer.

TACTIC 2: WORK IN THE UNITS THAT ARE USED IN THE ANSWER CHOICES

Word problems will often have more than one element involved. There may be square and linear units, or weight in pounds and weight in ounces. If you are asked how many square feet there are in an area, make sure you aren't doing the calculation in yards or in inches. Starting out in the right units can save you time, and keep you from choosing the wrong answer if you forget to do the conversion.

Make sure also that you are working in consistent units. If one side of a square measures 30 inches and the other measures 2 feet, don't try multiplying to find the area until you have both measurements in either feet or inches.

TACTIC 3: KNOW WHAT THE QUESTION IS ASKING

This may seem elementary, but often part of the problem is determining what it is you are supposed to solve for. Consider this problem:

> A kindergarten teacher had six quarts of orange juice. With the first two quarts she gave juice to 12 children. How many more children does she have juice for?
>
> (A) 4 (B) 36 (C) 72 (D) 24 (E) 8

The arithmetic in this problem is very simple. The only trick is to make sure you are solving the right problem. You are not being asked how much juice is left (the first answer choice), or how many children the teacher could give juice to (the second answer choice). The question asks how many MORE children she can give juice to with the remaining four quarts, and the answer is, of course, Choice D.

TACTIC 4: DO NOT ASSUME ANYTHING THAT IS NOT SPECIFICALLY STATED

For example, the SAT often has problems involving points on a line. If all the problem says is that three points are on a line, do NOT assume that they have to be in the order given. If *A*, *B*, and *C* are on a line, they could go *A*, *C*, *B* or *B*, *A*, *C* just as well as *A*, *B*, *C*. Beware also of positive and negative numbers. If a problem does not specifically state that an unknown is a positive number, it could just as well be a negative number or zero. Don't forget that the square root of a number can be positive or negative. Consider this problem.

Albert, Anthony, Andrew, and Arthur were given two dozen cookies. Albert ate 10 cookies, and Anthony ate 4. What is the maximum number of cookies that Arthur could have eaten?

(A) 14 (B) 2 (C) 9 (D) 10 (E) 24

You might choose answer (C) 9, reasoning that there were 10 cookies left, and if Andrew ate only one of them, there would be nine left for Arthur. But nowhere in the question does it say that Andrew got to eat any of the cookies at all. Therefore, it is possible that Andrew ate no cookies, and the maximum that Arthur could have eaten is (D) 10.

TACTIC 5: DO NOT PANIC WHEN FACED WITH COMPLEX PROBLEMS

When you are faced with complex problems involving several steps, just do them one step at a time. Sometimes you will discover that completing even one step turns what looked like an extremely complicated problem into a very simple one.

EXAMPLE:

Two thirds of a class are going on a class trip with the teacher. The pupils who are not going on this trip are divided equally among 4 other classes. If 3 pupils are thus sent to each class, how many pupils are going on the trip?

(A) 12 (B) 18 (C) 24 (D) 30 (E) 36

You would use the following steps to solve this problem:

1. Determine how many pupils are not going on the trip. $3 \times 4 = 12$.
2. Since $^2/_3$ of the class are going on the trip, then $^1/_3$ (or 12) are not going and $^2/_3$ or 24 are going.

Notice this also illustrates the need for answering the question given, not what you may expect the question to ask you to do. The question could have asked "How many pupils are there in this class?" or "How many pupils were not going on the trip?"

Some problems give you more information than you actually need, making them seem even more complex than they are. Learn to recognize irrelevant material, and do not be distracted by it. Do not assume that because you are given a piece of information you have to use it.

EXAMPLE:

Before starting on a trip I find that the gasoline tank is $^3/_4$ full. After traveling for 130 miles I find that the tank is $^1/_{10}$ full. I therefore stop to fill the tank. Since it took 18 gallons to fill the tank, what is the capacity of the tank in gallons?

(A) 10 (B) 15 (C) 18 (D) 20 (E) 22

This problem is full of extraneous information. The only significant information is that 18 gallons of gasoline represents $^9/_{10}$ of the full capacity of the tank. Here is the way to solve the problem:

Let x = the full capacity

Then $^9/_{10}x = 18$

$x = (18)(^{10}/_9)$

$x = 20$ gallons

TACTIC 6: KNOW IMPORTANT MATHEMATICAL DEFINITIONS, CONCEPTS, AND RULES

Learn the important mathematical definitions and rules at the end of this chapter, so that you can apply them automatically. For example, suppose you are given this problem:

Which of the following numbers is divisible by 12?

(A) 4653 (B) 4818 (C) 4501 (D) 4889 (E) 4404

You could try doing the necessary division with each number, or you could remember that an even number will only go evenly into another even number. That immediately eliminates Choices A, C, and D, and you will arrive at the correct answer, Choice E, much more quickly than you would have if you had done the arithmetic on each of the answer choices.

TACTIC 7: DO NOT PANIC IF A QUESTION HAS AN UNUSUAL SYMBOL

If a question has an unusual symbol with a specially designed definition, simply replace the symbol with a more familiar term and you will immediately recognize the problem as a standard question.

EXAMPLE:

> If $\boxed{x}$ is defined by the equation $\boxed{x} = \frac{\sqrt{x}}{4}$ whenever x is a whole number, then which of the following equals 3?
>
> (A) $\boxed{100}$ (B) $\boxed{12}$ (C) $\boxed{144}$ (D) $\boxed{256}$
> (E) $\boxed{36}$

On analysis you see that all this question is really asking is: If the square of a number divided by 4 equals 3, what is the number? And the answer is (C) 144. (Hint: In solving problems like these, where you work back from the answer choices, first do the answer choices that are easiest to do. For the example above you would start with $36 \rightarrow 6 \div 4 = 1\frac{1}{2}$, then $100 \rightarrow 10 \div 4 = 2\frac{1}{2}$, then $144 \rightarrow 12 \div 4 = 3$, which is your answer.)

Just as you shouldn't panic if you come across unusual symbols, don't panic when you are faced with mathematical terminology. Try putting the problem into simpler words. "*S* is a set of integers on the number line 1–100 inclusive" just means "*S* is all the numbers from 1 through 100."

TACTIC 8: USE THE TEST BOOKLET TO DO COMPUTATIONS AND TO DRAW DIAGRAMS

Write in the test booklet. Don't try to do all the computations in your head. On the geometry questions, draw diagrams if they will help you, or mark up the diagrams that are given. In problems like the following, drawing a diagram makes what would be a confusing question a relatively simple one.

EXAMPLE:

> City L is 3 miles south of city K. City M is 4 miles east of city L. What is the shortest distance between city K and city M?
>
> (A) 3 (B) 4 (C) 5 (D) 6 (E) 7

By drawing the diagram that follows, it is easy to recognize that we have here a 3-4-5 triangle, and that the answer is Choice C.

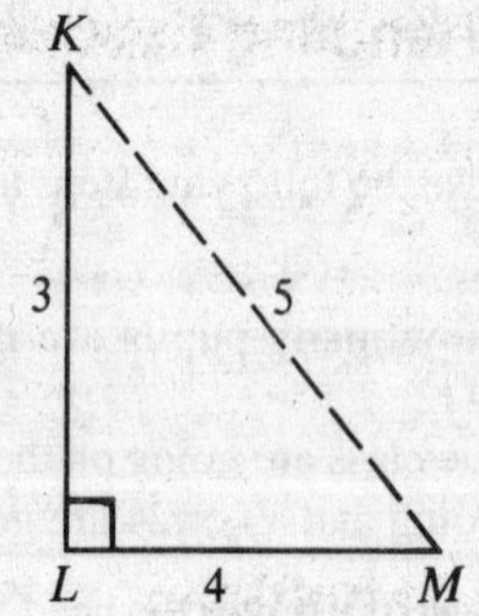

TACTIC 9: DO NOT SPEND TOO LONG ON A PROBLEM

If you have absolutely no idea how to solve a particular problem, do not waste time on it. Circle it, and leave it. If you have time at the end of the test, you can go back and try again. Remember that you get the same amount of credit for answering an easy question as you do for answering a difficult question, so don't spend too much time on a question that is difficult for you. The best method is to do the easy questions first, and then go back to the difficult questions (which you have circled) if you have time left.

Two hints to keep in mind if you are having trouble solving a problem:

1. If the problem has several unknowns, try substituting simple numbers for the unknowns.
2. For some of the questions, you have to try all the answers to see which one works. When you hit one of these, start with Choice E instead of Choice A. Most of the time, the correct answer on these seems to be toward the end of the choices.

LONG-RANGE STRATEGIES

You are most likely to do well on the mathematics section of the SAT if you know your math. All the tactics in the world cannot substitute for knowledge. In the long run, the ability to solve problems quickly and accurately is going to be far more useful than the ability to psych out the testers.

However, not all students are gifted mathematicians, and even those who are may have forgotten some of the topics they covered a year or two ago in algebra and geometry. Almost all of you could benefit from some review. The facts and formulas that follow in this chapter provide a minimal review for those of you who are running short on time. Go over these points and, as far as possible, commit them to memory.

In addition, spend as much time as you can on the review material in Chapter 11. This chapter is divided topically, so you can concentrate on those topics that you have forgotten, or that you know always gave you trouble.

IMPORTANT FACTS AND FORMULAS

Symbols

$=$ equals	$\simeq$ congruent
$\neq$ not equal to	$\sim$ similar
$>$ more than	$\perp$ perpendicular
$<$ less than	$\parallel$ parallel
$\geqq$ greater than or equal to	$\pm$ plus or minus
$\leqq$ less than or equal to	

Rules for Handling Exponents

$$x^a \cdot x^b = x^{a+b}$$
$$x^a \div x^b = x^{a-b}$$
$$(x^a)^b = x^{ab}$$
$$(xy)^a = x^a y^a$$
$$\left(\frac{x}{y}\right)^a = \frac{x^a}{y^a}$$
$$x^0 = 1 \text{ if } x \neq 0$$
$$x^{-a} = \frac{1}{x^a}$$
$$x^{\frac{1}{a}} = \sqrt[a]{x}$$

Important Definitions

Sum is the result of addition.
Difference is the result of subtraction.
Product is the result of multiplication.
In division,

$$\frac{\text{Dividend}}{\text{Divisor}} = \text{quotient} + \frac{\text{remainder}}{\text{divisor}}$$

A fraction is an indicated division.
A decimal is an implied fraction with a denominator of 10, 100, 1000,...
A percent is a fraction with a denominator of 100.
A ratio compares two quantities by dividing one by the other.
A proportion is an equation, both sides of which are fractions.
A *positive* number is one that is greater than zero; a *negative* number is one that is less than zero. The meaning and the use of signed numbers are basic in the study of algebra. Positive numbers are preceded by a plus sign (+); negative numbers, by a minus sign (−).

Important Formulas

$$\text{Average} = \frac{\text{sum of numbers}}{\text{quantity of numbers}}$$

(Rate) (time) = distance

$$\text{Time} = \frac{\text{distance}}{\text{rate}}$$

$$\text{Rate} = \frac{\text{distance}}{\text{time}}$$

$$\text{Percentage composition} = \frac{\text{quantity dissolved}}{\text{total quantity of mixture}} \times 100$$

$$\text{Part of task done} = \frac{\text{time actually worked}}{\text{time required to complete entire task}}$$

Arithmetic Concepts

Any quantity multiplied by zero is zero ($x \cdot 0 = 0$).
Any quantity except zero raised to the zero power is one ($x^0 = 1$ if $x \neq 0$).
If $x^2 = 4$, then $x = +2$ or -2.
Any fraction multiplied by its reciprocal equals 1:

$$\left(\frac{x}{y}\right)\left(\frac{y}{x}\right) = 1$$

Odd and Even Numbers

even + even = even
odd + odd = even
even + odd = odd
even × even = even
even × odd = even
odd × odd = odd

Algebra Concepts

Only *like* algebraic terms may be combined.

Always check your answer in the original equation.

In *algebraic expressions*, break problems down to their simplest form and try to eliminate any equivalent answer choices. In simplifying, remember to multiply and divide before adding and subtracting; simplify exponents and fractions; combine like terms.

If an expression has more than one set of parentheses, get rid of the inner parentheses first and work outward through the rest of the parentheses.

Any operation done to one side of an equation must be done to the other.

Geometry Concepts

Important Relationships

Right triangles

In a right triangle, $(\text{leg})^2 + (\text{leg})^2 = (\text{hypotenuse})^2$, or $a^2 + b^2 = c^2$.

In a 30° − 60° − 90° triangle:

the leg opposite the 30° angle equals ½ the hypotenuse.

the leg opposite the 60° angle equals ½ the hypotenuse times $\sqrt{3}$.

the ratio of the shorter leg to the hypotenuse is 1:2.

In a 45°–45°–90° triangle:

the hypotenuse equals a leg times $\sqrt{2}$.

the leg equals ½ the hypotenuse times $\sqrt{2}$.

Equilateral triangles

In an equilateral triangle, an altitude equals ½ the side times $\sqrt{3}$.

Areas of polygons

Area of a rectangle $= bh$

Area of a square $= s^2$

Area of a parallelogram $= bh$

Area of a triangle $= \frac{1}{2} bh$

Area of a right triangle $= \frac{1}{2}$ leg × leg

Circles

Circumference of a circle $= \pi D$ or $2\pi r$

Length of an arc $= \dfrac{n}{360} \times 2\pi r$

Area of a circle $= \pi r^2$

Coordinate geometry

Distance between two points =

$$\sqrt{(x_1 - x_2)^2 + (y_1 - y_2)^2}$$

Coordinates of midpoint of line =

$\frac{1}{2}(x_1 + x_2), \frac{1}{2}(y_1 + y_2)$

Basic quantities to know (where ≈ represents "approximately equals")

$\pi \approx 3.1416 \approx \dfrac{22}{7}$

$\sqrt{2} \approx 1.1414$

$\sqrt{3} \approx 1.732$

Important solutions of the Pythagorean theorem

3-4-5 triangle

5-12-13 triangle

1-1-$\sqrt{2}$ triangle (45°- 45°- 90°)

1-$\sqrt{3}$-2 triangle (30°-60°-90°)

Important Theorems

If two sides of a triangle are congruent, the angles opposite these sides are congruent. (Base angles of an isosceles triangle are congruent.)

The sum of the measure of the angles of a triangle is equal to a straight angle. (180°)

If two angles of a triangle are congruent, the sides opposite these angles are congruent.

Two right triangles are congruent if the hypotenuse and leg of one triangle are congruent to the hypotenuse and corresponding leg of the other.

In a circle, a diameter perpendicular to a chord bisects the chord and its two arcs.

An angle inscribed in a circle is measured by one-half its intercepted arc.

An angle formed by two chords intersecting within a circle is measured by one-half the sum of the intercepted arcs.

An angle formed by two secants meeting outside a circle is measured by one-half the difference of the intercepted arcs.

An angle formed by a tangent and a secant is measured by one-half the difference of the intercepted arcs.

An angle formed by the intersection of two tangents is measured by one-half the difference of the intercepted arcs.

If two triangles have the three angles of one congruent respectively to the three angles of the other, the triangles are similar.

If, in a right triangle, the altitude is drawn upon the hypotenuse:

A. the two triangles thus formed are similar to the given triangle and similar to each other.

B. the length of each leg of the given triangle is the mean proportional between the hypotenuse and the projection of that leg on the hypotenuse.

If two lines are cut by a transversal and a pair of alternate interior angles are congruent, the two lines are parallel.

The opposite sides of a parallelogram are congruent and the opposite angles are congruent.

The diagonals of a parallelogram bisect each other.

If the opposite sides of a quadrilateral are congruent, the figure is a parallelogram.

If two sides of a quadrilateral are congruent and parallel, the figure is a parallelogram.

In a circle or in congruent circles, congruent chords are equally distant from the center.

Tangents drawn to a circle from an external point are equal in length.

An angle formed by a tangent and a chord drawn from the point of contact is measured by one-half its intercepted arc.

If an angle of one triangle is congruent to an angle of another triangle and the sides including these angles are proportional, the triangles are similar.

If two chords intersect within a circle, the product of the segments of one chord is equal to the product of the segments of the other.

If from a point outside a circle a tangent and a secant are drawn to the circle, the tangent is the mean proportional between the secant and its external segment.

The areas of two similar triangles are to each other as the squares of any two corresponding sides.

If two sides of a triangle are not congruent, the angles opposite these sides are not congruent and the greater angle lies opposite the greater side.

If two angles of a triangle are not congruent, the sides opposite these angles are not congruent and the greater side lies opposite the greater angle.

PRACTICE EXERCISES

MATHEMATICS TEST A

1. Find the value of $\frac{x}{x-a}+\frac{a}{a-x}$ when x is 50 and a is 10.

(a) 0 (b) 1 (c) 10 (d) 5 (e) 50

1. Ⓐ Ⓑ Ⓒ Ⓓ Ⓔ

2. Suppose $z=\frac{3x}{y}$, what happens to z if x is doubled and y is tripled?

(a) doubled (b) tripled (c) halved (d) multiplied by 6 (e) multiplied by a factor of $\frac{2}{3}$.

2. Ⓐ Ⓑ Ⓒ Ⓓ Ⓔ

3. Suppose $x^2+y^2=2$ and $x^2-y^2=2$, find x^4-y^4.

(a) 0 (b) 2 (c) 4 (d) 5 (e) 8

3. Ⓐ Ⓑ Ⓒ Ⓓ Ⓔ

4. $\frac{8(11-2)-5(11-2)}{3}=?$

(a) 1 (b) 11 (c) 9 (d) 3 (e) 5

4. Ⓐ Ⓑ Ⓒ Ⓓ Ⓔ

5. Find x when $27 \cdot 27 = 3 \cdot 3 \cdot x$

(a) 9 (b) 27 (c) 81 (d) 243 (e) 36

5. Ⓐ Ⓑ Ⓒ Ⓓ Ⓔ

6. A certain type of bacteria triples in number every 20 minutes. At the end of five hours there are x bacteria in the colony. How many hours more will it take until there are $27x$?

(a) 1 (b) $1\frac{1}{3}$ (c) $1\frac{2}{3}$ (d) 2 (e) $\frac{2}{3}$

6. Ⓐ Ⓑ Ⓒ Ⓓ Ⓔ

7. What number must be multiplied by $\frac{1}{\sqrt{2}}$ to give $\sqrt{2}$?

(a) 2 (b) $\sqrt{2}$ (c) $\frac{1}{2}$ (d) $\frac{1}{\sqrt{2}}$ (e) $\frac{\sqrt{2}}{2}$

7. Ⓐ Ⓑ Ⓒ Ⓓ Ⓔ

8. For what value of x is $\frac{1}{x} = \frac{1}{x-2}$ a true statement? 8. Ⓐ Ⓑ Ⓒ Ⓓ Ⓔ

(a) 0 (b) 2 (c) −2 (d) 1 (e) no value possible

9. The expression $ax^5 + bx^3 - 4 = 0$ when x is −1. What is its value when x is 1? 9. Ⓐ Ⓑ Ⓒ Ⓓ Ⓔ

(a) 0 (b) 1 (c) 6 (d) −8 (e) −4

10. Find the area of a square if its diagonal is 6 inches. 10. Ⓐ Ⓑ Ⓒ Ⓓ Ⓔ

(a) 9 (b) 6 (c) 36 (d) 12 (e) 18

11. Suppose $a * b = c$ is only true if $b^c = a$. Find y when $64 * 4 = y$. 11. Ⓐ Ⓑ Ⓒ Ⓓ Ⓔ

(a) $\frac{1}{2}$ (b) 2 (c) 3 (d) 4 (e) $\frac{1}{4}$

12. The statement $3x - 1 \neq 2x$ is true for all values of x EXCEPT 12. Ⓐ Ⓑ Ⓒ Ⓓ Ⓔ

(a) $x \neq 1$ (b) $x = -1$ (c) $x = 1$ (d) $x > 1$ (e) $x < 1$

13. A bag contains 28 pounds of sugar which is to be separated into package containing 14 ounces each. How many such packages can be made? 13. Ⓐ Ⓑ Ⓒ Ⓓ Ⓔ

(a) 2 (b) 4 (c) 8 (d) 16 (e) 32

14. Find the value of $1^{3a} + 1^{2a}$ 14. Ⓐ Ⓑ Ⓒ Ⓓ Ⓔ

(a) 0 (b) 1 (c) 2 (d) 5 (e) cannot be determined

15. Suppose you know that $\sqrt{15}$ is approximately 3.87. Which of the following is the best approximation to $\sqrt{\frac{5}{3}}$? 15. Ⓐ Ⓑ Ⓒ Ⓓ Ⓔ

(a) 0.2 (b) 0.41 (c) 1.29 (d) 6.10 (e) 3.66

16. Which of the numbers in (a) through (e) is the greatest? 16. Ⓐ Ⓑ Ⓒ Ⓓ Ⓔ

(a) $\frac{1-\frac{1}{3}}{3}$ (b) $\frac{-3}{-\frac{1}{3}}$ (c) $\frac{-3}{\frac{1}{3}}$ (d) 0 (e) $\frac{3-\frac{1}{3}}{3}$

17. When x is 1, 2, 3, or 4, the expression $x^2 + x + 17$ has the values 19, 23, 29, and 37 respectively. All of these results are prime numbers. What is the least positive integer which will not yield a prime in the formula? 17. Ⓐ Ⓑ Ⓒ Ⓓ Ⓔ

(a) 5 (b) 7 (c) 11 (d) 13 (e) 17

18. Find the area of $\triangle ABC$. 18. Ⓐ Ⓑ Ⓒ Ⓓ Ⓔ

(a) $13\frac{1}{2}$ (b) 12 (c) 11 (d) 9 (e) $9\frac{1}{2}$

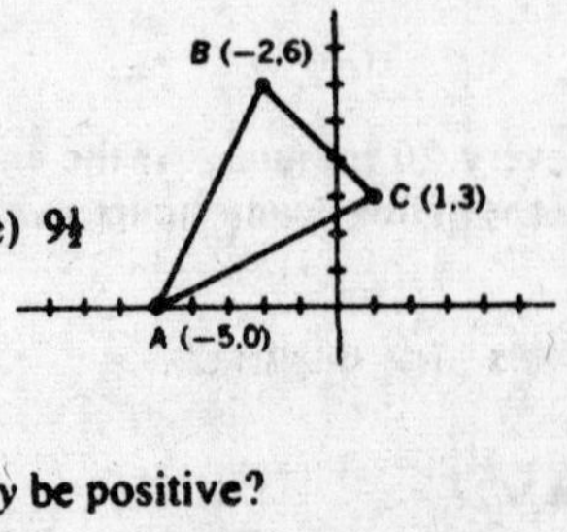

19. If $y = \frac{3x-6}{x}$, for what values of x will y be positive? 19. Ⓐ Ⓑ Ⓒ Ⓓ Ⓔ

(a) $x > 2$ or $x < 0$ (b) only when x is positive (c) only when x is negative (d) $-2 < x < 2$ (e) $-2 < x < 2$ but not zero

20. If AD and BC are parallel, what is the length of BC?

(a) x (b) $x+y$ (c) $x+2y$ (d) $2x+y$ (e) $2x+2y$

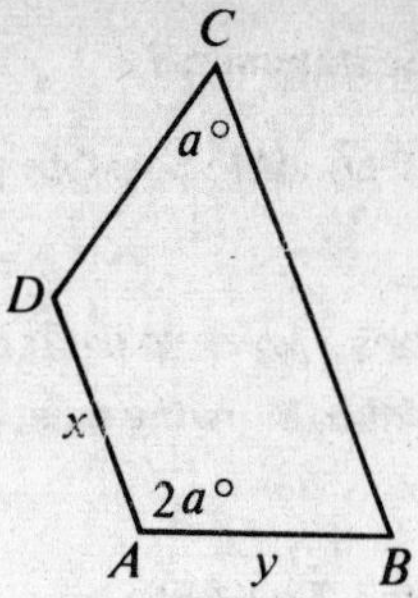

20. Ⓐ Ⓑ Ⓒ Ⓓ Ⓔ

21. Suppose $a * b = c$ is true if and only if c is the remainder after a is divided by b. Find the value of $\dfrac{5 * 3}{10 * 6}$.

21. Ⓐ Ⓑ Ⓒ Ⓓ Ⓔ

(a) 2 (b) $\frac{1}{2}$ (c) 4 (d) 3 (e) 1

22. If $(0.4)(y) = 5$, find $(4.44)(y)$.

(a) 5.055 (b) 0.555 (c) 555 (d) 55.5 (e) 5.55

22. Ⓐ Ⓑ Ⓒ Ⓓ Ⓔ

23. Find x if $\dfrac{1}{2-\dfrac{x}{1-x}} = \dfrac{1}{2}$.

23. Ⓐ Ⓑ Ⓒ Ⓓ Ⓔ

(a) 12 (b) -2 (c) 0 (d) 1 (e) -1

24. If $p > 1$, which of the following expressions decrease(s) as p increases?

I. $p+\dfrac{1}{p}$

II. $p^2 - 10p$

III. $\dfrac{1}{p+1}$

24. Ⓐ Ⓑ Ⓒ Ⓓ Ⓔ

(a) III only (b) I and III only (c) II and III only (d) all (e) none

25. If y and z are consecutive integers and $z^2 = x^2 + y^2$, which of the following is true?

25. Ⓐ Ⓑ Ⓒ Ⓓ Ⓔ

(a) $z = x+y$ (b) $x^2 = 1+2y$ (c) $y^2 = 2x+1$ (d) $z = 1+2x$
(e) $x = y+2z$

MATHEMATICS TEST B

1. If the circumference of a circle increases from π inches to 2π inches what change occurs in the area?

(a) remains the same (b) doubles (c) triples (d) quadruples
(e) is halved

1. Ⓐ Ⓑ Ⓒ Ⓓ Ⓔ

2. $31(m-n) - 32(m-n) + (m-n) = ?$

(a) $-n$ (b) $-m$ (c) 0 (d) 1 (e) m

2. Ⓐ Ⓑ Ⓒ Ⓓ Ⓔ

3. If $3x = 2y$ and $6y = 7z$, what is the ratio of x to z?

(a) 2:3 (b) 7:9 (c) 3:2 (d) 5:7 (e) 5:3 — 3. Ⓐ Ⓑ Ⓒ Ⓓ Ⓔ

4. If x must be greater than 4, which of the following must have the least value?

(a) $\frac{4}{x+1}$ (b) $\frac{4}{x-1}$ (c) $\frac{4}{x}$ (d) $\frac{x}{4}$ (e) $\frac{x+1}{4}$ — 4. Ⓐ Ⓑ Ⓒ Ⓓ Ⓔ

5. $\dfrac{\frac{1}{5}+\frac{1}{10}}{\frac{1}{15}+\frac{1}{5}} = ?$

(a) $\frac{7}{15}$ (b) $\frac{2}{3}$ (c) $\frac{9}{8}$ (d) 15 (e) 5 — 5. Ⓐ Ⓑ Ⓒ Ⓓ Ⓔ

6. Six consecutive integers are given. The sum of the first three is 27. What is the sum of the last three?

(a) 29 (b) 30 (c) 32 (d) 33 (e) 36 — 6. Ⓐ Ⓑ Ⓒ Ⓓ Ⓔ

7. Find all values of x for which $-x = \sqrt[3]{x}$.

(a) 1 (b) 0, and -1 (c) 0 only (d) -8 (e) no values are possible — 7. Ⓐ Ⓑ Ⓒ Ⓓ Ⓔ

8. If the points given in (a) through (e) are the endpoints of segments which have the other end at the origin, which segment has a mid-point which is farthest from the origin?

(a) (3, 3) (b) (2, 5) (c) (1, 6) (d) (0, 7) (e) (4, 3) — 8. Ⓐ Ⓑ Ⓒ Ⓓ Ⓔ

9. An arithmetic progression is a sequence of numbers for which each new number is found by adding a given number p to the previous number. In the arithmetic progression below, only two numbers are known.

_, _, 5, _, _, _, 17, __

What number comes after 17?

(a) 19 (b) 20 (c) 21 (d) 18 (e) 23 — 9. Ⓐ Ⓑ Ⓒ Ⓓ Ⓔ

10. Suppose $x > y$ and $xy < 0$, which of the following must be negative?

(a) y (b) x (c) $x-y$ (d) x^2-y^2 (e) $(y-x)^2$ — 10. Ⓐ Ⓑ Ⓒ Ⓓ Ⓔ

11. What would the result be if $\frac{x+10}{2}$ is subtracted from $\frac{x}{2}+10$?

(a) 5 (b) x (c) $\frac{x}{2}$ (d) 0 (e) $x+10$ — 11. Ⓐ Ⓑ Ⓒ Ⓓ Ⓔ

12. A mathematical law states that the sum of the first n odd counting numbers is n^2. Which of the following is an example of this law? — 12. Ⓐ Ⓑ Ⓒ Ⓓ Ⓔ

(a) $1+3=4$ (b) $1+9+16=26$ (c) $1+2=3$
(d) $1+3+5=1+2(4)^2$ (e) $1+4=5$

13. Find the area of triangle ABC if for each point (x, y) of line AB, $y = 2x - 8$.

(a) 100 (b) 121 (c) 144 (d) 169 (e) 132

13. Ⓐ Ⓑ Ⓒ Ⓓ Ⓔ

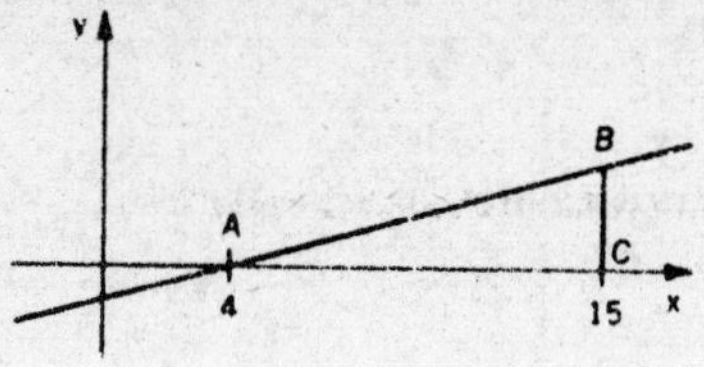

14. If the fraction

$$\frac{y^4 - y^2 + y + 1}{y^3 - y^2 + 1}$$

is written with no factors common to numerator and denominator, the result is?

(a) $y + 1$ (b) $y - 1$ (c) $1 - y^2$
(d) $y^2 + 1$ (e) $1 - y$

14. Ⓐ Ⓑ Ⓒ Ⓓ Ⓔ

15. $\frac{4^3 + 4^4}{4^3} = ?$

(a) 1 (b) 2 (c) 4 (d) 5 (e) 8

15. Ⓐ Ⓑ Ⓒ Ⓓ Ⓔ

16. Which of the following is the simplest form of $\dfrac{x - \frac{1}{y}}{y - \frac{1}{x}}$?

(a) x/y (b) y/x (c) $\dfrac{x-1}{y-1}$ (d) $\dfrac{y-1}{x-1}$ (e) $\dfrac{xy-1}{xy}$

16. Ⓐ Ⓑ Ⓒ Ⓓ Ⓔ

17. Suppose $a = b + 3$, what is the value of $(a - b)^3$?

(a) 1 (b) 8 (c) 27 (d) 64 (e) 0

17. Ⓐ Ⓑ Ⓒ Ⓓ Ⓔ

18. Suppose you have 72 green marbles and 108 red marbles to sell. You decide to separate them into packages of the same size, each of which contains either all red or all green. What is the greatest number you can put in each package?

(a) 3 (b) 18 (c) 12 (d) 24 (e) 36

18. Ⓐ Ⓑ Ⓒ Ⓓ Ⓔ

19. If the length of a rectangle is increased by 20 percent and the width is decreased by 20 percent, what percent change occurs in the area?

(a) remains the same (b) increases 5 percent (c) decreases 4 percent
(d) increases 2 percent (e) decreases 2 percent

19. Ⓐ Ⓑ Ⓒ Ⓓ Ⓔ

20. What percent of $\frac{1}{2}$ is $\frac{3}{4}$?

(a) 100% (b) 120% (c) 125% (d) 140% (e) 150%

20. Ⓐ Ⓑ Ⓒ Ⓓ Ⓔ

21. Which of the following is the square (second power) of $\sqrt{1 + \sqrt{1}}$?

(a) 1 (b) 2 (c) 4 (d) 3 (e) $1 + \sqrt{2}$

21. Ⓐ Ⓑ Ⓒ Ⓓ Ⓔ

22. Suppose $x = 1 + 3^a$ and $y = 1 + 3^{-a}$ which of the following is a formula for y in terms of x?

22. Ⓐ Ⓑ Ⓒ Ⓓ Ⓔ

(a) x (b) $x - 1$ (c) $\frac{1}{x-1}$ (d) $\frac{x}{x-1}$ (e) $x + 1$

23. If $\frac{p \times p \times p}{p + p + p} = 3$, find p.

23. Ⓐ Ⓑ Ⓒ Ⓓ Ⓔ

(a) $\frac{1}{3}$ (b) $\frac{1}{9}$ (c) 27 (d) ± 3 (e) 9

24. Suppose $S(x)$ is defined as follows:

24. Ⓐ Ⓑ Ⓒ Ⓓ Ⓔ

$S(x) = 1$ when $x > 1$,
$S(x) = x$ when $-1 \leq x \leq 1$, and
$S(x) = -1$ when $x < -1$.

What is the value of $S(5) + S(4) + S(0)$?

(a) 1 (b) 0 (c) 3 (d) 2 (e) -1

25. Find the value of $5 - [7 - (9 - 11)]$.

25. Ⓐ Ⓑ Ⓒ Ⓓ Ⓔ

(a) -4 (b) 3 (c) -2 (d) 7 (e) 5

ANSWER KEY

Mathematics Test A

1.	B	6.	A	11.	C	16.	B	21.	B
2.	E	7.	A	12.	C	17.	E	22.	D
3.	C	8.	E	13.	E	18.	A	23.	C
4.	C	9.	D	14.	C	19.	A	24.	A
5.	C	10.	E	15.	C	20.	B	25.	B

Mathematics Test B

1.	D	6.	E	11.	A	16.	A	21.	B
2.	C	7.	C	12.	A	17.	C	22.	D
3.	B	8.	D	13.	B	18.	E	23.	D
4.	A	9.	B	14.	A	19.	C	24.	D
5.	C	10.	A	15.	D	20.	E	25.	A

ANSWER EXPLANATIONS

Mathematics Test A

1. $a - x = -(x - a)$ so the fractions can be combined to get $\frac{x-a}{x-a} = 1$ regardless of the value of x and a (as long as x does not equal a, of course) (b).

2. The pitfall which traps many students is the 3 in the numerator which they cancel with the 3 which appears in the denominator when the denominator is tripled. If this is done the result is $\frac{2x}{y}$ which is still $\frac{2}{3}\left(\frac{3x}{y}\right)$ or $\frac{2}{3}z$. The obvious solution is the true one (e).

3. $x^4 - y^4 = (x^2 + y^2)(x^2 - y^2) = (2)(2)$ (c).

4. The calculation is not really lengthy but note: $\frac{8(11-2) - 5(11-2)}{3} = \frac{\cancel{3}(11-2)}{\cancel{3}} = 11 - 2 = 9$ (c).

5. $27 \cdot 27 = (3 \cdot 3)(9 \cdot 9)$. Thus $x = 9 \cdot 9 = 81$ (c).

6. Since the question asks "how many more?" you can ignore the first 5 hours. In 20 minutes x will triple to $3x$ and in 20 more minutes this will triple to $3(3x)$, and at end of one hour, it will be $(3)(3)(3x)$ or $27x$ (a).

7. Divide $\sqrt{2}$ by $\frac{1}{\sqrt{2}}$ to get $\sqrt{2} \cdot \frac{\sqrt{2}}{1} = 2$ (a).

8. To be true the denominators must be equal since the numerators are. But $x = x - 2$ can never be true for any x. Many students do not know how to interpret what they get when they try to solve an equation of this kind. If you subtract x from each side of $x = x - 2$ you get $x - x = -2$ or $(1 - 1)x = -2$. The latter is $0 \cdot x = -2$. But multiplying any number by 0 gives 0 (e).

9. This is rather difficult. You are trying to find the value of $a + b - 4$ which is what you get when you replace x by 1. But $a + b - 4 = a + b + 4 - 8$ and $a + b + 4 = 0$. The reason $a + b + 4 = 0$ is that $-a - b - 4 = 0$ which is what you get by replacing x by -1 in the original equation. Multiply each side of the latter by -1 and you get $a + b + 4 = 0$. This is an unusual question in that there are students who can find the correct answer very quickly and not be able to explain how they got it (d).

10. We have reviewed the formula for the area of a square in this text in terms of the diagonal, but it is not one most students remember. The square has diagonals which bisect each other, are perpendicular, and separate the square into four triangles of the same area. Thus you have four right triangles with legs of length 3, therefore areas of $\frac{9}{2}$ $4(\frac{9}{2}) = 18$ (e).

11. By direct substitution into the formula given you get $4^y = 64$. $64 = 4^3$ so $y = 3$ (c).

12. Any value which makes $3x - 1 \neq 2x$ true makes $3x - 1 = 2x$ false. The latter is true for $x = 1$ (c).

13. Changing pounds to ounces gives 28×16, but do not multiply it out since 14 will divide 28. $2 \times 16 = 32$ (e).

14. No matter what a is, $1^{3a} = 1$ and $1^{2a} = 1$ (c).

15. You must change $\sqrt{\frac{5}{3}}$ to a form that will use the given approximation of $\sqrt{15}$. $\sqrt{\frac{5}{3}} = \sqrt{\frac{5 \times 3}{3 \times 3}} = \frac{\sqrt{15}}{\sqrt{9}} = \frac{\sqrt{15}}{3} = \frac{3.87}{3} = 1.29$ (c).

16. (a), (b), (e) are positive so (c) and (d) can be eliminated since they aren't. (e) is greater than (a) since $3 - \frac{1}{3}$ is greater than $1 - \frac{1}{3}$. (b) is 9. (e) is $\frac{2\frac{2}{3}}{3}$ which is $\frac{1}{3}$ of $2\frac{2}{3}$ and hence less than 1. A routine and lengthy approach is to simplify each of them (b).

17. $17^2 + 17 + 17 = 17(17 + 1 + 1) = 17 \cdot 19$ (e). Substituting anything less than 17 for x will yield a value for $x^2 + x$ which does not have a factor of 17; hence $x^2 + x + 17$ will have no factors at all.

18. You cannot find any base or height by simple methods so draw perpendiculars to the x-axis from B and C and then add and subtract the necessary pieces.

(1) area of triangle $ABB' = \frac{1}{2}(3)(6) = 9$.
(2) area of trapezoid $BB'C'C = \frac{1}{2}(6 + 3)3 = 13\frac{1}{2}$.
(3) area of triangle $ACC' = \frac{1}{2}(6)(3) = 9$.
Add (1) and (2), then subtract (3) (a).

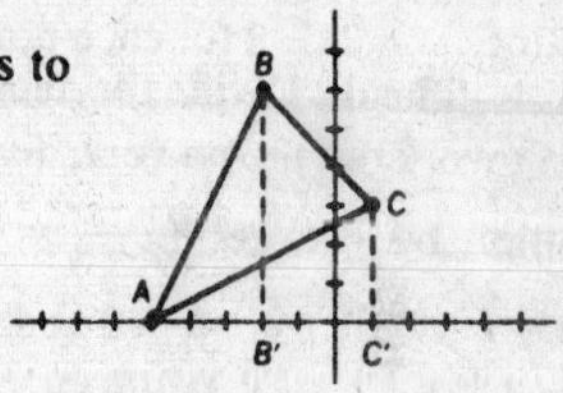

19. $\frac{3x - 6}{x} = 3 - \frac{6}{x}$ which will be positive as long as $3 > \frac{6}{x} \cdot \frac{6}{x}$ will be less than 3 when (1) x is negative, or (2) $x > 2$ (a).

20. Draw AP bisecting $\angle DAB$. $PC = x$ since $PADC$ is a parallelogram. $\angle APB$ has measure $a°$ since $\angle APB$ and $\angle C$ are corresponding angles. $PB = y$ since $\angle PAB$ and $\angle BPA$ have the same measure (b).

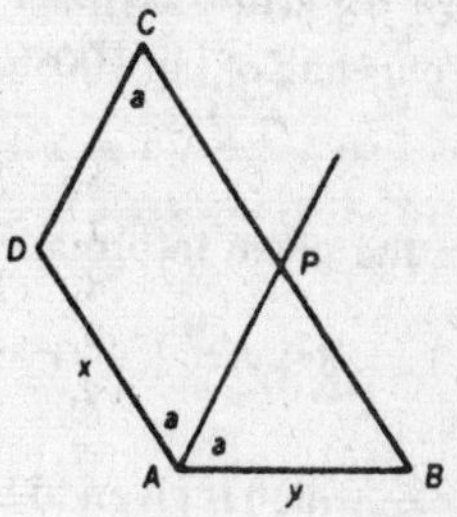

21. By direct division $5 * 3 = 2$ and $10 * 6 = 4$. $\frac{2}{4} = \frac{1}{2}$ (b)

22.
$$\begin{aligned} 0.4y &= 5 \\ 0.04y &= 0.5 \text{ (multiply by 0.1)} \\ + \quad 4y &= 50 \text{ (multiply original equation by 10)} \\ \hline 4.44y &= 55.5 \quad \text{(d)} \end{aligned}$$

23. The fractions can only be equal when $\frac{x}{1 - x} = 0$ which means $x = 0$ (c).

24. Only III (a).

25. $z = y + 1$ so $z^2 = y^2 + 2y + 1 = x^2 + y^2$. Thus $2y + 1 = x^2$ (b).

Mathematics Test B

1. Since the circumference is doubled, the radius is doubled. The area is based on the square of the radius. Squaring the factor of 2 thus introduced makes the area change by a factor of 4 (d).

2. $31(m - n) + (m - n) = 32(m - n)$. Thus the value of the expression is $32(m - n) - 32(m - n) = 0$ (c)

3. Multiply both sides of $3x = 2y$ by 3 to get $9x = 6y$. Since $6y = 7z$ then $9x = 7z$ by substitution. Divide the latter equation by $9z$ and you will get $\frac{x}{z} = \frac{7}{9}$ (b).

4. (d) and (e) can be excluded because greater values of x will increase the numerator and thereby the fraction. (a), (b) and (c) all have the same numerator so the least fraction will be the one with greatest denominator (a).

5. You might have added the fractions and divided the results, all of which wastes time. Multiply the original fraction by $\frac{30}{30}$ and you get $\frac{6+3}{2+6}$ (c).

6. The sum of the last three must be 9 more than the sum of the first three. You can see the pattern if we let x be the first of these integers.

$$\underbrace{x, x+1, x+2}_{3x+3}, \underbrace{x+3, x+4, x+5}_{3x+12} \quad \text{(e).}$$

7. This one is most easily done by first looking at the solutions. The numbers given can be tested very quickly in your head (c).

8. If the mid-point is farthest from the origin then the end-point will be as well, so you need not find any mid-points. You could crank out the distances by formula, but a quick sketch gets the results in less time.

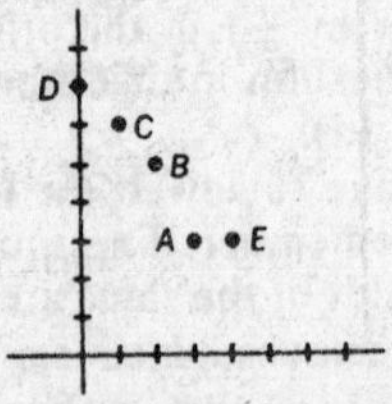

(d)

9. You can ignore the first two terms and get the result strictly from the definition given. The terms, starting with 5 are:

$$\_, \_, 5, 5+p, 5+2p, 5+3p, 5+4p.$$
$$5+4p = 17 \text{ so } p \text{ is 3 and the next term is 20.} \quad \text{(b)}$$

10. If xy is negative then one and only one of x and y is negative. Since $x > y$, it must be y (a).

11. $\frac{x+10}{2} = \frac{x}{2} + 5$ which will leave 5 when subtracted from $\frac{x}{2} + 10$ (a).

12. This is easy. Since each answer given uses only two or three terms ($n = 2$ or $n = 3$) you could write what the law states for the two cases and test.

$$1+3 = 2^2 \text{ and } 1+3+5 = 3^2 \text{ (a).}$$

13. This is easy. You have the length of the base, $15-4 = 11$, but need the height. The y-coordinate of b tells you the height. Since $y = 2x-8$ for each point of the line and $x = 15$ at B, $y = 22$. Area $= \frac{1}{2}(11)(22) = 121$ (b)

14. This is difficult. Divide the denominator into the numerator and the result is $y+1$ (a).

15. Don't work out the powers; divide first and you will get $1+4 = 5$ (d).

16. Multiply by $\frac{xy}{xy}$ to get $\frac{x^2y-x}{xy^2-y} = \frac{x(xy-1)}{y(xy-1)} = \frac{x}{y}$ (a).

17. If $a = b+3$ then $a-b = 3$ and $(a-b)^3 = 3^3$ (c).

18. $72 = 2\times2\times2\times3\times3$, $108 = 2\times2\times3\times3\times3$. By inspecting factors you can see that the greatest number which will divide both is $2\times2\times3\times3$ (e).

19. $(1.20L)(0.80W) = 0.96LW$ is the new area or a decrease of $0.04\,LW$ or 4 percent (c).

20. $\frac{3}{4}$ is $\frac{1}{2}$ plus half of $\frac{1}{2}$ or 100% plus 50% (e).

21. $\sqrt{1} = 1$ so $\sqrt{1+\sqrt{1}} = \sqrt{1+1} = \sqrt{2}$ which when squared gives 2 (b).

22. From the given information we can conclude:

$$x - 1 = 3^a; y = 1 + 3^{-a}; y = 1 + \frac{1}{3^a} = 1 + \frac{1}{x\text{-}1} = \frac{x-1}{x-1} + \frac{1}{x-1} = \frac{x}{x-1} \quad \text{(d)}.$$

23. $\frac{p^3}{3p} = \frac{p^2}{3}$ which is given to be 3. Thus $p^2 = 9$ and $p = 3$ (d).

24. From the three-part formula we can conclude $S(5) = 1, S(4) = 1, S(0) = 0$ so $1+1+0 = 2$ (d).

25. This question illustrates one of the pitfalls of spending too much time looking for non-routine methods of solution. The answer can be cranked out routinely in a few seconds.

$$5-[7-(9-11)] =$$
$$5-[7-(-2)] =$$
$$5-[7+2] =$$
$$5-9 = -4 \text{ (a).}$$

THE QUANTITATIVE COMPARISON QUESTION

10

- **Testing Tactics**
- **Long-Range Strategies**
- **Practice Exercises**
- **Answer Key**

TESTING TACTICS

About one third of the questions in the mathematics sections of the SAT are quantitative comparison questions. You may never have seen questions quite like these before, so they require some explanation. These questions do not ask you for the solution to a problem. Instead, you will be given two quantities. Sometimes you will also be given information about the two quantities to help you compare them. Then you must decide whether one of the quantities is greater than the other, or whether they are equal. Sometimes there will not be enough information for you to be able to make a decision. The directions for these questions are:

Questions 8–27 each consist of two quantities, one in Column A and one in Column B. You are to compare the two quantities and on the answer sheet blacken space

A if the quantity in Column A is greater;
B if the quantity in Column B is greater;
C if the two quantities are equal;
D If the relationship cannot be determined from the information given.

AN E RESPONSE WILL NOT BE SCORED.

EXAMPLES

	Column A	Column B	Answers
E1.	2×6	$2 + 6$	● Ⓑ Ⓒ Ⓓ Ⓔ
	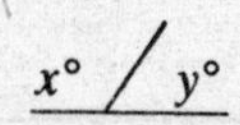		
E2.	$180 - x$	y	Ⓐ Ⓑ ● Ⓓ Ⓔ
E3.	$p - q$	$q - p$	Ⓐ Ⓑ Ⓒ ● Ⓔ

Notes:

1. In certain questions, information concerning one or both of the quantities to be compared is centered above the two columns.
2. In a given question, a symbol that appears in both columns represents the same thing in Column A as it does in Column B.
3. Letters such as x, n, and k stand for real numbers.

Read those directions again, and remind yourself that there are only FOUR possible answers to these questions. Every other question on the SAT has five answer choices. These are different. You must not choose (E) for your answer. If you do, your answer will not be scored, and you might as well have saved your time and skipped the question.

These questions reflect the contemporary emphasis on inequalities in school mathematics courses. In general, these questions require less time than the other mathematics questions, since they require less reading and, usually, less computation. You will, of course, have to do some problem-solving to find the correct answers to these questions, and most of the tactics that you would use for the regular multiple-choice questions can be used for these too. In addition, there are some tactics that apply particularly to the quantitative comparison questions.

TACTIC 1: DON'T ASSUME UNKNOWNS ARE POSITIVE NUMBERS

Be particularly careful not to forget about negative numbers and zero in these problems. What may look like a perfectly simple problem may actually be one that cannot be solved without more information, because you have no way of knowing if the numbers are positive or negative.

EXAMPLE:

Column A	Column B
$x + y$	$x - y$

Now if x and y are both positive numbers, the quantity in Column A is obviously larger. However, the problem does not specifically state that x and y are positive, so either or both could just as well be negative. Therefore, the correct answer is (D), the relationship cannot be determined.

TACTIC 2: DON'T ASSUME UNKNOWNS ARE WHOLE NUMBERS

Just as unknowns can represent either positive or negative numbers, so they can represent either whole numbers or fractions. Don't assume anything you haven't been told.

EXAMPLE:

Column A	Column B
Both x and y are positive numbers	
$\frac{x}{y}$	xy

You don't have to worry about positive and negative numbers here, but you haven't been told anything about whole numbers. If x and y are both whole numbers, the quantity in Column B is obviously larger; but if y is a fraction, the quantity in Column A is larger. You have another (D) answer.

Remember also, multiplication usually makes a number larger, but when you multiply it by a fraction less than 1, you make it smaller. And don't forget the reverse: when you divide a number by a fraction less than 1, you make it larger.

Here is a quick way to determine which of two fractions is larger when they have different denominators.

EXAMPLE:

Column A	Column B
$\frac{2}{3}$	$\frac{3}{4}$

Convert the two fractions so that they each have the same denominators and then evaluate their numerators, or change both numerators and evaluate their denominators. For example:

$$\frac{2}{3} = \frac{8}{12} \text{ and } \frac{3}{4} = \frac{9}{12} \text{ and } \frac{9}{12} > \frac{8}{12}$$

Or,

$$\frac{2}{3} = \frac{6}{9} \text{ and } \frac{3}{4} = \frac{6}{8} \text{ and } \frac{6}{8} > \frac{6}{9}$$

TACTIC 3: IF YOU ARE RUNNING OUT OF TIME, USE THESE SHORTCUTS TO IMPROVE YOUR GUESSING

1. Remember that the questions get harder as they go along. If a problem towards the end looks very easy, either you are a math whiz or the question is a trap. In fact, the answer is probably (D), "the relationship cannot be determined."

EXAMPLE:

Column A	Column B
$0.6x$	$0.07x$

If you looked at this question quickly, you might think they were testing you on your knowledge of decimals, and jump to the conclusion that the answer is (A) because 0.6 is larger than 0.07. But who told you that x represented a positive number? Who told you $x \neq 0$? The answer is (D).

2. If the question requires complicated computations, the answer is probably (C), the two quantities are equal. Think about this one for a moment, and you will see that this is the only way the test makers can make sure you don't get the right answer by mistake. If Column A had 256×639, and Column B had 229×732, and you did the arithmetic accurately, you would end up with 163,584 for Column A, and 167,628 for Column B, and you would be correct when you chose (B) for your answer. But if you made a mistake, and ended up with 163,554 for Column A, you would still choose the correct answer (B). The only way the test makers can make sure that a mistake in arithmetic will lead you to the wrong answer choice is to make (C) the correct answer.

3. When a problem involves straightforward computation, eliminate choice (D), which cannot possibly be correct. Even if you now have to guess, you have improved your chances of guessing correctly.

LONG-RANGE STRATEGIES

The preparation you do for the mathematics section as a whole will help you prepare for the quantitative comparison questions. The same areas of arithmetic, algebra, and geometry appear on both parts of the test. You can do the practice exercises that appear later in this chapter to help you get used to the format of these questions.

In addition, review the following principles involving inequalities:

1. You may add or subtract the same quantity from both sides of an inequality without altering its solution set.
   If $x > y$, then $x - y > 0$.
2. You may multiply or divide an inequality by the same POSITIVE quantity without altering its solution set.
   If $\frac{a}{4} > 1$, then $a > 4$.
3. If you multiply or divide an inequality by a NEGATIVE number, then you must reverse the direction of the inequality sign.
   If $-2x > 3$, then $x < \frac{-3}{2}$.
4. If unequal quantities are added to unequal quantities of the same order, the result is unequal in the same order.
   If $a > b$ and $c > d$, then $a + c > b + d$.
5. You may take the square root of both sides of the inequality without changing the direction of the inequality. (Note: You may only take square roots of a positive number.)
6. You may square both sides of an inequality if both sides are positive. The direction of the inequality remains the same. If both sides of an inequality are negative, you must switch the direction of the inequality.
7. If the first of three quantities is greater than the second, and the second is greater than the third, then the first is greater than the third.
   If $a > b$ and $b > c$, then $a > c$.
8. The sum of the lengths of any two sides of a triangle is greater than the length of the third side.
9. If two sides of a triangle are unequal, then the angles opposite those sides are unequal. The greater angle lies opposite the greater side.
10. The exterior angle of a triangle is greater than either remote interior angle.

$c > a$ and
$c > d$

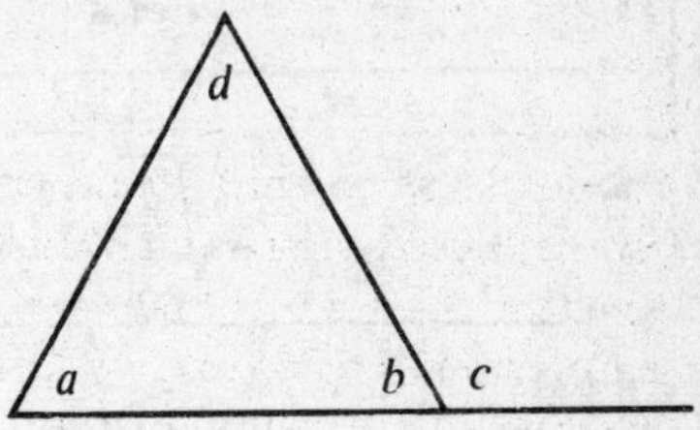

PRACTICE EXERCISES

Questions 1-142 each consist of two quantities, one in Column A and one in Column B. You are to compare the two quantities and on the answer sheet blacken space

A if the quantity in Column A is greater;
B if the quantity in Column B is greater;
C if the two quantities are equal;
D If the relationship cannot be determined from the information given.

AN E RESPONSE WILL NOT BE SCORED.

EXAMPLES

	Column A	Column B	Answers
E1.	2×6	$2 + 6$	● (B) (C) (D) (E)
E2.	$180 - x$	y	(A) (B) ● (D) (E)
E3.	$p - q$	$q - p$	(A) (B) (C) ● (E)

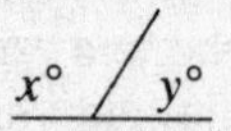

Notes:
1. In certain questions, information concerning one or both of the quantities to be compared is centered above the two columns.
2. In a given question, a symbol that appears in both columns represents the same thing in Column A as it does in Column B.
3. Letters such as x, n, and k stand for real numbers.

	COLUMN A		COLUMN B	
1.	3^2		2^3	**1.** (A) (B) (C) (D) (E)
2.	$\dfrac{6 + \frac{3}{4}}{2 - \frac{5}{4}}$		$(3)^2$	**2.** (A) (B) (C) (D) (E)
3.	⅓ of 8		66⅔% of 4	**3.** (A) (B) (C) (D) (E)
4.	$\sqrt{\frac{1}{4}} + \sqrt{\frac{1}{25}}$		$\sqrt{\frac{1}{4} + \frac{1}{25}}$	**4.** (A) (B) (C) (D) (E)
5.	$2x - 18y$	$x = 3$ and $y = \frac{1}{6}$	$3x - 36y$	**5.** (A) (B) (C) (D) (E)
6.	the average of $\sqrt{0.49}$, $\frac{3}{4}$, and 0.8		75%	**6.** (A) (B) (C) (D) (E)
7.	$2B(A + C)$	$B = 0$ $A > 1$ $C > 1$	$A(B + C)$	**7.** (A) (B) (C) (D) (E)

	COLUMN A	COLUMN B	
8.	$\frac{n + a}{a}$	$\frac{n}{a} + 1$	**8.** Ⓐ Ⓑ Ⓒ Ⓓ Ⓔ
9.	$\sqrt{\frac{1}{.25}}$	4	**9.** Ⓐ Ⓑ Ⓒ Ⓓ Ⓔ

10. $x < 0$ and $y < 0$

	COLUMN A	COLUMN B	
	$x + y$	$x - y$	**10.** Ⓐ Ⓑ Ⓒ Ⓓ Ⓔ

11. In triangle ABC $\angle ACB \doteq 60$

	COLUMN A	COLUMN B	
	$\angle B$	$\angle A$	**11.** Ⓐ Ⓑ Ⓒ Ⓓ Ⓔ
12.	Michael has 5 green marbles and the same number of red marbles. The number of red marbles in his collection is ½ the number of white marbles and ⅓ the number of blue ones.	Philip has 35 marbles in his collection.	**12.** Ⓐ Ⓑ Ⓒ Ⓓ Ⓔ
13.	The number of posts needed by Mr. A. to hold a wire fence 120 feet long if he places posts 12 feet apart in a straight line.	Mr. B uses 10 posts to support a similar wire fence.	**13.** Ⓐ Ⓑ Ⓒ Ⓓ Ⓔ

14. $0 < x < 10$
$0 < y < 12$

	COLUMN A	COLUMN B	
	x	y	**14.** Ⓐ Ⓑ Ⓒ Ⓓ Ⓔ

15. $a = 1$ and $b = -1$

	COLUMN A	COLUMN B	
	$\frac{x(a + b)}{v}$	$\frac{2x(a + b)}{v}$	**15.** Ⓐ Ⓑ Ⓒ Ⓓ Ⓔ

16. Triangle ABC

	COLUMN A	COLUMN B	
	$AB + BC$	AC	**16.** Ⓐ Ⓑ Ⓒ Ⓓ Ⓔ

17.

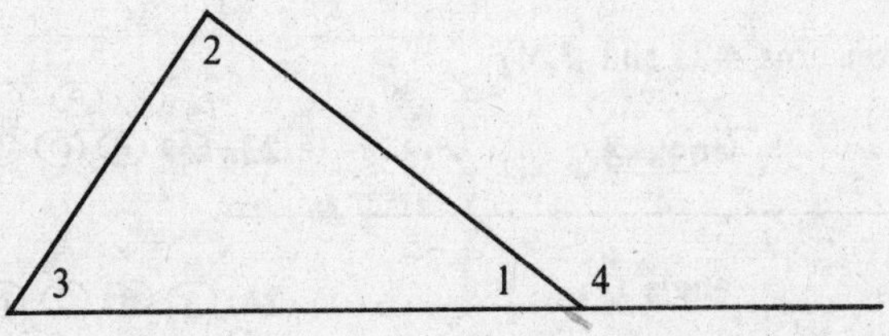

	COLUMN A	COLUMN B	
	$\angle 4$	$\angle 3$	**17.** Ⓐ Ⓑ Ⓒ Ⓓ Ⓔ

	COLUMN A	COLUMN B	

18.

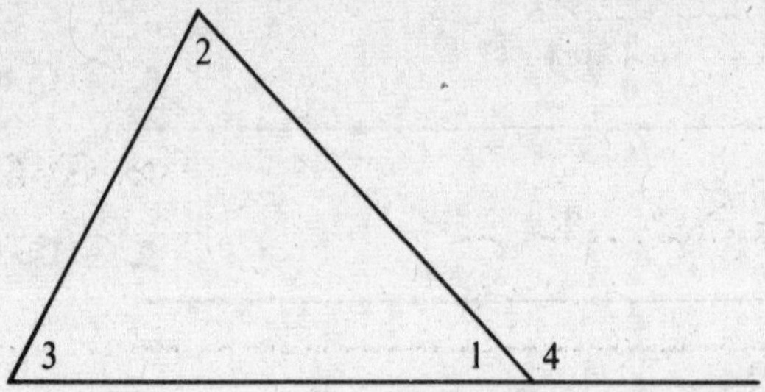

	$\angle 4 + \angle 1$	$\angle 1 + \angle 2 + \angle 3$	**18.** Ⓐ Ⓑ Ⓒ Ⓓ Ⓔ
19.	**Mark received either an 80% or a 90% on each of four physics tests.**	**Sara's average for these four physics tests was 85%.**	**19.** Ⓐ Ⓑ Ⓒ Ⓓ Ⓔ
20.	**Ann earns $10 a day for clerical work in the dean's office.**	**Joan earns $50 a week for work in the dean's office during vacation periods.**	**20.** Ⓐ Ⓑ Ⓒ Ⓓ Ⓔ
21.	**Last week Martin received $10 in commission for selling 100 copies of a magazine.**	**Last week Miguel sold 100 copies of this magazine. He received his basic salary of $5. per week plus a commission of 2¢ for each of the first 25 copies sold, 3¢ for each of the next 25 copies sold and 4¢ for each copy thereafter.**	**21.** Ⓐ Ⓑ Ⓒ Ⓓ Ⓔ

22.

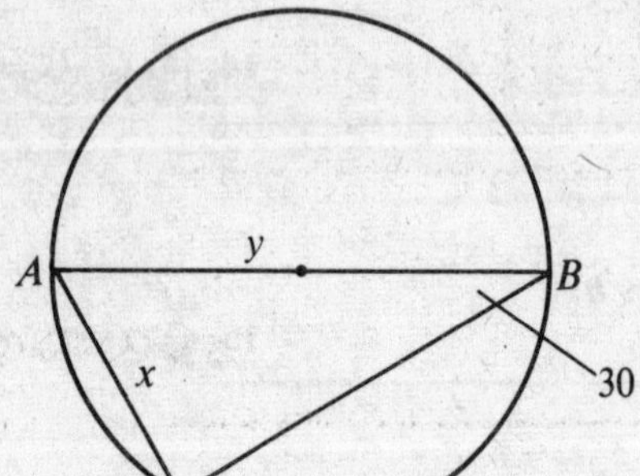

$\angle B \doteq 30$

	$2x$	y	**22.** Ⓐ Ⓑ Ⓒ Ⓓ Ⓔ

In triangle ABC, $AC < AB$ and $AC > BC$ (this concerns #23 and #24)

23.	angle B	angle A	**23.** Ⓐ Ⓑ Ⓒ Ⓓ Ⓔ
24.	angle B	angle C	**24.** Ⓐ Ⓑ Ⓒ Ⓓ Ⓔ

	COLUMN A	COLUMN B	
25.	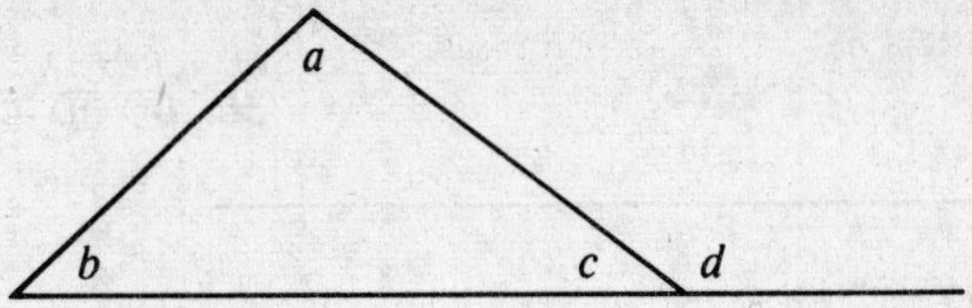 b	$d - c$	25. Ⓐ Ⓑ Ⓒ Ⓓ Ⓔ
26.	$(5)(144)(6)$	$(12^2)(5^2)$	26. Ⓐ Ⓑ Ⓒ Ⓓ Ⓔ
27.	$7 \times 5 \times 8 \times 9$	$63 \times 4 \times 10$	27. Ⓐ Ⓑ Ⓒ Ⓓ Ⓔ
28.	$\frac{(369)(72)}{(3)(4)(5)}$	$\frac{(10)(8)(369)}{(2)(3)(4)}$	28. Ⓐ Ⓑ Ⓒ Ⓓ Ⓔ
29.	$\frac{0.9}{2}$	$\frac{3}{10}$	29. Ⓐ Ⓑ Ⓒ Ⓓ Ⓔ
30.	$\sqrt{14.4}$	1.2	30. Ⓐ Ⓑ Ⓒ Ⓓ Ⓔ
31.	$\sqrt{\frac{1}{9} + \frac{1}{16}}$	$\sqrt{\frac{1}{16}} + \sqrt{\frac{1}{9}}$	31. Ⓐ Ⓑ Ⓒ Ⓓ Ⓔ
32.	$\frac{1}{0.5}$	$\sqrt{4}$	32. Ⓐ Ⓑ Ⓒ Ⓓ Ⓔ
33.	$\left(\frac{1}{0.07}\right)^2$	$\frac{1}{7}$	33. Ⓐ Ⓑ Ⓒ Ⓓ Ⓔ
34.	$3^{n+2} = 27$ n	3	34. Ⓐ Ⓑ Ⓒ Ⓓ Ⓔ
35.	$\sqrt{0.16}$	0.1π	35. Ⓐ Ⓑ Ⓒ Ⓓ Ⓔ

	COLUMN A		COLUMN B	
36.	$\frac{1}{\sqrt{25}}$		$\frac{1}{(0.5)}$	36. Ⓐ Ⓑ Ⓒ Ⓓ Ⓔ
37.	x	$3 - 2x < 9$	-3	37. Ⓐ Ⓑ Ⓒ Ⓓ Ⓔ
38.	$a \div b$	$a < 0$ and $b < 0$	$a + b$	38. Ⓐ Ⓑ Ⓒ Ⓓ Ⓔ
39.	$2y$	$x > 0$ and $y > 0$; $\frac{x}{y} > 2$	x	39. Ⓐ Ⓑ Ⓒ Ⓓ Ⓔ
40.	$\sqrt{0.25}$		$\frac{1}{4}$	40. Ⓐ Ⓑ Ⓒ Ⓓ Ⓔ
41.	0.425		$3\sqrt{0.0196}$	41. Ⓐ Ⓑ Ⓒ Ⓓ Ⓔ
42.	$\sqrt[3]{8} + 1^5$		$5\sqrt{8}$	42. Ⓐ Ⓑ Ⓒ Ⓓ Ⓔ
43.	5		$\sqrt{9} + \sqrt{16}$	43. Ⓐ Ⓑ Ⓒ Ⓓ Ⓔ
44.	$(0.3)^2$		$\sqrt{0.09}$	44. Ⓐ Ⓑ Ⓒ Ⓓ Ⓔ
45.	a^3		a^2	45. Ⓐ Ⓑ Ⓒ Ⓓ Ⓔ
46.	$n + 1$		$n - 1$	46. Ⓐ Ⓑ Ⓒ Ⓓ Ⓔ
47.	$10 - \frac{10}{0.1}$		-90	47. Ⓐ Ⓑ Ⓒ Ⓓ Ⓔ

	COLUMN A		COLUMN B	
48.	$\frac{5}{x}$	$x = \frac{1}{y+z}$	$5(y+z)$	**48.** Ⓐ Ⓑ Ⓒ Ⓓ Ⓔ
49.	$\frac{1}{z^5}$	$-10 < z < -1$	$\frac{1}{z^4}$	**49.** Ⓐ Ⓑ Ⓒ Ⓓ Ⓔ
50.	$b - a$	$1<a<5$ $1<b<5$	$a - b$	**50.** Ⓐ Ⓑ Ⓒ Ⓓ Ⓔ
51.	$\frac{x}{y} + 5$	$0 < x < 20$ $0 < y < 24$	$\frac{y}{x} + 10$	**51.** Ⓐ Ⓑ Ⓒ Ⓓ Ⓔ
52.	a	$a : b = 1$	b	**52.** Ⓐ Ⓑ Ⓒ Ⓓ Ⓔ
53.	$\sqrt{2}$		$\frac{2}{\sqrt{2}}$	**53.** Ⓐ Ⓑ Ⓒ Ⓓ Ⓔ
54.	$x^3 - 1$	$x < 0$	1	**54.** Ⓐ Ⓑ Ⓒ Ⓓ Ⓔ
55.	$\frac{\frac{a}{2}}{\frac{2}{a}}$	$a > 1$	$\frac{a^2}{2}$	**55.** Ⓐ Ⓑ Ⓒ Ⓓ Ⓔ
56.	x^2		x^3	**56.** Ⓐ Ⓑ Ⓒ Ⓓ Ⓔ

	COLUMN A		COLUMN B	
57.		$\frac{1}{x} = \sqrt{0.04}$		57. Ⓐ Ⓑ Ⓒ Ⓓ Ⓔ
	x		25	
58.	$(x+y)^2$		$(x-y)^2$	58. Ⓐ Ⓑ Ⓒ Ⓓ Ⓔ
59.	$\frac{a}{b}$		$\frac{a}{b} \cdot \frac{b}{a}$	59. Ⓐ Ⓑ Ⓒ Ⓓ Ⓔ
60.	$(y+10)-(y-2x-30)$		$(x+160)-(120-x)$	60. Ⓐ Ⓑ Ⓒ Ⓓ Ⓔ
61.	$\frac{x+y}{y}$		$\frac{x}{y}+1$	61. Ⓐ Ⓑ Ⓒ Ⓓ Ⓔ
62.		$x = 2,\ y = 1,\ z = 0$		62. Ⓐ Ⓑ Ⓒ Ⓓ Ⓔ
	$4x + 2y - 3z^2$		10	
63.	$\frac{x^2 - y^2}{x}$		$\frac{x^2 + 2xy + y^2}{x - y}$	63. Ⓐ Ⓑ Ⓒ Ⓓ Ⓔ
64.		$x = 2,\ y = 3$		64. Ⓐ Ⓑ Ⓒ Ⓓ Ⓔ
	$\dfrac{xy}{\frac{1}{x} + \frac{1}{y}}$		7	
65.		$a > 0$		65. Ⓐ Ⓑ Ⓒ Ⓓ Ⓔ
	$\frac{5a-3}{6a} + \frac{3a+7}{10a}$		$\frac{17a+3}{15a}$	
66.		$x + 13 = 4y$ $3x + 4y = 25$		66. Ⓐ Ⓑ Ⓒ Ⓓ Ⓔ
	x		y	

	COLUMN A		COLUMN B	
67.		$x^2 + 25 = 10x$ $y^2 + 36 = 12y$		67. Ⓐ Ⓑ Ⓒ Ⓓ Ⓔ
	x		y	
68.		$x = 2, y = 3, z = 4$		68. Ⓐ Ⓑ Ⓒ Ⓓ Ⓔ
	$\frac{x^2 + y^2}{z^2}$		$\frac{x + y}{z}$	
69.		$a - 2b = 11$ $5a + 4b = 27$		69. Ⓐ Ⓑ Ⓒ Ⓓ Ⓔ
	$5a$		35	
70.		$(x - y)^2 = 16$ $x^2 + y^2 = 58$		70. Ⓐ Ⓑ Ⓒ Ⓓ Ⓔ
	xy		$(x - y)^2$	
71.		$x\sqrt{0.01} = 1$		
	x		10	71. Ⓐ Ⓑ Ⓒ Ⓓ Ⓔ
72.	$\frac{x}{y} + \frac{a}{b}$		$\frac{xb + ya}{by}$	72. Ⓐ Ⓑ Ⓒ Ⓓ Ⓔ
73.	$(a + b)(a - b)$		$a^2 - b^2$	73. Ⓐ Ⓑ Ⓒ Ⓓ Ⓔ
74.		$x^2 = 4$ $y^2 = 9$		74. Ⓐ Ⓑ Ⓒ Ⓓ Ⓔ
	x		y	
75.	0.3%		$\frac{3}{1000}$	75. Ⓐ Ⓑ Ⓒ Ⓓ Ⓔ

	COLUMN A	COLUMN B	
76.	0.04% of 600	4% of 600	76. Ⓐ Ⓑ Ⓒ Ⓓ Ⓔ
77.	102	102% of 100	77. Ⓐ Ⓑ Ⓒ Ⓓ Ⓔ
78.	List price of $500 with discounts of 10% and 20%	List price of $490 less 20%	78. Ⓐ Ⓑ Ⓒ Ⓓ Ⓔ
79.	The average weight of Lori, Michael, and Sara is 45 pounds		79. Ⓐ Ⓑ Ⓒ Ⓓ Ⓔ
	The combined weight of Lori and Michael	The combined weight of Lori and Sara	
80.	Percent increase from 800 to 1400	Percent increase from 1400 to 2000	80. Ⓐ Ⓑ Ⓒ Ⓓ Ⓔ
81.	The distance covered in 3 hours at an average rate of 40 miles per hour	The distance covered traveling at 50 miles per hour for one hour and 30 miles per hour for the next 2 hours	81. Ⓐ Ⓑ Ⓒ Ⓓ Ⓔ
82.	The average rate of a motorcyclist who covers a mile in one minute and 20 seconds	The average rate of a motorist traveling for one hour and covering 45 miles	82. Ⓐ Ⓑ Ⓒ Ⓓ Ⓔ
83.	The work done by m men in h hours	The work done by n men in h hours	83. Ⓐ Ⓑ Ⓒ Ⓓ Ⓔ
84.	The record of a team that won W games and lost L games	The record of a team that won W games of the $W + L$ games played	84. Ⓐ Ⓑ Ⓒ Ⓓ Ⓔ
85.	Perimeter of square $ABCD = 8a$		85. Ⓐ Ⓑ Ⓒ Ⓓ Ⓔ
	Side of $ABCD$	$2a$	

	COLUMN A	COLUMN B	
86.	Side of square $ABCD = 4$		
	Area of $ABCD$	Perimeter of $ABCD$	**86.** Ⓐ Ⓑ Ⓒ Ⓓ Ⓔ

87.

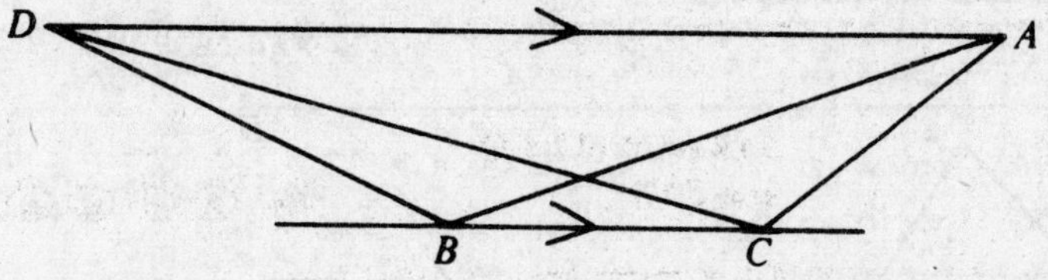

Area of $\Delta\, ABC$	Area of $\Delta\, DBC$

87. Ⓐ Ⓑ Ⓒ Ⓓ Ⓔ

88.

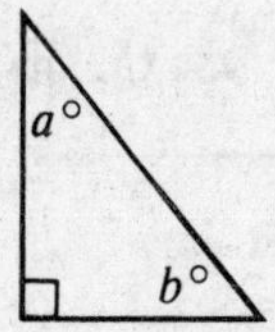

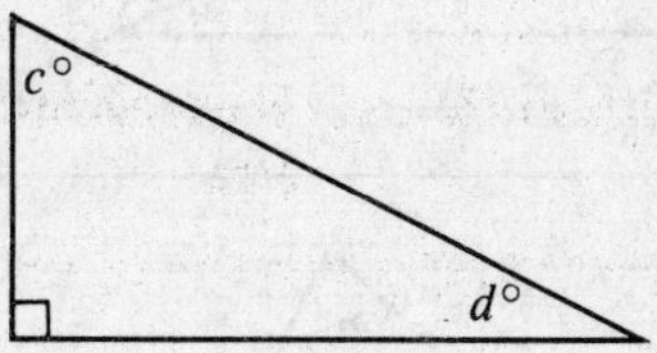

$a + b$	$c + d$

88. Ⓐ Ⓑ Ⓒ Ⓓ Ⓔ

89.

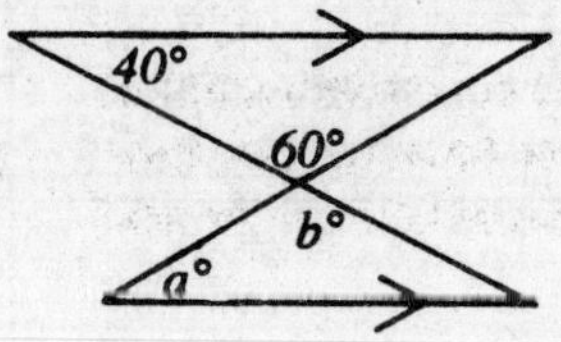

a	b

89. Ⓐ Ⓑ Ⓒ Ⓓ Ⓔ

90.

$a + b$	$c + d$

90. Ⓐ Ⓑ Ⓒ Ⓓ Ⓔ

91.

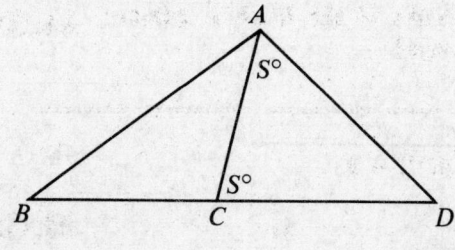

BD	$AD + BC$

91. Ⓐ Ⓑ Ⓒ Ⓓ Ⓔ

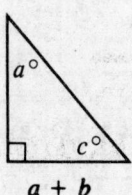

	COLUMN A		COLUMN B	

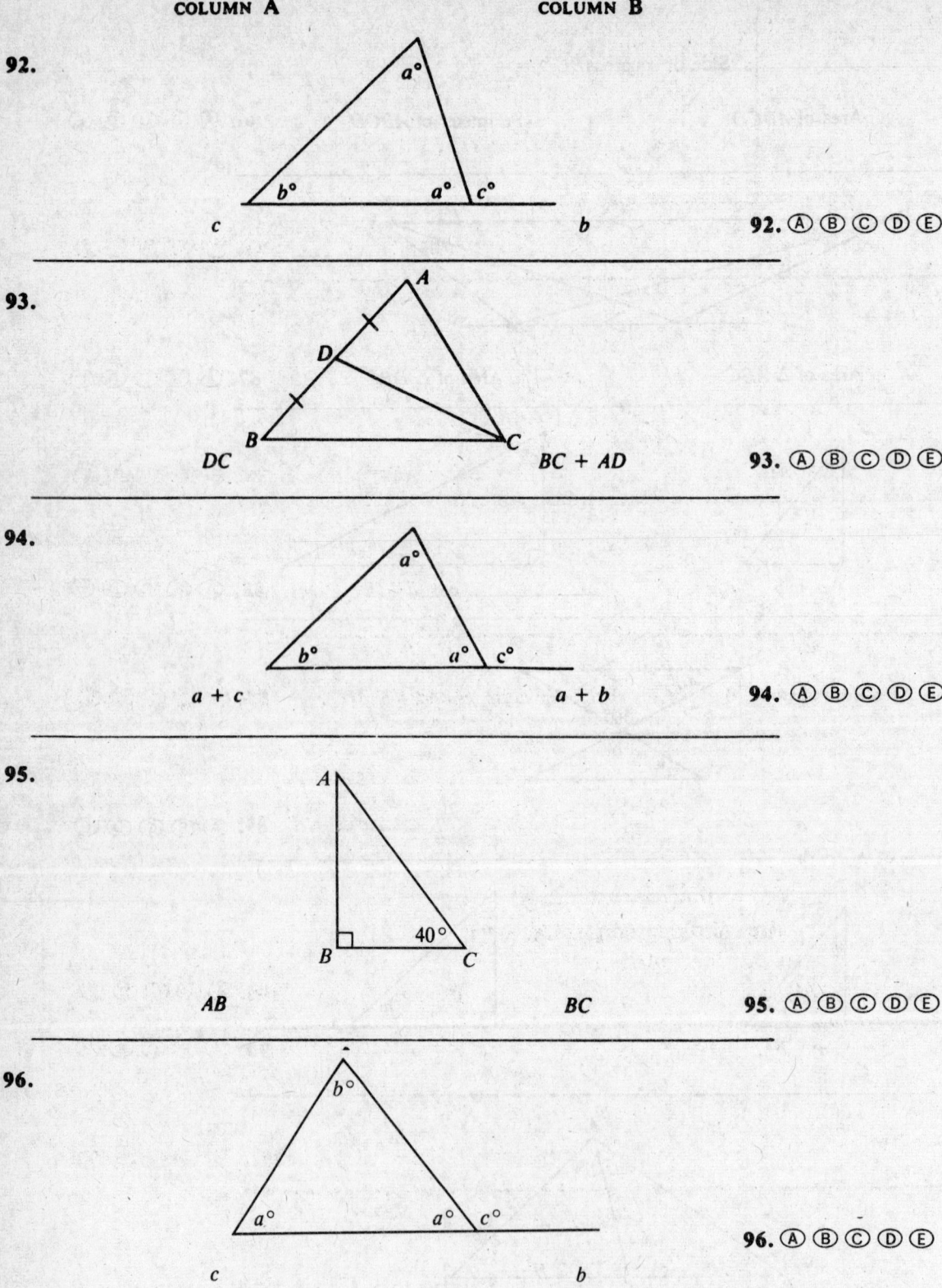

92.

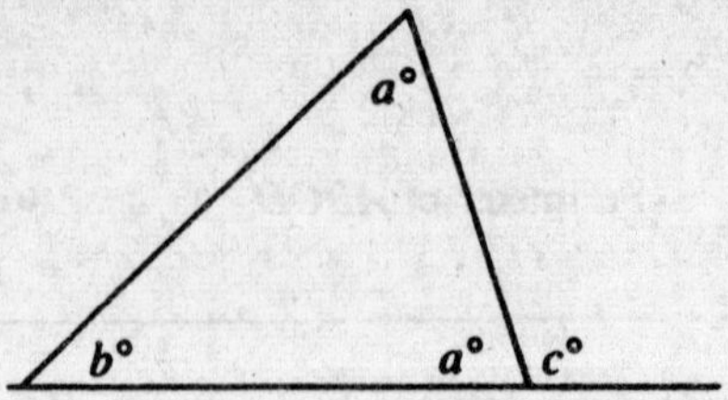

c | b | **92.** Ⓐ Ⓑ Ⓒ Ⓓ Ⓔ

93.

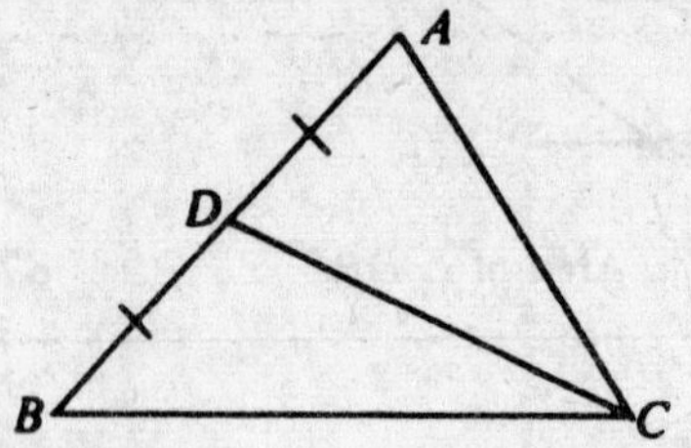

DC | $BC + AD$ | **93.** Ⓐ Ⓑ Ⓒ Ⓓ Ⓔ

94.

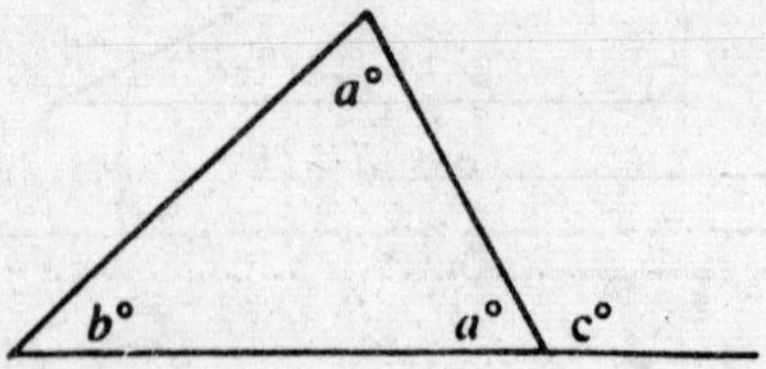

$a + c$ | $a + b$ | **94.** Ⓐ Ⓑ Ⓒ Ⓓ Ⓔ

95.

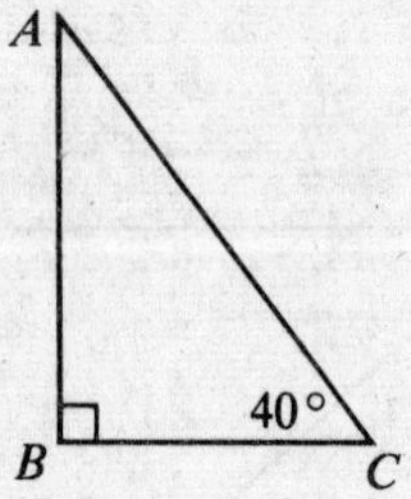

AB | BC | **95.** Ⓐ Ⓑ Ⓒ Ⓓ Ⓔ

96.

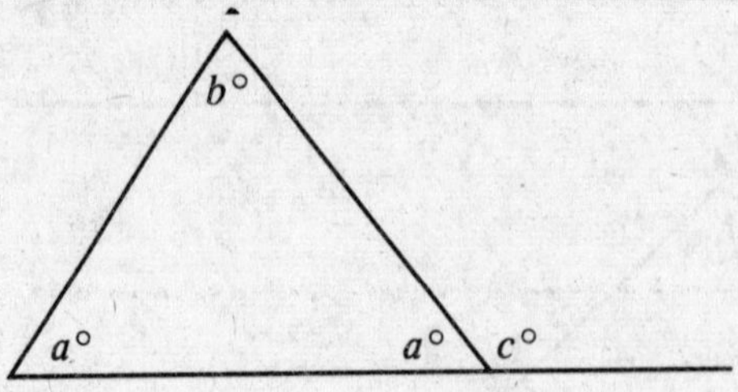

c | b | **96.** Ⓐ Ⓑ Ⓒ Ⓓ Ⓔ

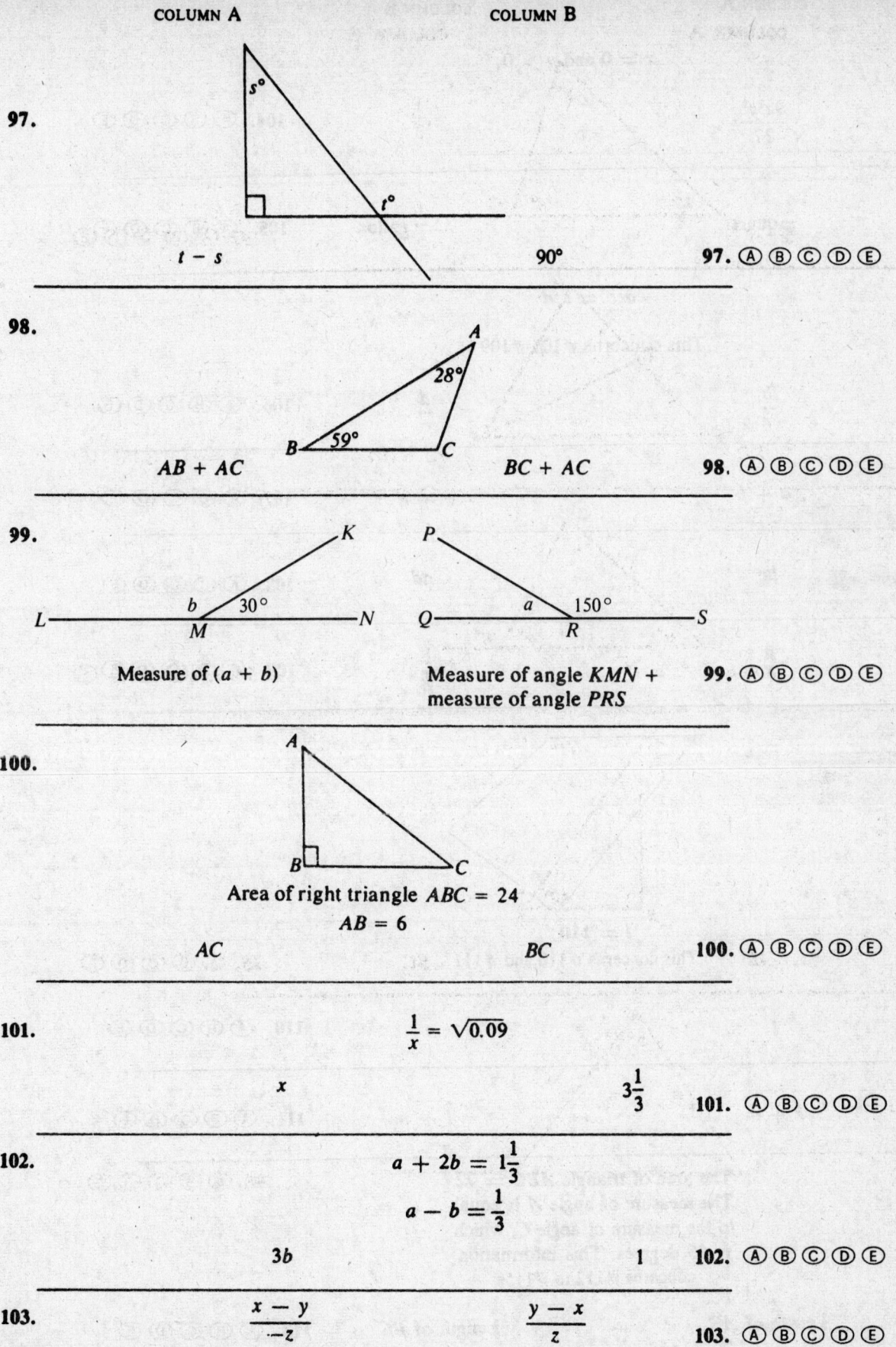

	COLUMN A	COLUMN B	

97.

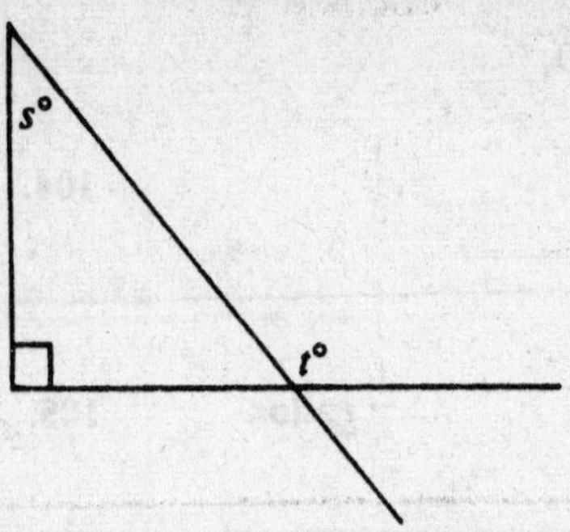

$t - s$	90°	97. Ⓐ Ⓑ Ⓒ Ⓓ Ⓔ

98.

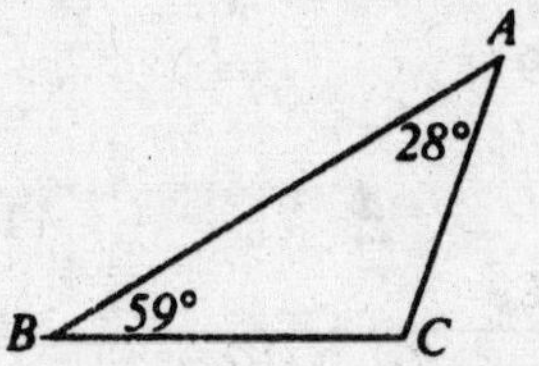

$AB + AC$	$BC + AC$	98. Ⓐ Ⓑ Ⓒ Ⓓ Ⓔ

99.

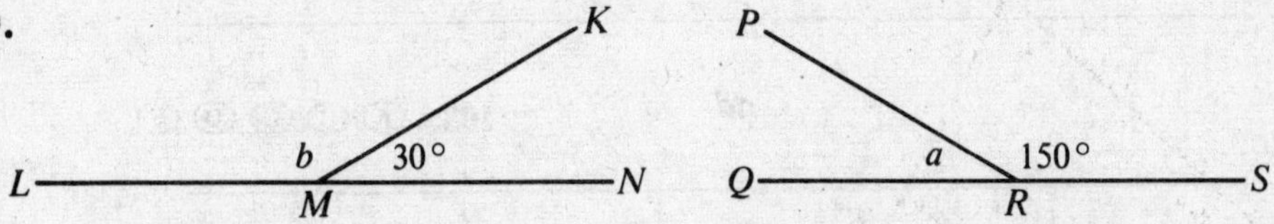

Measure of $(a + b)$	Measure of angle KMN + measure of angle PRS	99. Ⓐ Ⓑ Ⓒ Ⓓ Ⓔ

100.

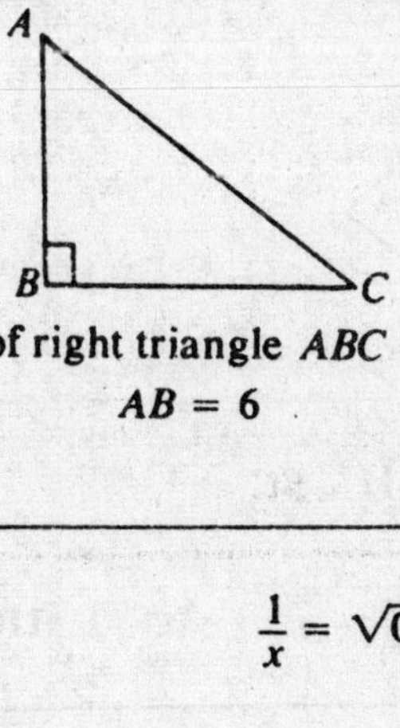

Area of right triangle $ABC = 24$

$AB = 6$

AC	BC	100. Ⓐ Ⓑ Ⓒ Ⓓ Ⓔ

101. $\frac{1}{x} = \sqrt{0.09}$

x	$3\frac{1}{3}$	101. Ⓐ Ⓑ Ⓒ Ⓓ Ⓔ

102. $a + 2b = 1\frac{1}{3}$

$a - b = \frac{1}{3}$

$3b$	1	102. Ⓐ Ⓑ Ⓒ Ⓓ Ⓔ

103. $\frac{x - y}{-z}$	$\frac{y - x}{z}$	103. Ⓐ Ⓑ Ⓒ Ⓓ Ⓔ

	COLUMN A		COLUMN B	
104.		$x = 0$ and $y > 0$		
	$\frac{9x^2y^2}{27}$		$\frac{1}{3}$	104. Ⓐ Ⓑ Ⓒ Ⓓ Ⓔ
105.	$\frac{4}{5}$ quart		$\frac{1}{5}$ gallon	105. Ⓐ Ⓑ Ⓒ Ⓓ Ⓔ
106.		$a:b = c:d$ This concerns #106-#109		
	$\frac{b}{a}$		$\frac{d}{c}$	106. Ⓐ Ⓑ Ⓒ Ⓓ Ⓔ
107.	$a + b$		$c + d$	107. Ⓐ Ⓑ Ⓒ Ⓓ Ⓔ
108.	bc		ad	108. Ⓐ Ⓑ Ⓒ Ⓓ Ⓔ
109.	$\frac{a}{c}$		$\frac{b}{d}$	109. Ⓐ Ⓑ Ⓒ Ⓓ Ⓔ

110.

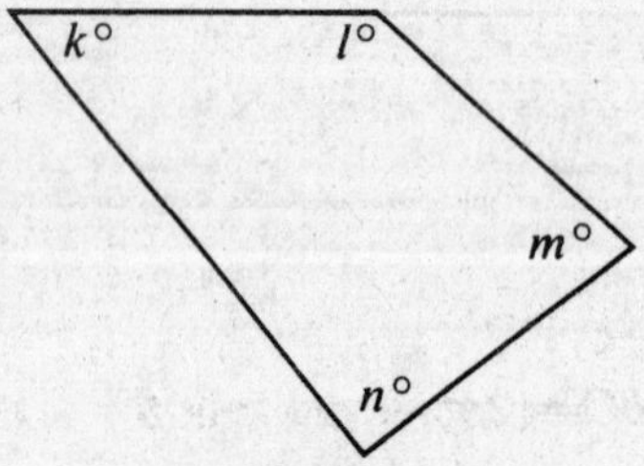

$l = 110$

This concerns #110 and #111

	COLUMN A		COLUMN B	
110.	l		n	110. Ⓐ Ⓑ Ⓒ Ⓓ Ⓔ
111.	$k + m$		$l + n$	111. Ⓐ Ⓑ Ⓒ Ⓓ Ⓔ
112.		The area of triangle $ABC = 72$ The measure of angle A is equal to the measure of angle C, which is 45 degrees. This information concerns #112 to #115		
	Length of AB		Length of BC	112. Ⓐ Ⓑ Ⓒ Ⓓ Ⓔ

	COLUMN A	COLUMN B	
113.	Length of *AB*	Length of *AC*	113. Ⓐ Ⓑ Ⓒ Ⓓ Ⓔ
114.	Length of *AB*	12	114. Ⓐ Ⓑ Ⓒ Ⓓ Ⓔ
115.	Length of *AC* + length of *BC*	Length of *AB*	115. Ⓐ Ⓑ Ⓒ Ⓓ Ⓔ
116.	The average of $\sqrt{0.81}$, 60%, $1\frac{1}{2}$	3	116. Ⓐ Ⓑ Ⓒ Ⓓ Ⓔ

---

117. $7x = 196$

	COLUMN A	COLUMN B	
	$\frac{x}{7}$	4	117. Ⓐ Ⓑ Ⓒ Ⓓ Ⓔ
118.	(2)(4)(6)(8)(10)(12)(14)	(16)(14)(12)(10)(8)(6)	118. Ⓐ Ⓑ Ⓒ Ⓓ Ⓔ

---

119. $A > B$
$B > C$

	COLUMN A	COLUMN B	
	$2A$	$B + C$	119. Ⓐ Ⓑ Ⓒ Ⓓ Ⓔ

---

120. $5 \times 5 \times 5 \times 5 = 10 \times 10 \times T$

	COLUMN A	COLUMN B	
	T	10	120. Ⓐ Ⓑ Ⓒ Ⓓ Ⓔ

---

121. $\frac{\text{Area of cirle } A}{\text{Area of circle } B} = \frac{1}{4}$

	COLUMN A	COLUMN B	
	Four times the radius of circle *A*	The radius of circle *B*	121. Ⓐ Ⓑ Ⓒ Ⓓ Ⓔ

---

122. Point *O* (5,3) is the center of a circle. Point *P* (5,7) lies on the circle

	COLUMN A	COLUMN B	
	The circumference of the circle	8π	122. Ⓐ Ⓑ Ⓒ Ⓓ Ⓔ

123.

ABC and *DEF* are straight lines
$a = 20$ and $b = 160$

	COLUMN A	COLUMN B	
	$a + x$	$x + y$	123. Ⓐ Ⓑ Ⓒ Ⓓ Ⓔ

	COLUMN A	COLUMN B	

124.

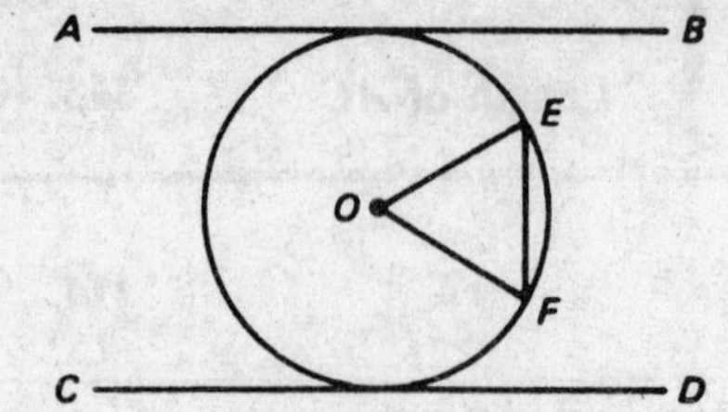

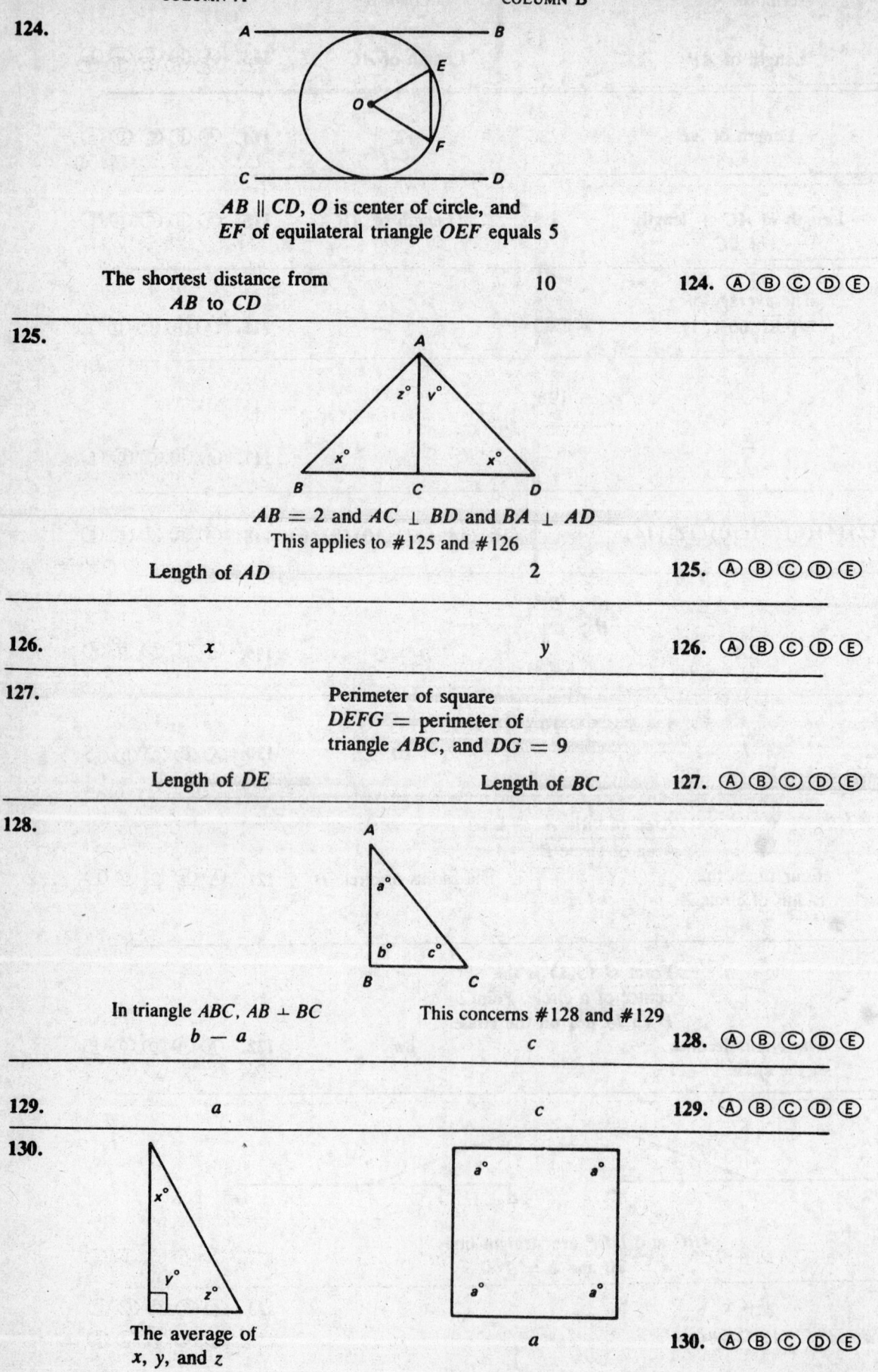

$AB \parallel CD$, O is center of circle, and EF of equilateral triangle OEF equals 5

The shortest distance from AB to CD — 10 — 124. Ⓐ Ⓑ Ⓒ Ⓓ Ⓔ

125.

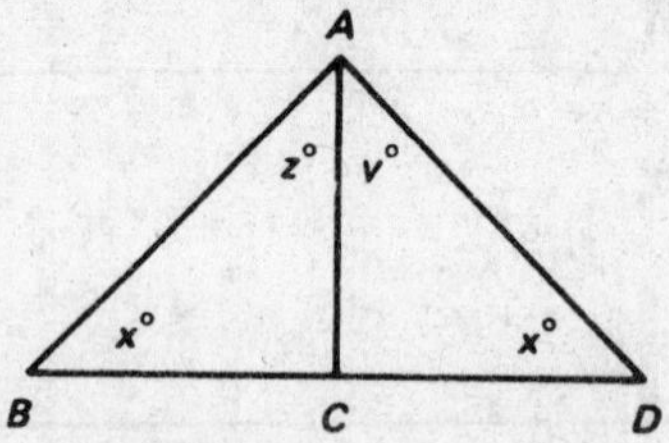

$AB = 2$ and $AC \perp BD$ and $BA \perp AD$

This applies to #125 and #126

Length of AD — 2 — 125. Ⓐ Ⓑ Ⓒ Ⓓ Ⓔ

---

126. x — y — 126. Ⓐ Ⓑ Ⓒ Ⓓ Ⓔ

127.

Perimeter of square $DEFG$ = perimeter of triangle ABC, and $DG = 9$

Length of DE — Length of BC — 127. Ⓐ Ⓑ Ⓒ Ⓓ Ⓔ

128.

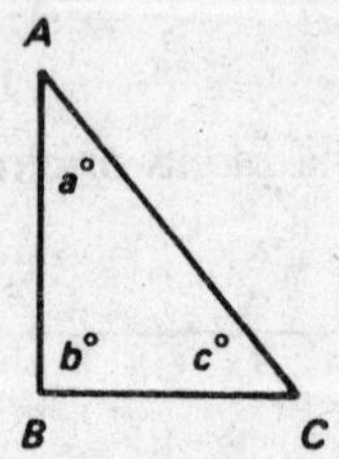

In triangle ABC, $AB \perp BC$ — This concerns #128 and #129

$b - a$ — c — 128. Ⓐ Ⓑ Ⓒ Ⓓ Ⓔ

---

129. a — c — 129. Ⓐ Ⓑ Ⓒ Ⓓ Ⓔ

130.

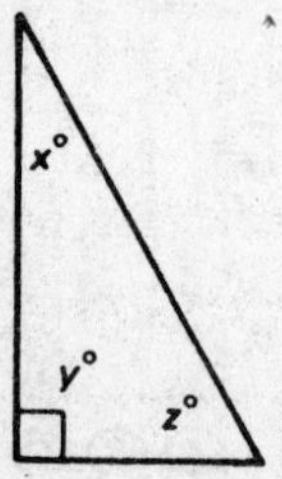

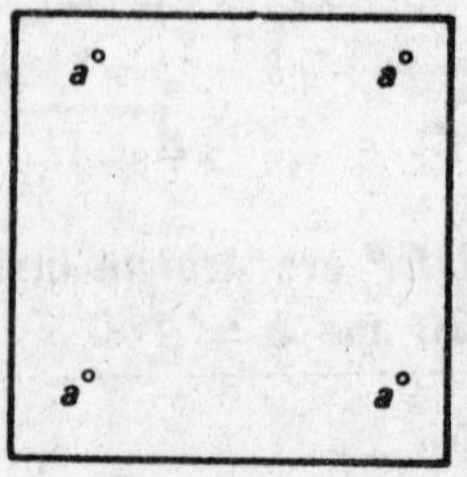

The average of x, y, and z — a — 130. Ⓐ Ⓑ Ⓒ Ⓓ Ⓔ

	COLUMN A		COLUMN B	
131.		$xy = 45$		
	$x + y$		14	**131.** Ⓐ Ⓑ Ⓒ Ⓓ Ⓔ
132.		$x^2 = 25$ $y^2 = 36$		
	x		y	**132.** Ⓐ Ⓑ Ⓒ Ⓓ Ⓔ
133.		$4a^3b^2c = 0$		
	a		b	**133.** Ⓐ Ⓑ Ⓒ Ⓓ Ⓔ

134.

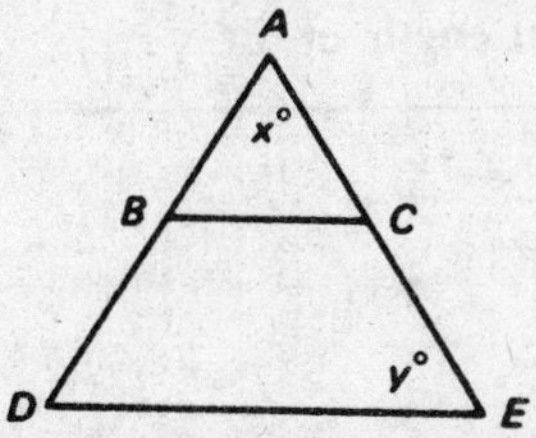

In triangle ABC, $AC = BC$
$BC \parallel DE$ and $x = 65$

x		y	**134.** Ⓐ Ⓑ Ⓒ Ⓓ Ⓔ

135.

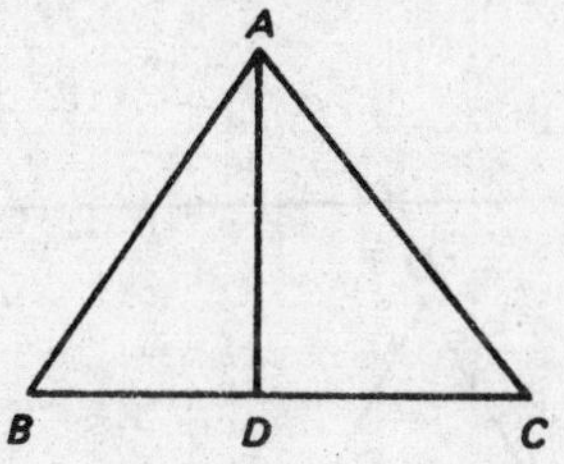

Area of $ABC = 20$ in^2
$AD = 5''$ and $AD \perp BC$

4 inches		Length of DC	**135.** Ⓐ Ⓑ Ⓒ Ⓓ Ⓔ

136.

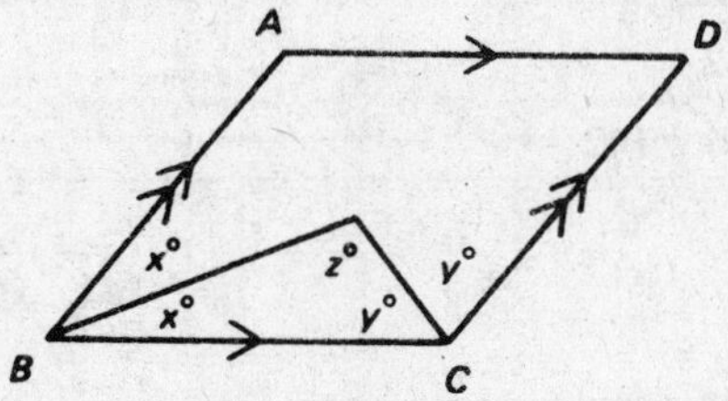

$y = 50$

$z - y$		40	**136.** Ⓐ Ⓑ Ⓒ Ⓓ Ⓔ

137.

The area of rectangle
$ABCD = 120$, and $AD = 40$

This concerns #137 and #138

$AD + DC$		$BC + AB$	**137.** Ⓐ Ⓑ Ⓒ Ⓓ Ⓔ

138.	$AB + BC$		AC	**138.** Ⓐ Ⓑ Ⓒ Ⓓ Ⓔ

COLUMN A		COLUMN B	

139.

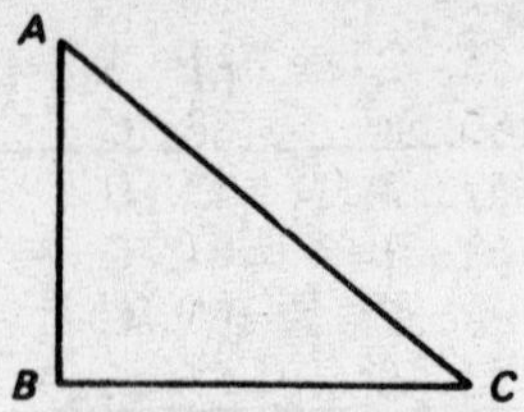

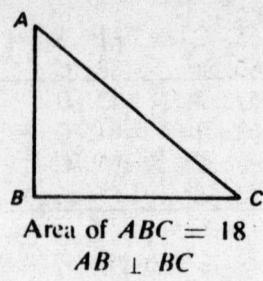

Area of $ABC = 18$
$AB \perp BC$

Length of AB	Length of BC	139. Ⓐ Ⓑ Ⓒ Ⓓ Ⓔ

140.

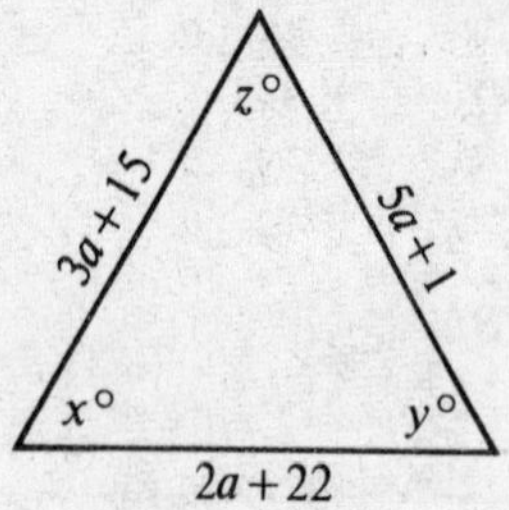

$x = y = z$

a	7	140. Ⓐ Ⓑ Ⓒ Ⓓ Ⓔ

141.

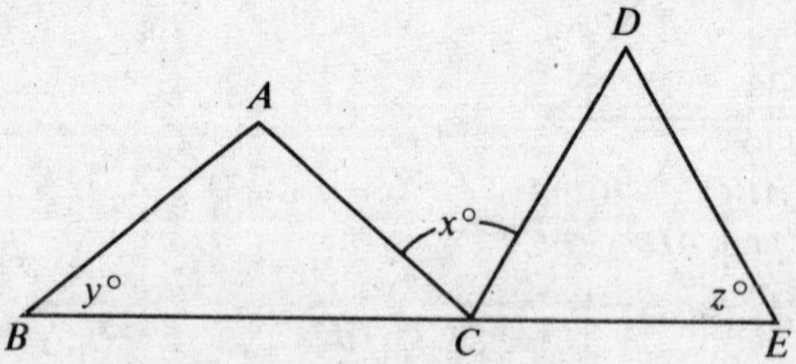

$AB = AC$, $DC = DE$,
$y = 59$, and $z = 62$
This concerns #141 and #142

x	y	141. Ⓐ Ⓑ Ⓒ Ⓓ Ⓔ

142.	x	z	142. Ⓐ Ⓑ Ⓒ Ⓓ Ⓔ

ANSWER KEY

1. **A**	17. **A**	33. **A**	49. **B**	65. **C**	81. **A**	97. **C**	113. **B**	129. **D**
2. **C**	18. **C**	34. **B**	50. **D**	66. **B**	82. **C**	98. **A**	114. **C**	130. **B**
3. **C**	19. **D**	35. **A**	51. **D**	67. **B**	83. **D**	99. **C**	115. **A**	131. **D**
4. **A**	20. **D**	36. **B**	52. **C**	68. **B**	84. **C**	100. **A**	116. **B**	132. **D**
5. **C**	21. **A**	37. **A**	53. **C**	69. **C**	85. **C**	101. **C**	117. **C**	133. **D**
6. **C**	22. **C**	38. **A**	54. **B**	70. **A**	86. **C**	102. **C**	118. **B**	134. **A**
7. **B**	23. **A**	39. **B**	55. **B**	71. **C**	87. **C**	103. **C**	119. **A**	135. **D**
8. **C**	24. **B**	40. **A**	56. **D**	72. **C**	88. **C**	104. **B**	120. **B**	136. **C**
9. **B**	25. **C**	41. **A**	57. **B**	73. **C**	89. **A**	105. **C**	121. **A**	137. **C**
10. **B**	26. **A**	42. **B**	58. **D**	74. **D**	90. **D**	106. **C**	122. **C**	138. **A**
11. **D**	27. **C**	43. **B**	59. **D**	75. **C**	91. **C**	107. **D**	123. **C**	139. **D**
12. **C**	28. **B**	44. **B**	60. **C**	76. **B**	92. **A**	108. **C**	124. **C**	140. **C**
13. **A**	29. **A**	45. **D**	61. **C**	77. **C**	93. **B**	109. **C**	125. **C**	141. **C**
14. **D**	30. **A**	46. **A**	62. **C**	78. **B**	94. **A**	110. **D**	126. **C**	142. **B**
15. **C**	31. **B**	47. **C**	63. **D**	79. **D**	95. **B**	111. **D**	127. **D**	
16. **A**	32. **C**	48. **C**	64. **A**	80. **A**	96. **A**	112. **C**	128. **C**	

REVIEWING MATHEMATICS 11

- **Arithmetic Review**
- **Algebra Review**
- **Geometry Review**
- **Practice Exercises**
- **Answer Keys**

The questions on a mathematics aptitude test, of course, are about mathematics. Thus, the better you are able to use basic mathematics, the better you will be able to do on the mathematics sections of the Scholastic Aptitude Test (SAT). The people who make up the mathematics sections of the SAT want to determine how fast you work, how accurately you can read questions and follow instructions, and how well you can understand basic mathematical concepts.

You can increase your grasp of basic mathematics through practice. In this chapter you will find a complete review of the mathematics covered on the SAT. You will also find practice exercises on a variety of math topics to help you sharpen your skill in handling basic mathematics.

FUNDAMENTAL OPERATIONS

The Real Numbers

The Real Numbers, often called Signed Numbers, are basic to the study of algebra. Even the best students make mistakes using them, however, and you should find review and drill helpful.

The real number system, which is used in elementary mathematics, contains positive numbers, negative numbers, and zero (zero is neither positive nor negative). For each real number there is a number which is its "opposite." Two numbers are opposite if their sum is zero. The opposite of a positive number is a negative number, and vice versa.

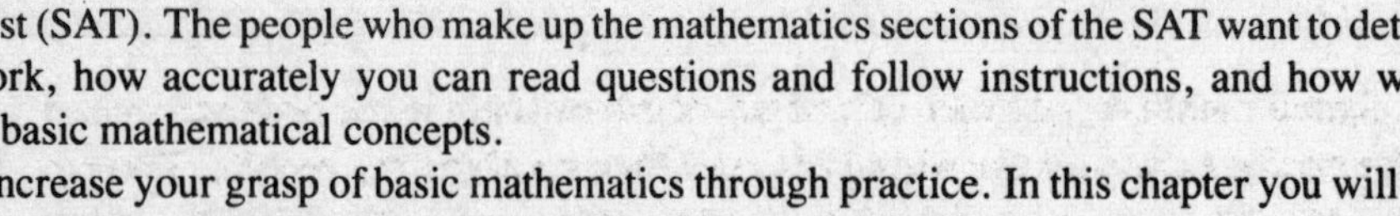

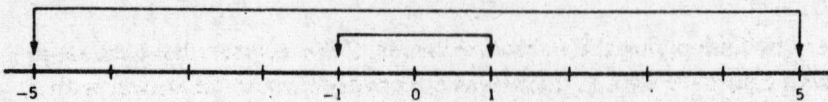

We indicate the opposite of a number by putting a negative sign (−) in front of it. Thus the opposite of 3 is −3 and $3 + (-3) = 0$. The opposite of −3 is $-(-3)$ which is another name for 3.

- • 1. The opposite of 7 is ?
- • 2. The opposite of −4 is ?

Be sure you know that $-(-a) = a$ for all real numbers. The opposite of 0 (written −0) is 0.

• *Answers given on page 378.*

Positive numbers are usually not written with a sign, but they can be written with a positive sign (+) when it is useful. Thus 3 and +3 mean the same thing.

Every simple signed number has two parts: a sign (+ or −) and a numeral representing its *absolute value*. The absolute value of an expression with variables in it can be tricky to work with but, for simple numerals, it is the value which is left when the sign is removed. Thus the absolute value of both 3 and −3 is just 3.

- 3. The absolute value of 11 is ?
- 4. The absolute value of −7 is ?

Signed numbers can be added, subtracted, multiplied, and divided. ***You must learn how to do all of the operations quickly in your head.***

To add numbers with the same sign, add their absolute values and write the result with the common sign.

- 5. $14+12=?$
- 6. $-8+(-9)=?$

To add numbers with opposite signs, find their absolute values, subtract the lesser absolute value from the greater, and then write the result with the same sign as that of the number with the greater absolute value. For example, to add −36 and +14, subtract 14 from 36 to get 22 and write the result as −22 since the −36 had the greater absolute value.

- 7. $+36+(-14)=?$
- 8. $-50+33=?$
- 9. $50+(-33)=?$
- 10. $16+(-16)=?$

To add three or more signed numbers you can, of course, combine them in the order given but it is simpler to add all the positives and all the negatives, and then combine the results. Thus to add $-22+37+64-18-46+13-85$, we add $37+64+13=114$ and $-22-18-46-85=-171$. Then we combine the results:

- 11. $-171+114=?$

Subtraction is based on the following property:

$$a-b=a+(-b)$$

This means that subtracting a number is the same as adding its opposite. The number being subtracted is called the *subtrahend,* so to subtract signed numbers, simply change the sign of the subtrahend and add.

- 12. $27-(-18)=27+18=?$
- 13. $-37-(-29)=-37+29=?$
- 14. $-26-14=-26+(-14)=?$
- 15. $42-(-42)=?$
- 16. $-18-15=?$

Multiply signed numbers by multiplying their absolute values. If the numbers have the same sign, write your answer with a positive sign. If their signs are opposite, write the answer with a negative sign.

- 17. $(+8)(-7)=?$
- 18. $(-4)(-3)=?$
- 19. $(12)(10)=?$
- 20. $(-7)(16)=?$

• *Answers given on page 378.*

Division follows the same rule: divide absolute values and choose a positive sign for your answer if the original signs were the same, or use a negative sign if they were opposite:

- • 21. $35 \div 7 = ?$
- • 22. $16 \div (-4) = ?$
- • 23. $-27 \div 3 = ?$
- • 24. $-36 \div (-9) = ?$

ALGEBRAIC OPERATIONS

The Language of Algebra

In algebra we use letters to represent numbers or sets of numbers. Such letters are called *variables*. When two variables, or a numeral and a variable, are written with no sign of operation between them, we mean that the numbers they represent are to be multiplied:

- • 25. $4abc$ means ?

When two or more numerals and variables represent numbers which are being multiplied to yield a product, these numerals and variables are called the *factors* of the product. *To factor* means to find the multipliers which yield the product. Thus 6 and 5 are factors of 30. Bear in mind, however, that 6 can also be factored into 2 times 3. To be completely factored, the number 30 must be written as $2 \times 3 \times 5$. The latter is called the *prime factorization* of 30. The numbers 2, 3, and 5 are called *primes* because they have no positive integers as factors except themselves and 1. Note, however, that 1 is not considered to be a prime even though it follows the definition.

Find the factors of the following:

- • 26. $15 = ?$
- • 27. $6ab = ?$
- • 28. $a^2 + 2ab + b^2 = ?$
- • 29. $a^2 - b^2 = ?$

Any factor of a product is called the *coefficient* of the remaining factors, but the usual use of this word is to designate the numerical factor.

Find the coefficients:

- • 30. The coefficient of $6ab$ is ?
- • 31. The coefficient of $-5x^2$ is ?
- • 32. The coefficient of x^4y^2 is ?

Exponents are used to indicate the number of times a numeral or variable is used as a factor.

- • 33. 2^5 means ?
- • 34. x^2y^4 means ?

When an exponent is not a positive integer (a number belonging to the set {1, 2, 3, 4, . . .}) it has a different use which we will review later.

A *monomial* is an expression consisting of one term; it is the product of a set of numerals and variables. Examples of monomials are $14x$, $6ab$, and $21/b$ (which can be written as $21(1/b)$, a product). If two monomials have the same variables as factors, and these variables have the same exponents, they are called *similar* or *like* terms.

Decide whether or not each of the following is a pair of like terms:

- • 35. $4a^2c$ and $5ac^2$
- • 36. $4a^2c$ and $5a^2c$
- • 37. $4a^2$ and $4c^2$

• *Answers given on page 378.*

A *binomial* is the sum or difference of two monomials. Decide whether each of these is a binomial:

• 38. $3x+4y$

• 39. $26x^2y-72xy$

A *trinomial* has three terms such as

$$9x^2+4xy-2y^3,\text{ and}$$

$$2x^7y-16x+2y.$$

Monomials, binomials and trinomials all belong to a family of expressions called *polynomials*. A polynomial may have any number of terms.

Addition and Subtraction

Most algebraic additions and subtractions are carried out with the aid of a simple pattern known as the *distributive law*:

$$ab+ac=a(b+c),$$

or its corollary:

$$ab-ac=a(b-c).$$

• 40. $2x+3x=(2+3)x=?$

• 41. $8x^2y+(-3x^2y)=[8+(-3)]x^2y=?$

• 42. $4x^2-6x^2=?$

• 43. $3abc^2+abc^2=(3+1)abc^2=?$

When adding polynomials you will make fewer mistakes if you arrange the like terms in vertical columns. For example, to add $3x^2+9x-4$ and $-7x^2-4x+8$, arrange your work as follows:

$$\begin{array}{r} 3x^2+9x-4 \\ \underline{-7x^2-4x+8} \\ -4x^2+5x+4 \end{array}$$

Add the following polynomials:

• 44. $(8x^3+3x^2-x+1)+(-2x^2+7x-3)$

When two polynomials are to be subtracted, arrange them in vertical columns according to like terms and change the sign of every term in the subtrahend. For example, to subtract $9x^2-3x-5$ from $2x^2+3x-8$, change the signs of the first polynomial as follows: $-9x^2+3x+5$, and then add.

$$\begin{array}{r} 2x^2+3x-8 \\ \underline{-9x^2+3x+5} \\ -7x^2+6x-3 \end{array}$$

Try the following exercise:

• 45. Subtract $3x^2+2x-5$ from $5x^2-10x-4$

Multiplication

Before you can multiply polynomials you must master the multiplication of variables, and thus you must understand a simple rule of exponents.

• 46. $x^2\cdot x^3=x\cdot x\cdot x\cdot x\cdot x=?$

• *Answers given on page 378.*

The positive integer used as an exponent counts the number of times the variable (its base) is used as a factor. When multiplying factors which have the same base, add their exponents.

- 47. $x^5 \cdot x^7 = ?$
- 48. $(x^2y)(x^3y^2) = ?$

To multiply monomials, multiply their coefficients and add the exponents of variables with the same base.

- 49. $(6x^2)(5x^4) = (6 \cdot 5)(x^2 \cdot x^4) = ?$
- 50. $(6x)(-5x^4) = ?$

To multiply a polynomial by a monomial, multiply each term of the polynomial by the monomial.

- 51. $3x^2(5x^3 + 2x - 3y) = ?$
- 52. $-4x^2y(2x^2 - 3xy - 4y^2) = ?$

To multiply a polynomial by a polynomial, multiply each term of one polynomial by each term of the other and combine like terms.

- 53. $(3x^2 - 2x - 7)(2x - 4) = ?$

A special case of multiplying polynomials is worth studying separately because of its use in factoring. To multiply a binomial by a binomial, note first how the pairs of terms are named:

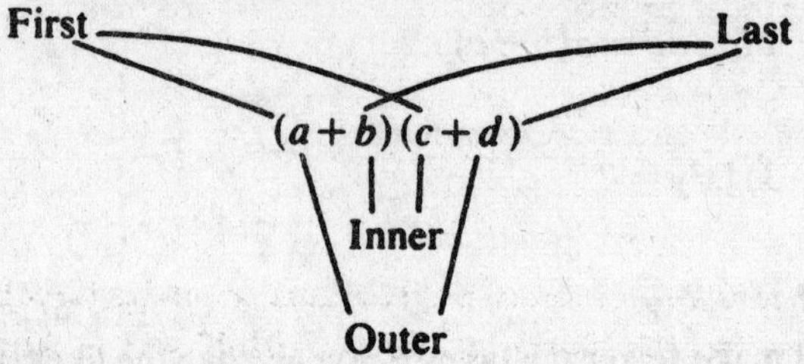

Multiply the binomials term by term in the order F, O, I, L. Frequently the O and I terms combine to make the product a trinomial or a binomial.

- 54. $(x+3)(x-2) = ?$
- 55. $(x-3)(x+3) = ?$

Removing Parentheses

Parentheses are used as grouping symbols and as indicators of multiplication. Often it is necessary to remove the parentheses to simplify expressions which have grouped terms. If the parentheses are preceded by a positive sign they may be removed with no further alteration.

- 56. $(x+y) + (3x-2y) = ?$

If the parentheses are preceded by a negative sign, then they may be removed only if the signs of each term inside the parentheses are changed to the opposite sign.

- 57. $(x+y) - (3x-2y) = x+y-3x+2y = ?$
- 58. $(3x^2+2x) - (4x^2-3x+5) = ?$

If the parentheses are preceded by a multiplier, carry out the multiplication first and then use one of the rules just mentioned.

- 59. $(x+y) - 5(x+y) = (x+y) - (5x+5y) = ?$
- 60. $4(3x^2+2x) - 8(x^2+3x-2) = ?$

• *Answers given on page 378.*

When additional grouping symbols are needed, we use brackets, [ ], and braces, { }. If grouping symbols appear within other sets, remove one set at a time starting with the innermost.

- • 61. $4x-\{2x-3[(x+2)-(3-x)]\}=$
  $4x-\{2x-3[x+2-3+x]\}=$
  $4x-\{2x-3[2x-1]\}=$
  $4x-\{2x-6x+3\}=?$

Division

To divide a monomial by a monomial, divide the coefficients algebraically and subtract exponents of factors which have the same base.

- • 62. $x^6 \div x^2 = ?$
- • 63. $-15x^6y^3 \div 3x^2y = ?$
- • 64. $-18x^3yz^2 \div (-6xyz) = ?$

To divide a polynomial by a monomial, divide each term of the dividend by the divisor.

- • 65. $(-18x^4-6x^3+2x^2)\div 2x^2=$
  $\dfrac{-18x^4-6x^3+2x^2}{2x^2}= \quad \dfrac{-18x^4}{2x^2}+\dfrac{-6x^3}{2x^2}+\dfrac{2x^2}{2x^2}=?$
- • 66. $\dfrac{6x^{3c}-8x^{2c}}{2x^c}=?$

Factoring

To factor an expression means to find two or more expressions whose product is the given expression. Every expression can be written as the product of itself and 1. Any expression which cannot be factored in any other way is called *prime*.

Type 1. **To factor a polynomial which has a common monomial factor, find the greatest monomial which will divide into each term of the polynomial. This is one factor. Divide the polynomial by this factor to obtain the other factor.**

- • 67. Factor $4x^3y^3-22xy^2$

Type 2. **To factor an expression which is the difference of two perfect squares, find the square root of each term. The sum of the two square roots is one factor and the difference of the two square roots is the other factor. This factoring rule can be easily visualized as:**

$$a^2-b^2=(a+b)(a-b).$$

- • 68. Factor x^2-64

Type 3. **Trinomials of the form ax^2+bx+c. When two binomials of the form $mx+n$ and $px+q$ are multiplied the result is a trinomial with the rather complicated-looking form:**

$$mpx^2+(mq+np)x+nq.$$

When the actual multiplication is carried out, of course, the result is not nearly so awesome since the real numbers m, n, p and q all combine to produce the simplified form

$$ax^2+bx+c.$$

For example: $(3x+2)(5x+7)=3\cdot 5\cdot x^2+(3\cdot 7+2\cdot 5)x+2\cdot 7$
But the latter is simply $15x^2+31x+14$.

Note that the first coefficient of the trinomial is the product of the first coefficients of the factors, and the last coefficient of the trinomial is the product of the last coefficients of the factors. The middle coefficient is the sum of the products of the first and last coefficients taken in a special order: the product of the inner terms and the product of the outer terms.

• *Answers given on page 378.*

To factor you must be able to guess how this process is reversed. Your clues are the factors of the first, ax^2, and last, c, terms of the trinomial ax^2+bx+c. Since several possible factorizations of ax^2 and c may be possible, some of your work will be by trial and error.

- • 69. Factor $x^2+8x+12$
  (Note that the factors of x^2 are just x and x, but the factors of 12 which you must try are, in pairs, 12 and 1, -12 and -1, 4 and 3, -4 and -3, 6 and 2, -6 and -2. Your job is to determine which of these will combine to give the coefficient of the middle term, 8.)
- • 70. Factor x^2-6x+8
- • 71. Factor $x^2-3x-10$

Roots and Radicals

If $x^2 = y$ then x is called a *square root* of y. Thus 10 is a square root of 100 since $10^2 = 100$. Also, -10 is a square root of 100 since $(-10)^2 = 100$. Every positive number has two square roots which are always the opposites of each other. Zero has only one square root, 0. Negative numbers have no square roots in the real number system.

The *principal square root* of a number is its positive square root if the number has two roots. This principal root is indicated by the radical sign, $\sqrt{}$. Thus $\sqrt{100} = 10$ and $\sqrt{49} = 7$.

The *negative square root* is indicated by a negative sign in front of the radical.

- • 72. $-\sqrt{100} = ?$

A *radical* is an indicated root of a number or expression. The number under the radical sign is called the *radicand*. The index of the root is written as a small number in the "vee" of the radical sign and indicates the number of equal factors which must be multiplied to give the radicand. Thus $\sqrt[3]{8}$ means:

$$\sqrt[3]{8}\cdot\sqrt[3]{8}\cdot\sqrt[3]{8} = 8.$$

Since $2\cdot 2\cdot 2 = 8$ it follows that $\sqrt[3]{8} = 2$.

Similarly, $\sqrt[5]{2}$ means:

$$\sqrt[5]{2}\cdot\sqrt[5]{2}\cdot\sqrt[5]{2}\cdot\sqrt[5]{2}\cdot\sqrt[5]{2} = 2.$$

But there is no whole number or ratio of integers for which the latter equation is true so $\sqrt[5]{2}$ is an irrational number.

Where no index is written as in $\sqrt{100}$ the number 2 is understood. Thus $\sqrt{100} = \sqrt[2]{100}$.

A *rational* number is a number which can be expressed as the ratio of two integers (where the denominator is not 0). Thus $2\frac{1}{3}$ is a rational number since $2\frac{1}{3} = \frac{7}{3}$.

An *irrational* number is a number which cannot be expressed as the ratio of two integers. Examples encountered in elementary mathematics include $\sqrt{2}$, $\sqrt[3]{5}$, and π.

Expressions involving radicals can often be simplified. Look first to see if there are factors which can be removed from the radicand.

- • 73. $\sqrt{8} = \sqrt{4\cdot 2} = \sqrt{4}\sqrt{2} = ?$
- • 74. $\sqrt{75} = \sqrt{25\cdot 3} = ?$
- • 75. $\sqrt[3]{54} = ?$

When all radicals in a sum or difference have been simplified, like radicals are combined.

- • 76. $2\sqrt{5}+5\sqrt{5} = (2+5)\sqrt{5} = ?$
- • 77. $6\sqrt{3}-3\sqrt{3} = (6-3)\sqrt{3} = ?$
- • 78. $\sqrt{50}+\sqrt{2} = ?$
- • 79. $3\sqrt{27}+\sqrt{108} = ?$
- • 80. $4\sqrt{32}-6\sqrt{8} = ?$

• *Answers given on page 378.*

To simplify the radicals we have actually used a law that looks like this:

$$\sqrt{ab} = \sqrt{a}\sqrt{b}$$

The same law when read from right to left tells how to multiply radicals.

- 81. $\sqrt{18}\sqrt{2} = \sqrt{18 \cdot 2} = ?$
- 82. $(2\sqrt{8})(3\sqrt{18}) = 2 \cdot 3\sqrt{8 \cdot 18} = ?$
- 83. $(\frac{2}{3}\sqrt{3})(9\sqrt{27}) = ?$
- 84. $(\frac{1}{3}\sqrt{8})(3\sqrt{2}) = ?$

To divide two radicals, first simplify each and then rationalize the denominator by multiplying numerator and denominator by whatever factors are necessary to make the denominator a rational number.

- 85. $\dfrac{\sqrt{75}}{\sqrt{3}} = \dfrac{5\sqrt{3}}{\sqrt{3}} = ?$
- 86. $\dfrac{\sqrt{6}}{\sqrt{3}} = \dfrac{\sqrt{6} \cdot \sqrt{3}}{\sqrt{3} \cdot \sqrt{3}} = \dfrac{\sqrt{18}}{3} = ?$
- 87. $\dfrac{\sqrt{5}}{\sqrt{2}} = \dfrac{\sqrt{5} \cdot \sqrt{2}}{\sqrt{2} \cdot \sqrt{2}} = ?$
- 88. $\dfrac{25\sqrt{32}}{5\sqrt{2}} = \dfrac{25 \cdot 4\sqrt{2}}{5\sqrt{2}} = ?$

Solving Equations

An equation is a mathematical sentence which states that two expressions name the same number. Thus $4x = 20$ is an equation which is true when x is 5 and false when x is anything else.

A root (or solution) of an equation is a number which makes the equation true when used in place of the variable. The root of the equation $4x = 20$ is 5. Some equations have more than one root. The roots of the equation $x^2 - 7x + 12 = 0$ are 4 and 3.

Addition, subtraction, multiplication, or division of each side of an equation by the same quantity results in a new equation which has the same roots. (Division by 0, of course, is excluded here as in every other place in mathematics). These operations are used on equations whose roots are not immediately apparent in order to find new equations which are simpler. In the examples below, solve for x:

- 89. $x - 4 = 12$

  Add 4 to each side.

  $(x - 4) + 4 = 12 + 4$

  $x = ?$
- 90. $x + 4 = 12$

  $x = ?$
- 91. $4x - 5 = 3x + 2$

  $x = ?$
- 92. $\dfrac{x}{4} = 12$

  $x = ?$
- 93. $4x = 12$

  $x = ?$

If each side of an equation is raised to the same power, the new equation will include the roots of the original, but may also have one or more additional roots which do not satisfy the original equation. As a very simple example, note that the only root of the equation $x = -3$ is -3 but that $x^2 = 9$, which is obtained by squaring each side, also has 3 as a solution.

• *Answers given on page 378-379.*

Thus, if you find it necessary to square both sides of an equation always check your solution set with the original equation and discard any of the added "extraneous" roots.

Solve for x:

• 94. $3\sqrt{x+2}-3=4$

Add 3 to each side and then divide each side by 3.

$\sqrt{x+2}=\frac{7}{3}$

Now square each side and subtract 2.

$x=?$

• 95. $\sqrt{x}+1=0$

$x=?$

When an equation has no roots we say its solution set is empty. Any set which is empty is indistinguishable from any other set which is empty. For example, the set of all married bachelors is the same as the set of four-sided triangles. Therefore we say there is only one empty set and designate it by $\emptyset$.

Often when working with formulas it is useful to rearrange the variables so that the quantity we seek is expressed in terms of the others.

For example,

• 96. The formula used to change centigrade degrees to Fahrenheit is:

$$F=\frac{9}{5}C+32.$$

Solve for C in terms of F.

$$C=?$$

• 97. The relationship between distance, rate, and time is given by:

$$d=rt.$$

Solve for r in terms of d and t.

$$r=?$$

USING ALGEBRA

Solving Problems by Equations

Many types of problems may be solved easily by changing the verbal statements into one or more equations. The five steps outlined below will help you to see how this is done.

1. Read the problem carefully and then determine the unknown quantity. Use a variable to represent this number.

2. If more than one unknown quantity is requested these will be related to each other in some way. In most cases, it is possible to represent each of these quantities in terms of the original variable.

3. One of the verbal statements in the problem can be readily translated into an equation. Write this equation.

4. Solve the equation.

5. Check your answer by applying it to the original statement.

For example: If 4 is subtracted from one-fourth of a number, the result is 20. Find the number.

Let $x=$ the number. Then the first sentence readily translates into the equation.

$$\frac{1}{4}x-4=20$$

• *Answers given on page 379.*

This equation is solved by first multiplying both sides by 4 and then adding 16 to each side.

$$x = 96$$

To check, note that $\frac{1}{4}$ of 96 is 24, and when 4 is subtracted from 24 the result is 20.

- • 98. Find two consecutive numbers whose sum is 43.
  Let $x =$ the first number and $x + 1$ will then represent the second. Thus the equation is $x + x + 1 = 43$. The numbers are ?
- • 99. A rectangular box is to be 4 feet long and 2 feet wide. How high must it be to have a volume of 24 cubic feet?
  Let h be the height and the equation will come from the formula $V = lwh$.
- • 100. The cost of a new highway was $88,000.00. The township agreed to pay twice as much as the state and the county was to pay 4 times as much as the township. How much did each pay?
- • 101. Mr. Smith, who is 28 years of age, has a son who is 4 years old. In how many years will Mr. Smith be 4 times as old as his son?
- • 102. A man changed a $1.00 bill and received 14 coins made up of nickels and dimes. How many nickels did he receive?

Inequalities and the Number Line

On the SAT you will be expected to know the meanings of the symbols > (is greater than), and < (is less than), as well as how to simplify mathematical sentences which use these symbols. The meanings should be intuitively clear from the descriptions above, but more formal definitions follow:

$a > b$ means that $a - b$ is a positive number.

$a < b$ means that $a - b$ is a negative number.

Insert the proper symbol in the place of the question mark:

- • 103. $6 \ ? -6$ because $6 - (-6) = 12$
- • 104. $8 \ ? \ 11$ because $8 - 11 = -3$
- • 105. $-4 \ ? -1$
- • 106 $-5 \ ? \ 0$

Many of the concepts of inequalities are easily understood by reference to a number line. Every point on a number line has a real number assigned to it and every real number is assigned to some point of the line. This matching can be done as follows:

On a horizontal line pick any two points. Label the one on the left 0 and the one on the right 1.

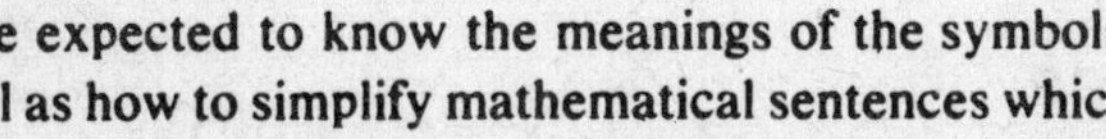

Set a compass to the distance between these points and mark off additional points to the right of 1,

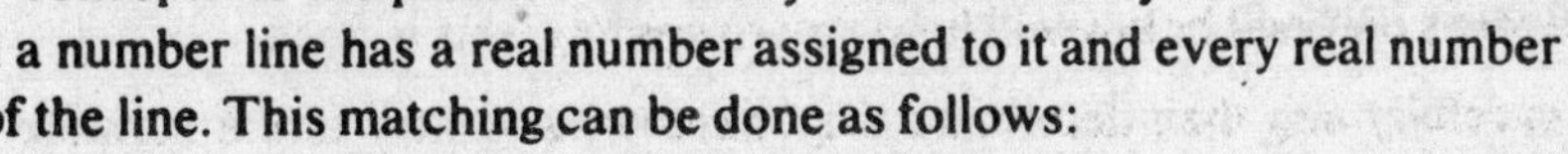

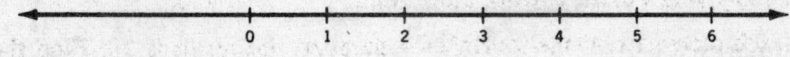

and to the left of 0.

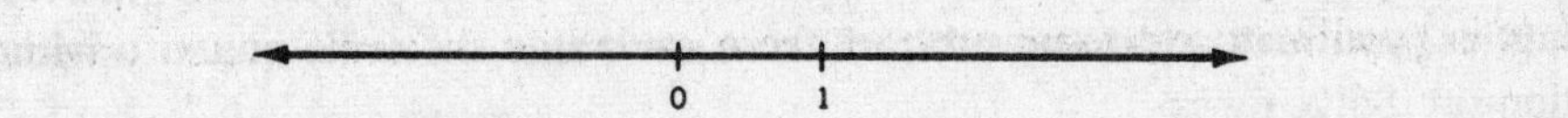

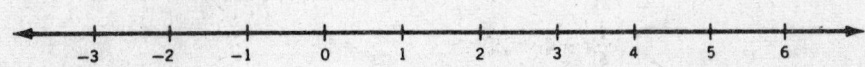

• *Answers given on page 379.*

The remaining rational numbers can be assigned by dividing up the segments connecting the integers in proportion to the fractional values.

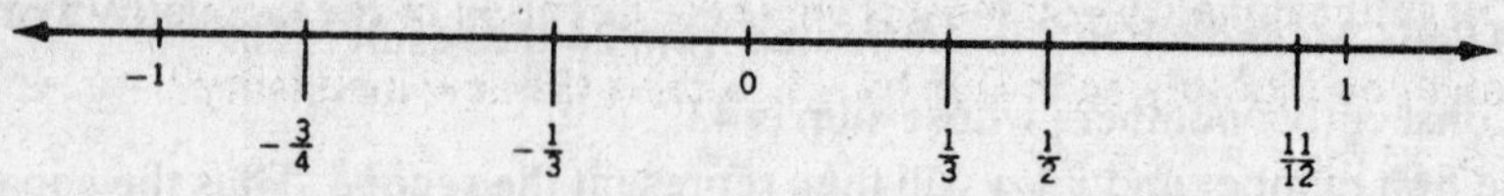

The irrational numbers can be assigned using geometric constructions. Some such constructions are based on the Pythagorean Theorem which states that in a right triangle with sides as labeled below,

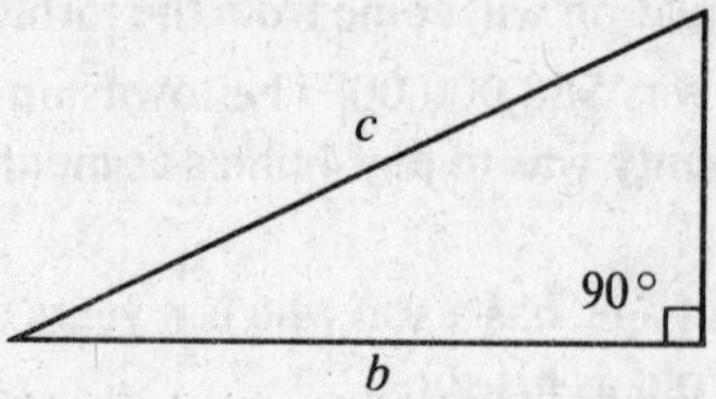

then

$$c^2 = a^2 + b^2.$$

We can use this fact to find the point corresponding to $\sqrt{2}$, for example, by constructing a triangle with one side on the number line and a hypotenuse equal to $\sqrt{2}$.

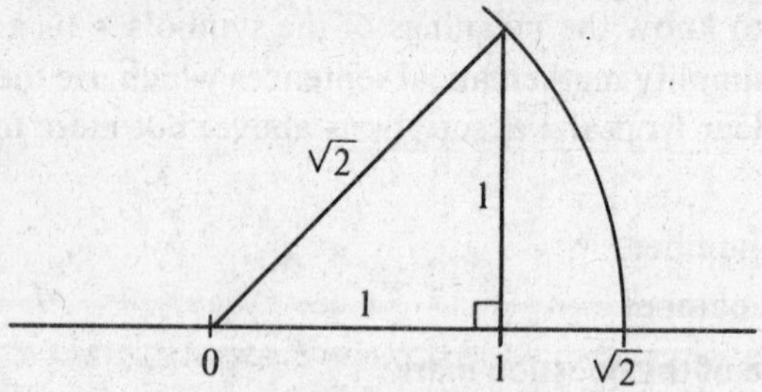

When a point and a number are paired in this way the number is called the *coordinate* of the point and the point is called the *graph* of the number.

The inequality symbols have simple number line meanings. Therefore, $a > b$ means "a is to the right of b" on the number line; $a < b$ means that "a is to the left of b."

Graph the following inequalities by darkening the points on the number line whose coordinates make the inequality true:

- **107. $x > 3$**
- **108. $x \geq 4$ ("x is greater than or equal to 4")**
- **109. $-2 < x < 5$ ("-2 is less than x and x is less than 5")**

To solve inequalities, you may add to or subtract from each side the same quantity without changing the solution set. Solve for x:

- **110. $x - 4 > 15$**

  Add 4 to each side.

  $x > ?$

- **111. $x + 5 \leq 3$**

  Subtract 5 from each side.

  $x \leq ?$

• *Answers given on page 379.*

The multiplication and division laws are slightly more complicated. Each side may be multiplied by or divided by a positive quantity with no change in the solution set. But if you multiply or divide by a negative quantity you must reverse the direction of the inequality symbol.

- • 112. If $3 < 4$ and you multiply each side by -1, what is the new inequality?
- • 113. Solve $3x > 12$ for x.

  $x > ?$
- • 114. Solve $-4x+6 < 30$ for x.

  $x\ ?\ -6$
- • 115. Solve for x:

  $x+3 < \frac{3}{2}x - 1$
- • 116. Solve for x:

  $3x \geqslant 7x-8$

Two inequalities may be added if the inequality signs have the same direction by simply adding the left sides, adding the right sides and keeping the same inequality sign. If they do not have the same direction, use the fact that $a > b$ means the same thing as $b < a$ to alter one of the inequalities until they do agree. Since $5 > 2$ and $8 > -1$, it follows that $5+8 > 2+(-1)$.

- • 117. If $x > 3$ and $y > 8$ then $x+y > ?$
- • 118. If $x > 16$ and $y < 15$, then

  $x-y > ?$

When it is necessary to determine which of two fractions is the greater, use the following rule: When both b and d are positive,

$$\frac{a}{b} > \frac{c}{d}$$

if and only if $ad > bc$. In other words, cross-multiply each denominator with the opposite numerator and decide which of these products is the greater. In the examples replace the ? with > or <.

- • 119. $\frac{7}{11}\ ?\ \frac{2}{3}$ since $3 \times 7 < 2 \times 11$
- • 120. $-\frac{8}{17}\ ?\ -\frac{5}{8}$ since $(-8)(8)\ ?\ (17)(-5)$.

A rule that students have found useful on past SAT examinations is the following:

If $\frac{1}{a} < \frac{1}{b}$ and a and b are both positive or both negative, then $a > b$.

In other words, the fractions may be inverted only if the inequality symbol is reversed when both fractions have the same sign.

If a and b do not have the same sign, then the inequality symbol keeps its direction.

- • 121. $\frac{1}{2} < \frac{3}{4}$ therefore $2\ ?\ \frac{4}{3}$.
- • 122. If $x > 0$ and $\frac{1}{x} < \frac{1}{2}$ then $x\ ?\ 2$.
- • 123. $\frac{1}{x-1} > \frac{1}{3}$ therefore $x-1\ ?\ 3$.

Many students find this last rule a difficult one to master but it can be helpful in dealing with problems which require non-routine thinking.

• *Answers given on page 379.*

PRACTICE EXERCISES

Operations Involving Whole Numbers *Answers given on page 382.*

Addition

1.	2.	3.	4.	5.	6.	7.	8.	9.
5	6	85	17	74	216	169	729	879
9	7	46	96	55	483	534	123	978
8	2	37	69	20	529	234	315	105
7	5	22	28	49	118	157	468	324
3	4	73	81	68	379	828	850	647
4	3							

10.	11.	12.	13.	14.	15.
927	7568	9060	2340	8075	9153
132	6930	7245	8196	3210	7080
513	8241	4618	5619	6109	1967
868	9060	379	257	7308	427
746	808		3284	215	3859

Subtraction

16.	17.	18.	19.	20.	21.	22.	23.	24.	25.
605	480	703	804	692	402	653	1683	4802	7642
72	67	89	89	105	174	597	678	346	2385

Multiplication

26.	27.	28.	29.	30.	31.	32.	33.	34.	35.
327	425	812	504	657	311	270	345	273	206
49	38	63	57	56	89	28	31	79	68

36. What is the product of 318 and 29?
37. What is the product of 17 and 289?
38. What is the product of 98 and 989?
39. What is the product of 850 and 93?
40. What is the product of 855 and 56?

Division

41. Divide 1817 by 79
42. Divide 1302 by 31
43. Divide 4968 by 69
44. Divide 952 by 28
45. Divide 2679 by 47
46. Divide 3185 by 65
47. Divide 2146 by 37
48. Divide 78884 by 82
49. Divide 18228 by 49
50. Divide 21504 by 56

Roots and Radicals *Answers given on page 382.*

1. $2\sqrt{3} + 3\sqrt{3} - 4\sqrt{3}$
2. $5\sqrt{32} + 2\sqrt{50}$
3. $10\sqrt{18} - 2\sqrt{50}$
4. $4\sqrt{28} - \sqrt{63} - \sqrt{7}$
5. $\frac{1}{4}\sqrt{96} + \frac{1}{5}\sqrt{150}$
6. $2\sqrt{45} - 3\sqrt{20} + \sqrt{80}$
7. $2\sqrt{75} - 3\sqrt{50} + 2\sqrt{98}$
8. $\frac{1}{3}\sqrt{27} - \frac{1}{2}\sqrt{12}$
9. $\sqrt{7} + 3\sqrt{28} + 2\sqrt{63}$
10. $\sqrt{500} + 2\sqrt{20} - 3\sqrt{45} + \sqrt{125}$

Simplify each of the following products

11. $(\sqrt{3})(\sqrt{12})$
12. $(\sqrt{21})(\sqrt{3})$
13. $(\sqrt{60})(\sqrt{5})$
14. $(3\sqrt{18})(\sqrt{3})$
15. $(3\sqrt{3})(\sqrt{6})$
16. $(2\sqrt{17})(3\sqrt{17})$

17. $(2\sqrt{3})(\sqrt{7})$

18. $\left(\frac{1}{5}\sqrt{9}\right)\left(5\sqrt{9}\right)$

19. $\left(\frac{1}{3}\sqrt{2}\right)\left(\sqrt{5}\right)$

20. $(2\sqrt{2})(8\sqrt{8})$

Simplify each of the following quotients:

21. $\sqrt{75} \div \sqrt{3}$

22. $\sqrt{24} \div \sqrt{2}$

23. $21\sqrt{75} \div 3\sqrt{3}$

24. $\frac{1}{3}\sqrt{54} \div \sqrt{3}$

25. $9\sqrt{27} \div 3\sqrt{27}$

26. $\dfrac{4\sqrt{20}}{\sqrt{5}}$

27. $\dfrac{3\sqrt{48}}{\sqrt{3}}$

28. $\dfrac{6\sqrt{54}}{2\sqrt{3}}$

29. $\dfrac{25\sqrt{21}}{5\sqrt{3}}$

30. $\dfrac{2\sqrt{18} + 4\sqrt{2}}{\sqrt{200}}$

Solving Equations *Answers given on page 382.*

1. Solve for x

$8x - (6x - 3) = 9$

2. Solve for a

$p = \dfrac{cn}{a}$

3. Solve for y

$10y - (3y + 11) = 45$

4. Solve for h

$A = \dfrac{h}{2}(b + b_1)$

5. Solve for z

$28z - 6(3z - 5) = 40$

6. Solve for a

$S = \dfrac{n}{2}(a + L)$

7. Solve for n

$2n - (24 - n) = 30$

8. Solve for d

$A = \dfrac{1}{4}\pi d^2$

9. Solve for x

$3 + 13x = 1 - 3x$

10. Solve for r

$i = Prt$

11. Solve for y

$cd = y\,(c + d)$

12. Solve for e

$S = 6e^2$

13. Solve for x

$2\sqrt{x + 1} = 3$

14. Solve for L

$P - 2L + 2W$

15. Solve for π

$A = \pi(R + r)(R - r)$

16. Solve for E

$I = \dfrac{E}{R}$

17. Solve for t

$s = \dfrac{at^2}{2}$

18. Solve for x

$\dfrac{6}{\sqrt{x + 5}} = \sqrt{x + 5}$

19. Solve for y

$3\sqrt{3y + 2} - 4 = 0$

20. Solve for s

$K = s^2$

Solving Verbal Problems Algebraically

Answers given on page 382.

1. The highest recorded temperature in South Dakota was 109 degrees and the lowest was −33 degrees. How many degrees difference is there between these two temperatures?

(a) 33 (b) 71 (c) 76 (d) 109 (e) 142

1. a b c d e

2. *A* is now $x - 10$ years old. How old will he be ten years from now?

(a) $x - 20$ (b) $x + 10$ (c) x (d) $10x - 10$ (e) $x + 20$

2. a b c d e

3. How many 3¢ stamps can be purchased for *c* cents?

(a) $3c$ (b) $\frac{c}{3}$ (c) $\frac{3}{c}$ (d) $300c$ (e) $\frac{3c}{100}$

3. a b c d e

4. A lending library charges *c* cents for the first week that a book is loaned and *f* cents for each day over one week. What is the cost for taking out a book for *d* days, where *d* is greater than 7?

(a) $c + fd$ (b) $c + f(d - 7)$ (c) cd (d) $7c + f(d - 7)$ (e) $cd + f$

4. a b c d e

5. At *c* cents per orange, what is the price in dollars for 1 dozen oranges?

(a) $12c$ (b) $\frac{c}{12}$ (c) $\frac{12}{100c}$ (d) $\frac{c}{100}$ (e) $\frac{12c}{100}$

5. a b c d e

6. What is the total weight, in ounces, of a package containing a book which weighs *p* pounds and the wrapping material weighs *n* ounces?

(a) $16p + n$ (b) $16n + p$ (c) $16(n + p)$ (d) $\frac{p}{16} + n$ (e) $n + \frac{16}{p}$

6. a b c d e

7. How many pupils are there in a class if two pupils remain after four rows of seats are filled, and nine pupils remain after three rows of seats are filled?

(a) 7 (b) 26 (c) 30 (d) 34 (e) 36

7. a b c d e

8. To send a parcel 200 miles by air mail the cost is 60 cents for the first pound and 48 cents for each additional pound. What is the cost (in cents) of sending a parcel weighing *p* pounds?

(a) $48p$ (b) $60p$ (c) $12p$ (d) $60 + 48p$ (e) $12 + 48p$

8. a b c d e

9. Mr. Jones receives a weekly salary of $*D* for a five-day work week. What is his daily salary after receiving a $5.00 per week increase?

(a) $D + 5$ (b) $5D$ (c) $\frac{D}{5} + 1$ (d) $\frac{D}{5} + 5$ (e) $5D + 5$

9. a b c d e

10. A picnic has 240 persons. There are 20 more men than women and there are 20 more adults than children. How many men are there at this picnic?

(a) 240 (b) 75 (c) 110 (d) 130 (e) 200

10. a b c d e

11. Eight years from now Miss Blank will be twice the age she was six years ago. What is her present age?

(a) 4 (b) 8 (c) 12 (d) 20 (e) 26

11. a b c d e

12. Saul and Gladys together had $100. After giving Gladys $10.00 he finds that he has $4.00 **more** than $\frac{1}{5}$ the amount Gladys now has. How much does Saul now have?

(a) $18.67 (b) $20.00 (c) $21.00 (d) $27.50 (e) $35.00

12. a b c d e

13. The numerator and denominator of a fraction are in the ratio of 2:3. If 6 is subtracted from the numerator, the result will be a fraction that has a value $\frac{2}{3}$ of the original fraction. The numerator of the original fraction is

(a) 4 (b) 6 (c) 9 (d) 18 (e) 27

13. a b c d e

14. One-half of the student body at the Danby School study French and one-third of the others study Spanish. The remaining 300 do not study any foreign language. How many students are there in the Danby School?

(a) 360 (b) 550 (c) 900 (d) 1350 (e) 1800

14. a b c d e

15. During the month of June the Forster-Gold Fruit Company sold twice as many apricots as pears, three times as many peaches as apricots and four times as many apples as peaches. If they sold 300 more peaches than apricots, how many apples were sold?

(a) 75 (b) 180 (c) 300 (d) 720 (e) 1800

15. a b c d e

16. Jill is twice as old as Shelly. In y years she will be $1\frac{1}{2}$ times as old. What is Shelly's age at present?

(a) $\frac{y}{4}$ (b) $\frac{2y}{3}$ (c) y (d) $\frac{3y}{2}$ (e) $3y$

16. a b c d e

17. The sum of six consecutive odd numbers exceeds twice the largest by 38. Find the sum of the six numbers.

(a) 42 (b) 50 (c) 57 (d) 60 (e) 72

17. a b c d e

18. The price of a balcony seat in the Avon Theatre is $\frac{1}{3}$ the price of a seat in the orchestra. When completely sold out the total receipts from the 600 orchestra seats and the 450 balcony seats are $4500. What is the price of one orchestra seat?

(a) $2.00 (b) $2.30 (c) $4.00 (d) $6.00 (e) $10.00

18. a b c d e

19. In 1950 there were twice as many radios as television sets in Manchester. By 1952, 200 more television sets had been purchased but the number of radios still exceeded the number of television sets by 40. How many radio sets were there in Manchester in 1952?

(a) 160 (b) 280 (c) 320 (d) 360 (e) 480

19. a b c d e

20. Fifteen houses line Indian Creek. The average space between each house exceeds the average width of each house by 80 feet. The sidewalk, 2920 feet in length begins at a point 30 feet before the first house and ends at a point 30 feet beyond the last house. What is the average width (in feet) of each house?

(a) 58 (b) 59 (c) 60 (d) 61 (e) 62

20. a b c d e

Inequalities and the Number Line *Answers given on page 383.*

Replace the question mark with either > or < in questions 1 through 10:

1. 3 ? 6 **2.** −3 ? −6 **3.** −3 ? 6 **4.** $-\frac{1}{2}\ ?\ -\frac{1}{4}$

5. If $x > 0$, $y > 0$, and $\frac{1}{x} > \frac{1}{y}$, then x ? y.

6. If $x > 0 > y$ and $\frac{1}{y} < \frac{1}{x}$ then y ? x.

7. If $x > y > 0$ then x^2 ? y^2.

8. If $y < x < 0$ then x^2 ? y^2.

9. If $x > 1$ then $x + \frac{1}{x}$? 2.

10. If $x > 1 > y$ then $x^2 + y^2$? 0.

Solve each of the following inequalities for x and graph the solution set on a number line:

11. $3x > 12$ **12.** $8x \leq 5$ **13.** $4x - 12 > 0$.

14. $x + 3 > 4x - 9$ **15.** $5 - 4x > 2x - 7$ **16.** $\frac{1}{x} < 5$

17. $\frac{1}{x} > 5$ **18.** $\frac{2}{x-1} > \frac{1}{2}$ **19.** $\frac{1}{x^2} > \frac{1}{4}$

20. $\frac{1}{-\sqrt{x}} < \frac{1}{9}$

FRACTIONS

A *fraction* is an indicated division. Thus $\frac{1}{2}$ means 1 divided by 2. In a fraction the top number is called the *numerator* and the bottom number, the *denominator*. An *improper fraction* is one in which the numerator is greater than the denominator. Thus, $\frac{12}{5}$ is an improper fraction.

A *mixed number* indicates the sum of a whole number and a proper fraction. Thus, $3\frac{1}{4}$ is a mixed number representing $3 + \frac{1}{4}$.

In many applications it is necessary to convert mixed numbers to improper fractions. This can be done by changing the whole number to a fraction with the same denominator as the fractional part has and then adding the two fractions. A shortcut that saves time is to multiply the whole number by the denominator and then add the numerator to get the numerator of the result. The denominator is unchanged.

• 124. $6\frac{1}{2} = \frac{6 \times 2 + 1}{2} = ?$

• 125. $9\frac{3}{8} = ?$

Convert an improper fraction to a mixed number by dividing the numerator by the denominator. Remember that $\frac{\text{dividend}}{\text{divisor}} = \text{quotient} + \frac{\text{remainder}}{\text{divisor}}$

• *Answers given on page 379-380.*

• 126. $\frac{24}{7}$ means $7\overline{)24}$

$$\begin{array}{r} 3 \\ 7\overline{)24} \\ \underline{21} \\ 3 \end{array}$$

Therefore: $\frac{24}{7} = ?$

$\frac{24}{7} = ?$

• 127. $\frac{15}{4} = ?$

Equivalent Fractions

Principle 1: $\frac{a}{b} = \frac{a}{b} \times \frac{c}{c} = \frac{ac}{bc}$ if c is not 0.

This principle says that we may multiply the numerator and denominator of a fraction by the same non-zero number without changing the value of the fraction.

• 128. $\frac{1}{4} = \frac{1 \times 3}{4 \times 3} = ?$

• 129. $\frac{1}{4} = \frac{1 \times 7}{4 \times 7} = ?$

By using this principle we can write any fraction with any denominator (except zero) that we choose without changing the value of the fraction.

Write each of the following with a denominator of 36:

• 130. $\frac{8}{12} = \frac{8 \times 3}{12 \times 3} = ?$

• 131. $\frac{1}{4} = ?$

• 132. $\frac{1}{3} = ?$

• 133. $\frac{4}{9} = ?$

Change to an equivalent fraction with a denominator of $x^2 - 4$:

• 134. $\frac{3}{x-2} = \frac{3(x+2)}{(x-2)(x+2)} = ?$

Principle 1 can also be used to simplify fractions by removing factors which appear in both the numerator and the denominator. This use can perhaps be seen better if the principle is rewritten as:

$$\frac{ac}{bc} = \frac{a}{b} \quad \text{if } c \text{ is not } 0.$$

It is easier to apply this principle when the numerator and denominator are first factored:

• 135. $\frac{4y-2}{2y^2-5y+2} = \frac{2(2y-1)}{(2y-1)(y-2)} = ?$

• 136. $\frac{2x-1}{2x^2-x} = ?$

• *Answers given on page 380.*

Signs of Fractions

Principle 2: $+\frac{a}{b} = +\frac{-a}{-b} = -\frac{-a}{+b} = -\frac{+a}{-b}$

This principle can be simply stated as follows: if any two of the three signs of a fraction are changed, the value of the fraction will remain unchanged.

Write each of the following without negative signs if possible:

• 137. $\frac{-2}{-3} = ?$

• 138. $-\frac{2}{-3} = ?$

• 139. $\frac{-a-3}{-4} = \frac{-(a+3)}{-4} = ?$

• 140. $-\frac{3-a}{-4} = ?$

Addition and Subtraction

Principle 3: $\frac{a}{c} + \frac{b}{c} = \frac{a+b}{c}$ and $\frac{a}{c} - \frac{b}{c} = \frac{a-b}{c}$.

In other words, the sum (or difference) of two fractions which have the same denominator is a fraction with the same denominator and with a numerator which is the sum (or difference) of the original numerators. If the fractions to be combined have different denominators, use Principle 1 to change them to the same denominator. After you have found a sum or difference be sure to reduce your answer to lowest terms.

• 141. $\frac{2}{7} + \frac{3}{7} + \frac{1}{7} = \frac{2+3+1}{7} = ?$

• 142. $\frac{1}{2} + \frac{1}{3} + \frac{1}{4} = \frac{6}{12} + \frac{4}{12} + \frac{3}{12} = ?$

• 143. $\frac{3}{6} - \frac{2}{6} = ?$

• 144. $\frac{11}{12} - \frac{3}{4} = ?$

• 145. $12\frac{3}{4} - 1\frac{7}{8} = \frac{51}{4} - \frac{15}{8} = ?$

• 146. $\frac{5}{3b} + \frac{2}{3b} + \frac{1}{3b} + \frac{4}{3b} = ?$

• 147. $\frac{2a}{b} - \frac{c}{b} - \frac{a}{2b} + \frac{4c}{3b} = ?$

• 148. $\frac{5}{a-3} + \frac{3}{3-a} = \frac{5}{a-3} + \frac{-3}{a-3} = ?$

Sometimes it is difficult to find the lowest common denominator (LCD) when combining fractions. Proceed according to the following steps:

a. Factor each denominator completely.
b. Form the LCD by using every factor which appears in any denominator.
c. Use each factor in the LCD as many times as it appears in the denominator in which it occurs the most times.

• *Answers given on page 380.*

For example, suppose 360 and 175 were the denominators of two fractions you wished to add.

$$360 = 2^3 \cdot 3^2 \cdot 5$$

$$175 = 5^2 \cdot 7$$

Thus the LCD must have 2, 3, 5 and 7 as its factors and LCD = $2^3 3^2 5^2 7$.

Find the LCD for each of the following:

- 149. $\frac{1}{18}+\frac{1}{12}=?$
- 150. $\frac{1}{a^3bc^2}-\frac{3}{2b^3c}=?$
- 151. $\frac{1}{(x-1)^2(x+1)}+\frac{3}{x^2-1}=?$

Multiplication

Principle 4: $\frac{a}{b}\times\frac{c}{d}=\frac{ac}{bd}$

To multiply fractions, multiply their numerators to obtain the numerator of the product and multiply their denominators to form the denominator.

- 152. $\frac{2}{7}\times\frac{3}{7}\times\frac{1}{7}=?$
- 153. $\frac{1}{2}\times\frac{1}{3}\times\frac{1}{4}=?$
- 154. $\frac{a}{b^2c}\times\frac{b}{ac^2}=?$

Often the product of fractions will have factors common to numerator and denominator as in example 154 above. As a shortcut these can be removed before the multiplication is done. If a factor appears in any numerator of the product, and in any denominator as well, it will not change the value of the product and can be removed from both.

- 155. $\frac{3}{4}\times\frac{20}{49}\times\frac{7}{25}=\frac{3}{\cancel{4}}\times\frac{\cancel{5}\cdot\cancel{4}}{7\cdot\cancel{7}}\times\frac{\cancel{7}}{\cancel{5}\cdot 5}$

  $=\frac{3}{1}\times\frac{1}{7}\times\frac{1}{5}$

  $=?$

- 156. $\left(\frac{8x-4}{12x}\right)\left(\frac{2x^2+x}{4x^2-1}\right)=$

  $\frac{4(2x-1)}{12x}\cdot\frac{x(2x+1)}{(2x+1)(2x-1)}=?$

To multiply mixed numbers, convert them to improper fractions first.

- 157. $2\frac{5}{6}\times 5\frac{2}{3}=\frac{17}{6}\times\frac{17}{3}=?$

Division

Principle 5: $\frac{a}{b}\div\frac{c}{d}=\frac{a}{b}\times\frac{d}{c}.$

To divide a fraction by a fraction, invert the divisor and then multiply according to Principle 4.

- 158. $\frac{1}{2}\div\frac{1}{3}=\frac{1}{2}\times\frac{3}{1}=?$
- 159. $\frac{2}{5}\div\frac{8}{15}=?$

• *Answers given on page 380.*

To divide mixed numbers, convert to improper fractions first.

• **160.** $2\frac{5}{6} \div 5\frac{2}{3} = \frac{17}{6} \div \frac{17}{3} = ?$

To divide fractions involving variables, be sure to factor after inverting and cancel any common factors before multiplying.

• **161.** $\frac{x+y}{x^2-xy} \div \frac{1}{x^2-y^2} =$

$$\frac{x+y}{x(x-y)} \cdot \frac{(x+y)(x-y)}{1} = ?$$

Simplifying Complex Fractions

A complex fraction is a fraction which has one or more fractions in its numerator or denominator. To simplify a complex fraction, find the LCD of all of the fractions found in the numerator and denominator. Then multiply the numerator and denominator of the complex fraction by this LCD. Your fraction will no longer be complex but may have factors common to numerator and denominator which can be removed.

• **162.** $\frac{\frac{1}{3}+\frac{5}{6}}{1-\left(\frac{1}{3}\right)\left(\frac{3}{4}\right)} = ?$ **(Note that LCD = 12)**

$$\frac{12\left(\frac{1}{3}+\frac{5}{6}\right)}{12\left(1-\frac{1}{3}\cdot\frac{3}{4}\right)} = ?$$

• **163.** $\frac{\frac{1}{x}+\frac{1}{y}}{\frac{1}{xy}} =$ **(LCD = xy)**

$$\frac{xy\left(\frac{1}{x}+\frac{1}{y}\right)}{xy\left(\frac{1}{xy}\right)} = ?$$

• **164.** $\frac{\frac{1}{a}}{1-\frac{1}{a}} = ?$

• **165.** $\frac{\frac{1}{y}-\frac{1}{x}}{1-\frac{y}{x}} = ?$

Solving Fractional Equations

To solve an equation involving fractions, change it to an equation with no fractions. This can be done by multiplying each side by the LCD of all of the fractions which appear in the equation.

Solve for x:

• **166.** $\frac{x}{4}+\frac{x}{3}=\frac{7}{12}$ **(LCD is 12)**

$$12\left(\frac{x}{4}+\frac{x}{3}\right) = 12\left(\frac{7}{12}\right)$$

$$x = ?$$

• *Answers given on page 380.*

• 167. $\frac{4x}{7+5x}=\frac{1}{3}$ (LCD is $3(7+5x)$)

• 168. $\frac{5}{x-2}+\frac{2}{2-x}=\frac{3}{2}$

$\left(\text{Note that } 2-x=-(x-2) \text{ so this equation is the same as } \frac{5}{x-2}-\frac{2}{x-2}=\frac{3}{2}\right)$

• 169. Solve for r: $\frac{1}{p}+\frac{1}{r}=\frac{1}{s}$ (LCD is prs)

• 170. Solve for a: $S=\frac{1}{2}n(a+1)$

Solving Problems Involving Fractions

The word "of" frequently indicates multiplication. For example, $\frac{1}{2}$ of 4 means $\frac{1}{2}\cdot 4=2$ and $\frac{2}{3}$ of $\frac{9}{10}$ means $\frac{2}{3}\times\frac{9}{10}=\frac{3}{5}$.

• 171. Find $\frac{7}{8}$ of 48.

• 172. What is $\frac{1}{4}$ of $\frac{4}{7}$?

• 173. Mr. Brown owns $\frac{4}{7}$ of the interest in a company and sells $\frac{1}{2}$ of this share to Mr. Wein. What part of the business does Mr. Wein own after this deal?

A fraction is commonly used to indicate the ratio of some part to the whole.

$$\frac{\text{part}}{\text{whole}}=\text{fractional part}$$

In many problems, the "part" follows the word "is" and the "whole" follows "of."

• 174. What fractional part of 32 is 20?
part = 20
whole = 32
fractional part = ?

• 175. In a class of 26 there are 16 girls. What fractional part of the class is made up of girls?

• 176. What fractional part of a quarter is a nickel?

• 177. $6=\frac{2}{3}x$
$x=?$

• 178. When 300 pupils are in a lecture hall only $\frac{2}{3}$ of the seats are occupied. How many seats are there?
Let x = the number of seats.

$$\frac{300}{x}=\frac{2}{3}$$

• 179. 5 is $\frac{1}{4}$ of what number?

PRACTICE EXERCISES

Operations Involving Fractions *Answers given on page 383-384.*

Do only the odd-numbered questions. If you discover that you are very weak in your work with fractions, then return to this section later, if you have the time, and work the even-numbered questions.

• *Answers given on page380-381.*

Addition

1. $\frac{1}{2}+\frac{1}{4}$ **2.** $\frac{1}{4}+\frac{5}{8}$ **3.** $\frac{1}{2}+\frac{1}{8}$ **4.** $\frac{2}{3}+\frac{5}{6}$ **5.** $\frac{1}{3}+\frac{1}{4}$ **6.** $\frac{1}{3}+\frac{1}{5}$

7. $\frac{1}{6}+\frac{1}{3}$ **8.** $\frac{1}{2}+\frac{1}{5}$ **9.** $\frac{2}{7}+\frac{1}{3}$ **10.** $\frac{1}{2}+\frac{1}{7}$ **11.** $\frac{1}{2}+\frac{1}{3}+\frac{1}{4}$ **12.** $\frac{1}{3}+\frac{3}{4}+\frac{5}{6}$

13. $\frac{1}{2}+\frac{5}{8}+\frac{1}{4}$ **14.** $\frac{1}{4}+\frac{1}{8}+\frac{1}{2}$ **15.** $\frac{1}{5}+\frac{2}{3}+\frac{1}{4}$

16. $$\begin{array}{r} 17\frac{5}{8} \\ 21\frac{3}{4} \\ \hline \end{array}$$

17. $$\begin{array}{r} 36\frac{5}{12} \\ 24\frac{2}{3} \\ \hline \end{array}$$

18. $$\begin{array}{r} 8\frac{5}{6} \\ 7\frac{5}{12} \\ 6\frac{2}{3} \\ \hline \end{array}$$

19. $$\begin{array}{r} 3\frac{1}{4} \\ \frac{1}{3} \\ \hline \end{array}$$

20. $7\frac{1}{2}+2\frac{1}{3}+3\frac{3}{8}+4\frac{3}{4}$

21. $$\begin{array}{r} 64\frac{3}{4} \\ 45\frac{2}{3} \\ \hline \end{array}$$

22. $15\frac{5}{6}+7\frac{1}{4}$ **23.** $8\frac{2}{3}+3\frac{5}{6}$

24. $9\frac{1}{2}+\frac{1}{10}$ **25.** $8\frac{1}{2}+\frac{1}{3}$

Subtraction

26. $\frac{2}{3}-\frac{1}{6}$ **27.** $\frac{7}{8}-\frac{1}{2}$ **28.** $\frac{1}{2}-\frac{3}{8}$ **29.** $\frac{3}{4}-\frac{1}{2}$ **30.** $\frac{3}{4}-\frac{1}{6}$ **31.** $\frac{2}{3}-\frac{1}{9}$

32. $\frac{5}{9}-\frac{1}{3}$ **33.** $\frac{7}{12}-\frac{1}{3}$

34. $$\begin{array}{r} 19\frac{2}{3} \\ -\,7\frac{1}{4} \\ \hline \end{array}$$

35. $$\begin{array}{r} 97\frac{1}{3} \\ -\,28\frac{5}{6} \\ \hline \end{array}$$

36. $$\begin{array}{r} 62 \\ -\,7\frac{5}{8} \\ \hline \end{array}$$

37. $$\begin{array}{r} 23\frac{1}{2} \\ -\,4\frac{4}{5} \\ \hline \end{array}$$

38. $9\frac{3}{4}-\frac{1}{2}$ **39.** $76\frac{3}{4}-67\frac{1}{3}$ **40.** $13\frac{7}{12}-2\frac{1}{3}$ **41.** $44\frac{1}{2}-3\frac{3}{4}$ **42.** $3\frac{1}{3}-2\frac{1}{2}$ **43.** $4\frac{1}{3}-1\frac{5}{6}$

44. $8\frac{1}{10}-6\frac{3}{5}$ **45.** $9\frac{1}{2}-\frac{2}{3}$

Multiplication

46. $\frac{3}{7}\times\frac{2}{3}$ **51.** $\frac{2}{5}\times\frac{5}{6}$ **56.** $4\frac{1}{6}\times 5\frac{1}{5}$ **61.** $3\frac{5}{8}\times 7\frac{2}{3}$

47. $\frac{5}{8}\times\frac{4}{5}$ **52.** $\frac{7}{8}\times 36$ **57.** $6\frac{1}{5}\times 7\frac{2}{3}$ **62.** $5\frac{1}{2}\times 9\frac{4}{5}$

48. $\frac{3}{8}\times\frac{4}{9}$ **53.** $55\times\frac{2}{5}$ **58.** $8\frac{5}{12}\times 1\frac{3}{5}$ **63.** $4\frac{4}{5}\times 2\frac{1}{12}$

49. $\frac{5}{6}\times\frac{2}{5}$ **54.** $7\frac{1}{2}\times 1\frac{2}{3}$ **59.** $9\frac{7}{10}\times 3\frac{5}{6}$ **64.** $6\frac{1}{10}\times 4\frac{5}{6}$

50. $\frac{1}{3}\times\frac{1}{4}$ **55.** $2\frac{2}{3}\times 3\frac{1}{10}$ **60.** $2\frac{4}{9}\times 5\frac{3}{8}$ **65.** $7\frac{2}{3}\times 8\frac{1}{2}$

Division

66. $\frac{2}{3} \div \frac{1}{3}$

67. $\frac{5}{8} \div \frac{1}{2}$

68. $\frac{2}{3} \div \frac{5}{6}$

69. $\frac{1}{4} \div \frac{1}{3}$

70. $\frac{3}{4} \div \frac{1}{8}$

71. $\frac{5}{12} \div \frac{5}{9}$

72. $\frac{7}{8} \div \frac{3}{4}$

73. $\frac{5}{9} \div \frac{1}{6}$

74. $\frac{5}{6} \div \frac{5}{9}$

75. $\frac{2}{3} \div \frac{1}{12}$

76. $3\frac{1}{3} \div \frac{2}{3}$

77. $5\frac{1}{3} \div \frac{5}{6}$

78. $7\frac{1}{6} \div \frac{1}{3}$

79. $9\frac{1}{9} \div \frac{2}{3}$

80. $4\frac{3}{8} \div \frac{1}{4}$

81. $2\frac{3}{4} \div 1\frac{1}{8}$

82. $6\frac{3}{10} \div 3\frac{1}{5}$

83. $8\frac{1}{6} \div 4\frac{1}{4}$

84. $2\frac{1}{3} \div 5\frac{2}{5}$

85. $3\frac{4}{9} \div 7\frac{2}{3}$

86. $5\frac{1}{3} \div 2\frac{1}{5}$

87. $14\frac{2}{3} \div 8\frac{5}{6}$

88. $18\frac{1}{6} \div 2\frac{1}{3}$

89. $10\frac{1}{4} \div 4\frac{5}{8}$

90. $12\frac{1}{6} \div 6\frac{1}{8}$

91. $25\frac{1}{2} \div 2\frac{1}{5}$

92. $16\frac{1}{2} \div 5\frac{1}{2}$

93. $14\frac{1}{6} \div 4\frac{1}{5}$

94. $13\frac{2}{3} \div 1\frac{1}{2}$

95. $18\frac{1}{2} \div 5\frac{1}{3}$

96. $\left(\frac{1}{4} + \frac{5}{8}\right) \div \left(\frac{1}{2} + \frac{3}{4}\right)$

97. $\left(\frac{1}{4} + \frac{1}{8}\right) \div \left(\frac{3}{8} + \frac{1}{2}\right)$

98. $\left(\frac{1}{8} + \frac{1}{2}\right) \div \left(\frac{1}{2} + \frac{1}{3}\right)$

99. $\left(\frac{2}{9} + \frac{1}{3}\right) \div \left(\frac{1}{3} + \frac{1}{4}\right)$

100. $\left(\frac{3}{4} + \frac{1}{3}\right) \div \left(\frac{2}{3} + \frac{5}{12}\right)$

Complex Fractions

101. $\dfrac{\frac{1}{2} - \frac{1}{4}}{\frac{3}{4} - \frac{1}{8}}$

102. $\dfrac{\frac{2}{3} - \frac{1}{6}}{\frac{7}{8} - \frac{1}{2}}$

103. $\dfrac{\frac{5}{12} - \frac{1}{6}}{\frac{5}{6} - \frac{2}{3}}$

104. $\dfrac{\frac{1}{2} - \frac{2}{5}}{\frac{1}{3} - \frac{1}{9}}$

105. $\dfrac{\frac{2}{3} - \frac{1}{4}}{\frac{1}{2} - \frac{1}{3}}$

106. $\dfrac{\frac{1}{4} + \frac{1}{6} + \frac{2}{3}}{\frac{2}{3} - \frac{1}{2}}$

107. $\dfrac{2\frac{1}{4} + 5\frac{5}{6}}{\frac{5}{6} - \frac{3}{4}}$

108. $\dfrac{6\frac{3}{4} + 6\frac{1}{2}}{\frac{3}{4} - \frac{2}{3}}$

109. $\dfrac{1\frac{2}{3} + 4\frac{3}{4}}{\frac{7}{8} - \frac{1}{4}}$

110. $\dfrac{3\frac{1}{3} + \frac{1}{4}}{\frac{2}{3} - \frac{1}{4}}$

111. $\dfrac{\frac{7}{8} - \frac{1}{2}}{\frac{1}{4} + \frac{1}{6} + \frac{2}{3}}$

112. $\dfrac{\frac{2}{3} - \frac{1}{6}}{\frac{1}{2} + \frac{3}{4} + \frac{3}{8}}$

113. $\dfrac{\frac{11}{12} - \frac{1}{4}}{2\frac{1}{4} + 5\frac{5}{6}}$

114. $\dfrac{2\frac{1}{2} - \frac{1}{5}}{\frac{1}{2} + \frac{3}{5}}$

115. $\dfrac{4 - 1\frac{7}{8}}{\frac{1}{8} + \frac{1}{2} + \frac{1}{4}}$

116. $\dfrac{\frac{14}{15} - \frac{3}{5}}{\frac{1}{2} \div \frac{3}{8}}$

117. $\dfrac{4\frac{1}{3} \div \frac{2}{3}}{10\frac{1}{2} + 9\frac{3}{4}}$

118. $\dfrac{6\frac{2}{3} + 4\frac{1}{2}}{8 \times \frac{1}{4}}$

119. $\dfrac{48 \times \frac{5}{12}}{4\frac{7}{12} + 2\frac{1}{3}}$

120. $\dfrac{\frac{2}{5} \times 35}{\frac{7}{8} + \frac{1}{3}}$

121. $\dfrac{4\frac{3}{4} \times \frac{2}{9}}{\frac{1}{2} \div \frac{1}{4}}$

122. $\dfrac{7\frac{3}{5} - 2\frac{1}{10}}{\frac{1}{4} \times 3\frac{3}{4}}$

123. $\dfrac{9\frac{7}{8} - 3\frac{11}{12}}{\frac{7}{10} \times \frac{5}{6}}$

124. $\dfrac{4\frac{2}{5} \div 5\frac{1}{2}}{8\frac{5}{6} - 8\frac{1}{2}}$

125. $\dfrac{2\frac{2}{5} \times 2\frac{1}{3}}{\frac{2}{3} \div \frac{2}{6}}$

Algebraic Fractions *Answers given on page 384.*

Reduce to lowest terms:

1. $\dfrac{3x + 3}{x^2 + 2x + 1}$

2. $\dfrac{2x^2 - 2}{x + 1}$

3. $\dfrac{3y + 3z}{4y + 4z}$

4. $\dfrac{5x + 5y}{5x + 5y}$

5. $\dfrac{x^2 - 25}{3x + 15}$

6. $\dfrac{a^2 - 16}{a^2 - 8a + 16}$

7. $\dfrac{5a + 10}{a^2 + 4a + 4}$

8. $\dfrac{x^2 - 3x - 4}{x^2 + 2x + 1}$

9. $\dfrac{x^2 + 5x - 6}{x^2 - 2x + 1}$

10. $\dfrac{x^2 - 8x + 15}{x^2 + x - 12}$

11. $\dfrac{\frac{1}{x} + \frac{1}{y}}{\frac{1}{xy}}$

12. $\dfrac{\frac{1}{x}}{\frac{1}{x} - x}$

13. $\dfrac{1 - \frac{1}{m}}{\frac{1}{m}}$

14. $\dfrac{x - 1}{1 - x^2}$

15. $\dfrac{b - \frac{1}{a}}{\frac{1}{a}}$

16. $\dfrac{1 - a^2}{a + 1}$

17. $\dfrac{\frac{a}{x}}{\frac{b}{x^2}}$

18. $\dfrac{\frac{1}{a^2} + \frac{1}{b^2}}{\frac{2}{ab}}$

19. $\dfrac{1 - \frac{1}{a}}{1 + \frac{1}{a}}$

20. $\dfrac{\frac{x}{y} + \frac{y}{x}}{\frac{1}{xy}}$

Combine into a single fraction:

21. $\dfrac{5x}{3} + \dfrac{x}{4}$

22. $\dfrac{5x}{3} + \dfrac{2x}{4}$

23. $\dfrac{5x - 3}{6x} + \dfrac{3x + 7}{10x}$

24. $\dfrac{x + 4}{3} + \dfrac{x + 5}{4}$

25. $\dfrac{5}{2a} - \dfrac{a - b}{6a^2}$

26. $\dfrac{3}{a - 5} + \dfrac{2}{5 - a}$

27. $\dfrac{5a}{4} - \dfrac{a}{3}$

28. $\dfrac{1}{x} - \dfrac{1}{y}$

29. $\dfrac{1}{5} + \dfrac{1}{x}$

30. $\dfrac{3}{x^2} - \dfrac{2}{x}$

Multiply:

31. $\dfrac{3a^2b}{2} \cdot \dfrac{8}{ab^2}$

32. $\dfrac{a^2 - b^2}{12a^3} \cdot \dfrac{6a}{a - b}$

33. $\dfrac{(x + 5)^2}{25} \cdot \dfrac{5}{(x + 5)}$

34. $\left(\dfrac{a}{b} + 2\right)\left(\dfrac{a}{b} - 2\right)$

35. $\left(5 + \dfrac{5}{3a}\right)\left(\dfrac{1}{a} + 3\right)$

36. $\left(\dfrac{1}{9} - x^2\right)\left(\dfrac{9}{1 - 3x}\right)$

37. $\left(\dfrac{1}{a^2} - \dfrac{1}{b^2}\right)\left(\dfrac{2ab}{a - b}\right)$

38. $\left(x + \dfrac{x^2}{y}\right)\left(\dfrac{y^2}{y^2 - x^2}\right)$

39. $\left(\dfrac{x^2 - 1}{x - 1}\right)\left(\dfrac{x - 1}{x + 1}\right)$

40. $\left(\dfrac{x^2 + 4}{x^2 - 4}\right)\left(\dfrac{(x - 2)}{x + 2}\right)$

Divide

41. $\left(2+\frac{x}{y}\right)\div\left(2-\frac{x^2}{y^2}\right)$

42. $\left(1-\frac{a}{b}\right)\div\left(b-\frac{a^2}{b}\right)$

43. $\left(\frac{x^2}{y^2}-16\right)\div\left(\frac{x}{y}-4\right)$

44. $\left(5+\frac{5}{3a}\right)\div\left(\frac{1}{9a}-a\right)$

45. $\left(\frac{1}{9}-x^2\right)\div\left(x-\frac{1}{3}\right)$

Simplify

46. $\dfrac{\frac{x^2-4y^2}{y^2}}{\frac{x+2y}{y}}$

47. $\dfrac{1-\frac{3}{x}}{1-\frac{9}{x^2}}$

48. $\dfrac{a+\frac{1}{4}}{a^2-\frac{1}{16}}$

49. $\dfrac{x-\frac{y^2}{x}}{1+\frac{y}{x}}$

50. $\dfrac{\frac{x}{y}-\frac{y}{x}}{\frac{y}{x}-1}$

Fractional Equations *Answers given on page 385.*

1. $\frac{x}{3}+\frac{x}{4}=\frac{7}{12}$ $x=(?)$
   (a) $\frac{1}{12}$ (b) 1 (c) $3\frac{1}{2}$ (d) 7 (e) 14

2. $\frac{x+2}{3}-\frac{x-2}{5}=2$ $x=(?)$
   (a) −7 (b) 2 (c) 3 (d) 7 (e) 15

3. $\frac{8}{20}=\frac{x}{30}$ $x=(?)$
   (a) 2 (b) $7\frac{1}{2}$ (c) 12 (d) 18 (e) 24

4. $\frac{2x+3}{3}-\frac{x-3}{5}=3$ $x=(?)$
   (a) −3 (b) $-\frac{11}{7}$ (c) 1 (d) 3 (e) 9

5. $\frac{27}{x}=\frac{3}{4}$ $x=(?)$
   (a) 3 (b) 4 (c) 12 (d) 36 (e) 108

6. $\frac{10}{1-2x}=2$ $x=(?)$
   (a) −3 (b) −2 (c) $-\frac{1}{2}$ (d) 2 (e) 3

7. $\frac{2}{3x+4}=\frac{1}{4x-3}$ $x=(?)$
   (a) $\frac{10}{11}$ (b) $\frac{2}{5}$ (c) 1 (d) 2 (e) 7

8. $\frac{rx-a}{x-1}=s$ $x=(?)$
   (a) $\frac{s-a}{s-r}$ (b) $\frac{a}{r}$ (c) $-\frac{a}{r}$ (d) $\frac{1-a}{s-r}$
   (e) $\frac{a-1}{s-r}$

9. $r=\frac{x}{1-x}$ $x=(?)$
   (a) 0 (b) 1 (c) r (d) $\frac{r}{r-1}$ (e) $\frac{r}{r+1}$

10. $\frac{x-3}{2x}=\frac{1}{3}$ $x=(?)$
    (a) −9 (b) $2\frac{2}{3}$ (c) 3 (d) $4\frac{1}{2}$ (e) 9

11. $\frac{2x}{3}+3=\frac{x}{3}$ $x=(?)$
    (a) −9 (b) −3 (c) −1 (d) $\frac{3}{5}$ (e) 9

12. $\frac{x^2+4x+2}{x^2+3x+7}=1$ $x=(?)$
    (a) 5 (b) 9 (c) $\frac{2}{7}$ (d) 1 (e) $\frac{5}{7}$

13. $\frac{t}{5u}=3, \frac{r}{2s}=5, \frac{s}{t}=2$ $\frac{u}{r}=(?)$
    (a) $\frac{1}{300}$ (b) $\frac{3}{20}$ (c) $\frac{3}{5}$ (d) $\frac{5}{3}$ (e) 30

14. $\sqrt{\frac{2+x^2}{2}}=3$ $x=(?)$
    (a) −4 (b) +4 (c) ±4 (d) 9 (e) 16

15. $\sqrt{\frac{9}{16}x^2} + \frac{3}{8}x + \frac{1}{16} = 4$

(a) 3 (b) 3½ (c) $\frac{17}{3}$ (d) 16 (e) 17

16. $\left(2+\frac{1}{x}\right)\left(\ ?\ \right)=\left(\frac{1}{x}\right)$

(a) −2 (b) $\frac{1}{2}$ (c) $\frac{1}{2x+1}$

(d) $\frac{2}{2x+1}$ (e) $\frac{2x+1}{x^2}$

17. $\frac{a}{3} = 2b,\ b = \frac{c}{2}$ $c = (?)$

(a) $\frac{a}{3}$ (b) $\frac{12}{a}$ (c) $\frac{3a}{4}$ (d) $\frac{4a}{3}$ (e) $3a$

18. $\frac{3}{x} = \frac{a+b}{c}$ $\frac{x}{3} = (?)$

(a) $\frac{c}{a+b}$ (b) $\frac{3c}{a+b}$ (c) $3c$

(d) $3c(a+b)$ (e) $3c+a+b$

19. $13 = \frac{13w}{1-w}$ $(2w)^2 = (?)$

(a) $\frac{1}{2}$ (b) $\frac{1}{4}$ (c) 1 (d) 2 (e) 4

20. $\frac{1}{2}x = k = \frac{2}{3}y$ $x + y = (?)k$

(a) $\frac{2}{5}$ (b) $\frac{3}{4}$ (c) $1\frac{1}{6}$

(d) $2\frac{1}{2}$ (e) $3\frac{1}{2}$

Verbal Problems Involving Fractions *Answers given on page 385.*

1. Ten merchants agreed to purchase uniforms for a local baseball team at a total cost of M dollars. After a disagreement, two merchants dropped out of the project. By how many dollars was the cost to each merchant increased?

(a) $\frac{M-20}{2}$ (b) $\frac{M}{40}$ (c) $\frac{M}{9}$ (d) $\frac{M}{2}$ (e) $2M$

1 a b c d e

2. Three-fourths of a gasoline storage tank is emptied by filling each of 5 trucks with the same amount of fuel. What part of the total capacity of the storage tank did each vehicle receive?

(a) $\frac{1}{5}$ (b) $\frac{1}{10}$ (c) $\frac{2}{15}$ (d) $\frac{3}{20}$ (e) $\frac{4}{15}$

2. a b c d e

3. A gasoline tank is $\frac{1}{2}$ full and has 8 gallons removed. The tank was then $\frac{1}{10}$ full. What is the capacity of the tank (in gallons)?

(a) 2.5 (b) 6.4 (c) 15.8 (d) 20 (e) 40

3. a b c d e

4. A motion was adopted by a vote of 5 to 3. What part of the total vote was against the motion?

(a) $\frac{3}{8}$ (b) $\frac{3}{5}$ (c) $\frac{5}{8}$ (d) $\frac{5}{3}$ (e) $\frac{8}{5}$

4. a b c d e

5. The indicator of an oil tank shows $\frac{1}{5}$ full. After the truck delivers 165 gallons of oil the indicator shows $\frac{4}{5}$ full. What is the capacity of the tank (in gallons)?

(a) 55 (b) 105 (c) 140 (d) 175 (e) 275

5. a b c d e

6. A man owned $\frac{5}{8}$ of an interest in a house. He sold $\frac{1}{5}$ of his interest, at cost, for $1,000. What is the total value of the house?

(a) $3,000 (b) $4,000 (c) $5,000 (d) $6,000 (e) $8,000

6. a b c d e

7. Of a man's salary, $\frac{1}{10}$ is spent for clothing, $\frac{1}{3}$ for food and for rent. What part of the salary is left for other expenditures and savings?

(a) $\frac{17}{30}$ (b) $\frac{3}{5}$ (c) $\frac{19}{30}$ (d) $\frac{2}{3}$ (e) $\frac{7}{10}$

7. a b c d e

8. A man leaves his estate to his wife and two sons. If the wife received $\frac{1}{3}$ of the estate and each son receives $\frac{1}{2}$ of the remainder, find the value of the entire estate if each son receives $4,000 as his share.

(a) $6,000 (b) $12,000 (c) $16,000 (d) $18,000 (e) $24,000

8. a b c d e

9. What part of a quarter is two pennies, two nickels and one dime?

(a) $\frac{1}{88}$ (b) $\frac{1}{5}$ (c) $\frac{3}{25}$ (d) $\frac{17}{25}$ (e) $\frac{22}{25}$

9. a b c d e

10. Sulfuric acid contains, by weight, 2 parts of hydrogen, 32 parts of sulfur and 64 parts of oxygen. What part, by weight, of sulfuric acid is sulfur?

(a) $\frac{1}{4}$ (b) $\frac{16}{49}$ (c) $\frac{8}{25}$ (d) $\frac{16}{33}$ (e) $\frac{16}{30}$

10. a b c d e

11. When the gasoline gauge of an automobile shows $\frac{1}{8}$ full it takes 14 gallons to completely fill the tank. What is the capacity of the gasoline tank (in gallons)?

(a) 15 (b) 16 (c) 18 (d) 20 (e) 98

11. a b c d e

12. A five foot stick is cut so that one part is $\frac{2}{3}$ of the other. How many inches is the shorter segment?

(a) 3 (b) $3\frac{1}{3}$ (c) $3\frac{1}{2}$ (d) 24 (e) 36

12. a b c d e

13. A baseball team won w games and lost l games. What fractional part of its games did it win?

(a) $\frac{l}{w}$ (b) $\frac{w-l}{w}$ (c) $\frac{w}{l}$ (d) $\frac{w+l}{w}$ (e) $\frac{w}{w+l}$

13. a b c d e

14. In a graduating class with the same number of boys and girls, $\frac{1}{8}$ of the girls and $\frac{5}{6}$ of the boys are honor students. What part of the class are boys who are not honor students?

(a) $\frac{1}{12}$ (b) $\frac{1}{6}$ (c) $\frac{7}{48}$ (d) $\frac{13}{48}$ (e) $\frac{35}{48}$

14. a b c d e

15. If a man's salary is $\$D$ per month and during a certain month he spends $\$a$, what fractional part of his salary does he save?

(a) $D - a$ (b) $\frac{D-a}{D}$ (c) $\frac{a}{D}$ (d) $\frac{D}{a}$ (e) $\frac{D-a}{a}$

15. a b c d e

16. A state convention contains r representatives. Town A has a representatives while Town B has b representatives. What part of the representatives are from Town A?

(a) $\frac{b}{r}$ (b) $\frac{a}{b}$ (c) $\frac{a}{b+r}$ (d) $\frac{a}{r}$ (e) $\frac{a}{a+r}$

16. a b c d e

17. A boy walked for $\frac{1}{2}$ hour and then got an automobile ride for $\frac{1}{3}$ of an hour. What part of an hour did the entire trip take?

(a) $\frac{1}{6}$ (b) $\frac{1}{5}$ (c) $\frac{2}{5}$ (d) $\frac{5}{6}$ (e) $\frac{3}{2}$

17. a b c d e

18. A manufacturer of a glassware product finds that $\frac{1}{20}$ of the items are damaged in shipment and not suitable for sale. How many items should be shipped so that a customer will have 190 items suitable for sale?

(a) 152 (b) 200 (c) 228 (d) 285 (e) 380

19. Three out of five boys in Centerville graduate from high school. One third of these boys go to junior college. What fractional part of the boys in Centerville go to junior college?

(a) $\frac{3}{40}$ (b) $\frac{1}{8}$ (c) $\frac{1}{5}$ (d) $\frac{5}{9}$ (e) $\frac{9}{5}$

20. If 10 parts of alcohol are mixed with 14 parts of xylol, what part of the mixture is alcohol?

(a) $\frac{1}{14}$ (b) $\frac{1}{7}$ (c) $\frac{5}{12}$ (d) $\frac{7}{12}$ (e) $\frac{7}{5}$

21. If $\frac{2}{3}$ of the men in a factory go on vacation in July and $\frac{1}{2}$ of the remainder take their vacations in August, what fraction of the men take their vacations at other times of the year?

(a) 0 (b) $\frac{1}{6}$ (c) $\frac{1}{3}$ (d) $\frac{2}{3}$ (e) $\frac{5}{6}$

22. Which of the following fractions is closest to $\frac{1}{4}$?

(a) $\frac{1}{5}$ (b) $\frac{3}{10}$ (c) $\frac{3}{20}$ (d) $\frac{7}{20}$ (e) $\frac{4}{15}$

23. Susan is four times as old as Paul and $1\frac{1}{2}$ times as old as Mary. What fraction of Paul's age is Mary?

(a) $\frac{3}{8}$ (b) $2\frac{2}{3}$ (c) $3\frac{3}{4}$ (d) 6 (e) $6\frac{1}{2}$

24. How many $\frac{1}{4}$ inch strips can be cut from a length of ribbon eight feet long?

(a) 24 (b) 32 (c) 200 (d) 320 (e) 384

25. 2 pints = 1 quart
4 quarts = 1 gallon
What part of a gallon is 6 pints?

(a) $\frac{1}{6}$ (b) $\frac{2}{3}$ (c) $\frac{3}{4}$ (d) $\frac{4}{3}$ (e) $\frac{3}{2}$

26. When the price of an article is reduced by $\frac{2}{7}$ of its former value, the number of articles sold is increased to $\frac{21}{10}$ of the original amount. The present daily receipts is what fraction of the former?

(a) $\frac{3}{5}$ (b) $1\frac{1}{2}$ (c) $1\frac{2}{3}$ (d) $2\frac{2}{5}$ (e) $2\frac{1}{2}$

27. Roy paints $\frac{1}{4}$ of a barn and Ronald paints $\frac{1}{8}$ of the remainder. What fraction of the barn is left unpainted?

(a) $\frac{1}{32}$ (b) $\frac{11}{32}$ (c) $\frac{21}{32}$ (d) $\frac{29}{32}$ (e) $\frac{31}{32}$

28. Milltown has 1600 phones of which $\frac{3}{4}$ are manually operated. If $\frac{1}{3}$ of these are replaced by dial phones and 300 additional dial phones are installed, what fraction of the phones are now manually operated?

(a) $\frac{8}{19}$ (b) $\frac{7}{16}$ (c) $\frac{11}{19}$ (d) $\frac{9}{16}$ (e) $\frac{1}{2}$

29. If $\frac{2}{3}$ of a yard of licorice is divided into 12 strips, what part of a foot would two strips be?

(a) $\frac{1}{9}$ (b) $\frac{1}{6}$ (c) $\frac{1}{3}$ (d) $\frac{1}{2}$ (e) $\frac{2}{3}$

a b c d e
29. || || || || ||

30. Each year a car depreciates a certain fraction of its value. During the first year it depreciates $\frac{1}{3}$ of its value, while during the second year it depreciates $\frac{1}{4}$ of its value, and during the third year it depreciates $\frac{1}{5}$ of its value. What fraction of its original value is the value of a car at the end of the third year?

(a) $\frac{2}{5}$ (b) $\frac{3}{5}$ (c) $\frac{13}{60}$ (d) $\frac{47}{60}$ (e) $\frac{29}{30}$

a b c d e
30. || || || || ||

DECIMALS

A decimal is an indicated fraction in which the denominator is 10, 100, 1000, 10.000 . . . etc.

$\frac{3}{10}$ is written as 0.3

$\frac{3}{100}$ is written as 0.03

$\frac{3}{1000}$ is written as 0.003

$33\frac{3}{100}$ is written as 33.03

If a number consists of a whole number and a fraction, the whole number is written before the decimal point and the fraction after it.

$3\frac{7}{10} = 3.7$

$3\frac{72}{100} = 3.72$

$37\frac{2}{10} = 37.2$

The value of a decimal is not changed by adding zeros at the end of the numeral.

Thus $0.5 = 0.50 = 0.500$ because $0.5 = \frac{5}{10}$,

$0.50 = \frac{50}{100}$, $0.500 = \frac{500}{1000}$

Addition

To add decimal numbers list the numbers to be added, making certain that the decimal points are under each other, and add in the usual manner. Thus:

$4.25 + 12 + 6.312 + 3.2 = ?$

```
  4.25
 12.
  6.312
  3.2
 ------
 25.762   Answer
```

Subtraction

Subtraction. List and subtract, as in the following:

From 8.6 take 2.73

```
  8.60
- 2.73
 -----
  5.87   Answer
```

Multiplication

Multiplication. The number of decimal places in the product is equal to the number of decimal places in the multiplicand and the multiplier.

```
   2.663    multiplicand (three decimal places)
 × 3.14     multiplier (two decimal places)
 -------
   10652
   2663
  7989
 -------
  836182    product
 8.36182    answer after placing the decimal five decimal
              places to the left.
```

Multiplication of decimals by 10, 100, 1000, 0.1, 0.01, 0.001 etc. can be carried out quickly by changing the position of the decimal point. To multiply by 10 we move the decimal point one place to the right; to multiply by 100 we move the decimal point two places to the right, etc. To multiply by 0.1 we move the decimal point one place to the left; to multiply by 0.01 we move the decimal point two places to the left, etc.

$(72.36)(10) = 723.6$

$(5.9824)(100) = 598.24$

$(0.27345)(1000) = 273.45$

$(0.003279)(10000) = 32.79$

$(437.21)(0.1) = 43.721$

$(324.79)(0.01) = 3.2479$

$(0.0324)(0.001) = 0.0000324$

Division

Division. Make the divisor a whole number by moving the decimal point the proper number of places to the right. Move the decimal point of the dividend the same number of places to the right. Place a decimal point in the quotient directly above the decimal point in the dividend.

Divide 9.683 by 4.21

```
        quotient              2.3
divisor ) dividend    4.21. ) 9.68.3
                              8 42
                              ----
                              1 26 3
                              1 26 3
                              ------
```

When the question is worded "find correct to two decimal places or to the nearest hundredth," it is necessary to carry the division to one more place than specified. Thus,

Divide correct to two decimal places: 27.5 ÷ 8

$$8\overline{)27.500}$$
$$3.437$$

If the digit just to the right of the desired decimal place is 5 or greater, we add 1 to the desired decimal place number. In the example above, 3.437 becomes 3.44. If the digit just to the right of the desired decimal place is less than 5, we drop it.

Divide 0.22 by 0.7, correct to two decimal places.

$$0.7.\overline{)0.2.200}$$
$$.314$$
$$.31$$

Division of decimals by 10, 100, 1000, can be carried out quickly by changing the position of the decimal point. To divide by 10 we move the decimal point one place to the left; to divide by 100 we move the decimal point two places to the left, etc.

72.36 ÷ 10 = 7.236
5.9824 ÷ 100 = 0.059824
0.27345 ÷ 1000 = 0.00027345
0.003279 ÷ 10000 = 0.0000003279

To convert a fraction to a decimal, simply perform the indicated division. The numerator is divided by the denominator.

What is the decimal equivalent of $\frac{7}{8}$?

$$\begin{array}{r} .875 \\ 8\overline{)7.000} \end{array}$$

What is the decimal equivalent of $\frac{3}{64}$?

$$\begin{array}{r} .046875 \\ 64\overline{)3.000000} \\ 2\ 56 \\ \hline 440 \\ 384 \\ \hline 560 \\ 512 \\ \hline 480 \\ 448 \\ \hline 320 \\ 320 \\ \hline \end{array}$$

Solving Equations Containing Decimals

To clear the equation of decimals, multiply both sides of the equation by 10, 100 etc.

Solve for x

$0.02x + 0.6 = x$

Multiply both sides of the equation by 100

$2x + 60 = 100x$

Subtract $2x$ from both sides of the equation

$60 = 98x$

Divide both sides of the equation by 98

$x = \frac{60}{98}$ Reduce $x = \frac{30}{49}$

PRACTICE EXERCISES

Decimals *Answers given on page 385.*

1. Add 47.63 + 97.863 + 854.8 + 0.2897
2. Add 3.876 + 48.7 + 96 + 833.97
3. Subtract 867.4 − 93.87
4. Subtract 97.637 from 121.86
5. Multiply 873.9 × 0.46
6. Multiply 2.7 × 0.023
7. Multiply 48.7 × 9.3
8. Divide correct to two decimal places 637.56 ÷ 8.3
9. Divide correct to two decimal places 42.93 ÷ 0.76
10. Divide correct to two decimal places 496 ÷ 6.9

Solve the following for y

11. $0.2y = 0.16$
12. $9y - 2.1 = 2.1 - 5y$
13. $2y + 3.4 = 6.8$
14. $8y + 7.3 = 9y - 5.7$
15. $23y - 39.2 = 2.8 + 2y$

PERCENT

A *percent* is a fraction with a denominator of 100. Instead of writing the denominator, we write the symbol %. Thus, to write a percent as a fraction, drop the % sign and write a fraction with the original number as the numerator and 100 as denominator. If a decimal is needed, this fraction can be very easily converted to a decimal by using the methods reviewed in the previous section.

$$1\% = \frac{1}{100} = 0.01$$

$$22\% = \frac{22}{100} = 0.22$$

$$3.7\% = \frac{3.7}{100} = 0.037$$

- 180. $75\% = ? = ?$
- 181. $\frac{1}{2}\% = ? = ?$
- 182. $a\% = ? = ?$

Some percents are used often enough that many students find it helpful to memorize the simplified fractions to which they are equivalent:

$33\frac{1}{3}\% = \frac{1}{3}$	$20\% = \frac{1}{5}$	$83\frac{1}{3}\% = \frac{5}{6}$
$66\frac{2}{3}\% = \frac{2}{3}$	$40\% = \frac{2}{5}$	$12\frac{1}{2}\% = \frac{1}{8}$
$25\% = \frac{1}{4}$	$60\% = \frac{3}{5}$	$37\frac{1}{2}\% = \frac{3}{8}$
$50\% = \frac{1}{2}$	$80\% = \frac{4}{5}$	$62\frac{1}{2}\% = \frac{5}{8}$
$75\% = \frac{3}{4}$	$16\frac{2}{3}\% = \frac{1}{6}$	$87\frac{1}{2}\% = \frac{7}{8}$

To change a percent to a decimal, drop the % sign and move the decimal point two places to the left. For example: 5% = 0.05

- 183. $83\% = ?$
- 184. $2.3\% = ?$

To change a decimal to a percent, move the decimal point two places to the right and attach a % sign: 0.0002 = 0.02%

- 185. $0.02 = ?\%$
- 186. $20 = ?\%$

To write a fraction as a percent, first change it to a decimal and then move the decimal point two places to the right and add the % sign: $\frac{2}{5} = 0.40 = 40\%$

- **187.** $\frac{3}{25} = ?\%$
- **188.** $\frac{7}{10} = ?\%$

Types of Percentage Problems

Most problems in which the information is given in terms of percents, or the answer is requested as a percent, can be handled by setting up a proportion. The formula below will help.

$$\frac{\text{part}}{\text{whole}} = y\% = \frac{y}{100}$$

- **189. 2 is what percent of 5?** $\frac{2}{5} = \frac{x}{100}$

$$x = ?$$

• *Answers given on page 381.*

• 190. What percent of 4 is 0.02? $\frac{0.02}{4} = \frac{x}{100}$

$x = ?$

• 191. Write a/b as a percent. $\frac{a}{b} = \frac{x}{100}$

$x = ?$

• 192. What percent of p is q? $\frac{q}{p} = \frac{x}{100}$

$x = ?$

• 193. t is what percent of v?

• 194. What is 20% of 15? $\frac{20}{100} = \frac{x}{15}$

$x = ?$

• 195. What is 300 percent of 7?
• 196. 15 is 20 percent of what number?
• 197. 7 is 5 percent of what number?
• 198. 140 is $66\frac{2}{3}$ percent of what number?

Verbal Problems Involving Percent

• 199. A book sold for \$4.80 after a 20 percent discount was taken off the list price. What was the list price?
If a 20 percent discount was taken, then \$4.80 is 80 percent of the list price. Let x be the list price and set up the proportion:

$$\frac{80}{100} = \frac{4.80}{x}$$

• 200. A company pays a salesman a commission of $16\frac{2}{3}$ percent and has \$20,000 left in proceeds. What was the value of the sales before the commission was deducted? (Hint: the \$20,000 represents $83\frac{1}{3}$ percent of the value.)

• 201. A radio sells for \$220. If this represents a profit of 10 percent of the cost for the seller, how much did he buy it for?
Let x = the original cost. Then 10 percent of x, which is $0.10x$, is the profit. Thus the 220 is cost + profit or 110 percent of x.

• 202. If the temperature rises from 72° to 80°, what is the percent of increase?
Let x percent be the percent of increase, which is a change of 8°. Therefore,

$$\frac{x}{100} = \frac{8}{72}.$$

PRACTICE EXERCISES

Percent *Answers given on page 385.*

1. What % is $\frac{3}{12}$?
2. What percent of 12 is 3?
3. $12\% = \frac{3}{?}$
4. What percent of 3 is 12?
5. $40\% = \frac{?}{5}$
6. How much is 40% of 5?

• *Answers given on page 381.*

7. $\frac{?}{40} = 5\%$

8. 3 is 6% of a certain number. What is the number?

9. $\frac{3}{?} = 6\%$

10. What percent of 6 is 3?

11. What percent of 3 is 6?

12. What percent of 7 is 5?

13. What percent of 5 is 7?

14. Calculate 5% of 7.

15. Calculate 7% of 5.

16. What fraction is equivalent to 325%?

17. 3% of a certain number is equal to 7. What is the number?

18. What is the fraction equivalent of .024%?

19. Find 600% of 0.075.

20. What % of 0.002 is 0.0004?

21. What is 0.007 percent of t?

22. 0.00003 = 330% of x. Find x.

23. Find 0.003% of 0.0012.

24. What % of m is n?

25. If b is larger than d, what is the difference between 6% of b and 5% of d?

Verbal Problems Involving Percent *Answers given on page 386.*

1. In a class of 550 students, 42% wish to go to college. How many students wish to attend college?

(a) 13 (b) 23 (c) 77 (d) 210 (e) 231

1. a b c d e

2. In a class of 20 boys and 28 girls what percent of the class are girls?

(a) 41.7 (b) 48 (c) 58.3 (d) 70 (e) 71

2. a b c d e

3. A man saved $24.00 or 37½% of his weekly salary. What was his weekly salary?

(a) $40 (b) $46 (c) $64 (d) $88 (e) $90

3. a b c d e

4. A man deposits $700.00 in a bank which pays 3% interest per year. How much money does he have at the end of the year?

(a) $21.00 (b) $679.00 (c) $702.10 (d) $721.00 (e) $910.00

4. a b c d e

5. How much money would a man have to invest at the rate of 5% per year, to have $1470.00 at the end of the year?

(a) $70.00 (b) $700.00 (c) $1400.00 (d) $1462.65 (e) $1540.00

5. a b c d e

6. Mr. Carson paid $4.80 for a book after receiving a discount of 20% of the list price. What was the list price?

(a) $3.60 (b) $3.84 (c) $5.76 (d) $6.00 (e) $8.64

6. a b c d e

7. Mr. Goodsale receives a salary of $6000 per year plus 5% of all his sales over $10,000 and a special bonus of $500 if his sales exceed $20,000. What are his earnings during a year when his sales total $21,000?

(a) $6050. (b) $6500. (c) $6550. (d) $7000. (e) $7050.

7. a b c d e

8. A radio sells for $220.00. What was the cost, if the rate of profit was 10% of the cost?

(a) $198.00 (b) $200.00 (c) $210.00 (d) $240.00 (e) $242.00

8. a b c d e

9. The population of a city was 63,900 in 1955, an increase of 6½% over a previous census. By how many persons did the population increase between these periods?

(a) 3900 (b) 59,747 (c) 60,000 (d) 67,800 (e) 68,153

9. a b c d e

10. A department store had an end-of-winter sale of overcoats at the following prices:

A—\$80. coats reduced to \$55.
B—\$85. coats reduced to \$60.
C—\$90. coats reduced to \$65.
D—\$95. coats reduced to \$70.
E—\$120. coats reduced to \$95.

Which group of coats was offered at the greatest rate of discount from its original price?

(a) A (b) B (c) C (d) D (e) E

10. a b c d e

11. If 54% of a town's population received the first two polio "shots" and 10% of these did not receive the third, what percent of the town took all three "shots"?

(a) 44 (b) 48.6 (c) 49.6 (d) 59.4 (e) 64

11. a b c d e

12. A class of 80 is 25% girls. If 10% of the boys and 20% of the girls attended a picnic, what percent of the class attended?

(a) 10 (b) 12 (c) $12\frac{1}{2}$ (d) 20 (e) 30

12. a b c d e

13. Q is what percent of 20% of 15?

(a) $\frac{Q}{300}$ (b) $\frac{3}{100Q}$ (c) $\frac{3Q}{100}$ (d) $\frac{100}{3Q}$ (e) $\frac{100Q}{3}$

13. a b c d e

14. In May the average price of a bushel of corn was 25% above that of April. In June it was 30% below that of May. If the average price of corn in April was \$1.60 a bushel, what was the decrease in the average price of a bushel of corn from May to June?

(a) \$0.20 (b) \$0.36 (c) \$0.48 (d) \$0.60 (e) \$0.72

14. a b c d e

15. On the average an inspector rejects 0.08% of the instruments as defective. How many instruments will he examine in order to reject 2?

(a) 25 (b) 250 (c) 2,500 (d) 25,000 (e) 250,000

15. a b c d e

16. Judy gave her sister Lucy \$12.00 which is 15% of her weekly earnings. How much does Judy have now?

(a) \$10.20 (b) \$68.00 (c) \$69.80 (d) \$80.00 (e) \$92.00

16. a b c d e

17. What is the value of n after it has been decreased by $16\frac{2}{3}\%$?

(a) $\frac{1}{6}n$ (b) $\frac{1}{3}n$ (c) $\frac{5}{6}n$ (d) $\frac{6}{7}n$ (e) $\frac{7}{6}n$

17. a b c d e

18. 8% of 36 is 72% of what number?

(a) 2.06 (b) 2.88 (c) 3.24 (d) 4 (e) 40

18. a b c d e

19. If the number of articles purchased is increased by 20% and the price of each is decreased by 25%, by what percent is the value of the purchase changed?

(a) +5% (b) −5% (c) +10% (d) −10% (e) zero

19. a b c d e

20. X is what percent of $\frac{4}{5}$ of X?

(a) 75% (b) 80% (c) 120% (d) 125% (e) 180%

20. a b c d e

VERBAL PROBLEMS

Averages

To find the average of a set of numbers, add them and divide by the number of members of the set. Suppose $x_1, x_2, x_3, \ldots, x_n$ are n numbers, then their average, $\bar{x}$, is given by the formula:

$$\bar{x} = \frac{x_1 + x_2 + x_3 + \cdots + x_n}{n}$$

• 203. A boy in a chemistry class reports the following readings on a thermometer during an experiment: 5°, 0°, −2°, 9°. What is the average temperature?

Note that the formula given above can be written in a different form if each side is multiplied by n, the number of members in the set being averaged.

$$n\bar{x} = x_1 + x_2 + x_3 + \cdots + x_n.$$

This new formula says that the sum of a set of numbers is the same as the result gotten by multiplying the number of members times the average of the set.

• 204. A student has an average of 80 percent for six semesters. What must he earn in the next semester if he wants his average to be 82 percent?
Since he will end up with seven scores which average 82 the total of the test scores will have to be 7(82). But this total is also represented by the sum of the first six scores, 6(80) plus the last score which you can indicate by x. Write an equation and find x.

If the averages of two different sets of numbers are to be combined, they must be weighted in proportion to the number of members of each set.

• 205. A student attended Central High School for two semesters and earned an average of 90 percent. He transfered to Union High School and averaged 85 percent for five semesters. What is his scholastic average for all seven semesters? (First find the sum of his grades for the seven terms using the same idea as in the previous example.)

• 206. If 3 boys each earn an average of $5 a day and 2 men each earn $12 per day, what are the average daily earnings of the group?

PRACTICE EXERCISES *Answers given on page 386.*

1. What average must a student earn in his seventh semester in order to attain a scholastic average of 80%, if his averages for his previous semesters were as follows: Semester I 71%, Semester II 75%, Semesters III and IV 80%, Semester V 86% and Semester VI 88%?

(a) 80% (b) 82% (c) 83% (d) 84% (e) 85%

1. a b c d e

2. What is the average of a, b and c?

(a) $\frac{abc}{3}$ (b) $\frac{a+b+c}{3}$ (c) $3abc$ (d) $\frac{abc}{a+b+c}$ (e) $\frac{a+b+c}{abc}$

2. a b c d e

3. What is average temperature reading for a 4-day period when the daily temperature readings were: 7, 0, −2, and 3?

(a) −2 (b) 2 (c) 2.6 (d) 3 (e) −3

3. a b c d e

• *Answers given on page 381.*

4. What is the average of $\frac{1}{2}, \frac{5}{6}, \frac{3}{4}, \frac{5}{12}$?

(a) $\frac{7}{8}$ (b) $\frac{2}{5}$ (c) $\frac{5}{8}$ (d) $1\frac{3}{8}$ (e) $2\frac{1}{2}$

4. a b c d e

5. What is the average of 0.6, 6.6; 0.4, 2.4?

(a) 1 (b) 2 (c) $2\frac{1}{2}$ (d) 10 (e) 12

5. a b c d e

6. Find the value of x if the average of 1.0, 0.8, 0.2 and x is exactly 0.6.

(a) 0.2 (b) 0.4 (c) 0.66 (d) 1.3 (e) 2.4

6. a b c d e

7. The average of two numbers is M and one number is N. The other number is

(a) $2N$ (b) $2M$ (c) $2M - 2$ (d) $2M - N$ (e) $M - N$

7. a b c d e

8. The readings in a freezer are 5°, −7° and 8°. What must the next reading be so that the average will be 1°?

(a) −5° (b) −2° (c) −1° (d) 1° (e) 10°

8. a b c d e

9. Mary purchases 3 lbs. of mixed nuts at 89 cents per pound. Jane purchases 2 lbs. of peanuts at 49 cents per pound. What is the average price per pound for the mixture of both purchases?

(a) 69¢ (b) 70¢ (c) 71¢ (d) 72¢ (e) 73¢

9. a b c d e

10. What is the average of $N - 2$, $-N$, $N + 2$, and $2N$?

(a) $\frac{3N}{4}$ (b) N (c) $2N$ (d) $\frac{N}{4}$ (e) $4N$

10. a b c d e

11. Mr. Rich bought 50 shares of Shurshot Corporation at $60 and two months later purchased 25 shares of this stock at $56. At what price should he purchase 25 additional shares in order to have an average of $58 per share?

(a) $53 (b) $54 (c) $55 (d) $56 (e) $57

11. a b c d e

12. What is the average of one tenth, one hundredth and one thousandth?

(a) 0.003 (b) 0.01 (c) 0.037 (d) 0.111 (e) 0.333

12. a b c d e

13. The average of two numbers is a. If the larger number is l, what is the smaller?

(a) $a - l$ (b) $2a - l$ (c) $l - \frac{1}{2}a$ (d) $l - a$ (e) $l - 2a$

13. a b c d e

14. The variations of several barometer readings on either side of 29 inches were +0.3, −0.8, −0.2, 0.0, and +0.2 inch. What is the average of these readings (in inches)?

(a) 28.875 (b) 28.9 (c) 29.0 (d) 29.1 (e) 29.125

14. a b c d e

15. The average of M numbers is A, and the average of N numbers is B. What is the average of all the numbers?

(a) $A + B$ (b) $\frac{A + B}{2}$ (c) $\frac{AM + BN}{2}$ (d) $\frac{AM + BN}{M + N}$ (e) $\frac{AM + BN}{A + B}$

15. a b c d e

Motion

To solve problems involving motion you must know and understand the formula:

$$\text{Distance} = \text{Rate} \times \text{Time or}$$
$$d = rt.$$

The distance an object travels is the product of its *average* speed (rate) and the time it is traveling. This formula can be readily converted to express time in terms of distance and rate by dividing each side by r,

$$t = \frac{d}{r}.$$

It can also be changed to a formula for rate by dividing it by t,

$$r = \frac{d}{t}.$$

You should memorize the original formula, $d = rt$, and know how to convert it quickly to the others.

- • 207. How many miles can be covered in 3 hours by a train traveling an average speed of 45 miles per hour? (Note: $t = 3$, $r = 45$, $d = ?$)

- • 208. A motorist covers 93 miles in 3 hours. What is his average rate during this trip?

$$d = rt, \text{ so}$$
$$93 = (r)(3)$$
$$r = ?$$

- • 209. How long will it take a plane to cover a distance of 900 miles if it maintains an average rate of 90 miles per hour?

$$d = 900, r = 90, \quad = ?$$

- • 210. A motorist travels for 3 hours at 45 miles per hour and for 2 hours at 40 miles per hour. What is his average rate for the entire trip?
(Find the total distance covered by finding the distance for each part and adding the results. Then substitute total distance and total time into the formula.)

- • 211. Two trains start from the same station at the same time but travel in opposite directions. Their hourly rates are 35 miles per hour and 55 miles per hour. After how many hours will the trains be 540 miles apart?
(Let x = the number of hours each train travels since both travel for exactly the same time. Then $35x$ is the first train's distance and $55x$ the second. Together they have traveled 540 miles.)

PRACTICE EXERCISES *Answers given on page 386.*

1. How many miles can a motorist travel from 9:55 A.M. to 10:15 A.M. at the rate of 40 miles per hour?

(a) $13\frac{1}{3}$ (b) 15 (c) 20 (d) 30 (e) 40

a b c d e
1. || || || || ||

2. What is the average speed (in miles per hour) of a plane that covers 120 miles in one hour and twenty minutes?

(a) 30 (b) 60 (c) 90 (d) 100 (e) 120

a b c d e
2. || || || || ||

3. A man walked into the woods at the rate of 4 miles an hour and returned over the same road at the rate of 3 miles an hour. If he completed the entire trip in $3\frac{1}{2}$ hours, how far (in miles) into the woods did he walk?

(a) 3 (b) 4 (c) 5 (d) 6 (e) 7

a b c d e
3. || || || || ||

• *Answers given on page 381.*

4. Mr. Bronson left his home at 8:00 A.M. and traveled at the average rate of 40 miles per hour until 11:30 A.M. What distance (in miles) did he cover during the period?

(a) 100 (b) 140 (c) 160 (d) 320 (e) 340

5. A salesman travels for 2 hours at 30 miles an hour and then covers 60 miles in the next 3 hours. What is the average rate for the entire trip?

(a) 18 (b) 24 (c) 36 (d) 45 (e) 90

6. What is the rate in miles per hour for a messenger who travels $\frac{2}{3}$ of a mile in 4 minutes?

(a) 10 (b) 24 (c) 26$\frac{2}{3}$ (d) 30 (e) 45

7. What is the distance covered by a jet plane that travels at the rate of *xy* miles per hour for 2 hours?

(a) $\frac{x}{2}$ (b) $\frac{x}{y}$ (c) $2xy$ (d) $\frac{xy}{2}$ (e) $\frac{y}{2}$

8. What is the rate of a plane that covers *xy* miles in *y* hours?

(a) x (b) $\frac{x}{y}$ (c) $2xy$ (d) $\frac{xy}{2}$ (e) y

9. At what time will a train, traveling at 50 miles per hour, arrive at the station, if it is 5 miles from the station at 5:00 P.M.?

(a) 5:05 (b) 5:06 (c) 5:10 (d) 5:50 (e) 5:55

10. A train traveling 100 miles at *m* miles per hour arrived at its destination 1 hour late. How many miles an hour should it have traveled to arrive on time?

(a) $\frac{100}{m}$ (b) $\frac{100-m}{m}$ (c) $\frac{100m}{100-m}$ (d) $\frac{100m}{100+m}$ (e) $\frac{100-m}{100m}$

11. A train covers the distance *d* between two cities in *h* hours arriving 2 hours late. What rate would permit the train to arrive on schedule?

(a) $h-2$ (b) $\frac{d}{h}-2$ (c) $\frac{d}{h-2}$ (d) $dh-2$ (e) $\frac{d}{h+2}$

12. A train travels from La Crosse to New Lisbon in 46 minutes. If the distance between the two cities is 59.8 miles, what is the average rate of the train in miles per hour?

(a) 46 (b) 47 (c) 48 (d) 61 (e) 78

13. How fast is a train moving if it covers *d* miles in *h* hours?

(a) $\frac{h}{d}$ (b) hd (c) $\frac{dh}{2}$ (d) $\frac{d}{h}$ (e) $\frac{h}{2d}$

14. A boat sails *m* miles upstream at the rate of *r* miles per hour. If the rate of the stream is *s* miles per hour, how long will it take the boat to return to its starting point?

(a) $\frac{m}{r}$ (b) $\frac{m}{r+2s}$ (c) $mr-s$ (d) $\frac{m}{s}+r$ (e) $\frac{m}{r+s}$

15. How many hours will a man require to travel *M* miles at the rate of *H* miles per hour?

(a) HM (b) $\frac{H}{M}$ (c) $\frac{M}{H}$ (d) $\frac{M}{2H}$ (e) $\frac{D}{2M}$

16. A train covered d miles the first hour, e miles the second hour and f miles the third hour. What was the average rate for the entire trip?

(a) $\frac{def}{3}$ (b) $3def$ (c) $3(def)$ (d) $3(d+e+f)$ (e) $\frac{1}{3}(d+e+f)$

16. a b c d e

17. A motorist traveled 60 miles at the rate of 30 miles per hour and returned over the same route at 40 miles per hour. What was the average rate for the entire trip?

(a) $26\frac{2}{3}$ (b) 30 (c) 34 (d) $37\frac{1}{2}$ (e) 60

17. a b c d e

18. How many minutes would it take a train to cover a distance of one mile if its average speed is 50 M.P.H.?

(a) 0.2 (b) 0.8 (c) 1.2 (d) 2 (e) 5

18. a b c d e

19. A boy rides his bicycle ten miles at an average rate of twelve miles an hour and twelve miles at an average rate of ten miles an hour. The average rate for the entire trip is approximately

(a) 2 (b) 10 (c) 11 (d) 21 (e) 22

19. a b c d e

20. How many miles can a motorist travel from 8:55 A.M. to 9:15 A.M. if his average rate is 36 miles per hour?

(a) 12 (b) 24 (c) 36 (d) 48 (e) 108

20. a b c d e

21. Mr. Quigley runs y yards in s seconds. What would his rate be (in yards per second) if he ran twice as far in 10 more seconds?

(a) $\frac{2+y}{100+s}$ (b) $\frac{y}{2(s+10)}$ (c) $\frac{2y}{10s}$ (d) $\frac{2y}{s+10}$ (e) $\frac{2y}{s-10}$

21. a b c d e

22. A wheel rotates 10 times each minute and moves 20 feet during each rotation. How many feet does the wheel move in one hour?

(a) 120 (b) 200 (c) 600 (d) 1200 (e) 12,000

22. a b c d e

23. Two automobiles travel in the same direction at 40 miles per hour and 50 miles per hour respectively. How many hours after they are alongside of each other will they be 18 miles apart?

(a) 0.36 (b) 0.40 (c) 0.45 (d) 1.80 (e) 2.50

23. a b c d e

24. A mile runner is clocked at 58 seconds after the first quarter mile (440 yds.) and 1 minute 56 seconds after he has run a half mile. What rate (in yards per second) must he maintain for the final two quarters if he is to run a four minute mile?

(a) 7.0 (b) 7.1 (c) 7.3 (d) 7.6 (e) 7.8

24. a b c d e

25. Mr. Beedle rides his bicycle at an average rate of m kilometers per minute. Mr. Coddle walks half the distance in three times the length of time. What is Mr. Coddle's rate in kilometers per minute?

(a) $\frac{m}{90}$ (b) $\frac{m}{40}$ (c) $\frac{m}{10}$ (d) $\frac{m}{6}$ (e) $\frac{2m}{3}$

25. a b c d e

26. Mr. Bailey travels m miles at a miles per hour and Mr. Barnes travels the same distance but at a slower rate of b miles per hour. What is the difference (in hours) between the time taken by Mr. Bailey and the time taken by Mr. Barnes?

(a) $\frac{m}{a-b}$ (b) $\frac{m}{ab}$ (c) $\frac{2m}{a-b}$ (d) $\frac{m(a-b)}{ab}$ (e) $\frac{m(b-a)}{ab}$

26. a b c d e

27. How much farther can a motorist traveling at 35 miles an hour for h hours travel than a motorist who travels at 40 miles an hour for $(h - 2)$ hours?

(a) $70 - 5h$ (b) $80 - 5h$ (c) 45 (d) $5h - 80$ (e) $5h + 80$

27. a b c d e

28. The "MISTRAL" connects Paris and Lyons, a distance of 320 miles. At an average rate of 78 miles per hour, how many minutes does the trip take?

(a) 244 (b) 245 (c) 246 (d) 408 (e) 410

28. a b c d e

29. The "SUD-EXPRESS" averages a rate of 73 miles per hour in its run from Paris to Bordeaux. What is the distance (in miles) between these two cities, if the trip takes 297 minutes?

(a) 246 (b) 361 (c) 365 (d) 369 (e) 407

29. a b c d e

30. If a wheel rotates 12 times each minute, how many degrees does it rotate in 5 seconds?

(a) 60 (b) 150 (c) 240 (d) 360 (e) 1800

30. a b c d e

31. By rail the trip from Boston to New York is 215 miles while by airplane it is 188 miles. How many hours shorter is the trip by plane traveling at 225 miles per hour than by train traveling at 54 miles per hour?

(a) 2.98 (b) 3.0 (c) 3.14 (d) 4.0 (e) 4.5

31. a b c d e

32. Mr. Walker travels a miles in b hours, and then c miles in d hours. How many hours would it take to travel 1000 miles if he maintains this average rate?

(a) $\frac{1000}{a+c}$ (b) $\frac{1000}{b+d}$ (c) $\frac{1000}{b+c+d}$ (d) $\frac{1000(b+d)}{a+c}$ (e) $\frac{a+c}{1000(b+d)}$

32. a b c d e

33. The elevator in an eleven-story office building travels at the rate of 1 floor per ¼ minute which allows time for picking up and discharging passengers. At the main floor and at the top floor the operator stops for one minute. How many complete trips will an operator make during a 7 hour period?

(a) 20 (b) 30 (c) 60 (d) 76 (e) 120

33. a b c d e

34. How many minutes would it take a police car to respond to a call d miles away if the police car travels at m miles per hour?

(a) $\frac{60m}{d}$ (b) $\frac{60d}{m}$ (c) $\frac{d}{m}$ (d) $\frac{dm}{60}$ (e) $\frac{60}{dm}$

34. a b c d e

35. Mr. Barrow travels from London to Tintern Abbey, a distance of 250 miles, in $5\frac{1}{2}$ hours. After resting for 20 minutes he returns to London in 4 hours and 40 minutes. What is his average rate (in miles per hour) for the round trip?

(a) 43 (b) 44 (c) 45 (d) 46 (e) 48

35. a b c d e

Ratio and Proportion

A ratio is an expression which compares two quantities by dividing one by the other. In a class of 10 girls and 13 boys, the ratio of girls to boys is $\frac{10}{13}$ or 10:13. The ratio of boys to girls is $\frac{13}{10}$ or 13:10.

Since a ratio may be written as a fraction, to find the maximum ratio among a given set of ratios, determine which fraction has the greatest value. In any ratio involving measured quantities the units of measure of the quantities compared must be the same.

• 212. A room is 120 inches long and 1.2 feet wide. Find the ratio of width to length. (First change everything to feet.)

• 213. Find the ratio of 2 ounces to 4 pounds. (Convert the 4 pounds to 64 ounces to get similar units.)

• 214. The ratio of two numbers is 7:3, and their difference is 20. Find the numbers. (Since the two numbers are not themselves 7 and 3, it follows that $\frac{7}{3}$ is a fraction which has been simplified by removing a common factor. Let n be this common factor and represent the numbers by $7n$ and $3n$.)

• 215. The ratio of two numbers is 16 to 33. The larger number is 264, find the smaller. (Let the common factor be n.)

• 216. Two numbers are in the ratio 5 to 8. When 2 is added to each, the ratio of the resulting numbers is 2 to 3. Find the numbers. (Let $5n$ and $8n$ be the numbers. Then the resulting numbers will be $5n+2$ and $8n+2$ and their ratio will equal the fraction $\frac{2}{3}$.)

A *proportion* is an equation both sides of which are fractions. For example, $\frac{1}{2} = \frac{5}{10}$ is a proportion. A proportion consists of four terms: the first and last are the *extremes*, the second and third are the *means*. In the example above, 1 and 10 are extremes, 2 and 5 are means. In any proportion the product of the means equals the product of the extremes.

Thus, if $$\frac{a}{b} = \frac{c}{d}$$

then, $$ad = bc.$$

• 217. Find the value of x if $\frac{4}{7} = \frac{16}{x}$

then $4x = 16 \times 7$

$x = ?$

• 218. If $7y = 3z$ then $(y/z) = ?$

(To undo this cross-multiplication divide both sides by $7z$.)

The principles used in ratios and proportions can help solve many verbal problems. First decide if a proportion exists. Then determine whether it is a *direct* or an *inverse* proportion as explained below.

Two variables, x and y, are directly proportional if their corresponding values have some constant ratio, k.

$$\frac{x}{y} = k \text{ or } x = ky.$$

Note that an increase in either x or y causes an increase in the other if k is positive.

Two variables, x and y, are inversely proportional if $x = (k/y)$ where k is a constant. The relation is usually written as $xy = k$. Note that an increase in one variable results in a decrease in the other when k is positive.

Problems which involve these ideas do not necessarily have to use the terms *inversely proportional* or *directly proportional*.

• 219. If m books cost d dollars, how much will x books cost?
The ratio m/d is the proportionality constant for a direct proportion between the number of books and their cost. Let y be the number of dollars in the cost of the x books, set up the proportion and solve for y.

• *Answers given on page 381.*

- **220. If $1\frac{1}{3}$ cups of molasses can be substituted for a cup of sugar in a recipe, how many cups of molasses should be used in a recipe requiring $1\frac{1}{2}$ cups of sugar.**
The constant of proportionality is the ratio of cups of molasses to cups of sugar.
- **221. The current and resistance in an electrical circuit are inversely proportional (if the voltage remains unchanged). If a circuit has a resistance of 200 ohms and a current of $1\frac{1}{2}$ amps, find the current when the resistance is 500 ohms. Use the formula $rc = k$ where r is the resistance and c is the current, and find k with the given information.**
- **222. The greater the number of people hired to do a certain job, the shorter the time it takes to complete the job. If ten men take 12 hours, how long will sixteen men take?**

PRACTICE EXERCISES *Answers given on page 386.*

1. A city street has four large apartment houses and 14 private homes. What is the ratio of apartment houses to private homes?

(a) $\frac{2}{5}$ (b) $\frac{2}{9}$ (c) $\frac{4\frac{1}{2}}{1}$ (d) $\frac{1}{3\frac{1}{2}}$ (e) $\frac{7}{2}$

2. A mixture of nuts contains 2 lbs. of cashew nuts and 2 ounces of peanuts. What is the ratio of peanuts to cashew nuts in the mixture?

(a) 1:16 (b) 1:1 (c) 8:1 (d) 16:1 (e) 4:1

3. A pound of candy which ordinarily is sold for $1.60 per pound is offered for 48 cents in a six ounce package. What is the ratio of the former price to the present price?

(a) 3:1 (b) 5:4 (c) 10:3 (d) 3:10 (e) 4:5

4. If 3 apples cost 19 cents, how many apples can be purchased for $1.52?

(a) 15 (b) 19 (c) 22 (d) 24 (e) 26

5. A boy makes a diagram of a plane to a scale of $\frac{1}{400}$ of actual size. If the diagram of the plane is 9.6 inches in length, what is the length, in feet, of the plane?

(a) 96 (b) 320 (c) 384 (d) 960 (e) 3840

6. On a map drawn to a scale $\frac{1}{2}$ inch = 200 miles, what is the distance between two cities which are $3\frac{1}{2}$ inches apart?

(a) 300 (b) 350 (c) 700 (d) 1200 (e) 1400

7. How many minutes will it take a train traveling at the rate of 45 miles per hour to cover a distance of $\frac{4}{5}$ of a mile?

(a) 1.07 (b) 1.7 (c) 10 (d) 16 (e) 7.4

8. A motorist on the Freeway covers 0.8 mile in a minute. What distance (in miles) could he travel in 6 seconds?

(a) 0.08 (b) 0.48 (c) 0.8 (d) 4.8 (e) 8

9. What is the average rate in miles per hour for a motorist who goes 2 miles in 3 minutes?

(a) 20 (b) 24 (c) 32 (d) 40 (e) $66\frac{2}{3}$

10. How many miles are there in $1\frac{3}{5}$ kilometers if 1 kilometer equals $\frac{5}{8}$ of a mile?

(a) $\frac{24}{64}$ (b) 1 (c) $1\frac{38}{40}$ (d) 2 (e) 24

• *Answers given on page 381.*

11. If rain is falling 2 inches per hour, how many inches will fall in 12 minutes?

(a) $\frac{1}{360}$ (b) $\frac{2}{5}$ (c) $2\frac{1}{2}$ (d) 5 (e) 600

11. a b c d e

12. A vertical pole 6 feet high casts a shadow 4 feet long. At the same time a tree casts a shadow 64 feet long. What is the height (in feet) of the tree?

(a) 44 (b) 72 (c) 96 (d) 192 (e) 256

12. a b c d e

13. If 2 cups of melted chocolate weigh 16 oz., how many cups of melted chocolate can be obtained from a package of chocolate weighing 1 lb. 8 oz.?

(a) 2.2 (b) 3 (c) 3.2 (d) 4 (e) 4.3

13. a b c d e

14. Six cups of shredded coconut weigh one pound. What is the weight in ounces of one cup of shredded coconut?

(a) 0.6 (b) 0.16 (c) 1.6 (d) 2.6 (e) 4.3

14. a b c d e

15. A package of dried currants weighs 10 ounces. If 3 cups of dried currants weigh one pound, how many packages will a baker need for a recipe which calls for 15 cups of dried currants?

(a) 5 (b) 8 (c) 10 (d) 50 (e) 80

15. a b c d e

16. There are 3 to 4 tablespoons of bread flour in one ounce. What is the maximum number of tablespoons of bread flour in 12 ounces?

(a) 8 (b) 12 (c) 36 (d) 42 (e) 48

16. a b c d e

17. One cup of condensed, sweetened milk weighs 11 ounces. How much milk will remain unused for a recipe requiring 2 cups of milk when a housewife opens 4 six ounce cans of condensed milk?

(a) 1 (b) 2 (c) 12 (d) 20 (e) 22

17. a b c d e

18. 2 tablespoons = 1 oz. liquid

4 tablespoons = $\frac{1}{4}$ cup

How many ounces are there in 1 cup?

(a) 4 (b) 8 (c) 16 (d) 24 (e) 32

18. a b c d e

19. If a apples cost d dollars, how many apples can be bought for x dollars?

(a) $\frac{ad}{x}$ (b) $\frac{d}{ax}$ (c) $\frac{dx}{a}$ (d) $\frac{a}{d}$ (e) $\frac{ax}{d}$

19. a b c d e

20. If cards are sold at the rate of 3 for 10¢ what will be the cost of 3 dozen such cards?

(a) $0.42 (b) $1.08 (c) $1.20 (d) $1.26 (e) $1.44

20. a b c d e

21. At the rate of 2 for 5 cents, how many envelopes can be purchased for 65 cents?

(a) 13 (b) 26 (c) 32 (d) 34 (e) 52

21. a b c d e

22. The blueprint of a room is drawn to the scale 1 inch equals 20 feet. If a room is actually 10 yards long, how long is the line of the blueprint drawn to represent the length of the room?

(a) $\frac{2}{3}$ inch (b) $1\frac{1}{2}$ inches (c) $1\frac{1}{3}$ inches (d) 2 inches (e) 6 inches

22. a b c d e

23. If 4 men can clear the snow near a school in 6 hours, how many hours will it take 12 men working at the same rate to perform this task?

(a) 2 (b) 8 (c) 12 (d) 18 (e) 24

23. a b c d e

24. If m men do a job in 10 days how long will it take 10 men to complete this task, assuming that they work at the same rate?

(a) $\frac{10}{m}$ (b) $\frac{100}{m}$ (c) $100m$ (d) $\frac{m}{100}$ (e) m

24. a b c d e

25. A dietitian has sufficient milk to feed 13 infants for 4 weeks. How many days will this supply last if 13 additional infants were added?

(a) 2 (b) 8 (c) 14 (d) 26 (e) 56

25. a b c d e

26. In planning for a picnic, a committee purchases enough frankfurters to allow each of the 18 persons 3 frankfurters. If nine additional persons come to the picnic, how many fewer frankfurters will each person be given?

(a) 1 (b) $1\frac{1}{3}$ (c) 2 (d) $2\frac{1}{4}$ (e) $2\frac{1}{2}$

26. a b c d e

27. How many inches is the shadow of an R foot pole, if an r inch ruler casts an s inch shadow at the same time?

(a) $\frac{12Rs}{r}$ (b) $\frac{Rs}{r}$ (c) $\frac{Rs}{12r}$ (d) $\frac{12R}{rs}$ (e) $\frac{rs}{R}$

27. a b c d e

28. If a $3\frac{2}{3}$ pound box of candy costs \$3.30, what is the price per pound of candy in the box?

(a) 90¢ (b) \$1.00 (c) \$1.10 (d) \$1.11 (e) \$1.21

28. a b c d e

29. A pound of commercial fertilizer occupies from 20 to 25 cubic inches while a pound of humus occupies from 40 to 55 cubic inches. What is the maximum ratio of the amount of commercial fertilizer to humus in a two ton truck carrying equal amounts of each?

(a) $\frac{1}{2}$ (b) $\frac{4}{11}$ (c) $\frac{5}{8}$ (d) $\frac{5}{11}$ (e) $\frac{9}{19}$

29. a b c d e

30. In a section of Mills City the ratio of private homes to apartment house dwellings is 5:3. If all the apartment house dwellings are brick structures and $\frac{1}{10}$ of the private homes are wooden structures, what is the maximum portion of houses that may be brick?

(a) $\frac{3}{8}$ (b) $\frac{5}{8}$ (c) $\frac{6}{13}$ (d) $\frac{8}{13}$ (e) $\frac{15}{16}$

30. a b c d e

31. Grass seed which formerly sold for 60¢ a pound is now packaged in two-pound packages and is sold for \$1.50 per package. What is the ratio of the old price to the present price of this seed?

(a) 1:5 (b) 2:5 (c) 3:5 (d) 4:5 (e) 5:4

31. a b c d e

32. A test tube holds x cubic centimeters of water. How many test tubes are necessary to hold y cubic centimeters of water?

(a) $\frac{y}{x}$ (b) $\frac{x}{y}$ (c) xy (d) $\frac{1}{y}$ (e) $\frac{1}{x}$

32. a b c d e

33. How many 3 cent stamps may be purchased for d dollars?

(a) $\frac{d}{3}$ (b) $\frac{3}{d}$ (c) $\frac{d}{300}$ (d) $\frac{3}{100d}$ (e) $\frac{100d}{3}$

33. a b c d e

34. If t tables cost d dollars, what will be the cost in dollars of x tables?

(a) $\frac{dx}{t}$ (b) $\frac{dt}{x}$ (c) dtx (d) $\frac{xt}{d}$ (e) $\frac{d}{t}$

34. a b c d e

35. The British gallon is equivalent to 1.20094 United States gallons. If an automobile travels 18 miles on a British gallon of gasoline, how many United States gallons would it use on a 216 mile trip?

(a) 10 (b) 12 (c) 14.4 (d) 21.6 (e) 3240

35. a b c d e

36. Mr. Lynch who owns $\frac{3}{7}$ of a business received $6000 as his share of the profit for a certain year. How much will Mr. Beane receive during this same year if Mr. Beanc owns $\frac{2}{7}$ of this business?

(a) $1400. (b) $1614. (c) $2000. (d) $2562. (e) $4000.

36. a b c d e

37. If 7 miles are equivalent to 11.27 kilometers then 9.66 kilometers are equivalent to

(a) 5 miles (b) 6 miles (c) 7 miles (d) 7.5 miles (e) 7.9 miles

37. a b c d e

38. Mr. Wilson left $32,000 and specified that the money should be divided so that the ratio of the wife's share to the son's share should be 5:3. The son received

(a) $4000 (b) $6400 (c) $10,667 (d) $12,000 (e) $20,000

38. a b c d e

39. An office worker is paid $56.00 for a 35 hour week. Up to 40 hours she is paid at the regular hourly rate. For overtime more than 40 hours she receives $1\frac{1}{2}$ times as much as the regular hourly rate. How many hours did she work during a particular week when she earned $88?

(a) 45 (b) 48.3 (c) 50 (d) 52 (e) 55

39. a b c d e

40. A furniture salesman averages $160 during a normal 40 hour week. During a special sale his rate of commission is increased by 25%. What is his average weekly commission during this period if he works 60 hours per week while the special sale is in progress?

(a) $192 (b) $240 (c) $300 (d) $320 (e) $427

40. a b c d e

41. At d cents per dozen what is the price in cents of x pencils?

(a) $\frac{x}{12d}$ (b) $\frac{12d}{x}$ (c) $\frac{12x}{d}$ (d) $12dx$ (e) $\frac{dx}{12}$

41. a b c d e

42. A trackman runs 100 yards in 9.8 seconds and then runs 440 yards in 49 seconds. What is the ratio of his average speed in the 440 yard run to his average speed in the 100 yard run?

(a) $\frac{49}{43}$ (b) $\frac{22}{25}$ (c) $\frac{11}{12}$ (d) $\frac{12}{11}$ (e) $\frac{25}{22}$

42. a b c d e

43. A "parsec" is approximately 3.26 light years or 19.2 trillion miles. Approximately how many trillion miles are equivalent to one light year?

(a) $\frac{1}{63}$ (b) $\frac{1}{6}$ (c) 6 (d) 19 (e) 63

43. a b c d e

44. If the official exchange ratio of French francs to dollars is 350:1 and the free exchange ratio is 400:1, how much profit would a man make if he could convert $70 to francs at the free rate and then convert these back to dollars at the official rate?

(a) $1 (b) $10 (c) $61.25 (d) $70 (e) $80

44. a b c d e

45. Approximately $8,000,000 in bills of $10,000 denomination are in circulation, and approximately $400,000,000 in $1,000 bills are in circulation in the United States. What is the ratio of the number of $10,000 bills in circulation to the number of $1,000 bills in circulation?

(a) 1:500 (b) 1:50 (c) 1:5 (d) 50:1 (e) 500:1

45. a b c d e

46. Mr. Power averages 12 television service calls a day and Mr. Fixit averages 16 service calls per day. If Mr. Power's average charge is $\frac{3}{2}$ as much as Mr. Fixit who earns $7200 per year, then the annual earnings of Mr. Power are

(a) $3600 (b) $6400 (c) $7200 (d) $8100 (e) $14,400

46. a b c d e

47. At 625 Italian lire per American dollar what is the value (in cents) of 100 lire?

(a) 6 (b) $6\frac{1}{4}$ (c) 16 (d) 62 (e) $62\frac{1}{2}$

47. a b c d e

48. In the dining room of a children's summer camp, a quart of milk can serve 4 campers or 3 staff members. If at one meal 40 campers and 12 staff members are being served, how much milk will remain unused if 16 quarts are brought into the dining room?

(a) 2 (b) $8\frac{1}{3}$ (c) 10 (d) $10\frac{2}{3}$ (e) 14

48. a b c d e

49. In Europe tire pressure is measured in kilograms per square centimeter. If 32 pounds per square inch corresponds to 2.24 kilograms per square centimeter, how many kilograms per square centimeter would be equivalent to 24 pounds per square inch?

(a) 1.54 (b) 1.68 (c) 1.82 (d) 1.96 (e) 3.4

49. a b c d e

50. Approximate Working Time (in minutes) Required to Produce

Commodity	U.S.S.R.	U.S.A.
1 Quart Milk	42	7
1 Pound of Potatoes	7	2

How many more times efficient is the U.S.A. than the U.S.S.R. in the production of one quart of milk than in the production of one pound of potatoes?

(a) 1.7 (b) 2.5 (c) 3.5 (d) 6 (e) 21

50. a b c d e

Mixtures and Solutions

The principles of fractions are used in solving problems involving mixtures or solutions. One useful formula is:

$$\frac{\text{Quantity of substance dissolved}}{\text{Total quantity of solution}} = \text{Fractional part of solution containing dissolved substance}$$

• 223. A ten-gallon solution of disinfectant contains 1 gallon of disinfectant. What is the percent concentration of the solution?

• *Answers given on page 381.*

• **224.** How many pounds of pure salt must be added to 30 pounds of a 2 percent solution of salt and water to increase it to a 10 percent solution?
(Since 2% of the 30 pounds is salt, there is 0.6 pound of salt. Add x pounds of salt to the solution and set up the ratio of the new amount of salt, $x + .6$, to the new amount of solution, $x + 30$.)

• **225.** How much water must be added to 3 quarts of a 10 percent solution of acid to reduce it to a 6 percent solution?
Let x be the amount of water added, then set up the ratio of quarts of acid to the new number of quarts of solution.

PRACTICE EXERCISES *Answers given on page 386.*

1. How much water must be added to 10 quarts of alcohol that is 95% pure in order to obtain a solution that is 50% pure?
(a) 0.5 (b) 5 (c) 9 (d) 10 (e) 15

1. a b c d e

2. An alloy of copper and tin is 20% copper. How many pounds of copper must be added to 20 pounds of the alloy in order that the resulting alloy may be 50% copper?
(a) 6 (b) 12 (c) 12.5 (d) 13 (e) 14

2. a b c d e

3. A certain grade of gun metal (a mixture of tin and copper) contains 16% tin. How much tin must be added to 410 pounds of this gun metal to make a mixture that is 18% tin?
(a) 5 (b) 6.5 (c) 7 (d) 8 (e) 10

3. a b c d e

4. Of 24 pounds of salt water, 8% is salt; of another mixture, 4% is salt. How many pounds of the second mixture should be added to the first mixture in order to get a mixture that is 5% salt?
(a) 18 (b) 36 (c) 54 (d) 63 (e) 72

4. a b c d e

5. How much water must be added to 100 cc of 80% solution of boric acid to reduce it to a 50% solution?
(a) 30 (b) 40 (c) 50 (d) 60 (e) 84

5. a b c d e

6. How many quarts of pure alcohol must be added to 10 quarts of a mixture that is 15% alcohol to make a mixture that will be 25% alcohol?
(a) $\frac{3}{4}$ (b) $1\frac{1}{3}$ (c) $1\frac{1}{4}$ (d) $2\frac{1}{2}$ (e) 4

6. a b c d e

7. A solution of 27 gallons of acid contains 9 gallons of pure acid. How much water (in gallons) should be added to produce a 25% solution of this acid?
(a) $6\frac{3}{4}$ (b) 9 (c) $15\frac{3}{4}$ (d) 18 (e) 27

7. a b c d e

8. A solution is made by mixing a quarts of pure salt with b quarts of water. What is the per cent solution of the salt?
(a) $\frac{a}{a+b}\%$ (b) $\frac{100a}{a+b}\%$ (c) $\frac{100a}{b}\%$ (d) $\frac{a+b}{100}\%$ (e) $100(a+b)\%$

8. a b c d e

9. A chemist has 80 pints of a 20% salt solution. How much pure salt must be added to produce a solution which is 30% pure salt?
(a) 4.6 (b) 8 (c) 11.4 (d) 16 (e) 27.4

9. a b c d e

• *Answers given on page 381.*

10. How much alcohol must be added to 80 pints of a solution of alcohol and iodine which is 20% iodine, in order to produce a 15% solution of iodine?

(a) 4.7 (b) 10.7 (c) 12 (d) 12.7 (e) 26.7

10. a b c d e

11. A pharmacist wishes to convert 100 ounces of a 3% tincture of iodine to a 2% tincture of iodine. How many ounces of alcohol should he add to his original solution?

(a) 1 (b) 50 (c) 67 (d) 100 (e) 150

11. a b c d e

12. 16 ounces of fresh orange juice contains 216 calories and 16 ounces of fresh grapefruit juice contains 174 calories. If an 8 ounce mixture of these two juices contains 94 calories, what fraction of the mixture is orange juice?

(a) $\frac{1}{3}$ (b) $\frac{47}{108}$ (c) $\frac{1}{2}$ (d) $\frac{2}{3}$ (e) $\frac{47}{54}$

12. a b c d e

13. When purchased in units of 25 the 50¢ "Corona Royals" sell for $9.75 and the 25¢ "Coronas" sell for $4.50. What is the cost of 70 "Coronas" and 30 "Corona Royals" at this special rate?

(a) $18.00 (b) $23.25 (c) $24.30 (d) $28.50 (e) $32.50

13. a b c d e

14. How many quarts of a 90% solution of alcohol should be mixed with a 75% solution of alcohol in order to make 20 quarts of a 78% solution?

(a) 4 (b) 9 (c) 11 (d) 15 (e) 16

14. a b c d e

15. A confectioner mixes 9 parts of a grade of candy which costs p¢ a pound with 4 parts of another grade of candy which costs $1\frac{1}{2}$ times as much. What is the cost (in cents) of one pound of this mixture?

(a) p (b) $\frac{15}{13}p$ (c) $\frac{35}{26}p$ (d) $\frac{3}{2}p$ (e) $15p$

15. a b c d e

16. A 64 pound mixture of sand and gravel is 25% sand. How many pounds of sand must be added to produce a mixture which is 40% gravel?

(a) 9.6 (b) 16 (c) 38.4 (d) 40 (e) 56

16. a b c d e

17. How many pounds of water must be added to 48 pounds of alcohol to make a solution which is 25% alcohol?

(a) 36 (b) 48 (c) 64 (d) 144 (e) 192

17. a b c d e

18. A six ounce can of frozen orange juice concentrate contains 300 calories while an eight ounce glass of fresh orange juice contains 100 calories. How many ounces of water should be added to a six ounce can of concentrate in order to produce a drink with the same caloric value per ounce as fresh orange juice? (Note: Water has no caloric value.)

(a) 18 (b) 24 (c) 400 (d) 3744 (e) 3750

18. a b c d e

19. A tobacconist sells "burley," a base tobacco at 12¢ per ounce, and a blend of aromatic tobaccos at 35¢ per ounce. What is the cost of a one pound mixture containing 10 ounces of burley and the rest aromatic blend?

(a) $1.65 (b) $3.30 (c) $3.40 (d) $6.80 (e) $4.70

19. a b c d e

20. A recipe for a cheese cake calls for 12 ounces of cottage cheese and 6 ounces of cream cheese. If there are 216 calories in 8 ounces of cottage cheese and 106 calories in 1 ounce of cream cheese, how many calories are there in 36 ounces of the cheese mixture?

(a) 960 (b) 972 (c) 1920 (d) 3816 (e) 4788

20. a b c d e

Work

Problems involving time spent working often require the use of fractions. For example, a student who has four hours of homework does $\frac{1}{4}$ of his task when he works one hour. A simple formula to remember is:

$$\frac{\text{Time spent working}}{\text{Time required to do job}} = \text{Fractional part of job done}$$

• 226. A man can paint a room in six hours. His son can paint the same room in eight hours if he works alone. How long will it take the man and his son if they work together?
(Let $x =$ the number of hours it will take them to finish working together. Then in each hour they complete $1/x$ of the job. This $1/x$ represents the $\frac{1}{6}$ which the man does and the $\frac{1}{8}$ that his son completes.)

• 227. Mr. Jones can do a job in 10 days. After working 3 days he hires a helper and the two complete the task in 5 days. How long would it have taken the helper to complete the task alone?
(Each day Mr. Jones does $1/10$ of the job. In three days he does $3/10$ and then does another $5/10$ while working with the helper. If x is the number of days the helper would take to do the job alone, then he does $1/x$ each day and $5/x$ in five days. The sum of these fractions must equal 1 since the job was completed.)

• 228. One garden hose can completely fill a portable swimming pool in 80 minutes. Another garden hose could fill the same pool in half the time. How long would it take to fill the pool using both hoses? (Let $x =$ the number of minutes needed to fill the pool using both hoses. Then $1/x$ will be the fractional part completed in 1 minute. This represents the combined effects of the $1/80$ from the first hose and the $1/40$ from the second.)

PRACTICE EXERCISES *Answers given on page 386.*

1. Mr. Jones can do a job in 8 days and his son can do it in 12 days. How long would it take them to do the job if they worked together?

   (a) 4.8 (b) 5 (c) 10 (d) 15 (e) 20

   1. a b c d e

2. A and B can paint a barn in 3 days. A can do it alone in 5 days. How many days would it take B to do this job alone?

   (a) 0.2 (b) 3.2 (c) 5.0 (d) 6.4 (e) 7.5

   2. a b c d e

3. A machine can cut some wood in 6 minutes and a man using a hand saw could do it in 18 minutes. After 4 minutes there is a power shortage and the wood must be cut by hand saw. How many minutes must the man work to complete the task?

   (a) 2 (b) 6 (c) 12 (d) 14 (e) 18

   3. a b c d e

4. Mr. Boone can do a job in 10 days. A helper joins him after three days and together they work for 4 days to complete the task. How long would it take the helper to do the job alone?

   (a) 3 (b) $5\frac{5}{7}$ (c) 6 (d) 7 (e) $13\frac{1}{3}$

   4. a b c d e

5. A pipe can fill a swimming pool in h hours. What part of the pool is filled in x hours?

   (a) hx (b) $\frac{h}{x}$ (c) $\frac{x}{h}$ (d) $h + x$ (e) $\frac{hx}{2}$

   5. a b c d e

• *Answers given on page 381.*

6. Three pipes are used to fill a pool with water. One pipe alone can fill it in 9 hours. Another can fill it in 6 hours. The third can fill it in 3 hours. How many minutes would it take to fill this pool if all three pipes are used simultaneously?

(a) 1.63 (b) 11 (c) 54 (d) 56.4 (e) 98

6. a b c d e

7. The secretary of a club can address the envelopes for a mailing in 40 minutes. His younger brother who could do the entire job alone in one hour assists him. How long would it take to address the envelopes if both boys work?

(a) 0.04 minutes (b) 0.4 minutes (c) 8 minutes (d) 24 minutes
(e) 50 minutes

7. a b c d e

8. Mr. Mitchell can do a job in 45 minutes while his son would require 2 hours to do this job. How long would it take to complete this task if Mr. Mitchell was assisted by his son?

(a) 18 minutes (b) 33 minutes (c) 35 minutes (d) 1 hour 21 minutes
(e) 1 hour 31 minutes

8. a b c d e

9. If a man working alone can do a job in h hours and his helper working alone can do it in k hours, how long would it take them to do this job if they worked together?

(a) $\frac{1}{hk}$ (b) $\frac{h+k}{hk}$ (c) $\frac{h+k}{2}$ (d) $\frac{hk}{2}$ (e) $\frac{hk}{h+k}$

9. a b c d e

10. Mr. Jones can mow his lawn in x hours. After 2 hours it begins to rain. What part of the lawn is left unmowed?

(a) $\frac{2-x}{x}$ (b) $\frac{x}{2}$ (c) $x-2$ (d) $\frac{x-2}{2}$ (e) $\frac{x-2}{x}$

10. a b c d e

11. If 10 men can do a piece of work in 20 days how long will it take 8 men to do the job if they work at the same rate?

(a) 4 (b) 14 (c) 16 (d) 18 (e) 25

11. a b c d e

12. A master painter can paint a house in m days, and his two workers require w_1 and w_2 days to paint a house. If the master works as fast as the two workers together, find m in terms of w_1 and w_2.

(a) 1 (b) $\frac{w_1+w_2}{w_1w_2}$ (c) $\frac{w_1w_2}{w_1+w_2}$ (d) $\frac{w_1}{w_2}$ (e) $\frac{w_2}{w_1}$

12. a b c d e

13. A father can do a job as fast as two sons working together. If one son does the job alone in three hours and the other does it alone in six hours, how many hours does it take the father to do the job alone?

(a) 1 (b) 2 (c) 3 (d) 4 (e) 5

13. a b c d e

14. Five men can paint a house in six days. If two of the men don't work, what will be the increase of time required to complete the job?

(a) 4 (b) 6 (c) 8 (d) 10 (e) 12

14. a b c d e

15. In a factory, a men work b hours a day and produce c articles each day. If d men are released, how many hours a day will the remaining men have to work to produce c articles each day?

(a) $\frac{ab}{d}$ (b) $\frac{ad}{b}$ (c) $\frac{a-d}{b}$ (d) $\frac{ab}{a-d}$ (e) $\frac{b(a-d)}{d}$

15. a b c d e

16. Mr. Berg who works twice as fast as Mr. Slocum receives an hourly rate of pay $1\frac{1}{3}$ times as much as Mr. Slocum. An efficiency expert calculates that an article produced by Mr. Berg has a labor cost of 12¢. What is the labor cost of an article produced by Mr. Slocum?

(a) 4¢ (b) 8¢ (c) 9¢ (d) 16¢ (e) 18¢

17. A regular postal clerk sorts 100 letters in c seconds while a part-time worker requires p seconds to sort 100 letters. How many seconds would it take them to sort 100 letters if they work together?

(a) $\frac{p+c}{2}$ (b) $\frac{p+c}{pc}$ (c) $\frac{pc}{p+c}$ (d) $\frac{100(p+c)}{pc}$ (e) $\frac{100pc}{p+c}$

18. Mrs. Crocker can do the dinner dishes in a quarter of an hour while her daughter Betty takes half an hour. What part of an hour would it take to do these dishes if they work together?

(a) $\frac{1}{8}$ (b) $\frac{1}{6}$ (c) $\frac{3}{16}$ (d) $\frac{3}{8}$ (e) $\frac{4}{3}$

19. John can paint a barn in 12 days. Joseph can do the same job in 3 days while James can paint the barn in 2 days. What part of the task would be completed in one day if the three boys worked together?

(a) $\frac{1}{17}$ (b) $\frac{3}{17}$ (c) $\frac{11}{12}$ (d) 1 (e) $\frac{12}{11}$

20. If three boys can paint a fence in two days, what part of the job can be completed by two boys in one day?

(a) $\frac{1}{3}$ (b) $\frac{2}{3}$ (c) $\frac{3}{4}$ (d) 1 (e) $\frac{4}{3}$

21. Mr. Smith works twice as fast as Mr. Slocum and three times as fast as Mr. Tyler. If Mr. Tyler can complete a job in 12 hours, what part of the job can Mr. Slocum do in 6 hours?

(a) $\frac{1}{12}$ (b) $\frac{1}{3}$ (c) $\frac{1}{2}$ (d) $\frac{3}{4}$ (e) 1

22. In one half the time, Mr. A can produce three times as much work as Mr. B. Mr. B can do in twice the time one third as much work as Mr. C. If Mr. C does a job in one hour, how many hours would it take Mr. A to do the same job?

(a) $\frac{1}{6}$ (b) $\frac{2}{3}$ (c) 1 (d) $\frac{3}{2}$ (e) 6

23. If three secretaries can type six manuscripts in twelve days, how many days would it take two secretaries to type three such manuscripts?

(a) 4 (b) 9 (c) 12 (d) 16 (e) 36

24. Snowhite Paint Co. contracts to paint three houses. Mr. Brown can paint a house in 6 days while Mr. Pinter would take 8 days and Mr. Slocum would take 12 days. After 8 days Mr. Brown goes on vacation and Mr. Pinter begins to work for a period of 6 days. How many days will it take Mr. Slocum to complete the contract?

(a) 7 (b) 8 (c) 11 (d) 12 (e) 13

25. Mr. Stanley mowed $\frac{3}{4}$ of his lawn in $1\frac{1}{4}$ hours. Mr. Samuels who works twice as fast finished mowing the lawn. How many minutes did Mr. Samuels work?

(a) $12\frac{1}{2}$ (b) 16 (c) 25 (d) 38 (e) 50

25. a b c d e

COORDINATE GEOMETRY

Many of the techniques of algebra can be applied to geometry when the points of a plane are assigned pairs of real numbers which indicate the positions of these points. This can be done by first drawing a pair of perpendicular number lines, *axes*, in the plane which intersect at the origin of each line.

One axis is drawn horizontal, the *x-axis*, and one vertical, the *y-axis*. The positive ray of the x-axis points to the right and the positive ray of the y-axis points up.

To label a given point in the plane, draw perpendicular lines from the point to each of the axes and find the number line coordinates on these axes. To avoid confusion we always record the x-coordinate first and the y-coordinate second, separating them with a comma and enclosing the pair of numbers in parentheses to indicate that the order of the numbers has special meaning.

• 229. In the following diagram, what are the coordinates of each point?

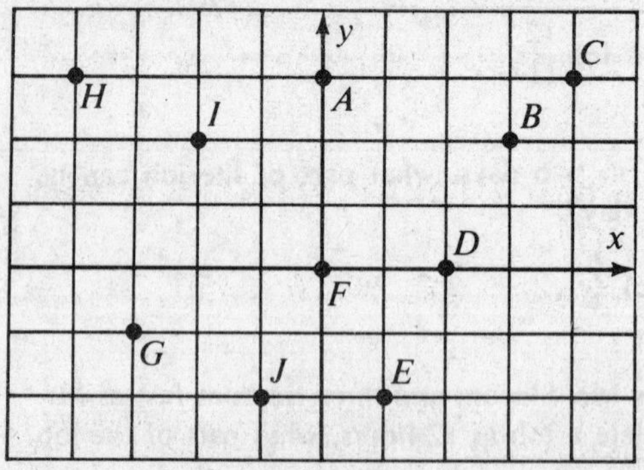

To find the distance between any two points use the distance formula. According to this formula, if point P_1 has coordinates (x_1, y_1) and the point P_2 is (x_2, y_2) then the distance between them is

$$\sqrt{(x_1 - x_2)^2 + (y_1 - y_2)^2}$$

• 230. Find the length of AC in the figure of example 229.

• 231. Find the length of FE in the figure of example 229.

To find the coordinates of the midpoint of a segment whose endpoints are given, use the midpoint formula. According to this formula, if point $P_1 = (x_1, y_1)$ and $P_2 = (x_2, y_2)$, the midpoint of the segment whose endpoints are P_1 and P_2 is:

$$\left(\frac{x_1 + x_2}{2}, \frac{y_1 + y_2}{2}\right)$$

• 232. If $(3, -1)$ and $(-4, 2)$ are the coordinates of the endpoints of a segment, find the coordinates of the midpoint.

• 233. If $(3, -1)$ is one endpoint of a segment and $(5, 0)$ is its midpoint, find the coordinates of the other endpoint.

• *Answers given on page 381.*

PRACTICE EXERCISES *Answers given on page 387.*

1. A line segment AB is drawn from point (2, 3) and point (4, 7). What are the coordinates of the midpoint?

(a) (5, 3) (b) (3, 5) (c) (6, 10) (d) (2, 4) (e) (4, 2)

1. a b c d e

2. What is the distance from point A (3, 4) to point B (−3, −4)?

(a) 0 (b) 5 (c) 10 (d) 13 (e) 14

2. a b c d e

3. Point P (4, 2) is the midpoint of line OPC, where O is at origin (O, O). The coordinates of C are

(a) (2, 1) (b) (4, 8) (c) (4, 4) (d) (8, 2) (e) (8, 4)

3. a b c d e

4. Point P (0, −4) is the midpoint of line AB where the coordinates of point A are (−2, −5). The coordinates of point B are

(a) (−4, −10) (b) (2, −5) (c) (2, 5) (d) (2, −3) (e) (2, 3)

4. a b c d e

5. The vertices of triangle ABC are (−1, 2), (−1, 1) and (−3, 2). Triangle ABC is

(a) obtuse (b) isosceles (c) right (d) equilateral
(e) either isosceles or equilateral

5. a b c d e

6. The vertices of triangle DEF are (1, 2), (−1, 1) and (−3, 2). Triangle DEF is

(a) equilateral (b) acute (c) either equilateral or obtuse (d) isosceles
(e) neither isosceles nor right

6. a b c d e

7. Triangle ABC has the following vertices: A (1, 1), B (9, 4) and C (1, 7). Which of the following statements is true?

(a) $AB = BC$ (b) $AB = AC$ (c) $AB > BC$ (d) $AB < BC$
(e) $AC = BC$

7. a b c d e

8. The vertices of triangle ABC are: A (2, 3), B (8, 3) and C (6, 7). Median BM is drawn. The coordinates of point M are

(a) (5, 4) (b) (4, 5) (c) (6, 4.5) (d) (4, 6) (e) (4, 6.5)

8. a b c d e

9. The vertices of square $ABCD$ are: (4, 0), (4, 4), (8, 4) and (8, 0). The area of $ABCD$ equals

(a) 2 (b) 4 (c) 8 (d) 12 (e) 16

9. a b c d e

10. The vertices of triangle ABC are (2, 2), (2, 6) and (6, 2). The area of triangle ABC is

(a) 8 (b) 10 (c) 12 (d) 14 (e) 16

10. a b c d e

11. What is the area of a square whose points (corners) are (0, 4), (4, 0), (0, −4) and (−4, 0)?

(a) 4 (b) 8 (c) 16 (d) 32 (e) 64

11. a b c d e

12. The area of a circle whose center is at (0, 0) is 9π. The circle passes through all of the following points EXCEPT

(a) (−3, 0) (b) (3, 0) (c) (0, 3) (d) (0, −3) (e) (3, 3)

12. a b c d e

13. Quadrilateral $ABCD$ has the following points as its vertices: (2, 2), (6, 2), (−2, −2) and (6, −2). The area of $ABCD$ is

(a) 4 (b) 8 (c) 24 (d) 32 (e) 64

13. a b c d e

14. AB is a diameter of a circle whose center is O. The coordinates of point A are $(-2, 0)$. The coordinates of point B are $(2, 0)$. The circle passes through a point whose coordinates are

(a) $(-2, -2)$ (b) $(-2, 2)$ (c) $(0, 4)$ (d) $(0, -2)$ (e) $(2, 2)$

14. a b c d e

15. A circle whose center is at origin O passes through point P (4, 3). The length of the radius of this circle is

(a) 3 (b) 3.5 (c) 4 (d) 4.5 (e) 5

15. a b c d e

16. The coordinates of a point equally distant from A(4,-2) and B(4,6) and on the y-axis are

(a) (0,2) (b) (0,4) (c) (0,8) (d) (2,0) (e) (2,2)

16. a b c d e

17. Triangle ABC is formed by joining point A(6,5), point B(-3,2), and point C(9,-4). If median AM is drawn, the coordinates of point M are

(a) (-1,3) (b) (-6,-2) (c) (-6,2) (d) (3,1) (e) (3,-1)

17. a b c d e

18. Line segment AB is drawn from point (-3,4) to point (-3,-4). Line segment CD is drawn from point (3,3) to point (3,-5). Which of the following is always true?

(a) $AB > CD$ (b) $AB < CD$ (c) $AB \parallel CD$ (d) AB intersects CD (e) $AB \perp CD$

18. a b c d e

19. If all points 3 units from (0,0) are joined, the result would be a

(a) square with perimeter of 12 units (b) triangle with area of $9\sqrt{3}$ (c) circle with diameter of 3 units (d) circle with radius of 3 units (e) rectangle with area of 9 units

19. a b c d e

20. The locus of points equidistant from a given line is a pair of lines that are

(a) perpendicular (b) equal (c) bisected (d) broken (e) parallel

20. a b c d e

21. The following points are joined: (-2,-2), (-1,-1), (1,1), (2,2). All of the following correctly describe the result EXCEPT

(a) The line formed is parallel to the x-axis. (b) A straight line is formed. (c) The line formed bisects the right angle formed by the coordinates of the axes. (d) Any point on the line formed is equidistant from the x-axis and the y-axis. (e) The line formed passes through the origin.

21. a b c d e

22. The perpendicular bisector of AB, where AB is formed by joining point (3,6) and point (3,0) is a line

(a) parallel to the y-axis, passing through (0,0) (b) parallel to the x-axis, passing through (3,3) (c) passing through (3,3) and (0,0) (d) intersecting AB at (3,0) (e) intersecting AB at (3,6)

22. a b c d e

23. Point (-2,6) is the center of a circle which is tangent to the x-axis. The coordinates of the point of tangency are

(a) (-2,0) (b) (0,4) (c) (-2,-6) (d) (0,-2) (e) (6,0)

23. a b c d e

24. What is the area of the triangle with vertices at (5,3), (11,3), and (8,8)?

(a) 7 (b) 15 (c) 24 (d) 30 (e) 64

24. a b c d e

25. *KL* is drawn from point (1,6) to point (1,-6). Of the following lines, which would be parallel to *KL*?

(a) from point (1,6) to point (6,1) (b) from point (-1,-6) to point (-6,-1) (c) from point (-1,-1) to point (-6,-6) (d) from point (-6,-6) to point (-6,6) (e) from point (1,1) to point (6,6)

25. a b c d e

GEOMETRY

Those questions appearing on the SAT which involve geometry make use of only elementary ideas concerning such simple plane figures as angles, lines, circles, and triangles and such simple solid figures as spheres and rectangular solids.

A list of geometric facts is given at the beginning of the math section of the SAT and just about all of the geometry questions can be worked using these facts as a basis. The more experience you have with the use of these facts, however, the easier you will find the questions and the quicker you will discover the methods needed to answer the questions.

The skills you need to practice involve: area, circumference, and arc measures of circles; angle relationships in triangles; the area of a triangle; the relationship between the sides of a right triangle; the area and perimeter of a rectangle; and the volumes of rectangular and spherical solids.

In order to help you visualize these relationships we have compiled a summary of facts and fundamental situations involving common geometric ideas. Be sure to master these concepts.

Points, Lines, and Planes

The building blocks of geometry are points, lines, and planes. A point indicates a position and has no length, width, or thickness. A line is a continuous set of points which is straight, infinitely long in two opposite directions, and has no width or thickness. A plane is a flat surface which extends in all directions but has no thickness.

Most geometric figures are formed by joining parts of lines—either line segments or rays. A line segment has two points of a line as endpoints and contains all points of the line which lie between the endpoints. A ray has one point of a line as an endpoint and contains all of the points which lie in a given side of the line.

In drawings, these figures appear like this:

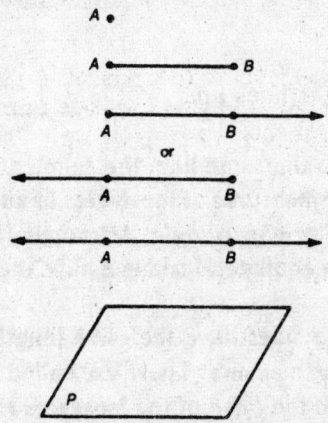

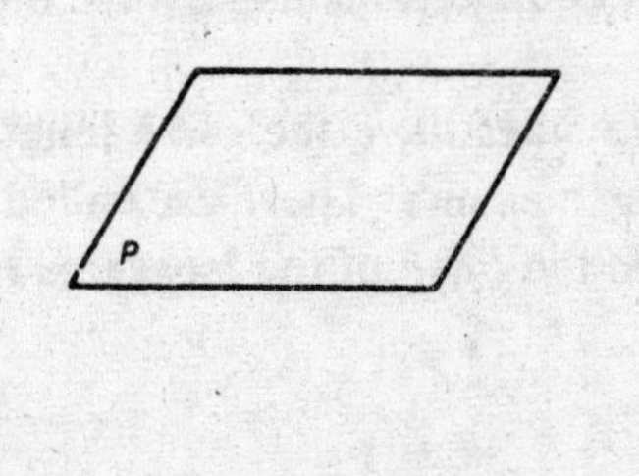

Angles and Triangles

If two different rays have the same endpoint, they form an angle.

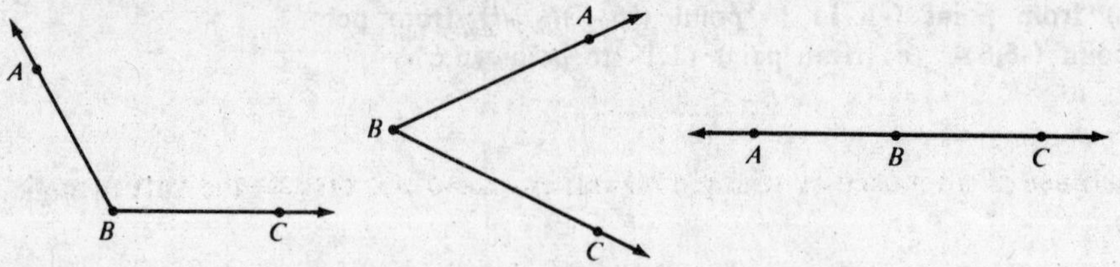

The common endpoint is called the *vertex* and the rays are called the *sides*.

The angle at right above has rays which are opposite to each other and lie along a straight line. Such an angle is called a *straight angle*. The measure in degrees of a straight angle is 180. Degree measures of other angles are proportional to the fractional part of a straight angle which they represent.

Two angles are *adjacent* if they have the same vertex and share a common side between them. Adjacent angles may not overlap. In the figure there is one pair of adjacent angles, ∠ ABC and ∠ CBD. Note that ∠ ABC and ∠ ABD are not adjacent since they overlap.

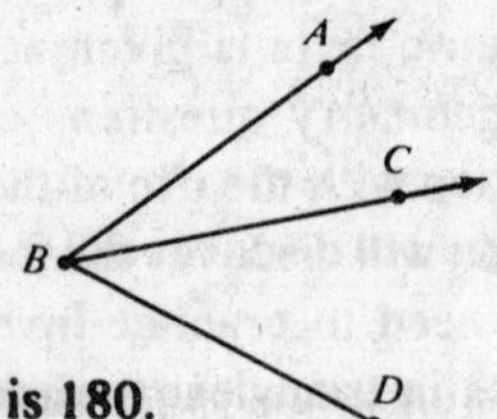

Two angles are *supplementary* if the sum of their degree measures is 180.

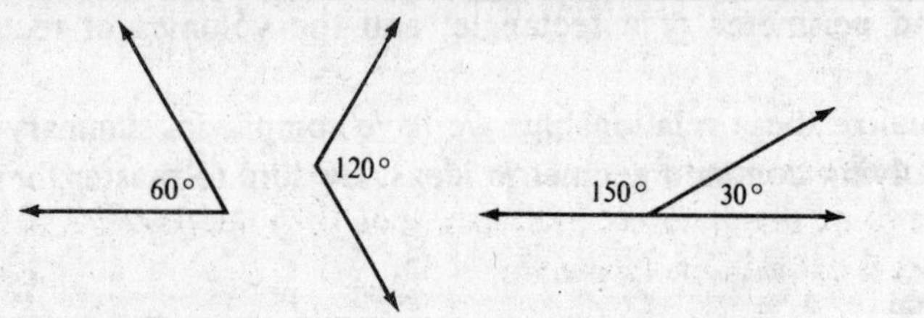

Two angles are *complementary* if the sum of their degree measures is 90.

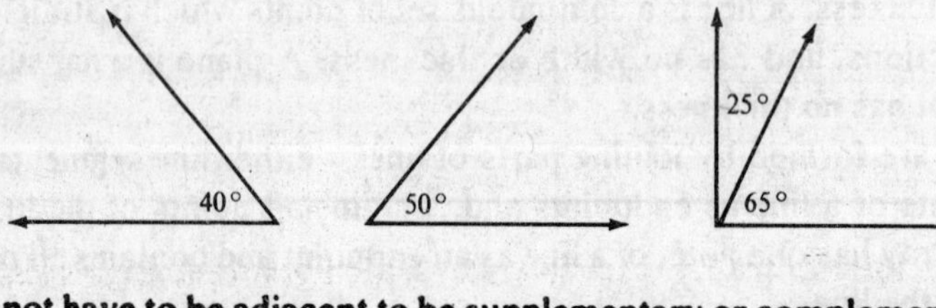

Note that two angles do not have to be adjacent to be supplementary or complementary.

An angle is a right angle if its measure is 90. Note that two adjacent right angles have sides which form a line.

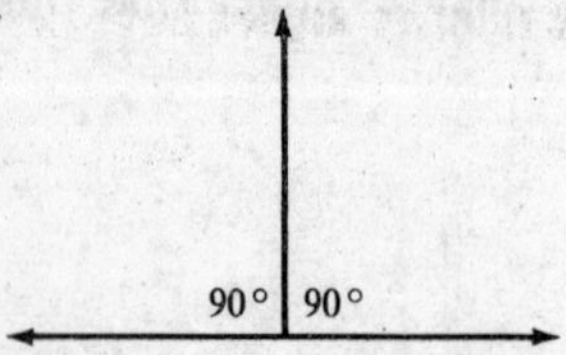

If two lines intersect to form right angles the lines are *perpendicular*.

If three points of a plane do not all lie on the same line, the segments which connect these points form a triangle. The sum of the degree measures of the angles of a triangle is 180.

If a triangle has a right angle, it is called a *right triangle*. A triangle is *equilateral* if all sides have the same length. All of the angles of an equilateral triangle have the same degree measure, 60.

An *isosceles triangle* is one in which two sides have the same length. The angles opposite the sides of equal length have the same degree measure. These are called the *base angles* and the side of the triangle which they share is called the *base* of the isosceles triangle.

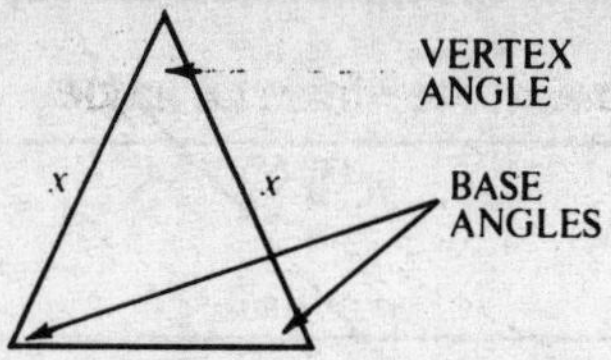

The altitude to the base of an isosceles triangle bisects the base and bisects the vertex angle.

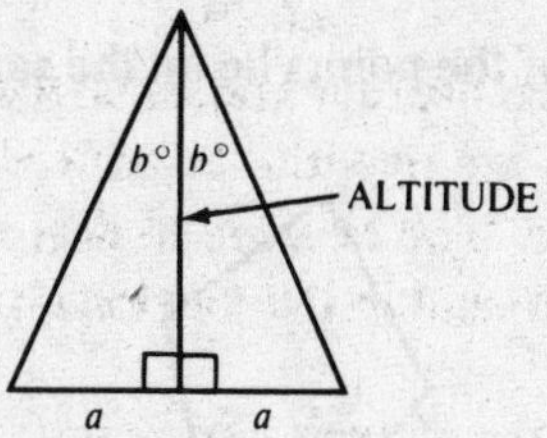

Line-Angle Relationships

Two intersecting lines form two pairs of vertical angles. Note that ∠1 and ∠2 are vertical angles, and ∠*a* and ∠*b* are vertical angles.

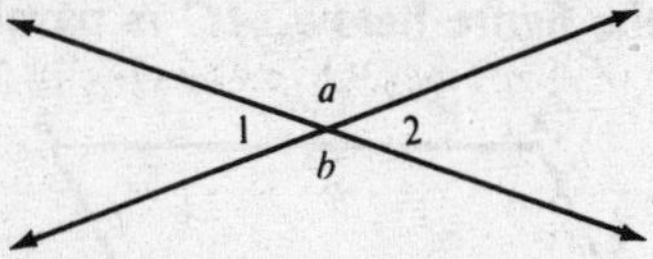

Vertical angles have the same degree measure.

If two lines which lie in the same plane do not intersect, then they are *parallel*. A line which intersects a pair of parallel lines is called a *transversal*.

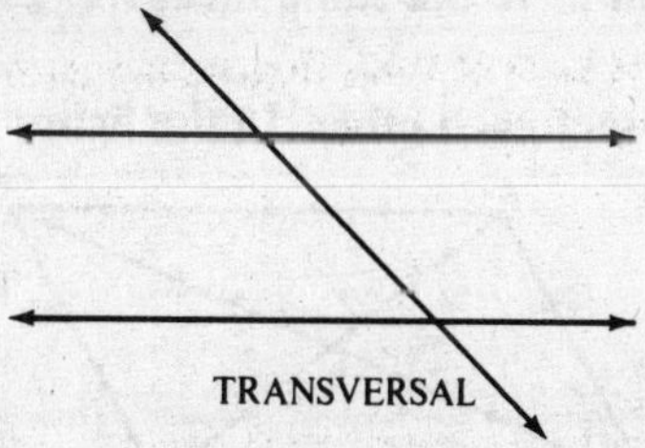

If a pair of parallel lines is intersected by a transversal, three important angle relationships exist:

(1) Alternate interior angles have the same measure:

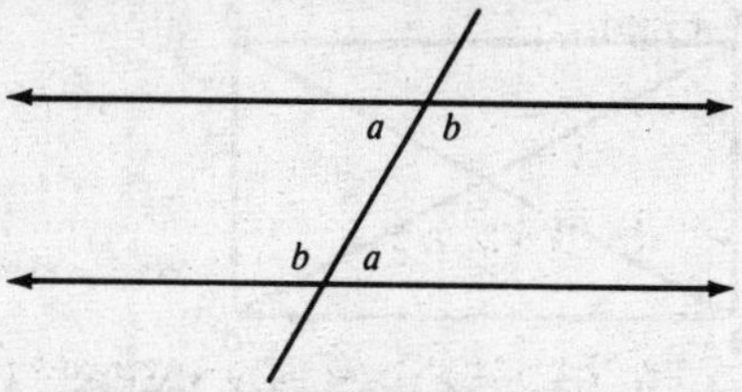

(2) Corresponding angles have the same measure:

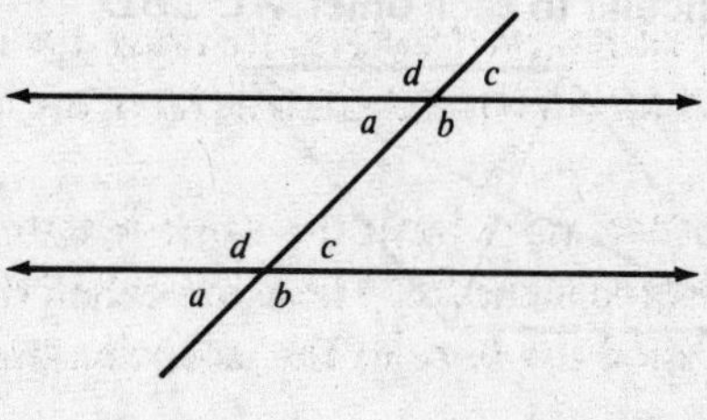

(3) Interior angles on the same side of the transversal are supplementary:

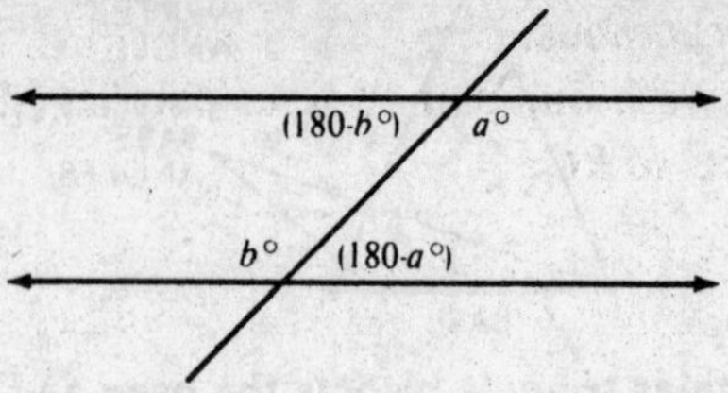

Quadrilaterals

If four points lie in a plane and no three of the points lie on the same line, the segments which connect these points form a quadrilateral.

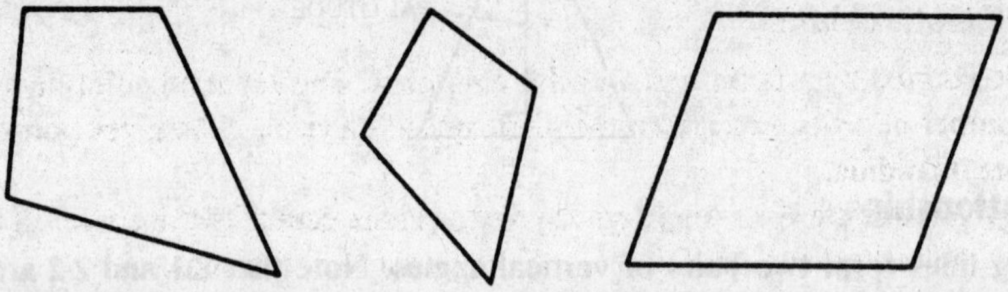

A *parallelogram* is a quadrilateral having opposite sides parallel. The opposite sides of a parallelogram are also equal in length. In the figure below, *AC* is parallel to and equal to *BD*; *AB* is parallel to and equal to *DC*.

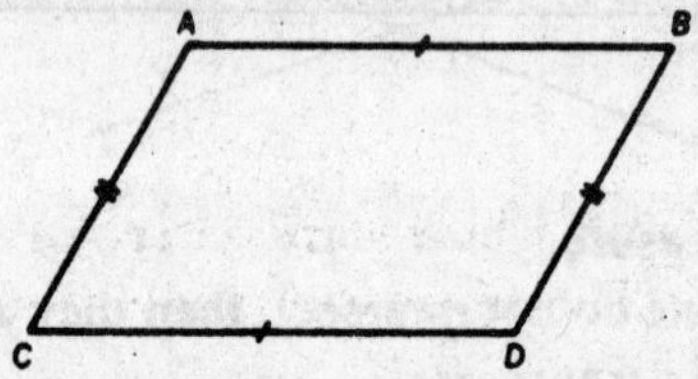

The opposite angles of a parallelogram have the same measure. ∠*A* has the same measure as ∠*D*. ∠*B* has the same measure as ∠*C*.

The diagonals of a parallelogram bisect each other. In the figure below, *AE* = *ED* and *BE* = *EC*.

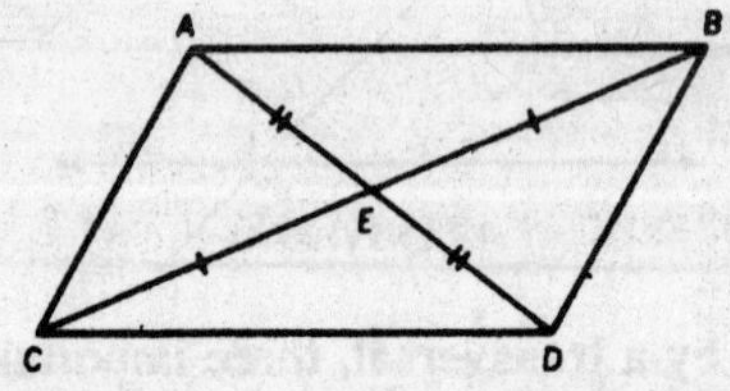

If a parallelogram has four right angles it is a *rectangle*. The diagonals of a rectangle are equal in length. *AC* = *BD*.

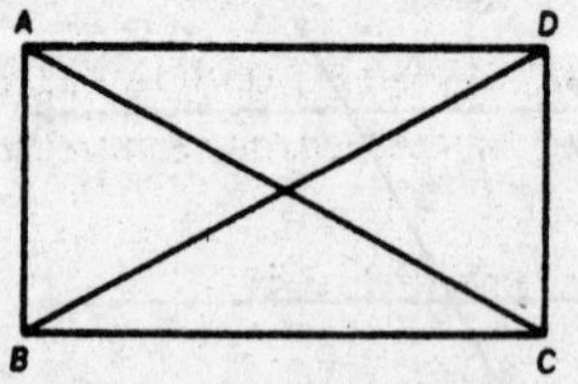

A *rhombus* is a parallelogram having all sides of the same length. *AB* = *BC* = *CD* = *AD*. The diagonals of a rhombus are perpendicular to each other. *AC* ⊥ *BD*.

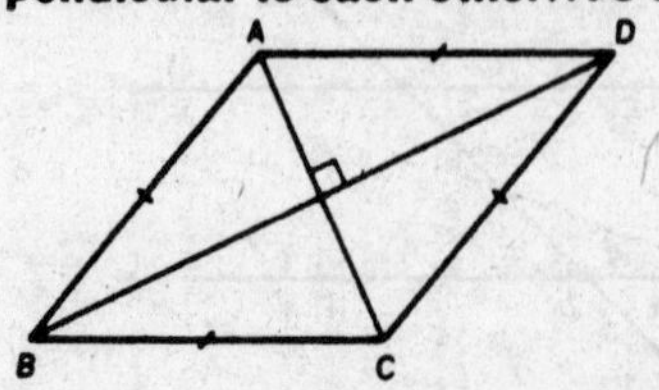

A *square* is a rectangle having all sides of the same length. Thus it has all of the properties of a parallelogram, a rectangle, and a rhombus.

A *trapezoid* is a quadrilateral having one pair of sides parallel (the *bases*) and the other pair non-parallel (the *legs*). AD is parallel to BC.

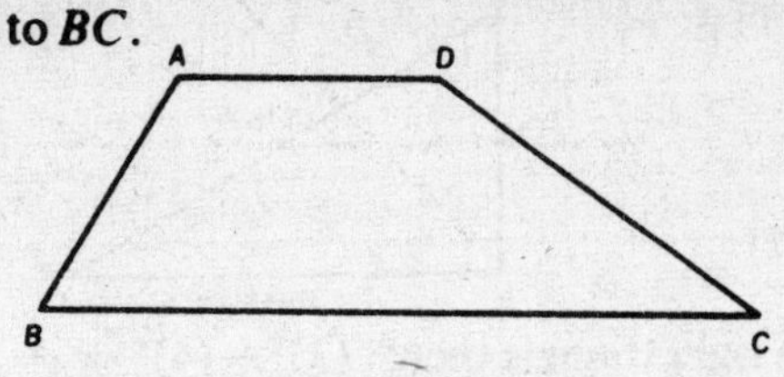

Angle-Circle Relationships

A *circle* is determined by a point and a positive number. The set of all points in a plane which are the given number of units away from the given point is a circle. The given point is its center, the given number its radius.

A *central angle* of a circle is an angle whose vertex is the center of the circle. The measure of the arc cut off by the central angle is the same as the measure of the angle.

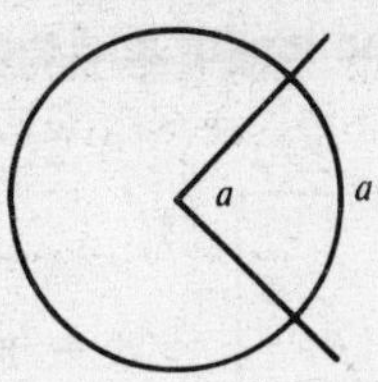

An *inscribed angle* of a circle is an angle whose vertex is a point of the circle and whose sides intersect two other points of the circle. The measure of an inscribed angle is half the measure of the arc it cuts off.

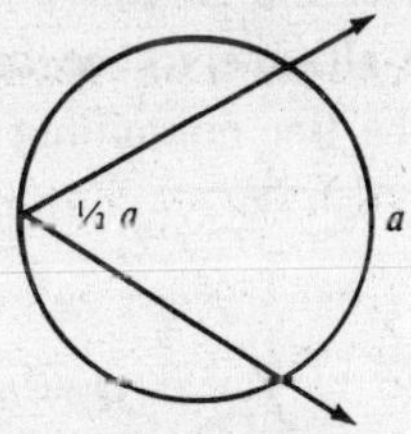

If an angle is inscribed in a semi-circle, it must be a right angle.

Relationships Between the Sides of Triangles

Two triangles are *similar* if all of their pairs of corresponding angles have the same measure. Roughly speaking, triangles are similar if they have the same shape but not necessarily the same size.

Corresponding sides of similar triangles are proportional.

$$\frac{AB}{A'B'} = \frac{AC}{A'C'} = \frac{BC}{B'C'}$$

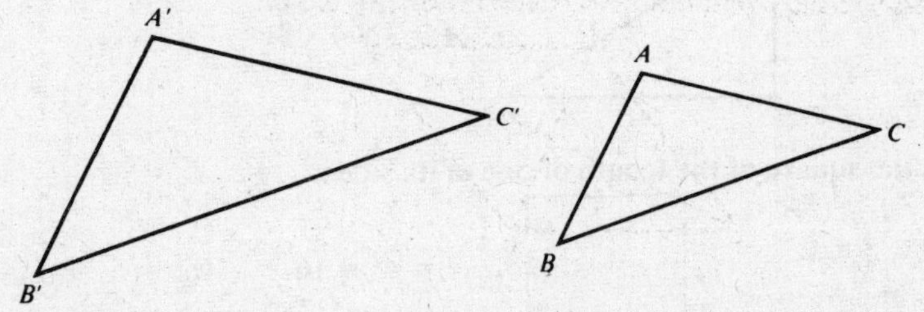

In a right triangle the square of the hypotenuse is equal to the sum of the squares of the legs.

$$(\text{leg})^2 + (\text{leg})^2 = (\text{hypotheneuse})^2$$

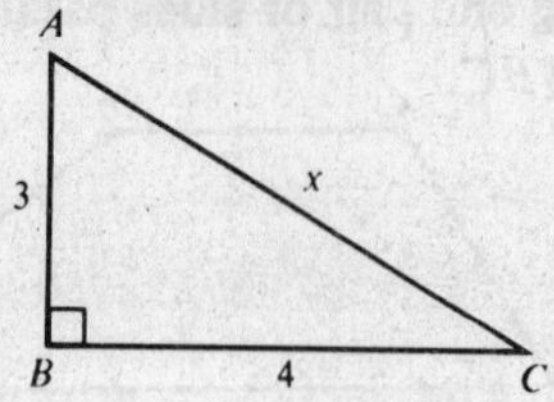

If the triangle shown above is a right triangle then: $(3)^2 + (4)^2 = x^2$

$$9 + 16 = x^2$$
$$25 = x^2$$
$$5 = x$$

Note that the *hypoteneuse* is the side opposite the right angle; it is always the longest side of the right triangle. Look for the relationship of 3:4:5 or 5:12:13 in right triangles and avoid lengthy computation.

Areas and Volumes

The area of a rectangle is the product of the length and the width. If the length is 4 and the width is 8, the area is $4 \times 8 = 32$.

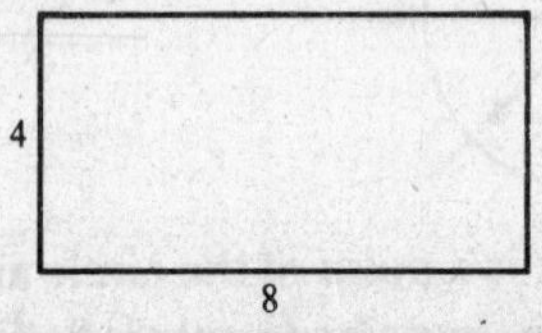

$$A = lw = 4 \times 8 = 32$$

The area of a parallelogram is the product of the lengths of the base and the altitude to that base. Any side can be used for the base. The altitude to the base is a segment from any point of the opposite side drawn perpendicular to the line containing the base.

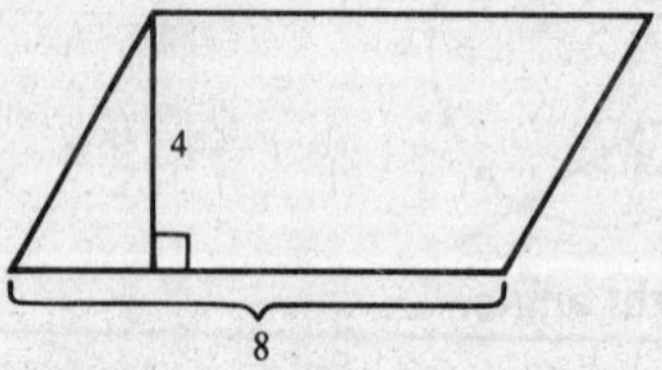

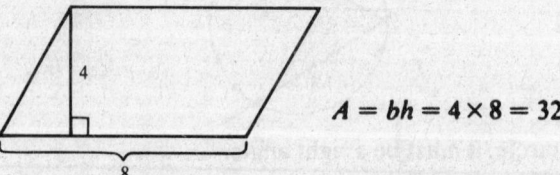

$$A = bh = 4 \times 8 = 32$$

The area of a triangle is equal to one-half the product of the lengths of a base and the altitude to that base. Any side may be a base. The altitude to the base is the segment from the vertex opposite to the base and perpendicular to the line containing the base.

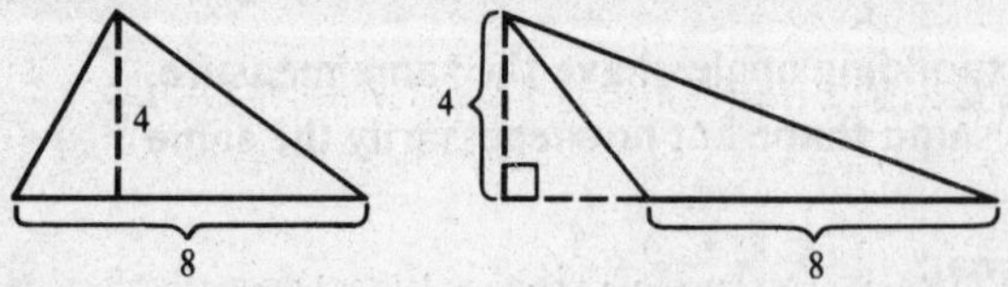

$$A = \tfrac{1}{2} \times 4 \times 8$$

The area of a right triangle is one-half the product of the lengths of its legs.

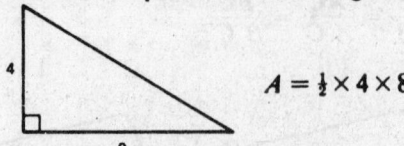

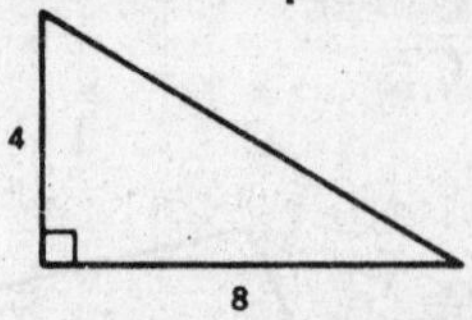

$$A = \tfrac{1}{2} \times 4 \times 8$$

The area of a square is the square of the length of one of its sides.

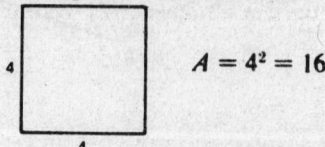

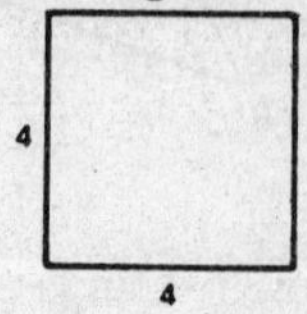

$$A = 4^2 = 16$$

The area of a square is also equal to one-half the square of the length of its diagonal.

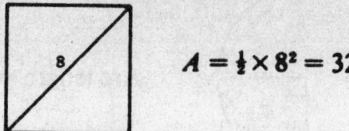

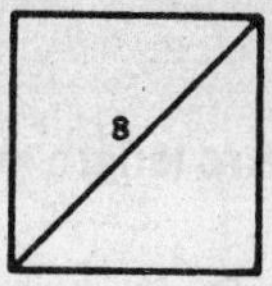

$$A = \frac{1}{2} \times 8^2 = 32$$

The ratio of the areas of two similar figures is equal to the square of the ratio of the lengths of any two corresponding linear parts (sides, altitudes, medians, or angle bisectors).

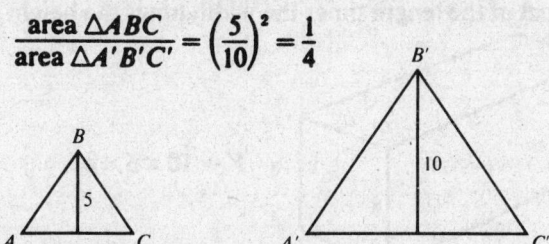

$$\frac{\text{area } \Delta ABC}{\text{area } \Delta A'B'C'} = \left(\frac{5}{10}\right)^2 = \frac{1}{4}$$

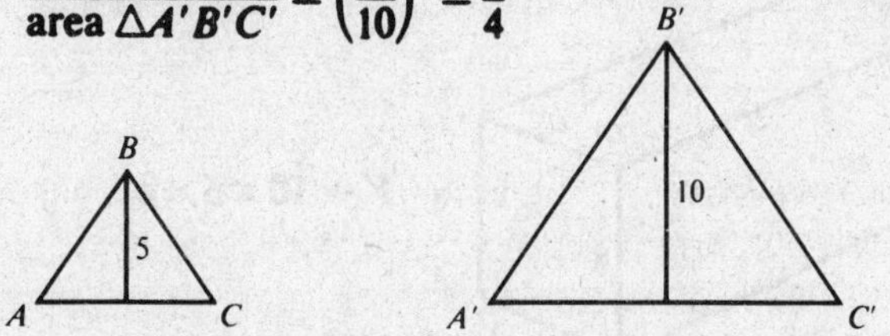

The circumference of (sometimes referred to as the "distance around") a circle is the product of the diameter and π. $C = \pi d$ or $C = 2\pi r$, if r is the radius.

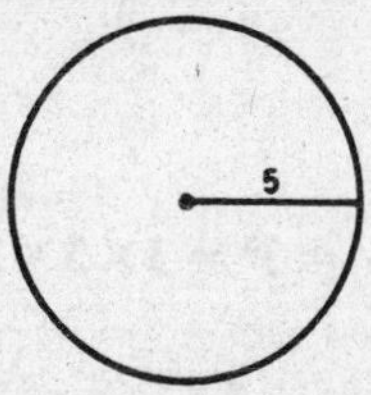

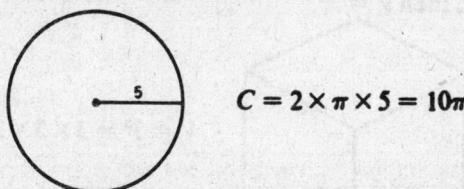

$$C = 2 \times \pi \times 5 = 10\pi$$

The area of a circle is equal to the product of π and the square of the radius. $A = \pi r^2$.

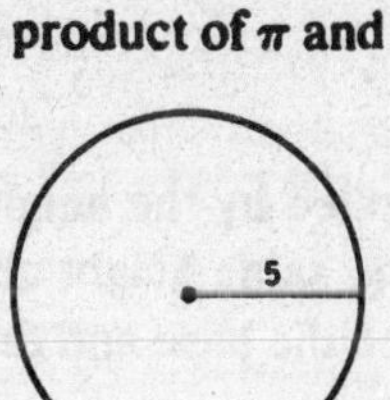

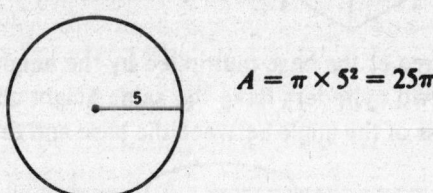

$$A = \pi \times 5^2 = 25\pi$$

A *sector* of a circle is a pie-shaped region bounded by a central angle and the arc it cuts off. Each sector of a circle represents some fractional part of the circular region. This fractional part can be found by formula.

$$\frac{\text{degree measure of central angle}}{360} = \text{fractional part of circle}$$

Hence a 60° angle cuts off a sector which represents $\frac{1}{6}$ of the circle and a 150° angle determines a sector which is $\frac{150}{360}$ or $\frac{5}{12}$ of the circle.

To find the area of the sector, find the area of the circle and multiply by the fractional part.

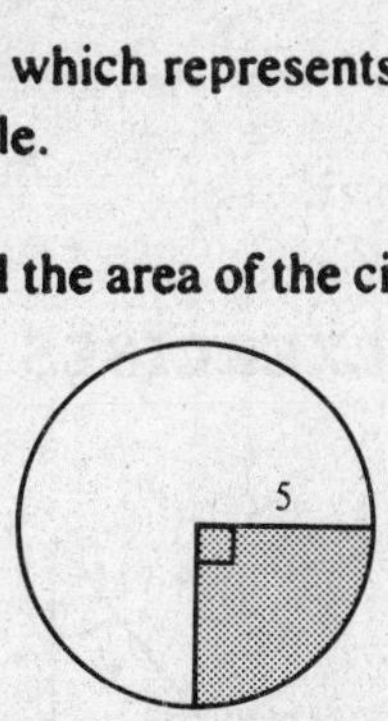

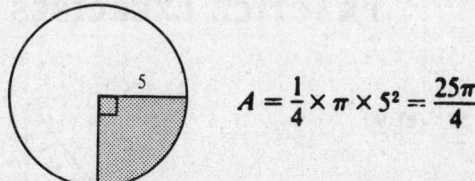

$$A = \frac{1}{4} \times \pi \times 5^2 = \frac{25\pi}{4}$$

To find the arc length of a sector find the circumference of the circle and multiply by the fractional part.

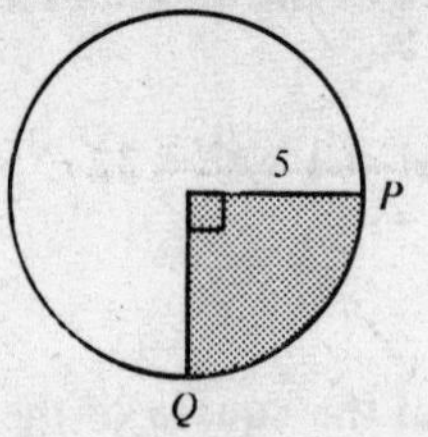

Arc length $= \frac{1}{4} \times 2\pi \times 5 = \frac{5\pi}{2}$

A *rectangular parallelepiped* is a solid figure all of whose faces are rectangles. It has six such faces. Its volume is the product of the length times the width times the height.

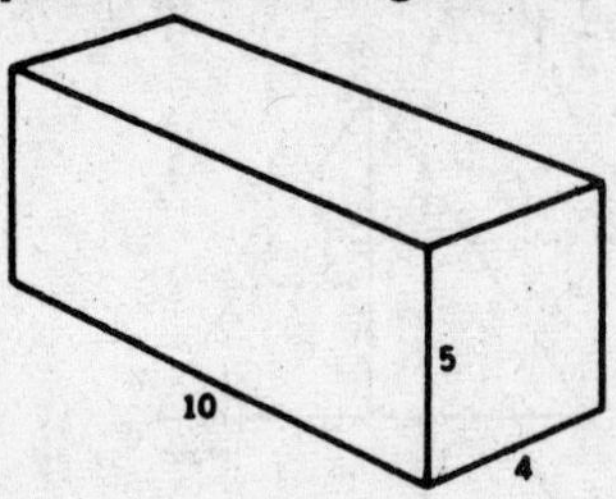

$V = 10 \times 5 \times 4$

A *cube* is a special kind of rectangular parallelepiped with length, width, and height all equal. If x is the length, width, or height, then $V = x^3$.

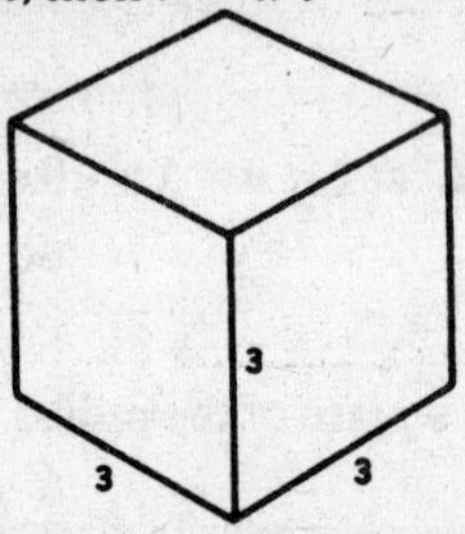

$V = 3^3 = 3 \times 3 \times 3 = 27$

The volume of a *cylinder* is the area of the base multiplied by the height. If the cylinder has a circular base, then $V = h(\pi r^2)$. If two cylinders have the same height and the same base, they will have the same volume regardless of the angle between the base and the line of centers.

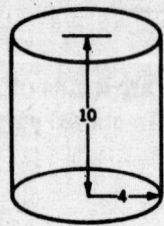

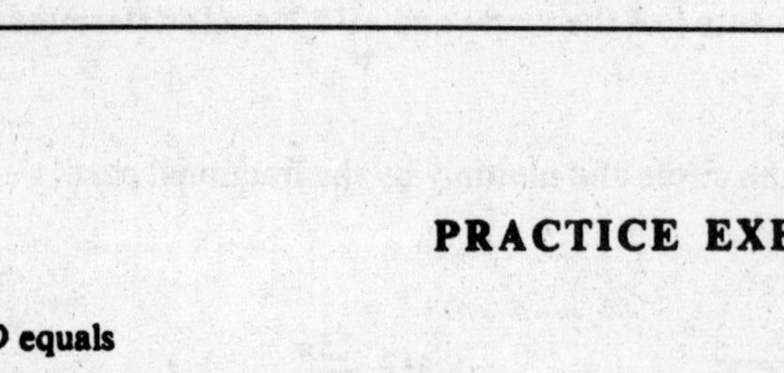

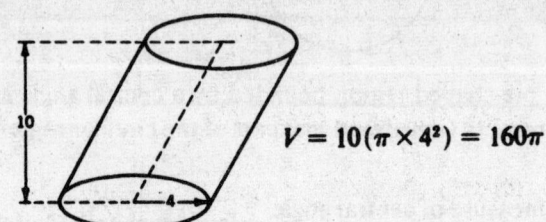

$V = 10(\pi \times 4^2) = 160\pi$

PRACTICE EXERCISES *Answers given on page 387.*

1. Angle *ECD* equals

(a) 20 (b) 25 (c) 40 (d) 50 (e) 90

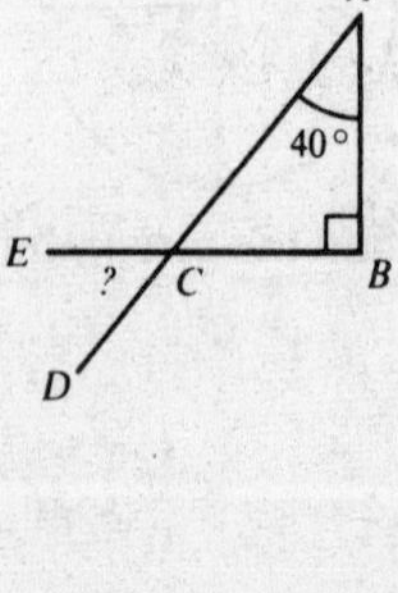

1. a b c d e

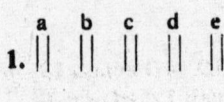

2. *AD* is perpendicular to *CD*. Angle *ADE* = 140°. Angle *EDC* equals

(a) 40° (b) 50° (c) 120° (d) 130° (e) 220°

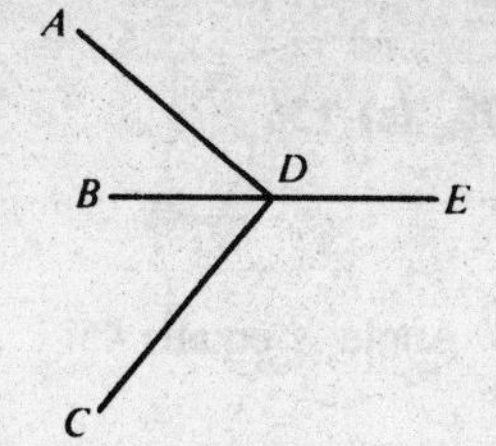

2. a b c d e

3. *AB* = *AC*, angle $B \doteq a$. Angle $A \doteq$ (?)

(a) $a - 180$ (b) $2a - 180$ (c) $180 - 2a$
(d) $180 - a$ (e) $\frac{180 - a}{2}$

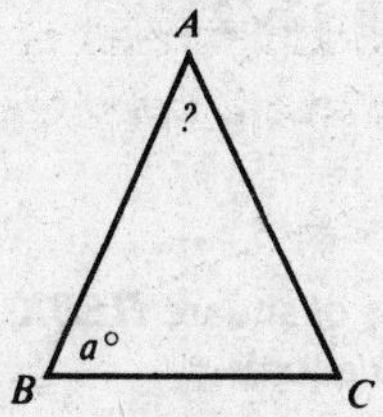

3. a b c d e

4. *AB* = *AC*, angle $A \doteq b$. Angle $B \doteq$ (?)

(a) $b - 180$ (b) $b - 90$ (c) $180 - 2b$
(d) $180 - b$ (e) $90 - \frac{b}{2}$

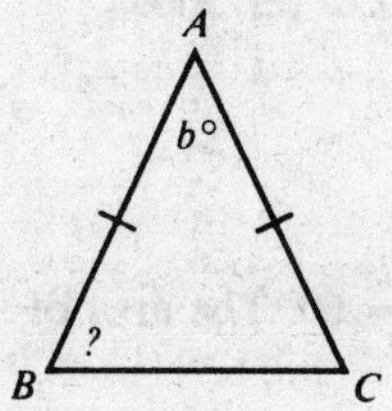

4. a b c d e

5. *AB* is parallel to *DC*. Angle *B* equals *a*°. Angle *c* equals (?)°

(a) a (b) $90 - a$ (c) $\frac{180 - a}{2}$ (d) $180 - a$
(e) $360 - a$

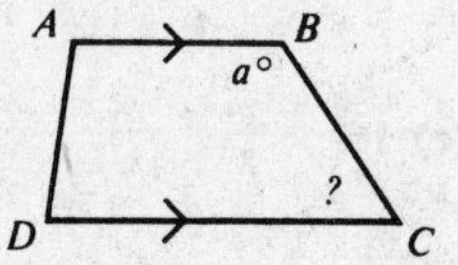

5. a b c d e

6. *CD* is perpendicular to *AB*. Angle *CDE* equals 40°. Angle *EDA* equals

(a) 40° (b) 50° (c) 90° (d) 130° (e) 140°

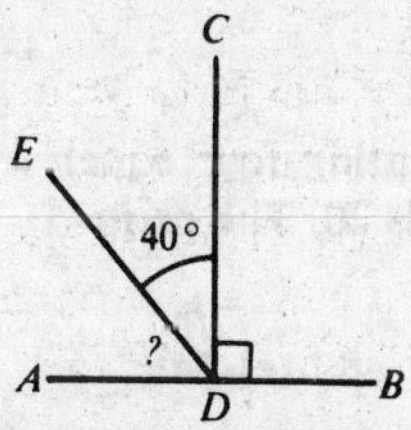

6. a b c d e

7. *AE* is perpendicular to *BE*. Angle *AEC* equals 25°. Angle *x* equals

(a) 25° (b) 65° (c) 75° (d) 115° (e) 155°

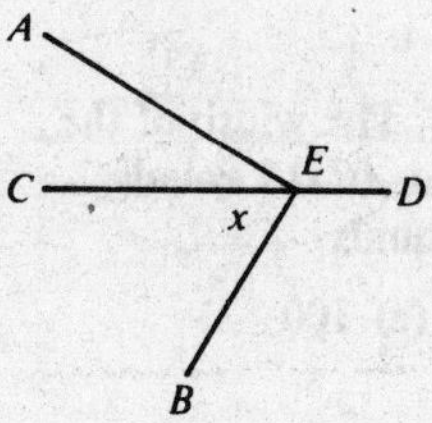

7. a b c d e

8. *DB* and *DC* are angle bisectors of isosceles triangle *ABC*. Angle *A* equals 70°. Angle *BDC* equals

(a) 55° (b) 70° (c) 110° (d) 125° (e) 140°

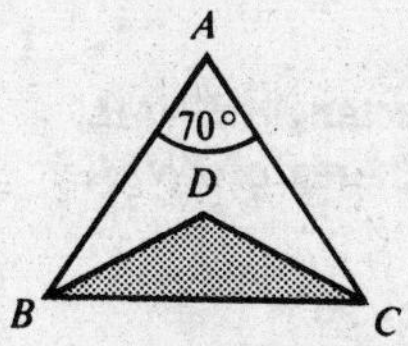

8. a b c d e

9. In triangle *ABD*, *AD* equals 13, *AB* equals *AD*. Altitude *AC* equals 12. *BD* equals

(a) 5 (b) 10 (c) 12 (d) 13 (e) 25

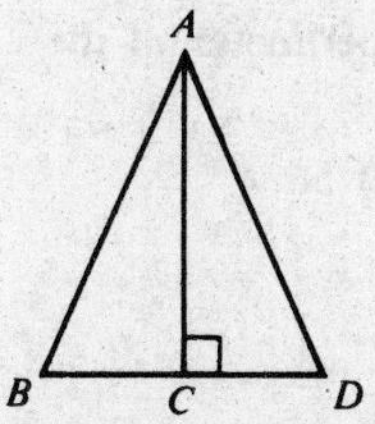

9. a b c d e

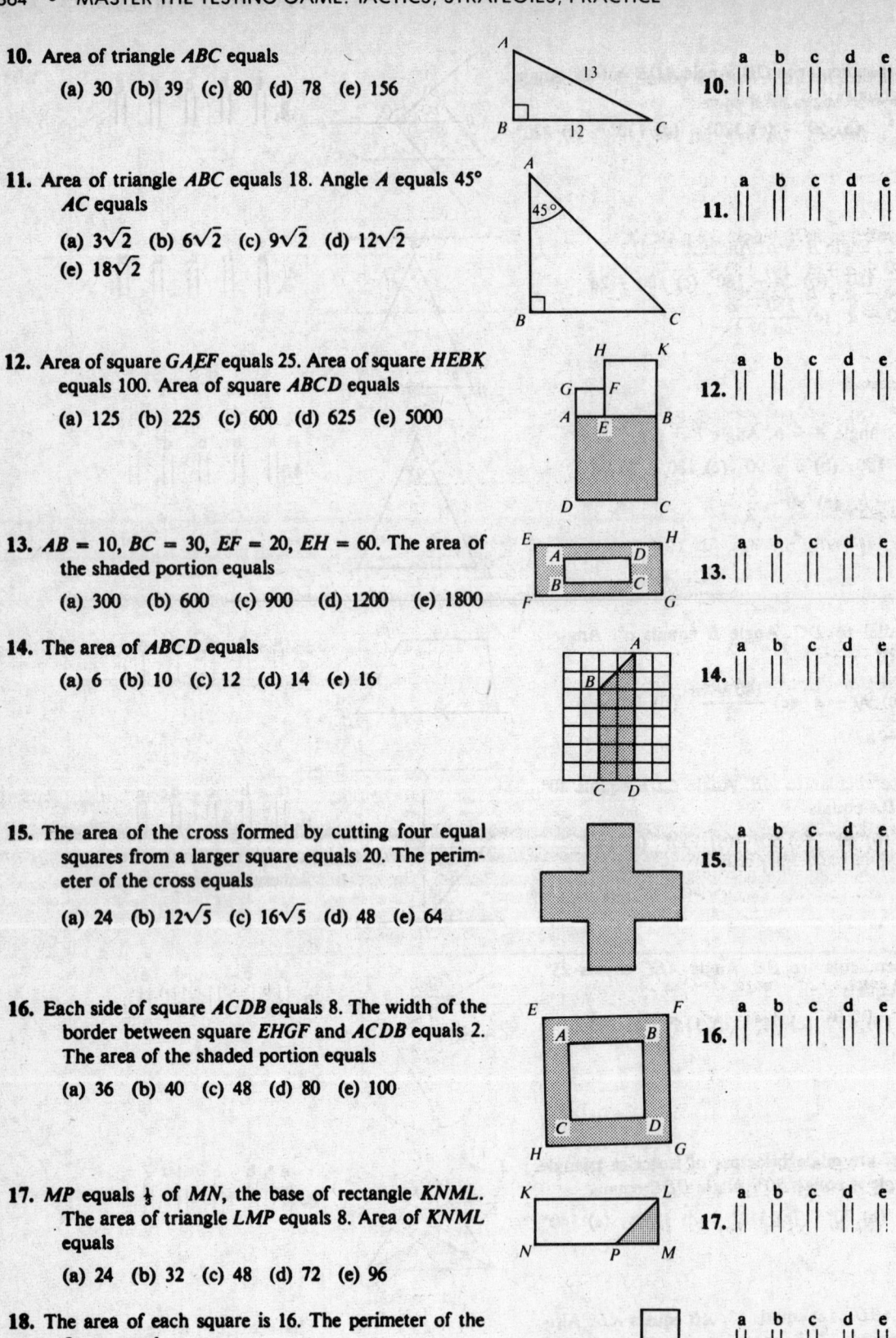

10. Area of triangle *ABC* equals

(a) 30 (b) 39 (c) 80 (d) 78 (e) 156

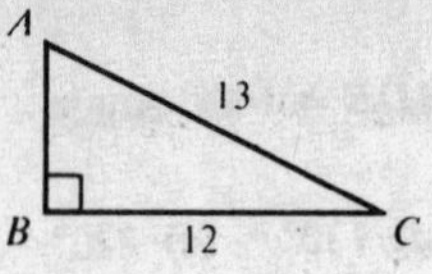

a b c d e
10.

11. Area of triangle *ABC* equals 18. Angle *A* equals 45° *AC* equals

(a) $3\sqrt{2}$ (b) $6\sqrt{2}$ (c) $9\sqrt{2}$ (d) $12\sqrt{2}$
(e) $18\sqrt{2}$

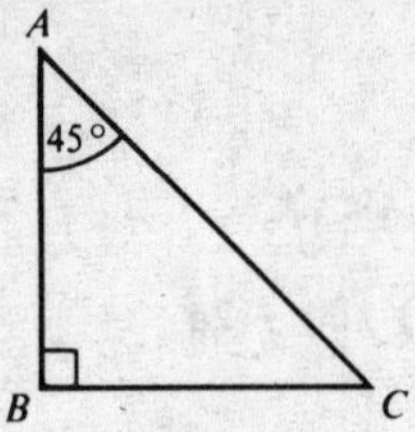

a b c d e
11.

12. Area of square *GAEF* equals 25. Area of square *HEBK* equals 100. Area of square *ABCD* equals

(a) 125 (b) 225 (c) 600 (d) 625 (e) 5000

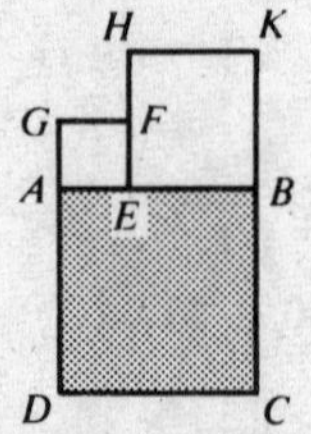

a b c d e
12.

13. *AB* = 10, *BC* = 30, *EF* = 20, *EH* = 60. The area of the shaded portion equals

(a) 300 (b) 600 (c) 900 (d) 1200 (e) 1800

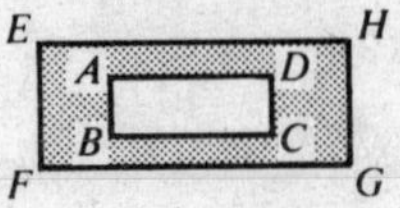

a b c d e
13.

14. The area of *ABCD* equals

(a) 6 (b) 10 (c) 12 (d) 14 (e) 16

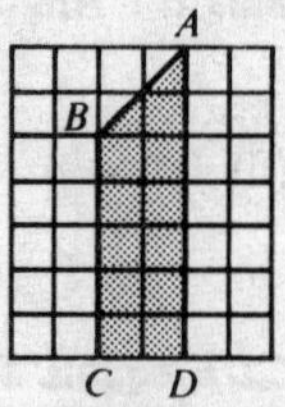

a b c d e
14.

15. The area of the cross formed by cutting four equal squares from a larger square equals 20. The perimeter of the cross equals

(a) 24 (b) $12\sqrt{5}$ (c) $16\sqrt{5}$ (d) 48 (e) 64

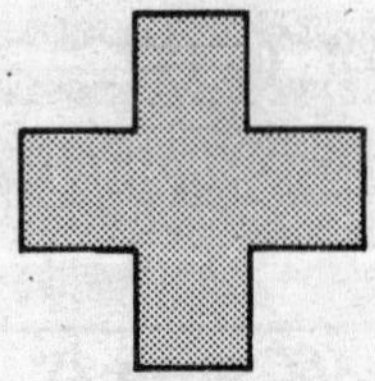

a b c d e
15.

16. Each side of square *ACDB* equals 8. The width of the border between square *EHGF* and *ACDB* equals 2. The area of the shaded portion equals

(a) 36 (b) 40 (c) 48 (d) 80 (e) 100

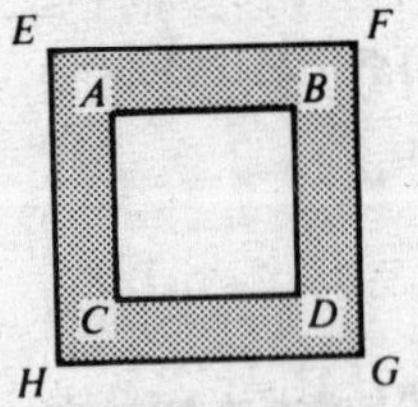

a b c d e
16.

17. *MP* equals $\frac{1}{3}$ of *MN*, the base of rectangle *KNML*. The area of triangle *LMP* equals 8. Area of *KNML* equals

(a) 24 (b) 32 (c) 48 (d) 72 (e) 96

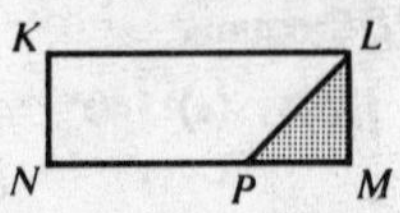

a b c d e
17.

18. The area of each square is 16. The perimeter of the figure equals

(a) 24 (b) 40 (c) 44 (d) 48 (e) 56

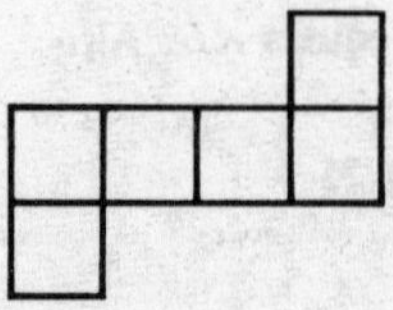

a b c d e
18.

19. *ED* is parallel to *BC*. Angle *A* equals 74°. Angle *B* equals 41°. Angle *AED* equals

(a) 41° (b) 65° (c) 74° (d) 106° (e) 115°

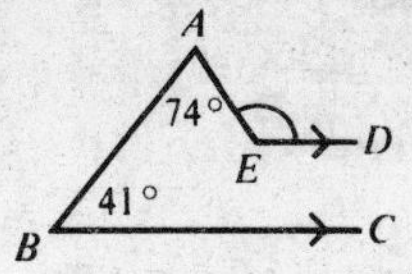

19. a b c d e

20. *KL* is parallel to *MN*. Angle *2* equals (?)°

(a) $180 - a + b$ (b) $180 + a + b$
(c) $360 - a + b$ (d) $360 - a - b$ (e) $b - a$

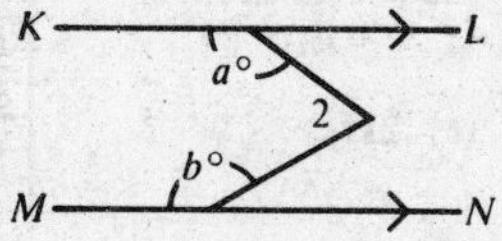

20. a b c d e

21. Angle *x* equals

(a) 40° (b) 45° (c) 50° (d) 85° (e) 125°

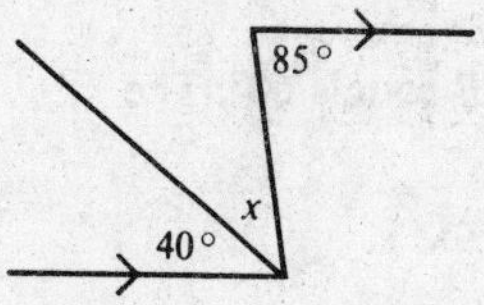

21. a b c d e

22. Angle *a* equals

(a) 30° (b) 60° (c) 70° (d) 150° (e) 160°

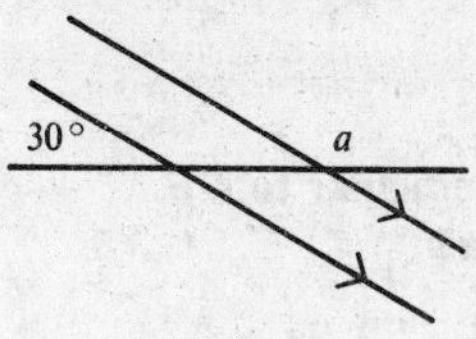

22. a b c d e

23. Angle *EGA* equals (?)°

(a) b (b) $b - 180$ (c) $90 - b$ (d) $180 - b$
(e) $\frac{360 - b}{2}$

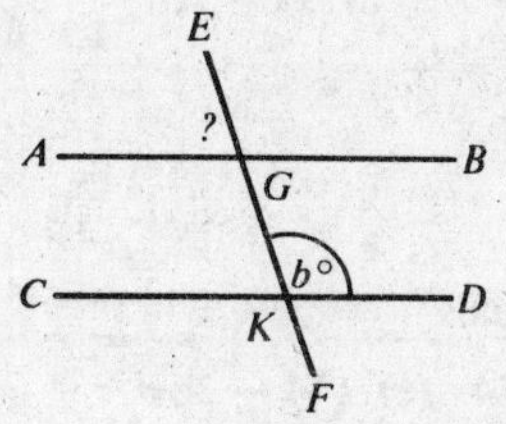

23. a b c d e

24. Circle *O* is inscribed in $\triangle ABC$. $BD = 4$, $AF = 3$, $EC = 5$. Perimeter of $\triangle ABC$ equals

(a) 12 (b) 15 (c) 17 (d) 24 (e) none of these

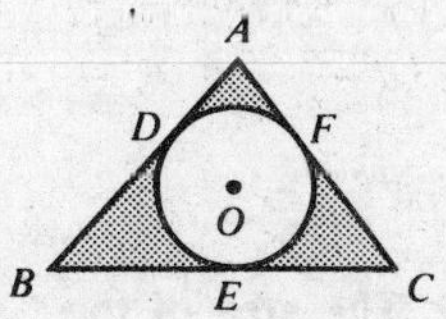

24. a b c d e

25. Arc *ACB* equals 120°. Angle *BAO* equals

(a) 12° (b) 30° (c) 45° (d) 60° (e) 120°

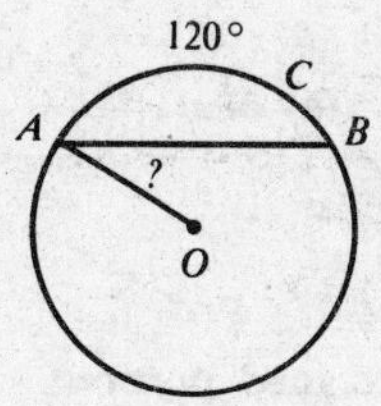

25. a b c d e

26. $AB = BC = CD = DE = EA$ and $AO = OB = OC = OD = OE$. $<BOA \doteq$ (?)

(a) 15 (b) 30 (c) 45 (d) 60 (e) 72

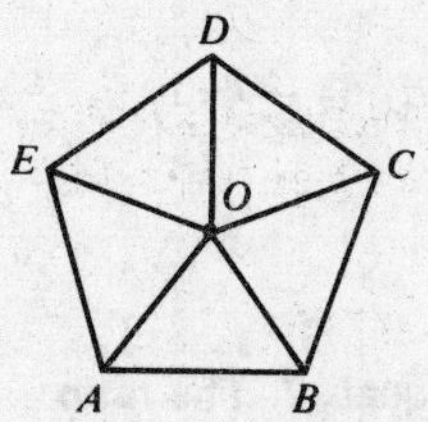

26. a b c d e

27. If the radius of the circle is increased by 50%, the area of the circle is increased by

(a) 25% (b) 50% (c) 100% (d) 125%
(e) 250%

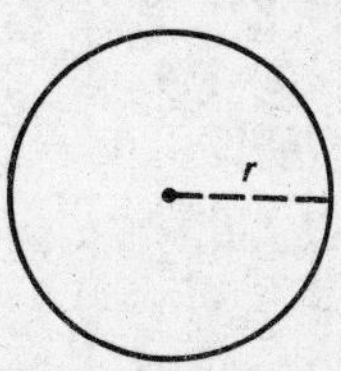

27. a b c d e

28. If the radius of the circle is increased by 50% the circumference is increased by

(a) 25% (b) 50% (c) 100% (d) 125%
(e) 250%

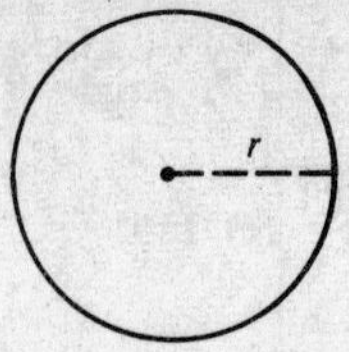

28. a b c d e

29. Area of circle O equals 9π square inches. The area of $ABCD$ is (?) square inches.

(a) 64 (b) 72 (c) 81 (d) 100 (e) 216

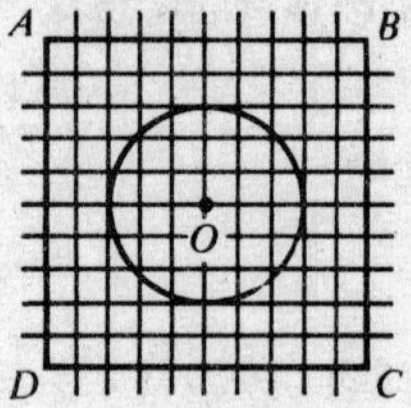

29. a b c d e

30. In circle O, OA equals 6. Angle AOB equals 60°. The area of the shaded portion equals

(a) 2π (b) $4\pi - \sqrt{3}$ (c) $6\pi - 9\sqrt{3}$
(d) $36\pi - 9\sqrt{3}$ (e) $36\pi - 36$

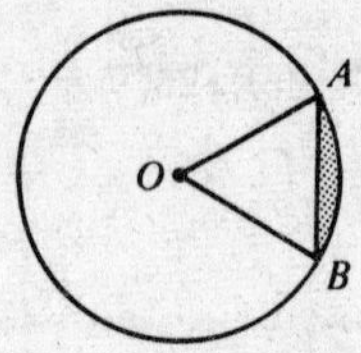

30. a b c d e

31. In circle O, OA equals 6. AO is perpendicular to OB. The area of the shaded portion equals

(a) 2π (b) $\pi - 2$ (c) $6\pi - 9\sqrt{3}$ (d) $9\pi - 18$
(e) $36\pi - 9\sqrt{3}$

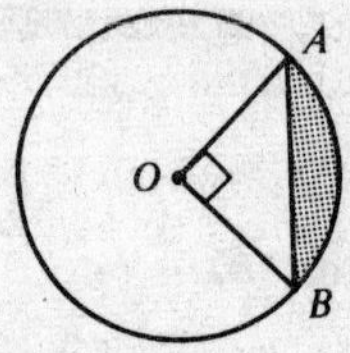

31. a b c d e

32. If r equals 2, the area of $ABCD$ equals

(a) 36 (b) 12π (c) 36π (d) 144 (e) $144 - 36\pi$

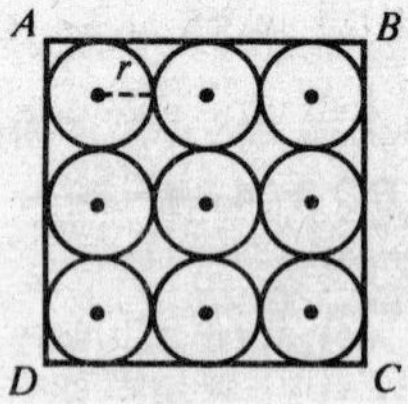

32. a b c d e

33. Radius OA equals 6. AB equals 2. The area of the shaded portion equals

(a) 4π (b) 18π (c) 28π (d) 32π (e) 36π

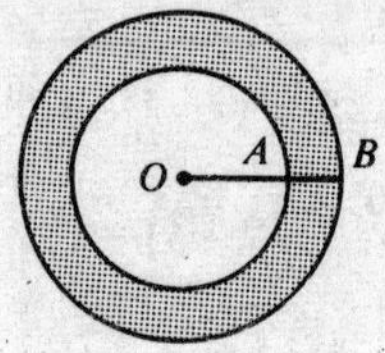

33. a b c d e

34. Radius r equals 2. The area of the shaded portion equals

(a) 16 (b) $16 - 2\pi$ (c) 48π (d) $64 - 4\pi$
(e) $64 - 16\pi$

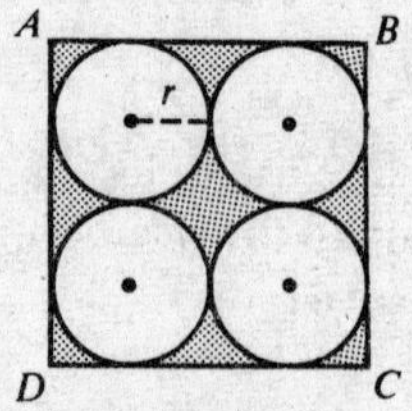

34. a b c d e

35. In circle O, OB equals 6 and AB equals 2. The ratio of the shaded portion to the small circle is

(a) 1:9 (b) 1:3 (c) 4:5 (d) 5:4 (e) 3:4

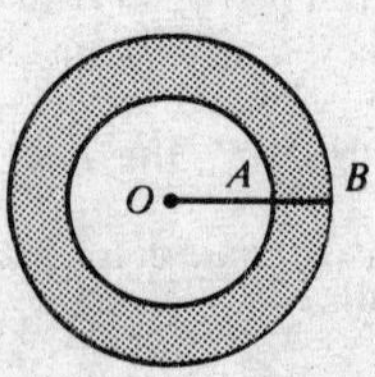

35. a b c d e

36. If AE is parallel to BC then angle E + angle D + angle C equals

(a) 60° (b) 100° (c) 180° (d) 360°
(e) none of these

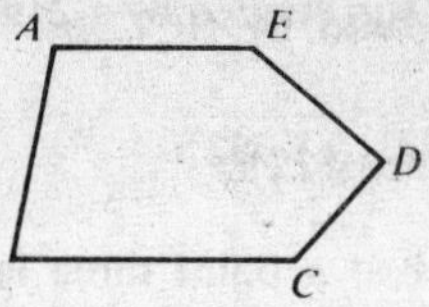

36. a b c d e

37. AB equals AC equals 5. BC equals 6. Altitude AD equals

(a) 4 (b) 5 (c) $5\sqrt{2}$ (d) $5\sqrt{3}$ (e) 6

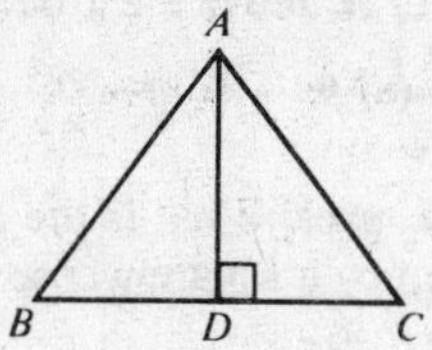

37. a b c d e

38. AB = radius OA; area of triangle AOB equals $4\sqrt{3}$. Area of circle O equals

(a) 4π (b) 8π (c) 16π (d) $24\sqrt{3}$ (e) $24\pi\sqrt{3}$

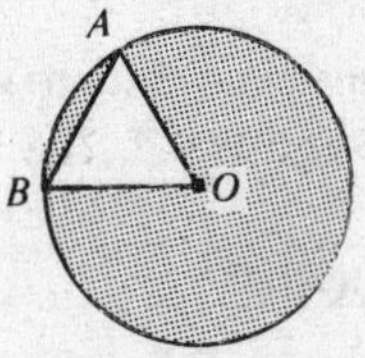

38. a b c d e

39. A rectangular fish tank is 3 feet long by 2 feet wide and contains water to a height of one foot. If all the water is poured into a second tank that is 4 feet long and 1 foot wide, how high will the water level be in the second tank?

(a) 0.5′ (b) 0.66′ (c) 1.5′ (d) 5.0′ (e) 6.0′

39. a b c d e

40. A room is 12 feet × 27 feet. What is the cost of carpeting the room at $11.00 per square yard?

(a) $29.70 (b) $396.00 (c) $45.64 (d) $225.00 (e) $1188.00

40. a b c d e

41. The length of a rectangle is $4l$ and the width is $3w$. What is its perimeter?

(a) $4l + 3w$ (b) $7lw$ (c) $12lw$ (d) $14lw$ (e) $8l + 6w$

41. a b c d e

42. A wheel which has an area of πs^2 rolls a distance of m feet. How many revolutions does it make?

(a) $\frac{\pi s^2}{m}$ (b) $\frac{m}{\pi s^2}$ (c) $\frac{m}{2\pi s}$ (d) $\frac{2\pi s}{m}$ (e) $2\pi sm$

42. a b c d e

43. The width of a rectangle is $\frac{4}{5}$ of its length. If its perimeter is 72, what is its area?

(a) 160 (b) 250 (c) 280 (d) 320 (e) 500

43. a b c d e

44. The length and width of a rectangle are l and w respectively. If each is increased by a units, the perimeter is increased by how many units?

(a) a (b) $2a$ (c) $4a$ (d) a^2 (e) $4a^2$

44. a b c d e

45. A square has the same area as a triangle whose base is 12 inches and whose altitude is 24 inches. Find the length of the side of the square.

(a) 6 (b) 12 (c) 36 (d) 144 (e) 288

45. a b c d e

46. A circular flower bed whose diameter is 4 feet is increased so that the diameter is 12 feet. How many times larger is the new flower bed?

(a) $\sqrt{8}$ (b) 3 (c) 8 (d) 9 (e) 64

46. a b c d e

47. A rectangular lot 50 feet by 100 feet is surrounded on all sides by a concrete walk 5 feet wide. Find the number of square feet in the surface of the walk.

(a) 1600 (b) 5250 (c) 5500 (d) 6100 (e) 6600

47. a b c d e

48. A picture 12 inches by 20 inches is surrounded by a 2 inch mat. Find the area of the mat.

(a) 68 (b) 96 (c) 112 (d) 144 (e) 352

48. a b c d e

49. A seesaw is balanced at its center at a point three feet above the ground. What is the highest one end can rise above the ground?

(a) 3 (b) $3\sqrt{2}$ (c) 5 (d) 6 (e) 9

49. a b c d e

50. The scale of a map is $\frac{3}{4}$ inch = 12 miles. What is the area (in square miles) of a plot represented on this map by a square whose side is one inch?

(a) 4 (b) 9 (c) 16 (d) 81 (e) 256

50. a b c d e

51. A wheel has a radius of $3\frac{1}{2}$ feet. How many revolutions will it make in traveling 242 feet? (Use $\pi = \frac{22}{7}$)

(a) 3.3 (b) 5.5 (c) 11 (d) 22 (e) 80

51. a b c d e

52. The ratio of the surface areas of 2 cubes is 1:4. What is the ratio of their volumes?

(a) 1:2 (b) 1:4 (c) $\frac{1}{2}$:4 (d) 1:8 (e) 1:16

52. a b c d e

53. The diameter of the front wheel of a tricycle is 8 inches and of each of the two back wheels 3 inches. How many revolutions has each of the back wheels made when the front wheel has turned 1,440°?

(a) $2\frac{2}{3}$ (b) 4 (c) $10\frac{2}{3}$ (d) 24 (e) 96

53. a b c d e

54. An angle is 30° more than one-half its complement. Find the angle.

(a) 20° (b) 30° (c) 50° (d) 60° (e) 75°

54. a b c d e

55. Two sides of a triangle are 12 and 8 inches respectively. If the altitude to the former is 4 inches, the altitude to the latter is

(a) $\frac{8}{3}$ (b) 3 (c) 6 (d) 12 (e) 24

55. a b c d e

56. What is the area of a circle inscribed in a square having a side of 6 inches?

(a) 6π (b) 9π (c) 16π (d) 18π (e) 36π

56. a b c d e

57. What is the area of a square inscribed in a circle whose area is 25π?

(a) 25 (b) 50 (c) 75 (d) 100 (e) 125

57. a b c d e

58. The circumference of the base of a cylinder is 16π inches. The height of the cylinder is equal to the diameter of the base. How many gallons does the cylinder hold? (231 cu. in. = 1 gal.)

(a) 1.10 (b) 3.5 (c) 4 (d) 13.9 (e) 16

58. a b c d e

59. What is the perimeter of a right triangle whose legs are 36 and 48?

(a) 60 (b) 84 (c) 120 (d) 132 (e) 144

59. a b c d e

60. The angles of a quadrilateral are in the ratio of 1:2:3:4. Find the largest angle.

(a) 72° (b) 90° (c) 120° (d) 144° (e) 180°

60. a b c d e

DATA INTERPRETATION

A *graph* is a pictorial representation of data that gives an overall view of facts, omitting minor details. General conclusions can be drawn after examining the data. The ability to interpret a pictorial representation of facts and figures is important for success in college level work. This justifies the inclusion of this type of question on the Scholastic Aptitude Test. In addition, this type of question lends itself to testing applications of basic principles of arithmetic, algebra, and geometry.

Some Hints on How to Cope with Graph Questions

1. Examine the entire graph. Get the general meaning of the picture.
2. Be careful to use the correct units in answering the question. Do not confuse decimals with percentages.
3. Avoid lengthy computation. Most of these questions are answered by estimating or applying the given choices to the facts presented.
4. Use information given and do not add information from your own background knowledge.
5. Make sure your conclusion is reasonable.

Types of Graphs

Line graphs are used to show how a quantity changes continuously. Very often the quantity is measured as time changes. If the line goes up, the quantity is increasing; if the line is horizontal, the quantity is not changing. To measure the height of a point on the graph it is not necessary to use a ruler. Use your pencil or a piece of paper as a straight edge. Graph V is a good illustration. Some graphs deal with two factors (graph II) in which case comparisons are made.

Bar graphs can either be vertical or horizontal (graph I). Quantities are compared by the height or length of the bar.

Circle graphs (III and IV) are used to show how various sectors share in the whole.

PRACTICE EXERCISES *Answers given on page 387.*

COST OF SEED PER FIFTY POUNDS

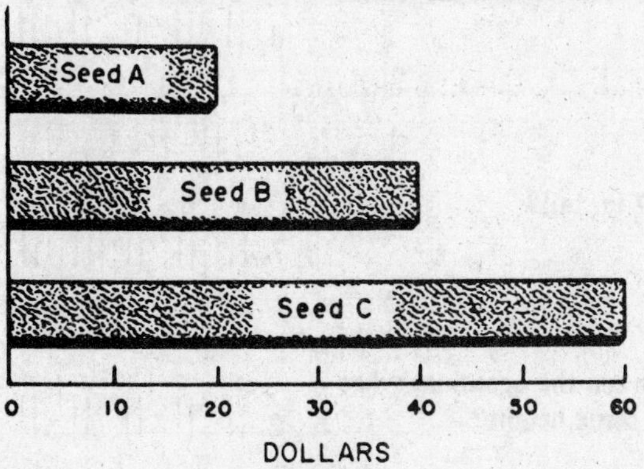

GRAPH I

QUESTIONS 1-4 REFER TO GRAPH I.

1. What is the cost of $12\frac{1}{2}$ pounds of Seed B?

   (a) $10. (b) $20. (c) $40. (d) $60. (e) $75.

1. a b c d e

2. How many pounds of Seed C would I get for $30?

(a) 12$\frac{1}{2}$ (b) 25 (c) 50 (d) 100 (e) 900

2. a b c d e

3. The price of one pound of Seed C is what per cent of the price of one pound of Seed B?

(a) 20% (b) 33$\frac{1}{3}$% (c) 66$\frac{2}{3}$% (d) 120% (e) 150%

3. a b c d e

4. What is the ratio of the price of 20 pounds of Seed B to the price of 20 pounds of Seed A?

(a) 1:1 (b) 1:2 (c) 2:1 (d) 2:3 (e) 4:1

4. a b c d e

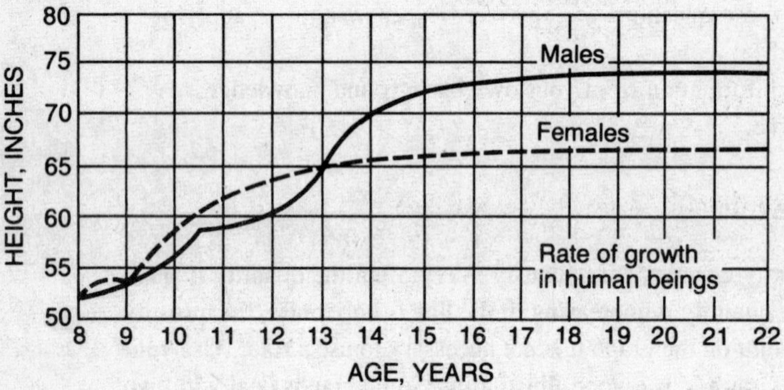

GRAPH II

QUESTIONS 5-9 REFER TO GRAPH II.

5. How many years old is the male when he reaches the height of an eleven-year-old female?

(a) 10 (b) 11 (c) 12 (d) 12.2 (e) 12.5

5. a b c d e

6. How many years old is the male when he is one-half foot taller than the female of the same age?

(a) 10.5 (b) 13 (c) 15 (d) 17 (e) 20

6. a b c d e

7. How many years old is the female when she is 4 ft. 7 in. tall?

(a) 9.2 (b) 9.5 (c) 9.6 (d) 13.3 (e) 21

7. a b c d e

8. According to this graph, how many years elapse between the occasions when males and females of the same age are also of the same height?

(a) 4 (b) 8 (c) 9 (d) 13 (e) 22

8. a b c d e

9. How old is the male when he is 20% taller than the female is at the age of 10.5 years?

(a) 10 (b) 10.5 (c) 14 (d) 14.5 (e) 15.2

9. a b c d e

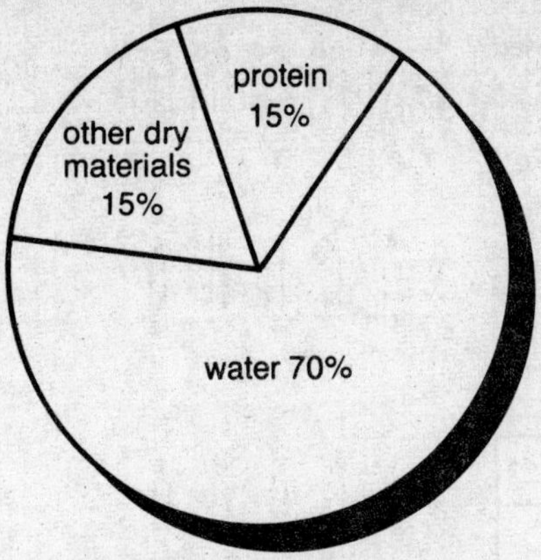

DISTRIBUTION OF MATERIALS
IN THE HUMAN BODY

GRAPH III

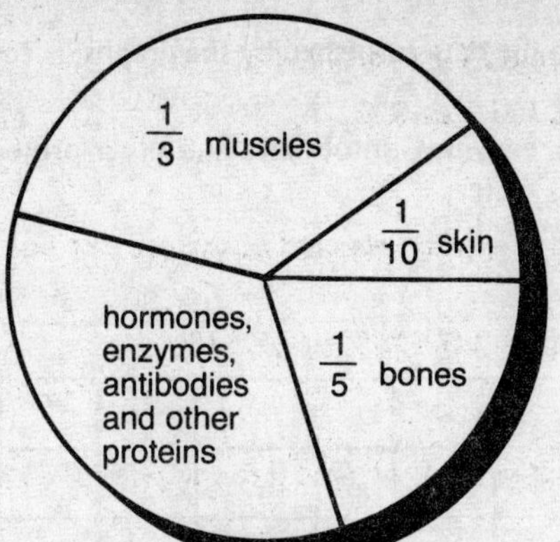

DISTRIBUTION OF PROTEINS
IN THE HUMAN BODY

GRAPH IV

QUESTIONS 10-17 REFER TO GRAPHS III, IV.

10. In terms of the total body weight, the distribution of materials other than water and proteins is equal to

(a) $\frac{1}{15}$ (b) $\frac{85}{100}$ (c) $\frac{1}{20}$ (d) $\frac{3}{20}$ (e) $\frac{1}{5}$

10. a b c d e

11. A person weighing 170 pounds would, according to these graphs, be composed of water weighing

(a) 17 pounds (b) 70 pounds (c) 100 pounds (d) 119 pounds (e) 153 pounds

11. a b c d e

12. How many degrees of the circle should be used to represent the distribution of protein?

(a) 15 (b) 45 (c) 54 (d) 60 (e) 90

12. a b c d e

13. What percent of the entire body weight is made up of skin?

(a) 0.15 (b) 1.0 (c) 1.5 (d) 10. (e) 15.0

13. a b c d e

14. If the weight of the bones of an individual is represented by x pounds, the weight of the skin of this individual is represented by

(a) $\frac{1}{x+5}$ (b) $\frac{1}{x-5}$ (c) $2x$ (d) $\frac{x}{2}$ (e) $\frac{x}{5}$

14. a b c d e

15. What part of the proteins in the body is made up of muscles and skin?

(a) $\frac{15}{1300}$ (b) $\frac{1}{130}$ (c) $\frac{1}{13}$ (d) $\frac{13}{30}$ (e) $\frac{1}{30}$

15. a b c d e

16. The ratio of the distribution of proteins in muscle to the distribution of protein in skin is

(a) 3:1 (b) 1:3 (c) 3:10 (d) $3\frac{1}{3}$:1 (e) 30:1

16. a b c d e

17. The human body, according to the data furnished by the graphs, is composed mainly of

(a) proteins (b) hormones, enzymes, antobodies and other proteins (c) muscles (d) bones (e) water

17. a b c d e

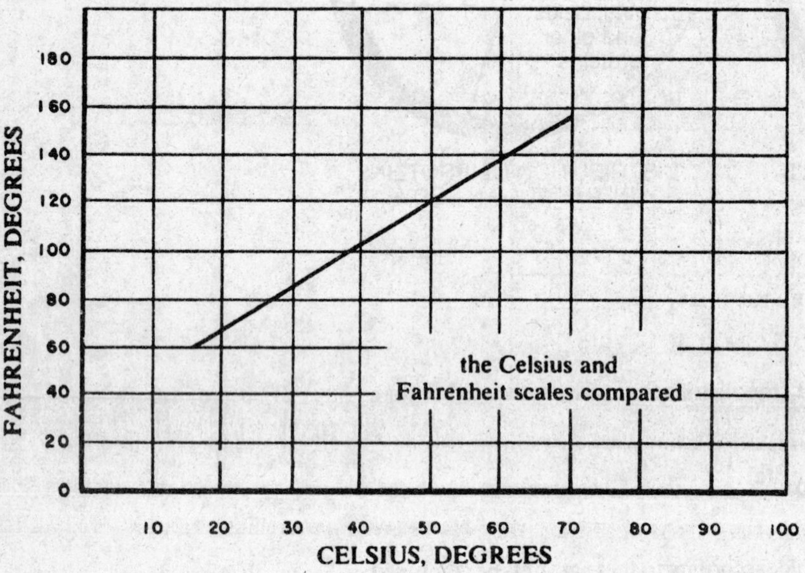

GRAPH V

QUESTIONS 18-20 REFER TO GRAPH V.

18. When the temperature is 10 degrees on the Celsius scale the number of degrees on the Fahrenheit scale is

(a) 10 (b) 32 (c) 42 (d) 50 (e) 68

18. a b c d e

19. Which of the following statements is not true?

19. a b c d e

(a) If the Fahrenheit temperature that is equivalent to a Celsius reading of 60° is decreased by 10%, the resulting Celsius temperature is approximately 55°.

(b) 90° on the Celsius scale corresponds to approximately 194° on the Fahrenheit scale.

(c) 90° on the Fahrenheit scale corresponds to approximately 32° on the Celsius scale.

(d) 0° on the Fahrenheit scale corresponds to approximately 0° on the Celsius scale.

(e) Fahrenheit degrees equal approximately $\frac{9}{5}$ Celsius plus 32°.

20. What will be the increase in the reading of the Fahrenheit scale when the Celsius reading is increased by 20°?

(a) 20° (b) 32° (c) 36° (d) 58° (e) 273°

20. a b c d e

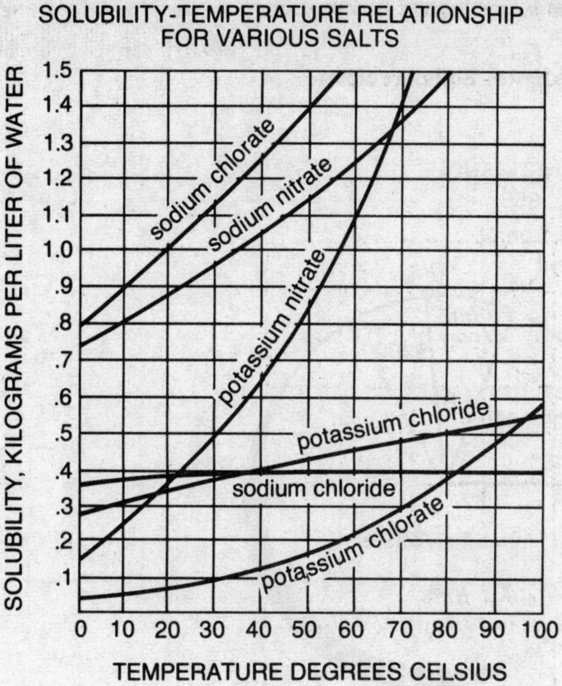

GRAPH VI

QUESTIONS 21-26 REFER TO GRAPH VI.

21. Which of the following salts has the greatest solubility?

(a) Potassium chlorate at 81°C.
(b) Potassium chloride at 45°C.
(c) Potassium nitrate at 29°C.
(d) Sodium chloride at 21°C.
(e) Sodium chloride at 85°C.

21. a b c d e

22. Approximately how many kilograms of potassium nitrate can be dissolved in ten liters of water at 23°C.?

(a) 0.04 (b) 0.4 (c) 0.35 (d) 3.0 (e) 4.0

22. a b c d e

23. By what per cent is the solubility of potassium chlorate in water increased as water is heated from 29°C. to 62°C.?

(a) 15 (b) 25 (c) 35 (d) 150 (e) 250

23. a b c d e

24. If one mole of potassium chloride weighs 0.07456 kilogram, approximately how many moles of potassium chloride can be dissolved in 100 liters of water at 36°C.?

(a) 0.002 (b) 0.2 (c) 5 (d) 50 (e) 500

24. a b c d e

25. For which of the following pairs of salts is there *not* a temperature between 10°C. and 90°C. at which the salts have the same solubility?

(a) Potassium chloride and sodium chloride
(b) Potassium nitrate and sodium nitrate
(c) Potassium chlorate and potassium nitrate
(d) Potassium chlorate and sodium chloride
(e) Potassium chloride and potassium nitrate

25. a b c d e

26. Which of the following salts has the greatest change in solubility (in kilograms per liter of water) between 15°C. and 25°C.?

(a) Potassium chlorate (b) Potassium nitrate (c) Sodium chlorate (d) Sodium chloride (e) Sodium nitrate

26. a b c d e

ANALYSIS OF ORDINARY LIFE INSURANCE PURCHASES IN THE U.S., 1955
[From 1956 Fact Book, permission of Institute of Life Insurance]

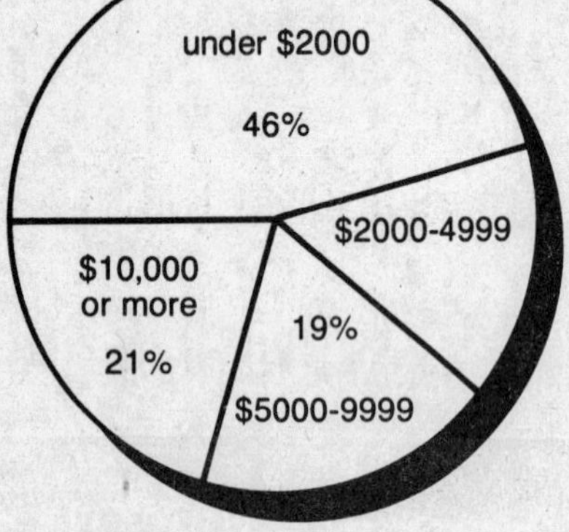

NUMBER OF POLICIES
Total Number of Policies — 7.5 Million
GRAPH VII

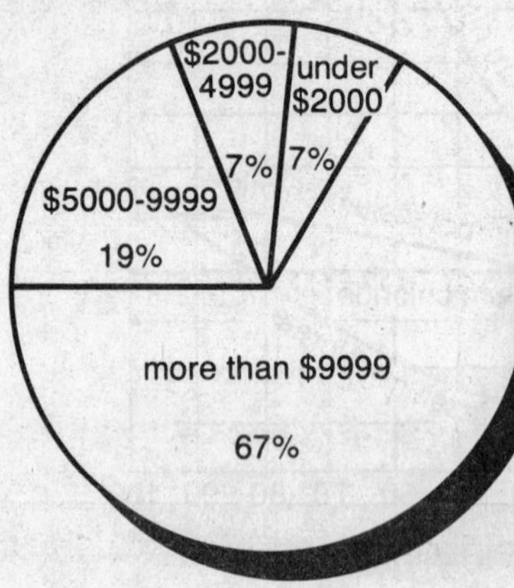

AMOUNT OF INSURANCE
Total Value of All Policies — $30.8 Billions
GRAPH VIII

QUESTIONS 27-31 REFER TO GRAPHS VII, VIII.

27. How many *more* ordinary life insurance policies were purchased for amounts of $2000 or more, than for amounts under $2000 in the United States in 1955? (Answer in millions.)

(a) 0.3 (b) 0.6 (c) 4.0 (d) 2864 (e) 2649

27. a b c d e

28. Approximately what part of the money invested in life insurance purchased in the United States in 1955 was for amounts less than $10,000?

(a) $\frac{1}{7}$ **(b)** $\frac{1}{5}$ **(c)** $\frac{1}{3}$ **(d)** $\frac{2}{3}$ **(e)** $\frac{4}{5}$

28. a b c d e

29. What was the average amount (in dollars) of all the ordinary life insurance policies purchased in the United States in 1955?

(a) 2310 (b) 2435 (c) 3428 (d) 4107 (e) 16,240

29. a b c d e

30. Of the insurance policies for amounts of more than $10,000 $\frac{8}{21}$ were for less than $25,000. How many policies of $25,000 or more were purchased? (Answer in millions.)

(a) 0.225 (b) 0.386 (c) 0.493 (d) 0.793 (e) 0.975

30. a b c d e

31. If the radius of each of the circles in the graph is 1, what is the perimeter enclosing the area representing the amount of ordinary life insurance over $9999 purchased in the United States in 1955?

(a) 2 **(b)** $\frac{2}{3}\pi$ **(c)** $\frac{2}{3}\pi + 2$ **(d)** $\frac{4}{3}\pi$ **(e)** $\frac{4}{3}\pi + 2$

31. a b c d e

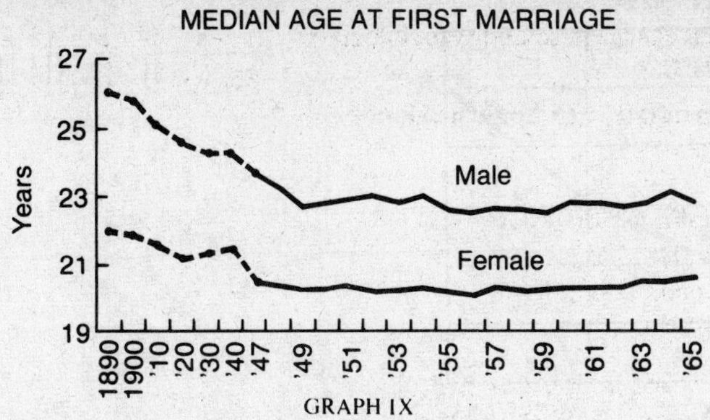

GRAPH IX

QUESTIONS 32-34 REFER TO GRAPH IX.

32. The median age for brides was lowest in

(a) 1940 (b) 1947 (c) 1956 (d) 1959 (e) 1965

32. a b c d e

33. The median age for bridegrooms was lowest in

(a) 1940 (b) 1947 (c) 1956 (d) 1959 (e) 1965

33. a b c d e

34. Of the following, the year in which there was the greatest difference in age between bride and bridegroom was

(a) 1900 (b) 1940 (c) 1947 (d) 1954 (e) 1964

34. a b c d e

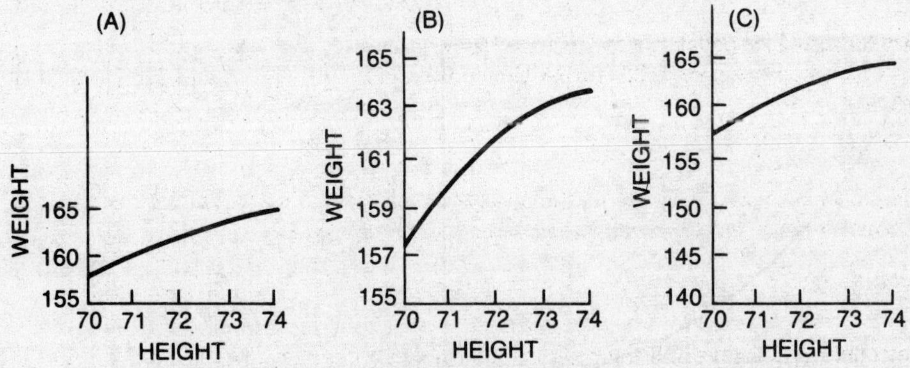

GRAPH X

QUESTION 35 REFERS TO GRAPH X.

Following is the average height in inches, and weight in pounds, of a given population.

Height	*Weight*
74	164
73	163
72	162
71	160
70	157

35. Which of the graphs above—*A*, *B*, or *C*—is the correct representation of the data?

(a) *A* (b) *B* (c) *C* (d) All are correct

35. a b c d

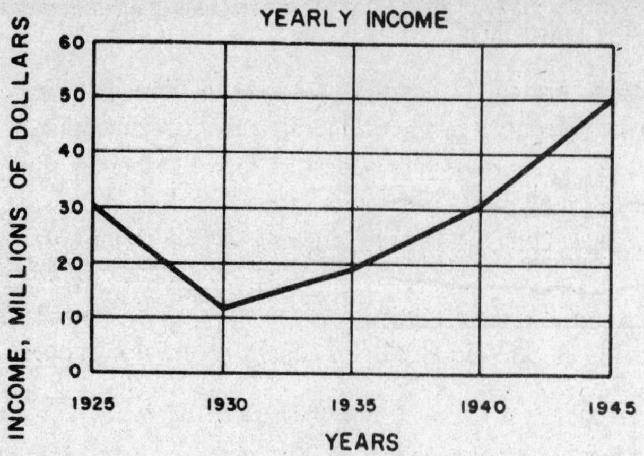

GRAPH XI

QUESTIONS 36-37 REFER TO GRAPH XI.

36. We are justified in concluding that

(a) higher prices were charged by the company in 1945.
(b) income of the company increased more rapidly in the 1935-1940 period than in the preceding five years.
(c) the number of sales of the company have been increasing since 1930.
(d) there was a depression in 1930.

36. a || b || c || d ||

37. About what was the average annual income of the company from 1930 to 1940?

(a) $15,000,000 (b) $20,000,000 (c) $25,000,000 (d) $30,000,000

37. a || b || c || d ||

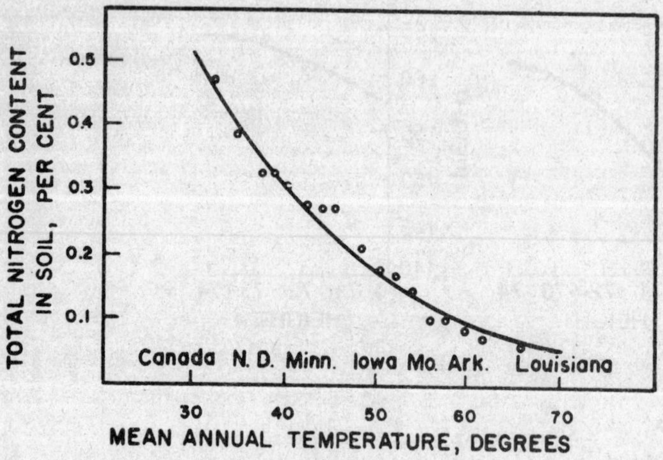

GRAPH XII

QUESTION 38 REFERS TO GRAPH XII.

38. The graph shows a relationship between mean annual temperature and nitrogen content of the soil. Which of the following statements can *best* be inferred from the graph?

(a) Heat "bakes out" nitrogen from the soil.
(b) Soils in the southern parts of the U. S. A. have lower nitrogen content than do northern midwestern soils.
(c) Southern farmers have greater need to fertilize thin soils than do Canadian farmers.
(d) Warmth may be substituted for nitrogen in raising farm crops.

38. a || b || c || d ||

NUMBER SEQUENCES

A *number sequence* is a succession of numbers arranged according to some definite pattern. Any number in this sequence is related to its preceding number according to a definite plan. In the relatively simple sequence, 3, 5, 7, 9, 11 . . . . . . two is added to each number in the sequence. Other relationships may involve the processes of subtraction, multiplication, division, squaring, extracting roots and, in the case of more difficult problems, it may involve a combination of these processes. For example, in the sequence 1, 2, 2, 5, 3, 10, 4, 17, 5 the second number in each pair is the square of the first number plus 1. Thus, 2 is $1^2 + 1$, 5 is $2^2 + 1$, 10 is $3^2 + 1$, etc. Similarly, in the sequence 3, 13, 53, 213 . . . . one is added to the product of the preceding number and 4.

PRACTICE EXERCISES *Answers given on page 387.*

Find the next number in each of the following sequences

1. 1, 3, 5, 7, 9 . . .
2. 3, 3, 6, 6, 9, 9, 12 . . .
3. 6, 11, 16, 21, 26 . . .
4. −9, −6, −3, 0 . . .
5. 36, 39, 39, 43, 43, 48, 48 . . .
6. $28\frac{1}{8}, 21\frac{1}{8}, 14\frac{1}{8}, 7\frac{1}{8}$ . . .
7. 5, 7, 11, 17, 25 . . .
8. −26, −20, −14, −8 . . .
9. 18, 26, 27, 35, 36, 44 . . .
10. 5, 6, 8, 11, 15, . . .
11. $7\frac{1}{2}, 6\frac{3}{4}, 6, 5\frac{1}{4}, 4\frac{1}{2}$ . . .
12. $9\frac{3}{4}, 9\frac{5}{8}, 9\frac{1}{2}, 9\frac{3}{8}$ . . .
13. 2.52, 3.02, 3.52, 4.02 . . .
14. 5.3, 6.4, 7.5, 8.6, 9.7 . . .
15. 11, 28, 79, 232 . . .
16. 5, 8, 9, 12, 13, 16 . . .
17. 7, 8, 10, 13, 17, 22 . . .
18. 79, 77, 75, 73, 71 . . .
19. 79, 74, 70, 67, 65 . . .
20. 21, 20, 18, 15, 11, 6 . . .
21. 13, 12, 10, 7 . . .
22. −5, 10, −20, 40, −80 . . .
23. −2, −4, −8, −16, −32 . . .
24. 1, 4, 9, 16, 25, 36, 49 . . .
25. 5, 10, 17, 26, 37 . . .
26. 2, 6, 14, 30, 62 . . .
27. 1782, 594, 198, 66 . . .
28. 4752, 792, 132 . . .
29. 99, 88, 77, 66, 55 . . .
30. 100, 81, 64, 49, 36 . . .
31. 5, 2, 5, 4, 5, 6, 5 . . .
32. 48, 24, 12, 6 . . .
33. 80, 2, 40, 2, 20, 2 . . .
34. 5, 8, 24, 27, 81, 84 . . .
35. 3, 5, 10, 12, 24, 26 . . .
36. 5, 6, 8, 11, 15, 20 . . .
37. 7, 14, 14, 21, 21, 28, 28 . . .
38. 3, 6, 5, 8, 7, 10, 9 . . .
39. 6, 10, 13, 17, 20, 24 . . .
40. 12, 16, 13, 17, 14, 18 . . .
41. 5, 6, 8, 11, 15, 20, 26 . . .
42. $\frac{1}{15}$, 0.2, 0.6, 1.8 . . .
43. 65, 60, 56, 53, 51 . . .
44. 256, 16, 4, 2 . . .
45. 400, 361, 324, 289, 256 . . .
46. 121, 144, 169, 196 . . .
47. 512, 343, 216, 125, 64 . . .
48. 2, 5, 15, 18, 54 . . .
49. 16, 256, 15, 225, 14, 196, 13 . . .
50. 4, 64, 5, 125, 6 . . .

ANSWER KEY—TEXT SAMPLES (Questions Indicated with •)

1. -7
2. $-(-4) = 4$
3. 11
4. 7
5. 26
6. -17
7. 22
8. -17
9. 17
10. 0
11. -57
12. 45
13. -8
14. -40
15. $42 + 42 = 84$
16. $-18 + (-15) = -33$
17. -56
18. 12
19. 120
20. -112
21. 5
22. -4
23. -9
24. 4
25. $4 \times a \times b \times c$
26. 5×3
27. $3 \times 2 \times a \times b$
28. $(a+b)(a+b)$
29. $(a+b)(a-b)$
30. 6
31. -5
32. $x^4y^2 = (1)(x^4y^2)$ thus coefficient is 1
33. $2 \times 2 \times 2 \times 2 \times 2 = 32$
34. $x \cdot x \cdot y \cdot y \cdot y \cdot y$
35. no
36. yes
37. no
38. yes
39. yes
40. $5x$
41. $5x^2y$
42. $(4-6)x^2 = -2x^2$
43. $4abc^2$
44. $8x^3 + x^2 + 6x - 2$
45. $(5x^2 - 10x - 4) + (-3x^2 - 2x + 5) = 2x^2 - 12x + 1$
46. x^5 by counting factors
47. $x^{5+7} = x^{12}$
48. $x^{2+3} \cdot y^{1+2} = x^5y^3$
49. $30x^{2+4} = 30x^6$
50. $(6)(-5)(x^1)(x^4) = -30x^5$
51. $(3x^2)(5x^3) + (3x^2)(2x) - (3x^2)(3y) = 15x^5 + 6x^3 - 9x^2y$
52. $(-4x^2y)(2x^2) - (-4x^2y)(3xy) - (-4x^2y)(4y^2) = -8x^4y + 12x^3y^2 + 16x^2y^3$
53. $(3x^2)(2x) - (2x)(2x) - (7)(2x) + (3x^2)(-4) + (-2x)(-4) + (-7)(-4) = 6x^3 - 4x^2 - 14x - 12x^2 + 8x + 28 = 6x^3 - 16x^2 - 6x + 28$
54. $x^2 - 2x + 3x - 6 = x^2 + x - 6$
55. $x^2 + 3x - 3x - 9 = x^2 - 9$
56. $x + y + 3x - 2y = x + 3x + y - 2y = 4x - y$
57. $x - 3x + y + 2y = -2x + 3y$
58. $3x^2 + 2x - 4x^2 + 3x - 5 = -x^2 + 5x - 5$
59. $x + y - 5x - 5y = -4x - 4y$
60. $(12x^2 + 8x) - (8x^2 + 24x - 16) = 12x^2 + 8x - 8x^2 - 24x + 16 = 4x^2 - 16x + 16$
61. $4x - \{-4x + 3\} = 4x + 4x - 3 = 8x - 3$
62. $x^{6-2} = x^4$
63. $\dfrac{-15}{3}x^{6-2}y^{3-1} = -5x^4y^2$
64. $\dfrac{-18}{-6}x^{3-1}y^{1-1}z^{2-1} = 3x^2z$ (Note that $y^0 = 1$ as long as y is any number except 0.)
65. $-9x^2 - 3x + 1$
66. $\dfrac{6x^{3c}}{2x^c} - \dfrac{8x^{2c}}{2x^c} = 3x^{3c-c} - 4x^{2c-c} = 3x^{2c} - 4x^c$
67. $2xy^2(2x^2y - 11)$
68. $(x-8)(x+8)$
69. $(x+6)(x+2)$
70. $(x-4)(x-2)$
71. $(x-5)(x+2)$
72. -10
73. $2\sqrt{2}$
74. $5\sqrt{3}$
75. $\sqrt[3]{27}\sqrt[3]{2} = 3\sqrt[3]{2}$
76. $7\sqrt{5}$
77. $3\sqrt{3}$
78. $5\sqrt{2} + \sqrt{2} = 6\sqrt{2}$
79. $3\sqrt{9}\sqrt{3} + \sqrt{36}\sqrt{3} = (3)(3)\sqrt{3} + 6\sqrt{3} = 15\sqrt{3}$
80. $4\sqrt{16}\sqrt{2} - 6\sqrt{4}\sqrt{2} = 4 \cdot 4\sqrt{2} - 6 \cdot 2\sqrt{2} = 4\sqrt{2}$
81. $\sqrt{36} = 6$
82. $6\sqrt{144} = 6 \cdot 12 = 72$
83. $(\frac{2}{3} \cdot 9)(\sqrt{81}) = 54$

84. $(\frac{1}{3} \cdot 3)(\sqrt{16}) = 4$

85. 5 (Remove common factor, $\sqrt{3}$.)

86. $\frac{\sqrt{18}}{3} = \frac{\sqrt{9}\sqrt{2}}{3} = \frac{3\sqrt{2}}{3} = \sqrt{2}$

87. $\frac{\sqrt{10}}{2}$

88. $\frac{100\sqrt{2}}{5\sqrt{2}} = 20$

89. 16

90. $x = 8$

91. $4x - 3x = 5 + 2; x = 7$

92. $x = 4 \cdot 12 = 48$

93. $x = \frac{12}{4} = 3$

94. $x + 2 = \frac{49}{9}; x = \frac{31}{9}$

95. $\sqrt{x} = -1; x = 1$, but 1 is extraneous since $\sqrt{1} + 1 = 2$. Thus no solution.

96. $F - 32 = \frac{9}{5}C; 5(F - 32) = 9C; \frac{5}{9}(F - 32) = C$

97. $r = \frac{d}{t}$

98. $2x + 1 = 43; x = 21$, numbers are 21 and 22.

99. $24 = 4 \times 2 \times h; h = 3$

100. Let x = amount state pays
$2x$ = amount township pays
$4(2x) = 8x$ = amount county pays
$x + 2x + 8x = 88{,}000; x = 8{,}000$
state: 8,000, township: 16,000, county: 64,000

101. Let x = number of years until Smith is 4 times as old as son. At that time Smith will be $28 + x$ and son, $4 + x$.
$(28 + x) = 4(4 + x)$
$x = 4$

102. Let x = number of nickels, then $14 - x$ will be number of dimes. $5x$ is value in cents of x nickels, $10(14 - x)$ will be value of dimes.
$5x + 10(14 - x) = 100$
$x = 8$
8 nickels, 6 dimes

103. $6 > -6$

104. $8 < 11$

105. $-4 < -1$ because $-4 - (-1) = -3$

106. $-5 < 0$ because $-5 - 0 = -5$

107. 

108. 

109. 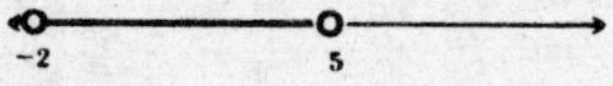

110. $x > 19$

111. $x < -2$

112. $-3 > -4$

113. $x > 4$

114. $-4x < 24;\ x > -6$ (Direction changed because each side was divided by a negative number, -4.)

115. $3 < \frac{1}{2}x - 1; 4 < \frac{1}{2}x; 8 < x$

116. $-4x \geq -8, x \leq 2$

117. Add left sides, add right sides: $x + y > 11$

118. $x > 16, -y > -15, x - y > 1$

119. $<$

120. $>$

121. $>$

122. $>$

123. $<$

124. $\frac{13}{2}$

125. $\frac{6\times9+5}{6}=\frac{59}{6}$
126. $3\frac{3}{7}$
127. $3\frac{3}{4}$
128. $\frac{3}{12}$
129. $\frac{7}{28}$
130. $\frac{24}{36}$
131. $\frac{1\times9}{4\times9}=\frac{9}{36}$
132. $\frac{1\times12}{3\times12}=\frac{12}{36}$.
133. $\frac{4\times4}{9\times4}=\frac{16}{36}$
134. $\frac{3x+6}{x^2-4}$
135. $\frac{2}{y-2}$
136. $\frac{2x-1}{x(2x-1)}=\frac{1}{x}$
137. $\frac{2}{3}$
138. $\frac{2}{3}$
139. $\frac{a+3}{4}$
140. $\frac{3-a}{4}$
141. $\frac{6}{7}$
142. $\frac{13}{12}$
143. $\frac{1}{6}$
144. $\frac{11}{12}-\frac{9}{12}=\frac{2}{12}=\frac{1}{6}$
145. $\frac{102}{8}-\frac{15}{8}=\frac{87}{8}$
146. $\frac{12}{3b}=\frac{4}{b}$
147. $\frac{12a}{6b}-\frac{6c}{6b}-\frac{3a}{6b}+\frac{8c}{6b}=\frac{9a+2c}{6b}$
148. $\frac{2}{a-3}$
149. $18=3\times3\times2, 12=2\times2\times3, \text{LCD}=2\times2\times3\times3=36$
150. $\text{LCD}=2a^3b^3c^2$
151. $x^2-1=(x+1)(x-1), \text{LCD}=(x-1)^2(x+1)$
152. $\frac{6}{343}$
153. $\frac{1}{24}$
154. $\frac{ab}{ab^2c^3}=\frac{1}{bc^3}$
155. $\frac{3}{35}$
156. $\frac{4}{12}\times1=\frac{1}{3}$
157. $\frac{289}{18}$
158. $\frac{3}{2}$
159. $\frac{2}{5}\times\frac{15}{8}=\frac{3}{4}$
160. $\frac{17}{6}\times\frac{3}{17}=\frac{1}{2}$
161. $\frac{(x+y)^2}{x}$
162. $\frac{\left(\frac{1}{3}+\frac{5}{6}\right)12}{\left(1-\frac{1}{3}\times\frac{3}{4}\right)12}=\frac{14}{9}$
163. $\frac{\left(\frac{1}{x}+\frac{1}{y}\right)xy}{\left(\frac{1}{xy}\right)xy}=y+x$
164. $\frac{\left(\frac{1}{a}\right)a}{\left(1-\frac{1}{a}\right)a}=\frac{1}{a-1}$
165. $\frac{\left(\frac{1}{y}-\frac{1}{x}\right)xy}{\left(1-\frac{y}{x}\right)xy}=\frac{x-y}{xy-y^2}=\frac{x-y}{y(x-y)}=\frac{1}{y}$
166. $3x+4x=7; x=1$
167. $3(4x)=1(7+5x); x=1$
168. $\text{LCD}=2(x-2); 2(5)-2(2)=3(x-2); x=4$

169. $rs+ps=pr; rs-pr=-ps; r(s-p)=-ps; r=\frac{-ps}{s-p}=\frac{-ps}{-(p-s)}=\frac{ps}{p-s}$

170. $2S=na+n; 2S-n=na; \frac{2S-n}{n}=a$

171. $\frac{7}{8}\times48=42$

172. $\frac{1}{4}\times\frac{4}{7}=\frac{1}{7}$

173. $\frac{1}{2}\cdot\frac{3}{7}=\frac{3}{14}$

174. $\frac{20}{32}=\frac{5}{8}$

175. $\frac{16}{26} = \frac{8}{13}$
176. $\frac{5}{25} = \frac{1}{5}$
177. $18 = 2x; x = 9$
178. $900 = 2x; x = 450$
179. $\frac{1}{4}x = 5; x = 20$
180. $\frac{75}{100} = .75$
181. $\frac{1/2}{100} = .005$
182. $\frac{a}{100}$ no decimal possible without knowing more about a.
183. .83
184. .023
185. 2%
186. 2,000%
187. 12%
188. 70%
189. $200 = 5x$; $40 = x$; therefore, 40%
190. $4x = 2$; $x = \frac{1}{2}$; therefore, $\frac{1}{2}$%
191. $100a = bx; x = \frac{100a}{b}$; therefore, $\frac{100a}{b}$ %
192. $\frac{100q}{p}$%
193. $\frac{t}{v} = \frac{x}{100}; x = \frac{100t}{v}$; therefore $\frac{100t}{v}$ %
194. $\frac{15 \times 20}{100} = 3$
195. $\frac{300}{100} = \frac{x}{7}; x = 21$
196. $\frac{20}{100} = \frac{15}{x}; x = 75$
197. $\frac{7}{x} = \frac{5}{100}; x = 140$
198. $\frac{140}{x} = \frac{66\frac{2}{3}}{100}; x = 210$
199. $80x = 480; x = 6$ (dollars)
200. $\frac{20{,}000}{x} = \frac{83\frac{1}{3}}{100}; x = 24{,}000$
201. $\frac{220}{x} = \frac{110}{100}; x = 200$
202. $72x = 800; x = 11\frac{1}{9}\%$
203. $\frac{5+0-2+9}{4} = 3$
204. $6(80) + x = 7(82); x = 94$
205. $\frac{2(90) + 5(85)}{7} = 86.4\%$
206. $\frac{3(5) + 2(12)}{5} = \$7.80$
207. $d = 3 \times 45 = 135$
208. $r = \frac{93}{3} = 31$
209. $900 = 90t; t = 10$
210. $\frac{3(45) + 2(40)}{5} = 43$
211. $35x + 55x = 540; x = 6$
212. $\frac{1.2}{10} = \frac{6}{50} = \frac{3}{25}$
213. $\frac{2}{64} = \frac{1}{32}$
214. $7n - 3n = 20; n = 5$; numbers are 35 and 15
215. $33n = 264; n = 8$; smaller $= 16n = 128$
216. $\frac{5n+2}{8n+2} = \frac{2}{3}; n = 2$; numbers are 10 and 16
217. $x = 28$
218. $\frac{7y}{7z} = \frac{3z}{7z}; \frac{y}{z} = \frac{3}{7}$
219. $\frac{m}{d} = \frac{x}{y}; y = \frac{xd}{m}$
220. $\frac{1\frac{1}{2}}{1} = \frac{x}{1\frac{1}{2}}; x = 2\frac{1}{4}$
221. $rc = k$; $(200)(1\frac{1}{2}) = k = 300$; $(500)(c) = 300$; $c = \frac{3}{5}$
222. $(10)(12) = k = 120$; $16x = 120$; $x = 7.5$
223. $\frac{1}{10}$
224. $\frac{x + .6}{x + 30} = \frac{1}{10}; x = 2\frac{2}{3}$
225. .3 quarts of acid in original solution. $3 + x$ quarts of new solution. $\frac{.3}{3 + x} = \frac{6}{100}; x = 2$
226. $\frac{1}{x} = \frac{1}{6} + \frac{1}{8}$
  LCD $= 24x$
  $24 = 4x + 3x$
  $x = 3\frac{3}{7}$
227. $\frac{5}{x} + \frac{5}{10} + \frac{3}{10} = 1$
  LCD $= 10x$
  $50 + 5x + 3x = 10x$
  $x = 25$
228. $\frac{1}{80} + \frac{1}{40} = \frac{1}{x}$
  LCD $= 80x$
  $x + 2x = 80$
  $x = 26\frac{2}{3}$
229. $A(0, 3)$, $B(3, 2)$, $C(4, 3)$, $D(2, 0)$, $E(1, -2)$, $F(0, 0)$, $G(-3, -1)$, $H(-4, 3)$, $I(-2, 2)$, $J(-1, -2)$
230. 4
231. $\sqrt{5}$
232. $\left(\frac{3+(-4)}{2}, \frac{-1+2}{2}\right) = \left(-\frac{1}{2}, \frac{1}{2}\right)$
233. Let (x, y) be the other endpoint.
  $\frac{x+3}{2} = 5; x = 7 \qquad \frac{y-1}{2} = 0; y = 1$

ANSWER KEY—PRACTICE EXERCISES

OPERATIONS INVOLVING WHOLE NUMBERS

1. 36
2. 27
3. 263
4. 291
5. 266
6. 1725
7. 1922
8. 2485
9. 2933
10. 3186
11. 32,607
12. 21,302
13. 19,696
14. 24,917
15. 22,486
16. 533
17. 413
18. 614
19. 715
20. 587
21. 228
22. 56
23. 1005
24. 4456
25. 5257
26. 16,023
27. 16,150
28. 51,156
29. 28,728
30. 36,792
31. 27,679
32. 7560
33. 10,695
34. 21,567
35. 14,008
36. 9222
37. 4913
38. 96,922
39. 79,050
40. 47,880
41. 23
42. 42
43. 72
44. 34
45. 57
46. 49
47. 58
48. 962
49. 372
50. 384

ROOTS AND RADICALS

1. $\sqrt{3}$
2. $30\sqrt{2}$
3. $20\sqrt{2}$
4. $4\sqrt{7}$
5. $2\sqrt{6}$
6. $4\sqrt{5}$
7. $10\sqrt{3} - \sqrt{2}$
8. 0
9. $13\sqrt{7}$
10. $10\sqrt{5}$
11. 6
12. $3\sqrt{7}$
13. $10\sqrt{3}$
14. $9\sqrt{6}$
15. $9\sqrt{2}$
16. 102
17. $2\sqrt{21}$
18. 9
19. $\frac{1}{3}\sqrt{10}$
20. 64
21. 5
22. $2\sqrt{3}$
23. 35
24. $\sqrt{2}$
25. 3
26. 8
27. 12
28. $9\sqrt{2}$
29. $5\sqrt{7}$
30. 1

SOLVING EQUATIONS

1. 3
2. $\frac{cn}{p}$
3. 8
4. $\frac{2A}{b + b_1}$
5. 1
6. $\frac{2S - nL}{n}$
7. 18
8. $\pm\sqrt{\frac{4A}{\pi}}$
9. $-\frac{1}{8}$
10. $\frac{i}{Pt}$
11. $\frac{cd}{c + d}$
12. $\pm\sqrt{\frac{s}{6}}$
13. $1\frac{1}{4}$
14. $\frac{P - 2W}{2}$
15. $\frac{A}{(R + r)(R - r)}$
16. IR
17. $\pm\sqrt{\frac{2s}{a}}$
18. 1
19. $-\frac{2}{27}$
20. $\pm\sqrt{k}$

SOLVING VERBAL PROBLEMS ALGEBRAICALLY

1. e
2. c
3. b
4. b
5. e
6. a
7. c
8. e
9. c
10. b
11. d
12. b
13. d
14. c
15. e
16. c
17. e
18. d
19. e
20. c

INEQUALITIES AND THE NUMBER LINE

1. $<$
2. $>$
3. $<$
4. $<$
5. $<$
6. $<$
7. $>$
8. $<$
9. $>$
10. $>$
11. $x > 4$;
12. $x \leq \frac{5}{8}$;
13. $x > 3$;
14. $x < 4$;
15. $x < 2$;
16. $x < 0$ or $x > \frac{1}{5}$;
17. $0 < x < \frac{1}{5}$;
18. $1 < x < 5$;
19. $-2 < x \leq 2$;
20. $-9 < \sqrt{x}$ is true for all values of $x \geq 0$ since $\sqrt{x}$ is always positive or 0.

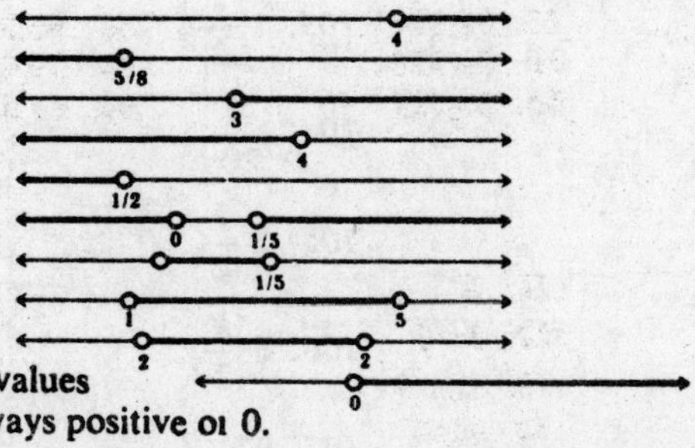

OPERATIONS INVOLVING FRACTIONS

ADDITION

1. $\frac{3}{4}$
2. $\frac{7}{8}$
3. $\frac{5}{8}$
4. $1\frac{1}{2}$
5. $\frac{7}{12}$
6. $\frac{8}{15}$
7. $\frac{1}{2}$
8. $\frac{7}{10}$
9. $\frac{13}{21}$
10. $\frac{9}{14}$
11. $1\frac{1}{12}$
12. $1\frac{11}{12}$
13. $1\frac{3}{8}$
14. $\frac{7}{8}$
15. $1\frac{7}{60}$
16. $39\frac{3}{8}$
17. $61\frac{1}{12}$
18. $22\frac{11}{12}$
19. $3\frac{7}{12}$
20. $17\frac{23}{24}$
21. $110\frac{5}{12}$
22. $23\frac{1}{12}$
23. $12\frac{1}{2}$
24. $9\frac{3}{5}$
25. $8\frac{5}{6}$

SUBTRACTION

26. $\frac{1}{2}$
27. $\frac{3}{8}$
28. $\frac{1}{8}$
29. $\frac{1}{4}$
30. $\frac{7}{12}$
31. $\frac{5}{9}$
32. $\frac{2}{9}$
33. $\frac{1}{4}$
34. $12\frac{5}{12}$
35. $68\frac{1}{2}$
36. $54\frac{3}{8}$
37. $18\frac{7}{10}$
38. $9\frac{1}{4}$
39. $9\frac{5}{12}$
40. $11\frac{1}{4}$
41. $40\frac{3}{4}$
42. $\frac{5}{6}$
43. $2\frac{1}{2}$
44. $1\frac{1}{2}$
45. $8\frac{5}{6}$

MULTIPLICATION

46. $\frac{2}{7}$
47. $\frac{1}{2}$
48. $\frac{1}{6}$
49. $\frac{1}{3}$
50. $\frac{1}{12}$
51. $\frac{1}{3}$
52. $31\frac{1}{2}$
53. 22
54. $12\frac{1}{2}$
55. $8\frac{4}{15}$
56. $21\frac{2}{3}$
57. $47\frac{8}{15}$
58. $13\frac{7}{15}$
59. $37\frac{11}{60}$
60. $13\frac{5}{36}$
61. $27\frac{19}{24}$
62. $53\frac{9}{10}$
63. 10
64. $29\frac{29}{60}$
65. $65\frac{1}{6}$

DIVISION

66. 2
67. $1\frac{1}{4}$
68. $\frac{4}{5}$

69. $\frac{3}{4}$

70. 6

71. $\frac{3}{4}$

72. $1\frac{1}{6}$

73. $3\frac{1}{3}$

74. $1\frac{1}{2}$

75. 8

76. 5

77. $6\frac{2}{5}$

78. $21\frac{1}{2}$

79. $13\frac{2}{3}$

80. $17\frac{1}{2}$

81. $2\frac{4}{9}$

82. $1\frac{31}{32}$

83. $1\frac{47}{51}$

84. $\frac{35}{81}$

85. $\frac{31}{69}$

86. $2\frac{14}{33}$

87. $1\frac{35}{53}$

88. $7\frac{11}{14}$

89. $2\frac{8}{37}$

90. $1\frac{145}{147}$

91. $11\frac{13}{22}$

92. 3

93. $3\frac{47}{126}$

94. $9\frac{1}{9}$

95. $3\frac{15}{32}$

96. $\frac{7}{10}$

97. $\frac{3}{7}$

98. $\frac{3}{4}$

99. $\frac{20}{21}$

100. 1

COMPLEX FRACTIONS

101. $\frac{2}{5}$

102. $1\frac{1}{3}$

103. $1\frac{1}{2}$

104. $\frac{9}{20}$

105. $2\frac{1}{2}$

106. $6\frac{1}{2}$

107. 97

108. 159

109. $10\frac{4}{15}$

110. $8\frac{3}{5}$

111. $\frac{9}{26}$

112. $\frac{4}{13}$

113. $\frac{8}{97}$

114. $2\frac{1}{11}$

115. $2\frac{3}{7}$

116. $\frac{1}{4}$

117. $\frac{26}{81}$

118. $5\frac{7}{12}$

119. $2\frac{74}{83}$

120. $11\frac{17}{29}$

121. $\frac{19}{36}$

122. $5\frac{13}{15}$

123. $10\frac{3}{14}$

124. $2\frac{2}{5}$

125. $2\frac{4}{5}$

ALGEBRAIC FRACTIONS

1. $\frac{3}{x+1}$

2. $2x-2$

3. $\frac{3}{4}$

4. 1

5. $\frac{x-5}{3}$

6. $\frac{a+4}{a-4}$

7. $\frac{5}{a+2}$

8. $\frac{x-4}{x+1}$

9. $\frac{x+6}{x-1}$

10. $\frac{x-5}{x+4}$

11. $x+y$

12. $\frac{1}{1-x^2}$

13. $m-1$

14. $-\frac{1}{x+1}$

15. $ab-1$

16. $1-a$

17. $\frac{ax}{b}$

18. $\frac{b^2 + a^2}{2ab}$

19. $\frac{a-1}{a+1}$

20. $x^2 + y^2$

21. $\frac{23x}{12}$

22. $\frac{13x}{6}$

23. $\frac{17x+3}{15x}$

24. $\frac{7x+31}{12}$

25. $\frac{14a+b}{6a^2}$

26. $\frac{1}{a-5}$

27. $\frac{11a}{12}$

28. $\frac{y-x}{xy}$

29. $\frac{x+5}{5x}$

30. $\frac{3-2x}{x^2}$

31. $\frac{12a}{b}$

32. $\frac{a+b}{2a^2}$

33. $\frac{x+5}{5}$

34. $\frac{a^2-4b^2}{b^2}$

35. $\frac{45a^2+30a+5}{3a^2}$

36. $1 + 3x$

37. $-\frac{2b+2a}{ab}$

38. $\frac{xy}{y-x}$

39. $x - 1$

40. $\frac{x^2+4}{x^2+4x+4}$

41. $\frac{2y^2+xy}{2y^2-x^2}$

42. $\frac{1}{b+a}$

43. $\frac{x+4y}{y}$

44. $\frac{15}{1-3a}$

45. $-\frac{3x+1}{3}$

46. $\frac{x-2y}{y}$

47. $\frac{x}{x+3}$

48. $\frac{4}{4a-1}$

49. $x - y$

50. $-\frac{x+y}{y}$

FRACTIONAL EQUATIONS

1. b
2. d
3. c
4. d
5. d
6. b
7. d
8. a
9. e
10. e
11. a
12. a
13. a
14. c
15. b
16. c
17. a
18. a
19. c
20. e

VERBAL PROBLEMS INVOLVING FRACTIONS

1. b
2. d
3. d
4. a
5. e
6. e
7. a
8. b
9. e
10. b
11. b
12. d
13. e
14. a
15. b
16. d
17. d
18. b
19. c
20. c
21. b
22. e
23. b
24. e
25. c
26. b
27. c
28. a
29. c
30. a

DECIMALS

1. 1000.5827
2. 982.546
3. 773.53
4. 24.223
5. 401.994
6. 0.0621
7. 452.91
8. 76.81
9. 56.49
10. 71.88
11. 0.8
12. 0.3
13. 1.7
14. 13
15. 2

PERCENT

1. 25%
2. 25%
3. 25
4. 400%
5. 2
6. 2
7. 2
8. 50
9. 50
10. 50%
11. 200%
12. 71.4%
13. 140%
14. 0.35
15. 0.35
16. $\frac{13}{4}$
17. $233\frac{1}{3}$
18. $\frac{24}{100000}$
19. 0.45
20. 20%
21. $0.00007t$
22. $\frac{1}{110000}$
23. 0.000000036
24. $\frac{100n}{m}$
25. $\frac{6b-5d}{100}$

VERBAL PROBLEMS INVOLVING PERCENT

1. e	5. c	9. a	13. e	17. c
2. c	6. d	10. a	14. d	18. d
3. c	7. e	11. b	15. c	19. d
4. d	8. b	12. c	16. b	20. d

AVERAGES

1. a	4. c	7. d	10. a	13. b
2. b	5. c	8. b	11. d	14. b
3. b	6. b	9. e	12. c	15. d

MOTION

1. a	8. a	15. c	22. e	29. b
2. c	9. b	16. e	23. d	30. d
3. d	10. c	17. a	24. b	31. c
4. b	11. c	18. c	25. d	32. d
5. b	12. e	19. c	26. e	33. c
6. a	13. d	20. a	27. b	34. b
7. c	14. b	21. d	28. c	35. e

RATIO AND PROPORTION

1. d	11. b	21. b	31. d	41. e
2. a	12. c	22. b	32. a	42. b
3. b	13. b	23. a	33. e	43. c
4. d	14. d	24. e	34. a	44. b
5. b	15. b	25. c	35. c	45. a
6. e	16. e	26. a	36. e	46. d
7. a	17. b	27. a	37. b	47. c
8. a	18. b	28. a	38. d	48. a
9. d	19. e	29. c	39. c	49. b
10. b	20. c	30. e	40. c	50. a

MIXTURES AND SOLUTION

1. c	5. d	9. c	13. c	17. d
2. b	6. b	10. e	14. a	18. a
3. e	7. b	11. b	15. b	19. b
4. e	8. b	12. a	16. e	20. c

WORK

1. a	6. e	11. e	16. d	21. d
2. e	7. d	12. c	17. c	22. c
3. b	8. b	13. b	18. b	23. b
4. e	9. e	14. a	19. c	24. c
5. c	10. e	15. d	20. a	25. a

COORDINATE GEOMETRY

1. b	*6.* d	*11.* d	*16.* a	*21.* a
2. c	*7.* a	*12.* e	*17.* c	*22.* b
3. e	*8.* b	*13.* c	*18.* c	*23.* a
4. d	*9.* e	*14.* d	*19.* d	*24.* b
5. c	*10.* a	*15.* e	*20.* e	*25.* d

GEOMETRY

1. d	*11.* b	*21.* b	*31.* d	*41.* e	*51.* c
2. d	*12.* b	*22.* d	*32.* d	*42.* c	*52.* d
3. c	*13.* c	*23.* d	*33.* c	*43.* d	*53.* c
4. e	*14.* c	*24.* d	*34.* e	*44.* c	*54.* c
5. d	*15.* a	*25.* b	*35.* d	*45.* b	*55.* c
6. b	*16.* d	*26.* e	*36.* d	*46.* d	*56.* b
7. b	*17.* c	*27.* d	*37.* a	*47.* a	*57.* b
8. d	*18.* e	*28.* b	*38.* c	*48.* d	*58.* d
9. b	*19.* e	*29.* d	*39.* c	*49.* d	*59.* e
10. a	*20.* d	*30.* c	*40.* b	*50.* e	*60.* d

DATA INTERPRETATION

1. a	*11.* d	*21.* c	*31.* e
2. b	*12.* c	*22.* e	*32.* c
3. e	*13.* c	*23.* d	*33.* d
4. c	*14.* d	*24.* e	*34.* a
5. e	*15.* d	*25.* c	*35.* d
6. c	*16.* d	*26.* b	*36.* b
7. a	*17.* e	*27.* b	*37.* b
8. a	*18.* d	*28.* c	*38.* b
9. e	*19.* d	*29.* d	
10. d	*20.* c	*30.* e	

NUMBER SEQUENCES

1. 11	*11.* $3\frac{3}{4}$	*20.* 0	*31.* 8	*42.* 5.4
2. 12	*12.* $9\frac{1}{4}$	*21.* 3	*32.* 3	*43.* 50
3. 31	*13.* 4.52	*22.* 160	*33.* 10	*44.* $\sqrt{2}$
4. 3	*14.* 10.8	*23.* −64	*34.* 252	*45.* 225
5. 54	*15.* 691	*24.* 64	*35.* 52	*46.* 225
6. $\frac{1}{8}$	*16.* 17	*25.* 50	*36.* 26	*47.* 27
7. 35	*17.* 28	*26.* 126	*37.* 35	*48.* 57
8. −2	*18.* 69	*27.* 22	*38.* 12	*49.* 169
9. 45	*19.* 64	*28.* 22	*39.* 27	*50.* 216
10. 20		*29.* 44	*40.* 15	
		30. 25	*41.* 33	

THE TEST OF STANDARD WRITTEN ENGLISH (TSWE) 12

- Testing Tactics
- 12 Common Grammar and Usage Errors
- Practice Exercises
- Answer Key

TESTING TACTICS

The Test of Standard Written English (TSWE) is not counted in your SAT score. It is scored separately, and is intended only to help colleges place students in the appropriate freshman English class. Therefore, you should probably not spend too much of your study time preparing for this section. At the same time, you don't want to approach it too casually. You don't want the college of your choice to think that your terrific verbal SAT score was a mistake.

In addition, this section tests you on your ability to recognize clear, correct standard written English, the kind of writing your college professors will expect on the papers you write for them. Therefore, this chapter contains material you really should know. If you have trouble with written English, you might want to review this chapter later on in an effort to improve your writing skills.

There are two different kinds of questions in this section, usage questions and sentence correction ones. Most of them are usage questions, in which you have to find the error in the underlined sections of a sentence. You do not have to correct the sentence or explain what is wrong. Here are the directions.

Usage Questions

Directions: The following sentences contain problems in grammar, usage, diction (choice of words), and idiom.

Some sentences are correct.

No sentence contains more than one error.

You will find that the error, if there is one, is underlined and lettered. Assume that elements of the sentence that are not underlined are correct and cannot be changed. In choosing answers, follow the requirements of standard written English.

If there is an error, select the one underlined part that must be changed to make the sentence correct and blacken the corresponding space on your answer sheet.

If there is no error, blacken answer space Ⓔ.

EXAMPLE:

The region has a climate so severe that (A) plants growing there (B) rarely had been (C) more than twelve inches high (D). No error (E)

SAMPLE ANSWER

Ⓐ Ⓑ ● Ⓓ Ⓔ

TACTIC 1: REMEMBER THAT THE ERROR, IF THERE IS ONE, MUST BE IN THE UNDERLINED PART OF THE SENTENCE

You don't have to worry about improvements that could be made to the rest of the sentence. The only errors you need to consider are those in the underlined parts. For example, if you have a sentence in which the subject is plural and the verb is singular, you could call either one the error. But if only the verb is underlined, the error for that sentence is the verb.

EXAMPLE:

> Mr. Brown is one of the commuters who takes the
> A B
> 7:30 train from Brooktown every morning. No error
> C D E

Since *who* refers to *commuters,* it is plural, and needs a plural verb, so the error is B. If you were writing this sentence yourself, you could correct it any number of other ways. You could say, "Mr. Brown is a commuter who takes..." or "Mr. Brown, a commuter, takes..." or "Mr. Brown, who is one of the commuters, takes..." However, the actual question doesn't offer you any of these possibilities. You have to choose from the underlined choices. Don't waste your time considering other ways to fix the sentence.

TACTIC 2: USE YOUR EAR FOR THE LANGUAGE

Remember, you don't have to name the error, or be able to explain why it is wrong. All you have to do is recognize that something is wrong. If a word sounds wrong to you, it probably is, even if you don't know why.

EXAMPLE:

> In my history class I learned why the American
> A B
> colonies opposed the British, how they organized the militia, and the work of the Continental
> C D
> Congress. No error
> E

The last part of this sentence probably sounds funny to you—awkward, strange, wooden. You may not know exactly what it is, but something sounds wrong here. If you followed your instincts and chose D as the error, you would be right. The error is a lack of parallel structure. The sentence is listing three things you learned, and they should all be in the same form. Since the first two are clauses, the third should be too: "In my history class I learned why the American colonies opposed the British, how they organized the militia, and how the Continental Congress worked."

TACTIC 3: LOOK FIRST FOR THE MOST COMMON ERRORS

Most of the sentences will have errors. If you are having trouble finding mistakes, check for some of the more common errors: subject-verb agreement, pronoun-antecedent problems, misuse of adjectives and adverbs, dangling modifiers. But only look for errors in the underlined parts of the sentence. This should not take very long.

EXAMPLE:

> Marilyn and I ran fast as we could, but we missed
> A B
> our train which made us late for work. No error
> C D E

Imagine that you have this sentence, and you can't see what is wrong with it. Start at the beginning and check each answer choice. *I* is part of the subject, so it is the right case. *Fast* can be an adverb, so it is being used correctly. *Which* is a pronoun, and needs a noun for its antecedent. The only available one is *train*, but that doesn't make sense. (The train didn't make us late—*missing* the train made us late.) So there is your error.

Once you have checked each answer choice, if you still can't find an error, choose E, "No error." A certain number of questions have no errors.

Sentence Correction Questions

In addition to the usage questions, there will also be a group of sentence correction questions. In these questions, you will have five different versions of the same sentence, and you must choose the best one. Here are the directions.

> Directions: In each of the following sentences, some part or all of the sentence is underlined. Below each sentence you will find five ways of phrasing the underlined part. Select the answer that produces the most effective sentence, one that is clear and exact, without awkwardness or ambiguity, and blacken the corresponding space on your answer sheet. In choosing answers, follow the requirements of standard written English. Choose the answer that best expresses the meaning of the original sentence.
>
> Answer (A) is always the same as the underlined part. Choose answer (A) if you think the original sentence needs no revision.
>
> EXAMPLE:
>
> Laura Ingalls Wilder published her first book and she was sixty-five years old then.
>
> (A) and she was sixty-five years old then
> (B) when she was sixty-five years old
> (C) at age sixty-five years old
> (D) upon reaching sixty-five years
> (E) at the time when she was sixty-five
>
> SAMPLE ANSWER
>
> Ⓐ ● Ⓒ Ⓓ Ⓔ

The tactics suggested for the usage questions will be helpful here, too. In addition, you can use the following suggestions.

TACTIC 4: IF YOU SPOT AN ERROR IN THE UNDERLINED SECTION, ELIMINATE ANY ANSWER THAT REPEATS IT

If something in the underlined section strikes you as an obvious error, you can immediately ignore any answer choices that repeat it. Remember, you still don't have to be able to explain what is wrong. You just need to find a correct equivalent. If the error you found is absent from more than one of the choices, look over those choices again to see if they add any new errors.

EXAMPLE:

> Being as I had studied for the test with a tutor, I was confident.
>
> (A) Being as I had studied for the test
> (B) Being as I studied for the test
> (C) Since I studied for the test
> (D) Since I had studied for the test
> (E) Because I studied for the test

Since you immediately recognize that *Being as* is not acceptable as a conjunction in standard written English, you can eliminate choices A and B right away. But you also know that both *since* and *because* are perfectly acceptable substitutes, so you have to look more closely at the remaining choices. The only other changes they make are in the tense of the verb. Since the studying occurred before the taking of the test, the past perfect tense, *had studied*, is correct, so the answer is Choice D. Even if you hadn't known that, you could have figured it out. Since *because* and *since* are both acceptable, and since choices C and E both use the same verb, *studied*, those two choices must be wrong. Otherwise, they would both be right, and the SAT doesn't have questions with two right answers.

TACTIC 5: FIND THE CHANGES IN THE ANSWERS

If you don't see the error in the underlined section, look at the answer choices to see what is changed. The changes will tell you what kind of problem is being tested in this question.

EXAMPLE:

> The panel narrowed the field of applicants to the three whom it thought were best qualified for the position because of training and experience.
> (A) whom it thought were
> (B) of whom it thought were
> (C) who it thought was
> (D) whom it thought was
> (E) who it thought were

You can see right away that you have to choose between *who* and *whom* and between *was* and *were*. You can immediately eliminate Choice B—any choice that turns the sentence into gibberish is the wrong answer. To decide the pronoun question, check on the way it is used in the sentence. In this sentence, it is the subject of the verb *was* or *were* and therefore it must be *who*. This leaves you with choices C and E. Now you want to know if you need a plural or a singular verb. Since *who* refers to *three*, it is plural, and needs the plural verb *were*. The correct answer is E.

TACTIC 6: MAKE SURE THAT ALL PARTS OF THE SENTENCE ARE LOGICALLY CONNECTED

Not all parts of a sentence are created equal. Some parts should be subordinated to the rest, connected with subordinating conjunctions or relative pronouns, not just added on with *and*. Overuse of *and* frequently makes sentences sound babyish.

EXAMPLE:

> The leader always had loyal supporters and they loved him.
> (A) and they loved him.
> (B) and they loving him.
> (C) what loved him.
> (D) who loved him.
> (E) which loved him.

The original version of this sentence doesn't have any grammatical errors, but it is a poor sentence because it doesn't connect its two clauses logically. The second clause is merely adding information about the supporters, so it should be turned into an adjective clause, introduced by a relative pronoun. Choices (D) and (E) both seem to fit, but you know that *which* should never be used to refer to people, so (D) is obviously the correct answer.

Similarly, those parts of a sentence that are logically equal should always be presented in similar form (parallel construction).

EXAMPLE:

> In this chapter we'll analyze both types of questions, suggest useful techniques for tackling them, providing some sample items for you to try.
> (A) suggest useful techniques for tackling them, providing some sample items for you to try.
> (B) suggest useful techniques for tackling them, providing some sample items which you can try.
> (C) suggest useful techniques for tackling them, and provide some sample items for you to try.
> (D) and suggest useful techniques for tackling them by providing some sample items for you to try.
> (E) having suggested useful techniques for tackling them and provided some sample items for you to try.

To answer questions like this correctly, you must pay attention to what the sentence means. You must first decide whether or not *analyzing*, *suggesting*, and *providing* are logically equal in importance here. Since they are—they are all activities that "we" will do—they should be given equal emphasis. Choice (C) is the one that correctly provides the parallel structure.

12 COMMON GRAMMAR AND USAGE ERRORS

Some errors are more common than others on the TSWE. Here are a dozen that appear frequently on the examination. Watch out for them when you do the practice exercises and when you take the SAT.

1. The Run-on Sentence

> Mary's party was very exciting, it lasted until two a.m.
>
> It is raining today, I need a raincoat.

You may also have heard this error called a comma splice. It can be corrected by making two sentences instead of one:

> Mary's party was very exciting. It lasted until two a.m.

or by using a semicolon in place of the comma:

> Mary's party was very exciting; it lasted until two a.m.

or by proper compounding:

> Mary's party was very exciting and lasted until two a.m.

You can also correct this error with proper subordination. The second example above could be corrected:

> Since it is raining today, I need a raincoat.
>
> It is raining today, so I need a raincoat.

2. The Sentence Fragment

> Since John was talking during the entire class, making it impossible for anyone to concentrate.

This is the opposite of the first error. Instead of too much in one sentence, here you have too little. Do not be misled by the length of the fragment. It must have a main clause before it can be a complete sentence. All you have in this example is the cause. You still need a result. For example, the sentence could be corrected:

> Since John was talking during the entire class, making it impossible for anyone to concentrate, the teacher made him stay after school.

3. Error in the Case of a Noun or Pronoun

> Between you and I, this test is not really very difficult.

Case problems usually involve personal pronouns, which are in the nominative case (*I, he, she, we, they, who)* when they are used as subjects or predicate nominatives, and in the objective case (*me, him, her, us, them, whom*) when they are used as direct objects, indirect objects, and objects of prepositions. In this example, if you realize that *between* is a preposition, you know that *I* should be changed to the objective *me* because it is the object of a preposition.

4. Error in Subject-Verb Agreement

> Harvard College, along with several other Ivy League schools, are sending students to the conference.

Phrases starting with *along with* or *as well as* or *in addition to* that are placed in between the subject and the verb do not affect the verb. The subject of this sentence is *Harvard College,* so the verb should be *is sending.*

> There is three bears living in that house.

Sentences that begin with *there* have the subject after the verb. The subject of this sentence is *bears,* so the verb should be *are.*

5. Error in Pronoun-Antecedent Agreement

> Every one of the girls on the team is trying to do their best.

Every pronoun must have a specific noun or noun substitute for an antecedent, and it must agree with that antecedent in number (singular or plural). In this example, *their* refers to *one* and must be singular:

> Every one of the girls on the team is trying to do her best.

6. Error in the Tense or Form of a Verb

> After the sun set behind the mountain, a cool breeze sprang up and brought relief from the heat.

Make sure the verbs in a sentence appear in the proper sequence of tenses, so that it is clear what happened when. Since according to the sentence, the breeze did not appear until after the sun had finished setting, the setting belongs in the past perfect tense:

> After the sun had set behind the mountain, a cool breeze sprang up and brought relief from the heat.

7. Failure to Use the Subjunctive Mood When Needed

If I was your parent, I would ground you for a month.

The subjunctive mood is not very common in English, but it is used to indicate a condition contrary to fact. Since I am not your parent, the subjunctive is needed in this example:

If I were your parent, I would ground you for a month.

8. Error in Comparison

I can go to California or Florida. I wonder which is best.

When you are comparing only two things, you should use the comparative form of the adjective, not the superlative:

I wonder which is better.

Comparisons must also be complete and logical.

The rooms on the second floor are larger than the first floor.

It would be a strange building that had rooms larger than an entire floor. Logically, this sentence should be corrected to:

The rooms on the second floor are larger than those on the first floor.

9. Misuse of Adjectives and Adverbs

She did good on the test.

They felt badly about leaving their friends.

These are the two most common ways that adjectives and adverbs are misused. In the first example, when you are talking about how someone did, you want the adverb *well*, not the adjective *good:*

She did well on the test.

In the second example, after a linking verb like *feel,* you want a predicate adjective to describe the subject:

They felt bad about leaving their friends.

10. Dangling Modifiers

Reaching for the book, the ladder slipped out from under him.

A participial phrase at the beginning of the sentence should describe the subject of the sentence. Since it doesn't make sense to think of a ladder reaching for a book, this participle is left dangling with nothing to modify. The sentence needs some rewriting:

When he reached for the book, the ladder slipped out from under him.

11. Lack of Parallel Structure

In his book on winter sports, the author discusses ice-skating, skiing, hockey, and how to fish in an ice-covered lake.

Logically, equal and similar ideas belong in similar form. This shows that they are equal. In this sentence, the author discusses four sports, and all four should be presented the same way:

In his book on winter sports, the author discusses ice skating, skiing, hockey, and fishing in an ice-covered lake.

12. Error in Diction or Idiom

The affects of the storm could be seen everywhere.

Your ear for the language will help you handle these errors, especially if you are accustomed to reading standard English. These questions test you on words that are frequently misused, on levels of usage (informal versus formal), and on standard English idioms. In this example, the verb *affect,* meaning "to influence," has been confused with the noun *effect,* meaning "result."

The effects of the storm could be seen everywhere.

PRACTICE EXERCISES

The test that follows will give you practice in answering the two types of questions you'll find on the TSWE: usage questions and sentence correction questions.

TSWE TEST

Directions: The following sentences contain problems in grammar, usage, diction (choice of words), and idiom.
Some sentences are correct.
No sentence contains more than one error.

You will find that the error, if there is one, is underlined and lettered. Assume that elements of the sentence that are not underlined are correct and cannot be changed. In choosing answers, follow the requirements of standard written English.

If there is an error, select the one underlined part that must be changed to make the sentence correct and blacken the corresponding space on your answer sheet.

If there is no error, blacken answer space Ⓔ.

EXAMPLE:

The region has a climate so severe that plants
A
growing there rarely had been more than twelve
B C
inches high. No error
D E

SAMPLE ANSWER

Ⓐ Ⓑ ● Ⓓ Ⓔ

1. The conditions governing the truce which
A
has been arranged by the United Nations has not
B C D
been revealed. No error
E

2. Each one of the dogs in the show require a
A B C
special kind of diet. No error
D E

3. By order of the Student Council, the wearing of
A B
slacks by we girls in school has been permitted.
C D
No error
E

4. The major difficulty confronting the authorities was
A
the reluctance of the people to talk; they had been
B C
warned not to say nothing to the police. No error
D E

5. We were already to leave for the amusement park
A
when John's car broke down; we were forced to
B C D
postpone our outing. No error
E

6. We have heard that the principal has decided whom
A B
the prize winners will be and will announce the
C D
names in the assembly today. No error
E

7. She sang like she wished the people in the next county
A B C
to hear her. No error
D E

8. Although the news had come as a surprise to all in
A B
the room, everyone tried to do their work as though
C D
nothing had happened. No error
E

9. The committee had intended both you and I to speak at
A B C
the assembly; however, only one of us will be able to
D
talk. No error
E

10. "At that moment," John reported, "the teacher
A B
said, 'Speak louder.'" No error
C D E

11. I wonder whether you're sure that scheme of
A B C
yours' will work. No error
D E

12. Everybody except Frank and me wanted him to be
A B C D
chosen class representative. No error
D E

13. He interviewed people whom he thought had
A B C
valuable information to present. No error
D E

14. I don't know if I should discuss this matter with her
A B C
or not. No error
D E

15. There was so much conversation in back of me that I
A B C
couldn't hear the actors on the stage. No error
D E

16. I am so exhausted I can't scarcely keep my eyes
A B C
open. No error
D E

17. She had forgotten all about the stranger's coming to
A B C
the door and inquiring about her brother. No error
D E

18. If anyone cares to join me in this campaign,
A B
either now or in the near future, they will be
C D
welcomed gratefully. No error
E

19. I will always remember you standing by me and
A B C
offering me encouragement. No error
D E

20. They are both excellent books, but this one is
A B C
best. No error
D E

21. June is my favorite month; the roses smell so sweetly
A B
and the birds sing so happily. No error
C D E

22. Having lost his money in the stock market, his friends
A B C
deserted him. No error
D E

23. The poems with which he occasionally deigned to
A
regale the fashionable world were invariably
B C
bad—stereotyped, bombastic, and even ludicrous.
D
No error
E

24. William Faulkner's great themes are the following;
A B C
courage, pride, pity. No error
D E

25. The affect of her remarks was startling; some of us
A B
were shocked; others, angry. No error
C D E

26. This book is too elementary; it can help neither you
A B
nor I. No error
C D E

27. Before we were called for breakfast, he had swum for
A B C D
fifteen minutes in the ocean. No error
E

28. After her fainting spell, she was told to lay down on
A B C
the couch for ten minutes. No error
D E

29. Although the books are altogether on the shelf, they
A B C
are not arranged in any kind of order. No error
D E

30. As soon as the sun had rose over the mountains, it
A B
became unbearably hot and stifling in the valley.
C D
No error
E

31. For modern man, the acquisition of facts is like a
A
habit-forming drug; the more he takes, the more
B
craving he has. No error
C D E

32. This play is different than the one we saw last
A B C D
night. No error
E

33. The house looked it's age, despite our efforts to
A B C
beautify it. No error
D E

34. It may be difficult to find an acceptable definition
A
of style; every critic has their own. No error
B C D E

35. Dozens of phrases can be offered to describe
A
style, but perhaps the best one is: "Style—it
B C
is the man." No error
D E

36. The laborer today has greater leisure, is less
A
provincial, enjoying the fruits of his labors to a
B C
far greater degree than was hitherto possible.
D
No error
E

37. In a way we may say that we have reached the end of
A B C
the industrial Revolution. No error
D E

38. This is oneof the paintings which is going to be sold
A B C
at auction this afternoon. No error
D E

39. When he begun to sing, all of us became quiet.
A B C D
No error
E

40. Take heart, Harold: we all make mistakes at one time
A B C
or another. No error
D E

41. In his poems he wanted to make many things happen
A B C
simultaneously. No error
D E

42. He works more diligent now that he has become the
A B C D
foreman. No error
E

43. Reading about the massacre, it was difficult to understand
A B
the motive of the killers. No error
C D E

44. We have constantly tried to win his good will
A
by entertaining him and providing him with luxuries,
B
which gives us the inside track. No error
C D E

45. Irregardles of the information you have submitted, I
A B
must deny your request. No error
C D E

46. Occurring in April, we were surprised by the
A B C
unexpected snow storm. No error
D E

47. "I maintain," the speaker claimed, "That we are
A B C
doomed to failure." No error
D E

48. What I find objectionable is him going to the store
A B C
without permission. No error
D E

49. The door being locked and bolted, the police were
A B
forced to break into the apartment through the
C D
bedroom window. No error
E

50. Had you come on time, you'd have heard a most vivid
A B C
account of his adventures in the Sierras. No error
D E

51. Your loud and incessant chatter aggravates your
A B C
father who is trying to concentrate. No error
D E

52. He was awarded the coveted gold medal by the
A B
principle of the Theodore Roosevelt High School.
C D
No error
E

53. It is not I who am to blame for the many
A B C
inconveniences you have suffered. No error
D E

54. Never (A) before in the history of our school, (B) has (C) there been such promising students. (D) No error (E)

55. At what time (A) will the performance (B) end," the theater-goer (C) asked as he entered the theater? (D) No error (E)

56. I have scarcely no (A) qualms (B) about (C) the righteousness of our cause; we are justified in our efforts to depose our oppressor. (D) No error (E)

57. The reason (A) for my prolonged absence (B) from class was (C) because I was ill for three weeks. (D) No error (E)

58. If I would have studied (A) for this examination, I would have won (B) the medal; as it was, (C) I received a very good grade without even (D) trying. No error (E)

59. As (A) I read this book, I get (B) the impression that the author writes like (C) he actually lived the way (D) his characters do. No error (E)

60. If I were (A) you, (B) I would never permit him (C) to take part (D) in such an exhausting and painful activity. No error (E)

Directions: In each of the following sentences, some part or all of the sentence is underlined. Below each sentence you will find five ways of phrasing the underlined part. Select the answer that produces the most effective sentence, one that is clear and exact, without awkwardness or ambiguity, and blacken the corresponding space on your answer sheet. In choosing answers, follow the requirements of standard written English. Choose the answer that best expresses the meaning of the original sentence.

Answer (A) is always the same as the underlined part. Choose answer (A) if you think the original sentence needs no revision.

EXAMPLE:

Laura Ingalls Wilder published her first book and she was sixty-five years old then.

(A) and she was sixty-five years old then
(B) when she was sixty-five years old
(C) at age sixty-five years old
(D) upon reaching sixty-five years
(E) at the time when she was sixty-five

SAMPLE ANSWER

Ⓐ ● Ⓒ Ⓓ Ⓔ

---

61. The child is neither encouraged to be critical or to examine all the evidence for his opinion.
(A) neither encouraged to be critical or to examine
(B) neither encouraged to be critical nor to examine
(C) either encouraged to be critical or to examine
(D) encouraged either to be critical nor to examine
(E) not encouraged either to be critical or to examine

62. The process by which the community influence the actions of its members is known as social control.
(A) influence the actions of its members
(B) influences the actions of its members
(C) had influenced the actions of its members
(D) influences the actions of their members
(E) will influence the actions of its members

63. To be sure, there would be scarcely no time left over for other things if school children would have been expected to have considered all sides of every matter on which they hold opinions.
(A) would have been expected to have considered
(B) should have been expected to have considered
(C) were expected to consider
(D) will be expected to have been considered
(E) were expected to be considered

64. Depending on skillful suggestion, argument is seldom used in advertising.
(A) Depending on skillful suggestion, argument is seldom used in advertising.
(B) Argument is seldom used by advertisers, who depend instead on skillful suggestion.
(C) Skillful suggestion is depended on by advertisers instead of argument.
(D) Suggestion, which is more skillful, is used in place of argument by advertisers.
(E) Instead of suggestion, depending on argument is used by skillful advertisers.

65. When this war is over, no nation will either be isolated in war or peace.
(A) either be isolated in war or peace
(B) be either isolated in war or peace
(C) be isolated in neither war nor peace
(D) be isolated either in war or in peace
(E) be isolated neither in war or peace

66. Each will be within trading distance of all the others and will be able to strike them.
(A) within trading distance of all the others and will be able to strike them
(B) near enough to trade with and strike all the others
(C) trading and striking the others
(D) within trading and striking distance of all the others
(E) able to strike and trade with all the others

67. Examining the principal movements sweeping through the world, it can be seen that they are being accelerated by the war.
(A) Examining the principal movements sweeping through the world, it can be seen
(B) Having examined the principal movements sweeping through the world
(C) Examining the principal movements sweeping through the world can be seen
(D) Examining the principal movements sweeping through the world, we can see
(E) It can be seen examining the principal movements sweeping through the world

68. However many mistakes have been made in our past, the tradition of America, not only the champion of freedom but also fair play, still lives among millions who can see light and hope scarcely anywhere else.
(A) not only the champion of freedom but also fair play
(B) the champion of not only freedom but also of fair play
(C) the champion not only of freedom but also of fair play
(D) not only the champion but also freedom and fair play
(E) not the champion of freedom only, but also fair play

69. In giving expression to the play instincts of the human race, new vigor and effectiveness are afforded by recreation to the body and to the mind.
(A) new vigor and effectiveness are afforded by recreation to the body and to the mind
(B) recreation affords new vigor and effectiveness to the body and to the mind
(C) there are afforded new vigor and effectiveness to the body and to the mind
(D) by recreation the body and mind are afforded new vigor and effectiveness
(E) the body and the mind afford new vigor and effectiveness to themselves by recreation

70. Play being recognized as an important factor in improving mental and physical health and thereby reducing human misery and poverty.
(A) Play being recognized as
(B) By recognizing play as
(C) Their recognizing play as
(D) Recognition of it being
(E) Play is recognized as

71. The fourteen-hour day not only has been reduced to one of ten hours but also, in some lines of work, to one of eight or even six.
(A) The fourteen-hour day not only has been reduced
(B) Not only the fourteen-hour day has been reduced
(C) Not the fourteen-hour day only has been reduced
(D) The fourteen-hour day has not only been reduced
(E) The fourteen-hour day has been reduced not only

72. The trend toward a decrease is further evidenced in the longer week end already given to employees in many business establishments.
(A) already
(B) all ready
(C) allready
(D) ready
(E) all in all

73. Using it wisely, leisure promotes health, efficiency and happiness.
(A) Using it wisely
(B) If used wisely
(C) Having used it wisely
(D) Because of its wise use
(E) Because of usefulness

74. Americans are learning that their concept of a research worker toiling alone in his laboratory and who discovers miraculous cures has been highly idealized and glamorized.
   (A) toiling alone in his laboratory and who discovers miraculous cures
   (B) toiling in his laboratory by himself and discovers miraculous cures
   (C) toiling alone in his laboratory to discover miraculous cures
   (D) who toil alone in the laboratory and discover miraculous cures
   (E) toiling in his laboratory to discover miraculous cures by himself

75. The game was scoreless for 15 innings, it lasted five hours before the winning run was scored.
   (A) innings, it
   (B) innings. it
   (C) innings; it
   (D) innings: it
   (E) innings for it

ANSWER KEY

1. **D**	16. **B**	31. **C**	46. **A**	61. **E**
2. **C**	17. **E**	32. **B**	47. **C**	62. **B**
3. **C**	18. **D**	33. **A**	48. **C**	63. **C**
4. **D**	19. **B**	34. **C**	49. **E**	64. **B**
5. **A**	20. **D**	35. **E**	50. **E**	65. **D**
6. **B**	21. **B**	36. **C**	51. **C**	66. **D**
7. **A**	22. **A**	37. **D**	52. **C**	67. **D**
8. **C**	23. **E**	38. **C**	53. **E**	68. **C**
9. **C**	24. **C**	39. **A**	54. **C**	69. **B**
10. **E**	25. **A**	40. **B**	55. **D**	70. **E**
11. **D**	26. **D**	41. **E**	56. **A**	71. **E**
12. **E**	27. **E**	42. **B**	57. **D**	72. **A**
13. **B**	28. **B**	43. **A**	58. **A**	73. **B**
14. **B**	29. **B**	44. **C**	59. **C**	74. **C**
15. **B**	30. **B**	45. **A**	60. **E**	75. **C**

ANSWER EXPLANATIONS

1. D. Should be *have.* The verb agrees with the subject *(conditions)* in person and number.

2. C. Should be *requires.* Verb should agree with the subject *(each one).*

3. C. Should be *us.* The expression *us girls* is the object of the preposition *by.*

4. D. Should be *anything. Not to say nothing* is a double negative.

5. A. Should be *all ready.* Adjective form is *all ready;* adverbial form is *already.*

6. B. Should be *who.* The pronoun is the predicate complement of *will be* and is in the nominative case.

7. A. Should be *as though. Like* is a preposition and should not be followed by a clause.

8. C. Should be *his* instead of *their.* The antecedent of the pronoun is *everyone* (singular).

9. C. Should be *me.* Subjects of infinitives are in the objective case.

10. E. Sentence is correct.

11. D. Should be *yours* (without the apostrophe).

12. E. Sentence is correct.

13. B. Should be *who.* The pronoun is the subject of *had.*

14. B. Should be *whether. Whether* is used when a choice is indicated.

15. B. Error in diction. Change *in back of* to *behind.*

16. B. Should be *can. Can't scarcely* is a double negative.

17. E. Sentence is correct.

18. D. Should be *he.* The antecedent of the pronoun is *anyone* (singular).

19. B. Should be *your.* The pronoun preceding a participle should be in the possessive case.

20. D. Should be *better.* Do not use the superlative when comparing two things.

21. B. Should be *sweet. Smell* is a verb that quires a predicate adjective.

22. A. *Having lost* is a dangling participle. Change participial phrase to a clause (*Because he lost his money...*).

23. E. Sentence is correct.

24. C. Error in punctuation. *Following:* is correct.

25. A. Should be *effect. Affect* is a verb and should not be used as a noun.

26. D. Should be *me.* Pronoun is the object of the verb *can help.*

27. E. Sentence is correct.

28. B. Should be *lie.* The verb, *to lie,* means to rest, to recline.

29. B. Should be *all together. All together* means in a group; *altogether,* entirely.

30. B. Should be *had risen.* The past participle of the verb *to rise* is *risen.*

31. C. Lack of parallel structure. The sentence is better as: *The more he takes, the more he craves.*

32. B. *Different from* is the preferred form.

33. A. *It's* is the contraction for *it is.* The possessive pronoun is *its.*

34. C. Error in agreement. *Their* should be *his* (singular) to agree with *critic* (singular).

35. E. Sentence is correct.

36. C. Lack of parallel structure. Substitute a verb for the participle to parallel the preceding verbs. Sentence is better as: *The laborer today has greater leisure, is less provincial, and enjoys....*

37. D. Error in capitalization. *Industrial* is correct.

38. C. Error in agreement between pronoun and verb. The antecedent of *which* is paintings (plural). *Which* (plural) should be followed by *are going* (plural).

39. A. Error in tense. *Began* is the past of *begin.*

40. B. Error in punctuation. A semicolon should be used after *Harold.*

41. E. Sentence is correct.

42. B. Improper modifier. The adverb *diligently* is correct.

43. A. Dangling participle. Change *Reading* to *As we read.*

44. C. *Which* should not refer to an entire sentence. It is advisable to write this as two sentences. End the first sentence with *luxuries* and begin the second sentence with *This* (instead of *which*).

45. A. There is no such word as *irregardless.*

46. A. *Occurring* is a dangling participle. Change to: *Because it occurred in April.*

47. C. Improper capitalization. *That* should not be capitalized.

48. C. Error in case. A pronoun preceding a participle should be in the possessive case. Change *him* to *his.*

49. E. Sentence is correct.

50. E. Sentence is correct.

51. C. *Aggravate* does not mean to worry or to irritate.

52. C. Substitute *principal* for *principle.*

53. E. Sentence is correct.

54. C. Agreement between subject and verb. The subject of the sentence is *students* (plural). The verb should be *have been.*

55. D. Improper punctuation of direct discourse. The question mark should come at the end of the quotation. *"At what time will the performance end?" the theater-goer asked.*

56. A. *Scarcely no* is a double negative. Change to *scarcely any.*

57. D. Improper use of *because.* Change to *The reason... was that....*

58. A. Improper sequence of tenses. Change to *had studied.*

59. C. *Like* is not a conjunction. Substitute *as though.*

60. E. Sentence is correct.

61. E. This question involves two aspects of correct English. *Neither* should be followed by *nor; either* by *or*. Choices A and D are, therefore, incorrect. The words *neither... nor* and *either... or* should be placed before the two items being discussed—*to be critical* and *to criticize*. Choice E meets both requirements.

62. B. This question tests agreement. Agreement between subject and verb and pronoun and antecedent are both involved. *Community* (singular) needs a singular verb, *influences*. Also, the pronoun which refers to *community* should be singular (*its*). Choice B is best.

63. C. *Would have been expected* is incorrect as a verb in a clause introduced by the conjunction *if. Had been expected* or *were expected* is preferable. *To have considered* does not follow correct sequence of tense and should be changed to *to consider*. Choice E changes the thought of the sentence and is illogical. Choice C is best.

64. B. As presented, the sentence contains a dangling participle, *depending*. Choice B corrects this error. The other choices change the emphasis presented by the author.

65. D. This question is similar to question 1. Either... or should precede the two choices offered (*in war* and *in peace*). Choice D.

66. D. Choice D. This phrase expresses the thought more compactly than the other four choices.

67. D. Choices A and B are incorrect because of the dangling participle. Choice C is incoherent. Choice D is better than Choice E because it is more compact.

68. C. Choice C. Parallel structure requires the *not only ... but also* construction immediately precede the words they limit.

69. B. Given a choice, most authorities recommend the use of the active voice whenever possible. Thus, *affords* in Choice B is stronger than are afforded in Choices A, C, and D. The meaning of the sentence is changed in Choice E.

70. E. This is an incomplete sentence or fragment. The sentence needs a verb to establish a principal clause. Choice E provides the verb (*is recognized*) and presents the only complete sentence in the group.

71. E. Since the words *but also* precede a phrase (*to one of eight or even six*), the words *not only* should precede a phrase (*to one of ten hours*). This error in parallel structure is corrected in Choice E.

72. A. Choice A. *Already* is an adverb; *all ready*, is an adjectival construction. *Allready* is a misspelling. Choices D and E do not convey the thought of the sentence.

73. B. One way of correcting a dangling participle is to change the participial phrase to a clause. Choices B and D substitute clauses for the phrase. However, Choice D changes the meaning of the sentence. Choice B is correct.

74. C. In the underlined phrase, we find two modifiers of *worker—toiling* and *who discovers*. The first is an adjective and the second a clause. This results in an error in parallel structure. Choice C corrects this by eliminating one of the modifiers of *worker*. Choice E does the same thing but creates a change in the thought of the sentence. Choice D corrects the error in parallel structure but introduces an error in agreement between subject and verb—*who*, (singular) and *toil* (plural).

75. C. The punctuation in Choices A, B, and D creates a run-on sentence. In Choice E the conjunction *for* makes the sentence incoherent.

PART FOUR

TEST YOURSELF

SIX MODEL SCHOLASTIC APTITUDE TESTS

13

- **6 Model Tests**
- **Answer Keys**
- **Self-Evaluations**
- **Answer Explanations**

You are now about to take a major step in preparing yourself to handle an actual SAT. Before you are 6 Model Tests patterned after current published SATs. Up to now, you've concentrated on specific areas and on general testing techniques. You've mastered tactics and worked on drills. Now you have a chance to test yourself—thoroughly, repeatedly—before you walk in that test center door.

These 6 Model Tests resemble the actual SAT in format, in difficulty, and in content. When you take them, take them as if they *were* the actual SAT.

BUILD YOUR STAMINA

Don't start and stop and take time out for a soda or for an important phone call. To do well on the SAT, you have to focus on the test, the test, and nothing but the test for hours at a time. Most high school students have never had to sit through a three-hour examination before they take their first SAT. To survive a three-hour exam takes *stamina*, and, as marathon runners know, the only way to build stamina is to put in the necessary time.

REFINE YOUR SKILLS

You know how to maximize your score by tackling easy questions first and by eliminating wrong answers whenever you can. Put these skills into practice. If you find yourself spending too much time on any one question, skip it and move on. Remember to check frequently to make sure you are answering the questions in the right spots. This is a great chance for you to get these skills down pat.

SPOT YOUR WEAK POINTS

Do you need a bit more drill in a particular area? After you take each test, consult the self-evaluation section for that test to pinpoint any areas that need work. One more look at a couple of testing tactics may be all that you need.

TAKE A DEEP BREATH—AND SMILE!

It's hard to stay calm when those around you are tense, and you're bound to run into some pretty tense people when you take the SAT. (Not everyone works through this book, unfortunately.) So you may experience a slight case of "exam nerves" on the big day. Don't worry about it:

1. Being keyed up for an examination isn't always bad: you may outdo yourself because you are so worked up.

2. Total panic is unlikely to set in: you know too much.

You know you can handle a three-hour test.

You know you can handle the sorts of questions you'll find on the SAT.

You know you can omit several questions and *still* score high. Answer only 50-60% of the questions correctly and you'll still get an average or better than average score (and dozens of solid, well-known colleges are out there right now, looking for serious students with just that kind of score). Answer more than that correctly and you should wind up with a superior score.

MAKE YOUR PRACTICE PAY—APPROXIMATE THE TEST

1. Complete an entire Model Test at one sitting.
2. Use a clock or timer.
3. Allow *precisely* 30 minutes for each section. (If you have time left over, review your answers or recheck the way you've marked your answer sheet.)
4. After each section, give yourself a five-minute break.
5. Allow no talking in the test room.
6. Work rapidly without wasting time.

Remove answer sheet by cutting on dotted line

ANSWER SHEET—TEST 1

SECTION 1

1. Ⓐ Ⓑ Ⓒ Ⓓ Ⓔ	11. Ⓐ Ⓑ Ⓒ Ⓓ Ⓔ	21. Ⓐ Ⓑ Ⓒ Ⓓ Ⓔ	31. Ⓐ Ⓑ Ⓒ Ⓓ Ⓔ	41. Ⓐ Ⓑ Ⓒ Ⓓ Ⓔ
2. Ⓐ Ⓑ Ⓒ Ⓓ Ⓔ	12. Ⓐ Ⓑ Ⓒ Ⓓ Ⓔ	22. Ⓐ Ⓑ Ⓒ Ⓓ Ⓔ	32. Ⓐ Ⓑ Ⓒ Ⓓ Ⓔ	42. Ⓐ Ⓑ Ⓒ Ⓓ Ⓔ
3. Ⓐ Ⓑ Ⓒ Ⓓ Ⓔ	13. Ⓐ Ⓑ Ⓒ Ⓓ Ⓔ	23. Ⓐ Ⓑ Ⓒ Ⓓ Ⓔ	33. Ⓐ Ⓑ Ⓒ Ⓓ Ⓔ	43. Ⓐ Ⓑ Ⓒ Ⓓ Ⓔ
4. Ⓐ Ⓑ Ⓒ Ⓓ Ⓔ	14. Ⓐ Ⓑ Ⓒ Ⓓ Ⓔ	24. Ⓐ Ⓑ Ⓒ Ⓓ Ⓔ	34. Ⓐ Ⓑ Ⓒ Ⓓ Ⓔ	44. Ⓐ Ⓑ Ⓒ Ⓓ Ⓔ
5. Ⓐ Ⓑ Ⓒ Ⓓ Ⓔ	15. Ⓐ Ⓑ Ⓒ Ⓓ Ⓔ	25. Ⓐ Ⓑ Ⓒ Ⓓ Ⓔ	35. Ⓐ Ⓑ Ⓒ Ⓓ Ⓔ	45. Ⓐ Ⓑ Ⓒ Ⓓ Ⓔ
6. Ⓐ Ⓑ Ⓒ Ⓓ Ⓔ	16. Ⓐ Ⓑ Ⓒ Ⓓ Ⓔ	26. Ⓐ Ⓑ Ⓒ Ⓓ Ⓔ	36. Ⓐ Ⓑ Ⓒ Ⓓ Ⓔ	46. Ⓐ Ⓑ Ⓒ Ⓓ Ⓔ
7. Ⓐ Ⓑ Ⓒ Ⓓ Ⓔ	17. Ⓐ Ⓑ Ⓒ Ⓓ Ⓔ	27. Ⓐ Ⓑ Ⓒ Ⓓ Ⓔ	37. Ⓐ Ⓑ Ⓒ Ⓓ Ⓔ	47. Ⓐ Ⓑ Ⓒ Ⓓ Ⓔ
8. Ⓐ Ⓑ Ⓒ Ⓓ Ⓔ	18. Ⓐ Ⓑ Ⓒ Ⓓ Ⓔ	28. Ⓐ Ⓑ Ⓒ Ⓓ Ⓔ	38. Ⓐ Ⓑ Ⓒ Ⓓ Ⓔ	48. Ⓐ Ⓑ Ⓒ Ⓓ Ⓔ
9. Ⓐ Ⓑ Ⓒ Ⓓ Ⓔ	19. Ⓐ Ⓑ Ⓒ Ⓓ Ⓔ	29. Ⓐ Ⓑ Ⓒ Ⓓ Ⓔ	39. Ⓐ Ⓑ Ⓒ Ⓓ Ⓔ	49. Ⓐ Ⓑ Ⓒ Ⓓ Ⓔ
10. Ⓐ Ⓑ Ⓒ Ⓓ Ⓔ	20. Ⓐ Ⓑ Ⓒ Ⓓ Ⓔ	30. Ⓐ Ⓑ Ⓒ Ⓓ Ⓔ	40. Ⓐ Ⓑ Ⓒ Ⓓ Ⓔ	50. Ⓐ Ⓑ Ⓒ Ⓓ Ⓔ

SECTION 2

1. Ⓐ Ⓑ Ⓒ Ⓓ Ⓔ	11. Ⓐ Ⓑ Ⓒ Ⓓ Ⓔ	21. Ⓐ Ⓑ Ⓒ Ⓓ Ⓔ	31. Ⓐ Ⓑ Ⓒ Ⓓ Ⓔ	41. Ⓐ Ⓑ Ⓒ Ⓓ Ⓔ
2. Ⓐ Ⓑ Ⓒ Ⓓ Ⓔ	12. Ⓐ Ⓑ Ⓒ Ⓓ Ⓔ	22. Ⓐ Ⓑ Ⓒ Ⓓ Ⓔ	32. Ⓐ Ⓑ Ⓒ Ⓓ Ⓔ	42. Ⓐ Ⓑ Ⓒ Ⓓ Ⓔ
3. Ⓐ Ⓑ Ⓒ Ⓓ Ⓔ	13. Ⓐ Ⓑ Ⓒ Ⓓ Ⓔ	23. Ⓐ Ⓑ Ⓒ Ⓓ Ⓔ	33. Ⓐ Ⓑ Ⓒ Ⓓ Ⓔ	43. Ⓐ Ⓑ Ⓒ Ⓓ Ⓔ
4. Ⓐ Ⓑ Ⓒ Ⓓ Ⓔ	14. Ⓐ Ⓑ Ⓒ Ⓓ Ⓔ	24. Ⓐ Ⓑ Ⓒ Ⓓ Ⓔ	34. Ⓐ Ⓑ Ⓒ Ⓓ Ⓔ	44. Ⓐ Ⓑ Ⓒ Ⓓ Ⓔ
5. Ⓐ Ⓑ Ⓒ Ⓓ Ⓔ	15. Ⓐ Ⓑ Ⓒ Ⓓ Ⓔ	25. Ⓐ Ⓑ Ⓒ Ⓓ Ⓔ	35. Ⓐ Ⓑ Ⓒ Ⓓ Ⓔ	45. Ⓐ Ⓑ Ⓒ Ⓓ Ⓔ
6. Ⓐ Ⓑ Ⓒ Ⓓ Ⓔ	16. Ⓐ Ⓑ Ⓒ Ⓓ Ⓔ	26. Ⓐ Ⓑ Ⓒ Ⓓ Ⓔ	36. Ⓐ Ⓑ Ⓒ Ⓓ Ⓔ	46. Ⓐ Ⓑ Ⓒ Ⓓ Ⓔ
7. Ⓐ Ⓑ Ⓒ Ⓓ Ⓔ	17. Ⓐ Ⓑ Ⓒ Ⓓ Ⓔ	27. Ⓐ Ⓑ Ⓒ Ⓓ Ⓔ	37. Ⓐ Ⓑ Ⓒ Ⓓ Ⓔ	47. Ⓐ Ⓑ Ⓒ Ⓓ Ⓔ
8. Ⓐ Ⓑ Ⓒ Ⓓ Ⓔ	18. Ⓐ Ⓑ Ⓒ Ⓓ Ⓔ	28. Ⓐ Ⓑ Ⓒ Ⓓ Ⓔ	38. Ⓐ Ⓑ Ⓒ Ⓓ Ⓔ	48. Ⓐ Ⓑ Ⓒ Ⓓ Ⓔ
9. Ⓐ Ⓑ Ⓒ Ⓓ Ⓔ	19. Ⓐ Ⓑ Ⓒ Ⓓ Ⓔ	29. Ⓐ Ⓑ Ⓒ Ⓓ Ⓔ	39. Ⓐ Ⓑ Ⓒ Ⓓ Ⓔ	49. Ⓐ Ⓑ Ⓒ Ⓓ Ⓔ
10. Ⓐ Ⓑ Ⓒ Ⓓ Ⓔ	20. Ⓐ Ⓑ Ⓒ Ⓓ Ⓔ	30. Ⓐ Ⓑ Ⓒ Ⓓ Ⓔ	40. Ⓐ Ⓑ Ⓒ Ⓓ Ⓔ	50. Ⓐ Ⓑ Ⓒ Ⓓ Ⓔ

SECTION 3

1. Ⓐ Ⓑ Ⓒ Ⓓ Ⓔ	11. Ⓐ Ⓑ Ⓒ Ⓓ Ⓔ	21. Ⓐ Ⓑ Ⓒ Ⓓ Ⓔ	31. Ⓐ Ⓑ Ⓒ Ⓓ Ⓔ	41. Ⓐ Ⓑ Ⓒ Ⓓ Ⓔ
2. Ⓐ Ⓑ Ⓒ Ⓓ Ⓔ	12. Ⓐ Ⓑ Ⓒ Ⓓ Ⓔ	22. Ⓐ Ⓑ Ⓒ Ⓓ Ⓔ	32. Ⓐ Ⓑ Ⓒ Ⓓ Ⓔ	42. Ⓐ Ⓑ Ⓒ Ⓓ Ⓔ
3. Ⓐ Ⓑ Ⓒ Ⓓ Ⓔ	13. Ⓐ Ⓑ Ⓒ Ⓓ Ⓔ	23. Ⓐ Ⓑ Ⓒ Ⓓ Ⓔ	33. Ⓐ Ⓑ Ⓒ Ⓓ Ⓔ	43. Ⓐ Ⓑ Ⓒ Ⓓ Ⓔ
4. Ⓐ Ⓑ Ⓒ Ⓓ Ⓔ	14. Ⓐ Ⓑ Ⓒ Ⓓ Ⓔ	24. Ⓐ Ⓑ Ⓒ Ⓓ Ⓔ	34. Ⓐ Ⓑ Ⓒ Ⓓ Ⓔ	44. Ⓐ Ⓑ Ⓒ Ⓓ Ⓔ
5. Ⓐ Ⓑ Ⓒ Ⓓ Ⓔ	15. Ⓐ Ⓑ Ⓒ Ⓓ Ⓔ	25. Ⓐ Ⓑ Ⓒ Ⓓ Ⓔ	35. Ⓐ Ⓑ Ⓒ Ⓓ Ⓔ	45. Ⓐ Ⓑ Ⓒ Ⓓ Ⓔ
6. Ⓐ Ⓑ Ⓒ Ⓓ Ⓔ	16. Ⓐ Ⓑ Ⓒ Ⓓ Ⓔ	26. Ⓐ Ⓑ Ⓒ Ⓓ Ⓔ	36. Ⓐ Ⓑ Ⓒ Ⓓ Ⓔ	46. Ⓐ Ⓑ Ⓒ Ⓓ Ⓔ
7. Ⓐ Ⓑ Ⓒ Ⓓ Ⓔ	17. Ⓐ Ⓑ Ⓒ Ⓓ Ⓔ	27. Ⓐ Ⓑ Ⓒ Ⓓ Ⓔ	37. Ⓐ Ⓑ Ⓒ Ⓓ Ⓔ	47. Ⓐ Ⓑ Ⓒ Ⓓ Ⓔ
8. Ⓐ Ⓑ Ⓒ Ⓓ Ⓔ	18. Ⓐ Ⓑ Ⓒ Ⓓ Ⓔ	28. Ⓐ Ⓑ Ⓒ Ⓓ Ⓔ	38. Ⓐ Ⓑ Ⓒ Ⓓ Ⓔ	48. Ⓐ Ⓑ Ⓒ Ⓓ Ⓔ
9. Ⓐ Ⓑ Ⓒ Ⓓ Ⓔ	19. Ⓐ Ⓑ Ⓒ Ⓓ Ⓔ	29. Ⓐ Ⓑ Ⓒ Ⓓ Ⓔ	39. Ⓐ Ⓑ Ⓒ Ⓓ Ⓔ	49. Ⓐ Ⓑ Ⓒ Ⓓ Ⓔ
10. Ⓐ Ⓑ Ⓒ Ⓓ Ⓔ	20. Ⓐ Ⓑ Ⓒ Ⓓ Ⓔ	30. Ⓐ Ⓑ Ⓒ Ⓓ Ⓔ	40. Ⓐ Ⓑ Ⓒ Ⓓ Ⓔ	50. Ⓐ Ⓑ Ⓒ Ⓓ Ⓔ

SECTION 4

1. Ⓐ Ⓑ Ⓒ Ⓓ Ⓔ	11. Ⓐ Ⓑ Ⓒ Ⓓ Ⓔ	21. Ⓐ Ⓑ Ⓒ Ⓓ Ⓔ	31. Ⓐ Ⓑ Ⓒ Ⓓ Ⓔ	41. Ⓐ Ⓑ Ⓒ Ⓓ Ⓔ
2. Ⓐ Ⓑ Ⓒ Ⓓ Ⓔ	12. Ⓐ Ⓑ Ⓒ Ⓓ Ⓔ	22. Ⓐ Ⓑ Ⓒ Ⓓ Ⓔ	32. Ⓐ Ⓑ Ⓒ Ⓓ Ⓔ	42. Ⓐ Ⓑ Ⓒ Ⓓ Ⓔ
3. Ⓐ Ⓑ Ⓒ Ⓓ Ⓔ	13. Ⓐ Ⓑ Ⓒ Ⓓ Ⓔ	23. Ⓐ Ⓑ Ⓒ Ⓓ Ⓔ	33. Ⓐ Ⓑ Ⓒ Ⓓ Ⓔ	43. Ⓐ Ⓑ Ⓒ Ⓓ Ⓔ
4. Ⓐ Ⓑ Ⓒ Ⓓ Ⓔ	14. Ⓐ Ⓑ Ⓒ Ⓓ Ⓔ	24. Ⓐ Ⓑ Ⓒ Ⓓ Ⓔ	34. Ⓐ Ⓑ Ⓒ Ⓓ Ⓔ	44. Ⓐ Ⓑ Ⓒ Ⓓ Ⓔ
5. Ⓐ Ⓑ Ⓒ Ⓓ Ⓔ	15. Ⓐ Ⓑ Ⓒ Ⓓ Ⓔ	25. Ⓐ Ⓑ Ⓒ Ⓓ Ⓔ	35. Ⓐ Ⓑ Ⓒ Ⓓ Ⓔ	45. Ⓐ Ⓑ Ⓒ Ⓓ Ⓔ
6. Ⓐ Ⓑ Ⓒ Ⓓ Ⓔ	16. Ⓐ Ⓑ Ⓒ Ⓓ Ⓔ	26. Ⓐ Ⓑ Ⓒ Ⓓ Ⓔ	36. Ⓐ Ⓑ Ⓒ Ⓓ Ⓔ	46. Ⓐ Ⓑ Ⓒ Ⓓ Ⓔ
7. Ⓐ Ⓑ Ⓒ Ⓓ Ⓔ	17. Ⓐ Ⓑ Ⓒ Ⓓ Ⓔ	27. Ⓐ Ⓑ Ⓒ Ⓓ Ⓔ	37. Ⓐ Ⓑ Ⓒ Ⓓ Ⓔ	47. Ⓐ Ⓑ Ⓒ Ⓓ Ⓔ
8. Ⓐ Ⓑ Ⓒ Ⓓ Ⓔ	18. Ⓐ Ⓑ Ⓒ Ⓓ Ⓔ	28. Ⓐ Ⓑ Ⓒ Ⓓ Ⓔ	38. Ⓐ Ⓑ Ⓒ Ⓓ Ⓔ	48. Ⓐ Ⓑ Ⓒ Ⓓ Ⓔ
9. Ⓐ Ⓑ Ⓒ Ⓓ Ⓔ	19. Ⓐ Ⓑ Ⓒ Ⓓ Ⓔ	29. Ⓐ Ⓑ Ⓒ Ⓓ Ⓔ	39. Ⓐ Ⓑ Ⓒ Ⓓ Ⓔ	49. Ⓐ Ⓑ Ⓒ Ⓓ Ⓔ
10. Ⓐ Ⓑ Ⓒ Ⓓ Ⓔ	20. Ⓐ Ⓑ Ⓒ Ⓓ Ⓔ	30. Ⓐ Ⓑ Ⓒ Ⓓ Ⓔ	40. Ⓐ Ⓑ Ⓒ Ⓓ Ⓔ	50. Ⓐ Ⓑ Ⓒ Ⓓ Ⓔ

SECTION 5

1. Ⓐ Ⓑ Ⓒ Ⓓ Ⓔ	11. Ⓐ Ⓑ Ⓒ Ⓓ Ⓔ	21. Ⓐ Ⓑ Ⓒ Ⓓ Ⓔ	31. Ⓐ Ⓑ Ⓒ Ⓓ Ⓔ	41. Ⓐ Ⓑ Ⓒ Ⓓ Ⓔ
2. Ⓐ Ⓑ Ⓒ Ⓓ Ⓔ	12. Ⓐ Ⓑ Ⓒ Ⓓ Ⓔ	22. Ⓐ Ⓑ Ⓒ Ⓓ Ⓔ	32. Ⓐ Ⓑ Ⓒ Ⓓ Ⓔ	42. Ⓐ Ⓑ Ⓒ Ⓓ Ⓔ
3. Ⓐ Ⓑ Ⓒ Ⓓ Ⓔ	13. Ⓐ Ⓑ Ⓒ Ⓓ Ⓔ	23. Ⓐ Ⓑ Ⓒ Ⓓ Ⓔ	33. Ⓐ Ⓑ Ⓒ Ⓓ Ⓔ	43. Ⓐ Ⓑ Ⓒ Ⓓ Ⓔ
4. Ⓐ Ⓑ Ⓒ Ⓓ Ⓔ	14. Ⓐ Ⓑ Ⓒ Ⓓ Ⓔ	24. Ⓐ Ⓑ Ⓒ Ⓓ Ⓔ	34. Ⓐ Ⓑ Ⓒ Ⓓ Ⓔ	44. Ⓐ Ⓑ Ⓒ Ⓓ Ⓔ
5. Ⓐ Ⓑ Ⓒ Ⓓ Ⓔ	15. Ⓐ Ⓑ Ⓒ Ⓓ Ⓔ	25. Ⓐ Ⓑ Ⓒ Ⓓ Ⓔ	35. Ⓐ Ⓑ Ⓒ Ⓓ Ⓔ	45. Ⓐ Ⓑ Ⓒ Ⓓ Ⓔ
6. Ⓐ Ⓑ Ⓒ Ⓓ Ⓔ	16. Ⓐ Ⓑ Ⓒ Ⓓ Ⓔ	26. Ⓐ Ⓑ Ⓒ Ⓓ Ⓔ	36. Ⓐ Ⓑ Ⓒ Ⓓ Ⓔ	46. Ⓐ Ⓑ Ⓒ Ⓓ Ⓔ
7. Ⓐ Ⓑ Ⓒ Ⓓ Ⓔ	17. Ⓐ Ⓑ Ⓒ Ⓓ Ⓔ	27. Ⓐ Ⓑ Ⓒ Ⓓ Ⓔ	37. Ⓐ Ⓑ Ⓒ Ⓓ Ⓔ	47. Ⓐ Ⓑ Ⓒ Ⓓ Ⓔ
8. Ⓐ Ⓑ Ⓒ Ⓓ Ⓔ	18. Ⓐ Ⓑ Ⓒ Ⓓ Ⓔ	28. Ⓐ Ⓑ Ⓒ Ⓓ Ⓔ	38. Ⓐ Ⓑ Ⓒ Ⓓ Ⓔ	48. Ⓐ Ⓑ Ⓒ Ⓓ Ⓔ
9. Ⓐ Ⓑ Ⓒ Ⓓ Ⓔ	19. Ⓐ Ⓑ Ⓒ Ⓓ Ⓔ	29. Ⓐ Ⓑ Ⓒ Ⓓ Ⓔ	39. Ⓐ Ⓑ Ⓒ Ⓓ Ⓔ	49. Ⓐ Ⓑ Ⓒ Ⓓ Ⓔ
10. Ⓐ Ⓑ Ⓒ Ⓓ Ⓔ	20. Ⓐ Ⓑ Ⓒ Ⓓ Ⓔ	30. Ⓐ Ⓑ Ⓒ Ⓓ Ⓔ	40. Ⓐ Ⓑ Ⓒ Ⓓ Ⓔ	50. Ⓐ Ⓑ Ⓒ Ⓓ Ⓔ

SECTION 6

1. Ⓐ Ⓑ Ⓒ Ⓓ Ⓔ	11. Ⓐ Ⓑ Ⓒ Ⓓ Ⓔ	21. Ⓐ Ⓑ Ⓒ Ⓓ Ⓔ	31. Ⓐ Ⓑ Ⓒ Ⓓ Ⓔ	41. Ⓐ Ⓑ Ⓒ Ⓓ Ⓔ
2. Ⓐ Ⓑ Ⓒ Ⓓ Ⓔ	12. Ⓐ Ⓑ Ⓒ Ⓓ Ⓔ	22. Ⓐ Ⓑ Ⓒ Ⓓ Ⓔ	32. Ⓐ Ⓑ Ⓒ Ⓓ Ⓔ	42. Ⓐ Ⓑ Ⓒ Ⓓ Ⓔ
3. Ⓐ Ⓑ Ⓒ Ⓓ Ⓔ	13. Ⓐ Ⓑ Ⓒ Ⓓ Ⓔ	23. Ⓐ Ⓑ Ⓒ Ⓓ Ⓔ	33. Ⓐ Ⓑ Ⓒ Ⓓ Ⓔ	43. Ⓐ Ⓑ Ⓒ Ⓓ Ⓔ
4. Ⓐ Ⓑ Ⓒ Ⓓ Ⓔ	14. Ⓐ Ⓑ Ⓒ Ⓓ Ⓔ	24. Ⓐ Ⓑ Ⓒ Ⓓ Ⓔ	34. Ⓐ Ⓑ Ⓒ Ⓓ Ⓔ	44. Ⓐ Ⓑ Ⓒ Ⓓ Ⓔ
5. Ⓐ Ⓑ Ⓒ Ⓓ Ⓔ	15. Ⓐ Ⓑ Ⓒ Ⓓ Ⓔ	25. Ⓐ Ⓑ Ⓒ Ⓓ Ⓔ	35. Ⓐ Ⓑ Ⓒ Ⓓ Ⓔ	45. Ⓐ Ⓑ Ⓒ Ⓓ Ⓔ
6. Ⓐ Ⓑ Ⓒ Ⓓ Ⓔ	16. Ⓐ Ⓑ Ⓒ Ⓓ Ⓔ	26. Ⓐ Ⓑ Ⓒ Ⓓ Ⓔ	36. Ⓐ Ⓑ Ⓒ Ⓓ Ⓔ	46. Ⓐ Ⓑ Ⓒ Ⓓ Ⓔ
7. Ⓐ Ⓑ Ⓒ Ⓓ Ⓔ	17. Ⓐ Ⓑ Ⓒ Ⓓ Ⓔ	27. Ⓐ Ⓑ Ⓒ Ⓓ Ⓔ	37. Ⓐ Ⓑ Ⓒ Ⓓ Ⓔ	47. Ⓐ Ⓑ Ⓒ Ⓓ Ⓔ
8. Ⓐ Ⓑ Ⓒ Ⓓ Ⓔ	18. Ⓐ Ⓑ Ⓒ Ⓓ Ⓔ	28. Ⓐ Ⓑ Ⓒ Ⓓ Ⓔ	38. Ⓐ Ⓑ Ⓒ Ⓓ Ⓔ	48. Ⓐ Ⓑ Ⓒ Ⓓ Ⓔ
9. Ⓐ Ⓑ Ⓒ Ⓓ Ⓔ	19. Ⓐ Ⓑ Ⓒ Ⓓ Ⓔ	29. Ⓐ Ⓑ Ⓒ Ⓓ Ⓔ	39. Ⓐ Ⓑ Ⓒ Ⓓ Ⓔ	49. Ⓐ Ⓑ Ⓒ Ⓓ Ⓔ
10. Ⓐ Ⓑ Ⓒ Ⓓ Ⓔ	20. Ⓐ Ⓑ Ⓒ Ⓓ Ⓔ	30. Ⓐ Ⓑ Ⓒ Ⓓ Ⓔ	40. Ⓐ Ⓑ Ⓒ Ⓓ Ⓔ	50. Ⓐ Ⓑ Ⓒ Ⓓ Ⓔ

MODEL SAT TEST 1

SECTION 1 VERBAL ABILITY

45 QUESTIONS - 30 MINUTES

For each question in this section, choose the best answer and blacken the corresponding space on the answer sheet.

Each question below consists of a word in capital letters, followed by five lettered words or phrases. Choose the word or phrase that is most nearly opposite in meaning to the word in capital letters. Since some of the questions require you to distinguish fine shades of meaning, consider all the choices before deciding which is best.

Example:

GOOD: (A) sour (B) bad (C) red (D) hot (E) ugly

Ⓐ ● Ⓒ Ⓓ Ⓔ

1. FERTILE:
(A) useful
(B) hospitalized
(C) gloomy
(D) barren
(E) isolated

2. STOLID:
(A) burglarized
(B) unstable
(C) petulant
(D) giddy
(E) insufficient

3. ACTOR:
(A) spectator
(B) singer
(C) lecturer
(D) benefactor
(E) editor

4. ORNATE:
(A) wanton
(B) severe
(C) bizarre
(D) fruitful
(E) superfluous

5. SYCOPHANT:
(A) mastadon
(B) coward
(C) preacher
(D) healer
(E) leader

6. CONSUMMATE:
(A) convict
(B) undertake
(C) starve
(D) reveal
(E) fashion

7. CRAVEN:
(A) unsafe
(B) white
(C) spoken
(D) noble
(E) indifferent

8. NEOPHYTE:
(A) dancer
(B) expert
(C) menace
(D) singer
(E) fencer

9. ERRATIC:
(A) dominant
(B) predictable
(C) peaceful
(D) perishable
(E) holy

10. VITUPERATIVE:
(A) anxious
(B) laudatory
(C) irritated
(D) steady
(E) hortative

11. EXPATIATE:
(A) alienate
(B) approve
(C) demonstrate
(D) summarize
(E) return

12. AVERSE:
(A) eager
(B) offended
(C) frantic
(D) finished
(E) greedy

13. IMBECILITY:
(A) crime
(B) intelligence
(C) assurance
(D) belligerence
(E) culpability

14. OBLITERATE:
(A) dazzle
(B) establish
(C) prefer
(D) conclude
(E) contact

15. SCHISM:
(A) union
(B) undertaking
(C) failure
(D) plot
(E) doctrine

Each sentence below has one or two blanks, each blank indicating that something has been omitted. Beneath the sentence are five lettered words or sets of words. Choose the word or set of words that best fits the meaning of the sentence as a whole.

Example:

Although its publicity has been ----, the film itself is intelligent, well-acted, handsomely produced, and altogether ----.

(A) tasteless..respectable (B) extensive..moderate (C) sophisticated..amateur (D) risqué..crude (E) perfect..spectacular

● Ⓑ Ⓒ Ⓓ Ⓔ

16. The present expansion of the military strength of our neighboring country must fill us with ______.
(A) awe
(B) amazement
(C) admiration
(D) apprehension
(E) anger

17. The candidate's speech was filled with empty promises, ______, and cliches.
(A) candor
(B) platitudes
(C) anger
(D) ingenuity
(E) threats

18. By dint of much practice, he became ______ and was able to sign his name with either hand.
(A) practical
(B) tricky
(C) ambiguous
(D) ambidextrous
(E) ambivalent

19. This work, published ______, revived our interest in the author who had just died.
(A) posthumously
(B) anonymously
(C) privately
(D) prominently
(E) synthetically

20. The hypocrite ______ feelings which he does not possess but which he feels he should display.
(A) depicts
(B) decries
(C) betrays
(D) simulates
(E) intensifies

Each passage below is followed by questions based on its content. Answer all questions following a passage on the basis of what is stated or implied in that passage.

If you watch a lamp which is turned very rapidly on and off, and you keep your eyes open, "persistence of vision" will bridge the gaps of darkness between the flashes of light, and the lamp will seem to be continuously lit. This "optical afterglow" explains the magic produced by the stroboscope, a new instrument which seems to freeze the swiftest motions while they are still going on, and to stop time itself dead in its tracks. The "magic" is all in the eye of the beholder.

21. The "magic" of the stroboscope is due to
(A) continuous lighting
(B) intense cold
(C) slow motion
(D) behavior of the human eye
(E) a lapse of time

22. "Persistence of vision" is explained by
(A) darkness
(B) winking
(C) rapid flashes
(D) gaps
(E) afterimpressions

For centuries we have enjoyed certain blessings: a stable law, before which the poor man and the rich man were equal; freedom within that law to believe what we pleased; a system of government which gave the ultimate power to the ordinary man. We have lived by toleration, rational compromise and freely expressed opinion, and we have lived very well. But we have come to take these things for granted; like the air we breathe. They have lost all glamour for us since they have become too familiar. Indeed it is a mark of the intellectual to be rather critical and contemptuous of them. Young men have acquired a cheap reputation by sneering at the liberal spirit in politics, and questioning the value of free discussion, toleration, and compromise.

23. The title that best expresses the ideas of this paragraph is:
(A) The value of free discussion
(B) Respect for law
(C) The weakness of the democratic way of life
(D) Characteristics of democracy
(E) Unappreciated advantages of democratic life

24. The writer resents the growing criticism of freedom—an attitude which results from
(A) questioning the rightness of democracy
(B) being too accustomed to freedom
(C) too much freedom of speech
(D) living in poverty too long
(E) the conservatism of young intellectuals

25. The writer's attitude toward young intellectuals is
(A) indifferent
(B) critical
(C) very contemptuous
(D) generous
(E) angry

A moment's reflection will make it clear that one can not live a full, free, influential life in America without argument. No doubt people often argue on insufficient evidence and for insufficient reasons; no doubt they often argue on points about which they should rather be thinking and studying; no doubt they sometimes fancy they are arguing when they are merely wrangling and disputing. But this is only proof that argument is employed badly, that it is misused rather than used skillfully. Argument, at the right moment and for the right purpose and in the right way, is undoubtedly one of the most useful instruments in American life; it is an indispensable means of expressing oneself and impressing others.

26. The title that best expresses the ideas of this paragraph is:
(A) The usefulness of argument
(B) Principles of argument
(C) How to win arguments
(D) Misuses of argument
(E) Need for evidence in argument

27. Argument is an important factor in American life because it gives people a chance to
(A) talk about things of which they know little
(B) influence the ideas of others
(C) develop sufficient evidence
(D) have friendly conversations
(E) use argument at the right time and in the right way

28. Argument is being used unwisely when it results in
(A) understanding
(B) compromise
(C) deliberation
(D) bickering
(E) differences of opinion

In no field of history has the search for logical explanation been so diligent as in the study of the decline and fall of the Roman Empire. This is the only known instance of the decay of a more or less universal civilization, which might serve as something of an object lesson to our own; accordingly it has been very thoroughly studied, and the attempt to explain it has engaged some of the ablest historians who ever wrote. Almost any orator or politician can tell you why Rome fell, but the men who know most about it are not so ready with glib explanations. Even they must admit at critical moments the decisive interposition of Chance.

29. The fall of the Roman Empire has been thoroughly studied because
(A) it may serve as a lesson to us
(B) it affected the lives of so many people
(C) it was so unusual
(D) Rome was the greatest empire the world has known
(E) detailed records were readily available

30. People who know most about the fall of the Roman Empire
(A) think politicians were its chief cause
(B) are uncertain as to its cause
(C) prepare object lessons from it
(D) give ready explanations of it
(E) have been able to learn little about it

Select the word or set of words that best completes each of the following sentences.

31. These are parlous times and we cannot afford to be too ______ about the future.
(A) pessimistic
(B) sanguine
(C) sanguinary
(D) salubrious
(E) acclimated

32. A ______ person is not ______.
(A) wanton—restrained
(B) dissolute—dissipated
(C) continent—dissolute
(D) prodigal—extravagant
(E) talkative—garrulous

33. He is so ______ that he cannot be disturbed by ______ matters.
(A) involved—simple
(B) excited—unrelated
(C) spiritual—mundane
(D) simple—complicated
(E) happy—current

34. ______ all his attempts to master the assignment, he failed.
(A) After
(B) Because of
(C) Despite
(D) Neglecting
(E) Describing

35. He was able to mislead the gullible with his ______ arguments.
(A) cogent
(B) specious
(C) incontrovertible
(D) simple
(E) contentious

Each question below consists of a related pair of words or phrases, followed by five lettered pairs of words or phrases. Select the lettered pair that best expresses a relationship similar to that expressed in the original pair.

Example:

YAWN : BOREDOM :: (A) dream : sleep (B) anger : madness (C) smile : amusement (D) face : expression (E) impatience : rebellion

Ⓐ Ⓑ ● Ⓓ Ⓔ

36. WORDS : WRITER ::
(A) honor : thieves
(B) mortar : bricklayer
(C) child : teacher
(D) batter : baker
(E) laws : policeman

37. ARIA : DIVA ::
(A) pool : swimmer
(B) soliloquy : actor
(C) opera : operetta
(D) solo : chorus
(E) one : two

38. BUOY : CHANNEL ::
(A) laws : society
(B) laws : transgressor
(C) laws : courts
(D) laws : lawyers
(E) laws : conduct

39. BIOGRAPHY : AUTOBIOGRAPHY
(A) mobile : automobile
(B) testimony : confession
(C) dead : living
(D) author : performer
(E) memoirs : history

40. BASEMENT : ATTIC ::
(A) pinnacle : apex
(B) nadir : zenith
(C) nadir : foundation
(D) zenith : apex
(E) zenith : root

41. ANGER : CHOLERIC ::
(A) wrath : ironic
(B) love : bucolic
(C) island : volcanic
(D) greed : avaricious
(E) pride : malicious

42. SHRUG : INDIFFERENCE ::
(A) grin : deference
(B) wave : fatigue
(C) nod : assent
(D) blink : scorn
(E) scowl : desire

43. SUCCESS : COMPLACENT ::
(A) stress : efficient
(B) courage : timorous
(C) disdain : pertinent
(D) pity : humorous
(E) rejection : despondent

44. INTEREST : USURY ::
(A) frugality : parsimony
(B) pleasure : use
(C) think : enjoy
(D) anger : wrath
(E) situation : position

45. GRAIN : SILO ::
(A) English : American
(B) seed : plant
(C) water : bucket
(D) druggist : doctor
(E) furlong : mile

S T O P

IF YOU FINISH BEFORE TIME IS CALLED, YOU MAY CHECK YOUR WORK ON THIS SECTION ONLY. DO NOT WORK ON ANY OTHER SECTION IN THE TEST.

SECTION 2 MATH ABILITY

25 QUESTIONS - 30 MINUTES

In this section solve each problem, using any available space on the page for scratchwork. Then decide which is the best of the choices given and blacken the corresponding space on the answer sheet.

The following information is for your reference in solving some of the problems.

Circle of radius r: Area $= \pi r^2$; Circumference $= 2\pi r$
The number of degrees of arc in a circle is 360.
The measure in degrees of a straight angle is 180.

Definitions of symbols:

$=$ is equal to
$\neq$ is unequal to
$<$ is less than
$>$ is greater than
$\leqq$ is less than or equal to
$\geqq$ is greater than or equal to
$\parallel$ is parallel to
$\perp$ is perpendicular to

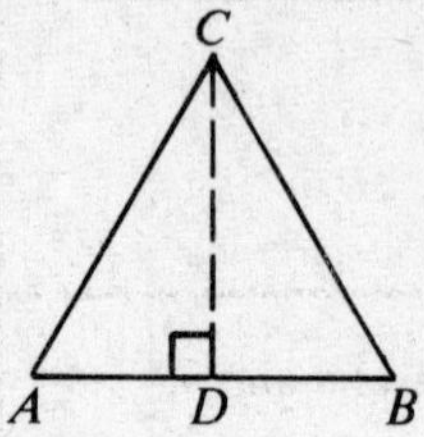

Triangle: The sum of the measures in degrees of the angles of a triangle is 180.
If $\angle CDA$ is a right angle, then

(1) area of $\triangle ABC = \frac{AB \times CD}{2}$

(2) $AC^2 = AD^2 + DC^2$

Note: Figures that accompany problems in this test are intended to provide information useful in solving the problems. They are drawn as accurately as possible EXCEPT when it is stated in a specific problem that its figure is not drawn to scale. All figures lie in a plane unless otherwise indicated. All numbers used are real numbers.

1. If $\frac{5y + 4x}{3} = 7$, what is the value of x expressed in terms of y?

(A) $\frac{7 - 5y}{12}$
(B) $\frac{21 - 5y}{4}$
(C) $\frac{21 - 15y}{4}$
(D) $\frac{5y - 21}{4}$
(E) $\frac{21}{5y}$

2. What is the value of the expression $\frac{a + b}{a - b}$ when a equals $\frac{2}{3}$ and b equals $\frac{5}{7}$?

(A) -29
(B) $-\frac{14}{15}$
(C) $-2\frac{1}{3}$
(D) -1
(E) $+29$

3. In a library system having six branches there are 60 workers employed. If no library has less than seven workers and no more than 18, what is the minimum number of workers in any two of these branches?

(A) 10
(B) 14
(C) 20
(D) 25
(E) 36

4. If $F = \frac{Gm_1m_2}{r^2}$ what is the value of m_1 expressed in terms of F, G, m_2, and r?

(A) $\frac{Gm_2}{r^2}$
(B) $\frac{FG}{m_2r^2}$
(C) $\frac{FGm_2}{r^2}$
(D) FGm_2r^2
(E) $\frac{Fr^2}{Gm_2}$

5. If $\frac{x}{16} = 0.375$, what is the numerical value of x?

(A) 2
(B) 3
(C) 4
(D) 5
(E) 6

6. If two halves of $2\frac{1}{2}$ are added to $2\frac{1}{2}$, the result is

(A) $2\frac{1}{2}$
(B) 3
(C) 5
(D) $5\frac{1}{2}$
(E) 6

7. To represent a family budget on a circle graph, how many degrees of the circle should be used to represent an item which is 20% of the total budget?
(A) 20
(B) 36
(C) 60
(D) 72
(E) 90

8. C is the midpoint of line segment AE. B and D are on line AE so that $AB = BC$ and $CD = DE$. What percent of AC is AD?
(A) 33
(B) 50
(C) 66
(D) 133
(E) 150

9. If $\frac{a}{b} = c$ and $\frac{x}{a} = c$, find a in terms of x and b.
(A) $x + b$
(B) $\pm xb$
(C) $\pm\sqrt{xb}$
(D) $\pm\sqrt{x + b}$
(E) $(x + b)^2$

10. If 0.6 is the average of 0.2, 0.8, 1.0, and x, what is the numerical value of x?
(A) 0.2
(B) 0.4
(C) 0.67
(D) 1.3
(E) 2.4

11. If $\frac{2x}{5} = 9$, what is the value of $\frac{2x}{9}$?
(A) $\frac{4}{5}$
(B) $2\frac{1}{2}$
(C) 5
(D) $16\frac{1}{5}$
(E) $22\frac{1}{2}$

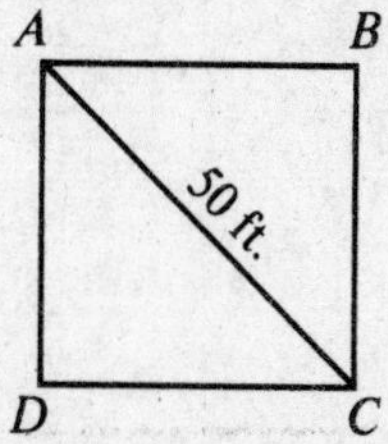

12. In the figure above, the distance from A to C in the square field $ABCD$ is 50 feet. What is the area of field $ABCD$ in square feet?
(A) $25\sqrt{2}$
(B) 625
(C) 1250
(D) 2500
(E) 5000

13. If a man was r years old s years ago, how many years old will he be t years from now?
(A) $rs + t$
(B) $r - s + t$
(C) $r + s + t$
(D) rst
(E) $s - r + t$

14. For what value of y does $\frac{y}{16\frac{1}{3}}$ equal $\frac{3}{y}$?
(A) $\frac{3}{7}$
(B) $\frac{7}{3}$
(C) $4\sqrt{3}$
(D) 7
(E) none of these

15. A man binds 112 books in one day, and his assistant works one quarter as fast. How many days would it take them to bind 560 books, if each works alone on alternate days?
(A) $\frac{1}{8}$
(B) $\frac{1}{2}$
(C) 2
(D) 4
(E) 8

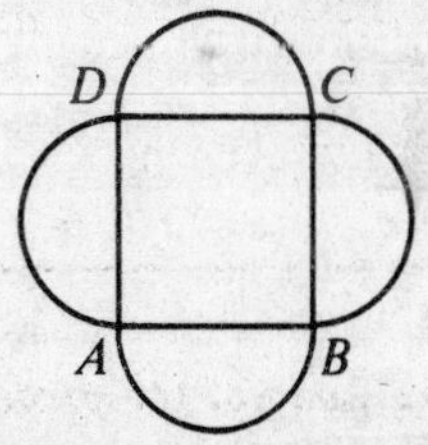

16. In the figure above, $ABCD$ is a square and semi-circles are constructed on each side of the square. If AB is 2, what is the area of the entire figure?
(A) $2 + 4\pi$
(B) $2 - 4\pi$
(C) $4 + 8\pi$
(D) $4 - 2\pi$
(E) $4 + 2\pi$

17. There are 45 pupils in a certain physics class. If two thirds of the pupils are boys, and one half of the boys are blue-eyed, how many blue-eyed boys are in the class?
(A) 15
(B) 30
(C) 34
(D) 38
(E) 43

R	1	2	3	4	5	6
S	2	5	8	11	14	17

18. Which of the following equations gives the relationship between R and S in the table above?
(A) $S = 2R$
(B) $S = R^2 + 1$
(C) $S = R^2 - 1$
(D) $S = 3R - 1$
(E) $S = 2R + 5$

19. An automobile passes City X at 9:55 A.M. and City Y at 10:15 A.M. City X is 30 miles from City Y. What is the average rate of the automobile in miles per hour?
(A) 10
(B) 30
(C) 90
(D) 120
(E) 360

20. How many three-pound weights are needed to balance twelve four-pound weights?
(A) 4
(B) 9
(C) 13
(D) 16
(E) 48

21. To which of the following is $\frac{a}{b} - \frac{a}{c}$ equal?
(A) $\frac{a}{b - c}$
(B) $\frac{1}{b - c}$
(C) $\frac{1}{bc}$
(D) $\frac{ab - ac}{bc}$
(E) $\frac{ac - ab}{bc}$

22. If $r = \frac{s}{3}$ and $4r = 5t$, what is s in terms of t?
(A) $\frac{4t}{15}$
(B) $\frac{15t}{4}$
(C) $4t$
(D) $5t$
(E) $60t$

23. If $\frac{n}{7} + \frac{n}{5} = \frac{12}{35}$, what is the numerical value of n?
(A) 1
(B) $\sqrt{12}$
(C) 6
(D) 17.5
(E) 35

24. A can of food feeds 3 kittens or 2 adult cats. If I have 8 cans of food, and I feed 12 kittens, how many adult cats can I feed with the remainder?
(A) 2
(B) 4
(C) 8
(D) 12
(E) 18

25. 234, 256, 273, 281, 218x.
Of the numbers listed above (assuming that x is greater than 1), which one of the following cannot possibly be the average of the five numbers?
(A) 218
(B) 255
(C) 271
(D) 281
(E) 2,839

S T O P

IF YOU FINISH BEFORE TIME IS CALLED, YOU MAY CHECK YOUR WORK ON THIS SECTION ONLY. DO NOT WORK ON ANY OTHER SECTION IN THE TEST.

SECTION 3 TEST OF STANDARD WRITTEN ENGLISH

50 QUESTIONS - 30 MINUTES

The questions in this section measure skills that are important to writing well. In particular, they test your ability to recognize and use language that is clear, effective, and correct according to the requirements of standard written English, the kind of English found in most college textbooks.

Directions: The following sentences contain problems in grammar, usage, diction (choice of words), and idiom.

Some sentences are correct.

No sentence contains more than one error.

You will find that the error, if there is one, is underlined and lettered. Assume that elements of the sentence that are not underlined are correct and cannot be changed. In choosing answers, follow the requirements of standard written English.

If there is an error, select the one underlined part that must be changed to make the sentence correct and blacken the corresponding space on your answer sheet.

If there is no error, blacken answer space (E).

EXAMPLE:

The region has a climate so severe that (A) plants growing there (B) rarely had been (C) more than twelve inches high. (D) No error (E)

SAMPLE ANSWER

(A) (B) ● (D) (E)

1. Being that (A) my car is getting its annual tune-up, I (B) will not be (C) able to pick you up (D) tomorrow morning. No error (E)

2. The teacher with her two aides (A) have complete control (B) of the situation; I look forward (C) to a very uneventful (D) trip. No error (E)

3. We were delighted (A) with the news of our son (B) winning (C) his first race. (D) No error (E)

4. We can't (A) hardly believe that the situation is so serious (B) as to justify (C) such precautions as you have taken. (D) No error (E)

5. Stroking (A) his (B) beard thoughtfully, a feeling of awe (C) filled (D) the room. No error (E)

6. The teacher wants us all (A)—Frank, Helen, you, (B) and I (C)—to visit (D) John in the hospital. No error (E)

7. He found (A) the climate of Arizona very healthy (B) and decided to move (C) to Phoenix as soon as (D) possible. No error (E)

8. You are being quite (A) cynical when you say (B) that the reason why (C) we have such a large turnout is because (D) we are serving refreshments. No error (E)

9. This award, I can assure (A) you, will be given to whoever (B) performs best (C) in today's (D) game. No error (E)

10. Had I started (A) packing earlier, (B) I would be finished (C) now and not be (D) the cause of this delay. No error (E)

11. Although (A) I am playing (B) golf for more than (C) three years, I cannot manage to break (D) 90. No error (E)

12. The lieutenant reminded (A) his men that the only information to be given (B) to the captors was each (C) individual's name, rank, and what his serial number was. (D) No error (E)

13. The data which (A) he presented (B) were (C) not pertinent to the matter under (D) discussion. No error (E)

14. All the members of the club but him (A) have paid (B) their dues; we must seek ways to make him (C) understand the need (D) for prompt payment. No error (E)

15. "I am not," she said emphatically, (A) "Going (B) to betray her confidence by telling (C) you what I know." (D) No error (E)

16. I have found (A) that a mild salt solution is more affective (B) than the commercial preparations available (C) in drug stores in the treatment of this (D) ailment. No error (E)

17. The teacher ordered (A) the student to go to the dean's (B) office, which (C) surprised us because she usually (D) handled her own discipline problems. No error (E)

18. Everyone in the community must (A) indicate their (B) opinion by writing to the proper (C) authorities in Congress and in City Hall. (D) No error (E)

19. He is not the kind of a person (A) who accepts such treatment passively; (B) he (C) is certain to seek (D) revenge. No error (E)

20. If (A) you had told (B) me that you couldn't do the homework, I would have (C) come to your house to explain (D) it to you. No error (E)

21. If (A) I have to make a choice between (B) John, Henry, or Ruth, I think I'll (C) select Henry because of his self (D) control during moments of stress. No error (E)

22. This (A) new information is so important (B) that we must inform the authorities; bring (C) this to the office at once and give it (D) to Mr. Brown. No error (E)

23. Unless (A) two or more members object to him (B) joining the club, we shall have to accept (C) his application for (D) membership. No error (E)

24. John, together with (A) the other members of the Alumni (B) Association, hopes (C) to establish an annual (D) varsity-alumni basketball game. No error (E)

25. I feel (A) badly (B) about the present conflict (C) because I do not know how to resolve it without hurting (D) either you or him. No error (E)

Directions: In each of the following sentences, some part or all of the sentence is underlined. Below each sentence you will find five ways of phrasing the underlined part. Select the answer that produces the most effective sentence, one that is clear and exact, without awkwardness or ambiguity, and blacken the corresponding space on your answer sheet. In choosing answers, follow the requirements of standard written English. Choose the answer that best expresses the meaning of the original sentence.

Answer (A) is always the same as the underlined part. Choose answer (A) if you think the original sentence needs no revision.

EXAMPLE:

Laura Ingalls Wilder published her first book and she was sixty-five years old then.

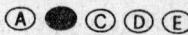

(A) and she was sixty-five years old then
(B) when she was sixty-five years old
(C) at age sixty-five years old
(D) upon reaching sixty-five years
(E) at the time when she was sixty-five

SAMPLE ANSWER

Ⓐ ● Ⓒ Ⓓ Ⓔ

26. Before considering an applicant for this job, he must have a degree in electrical engineering as well as three years experience in the field.
(A) Before considering an applicant for this job, he must
(B) Before considering an applicant for this job, he should
(C) We will not consider an applicant for this job unless he
(D) To consider an applicant for this job, he must
(E) We will not consider an applicant for this job if he does not

27. At one time numbered among the conservative bishops of El Salvador, the ruling military junta considered Bishop Oscar Romero to be a "safe" choice when he was installed as Archbishop of San Salvador in 1977.
(A) the ruling military junta considered Bishop Oscar Romero to be a "safe" choice
(B) the ruling military junta considered Bishop Oscar Romero was being a "safe" choice
(C) the ruling military junta had considered Bishop Oscar Romero to be a "safe" choice
(D) Bishop Oscar Romero was considered by the ruling military junta to be a "safe" choice
(E) Bishop Oscar Romero had been being considered to be a "safe" choice by the ruling military junta

28. She was told to give the award to whomever she thought had contributed most to the welfaré of the student body.
(A) to whomever she thought
(B) to whoever she thought
(C) to the senior whom she thought
(D) to whomsoever
(E) to him whom she thought

29. Irregardless of the outcome of this dispute, our two nations will remain staunch allies.
(A) Irregardless of the outcome
(B) Regardless of how the outcome
(C) With regard to the outcome
(D) Regardless of the outcome
(E) Disregarding the outcome

30. With the onset of winter the snows began to fall, we were soon forced to remain indoors most of the time.
(A) the snows began to fall, we were soon forced to remain indoors
(B) the snows began to fall: we were soon forced to remain indoors
(C) the snows began to fall: we were soon forced to remain indoors
(D) the snows began to fall, and We were soon forced to remain indoors
(E) the snows began to fall; We were soon forced to remain indoors

31. Since he is lying the book on the table where it does not belong.
(A) Since he is lying the book on the table where it does not belong
(B) He is lying the book on the table where it does not belong
(C) Because he is laying the book on the table where it does not belong
(D) Since he is laying the book on the table where it does not belong
(E) He is laying the book on the table where it does not belong.

32. Mary is as fast as, if not faster than anyone in her class and should be on the team.
(A) as fast as, if not faster than anyone
(B) as fast, if not faster than anyone else
(C) as fast, if not more fast than anyone
(D) as fast as, if not faster than anyone else
(E) as swift as, if not faster than anyone

33. Senator Dole is one of the legislators who are going to discuss the budget with the President.
(A) one of the legislators who are going
(B) one of the legislators who is going
(C) one of the legislators who has gone
(D) the legislator who is going
(E) the legislator who has gone

34. Before the search party reached the scene of the accident, the rain began to fall, making rescue efforts more difficult.
(A) the rain began to fall
(B) the rain had began to fall
(C) it began to rain
(D) the rain had begun to fall
(E) it started to rain

35. In 1980 the Democrats lost not only the executive branch but also their majority in the United States Senate.
(A) lost not only the executive branch but also their majority
(B) lost not only the executive branch but also its majority
(C) not only lost the executive branch but their majority also
(D) lost the executive branch but also their majority
(E) lost not only the executive branch but their majority also

36. Although serfs were lucky to drink their ale from cracked wooden bowls, nobles customarily drunk their wine from elaborately chased drinking horns.
(A) drunk their wine from
(B) have drinked their wine from
(C) drank their wine from
(D) had drunken their wine from
(E) drinking their wine from

37. "Araby," along with several other stories from Joyce's *Dubliners*, are going to be read at Town Hall by noted Irish actress Siobhan McKenna.
(A) are going to be read
(B) were going to be read
(C) are gone to be read
(D) is going to be read
(E) is gone to be read

38. For many students, keeping a journal during college seems satisfying their need for self-expression.
(A) keeping a journal during college seems satisfying their need
(B) keeping a journal during college seems to satisfy their need
(C) keeping a journal during college seeming satisfying their need
(D) to keep a journal during college seems satisfying their need
(E) the keeping of a journal during college seems satisfying their need

39. Peter Martin began to develop his own choreographic style, but he was able to free himself from the influence of Balanchine.
(A) style, but he was able to
(B) style; but he was able to
(C) style only when he was able to
(D) style only when he is able to
(E) style: only when he was able to

40. In general, the fate of Latin American or East Asian countries will affect America more than it does Britain or France.
(A) will affect America more than it does
(B) will effect America more than it does
(C) will affect America more than they do
(D) will effect America more than they do
(E) will affect America more than they would

Note: The remaining questions are like those at the beginning of the section.

Directions: For each sentence in which you find an error, select the one underlined part that must be changed to make the sentence correct and blacken the corresonding space on your answer sheet.

If there is no error, blacken answer space Ⓔ.

EXAMPLE:

The region has a climate so severe that plants
A
growing there rarely had been more than twelve
B C
inches high. No error
D E

SAMPLE ANSWER

Ⓐ Ⓑ ● Ⓓ Ⓔ

41. To invest intelligently for the future, mutual funds
A B
provide an excellent means for the average
C D
investor. No error
E

42. No one but he knew which questions were going to
A B C D
be asked on this test. No error
E

43. "How far is it to Portsmouth?" the motorist asked.
A B
"I need to know in order to decide whether to
C
travel on or to remain at this motel over night."
D
No error
E

44. We have spent all together too much money on this
A B
project; we have exceeded our budget and
C
can expect no additional funds until the beginning
D
of the new year. No error
E

45. A celebration like this only comes once every two
A B C D
years. No error
E

46. The climate of Israel is somewhat like
A B C
southern California. No error
D E

47. The only food the champion requested was steak and
A B C
potatoes. No error
D E

48. He was the author whom I believed was
A B
most likely to receive the coveted award.
C D
No error
E

49. Postal regulations forbid your company sending this
A B
kind of material as parcel post. No error
C D E

50. Please give this scholarship to whoever in the grad-
A
uating class has done the most to promote goodwill
B C
in the community. No error
D E

S T O P

IF YOU FINISH BEFORE TIME IS CALLED, YOU MAY CHECK YOUR WORK ON THIS SECTION ONLY. DO NOT WORK ON ANY OTHER SECTION IN THE TEST.

SECTION 4 VERBAL ABILITY

40 QUESTIONS - 30 MINUTES

For each question in this section, choose the best answer and blacken the corresponding space on the answer sheet.

Each question below consists of a word in capital letters, followed by five lettered words or phrases. Choose the word or phrase that is most nearly opposite in meaning to the word in capital letters. Since some of the questions require you to distinguish fine shades of meaning, consider all the choices before deciding which is best.

Example:

GOOD: (A) sour (B) bad (C) red (D) hot (E) ugly

Ⓐ ● Ⓒ Ⓓ Ⓔ

1. GARRULOUS:
   (A) flamboyant
   (B) tautological
   (C) pithy
   (D) incongruous
   (E) insipid

2. GARGANTUAN:
   (A) mortal
   (B) lilliputian
   (C) manual
   (D) simian
   (E) leonine

3. MENIAL:
   (A) sanguine
   (B) physical
   (C) indifferent
   (D) supercilious
   (E) sycophantic

4. QUIXOTIC:
   (A) slow
   (B) feasible
   (C) vapid
   (D) fashionable
   (E) irritable

5. NOISOME:
   (A) boisterous
   (B) sensible
   (C) silent
   (D) fragrant
   (E) handsome

6. BELLICOSE:
   (A) ugly
   (B) outrageous
   (C) stupid
   (D) epigrammatic
   (E) pacific

7. FAMISHED:
   (A) sated
   (B) exiled
   (C) suited
   (D) unknown
   (E) thirsty

8. YIELDING:
   (A) flat
   (B) affluent
   (C) impenetrable
   (D) redolent
   (E) compromised

9. SCRUPULOUS:
   (A) reticent
   (B) remiss
   (C) intrepid
   (D) introvert
   (E) extrovert

10. MOLLIFY:
    (A) annoy
    (B) sympathize
    (C) alter
    (D) intimidate
    (E) liquefy

Each sentence below has one or two blanks, each blank indicating that something has been omitted. Beneath the sentence are five lettered words or sets of words. Choose the word or set of words that best fits the meaning of the sentence as a whole.

Example:

Although its publicity has been ----, the film itself is intelligent, well-acted, handsomely produced, and altogether ----.

(A) tasteless..respectable (B) extensive..moderate (C) sophisticated..amateur (D) risqué..crude (E) perfect..spectacular

● Ⓑ Ⓒ Ⓓ Ⓔ

11. It is difficult to translate a foreign text literally because we cannot capture the ______ of the original passage exactly.
    (A) rhythms
    (B) explanations
    (C) connotations
    (D) text
    (E) ideas

12. For a while, it was fashionable to deprecate the values of _______ because the people wanted efficiency in government.
(A) anarchy
(B) autocracy
(C) democracy
(D) technical skill
(E) feudalism

13. It is remarkable that a man so in the public eye, so highly praised and imitated, can retain his _______ and reticence.
(A) magniloquence
(B) dogmas
(C) bravado
(D) idiosyncrasies
(E) humility

14. The clergy realized that they had to use the _______ to bring the Gospel to the _______.
(A) extraordinary—natives
(B) sermon—neighborhood
(C) vernacular—laity
(D) army—downfall
(E) bishop—people

15. The doctor felt that the _______ was using up valuable time that he needed for really sick patients.
(A) kleptomaniac
(B) hypochondriac
(C) dipsomaniac
(D) invalid
(E) psychiatrist

Each question below consists of a related pair of words or phrases, followed by five lettered pairs of words or phrases. Select the lettered pair that best expresses a relationship similar to that expressed in the original pair.
Example:
YAWN : BOREDOM :: (A) dream : sleep
(B) anger : madness (C) smile : amusement
(D) face : expression (E) impatience : rebellion
Ⓐ Ⓑ ● Ⓓ Ⓔ

16. HEART : PUMP ::
(A) lungs : collapse
(B) appendix : burst
(C) stomach : digest
(D) intestine : twist
(E) teeth : ache

17. STANZA : POEM ::
(A) flag : anthem
(B) scene : play
(C) staircase : step
(D) program : recital
(E) rhyme : prose

18. AMULET : EVIL ::
(A) fort : attack
(B) fire : hose
(C) eggs : rotten
(D) police : law
(E) talisman : good

19. MASTER : SERVANT ::
(A) judge : jury
(B) monarch : vassal
(C) serf : noble
(D) capital : labor
(E) landlord : tenant

20. MONGREL : COLLIE ::
(A) man : god
(B) man : angel
(C) alloy : iron
(D) anger : piety
(E) variety : motley

21. MASON : TROWEL ::
(A) potter : clay
(B) doctor : degree
(C) carpenter : adze
(D) preacher : sermon
(E) sculptor : museum

22. AMASS : WEALTH ::
(A) lavish : bribes
(B) garner : grain
(C) disperse : enemy
(D) refund : deposit
(E) weigh : value

23. NOTORIOUS : MALEFACTOR ::
(A) conspicuous : leader
(B) egregious : philanthropist
(C) reprehensible : altruist
(D) renowned : benefactor
(E) criminal : alias

24. CONNOISSEUR : PAINTING ::
(A) egotist : self
(B) gourmet : viands
(C) miser : gold
(D) jury : criminal
(E) artist : critic

25. CARTOGRAPHER : GAZETTEER ::
(A) conductor : newspaper
(B) novice : expert
(C) author : composer
(D) lexicographer : dictionary
(E) lexicographer : thesaurus

Each passage below is followed by questions based on its content. Answer all questions following a passage on the basis of what is stated or implied in that passage.

The money-changers have two irregular modes of making a profit by their traffic: if they state the fair price of silver to the customer, they cheat him in the weight, if their scales and their method of weighing are accurate, they diminish the price of the silver accordingly. But when they have to do with Tartars, they employ neither of these methods of fraud; on the contrary, they weigh the silver scrupulously, and sometimes allow a little overweight, and even they pay them above the market price, in fact, they appear to be quite losers by the transaction, and so they would be, if the weight and the price of the silver alone were considered, their advantage is derived, in these cases, from their manner of calculating the amount. When they come to reduce the silver into sapeks, they do indeed reduce it, making the most flagrant miscalculations, which the Tartars, who can count nothing beyond their beard, are quite incapable of detecting, and which they, accordingly, adopt implicitly, and even with satisfaction, always considering they have sold their bullion well, since they know the full weight has been allowed, and that the full market price has been given.

26. Money-changers cheat Tartars
(A) by manipulating their scales
(B) by weighing the silver scrupulously
(C) by paying unfair prices for each unit of silver
(D) by allowing them a little overweight of bullion
(E) by deliberate miscalculations

27. Which of the following is true?
(A) Tartars hide valuables under their beards
(B) Tartars are careful about weight and market price
(C) Tartars sell sapeks for silver
(D) Tartars cheat their customers by employing fraudulent methods of weighing their goods
(E) Tartars seek an unfair price for their sapeks

28. According to this passage
(A) money-changers are aware of the fact that Tartars are poor mathematicians
(B) money-changers have fixed prices
(C) money-changers convert bullion into pure silver
(D) money-changers reduce silver
(E) there are only two ways by which money-changers can make an illegitimate profit; namely, by cheating the weight or paying an unfair price

Free unrhymed verse has been practiced for some thousands of years and reaches back to the incantation which linked verse with the ritual dance. It produced a communal emotion; the aim of the cadenced phrases was to create a state of mind. The general coloring of free rhythms in the poetry of today is very different. The predominant pattern of poetry today is that of speech rhythm, composed in the sequence of the musical phrase, not in the sequence of metronome, the regular beat. In the twenties, conventional rhyme fell into almost complete disuse. This liberation from rhyme became as well a liberation of rhyme. Freed of its exacting task of supporting lame verse, it could be applied with greater effect where wanted for some special effect. Such break in the tradition of rhymed verse had the healthy effect of giving it a fresh start, released from the hampering convention of too familiar cadences. This refreshing and subtilizing of the use of rhyme can be seen everywhere in the poetry of today.

29. The title that best expresses the ideas of this paragraph is:
(A) Primitive poetry
(B) The origin of poetry
(C) Rhyme and rhythm in modern verse
(D) Classification of poetry
(E) Purposes in all poetry

30. Free verse had its origin in primitive
(A) fairy tales
(B) literature
(C) warfare
(D) chants
(E) courtship

31. The object of early free verse was to
(A) influence the mood of the people
(B) convey ideas
(C) produce mental pictures
(D) create pleasing sounds
(E) provide enjoyment

Of all the strange experiences that may await the astronaut, none will be quite so strange, the experts agree, as weightlessness. This phenomenon will occur as soon as the spaceship reaches a speed at which the rocket's centrifugal force cancels the pull of the earth's gravity, and when it does, the space man, whether settling into orbit or making for Venus or Mars, will know for certain that he has arrived in outer space. He will weigh nothing. The air in his cabin will weigh nothing. The warm carbon dioxide he breathes out, being no lighter than the air in the cabin, will not rise, so he will have to exhale forcibly. Momentum, the force, whirling the ship on its course, will rule its interior as well, and with possibly weird results. All objects that are not in some way fastened down — a map, a flashlight, a pencil — will float freely, subjecting the space man to a haphazard crossfire. If he were to drink water from an ordinary tumbler, the water might dash into his nostrils, float there, and drown him. Ordinary tumblers will not be used, however: plastic squeeze bottles will. ("The proper-size orifice is being worked out," I was told by Major Henry G. Wise, of the Human Factors Division, Air Force Directorate of Research and Development.) Far more startling than the movement of objects, though, will be the space man's own movements. Normally in making a movement of any kind, a man has to overcome the body's inertia plus its weight; a weightless man has only the inertia to overcome, and the chances are that it will take a long time for his muscles to grow accustomed to the fact. "What would be a normal step on earth would . . . send the 'stepper' sailing across the cabin or somersaulting wildly in the air," the Air University Command and Staff School study declares. "A mere sneeze could propel the victim violently against the cabin wall and result in possible injury."

32. The best title for this passage is
(A) Miracles in the air
(B) New scientific frontiers
(C) Overcoming inertia
(D) Momentum and the astronaut
(E) Loss of weight in space

33. Sneezing in a spacecraft is dangerous because
(A) the force of the sneeze may propel the astronaut into the wall of the craft
(B) the astronaut may choke
(C) the astronaut is weightless
(D) the astronaut is influenced by the momentum of the craft
(E) the astronaut may develop a nose bleed

34. Weightless occurs when
(A) carbon dioxide rises
(B) the rocket's centripetal force cancels the pull of the earth's gravity
(C) the missile's trajectory escapes the range of the earth's gravity
(D) the rocket's speed offsets the force of gravity
(E) inertia equals the speed of the missile

35. From this passage, we learn that
(A) warm carbon dioxide is heavier than air
(B) warm carbon dioxide is no heavier than air
(C) warm carbon dioxide is lighter than air
(D) air has no weight
(E) man's muscles are not accustomed to inertia

36. The Human Factors Division of the Air Force is studying
(A) warm carbon dioxide
(B) momentum of floating bodies
(C) centrifugal force
(D) colds in the stratosphere
(E) proper devices for drinking

Throughout extensive areas of the tropics the tall and stately primeval forest has given way to eroded land, scrub and the jumble of secondary growth. Just as the virgin forests of Europe and North America were laid low by man's improvidence, so those of the tropics are now vanishing — only their destruction may be encompassed in decades instead of centuries. A few authorities hold that, except for government reserves, the earth's great rain forests may vanish within a generation. The economic loss will be incalculable, for the primary rain forests are rich sources of timber (mahogany, teak) and such by-products as resins, gums, cellulose, camphor and rattans. No one, indeed, can compute their resources, for of the thousands of species that compose the forest cover, there are only a few whose physical and chemical properties have been studied with a view to commercial use.

Most important of all, the primeval rain forest is a reservoir of specimens, a dynamic center of evolution whence the rest of the world's plant life has been continually enriched with new forms. These extensive reserves must be defended from the acquisitive hand of man, whose ruthless ax would expose them to the ravages of sun and rain.

37. The primary reason for conservation of the great rain forests is that they
(A) are areas of botanical evolution
(B) are not ready for man's ruthless ax
(C) are the chief source of income of governments
(D) provide major sources of material for chemical industries
(E) need further development before they can be used commercially

38. As used in the passage, the word "primeval" (paragraph 2, line 1) means
(A) of first importance
(B) commercial
(C) gorgeous
(D) untouched
(E) thick

39. The ideas of the author would probably be most strongly supported by
(A) lumber company representatives
(B) conservationists and botanists
(C) chemical manufacturers
(D) government representatives
(E) the "man on the street"

40. The resources of the rain forests are
(A) incalculable
(B) purely chemical
(C) somewhat limited
(D) uncommercial
(E) of interest only to scientists

S T O P

IF YOU FINISH BEFORE TIME IS CALLED, YOU MAY CHECK YOUR WORK ON THIS SECTION ONLY. DO NOT WORK ON ANY OTHER SECTION IN THE TEST.

SECTION 5 MATH ABILITY

35 QUESTIONS - 30 MINUTES

In this section solve each problem, using any available space on the page for scratchwork. Then decide which is the best of the choices given and blacken the corresponding space on the answer sheet.

The following information is for your reference in solving some of the problems.

Circle of radius r: Area $= \pi r^2$; Circumference $= 2\pi r$
The number of degrees of arc in a circle is 360.
The measure in degrees of a straight angle is 180.

Definitions of symbols:

$=$ is equal to
$\neq$ is unequal to
$<$ is less than
$>$ is greater than
$\leq$ is less than or equal to
$\geq$ is greater than or equal to
$\parallel$ is parallel to
$\perp$ is perpendicular to

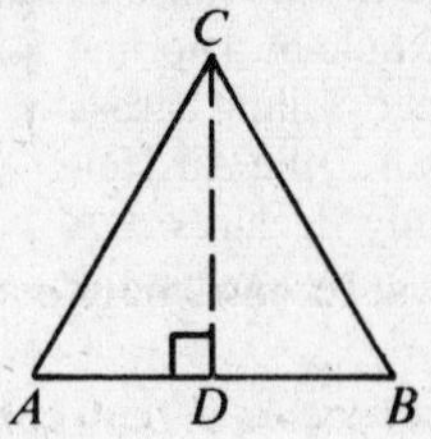

Triangle: The sum of the measures in degrees of the angles of a triangle is 180.
If $\angle CDA$ is a right angle, then
(1) area of $\triangle ABC = \frac{AB \times CD}{2}$
(2) $AC^2 = AD^2 + DC^2$

Note: Figures that accompany problems in this test are intended to provide information useful in solving the problems. They are drawn as accurately as possible EXCEPT when it is stated in a specific problem that its figure is not drawn to scale. All figures lie in a plane unless otherwise indicated. All numbers used are real numbers.

1. If $\frac{1}{r} = 3$ and $s = 3$ what is r in terms of s?
(A) s
(B) $3 - s$
(C) $\frac{1}{s}$
(D) $-s$
(E) $9s$

2. If two parts of sand are mixed with three parts of gravel, what part of the total mixture is sand?
(A) $\frac{1}{3}$
(B) $\frac{2}{5}$
(C) $\frac{3}{5}$
(D) $\frac{2}{3}$
(E) $\frac{3}{2}$

3. If $2.3y = 46$, what is the value of y?
(A) 2
(B) 20
(C) 105.5
(D) 200
(E) 1058

4. $\frac{8}{10} - \frac{12}{15} = (?)$
(A) -1
(B) 0
(C) 1
(D) $\frac{4}{15}$
(E) $\frac{8}{5}$

5. Which of the following is the equivalent of $\frac{1}{N + \frac{1}{N}}$?
(A) 1
(B) $\frac{1}{2N}$
(C) $\frac{2}{N}$
(D) $\frac{N}{N+1}$
(E) $\frac{N}{N^2+1}$

6. Which of the following fractions has the smallest value?
(A) $\frac{5}{4}$
(B) $\frac{6}{5}$
(C) $\frac{13}{10}$
(D) $\frac{29}{25}$
(E) $\frac{59}{50}$

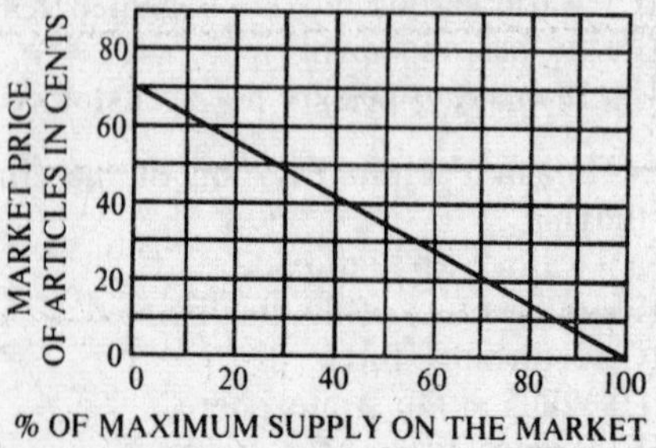

7. When 30% of the maximum supply of a certain article is on the market, what is the price (in cents) of the article according to the graph above?
(A) 47
(B) 49
(C) 52
(D) 56
(E) 66

Questions 8–27 each consist of two quantities, one in Column A and one in Column B. You are to compare the two quantities and on the answer sheet blacken space

- A if the quantity in Column A is greater;
- B if the quantity in Column B is greater;
- C if the two quantities are equal;
- D If the relationship cannot be determined from the information given.

AN E RESPONSE WILL NOT BE SCORED.

EXAMPLES

	Column A	Column B	Answers
E1.	2×6	$2 + 6$	● Ⓑ Ⓒ Ⓓ Ⓔ

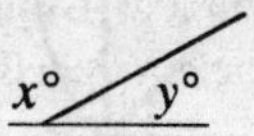

	Column A	Column B	Answers
E2.	$180 - x$	y	Ⓐ Ⓑ ● Ⓓ Ⓔ
E3.	$p - q$	$q - p$	Ⓐ Ⓑ Ⓒ ● Ⓔ

Notes:

1. In certain questions, information concerning one or both of the quantities to be compared is centered above the two columns.
2. In a given question, a symbol that appears in both columns represents the same thing in Column A as it does in Column B.
3. Letters such as x, n, and k stand for real numbers.

	Column A	Column B
	$\frac{1}{x} < 0$	
8.	x	1
	$x = y^2 - 1 = 3$	
9.	x	y
	$x^2 = 25$	
10.	x	5
11.	$\dfrac{\frac{1}{x} \div \frac{1}{1}}{x}$	$\frac{1}{x} \cdot \frac{1}{x}$
	$0 < x < 31$; x is divisible by 3 and 9	
12.	x	27
13.	$\frac{1}{3}$ of (4 yards, 2 feet)	1 yard, 4 feet
	$x^n = 1$	
14.	x	1
	$x > 1$	
15.	$\sqrt{\frac{2x}{y}} \times \sqrt{\frac{xy}{2}}$	x
	$x = \frac{1}{2}$	
16.	$\dfrac{\frac{3}{4}}{1 + x}$	x

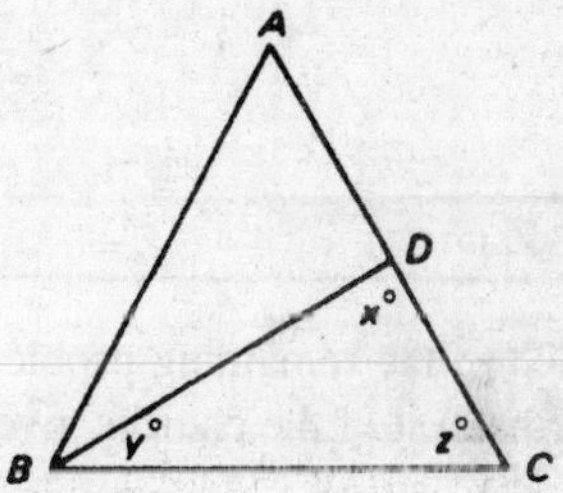

Note: This concerns #17 and #18

$DC = \frac{1}{2} AC = \frac{1}{2} BC = \frac{1}{2} AB$

	Column A	Column B
17.	$(BC)^2$	$(DC)^2 + (BD)^2$
18.	$2y$	z

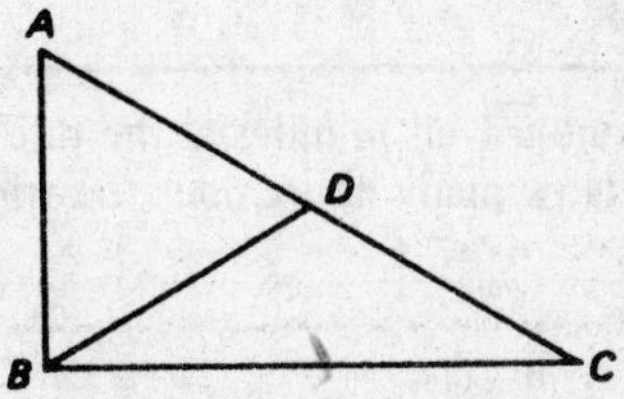

Note: This concerns #19–21

$AB = BD = AD$ and $AB \perp BC$

	Column A	Column B
19.	BC	DC
20.	BD	BC
21.	BD	DC

Column A	Column B

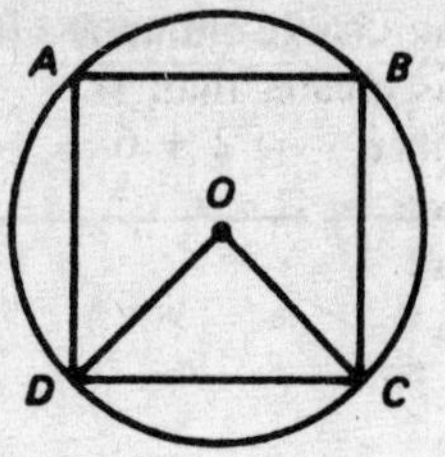

Note: This concerns #22 and #23

$DO \perp OC$ and area of triangle $DOC = 12.5$

	Column A	Column B
22.	Area of circle O	25π
23.	Length of DC	$5\sqrt{2}$

In triangle ABC, $m \angle A > m \angle B$, and $\angle C \triangleq 60$

24.	Side CB	Side AB

Column A	Column B

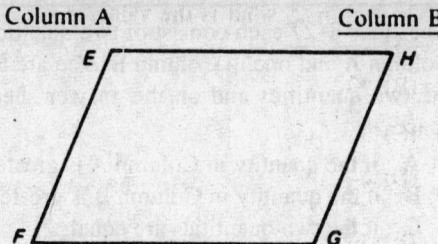

Note: This concerns #25 and #26

In parallelogram $EFGH$, $EF + EH = 20$

	Column A	Column B
25.	EH	FG
26.	Perimeter of $EFGH$	40

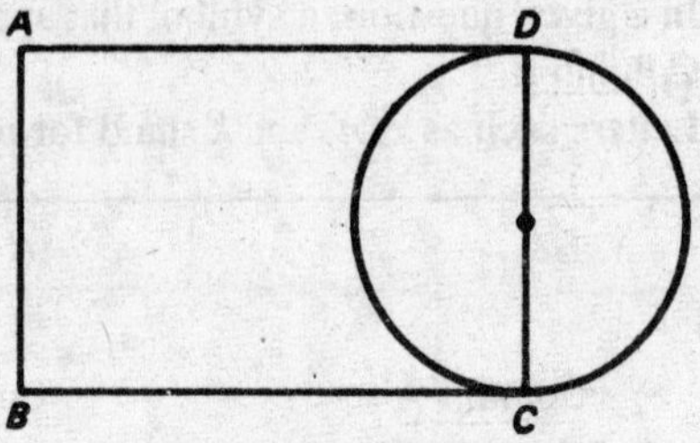

BC of rectangle $ABCD = 2.5\pi$

DC, diameter $= 10$

27.	Area of $ABCD$	Area of circle

Solve each of the remaining problems in this section using any available space for scratchwork. Then decide which is the best of the choices given and blacken the corresponding space on the answer sheet.

28. $42:63 = 28:x \quad x = ?$

(A) $\frac{6}{7}$

(B) $18\frac{2}{3}$

(C) 40

(D) 41

(E) 42

29. An airplane travels m miles at the rate of h miles per hour. How many hours does the trip take?

(A) $\frac{h}{m}$

(B) $h + m$

(C) $\frac{m}{h}$

(D) $-m + h$

(E) $m - h$

30. A nurse gives her patient one tablet every 45 minutes. How many tablets will she need for her nine-hour tour of duty, if she gives the patient a tablet at the beginning and end of her tour?

(A) 8

(B) 10

(C) 11

(D) 12

(E) 13

31. If an airplane starts at point R and travels 14 miles directly north to S, then 48 miles directly west to T, what is the straight line distance from T to R in miles?

(A) 25

(B) 34

(C) 50

(D) 62

(E) 2500

32. If $2x - 3 = 2$, what is the value of $x - \frac{1}{2}$?

(A) 2

(B) $2\frac{1}{2}$

(C) 3

(D) $4\frac{1}{2}$

(E) $5\frac{1}{2}$

33. $\frac{2}{s-t} - \frac{3}{t-s}$ is equal to

(A) $\frac{1}{s^2 + 2st + t^2}$

(B) $\frac{-1}{s-t}$

(C) $\frac{-1}{t-s}$

(D) $\frac{5}{s-t}$

(E) $\frac{5}{t-s}$

34. If the taxi fare is c cents for the first quarter of a mile and s cents for each additional quarter of a mile, what is the charge (in cents) for a trip of x miles (where x is greater than 1)?

(A) $c + s(4x - 1)$

(B) $c + s(x - 1)$

(C) $c + sx$

(D) sx

(E) $(c - 1)s + x$

35. The water in a fish tank 1¼ feet by 8 inches is 7 inches high. If it is poured into a tank 13 inches by 20 inches, what height will it reach in the larger tank?

(A) 0.27″

(B) 0.31″

(C) 1.7″

(D) 3.2″

(E) 4.6″

S T O P

IF YOU FINISH BEFORE TIME IS CALLED, YOU MAY CHECK YOUR WORK ON THIS SECTION ONLY. DO NOT WORK ON ANY OTHER SECTION IN THE TEST.

SECTION 6 VERBAL ABILITY

45 QUESTIONS - 30 MINUTES

For each question in this section, choose the best answer and blacken the corresponding space on the answer sheet.

Each question below consists of a word in capital letters, followed by five lettered words or phrases. Choose the word or phrase that is most nearly opposite in meaning to the word in capital letters. Since some of the questions require you to distinguish fine shades of meaning, consider all the choices before deciding which is best.

Example:

GOOD: (A) sour (B) bad (C) red (D) hot (E) ugly

Ⓐ ● Ⓒ Ⓓ Ⓔ

1. APATHETIC:
   (A) sad
   (B) gloomy
   (C) eager
   (D) angry
   (E) insolent

2. GRAPHIC:
   (A) leaden
   (B) literary
   (C) elementary
   (D) dull
   (E) enlarged

3. DASTARD:
   (A) neighbor
   (B) knight
   (C) hero
   (D) ancestor
   (E) lover

4. EPHEMERAL:
   (A) relevant
   (B) waspish
   (C) intelligent
   (D) active
   (E) permanent

5. CASTIGATE:
   (A) enthrone
   (B) classify
   (C) close
   (D) praise
   (E) rehabilitate

6. FESTER:
   (A) soothe
   (B) heal
   (C) stain
   (D) erase
   (E) decelerate

7. HILARITY:
   (A) depth
   (B) fog
   (C) anger
   (D) gloom
   (E) abundance

8. INEVITABLE:
   (A) infrequent
   (B) visible
   (C) vital
   (D) enviable
   (E) avoidable

9. RESTRAINT:
   (A) excess
   (B) renewal
   (C) woe
   (D) wakefulness
   (E) division

10. INARTICULATE:
    (A) distinct
    (B) remote
    (C) sudden
    (D) favorable
    (E) zestful

11. INSIPID:
    (A) sparkling
    (B) thirsty
    (C) blooming
    (D) inspired
    (E) constant

12. RECONDITE:
    (A) ambushed
    (B) popular
    (C) unkempt
    (D) outlandish
    (E) auxiliary

13. SENTENTIOUS:
(A) roundabout
(B) rewarding
(C) adverbial
(D) impoverished
(E) lamentable

14. AFFLUENT:
(A) argumentative
(B) appeasing
(C) impoverished
(D) vicarious
(E) vigilant

15. FELICITOUS:
(A) inappropriate
(B) expert
(C) congratulatory
(D) articulate
(E) frantic

Each sentence below has one or two blanks, each blank indicating that something has been omitted. Beneath the sentence are five lettered words or sets of words. Choose the word or set of words that best fits the meaning of the sentence as a whole.

Example:

Although its publicity has been ----, the film itself is intelligent, well-acted, handsomely produced, and altogether ----.

(A) tasteless..respectable (B) extensive..moderate (C) sophisticated..amateur (D) risqué..crude (E) perfect..spectacular

● Ⓑ Ⓒ Ⓓ Ⓔ

16. _______ tools are used to _______ instruments.
(A) Delicate—manufacture
(B) Abrasive—edge
(C) Sharp—stultify
(D) Expensive—desecrate
(E) Authentic—sharpen

17. Like people who continue to live near an active volcano, many of us are _______ about the _______ of atomic warfare and its attendant destruction.
(A) worried—possibility
(B) unconcerned—threat
(C) excited—power
(D) cheered—possession
(E) irritated—news

18. This is the _______ and the _______, the Alpha and Omega of our tribulations.
(A) Scylla–Charybdis
(B) Pyramus—Thisbe
(C) beginning—end
(D) cause—effect
(E) Joan—Darby

19. I regret that we shall be unable to _______ all who have applied for rooms.
(A) correlate
(B) accommodate
(C) elucidate
(D) saturate
(E) intimidate

20. The _______ tables of the insurance companies indicate that the life expectancy of Americans is _______.
(A) statistical—stimulating
(B) accounting—good
(C) authorial—waning
(D) statistical-inhibiting
(E) actuarial—waxing

Each passage below is followed by questions based on its content. Answer all questions following a passage on the basis of what is stated or implied in that passage.

Before taking up the subject of primitivism in United States painting, we must first consider whether there actually is such a thing as United States painting. Perhaps the U.S. art form merely belongs to the sum total of Western or, more precisely, European painting. The mere fact that there are painters in the United States does not necessarily imply the existence of a distinctive U.S. art form.

We believe, however, that painting has a native and singular flavor that sets it apart. True enough, some painters like Whistler, Sargent, and Mary Cassatt belong to the English or French school, but they are the exception. Almost all U.S. artists have developed on their own. They have been self-taught artists who have perfected their talents to a greater or lesser degree. Those who felt the imperious need to visit Europe did so when they had already achieved maturity. For them the Old World influence served more to improve their techniques than to modify their already existing styles. For some artists, for example Grant Wood, a European tour stimulated awareness of their own national roots, and convinced them that their true place was in their own country and in their own setting.

Many factors point to the existence of an indigenous U.S. school, similar to the European schools, but with a special stamp of its own. By way of introduction a brief review of the pioneer painters who came to the New World is in order.

21. The title below that best expresses the ideas of this passage is
   (A) An indigenous art form in America
   (B) Europe's influence on American painters
   (C) Grant Wood's experience
   (D) American pioneer painters
   (E) Self-taught American artists

22. The author believes that
   (A) Grant Wood modified his style during his European visit
   (B) Whistler is not typical of most American artists
   (C) a European tour is a "must" for American artists
   (D) a native school of art is unlikely
   (E) American painting must be considered in the light of European culture

23. In the paragraph following this passage, we may expect a discussion of
   (A) primitivism
   (B) English and French influence on Sargent
   (C) Grant Wood's independence
   (D) painters who migrated to America
   (E) an indigenous American school

24. The author maintains that Whistler, Sargent, and Mary Cassatt are exceptions because
   (A) they developed on their own
   (B) their styles were modified by their European contacts
   (C) they became aware of their national roots
   (D) they were self-taught
   (E) they were immature when they visited Europe

For me, scientific knowledge is divided into mathematical sciences, natural sciences or sciences dealing with the natural world (physical and biological sciences), and sciences dealing with mankind (psychology, sociology, all the sciences of cultural achievements, every kind of historical knowledge). Apart from these sciences is philosophy, about which we will talk later. In the first place, all this is pure or theoretical knowledge, sought only for the purpose of understanding, in order to fulfill the need to understand that is intrinsic and consubstantial to man. What distinguishes man from animal is that he knows and needs to know. If man did not know that the world existed, and that the world was of a certain kind, that he was in the world and that he himself was of a certain kind, he wouldn't be man. The technical aspects or applications of knowledge are equally necessary for man and are of the greatest importance, because they also contribute to defining him as man and permit him to pursue a life increasingly more truly human.

But even while enjoying the results of technical progress, he must defend the primacy and autonomy of pure knowledge. Knowledge sought directly for its practical applications will have immediate and foreseeable success, but not the kind of important result whose revolutionary scope is in large part unforeseen, except by the imagination of the Utopians. Let me recall a well-known example. If the Greek mathematicians had not applied themselves to the investigation of conic sections, zealously and without the least suspicion that it might someday be useful, it would not have been possible centuries later to navigate far from shore. The first men to study the nature of electricity could not imagine that their experiments, carried on because of mere intellectual curiosity, would eventually lead to modern electrical technology, without which we can scarcely conceive of contemporary life. Pure knowledge is valuable for its own sake, because the human spirit cannot resign itself to ignorance. But, in addition, it is the foundation for practical results that would not have been reached if this knowledge had not been sought disinterestedly.

25. The most important advances made by mankind come from
(A) technical applications
(B) apparently useless information
(C) the natural sciences
(D) philosophy
(E) the biological sciences

26. The author does not include among the sciences the study of
(A) chemistry
(B) astronomy
(C) economics
(D) anthropology
(E) literature

27. In the paragraph which follows this passage, we may expect the author to discuss
(A) the value of technical research
(B) the value of pure research
(C) philosophy
(D) unforeseen discoveries
(E) scientific foundations

28. The author points out that the Greeks who studied conic sections
(A) were mathematicians
(B) were interested in navigation
(C) were unaware of the value of their studies
(D) worked with electricity
(E) resigned

29. The title below that best expresses the ideas of this passage is
(A) Technical Progress
(B) A Little Learning Is a Dangerous Thing
(C) Man's Distinguishing Characteristics
(D) Learning for Its Own Sake
(E) The Difference between Science and Philosophy

30. The practical scientist
(A) knows the value of what he will discover
(B) is interested in the unknown
(C) knows that the world exists
(D) is a philosopher
(E) conceives of contemporary life

Select the word or set of words that best completes each of the following sentences.

31. Thomas Hardy's novels are said to suffer from the "long arm of coincidence" because too many events seem to have a ______ rather than a ______ connection.
(A) surprising factual (B) exhilarating—central
(C) fortuitous—causal (D) causal—actual
(E) realistic—casual

32. By developing skill in the use of sign language, he was able to overcome his ______ difficulties during his recent trip to Japan.
(A) peripatetic (B) linguistic (C) persistent
(D) monetary (E) personal

33. I am confident that the judge will realize that the prisoner is accused of mere ______ rather than major offenses and will set bail accordingly.
(A) felonies (B) details (C) peccadilloes
(D) insinuations (E) embezzlement

34. A person who is ______ is not ______.
(A) disheveled—tardy (B) meticulous—careless
(C) facetious—silly (D) sanguine—optimistic
(E) gullible—credulous

35. Your ______ in the face of all the evidence we have presented is proof of our statement that you have an ______ mind.
(A) gullibility—informed
(B) incredulity—open
(C) acquiescence—acquisitive
(D) skepticism—indifferent
(E) incredulity—opinionated

Each question below consists of a related pair of words or phrases, followed by five lettered pairs of words or phrases. Select the lettered pair that best expresses a relationship similar to that expressed in the original pair.

Example:

YAWN : BOREDOM :: (A) dream : sleep
(B) anger : madness (C) smile : amusement
(D) face : expression (E) impatience : rebellion

Ⓐ Ⓑ ● Ⓓ Ⓔ

36. NOVELIST : PLOT ::
(A) dramatist : acts
(B) architect : blueprint
(C) sculptor : chisel
(D) magician: legerdemain
(E) composer : notes

37. SLINK : STEALTH ::
(A) whine : querulousness
(B) snarl : mockery
(C) disguise : alias
(D) praise : friendship
(E) fashion : style

38. ABHOR : DISLIKE ::
(A) chastise : punish
(B) vanquish : defeat
(C) qualify : limit
(D) demolish : damage
(E) like : love

39. SEDULOUS : DILIGENT ::
(A) ambitious : vain
(B) haughty : obsequious
(C) lush : barren
(D) ingenuous : naive
(E) ingenuous : clever

40. WINCE : PAIN ::
(A) pardon : tolerance
(B) blush : embarrassment
(C) cry : anger
(D) sing : gaiety
(E) march : patriotism

41. HECKLER : JEER ::
(A) snob : flatter
(B) grumbler : complain
(C) mentor : repent
(D) laughingstock : mock
(E) miser : weep

42. STANCH : BLEEDING ::
(A) dam : flood
(B) divert : traffic
(C) squander : money
(D) induce : nausea
(E) color : facts

43. DREGS : WINE ::
(A) wheat : chaff
(B) nectar : ambrosia
(C) fruit : grapes
(D) gold : ore
(E) slag : iron

44. AMUSING : UPROARIOUS ::
(A) puzzling : dumbfounding
(B) quiet : noisy
(C) intractable : stubborn
(D) petty : narrow-minded
(E) exhausted : weary

45. CARAPACE : TURTLE ::
(A) speed : hare
(B) chameleon : lizard
(C) amphibian : frog
(D) shell : snail
(E) kennel : dog

S T O P

IF YOU FINISH BEFORE TIME IS CALLED, YOU MAY CHECK YOUR WORK ON THIS SECTION ONLY. DO NOT WORK ON ANY OTHER SECTION IN THE TEST.

ANSWER KEY

Note: The answers to the math sections are keyed to the corresponding review areas in Chapter 11. The numbers in parentheses after each answer refer to topics as listed below. (Note that to review for number 16, Quantitative Comparison, study Chapter 10.)

1. Fundamental Operations
2. Algebraic Operations
3. Using Algebra
4. Roots and Radicals
5. Inequalities
6. Fractions
7. Decimals
8. Percent
9. Averages
10. Motion
11. Ratio and Proportion
12. Mixtures and Solutions
13. Work
14. Coordinate Geometry
15. Geometry
16. Quantitative Comparison
17. Data Interpretation

SECTION 1 VERBAL

1.	D	10.	B	19.	A	28.	D	37.	B
2.	D	11.	D	20.	D	29.	A	38.	E
3.	A	12.	A	21.	D	30.	B	39.	B
4.	B	13.	B	22.	E	31.	B	40.	B
5.	E	14.	B	23.	E	32.	C	41.	D
6.	B	15.	A	24.	B	33.	C	42.	C
7.	D	16.	D	25.	C	34.	C	43.	E
8.	B	17.	B	26.	A	35.	B	44.	A
9.	B	18.	D	27.	B	36.	D	45.	C

SECTION 2 MATH

1.	B (2)	6.	C (1)	11.	C (2,6)	16.	E (15)	21.	E (2,6)
2.	A (2)	7.	D (15)	12.	C (15)	17.	A (6)	22.	B (2)
3.	B (7)	8.	E (15)	13.	C (3)	18.	D (2)	23.	A (2)
4.	E (2)	9.	C (2)	14.	D (2)	19.	C (10)	24.	C (11,17)
5.	E (2)	10.	B (8,9)	15.	E (1,17)	20.	D (1)	25.	A (9)

SECTION 3 TEST OF STANDARD WRITTEN ENGLISH

1.	A	11.	B	21.	B	31.	E	41.	A
2.	B	12.	D	22.	C	32.	D	42.	B
3.	B	13.	E	23.	B	33.	A	43.	E
4.	A	14.	E	24.	E	34.	A	44.	A
5.	A	15.	B	25.	B	35.	A	45.	C
6.	C	16.	B	26.	E	36.	C	46.	D
7.	B	17.	C	27.	D	37.	D	47.	E
8.	D	18.	B	28.	B	38.	B	48.	A
9.	E	19.	A	29.	D	39.	C	49.	B
10.	E	20.	E	30.	B	40.	A	50.	E

SECTION 4 VERBAL

1.	C	9.	B	17.	B	25.	D	33.	A
2.	B	10.	A	18.	A	26.	E	34.	D
3.	D	11.	C	19.	B	27.	B	35.	C
4.	B	12.	C	20.	C	28.	A	36.	E
5.	D	13.	E	21.	C	29.	C	37.	A
6.	E	14.	C	22.	B	30.	D	38.	D
7.	A	15.	B	23.	D	31.	A	39.	B
8.	C	16.	C	24.	B	32.	E	40.	C

SECTION 5 MATH

1. C (2)	8. B (5,16)	15. C (4,16)	22. C (15,16)	29. C (10)
2. B (6)	9. A (2,16)	16. C (2,6,16)	23. C (15,16)	30. E (1)
3. B (2)	10. D (2,16)	17. C (15,16)	24. A (15,16)	31. C (15)
4. B (6)	11. C (2,6,16)	18. C (15,16)	25. C (15,16)	32. A (2)
5. E (6)	12. D (5,16)	19. A (15,16)	26. C (15,16)	33. D (2,6)
6. D (6)	13. B (1,16)	20. B (15,16)	27. C (15,16)	34. A (3)
7. B (8,18)	14. D (4,16)	21. C (15,16)	28. E (11)	35. D (15)

SECTION 6 VERBAL

1. C	10. A	19. B	28. C	37. A
2. D	11. A	20. E	29. D	38. D
3. C	12. B	21. A	30. A	39. D
4. E	13. A	22. B	31. C	40. B
5. D	14. C	23. D	32. B	41. B
6. B	15. A	24. B	33. C	42. A
7. D	16. B	25. B	34. B	43. E
8. E	17. B	26. E	35. E	44. A
9. A	18. C	27. C	36. B	45. D

SELF-EVALUATION

The model SAT test you have just completed has the same format as the actual SAT. As you take more of the model tests in this chapter, you will lose any SAT "stage fright" you might have.

Use the steps that follow to evaluate your performance on Model SAT Test 1. (Note: You'll find the charts referred to in steps 1–5 on the next three pages.)

STEP 1 Use the Answer Key to check your answers for each section.

STEP 2 For each section, count the number of correct and incorrect answers (remember that you don't count omitted answers), and enter the numbers on the appropriate lines of the chart "Obtaining Your Raw Score." Then do the indicated calculations to get your Raw Verbal Score, your Raw TSWE Score, and your Raw Math Score.

STEP 3 Consult the chart "Evaluate Your Performance" to see how well you did.

STEP 4 To pinpoint the specific areas in which you need to improve, circle the numbers of the questions that you either left blank or got wrong on the "Identify Your Weaknesses" charts. This will tell you where to concentrate your efforts to get the most out of your study time. The chart for the math sections gives you page references for review and practice by skill areas. The charts for the verbal and TSWE sections refer you to the appropriate chapters to study for each question type.

STEP 5 Do the review and practice indicated on the charts wherever you had a concentration of circles.

Remember that in addition to evaluating your scores, you should read all of the answer explanations for questions you answered incorrectly, questions you omitted, and questions you answered correctly but found difficult. Reviewing the answer explanations will help you understand concepts and strategies, and may point out shortcuts.

OBTAINING YOUR RAW SCORE

Verbal

Section 1 ______________ – 1/4 (______________) = ______________ (A)
number correct number incorrect

Section 4 ______________ – 1/4 (______________) = ______________ (B)
number correct number incorrect

Section 6 ______________ – 1/4 (______________) = ______________ (C)
number correct number incorrect

Raw Verbal Score = (A) + (B) + (C) = ______________

TSWE

Section 3 ______________ – 1/4 (______________) = Raw TSWE Score = ______________
number correct number incorrect

Math

Section 2 ______________ – 1/4 (______________) = ______________ (D)
number correct number incorrect

Section 5 (1-7, 28-35) ______________ – 1/4 (______________) = ______________ (E)
number correct number incorrect

Section 5 (8-27) ______________ – 1/3 (______________) = ______________ (F)
number correct number incorrect

Raw Math Score = (D) + (E) + (F) = ______________

EVALUATE YOUR PERFORMANCE

	Verbal	TSWE	Math
Excellent	111-130	45-50	52-60
Very Good	91-110	39-44	45-51
Good	81-90	34-38	36-44
Average	61-80	25-33	30-35
Below Average	40-60	15-24	25-29
Unsatisfactory	below 40	below 15	below 25

IDENTIFY YOUR WEAKNESSES
Verbal

Question Type	Question Numbers			Chapter to Study
	Section 1	Section 4	Section 6	
Antonym	1, 2, 3, 4, 5, 6, 7, 8, 9, 10, 11, 12, 13, 14, 15	1, 2, 3, 4, 5, 6, 7, 8, 9, 10	1, 2, 3, 4, 5, 6, 7, 8, 9, 10, 11, 12, 13, 14, 15	Chapter 4
Analogy	36, 37, 38, 39, 40, 41, 42, 43, 44, 45	16, 17, 18, 19, 20, 21, 22, 23, 24, 25	36, 37, 38, 39, 40, 41, 42, 43, 44, 45	Chapter 5
Sentence Completion	16, 17, 18, 19, 20, 31, 32, 33, 34, 35	11, 12, 13, 14, 15	16, 17, 18, 19, 20, 31, 32, 33, 34, 35	Chapter 6
Reading Comprehension	21, 22, 23, 24, 25, 26, 27, 28, 29, 30	26, 27, 28, 29, 30, 31, 32, 33, 34, 35, 36, 37, 38, 39, 40	21, 22, 23, 24, 25, 26, 27, 28, 29, 30	Chapter 7

TSWE

Question Type	Question Numbers	Chapter to Study
Usage	1, 2, 3, 4, 5, 6, 7, 8, 9, 10, 11, 12, 13, 14, 15, 16, 17, 18, 19, 20, 21, 22, 23, 24, 25, 41, 42, 43, 44, 45, 46, 47, 48, 49, 50	Chapter 12
Sentence Correction	26, 27, 28, 29, 30, 31, 32, 33, 34, 35, 36, 37, 38, 39, 40	Chapter 12

Math

Skill Area	Question Numbers		Pages to Study
	Section 2	Section 5	
Fundamental Operations	6, 15, 20	13, 30	300–302
Algebraic Operations	1, 2, 4, 5, 9, 11, 14, 18, 21, 22, 23	1, 3, 9, 10, 11, 14, 15, 16, 32, 33	302–308
Using Algebra	13	34	308–316
Fractions	11, 17, 21	2, 4, 5, 6, 8, 11, 16, 33	316–329
Decimals and Percents	3	7	329–334
Verbal Problems	10, 19, 25	29	335–352
Ratio and Proportion	24	28	340–346
Geometry	7, 8, 12, 16	17, 18, 19, 20, 22, 23, 24, 25, 26, 27, 31, 35	355–368
Inequalities		8, 12	309–311; 315–316
Quantitative Comparison		8, 9, 10, 11, 12, 13, 14, 15, 16, 17, 18, 19, 20, 21, 22, 23, 24, 25, 26, 27	279–299
Data Interpretation		7	369–376
Roots and Radicals		14, 15	306–307; 312–313

ANSWER EXPLANATIONS

SECTION 1

1. D. The opposite of *fertile* (fruitful) is *barren.*

2. D. The opposite of *stolid* (unemotional) is giddy.

3. A. The opposite of *actor* (a person who performs) is *spectator.*

4. B. The opposite of *ornate* (much adorned) is plain or *severe.*

5. E. A *sycophant* is a flattering follower. *Leader* is the best opposite.

6. B. The opposite of *consummate* (complete) is to begin or *undertake.*

7. D. The opposite of *craven* (of abject spirit, cowardly) is *noble.*

8. B. A *neophyte* is a beginner and not *expert.*

9. B. The opposite of *erratic* (odd, capricious) is *predictable.*

10. B. The opposite of *vituperative* (abusing, reviling) is *laudatory* (praising).

11. D. The opposite of *expatiate* (to expand upon) is *summarize* (to make a concise statement of).

12. A. *Averse* (unwilling) and *eager* (desirous) are opposites.

13. B. The opposite of *imbecility* (lack of mental ability is *intelligence.*

14. B. The opposite of *obliterate* (wipe out) is build up or *establish.*

15. A. The opposite of *schism* (division or split) is *union.*

16. D. It is logical to become fearful or *apprehensive* when a neighboring country begins to expand its military forces.

17. B. *Platitudes* (trite remarks) parallels *empty promises* and *cliches.*

18. D. A person who performs well with either hand is *ambidextrous.*

19. A. A book issued *posthumously* is published after the author's death.

20. D. A hypocrite pretends or *simulates* emotions which he does not feel.

21. D. The last sentence of the passage supports Choice D.

22. E. The phrase "optical afterglow" supports Choice E.

23. E. The passage points out the values of democratic life and indicates how it is derided. Choice E emphasizes the fact that we fail to appreciate our advantages.

24. B. The statement that "they have become too familiar" supports Choice B.

25. C. Since the author uses words like "cheap" and "sneering," we may assume that he is *very contemptuous.*

26. A. The opening and closing sentences emphasize the value of argument (Choice A).

27. B. The last sentence emphasizes that argument is an "indispensable means of . . . . impressing others."

28. D. The author states that argument is used badly when it results in mere wrangling and disputing.

29. A. Choice A is supported in the second sentence.

30. B. The last two sentences of the passage support Choice B.

31. B. If the times are *parlous* (difficult, disconcerting), a person cannot afford to be optimistic or *sanguine.*

32. C. A *continent* person is highly moral and is not *dissolute* (morally lax).

33. C. *Mundane* or earthly matters will not concern a person who is *spiritual* (not concerned with earthly matters, highly religious).

34. C. The failure occurred in spite of his efforts. *Despite* is best.

35. B. Gullible people will be fooled by *specious* (seemingly plausible) arguments.

36. D. Just as *words* are the material with which a *writer* works, *batter* (the mixture of ingredients in a cake) is the materials with which a *baker* works.

37. B. An *aria* (operatic song) is performed by a *diva* (great female singer). A *soliloquy* is delivered by an *actor.*

38. E. A *buoy* indicates the proper *channel* for a ship to follow; *laws* indicate the proper *conduct* for people or society to follow.

39. B. An *autobiography* is a personal statement about one's own life and is similar to a *confession.* A *biography* is written about someone else and is similar to *testimony* about another person's conduct.

40. B. The *basement* is the lowest portion of a house and can be matched by *nadir,* the lowest point. Similarly, the *attic* is the highest portion of a house and can be matched by *zenith.*

41. D. A person characterized by *anger* is defined as *choleric*; one characterized by *greed*, as *avaricious*.

42. C. A *shrug* shows *indifference*; a *nod* indicates *assent*.

43. E. *Success* may make one satisfied or *complacent; rejection* may make one *despondent* (dejected; depressed).

44. A. *Usury* is an excessive or extreme form of *interest*; *parsimony* (stinginess) is an extreme form of *frugality* (thrift).

45. C. *Grain is* kept in a *silo*; *water* is kept in a *bucket.*

SECTION 2

1. B. Cross multiply: $5v + 4x = 21$
Subtract $5v$ $\quad 4x = 21 - 5v$
Divide by 4 $\quad x = \dfrac{21 - 5v}{4}$

2. A. Substitute values

$$\frac{\frac{2}{3}+\frac{5}{7}}{\frac{2}{3}-\frac{5}{7}} = \frac{\frac{14}{21}+\frac{15}{21}}{\frac{14}{21}-\frac{15}{21}} = \frac{\frac{29}{21}}{\frac{-1}{21}} = \frac{29}{-1} = -29$$

3. B. The minimum number of workers in two libraries can be 7 × 2 or 14, for there will be 60 − 14 or 46 workers remaining for the other 4 branches. These 46 workers can be assigned to the 4 libraries without exceeding the specified maximum of 18 in any one library.

4. E. $\dfrac{F}{1} = \dfrac{Gm_1m_2}{r^2}$

Cross multiply $\quad Fr^2 = Gm_1m_2$

Divide by Gm_2 $\quad \dfrac{Fr^2}{Gm_2} = m_1$

5. E. Cross multiply. $x = 16 \times .375$
$x = 6$

6. C. Two halves of $2\frac{1}{2} = 2\frac{1}{2}$

$2\frac{1}{2}$ plus $2\frac{1}{2} = 5$

7. D. There are 360° in a circle. 20% (or $\frac{1}{5}$) of 360° = 72°

8. E. *AD* is larger than *AC*. It is $\frac{3}{2}$ as large or $1\frac{1}{2}$ or 150%

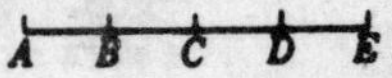

9. C. $\frac{a}{b}$ and $\frac{x}{a}$ are each equal to c and therefore equal to each other. $\quad \dfrac{a}{b} = \dfrac{x}{a}$

Cross multiply: $\quad a^2 = bx$

Extract $\sqrt{\ }$ of both sides: $\quad a = \pm\sqrt{bx}$

10. B. Since 0.6 is the average

$$\frac{0.2 + 0.8 + 1.0 + x}{4} = 0.6$$

Cross multiply: $\quad 2.4 = 2 + x$
$x = 0.4$

11. C. In a proportion, the two means (or extremes) may be interchanged.
Since $\frac{2x}{5} = \frac{9}{1}$, interchanging the means, 9 and 5, we get $\frac{2x}{9} = \frac{5}{1}$ or 5

12. C. In right triangle *ADC*
$x^2 + x^2 = 50^2$
$2x^2 = 2500$
$x^2 = 1250$
Area of square $= s^2$, where s = side of square
Area of square $= x^2$ or 1250

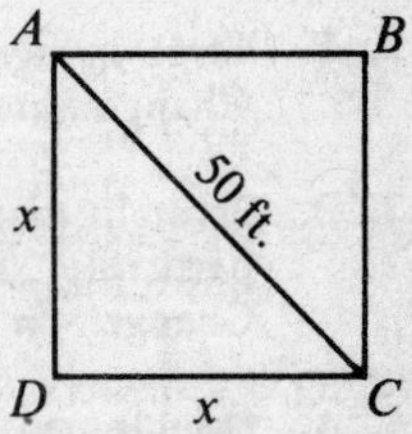

13. C. If the man was r years old s years ago, he is now $r + s$ years; t years hence he will be $r + s + t$

14. D. $\frac{y}{16\frac{1}{3}} = \frac{3}{y}$

$\frac{y}{\frac{49}{3}} = \frac{3}{y}$

$y^2 = 49$

$y = \pm 7$; $+7$ is one of the choices.

15. E. A man binds 112 books in one day and his assistant works one quarter as fast and binds 28 books in one day. Since they work on alternate days, they produce an average of $\frac{112 + 28}{2}$ or 70 books each day, so it takes $\frac{560}{70}$ or 8 days to produce 560 books.

16. E. Each side = 2
Area of square = 4
The four semi-circles equal 2 circles with diameter = 2, radius = 1
The area of one circle = $\pi(1)^2$ or π
The area of two circles = 2π
Therefore the area of the entire figure is $4 + 2\pi$

17. A. Since there are 45 pupils in the class, and two thirds are boys, there are 30 boys in the class. If one half of the boys are blue-eyed, 15 boys are blue-eyed.

18. D. The best way to do this is to start with the answer (A) and substitute the values of the table in each of the possible answers. (A) is not correct because when $R = 2$, S does not equal 5. (B) is not the correct answer because when $R = 3$, S does not $= 8$. (C) is not correct because when $R = 1$, S does not $= 2$. $S = 3R - 1$ is satisfied by all values in the table. $(3 \times 1) - (1) = 2$, $(3 \times 2) - 1 = 5$, $(3 \times 3) - 1 = 8$, $(4 \times 3) - 1 = 11$, $(5 \times 3) - 1 = 14$, and $(6 \times 3) - 1 = 17$. (E) is not correct because when $R = 1$, S does not $= 2$.

19. C. The auto travels 30 miles from X to Y in 20 minutes. At this rate the car averages 90 miles in 60 minutes or 1 hour.

20. D. Twelve four-pound weights weigh 48 pounds. It takes 16 three-pound weights to weigh 48 pounds.

21. E. $\frac{a}{b} - \frac{a}{c}$

Use bc as a common denominator: $\frac{ac - ab}{bc}$

22. B. $4r = 5t$ $\qquad 4r = 5t$

Divide by 4: $\qquad r = \frac{5t}{4}$

Since $\qquad r = \frac{s}{3}$

Then $\qquad \frac{s}{3} = \frac{5t}{4}$ (since they each equal r)

Cross multiply: $4s = 15t$

Divide by 4: $\qquad s = \frac{15t}{4}$

23. A. $\frac{n}{7} + \frac{n}{5} = \frac{12}{35}$

Multiply each side by 35: $5n + 7n = 12$

$12n = 12$

$n = 1$

24. C. 12 kittens consume 4 cans. The remaining 4 cans can feed 8 cats.

25. A. Since x is greater than 1, $218x$ is greater than 218. Since none of the numbers is less than 218, it is impossible for the average of the numbers to be 218. The average of a group of numbers cannot be less than the smallest of the numbers nor greater than the largest of the numbers. If x is large, the average of the numbers may be 2839.

SECTION 3

1. A. Error in diction. Change *Being that* to *Since.*

2. B. Error in agreement between subject and verb. Change *have control* to *has control.*

3. B. Error in case. A noun or pronoun preceding a participle should be in the possessive case. Change *son to son's.*

4. A. Double negative. Change *can't* to *can.*

5. A. Dangling participle. Change participle to a subordinate clause, *As he stroked his beard thoughtfully.*

6. C. Error in case. Change *I* to *me.*

7. B. Error in diction. Change *healthy* to *healthful.*

8. D. Change *reason . . . is because* to *reason . . . that.*

9. E. Sentence is correct.

10. E. Sentence is correct.

11. B. Error in tense. Change *am playing* to *have been playing.*

12. D. Lack of parallel structure. Change the clause *what his serial number was* to a noun (*serial number*) to match the other items mentioned in the sentence.

13. E. Sentence is correct.

14. E. Sentence is correct.

15. B. Error in capitalization in a direct quotation. Should be "*going.* . . .

16. B. Error in diction. Change *affective* to *effective.*

17. C. The pronoun *which* should not refer to a clause. Change by writing the statement as two sentences: *The teacher ordered the student to go to the dean's office. This (order) surprised us.* . . .

18. B. Error in agreement. Change *their* to *his.*

19. A. Avoid the expression *kind of a person.* Omit the article (*a*).

20. E. Sentence is correct.

21. B. Error in diction. *Among* should be used when three or more items are being considered.

22. C. Error in diction. Change *bring* to *take.*

23. B. Error in case. Change *him* to *his.*

24. E. Sentence is correct.

25. B. The verb *feels* should be followed by an adjective (*bad*).

26. E. The dangling modifier is corrected in Choice E.

27. D. Choice D corrects the dangling modifier of the original sentence.

28. B. The error in case is corrected in Choice B. *Whoever* is the subject of the verb *had contributed.*

29. D. *Irregardless* is a nonstandard use of *regardless.*

30. B. The run-on sentence is corrected in Choice B.

31. E. In this question we find two errors. Both the sentence fragment and the misuse of the intransitive verb *lie* are corrected in Choice E.

32. D. The faulty comparison is corrected in Choice D.

33. A. The original sentence is correct. The subject of *are going* is *legislators* (plural). Therefore, Choices B and C are incorrect. Choices D and E change the meaning of the original sentence.

34. A. The correct use of the subjunctive mood to indicate a condition contrary to fact is found in Choice A.

35. A. Choice B introduces an error in agreement. Choices C, D, and E misuse the *not only* . . . *but also* construction.

36. C. Choice C uses *drank,* the correct form of the irregular verb *drink.*

37. D. The phrase *along with several other stories* is not part of the subject of the sentence. The subject is *"Araby"* (singular); the verb should be *is going to be read* (singular).

38. B. *Seems satisfying their need* is unidiomatic. *Seems to satisfy their need* is correct (Choice B).

39. C. Choice C corrects the error in conjunction use.

40. A. The original sentence is correct. The singular pronoun *it* refers to the subject of the main clause, *fate* (singular).

41. A. Dangling construction. One way to correct this error is to provide a word for the infinitive (*To invest*) to modify. *To invest intelligently, the average investor should consider.* . . .

42. B. Error in case. *But,* as used in this sentence, is a preposition meaning *except.* Change *he* to *him.*

43. E. Sentence is correct.

44. A. Error in diction. *Altogether* is correct.

45. C. Misplaced modifier. The word *only* should be placed in front of *once.*

46. D. Improper comparison. Change *southern California* to *that of southern California.*

47. E. Sentence is correct.

48. A. Error in case. Change *whom* to *who.*

49. B. Error in case. Change *company* to *company's.*

50. E. Sentence is correct.

SECTION 4

1. C. *Garrulous* (overly talkative) is the opposite of *pithy* (concise).

2. B. *Gargantuan* (large, gigantic) is the opposite of *Lilliputian* (tiny).

3. D. *Menial* describes a person who does lowly domestic work. Such a person would not be haughty or *supercilious*.

4. B. *Quixotic* (impractical, visionary) is the opposite of *feasible* (practical).

5. D. The opposite of *noisome* (foul-smelling) is *fragrant*.

6. E. The opposite of *bellicose* (warlike) is *pacific* (peaceful).

7. A. The opposite of *famished* (starved) is *sated* (stuffed).

8. C. A person or thing that is *yielding* gives way easily or is soft. Its opposite is hard or *impenetrable*.

9. B. The opposite of *scrupulous* (careful in attending to details) is *remiss* (careless).

10. A. The opposite of *mollify* (appease, placate) is *annoy*.

11. C. *Connotations* (the implications or overtones a word carries in addition to its primary meaning) are most difficult to translate.

12. C. Critics of democracy as a form of government maintain that it often is slow, cumbersome, and *inefficient*.

13. E. *Humility* parallels *reticence*.

14. C. To acquaint the general public (*laity*) with the stories of the Bible, the clergy and missionaries had to tell the stories in the native tongue or the *vernacular*.

15. B. A *hypochondriac* suffers from unwarranted fear of illness.

16. C. The function of the *heart* is to *pump*; the function of the *stomach* is to *digest*.

17. B. A *stanza* is a subdivision of a *poem*; a *scene* is a subdivision of a *play*.

18. A. An *amulet* is a charm designed to repel *evil*; a *fort* is a stronghold designed to repel *attack*.

19. B. A *servant* serves his *master*; a *vassal* serves his *monarch*.

20. C. A *mongrel* is of mixed breed while a *collie* is a pure breed. An alloy is a mixture of metals; iron is a single metal.

21. C. A *trowel* is a tool used by a *mason*; an *adze*, a tool used by a *carpenter*.

22. B. One seeks to *amass* or gather *wealth* to preserve it; one seeks to *garner grain* to store it.

23. D. A suitable adjective describing a known *malefactor* is *notorious;* a suitable adjective describing a known *benefactor* is *renowned.*

24. B. A *connoisseur* is a critical judge of *paintings*, etc. A *gourmet* is an expert in the field of food or *viands*.

25. D. A *cartographer* (map drawer) would be connected with a *gazetteer* (geographical dictionary). A *lexicographer* is a writer of *dictionaries*.

26. E. The last sentence discusses how merchants use miscalculations to cheat the Tartars.

27. B. The last sentence supports Choice B.

28. A. The last sentence supports Choice A.

29. C. After the first two sentences, the entire passage is devoted to a discussion of the place and purpose of rhythm and rhyme in modern poetry.

30. D. The first sentence states that free verse "reaches back to the incantations" or chants.

31. A. Choice A is supported by the second sentence.

32. E. The passage discusses aspects of weightlessness in space.

33. A. The last sentence supports Choice A.

34. D. The second sentence supports Choice D. Note that Choice B is incorrect because of the use of "centripetal" instead of "centrifugal."

35. C. Throughout the passage, the author tells us of things that will not happen in a state of weightlessness. "Warm carbon dioxide will not rise" in the cabin. By inference, we may assume that warm carbon dioxide does rise on earth and is lighter than air.

36. E. The sentence in parentheses (sentence 10) supports Choice E.

37. A. The opening sentence of the second paragraph supports Choice A.

38. D. The rain forest is still "primeval" because it has been untouched.

39. B. The author's contention that these forests should be preserved would be supported by conservationists and botanists.

40. C. Although the author mentions the magnitude of the forests, he predicts that they can be wiped out. They are, therefore, limited.

SECTION 5

1. C. s equals $\frac{1}{r}$ since each equals 3. Things equal to the same thing are equal to each other.

$$s = \frac{1}{r}$$

Cross multiply: $rs = 1$

Divide by s: $r = \frac{1}{s}$

2. B. If two parts of sand are mixed with three parts of gravel, there are five parts of mixture. Since there are 2 parts of sand, $\frac{2}{5}$ of the mixture is sand.

3. B. $2.3y = 46$

Multiply by 10: $23y = 460$

Divide by 23: $y = 20$

4. B. Reduce the fractions: $\frac{8}{10} = \frac{4}{5}$ and $\frac{12}{15} = \frac{4}{5}$

$$\frac{4}{5} - \frac{4}{5} = 0$$

5. E. $\dfrac{1}{N + \frac{1}{N}} = \dfrac{1}{\frac{N^2}{N} + \frac{1}{N}}$ or $\dfrac{1}{\frac{N^2+1}{N}}$ or $\dfrac{N}{N^2+1}$

6. D. 100 is the common denominator.

$\frac{5}{4} = \frac{125}{100}$ $\frac{6}{5} = \frac{120}{100}$ $\frac{13}{10} = \frac{130}{100}$

$\frac{29}{25} = \frac{116}{100}$ $\frac{59}{50} = \frac{118}{100}$

The smallest fraction is $\frac{116}{100}$ or $\frac{29}{25}$

7. B. By looking at the graph half-way between 20 and 40 on the horizontal axis we may see that the market price is slightly less than 50 or 49.

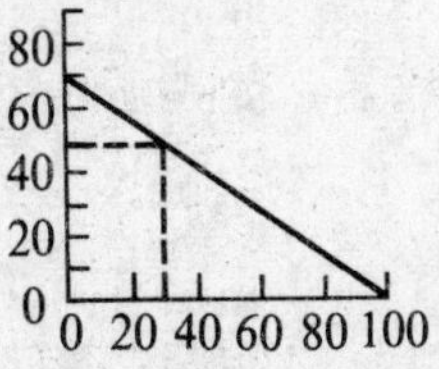

8. B. Since the value of the fraction is negative, the denominator must be negative since the numerator has a positive value. Therefore the value of x is less than 1.

9. A. $y^2 - 1 = 3$

$y^2 = 4$

$y = \pm 2$

Since $x = 3$, then x is larger than y.

10. D. Since $x^2 = 25$, $x = \pm 5$. If $x = +5$, then the correct choice would be (C).
However, if $x = -5$, then the correct choice would be (A).

11. C. In column A, $\dfrac{1}{x} \div \dfrac{1}{\frac{1}{x}}$ or, $\dfrac{1}{x} \div \dfrac{x}{1}$

or, $\dfrac{1}{x} \cdot \dfrac{1}{x}$ or, $\dfrac{1}{x^2}$

In column B, $\dfrac{1}{x} \cdot \dfrac{1}{x} = \dfrac{1}{x^2}$

12. D. x could be 9, 18, or 27.

13. B. 4 yards = 12 feet

4 yards, 2 feet = 14 feet

$\frac{1}{3}$ of (4 yards, 2 feet) = $\frac{14}{3} = 4\frac{2}{3}$ feet

1 yard, 4 feet = 7 feet

14. D. If n has a value of zero, then x could have any positive value.
If n has a value of 1, then x could be equal to 1.
If n has an even integral value, then x could be ± 1.

15. C. $\sqrt{\dfrac{2x}{y}} \cdot \sqrt{\dfrac{xy}{2}} = \sqrt{\dfrac{2x^2y}{2y}} = \sqrt{x^2} = x$

16. C. $\dfrac{\frac{3}{4}}{1 + \frac{1}{2}}$ or $\dfrac{\frac{3}{4}}{\frac{3}{2}}$ or $\dfrac{3}{4} \div \dfrac{3}{2}$ or $\dfrac{\cancel{3}}{\cancel{4}_2} \cdot \dfrac{\cancel{2}^1}{\cancel{3}} = \dfrac{1}{2}$

17. C. If $\frac{1}{2}AC = \frac{1}{2}BC = \frac{1}{2}AB$, then $AC = AB = BC$. The triangle is equilateral and $z = 60$. Since BD divides AC so that $AD = DC$, it is also perpendicular, forming right triangle BDC, and $x = 90$. This question is an application of the Pythagorean Theorem.

18. C. $y = 30$ and $z = 60$.

19. A. ABD is equilateral. $x = y = w = 60$. Since $AB \perp BC$, $y + z = 90$, and $z = 30$. BC lies opposite v which equals 120° and DC lies opposite the 30° angle. Therefore, $BC > DC$.

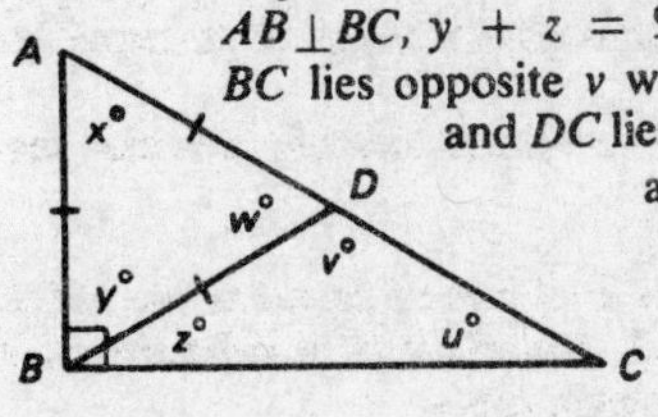

20. B. In triangle ABC, since the measure of angle $ABC = 90$, and $x = 60$, then $u = 30$. BD lies opposite the 30° angle and BC lies opposite a 120° angle (angle v). Therefore, BC>BD.

21. C. BD lies opposite $u°$, a 30° angle, and DC lies opposite $z°$, a 30° angle. $BD = DC$.

22. C. Radii OD and OC are equal legs of right triangle DOC. Area of $DOC = 1/2$ (leg) (leg) $= 12.5$ or $(\text{leg})^2 = 25$. Therefore, leg $= 5$. Since leg (or radius) equals 5, the area of the circle equals 25π.

23. C. DC is the hypotenuse of isosceles right triangle DOC. By the Pythagorean Theorem $(DC)^2 = (5)^2 + (5)^2$ or $(DC)^2 = 50$ or $DC = \sqrt{50}$ or $5\sqrt{2}$.

24. A. Since the measure of angle C is 60, then the measure of angle A + angle B is 120, and therefore the measure of angle A is more than $\frac{1}{2}$ of 120, since A is larger than B (given). Side CB lies opposite the angle with a measure of more than 60° and is therefore larger than side AB, which lies opposite the angle with a measure of 60°.

25. C. Since this is a parallelogram, $EH = FG$.

26. C. $EF + EH = \frac{1}{2}$ the perimeter.

27. C. The area of $ABCD = (BC)\ (DC)$ or $(2.5\pi)(10)$ or 25π. The area of the circle $= \pi r^2$. Since the diameter $= 10$, the radius $= 5$ and the area $= \pi r^2$ or 25π.

28. E. $42 : 63 = 28 : x$

or $\frac{42}{63} = \frac{28}{x}$

Reduce the fraction: $\frac{42}{63} = \frac{2}{3}$

Therefore $\frac{2}{3} = \frac{28}{x}$

$2x = 84$

$x = 42$

29. C. Recall the formula: $\frac{\text{Distance}}{\text{Rate}} = \text{Time}$

Substitute: $\frac{m}{h} = \text{Time}$

30. E. There are 9×60 or 540 minutes in 9 hours. The nurse needs a tablet when she begins and one every 45 minutes for 540 minutes. There are $\frac{540}{45}$ or 12 tablets needed for the nine hour period. Adding the tablet she gives at the beginning, she needs 13 tablets.

31. C. Applying the Pythagorean Theorem to this right triangle:

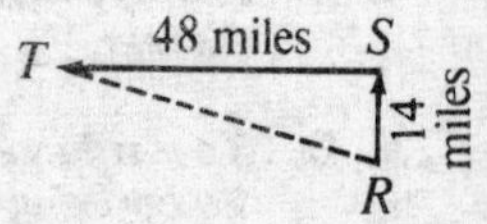

$(TR)^2 = (ST)^2 + (SR)^2$

The straight line distance RT is $\sqrt{14^2 + 48^2}$ or 50.

32. A. $2x - 3 = 2$

Add 3: $2x = 5$

Divide by 2: $x = \frac{5}{2}$

Find $x - \frac{1}{2}$ by substitution. $\frac{5}{2} - \frac{1}{2} = 2$

33. D. If both fractions have similiar denominators the problem is simplified.

$\frac{3}{t-s}$ or $\frac{3}{-s+t} = \frac{-3}{s-t}$

because the numerator and denominator are multiplied by -1. The problem now is

$\frac{2}{s-t} - \frac{-3}{s-t}$ or $\frac{5}{s-t}$

34. A. There are $4x$ quarter-miles in a trip of x miles. c cents is the charge for the first quarter-mile. The remaining quarter miles $(4x - 1)$ are s cents each or $s(4x - 1)$ cents. The total cost for the trip is $c + s(4x - 1)$ cents.

35. D. The dimensions of the first tank are 7 inches, 8 inches and one and one quarter feet (15 inches). The volume is $7 \times 8 \times 15$ cubic inches or 840 cubic inches. The volume (840 cubic inches) occupied in the second tank equals 13 inches $\times$ 20 inches $\times$ H inches or $260H$ cubic inches.

Since $260H = 840$, H equals $\frac{42}{13}$ or 3.2.

SECTION 6

1. C. The opposite of *apathetic* (indifferent) is *eager*.

2. D. The opposite of *graphic* (vivid) is *dull*.

3. C. A *dastard* is a coward. Its opposite is *hero*.

4. E. The opposite of *ephemeral* (short-lived) is *permanent*.

5. D. To *castigate* is to punish with blows or words. Its opposite is *praise*.

6. B. The opposite of *fester* (rot; grow putrid) is *heal*.

7. D. The opposite of *hilarity* (merriment) is *gloom*.

8. E. The opposite of *inevitable* (inescapable) is *avoidable*.

9. A. The opposite of *restraint* (moderation) is *excess*.

10. A. The opposite of *inarticulate* (unintelligible) is *distinct*.

11. A. The opposite of *insipid* (flavorless, dull) is *sparkling*.

12. B. The best opposite of *recondite* (abstruse, not too well known) is *popular*.

13. A. A *sententious* statement is pithy and aphoristic. Its opposite is *roundabout*.

14. C. The opposite of *affluent* (wealthy) is *impoverished* (poor).

15. A. A *felicitous* remark is apt and well-chosen. Its opposite is *inappropriate*.

16. B. To sharpen (*edge*) tools and instruments, *abrasive* tools are used.

17. B. Many writers have commented about the lack of concern that people who live in areas of danger (volcanoes, tornadoes, earthquakes) display.

18. C. *Alpha* and *Omega* are the first and last letters of the Greek alphabet. Parallelism justifies the choice of *beginning* and *end*.

19. B. To be unable to provide rooms for people is to be unable to *accommodate* them.

20. E. *Actuarial* (pertaining to statistics of mortality rates) tables indicate that the life expectancy of Americans is on the rise or *waxing*.

21. A. The author develops the concept that there is an indigenous American school of painting. Choice A is best.

22. B. The second sentence of paragraph 2 supports Choice B.

23. D. The last sentence of the passage indicates that Choice D (painters who migrated to America) is the logical selection.

24. B. The author maintains that most American artists "developed on their own." Whistler, Sargent, and Mary Cassatt are exceptions to this general rule; they were affected by their European visit. Choice B is best.

25. B. The illustrations given by the author in the second paragraph indicate how "useless" study of conic sections and electricity has been of unexpected and tremendous value to man. Choice B is best.

26. E. In the opening sentence the author mentions Choices A, B, C, and D. He does not mention *literature* (Choice E).

27. C. In the first paragraph, the author mentions *philosophy* and adds "about which we will talk later." We may assume that he will begin his discussion as soon as possible.

28. C. In the second paragraph we are told that the Greeks studied conic sections "without the least suspicion that it might someday be useful." This supports Choice C.

29. D. The author is stressing the value of pure research or "learning for its own sake."

30. A. Sentence 2 of the second paragraph tells us that the practical scientist knows what the value of his discoveries will be. We are told that the results are forseeable (Choice A).

31. C. Since *fortuitous* (due to chance, by accident) relates most closely with *coincidence*, we can support Choice C.

32. B. Sign language is useful when words are unavailable or when a person has *linguistic* difficulties.

33. C. *Peccadilloes* are minor offenses.

34. B. A *meticulous* person is precise and careful.

35. E. Disbelief or *incredulity* in the face of strong evidence indicates a closed or *opinionated* mind.

36. B. Just as a *novelist* uses a *plot* as a plan for the novel he is writing, the *architect* prepares a *blueprint* as a guide for his further work.

37. A. To *slink* is to walk with *stealth;* to *whine* is an act of *querulousness*.

38. D. ***Abhor*** **(hate) is more extreme than *dislike; demolish,* more extreme than *damage.***

39. D. ***Sedulous*** **and *diligent* are synonyms; likewise, *ingenuous* and *naive* are synonyms.**

40. B. **Those who *wince* indicate *pain;* those who *blush, embarrassment.***

41. B. A *heckler* is someone who *jeers;* a *grumbler,* someone who *complains.*

42. A. One must *stanch bleeding* to check the flow of blood; one must *dam* a *flood* to prevent an overflow of water.

43. E. **Just as the *dregs* (sediment) must be separated from *wine, slag* must be separated from *iron.***

44. A. Something *uproarious* is extremely *amusing;* something *dumbfounding,* extremely *puzzling.*

45. D. A *carapace* (hard case) protects a *turtle;* a *shell* protects a *snail.*

ANSWER SHEET—TEST 2

SECTION 1

1. Ⓐ Ⓑ Ⓒ Ⓓ Ⓔ	11. Ⓐ Ⓑ Ⓒ Ⓓ Ⓔ	21. Ⓐ Ⓑ Ⓒ Ⓓ Ⓔ	31. Ⓐ Ⓑ Ⓒ Ⓓ Ⓔ	41. Ⓐ Ⓑ Ⓒ Ⓓ Ⓔ
2. Ⓐ Ⓑ Ⓒ Ⓓ Ⓔ	12. Ⓐ Ⓑ Ⓒ Ⓓ Ⓔ	22. Ⓐ Ⓑ Ⓒ Ⓓ Ⓔ	32. Ⓐ Ⓑ Ⓒ Ⓓ Ⓔ	42. Ⓐ Ⓑ Ⓒ Ⓓ Ⓔ
3. Ⓐ Ⓑ Ⓒ Ⓓ Ⓔ	13. Ⓐ Ⓑ Ⓒ Ⓓ Ⓔ	23. Ⓐ Ⓑ Ⓒ Ⓓ Ⓔ	33. Ⓐ Ⓑ Ⓒ Ⓓ Ⓔ	43. Ⓐ Ⓑ Ⓒ Ⓓ Ⓔ
4. Ⓐ Ⓑ Ⓒ Ⓓ Ⓔ	14. Ⓐ Ⓑ Ⓒ Ⓓ Ⓔ	24. Ⓐ Ⓑ Ⓒ Ⓓ Ⓔ	34. Ⓐ Ⓑ Ⓒ Ⓓ Ⓔ	44. Ⓐ Ⓑ Ⓒ Ⓓ Ⓔ
5. Ⓐ Ⓑ Ⓒ Ⓓ Ⓔ	15. Ⓐ Ⓑ Ⓒ Ⓓ Ⓔ	25. Ⓐ Ⓑ Ⓒ Ⓓ Ⓔ	35. Ⓐ Ⓑ Ⓒ Ⓓ Ⓔ	45. Ⓐ Ⓑ Ⓒ Ⓓ Ⓔ
6. Ⓐ Ⓑ Ⓒ Ⓓ Ⓔ	16. Ⓐ Ⓑ Ⓒ Ⓓ Ⓔ	26. Ⓐ Ⓑ Ⓒ Ⓓ Ⓔ	36. Ⓐ Ⓑ Ⓒ Ⓓ Ⓔ	46. Ⓐ Ⓑ Ⓒ Ⓓ Ⓔ
7. Ⓐ Ⓑ Ⓒ Ⓓ Ⓔ	17. Ⓐ Ⓑ Ⓒ Ⓓ Ⓔ	27. Ⓐ Ⓑ Ⓒ Ⓓ Ⓔ	37. Ⓐ Ⓑ Ⓒ Ⓓ Ⓔ	47. Ⓐ Ⓑ Ⓒ Ⓓ Ⓔ
8. Ⓐ Ⓑ Ⓒ Ⓓ Ⓔ	18. Ⓐ Ⓑ Ⓒ Ⓓ Ⓔ	28. Ⓐ Ⓑ Ⓒ Ⓓ Ⓔ	38. Ⓐ Ⓑ Ⓒ Ⓓ Ⓔ	48. Ⓐ Ⓑ Ⓒ Ⓓ Ⓔ
9. Ⓐ Ⓑ Ⓒ Ⓓ Ⓔ	19. Ⓐ Ⓑ Ⓒ Ⓓ Ⓔ	29. Ⓐ Ⓑ Ⓒ Ⓓ Ⓔ	39. Ⓐ Ⓑ Ⓒ Ⓓ Ⓔ	49. Ⓐ Ⓑ Ⓒ Ⓓ Ⓔ
10. Ⓐ Ⓑ Ⓒ Ⓓ Ⓔ	20. Ⓐ Ⓑ Ⓒ Ⓓ Ⓔ	30. Ⓐ Ⓑ Ⓒ Ⓓ Ⓔ	40. Ⓐ Ⓑ Ⓒ Ⓓ Ⓔ	50. Ⓐ Ⓑ Ⓒ Ⓓ Ⓔ

SECTION 2

1. Ⓐ Ⓑ Ⓒ Ⓓ Ⓔ	11. Ⓐ Ⓑ Ⓒ Ⓓ Ⓔ	21. Ⓐ Ⓑ Ⓒ Ⓓ Ⓔ	31. Ⓐ Ⓑ Ⓒ Ⓓ Ⓔ	41. Ⓐ Ⓑ Ⓒ Ⓓ Ⓔ
2. Ⓐ Ⓑ Ⓒ Ⓓ Ⓔ	12. Ⓐ Ⓑ Ⓒ Ⓓ Ⓔ	22. Ⓐ Ⓑ Ⓒ Ⓓ Ⓔ	32. Ⓐ Ⓑ Ⓒ Ⓓ Ⓔ	42. Ⓐ Ⓑ Ⓒ Ⓓ Ⓔ
3. Ⓐ Ⓑ Ⓒ Ⓓ Ⓔ	13. Ⓐ Ⓑ Ⓒ Ⓓ Ⓔ	23. Ⓐ Ⓑ Ⓒ Ⓓ Ⓔ	33. Ⓐ Ⓑ Ⓒ Ⓓ Ⓔ	43. Ⓐ Ⓑ Ⓒ Ⓓ Ⓔ
4. Ⓐ Ⓑ Ⓒ Ⓓ Ⓔ	14. Ⓐ Ⓑ Ⓒ Ⓓ Ⓔ	24. Ⓐ Ⓑ Ⓒ Ⓓ Ⓔ	34. Ⓐ Ⓑ Ⓒ Ⓓ Ⓔ	44. Ⓐ Ⓑ Ⓒ Ⓓ Ⓔ
5. Ⓐ Ⓑ Ⓒ Ⓓ Ⓔ	15. Ⓐ Ⓑ Ⓒ Ⓓ Ⓔ	25. Ⓐ Ⓑ Ⓒ Ⓓ Ⓔ	35. Ⓐ Ⓑ Ⓒ Ⓓ Ⓔ	45. Ⓐ Ⓑ Ⓒ Ⓓ Ⓔ
6. Ⓐ Ⓑ Ⓒ Ⓓ Ⓔ	16. Ⓐ Ⓑ Ⓒ Ⓓ Ⓔ	26. Ⓐ Ⓑ Ⓒ Ⓓ Ⓔ	36. Ⓐ Ⓑ Ⓒ Ⓓ Ⓔ	46. Ⓐ Ⓑ Ⓒ Ⓓ Ⓔ
7. Ⓐ Ⓑ Ⓒ Ⓓ Ⓔ	17. Ⓐ Ⓑ Ⓒ Ⓓ Ⓔ	27. Ⓐ Ⓑ Ⓒ Ⓓ Ⓔ	37. Ⓐ Ⓑ Ⓒ Ⓓ Ⓔ	47. Ⓐ Ⓑ Ⓒ Ⓓ Ⓔ
8. Ⓐ Ⓑ Ⓒ Ⓓ Ⓔ	18. Ⓐ Ⓑ Ⓒ Ⓓ Ⓔ	28. Ⓐ Ⓑ Ⓒ Ⓓ Ⓔ	38. Ⓐ Ⓑ Ⓒ Ⓓ Ⓔ	48. Ⓐ Ⓑ Ⓒ Ⓓ Ⓔ
9. Ⓐ Ⓑ Ⓒ Ⓓ Ⓔ	19. Ⓐ Ⓑ Ⓒ Ⓓ Ⓔ	29. Ⓐ Ⓑ Ⓒ Ⓓ Ⓔ	39. Ⓐ Ⓑ Ⓒ Ⓓ Ⓔ	49. Ⓐ Ⓑ Ⓒ Ⓓ Ⓔ
10. Ⓐ Ⓑ Ⓒ Ⓓ Ⓔ	20. Ⓐ Ⓑ Ⓒ Ⓓ Ⓔ	30. Ⓐ Ⓑ Ⓒ Ⓓ Ⓔ	40. Ⓐ Ⓑ Ⓒ Ⓓ Ⓔ	50. Ⓐ Ⓑ Ⓒ Ⓓ Ⓔ

SECTION 3

1. Ⓐ Ⓑ Ⓒ Ⓓ Ⓔ	11. Ⓐ Ⓑ Ⓒ Ⓓ Ⓔ	21. Ⓐ Ⓑ Ⓒ Ⓓ Ⓔ	31. Ⓐ Ⓑ Ⓒ Ⓓ Ⓔ	41. Ⓐ Ⓑ Ⓒ Ⓓ Ⓔ
2. Ⓐ Ⓑ Ⓒ Ⓓ Ⓔ	12. Ⓐ Ⓑ Ⓒ Ⓓ Ⓔ	22. Ⓐ Ⓑ Ⓒ Ⓓ Ⓔ	32. Ⓐ Ⓑ Ⓒ Ⓓ Ⓔ	42. Ⓐ Ⓑ Ⓒ Ⓓ Ⓔ
3. Ⓐ Ⓑ Ⓒ Ⓓ Ⓔ	13. Ⓐ Ⓑ Ⓒ Ⓓ Ⓔ	23. Ⓐ Ⓑ Ⓒ Ⓓ Ⓔ	33. Ⓐ Ⓑ Ⓒ Ⓓ Ⓔ	43. Ⓐ Ⓑ Ⓒ Ⓓ Ⓔ
4. Ⓐ Ⓑ Ⓒ Ⓓ Ⓔ	14. Ⓐ Ⓑ Ⓒ Ⓓ Ⓔ	24. Ⓐ Ⓑ Ⓒ Ⓓ Ⓔ	34. Ⓐ Ⓑ Ⓒ Ⓓ Ⓔ	44. Ⓐ Ⓑ Ⓒ Ⓓ Ⓔ
5. Ⓐ Ⓑ Ⓒ Ⓓ Ⓔ	15. Ⓐ Ⓑ Ⓒ Ⓓ Ⓔ	25. Ⓐ Ⓑ Ⓒ Ⓓ Ⓔ	35. Ⓐ Ⓑ Ⓒ Ⓓ Ⓔ	45. Ⓐ Ⓑ Ⓒ Ⓓ Ⓔ
6. Ⓐ Ⓑ Ⓒ Ⓓ Ⓔ	16. Ⓐ Ⓑ Ⓒ Ⓓ Ⓔ	26. Ⓐ Ⓑ Ⓒ Ⓓ Ⓔ	36. Ⓐ Ⓑ Ⓒ Ⓓ Ⓔ	46. Ⓐ Ⓑ Ⓒ Ⓓ Ⓔ
7. Ⓐ Ⓑ Ⓒ Ⓓ Ⓔ	17. Ⓐ Ⓑ Ⓒ Ⓓ Ⓔ	27. Ⓐ Ⓑ Ⓒ Ⓓ Ⓔ	37. Ⓐ Ⓑ Ⓒ Ⓓ Ⓔ	47. Ⓐ Ⓑ Ⓒ Ⓓ Ⓔ
8. Ⓐ Ⓑ Ⓒ Ⓓ Ⓔ	18. Ⓐ Ⓑ Ⓒ Ⓓ Ⓔ	28. Ⓐ Ⓑ Ⓒ Ⓓ Ⓔ	38. Ⓐ Ⓑ Ⓒ Ⓓ Ⓔ	48. Ⓐ Ⓑ Ⓒ Ⓓ Ⓔ
9. Ⓐ Ⓑ Ⓒ Ⓓ Ⓔ	19. Ⓐ Ⓑ Ⓒ Ⓓ Ⓔ	29. Ⓐ Ⓑ Ⓒ Ⓓ Ⓔ	39. Ⓐ Ⓑ Ⓒ Ⓓ Ⓔ	49. Ⓐ Ⓑ Ⓒ Ⓓ Ⓔ
10. Ⓐ Ⓑ Ⓒ Ⓓ Ⓔ	20. Ⓐ Ⓑ Ⓒ Ⓓ Ⓔ	30. Ⓐ Ⓑ Ⓒ Ⓓ Ⓔ	40. Ⓐ Ⓑ Ⓒ Ⓓ Ⓔ	50. Ⓐ Ⓑ Ⓒ Ⓓ Ⓔ

Remove answer sheet by cutting on dotted line

SECTION 4

1. Ⓐ Ⓑ Ⓒ Ⓓ Ⓔ	11. Ⓐ Ⓑ Ⓒ Ⓓ Ⓔ	21. Ⓐ Ⓑ Ⓒ Ⓓ Ⓔ	31. Ⓐ Ⓑ Ⓒ Ⓓ Ⓔ	41. Ⓐ Ⓑ Ⓒ Ⓓ Ⓔ
2. Ⓐ Ⓑ Ⓒ Ⓓ Ⓔ	12. Ⓐ Ⓑ Ⓒ Ⓓ Ⓔ	22. Ⓐ Ⓑ Ⓒ Ⓓ Ⓔ	32. Ⓐ Ⓑ Ⓒ Ⓓ Ⓔ	42. Ⓐ Ⓑ Ⓒ Ⓓ Ⓔ
3. Ⓐ Ⓑ Ⓒ Ⓓ Ⓔ	13. Ⓐ Ⓑ Ⓒ Ⓓ Ⓔ	23. Ⓐ Ⓑ Ⓒ Ⓓ Ⓔ	33. Ⓐ Ⓑ Ⓒ Ⓓ Ⓔ	43. Ⓐ Ⓑ Ⓒ Ⓓ Ⓔ
4. Ⓐ Ⓑ Ⓒ Ⓓ Ⓔ	14. Ⓐ Ⓑ Ⓒ Ⓓ Ⓔ	24. Ⓐ Ⓑ Ⓒ Ⓓ Ⓔ	34. Ⓐ Ⓑ Ⓒ Ⓓ Ⓔ	44. Ⓐ Ⓑ Ⓒ Ⓓ Ⓔ
5. Ⓐ Ⓑ Ⓒ Ⓓ Ⓔ	15. Ⓐ Ⓑ Ⓒ Ⓓ Ⓔ	25. Ⓐ Ⓑ Ⓒ Ⓓ Ⓔ	35. Ⓐ Ⓑ Ⓒ Ⓓ Ⓔ	45. Ⓐ Ⓑ Ⓒ Ⓓ Ⓔ
6. Ⓐ Ⓑ Ⓒ Ⓓ Ⓔ	16. Ⓐ Ⓑ Ⓒ Ⓓ Ⓔ	26. Ⓐ Ⓑ Ⓒ Ⓓ Ⓔ	36. Ⓐ Ⓑ Ⓒ Ⓓ Ⓔ	46. Ⓐ Ⓑ Ⓒ Ⓓ Ⓔ
7. Ⓐ Ⓑ Ⓒ Ⓓ Ⓔ	17. Ⓐ Ⓑ Ⓒ Ⓓ Ⓔ	27. Ⓐ Ⓑ Ⓒ Ⓓ Ⓔ	37. Ⓐ Ⓑ Ⓒ Ⓓ Ⓔ	47. Ⓐ Ⓑ Ⓒ Ⓓ Ⓔ
8. Ⓐ Ⓑ Ⓒ Ⓓ Ⓔ	18. Ⓐ Ⓑ Ⓒ Ⓓ Ⓔ	28. Ⓐ Ⓑ Ⓒ Ⓓ Ⓔ	38. Ⓐ Ⓑ Ⓒ Ⓓ Ⓔ	48. Ⓐ Ⓑ Ⓒ Ⓓ Ⓔ
9. Ⓐ Ⓑ Ⓒ Ⓓ Ⓔ	19. Ⓐ Ⓑ Ⓒ Ⓓ Ⓔ	29. Ⓐ Ⓑ Ⓒ Ⓓ Ⓔ	39. Ⓐ Ⓑ Ⓒ Ⓓ Ⓔ	49. Ⓐ Ⓑ Ⓒ Ⓓ Ⓔ
10. Ⓐ Ⓑ Ⓒ Ⓓ Ⓔ	20. Ⓐ Ⓑ Ⓒ Ⓓ Ⓔ	30. Ⓐ Ⓑ Ⓒ Ⓓ Ⓔ	40. Ⓐ Ⓑ Ⓒ Ⓓ Ⓔ	50. Ⓐ Ⓑ Ⓒ Ⓓ Ⓔ

SECTION 5

1. Ⓐ Ⓑ Ⓒ Ⓓ Ⓔ	11. Ⓐ Ⓑ Ⓒ Ⓓ Ⓔ	21. Ⓐ Ⓑ Ⓒ Ⓓ Ⓔ	31. Ⓐ Ⓑ Ⓒ Ⓓ Ⓔ	41. Ⓐ Ⓑ Ⓒ Ⓓ Ⓔ
2. Ⓐ Ⓑ Ⓒ Ⓓ Ⓔ	12. Ⓐ Ⓑ Ⓒ Ⓓ Ⓔ	22. Ⓐ Ⓑ Ⓒ Ⓓ Ⓔ	32. Ⓐ Ⓑ Ⓒ Ⓓ Ⓔ	42. Ⓐ Ⓑ Ⓒ Ⓓ Ⓔ
3. Ⓐ Ⓑ Ⓒ Ⓓ Ⓔ	13. Ⓐ Ⓑ Ⓒ Ⓓ Ⓔ	23. Ⓐ Ⓑ Ⓒ Ⓓ Ⓔ	33. Ⓐ Ⓑ Ⓒ Ⓓ Ⓔ	43. Ⓐ Ⓑ Ⓒ Ⓓ Ⓔ
4. Ⓐ Ⓑ Ⓒ Ⓓ Ⓔ	14. Ⓐ Ⓑ Ⓒ Ⓓ Ⓔ	24. Ⓐ Ⓑ Ⓒ Ⓓ Ⓔ	34. Ⓐ Ⓑ Ⓒ Ⓓ Ⓔ	44. Ⓐ Ⓑ Ⓒ Ⓓ Ⓔ
5. Ⓐ Ⓑ Ⓒ Ⓓ Ⓔ	15. Ⓐ Ⓑ Ⓒ Ⓓ Ⓔ	25. Ⓐ Ⓑ Ⓒ Ⓓ Ⓔ	35. Ⓐ Ⓑ Ⓒ Ⓓ Ⓔ	45. Ⓐ Ⓑ Ⓒ Ⓓ Ⓔ
6. Ⓐ Ⓑ Ⓒ Ⓓ Ⓔ	16. Ⓐ Ⓑ Ⓒ Ⓓ Ⓔ	26. Ⓐ Ⓑ Ⓒ Ⓓ Ⓔ	36. Ⓐ Ⓑ Ⓒ Ⓓ Ⓔ	46. Ⓐ Ⓑ Ⓒ Ⓓ Ⓔ
7. Ⓐ Ⓑ Ⓒ Ⓓ Ⓔ	17. Ⓐ Ⓑ Ⓒ Ⓓ Ⓔ	27. Ⓐ Ⓑ Ⓒ Ⓓ Ⓔ	37. Ⓐ Ⓑ Ⓒ Ⓓ Ⓔ	47. Ⓐ Ⓑ Ⓒ Ⓓ Ⓔ
8. Ⓐ Ⓑ Ⓒ Ⓓ Ⓔ	18. Ⓐ Ⓑ Ⓒ Ⓓ Ⓔ	28. Ⓐ Ⓑ Ⓒ Ⓓ Ⓔ	38. Ⓐ Ⓑ Ⓒ Ⓓ Ⓔ	48. Ⓐ Ⓑ Ⓒ Ⓓ Ⓔ
9. Ⓐ Ⓑ Ⓒ Ⓓ Ⓔ	19. Ⓐ Ⓑ Ⓒ Ⓓ Ⓔ	29. Ⓐ Ⓑ Ⓒ Ⓓ Ⓔ	39. Ⓐ Ⓑ Ⓒ Ⓓ Ⓔ	49. Ⓐ Ⓑ Ⓒ Ⓓ Ⓔ
10. Ⓐ Ⓑ Ⓒ Ⓓ Ⓔ	20. Ⓐ Ⓑ Ⓒ Ⓓ Ⓔ	30. Ⓐ Ⓑ Ⓒ Ⓓ Ⓔ	40. Ⓐ Ⓑ Ⓒ Ⓓ Ⓔ	50. Ⓐ Ⓑ Ⓒ Ⓓ Ⓔ

SECTION 6

1. Ⓐ Ⓑ Ⓒ Ⓓ Ⓔ	11. Ⓐ Ⓑ Ⓒ Ⓓ Ⓔ	21. Ⓐ Ⓑ Ⓒ Ⓓ Ⓔ	31. Ⓐ Ⓑ Ⓒ Ⓓ Ⓔ	41. Ⓐ Ⓑ Ⓒ Ⓓ Ⓔ
2. Ⓐ Ⓑ Ⓒ Ⓓ Ⓔ	12. Ⓐ Ⓑ Ⓒ Ⓓ Ⓔ	22. Ⓐ Ⓑ Ⓒ Ⓓ Ⓔ	32. Ⓐ Ⓑ Ⓒ Ⓓ Ⓔ	42. Ⓐ Ⓑ Ⓒ Ⓓ Ⓔ
3. Ⓐ Ⓑ Ⓒ Ⓓ Ⓔ	13. Ⓐ Ⓑ Ⓒ Ⓓ Ⓔ	23. Ⓐ Ⓑ Ⓒ Ⓓ Ⓔ	33. Ⓐ Ⓑ Ⓒ Ⓓ Ⓔ	43. Ⓐ Ⓑ Ⓒ Ⓓ Ⓔ
4. Ⓐ Ⓑ Ⓒ Ⓓ Ⓔ	14. Ⓐ Ⓑ Ⓒ Ⓓ Ⓔ	24. Ⓐ Ⓑ Ⓒ Ⓓ Ⓔ	34. Ⓐ Ⓑ Ⓒ Ⓓ Ⓔ	44. Ⓐ Ⓑ Ⓒ Ⓓ Ⓔ
5. Ⓐ Ⓑ Ⓒ Ⓓ Ⓔ	15. Ⓐ Ⓑ Ⓒ Ⓓ Ⓔ	25. Ⓐ Ⓑ Ⓒ Ⓓ Ⓔ	35. Ⓐ Ⓑ Ⓒ Ⓓ Ⓔ	45. Ⓐ Ⓑ Ⓒ Ⓓ Ⓔ
6. Ⓐ Ⓑ Ⓒ Ⓓ Ⓔ	16. Ⓐ Ⓑ Ⓒ Ⓓ Ⓔ	26. Ⓐ Ⓑ Ⓒ Ⓓ Ⓔ	36. Ⓐ Ⓑ Ⓒ Ⓓ Ⓔ	46. Ⓐ Ⓑ Ⓒ Ⓓ Ⓔ
7. Ⓐ Ⓑ Ⓒ Ⓓ Ⓔ	17. Ⓐ Ⓑ Ⓒ Ⓓ Ⓔ	27. Ⓐ Ⓑ Ⓒ Ⓓ Ⓔ	37. Ⓐ Ⓑ Ⓒ Ⓓ Ⓔ	47. Ⓐ Ⓑ Ⓒ Ⓓ Ⓔ
8. Ⓐ Ⓑ Ⓒ Ⓓ Ⓔ	18. Ⓐ Ⓑ Ⓒ Ⓓ Ⓔ	28. Ⓐ Ⓑ Ⓒ Ⓓ Ⓔ	38. Ⓐ Ⓑ Ⓒ Ⓓ Ⓔ	48. Ⓐ Ⓑ Ⓒ Ⓓ Ⓔ
9. Ⓐ Ⓑ Ⓒ Ⓓ Ⓔ	19. Ⓐ Ⓑ Ⓒ Ⓓ Ⓔ	29. Ⓐ Ⓑ Ⓒ Ⓓ Ⓔ	39. Ⓐ Ⓑ Ⓒ Ⓓ Ⓔ	49. Ⓐ Ⓑ Ⓒ Ⓓ Ⓔ
10. Ⓐ Ⓑ Ⓒ Ⓓ Ⓔ	20. Ⓐ Ⓑ Ⓒ Ⓓ Ⓔ	30. Ⓐ Ⓑ Ⓒ Ⓓ Ⓔ	40. Ⓐ Ⓑ Ⓒ Ⓓ Ⓔ	50. Ⓐ Ⓑ Ⓒ Ⓓ Ⓔ

Remove answer sheet by cutting on dotted line

MODEL SAT TEST 2

SECTION 1 VERBAL ABILITY

40 QUESTIONS - 30 MINUTES

For each question in this section, choose the best answer and blacken the corresponding space on the answer sheet.

Each question below consists of a word in capital letters, followed by five lettered words or phrases. Choose the word or phrase that is most nearly opposite in meaning to the word in capital letters. Since some of the questions require you to distinguish fine shades of meaning, consider all the choices before deciding which is best.

Example:

GOOD: (A) sour (B) bad (C) red (D) hot (E) ugly

Ⓐ ● Ⓒ Ⓓ Ⓔ

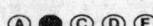

1. LICENTIOUS:
   (A) moral
   (B) permitted
   (C) banal
   (D) beginning
   (E) mundane

2. RECALCITRANT:
   (A) bellicose
   (B) late
   (C) stone-like
   (D) mangy
   (E) tractable

3. IMPASSIVE:
   (A) strange
   (B) meager
   (C) stationary
   (D) agitated
   (E) noble

4. PROFLIGATE:
   (A) incompetent
   (B) despondent
   (C) staid
   (D) masterly
   (E) active

5. PROLIX:
   (A) contrary
   (B) tapered
   (C) terse
   (D) insignificant
   (E) angry

6. PRODIGIOUS:
   (A) intellectual
   (B) adult
   (C) microscopic
   (D) intense
   (E) religious

7. SPECIOUS:
   (A) typical
   (B) narrow
   (C) golden
   (D) veracious
   (E) earthly

8. SEDULOUS:
   (A) imitative
   (B) seditious
   (C) heavy
   (D) indolent
   (E) contrary

9. EFFETE:
   (A) festive
   (B) bland
   (C) energetic
   (D) elaborate
   (E) anxious

10. NOCTURNAL:
    (A) musical
    (B) heavenly
    (C) lunar
    (D) deadly
    (E) daily

Each sentence below has one or two blanks, each blank indicating that something has been omitted. Beneath the sentence are five lettered words or sets of words. Choose the word or set of words that best fits the meaning of the sentence as a whole.

Example:

Although its publicity has been ----, the film itself is intelligent, well-acted, handsomely produced, and altogether ----.

(A) tasteless..respectable (B) extensive..moderate (C) sophisticated..amateur (D) risqué..crude (E) perfect..spectacular

● Ⓑ Ⓒ Ⓓ Ⓔ

11. If one is tempted to reflect on the type of language which is used in polite society, and, more _______, if one is inclined to interpret it literally, one must conclude that social intercourse involves a collection of _______ and a tissue of lies.
(A) thoughtfully—saws
(B) especially—maxims.
(C) essentially—aphorisms
(D) particularly—inanities
(E) violently—proverbs

12. It is said that the custom of shaking hands originated when primitive men held out empty hands to indicate that they had no _______ weapons and were thus _______ disposed.
(A) lethal—clearly
(B) concealed—amicably
(C) hidden—harmoniously
(D) murderous—well
(E) secret—finally

13. In order to control and defeat the dreadful diseases which plague humanity, _______ activity is necessary.
(A) concerted
(B) vital
(C) constant
(D) full
(E) indomitable

14. A leader, young or old, must have character traits which inspire others to accept his leadership. He must display courage, intelligence, and _______.
(A) wisdom
(B) bravery
(C) timorousness
(D) imbecility
(E) integrity

15. Such homely virtues as _______, hard work, and simplicity appear old-fashioned in these days.
(A) parsimony
(B) asceticism
(C) prodigality
(D) thrift
(E) wantonness

Each question below consists of a related pair of words or phrases, followed by five lettered pairs of words or phrases. Select the lettered pair that best expresses a relationship similar to that expressed in the original pair.

Example:

YAWN : BOREDOM :: (A) dream : sleep (B) anger : madness (C) smile : amusement (D) face : expression (E) impatience : rebellion

Ⓐ Ⓑ ● Ⓓ Ⓔ

16. POLICEMAN : CRIMINAL ::
(A) patient : doctor
(B) officer : private
(C) educator : scholar
(D) evangelist : sinner
(E) doctor : patient

17. THERMOMETER : HEAT ::
(A) filament : light
(B) chronometer : color
(C) odometer : waves
(D) Geiger counter : radiation
(E) barometer : electricity

18. SIP : GULP ::
(A) giggle : guffaw
(B) devour : eat
(C) marry : divorce
(D) fret : worry
(E) hunt : fish

19. CREST : TROUGH ::
(A) apex : summit
(B) crown : throne
(C) acme : zenith
(D) peak : valley
(E) honor : noble

20. TITANIC : LILLIPUTIAN ::
(A) gigantic : monstrous
(B) disastrous : ingenious
(C) oceanic : terrestrial
(D) obese : emaciated
(E) powerful : wicked

21. SCOLD : REBUKE ::
(A) dislike : loathe
(B) implore : request
(C) fondle : caress
(D) delete : insert
(E) suffer : retain

22. AIRPLANE : HANGAR ::
(A) ship : channel
(B) jet : runway
(C) helicopter : pad
(D) motorcycle : sidecar
(E) automobile : garage

23. SPINE : CACTUS ::
(A) backbone : man
(B) quill : porcupine
(C) root : oak
(D) pit : olive
(E) binding : book

24. CANDLE : TALLOW ::
(A) banana : peel
(B) temple : altar
(C) statue : bronze
(D) fireplace : hearth
(E) furniture : polish

25. MARSUPIAL : OPOSSUM ::
(A) rodent : squirrel
(B) fish : whale
(C) kangaroo : hare
(D) unicorn : lion
(E) carnivore : herbivore

Each passage below is followed by questions based on its content. Answer all questions following a passage on the basis of what is stated or implied in that passage.

It is no secret that I am not one of those naturalists who suffer from cities, or affect to do so, nor do I find a city unnatural or uninteresting, or a rubbish heap of follies. It has always seemed to me there is something more than mechanically admirable about a train that arrives on time, a fire department that comes when you call it, a light that leaps into the room at a touch, and a clinic that will fight for the health of a penniless man and mass for him the agencies of mercy, the X-ray, the precious radium, the anesthetics and the surgical skill. For, beyond any pay these services receive, stands out the pride in perfect performance. And above all, I admire the noble impersonality of civilization that does not inquire where the recipient stands on religion or politics or race. I call this beauty, and I call it spirit — not some mystical soulfulness that nobody can define, but the spirit of man, that has been a million years a-growing.

26. The title that best expresses the ideas of this paragraph is:
(A) The spirit of the city
(B) Advantages of a city home
(C) Disagreement among naturalists
(D) Admirable characteristics of cities
(E) Tolerance in the city

27. The services rendered by city agencies are given
(A) only for pay
(B) on time
(C) only to people having a certain political background
(D) to everybody
(E) to the spirit of man

28. The author makes a defense of
(A) cities
(B) prompt trains
(C) rural life
(D) nature
(E) free clinics

29. The aspect of city life most commendable to this author is its
(A) punctuality
(B) free benefits
(C) impartial service
(D) mechanical improvement
(E) health clinics

30. The author implies that efficient operation of public utilities is
(A) expensive
(B) of no special interest
(C) admired by most naturalists
(D) mechanically commendable
(E) spiritual in quality

The history of mammals dates back at least to Triassic time. Development was retarded, however, until the sudden acceleration of evolutional change that occurred in the oldest Paleocene. This led in Eocene time to increase in average size, larger mental capacity, and special adaptations for different modes of life. In the Oligocene Epoch, there was further improvement, with some appearance of some new lines and extinction of others. Miocene and Pliocene time was marked by culmination of several groups and continued approach toward modern characters. The peak of the career of mammals in variety and average large size was attained in the Miocene.

The adaptation of mammals to almost all possible modes of life parallels that of the reptiles in Mesozoic time, and except for greater intelligence, the mammals do not seem to have done much better than corresponding reptilian forms. The bat is doubtless a better flying animal than the pterosaur, but the dolphin and whale are hardly more fishlike than the ichthyosaur. Many swift-running mammals of the plains, like the horse and the antelope, must excel any of the dinosaurs. The tyrannosaur was a more ponderous and powerful carnivore than any flesh-eating mammal, but the lion or tiger is probably a more efficient and dangerous beast of prey because of a superior brain. The significant point to observe is that different branches of the mammals gradually fitted themselves for all sorts of life, grazing on the plains and able to run swiftly (horse, deer, bison), living in rivers and swamps (hippopotamus, beaver), dwelling in trees (sloth, monkey), digging underground (mole, rodent), feeding on flesh in the forest (tiger) and plain (wolf), swimming in the sea (dolphin, whale, seal) and flying in the air (bat). Man is able by mechanical means to conquer the physical world and adapt himself to almost any set of conditions.

This adaptation produces gradual changes of form and structure. It is biologically characteristic of the youthful, plastic stage of a group. Early in its career, an animal assemblage seems to possess capacity for change, which, as the unit becomes old and fixed, disappears. The generalized types of organisms retain longest the ability to make adjustments when required, and it is from them that new, fecund stocks take origin — certainly not from any specialized end products. So, in the mammals, we witness the birth, plastic spread in many directions, increasing specialization, and in some branches, the extinction, which we have learned from observation of the geological record of life is a characteristic of the evolution of life.

31. The arboreal mammal mentioned in the passage is the
(A) bison
(B) deer
(C) beaver
(D) mole
(E) sloth

32. From this passage, we may conclude that the pterosaur
(A) resembled the bat
(B) was a mammal that lived in the Mesozoic period
(C) was a flying reptile
(D) lived in the sea
(E) evolved during the Miocene period

33. The greatest number of forms of mammalian life is found in the
(A) Triassic period
(B) Eocene period
(C) Oligocene epoch
(D) Pliocene period
(E) Miocene period

34. That the mammals which succeeded the reptiles in geologic time were superior is illustrated by the statement that
(A) the tiger has a brain that surpasses that of the tyrannosaur
(B) the deer runs more swiftly than the lion
(C) the whale is more fishlike than the ichthyosaur
(D) the tiger is more powerful than the carnivorous reptiles
(E) the dinosaurs were slow moving animals

35. *Saur* in such words as pterosaur, dinosaur, and tyrannosaur probably means
(A) large
(B) reptilian
(C) living in Mesozoic time
(D) inefficient
(E) defunct

36. The statements made by the writer are based on evidence
(A) developed by Charles Darwin
(B) found by comparing animals and reptiles
(C) found by going to different time periods
(D) that cannot be definitely established
(E) gained by studying fossil remains

37. Man has been able to adjust himself to his environment better than other animals
(A) because he is stronger
(B) because he can swim and walk
(C) because he was developed in Pliocene time
(D) because he can adjust to his environment
(E) because he can utilize mechanical devices

We now know that what constitutes practically all of matter is empty space; relatively enormous voids in which revolve with lightning velocity infinitesimal particles so utterly small that they have never been seen or photographed. The existence of these particles has been demonstrated by mathematical physicists and their operations determined by ingenious laboratory experiments. It was not until 1911 that experiments by Sir Ernest Rutherford revealed the architecture of the mysterious atom. Moseley, Bohr, Fermi, Millikan, Compton, Urey, and others have also worked on the problem. Matter is composed of molecules whose average diameter is about 1/125 millionth of an inch. Molecules are composed of atoms so small that about five million could be placed in a row on the period at the end of this sentence. Long thought to be the ultimate, indivisible constituent of matter, the atom has been found to consist roughly of a proton, the positive electrical element in the atomic nucleus, surrounded by electrons, the negative electric elements swirling about the proton.

38. The center of the atom, according to this passage,
(A) contains one electron
(B) was seen as early as 1911
(C) has not yet been seen by the naked eye
(D) is about the size of a period
(E) might be photographed under microscopes

39. The paragraph indicates that the atom
(A) is the smallest particle
(B) is very little larger than a molecule
(C) is composed of several particles
(D) has been seen
(E) is empty space

40. Scientists agree that molecules are
(A) voids
(B) the most mysterious particles
(C) not divisible
(D) not basically composed of electric elements
(E) huge compared with electrons

S T O P

IF YOU FINISH BEFORE TIME IS CALLED, YOU MAY CHECK YOUR WORK ON THIS SECTION ONLY. DO NOT WORK ON ANY OTHER SECTION IN THE TEST.

SECTION 2 MATH ABILITY

25 QUESTIONS - 30 MINUTES

In this section, solve each problem, using any available space on the page for scratchwork. Then decide which is the best of the choices given and blacken the corresponding space on the answer sheet.

The following information is for your reference in solving some of the problems.

Circle of radius r: Area $= \pi r^2$; Circumference $= 2\pi r$
The number of degrees of arc in a circle is 360.
The measure in degrees of a straight angle is 180.

Definitions of symbols:

$=$ is equal to	$\leq$ is less than or equal to
$\neq$ is unequal to	$\geq$ is greater than or equal to
$<$ is less than	$\parallel$ is parallel to
$>$ is greater than	$\perp$ is perpendicular to

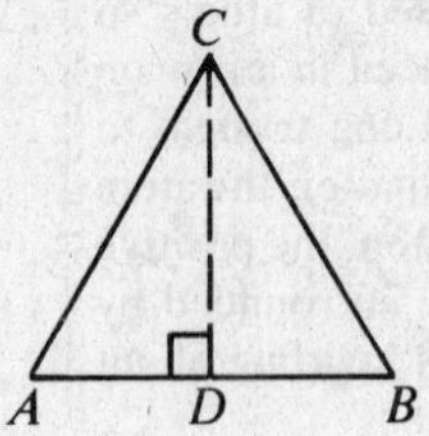

Triangle: The sum of the measures in degrees of the angles of a triangle is 180.
If $\angle CDA$ is a right angle, then
(1) area of $\triangle ABC = \frac{AB \times CD}{2}$
(2) $AC^2 = AD^2 + DC^2$

Note: Figures that accompany problems in this test are intended to provide information useful in solving the problems. They are drawn as accurately as possible EXCEPT when it is stated in a specific problem that its figure is not drawn to scale. All figures lie in a plane unless otherwise indicated. All numbers used are real numbers.

1. By how much does $r - s$ exceed $s - r$?
(A) $\frac{r - s}{s - r}$
(B) $2(r - s)$
(C) $2(s - r)$
(D) $r - s$
(E) -1

2. $\frac{\frac{1}{3} - \frac{1}{12}}{\frac{1}{4}} = ?$
(A) $\frac{-4}{9}$
(B) 0
(C) $\frac{1}{4}$
(D) 1
(E) $\frac{5}{3}$

3. $ax + b - y = 0 \quad b = ?$
(A) $y - ax$
(B) $y + ax$
(C) $ax - y$
(D) $\frac{y}{ax}$
(E) $\frac{-ax}{y}$

4. The temperature in a home freezer varied from $-25°$ to $+3°$. How many degrees difference is there between the two readings?
(A) 14
(B) 22
(C) 25
(D) 27
(E) 28

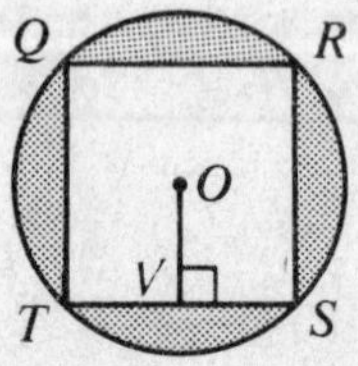

5. In the figure above, square $QRST$ is inscribed in circle O. $OV \perp TS$; $OV = 1$.
The area of the shaded portion is
(A) $\pi - 4$
(B) $4\pi - 4$
(C) $2\pi - 4$
(D) $4\pi - 2$
(E) $2\pi - 2$

6. Three times a number less seven is thirty-two. What is twice the number?
(A) 13
(B) 17
(C) 26
(D) 32
(E) 39

7. The Japanese ken is equivalent to 5.97 feet. How many feet are there in 59.7 ken?
(A) 0.1
(B) 10
(C) 248
(D) 356
(E) 360

8. What was the grade a student received on his first examination, if his other grades were 70, 80, and 90, and his average on the four was 75?
(A) 60
(B) 75
(C) 85
(D) 90
(E) 100

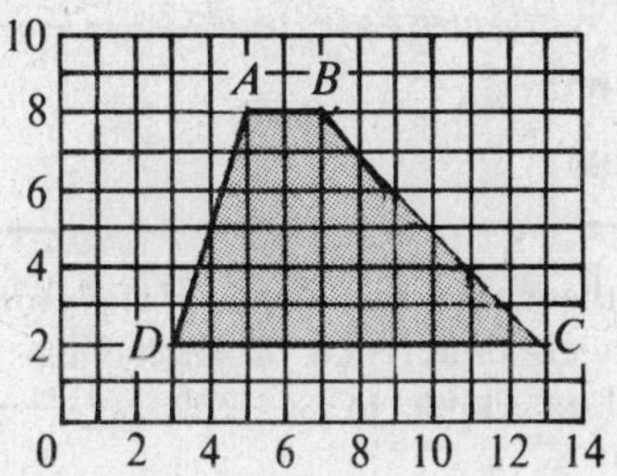

9. In the figure above, what is the area of *ABCD*?
(A) 24
(B) 30
(C) 35
(D) 36
(E) 48

10. If p pencils cost c cents, how many pencils can be bought for d dollars?
(A) $\frac{dp}{c}$
(B) $\frac{100c}{dp}$
(C) $\frac{100cp}{d}$
(D) $\frac{100cd}{p}$
(E) $\frac{100dp}{c}$

11. A train covers the distance d between two cities in h hours arriving 2 hours late. What rate would permit the train to arrive on schedule?
(A) $h - 2$
(B) $\frac{d}{h} - 2$
(C) $\frac{d}{h - 2}$
(D) $dh - 2$
(E) $\frac{d}{h + 2}$

12. $\frac{1.116963}{0.369}$ is exactly equal to
(A) 3.023
(B) 3.024
(C) 3.025
(D) 3.026
(E) 3.027

13. Mr. Stanley will be x years old 5 years hence. How old was he five years ago?
(A) $x - 5$
(B) $x + 10$
(C) $x - 10$
(D) $5x - 5$
(E) $7x$

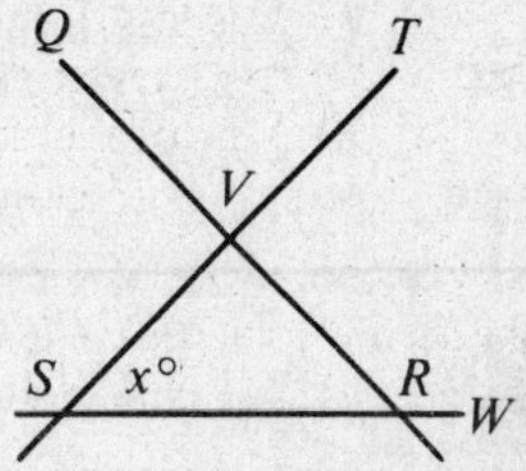

14. In the figure above, line QR is perpendicular to line ST at V.
$\angle VSR \hat{=} x$
$\angle VRW \hat{=}$ (?)
(A) $90 - x$
(B) $90 + x$
(C) $x - 90$
(D) $180 - x$
(E) 135

15. To send a parcel to Zone 7 the cost is 30¢ for the first pound and 15.5¢ for each additional pound. What is the cost of sending a package weighing 48 ounces to Zone 7? (16 oz. = 1 lb.)
(A) 46¢
(B) 59¢
(C) 61¢
(D) 64¢
(E) 90¢

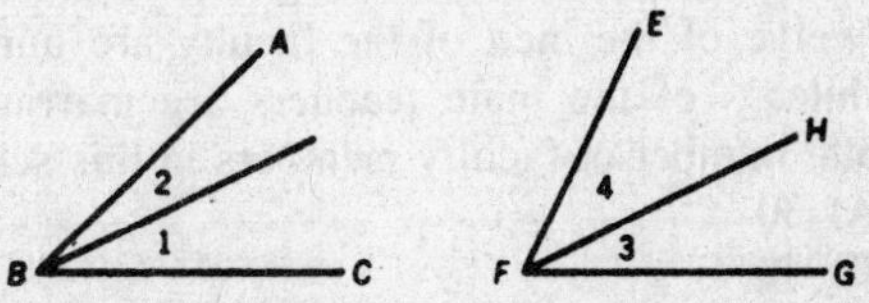

16. In the figures above, $\angle EFG > \angle ABC$ and the ratio of the measure of angle 1 to the measure of angle 3 is 1 : 1, therefore
(A) $\angle 1 + \angle 2 = \angle 3 + \angle 4$
(B) $\angle 2 = \angle 4$
(C) $\angle 2 > \angle 4$
(D) $\angle 2 < \angle 4$
(E) $(\angle 1 + \angle 2 + \angle 3 + \angle 4) = 180°$

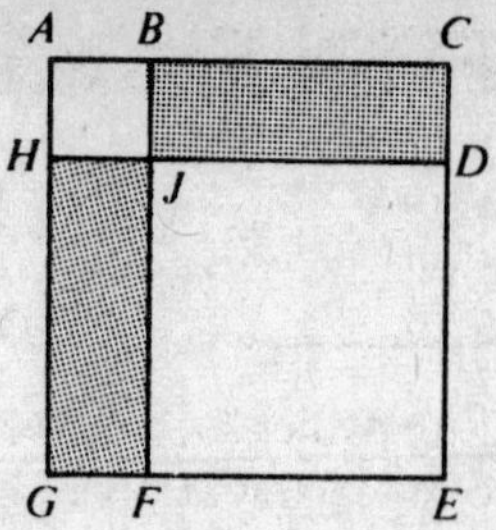

17. In the figure above, *ABJH, JDEF, ACEG* are squares.

$\frac{BC}{AB} = 3$

$\frac{\text{Area } BCDJ}{\text{Area } HJFG} = ?$

(A) $\frac{1}{9}$
(B) $\frac{1}{3}$
(C) 1
(D) 3
(E) 9

18. $r = 18$

$\frac{r}{s} = \frac{6}{y}$

$\frac{y}{s} = ?$

(A) $\frac{1}{3}$
(B) $3\frac{1}{6}$
(C) $3\frac{1}{3}$
(D) 6
(E) 18

19. Because of a decrease of available manpower, a toy factory reduced its monthly output by 20%. What is the necessary per cent increase of manpower to bring the output up to normal production?
(A) 20
(B) 25
(C) 50
(D) 120
(E) 125

20. Two thirds of the faculty of a high school are women. Twelve of the men of the faculty are unmarried while ⅗ of the male teachers are married. The total number of faculty members in this school is
(A) 30
(B) 50
(C) 60
(D) 72
(E) 90

21. The state of Oklahoma had eight Congressmen in 1940 and six in 1950. What was the per cent change in their representation?
(A) −75
(B) $-33\frac{1}{3}$
(C) −25
(D) +25
(E) +75

22. 10% of r = 20% of s
20% of s = 30% of t
100% of r = x% of t
$x = ?$
(A) 20
(B) $33\frac{1}{3}$
(C) 40
(D) $166\frac{2}{3}$
(E) 300

23. What is the maximum number of glass tumblers (each with a circumference of 4π inches) that can be placed on a table 48″ × 32″?
(A) 36
(B) 48
(C) 92
(D) 96
(E) 192

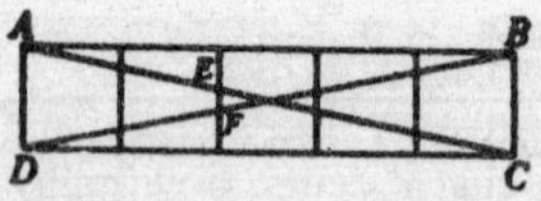

24. In the figure above, rectangle *ABCD* is made up of five squares of equal area. *AD* = 30. Find *EF*.
(A) 6
(B) 8
(C) 10
(D) 12
(E) 20

25. A corporation has 8 departments each with 10–16 bureaus. In each bureau there are at least 40 but no more than 60 workers. If 10% of the workers in each bureau are typists, what is the minimum number of typists in a department?
(A) 40
(B) 65
(C) 96
(D) 320
(E) 768

S T O P

IF YOU FINISH BEFORE TIME IS CALLED, YOU MAY CHECK YOUR WORK ON THIS SECTION ONLY. DO NOT WORK ON ANY OTHER SECTION IN THE TEST.

SECTION 3 TEST OF STANDARD WRITTEN ENGLISH

50 QUESTIONS - 30 MINUTES

The questions in this section measure skills that are important to writing well. In particular, they test your ability to recognize and use language that is clear, effective, and correct according to the requirements of standard written English, the kind of English found in most college textbooks.

Directions: The following sentences contain problems in grammar, usage, diction (choice of words), and idiom.

Some sentences are correct.

No sentence contains more than one error.

You will find that the error, if there is one, is underlined and lettered. Assume that elements of the sentence that are not underlined are correct and cannot be changed. In choosing answers, follow the requirements of standard written English.

If there is an error, select the one underlined part that must be changed to make the sentence correct and blacken the corresponding space on your answer sheet.

If there is no error, blacken answer space Ⓔ.

EXAMPLE:

The region has a climate so severe that (A) plants growing there (B) rarely had been (C) more than twelve inches high (D). No error (E)

SAMPLE ANSWER

Ⓐ Ⓑ ● Ⓓ Ⓔ

1. Your (A) argument is no different (B) from (C) the last speaker (D) who opposed the legislation. No error (E)

2. Please help me decide which (A) of the two activities to choose—going to the theater with John or (B) to attend (C) tonight's (D) dinner-dance at the hotel. No error (E)

3. Shirley is very (A) fidgety, (B) which (C) is an annoying trait. (D) No error (E)

4. Every woman in the ward (A) hoped (B) that their (C) child would be a normal and healthy (D) baby. No error (E)

5. When I have to (A) decide which (B) of two applicants for a job to hire, I find myself (C) giving the position to the one who uses the best (D) English. No error (E)

6. That (A) is the kind of a house (B) in which (C) I should (D) like to live. No error (E)

7. When you go shopping, (A) will you please bring (B) this note to (C) the manager of the grocery (D) department? No error (E)

8. Charles asked (A) would I go (B) to the ball game with (C) him. (D) No error (E)

9. We were particularly (A) frightened of John (B) driving (C) the car (D) in the race. No error (E)

10. Because (A) I was seated on the dais (B) just in back of (C) the speaker, I could see the audience's (D) reaction to his vituperative remarks. No error (E)

11. During (A) the recent gasoline shortage, the amount of (B) accidents on our highways decreased (C) markedly. (D) No error (E)

12. Having secured (A) the ball on a fumble, we (B) took (C) advantage of our opponent's (D) error and scored a field goal. No error (E)

13. This (A) is one (B) of the things (C) that annoy (D) me. No error (E)

14. Although (A) I am willing to go along (B) with your idea, I cannot enthuse (C) over its chances (D) of success. No error (E)

15. I was aggravated (A) by the child's (B) rudeness to the visiting (C) dignitaries who had come (D) to visit our school. No error (E)

16. A complete system (A) of checks and balances have been (B) incorporated (C) in our (D) Constitution. No error (E)

17. She is the only (A) one of my friends who (B) plan (C) to (D) attend the graduation exercises. No error (E)

18. Due to (A) the excessively (B) high interest rate on installment buying, it is advisable (C) to purchase things on a cash (D) basis. No error (E)

19. The boys whom (A) I predicted (B) would win (C) the contest have lived up (D) to my expectations. No error (E)

20. When asked how long she had been (A) a resident of the state, she replied, (B) "I am living (C) in this state for (D) five years." No error (E)

21. Owing to (A) unfavorable weather, (B) the party had to be (C) postponed for (D) a week. No error (E)

22. Neither (A) of the three applicants meets (B) the requirements (C) for this position. (D) No error (E)

23. When descending (A) from 37,000 feet to make our (B) landing, the pressure (C) affected (D) our ears. No error (E)

24. I am not certain (A) if (B) I should discuss (C) my promotion (D) with him or not. No error (E)

25. He had a keen (A) interest and (B) wide (C) knowledge of his esoteric (D) subject. No error (E)

Directions: In each of the following sentences, some part or all of the sentence is underlined. Below each sentence you will find five ways of phrasing the underlined part. Select the answer that produces the most effective sentence, one that is clear and exact, without awkwardness or ambiguity, and blacken the corresponding space on your answer sheet. In choosing answers, follow the requirements of standard written English. Choose the answer that best expresses the meaning of the original sentence.

Answer (A) is always the same as the underlined part. Choose answer (A) if you think the original sentence needs no revision.

EXAMPLE:

Laura Ingalls Wilder published her first book and she was sixty-five years old then.

(A) and she was sixty-five years old then
(B) when she was sixty-five years old
(C) at age sixty-five years old
(D) upon reaching sixty-five years
(E) at the time when she was sixty-five

SAMPLE ANSWER

Ⓐ ● Ⓒ Ⓓ Ⓔ

26. Although I calculate that he will be here any minute, I cannot wait much longer for him to arrive.
(A) Although I calculate that he will be here
(B) Although I reckon that he will be here
(C) Because I calculate that he will be here
(D) Although I am confident that he will be here
(E) Because I am confident that he will be here

27. The scouts were told to take an overnight hike, pitch camp, prepare dinner, and that they should be in bed by 9 p.m.
(A) to take an overnight hike, pitch camp, prepare dinner, and that they should be in bed by 9 p.m.
(B) to take an overnight hike, pitch camp, prepare dinner, and that they should go to bed by 9 p.m.
(C) to take an overnight hike, pitch camp, prepare dinner, and be in bed by 9 p.m.
(D) to take an overnight hike, pitching camp, preparing dinner and going to bed by 9 p.m.
(E) to engage in an overnight hike, pitch camp, prepare dinner, and that they should be in bed by 9 p.m.

28. We want the teacher to be him who has the best rapport with the students.
(A) We want the teacher to be him
(B) We want the teacher to be he
(C) We want him to be the teacher
(D) We desire that the teacher be him
(E) We anticipate that the teacher will be him

29. Did Alexander Pope write, "To err is human; to forgive, divine?"
(A) write, "To err is human; to forgive, divine?"
(B) write that "To err is human; to forgive, divine?"
(C) write, "To err is human; to forgive, divine"?
(D) write: "To err is human; to forgive, divine?"
(E) write, "To err is human, to forgive divine"?

30. If he were to win the medal, I for one would be disturbed.
(A) If he were to win the medal,
(B) If he was to win the medal,
(C) If he wins the medal,
(D) If he is the winner of the medal,
(E) In the event that he wins the medal,

31. She not only was competent but also friendly in nature.
(A) She not only was competent but also friendly
(B) She not was only competent but friendly also
(C) She not only was competent but friendly also
(D) She was not only competent but also friendly
(E) She was not only competent but friendly also

32. The dean informed us that the applicant had not and never will be accepted by the college because of his high school record.
(A) applicant had not and never will be accepted by the college because of his high school record.
(B) applicant had not and never would be accepted by the college because of his High School record.
(C) applicant had not been and never will be accepted by the college because of his high school record.
(D) applicant had not been and never would be accepted by the college because of his High School record.
(E) applicant had not been and never would be accepted by the college because of his high school record.

33. The government's failing to keep it's pledges will earn the distrust of all the other nations in the alliance.
(A) government's failing to keep it's pledges
(B) government failing to keep it's pledges
(C) government's failing to keep its pledges
(D) government failing to keep its pledges
(E) governments failing to keep their pledges

34. Her brother along with her parents insist that she remain in school.
(A) insist
(B) insists
(C) are insisting
(D) were insisting
(E) have insisted

35. Most students like to read these kind of books during their spare time.
(A) these kind of books
(B) these kind of book
(C) this kind of books
(D) this kinds of books
(E) those kind of books

36. The breakdown of the year-long talks between King Hussein and Yasser Arafat does not spell eminent war.
(A) does not spell eminent war
(B) do not spell eminent war
(C) does not spell imminent war
(D) do not spell imminent war
(E) are not spelling eminent war

37. Employers have begun to provide health club facilities for their employees because exercise builds stamina, decreases tension, and absenteeism is reduced.
(A) decreases tension, and absenteeism is reduced
(B) tension is decreased, and absenteeism reduced
(C) decreases tension, and reducing absenteeism
(D) decreases tension, and reduces absenteeism
(E) decreasing tension, and absenteeism is reduced

38. We are more concerned that the best possible candidate be hired than that bureaucratic affirmative action rules be followed to the letter.
(A) than that bureaucratic affirmative action rules be followed
(B) and not about following bureaucratic affirmative action rules
(C) than that one should follow bureaucratic affirmative action rules
(D) than your following bureaucratic affirmative action rules
(E) and not in any bureaucratic affirmative action rules being followed

39. Bernard Malamud was a forty-year-old college professor in Oregon and his short story "The Magic Barrel" was published in *The Partisan Review.*
(A) Oregon and his short story "The Magic Barrel"
(B) Oregon, his short story "The Magic Barrel"
(C) Oregon; his short story "The Magic Barrel"
(D) Oregon when his short story "The Magic Barrel"
(E) Oregon, furthermore, his short story "The Magic Barrel"

40. In keeping with the hallowed Russian tradition of putting on a show to impress the visitors, the capital being painted and festooned with banners and portraits of Marx and Lenin.
(A) the capital being painted and festooned
(B) the capital been painted and festooned
(C) the capital painted and being festooned
(D) the capital's painting and festooning
(E) the capital has been painted and festooned

Note: The remaining questions are like those at the beginning of the section.

Directions: For each sentence in which you find an error, select the one underlined part that must be changed to make the sentence correct and blacken the corresonding space on your answer sheet.

If there is no error, blacken answer space Ⓔ.

EXAMPLE:

The region has a climate so severe that (A) plants growing there (B) rarely had been (C) more than twelve inches high (D). No error (E)

SAMPLE ANSWER

Ⓐ Ⓑ ● Ⓓ Ⓔ

41. Everything (A) depended on Joneses (B) arriving (C) on time for the crucial (D) discussion. No error (E)

42. Although (A) he is (B) in this country only (C) two years, he talks like (D) a native. No error (E)

43. These cars are (A) not ready for delivery as they (B) come off of (C) the assembly line; they must be tested before they (D) can be sold. No error (E)

44. The technique discussed (A) in this article enables (B) a student to learn more quickly (C) and to remember for a longer period (D) of time. No error (E)

45. Everybody (A) but you (B) and he (C) has (D) joined the school organization. No error (E)

46. The population (A) of California is (B) larger than (C) any state (D) in the United States. No error (E)

47. Reading quickly, (A) the book was (B) soon (C) finished and returned (D) to the library. No error (E)

48. He is wiser (A) than (B) us (C) all (D). No error (E)

49. You can scarcely (A) see the birds in the trees because (B) of their (C) protective coloration (D). No error (E)

50. The man who (A) is laying (B) in the aisle (C) needs (D) medical attention immediately. No error (E)

S T O P

IF YOU FINISH BEFORE TIME IS CALLED, YOU MAY CHECK YOUR WORK ON THIS SECTION ONLY. DO NOT WORK ON ANY OTHER SECTION IN THE TEST.

SECTION 4 VERBAL ABILITY

45 QUESTIONS - 30 MINUTES

For each question in this section, choose the best answer and blacken the corresponding space on the answer sheet.

Each question below consists of a word in capital letters, followed by five lettered words or phrases. Choose the word or phrase that is most nearly opposite in meaning to the word in capital letters. Since some of the questions require you to distinguish fine shades of meaning, consider all the choices before deciding which is best.

Example:

GOOD: (A) sour (B) bad (C) red (D) hot (E) ugly

Ⓐ ● Ⓒ Ⓓ Ⓔ

1. PHLEGMATIC:
   (A) tired
   (B) fancy
   (C) repetitious
   (D) active
   (E) smooth

2. SALUTARY:
   (A) harmful
   (B) respectful
   (C) disrespectful
   (D) valedictory
   (E) anxious

3. CALLOUS:
   (A) concerned
   (B) blameless
   (C) irritated
   (D) noxious
   (E) careless

4. DEMURE:
   (A) objective
   (B) emotional
   (C) demonstrative
   (D) illiterate
   (E) intolerant

5. ORTHODOX:
   (A) right
   (B) left
   (C) massive
   (D) plain
   (E) heretical

6. DISSUADE:
   (A) exhort
   (B) extract
   (C) diminish
   (D) divide
   (E) antagonize

7. SUCCOR:
   (A) hindrance
   (B) tart
   (C) fakir
   (D) levity
   (E) growth

8. LAUDATORY:
   (A) imposing
   (B) quiet
   (C) defamatory
   (D) clandestine
   (E) unhatched

9. LACKADAISICAL:
   (A) sleepy
   (B) enthusiastic
   (C) monthly
   (D) livid
   (E) fortunate

10. SUAVE:
    (A) tactless
    (B) democratic
    (C) sourish
    (D) astute
    (E) authoritative

11. FERVENT:
    (A) noisome
    (B) futile
    (C) fantastic
    (D) old
    (E) indifferent

12. SACRILEGIOUS:
    (A) stupid
    (B) flagrant
    (C) sanctifying
    (D) devoted
    (E) reflective

13. URBANE:
(A) open
(B) rural
(C) naive
(D) cautious
(E) reckless

14. DEFERENCE:
(A) support
(B) vanity
(C) postponement
(D) value
(E) disrespect

15. PUNY:
(A) rewarding
(B) gigantic
(C) serious
(D) obese
(E) silent

Each sentence below has one or two blanks, each blank indicating that something has been omitted. Beneath the sentence are five lettered words or sets of words. Choose the word or set of words that <u>best</u> fits the meaning of the sentence as a whole.

Example:

Although its publicity has been ----, the film itself is intelligent, well-acted, handsomely produced, and altogether ----.

(A) tasteless..respectable (B) extensive..moderate
(C) sophisticated..amateur (D) risqué..crude
(E) perfect..spectacular

● Ⓑ Ⓒ Ⓓ Ⓔ

16. To relieve his stomach distress, the doctor suggested that he take a ________.
(A) palliative
(B) paregoric
(C) ministration
(D) mendicant
(E) migraine

17. You talk as though you were ________.
(A) ubiquitous
(B) omnipresent
(C) omniscient
(D) omnivorous
(E) nurtured

18. If you need additional ________, the person who reaches his quota will get a trip to Europe.
(A) objective
(B) aims
(C) impetus
(D) incentive
(E) prompting

19. A pessimist has a ________ outlook on life.
(A) salubrious
(B) contemptuous
(C) intense
(D) placid
(E) lugubrious

20. The evidence is not ________ to the issue at hand.
(A) germane
(B) consistent
(C) inchoate
(D) luminous
(E) manifest

Each passage below is followed by questions based on its content. Answer all questions following a passage on the basis of what is stated or implied in that passage.

Our ignorance of the complex subject of social insurance was and remains colossal. For years American business leaders delighted in maligning the British social insurance schemes. Our industrialists condemned them without ever finding out what they were about. Even our universities displayed no interest. Contrary to the interest in this subject taken by organized labor abroad, our own labor movements bitterly opposed the entire program of social insurance up to a few years ago. Since the success of any reform depends largely upon a correct public understanding of the principles involved, the adoption of social insurance measures presented peculiar difficulties for the United States under our Federal type of government of limited powers, our constitutional and judicial handicaps, our long conditioning to individualism, the traditional hostility to social reform by both capital and labor, the general inertia, and our complete lack of trained administrative personnel without which even the best law can be ineffective. Has not bitter experience taught us that far more important than the passage of a law, which is at best only a declaration of intention, is a ready public opinion prepared to enforce it?

21. According to this writer, what attitude have we shown in this country toward social insurance?
(A) We have been extremely doubtful that it will work, but have been willing to give it a chance.
(B) We have opposed it on the grounds of a careful study of its defects.
(C) We have shown an unintelligent and rather blind antagonism toward it.
(D) We have been afraid that it would not work under our type of government.
(E) We have resented it because of the extensive propaganda in favor of it.

22. To what does the phrase, "our long conditioning to individualism," refer?
(A) Our habit of depending upon ourselves
(B) Our increasing dependence on the Federal Government
(C) Our long distrust of "big business"
(D) Our policies of high protective tariff
(E) Our unwillingness to accept reforms

23. Which of these ideas is expressed in this passage?
(A) The surest way to cure a social evil is to get people to pass a law against it.
(B) Legislation alone cannot effect social reforms.
(C) The American people are seriously uninformed about all social problems.
(D) Our type of government makes social reform practically impossible.
(E) Capital and labor retard social progress.

The artist of the Renaissance was an all-round man. From his studio one could order a painting for the church altar, a carved wedding chest, a silver ewer, or a crucifix. The master of the workshop might be sculpturing a Venus for the Duke's garden while his apprentices were roughing-out a reredos for the new chapel. Many of the well-known painters of that golden period were goldsmiths, armorers, workers in glass, enamel or iron. The engineer was artist and the artist was engineer. The great Leonardo, famous today as the painter of *The Last Supper* and *Mona Lisa*, was perhaps equally well known in the 16th century for his engineering projects and his scientific experiments. Our own Thomas A. Edison pronounced him the greatest inventive genius of his time.

24. The title that best expresses the ideas of this paragraph is:
(A) The great Leonardo
(B) Edison and 16th century scientists
(C) The golden period
(D) Masters and apprentices
(E) Renaissance artists

25. Leonardo was famed as
(A) a scientist
(B) an electrician
(C) a worker in glass
(D) a railroad engineer
(E) an apprentice

26. Artists of the Renaissance were
(A) numerous
(B) many-sided
(C) honest
(D) wealthy
(E) lacking in thoroughness

The same high mental faculties which first led man to believe in unseen spiritual agencies, then in fetichism, polytheism, and ultimately in monotheism, would infallibly lead him, as long as his reasoning powers remained poorly developed, to various strange superstitions and customs. Many of these are terrible to think of—such as the sacrifice of human beings to a blood-loving god; the trial of innocent persons by the ordeal of poison or fire; witchcraft, etc.—yet it is well occasionally to reflect on these superstitions, for they show us what an infinite debt of gratitude we owe to the improvement of our reason to science, and to our accumulated knowledge.

27. According to this author we owe a debt of gratitude to science for our
(A) accumulated knowledge
(B) higher mental faculties
(C) present judicial system of protecting the innocent
(D) departure from primitive superstitions
(E) powers of reflection

28. This passage most likely is part of a treatise on
(A) witchcraft
(B) theology
(C) scientific method
(D) anthropology
(E) organic evolution

29. Select the statement which is true.
(A) Monotheism motivated primitive people to the sacrifice of human beings.
(B) Monotheism evolved with the development of the intellect.
(C) Monotheism preceded the belief in unseen spiritual forces.
(D) Monotheism was caused by the poor reasoning power of Man.
(E) Monotheism preceded fetichism.

30. From this passage we may infer that
(A) polytheism believed that there was a blood-loving god
(B) we can best appreciate the blessings of this century by examining the customs and superstitions of Primitive Man
(C) trial of innocent persons by the ordeal of poison was practiced until the development of modern religious concepts
(D) the author would condone witchcraft
(E) development of reasoning power had no effect on social customs

Select the word or set of words that best completes each of the following sentences.

31. The question is whether night baseball will prove a boon or a ______ to the game.
(A) favor
(B) benefit
(C) bonanza
(D) panacea
(E) disaster

32. His employers could not complain about his work because he was ______ in the performance of his duties.
(A) derelict
(B) penetrating
(C) diversified
(D) assiduous
(E) mandatory

33. He is much too ______ in his writings; he writes a page when a sentence should suffice.
(A) devious
(B) pithy
(C) verbose
(D) benignant
(E) pleasant

34. Although I am not a (an) ______, I am interested in the derivation of words.
(A) entomologist
(B) graphologist
(C) historian
(D) numismatist
(E) lexicographer

35. The ______ pack of wolves ______ the herd of cattle in their search for a stray calf.
(A) voracious–stalked
(B) mendacious—pursued
(C) meandering—harassed
(D) pacific—pursued
(E) nocturnal—followed

Each question below consists of a related pair of words or phrases, followed by five lettered pairs of words or phrases. Select the lettered pair that best expresses a relationship similar to that expressed in the original pair.

Example:

YAWN : BOREDOM :: (A) dream : sleep (B) anger : madness (C) smile : amusement (D) face : expression (E) impatience : rebellion

Ⓐ Ⓑ ● Ⓓ Ⓔ

36. OSTRACISM : CENSURE ::
(A) love : marriage
(B) success : promotion
(C) applause : approval
(D) editing : criticism
(E) loyalty : tribute

37. COBBLER : SHOES ::
(A) mechanic : automobile
(B) carpenter : saw
(C) apothecary : drugs
(D) spy : plans
(E) interrogator : questions

38. PROPITIATE : APPEASE ::
(A) disturb : agitate
(B) inaugurate : terminate
(C) illiterate : articulate
(D) mollify : incite
(E) irritate : soothe

39. LACONIC : VOLUBLE ::
(A) spartan : stern
(B) false : deceitful
(C) quiet : taciturn
(D) frozen : boiling
(E) noisy : shrill

40. ROOSTER : HEN ::
(A) duck : drake
(B) dog : cat
(C) gander : gosling
(D) swan : drake
(E) gander : goose

41. VIOLA : INSTRUMENT ::
(A) color : sound
(B) spectrum : shade
(C) trumpet : drum
(D) chisel : tool
(E) fiddle : bass

42. QUART : PINT ::
(A) liter : meter
(B) pound : ton
(C) yard : inch
(D) minute : hour
(E) minute : second

43. ASSURANCE : FEAR ::
(A) opiate : pain
(B) opiate : dreams
(C) cigarette : nerves
(D) confidence : man
(E) narcotic : drug

44. TIME : SCYTHE ::
(A) liberty : sickle
(B) justice : scales
(C) honesty : badge
(D) ignorance : chains
(E) freedom : mountain top

45. FELICITY : SORROW ::
(A) agility : skill
(B) agility : clumsiness
(C) concept : scheme
(D) congratulations : benediction
(E) ignorance : bliss

S T O P

IF YOU FINISH BEFORE TIME IS CALLED, YOU MAY CHECK YOUR WORK ON THIS SECTION ONLY. DO NOT WORK ON ANY OTHER SECTION IN THE TEST.

SECTION 5 MATH ABILITY

35 QUESTIONS - 30 MINUTES

In this section solve each problem, using any available space on the page for scratchwork. Then decide which is the best of the choices given and blacken the corresponding space on the answer sheet.

The following information is for your reference in solving some of the problems.

Circle of radius r: Area $= \pi r^2$; Circumference $= 2\pi r$

The number of degrees of arc in a circle is 360.

The measure in degrees of a straight angle is 180.

Definitions of symbols:

$=$ is equal to

$\neq$ is unequal to

$<$ is less than

$>$ is greater than

$\leqq$ is less than or equal to

$\geqq$ is greater than or equal to

$\parallel$ is parallel to

$\perp$ is perpendicular to

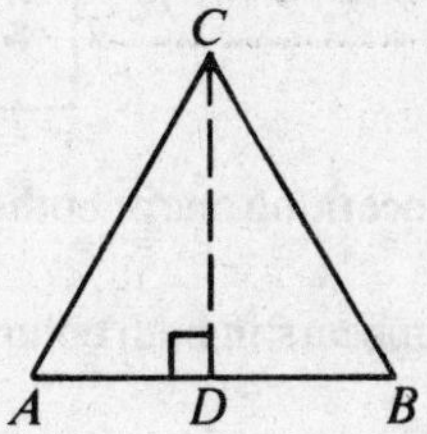

Triangle: The sum of the measures in degrees of the angles of a triangle is 180.

If $\angle CDA$ is a right angle, then

(1) area of $\triangle ABC = \frac{AB \times CD}{2}$

(2) $AC^2 = AD^2 + DC^2$

Note: Figures that accompany problems in this test are intended to provide information useful in solving the problems. They are drawn as accurately as possible EXCEPT when it is stated in a specific problem that its figure is not drawn to scale. All figures lie in a plane unless otherwise indicated. All numbers used are real numbers.

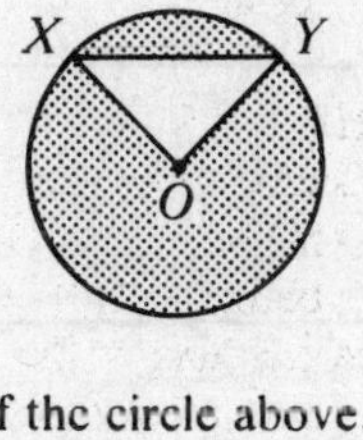

1. O is the center of the circle above. XO is perpendicular to YO and the area of triangle XOY is 32. What is the area of circle O?
   (A) 16π
   (B) 32π
   (C) 64π
   (D) 128π
   (E) 256π

2. By how many sixteenths is $\frac{1}{3}$ of $\frac{3}{4}$ more than $\frac{1}{4}$ of $\frac{3}{4}$?
   (A) 1
   (B) 3
   (C) 5
   (D) 6
   (E) 14

3. The length of a rectangle is l and the width is w. If the width is increased by 2 units, by how many units will the perimeter be increased?
   (A) 2
   (B) 4
   (C) $2w$
   (D) $2w + 2$
   (E) $2w + 4$

4. Which of the following signs inserted in the parentheses will make the statement below correct?

$$\frac{6}{14}\ (\quad)\ \frac{9}{21} = \frac{3}{7}$$

   (A) $+$
   (B) $-$
   (C) $\times$
   (D) $\div$
   (E) $=$

5. If 7 lbs. of variety p tea is worth 5 lbs. of variety q tea and 3 lbs. of variety p tea is worth x lbs. of variety q tea, then the numerical value of x is
   (A) $\frac{5}{7}$
   (B) $1\frac{2}{3}$
   (C) $2\frac{1}{7}$
   (D) $3\frac{5}{7}$
   (E) $4\frac{1}{5}$

6. If the average of the ages of three men is 44 years, and if no one of them is less than 42 years old, what is the maximum age (in years) of any one man?
   (A) 44
   (B) 46
   (C) 48
   (D) 49
   (E) 50

7. What is the radius of a circle if it is equal in area to a triangle with an altitude of 4π and a base of 16?
   (A) 4
   (B) $4\sqrt{2}$
   (C) 8
   (D) $4\sqrt{2\pi}$
   (E) 8π

Questions 8–27 each consist of two quantities, one in Column A and one in Column B. You are to compare the two quantities and on the answer sheet blacken space

- A if the quantity in Column A is greater;
- B if the quantity in Column B is greater;
- C if the two quantities are equal;
- D If the relationship cannot be determined from the information given.

AN E RESPONSE WILL NOT BE SCORED.

EXAMPLES

	Column A	Column B	Answers
E1.	2×6	$2 + 6$	● Ⓑ Ⓒ Ⓓ Ⓔ
E2.	$180 - x$	y	Ⓐ Ⓑ ● Ⓓ Ⓔ
E3.	$p - q$	$q - p$	Ⓐ Ⓑ Ⓒ ● Ⓔ

Diagram for E2:

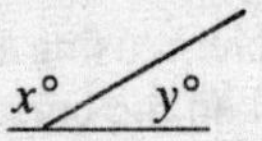

Notes:

1. In certain questions, information concerning one or both of the quantities to be compared is centered above the two columns.
2. In a given question, a symbol that appears in both columns represents the same thing in Column A as it does in Column B.
3. Letters such as x, n, and k stand for real numbers.

	Column A	Column B
8.	$\frac{n+7}{3} + \frac{n-3}{4}$	$\frac{7n+19}{7}$
	$5 \times 5 \times 5 \times R = 3 \times 3 \times 3 \times 3$	
9.	5	R
	$a > c \quad b < d$; a, b, c and d are positive integers	
10.	$\frac{a}{b}$	$\frac{c}{d}$
11.	$9 \times 682 \times 7$	$10 \times 682 \times 6$
	$-10 < r < -1$	
12.	$\frac{1}{r^7}$	$\frac{1}{r^6}$
13.	$\frac{c^2d^2e^2}{c^3d^3e^3}$	$\frac{cde}{3}$
	$n^2 > 0$	
14.	n	0
	$x \neq 0$; $x^2 = xy$	
15.	x	y
16.	$\frac{1}{2} + \frac{1}{3}$	$\frac{2}{5}$
17.	0.4%	$\frac{4}{1000}$
18.	0.0005	$\frac{1}{2}$%
19.	The number of posts needed for a fence 144 feet long and posts are placed 12 feet apart.	12 posts
	The houses on Jordan Drive are numbered as follows: west side (1801–1837) with consecutive odd numbers; east side has 18 houses	
20.	Number of houses on the west side	Number of houses on the east side

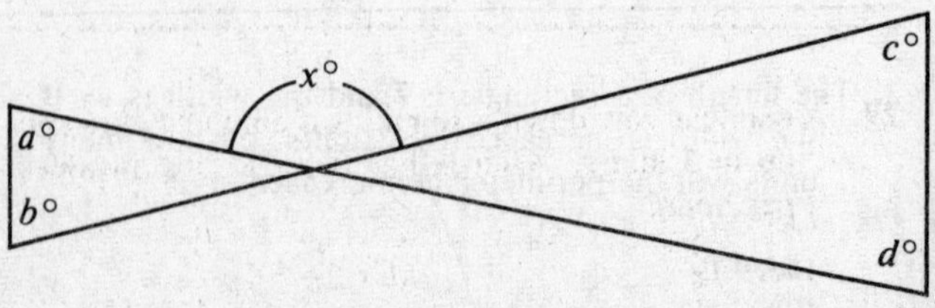

$2x$

	Column A	Column B
21.	$a + b + c + d$	$2x$

	Column A	Column B

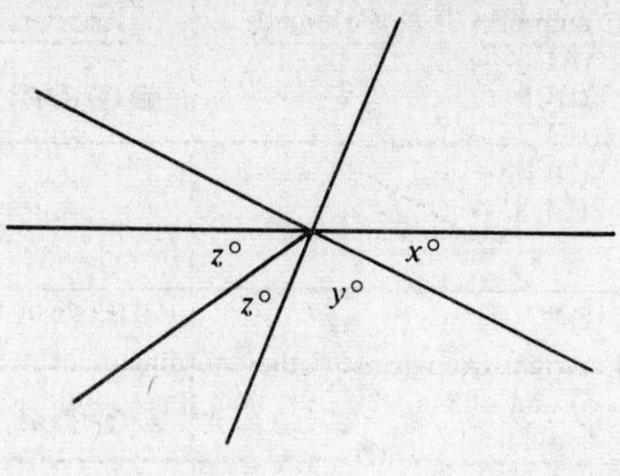

22. $x + y$ | $y + z$

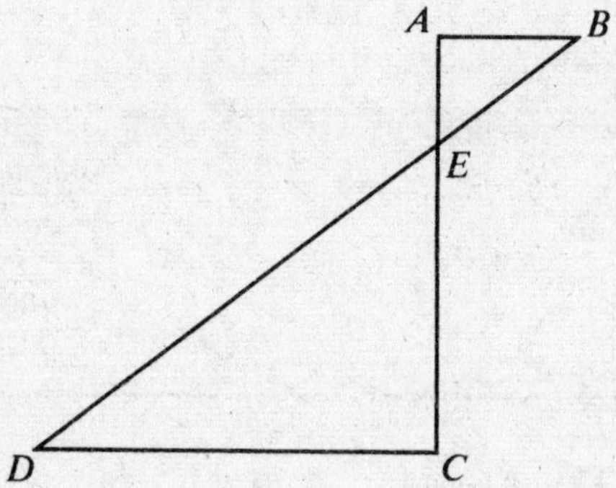

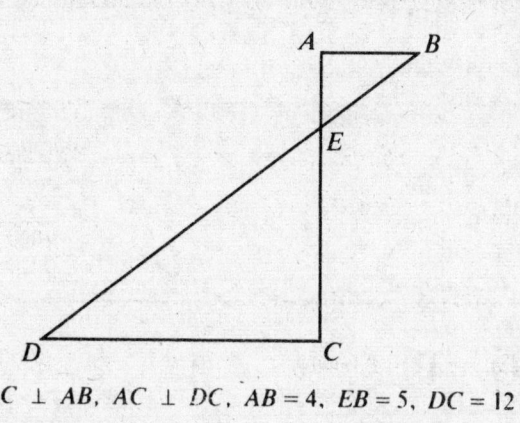

$AC \perp AB$, $AC \perp DC$, $AB = 4$, $EB = 5$, $DC = 12$

23. AC | DC

	Column A	Column B

Radius of circle A = $\frac{1}{2}$ radius of circle B

24. Circumference of circle B | Twice the circumference of circle A

Henry Aaron made 99 hits in 200 times at bat

25. The batting average of Bob Smith who made 20 fewer hits than Henry Aaron | The batting average of Cleon Jones who made 19 fewer hits than Henry Aaron

Three gold coins and one silver coin are worth as much as 5 silver coins and two gold coins

26. 4 of these silver coins | 1 of these gold coins

27. $\frac{288}{3}$ inches | $2\frac{2}{3}$ yards

Solve each of the remaining problems in this section using any available space for scratchwork. Then decide which is the best of the choices given and blacken the corresponding space on the answer sheet.

28. Mr. A owes Mr. B \$70 and Mr. B owes Mr. A \$60. If Mr. A gives Mr. B a \$50 bill, how many dollars in change should Mr. B give Mr. A?
(A) 10
(B) 20
(C) 30
(D) 40
(E) 60

29. A man can row down a 10 mile stream in 2 hours and up in 5 hours. What is his average rate, in miles per hour?
(A) $1\frac{3}{7}$
(B) $3\frac{1}{2}$
(C) $2\frac{6}{7}$
(D) 3
(E) 7

30. Base RT of triangle RST is $\frac{4}{5}$ of altitude SV. If SV equals c, which of the following is an expression for the area of the triangle RST?
(A) $\frac{2c}{5}$
(B) $\frac{2c^2}{5}$
(C) $\frac{c^2}{2}$
(D) $\frac{4c^2}{5}$
(E) $\frac{8c^2}{5}$

31. If a pipe fills a tank in h hours, what part of the tank does it fill in two hours?
(A) $\frac{2}{h}$
(B) $\frac{h}{2}$
(C) $2h$
(D) $h + 2$
(E) $h - 2$

32. If $2p$ painters can paint $2h$ houses in $2w$ weeks, how many painters would it take to paint $4h$ houses in $4w$ weeks?
(A) p
(B) $2p$
(C) $4p$
(D) $8p$
(E) $16p$

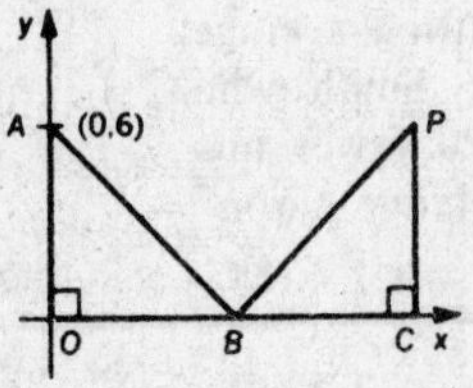

33. In the diagram above, AOB and PCB are right isosceles triangles with equal areas. What are the coordinates of point P?
(A) (6, 0)
(B) (6, 12)
(C) (12, 0)
(D) (0, 12)
(E) (12, 6)

34. The center of square $ABCD$ is located at point (3, 3) and two of its sides are along the x and y axes. The area of $ABCD$ is
(A) 6
(B) 9
(C) 24
(D) 36
(E) 81

35. For right triangle ABC the coordinates of A are (3, 5) and of C (−2, −2), then the coordinates of B could be
(A) (−2, 3)
(B) (3, −2)
(C) (2, 5)
(D) (−2, 8)
(E) (5, −2)

S T O P

IF YOU FINISH BEFORE TIME IS CALLED, YOU MAY CHECK YOUR WORK ON THIS SECTION ONLY. DO NOT WORK ON ANY OTHER SECTION IN THE TEST.

SECTION 6 MATH ABILITY

25 QUESTIONS - 30 MINUTES

In this section solve each problem, using any available space on the page for scratchwork. Then decide which is the best of the choices given and blacken the corresponding space on the answer sheet.

The following information is for your reference in solving some of the problems.

Circle of radius r: Area $= \pi r^2$; Circumference $= 2\pi r$
The number of degrees of arc in a circle is 360.
The measure in degrees of a straight angle is 180.

Definitions of symbols:

$=$ is equal to	$\leq$ is less than or equal to
$\neq$ is unequal to	$\geq$ is greater than or equal to
$<$ is less than	$\parallel$ is parallel to
$>$ is greater than	$\perp$ is perpendicular to

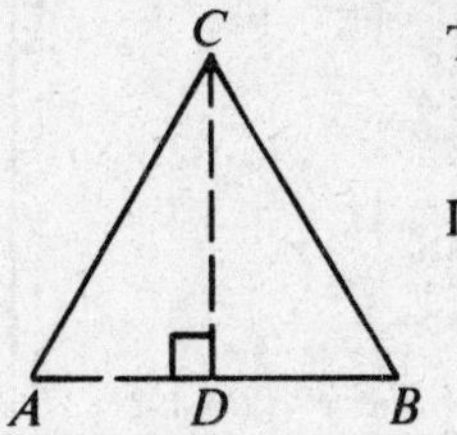

Triangle: The sum of the measures in degrees of the angles of a triangle is 180.
If $\angle CDA$ is a right angle, then
(1) area of $\triangle ABC = \frac{AB \times CD}{2}$
(2) $AC^2 = AD^2 + DC^2$

Note: Figures that accompany problems in this test are intended to provide information useful in solving the problems. They are drawn as accurately as possible EXCEPT when it is stated in a specific problem that its figure is not drawn to scale. All figures lie in a plane unless otherwise indicated. All numbers used are real numbers.

1. $12 = 1\frac{1}{3}(?)$
   (A) 3
   (B) 4
   (C) 8
   (D) 9
   (E) 16

2. If one pie serves seven people, how many pies are needed to serve a banquet of 91 people?
   (A) 7
   (B) 9
   (C) 13
   (D) 15
   (E) 637

3. Which of the following is the next smaller than $\frac{1}{2}$?
   (A) $\frac{1}{5}$
   (B) $\frac{2}{5}$
   (C) $\frac{3}{5}$
   (D) $\frac{16}{25}$
   (E) $\frac{13}{25}$

4. $\frac{a+b}{a-b} \div \frac{b+a}{b-a} = ?$
   (A) -1
   (B) 0
   (C) 1
   (D) $a + b$
   (E) $a - b$

5. How many feet are there in 7.2 inches?
   (A) $\frac{1}{6}$
   (B) $\frac{7}{12}$
   (C) $\frac{3}{5}$
   (D) $\frac{5}{3}$
   (E) 6

6. Which is the smallest of the following?
   (A) $\frac{1}{0.4}$
   (B) $\frac{5}{8}$
   (C) $(0.2)^2$
   (D) $\frac{9}{100}$
   (E) $\sqrt{1.44}$

7. A car uses a gallon of gasoline in traveling 15 miles. Another automobile can travel m miles on a gallon of gasoline. How many miles can the second travel on the amount of gasoline required by the first car in going 60 miles?
   (A) $\frac{m}{4}$
   (B) m
   (C) $4m$
   (D) $\frac{m}{9}$
   (E) $9m$

8. A box of 12 tablets costs 21 cents. The same brand is packaged in bottles containing 100 tablets and sells for $1.50 per bottle. How much is saved per dozen, by purchasing the larger amount?
(A) 3¢
(B) 4¢
(C) 30¢
(D) 36¢
(E) 40¢

9. A man can do $\frac{1}{8}$ of a piece of work in one day. How much of it can he do in x days?
(A) $\frac{x}{8}$
(B) $\frac{8}{x}$
(C) $x + 8$
(D) $8 - x$
(E) $8x$

10. If the length of a rectangle is $3u + 2v$, and its perimeter is $10u + 6v$, what is its width?
(A) $v + 2u$
(B) $2v + 4u$
(C) $2v + \frac{7}{2}u$
(D) $4v + 7u$
(E) $6v + 10u$

11. $W = i^2r$
$r = \frac{E}{i}$
Find E in terms of W and r.
(A) $\frac{1}{Wr}$
(B) Wr
(C) $\sqrt{Wr}$
(D) $\frac{W}{r}$
(E) w^2r^2

12. At 10 A.M. water begins to pour into a cylindrical can 14 inches high and 4 inches in diameter at the rate of 8 cubic inches every 10 minutes. At what time will it begin to overflow? (Use $\pi = 22/7$.)
(A) 1:20 P.M.
(B) 1:40 P.M.
(C) 3:40 P.M.
(D) 6:20 P.M.
(E) 6:40 P.M.

13. The length of a rectangle is increased by 50%. By what per cent would the width have to be decreased to maintain the same area?
(A) $33\frac{1}{3}$
(B) 50
(C) $66\frac{2}{3}$
(D) 150
(E) 200

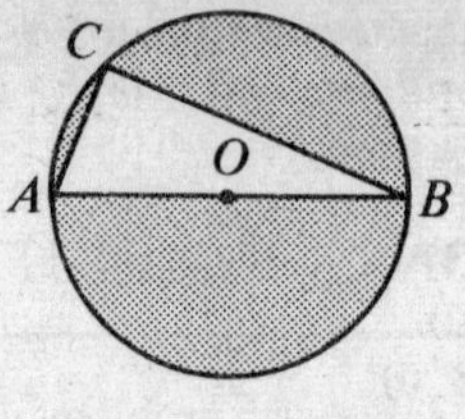

14. In the figure above, radius $OA = 6.5$
Chord $AC = 5$
Area of triangle ABC equals
(A) 16
(B) 18
(C) 24
(D) 30
(E) 36

15. A man travels in his yacht downstream at d knots and returns the same distance upstream at u knots. What is his average rate (in knots) for the round trip?
(A) $\frac{du}{2}$
(B) $\frac{d+u}{2}$
(C) $\frac{du}{d+2}$
(D) $\frac{2du}{d+u}$
(E) $\frac{d+u}{2du}$

16. $ab - 2cd = p$
$ab - 2cd = q$
$6cd - 3ab = r$
$\frac{p}{r} = ?$
(A) -3
(B) $-\frac{1}{3}$
(C) $\frac{1}{3}$
(D) 1
(E) 3

17. In a certain office, $\frac{1}{3}$ of the workers are women, $\frac{1}{2}$ of the women are married, and $\frac{1}{3}$ of the married women have children. If $\frac{3}{4}$ of the men are married and $\frac{2}{3}$ of the married men have children, what part of the workers are without children?
(A) $\frac{5}{18}$
(B) $\frac{4}{9}$
(C) $\frac{17}{36}$
(D) $\frac{11}{18}$
(E) $\frac{2}{3}$

18. The distance between point P (3, 0) and point Q is 5. The coordinates of point Q could be any of the following except
(A) (3, −5)
(B) (3, 5)
(C) (8, 0)
(D) (−8, 0)
(E) (−2, 0)

---

19. The coordinates of A and B are $(2a, 2b)$ and $(4a, 6b)$, respectively. The coordinates of the midpoint of AB in terms of a and b are
(A) $(3a, 4b)$
(B) $(3b, 4a)$
(C) $(6a, 8b)$
(D) $(6b, 8a)$
(E) $(3a, 6b)$

---

20. The vertices of rectangle $ABCD$ are the points A (0,0), B (8,0), C (8, k), D (0,5). k equals
(A) 4
(B) 5
(C) 6
(D) 3
(E) 2

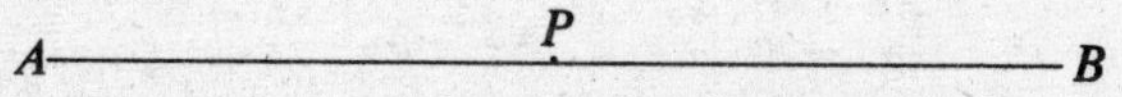

21. Point P is the midpoint of line segment AB above. If $AP = 2x + y$ and $PB = 3x - y$, then x equals
(A) $+y$
(B) $+2y$
(C) $-2y$
(D) $2/5\ y$
(E) $-2/5\ y$

22. Which of the following represents the number 69.999 rounded off to the nearest tenth?
(A) 69
(B) 69.9
(C) 69.99
(D) 70.0
(E) 70.09

---

23. Which of the following is equivalent to

$$1000 + 1 + \frac{1}{1000}?$$

(A) 1000.1
(B) 1000.01
(C) 1001.01
(D) 1001.001
(E) 1001.0001

---

24. What is the radius of a circle with a circumference of $2\pi^2$?
(A) π
(B) 2π
(C) $\pi/2$
(D) π^2
(E) 4π

---

25. The sum of 3 positive consecutive integers is a. In terms of a the smallest of these integers may be expressed as
(A) $\frac{a}{3} - 6$
(B) $a-6$
(C) $\frac{a-6}{3}$
(D) $\frac{a}{3}$
(E) $\frac{a+6}{3}$

ANSWER KEY

Note: The answers to the math sections are keyed to the corresponding review areas in Chapter 11. The numbers in parentheses after each answer refer to topics as listed below. (Note that to review for number 16, Quantitative Comparison, study Chapter 10.)

1. Fundamental Operations
2. Algebraic Operations
3. Using Algebra
4. Roots and Radicals
5. Inequalities
6. Fractions
7. Decimals
8. Percent
9. Averages
10. Motion
11. Ratio and Proportion
12. Mixtures and Solutions
13. Work
14. Coordinate Geometry
15. Geometry
16. Quantitative Comparison
17. Data Interpretation

SECTION 1 VERBAL

1.	A	9.	C	17.	D	25.	A	33.	E
2.	E	10.	E	18.	A	26.	D	34.	A
3.	D	11.	D	19.	D	27.	D	35.	B
4.	C	12.	B	20.	D	28.	A	36.	E
5.	C	13.	A	21.	C	29.	C	37.	E
6.	C	14.	E	22.	E	30.	E	38.	C
7.	D	15.	D	23.	B	31.	E	39.	C
8.	D	16.	D	24.	C	32.	C	40.	E

SECTION 2 MATH

1.	B (2)	6.	C (3)	11.	C (10)	16.	D (15)	21.	C (8)
2.	D (6)	7.	D (11)	12.	E (1,6)	17.	C (15)	22.	E (2,8)
3.	A (2)	8.	A (9)	13.	C (3)	18.	A (2)	23.	D (15)
4.	E (3)	9.	D (15)	14.	B (15)	19.	B (8)	24.	A (15)
5.	C (15)	10.	E (11)	15.	C (3)	20.	E (6)	25.	A (8,17)

SECTION 3 TEST OF STANDARD WRITTEN ENGLISH

1.	D	11.	B	21.	E	31.	D	41.	B
2.	C	12.	E	22.	A	32.	E	42.	B
3.	C	13.	E	23.	A	33.	C	43.	C
4.	C	14.	C	24.	B	34.	B	44.	E
5.	D	15.	A	25.	B	35.	C	45.	C
6.	B	16.	B	26.	D	36.	C	46.	D
7.	B	17.	D	27.	C	37.	D	47.	A
8.	B	18.	A	28.	A	38.	A	48.	C
9.	B	19.	A	29.	C	39.	D	49.	E
10.	C	20.	C	30.	A	40.	E	50.	B

SECTION 4 VERBAL

1.	D	10.	A	19.	E	28.	C	37.	A
2.	A	11.	E	20.	A	29.	B	38.	A
3.	A	12.	C	21.	C	30.	B	39.	D
4.	C	13.	C	22.	A	31.	E	40.	E
5.	E	14.	E	23.	B	32.	D	41.	D
6.	A	15.	B	24.	E	33.	C	42.	E
7.	A	16.	B	25.	A	34.	E	43.	A
8.	C	17.	C	26.	B	35.	A	44.	A
9.	B	18.	D	27.	D	36.	C	45.	B

SECTION 5 MATH

1. **C (15)**	8. **D (2,16)**	15. **C (2,16)**	22. **D (15,16)**	29. **C (10)**
2. **A (6)**	9. **A (1,16)**	16. **A (1,6,16)**	23. **C (15,16)**	30. **B (15)**
3. **B (15)**	10. **A (5,16)**	17. **C (6,8,16)**	24. **C (15,16)**	31. **A (13)**
4. **E (6)**	11. **A (1,16)**	18. **B (7,8,16)**	25. **D (6,16)**	32. **B (11,13)**
5. **C (17)**	12. **B (5,16)**	19. **A (1,16)**	26. **C (3,16)**	33. **E (14)**
6. **C (9)**	13. **D (4,16)**	20. **A (1,16)**	27. **C (1,16)**	34. **D (14)**
7. **B (15)**	14. **D (5,16)**	21. **C (15,16)**	28. **D (1)**	35. **B (14)**

SECTION 6 MATH

1. **D (1,6)**	6. **C (1)**	11. **C (2)**	16. **B (2)**	21. **B (2)**
2. **C (11)**	7. **C (11,13)**	12. **B (11,15)**	17. **D (6)**	22. **D (1)**
3. **B (6)**	8. **A (15)**	13. **A (8,15)**	18. **D (14)**	23. **D (6,7)**
4. **A (2,6)**	9. **A (2)**	14. **D (15)**	19. **A (14)**	24. **A (15)**
5. **C (11)**	10. **A (11,15)**	15. **D (10)**	20. **B (14)**	25. **C (3)**

SELF-EVALUATION

The model SAT test you have just completed has the same format as the actual SAT. As you take more of the model tests in this chapter, you will lose any SAT "stage fright" you might have.

Use the steps that follow to evaluate your performance on Model SAT Test 2. (Note: You'll find the charts referred to in steps 1–5 on the next three pages.)

STEP 1 Use the Answer Key to check your answers for each section.

STEP 2 For each section, count the number of correct and incorrect answers (remember that you don't count omitted answers), and enter the numbers on the appropriate lines of the chart "Obtaining Your Raw Score." Then do the indicated calculations to get your Raw Verbal Score, your Raw TSWE Score, and your Raw Math Score.

STEP 3 Consult the chart "Evaluate Your Performance" to see how well you did.

STEP 4 To pinpoint the specific areas in which you need to improve, circle the numbers of the questions that you either left blank or got wrong on the "Identify Your Weaknesses" charts. This will tell you where to concentrate your efforts to get the most out of your study time. The chart for the math sections gives you page references for review and practice by skill areas. The charts for the verbal and TSWE sections refer you to the appropriate chapters to study for each question type.

STEP 5 Do the review and practice indicated on the charts wherever you had a concentration of circles.

Remember that in addition to evaluating your scores, you should read all of the answer explanations for questions you answered incorrectly, questions you omitted, and questions you answered correctly but found difficult. Reviewing the answer explanations will help you understand concepts and strategies, and may point out shortcuts.

OBTAINING YOUR RAW SCORE

Verbal

Section 1 ________ (number correct) − 1/4 (________ number incorrect) = ________ (A)

Section 4 ________ (number correct) − 1/4 (________ number incorrect) = ________ (B)

Raw Verbal Score = (A) + (B) = ________

TSWE

Section 3 ________ (number correct) − 1/4 (________ number incorrect) = Raw TSWE Score = ________

Math

Section 2 ________ (number correct) − 1/4 (________ number incorrect) = ________ (C)

Section 5 (1-7, 28-35) ________ (number correct) − 1/4 (________ number incorrect) = ________ (D)

Section 5 (8-27) ________ (number correct) − 1/3 (________ number incorrect) = ________ (E)

Section 6 ________ (number correct) − 1/4 (________ number incorrect) = ________ (F)

Raw Math Score = (D) + (E) + (F) = ________

EVALUATE YOUR PERFORMANCE

	Verbal	TSWE	Math
Excellent	75-85	45-50	70-85
Very Good	65-74	39-44	60-69
Good	50-64	34-38	50-59
Average	40-49	25-33	40-49
Below Average	28-39	15-24	30-39
Unsatisfactory	below 28	below 15	below 30

IDENTIFY YOUR WEAKNESSES
Verbal

Question Type	Question Numbers		Chapter to Study
	Section 1	Section 4	
Antonym	1, 2, 3, 4, 5, 6, 7, 8, 9, 10	1, 2, 3, 4, 5, 6, 7, 8, 9, 10, 11, 12, 13, 14, 15	Chapter 4
Analogy	16, 17, 18, 19, 20, 21, 22, 23, 24, 25	36, 37, 38, 39, 40, 41, 42, 43, 44, 45	Chapter 5
Sentence Completion	11, 12, 13, 14, 15	16, 17, 18, 19, 20, 31, 32, 33, 34, 35	Chapter 6
Reading Comprehension	26, 27, 28, 29, 30, 31, 32, 33, 34, 35, 36, 37, 38, 39, 40	21, 22, 23, 24, 25, 26, 27, 28, 29, 30	Chapter 7

TSWE

Question Type	Question Numbers	Chapter to Study
Usage	1, 2, 3, 4, 5, 6, 7, 8, 9, 10, 11, 12, 13, 14, 15, 16, 17, 18, 19, 20, 21, 22, 23, 24, 25, 41, 42, 43, 44, 45, 46, 47, 48, 49, 50	Chapter 12
Sentence Correction	26, 27, 28, 29, 30, 31, 32, 33, 34, 35, 36, 37, 38, 39, 40	Chapter 12

Math

Skill Area	Question Numbers			Pages to Study
	Section 2	Section 5	Section 6	
Fundamental Operations	12	9, 11, 16, 19, 20, 27, 28	1, 6, 22	300–302
Algebraic Operations	1, 3, 18	5, 8, 15	4, 9, 11, 16, 21	302–308
Using Algebra	4, 6, 13, 15, 22, 26	26	25	308–316
Fractions	2, 12, 20	2, 4, 16, 17, 18, 25	1, 3, 4, 17, 23	316–329
Decimals and Percents	19, 21, 22, 25	17, 18	13, 23	329–334
Verbal Problems	8, 11	6, 29, 31, 32	7, 15	335–352
Ratio and Proportion	7, 10	32	2, 5, 7, 10, 12	340–346
Geometry	5, 9, 14, 16, 17, 23, 24	1, 3, 7, 21, 22, 23, 24, 30	8, 10, 12, 13, 14, 18, 19, 20, 24	355–368
Coordinate Geometry		33, 34, 35	18, 19, 20	352–355
Inequalities		10, 12, 14		309–311; 315–316
Quantitative Comparison		8, 9, 10, 11, 12, 13, 14, 15, 16, 17, 18, 19, 20, 21, 22, 23, 24, 25, 26, 27		279–299
Roots and Radicals		4, 13		306–307; 312–313

ANSWER EXPLANATIONS

SECTION 1

1. A. The opposite of *licentious* (immoral) is *moral.*

2. E. The opposite of *recalcitrant* (refusing compliance) is *tractable* (willing to conform or comply).

3. D. The opposite of *impassive* (devoid of emotion) is *agitated.*

4. C. The opposite of *profligate* (dissolute) is *staid* (sober).

5. C. The opposite of *prolix* (long-winded) is *terse* (concise.)

6. C. The opposite of *prodigious* (enormous) is *microscopic* (tiny).

7. D. The opposite of *specious* (seemingly plausible) is *veracious* (true).

8. D. The opposite of *sedulous* (persevering) is *indolent* (lazy).

9. C. The opposite of *effete* (worn out) is *energetic.*

10. E. The opposite of *nocturnal* (nightly) is *daily.*

11. D. *Inaninities* (words which are empty and senseless) is the only word which can go with the expression "a pack of lies." *Saws, maxims, aphorisms* and *proverbs* cannot be called *lies.*

12. B. The showing of a lack of *concealed* weapons revealed that people were friendly or *amicably* disposed.

13. A. This question calls for judgment since all the choices seem good. However, a *concerted* or joint effort where everyone does his best is most likely to produce the desired results.

14. E. We can eliminate Choices C and D because they are undesirable traits. Choices A and B are synonyms of things mentioned in the sentence and are repetitious. Choice E presents a new and desirable trait.

15. D. *Thrift* is a virtue not mentioned in the sentence.

16. D. The *policeman* fights the *criminal* and the *evangelist* fights the *sinner.*

17. D. A *thermometer* measures temperature or *heat;* a *Geiger counter* measures *radiation.*

18. A. To *gulp* is more extreme than to *sip;* to *guffaw* is more extreme than to *giggle.*

19. D. The *crest* of a wave may be compared to a *peak* and the *trough* to a *valley.*

20. D. *Titanic* (enormous) and *lilliputian* (puny) are antonyms, as are *obese* and *emaciated.*

21. C. *Scold* and *rebuke* are synonyms, as are *fondle* and *caress.*

22. E. An *airplane* is serviced in a *hangar;* an *automobile,* in a *garage.*

23. B. A *spine* is a sharp-pointed outgrowth on a *cactus;* a *quill,* a sharp-pointed bristle on a *porcupine.*

24. C. A *candle* may be made of *tallow;* a *statue,* of *bronze.*

25. A. One example of a *marsupial* is an *opossum;* of a *rodent,* a *squirrel.*

26. D. Throughout the passage, the author mentions characteristics of a city which he finds admirable.

27. D. The reference to the "penniless man" and "noble impersonality" indicates that the services are given to everybody.

28. A. This passage is a defense of cities.

29. C. The use of the expression, "and above all" in the next-to-last sentence emphasizes the author's pleasure with the impartial service.

30. E. The last sentence justifies Choice E.

31. E. In the second paragraph, the author mentions two arboreal (living in trees) mammals—the sloth and the monkey.

32. C. In the second paragraph the author shows how the adaptation of mammals parallels that of ancient reptiles. As an illustration, he compares the flying abilities of the bat (a mammal) with those of the ptersosaur (a reptile).

33. E. See the last sentence of the first paragraph.

34. A. In the second paragraph, the author points out the superiority of the mammals to the reptiles and in the discussion of the tyrannosaur and the tiger, the author attributes the tiger's superiority to a "superior brain."

35. B. Since these three animals were reptiles, we may assume that *saur* means reptile.

36. E. The last sentence of the passage supports Choice E.

37. E. The last sentence of the second paragraph supports Choice E.

38. C. Choice C is supported by the opening sentence.

39. C. The particles that make up the atom are mentioned in the opening and closing sentences.

40. E. Molecules are much larger than atoms and even larger than electrons.

SECTION 2

1. B. $(r - s) - (s - r)$
$r - s - s + r$
$2r - 2s$ (Combine similar terms)
$2(r - s)$ (Factor)

2. D. $\left(\frac{1}{3} - \frac{1}{12}\right) \div \left(\frac{1}{4}\right)$

$\frac{3}{12} \div \frac{1}{4}$

$\frac{\cancel{3}}{\cancel{12}_{\,3}} \cdot \frac{\cancel{4}}{1} = 1$

3. A. $ax + b - y = 0$
$ax + b = y$
$b = y - ax$

4. E. From $-25°$ to $0° = 25°$
From $0°$ to $+3° = 3°$
Total $= 28°$

5. C. Draw $OA \perp QR$
AV = side of square = 2
Area of square = 4
Draw radius OS

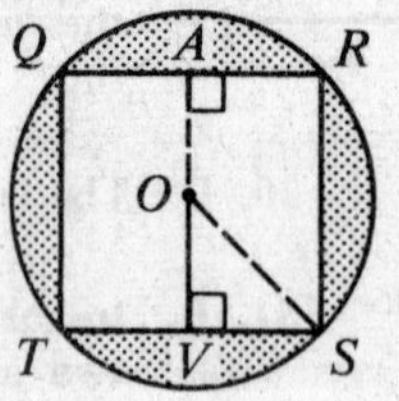

$VS = \frac{1}{2} ST$ (side of square)
$= 1$ (radius drawn $\perp$ chord bisects chord)
In right triangle OVS,
$(OV)^2 + (VS)^2 = (OS)^2$
or $1 + 1 = (OS)^2$
$2 = (OS)^2$
$\sqrt{2} = OS$ (radius of circle)
Area of circle $= \pi(\sqrt{2})^2$ or 2π
Area of circle − Area of square = Area of shaded portion
$2\pi - 4$ = Area of shaded portion

6. C. Let x = the number
$3x - 7 = 32$ (given)
$3x = 39$
$x = 13$
Twice the number, or $2x$, $= 26$

7. D. $\frac{\text{Ken}}{\text{feet}} = \frac{1}{5.97} = \frac{59.7}{x}$
$x = (5.97)(59.7)$ (in a proportion, the product of the means equals the product of the extremes)
$x = 356.409$ or 356 feet

8. A. Since average = 75,
Sum of all grades $= (75)(4) = 300$
Sum of three grades $= \underline{240}$ (given)
Grade on first examination $= 60$

9. D. Draw altitudes AE, BF
Area of figure =
$\triangle AED + \triangle BFC +$ rectangle $AEFB$

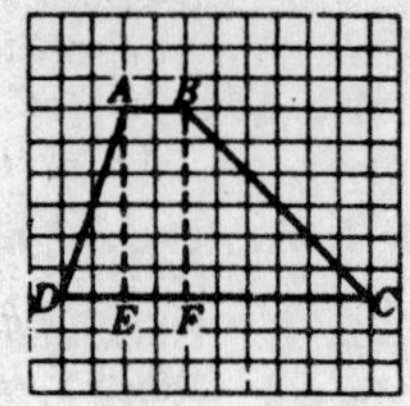

Area of $\triangle AED$ =
$\frac{bh}{2}$ or $\frac{(2 \text{ units})(6 \text{ units})}{2}$ or 6 square units

Area of $\triangle BFC$ =
$\frac{bh}{2}$ or $\frac{(6 \text{ units})(6 \text{ units})}{2}$ or 18 square units

Area of rectangle $AEFB$ =
bh or (2 units)(6 units) or 12 square units
Sum = 36 square units

OR, apply formula for area of trapezoid
Area $= \frac{1}{2} h(b + b_1)$
Area $= \frac{1}{2}(6)(10 + 2)$
Area = 36 square units

10. E. Let x = number of pencils that can be bought for d dollars (or $100d$ cents)
$\frac{\text{number of pencils}}{\text{cost per pencil, in cents}} = \frac{p}{c} = \frac{x}{100d}$
$cx = 100dp$ (in a proportion, the product of the means equals the product of the extremes)
$x = \frac{100dp}{c}$ (divide by c)

11. C. $\frac{\text{Distance}}{\text{Time}} = \text{Rate}$
$\frac{d}{h}$ = rate of train that resulted in arrival two hours late
$h - 2$ = time that would result in arrival on schedule
$\frac{d}{h-2}$ = rate that would result in arrival on schedule

12. E. Since the question indicates that the quotient is *exactly* one of the answers, the correct answer must obviously have as its last digit a 7 which when multiplied by the 9 (the last digit of the denominator) will yield a 3 (last digit of the numerator).

13. C. Mr. Stanley is now $x - 5$ years old. Mr. Stanley was $(x - 5) - 5$ years old five years ago.
$(x - 5) - 5 = x - 10$

14. B. Angle SVR is a right angle
Angle $SVR = 90°$
Angle $VSR = x°$
Angles $SVR + VSR + VRS = 180°$
(The sum of the angles of a triangle equals 180°)
Angle $VRS = 180° - (90° + x)$ or $90° - x°$
Angle VRS + Angle $VRW = 180°$
Angle $VRW = 180° - (90° - x°)$
or $180° - 90° + x°$
or $90° + x°$
OR,
Angle VRW = Angle SVR + Angle VSR
(the exterior angle of a triangle equals the sum of both remote interior angles)
Angle $VRW = 90° + x°$

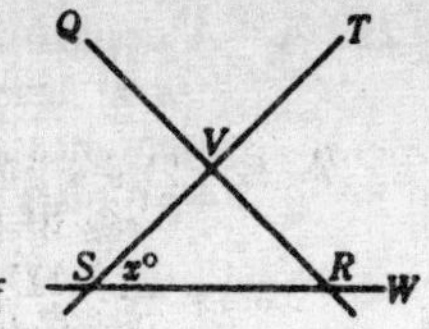

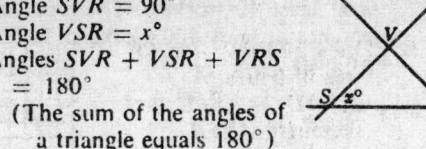

15. C. 48 ounces = 3 pounds
Cost of first pound = 30¢
Cost of 2 pounds = 31¢

Total cost = 61¢

16. D. $\angle 1 + \angle 2 = \angle ABC$ and $\angle 3 + \angle 4 = \angle EFG$. Since $\angle 1 = \angle 3$, we are applying the principle: if equal quantities are subtracted from unequal quantities, the remainders are unequal in the same order.

17. C. Let $x = AB$
Then $BC = 3x \left(\frac{BC}{AC} = 3\right)$
$AC = 4x$ (side of square)
Area of $BCDJ = 3x^2$
Area of $HJFG = 3x^2$

$$\frac{\text{Area of } BCDJ}{\text{Area of } HJFG} = \frac{3x^2}{3x^2} = \frac{1}{1}$$

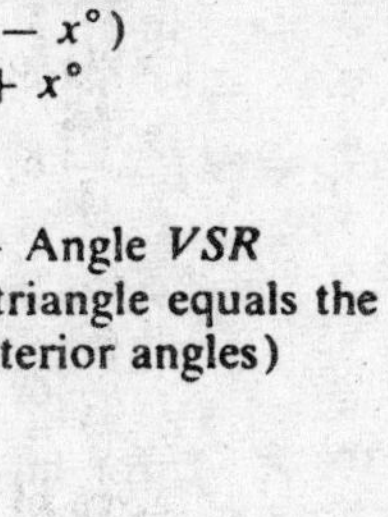

18. A. $r = 18$

$\frac{r}{s} = \frac{6}{y}$

$\frac{18}{s} = \frac{6}{y}$ (substitution)

$18y = 6s$

$y = \frac{6s}{18}$ or $\frac{s}{3}$ (division by 18)

$\frac{y}{s} = \frac{1}{3}$ (division by s)

19. B. Let $x\%$ or $\frac{x}{100}$ = increase of manpower required to return to normal (100%) production
80% (present production) + $x\%$ of present output = 100% (normal output)

$$\frac{80}{100} + \left(\frac{x}{100} \cdot \frac{80}{100}\right) = 100\%$$

$$\frac{4}{5} + \frac{4x}{500} = 1$$
$$400 + 4x = 500$$
$$4x = 100$$
$$x = 25\%$$

20. E. If $\frac{2}{3}$ of the faculty are women, $\frac{1}{3}$ are men.

If $\frac{3}{5}$ of the male teachers are married, $\frac{2}{5}$ are unmarried.

Then $\frac{2}{5}$ of $\frac{1}{3}$ or $\frac{2}{15}$ of the faculty are unmarried men.

Let x = total number of faculty members.

$\frac{2}{15}$ of x = number of unmarried male teachers

$\frac{2x}{15} = 12$

$2x = 180$
$x = 90$

21. C. $\frac{\text{Change}}{\text{Original}} \times 100$ = Per cent change

$\frac{-2}{8}$ or $\left(-\frac{1}{4}\right) \times 100$ = Per cent change

-25% = change

22. E. $0.1r = 0.2s$
$0.2s = 0.3t$
$0.1r = 0.3t$ (things equal to the same thing are equal to each other)
$r = 3t$ (multiply by 10)
or, $100\%\ r = 300\%\ t$ (conversion to per cent)

23. D. (Diameter)(π) = Circumference
(Diameter)(π) = 4π inches
Diameter = $\frac{4\pi}{\pi}$ or 4 inches (division)
Since the length is 48 inches there will be a maximum of 12 tumblers placed across the length. Since the width is 32 inches there will be a maximum of 8 tumblers placed across the width of the table. Total number of tumblers will be 12 × 8 or 96.

24. A. Triangle AGD is similar to triangle GEF (They have a common angle and EF is parallel to AD)

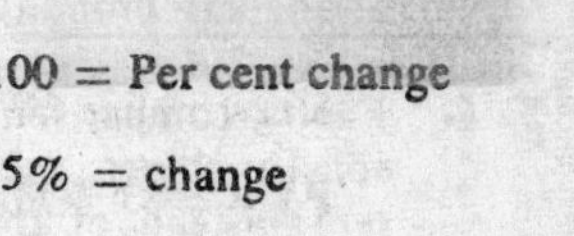

Altitude of triangle AGD equals

$DH + HK + \frac{1}{2}KP$ or 75

Altitude of triangle GEF equals $\frac{1}{2}KP$ or 15

$$\frac{\text{Altitude of } AGD}{\text{Altitude of } GEF} = \frac{75}{15} = \frac{5}{1}$$

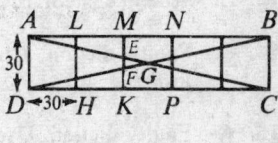

Therefore, $\frac{\text{Base of } AGD}{\text{Base of } GEF} = \frac{5}{1}$

Let $x = EF$

$$\frac{AD}{EF} = \frac{5}{1} = \frac{30}{x}$$

$$5x = 30$$

$$x = 6$$

25. A. A department has at least 10 bureaus. A bureau has at least 40 workers. Therefore one department has at least 400 workers. 10% of 400 = 40 typists.

SECTION 3

1. D. Faulty comparison. Do not compare a person with a thing. Correct form: *Your argument is no different from that of the last speaker . . . .*

2. C. Violation of parallel structure. Change *to attend* to *attending.*

3. C. Faulty reference. *Which* should not refer to a clause.

4. C. Lack of agreement. Woman (singular) requires a singular pronoun.

5. D. Faulty comparison. When comparing two persons or things, use the comparative form (*better*) instead of the superlative (*best*).

6. B. Faulty diction. Omit the article (*a*) in *this kind of a . . . .*

7. B. Faulty diction. Use *take* instead of *bring.*

8. B. Faulty diction. Change *would I go* to *whether I would go.*

9. B. Wrong case. Change *John* to *John's.*

10. C. Faulty diction. Use *behind* instead of *in back of.*

11. B. Faulty diction. Change *amount* to *number.*

12. E. Sentence is correct.

13. E. Sentence is correct.

14. C. Faulty diction. Change *enthuse* to *be enthusiastic.*

15. A. Faulty diction. Use *annoyed* or *irritated* instead of *aggravated.*

16. B. Error in agreement. *A system has been incorporated* is correct.

17. D. Error in agreement. The antecedent of *who* is *one*. Change *plan* to *plans.*

18. A. Error in diction. Do not use *due to* when you mean *because of.*

19. A. Error in case. Use *who* because it is the subject of *would win.*

20. C. Error in tense. Substitute *have lived* for *am living.*

21. E. Sentence is correct.

22. A. Faulty diction. Do not use *neither* when discussing more than two items. Substitute *none.*

23. A. Dangling participle. Change to a subordinate clause—*When we descended . . . .*

24. B. Faulty diction. Use *if* to indicate a condition. Substitute *whether.*

25. B. Omission of important word. Sentence is better as: *He had a keen interest in and a wide knowledge of his esoteric subject.*

26. D. Do not use *calculate* when you mean *think.*

27. C. This sentence does not violate parallel structure.

28. A. Sentence is correct.

29. C. Improper punctuation of direct quotation. Choice C is correct.

30. A. Sentence is correct.

31. D. This choice eliminates the error in parallel structure.

32. E. Omission of important word and error in verb tense are corrected in choice E.

33. C. Error in the possessive form of *government* and *it.*

34. B. Error in agreement. *Her brother . . . insists* is correct.

35. C. Error in agreement. *Kind* is singular and requires a singular modifier (*this*).

36. C. Do not use *eminent* (outstanding) in place of *imminent* (impending; near at hand).

37. D. Changing *absenteeism is reduced* to *reduces absenteeism* maintains parallel structure.

38. A. The sentence's use of parallel structure is effective and correct.

39. D. The addition of *when* makes the sentence more effective by tightening up the relationship between the clauses.

40. E. This choice corrects the sentence fragment.

41. B. Wrong case. The possessive case of *Jones* is *Jones's*.

42. B. **Wrong tense. Change *is* to *has been*.**

43. C. Faulty diction. Delete *of*.

44. E. Sentence is correct.

45. C. Error in case. Substitute *him* for *he*.

46. D. Faulty comparison. Change *any state* to *that of any other state*.

47. A. Dangling participle. Change *Reading quickly* to *Because he was a quick reader*.

48. C. Incorrect case. Change *us* to *we*.

49. E. Sentence is correct.

50. B. **Wrong word. Use *lying* instead of *laying*.**

SECTION 4

1. D. The opposite of *phlegmatic* (sluggish) is *active*.

2. A. The opposite of *salutary* (wholesome, beneficial) is *harmful*.

3. A. The opposite of *callous* (uncaring) is *concerned*.

4. C A *demure* (markedly quiet and unexcited) person is not *demonstrative*.

5. E. The opposite of *orthodox* (holding correct views) is *heretical* (unorthodox).

6. A The opposite of *dissuade* (discourage) is *exhort* (urge on).

7. A. The opposite of *succor* (aid, assistance) is *hindrance*.

8. C. A *laudatory* (admiring) remark is not *defamatory*.

9. B. A *lackadaisical* person lacks enthusiasm. He is not *enthusiastic*.

10. A. A *suave* individual is polite and polished. He would not be *tactless*.

11. E. The opposite of *fervent* (showing intensity of feeling) is *indifferent*.

12. C. *Sacrilegious* (profaning something sacred) is the opposite of *sanctifying* (making holy).

13. C. *Urbane* (sophisticated) and *naive* (unsophisticated) are opposites.

14. E. *Deference* (respectful regard) and *disrespect* are opposites.

15. B. *Puny* (small) and *gigantic* (large) are opposites.

16. B. A *paregoric* would be the most suitable remedy.

17. C. *Omniscient* means all-knowing.

18. D. The bonus of a trip to Europe would provide an *incentive*.

19. E. A pessimist has a doleful or *lugubrious* outlook.

20. A. *Germane*, meaning pertinent, is the only appropriate choice.

21. C. The passage describes the extreme lack of interest in and knowledge of social insurance. Choice C sums this up.

22. A. Americans have always been proud of our "rugged individualism." Choice A is best.

23. B. **The last sentence supports Choice B.**

24. E. **The passage discusses the versatility of all Renaissance artists. Choice E is best.**

25. A. **The next-to-the-last sentence discusses Leonardo's fame as an engineer and scientist.**

26. B. Another way of describing an "all-around Man" (sentence 1) is that he is "many-sided."

27. D. The last portion of the paragraph reminds us of the "terrible" things we did because of superstition.

28. C. Since the passage ends with a note of gratitude to science, we may assume that the author will continue to discuss science and scientific methods.

29. B. The opening sentence supports Choice B.

30. B. The use of the words "it is well to reflect occasionally" in the last sentence supports Choice B. An examination of the other choices reveals that they are all false according to the passage.

31. E. The word *or* in the sentence indicates that we need a contrast to *boon* (blessing). *Disaster* provides such a contrast.

32. D. *Assiduous* means diligent.

33. C. *Verbose* means overly wordy.

34. E. A *lexicographer* (writer of dictionaries) would be interested in the derivation of words.

35. A. *Voracious* (craving or eating large quantities of food) animals *stalk* (pursue stealthily) their prey.

36. C. *Ostracism* (banishment from society) is a form of *censure* (expression of disapproval). *Applause* is a demonstration of *approval.*

37. A. A *cobbler* repairs *shoes* and a *mechanic* repairs *automobiles.*

38. A. *Propitiate* and *appease* are synonyms; likewise, *disturb* and *agitate* are synonyms.

39. D. *Laconic* and *voluble* are antonyms; likewise *frozen* and *boiling* are antonyms.

40. E. *Rooster* and *gander* are male; *hen* and *goose,* female.

41. D. A *viola* is a kind of *instrument;* a *chisel,* a kind of *tool.*

42. E. In measuring liquids, (liquid measure) *pint* immediately precedes *quart;* in measuring time, *second* immediately precedes *minute.*

43. A. *Assurance* will allay *fear* and an *opiate* will allay *pain.*

44. A. The symbol of *time* is a bearded gentleman carrying a *scythe;* the symbol of *justice* is a blindfolded lady carrying a *scale.*

45. B. *Felicity* (bliss) and *sorrow* are antonyms; *agility* and *clumsiness* are antonyms.

SECTION 5

1. C. Area of triangle $XOY =$

$\frac{1}{2}bh$ or $\frac{1}{2}(XO)(YO)$

Since $YO = XO = r$

$$32 = \frac{1}{2}r^2$$

$$r^2 = 64$$

Area of circle $= \pi r^2 = 64\pi$

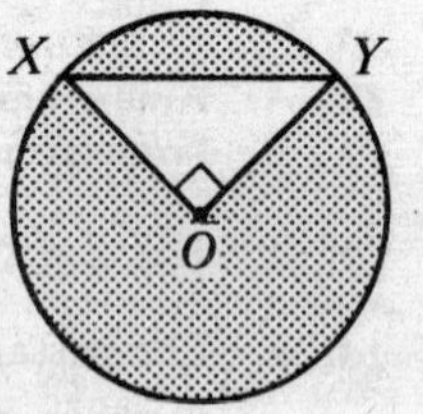

2. A. $\frac{1}{3}$ of $\frac{3}{4}$ is $\frac{3}{12}$ or $\frac{1}{4}$ or $\frac{4}{16}$

$\frac{1}{4}$ of $\frac{3}{4}$ is $\frac{3}{16}$

$\frac{4}{16}$ is $\frac{1}{16}$ more than $\frac{3}{16}$

3. B. The perimeter of a rectangle is twice the width plus twice the length. The original perimeter was $2l + 2w$ and the increased perimeter was $2l + 2(w + 2)$ or $2l + 2w + 4$. The perimeter is increased by 4 units.

4. E. Reduce the fractions:

$\frac{6}{14} = \frac{3}{7} \quad \frac{9}{21} = \frac{3}{7}; \quad \frac{3}{7} (\ ) \frac{3}{7} = \frac{3}{7}$

The answer is obviously =.

5. C.

$$7p = 5q$$

$$3p = xq$$

Therefore: $\frac{7p}{3p} = \frac{5q}{xq}$ (by division)

$$\frac{7}{3} = \frac{5}{x}$$

$$7x = 15$$

$$x = 2\frac{1}{7}$$

6. C. The average of the ages of the three men is 44, so the sum of their ages is 44×3 or 132 years. If two men are 42, the sum of their ages is 84. The maximum age of the third man is $132 - 84$ or 48 years.

7. B. Area of circle = Area of triangle

$$\pi r^2 = \frac{1}{2}bh$$

$$\pi r^2 = \frac{1}{2}16)(4\pi)$$

$$r^2 = 32$$

$$r = \sqrt{32} \text{ or } \sqrt{16} \cdot \sqrt{2} \text{ or } 4\sqrt{2}$$

8. D. $\frac{n+7}{3} + \frac{n-3}{4}$

$$\frac{4n + 28 + 3n - 9}{12}$$

$$\frac{7n + 19}{12}$$

The numerators are the same but the fraction in column *B* has a smaller denominator.
If 7n + 19 has a positive value, column *B* would be the larger; however, if 7n + 19 has a negative value, column *A* would be the larger.

9. A. $125\ R = 81$

$$R = \frac{81}{125}$$

$$5 > R$$

10. A. Since $a > c$ and $b < d$ the fraction in column A has a larger numerator and a smaller denominator than the fraction in column B.

11. A. Since both columns have 682 in common, consider only 9×7 in column A and 10×6 in column B. $63 > 60$

12. B. The value of r is between -1 and -10. For any of these values r^7 would be negative. For example, if $r = -2$ then

$$\frac{1}{r^7} = \frac{1}{-128} \text{ or } -\frac{1}{128}$$

For any of these values for r, r^6 would have a positive value. For example, if $r = -2$, then

$$\frac{1}{r^6} = \frac{1}{64} \qquad \frac{1}{64} > -\frac{1}{128}$$

13. D. $\frac{c^2d^2e^2}{c^3d^3e^3}$ or $\frac{1}{cde}$ may be larger than, smaller than, or equal to $\frac{cde}{3}$ depending upon the values of $c,d,$ and e.

14. D. Since $n^2 > 0$, n may have a negative value, and $n < 0$. Since $n^2 > 0$, n may have a positive value in which case $n > 0$.

15. C. $x^2 = xy$. Divide by x and $x = y$.

16. A. $\frac{1}{2} + \frac{1}{3} = \frac{5}{6} = \frac{25}{30} \qquad \frac{2}{5} = \frac{12}{30}$

17. C. $0.4\% = \frac{0.4}{100} = \frac{4}{1000}$

18. B. $\frac{1}{2}\% = 0.5\% = 0.005$
$0.005 > 0.0005$

19. A. The length of the fence (144 feet) ÷ the distance between the posts (12 feet) equals 12 spaces between posts. However, the first space has 2 posts and an additional post will appear at each subsequent space.

20. A. There are 19 houses on the west side. From #1 to #37 there are 19 odd numbers.

21. C. The exterior angle of a triangle equals the sum of the measure of both remote interior angles. Therefore, $x = a + b$ and $x = c + d$. By addition, $2x = a + b + c + d$.

22. D. y is common to both columns. Consider x and z. No information is given about their relationship.

23. C. Since vertical angles 1 and 2 are equal, right triangle *ABE* is similar to right triangle *DEC*,

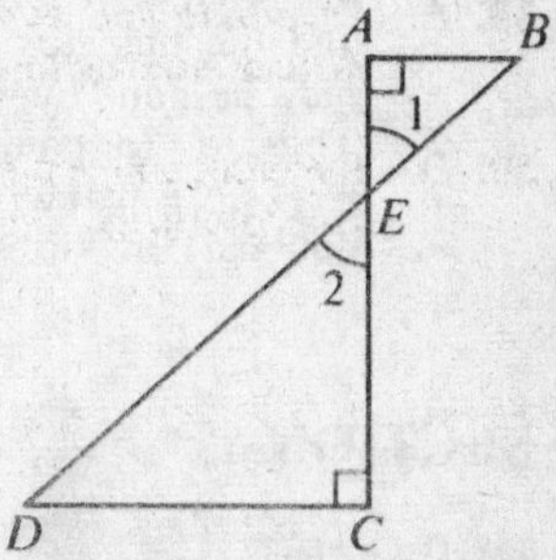

and $\frac{AB}{DC} = \frac{AE}{EC}$

In *ABE*, hypotenuse $BE = 5$, and $AB = 4$ then leg $AE = 3$. In DEC, if $AB = 4$, and $DC = 12$, and since $AE = 3$, then $EC = 9$, and $AC = AE + EC = 3 + 9 = 12$.

24. C. Circumference $= 2\pi r$. If the radius of $A = \frac{1}{2}$ radius of B, then circumference of $A = \frac{1}{2}$ circumference of B. This may be stated as follows: twice the circumference of A = the circumference of B.

25. D. For Bob and Cleon the number of times at bat are not given. The batting average depends upon the number of hits as compared with the total times at bat.

26. C. Let g = the value of each gold coin and let s = the value of each silver coin. Then,
$3g + 1s = 5s + 2g$ (given)
$1g = 4s$

27. C. 2 yards = 72 inches
$\frac{2}{3}$ yards = 24 inches

$\frac{288}{3}$ inches = 96 inches

$2\frac{2}{3}$ yards = 96 inches

28. D. Mr. *A* owes Mr. *B* \$70 and Mr. *B* owes Mr. *A* \$60, so Mr. *A* owes Mr. *B* \$10. If Mr. *A* gives Mr. *B* \$50 (\$40 more than he owes Mr. *B*), Mr. *B* must give Mr. *A* \$40 in change.

29. C. Average rate equals (total) distance divided by (total) time. The total distance up and down is 20 miles and the time is 5 plus 2 or 7 hours.
The average rate is $\frac{20}{7}$ or $2\frac{6}{7}$ miles per hour.

30. B. Area of triangle

$= \frac{1}{2}$ base × altitude

$= \frac{1}{2}\left(\frac{4}{5}c\right)(c)$

$= \frac{2c^2}{5}$

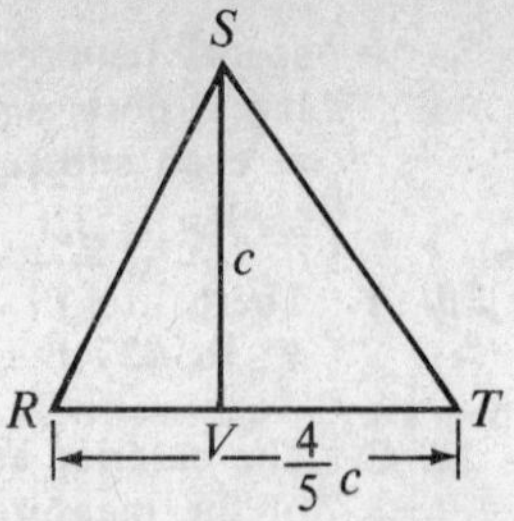

31. A. Substitute a number for the letter. If the tank fills in 7 ($h = 7$) hours, $\frac{2}{7}$ of it fills in 2 hours. Substituting h for 7, $\frac{2}{h}$ of it fills in 2 hours.

32. B. If the amount of work to be done is doubled, and the time for the work is doubled, the job may be done by the same number of workers. Thus, if $2p$ painters paint $2h$ houses in $2w$ weeks, $2p$ painters can paint $4h$ houses (work doubled) in $4w$ weeks (time doubled).

33. E. Since the areas are equal $PC = AO$ and $OB = BC$. Since the triangles are isosceles $AO = OB$ and $BC = PC$.

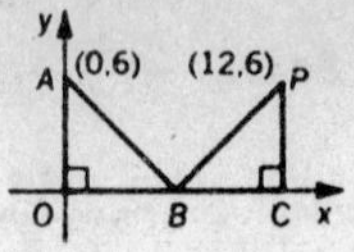

34. D. Observe the location of the center of the square. Each side of the square is twice the distance to the axes or 6 units. Area equals $(\text{side})^2$ or 36.

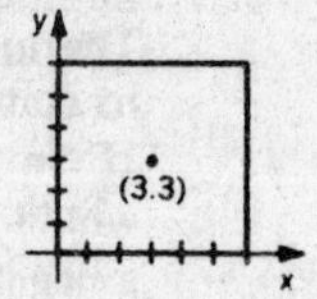

35. B. Locate point C and point A. Draw AC. Draw CD parallel to the x axis. Draw AB perpendicular to CD. Coordinates of B (3, −2).

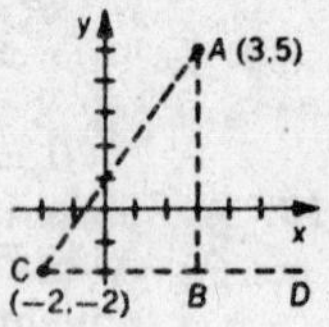

SECTION 6

1. D. $12 = 1\frac{1}{3}(x)$

$12 = \frac{4}{3}x$

$\frac{4}{3}x = 12$

$4x = 36$

$x = 9$

2. C. $\frac{\text{quantity of pie}}{\text{number of people served}} = \frac{1}{7} = \frac{x}{91}$

$7x = 91$

$x = 13$

3. B. $\frac{1}{5} = 20\%$; $\frac{2}{5} = 40\%$; $\frac{3}{5} = 60\%$;

$\frac{16}{25} = 64\%$; $\frac{13}{25} = 52\%$

$\frac{2}{5}$ is next smaller than $\frac{1}{2}$ or 50%

4. A. $\frac{a+b}{a-b} \div \frac{b+a}{b-a}$

$\frac{a+b}{a-b} \cdot \frac{b-a}{b+a}$

$\frac{a+b}{a-b} \cdot \frac{-a+b}{a+b}$

$\frac{a+b}{a-b} \cdot -\frac{a-b}{a+b}$

$\frac{a+b}{\cancel{a-b}} \cdot -\frac{\cancel{a-b}}{a+b}$ or −1

5. C. $\frac{\text{feet}}{\text{inches}} = \frac{1}{12} = \frac{x}{7.2}$

$12x = 7.2$

$120x = 72$

$x = \frac{72}{120}$ or $\frac{3}{5}$

6. C. $\frac{1}{0.4} = \frac{10}{4} = 2\frac{1}{2}$ or 250%

$\frac{5}{8} = 62\frac{1}{2}\%$

$(0.2)^2 = 0.04 = 4\%$

$\frac{9}{100} = 9\%$

$\sqrt{1.44} = 1.2 = 120\%$

4% or $(0.2)^2$ is smallest

7. C. First car uses 1 gallon for 15 miles. Therefore, it uses 4 gallons for 60 miles. Since the second car can travel m miles on one gallon, it can travel $4m$ miles on 4 gallons.

8. A. When purchased in box of 12, cost per tablet is $\frac{21¢}{12}$ or $1\frac{3}{4}¢$

When purchased in bottle of 100, cost per tablet is $\frac{\$1.50}{100}$ or $1\frac{1}{2}¢$

Saving per tablet by purchasing in bottle is $1\frac{3}{4}¢ - 1\frac{1}{2}¢$ or $\frac{1}{4}¢$

Therefore saving per dozen $= 12\left(\frac{1}{4}¢\right)$ or 3¢

9. A. If a man does $\frac{1}{8}$ of his work in one day, in x days he will do x times as much or $\frac{x}{8}$.

10. A. Perimeter of rectangle = 2 (Length) + 2 (Width)

Let x = the width

Perimeter of rectangle $= 2(3u + 2v) + 2x$

Perimeter of rectangle $= 6u + 4v + 2x$

$10u + 6v = 6u + 4v + 2x$

$4u + 2v = 2x$

$x = 2u + v$

11. C.

$r = \frac{E}{i}$

$ir = E$

$i = \frac{E}{r}$

$W = i^2r$

$W = \frac{E}{r} \cdot \frac{E}{r} \cdot r$ (Substitution)

$W = \frac{E^2}{r}$

$Wr = E^2$

$E = \sqrt{Wr}$

12. B. Volume of water in can = (area of base) (height)

Volume of water in can = $(\pi)(\text{radius})^2$ (height)

Volume of water in can = $(\frac{22}{7})(4)(14)$ or 176 cubic inches

To find time for 176 cubic inches we have a direct proportion

Let x = number of minutes required for 176 cubic inches

$\frac{\text{cubic inches}}{\text{minutes}} = \frac{8}{10} = \frac{176}{x}$

$8x = 1760$

$x = 220$ minutes

Since 220 minutes equals 3 hours and 40 minutes, the water which began to flow at 10 A.M. will begin to overflow at 1:40 P.M.

13. A. Area of original rectangle $= lw$

Length of new rectangle $= l + \frac{1}{2}l$

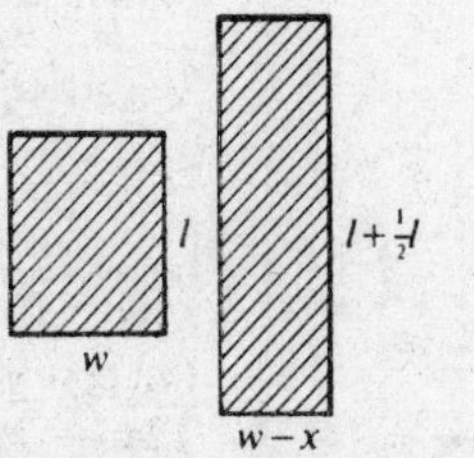

Let x = decrease in width

Width of new rectangle $= w - x$

Area of new rectangle $= (l + \frac{1}{2}l)\ (w - x) = lw$

$(\frac{3}{2}l)(w - x) = lw$

$\frac{3lw}{2} - \frac{3lx}{2} = lw$

$3lw - 3lx = 2lw$

$-3lx = 2lw - 3lw$

$-3lx = -lw$

$-3x = -\frac{lw}{l}$

$3x = w$

$x = \frac{1}{3}w$ or $33\frac{1}{3}\%\,w$

14. D. Radius $AO = 6.5$

Diameter $AB = 13$

Angle C is a right angle (an angle inscribed in a semi-circle is a right angle)

Triangle ABC is a right triangle

$(13)^2 = (5)^2 + (CB)^2$

$169 = 25 + (CB)^2$

$(CB)^2 = 144$

$CB = 12$

Area of triangle $ABC = \frac{1}{2}(AC)(CB)$

Area of triangle $ABC = \frac{1}{2}(5)(12)$ or 30

15. D. Let x = distance (one way) traveled by yacht.

$\frac{\text{Distance}}{\text{Rate}} = \text{Time}$

$\frac{x}{d}$ = Time (downstream)

$\frac{x}{u}$ = Time (upstream)

$\frac{x}{d} + \frac{x}{u}$ or $\frac{ux + dx}{du}$ (Total time)

$2x$ = total distance

$\frac{\text{Total distance}}{\text{Total time}}$ = average rate for the round trip

$\frac{2x}{\frac{ux + dx}{du}}$ = average rate for the round trip

$= 2x \div \frac{ux + dx}{du}$

$= 2x \cdot \frac{du}{ux + dx}$

$= 2x \cdot \frac{du}{x(u + d)}$

$= 2x \cdot \frac{du}{x(u + d)}$

$= \frac{2du}{u + d}$

16. B.

$p = ab - 2cd$
$3p = 3ab - 6cd$
$-3p = -3ab + 6cd$
$r = -3ab + 6cd$
$-3p = r$ (things equal to the same thing are equal to each other)

$\frac{-3p}{r} = 1$ (division by r)

$\frac{p}{r} = -\frac{1}{3}$ (division by -3)

$ab - 2cd = q$ is irrelevant

17. D. $\frac{1}{2}$ of $\frac{1}{3}$ or $\frac{1}{6}$ of the workers are married women

$\frac{1}{3}$ of $\frac{1}{6}$ or $\frac{1}{18}$ of the women workers have children

Since $\frac{1}{3}$ of the workers are women, $\frac{2}{3}$ of the workers are men

$\frac{3}{4}$ of $\frac{2}{3}$ or $\frac{1}{2}$ of the workers are married men

$\frac{2}{3}$ of $\frac{1}{2}$ or $\frac{1}{3}$ of the male workers have children

$\frac{1}{18} + \frac{1}{3}$ or $\frac{7}{18}$ of the workers have children

Therefore $\frac{11}{18}$ of the workers do not have children

18. D. If two points have one coordinate the same, the distance between them is the difference between the two other coordinates.
(*A*) $0 - (-5) = 5$ (*B*) $5 - 0 = 5$
(*C*) $8 - 3 = 5$ (*D*) $3 - (-8) \neq 5$
(*E*) $3 - (-2) = 5$

19. A. Use the formulas:

$x \text{ mid.} = \frac{x_1 + x_2}{2}$ and $y \text{ mid.} = \frac{y_1 + y_2}{2}$.

In this case, $x_1 = 2a$, $x_2 = 4a$, $y_1 = 2b$, $y_2 = 6b$.

$x \text{ mid.} = \frac{2a + 4a}{2} = \frac{6a}{2} = 3a$

$y \text{ mid.} = \frac{2b + 6b}{2} = \frac{8b}{2} = 4b$

20. **B.** k is the y-coordinate of point C.
Point C is the same distance above the x-axis as is point D. The y-coordinate of point D is 5. Therefore, the y-coordinate of point C is 5. Thus, $k = 5$.

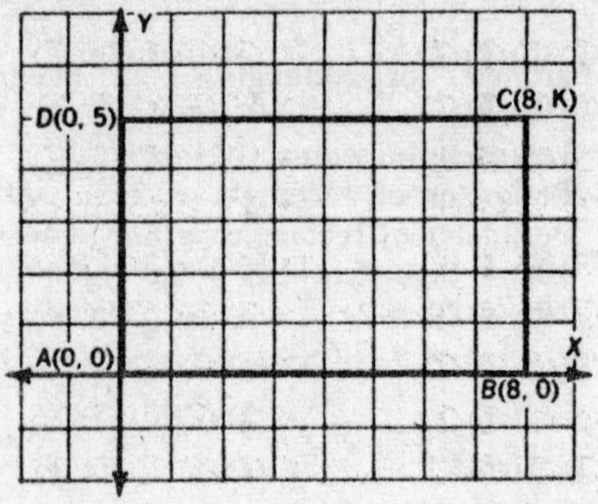

21. B. $3x - y = 2x + y$
$x - y = y$ (subtract $2x$)
$x = 2y$ (add y)

22. D. Since the hundredths unit (9) is more than 5, the tenths unit is raised from 9 to 10 so that the digit 69 becomes 70, and the number 69.999 becomes 70.0 to the nearest tenth.

23. D. Since 1000 + 1 = 1001 and the fraction $\frac{1}{1000}$ written as a decimal is .001 the correct answer is 1001.001.

24. A. (2) (π) (radius) = circumference
(2) (π) (radius) = $2\pi^2$ (given)
radius = π (divide by 2π)

25. C. Let x = the smallest integer
then $x + 2$ = the next consecutive positive integer
and $x + 4$ = the next consecutive positive integer
$3x + 6$ = sum of the three integers
$3x + 6 = a$ (given)
$3x = a - 6$
$x = \frac{a-6}{3}$

ANSWER SHEET—TEST 3

SECTION 1

1. Ⓐ Ⓑ Ⓒ Ⓓ Ⓔ	11. Ⓐ Ⓑ Ⓒ Ⓓ Ⓔ	21. Ⓐ Ⓑ Ⓒ Ⓓ Ⓔ	31. Ⓐ Ⓑ Ⓒ Ⓓ Ⓔ	41. Ⓐ Ⓑ Ⓒ Ⓓ Ⓔ
2. Ⓐ Ⓑ Ⓒ Ⓓ Ⓔ	12. Ⓐ Ⓑ Ⓒ Ⓓ Ⓔ	22. Ⓐ Ⓑ Ⓒ Ⓓ Ⓔ	32. Ⓐ Ⓑ Ⓒ Ⓓ Ⓔ	42. Ⓐ Ⓑ Ⓒ Ⓓ Ⓔ
3. Ⓐ Ⓑ Ⓒ Ⓓ Ⓔ	13. Ⓐ Ⓑ Ⓒ Ⓓ Ⓔ	23. Ⓐ Ⓑ Ⓒ Ⓓ Ⓔ	33. Ⓐ Ⓑ Ⓒ Ⓓ Ⓔ	43. Ⓐ Ⓑ Ⓒ Ⓓ Ⓔ
4. Ⓐ Ⓑ Ⓒ Ⓓ Ⓔ	14. Ⓐ Ⓑ Ⓒ Ⓓ Ⓔ	24. Ⓐ Ⓑ Ⓒ Ⓓ Ⓔ	34. Ⓐ Ⓑ Ⓒ Ⓓ Ⓔ	44. Ⓐ Ⓑ Ⓒ Ⓓ Ⓔ
5. Ⓐ Ⓑ Ⓒ Ⓓ Ⓔ	15. Ⓐ Ⓑ Ⓒ Ⓓ Ⓔ	25. Ⓐ Ⓑ Ⓒ Ⓓ Ⓔ	35. Ⓐ Ⓑ Ⓒ Ⓓ Ⓔ	45. Ⓐ Ⓑ Ⓒ Ⓓ Ⓔ
6. Ⓐ Ⓑ Ⓒ Ⓓ Ⓔ	16. Ⓐ Ⓑ Ⓒ Ⓓ Ⓔ	26. Ⓐ Ⓑ Ⓒ Ⓓ Ⓔ	36. Ⓐ Ⓑ Ⓒ Ⓓ Ⓔ	46. Ⓐ Ⓑ Ⓒ Ⓓ Ⓔ
7. Ⓐ Ⓑ Ⓒ Ⓓ Ⓔ	17. Ⓐ Ⓑ Ⓒ Ⓓ Ⓔ	27. Ⓐ Ⓑ Ⓒ Ⓓ Ⓔ	37. Ⓐ Ⓑ Ⓒ Ⓓ Ⓔ	47. Ⓐ Ⓑ Ⓒ Ⓓ Ⓔ
8. Ⓐ Ⓑ Ⓒ Ⓓ Ⓔ	18. Ⓐ Ⓑ Ⓒ Ⓓ Ⓔ	28. Ⓐ Ⓑ Ⓒ Ⓓ Ⓔ	38. Ⓐ Ⓑ Ⓒ Ⓓ Ⓔ	48. Ⓐ Ⓑ Ⓒ Ⓓ Ⓔ
9. Ⓐ Ⓑ Ⓒ Ⓓ Ⓔ	19. Ⓐ Ⓑ Ⓒ Ⓓ Ⓔ	29. Ⓐ Ⓑ Ⓒ Ⓓ Ⓔ	39. Ⓐ Ⓑ Ⓒ Ⓓ Ⓔ	49. Ⓐ Ⓑ Ⓒ Ⓓ Ⓔ
10. Ⓐ Ⓑ Ⓒ Ⓓ Ⓔ	20. Ⓐ Ⓑ Ⓒ Ⓓ Ⓔ	30. Ⓐ Ⓑ Ⓒ Ⓓ Ⓔ	40. Ⓐ Ⓑ Ⓒ Ⓓ Ⓔ	50. Ⓐ Ⓑ Ⓒ Ⓓ Ⓔ

SECTION 2

1. Ⓐ Ⓑ Ⓒ Ⓓ Ⓔ	11. Ⓐ Ⓑ Ⓒ Ⓓ Ⓔ	21. Ⓐ Ⓑ Ⓒ Ⓓ Ⓔ	31. Ⓐ Ⓑ Ⓒ Ⓓ Ⓔ	41. Ⓐ Ⓑ Ⓒ Ⓓ Ⓔ
2. Ⓐ Ⓑ Ⓒ Ⓓ Ⓔ	12. Ⓐ Ⓑ Ⓒ Ⓓ Ⓔ	22. Ⓐ Ⓑ Ⓒ Ⓓ Ⓔ	32. Ⓐ Ⓑ Ⓒ Ⓓ Ⓔ	42. Ⓐ Ⓑ Ⓒ Ⓓ Ⓔ
3. Ⓐ Ⓑ Ⓒ Ⓓ Ⓔ	13. Ⓐ Ⓑ Ⓒ Ⓓ Ⓔ	23. Ⓐ Ⓑ Ⓒ Ⓓ Ⓔ	33. Ⓐ Ⓑ Ⓒ Ⓓ Ⓔ	43. Ⓐ Ⓑ Ⓒ Ⓓ Ⓔ
4. Ⓐ Ⓑ Ⓒ Ⓓ Ⓔ	14. Ⓐ Ⓑ Ⓒ Ⓓ Ⓔ	24. Ⓐ Ⓑ Ⓒ Ⓓ Ⓔ	34. Ⓐ Ⓑ Ⓒ Ⓓ Ⓔ	44. Ⓐ Ⓑ Ⓒ Ⓓ Ⓔ
5. Ⓐ Ⓑ Ⓒ Ⓓ Ⓔ	15. Ⓐ Ⓑ Ⓒ Ⓓ Ⓔ	25. Ⓐ Ⓑ Ⓒ Ⓓ Ⓔ	35. Ⓐ Ⓑ Ⓒ Ⓓ Ⓔ	45. Ⓐ Ⓑ Ⓒ Ⓓ Ⓔ
6. Ⓐ Ⓑ Ⓒ Ⓓ Ⓔ	16. Ⓐ Ⓑ Ⓒ Ⓓ Ⓔ	26. Ⓐ Ⓑ Ⓒ Ⓓ Ⓔ	36. Ⓐ Ⓑ Ⓒ Ⓓ Ⓔ	46. Ⓐ Ⓑ Ⓒ Ⓓ Ⓔ
7. Ⓐ Ⓑ Ⓒ Ⓓ Ⓔ	17. Ⓐ Ⓑ Ⓒ Ⓓ Ⓔ	27. Ⓐ Ⓑ Ⓒ Ⓓ Ⓔ	37. Ⓐ Ⓑ Ⓒ Ⓓ Ⓔ	47. Ⓐ Ⓑ Ⓒ Ⓓ Ⓔ
8. Ⓐ Ⓑ Ⓒ Ⓓ Ⓔ	18. Ⓐ Ⓑ Ⓒ Ⓓ Ⓔ	28. Ⓐ Ⓑ Ⓒ Ⓓ Ⓔ	38. Ⓐ Ⓑ Ⓒ Ⓓ Ⓔ	48. Ⓐ Ⓑ Ⓒ Ⓓ Ⓔ
9. Ⓐ Ⓑ Ⓒ Ⓓ Ⓔ	19. Ⓐ Ⓑ Ⓒ Ⓓ Ⓔ	29. Ⓐ Ⓑ Ⓒ Ⓓ Ⓔ	39. Ⓐ Ⓑ Ⓒ Ⓓ Ⓔ	49. Ⓐ Ⓑ Ⓒ Ⓓ Ⓔ
10. Ⓐ Ⓑ Ⓒ Ⓓ Ⓔ	20. Ⓐ Ⓑ Ⓒ Ⓓ Ⓔ	30. Ⓐ Ⓑ Ⓒ Ⓓ Ⓔ	40. Ⓐ Ⓑ Ⓒ Ⓓ Ⓔ	50. Ⓐ Ⓑ Ⓒ Ⓓ Ⓔ

SECTION 3

1. Ⓐ Ⓑ Ⓒ Ⓓ Ⓔ	11. Ⓐ Ⓑ Ⓒ Ⓓ Ⓔ	21. Ⓐ Ⓑ Ⓒ Ⓓ Ⓔ	31. Ⓐ Ⓑ Ⓒ Ⓓ Ⓔ	41. Ⓐ Ⓑ Ⓒ Ⓓ Ⓔ
2. Ⓐ Ⓑ Ⓒ Ⓓ Ⓔ	12. Ⓐ Ⓑ Ⓒ Ⓓ Ⓔ	22. Ⓐ Ⓑ Ⓒ Ⓓ Ⓔ	32. Ⓐ Ⓑ Ⓒ Ⓓ Ⓔ	42. Ⓐ Ⓑ Ⓒ Ⓓ Ⓔ
3. Ⓐ Ⓑ Ⓒ Ⓓ Ⓔ	13. Ⓐ Ⓑ Ⓒ Ⓓ Ⓔ	23. Ⓐ Ⓑ Ⓒ Ⓓ Ⓔ	33. Ⓐ Ⓑ Ⓒ Ⓓ Ⓔ	43. Ⓐ Ⓑ Ⓒ Ⓓ Ⓔ
4. Ⓐ Ⓑ Ⓒ Ⓓ Ⓔ	14. Ⓐ Ⓑ Ⓒ Ⓓ Ⓔ	24. Ⓐ Ⓑ Ⓒ Ⓓ Ⓔ	34. Ⓐ Ⓑ Ⓒ Ⓓ Ⓔ	44. Ⓐ Ⓑ Ⓒ Ⓓ Ⓔ
5. Ⓐ Ⓑ Ⓒ Ⓓ Ⓔ	15. Ⓐ Ⓑ Ⓒ Ⓓ Ⓔ	25. Ⓐ Ⓑ Ⓒ Ⓓ Ⓔ	35. Ⓐ Ⓑ Ⓒ Ⓓ Ⓔ	45. Ⓐ Ⓑ Ⓒ Ⓓ Ⓔ
6. Ⓐ Ⓑ Ⓒ Ⓓ Ⓔ	16. Ⓐ Ⓑ Ⓒ Ⓓ Ⓔ	26. Ⓐ Ⓑ Ⓒ Ⓓ Ⓔ	36. Ⓐ Ⓑ Ⓒ Ⓓ Ⓔ	46. Ⓐ Ⓑ Ⓒ Ⓓ Ⓔ
7. Ⓐ Ⓑ Ⓒ Ⓓ Ⓔ	17. Ⓐ Ⓑ Ⓒ Ⓓ Ⓔ	27. Ⓐ Ⓑ Ⓒ Ⓓ Ⓔ	37. Ⓐ Ⓑ Ⓒ Ⓓ Ⓔ	47. Ⓐ Ⓑ Ⓒ Ⓓ Ⓔ
8. Ⓐ Ⓑ Ⓒ Ⓓ Ⓔ	18. Ⓐ Ⓑ Ⓒ Ⓓ Ⓔ	28. Ⓐ Ⓑ Ⓒ Ⓓ Ⓔ	38. Ⓐ Ⓑ Ⓒ Ⓓ Ⓔ	48. Ⓐ Ⓑ Ⓒ Ⓓ Ⓔ
9. Ⓐ Ⓑ Ⓒ Ⓓ Ⓔ	19. Ⓐ Ⓑ Ⓒ Ⓓ Ⓔ	29. Ⓐ Ⓑ Ⓒ Ⓓ Ⓔ	39. Ⓐ Ⓑ Ⓒ Ⓓ Ⓔ	49. Ⓐ Ⓑ Ⓒ Ⓓ Ⓔ
10. Ⓐ Ⓑ Ⓒ Ⓓ Ⓔ	20. Ⓐ Ⓑ Ⓒ Ⓓ Ⓔ	30. Ⓐ Ⓑ Ⓒ Ⓓ Ⓔ	40. Ⓐ Ⓑ Ⓒ Ⓓ Ⓔ	50. Ⓐ Ⓑ Ⓒ Ⓓ Ⓔ

SECTION 4

1. Ⓐ Ⓑ Ⓒ Ⓓ Ⓔ	11. Ⓐ Ⓑ Ⓒ Ⓓ Ⓔ	21. Ⓐ Ⓑ Ⓒ Ⓓ Ⓔ	31. Ⓐ Ⓑ Ⓒ Ⓓ Ⓔ	41. Ⓐ Ⓑ Ⓒ Ⓓ Ⓔ
2. Ⓐ Ⓑ Ⓒ Ⓓ Ⓔ	12. Ⓐ Ⓑ Ⓒ Ⓓ Ⓔ	22. Ⓐ Ⓑ Ⓒ Ⓓ Ⓔ	32. Ⓐ Ⓑ Ⓒ Ⓓ Ⓔ	42. Ⓐ Ⓑ Ⓒ Ⓓ Ⓔ
3. Ⓐ Ⓑ Ⓒ Ⓓ Ⓔ	13. Ⓐ Ⓑ Ⓒ Ⓓ Ⓔ	23. Ⓐ Ⓑ Ⓒ Ⓓ Ⓔ	33. Ⓐ Ⓑ Ⓒ Ⓓ Ⓔ	43. Ⓐ Ⓑ Ⓒ Ⓓ Ⓔ
4. Ⓐ Ⓑ Ⓒ Ⓓ Ⓔ	14. Ⓐ Ⓑ Ⓒ Ⓓ Ⓔ	24. Ⓐ Ⓑ Ⓒ Ⓓ Ⓔ	34. Ⓐ Ⓑ Ⓒ Ⓓ Ⓔ	44. Ⓐ Ⓑ Ⓒ Ⓓ Ⓔ
5. Ⓐ Ⓑ Ⓒ Ⓓ Ⓔ	15. Ⓐ Ⓑ Ⓒ Ⓓ Ⓔ	25. Ⓐ Ⓑ Ⓒ Ⓓ Ⓔ	35. Ⓐ Ⓑ Ⓒ Ⓓ Ⓔ	45. Ⓐ Ⓑ Ⓒ Ⓓ Ⓔ
6. Ⓐ Ⓑ Ⓒ Ⓓ Ⓔ	16. Ⓐ Ⓑ Ⓒ Ⓓ Ⓔ	26. Ⓐ Ⓑ Ⓒ Ⓓ Ⓔ	36. Ⓐ Ⓑ Ⓒ Ⓓ Ⓔ	46. Ⓐ Ⓑ Ⓒ Ⓓ Ⓔ
7. Ⓐ Ⓑ Ⓒ Ⓓ Ⓔ	17. Ⓐ Ⓑ Ⓒ Ⓓ Ⓔ	27. Ⓐ Ⓑ Ⓒ Ⓓ Ⓔ	37. Ⓐ Ⓑ Ⓒ Ⓓ Ⓔ	47. Ⓐ Ⓑ Ⓒ Ⓓ Ⓔ
8. Ⓐ Ⓑ Ⓒ Ⓓ Ⓔ	18. Ⓐ Ⓑ Ⓒ Ⓓ Ⓔ	28. Ⓐ Ⓑ Ⓒ Ⓓ Ⓔ	38. Ⓐ Ⓑ Ⓒ Ⓓ Ⓔ	48. Ⓐ Ⓑ Ⓒ Ⓓ Ⓔ
9. Ⓐ Ⓑ Ⓒ Ⓓ Ⓔ	19. Ⓐ Ⓑ Ⓒ Ⓓ Ⓔ	29. Ⓐ Ⓑ Ⓒ Ⓓ Ⓔ	39. Ⓐ Ⓑ Ⓒ Ⓓ Ⓔ	49. Ⓐ Ⓑ Ⓒ Ⓓ Ⓔ
10. Ⓐ Ⓑ Ⓒ Ⓓ Ⓔ	20. Ⓐ Ⓑ Ⓒ Ⓓ Ⓔ	30. Ⓐ Ⓑ Ⓒ Ⓓ Ⓔ	40. Ⓐ Ⓑ Ⓒ Ⓓ Ⓔ	50. Ⓐ Ⓑ Ⓒ Ⓓ Ⓔ

SECTION 5

1. Ⓐ Ⓑ Ⓒ Ⓓ Ⓔ	11. Ⓐ Ⓑ Ⓒ Ⓓ Ⓔ	21. Ⓐ Ⓑ Ⓒ Ⓓ Ⓔ	31. Ⓐ Ⓑ Ⓒ Ⓓ Ⓔ	41. Ⓐ Ⓑ Ⓒ Ⓓ Ⓔ
2. Ⓐ Ⓑ Ⓒ Ⓓ Ⓔ	12. Ⓐ Ⓑ Ⓒ Ⓓ Ⓔ	22. Ⓐ Ⓑ Ⓒ Ⓓ Ⓔ	32. Ⓐ Ⓑ Ⓒ Ⓓ Ⓔ	42. Ⓐ Ⓑ Ⓒ Ⓓ Ⓔ
3. Ⓐ Ⓑ Ⓒ Ⓓ Ⓔ	13. Ⓐ Ⓑ Ⓒ Ⓓ Ⓔ	23. Ⓐ Ⓑ Ⓒ Ⓓ Ⓔ	33. Ⓐ Ⓑ Ⓒ Ⓓ Ⓔ	43. Ⓐ Ⓑ Ⓒ Ⓓ Ⓔ
4. Ⓐ Ⓑ Ⓒ Ⓓ Ⓔ	14. Ⓐ Ⓑ Ⓒ Ⓓ Ⓔ	24. Ⓐ Ⓑ Ⓒ Ⓓ Ⓔ	34. Ⓐ Ⓑ Ⓒ Ⓓ Ⓔ	44. Ⓐ Ⓑ Ⓒ Ⓓ Ⓔ
5. Ⓐ Ⓑ Ⓒ Ⓓ Ⓔ	15. Ⓐ Ⓑ Ⓒ Ⓓ Ⓔ	25. Ⓐ Ⓑ Ⓒ Ⓓ Ⓔ	35. Ⓐ Ⓑ Ⓒ Ⓓ Ⓔ	45. Ⓐ Ⓑ Ⓒ Ⓓ Ⓔ
6. Ⓐ Ⓑ Ⓒ Ⓓ Ⓔ	16. Ⓐ Ⓑ Ⓒ Ⓓ Ⓔ	26. Ⓐ Ⓑ Ⓒ Ⓓ Ⓔ	36. Ⓐ Ⓑ Ⓒ Ⓓ Ⓔ	46. Ⓐ Ⓑ Ⓒ Ⓓ Ⓔ
7. Ⓐ Ⓑ Ⓒ Ⓓ Ⓔ	17. Ⓐ Ⓑ Ⓒ Ⓓ Ⓔ	27. Ⓐ Ⓑ Ⓒ Ⓓ Ⓔ	37. Ⓐ Ⓑ Ⓒ Ⓓ Ⓔ	47. Ⓐ Ⓑ Ⓒ Ⓓ Ⓔ
8. Ⓐ Ⓑ Ⓒ Ⓓ Ⓔ	18. Ⓐ Ⓑ Ⓒ Ⓓ Ⓔ	28. Ⓐ Ⓑ Ⓒ Ⓓ Ⓔ	38. Ⓐ Ⓑ Ⓒ Ⓓ Ⓔ	48. Ⓐ Ⓑ Ⓒ Ⓓ Ⓔ
9. Ⓐ Ⓑ Ⓒ Ⓓ Ⓔ	19. Ⓐ Ⓑ Ⓒ Ⓓ Ⓔ	29. Ⓐ Ⓑ Ⓒ Ⓓ Ⓔ	39. Ⓐ Ⓑ Ⓒ Ⓓ Ⓔ	49. Ⓐ Ⓑ Ⓒ Ⓓ Ⓔ
10. Ⓐ Ⓑ Ⓒ Ⓓ Ⓔ	20. Ⓐ Ⓑ Ⓒ Ⓓ Ⓔ	30. Ⓐ Ⓑ Ⓒ Ⓓ Ⓔ	40. Ⓐ Ⓑ Ⓒ Ⓓ Ⓔ	50. Ⓐ Ⓑ Ⓒ Ⓓ Ⓔ

SECTION 6

1. Ⓐ Ⓑ Ⓒ Ⓓ Ⓔ	11. Ⓐ Ⓑ Ⓒ Ⓓ Ⓔ	21. Ⓐ Ⓑ Ⓒ Ⓓ Ⓔ	31. Ⓐ Ⓑ Ⓒ Ⓓ Ⓔ	41. Ⓐ Ⓑ Ⓒ Ⓓ Ⓔ
2. Ⓐ Ⓑ Ⓒ Ⓓ Ⓔ	12. Ⓐ Ⓑ Ⓒ Ⓓ Ⓔ	22. Ⓐ Ⓑ Ⓒ Ⓓ Ⓔ	32. Ⓐ Ⓑ Ⓒ Ⓓ Ⓔ	42. Ⓐ Ⓑ Ⓒ Ⓓ Ⓔ
3. Ⓐ Ⓑ Ⓒ Ⓓ Ⓔ	13. Ⓐ Ⓑ Ⓒ Ⓓ Ⓔ	23. Ⓐ Ⓑ Ⓒ Ⓓ Ⓔ	33. Ⓐ Ⓑ Ⓒ Ⓓ Ⓔ	43. Ⓐ Ⓑ Ⓒ Ⓓ Ⓔ
4. Ⓐ Ⓑ Ⓒ Ⓓ Ⓔ	14. Ⓐ Ⓑ Ⓒ Ⓓ Ⓔ	24. Ⓐ Ⓑ Ⓒ Ⓓ Ⓔ	34. Ⓐ Ⓑ Ⓒ Ⓓ Ⓔ	44. Ⓐ Ⓑ Ⓒ Ⓓ Ⓔ
5. Ⓐ Ⓑ Ⓒ Ⓓ Ⓔ	15. Ⓐ Ⓑ Ⓒ Ⓓ Ⓔ	25. Ⓐ Ⓑ Ⓒ Ⓓ Ⓔ	35. Ⓐ Ⓑ Ⓒ Ⓓ Ⓔ	45. Ⓐ Ⓑ Ⓒ Ⓓ Ⓔ
6. Ⓐ Ⓑ Ⓒ Ⓓ Ⓔ	16. Ⓐ Ⓑ Ⓒ Ⓓ Ⓔ	26. Ⓐ Ⓑ Ⓒ Ⓓ Ⓔ	36. Ⓐ Ⓑ Ⓒ Ⓓ Ⓔ	46. Ⓐ Ⓑ Ⓒ Ⓓ Ⓔ
7. Ⓐ Ⓑ Ⓒ Ⓓ Ⓔ	17. Ⓐ Ⓑ Ⓒ Ⓓ Ⓔ	27. Ⓐ Ⓑ Ⓒ Ⓓ Ⓔ	37. Ⓐ Ⓑ Ⓒ Ⓓ Ⓔ	47. Ⓐ Ⓑ Ⓒ Ⓓ Ⓔ
8. Ⓐ Ⓑ Ⓒ Ⓓ Ⓔ	18. Ⓐ Ⓑ Ⓒ Ⓓ Ⓔ	28. Ⓐ Ⓑ Ⓒ Ⓓ Ⓔ	38. Ⓐ Ⓑ Ⓒ Ⓓ Ⓔ	48. Ⓐ Ⓑ Ⓒ Ⓓ Ⓔ
9. Ⓐ Ⓑ Ⓒ Ⓓ Ⓔ	19. Ⓐ Ⓑ Ⓒ Ⓓ Ⓔ	29. Ⓐ Ⓑ Ⓒ Ⓓ Ⓔ	39. Ⓐ Ⓑ Ⓒ Ⓓ Ⓔ	49. Ⓐ Ⓑ Ⓒ Ⓓ Ⓔ
10. Ⓐ Ⓑ Ⓒ Ⓓ Ⓔ	20. Ⓐ Ⓑ Ⓒ Ⓓ Ⓔ	30. Ⓐ Ⓑ Ⓒ Ⓓ Ⓔ	40. Ⓐ Ⓑ Ⓒ Ⓓ Ⓔ	50. Ⓐ Ⓑ Ⓒ Ⓓ Ⓔ

MODEL SAT TEST 3

SECTION 1 MATH ABILITY

25 QUESTIONS - 30 MINUTES

In this section solve each problem, using any available space on the page for scratchwork. Then decide which is the best of the choices given and blacken the corresponding space on the answer sheet.

The following information is for your reference in solving some of the problems.

Circle of radius r: Area $= \pi r^2$; Circumference $= 2\pi r$
The number of degrees of arc in a circle is 360.
The measure in degrees of a straight angle is 180.

Definitions of symbols:

$=$ is equal to	$\leq$ is less than or equal to
$\neq$ is unequal to	$\geq$ is greater than or equal to
$<$ is less than	$\parallel$ is parallel to
$>$ is greater than	$\perp$ is perpendicular to

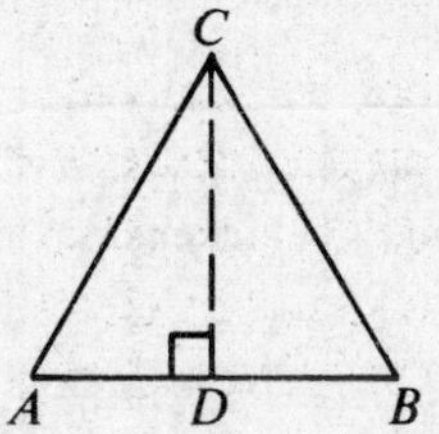

Triangle: The sum of the measures in degrees of the angles of a triangle is 180.
If $\angle CDA$ is a right angle, then

(1) area of $\triangle ABC = \dfrac{AB \times CD}{2}$

(2) $AC^2 = AD^2 + DC^2$

Note: Figures that accompany problems in this test are intended to provide information useful in solving the problems. They are drawn as accurately as possible EXCEPT when it is stated in a specific problem that its figure is not drawn to scale. All figures lie in a plane unless otherwise indicated. All numbers used are real numbers.

1. What is the thickness of a pipe that has an outer diameter of 2.5 inches and an inner diameter of 2.1 inches?
   (A) 0.2″
   (B) 0.4″
   (C) 0.8″
   (D) 3.2″
   (E) 4.6″

2. 9% of what number is 27?
   (A) 24
   (B) 30
   (C) 243
   (D) 300
   (E) 330

3. $\dfrac{?}{64} = 0.875$
   (A) 48
   (B) 54
   (C) 56
   (D) 58
   (E) 62

4. What is the value of x, if $\dfrac{a+b}{a-b} = \dfrac{x}{b-a}$?
   (A) $-a - b$
   (B) -1
   (C) $a - b$
   (D) $a + b$
   (E) $a^2 - b^2$

5. If the total cost of a oranges is D dollars, what is the cost (in cents) of x oranges?
   (A) $\dfrac{100Dx}{a}$
   (B) $\dfrac{100D}{ax}$
   (C) $\dfrac{100D}{x}$
   (D) $\dfrac{Dx}{100a}$
   (E) $\dfrac{Da}{100x}$

6. A fence 320 feet long has wooden posts each 40 feet apart. How many posts are there?
(A) 7
(B) 8
(C) 9
(D) 10
(E) 11

7. If $x = -2$ and $\frac{1}{y} = -4$, what is the value of y in terms of x?
(A) $x - 6$
(B) $2x$
(C) $\frac{x}{2}$
(D) $\frac{1}{2x}$
(E) $x + 6$

8. How many eighths are there in $37\frac{1}{2}\%$?
(A) 3
(B) 4
(C) 4.8
(D) 5
(E) 7

9. A bag of chicken feed will feed 18 chickens for 54 days. For how many days will it feed 12 chickens?
(A) 36
(B) 37
(C) 53
(D) 72
(E) 81

10. A picture in an art museum is six feet wide and eight feet long. If its frame has a width of six inches, what is the ratio of the area of the frame to the area of the picture?
(A) $\frac{5}{16}$
(B) $\frac{5}{4}$
(C) $\frac{4}{5}$
(D) $\frac{5}{12}$
(E) $\frac{3\frac{1}{5}}{1}$

11. To indicate on a circle graph that $\frac{2}{5}$ of a graduating class is going to college, how many degrees should there be in the central angle of the portion drawn to represent this group?
(A) 36
(B) 40
(C) 72
(D) 80
(E) 144

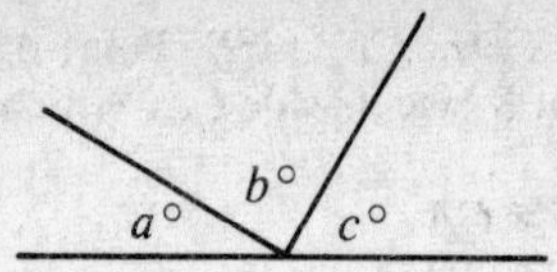

12. In the figure above, a, b and c are in the ratio of 1:3:2. Find b.
(A) 30
(B) 50
(C) 60
(D) 90
(E) 120

13. A minor league baseball team plays 154 games in a season. On a certain date a team has won 40 and lost 20 games. How many of the remaining games must they win to finish the season winning approximately 65% of the games?
(A) 60
(B) 80
(C) 90
(D) 94
(E) 100

14. At 13° Celsius a cubic centimeter of uranium weighs 18.7 grams. What is the weight (in grams) of 0.01 cubic centimeter of uranium at 13° Celsius?
(A) 1
(B) 0.187
(C) 18.7
(D) 100
(E) 1870

15. The number of pupils in a classroom can be arranged in r rows of s seats in each row leaving two seats vacant. Express in terms of r and s the number of pupils in the classroom.
(A) $2 - rs$
(B) $2r - s$
(C) $2s - r$
(D) $rs + 2$
(E) $rs - 2$

16. Potassium nitrate is composed of 39 parts potassium, 14 parts of nitrogen and 48 parts of oxygen. Find the percentage of potassium in potassium nitrate.
(A) 14
(B) 39
(C) 45
(D) 48
(E) 62

17. In triangle CDE, $CE > CD$. Point A bisects side CD and point B bisects side CE. Which of the following is true?
(A) $CB > CA$
(B) $CB = CA$
(C) $CB < CA$
(D) $CB = AD$
(E) $AD = BE$

18. $\frac{0.24x}{6} + 7 = 10$
$x = ?$
(A) $\frac{3}{4}$
(B) 7.5
(C) 11
(D) 22
(E) 75

19. After reaching a low of $-16°$F at 11 P.M., the temperature began rising at an average of 3 degrees an hour. What was the thermometer reading at 2 A.M.?
(A) $-25°$
(B) $-10°$
(C) $-7°$
(D) $+7°$
(E) $+9°$

20. If the registration of a school increased from 300 to 1200, what is the per cent of increase in registration?
(A) 30%
(B) 40%
(C) 75%
(D) 300%
(E) 400%

21. $\frac{1}{2} + \frac{2}{3} + \frac{3}{y} = \frac{23}{12}$
$y = ?$
(A) 2
(B) 3
(C) 4
(D) 9
(E) 12

22. For a nine-week period a man working 5 days per week earned $454.50. What were his earnings per day?
(A) $9.90
(B) $10.00
(C) $10.10
(D) $11.00
(E) $11.10

23. In 43 oz. of sulfanilamide there are 8 oz. of sulfur. How many ounces of sulfur are necessary to make 172 oz. of sulfanilamide?
(A) 32
(B) 32.4
(C) 33
(D) 40
(E) 41

24. $x - 7 = 0$
$y^2 = 25$
$xy = ?$
(A) $\sqrt{35}$
(B) -35
(C) ± 35
(D) 35.7
(E) $\sqrt{175}$

25. On a trip a man travels at the rate of 40 miles an hour for the first 100 miles and then averages 50 miles an hour for the next 100 miles. What is the average speed (in miles per hour) for the first 200 miles of this trip?
(A) 22.2
(B) 22.5
(C) 44.4
(D) 45
(E) 90

STOP

IF YOU FINISH BEFORE TIME IS CALLED, YOU MAY CHECK YOUR WORK ON THIS SECTION ONLY. DO NOT WORK ON ANY OTHER SECTION IN THE TEST.

SECTION 2 TEST OF STANDARD WRITTEN ENGLISH

50 QUESTIONS - 30 MINUTES

The questions in this section measure skills that are important to writing well. In particular, they test your ability to recognize and use language that is clear, effective, and correct according to the requirements of standard written English, the kind of English found in most college textbooks.

Directions: The following sentences contain problems in grammar, usage, diction (choice of words), and idiom.

Some sentences are correct.

No sentence contains more than one error.

You will find that the error, if there is one, is underlined and lettered. Assume that elements of the sentence that are not underlined are correct and cannot be changed. In choosing answers, follow the requirements of standard written English.

If there is an error, select the one underlined part that must be changed to make the sentence correct and blacken the corresponding space on your answer sheet.

If there is no error, blacken answer space (E).

EXAMPLE:

The region has a climate so severe that [A] plants growing there [B] rarely had been [C] more than twelve inches high [D]. No error [E]

SAMPLE ANSWER

(A) (B) ● (D) (E)

1. After raining [A] steadily [B] for five days, the football field was [C] a sea [D] of mud. No error [E]

2. The prospective [A] purchaser of the house left the premises because he was asked [B] to pay a considerable [C] higher [D] price than he was able to afford. No error [E]

3. The newly [A] organized football association [B] has [C] added two new teams to their [D] league. No error [E]

4. While traveling [A] with my [B] aunt through [C] our National Parks, she was frightened [D] by a bear. No error [E]

5. Before we adopt [A] this legislation, we ought [B] to consider the affect [C] the new law will have on our retired and disabled [D] citizens. No error [E]

6. They are more [A] talented and better [B] trained than [C] we. [D] No error [E]

7. Do [A] you know whom [B] the writer [C] of that speech was? [D] No error [E]

8. I do not believe [A] that [B] it was [C] she [D] who called me at midnight. No error [E]

9. We must regard any statement about this
A
controversy, whatever the source, as gossip
B C
until they are confirmed. No error
D E

10. After his heart attack, he was ordered to lay in bed
A B C
and rest for two weeks. No error
D E

11. The Edsel is one of those cars which has been
A B C
discontinued by the manufacturers. No error
D E

12. Neither the teachers nor the principal are being
A B C
considered for promotion at this time. No error
D E

13. That book is liable to become a best seller because
A B
it is well-written, full of suspense, and very
C D
entertaining. No error
E

14. Choosing between you and he is very difficult;
A B C
both of you are fully qualified. No error
D E

15. Henry Aaron has established an enviable record, it
A B C
probably will not be broken during the next fifty
D
years. No error
E

16. His three children, Ruth, Frank, and Ellis, are very
A
talented youngsters but the latter shows the most
B C D
promise. No error
E

17. Mathematics is not his favorite subject; he finds
A B
them too confusing. No error
C D E

18. Mr. Brown is our best salesman; last year he
A
almost sold two million dollars worth of
B C
insurance. No error
D E

19. Our trip to London was a disappointment. Our
A
accommodations were uncomfortable and the
B C
food unappetizing. No error
D E

20. Neither John nor Henry handed in their
A B C
assignments on time. No error
D E

21. I was surprised and pleased when I was informed
A B C
of me winning the contest. No error
D E

22. I am sure he would apologize if he was in the same
A B C
situation as you are. No error
D E

23. He worked in the lumber camps during the summer
A
not because of the money but because he wanted
B C
to strengthen his muscles by doing hard physical
D
labor. No error
E

24. Because we had been warned about the danger
A
involved in walking on the railroad trestle.
B C D
No error
E

25. We admired his many attempts bravely to enter the
A B C D
burning building. No error
E

Directions: In each of the following sentences, some part or all of the sentence is underlined. Below each sentence you will find five ways of phrasing the underlined part. Select the answer that produces the most effective sentence, one that is clear and exact, without awkwardness or ambiguity, and blacken the corresponding space on your answer sheet. In choosing answers, follow the requirements of standard written English. Choose the answer that best expresses the meaning of the original sentence.

Answer (A) is always the same as the underlined part. Choose answer (A) if you think the original sentence needs no revision.

EXAMPLE:

Laura Ingalls Wilder published her first book and she was sixty-five years old then.

(A) and she was sixty-five years old then
(B) when she was sixty-five years old
(C) at age sixty-five years old
(D) upon reaching sixty-five years
(E) at the time when she was sixty-five

SAMPLE ANSWER

Ⓐ ● Ⓒ Ⓓ Ⓔ

26. As a retired executive, he is now busier than ever; he makes his living by speaking before business and philanthropic groups, writing books and articles, and he is a director of three major corporations.
(A) by speaking before business and philanthropic groups, writing books and articles, and he is a director of
(B) by speaking before business and philanthropic groups, and he writes books and articles as well as being a director of
(C) by speaking before business and philanthropic groups, and he writes books and articles, and directs
(D) by speaking before business and philanthropic groups, writing books and articles, and directing
(E) by speaking before business and philanthropic groups, in addition to writing books and articles, and he is a director of

27. Fifty-three thousand shouting enthusiasts filled the stadium, they had come to watch the first game of the season and to cheer the home team.
(A) enthusiasts filled the stadium, they had come
(B) enthusiasts filled the stadium. they had come
(C) enthusiasts, filling the stadium, had come
(D) enthusiasts filled the stadium; and had come
(E) enthusiasts filling the stadium, who had come

28. During the judging of the animals at the show, the judges could not decide whether Brown's collie or Jones's terrier was the best dog.
(A) whether Brown's collie or Jones's terrier was the best
(B) if Brown's collie or Joneses terrier was the better
(C) whether Brown's collie or Jones's terrier was the better
(D) if Brown's collie or Jones's terrier was the best
(E) if Browns' collie or Joneses' terrier was the best

29. Finally reviewing the extensive evidence against the defendant, he was found guilty.
(A) Finally reviewing the extensive evidence against the defendant,
(B) Reviewing the extensive evidence against the defendant,
(C) The jury finally reviewed the evidence against the defendant,
(D) When the jury finally reviewed the extensive evidence against the defendant,
(E) The jury finally reviewed the evidence against the defendant

30. Had I been at the scene of the accident, I could have administered first aid to the victims.
(A) Had I been at the scene of the accident,
(B) If I were at the scene of the accident
(C) If I was at the scene of the accident
(D) I should have been at the scene of the accident,
(E) I should have been at the scene of the accident.

31. It is not for you to assume responsibility; it is, rather, me who is the guilty person in this matter.
(A) me who is
(B) me who am
(C) I who is
(D) I who are
(E) I who am

32. Jason has been in Paris since the first of this month and does not intend to leave for London until his sister arrives.
(A) has been
(B) is
(C) will be
(D) was
(E) had been

33. Being a successful reporter demands powers of observation, fluency, and persistence.
(A) Being a successful reporter demands
(B) Being a successful reporter who demands
(C) To be a successful reporter who demands
(D) Being a successful reporter demanding
(E) To be a successful reporter demanding

34. I don't object to John paying the bill as long as he doesn't expect any favors from me in return.
(A) John paying the bill as long as
(B) John paying the bill providing
(C) John paying the bill if
(D) John's paying the bill as long as
(E) Johns' paying the bill as long as

35. At least, you are original: I have never heard that kind of an excuse until now.
(A) that kind of an excuse
(B) that sort of an excuse
(C) that kinds of excuse
(D) them kinds of excuses
(E) that kind of excuse

36. The President has established a special commission for the space program; the purpose being to investigate the causes of the Challenger disaster.
(A) program; the purpose being to
(B) program; whose purpose is to
(C) program, the purpose is to
(D) program to
(E) program; in order to

37. The growing impoverishment of women and children in American society distresses Senator Moynihan, and he is also infuriated.
(A) distresses Senator Moynihan, and he is also infuriated.
(B) distresses Senator Moynihan, infuriating him.
(C) distresses and infuriates Senator Moynihan.
(D) is distressing to Senator Moynihan, making him furious.
(E) is a cause of distress to Senator Moynihan, and of fury.

38. Paul Gauguin was married and had family responsibilities and he ran away to the South Seas to paint.
(A) Paul Gauguin was married and had family responsibilities and he
(B) Although being married and having family responsibilities, Paul Gauguin
(C) Although Paul Gauguin was married and had family responsibilities, he
(D) Being married, and therefore having family responsibilities, Paul Gauguin
(E) Despite Paul Gauguin was married and had family responsibilities, he

39. When Harriet Tubman decided to help runaway slaves escape to the North, she knew that her mission would bring her into danger in both South and North.
(A) When Harriet Tubman decided to help runaway slaves escape
(B) When Harriet Tubman decides to help runaway slaves escape
(C) When Harriet Tubman decided about helping runaway slaves escape
(D) After the decision by Harriet Tubman to help runaway slaves escape
(E) After Harriet Tubman's making of the decision to help runaway slaves escape

40. A key difference between mice and voles is tail length, a mouse's tail is twice as long as the tail of a vole.
(A) length, a mouse's tail is
(B) length; a mouse's tail is
(C) length, the tail of a mouse is
(D) length; a mouse's tail, it is
(E) length, mices's tails are

Note: The remaining questions are like those at the beginning of the section.

Directions: For each sentence in which you find an error, select the one underlined part that must be changed to make the sentence correct and blacken the corresonding space on your answer sheet.
If there is no error, blacken answer space E.

EXAMPLE:

The region has a climate so severe that plants
A
growing there rarely had been more than twelve
B C
inches high. No error
D E

SAMPLE ANSWER

Ⓐ Ⓑ ● Ⓓ Ⓔ

41. Rummaging through the attic, an album of our trip
A B C
to Europe was found. No error
D E

42. He read excerpts from "King Lear" and "Romeo
A B
and Juliet" to illustrate the changes in
C
Shakespeares style. No error
D E

43. If you omit the names of John and myself from the
A B C
list of people who deserve to be on the team,
D
you will spoil our chances for victory. No error
E

44. Was it they who were involved in the recent
A B C D
unruly demonstration? No error
E

45. The messenger reported that "The enemy
A B C
has been defeated and we can rejoice." No error
D E

46. She is the only one of the applicants who are fully
A B C
qualified for the position. No error
D E

47. Was it Lowell or Longfellow who wrote
A B C
"Hiawatha?" No error
D E

48. Neither the passengers nor the bus driver were
A B C
able to identify the youngsters who had created
D
the disturbance. No error
E

49. "You Can't Take It with You" has for its theme
A
the thought that no one wants to leave their
B C
money behind when death comes. No Error.
D E

50. Much more experimental data are required before
A B C D
we can accept this theory. No error
E

S T O P

IF YOU FINISH BEFORE TIME IS CALLED, YOU MAY CHECK YOUR WORK ON THIS SECTION ONLY
DO NOT WORK ON ANY OTHER SECTION IN THE TEST.

SECTION 3 VERBAL ABILITY

45 QUESTIONS - 30 MINUTES

For each question in this section, choose the best answer and blacken the corresponding space on the answer sheet.

Each question below consists of a word in capital letters, followed by five lettered words or phrases. Choose the word or phrase that is most nearly opposite in meaning to the word in capital letters. Since some of the questions require you to distinguish fine shades of meaning, consider all the choices before deciding which is best.

Example:

GOOD: (A) sour (B) bad (C) red (D) hot (E) ugly

Ⓐ ● Ⓒ Ⓓ Ⓔ

1. RIBALD :
   (A) refined
   (B) sensory
   (C) insignificant
   (D) hairy
   (E) impolitic

2. DIATRIBE :
   (A) monologue
   (B) hypocrisy
   (C) praise
   (D) clan
   (E) autocracy

3. SIMULATED :
   (A) depressed
   (B) genuine
   (C) gladdened
   (D) reckoned
   (E) understanding

4. DIABOLIC :
   (A) acidy
   (B) tart
   (C) dull
   (D) seraphic
   (E) clear

5. REVERE :
   (A) awake
   (B) protrude
   (C) divert
   (D) dishonor
   (E) pretend

6. PUERILE :
   (A) adult
   (B) safe
   (C) perfect
   (D) girlish
   (E) attractive

7. VENERABLE :
   (A) disgraceful
   (B) loving
   (C) costly
   (D) cheap
   (E) attractive

8. DISPARAGE :
   (A) mince
   (B) praise
   (C) tolerate
   (D) cultivate
   (E) endow

9. UNMARRED :
   (A) wed
   (B) scared
   (C) fought
   (D) spoiled
   (E) irritated

10. DISSIDENCE :
    (A) noise
    (B) glamor
    (C) treason
    (D) agreement
    (E) attraction

11. ANOMALOUS :
    (A) needed
    (B) regular
    (C) outstanding
    (D) protected
    (E) ready

12. QUELL :
    (A) purchase
    (B) develop
    (C) destroy
    (D) incur
    (E) incite

13. DISCERNIBLE :
(A) distinguished
(B) shabby
(C) intelligent
(D) imprudent
(E) imperceptible

14. NUGATORY :
(A) golden
(B) leaden
(C) affirmative
(D) effective
(E) opinionated

15. LASSITUDE :
(A) discovery
(B) undone work
(C) width
(D) breath
(E) liveliness

Each sentence below has one or two blanks, each blank indicating that something has been omitted. Beneath the sentence are five lettered words or sets of words. Choose the word or set of words that best fits the meaning of the sentence as a whole.

Example:

Although its publicity has been ----, the film itself is intelligent, well-acted, handsomely produced, and altogether ----.

(A) tasteless..respectable (B) extensive..moderate (C) sophisticated..amateur (D) risqué..crude (E) perfect..spectacular

● Ⓑ Ⓒ Ⓓ Ⓔ

16. Disturbed by the ______ nature of the plays being presented, the Puritans closed the theaters in 1642.
(A) mediocre
(B) fantastic
(C) moribund
(D) salacious
(E) witty

17. The columnist was very gentle when he mentioned his friends, but he was bitter and even ______ when he discussed people who irritated him.
(A) laconic
(B) splenetic
(C) remorseful
(D) militant
(E) stoical

18. ______ with the waters of the melting snow, the rivers threatened to overflow their banks.
(A) Ineffable
(B) Chilled
(C) Turgid
(D) Profound
(E) Berserk

19. The sergeant suspected that the private was ______ in order to avoid going on the strenuous campaign scheduled for that morning.
(A) malingering
(B) proselytizing
(C) arrant
(D) agnostic
(E) piqued

20. Since you have convinced me of my error in ordering his execution, I am going to ______ the order for his death.
(A) reaffirm
(B) reiterate
(C) reject
(D) rescind
(E) expiate

Each passage below is followed by questions based on its content. Answer all questions following a passage on the basis of what is stated or implied in that passage.

Just why some individuals choose one way of adjusting to their difficulties and others choose other ways is not known. Yet what an individual does when he is thwarted remains a reasonably good key to the understanding of his personality. If his responses to thwartings are emotional explosions and irrational excuses, he is tending to live in an unreal world. He may need help to regain the world of reality, the cause-and-effect world recognized by generations of thinkers and scientists. Perhaps he needs encouragement to redouble his efforts. Perhaps, on the other hand, he is striving for the impossible and needs to substitute a worthwhile activity within the range of his abilities. It is the part of wisdom to learn the nature of the world and of oneself in relation to it and to meet each situation as intelligently and as adequately as one can.

21. The title that best expresses the ideas of this paragraph is:
(A) Adjusting to life
(B) Escape from reality
(C) The importance of personality
(D) Emotional control
(E) The real nature of the world

22. The writer argues that all should
(A) substitute new activities for old
(B) redouble their efforts
(C) analyze their relation to the world
(D) seek encouragement from others
(E) avoid thwartings

Of the 197 million square miles making up the surface of the globe, 71 per cent is covered by interconnecting bodies of marine water; the Pacific Ocean alone covers half the Earth and averages near 14,000 feet in depth. The *continents* — Eurasia, Africa, North America, South America, Australia, and Antarctica — are the portions of the *continental masses* rising above sea level. The submerged borders of the continental masses are the *continental shelves*, beyond which lie the deep-sea basins.

The oceans attain their greatest depths not in their central parts, but in certain elongated furrows, or long narrow troughs, called *deeps*. These profound troughs have a peripheral arrangement, notably around the borders of the Pacific and Indian oceans. The position of the deeps near the continental masses suggests that the deeps, like the highest mountains, are of recent origin, since otherwise they would have been filled with waste from the lands. This suggestion is strengthened by the fact that the deeps are frequently the sites of world-shaking earthquakes. For example, the "tidal wave" that in April, 1946, caused widespread destruction along Pacific coasts resulted from a strong earthquake on the floor of the Aleutian Deep.

The topography of the ocean floors is none too well known, since in great areas the available soundings are hundreds or even thousands of miles apart. However, the floor of the Atlantic is becoming fairly well known as a result of special surveys since 1920. A broad, well-defined ridge — the Mid-Atlantic ridge — runs north and south between Africa and the two Americas, and numerous other major irregularities diversify the Atlantic floor. Closely spaced soundings show that many parts of the oceanic floors are as rugged as mountainous regions of the continents. Use of the recently perfected method of echo sounding is rapidly enlarging our knowledge of submarine topography. During World War II great strides were made in mapping submarine surfaces, particularly in many parts of the vast Pacific basin.

The continents stand on the average 2870 feet — slightly more than half a mile — above sea level. North America averages 2300 feet; Europe averages only 1150 feet; and Asia, the highest of the larger continental subdivisions, averages 3200 feet. The highest point on the globe, Mount Everest in the Himalayas, is 29,000 feet above the sea; and as the greatest known depth in the sea is over 35,000 feet, the maximum *relief* (that is, the difference in altitude between the lowest and highest points) exceeds 64,000 feet, or exceeds 12 miles. The continental masses and the deep-sea basins are relief features of the first order; the deeps, ridges, and volcanic cones that diversify the sea floor, as well as the plains, plateaus, and mountains of the continents, are relief features of the second order. The lands are unendingly subject to a complex of activities summarized in the term *erosion*, which first sculptures them in great detail and then tends to reduce them ultimately to sea level. The modeling of the landscape by weather, running water, and other agents is apparent to the keenly observant eye and causes thinking people to speculate on what must be the final result of the ceaseless wearing down of the lands. Long before there was a science of geology, Shakespeare wrote "the revolution of the times makes mountains level."

23. The highest point on North America is
(A) 2300 feet above sea level
(B) in Mexico
(C) not mentioned in the passage
(D) 2870 feet above sea level
(E) higher than the highest point in Europe

24. The largest ocean is the
(A) Atlantic
(B) Pacific
(C) Indian
(D) Aleutian Deep
(E) Arctic

25. The science of geology was started
(A) by the Greeks
(B) in 1920
(C) during World War II
(D) April 1946
(E) after 1600

26. The peripheral furrows or *deeps* are found
(A) only in the Pacific and Indian oceans
(B) near earthquakes
(C) near the shore
(D) in the center of the ocean
(E) to be 14,000 feet in depth in the Pacific

27. The highest mountains are
(A) oldest
(B) in excess of 12 miles
(C) near the *deeps*
(D) relief features of the first order
(E) of recent origin

28. The continental masses
(A) comprise 29 per cent of the earth's surface
(B) consist of six continents
(C) rise above sea level
(D) are partially submerged
(E) are relief features of the second order

29. The *deeps* are subject to change caused by
(A) earthquakes
(B) erosion
(C) soundings
(D) weathering
(E) waste

30. From this selection, we may conclude that earthquakes
(A) occur in the *deeps*
(B) occur more frequently in newly formed land or sea formations
(C) cause erosion
(D) will ultimately "make mountains level"
(E) are caused by the weight of the water

Select the word or set of words that <u>best</u> completes each of the following sentences.

31. I intend to wait for a more _______ occasion before I announce my plans.
(A) propitious
(B) prodigious
(C) pronounced
(D) pathetic
(E) positive

32. Your _______ attitude will alienate any supporters you may have won to your cause.
(A) fascinating
(B) altruistic
(C) logical
(D) truculent
(E) tortuous

33. In such a _______ grouping, a wide range of talent must be expected.
(A) casual
(B) formal
(C) homogeneous
(D) heathenish
(E) heterogeneous

34. A person who is _______ cannot be accused of being _______.
(A) dexterous — gauche
(B) glib — ribald
(C) magnanimous — charitable
(D) impolitic — partial
(E) reticent — shy

35. The size of the _______ controls the amount of _______ admitted.
(A) debt — interest
(B) aperture — light
(C) car — speed
(D) platform — people
(E) debt — mortgage

Each question below consists of a related pair of words or phrases, followed by five lettered pairs of words or phrases. Select the lettered pair that <u>best</u> expresses a relationship similar to that expressed in the original pair.
Example:
YAWN : BOREDOM :: (A) dream : sleep
(B) anger : madness (C) smile : amusement
(D) face : expression (E) impatience : rebellion
Ⓐ Ⓑ ● Ⓓ Ⓔ

36. HAGGARD : OBESE ::
(A) lonesome : pathetic
(B) gaunt : corpulent
(C) jocund : gay
(D) defiant : belligerent
(E) error : eraser

37. DAY : WEEK ::
(A) week : year
(B) second : hour
(C) week : month
(D) ephemeral : permanent
(E) time : duration

38. SPITZ : DOG ::
(A) philosopher : stone
(B) whale : fish
(C) growth : cancer
(D) whale : mammal
(E) reptile : crocodile

39. LARGE : IMMENSE ::
(A) zero : infinity
(B) mauled : battered
(C) dislike : hatred
(D) turgid : bloated
(E) quest : voyage

40. POISON : DEATH ::
(A) purgative : disease
(B) experience : knowledge
(C) growth : maturation
(D) beauty : cosmetics
(E) truth : beauty

41. CHAUVINISM : COUNTRY ::
(A) frugality : money
(B) patriotism : country
(C) gluttony : food
(D) jingoism : loyalty
(E) criticism : book

42. FRUGAL : PARSIMONIOUS ::
(A) joy : ecstasy
(B) caution : wisdom
(C) honor : loyalty
(D) poor : miserly
(E) eager : anxious

43. PRIDE : LION ::
(A) bevy : quail
(B) lair : bear
(C) fish : minnow
(D) flag : banner
(E) anger : symbol

44. FROWN : DISPLEASURE ::
(A) blush : pallor
(B) smile : commiseration
(C) sneer : contempt
(D) snore : relief
(E) smirk : regret

45. CONVENTION : MORES ::
(A) antics : caprice
(B) corruption : maggots
(C) popularity : ephemeral
(D) books : library
(E) honesty : falsity

S T O P

IF YOU FINISH BEFORE TIME IS CALLED, YOU MAY CHECK YOUR WORK ON THIS SECTION ONLY. DO NOT WORK ON ANY OTHER SECTION IN THE TEST.

SECTION 4 VERBAL ABILITY

40 QUESTIONS - 30 MINUTES

For each question in this section, choose the best answer and blacken the corresponding space on the answer sheet.

Each question below consists of a word in capital letters, followed by five lettered words or phrases. Choose the word or phrase that is most nearly <u>opposite</u> in meaning to the word in capital letters. Since some of the questions require you to distinguish fine shades of meaning, consider all the choices before deciding which is best.

Example:

GOOD: (A) sour (B) bad (C) red (D) hot (E) ugly Ⓐ ● Ⓒ Ⓓ Ⓔ

1. FURTIVE :
   (A) nearer
   (B) reluctant
   (C) apathetic
   (D) open
   (E) affable

2. PELLUCID :
   (A) turbid
   (B) liquid
   (C) capsular
   (D) handwritten
   (E) fancy

3. ORAL :
   (A) verbal
   (B) written
   (C) demonstrated
   (D) shouted
   (E) whispered

4. TERSE :
   (A) angry
   (B) quiet
   (C) verbose
   (D) shouted
   (E) whispered

5. ASCETIC :
   (A) wanton
   (B) sweet
   (C) diverse
   (D) manly
   (E) irreligious

6. FALLOW :
   (A) ruddy
   (B) mature
   (C) cultivated
   (D) decorated
   (E) visible

7. LENIENCY :
   (A) wealth
   (B) severity
   (C) status
   (D) brevity
   (E) defense

8. TRIVIA :
   (A) important matters
   (B) abstract matters
   (C) local concerns
   (D) specialized concerns
   (E) value judgments

9. EXTRICATE :
   (A) ensnare
   (B) simplify
   (C) leave whole
   (D) copy
   (E) indicate

10. INADVERTENT :
    (A) stubborn
    (B) intentional
    (C) dizzy
    (D) mysterious
    (E) cautious

Each sentence below has one or two blanks, each blank indicating that something has been omitted. Beneath the sentence are five lettered words or sets of words. Choose the word or set of words that best fits the meaning of the sentence as a whole.

Example:

Although its publicity has been ----, the film itself is intelligent, well-acted, handsomely produced, and altogether ----.

(A) tasteless..respectable (B) extensive..moderate (C) sophisticated..amateur (D) risqué..crude (E) perfect..spectacular

● Ⓑ Ⓒ Ⓓ Ⓔ

11. The introduction of fabrics made from rayon, nylon, and other ______ fibers has made many changes in our civilization.
(A) magic
(B) washable
(C) technical
(D) synthetic
(E) natural

12. Underlying historical events which influenced two great American peoples, citizens of Canada and of the United States, to work out their many problems through the years with such harmony and ______ benefit constitute a story which is both colorful and fascinating.
(A) mutual
(B) reciprocal
(C) quiet
(D) fascinating
(E) true

13. To many thoughtful people, the tremendous coverage of sporting events by television stations presents a ______. The instrument which has made us a sports-conscious nation is also the instrument which may destroy amateur and professional athletics in this country.
(A) nuance
(B) enigma
(C) handicap
(D) paradox
(E) *cul-de-sac*

14. Because he was accused of committing such a ______ crime, bail was set at a very ______ figure.
(A) vindicable — reasonable
(B) heinous — low
(C) violent — justifiable
(D) ordinary — exorbitant
(E) magnanimous — high

15. To be ______ is to be ______.
(A) pugnacious — supercilious
(B) obsequious — servile
(C) contradictory — hostile
(D) puerile — strong
(E) effete — violent

Each question below consists of a related pair of words or phrases, followed by five lettered pairs of words or phrases. Select the lettered pair that best expresses a relationship similar to that expressed in the original pair.

Example:

YAWN : BOREDOM :: (A) dream : sleep (B) anger : madness (C) smile : amusement (D) face : expression (E) impatience : rebellion

Ⓐ Ⓑ ● Ⓓ Ⓔ

16. AUTOMOBILE : GASOLINE ::
(A) fire : fuel
(B) man : energy
(C) airplane : propeller
(D) man : food
(E) disease : germs

17. COMPOSER : SYMPHONY ::
(A) tragedy : playwright
(B) actor : comedy
(C) conductor : orchestra
(D) director : movie
(E) poet : sonnet

18. ALLAY : PAIN ::
(A) mollify : fright
(B) cancel : order
(C) arbitrate : dispute
(D) mitigate : offense
(E) testify : court

19. EXPURGATE : PASSAGE ::
(A) burn : book
(B) filter : water
(C) abridge : text
(D) cancel : plan
(E) irritate : wound

20. WEARISOME : REFRESHING ::
(A) choleric : apoplectic
(B) tedious : dull
(C) original : scintillating
(D) lengthy : brief
(E) truthful : courageous

21. EVANESCENT : TEMPORARY ::
(A) shining : brief
(B) ephemeral : transient
(C) emanating : permanent
(D) lethargic : napping
(E) laconic : brief

22. EXERTION : FATIGUE ::
(A) school : graduation
(B) exercise : muscles
(C) carelessness : accident
(D) effort : results
(E) maximum : tiredness

23. PARIAH : FAVORITE ::
(A) appetizer : dessert
(B) equal : pet
(C) peer : sycophant
(D) liar : mendicant
(E) outcast : pet

24. DAMPEN : DRENCH ::
(A) wanton : wench
(B) gambol : play
(C) simmer : boil
(D) rain : snow
(E) moist : misty

25. ENMITY : HATE ::
(A) emulation : jealousy
(B) glory : envy
(C) intimidation : fear
(D) arbitration : love
(E) comity : friendship

Each passage below is followed by questions based on its content. Answer all questions following a passage on the basis of what is stated or implied in that passage.

The total impression made by any work of fiction can not be rightly understood without a sympathetic perception of the artistic aims of the writer. Consciously or unconsciously, he has accepted certain facts, and rejected or suppressed other facts, in order to give unity to the particular aspect of human life which he is depicting. No novelist possesses the impartiality, the indifference, the infinite tolerance of Nature. Nature displays to us, with complete unconcern, the beautiful and the ugly, the precious and the trivial, the pure and the impure. But a writer must select the aspects of Nature and human nature that are demanded by the work in hand. He is forced to select, to combine, to create.

26. The title that best expresses the ideas of this paragraph is:
(A) Unity in disunity
(B) The tolerance and impartiality of Nature
(C) The novelist's failure
(D) Understanding fiction
(E) Nature, the true novelist

27. A novelist chooses for his story material which will
(A) prove his impartiality
(B) further his general purpose
(C) completely copy Nature
(D) create a beautiful effect
(E) display his unconcern

28. A reader must
(A) detect trivialities
(B) understand all aspects of Nature
(C) discover the aim of the novelist
(D) maintain a tolerant attitude
(E) reject certain facts

There is an enormous difference in the ways in which various public officials respond to public pressures, and in the means and methods they employ to deal with them. The best possess understanding of the forces that must be taken into account, determination not to be swerved from the path of public interest, a willingness to make enemies along with a gift for avoiding them, and faith that public support will be forthcoming for the correct course. The poorest are overhesitant, evasive, preoccupied with their relationships with their colleagues, superiors, the press or the political support on which they lean. They will make no move unless the gallery is packed. They confront all embarrassments with a stale general formula.

29. The title that best expresses the ideas of this paragraph is:
(A) Political pressure groups
(B) Mistakes for public officials to avoid
(C) Characteristics of public officials
(D) Gaining political support
(E) Avoiding political enemies

30. The best public officials
(A) insist on unanimous support for their ideas
(B) uniformly follow well-established general procedures
(C) respond to pressure groups
(D) have confidence in the public
(E) are cautious

31. A fault of poor public officials *not* mentioned or implied in the selection is
(A) dishonesty
(B) lack of candor
(C) indecision
(D) timidity
(E) lack of independence

If Shakespeare needs any excuse for the exuberance of language (the high key in which he pitched most of his dramatic dialogue) it should be remembered that he was doing on the plastic stage of his own day what on the pictorial stage of our day is not so much required. Shakespeare's dramatic figures stood out on a platform-stage, without background, with the audience on three sides of it. And the whole of his atmosphere and environment had to come from the gestures and language of the actors. When they spoke, they provided their own scenery, which we now provide for them. They had to do a good deal more (when they spoke) than actors have to do today in order to give the setting. They carried the scenery on their backs, as it were, and spoke it in words.

32. The title that best expresses the ideas of this paragraph is:
(A) The scenery of the Elizabethan stage
(B) The importance of actors in the Shakespearean drama
(C) The influence of the Elizabethan stage on Shakespeare's style
(D) The importance of words
(E) Suitable gestures for the Elizabethan stage

33. In comparison with actors of Shakespeare's time, actors of today
(A) carry the settings in their words
(B) pitch their voices in a lower key
(C) depend more on elaborate settings
(D) have to do more to make the setting clear
(E) use many gestures

34. The nature of the stage for which Shakespeare wrote made it necessary for him to
(A) employ only highly dramatic situations
(B) depend on scenery owned by the actors themselves
(C) have the actors shift the scenery
(D) create atmosphere through the dialogue
(E) restrict backgrounds to familiar types of scenes

When it was found that oxygen or pure vital air would not cure consumption as was expected, but rather aggravated its symptoms, trial was made of an air of the most opposite kind. I wish we had acted with the same philosophical spirit in our attempts to cure the disease of poverty, and having found that the pouring in of fresh supplies of labor only tended to aggravate the symptoms, had tried what would be the effect of withholding a little these supplies.

35. According to this paragraph
(A) too much of anything may prove detrimental
(B) it is best to fight fire with fire
(C) philosophers exaggerate the ills of poverty
(D) you cannot have too much of anything
(E) a new broom sweeps clean

36. The term "consumption" is used here to signify
(A) the process of using up economic goods
(B) a type of social ill
(C) a wasting away of tissue
(D) an insufficiency of vital air
(E) a consumer in an economic world

37. "Vital" is used by the author to mean
(A) fundamental
(B) sound
(C) essential
(D) organic
(E) oxygen

The ordinary form of mercury thermometer is used for temperatures ranging from −40°F. to 500°F. For measuring temperatures below −40°F. thermometers filled with alcohol are used. These are, however, not satisfactory for use at high temperatures. When a mercury thermometer is used for temperatures above 500°F., the space above the mercury is filled with some inert gas, usually nitrogen or carbon dioxide, placed in the thermometer under pressure. As the mercury rises, the gas pressure is increased, so that it is possible to use these thermometers for temperatures as high as 1,000°F. This is the limit, however, as the melting point of glass is comparatively low. For temperatures exceeding 800°F., some form of pyrometer is generally used. The simplest of these is the metallic or mechanical pyrometer. This consists of two metals having different rates of expansion, such as iron and brass, attached to each other at one end and with the other ends free. By a system of levers and gears the expansion of the metals is made to move a hand over a dial graduated in degrees. This should not be used for temperatures exceeding 1,000°F. to 1,200°F.

38. According to the passage, what chiefly determines the upper temperature at which mercury thermometers can be used?
(A) Weight of mercury
(B) Gas pressure
(C) Melting point of glass
(D) Amount of gas
(E) Rates of expansion

39. What topic is treated in this passage?
(A) Manufacturing of thermometers
(B) Mercury thermometers
(C) Temperatures
(D) Temperature ranges
(E) Measuring temperatures

40. With what, besides mercury, would a thermometer be filled if it were designed to be used for measuring temperatures of about 500°F.?
(A) Pyrometer
(B) Inert gas
(C) Iron and brass
(D) Gas
(E) Alcohol

S T O P

IF YOU FINISH BEFORE TIME IS CALLED, YOU MAY CHECK YOUR WORK ON THIS SECTION ONLY. DO NOT WORK ON ANY OTHER SECTION IN THE TEST.

SECTION 5 MATH ABILITY

35 QUESTIONS - 30 MINUTES

In this section solve each problem, using any available space on the page for scratchwork. Then decide which is the best of the choices given and blacken the corresponding space on the answer sheet.

The following information is for your reference in solving some of the problems.

Circle of radius r: Area $= \pi r^2$; Circumference $= 2\pi r$
The number of degrees of arc in a circle is 360.
The measure in degrees of a straight angle is 180.

Definitions of symbols:

$=$ is equal to	$\leq$ is less than or equal to
$\neq$ is unequal to	$\geq$ is greater than or equal to
$<$ is less than	$\parallel$ is parallel to
$>$ is greater than	$\perp$ is perpendicular to

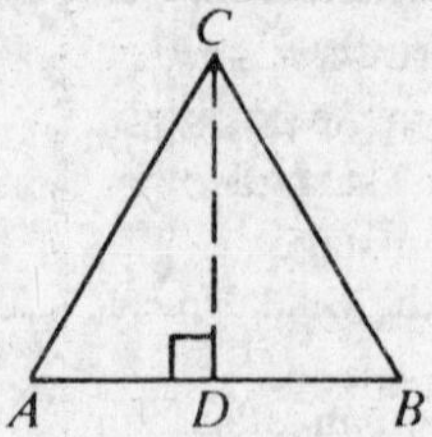

Triangle: The sum of the measures in degrees of the angles of a triangle is 180.
If $\angle CDA$ is a right angle, then

(1) area of $\triangle ABC = \frac{AB \times CD}{2}$

(2) $AC^2 = AD^2 + DC^2$

Note: Figures that accompany problems in this test are intended to provide information useful in solving the problems. They are drawn as accurately as possible EXCEPT when it is stated in a specific problem that its figure is not drawn to scale. All figures lie in a plane unless otherwise indicated. All numbers used are real numbers.

1. Point B is on line segment AC and point E is on line segment DF. If $AB > DE$ and $BC = EF$, then
   (A) $AC < DF$
   (B) $AC = DF$
   (C) $AC > DF$
   (D) $DF > AC$
   (E) $EF > DF$

2. A student attending a school for 3 semesters has a scholastic average of 85%. He transfers to another school and after 4 semesters earns an average of 90% in this school. What is his average for his work in both schools?
   (A) 82%
   (B) 87%
   (C) 87.5%
   (D) 87.9%
   (E) 88%

3. Three boys have marbles in the ratio of 19:5:3. If the boy with the least number has 9 marbles, how many marbles does the boy with the greatest number have?
   (A) 27
   (B) 33
   (C) 57
   (D) 81
   (E) 171

4. The distance between Portland, Oregon and Santa Fe, New Mexico is 1800 miles. How long (in hours) would it take a train with an average speed of 60 miles per hours to make the trip?
   (A) 30
   (B) 39
   (C) 48
   (D) 300
   (E) 480

5. If the cost of 500 articles is d dollars, how many of these articles can be bought for x dollars?
   (A) $\frac{500d}{x}$
   (B) $\frac{500}{dx}$
   (C) $\frac{dx}{500}$
   (D) $\frac{500x}{d}$
   (E) $\frac{d}{500x}$

6. What is the total cost (in cents) of n 2-cent stamps, and p 3-cent stamps?
   (A) $2n + 3p$
   (B) $5n + p$
   (C) $5(n + p)$
   (D) $2(n + p)$
   (E) $3(n + p)$

7. A candy dealer makes up a mixture of 3 parts of candy costing him 60¢ a pound with 2 parts of candy costing him 70¢ a pound, and 2 parts of candy costing him 50¢ a pound. At what price per pound should he sell this mixture to make a profit of 25%?
   (A) 50¢
   (B) 60¢
   (C) 65¢
   (D) 70¢
   (E) 75¢

Questions 8–27 each consist of two quantities, one in Column A and one in Column B. You are to compare the two quantities and on the answer sheet blacken space

- A if the quantity in Column A is greater;
- B if the quantity in Column B is greater;
- C if the two quantities are equal;
- D If the relationship cannot be determined from the information given.

AN E RESPONSE WILL NOT BE SCORED.

EXAMPLES

	Column A	Column B	Answers
E1.	2×6	$2 + 6$	● Ⓑ Ⓒ Ⓓ Ⓔ
	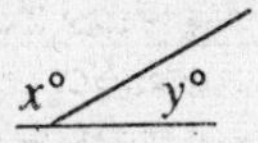		
E2.	$180 - x$	y	Ⓐ Ⓑ ● Ⓓ Ⓔ
E3.	$p - q$	$q - p$	Ⓐ Ⓑ Ⓒ ● Ⓔ

Notes:

1. In certain questions, information concerning one or both of the quantities to be compared is centered above the two columns.
2. In a given question, a symbol that appears in both columns represents the same thing in Column A as it does in Column B.
3. Letters such as x, n, and k stand for real numbers.

	Column A	Column B
8.	$3\frac{1}{2}\%$	$\frac{35}{1000}$
9.	$\sqrt{0.04}$	$(0.2)^2$
10.	$(\frac{1}{2})(\frac{7}{8})$	$87\frac{1}{2}\%$
11.	$(\frac{1}{2})^2$	23%
12.	0.3	$\frac{0.7}{2}$
13.	$\frac{X}{Y}$	$\frac{X}{Y} \cdot \frac{Y}{X}$

$-1 < a < 1$
$-1 < b < 0$

	Column A	Column B
14.	a	b

	Column A	Column B
15.	$\dfrac{2x - \dfrac{y-5}{6}}{\dfrac{y-5}{3} - 4x}$	-0.5

Circleville is 23 kilometers from Center City and Centerville is 46 kilometers from Center City.

	Column A	Column B
16.	Distance from Circleville to Centerville	23 kilometers

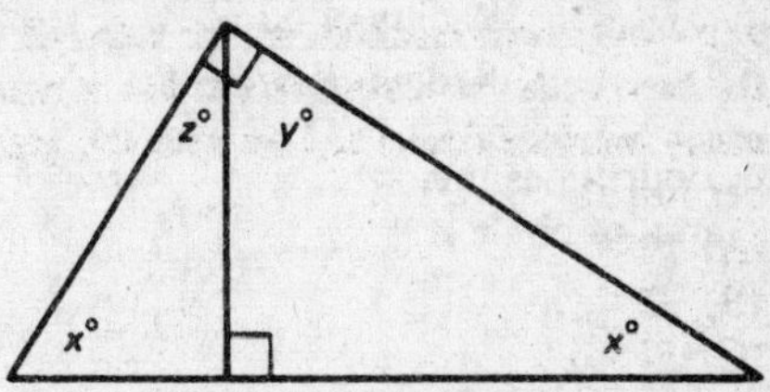

This concerns #17 and #18

	Column A	Column B
17.	z	45

	Column A	Column B
18.	45	x

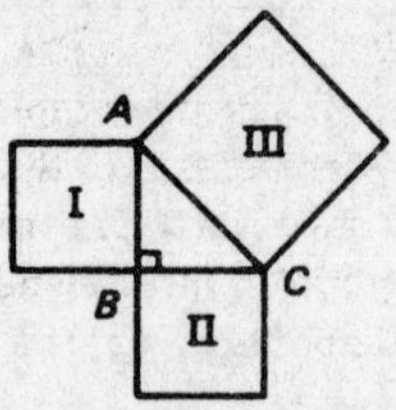

Squares I, II, and III are on the sides of isosceles right triangle ABC, whose area is 12.5. This concerns #19 and #20

	Column A	Column B
19.	Area of square III	Twice the area of triangle ABC
20.	Twice the area of square I	Area of square III

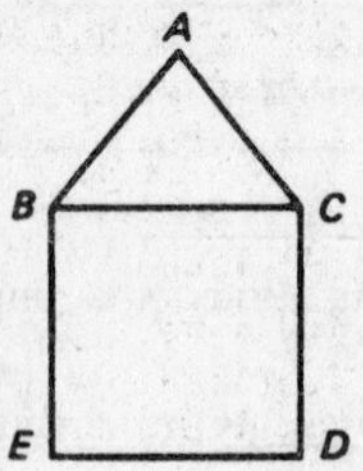

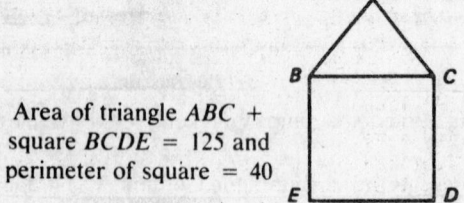

Area of triangle ABC + square $BCDE$ = 125 and perimeter of square = 40

	Column A	Column B
21.	The shortest distance from point A to ED	Twice the length of EB

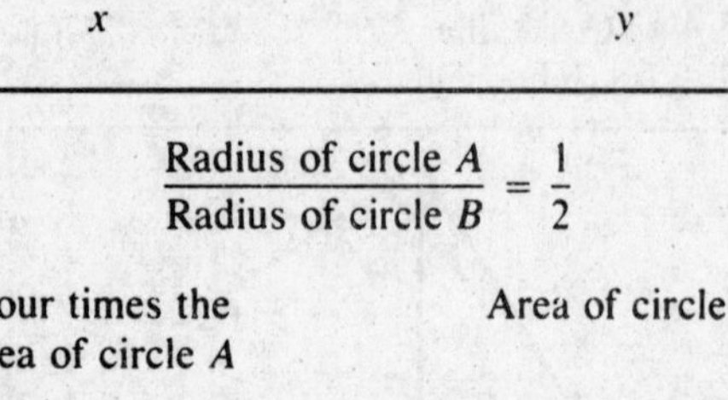

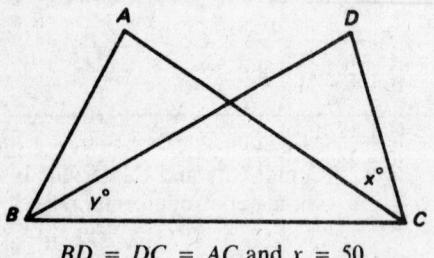

$BD = DC = AC$ and $x = 50$

	Column A	Column B
22.	x	y

$$\frac{\text{Radius of circle } A}{\text{Radius of circle } B} = \frac{1}{2}$$

	Column A	Column B
23.	Four times the area of circle A	Area of circle B

Ratio of the circumference of the small circle to the circumference of the larger circle is 1:2

	Column A	Column B
24.	Twice the area of the smaller circle	Area of the larger circle

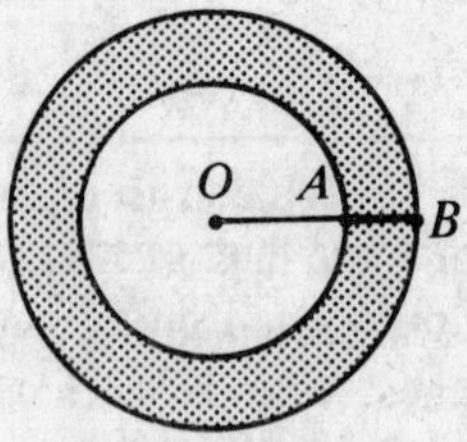

$OB - OA = 4$
Area of unshaded section $= 9\pi$
This concerns #25 and #26

	Column A	Column B
25.	Four times the area of the unshaded section	Area of the shaded portion
26.	Seven times the circumference of the inner circle	Three times the circumference of the outer circle

$0.1y + 0.01y = 2.2$

	Column A	Column B
27.	$0.1y$	20

Solve each of the remaining problems in this section using any available space for scratchwork. Then decide which is the best of the choices given and blacken the corresponding space on the answer sheet.

28. If 8 men can do a job in 12 days, what is the percentage increase in the number of days required to do the job when 2 men are released?
(A) 25
(B) 33⅓
(C) 50
(D) 67
(E) 75

29. One side of a rectangle is x inches. If the perimeter is p inches, what is the length (in inches) of the other side? Answer in terms of p and x.
(A) $p - x$
(B) $p - 2x$
(C) $\frac{p - x}{2}$
(D) $\frac{p - 2x}{2}$
(E) $2p - 2x$

30. $\frac{ca^2 - cb^2}{-a - b}$ is equivalent to $cb + ?$
(A) ac
(B) $-ca$
(C) 1
(D) -1
(E) c

31. 1 furlong = 220 yards = ⅛ statute mile
How many yards are there in one statute mile?
(A) $27\frac{1}{2}$
(B) 275
(C) 880
(D) 1760
(E) 5280

32. $x^2 + y^2 = 8$
$xy = 7$
$(x + y)^2 = ?$
(A) 14
(B) 16
(C) 22
(D) 30
(E) 49

33. A student does ⅓ of his homework and then goes to dinner. After dinner he completes ¾ of the remainder of his assignments and then decides to go to a basketball game. What part of his homework will be left uncompleted if he spends no additional time on his assignments?
(A) $\frac{1}{6}$
(B) $\frac{5}{12}$
(C) $\frac{1}{2}$
(D) $\frac{7}{12}$
(E) $\frac{2}{3}$

34. A train traveling at 30 miles per hour is stopped 1½ miles from its destination at 1:00 P.M. At what time would the train have arrived at its destination if it were not for the delay?
(A) 1:02
(B) 1:03
(C) 1:04
(D) 1:45
(E) 2:20

35. If it takes 9 men 15 days to complete a task, how many days would be required to complete this task if three additional men were employed?
(A) $4\frac{3}{4}$
(B) 10
(C) $11\frac{1}{4}$
(D) 12
(E) 16

S T O P

IF YOU FINISH BEFORE TIME IS CALLED, YOU MAY CHECK YOUR WORK ON THIS SECTION ONLY.
DO NOT WORK ON ANY OTHER SECTION IN THE TEST.

SECTION 6 VERBAL ABILITY

40 QUESTIONS - 30 MINUTES

For each question in this section, choose the best answer and blacken the corresponding space on the answer sheet.

Each question below consists of a word in capital letters, followed by five lettered words or phrases. Choose the word or phrase that is most nearly opposite in meaning to the word in capital letters. Since some of the questions require you to distinguish fine shades of meaning, consider all the choices before deciding which is best.

Example:

GOOD: (A) sour (B) bad (C) red (D) hot (E) ugly

Ⓐ ● Ⓒ Ⓓ Ⓔ

1. FEALTY :
   (A) mass
   (B) holiness
   (C) feudalism
   (D) treachery
   (E) sovereignty

2. INCENSED :
   (A) edited
   (B) appeased
   (C) perfumed
   (D) frightened
   (E) anticipated

3. INNUENDO :
   (A) interrogation
   (B) accusation
   (C) aptitude
   (D) aggression
   (E) pianissimo

4. AMASS :
   (A) protract
   (B) distribute
   (C) startle
   (D) embellish
   (E) delude

5. SQUALID :
   (A) equal
   (B) objective
   (C) calm
   (D) undefiled
   (E) shrunken

6. MENDACIOUS :
   (A) beggarly
   (B) regal
   (C) veracious
   (D) voracious
   (E) violent

7. SCARCITY :
   (A) plethora
   (B) mediocrity
   (C) loss
   (D) lateness
   (E) courage

8. HARMONIOUS :
   (A) organlike
   (B) halcyon
   (C) discordant
   (D) sugary
   (E) bellicose

9. EPIGRAMMATIC :
   (A) intelligent
   (B) mournful
   (C) destitute
   (D) verbose
   (E) incorrect

10. ORIGINAL :
   (A) banal
   (B) controlled
   (C) futile
   (D) authentic
   (E) false

Each sentence below has one or two blanks, each blank indicating that something has been omitted. Beneath the sentence are five lettered words or sets of words. Choose the word or set of words that best fits the meaning of the sentence as a whole.

Example:

Although its publicity has been ----, the film itself is intelligent, well-acted, handsomely produced, and altogether ----.

(A) tasteless..respectable (B) extensive..moderate (C) sophisticated..amateur (D) risqué..crude (E) perfect..spectacular

● Ⓑ Ⓒ Ⓓ Ⓔ

11. The audience was annoyed by the ________ remarks of the speaker; they were as lengthy as they were meaningless.
(A) sarcastic
(B) pithy
(C) lamentable
(D) inane
(E) sententious

12. He bore the pain ________ and did not wince or whimper when the incision was made.
(A) histrionically
(B) stoically
(C) realistically
(D) nobly
(E) graciously

13. People noticed his ________ because he was ________ to everyone he met.
(A) superficiality — courteous
(B) naivete — unkind
(C) servility — sarcastic
(D) meekness — obsequious
(E) arrogance — reconciliatory

14. Many police officers feel that the ________ shown by judges to first offenders ________ many young people to embark on a career of crime.
(A) tolerance — deters
(B) indifference — causes
(C) clemency — encourages
(D) understanding — deters
(E) penalties — encourages

15. To be ________ is to be ________.
(A) dishonest — hypercritical
(B) lucky — fortuitous
(C) credible — gullible
(D) mendacious — poor
(E) repetitious — redundant

16. We shall not be able to use your alibi in court unless we can find someone to ________ your statement.
(A) avouch
(B) challenge
(C) impugn
(D) corroborate
(E) refute

17. To be successful, a salesman cannot afford to be ________.
(A) extravagant
(B) diffident
(C) solicitous
(D) ubiquitous
(E) omniscient

18. The social worker sought the aid of wealthy benefactors as she sought to ________ the terrible living conditions of the poor people in the slums.
(A) evaluate
(B) remove
(C) ameliorate
(D) assay
(E) depict

19. A ________ at all times, he was suspicious of the ________ actions of others.
(A) misogynist — philanthropic
(B) cynic — altruistic
(C) satirist — philanthropic
(D) sentimentalist — humane
(E) hypocrite — overt

20. To take a ________ attitude often is to ________ any chance of favorable relationships.
(A) kindly — deny
(B) pertinent — violate
(C) sincere — reduce
(D) patronizing — eliminate
(E) promising — negate

Each question below consists of a related pair of words or phrases, followed by five lettered pairs of words or phrases. Select the lettered pair that best expresses a relationship similar to that expressed in the original pair.

Example:

YAWN : BOREDOM :: (A) dream : sleep
(B) anger : madness (C) smile : amusement
(D) face : expression (E) impatience : rebellion

Ⓐ Ⓑ ● Ⓓ Ⓔ

21. GAUNTLET : HAND ::
(A) buskin : foot
(B) helmet : protection
(C) talisman : amulet
(D) buskin : head
(E) amulet : foot

22. OLFACTORY : NOSE ::
(A) visible : eyes
(B) gustatory : tongue
(C) ambulatory : legs
(D) tactile : eyes
(E) gustatory : ears

23. ALLOY : METAL ::
(A) tin : lead
(B) hybrid : mongrel
(C) medley : ore
(D) cake : ingredients
(E) gold : brass

24. BIZARRE : EXOTIC ::
(A) egregious : esoteric
(B) ordinary : commonplace
(C) modish : outlandish
(D) routine : exciting
(E) behavior : dancing

25. FRIVOLOUS : SERIOUSNESS ::
(A) acute : perception
(B) meticulous : organization
(C) outspoken : reticence
(D) lavish : money
(E) industrious : perseverance

26. BRONZE : PATINA ::
(A) wood : veneer
(B) plaque : honor
(C) mold : yeast
(D) iron : rust
(E) lead : tin

27. DOLLAR : DIME ::
(A) week : day
(B) hour : minute
(C) meter : centimeter
(D) degree : minute
(E) decade : year

28. CARDIOLOGY : HEART ::
(A) pathology : maps
(B) apology : sorrow
(C) tautology : education
(D) pharmacology : drugs
(E) orthography : religion

29. TURNCOAT : TREACHEROUS ::
(A) seamstress : generous
(B) firebrand : mysterious
(C) mountebank : serious
(D) spoilsport : notorious
(E) killjoy : lugubrious

30. MELLIFLUOUS : CACOPHONOUS ::
(A) vinegary : honeyed
(B) fragrant : noisome
(C) sweet : euphonious
(D) sad : discordant
(E) plentiful : rare

Each passage below is followed by questions based on its content. Answer all questions following a passage on the basis of what is stated or implied in that passage.

The establishment of the Third Reich influenced events in American history by starting a chain of events which culminated in war between Germany and the United States. The complete destruction of democracy, the persecution of Jews, the war on religion, the cruelty and barbarism of the Nazis, and especially, the plans of Germany and her allies, Italy and Japan, for world conquest caused great indignation in this country and brought on fear of another world war. While speaking out against Hitler's atrocities, the American people generally favored isolationist policies and neutrality. The Neutrality Acts of 1935 and 1936 prohibited trade with any belligerents or loans to them. In 1937 the President was empowered to declare an arms embargo in wars between nations at his discretion.

American opinion began to change somewhat after President Roosevelt's "quarantine the aggressor" speech at Chicago (1937) in which he severely criticized Hitler's policies. Germany's seizure of Austria and the Munich Pact for the partition of Czechoslovakia (1938) also aroused the American people. The conquest of Czechoslovakia in March, 1939 was another rude awakening to the menace of the Third Reich. In August, 1939 came the shock of the Nazi-Soviet Pact and in September the attack on Poland and the outbreak of European war. The United States attempted to maintain neutrality in spite of sympathy for the democracies arrayed against the Third Reich. The Neutrality Act of 1939 repealed the arms embargo and permitted "cash and carry" exports of arms to belligerent nations. A strong national defense program was begun. A draft act was passed (1940) to strengthen the military services. A Lend-Lease Act (1941) authorized the President to sell, exchange, or lend materials to any country deemed necessary by him for the defense of the United States. Help was given to Britain by exchanging certain over-age destroyers for the right to establish American bases in British territory in the Western Hemisphere. In August, 1941, President Roosevelt and Prime Minister Churchill met and issued the Atlantic Charter which proclaimed the kind of a world which should be established after the war. In December, 1941, Japan launched the unprovoked attack on the United States at Pearl Harbor. Immediately thereafter, Germany declared war on the United States.

31. One item occurring before 1937 that the author does NOT mention in his list of actions that alienated the American public was
(A) the persecution of religious groups
(B) Nazi barbarism
(C) the pacts with Italy
(D) German plans for conquest
(E) the burning of the Reichstag

32. The Neutrality Act of 1939
(A) restated America's isolationist policies
(B) proclaimed American Neutrality
(C) permitted the selling of arms to belligerent nations
(D) was a cause of our entrance into World War II
(E) started our national defense program

33. We entered the war against Germany
(A) because Pearl Harbor was attacked
(B) after peaceful efforts had failed
(C) because Germany declared war
(D) because Japan was an ally of Germany
(E) after Germany had signed the Nazi-Soviet Pact

34. An event which did not occur in 1939 was
(A) the invasion of Poland
(B) the invasion of Czechoslovakia
(C) the passing of the Neutrality Act
(D) the passing of the Lend-Lease Act
(E) the outbreak of the war in Europe

35. The Lend-Lease Act was designed to
(A) strengthen our national defense
(B) provide battleships to the Allies
(C) help the British
(D) promote the Atlantic Charter
(E) avenge Pearl Harbor

36. During the years 1933–1936, American policy may be described as being
(A) watchful
(B) isolationist
(C) pacific
(D) incorrect
(E) discretionary

The *range in frequencies* of musical sounds is approximately 20–20,000 cycles per second (cy/sec). Some people can hear higher frequencies than others. Longitudinal waves whose frequencies are higher than those within the audible range are called *ultrasonic* frequencies. Ultrasonic frequencies are used in sonar for such purposes as submarine detection and depth finding. Ultrasonic frequencies are also being tried for sterilizing food since these frequencies kill some bacteria. Sound waves of all frequencies in the audible range travel at the same speed in the same medium. In the audible range, the higher the frequency of the sound the higher is the *pitch*. The term *supersonic* refers to speed greater than sound. An airplane traveling at supersonic speed is moving at a speed greater than the speed of sound in air at that temperature. *Mach 1* means a speed equal to that of sound; *Mach 2* means a speed equal to twice that of sound, etc.

Musical sounds have three basic *characteristics*: pitch, loudness, and quality or timbre. As was indicated above, *pitch* is determined largely by the frequency of the wave reaching the ear. The higher the frequency the higher is the pitch. *Loudness* depends on the amplitude of the wave reaching the ear. For a given frequency, the greater the amplitude of the wave the louder the sound. To discuss quality of sound we need to clarify the concept of overtones. Sounds are produced by vibrating objects; if these objects are given a gentle push, they usually vibrate at one definite frequency producing a pure tone. This is the way a tuning fork is usually used. When objects vibrate freely after a force is momentarily applied, they are said to produce their *natural frequency*. Some objects, like strings and air columns, can vibrate naturally at more than one frequency at a time. The lowest frequency which an object can produce when vibrating freely is known as the object's *fundamental frequency*; other frequencies that the object can produce are known as its *overtones*. The *quality* of a sound depends on the number and relative amplitude of the overtones present in the wave reaching the ear.

37. A soprano would probably have a frequency of
(A) 200 cy/sec
(B) 500 cy/sec
(C) 5000 cy/sec
(D) 10,000 cy/sec
(E) 20,000 cy/sec

38. The timbre of a musical sound is dependent on
(A) fundamentals
(B) amplitude
(C) frequency
(D) overtones
(E) speed

39. Which of the following individuals would be likely to use terms like Mach 5 or Mach 9?
(A) a jet pilot
(B) a musician
(C) an astronaut
(D) a submarine navigator
(E) a biologist

40. Ultrasonic frequencies are
(A) inaudible
(B) excessively fast
(C) characterized by a great amplitude
(D) death rays
(E) overtones

S T O P

IF YOU FINISH BEFORE TIME IS CALLED, YOU MAY CHECK YOUR WORK ON THIS SECTION ONLY. DO NOT WORK ON ANY OTHER SECTION IN THE TEST.

ANSWER KEY

Note: The answers to the math sections are keyed to the corresponding review areas in Chapter 11. The numbers in parentheses after each answer refer to topics as listed below. (Note that to review for number 16, Quantitative Comparison, study Chapter 10.)

1. Fundamental Operations
2. Algebraic Operations
3. Using Algebra
4. Roots and Radicals
5. Inequalities
6. Fractions
7. Decimals
8. Percent
9. Averages
10. Motion
11. Ratio and Proportion
12. Mixtures and Solutions
13. Work
14. Coordinate Geometry
15. Geometry
16. Quantitative Comparison
17. Data Interpretation

SECTION 1 MATH

1.	**A (1)**	6.	**C (1)**	11.	**E (15)**	16.	**B (12)**	21.	**C (2)**
2.	**D (8)**	7.	**D (2)**	12.	**D (11,15)**	17.	**A (5,15)**	22.	**C (1)**
3.	**C (6,7)**	8.	**A (6,8)**	13.	**A (8)**	18.	**E (2)**	23.	**A (3,12)**
4.	**A (2)**	9.	**E (11)**	14.	**B (11)**	19.	**C (1)**	24.	**C (2)**
5.	**A (11)**	10.	**A (15)**	15.	**E (3)**	20.	**D (8)**	25.	**C (10)**

SECTION 2 TEST OF STANDARD WRITTEN ENGLISH

1.	**A**	11.	**C**	21.	**D**	31.	**E**	41.	**A**
2.	**C**	12.	**C**	22.	**C**	32.	**A**	42.	**D**
3.	**D**	13.	**B**	23.	**B**	33.	**A**	43.	**B**
4.	**A**	14.	**B**	24.	**D**	34.	**D**	44.	**E**
5.	**C**	15.	**C**	25.	**C**	35.	**E**	45.	**B**
6.	**E**	16.	**B**	26.	**D**	36.	**D**	46.	**C**
7.	**B**	17.	**C**	27.	**C**	37.	**C**	47.	**D**
8.	**E**	18.	**B**	28.	**C**	38.	**C**	48.	**C**
9.	**D**	19.	**E**	29.	**D**	39.	**A**	49.	**C**
10.	**C**	20.	**C**	30.	**A**	40.	**B**	50.	**E**

SECTION 3 VERBAL

1.	**A**	10.	**D**	19.	**A**	28.	**D**	37.	**C**
2.	**C**	11.	**B**	20.	**D**	29.	**A**	38.	**D**
3.	**B**	12.	**E**	21.	**A**	30.	**B**	39.	**C**
4.	**D**	13.	**E**	22.	**C**	31.	**A**	40.	**B**
5.	**D**	14.	**D**	23.	**C**	32.	**D**	41.	**C**
6.	**A**	15.	**E**	24.	**B**	33.	**E**	42.	**A**
7.	**A**	16.	**D**	25.	**E**	34.	**A**	43.	**A**
8.	**B**	17.	**B**	26.	**C**	35.	**B**	44.	**C**
9.	**D**	18.	**C**	27.	**E**	36.	**B**	45.	**A**

SECTION 4 VERBAL

1.	**D**	9.	**A**	17.	**E**	25.	**C**	33.	**C**
2.	**A**	10.	**B**	18.	**D**	26.	**D**	34.	**D**
3.	**B**	11.	**D**	19.	**B**	27.	**B**	35.	**A**
4.	**C**	12.	**A**	20.	**D**	28.	**C**	36.	**C**
5.	**A**	13.	**D**	21.	**B**	29.	**C**	37.	**C**
6.	**C**	14.	**A**	22.	**C**	30.	**D**	38.	**C**
7.	**B**	15.	**B**	23.	**E**	31.	**A**	39.	**E**
8.	**A**	16.	**D**	24.	**C**	32.	**C**	40.	**B**

SECTION 5 MATH

1. **C (5,15)**	8. **C (6,8,16)**	15. **C (2,6,16)**	22. **B (15,16)**	29. **D (15)**
2. **D (9)**	9. **A (4,16)**	16. **D (1,16)**	23. **C (15,16)**	30. **B (2)**
3. **C (11)**	10. **B (6,8,16)**	17. **C (15,16)**	24. **B (15,16)**	31. **D (11)**
4. **A (10)**	11. **A (4,8,16)**	18. **C (15,16)**	25. **B (15,16)**	32. **C (2)**
5. **D (11)**	12. **B (6,7,16)**	19. **A (15,16)**	26. **C (15,16)**	33. **A (6)**
6. **A (1)**	13. **D (6,16)**	20. **C (15,16)**	27. **B (2,7,16)**	34. **B (10)**
7. **E (12)**	14. **D (5,16)**	21. **B (15,16)**	28. **B (13)**	35. **C (11,13)**

SECTION 6 VERBAL

1. **D**	9. **D**	17. **B**	25. **C**	33. **C**
2. **B**	10. **A**	18. **C**	26. **D**	34. **D**
3. **B**	11. **D**	19. **B**	27. **E**	35. **A**
4. **B**	12. **B**	20. **D**	28. **D**	36. **B**
5. **D**	13. **D**	21. **A**	29. **E**	37. **D**
6. **C**	14. **C**	22. **B**	30. **B**	38. **D**
7. **A**	15. **E**	23. **D**	31. **E**	39. **C**
8. **C**	16. **D**	24. **B**	32. **C**	40. **A**

SELF-EVALUATION

The model SAT test you have just completed has the same format as the actual SAT. As you take more of the model tests in this chapter, you will lose any SAT "stage fright" you might have.

Use the steps that follow to evaluate your performance on Model SAT Test 3. (Note: You'll find the charts referred to in steps 1–5 on the next three pages.)

STEP 1 Use the Answer Key to check your answers for each section.

STEP 2 For each section, count the number of correct and incorrect answers (remember that you don't count omitted answers), and enter the numbers on the appropriate lines of the chart "Obtaining Your Raw Score." Then do the indicated calculations to get your Raw Verbal Score, your Raw TSWE Score, and your Raw Math Score.

STEP 3 Consult the chart "Evaluate Your Performance" to see how well you did.

STEP 4 To pinpoint the specific areas in which you need to improve, circle the numbers of the questions that you either left blank or got wrong on the "Identify Your Weaknesses" charts. This will tell you where to concentrate your efforts to get the most out of your study time. The chart for the math sections gives you page references for review and practice by skill areas. The charts for the verbal and TSWE sections refer you to the appropriate chapters to study for each question type.

STEP 5 Do the review and practice indicated on the charts wherever you had a concentration of circles.

Remember that in addition to evaluating your scores, you should read all of the answer explanations for questions you answered incorrectly, questions you omitted, and questions you answered correctly but found difficult. Reviewing the answer explanations will help you understand concepts and strategies, and may point out shortcuts.

OBTAINING YOUR RAW SCORE

Verbal

Section 3 ________ – 1/4 (________) = ________ (A)
number correct number incorrect

Section 4 ________ – 1/4 (________) = ________ (B)
number correct number incorrect

Section 6 ________ – 1/4 (________) = ________ (C)
number correct number incorrect

Raw Verbal Score = (A) + (B) + (C) = ________

TSWE

Section 2 ________ – 1/4 (________) = Raw TSWE Score = ________
number correct number incorrect

Math

Section 1 ________ – 1/4 (________) = ________ (D)
number correct number incorrect

Section 5 (1-7, 28-35) ________ – 1/4 (________) = ________ (E)
number correct number incorrect

Section 5 (8-27) ________ – 1/3 (________) = ________ (F)
number correct number incorrect

Raw Math Score = (D) + (E) + (F) = ________

EVALUATE YOUR PERFORMANCE

	Verbal	TSWE	Math
Excellent	106-125	45-50	52-60
Very Good	91-105	39-44	45-51
Good	81-90	34-38	36-44
Average	61-80	25-33	30-35
Below Average	41-60	15-24	25-29
Unsatisfactory	below 40	below 15	below 25

IDENTIFY YOUR WEAKNESSES
Verbal

Question Type	Question Numbers			Chapter to Study
	Section 3	Section 4	Section 6	
Antonym	1, 2, 3, 4, 5, 6, 7, 8, 9, 10, 11, 12, 13, 14, 15	1, 2, 3, 4, 5, 6, 7, 8, 9, 10	1, 2, 3, 4, 5, 6, 7, 8, 9, 10	Chapter 4
Analogy	36, 37, 38, 39, 40, 41, 42, 43, 44, 45	16, 17, 18, 19, 20, 21, 22, 23, 24, 25	16, 17, 18, 19, 20, 21, 22, 23, 24, 25	Chapter 5
Sentence Completion	16, 17, 18, 19, 20, 31, 32, 33, 34, 35	11, 12, 13, 14, 15	11, 12, 13, 14, 15	Chapter 6
Reading Comprehension	21, 22, 23, 24, 25, 26, 27, 28, 29, 30	26, 27, 28, 29, 30, 31, 32, 33, 34, 35, 36, 37, 38, 39, 40	26, 27, 28, 29, 30, 31, 32, 33, 34, 35, 36, 37, 38, 39, 40	Chapter 7

TSWE

Question Type	Question Numbers	Chapter to Study
Usage	1, 2, 3, 4, 5, 6, 7, 8, 9, 10, 11, 12, 13, 14, 15, 16, 17, 18, 19, 20, 21, 22, 23, 24, 25, 41, 42, 43, 44, 45, 46, 47, 48, 49, 50	Chapter 12
Sentence Correction	26, 27, 28, 29, 30, 31, 32, 33, 34, 35, 36, 37, 38, 39, 40	Chapter 12

Math

Skill Area	Question Numbers		Pages to Study
	Section 1	Section 5	
Fundamental Operations	1, 6, 19, 22	6, 16	300–302
Algebraic Operations	4, 7, 18, 21, 24	15, 27, 30, 32	302–308
Using Algebra	15, 23		308–316
Fractions	3, 8	8, 10, 12, 13, 15, 33	316–329
Decimals and Percents	2, 3, 8, 13, 20	8, 10, 11, 12, 27	329–334
Verbal Problems	5, 9, 14, 15, 16, 23, 25	2, 3, 4, 5, 7, 28, 31, 34, 35	335–352
Ratio and Proportion	12	3, 5, 31, 35	340–346
Geometry	10, 11, 12, 17	1, 17, 18, 19, 20, 21, 22, 23, 24, 25, 26, 29	355–368
Inequalities	17	1, 14	309–311; 315–316
Quantitative Comparison		8, 9, 10, 11, 12, 13, 14 15, 16, 17, 18, 19, 20, 21, 22, 23, 24, 25, 26, 27	279–299
Roots and Radicals		9, 11	306–307; 312–313

ANSWER EXPLANATIONS

SECTION 1

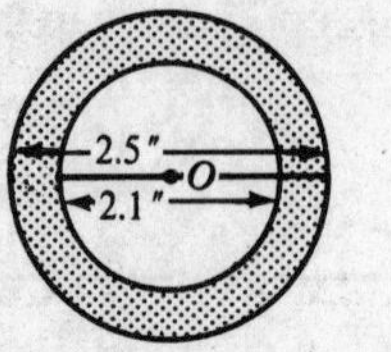

1. A. Shaded area represents thickness of pipe. Difference of radii equals thickness of pipe.
Radius of outer dimension = 1.25″
Radius of inner dimension = 1.05″
Difference = 0.2″

2. D. Let x = the number
$.09x = 27$
$9x = 2700$
$x = 300$

3. C. $.875 = 87\frac{1}{2}\% = \frac{7}{8}$
$\frac{x}{64} = \frac{7}{8}$
$8x = 448$
$x = 56$

4. A. $\frac{a+b}{a-b} = \frac{x}{b-a}$

$\frac{a+b}{a-b} = \frac{x}{-a+b}$

$\frac{a+b}{a-b} = \frac{-x}{a-b}$ [multiply numerator and denominator by -1]

$a + b = -x$ [multiply both sides of the equation by $(a - b)$]

$x = -a - b$ [multiply by -1]

5. A. D dollars = $100D$ cents

$\frac{\text{number of oranges}}{\text{cost in cents}} = \frac{a}{100D} = \frac{x}{?}$

Let y = cost (in cents) of x oranges

$\frac{a}{100D} = \frac{x}{y}$
$ay = 100Dx$
$y = \frac{100Dx}{a}$

6. C. $\frac{\text{Length of fence}}{\text{Distance between posts}} = $ Number of spaces between posts

$\frac{320 \text{ feet}}{40 \text{ feet}} = 8$ spaces

Since in the first space there are 2 posts and one post for each additional space there will be 9 posts.

7. D. $\frac{1}{y} = -4$

$\frac{1}{2y} = -2$ (divide by 2)

$x = -2$ (given)

$x = \frac{1}{2y}$ (Things equal to the same thing are equal to each other)

$2xy = 1$ (multiply by $2y$)

$y = \frac{1}{2x}$ (divide by $2x$)

8. A. Students who have memorized fraction–per cent equivalents recognize the fact that there are three eighths in $37\frac{1}{2}\%$

OR, Let x = number of eights in $37\frac{1}{2}\%$

$\frac{x}{8} = 37\frac{1}{2}\%$

$\frac{x}{8} = \frac{37.5}{100}$

$100x = 300$

$x = 3$

9. E. This is an inverse proportion.
Let x = number of days that a bag of feed can take care of 12 chickens

$\frac{18 \text{ chickens}}{12 \text{ chickens}} = \frac{x}{54 \text{ days}}$

$12x = (54)(18)$
$12x = 972$
$x = 81$ days

10. A. Area of outside rectangle minus area of inside rectangle equals area of frame. Area of inside rectangle (picture) = $(6')(8')$ or 48 square feet.

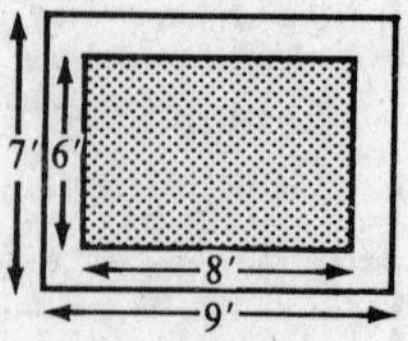

Area of outside rectangle $=(7')(9')$ or 63 square feet. Area of frame = 15 square feet.

$\frac{\text{Area of frame}}{\text{Area of picture}} = \frac{15 \text{ square feet}}{48 \text{ square feet}} = \frac{15}{48} = \frac{5}{16}$

11. E. $\frac{2}{5}$ of 360° or $\frac{2}{5} \times 360°$ or 144°

12. D. $a + b + c = 180°$
Let x = base of ratios
$x + 3x + 2x = 180°$
$6x = 180°$
$x = 30°$
$a, b,$ and c = 30, 90, and 60 respectively
Angle $b = 90$

13. A. Let x = number of remaining games that must be won

$$\frac{\text{Total games won}}{\text{Total games played}} = \text{Per cent games won}$$

$$\frac{40 + x}{154} = \frac{65}{100}$$

$4000 + 100x = 10010$
$100x = 6010$
$x = 60$ games

14. B. $$\frac{\text{Volume (in cubic centimeters)}}{\text{Weight (in grams)}} = \frac{1}{18.7} = \frac{.01}{x}$$

$x = (18.7)\ (.01)$
$x = .187$

15. E. If all seats were occupied there would be rs pupils. Since 2 seats remain vacant, there are $rs - 2$ students in the classroom.

16. B $$\frac{\text{Parts of Potassium}}{\text{Parts of Potassium + Nitrogen + Oxygen}} =$$

Part of potassium in potassium nitrate

$$\frac{39}{39 + 14 + 48} \text{ or } \frac{39}{101} \text{ or } .386 \text{ or } 39\%$$

17. A. CB is one-half of CE and CA is one-half of CD. Since $CE > CD$, then one-half of CE (or CB) > one-half of CD (or CA). Doubles, triples, halves, thirds . . . etc. of unequal quantities are unequal in the same order.

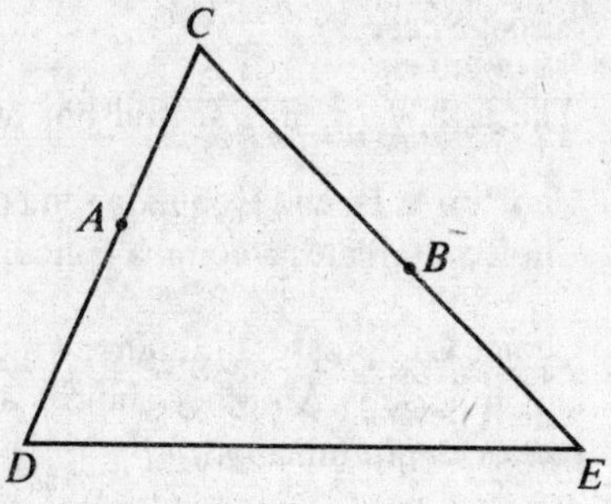

18. E. $$\frac{0.24x}{6} + 7 = 10$$

$\frac{0.24x}{6} = 3$ (subtract 7)

$0.04x = 3$ (divide numerator and denominator by 6)

$4x = 300$ (multiply by 100)
$x = 75$ (divide by 4)

19. C. Time elapsed from 11 P.M. to 2 A.M. = 3 hours
Rise in temperature = (3 degrees)(3) = 9° F.
$-16°\text{F.} + 9°\text{F.} \doteq -7°\text{F.}$

20. D. $$\frac{\text{Increase}}{\text{Original}} \times 100 = \text{Per cent increase}$$

$$\frac{900}{300} \times 100 = 300\%$$

21. C. $$\frac{1}{2} + \frac{2}{3} + \frac{3}{y} = \frac{23}{12}$$

$$\frac{1}{2} + \frac{2}{3} + \frac{3}{y} = \frac{23}{12} \quad \text{(multiply by 12 } y\text{)}$$

$6y + 8y + 36 = 23y$
$6y + 8y - 23y = -36$
$-9y = -36$
$y = 4$

22. C. During the nine-week period the man worked 45 days. Since the total earnings were $454.50, the earnings per day were
$$\frac{\$454.50}{45} \text{ or } \$10.10$$

23. A. Let x = number of ounces of sulfur necessary to make 172 oz. of sulfanilamide

$$\frac{\text{Quantity of sulfur (oz.)}}{\text{Quantity of sulfanilamide (oz.)}} = \frac{8}{43} = \frac{x}{172}$$

$43x = (172)(8)$
$43x = 1376$
$x = 32$

24. C. $x - 7 = 0$; $x = 7$ $\qquad y^2 = 25$; $y = \pm 5$
$xy = (7)(\pm 5)$
$xy = \pm 35$

25. C. $$\frac{\text{Distance}}{\text{Rate}} = \text{Time}$$

$\frac{100}{40} = 2\frac{1}{2}$ hours (time for first part of trip)

$\frac{100}{50} = 2$ hours (time for second part of trip)

Total Time $= 4\frac{1}{2}$ hours

Total Distance = 200 miles

$$\frac{\text{Distance}}{\text{Time}} = \text{Rate}$$

$\frac{200}{4\frac{1}{2}} = 44.4$ miles per hour

SECTION 2

1. A. Dangling participle. Change participial phrase to a clause, *After the rain had fallen steadily for five days . . . .*

2. C. Misuse of adjective for adverb. Change considerable to considerably.

3. D. Error in agreement between pronoun and antecedent. Change *their* to *its*.

4. A. Dangling participle. Change to clause, *While my aunt and I were traveling through . . . .*

5. C. Error in diction. Use *effect* instead of *affect*.

6. E. Sentence is correct.

7. B. Error in case. Change *whom* to *who* (subject of *was*).

8. E. Sentence is correct.

9. D. Error in agreement. Change *they are* to *it is*.

10. C. Wrong word. Use *lie* instead of *lay*.

11. C. Error in agreement. The antecedent of *which* is *cars* (plural). *Which* therefore requires a plural verb (*Have been*).

12. C. Error in agreement. In a neither-nor construction the verb agrees with the noun or pronoun which comes immediately before the verb. *Principal is being considered* is correct.

13. B. Error in diction. Change *liable* to *likely*.

14. B. Error in case. Change *he* to *him*.

15. C. This is a run-on or comma fault sentence. Change *record,* to *record;* or *record. It.*

16. B. Error in diction. Latter should not be used to refer to more than two items. Change *later* to *Ellis*.

17. C. Error in agreement. Change *them* to *it*.

18. B. Misplaced modifier. The thought of the sentence is conveyed correctly by *sold almost two million*.

19. E. Sentence is correct.

20. C. Error in agreement. Change *their* to *his*.

21. D. Error in case. Change *me* to *my*.

22. C. The subjunctive mood is needed in a condition contrary to fact statement. Change *was* to *were*.

23. B. Lack of parallel structure. Change *not because of the money* to *not because he needed the money* (a clause) to parallel the clause that follows *but*.

24. D. Incomplete sentence. Change *trestle* to *trestle,* and add a principal clause.

25. C. Misuse of adverb for adjective. Change *his many attempts bravely to enter* to *his many brave attempts to enter*.

26. D. Parallel structure is maintained in Choice D. The parallelism is violated in the other choices.

27. C. Choices A, B, D, and E are run-on sentences.

28. C. When comparing two things, you should use the comparative degree *(better)* rather than the superlative degree *(best)*. In Choice B, *Joneses* is incorrect.

29. D. Choices A and B have dangling modifiers. Choices C and E create run-on sentences.

30. A. The sentence uses the subjunctive mood correctly.

31. E. The errors in case and agreement are corrected in Choice E. *I* should be used instead of *me* because it is the predicate nominative of the verb *is*. *Who,* having as its antecedent the pronoun *I,* is a first person singular pronoun. The first person singular verb *am* should be used.

32. A. The present perfect tense is correctly used in Choice A.

33. A. Choices B, C, D, and E are sentence fragments.

34. D. A noun preceding a gerund should be in the possessive case.

35. E. The article *(a, an)* should not follow *kind of*.

36. D. Choices A, B, and E contain sentence fragments; Choice C creates a comma splice.

37. C. Choice C expresses the author's meaning directly and concisely. All other choices are either indirect or ungrammatical.

38. C. The subordinating conjunction *Although* best connects the sentence's two clauses.

39. A. The past tense and the subordinating conjunction *When* are correctly used in Choice A.

40. B. Choices A, C, and E are run-on sentences; Choice D is unidiomatic.

41. A. Dangling participle. Change *Rummaging* to *While we were rummaging*.

42. D. Lack of apostrophe. Should be *Shakespeare's*.

43. B. The reflexive pronoun *myself* cannot be used without the pronoun *I* or *me* to refer to. Change *myself* to *me*.

44. E. Sentence is correct.

45. B. Incorrect word. Eliminate *that*.

46. C. Error in agreement. The antecedent of *who* is *one*. Therefore, *who is* is correct.

47. D. Improper punctuation using quotation marks. The question mark should not be within the set of quotation marks. Correct form is *who wrote "Hiawatha"?*

48. C. Error in agreement. In a *neither . . . nor* sentence, the verb agrees with the noun or pronoun which immediately precedes it. Change *were* to *was*.

49. C. Error in agreement. Change *their* to *his*.

50. E. Sentence is correct.

SECTION 3

1. A. The opposite of *ribald* (profane, indecent) is *refined*.

2. C. The opposite of *diatribe* (denunciatory speech) is *praise*.

3. B. The opposite of *simulated* (feigned, counterfeit) is *genuine*.

4. D. The opposite of *diabolic* (devilish) is *seraphic* (angelic).

5. D. The opposite of *revere* (respect) is *dishonor*.

6. A. The opposite of *puerile* (childlike) is *adult* (mature).

7. A. The opposite of *venerable* (entitled to respect) is *disgraceful*.

8. B. The opposite of *disparage* (speak slightingly of) is *praise*.

9. D. The opposite of *unmarred* (not scarred or spoiled) is *spoiled*.

10. D. The opposite of *dissidence* (state of disagreement) is *agreement*.

11. B. *Anomalous* (deviating from the normal) and *regular* are opposites.

12. E. *Quell* (to put down) and *incite* (to stir up) are opposites.

13. E. *Discernible* (able to be perceived) and *imperceptible* (not perceived by the senses) are opposites.

14. D. The best opposite of *nugatory* (trifling, futile) is *effective*.

15. E. The opposite of *lassitude* (languor, lack of liveliness) is *liveliness*.

16. D. Puritans would be offended by *salacious* (lecherous) material.

17. B. *Splenetic* (morose, ill-tempered) goes best with *bitter*.

18. C. *Turgid* (swollen) rivers are likely to overflow their banks.

19. A. *Malingering* means pretending illness to avoid duty.

20. D. *Rescind* means to cancel or withdraw.

21. A. Throughout the paragraph, the author analyzes the way a person adjusts to life.

22. C. The last sentence justifies the selection of Choice C.

23. C. The author mentions the average height of the continents but does not mention the highest point on any continent except Asia.

24. B. We are told that 71% of the earth is covered by water and that the Pacific Ocean covers half of the earth. The Pacific is obviously the largest ocean.

25. E. The last sentence of the passage informs us that Shakespeare, who lived from 1564 to 1616, wrote long before there was a science of geology.

26. C. The peripheral furrows or *deeps* are discussed in the second paragraph. We are told that these deeps are near the continental masses.

27. E. The third sentence of the second paragraph informs us that the highest mountains are of recent origin.

28. D. The last sentence of the first paragraph discusses the submerged portions of the continental masses.

29. A. In the second paragraph, we are told that earthquakes frequently occur in the *deeps*.

30. B. We can support Choice B because the *deeps*, the site of frequent earthquakes, are of recent origin.

31. A. *Propitious* means favorable.

32. D. A *truculent* (bellicose, aggressive) attitude will alienate people.

33. E. A wide range will be obtained in a *heterogeneous* (diverse) group.

34. A. *Dexterous* (adroit, skilful) and *gauche* (clumsy) are opposites and fit in the sentence.

35. B. The *aperture* (opening) of a camera lens controls the amount of *light* admitted.

36. B. *Haggard* and *gaunt* are synonyms; *obese* and *corpulent* are synonyms.

37. C. In the time table, *day* is followed by *week*, and *week* is followed by *month*.

38. D. A *spitz* is a kind of *dog* and a *whale* is a kind of *mammal*.

39. C. The relationship is one of degree. *Immense* is extremely *large; hatred* is extreme *dislike*.

40. B. *Death* may result from *poison*; *knowledge* may result from *experience*.

41. C. *Chauvinism* is jingoism or extreme love of *country; gluttony*, extreme desire for *food*.

42. A. A *parsimonious* (stingy) person is extremely *frugal; ecstasy* is extreme *joy*.

43. A. A *pride* is a group of *lions*; a *bevy*, a group of *quail*.

44. C. A *frown* shows *displeasure*; a *sneer* shows *contempt*.

45. A. *Convention* and *mores* are synonyms; *antics* and *caprice* are synonyms.

SECTION 4

1. D. The opposite of *furtive* (stealthy) is *open*.

2. A. The opposite of *pellucid* (limpid, clear) is *turbid* (muddy).

3. B. The opposite of *oral* (spoken) is *written*.

4. C. The opposite of *terse* (compact, concise) is *verbose* (overly wordy).

5. A. *Ascetic* (severely abstinent) is the opposite of *wanton* (immoral).

6. C. The opposite of *fallow* (unsown) is *cultivated*.

7. B. The opposite of *leniency* (mercy) is *severity*.

8. A. The opposite of *trivia* (unimportant matters) is *important matters*.

9. A. The opposite of *extricate* (disentangle) is *ensnare*.

10. B. The opposite of *indavertent* (unintentional) is *intentional*.

11. D. Rayon and nylon are manufactured or *synthetic* fabrics.

12. A. The benefit discussed in this sentence accrued to both countries and was *mutual*.

13. D. Television by its coverage may create interest in a sport; by excessive coverage, it may kill interest in that sport. This contradiction or *paradox* has been observed in boxing.

14. A. A *vindicable* crime is one which may be justified or excused; *bail*, logically, could be set at a reasonable figure.

15. B. An *obsequious* person is fawning and *servile*.

16. D. *Gasoline* provides the energy for an *automobile; food*, the energy for *man*.

17. E. A *symphony* is written by a *composer*; a *sonnet*, by a *poet*.

18. D. To *allay pain* is to lessen it; to *mitigate* an *offense* is to reduce its severity.

19. B. To *expurgate* a *passage* is to remove it from a work because it is objectionable; to *filter water* is to remove objectionable particles.

20. D. *Wearisome* and *refreshing* are opposites; *lengthy* and *brief* are opposites.

21. B. *Evanescent* and *ephemeral* are synonyms; *temporary* and *transient* are synonyms.

22. C. *Exertion* causes *fatigue; carelessness* causes *accidents*.

23. E. *Pariah* and *outcast* are synonyms; *favorite* and *pet* are synonyms.

24. C. To *dampen* something is less intense than to *drench* it; to *simmer* something is less intense than to *boil* it.

25. C. People *hate* when they display *enmity;* they *fear* when they show *intimidation*.

26. D. The passage is concerned with the limitations imposed on a writer of fiction and the realization that we must be aware of these limitations if we are to understand fiction fully.

27. B. The next-to-last sentence supports Choice B.

28. C. The opening sentence supports choice C.

29. C. The passage describes the characteristics of the best and poorest public officials.

30. D. The author states that the best have "faith that public support will be forthcoming."

31. A. The author does not mention dishonesty.

32. C. The passage discusses the limitations of the Elizabethan stage and the ways Shakespeare's style was influenced by these limitations.

33. C. Today, actors do not have to provide the background: they rely on elaborate sets.

34. D. The third sentence supports Choice D.

35. A. The author supports his statement about the harm too much of anything can produce with the analogy to the use of excessive oxygen in the treatment of consumption.

36. C. *Consumption* is the common name for tuberculosis, a wasting away of tissues.

37. C. *Essential* is the best synonym for "vital" as used in this passage.

38. C. Sentence 6 informs us that "the melting point of glass is comparatively low."

39. E. The passage deals with the various means of measuring temperatures.

40. B. Sentence 4 discusses the use of "inert gas" in mercury thermometers.

SECTION 5

1. C. If equal quantities are added to unequal quantities the sums are unequal in the same order.

2. D. This is an example of weighted average

85% × 3 = 255
90% × 4 = 360
Sum = 615
Number of cases = 7

$$\frac{615}{7} = 87.85\% \text{ or } 87.9\%$$

3. C. According to the information furnished, the ratio of the number of marbles of the boy with the greatest number to those of the boy with the least number is 19 : 3. Since the boy with least number actually has 9 marbles (3 × 3), then the boy with the greatest number has 19 × 3 or 57 marbles.

$$\frac{\text{boy}}{\text{marbles}} = \frac{3}{9} = \frac{19}{x}$$

$$3x = 171$$

$$x = 57$$

4. A.

$$\frac{\text{Distance}}{\text{Rate}} = \text{Time}$$

$$\frac{1800 \text{ miles}}{60 \text{ miles per hour}} = 30 \text{ hours}$$

5. D. Let y = number of articles that can be bought for x dollars

$$\frac{\text{number of articles}}{\text{cost in dollars}} = \frac{500}{d} = \frac{y}{x}$$

$$dy = 500x$$

$$y = \frac{500x}{d}$$

6. A. Cost of n 2 cent stamps = $2n$ cents
Cost of p 3 cent stamps = $3p$ cents
Total cost = $2n + 3p$ cents

7. E. Assume that a *part* represents a pound

3 pounds at 60¢ a pound cost	$1.80
2 pounds at 70¢ a pound cost	1.40
2 pounds at 50¢ a pound cost	1.00
Total cost of mixture =	$4.20
Number of pounds in mixture =	7
Cost per pound	= 60¢
Profit per pound (25%)	= 15¢
Selling price	= 75¢

8. C. $3\frac{1}{2}\% = 3.5\% = \frac{3.5}{100} = \frac{35}{1000}$

9. A. $\sqrt{0.04} = 0.2$
$(0.2)^2 = 0.04$
$0.2 > 0.04$

10. B. $\frac{7}{8} = 87\frac{1}{2}\%$
$\left(\frac{1}{2}\right)\left(\frac{7}{8}\right) = 43 + \%$

11. A. $\left(\frac{1}{2}\right)^2 = \left(\frac{1}{4}\right) = 25\%$

12. B. $\frac{0.7}{2} = \frac{7}{20} = .35$
$0.35 > 0.3$

13. D. $\frac{X}{Y} \cdot \frac{Y}{X} = 1$
$\frac{X}{Y}$ may be equal to, smaller than, or larger than 1.

14. D. *a* could be equal to zero, or some positive fraction less than 1, or some negative fraction more than −1.
b could be some negative fraction more than −1.

15. C. $\left(2x - \frac{y-5}{6}\right) \div \left(\frac{y-5}{3} - 4x\right)$

$\frac{12x - y + 5}{6} \div \frac{y - 5 - 12x}{3}$

$\frac{12x - y + 5}{2\not{6}} \cdot \frac{\not{3}^{1}}{y - 5 - 12x}$

$\frac{12x - y + 5}{2} \cdot \frac{1}{-12x + y - 5}$

$\frac{\not{12x - y + 5}}{2} \cdot \frac{1}{-1(\not{12x - y + 5})}$ or, $-\frac{1}{2}$ or -0.5

16. D. Center City is located at point O. Circleville could be located at any point on the circumference of the circle with the radius of 23 kilometers. Centerville could be located at any point on the circumference with radius of 46 kilometers. The distance from Circleville and Centerville could be the straight line distance from any point on the circumference of one of these circles to the other circle. Obviously there are innumerable possibilities, some equal to 23 kilometers and some greater than 23 kilometers.

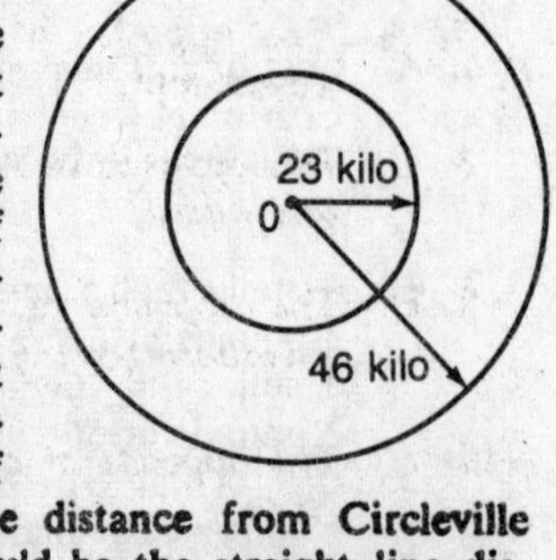

17. C. In right triangle *ABC*, $x = 45$. In right triangle *ADC*, $y = 45$. Therefore, $z = 45$.

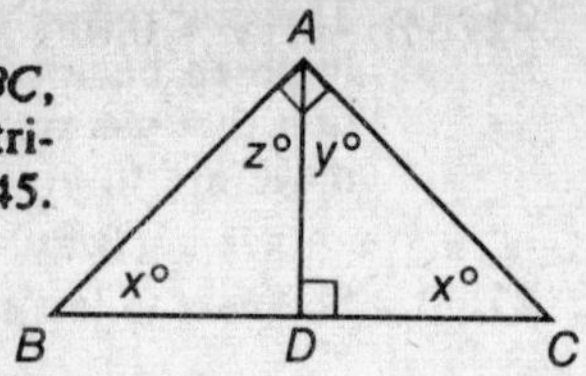

18. C. In right triangle *ABC*, since the acute angles are equal to ½ of 90°, $x = 45$.

19. A. The area of triangle $ABC = \frac{1}{2}(\text{leg} \times \text{leg}) = 12.5$ or, $(\text{leg})^2 = 25$. Therefore leg $= 5$.
Area of square I or II $= 5^2$ or 25.
Since $AB = BC = 5$, hypotenuse $AC = 5\sqrt{2}$
Area of square III $= (5\sqrt{2})^2$ or 50
Twice the area of ABC = 25 (given).

20. C. (see #19)

21. B. Each side of square $BCDE = 10$
Area of $ABC = 125 - 100$ or 25
Area of $ABC = \frac{1}{2}(BC)(AF) = 25$
$\frac{1}{2}(10)(AF) = 25$
$AF = 5$
$FG = BE = CD = 10$
$AFG = 15$ and $2(EB) = 20$

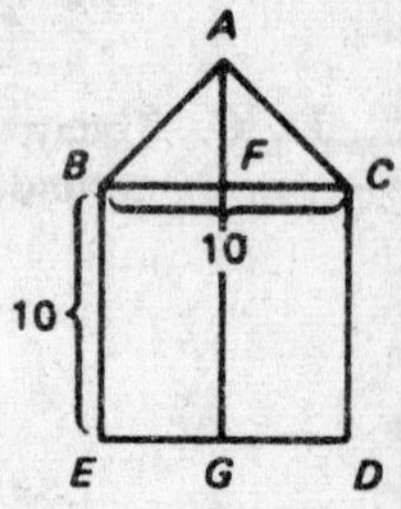

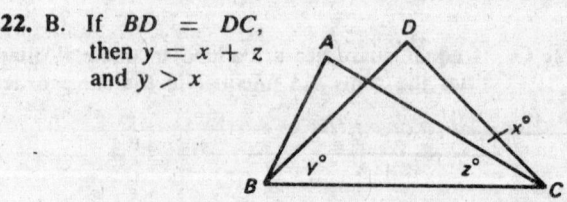

22. B. If $BD = DC$, then $y = x + z$ and $y > x$

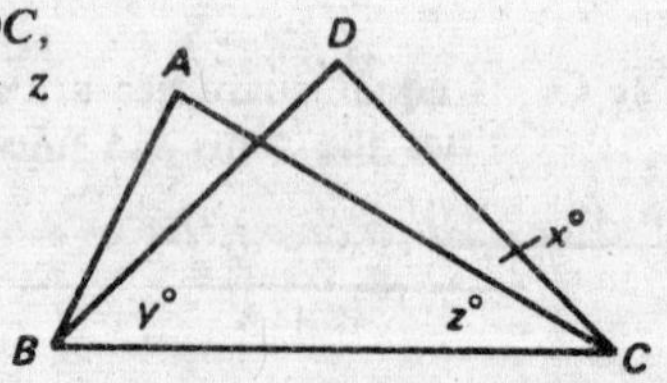

23. C. Area of circle $= \pi r^2$
If the radius of circle *B* is twice the radius of circle *A*, then area of circle *B* is four times the area of circle *A*. Stated differently, four times the area of circle *A* = the area of circle *B*.

24. B. Circumference $= 2\pi r$
If the circumference of one circle is twice another circle then the radius of the larger circle is twice the smaller circle, but the area of the larger circle would be four times the area of the smaller circle.

25. B. Since the area of the unshaded section $= 9\pi$, the radius $OA = 3$. Since $OB - OA = 4$, $OB = 7$. The area of the shaded plus the unshaded portion $= 49\pi$. The shaded portion $= 49\pi - 9\pi$ or 40π. Four times the unshaded section $= 36\pi$.

26. C. The circumference of the inner circle $= 6\pi$. $(7)(6\pi) = 42\pi$. The circumference of outer circle $= 14\pi$. $(3)(14\pi) = 42\pi$.

27. B. $0.1y + 0.01y = 2.2$
$10y + 1y = 220$
$11y = 220$
$y = 20$
$0.1y = 2$

28. B. $\frac{8 \text{ men}}{6 \text{ men}} = \frac{x \text{ days}}{12 \text{ days}}$ (an inverse proportion)
$6x = 96$
$x = 16$ days (time required when 2 men are released)
Increase in time is 4 days
$\frac{4 \text{ days (increase)}}{12 \text{ days (original)}} = \frac{1}{3} = 33\frac{1}{3}\%$

29. D. Perimeter = 2(length + width)
Let y = width
$p = 2(x + y)$
$p = 2x + 2y$
$2y = p - 2x$
$y = \frac{p - 2x}{2}$

30. B. $\frac{ca^2 - cb^2}{-a - b}$

$-\frac{ca^2 - cb^2}{a + b}$ (multiply numerator and denominator by -1)

$-\frac{c(a^2 - b^2)}{a + b}$ (factor)

$-\frac{c(a + b)(a - b)}{a + b}$ (factor and divide by $a + b$)

$-c(a - b)$
$-ac + bc$ or $bc - ac$ (remove parentheses)

31. D. $\frac{\text{yards}}{\text{statute miles}} = \frac{220}{\frac{1}{8}} = \frac{x}{1}$

$\frac{1}{8}x = 220$

$x = 1760$ (multiply by 8)

32. C. $(x + y)^2 = x^2 + 2xy + y^2$
$x^2 + y^2 = 8$ (given)
$xy = 7$ (given)
$2xy = 14$ (multiplication)
$x^2 + 2xy + y^2 = 8 + 14$ or 22

33. A. Before dinner $\frac{2}{3}$ of his homework is not done.

After dinner he does $\left(\frac{3}{4}\right)$ of $\left(\frac{2}{3}\right)$ or $\frac{1}{2}$.

Since $\frac{1}{3}$ was done before dinner and $\frac{1}{2}$ was done after dinner $\frac{1}{3} + \frac{1}{2}$ or $\frac{5}{6}$ of his homework was done. Therefore $\frac{1}{6}$ of his homework was left uncompleted.

34. B. The train had a distance of $1\frac{1}{2}$ miles to cover

$\frac{\text{Distance}}{\text{Rate}} = \text{Time}$

$\frac{1.5 \text{ miles}}{30 \text{ miles per hour}} = \frac{1}{20}$ of hour or 3 minutes

Since it was stopped at 1:00 P.M., it would have arrived at 1:03 P.M.

35. C. This is an inverse proportion
Let x = days required with 9 + 3 men
$\frac{9 \text{ men}}{12 \text{ men}} = \frac{x}{15 \text{ days}}$
$12x = 135$
$x = 11\frac{1}{4}$ days

SECTION 6

1. D. The opposite of *fealty* (fidelity) is *treachery*.

2. B. The opposite of *incensed* (angered) is *appeased*.

3. B. An *innuendo* is a suggestion or hint. Its opposite is *accusation*.

4. B. The opposite of *amass* (gather) is *distribute*.

5. D. The opposite of *squalid* (filthy) is *undefiled*.

6. C. The opposite of *mendacious* (telling falsehoods) is *veracious* (truthful).

7. A. The opposite of *scarcity* (lack) is *plethora* (oversupply).

8. C. The opposite of *harmonious* (in agreement) is *discordant*.

9. D. The opposite of *epigrammatic* (pithy, witty) is *verbose* (overly wordy).

10. A. The opposite of *original* (fresh, new) is *banal* (trite).

11. D. Parallelism calls for *inane* (empty, senseless) to match *meaningless*.

12. B. *Stoically* describes how a person bears pain with great courage.

13. D. An *obsequious* person (fawning, servile) will display *meekness* (submissiveness).

14. C. Law enforcement officers blame the light or suspended sentences that judges often give to first offenders for much of juvenile crime. They feel that judges should show less *clemency* to all criminals.

15. E. *Redundant* means *repetitious*.

16. D. An alibi must be confirmed or *corroborated* to be believed.

17. B. *Diffidence* (shyness) is not a desirable trait for a salesman.

18. C. To *ameliorate* (better, improve) living conditions is a logical and practical goal for social workers.

19. B. A *cynic* would be skeptical of people who were motivated by unselfish or *altruistic* motives.

20. D. A *patronizing* (condescending) attitude often alienates people.

21. A. Just as a *gauntlet* (glove) is worn on the *hand*, a *buskin* (shoe used by Greek actors) is worn on the *foot*.

22. B. *Olfactory* refers to the sense of smell; the organ involved in this is the *nose*. *Gustatory* refers to the sense of taste; the organ involved is the *tongue*.

23. D. An *alloy* is a mixture of metals. A *cake* is a mixture of ingredients.

24. B. *Bizarre* and *exotic* are synonyms; *ordinary* and *commonplace* are synonyms.

25. C. Someone *frivolous* lacks *seriousness*; someone *outspoken* lacks *reticence*.

26. D. Ancient *bronze* works are coated with a greenish rust called *patina*. Exposed *iron* also becomes coated with *rust*.

27. E. A *dime* is one-tenth of a *dollar* and a *year* is one-tenth of a *decade*.

28. D *Cardiology* is the study of the *heart; pharmacology* is the science of *drugs*.

29. E. A *turncoat* is by definition *treacherous*; a *killjoy* is by definition *lugubrious* or gloomy.

30. B. *Mellifluous* (sweet-sounding) and *cacophonous* (ugly sounding; discordant) are opposites. *Fragrant* (pleasant-smelling) and *noisome* (foul-smelling) are opposites.

31. E. Choices A, B, C, D are mentioned in the first paragraph.

32. C. This choice is stated in the second paragraph.

33. C. The last sentence supports Choice C.

34. D. Choice D is stated in the second paragraph.

35. A. The justification for the Lend-Lease Act was that it improved our national defense.

36. B. The third sentence of the first paragraph supports Choice B.

37. D. Since the highest frequency humans can hear is approximately 20,000 cy/sec., we can assume that sopranos reach this range. However, since they are audible to most people, we have to accept Choice D as being the highest that people can hear comfortably.

38. D. In the first sentence of Paragraph 2, we are told that quality and timbre are synonyms. In the last sentence of Paragraph 2, we learn that quality depends on overtones. Choice D is best.

39. C. Astronauts, traveling at speeds of thousands of miles per hour, would be traveling many times faster than the speed of sound. Choice C is logical.

40. A. The third sentence of Paragraph 1 supports Choice A.

Remove answer sheet by cutting on dotted line

ANSWER SHEET—TEST 4

SECTION 1

1. Ⓐ Ⓑ Ⓒ Ⓓ Ⓔ	11. Ⓐ Ⓑ Ⓒ Ⓓ Ⓔ	21. Ⓐ Ⓑ Ⓒ Ⓓ Ⓔ	31. Ⓐ Ⓑ Ⓒ Ⓓ Ⓔ	41. Ⓐ Ⓑ Ⓒ Ⓓ Ⓔ
2. Ⓐ Ⓑ Ⓒ Ⓓ Ⓔ	12. Ⓐ Ⓑ Ⓒ Ⓓ Ⓔ	22. Ⓐ Ⓑ Ⓒ Ⓓ Ⓔ	32. Ⓐ Ⓑ Ⓒ Ⓓ Ⓔ	42. Ⓐ Ⓑ Ⓒ Ⓓ Ⓔ
3. Ⓐ Ⓑ Ⓒ Ⓓ Ⓔ	13. Ⓐ Ⓑ Ⓒ Ⓓ Ⓔ	23. Ⓐ Ⓑ Ⓒ Ⓓ Ⓔ	33. Ⓐ Ⓑ Ⓒ Ⓓ Ⓔ	43. Ⓐ Ⓑ Ⓒ Ⓓ Ⓔ
4. Ⓐ Ⓑ Ⓒ Ⓓ Ⓔ	14. Ⓐ Ⓑ Ⓒ Ⓓ Ⓔ	24. Ⓐ Ⓑ Ⓒ Ⓓ Ⓔ	34. Ⓐ Ⓑ Ⓒ Ⓓ Ⓔ	44. Ⓐ Ⓑ Ⓒ Ⓓ Ⓔ
5. Ⓐ Ⓑ Ⓒ Ⓓ Ⓔ	15. Ⓐ Ⓑ Ⓒ Ⓓ Ⓔ	25. Ⓐ Ⓑ Ⓒ Ⓓ Ⓔ	35. Ⓐ Ⓑ Ⓒ Ⓓ Ⓔ	45. Ⓐ Ⓑ Ⓒ Ⓓ Ⓔ
6. Ⓐ Ⓑ Ⓒ Ⓓ Ⓔ	16. Ⓐ Ⓑ Ⓒ Ⓓ Ⓔ	26. Ⓐ Ⓑ Ⓒ Ⓓ Ⓔ	36. Ⓐ Ⓑ Ⓒ Ⓓ Ⓔ	46. Ⓐ Ⓑ Ⓒ Ⓓ Ⓔ
7. Ⓐ Ⓑ Ⓒ Ⓓ Ⓔ	17. Ⓐ Ⓑ Ⓒ Ⓓ Ⓔ	27. Ⓐ Ⓑ Ⓒ Ⓓ Ⓔ	37. Ⓐ Ⓑ Ⓒ Ⓓ Ⓔ	47. Ⓐ Ⓑ Ⓒ Ⓓ Ⓔ
8. Ⓐ Ⓑ Ⓒ Ⓓ Ⓔ	18. Ⓐ Ⓑ Ⓒ Ⓓ Ⓔ	28. Ⓐ Ⓑ Ⓒ Ⓓ Ⓔ	38. Ⓐ Ⓑ Ⓒ Ⓓ Ⓔ	48. Ⓐ Ⓑ Ⓒ Ⓓ Ⓔ
9. Ⓐ Ⓑ Ⓒ Ⓓ Ⓔ	19. Ⓐ Ⓑ Ⓒ Ⓓ Ⓔ	29. Ⓐ Ⓑ Ⓒ Ⓓ Ⓔ	39. Ⓐ Ⓑ Ⓒ Ⓓ Ⓔ	49. Ⓐ Ⓑ Ⓒ Ⓓ Ⓔ
10. Ⓐ Ⓑ Ⓒ Ⓓ Ⓔ	20. Ⓐ Ⓑ Ⓒ Ⓓ Ⓔ	30. Ⓐ Ⓑ Ⓒ Ⓓ Ⓔ	40. Ⓐ Ⓑ Ⓒ Ⓓ Ⓔ	50. Ⓐ Ⓑ Ⓒ Ⓓ Ⓔ

SECTION 2

1. Ⓐ Ⓑ Ⓒ Ⓓ Ⓔ	11. Ⓐ Ⓑ Ⓒ Ⓓ Ⓔ	21. Ⓐ Ⓑ Ⓒ Ⓓ Ⓔ	31. Ⓐ Ⓑ Ⓒ Ⓓ Ⓔ	41. Ⓐ Ⓑ Ⓒ Ⓓ Ⓔ
2. Ⓐ Ⓑ Ⓒ Ⓓ Ⓔ	12. Ⓐ Ⓑ Ⓒ Ⓓ Ⓔ	22. Ⓐ Ⓑ Ⓒ Ⓓ Ⓔ	32. Ⓐ Ⓑ Ⓒ Ⓓ Ⓔ	42. Ⓐ Ⓑ Ⓒ Ⓓ Ⓔ
3. Ⓐ Ⓑ Ⓒ Ⓓ Ⓔ	13. Ⓐ Ⓑ Ⓒ Ⓓ Ⓔ	23. Ⓐ Ⓑ Ⓒ Ⓓ Ⓔ	33. Ⓐ Ⓑ Ⓒ Ⓓ Ⓔ	43. Ⓐ Ⓑ Ⓒ Ⓓ Ⓔ
4. Ⓐ Ⓑ Ⓒ Ⓓ Ⓔ	14. Ⓐ Ⓑ Ⓒ Ⓓ Ⓔ	24. Ⓐ Ⓑ Ⓒ Ⓓ Ⓔ	34. Ⓐ Ⓑ Ⓒ Ⓓ Ⓔ	44. Ⓐ Ⓑ Ⓒ Ⓓ Ⓔ
5. Ⓐ Ⓑ Ⓒ Ⓓ Ⓔ	15. Ⓐ Ⓑ Ⓒ Ⓓ Ⓔ	25. Ⓐ Ⓑ Ⓒ Ⓓ Ⓔ	35. Ⓐ Ⓑ Ⓒ Ⓓ Ⓔ	45. Ⓐ Ⓑ Ⓒ Ⓓ Ⓔ
6. Ⓐ Ⓑ Ⓒ Ⓓ Ⓔ	16. Ⓐ Ⓑ Ⓒ Ⓓ Ⓔ	26. Ⓐ Ⓑ Ⓒ Ⓓ Ⓔ	36. Ⓐ Ⓑ Ⓒ Ⓓ Ⓔ	46. Ⓐ Ⓑ Ⓒ Ⓓ Ⓔ
7. Ⓐ Ⓑ Ⓒ Ⓓ Ⓔ	17. Ⓐ Ⓑ Ⓒ Ⓓ Ⓔ	27. Ⓐ Ⓑ Ⓒ Ⓓ Ⓔ	37. Ⓐ Ⓑ Ⓒ Ⓓ Ⓔ	47. Ⓐ Ⓑ Ⓒ Ⓓ Ⓔ
8. Ⓐ Ⓑ Ⓒ Ⓓ Ⓔ	18. Ⓐ Ⓑ Ⓒ Ⓓ Ⓔ	28. Ⓐ Ⓑ Ⓒ Ⓓ Ⓔ	38. Ⓐ Ⓑ Ⓒ Ⓓ Ⓔ	48. Ⓐ Ⓑ Ⓒ Ⓓ Ⓔ
9. Ⓐ Ⓑ Ⓒ Ⓓ Ⓔ	19. Ⓐ Ⓑ Ⓒ Ⓓ Ⓔ	29. Ⓐ Ⓑ Ⓒ Ⓓ Ⓔ	39. Ⓐ Ⓑ Ⓒ Ⓓ Ⓔ	49. Ⓐ Ⓑ Ⓒ Ⓓ Ⓔ
10. Ⓐ Ⓑ Ⓒ Ⓓ Ⓔ	20. Ⓐ Ⓑ Ⓒ Ⓓ Ⓔ	30. Ⓐ Ⓑ Ⓒ Ⓓ Ⓔ	40. Ⓐ Ⓑ Ⓒ Ⓓ Ⓔ	50. Ⓐ Ⓑ Ⓒ Ⓓ Ⓔ

SECTION 3

1. Ⓐ Ⓑ Ⓒ Ⓓ Ⓔ	11. Ⓐ Ⓑ Ⓒ Ⓓ Ⓔ	21. Ⓐ Ⓑ Ⓒ Ⓓ Ⓔ	31. Ⓐ Ⓑ Ⓒ Ⓓ Ⓔ	41. Ⓐ Ⓑ Ⓒ Ⓓ Ⓔ
2. Ⓐ Ⓑ Ⓒ Ⓓ Ⓔ	12. Ⓐ Ⓑ Ⓒ Ⓓ Ⓔ	22. Ⓐ Ⓑ Ⓒ Ⓓ Ⓔ	32. Ⓐ Ⓑ Ⓒ Ⓓ Ⓔ	42. Ⓐ Ⓑ Ⓒ Ⓓ Ⓔ
3. Ⓐ Ⓑ Ⓒ Ⓓ Ⓔ	13. Ⓐ Ⓑ Ⓒ Ⓓ Ⓔ	23. Ⓐ Ⓑ Ⓒ Ⓓ Ⓔ	33. Ⓐ Ⓑ Ⓒ Ⓓ Ⓔ	43. Ⓐ Ⓑ Ⓒ Ⓓ Ⓔ
4. Ⓐ Ⓑ Ⓒ Ⓓ Ⓔ	14. Ⓐ Ⓑ Ⓒ Ⓓ Ⓔ	24. Ⓐ Ⓑ Ⓒ Ⓓ Ⓔ	34. Ⓐ Ⓑ Ⓒ Ⓓ Ⓔ	44. Ⓐ Ⓑ Ⓒ Ⓓ Ⓔ
5. Ⓐ Ⓑ Ⓒ Ⓓ Ⓔ	15. Ⓐ Ⓑ Ⓒ Ⓓ Ⓔ	25. Ⓐ Ⓑ Ⓒ Ⓓ Ⓔ	35. Ⓐ Ⓑ Ⓒ Ⓓ Ⓔ	45. Ⓐ Ⓑ Ⓒ Ⓓ Ⓔ
6. Ⓐ Ⓑ Ⓒ Ⓓ Ⓔ	16. Ⓐ Ⓑ Ⓒ Ⓓ Ⓔ	26. Ⓐ Ⓑ Ⓒ Ⓓ Ⓔ	36. Ⓐ Ⓑ Ⓒ Ⓓ Ⓔ	46. Ⓐ Ⓑ Ⓒ Ⓓ Ⓔ
7. Ⓐ Ⓑ Ⓒ Ⓓ Ⓔ	17. Ⓐ Ⓑ Ⓒ Ⓓ Ⓔ	27. Ⓐ Ⓑ Ⓒ Ⓓ Ⓔ	37. Ⓐ Ⓑ Ⓒ Ⓓ Ⓔ	47. Ⓐ Ⓑ Ⓒ Ⓓ Ⓔ
8. Ⓐ Ⓑ Ⓒ Ⓓ Ⓔ	18. Ⓐ Ⓑ Ⓒ Ⓓ Ⓔ	28. Ⓐ Ⓑ Ⓒ Ⓓ Ⓔ	38. Ⓐ Ⓑ Ⓒ Ⓓ Ⓔ	48. Ⓐ Ⓑ Ⓒ Ⓓ Ⓔ
9. Ⓐ Ⓑ Ⓒ Ⓓ Ⓔ	19. Ⓐ Ⓑ Ⓒ Ⓓ Ⓔ	29. Ⓐ Ⓑ Ⓒ Ⓓ Ⓔ	39. Ⓐ Ⓑ Ⓒ Ⓓ Ⓔ	49. Ⓐ Ⓑ Ⓒ Ⓓ Ⓔ
10. Ⓐ Ⓑ Ⓒ Ⓓ Ⓔ	20. Ⓐ Ⓑ Ⓒ Ⓓ Ⓔ	30. Ⓐ Ⓑ Ⓒ Ⓓ Ⓔ	40. Ⓐ Ⓑ Ⓒ Ⓓ Ⓔ	50. Ⓐ Ⓑ Ⓒ Ⓓ Ⓔ

SECTION 4

1. Ⓐ Ⓑ Ⓒ Ⓓ Ⓔ	11. Ⓐ Ⓑ Ⓒ Ⓓ Ⓔ	21. Ⓐ Ⓑ Ⓒ Ⓓ Ⓔ	31. Ⓐ Ⓑ Ⓒ Ⓓ Ⓔ	41. Ⓐ Ⓑ Ⓒ Ⓓ Ⓔ
2. Ⓐ Ⓑ Ⓒ Ⓓ Ⓔ	12. Ⓐ Ⓑ Ⓒ Ⓓ Ⓔ	22. Ⓐ Ⓑ Ⓒ Ⓓ Ⓔ	32. Ⓐ Ⓑ Ⓒ Ⓓ Ⓔ	42. Ⓐ Ⓑ Ⓒ Ⓓ Ⓔ
3. Ⓐ Ⓑ Ⓒ Ⓓ Ⓔ	13. Ⓐ Ⓑ Ⓒ Ⓓ Ⓔ	23. Ⓐ Ⓑ Ⓒ Ⓓ Ⓔ	33. Ⓐ Ⓑ Ⓒ Ⓓ Ⓔ	43. Ⓐ Ⓑ Ⓒ Ⓓ Ⓔ
4. Ⓐ Ⓑ Ⓒ Ⓓ Ⓔ	14. Ⓐ Ⓑ Ⓒ Ⓓ Ⓔ	24. Ⓐ Ⓑ Ⓒ Ⓓ Ⓔ	34. Ⓐ Ⓑ Ⓒ Ⓓ Ⓔ	44. Ⓐ Ⓑ Ⓒ Ⓓ Ⓔ
5. Ⓐ Ⓑ Ⓒ Ⓓ Ⓔ	15. Ⓐ Ⓑ Ⓒ Ⓓ Ⓔ	25. Ⓐ Ⓑ Ⓒ Ⓓ Ⓔ	35. Ⓐ Ⓑ Ⓒ Ⓓ Ⓔ	45. Ⓐ Ⓑ Ⓒ Ⓓ Ⓔ
6. Ⓐ Ⓑ Ⓒ Ⓓ Ⓔ	16. Ⓐ Ⓑ Ⓒ Ⓓ Ⓔ	26. Ⓐ Ⓑ Ⓒ Ⓓ Ⓔ	36. Ⓐ Ⓑ Ⓒ Ⓓ Ⓔ	46. Ⓐ Ⓑ Ⓒ Ⓓ Ⓔ
7. Ⓐ Ⓑ Ⓒ Ⓓ Ⓔ	17. Ⓐ Ⓑ Ⓒ Ⓓ Ⓔ	27. Ⓐ Ⓑ Ⓒ Ⓓ Ⓔ	37. Ⓐ Ⓑ Ⓒ Ⓓ Ⓔ	47. Ⓐ Ⓑ Ⓒ Ⓓ Ⓔ
8. Ⓐ Ⓑ Ⓒ Ⓓ Ⓔ	18. Ⓐ Ⓑ Ⓒ Ⓓ Ⓔ	28. Ⓐ Ⓑ Ⓒ Ⓓ Ⓔ	38. Ⓐ Ⓑ Ⓒ Ⓓ Ⓔ	48. Ⓐ Ⓑ Ⓒ Ⓓ Ⓔ
9. Ⓐ Ⓑ Ⓒ Ⓓ Ⓔ	19. Ⓐ Ⓑ Ⓒ Ⓓ Ⓔ	29. Ⓐ Ⓑ Ⓒ Ⓓ Ⓔ	39. Ⓐ Ⓑ Ⓒ Ⓓ Ⓔ	49. Ⓐ Ⓑ Ⓒ Ⓓ Ⓔ
10. Ⓐ Ⓑ Ⓒ Ⓓ Ⓔ	20. Ⓐ Ⓑ Ⓒ Ⓓ Ⓔ	30. Ⓐ Ⓑ Ⓒ Ⓓ Ⓔ	40. Ⓐ Ⓑ Ⓒ Ⓓ Ⓔ	50. Ⓐ Ⓑ Ⓒ Ⓓ Ⓔ

SECTION 5

1. Ⓐ Ⓑ Ⓒ Ⓓ Ⓔ	11. Ⓐ Ⓑ Ⓒ Ⓓ Ⓔ	21. Ⓐ Ⓑ Ⓒ Ⓓ Ⓔ	31. Ⓐ Ⓑ Ⓒ Ⓓ Ⓔ	41. Ⓐ Ⓑ Ⓒ Ⓓ Ⓔ
2. Ⓐ Ⓑ Ⓒ Ⓓ Ⓔ	12. Ⓐ Ⓑ Ⓒ Ⓓ Ⓔ	22. Ⓐ Ⓑ Ⓒ Ⓓ Ⓔ	32. Ⓐ Ⓑ Ⓒ Ⓓ Ⓔ	42. Ⓐ Ⓑ Ⓒ Ⓓ Ⓔ
3. Ⓐ Ⓑ Ⓒ Ⓓ Ⓔ	13. Ⓐ Ⓑ Ⓒ Ⓓ Ⓔ	23. Ⓐ Ⓑ Ⓒ Ⓓ Ⓔ	33. Ⓐ Ⓑ Ⓒ Ⓓ Ⓔ	43. Ⓐ Ⓑ Ⓒ Ⓓ Ⓔ
4. Ⓐ Ⓑ Ⓒ Ⓓ Ⓔ	14. Ⓐ Ⓑ Ⓒ Ⓓ Ⓔ	24. Ⓐ Ⓑ Ⓒ Ⓓ Ⓔ	34. Ⓐ Ⓑ Ⓒ Ⓓ Ⓔ	44. Ⓐ Ⓑ Ⓒ Ⓓ Ⓔ
5. Ⓐ Ⓑ Ⓒ Ⓓ Ⓔ	15. Ⓐ Ⓑ Ⓒ Ⓓ Ⓔ	25. Ⓐ Ⓑ Ⓒ Ⓓ Ⓔ	35. Ⓐ Ⓑ Ⓒ Ⓓ Ⓔ	45. Ⓐ Ⓑ Ⓒ Ⓓ Ⓔ
6. Ⓐ Ⓑ Ⓒ Ⓓ Ⓔ	16. Ⓐ Ⓑ Ⓒ Ⓓ Ⓔ	26. Ⓐ Ⓑ Ⓒ Ⓓ Ⓔ	36. Ⓐ Ⓑ Ⓒ Ⓓ Ⓔ	46. Ⓐ Ⓑ Ⓒ Ⓓ Ⓔ
7. Ⓐ Ⓑ Ⓒ Ⓓ Ⓔ	17. Ⓐ Ⓑ Ⓒ Ⓓ Ⓔ	27. Ⓐ Ⓑ Ⓒ Ⓓ Ⓔ	37. Ⓐ Ⓑ Ⓒ Ⓓ Ⓔ	47. Ⓐ Ⓑ Ⓒ Ⓓ Ⓔ
8. Ⓐ Ⓑ Ⓒ Ⓓ Ⓔ	18. Ⓐ Ⓑ Ⓒ Ⓓ Ⓔ	28. Ⓐ Ⓑ Ⓒ Ⓓ Ⓔ	38. Ⓐ Ⓑ Ⓒ Ⓓ Ⓔ	48. Ⓐ Ⓑ Ⓒ Ⓓ Ⓔ
9. Ⓐ Ⓑ Ⓒ Ⓓ Ⓔ	19. Ⓐ Ⓑ Ⓒ Ⓓ Ⓔ	29. Ⓐ Ⓑ Ⓒ Ⓓ Ⓔ	39. Ⓐ Ⓑ Ⓒ Ⓓ Ⓔ	49. Ⓐ Ⓑ Ⓒ Ⓓ Ⓔ
10. Ⓐ Ⓑ Ⓒ Ⓓ Ⓔ	20. Ⓐ Ⓑ Ⓒ Ⓓ Ⓔ	30. Ⓐ Ⓑ Ⓒ Ⓓ Ⓔ	40. Ⓐ Ⓑ Ⓒ Ⓓ Ⓔ	50. Ⓐ Ⓑ Ⓒ Ⓓ Ⓔ

SECTION 6

1. Ⓐ Ⓑ Ⓒ Ⓓ Ⓔ	11. Ⓐ Ⓑ Ⓒ Ⓓ Ⓔ	21. Ⓐ Ⓑ Ⓒ Ⓓ Ⓔ	31. Ⓐ Ⓑ Ⓒ Ⓓ Ⓔ	41. Ⓐ Ⓑ Ⓒ Ⓓ Ⓔ
2. Ⓐ Ⓑ Ⓒ Ⓓ Ⓔ	12. Ⓐ Ⓑ Ⓒ Ⓓ Ⓔ	22. Ⓐ Ⓑ Ⓒ Ⓓ Ⓔ	32. Ⓐ Ⓑ Ⓒ Ⓓ Ⓔ	42. Ⓐ Ⓑ Ⓒ Ⓓ Ⓔ
3. Ⓐ Ⓑ Ⓒ Ⓓ Ⓔ	13. Ⓐ Ⓑ Ⓒ Ⓓ Ⓔ	23. Ⓐ Ⓑ Ⓒ Ⓓ Ⓔ	33. Ⓐ Ⓑ Ⓒ Ⓓ Ⓔ	43. Ⓐ Ⓑ Ⓒ Ⓓ Ⓔ
4. Ⓐ Ⓑ Ⓒ Ⓓ Ⓔ	14. Ⓐ Ⓑ Ⓒ Ⓓ Ⓔ	24. Ⓐ Ⓑ Ⓒ Ⓓ Ⓔ	34. Ⓐ Ⓑ Ⓒ Ⓓ Ⓔ	44. Ⓐ Ⓑ Ⓒ Ⓓ Ⓔ
5. Ⓐ Ⓑ Ⓒ Ⓓ Ⓔ	15. Ⓐ Ⓑ Ⓒ Ⓓ Ⓔ	25. Ⓐ Ⓑ Ⓒ Ⓓ Ⓔ	35. Ⓐ Ⓑ Ⓒ Ⓓ Ⓔ	45. Ⓐ Ⓑ Ⓒ Ⓓ Ⓔ
6. Ⓐ Ⓑ Ⓒ Ⓓ Ⓔ	16. Ⓐ Ⓑ Ⓒ Ⓓ Ⓔ	26. Ⓐ Ⓑ Ⓒ Ⓓ Ⓔ	36. Ⓐ Ⓑ Ⓒ Ⓓ Ⓔ	46. Ⓐ Ⓑ Ⓒ Ⓓ Ⓔ
7. Ⓐ Ⓑ Ⓒ Ⓓ Ⓔ	17. Ⓐ Ⓑ Ⓒ Ⓓ Ⓔ	27. Ⓐ Ⓑ Ⓒ Ⓓ Ⓔ	37. Ⓐ Ⓑ Ⓒ Ⓓ Ⓔ	47. Ⓐ Ⓑ Ⓒ Ⓓ Ⓔ
8. Ⓐ Ⓑ Ⓒ Ⓓ Ⓔ	18. Ⓐ Ⓑ Ⓒ Ⓓ Ⓔ	28. Ⓐ Ⓑ Ⓒ Ⓓ Ⓔ	38. Ⓐ Ⓑ Ⓒ Ⓓ Ⓔ	48. Ⓐ Ⓑ Ⓒ Ⓓ Ⓔ
9. Ⓐ Ⓑ Ⓒ Ⓓ Ⓔ	19. Ⓐ Ⓑ Ⓒ Ⓓ Ⓔ	29. Ⓐ Ⓑ Ⓒ Ⓓ Ⓔ	39. Ⓐ Ⓑ Ⓒ Ⓓ Ⓔ	49. Ⓐ Ⓑ Ⓒ Ⓓ Ⓔ
10. Ⓐ Ⓑ Ⓒ Ⓓ Ⓔ	20. Ⓐ Ⓑ Ⓒ Ⓓ Ⓔ	30. Ⓐ Ⓑ Ⓒ Ⓓ Ⓔ	40. Ⓐ Ⓑ Ⓒ Ⓓ Ⓔ	50. Ⓐ Ⓑ Ⓒ Ⓓ Ⓔ

Remove answer sheet by cutting on dotted line

MODEL SAT TEST 4

SECTION 1 MATH ABILITY

35 QUESTIONS - 30 MINUTES

In this section, solve each problem, using any available space on the page for scratchwork. Then decide which is the best of the choices given and blacken the corresponding space on the answer sheet.

The following information is for your reference in solving some of the problems.

Circle of radius r: Area $= \pi r^2$; Circumference $= 2\pi r$

The number of degrees of arc in a circle is 360.

The measure in degrees of a straight angle is 180.

Definitions of symbols:

$=$ is equal to
$\neq$ is unequal to
$<$ is less than
$>$ is greater than
$\leqq$ is less than or equal to
$\geqq$ is greater than or equal to
$\parallel$ is parallel to
$\perp$ is perpendicular to

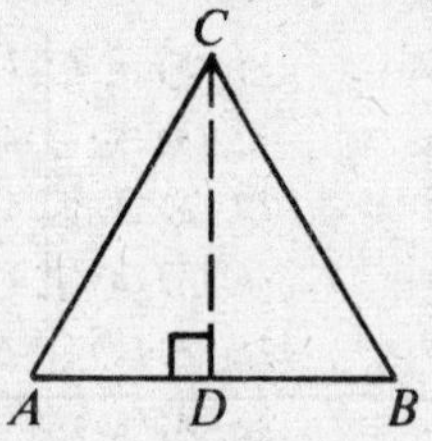

Triangle: The sum of the measures in degrees of the angles of a triangle is 180.

If $\angle CDA$ is a right angle, then

(1) area of $\triangle ABC = \frac{AB \times CD}{2}$

(2) $AC^2 = AD^2 + DC^2$

Note: Figures that accompany problems in this test are intended to provide information useful in solving the problems. They are drawn as accurately as possible EXCEPT when it is stated in a specific problem that its figure is not drawn to scale. All figures lie in a plane unless otherwise indicated. All numbers used are real numbers.

1. $r = \frac{rs}{1 - s}$

$s^2 + 2s + 1 = ?$

(A) 2
(B) $2\frac{1}{4}$
(C) $2\frac{1}{2}$
(D) 22
(E) 24

2. A merchant paid \$30.00 for an article. He wishes to place a price tag on it so that he can offer a 10% discount on the price marked on the tag and still make a profit of 20% on the cost. What price should he mark on the tag?

(A) \$33.00
(B) \$36.00
(C) \$39.60
(D) \$40.00
(E) \$42.40

3. Ten minutes after a plane leaves the airport, it is reported that the plane is 40 miles away. What is the average speed of the plane, in miles per hour?

(A) 66
(B) 240
(C) 400
(D) 600
(E) 660

4. A typist can complete a task in three hours. What part of her job can she do from 8:55 to 9:15?

(A) $\frac{1}{6}$
(B) $\frac{1}{3}$
(C) $\frac{2}{3}$
(D) $\frac{1}{5}$
(E) $\frac{1}{9}$

5. What part of a quarter is two pennies, two nickels and one dime?

(A) $\frac{3}{25}$

(B) $\frac{22}{25}$

(C) $\frac{1}{22}$

(D) $\frac{1}{5}$

(E) $\frac{3}{5}$

6. A man binds s sets of books in d days. If there are b books in a set, how many books does the man bind in one day?

(A) $\frac{d}{bs}$

(B) $\frac{s}{bd}$

(C) $\frac{bd}{s}$

(D) $\frac{bs}{d}$

(E) $\frac{ds}{b}$

7. If the radius of a wheel is f feet, how many revolutions does the wheel make per mile? (1 mile equals 5,280 feet.) Answer in terms of π and f.

(A) $5280f$

(B) $\frac{2640}{\pi f}$

(C) $5280\pi f^2$

(D) $\frac{\pi f}{2640}$

(E) $\frac{\pi f^2}{5280}$

Questions 8–27 each consist of two quantities, one in Column A and one in Column B. You are to compare the two quantities and on the answer sheet blacken space

A if the quantity in Column A is greater;
B if the quantity in Column B is greater;
C if the two quantities are equal;
D If the relationship cannot be determined from the information given.

AN E RESPONSE WILL NOT BE SCORED.

EXAMPLES

	Column A	Column B	Answers
E1.	2×6	$2 + 6$	● Ⓑ Ⓒ Ⓓ Ⓔ
E2.	$180 - x$	y	Ⓐ Ⓑ ● Ⓓ Ⓔ
E3.	$p - q$	$q - p$	Ⓐ Ⓑ Ⓒ ● Ⓔ

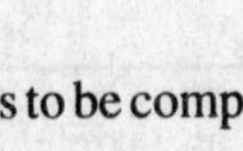

Notes:
1. In certain questions, information concerning one or both of the quantities to be compared is centered above the two columns.
2. In a given question, a symbol that appears in both columns represents the same thing in Column A as it does in Column B.
3. Letters such as x, n, and k stand for real numbers.

	Column A	Column B
8.	$\frac{1}{7}$	.0142
9.	$\sqrt{\frac{1}{0.25}}$	2
10.	5% of 500	2.5
11.	Time elapsed from 2:55 P.M. to 3:15 P.M. on the same afternoon	$\frac{1}{3}$ hour

	Column A	Column B
	$\frac{(15)(16)}{x} = (5)(4)(3)$	
12.	x	4
	Area of square $ABCD = 25$	
13.	$AB + BC + CD$	20
	Area of isosceles right triangle $ABC = 18$	
14.	Length of leg AB	Length of hypotenuse AC

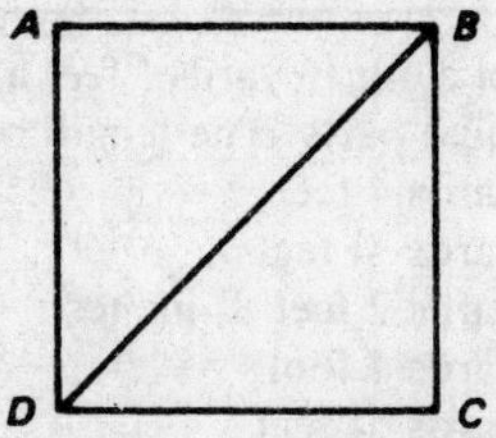

ABCD is a square   Diagonal $BD = 6\sqrt{2}$

This concerns #15 and #16

	Column A	Column B
15.	Perimeter of $ABCD$	24
16.	Area of ABD	18
	In triangle ABC, $AB = BC$, and the measure of angle B = the measure of angle C	
17.	The measure of angle B + the measure of angle C	The measure of angle B + the measure of angle A
	$36 - 7x = 8$	
18.	7	x
	$z > 0$	
19.	$\frac{z+6}{8}$	$\frac{z+3}{4}$
	In $\triangle ABC$ $AB = 5$ $BC = 8$	
20.	Area of ABC	20
21.	ABC is an equilateral triangle $AB = 5x$; $BC = 2y$	
	value of AC	$\frac{2}{5}y$
	$\frac{3a}{4} = 9$	
22.	$6a$	36
	$z = 0$	
23.	$x(y + z)$	xy
	$x^2 + y^2 = 12$, $xy = 9$	
24.	$(x + y)^2$	12
25.	Square with area of 25 square units	Square with perimeter of 20 units
	$x^2 - 7x + 12 = 0$	
26.	x	5
27.	Area of rectangle $ABCD$ with perimeter 36 units	Area of rectangle $EFGH$ with perimeter 36 units

Solve each of the remaining problems in this section using any available space for scratchwork. Then decide which is the best of the choices given and blacken the corresponding space on the answer sheet.

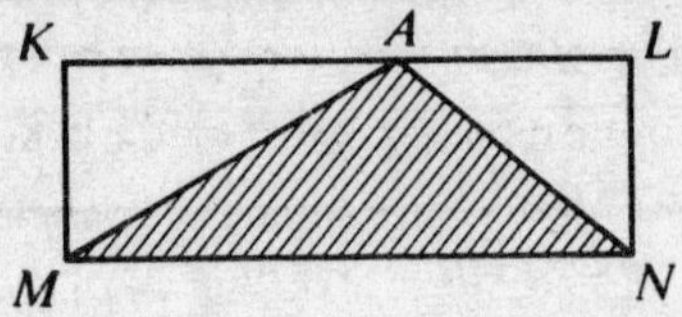

28. In the figure above, the area of a rectangle $KLNM$ equals 100. Base NM equals 20. What is the area of triangle ANM if A is any point on KL?
(A) 25
(B) 50
(C) 75
(D) 100
(E) cannot be determined

29. What fraction must be subtracted from the sum of $\frac{1}{2}$ and $\frac{1}{3}$ to have an average of $\frac{1}{6}$?
(A) $\frac{1}{3}$
(B) $\frac{2}{5}$
(C) $\frac{1}{6}$
(D) $\frac{5}{6}$
(E) 1

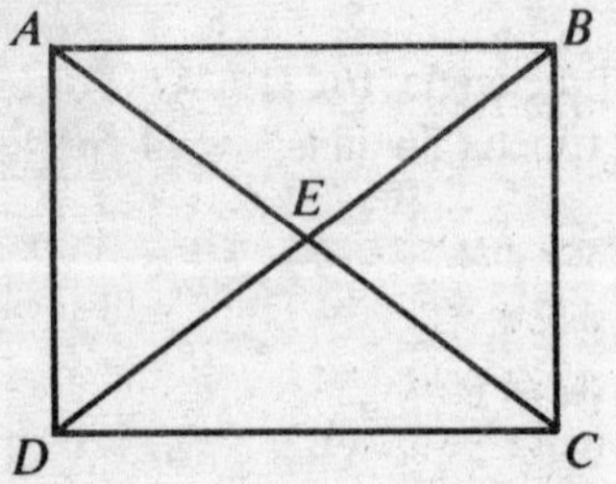

30. In the figure above, $ABCD$ is a rectangle. $AD = 12$. $AB = 16$. $DE = ?$
(A) 8
(B) 10
(C) 14
(D) 15
(E) 20

31. An Erlenmeyer flask can hold 0.6 liter. How many flasks are necessary to hold 3.6 liters?
(A) 3
(B) 4.2
(C) 6
(D) 12
(E) 21.6

32. $\frac{3}{rs} = \frac{1}{2t}$; $r = s^2$. Find s in terms of t.
(A) $\sqrt[3]{6t}$
(B) $\sqrt{6t}$
(C) $\sqrt{\frac{6}{t}}$
(D) $\frac{t}{6}$
(E) $6t$

33. A length of cloth 13 yards 5 feet and 1 inch is cut into three equal parts. The length of each piece is
(A) 4 yards 4 feet
(B) 4 yards $4\frac{1}{3}$ feet
(C) 4 yards 2 feet $8\frac{1}{3}$ inches
(D) 4 yards 1 foot
(E) 4 yards $5\frac{1}{3}$ feet

34. Point M is the midpoint of line KL and point C is the midpoint of line AB. If $KM > AC$ then which of the following is true?
(A) $KL < AB$
(B) $KL > AB$
(C) $KL < ML$
(D) $CB = AB$
(E) $AC = AB$

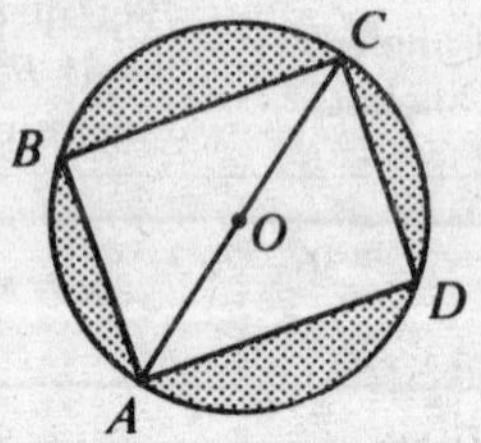

35. In the figure above, O is the center of the circle. BC is parallel to AD. $OA = 5$, $CB = 8$, $\frac{AB}{AD} = ?$
(A) $\frac{3}{4}$
(B) $\frac{4}{5}$
(C) 1
(D) $\frac{5}{4}$
(E) $\frac{4}{3}$

S T O P

IF YOU FINISH BEFORE TIME IS CALLED, YOU MAY CHECK YOUR WORK ON THIS SECTION ONLY. DO NOT WORK ON ANY OTHER SECTION IN THE TEST.

SECTION 2 VERBAL ABILITY

40 QUESTIONS - 30 MINUTES

For each question in this section, choose the best answer and blacken the corresponding space on the answer sheet.

Each question below consists of a word in capital letters, followed by five lettered words or phrases. Choose the word or phrase that is most nearly opposite in meaning to the word in capital letters. Since some of the questions require you to distinguish fine shades of meaning, consider all the choices before deciding which is best.

Example:

GOOD: (A) sour (B) bad (C) red (D) hot (E) ugly Ⓐ ● Ⓒ Ⓓ Ⓔ

1. BENEDICTION:
   (A) curse
   (B) psalm
   (C) verse
   (D) maltreatment
   (E) pledge

2. VACILLATING:
   (A) firm
   (B) soothing
   (C) irritating
   (D) ill
   (E) indolent

3. HEINOUS:
   (A) loquacious
   (B) multifarious
   (C) limited
   (D) noble
   (E) arterial

4. PUGNACIOUS:
   (A) devious
   (B) canine
   (C) arbitrary
   (D) conciliatory
   (E) defeated

5. PERTURBED:
   (A) boiled
   (B) whipped
   (C) polite
   (D) soothed
   (E) intruded

6. SCANTY:
   (A) clean
   (B) outer
   (C) profuse
   (D) serious
   (E) remodeled

7. GAUCHE:
   (A) righteous
   (B) measured
   (C) merry
   (D) adroit
   (E) indignant

8. ENLIGHTEN:
   (A) obscure
   (B) shorten
   (C) weigh down
   (D) take away
   (E) escape

9. CONTAMINATE:
   (A) make official
   (B) make pure
   (C) make peaceful
   (D) give back
   (E) devour

10. COMBUSTIBLE:
    (A) whole
    (B) edible
    (C) fragile
    (D) flameproof
    (E) serene

Each sentence below has one or two blanks, each blank indicating that something has been omitted. Beneath the sentence are five lettered words or sets of words. Choose the word or set of words that best fits the meaning of the sentence as a whole.

Example:

Although its publicity has been ----, the film itself is intelligent, well-acted, handsomely produced, and altogether ----.

(A) tasteless..respectable (B) extensive..moderate (C) sophisticated..amateur (D) risqué..crude (E) perfect..spectacular

● Ⓑ Ⓒ Ⓓ Ⓔ

11. An ______ is a personal ______.
(A) idiom—phrase
(B) allusion—deception
(C) idiosyncrasy—peculiarity
(D) aphorism—saying
(E) activity—deed

12. At such a serious moment in our history, your ______ is inappropriate and in bad taste.
(A) questioning
(B) levity
(C) attire
(D) moodiness
(E) maturation

13. The bombastic orator addressed the audience in ______ phrases which brought smiles to the faces of the more ______ listeners.
(A) trite—happy
(B) colorful—patriotic
(C) passionate—cultured
(D) flamboyant—sophisticated
(E) funny—attentive

14. Initiated into the tribe, the explorer hoped finally to be permitted to attend the ______ rites of the primitive people.
(A) hunting
(B) esoteric
(C) public
(D) barbaric
(E) cannibalistic

15. A prison term could not deter him from his ______ ways for with him stealing was a disease.
(A) criminal
(B) wayward
(C) impossible
(D) sinful
(E) larcenous

Each question below consists of a related pair of words or phrases, followed by five lettered pairs of words or phrases. Select the lettered pair that best expresses a relationship similar to that expressed in the original pair.

Example:

YAWN : BOREDOM :: (A) dream : sleep (B) anger : madness (C) smile : amusement (D) face : expression (E) impatience : rebellion

Ⓐ Ⓑ ● Ⓓ Ⓔ

16. CONSCIENCE : SIN ::
(A) law : crime
(B) brake : automobile
(C) confession : repentance
(D) fence : trespasser
(E) indolence : work

17. SANDAL : SOMBRERO ::
(A) trousers : shirt
(B) shoes : sash
(C) moccasins: cap
(D) leather : hide
(E) peasant : noble

18. DOG : MAMMAL ::
(A) wolf : carnivorous
(B) cat : feline
(C) man : intelligent
(D) crab : crustacean
(E) kennel : house

19. SILO : CORN ::
(A) vault : valuables
(B) wheat : granary
(C) shoes : bunion
(D) mineral : vegetable
(E) oil : grain

20. NECROMANCY : DEMONS ::
(A) fortune-telling : gypsies
(B) magic : carpets
(C) romance : flowers
(D) sorcery : spirits
(E) alchemy : gold

21. VISIONARY : PRACTICAL ::
(A) dilletante : amateurish
(B) braggart : modest
(C) rebel : revolutionary
(D) connoisseur : cultivated
(E) retainer : loyal

22. LINIMENT : ACHE ::
(A) cotton : bandage
(B) antiseptic : symptom
(C) salve : sore
(D) injection : syringe
(E) vaccine : remedy

23. INSUBORDINATION : PUNISHMENT ::
(A) abstinence : crime
(B) tolerance : segregation
(C) autonomy : government
(D) disobedience : reward
(E) diligence : promotion

24. EPHEMERAL : MAYFLY ::
(A) torrid : zone
(B) graceful : gazelle
(C) herbivorous : tiger
(D) expensive : elephant
(E) experimental : animal

25. TUMBLER : BEVERAGE ::
(A) quiver : arrows
(B) juggler : orange
(C) quibbler : revenge
(D) magician : prestidigitation
(E) gambler : lottery

Each passage below is followed by questions based on its content. Answer all questions following a passage on the basis of what is stated or implied in that passage.

Are we getting more than our usual share of snow in this part of the country, or less? It's hard to say one way or the other. Only within recent years has there been enough interest in snow, especially from the sport angle, to bring about careful recording of snow depths. Most weather records lump snow and rain under the noncommital head of "precipitation." We do know that, because of a general trend to higher temperatures over the last half-century or so, the winter precipitation in this part of the world has had an increasing tendency in recent years to take the form of rain. Whether this trend will continue this winter and in future winters is anybody's guess. The process of sublimation that leads to the precipitation of snow is one that man can not at all control and one that man has only a limited ability to predict.

26. The title that best expresses the ideas of this paragraph is:
(A) A possible trend in weather
(B) Popularity of winter sports
(C) Snow and winter sports
(D) Weather prediction
(E) What meteorological records show

27. We do not know whether or not we are getting more snow than usual because
(A) formerly snowfall and rain were not reported separately
(B) weather reports are inaccurate
(C) winters are getting warmer
(D) we can not predict weather accurately
(E) winter sports are relatively recent

28. During the last 50 years there has been
(A) an increase in average annual snowfall
(B) more interest in winter sports
(C) an increase in precipitation
(D) less snow and more rain
(E) a tendency toward colder winters

The Cardinal and Daniel de Bosola enter from the right. In appearance, the Cardinal is something between an El Greco cardinal and a Van Dyke noble lord. He has the tall, spare form — the elongated hands and features — of the former; the trim pointed beard, the imperial repose, the commanding authority of the latter. But the El Greco features are not really those of asceticism or inner mystic spirituality. They are the index to a cold, refined but ruthless cruelty in a highly civilized controlled form. Neither is the imperial repose an aloof mood of proud detachment. It is a refined expression of a satanic pride of place and talent. To a degree, the Cardinal's coldness is artificially cultivated. He has defined himself against his younger brother the Duke and is the opposite to the overwrought emotionality of the latter. But the Cardinal's aloof mood is not one of bland detachment. It is the deliberate detachment of a methodical man who collects his thoughts and emotions into the most compact and formidable shape — that when he strikes, he may strike with the more efficient and devastating force. His easy movements are those of the slowly circling eagle just before the swift descent with the exposed talons. Above all else, he is a man who never for a moment doubts his destined authority as a governor. He derisively and sharply rebukes his brother the Duke as easily and readily as his mistress Julia. If he has betrayed Bosola, he uses his brother as the tool to recover his "familiar." His court dress is a long brilliant scarlet cardinal's gown with white cuffs and a white collar turned back over the red, both collar and cuffs being elaborately scalloped and embroidered. He wears a small cape, reaching only to the elbows. His cassock is buttoned to the ground, giving a heightened effect to his already tall presence. Richelieu would have adored his neatly trimmed beard. A richly jeweled and ornamented cross lies on his breast, suspended from his neck by a gold chain. Bosola is the Renaissance ' familiar ' dressed conventionally in sombre black with a white collar. He wears a chain about his neck, a suspended ornament, and a sword. Although a "bravo," he must not be thought of as a leather-jacketed, heavy-booted tough, squat and swarthy. Still less is he a sneering, leering, melodramatic villain of the Victorian gaslight tradition. Like his black-and-white clothes, he is a colorful contradiction, a scholar-assassin, a humanist-hangman; introverted and introspective, yet ruthless in action; moody and reluctant, yet violent. He is a man of scholarly taste and subtle intellectual discrimination doing the work of a hired ruffian. In general effect, his impersonator must achieve suppleness and subtlety of nature, a highly complex, compressed, yet well restrained intensity of temperament. Like Duke Ferdinand, he is inwardly tormented, but not by undiluted passion. His dominant emotion is an intellectualized one; that of disgust at a world filled with knavery and folly, but in which he must play a part and that a lowly, despicable one. He is the kind of rarity that Browning loved to depict in his Renaissance monologues.

29. The actor portraying Bosola must depict the character
(A) as a familiar person
(B) as a sneering villain
(C) as a complicated yet restrained individual
(D) with subtlety and intensity
(E) as a highly civilized individual

30. The writer of this passage assumes that the reader is
(A) familiar with Renaissance poetry
(B) disgusted with a world filled with knavery and folly
(C) familiar with the paintings of El Greco
(D) familiar with the writings of Van Dyke and El Greco
(E) impressed by literary references

31. In this passage, we learn that
(A) the Cardinal is a man of inner mystic spirituality
(B) Bosola is a man of overwrought emotionality
(C) Van Dyke's characters lived ascetic lives
(D) Duke Ferdinand is tormented by passion
(E) the Cardinal was envied by Richelieu

32. El Greco
(A) depicted cruel and highly civilized characters
(B) depicts the Cardinal as a man of satanic pride
(C) is famous for his Cardinal-like appearance
(D) can be recognized by the elongated features of his characters
(E) was opposed by Van Dyke

33. Bosola is most like
(A) El Greco
(B) Van Dyke
(C) Browning
(D) an eagle
(E) Ferdinand

34. As used in this passage, the word *familiar* most nearly means
(A) frequent
(B) an intimate companion
(C) an acquaintance
(D) a customary role
(E) a domestic servant

When light passes through a medium which contains particles that are small compared with the wave length of the light, a part of the light is scattered by the particles in all directions, and the ratio of the intensities of the scattered and incident lights varies inversely as the fourth power of the wave length. The molecules of the air, and also the particles of dust suspended in it, have this effect upon sunlight and starlight; and so the light that reaches the eye directly through the air has been deprived of some of its shorter waves (composing the violet end of the spectrum), and the heavenly bodies appear of a redder or yellower hue than they would if the Earth had no atmosphere. Just before sunset, the sunlight passes through a greater depth of air than near the middle of the day, and its redness is increased both by this cause and by the greater dustiness of the air at that time of the day. The brilliant colors of sunset clouds are due to their illumination by light that has passed through different depths of air. On the other hand, when we turn to directions nearly at right angles to that of the Sun, we receive light that has been scattered by particles in the air, and which is therefore blue or, in the pure sky of high altitudes, a deep violet. The illumination and color of the sky are thus due to the scattering of light by the small particles of the air. If the Earth had no atmosphere, the sky would be black and the stars could be seen at all times, day or night.

35. Where there is no atmosphere,
(A) the stars are visible day and night
(B) light is scattered in all directions
(C) there is a red hue in the sky
(D) there is a greater dustiness in the air
(E) there is a violet hue in the sky

36. Starlight has a reddish hue because
(A) it has traveled through space which has no atmosphere
(B) it has been deprived of some of the shorter waves
(C) the particles in the air reflect the light
(D) the violet end of the spectrum is exposed
(E) incident light varies inversely as the fourth power of the wave length

37. Passengers traveling in a jet plane at altitudes of 30,000 feet or higher may expect to see skies that are
(A) yellowish
(B) blue
(C) black
(D) cloudy
(E) filled with stars

38. At sunset,
(A) there is a greater depth of air
(B) sunset clouds appear
(C) the atmosphere is denser
(D) there is more dust in the atmosphere
(E) the atmosphere scatters the light

39. From this passage, we may conclude that
(A) short wave lengths pass through the atmosphere more readily than long wave lengths
(B) the molecules in the air absorb some of the light
(C) the reddish colors are at the short end of the spectrum
(D) the reddish colors are at the long end of the spectrum
(E) at sunrise the light is at right angles to the Sun

40. The light seen when we turn to directions at right angles to the Sun is
(A) incident light
(B) scattered light
(C) absorbed
(D) reflected
(E) brilliant

S T O P

IF YOU FINISH BEFORE TIME IS CALLED, YOU MAY CHECK YOUR WORK ON THIS SECTION ONLY. DO NOT WORK ON ANY OTHER SECTION IN THE TEST.

SECTION 3 MATH ABILITY

25 QUESTIONS - 30 MINUTES

In this section solve each problem, using any available space on the page for scratchwork. Then decide which is the best of the choices given and blacken the corresponding space on the answer sheet.

The following information is for your reference in solving some of the problems.

Circle of radius r: Area $= \pi r^2$; Circumference $= 2\pi r$
The number of degrees of arc in a circle is 360.
The measure in degrees of a straight angle is 180.

Definitions of symbols:

$=$ is equal to	$\leq$ is less than or equal to
$\neq$ is unequal to	$\geq$ is greater than or equal to
$<$ is less than	$\parallel$ is parallel to
$>$ is greater than	$\perp$ is perpendicular to

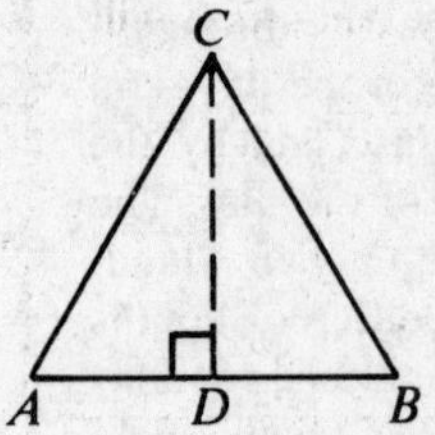

Triangle: The sum of the measures in degrees of the angles of a triangle is 180.

If $\angle CDA$ is a right angle, then

(1) area of $\triangle ABC = \frac{AB \times CD}{2}$

(2) $AC^2 = AD^2 + DC^2$

Note: Figures that accompany problems in this test are intended to provide information useful in solving the problems. They are drawn as accurately as possible EXCEPT when it is stated in a specific problem that its figure is not drawn to scale. All figures lie in a plane unless otherwise indicated. All numbers used are real numbers.

1. $1\frac{1}{4}(?) = \frac{1}{2}$

(A) $\frac{5}{8}$
(B) $\frac{2}{5}$
(C) $\frac{3}{4}$
(D) $\frac{5}{4}$
(E) $\frac{5}{2}$

2. How many nickels are there in q quarters?

(A) $\frac{q}{5}$
(B) $\frac{q}{4}$
(C) $5q$
(D) $25q$
(E) $\frac{5q}{100}$

3. A man runs y yards in m minutes. What is his rate in yards per hour?

(A) $\frac{y}{60m}$
(B) $\frac{m}{60y}$
(C) $60my$
(D) $\frac{60y}{m}$
(E) $\frac{60m}{y}$

4. $\frac{1}{2} + \frac{3}{4} \div \left(\frac{5}{6} \times \frac{7}{8}\right) - \frac{9}{10} = ?$

(A) $\frac{22}{35}$
(B) $\frac{57}{70}$
(C) $\frac{35}{22}$
(D) $\frac{12}{7}$
(E) 22

5. What is the maximum total weight of ten eggs, if four of them weigh 15 to 25 ounces each, and the others weigh from 20 to 25 ounces each?

(A) 180 oz.
(B) 210 oz.
(C) 220 oz.
(D) 225 oz.
(E) 250 oz.

6. In making tuna fish salad a recipe calls for 2 cups of fish to $\frac{1}{8}$ cup of chopped celery. How many cups of celery should be used for 8 cups of tuna fish?

(A) $\frac{1}{8}$
(B) $\frac{1}{4}$
(C) $\frac{1}{2}$
(D) 2
(E) 4

7. $x\sqrt{0.09} = 3$; $x = ?$

(A) $\frac{1}{10}$
(B) $\frac{3}{10}$
(C) $\frac{1}{3}$
(D) 1
(E) 10

8. A clock loses ten minutes each day. How many days will it take to reach a point where the clock will indicate the correct time?

(A) 36
(B) 72
(C) 120
(D) 132
(E) 144

9. How many 2-cent stamps may be purchased for c cents?

(A) $\frac{2}{c}$
(B) c
(C) $2c$
(D) $\frac{c}{2}$
(E) $c - 2$

10. What is the value of $\frac{3y^2 - x^2}{\frac{1}{2}a^3}$ when $x = -2$, $y = 3$, and $a = -1$?

(A) 0
(B) 1
(C) 8
(D) −8
(E) −46

11. $abc = dbc + e$
$bc = ?$

(A) $\frac{e}{a - d}$
(B) $bc + e$
(C) $\frac{abc + e}{a}$
(D) ae
(E) $\frac{ae}{d}$

12. A man works d days and earns w dollars more than p dollars. What are his average earnings per day?

(A) $\frac{p}{w + d}$
(B) $\frac{d + p}{w}$
(C) $\frac{d + w}{p}$
(D) $\frac{p + d}{w}$
(E) $\frac{p + w}{d}$

13. The distance between Montreal and Washington, D.C., is 600 miles. A train leaving Washington at 7:00 A.M. arrives at 3 P.M. What is the average rate of the train in M.P.H.?

(A) 24
(B) 37.5
(C) 48
(D) 75
(E) 150

14. Bath towels formerly sold for 80¢ each are now offered at $9.00 per dozen. What is the ratio of the old price to the new price?

(A) 5:1
(B) 16:15
(C) 15:16
(D) 8:45
(E) 45:8

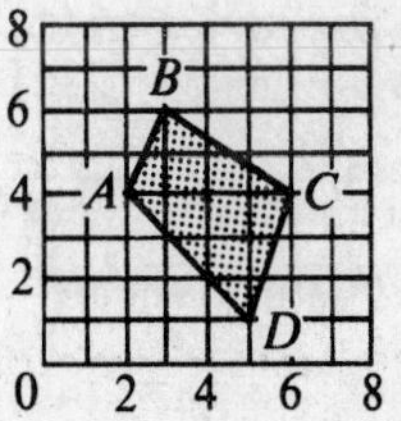

15. In the figure above, what is the area of *ABCD*?

(A) 5
(B) 8
(C) 10
(D) 16
(E) 20

16. A pond 100 feet in diameter is surrounded by a circular grass walk which is 2 feet wide. How many square feet of grass are there on the walk? (Answer in terms of π.)

(A) 98π
(B) 100π
(C) 102π
(D) 202π
(E) 204π

17. A boy's marks are 70, 90, 65, 85, and 75. What must his mark be on the next test to raise his average to 80%?
(A) 73
(B) 81
(C) 90
(D) 92.5
(E) 95

18. $\sqrt{x^2y^2 + x^3y^4} = 3xy$
$xy^2 = ?$
(A) $1\frac{1}{2}$
(B) 4
(C) 8
(D) 16
(E) 64

19. A cashier gave a man change for a dollar in dimes and quarters. How many coins did the man receive?
(A) 4
(B) 6
(C) 7
(D) 9
(E) 10

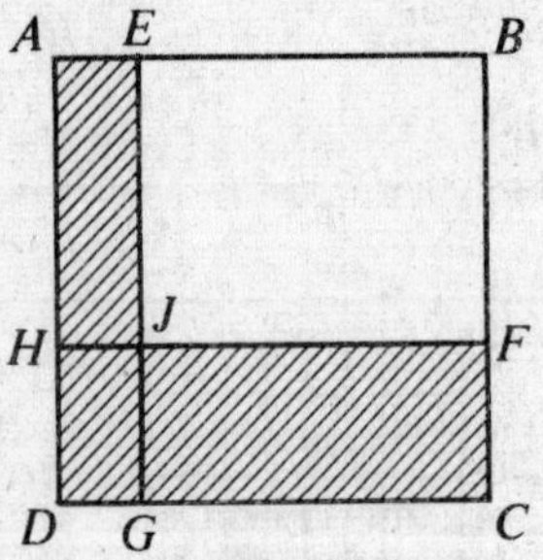

20. In the figure, $ABCD$ is a square
$AE = 2$
$GC = 8$
Shaded area = 44
Area of $FBEJ$ = ?
(A) 36
(B) 56
(C) 64
(D) 68
(E) 80

21. If the degree measures of the angles of an isosceles triangle are $x + 24$, $4x - 12$, and $\frac{3x}{2} + 12$, how many degrees are there in the vertex angle of the triangle?
(A) 24
(B) 30
(C) 48
(D) 84
(E) 108

22. A man travels a distance of 70 miles in $2\frac{1}{2}$ hours. How much faster on the average must he travel to make such a trip in $\frac{3}{4}$ hour less time?
(A) 12
(B) 23
(C) 24
(D) 28
(E) 37

23. Which of the following is an equation of the locus of points in the coordinate plane which are at a distance of 5 units from the origin?
(A) $x = 5$
(B) $y = 5$
(C) $x^2 + y^2 = 5$
(D) $x^2 + y^2 = 25$
(E) $x^2 + y^2 = 0$

24. If the coordinates of point A are $(1, -2)$ and the coordinates of point B are $(-4, -5)$, the length of AB is
(A) 9
(B) $\sqrt{34}$
(C) $\sqrt{58}$
(D) $\sqrt{74}$
(E) $\sqrt{15}$

25. The locus of points in a plane at a given distance d from a given line in that plane is
(A) one line
(B) two lines
(C) one circle
(D) two circles
(E) many circles

S T O P

IF YOU FINISH BEFORE TIME IS CALLED, YOU MAY CHECK YOUR WORK ON THIS SECTION ONLY. DO NOT WORK ON ANY OTHER SECTION IN THE TEST.

SECTION 4 VERBAL ABILITY

45 QUESTIONS - 30 MINUTES

For each question in this section, choose the best answer and blacken the corresponding space on the answer sheet.

Each question below consists of a word in capital letters, followed by five lettered words or phrases. Choose the word or phrase that is most nearly opposite in meaning to the word in capital letters. Since some of the questions require you to distinguish fine shades of meaning, consider all the choices before deciding which is best.

Example:

GOOD: (A) sour (B) bad (C) red (D) hot (E) ugly

Ⓐ ● Ⓒ Ⓓ Ⓔ

1. TAUT:
   (A) unschooled
   (B) practiced
   (C) eventual
   (D) loose
   (E) crime

2. PRONE:
   (A) available
   (B) disproved
   (C) haggard
   (D) shrewish
   (E) disinclined

3. SEGREGATE:
   (A) educate
   (B) unite
   (C) falsify
   (D) tolerate
   (E) restore

4. CIRCUMSPECT:
   (A) disregarded
   (B) rash
   (C) angular
   (D) idle
   (E) restored

5. NADIR:
   (A) radar
   (B) potentate
   (C) weakling
   (D) peak
   (E) rascal

6. PARAGON:
   (A) horrible example
   (B) house of worship
   (C) cause of dispute
   (D) hexagon
   (E) circle

7. WONTED:
   (A) undesired
   (B) tractable
   (C) unaccustomed
   (D) unfulfilled
   (E) wicked

8. CALLOW:
   (A) experienced
   (B) young
   (C) frenzied
   (D) articulate
   (E) magnificent

9. ENCOMIUM:
   (A) recompense
   (B) fine
   (C) loss
   (D) opprobrium
   (E) adumbration

10. JAUNDICED:
    (A) diseased
    (B) summery
    (C) vigorous
    (D) illicit
    (E) tolerant

11. INVIDIOUS:
    (A) visible
    (B) creating good will
    (C) unable to divide
    (D) loyal
    (E) subtle

12. PROXIMITY:
    (A) substitution
    (B) caution
    (C) essence
    (D) relief
    (E) distance

13. ALOOF:
(A) happy
(B) deadly
(C) gregarious
(D) manly
(E) varied

14. VIVACIOUS:
(A) lethargic
(B) hungry
(C) impatient
(D) inquisitive
(E) deadly

15. COLLABORATE:
(A) work alone
(B) depart
(C) fashion
(D) discard
(E) quit

Each sentence below has one or two blanks, each blank indicating that something has been omitted. Beneath the sentence are five lettered words or sets of words. Choose the word or set of words that best fits the meaning of the sentence as a whole.

Example:

Although its publicity has been ----, the film itself is intelligent, well-acted, handsomely produced, and altogether ----.

(A) tasteless..respectable (B) extensive..moderate (C) sophisticated..amateur (D) risqué..crude (E) perfect..spectacular

● Ⓑ Ⓒ Ⓓ Ⓔ

16. At the church the visitors ______ with the ______ parents of the children drowned in the lake.
(A) mingled—grieving
(B) chatted—enconsed
(C) commiserated—bereaved
(D) lamented—wailing
(E) spoke—sorrowing

17. In times of war, we must take precautions against acts of ______ as well as of direct violence.
(A) heinousness
(B) viciousness
(C) subterfuge
(D) sabotage
(E) infiltration

18. When the colonel learned that headquarters had been unable to send him reinforcements, he ______ the order for the scheduled attack.
(A) countermanded
(B) relinquished
(C) rephrased
(D) vitiated
(E) invalidated

19. News of the attack on Pearl Harbor ______ the nation into action.
(A) startled
(B) compelled
(C) assuaged
(D) soothed
(E) galvanized

20. Now that I realize the extent of your ______, I feel that it will be impossible for me to trust you implicitly in the future.
(A) chicanery
(B) lapse
(C) ingenuousness
(D) inconsistency
(E) inclemency

Each passage below is followed by questions based on its content. Answer all questions following a passage on the basis of what is stated or implied in that passage.

The annual survey of chemistry published by the American Chemical Society attributes the vast change in warfare to the airplanes and, above all, to the motor fuels of today. We never think of gasoline as an explosive, yet it has to some extent taken the place of the artillery propellants of a quarter of a century ago. A bomber is hardly a gun, but it certainly performs the function of one, with a range of many hundred miles.

About fifteen years ago we began to hear of iso-octane, a fuel used to measure antiknock qualities of high-compression gasoline. It was ideal for airplanes, but quantity production was not practical. Now we make lakes of it. Its performance is so remarkable that the planes propelled by it can carry loads that would have been inconceivable only ten years ago. As a result, octane numbers and indexes of antiknock properties have lost much of their former significance. It will probably be necessary to adopt some new standard. If we relate size and weight of engine to octane number, a truer picture of what aviation fuels really are is obtained. For each pound of weight, aviation engines of today produce respectively 100 per cent and 50 per cent more power than could those of 1918 and 1930.

21. The title that best expresses the ideas of this selection is:
(A) The chemist speeds the airplane
(B) Mass production of iso-octane
(C) Improving the gasoline engine
(D) Changing methods in warfare
(E) Gasoline as an explosive

22. Per pound of weight, the average engine now produces
(A) very much iso-octane
(B) high compression
(C) twice as much power as in 1930
(D) double the power of 1918
(E) 100 per cent efficiency

23. The proposed standard for measuring the quality of motor fuels is the
(A) ratio of power to weight
(B) antiknock index
(C) iso-octane number
(D) load-carrying ability
(E) relation of engine weight and size to octane number

24. The writer suggests that gasoline may be considered an explosive because
(A) it produces high compression
(B) modern bombing planes are essentially long range guns
(C) guns now have greater range
(D) iso-octane is now manufactured in quantity
(E) it has replaced explosives in cannons

Escape of coffee aroma vapors and gases does not in itself impair the flavor of coffee, according to new researches reported in Industrial and Engineering Chemistry. Oxygen is the chief culprit in staling. Tests showed that roasted coffee is best preserved in tightly sealed vacuum cans. If oxygen is present the coffee deteriorates even though the sealing is tight. The tests were made with the aid of professional coffee tasters. Samples hermetically sealed in a vacuum remained fresh throughout the test period of forty-eight days. Coffee swept continuously for fifty-five days with dry nitrogen remained comparatively fresh and showed that the evolution of gas has no detectable effect on flavor.

25. The title that best expresses the ideas of this paragraph is:
(A) Methods of storing coffee
(B) The chemistry of coffee
(C) Deterioration of coffee
(D) Research in coffee
(E) Experiments in keeping coffee fresh

26. Coffee will retain its flavor best when
(A) oxygen is excluded
(B) it is kept in tightly sealed containers
(C) it is kept in a vacuum for more than 48 days
(D) the gases are not allowed to escape
(E) it is roasted

27. In a special experiment, coffee was kept fresh by means of
(A) oxygen
(B) nitrogen
(C) coffee gases
(D) airtight containers
(E) constant testing

Loveliest of trees, the cherry now
Is hung with bloom along the bough,
And stands about the woodland ride
Wearing white for Eastertide.

Now, of my threescore years and ten,
Twenty will not come again,
And take from seventy springs a score,
It only leaves me fifty more.

And since to look at things in bloom
Fifty springs are little room,
About the woodlands I will go
To see the cherry hung with snow.

28. How old was the poet when he wrote this poem?
(A) 20
(B) 40
(C) 50
(D) 70
(E) One cannot tell

29. Which of these words is used as a descriptive figure of speech rather than in its usual meaning?
(A) "snow" (last line)
(B) "twenty" (sixth line)
(C) "woodlands" (next to last line)
(D) "bloom" (second line)
(E) "bough" (second line)

30. What feeling does the poet express in this passage?
(A) Delight in beauty
(B) Religious faith
(C) Anticipation of death
(D) Enjoyment of old age
(E) Worship of nature

Select the word or set of words that best completes each of the following sentences.

31. Unlike the highly emotional poets of the previous century, the 18th century poets were _______ and interested in moralizing.
(A) lyrical
(B) distraught
(C) didactic
(D) strange
(E) warped

32. After three years in Paris, he was filled with _______ and longed for the familiar scenes of New York City.
(A) ennui
(B) chagrin
(C) nostalgia
(D) lethargy
(E) anxiety

33. Despite his obvious unwillingness, the promoters were still hopeful of _______ him into signing the contract.
(A) ensnaring
(B) influencing
(C) enjoining
(D) deluding
(E) inveigling

34. No hero of ancient or modern days can surpass the Indian with his lofty contempt of death and the _______ with which he sustains its cruelest affliction.
(A) distress
(B) fortitude
(C) guile
(D) grace
(E) reverence

35. Not only the _______ are fooled by propaganda; we can all be _______ if we are not wary.
(A) ignorant—distressed
(B) gullible—misled
(C) people—puzzled
(D) masses—scorned
(E) uncultured—cultivated

Each question below consists of a related pair of words or phrases, followed by five lettered pairs of words or phrases. Select the lettered pair that best expresses a relationship similar to that expressed in the original pair.

Example:

YAWN : BOREDOM :: (A) dream : sleep
(B) anger : madness (C) smile : amusement
(D) face : expression (E) impatience : rebellion

Ⓐ Ⓑ ● Ⓓ Ⓔ

36. JOURNALIST : TYPEWRITER ::
(A) surgeon : bones
(B) carpenter : lumber
(C) poet : beauty
(D) floorwalker : flower
(E) electrician : pliers

37. POET : ECLOGUE ::
(A) philosopher : nature
(B) dramatist : scenery
(C) sculptor : marble
(D) seamstress : gown
(E) teacher : truth

38. PORTENTOUS : OMINOUS ::
(A) heavy : threatening
(B) magnificent : treacherous
(C) significant : pertinent
(D) good : evil
(E) showy : serious

39. MURAL : WALL ::
(A) statue : courtyard
(B) painting : portrait
(C) lithograph : stone
(D) etching : paper
(E) water color : tempera

40. MUTTON : SHEEP ::
(A) veal : lamb
(B) pig : pork
(C) hide : steer
(D) beef : steer
(E) veal : cow

41. TETHER : HORSE ::
(A) feed : dog
(B) cage : tiger
(C) captive : animal
(D) lasso : calf
(E) manacle : prisoner

42. LIBRETTO : SCORE ::
(A) opera : game
(B) author : composer
(C) drama : opera
(D) painter : sculptor
(E) architect : blueprint

43. REVELATION : PROPHET ::
(A) awl : carpenter
(B) canvas : painter
(C) bust : sculptor
(D) guitar : singer
(E) wrench : plumber

44. ENTRY : DIARY ::
(A) sonnet : ballad
(B) paragraph : prose
(C) missive : epistle
(D) episode : serial
(E) book : leaf

45. VIRTUOSO : EXPERIENCED ::
(A) tyro : untried
(B) democrat : dictatorial
(C) saint : dissolute
(D) leader : deferential
(E) evildoer : repentant

S T O P

IF YOU FINISH BEFORE TIME IS CALLED, YOU MAY CHECK YOUR WORK ON THIS SECTION ONLY. DO NOT WORK ON ANY OTHER SECTION IN THE TEST.

SECTION 5 MATH ABILITY

35 QUESTIONS - 30 MINUTES

In this section solve each problem, using any available space on the page for scratchwork. Then decide which is the best of the choices given and blacken the corresponding space on the answer sheet.

The following information is for your reference in solving some of the problems.

Circle of radius r: Area $= \pi r^2$; Circumference $= 2\pi r$
The number of degrees of arc in a circle is 360.
The measure in degrees of a straight angle is 180.

Definitions of symbols:

$=$ is equal to	$\leq$ is less than or equal to
$\neq$ is unequal to	$\geq$ is greater than or equal to
$<$ is less than	$\parallel$ is parallel to
$>$ is greater than	$\perp$ is perpendicular to

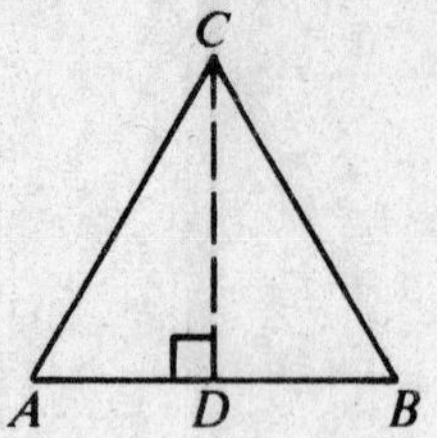

Triangle: The sum of the measures in degrees of the angles of a triangle is 180.

If $\angle CDA$ is a right angle, then

(1) area of $\triangle ABC = \frac{AB \times CD}{2}$

(2) $AC^2 = AD^2 + DC^2$

Note: Figures that accompany problems in this test are intended to provide information useful in solving the problems. They are drawn as accurately as possible EXCEPT when it is stated in a specific problem that its figure is not drawn to scale. All figures lie in a plane unless otherwise indicated. All numbers used are real numbers.

1. How many thirds are there in $\frac{5}{8}$?
   (A) $\frac{5}{24}$
   (B) $\frac{15}{8}$
   (C) $\frac{8}{15}$
   (D) $4\frac{1}{5}$
   (E) 15

2. $3 + \frac{3}{0.3} = ?$
   (A) 3.1
   (B) 3.9
   (C) 4
   (D) 4.11
   (E) 13

3. $\frac{(18)(24)}{(12)(16)} \div \frac{(18)}{(16)} = ?$
   (A) $\frac{1}{2}$
   (B) 2
   (C) $\frac{81}{32}$
   (D) $\frac{9}{4}$
   (E) 4

4. $\frac{?}{32} = 0.625$
   (A) 16
   (B) 20
   (C) 22
   (D) 24
   (E) 26

5. $\frac{1}{1-p} \div \frac{1}{p-1} = ?$
   (A) 0
   (B) -1
   (C) 1
   (D) p
   (E) $-p$

6. $\frac{2.6z}{6} = 65$

   $z = ?$
   (A) 15
   (B) 28.16
   (C) 30
   (D) 60
   (E) 150

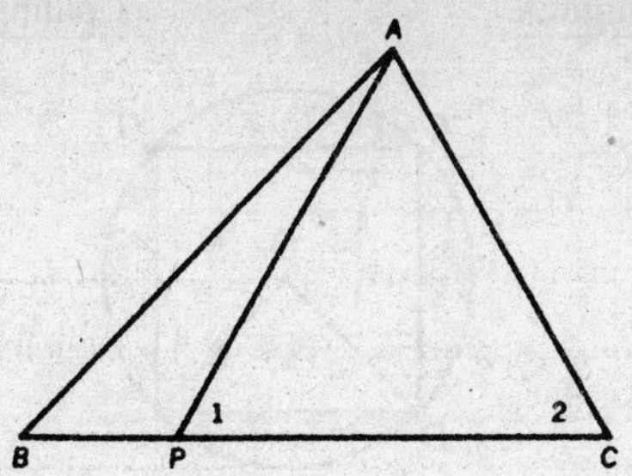

7. In the figure above, triangle ABC, AP is drawn so that $\angle 1 = \angle 2$. Which of the following is true if $AB > AC$?
(A) $AP > AB$
(B) $AP = AB$
(C) $BC < PC$
(D) $AP + AC < AB$
(E) $AP < AB$

Questions 8–27 each consist of two quantities, one in Column A and one in Column B. You are to compare the two quantities and on the answer sheet blacken space

A if the quantity in Column A is greater;
B if the quantity in Column B is greater;
C if the two quantities are equal;
D If the relationship cannot be determined from the information given.

AN E RESPONSE WILL NOT BE SCORED.

EXAMPLES

	Column A	Column B	Answers
E1.	2×6	$2 + 6$	● Ⓑ Ⓒ Ⓓ Ⓔ
E2.	$180 - x$	y	Ⓐ Ⓑ ● Ⓓ Ⓔ
E3.	$p - q$	$q - p$	Ⓐ Ⓑ Ⓒ ● Ⓔ

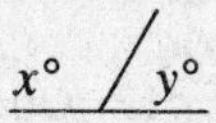

Notes:
1. In certain questions, information concerning one or both of the quantities to be compared is centered above the two columns.
2. In a given question, a symbol that appears in both columns represents the same thing in Column A as it does in Column B.
3. Letters such as x, n, and k stand for real numbers.

	Column A	Column B
8.	$\dfrac{\frac{1}{4} - \frac{3}{16}}{\frac{1}{8}}$	2
9.	$\dfrac{\text{3 yards, 1 foot, 3 inches}}{3}$	40 inches

$x^n = 1$
$n > 0$

	Column A	Column B
10.	x	1
11.	a^6	$6a^5$

$0 < x < 99$
x is divisible by 2, 5, 8

	Column A	Column B
12.	x	40

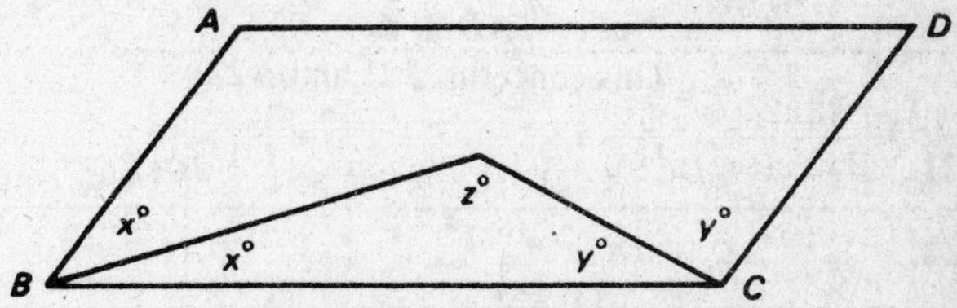

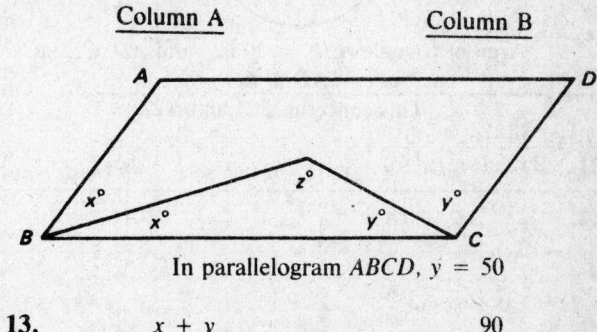

In parallelogram $ABCD$, $y = 50$

	Column A	Column B
13.	$x + y$	90

In triangle, ABC, the measure of angle A is greater than the measure of angle B, and angle C has a measure of 60°

	Column A	Column B
14.	Length of side AC	Length of side AB

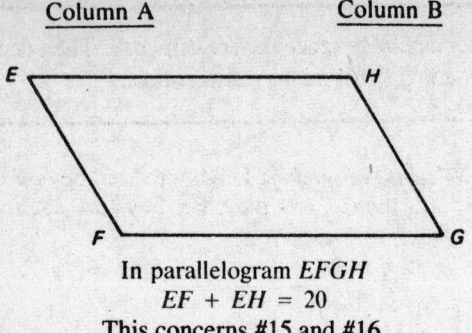

In parallelogram *EFGH*
$EF + EH = 20$
This concerns #15 and #16

	Column A	Column B
15.	$HG + FG$	$\frac{1}{2}$ perimeter of *EFGH*
16.	Length of *EH*	Length of *HG*

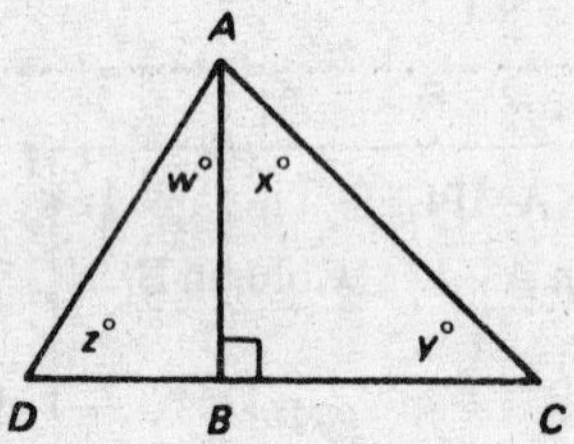

$AB = BC$
$AB \perp DC$
This concerns #17–#20

	Column A	Column B
17.	y	z
18.	x	y
19.	$w + z$	$x + y$
20.	w	z

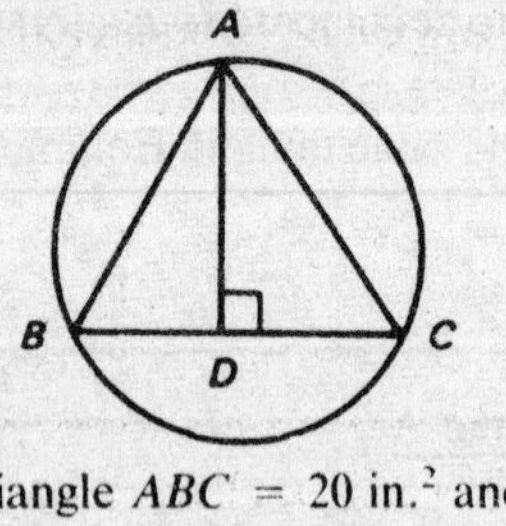

Area of triangle $ABC = 20$ in.^{2} and $AD = 5$ in.
$AD \perp BC$
This concerns #21 and #22

	Column A	Column B
21.	DC	BD
22.	$AD + DC$	AC

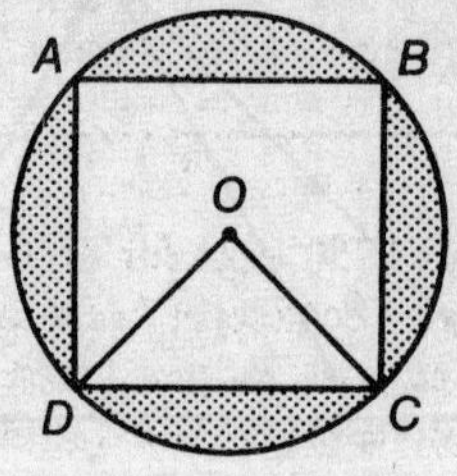

Square *ABCD* is inscribed in circle *O*.
Area of triangle *OCD* is 8 units. ($\sqrt{2} = 1.4$)
This concerns #23 and #24

	Column A	Column B
23.	22	Perimeter of *ABCD*
24.	Area of shaded portion	$16\pi - 32$

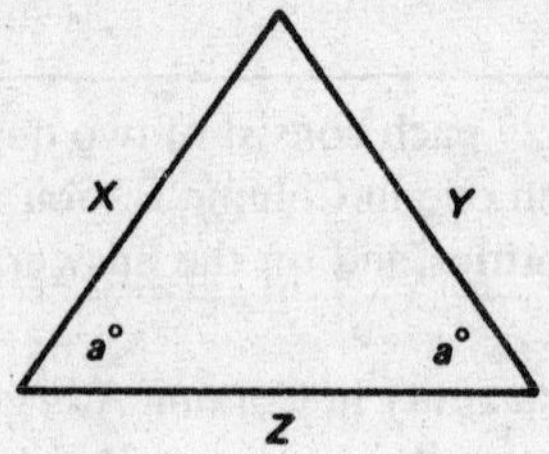

	Column A	Column B
25.	$\left(\frac{X}{Z}\right)\left(\frac{Z}{Y}\right)$	0

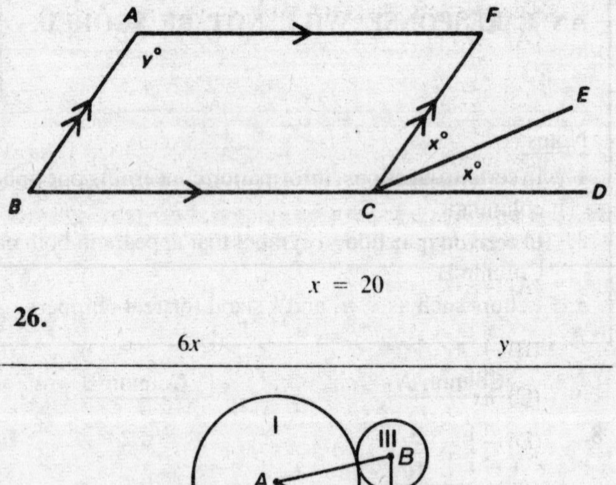

$x = 20$

	Column A	Column B
26.	$6x$	y

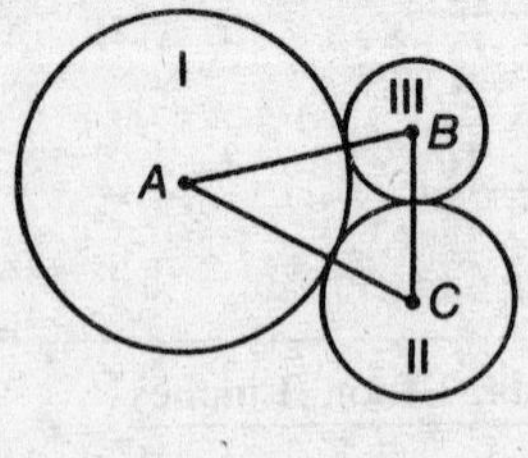

A, *B*, and *C* are centers of circles I, II, and III respectively
Area of circle I $= 25\pi$, Area of circle II $= 16\pi$,
Area of circle III $= 9\pi$

	Column A	Column B
27.	Perimeter of triangle *ABC*	12

Solve each of the remaining problems in this section using any available space for scratchwork. Then decide which is the best of the choices given and blacken the corresponding space on the answer sheet.

28. A man buys 2750 eggs for \$100.00, and loses 350 of these eggs because of breakage. If he sells the remaining eggs at 70¢ per dozen, what per cent of his original investment is his profit?
(A) 14
(B) 20
(C) 40
(D) 45
(E) 50

29. A broad jumper makes an average standing jump of eight feet. In how many jumps will he cover y yards?
(A) $\frac{y}{8}$
(B) $\frac{3y}{8}$
(C) $8y$
(D) $\frac{8y}{3}$
(E) $24y$

30. Of a man's salary, $\frac{1}{10}$ is spent for clothing, $\frac{1}{3}$ for food and $\frac{1}{5}$ for rent. What per cent of the salary is left for other expenditures and savings?
(A) $36\frac{2}{3}$
(B) $37\frac{2}{3}$
(C) $42\frac{1}{3}$
(D) $46\frac{2}{3}$
(E) $63\frac{1}{3}$

31. If a pipe fills a cistern in h hours, how much of the cistern does it fill in one hour?
(A) $\frac{1}{h}$
(B) $\frac{x}{h}$
(C) hx
(D) $\frac{h}{x}$
(E) h

32. What is the average height of three boys if one boy is x inches, and the other boys are each y inches tall?
(A) $x + 2y$
(B) $\frac{x + y}{3}$
(C) $\frac{x + 2y}{3}$
(D) $\frac{x + 3y}{3}$
(E) $\frac{2y - x}{3}$

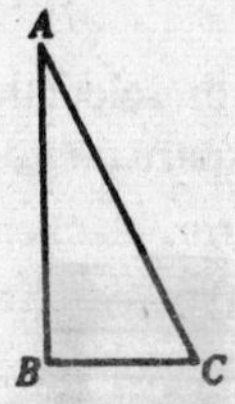

33. In the figure above, BC equals one half of AB. The area of right triangle ABC equals 64 square feet. Find hypotenuse AC to the nearest foot
(A) 12
(B) 14
(C) 18
(D) 24
(E) 32

34. A certain grade of eggs has a weight of 24 to 26 ounces per dozen. What is the minimum weight (in ounces) of 69 such eggs?
(A) 115
(B) 137
(C) 138
(D) 139
(E) 140

35. The center of a basketball team is 6'3". the two guards are each 6'. One forward is 5'10" and the other is 5'11". What is the average height of the basketball team?
(A) 5.2'
(B) 5.56'
(C) 5.6'
(D) 6'
(E) 6.2'

S T O P

IF YOU FINISH BEFORE TIME IS CALLED, YOU MAY CHECK YOUR WORK ON THIS SECTION ONLY. DO NOT WORK ON ANY OTHER SECTION IN THE TEST.

SECTION 6 TEST OF STANDARD WRITTEN ENGLISH

50 QUESTIONS - 30 MINUTES

The questions in this section measure skills that are important to writing well. In particular, they test your ability to recognize and use language that is clear, effective, and correct according to the requirements of standard written English, the kind of English found in most college textbooks.

Directions: The following sentences contain problems in grammar, usage, diction (choice of words), and idiom.

Some sentences are correct.

No sentence contains more than one error.

You will find that the error, if there is one, is underlined and lettered. Assume that elements of the sentence that are not underlined are correct and cannot be changed. In choosing answers, follow the requirements of standard written English.

If there is an error, select the one underlined part that must be changed to make the sentence correct and blacken the corresponding space on your answer sheet.

If there is no error, blacken answer space Ⓔ.

EXAMPLE:

The region has a climate so severe that (A) plants growing there (B) rarely had been (C) more than twelve inches high (D). No error (E)

SAMPLE ANSWER

Ⓐ Ⓑ ● Ⓓ Ⓔ

1. She finds talking to her friends on the telephone (A) a pleasure (B) and to write (C) letters an inconvenience. (D) No error (E)

2. The ad stated (A) that a piano was needed (B) for the school play (C) in good condition. (D) No error (E)

3. The fishing fleet (A) left (B) the harbor when the fishermen heard that a school of bluefish were (C) near (D) the wreck. No error (E)

4. While transacting (A) business in Paris, the American (B) ambassador (C) was very helpful. (D) No error (E)

5. A minority group comprising (A) 30% of the community and (B) represented by only (C) one member (D) out of 25 on the City Council. No error (E)

6. The azaleas in my (A) neighbor's (B) garden are (C) so (D) colorful. No error (E)

7. Among (A) George, Henry, and I, (B) there (C) can be no (D) secrets. No error (E)

8. Neither (A) the reporters nor (B) the editor were (C) satisfied with the salary offer made by (D) the publisher. No error (E)

9. The workers (A) who (B) I see in the subway every (C) afternoon seem tired and dejected. (D) No error (E)

10. The article was rejected (A) because of its length, verbosity, (B) and because it presented (C) only (D) one point of view. No error (E)

11. Mr. Jones's decision to retire came as a shock to
A B C D
all who respected his ability. No error
E

12. When she spoke with the police, she reported her
loss; she stated that a large quantity of clothing
A B
and valuable books were missing. No error
C D E

13. I only bought what was necessary. I was not
A B C
extravagant. No error
D E

14. Bailing vigorously, we managed to remain afloat
A B C D
until we were rescued by the Coast Guard.
No error
E

15. We had ought to finish our trip before dark because
A B
it gets very cold after the sun goes down.
C D
No error
E

16. Does that remark infer that you are displeased with
A B C
the way I am managing the business? No error
D E

17. I am sure that he has been here and did what was
A B C D
expected of him. No error
E

18. Because of its efficacy in treating many ailments
A
and because it has brought about miraculous
B
cures, penicillin has become an important
C
addition to the druggist's stock. No error
D E

19. Would I were able to go with you! No error
A B C D E

20. It is not you who are at fault; rather, it is I who is
A B C D
to blame. No error
E

21. I cannot force myself to like that kind of a person
A B C
because his smugness repels me. No error
D E

22. You should take your umbrella when you go out
A B
because it is liable to rain this afternoon.
C D
No error
E

23. The ideal that Arthur and his knights were in quest
A B
of were a better world order. No error
C D E

24. Please notify all those whom you think should have
A B C D
this information. No error
E

25. I believe that story about the fight because he
A B
himself has told us the story was true. No error
C D E

Directions: In each of the following sentences, some part or all of the sentence is underlined. Below each sentence you will find five ways of phrasing the underlined part. Select the answer that produces the most effective sentence, one that is clear and exact, without awkwardness or ambiguity, and blacken the corresponding space on your answer sheet. In choosing answers, follow the requirements of standard written English. Choose the answer that best expresses the meaning of the original sentence.

Answer (A) is always the same as the underlined part. Choose answer (A) if you think the original sentence needs no revision.

EXAMPLE:

Laura Ingalls Wilder published her first book and she was sixty-five years old then.

(A) and she was sixty-five years old then
(B) when she was sixty-five years old
(C) at age sixty-five years old
(D) upon reaching sixty-five years
(E) at the time when she was sixty-five

SAMPLE ANSWER

Ⓐ ● Ⓒ Ⓓ Ⓔ

26. In the normal course of events, John will graduate high school and enter college in two years.
(A) John will graduate high school and enter
(B) John will graduate from High School and enter
(C) John will be graduated from High School and enter
(D) John will be graduated from high school and enter
(E) John will have graduated from high school and enter

27. The teacher asked, "Have you read 'What makes Sammy Run'?"
(A) "Have you read 'What makes Sammy Run'?"
(B) "Have you read 'What makes Sammy Run?'"
(C) "Have you read 'What Makes Sammy Run'?"
(D) "Have you read 'What Makes Sammy Run?'"
(E) "Have you read What Makes Sammy Run?"

28. With the exception of Frank and I, everyone in the class finished the assignment before the bell rang.
(A) Frank and I, everyone in the class finished
(B) Frank and me, everyone in the class finished
(C) Frank and me, everyone in the class had finished
(D) Frank and I, everyone in the class had finished
(E) Frank and me everyone in the class finished

29. Many middle class individuals find that they cannot obtain good medical attention, despite they need it badly.
(A) despite they need it badly.
(B) despite their bad need of it.
(C) in spite of they need it badly.
(D) however much they need it.
(E) therefore, they need it badly.

30. During the winter of 1973, Americans discovered the need to conserve energy and attempts were made to meet the crisis.
(A) discovered the need to conserve energy and attempts were made to meet the crisis.
(B) discovered the need to conserve energy and that the crisis had to be met.
(C) discovered the need to conserve energy and to meet the crisis.
(D) needed to conserve energy and to meet the crisis.
(E) needed to conserve energy and attempts were made to meet the crisis.

31. When one eats in this restaurant, you often find that the prices are high and that the food is poorly prepared.
(A) When one eats in this restaurant, you often find
(B) When you eat in this restaurant, one often finds
(C) As you eat in this restaurant, you often find
(D) If you eat in this restaurant, you often find
(E) When one ate in this restaurant, he often found

32. Ever since the bombing of Cambodia, there has been much opposition from they who maintain that it was an unauthorized war.
(A) from they who maintain that it was an unauthorized war.
(B) from they who maintain that it had been an unauthorized war.
(C) from those who maintain that it was unauthorized.
(D) from they maintaining that it was unauthorized.
(E) from they maintaining that it had been unauthorized.

33. John was imminently qualified for the position because he had studied computer programming and how to operate an IBM machine.
(A) imminently qualified for the position because he had studied computer programming and how to operate an IBM machine.
(B) imminently qualified for the position because he had studied computer programming and the operation of an IBM machine.
(C) eminently qualified for the position because he had studied computer programming and how to operate an IBM machine.
(D) eminently qualified because he had studied computer programming and the operation of an IBM machine.
(E) eminently qualified because he had studied computer programming and how to operate an IBM machine.

34. I am not to eager to go to this play because it did not get good reviews.
(A) I am not to eager to go to this play because it did not get good reviews.
(B) Because of its poor reviews, I am not to eager to go to this play.
(C) Because of its poor revues, I am not to eager to go to this play.
(D) I am not to eager to go to this play because the critics did not give it good reviews.
(E) I am not too eager to go to this play because of its poor reviews.

35. "I am not going to the reception honoring him," the senator said, "everyone knows I do not support his point of view."
(A) honoring him," the senator said, "everyone knows I do not support his point of view."
(B) honoring him," the senator said. "Everyone knows I do not support his point of view."
(C) in his honor" the senator said. "Everyone knows I do not support his point of view".
(D) honoring him." the senator said. "everyone knows I do not support his point of view.
(E) "honoring him," the senator said. "Everyone knows I do not support his point of view."

36. The form of terrorism that makes diplomats its target reached Sweden in 1975, the West German embassy in Stockholm was seized by Germans linked to the Baader-Meinhof gang.
(A) 1975, the West German embassy in Stockholm was seized
(B) 1975, and the West German embassy in Stockholm was seized
(C) 1975, despite the West German embassy in Stockholm was seized
(D) 1975, when the West German embassy in Stockholm was seized
(E) 1975, the West German embassy in Stockholm's being seized

37. It would have been wrong, even had it been possible, to force a parliamentary democracy down the throat of the Iranians.
(A) wrong, even had it been possible,
(B) wrong; even had it been possible,
(C) wrong, it had been even possible,
(D) wrong, even if possible it had been,
(E) wrong: even if it had been possible,

38. The number of California condors, decimated by increasing human intrusions into traditional condor breeding grounds, are currently given as fewer than thirty.
(A) are currently given as fewer than thirty
(B) currently are given as fewer than thirty
(C) is currently given as fewer than thirty
(D) were given currently as fewer than thirty
(E) are currently going to be given as fewer than thirty

39. Many economists maintain that the current low interest rates not only promote investment in the stock market but also made it more profitable.
(A) but also made it more profitable
(B) but also makes it more profitable
(C) but also made it more able to profit
(D) but made it also more profitable
(E) but also make it more profitable

40. The giving of foreign aid is a tool of national policy, the hoped-for return is often indirect and long term.
(A) policy, the hoped-for return is often indirect and long term
(B) policy, however the hoped-for return is often indirect and long term
(C) policy, though the hoped-for return is often indirect and long term
(D) policy; albeit the hoped-for return is often indirect and long term
(E) policy; despite the hoped-for return is often indirect and long term

<u>Note:</u> The remaining questions are like those at the beginning of the section.

<u>Directions:</u> For each sentence in which you find an error, select the one underlined part that must be changed to make the sentence correct and blacken the corresonding space on your answer sheet.

If there is no error, blacken answer space Ⓔ.

EXAMPLE:

The region has a climate <u>so severe that</u> (A) plants <u>growing there</u> (B) rarely <u>had been</u> (C) more than twelve inches <u>high.</u> (D) <u>No error</u> (E)

SAMPLE ANSWER

Ⓐ Ⓑ ● Ⓓ Ⓔ

41. He <u>can't hardly</u> (A) do <u>anything</u> (B) with his right hand <u>ever</u> (C) since he <u>had</u> (D) his stroke. <u>No error</u> (E)

42. <u>Although</u> (A) many people complain about his attitude, <u>it</u> (B) <u>seems</u> (C) perfectly <u>alright</u> (D) to me. <u>No error</u> (E)

43. This <u>compact</u> (A) car which I <u>rented</u> (B) gives a different <u>kind of ride</u> (C) <u>than</u> (D) the heavier car I drive in the city. <u>No error</u> (E)

44. You will be <u>amazed</u> (A) at the great <u>amount</u> (B) of <u>people</u> (C) who will support you <u>as soon as</u> (D) they learn the facts in this case. <u>No error</u> (E)

45. <u>In</u> (A) the tennis match Don <u>was paired</u> (B) with <u>Bill;</u> (C) <u>Ed.</u> (D) with Al. <u>No error</u> (E)

46. The ship had <u>almost</u> (A) completely <u>sank</u> (B) <u>by the time</u> (C) the rescuers <u>arrived</u> (D) on the scene. <u>No error</u> (E)

47. <u>Since</u> (A) you do not participate in <u>any</u> (B) of the class activities, I must <u>conclude</u> (C) that you are <u>disinterested.</u> (D) <u>No error</u> (E)

48. He was <u>very</u> (A) <u>mad</u> (B) when he heard the rumors about his <u>daughter's</u> (C) behavior at the <u>school</u> (D) dance. <u>No error</u> (E)

49. <u>Turning</u> (A) the pages <u>rapidly</u> (B) does not <u>guarantee</u> (C) <u>rapid</u> (D) comprehension. <u>No error</u> (E)

50. <u>If</u> (A) he <u>had kept</u> (B) his eyes <u>open,</u> (C) he <u>would not have fallen</u> (D) into that trap. <u>No error</u> (E)

S T O P

IF YOU FINISH BEFORE TIME IS CALLED, YOU MAY CHECK YOUR WORK ON THIS SECTION ONLY. DO NOT WORK ON ANY OTHER SECTION IN THE TEST.

ANSWER KEY

Note: The answers to the math sections are keyed to the corresponding review areas in Chapter 11. The numbers in parentheses after each answer refer to topics as listed below. (Note that to review for number 16, Quantitative Comparison, study Chapter 10.)

1. Fundamental Operations
2. Algebraic Operations
3. Using Algebra
4. Roots and Radicals
5. Inequalities
6. Fractions
7. Decimals
8. Percent
9. Averages
10. Motion
11. Ratio and Proportion
12. Mixtures and Solutions
13. Work
14. Coordinate Geometry
15. Geometry
16. Quantitative Comparison
17. Data Interpretation

SECTION 1 MATH

1.	**B (2)**	8.	**A (1,16)**	15.	**C (15,16)**	22.	**A (2,16)**	29.	**A (9)**
2.	**D (8)**	9.	**C (4,16)**	16.	**C (15,16)**	23.	**C (2,16)**	30.	**B (15)**
3.	**B (10)**	10.	**A (8,16)**	17.	**C (15,16)**	24.	**A (2,16)**	31.	**C (11)**
4.	**E (1,6)**	11.	**C (1,6,16)**	18.	**A (2,16)**	25.	**C (15,16)**	32.	**A (2,4)**
5.	**B (6)**	12.	**C (2,16)**	19.	**B (2,16)**	26.	**B (2,16)**	33.	**C (1)**
6.	**D (11,13)**	13.	**B (15,16)**	20.	**D (15,16)**	27.	**D (15,16)**	34.	**B (5,15)**
7.	**B (15)**	14.	**B (15,16)**	21.	**A (2,16)**	28.	**B (15)**	35.	**A (15)**

SECTION 2 VERBAL

1.	**A**	9.	**B**	17.	**C**	25.	**A**	33.	**E**
2.	**A**	10.	**D**	18.	**D**	26.	**A**	34.	**E**
3.	**D**	11.	**C**	19.	**A**	27.	**A**	35.	**A**
4.	**D**	12.	**B**	20.	**D**	28.	**D**	36.	**B**
5.	**D**	13.	**D**	21.	**B**	29.	**C**	37.	**B**
6.	**C**	14.	**B**	22.	**C**	30.	**C**	38.	**D**
7.	**D**	15.	**E**	23.	**E**	31.	**D**	39.	**D**
8.	**A**	16.	**E**	24.	**B**	32.	**D**	40.	**B**

SECTION 3 MATH

1.	**B (6)**	6.	**C (11)**	11.	**A (2)**	16.	**E (15)**	21.	**D (15)**
2.	**C (1,11)**	7.	**E (2,4)**	12.	**E (3)**	17.	**E (9)**	22.	**A (10)**
3.	**D (10,11)**	8.	**B (3,11)**	13.	**D (10)**	18.	**C (2,4)**	23.	**D (14)**
4.	**A (1,6)**	9.	**D (11)**	14.	**B (11)**	19.	**C (17)**	24.	**B (14)**
5.	**E (1)**	10.	**E (2,4)**	15.	**C (15)**	20.	**B (15)**	25.	**B (14)**

SECTION 4 VERBAL

1.	**D**	10.	**B**	19.	**E**	28.	**A**	37.	**D**
2.	**E**	11.	**B**	20.	**A**	29.	**A**	38.	**C**
3.	**B**	12.	**E**	21.	**A**	30.	**A**	39.	**D**
4.	**B**	13.	**C**	22.	**D**	31.	**C**	40.	**D**
5.	**D**	14.	**A**	23.	**E**	32.	**C**	41.	**E**
6.	**A**	15.	**A**	24.	**B**	33.	**E**	42.	**B**
7.	**C**	16.	**C**	25.	**E**	34.	**B**	43.	**C**
8.	**A**	17.	**D**	26.	**A**	35.	**B**	44.	**D**
9.	**D**	18.	**A**	27.	**B**	36.	**E**	45.	**A**

SECTION 5 MATH

1. **B (6)**	8. **B (6,16)**	15. **C (15,16)**	22. **A (15,16)**	29. **B (11)**
2. **E (6,7)**	9. **A (1,16)**	16. **D (15,16)**	23. **B (15,16)**	30. **A (6,8)**
3. **B (1,6)**	10. **D (4,16)**	17. **D (15,16)**	24. **C (15,16)**	31. **A (11,13)**
4. **B (6,7)**	11. **D (4,16)**	18. **C (15,16)**	25. **A (15,16)**	32. **C (9)**
5. **B (2)**	12. **D (5,16)**	19. **C (15,16)**	26. **B (15,16)**	33. **C (15)**
6. **E (1,8)**	13. **C (15,16)**	20. **D (15,16)**	27. **A (15,16)**	34. **C (1)**
7. **E (5,15)**	14. **B (15,16)**	21. **D (15,16)**	28. **C (1,8)**	35. **D (9)**

SECTION 6 TEST OF STANDARD WRITTEN ENGLISH

1. **C**	11. **E**	21. **C**	31. **C**	41. **A**
2. **D**	12. **D**	22. **C**	32. **C**	42. **D**
3. **C**	13. **A**	23. **C**	33. **D**	43. **D**
4. **A**	14. **E**	24. **C**	34. **E**	44. **B**
5. **B**	15. **A**	25. **E**	35. **B**	45. **E**
6. **D**	16. **B**	26. **D**	36. **D**	46. **B**
7. **B**	17. **C**	27. **C**	37. **A**	47. **D**
8. **C**	18. **B**	28. **C**	38. **C**	48. **B**
9. **B**	19. **E**	29. **D**	39. **E**	49. **E**
10. **C**	20. **D**	30. **C**	40. **C**	50. **E**

SELF-EVALUATION

The model SAT test you have just completed has the same format as the actual SAT. As you take more of the model tests in this chapter, you will lose any SAT "stage fright" you might have.

Use the steps that follow to evaluate your performance on Model SAT Test 4. (Note: You'll find the charts referred to in steps 1–5 on the next three pages.)

STEP 1 Use the Answer Key to check your answers for each section.

STEP 2 For each section, count the number of correct and incorrect answers (remember that you don't count omitted answers), and enter the numbers on the appropriate lines of the chart "Obtaining Your Raw Score." Then do the indicated calculations to get your Raw Verbal Score, your Raw TSWE Score, and your Raw Math Score.

STEP 3 Consult the chart "Evaluate Your Performance" to see how well you did.

STEP 4 To pinpoint the specific areas in which you need to improve, circle the numbers of the questions that you either left blank or got wrong on the "Identify Your Weaknesses" charts. This will tell you where to concentrate your efforts to get the most out of your study time. The chart for the math sections gives you page references for review and practice by skill areas. The charts for the verbal and TSWE sections refer you to the appropriate chapters to study for each question type.

STEP 5 Do the review and practice indicated on the charts wherever you had a concentration of circles.

Remember that in addition to evaluating your scores, you should read all of the answer explanations for questions you answered incorrectly, questions you omitted, and questions you answered correctly but found difficult. Reviewing the answer explanations will help you understand concepts and strategies, and may point out shortcuts.

OBTAINING YOUR RAW SCORE

Verbal

Section 2 ______________ − 1/4 (______________) = ______________ (A)
number correct number incorrect

Section 4 ______________ − 1/4 (______________) = ______________ (B)
number correct number incorrect

Raw Verbal Score = (A) + (B) = ______________

TSWE

Section 6 ______________ − 1/4 (______________) = Raw TSWE Score = ______________
number correct number incorrect

Math

Section 1 (1-7, 28-35) ______________ − 1/4 (______________) = ______________ (C)
number correct number incorrect

Section 1 (8-27) ______________ − 1/3 (______________) = ______________ (D)
number correct number incorrect

Section 3 ______________ − 1/4 (______________) = ______________ (E)
number correct number incorrect

Section 5 (1-7, 28-35) ______________ − 1/4 (______________) = ______________ (F)
number correct number incorrect

Section 5 (8-27) ______________ − 1/3 (______________) = ______________ (G)
number correct number incorrect

Raw Math Score = (C) + (D) + (E) + (F) + (G) = ______________

EVALUATE YOUR PERFORMANCE

	Verbal	TSWE	Math
Excellent	75-85	45-50	80-95
Very Good	65-74	39-44	70-79
Good	50-64	34-38	60-69
Average	40-49	25-33	50-59
Below Average	28-39	15-24	40-49
Unsatisfactory	below 28	below 15	below 40

IDENTIFY YOUR WEAKNESSES
Verbal

Question Type	Question Numbers		Chapter to Study
	Section 2	Section 4	
Antonym	1, 2, 3, 4, 5, 6, 7, 8, 9, 10	1, 2, 3, 4, 5, 6, 7, 8, 9, 10, 11, 12, 13, 14, 15	Chapter 4
Analogy	16, 17, 18, 19, 20, 21, 22, 23, 24, 25	36, 37, 38, 39, 40, 41, 42, 43, 44, 45	Chapter 5
Sentence Completion	11, 12, 13, 14, 15	16, 17, 18, 19, 20, 31, 32, 33, 34, 35	Chapter 6
Reading Comprehension	26, 27, 28, 29, 30, 31, 32, 33, 34, 35, 36, 37, 38, 39, 40	21, 22, 23, 24, 25, 26, 27, 28, 29, 30	Chapter 7

TSWE

Question Type	Question Numbers	Chapter to Study
Usage	1, 2, 3, 4, 5, 6, 7, 8, 9, 10, 11, 12, 13, 14, 15, 16, 17, 18, 19, 20, 21, 22, 23, 24, 25, 41, 42, 43, 44, 45, 46, 47, 48, 49, 50	Chapter 12
Sentence Correction	26, 27, 28, 29, 30, 31, 32, 33, 34, 35, 36, 37, 38, 39, 40	Chapter 12

Math

Skill Area	Question Numbers			Pages to Study
	Section 1	Section 3	Section 5	
Fundamental Operations	4, 8, 11, 33	2, 4, 5, 19	3, 6, 9, 28, 34	300–302
Algebraic Operations	1, 12, 18, 19, 21, 22, 23, 24, 26, 32	7, 10, 11, 18	5	302–308
Using Algebra		8, 12		308–316
Fractions	4, 5, 11	1, 4	1, 2, 3, 4, 8, 30	316–329
Decimals and Percents	2, 10		2, 4, 6, 28, 30	329–334
Verbal Problems	3, 6, 29	3, 13, 17, 22	32, 35	335–352
Ratio and Proportion	6, 31	2, 3, 6, 8, 9, 14	29, 31	340–346
Geometry	7, 13, 14, 15, 16, 17, 20, 25, 27, 28, 30, 34	15, 16, 20, 21	7, 13, 14, 15, 16, 17, 18, 19, 20, 21, 22, 23, 24, 25, 26, 27, 33	355–368
Coordinate Geometry		23, 24, 25		352–355
Inequalities	34		7,12	309–311; 315–316
Quantitative Comparison	8, 9, 10, 11, 12, 13, 14, 15, 16, 17, 18, 19, 20, 21, 22, 23, 24, 25, 26, 27		8, 9, 10, 11, 12, 13, 14, 15, 16, 17, 18, 19, 20, 21, 22, 23, 24, 25, 26, 27	279–299
Roots and Radicals	9, 32	7, 10, 18	10, 11	306–307; 312–313

ANSWER EXPLANATIONS

SECTION 1

1. B. $r = \frac{rs}{1 - s}$

$rs = r(1 - s)$ [multiplied by $(1 - s)$]
$s = 1 - s$ (divide by r)
$2s = 1$ (add s)
$s = \frac{1}{2}$ (divide by 2)

Substitute $s = \frac{1}{2}$
$s^2 + 2s + 1 = ?$
$\left(\frac{1}{2}\right)^2 + (2)\left(\frac{1}{2}\right) + 1 = ?.$
$\frac{1}{4} + 1 + 1 = 2\frac{1}{4}$

2. D. Profit = 20% of \$30.00 (Cost) or \$6.00
Selling Price = \$36.00
Tag Price − Discount = Selling Price
Let x = Tag Price (in dollars)
$x - 10\%\ x = \$36.00$
$x - .1x = \$36.00$
$10x - 1x = 360$ (multiply by 10)
$9x = 360$
$x = \$40$

3. B. Time equals 10 minutes or $\frac{1}{6}$ hour
Distance equals 40 miles

Average rate = $\frac{\text{Distance}}{\text{Time}}$

Average rate = $\frac{40 \text{ miles}}{\frac{1}{6}\text{ hour}}$ or 240 miles per hour

4. E. The typist worked for 20 minutes or $\frac{1}{3}$ hour

$\frac{1 \text{ (or the complete task)}}{3 \text{ hours}} = \frac{\text{Part of task done}}{\frac{1}{3}\text{ hour}}$

Let x = part of task done

$\frac{1}{3} = \frac{x}{\frac{1}{3}}$

$3x = \frac{1}{3}$

$x = \frac{1}{9}$ (divide by 3)

5. B. $\frac{\text{2 pennies + 2 nickels + one dime}}{\text{1 quarter}} = \frac{22¢}{25¢} = \frac{22}{25}$

6. D. Let x = number of sets of books the man binds in one day

$\frac{s \text{ sets}}{d \text{ days}} = \frac{x \text{ sets}}{1 \text{ day}}$

$dx = s$

$x = \frac{s}{d}$

Since there are b books in one set, there are $(b)\left(\frac{s}{d}\right)$ or $\frac{bs}{d}$ books in $\frac{s}{d}$ sets

7. B. $\frac{\text{Distance covered by moving wheel}}{\text{Circumference}} =$ Number of revolutions made

Since radius equals f feet,
Circumference = 2π radius or $2\pi f$

$\frac{5280 \text{ feet}}{2\pi f \text{ feet}}$ or $\frac{2640}{\pi f}$ feet

8. A. $\frac{1}{7} = 0.142+$ $\qquad 0.142 > 0.0142$

9. C. $\sqrt{\frac{1}{0.25}} = \sqrt{\frac{100}{25}} = \sqrt{4} = 2$

10. A. 5% of 500 = 25

11. C. Between 2:55 and 3:15, 20 minutes (or $\frac{1}{3}$ of an hour) elapse.

12. C. Since 15 is common to both columns, consider only $\frac{16}{x} = 4$. Since $4x = 16$, $x = 4$.

13. B. Since the area = 25, each side = 5
The sum of three sides of the square = 15.

14. B. $\frac{x^2}{2} = 18$
$x^2 = 36$
$x = 6$
Therefore $AC = 6\sqrt{2}$
$6\sqrt{2} > 6$

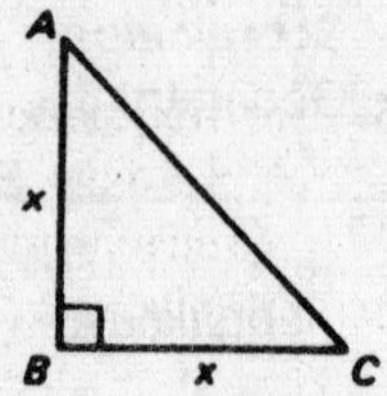

15. C. $AB = 6$
Perimeter = 24

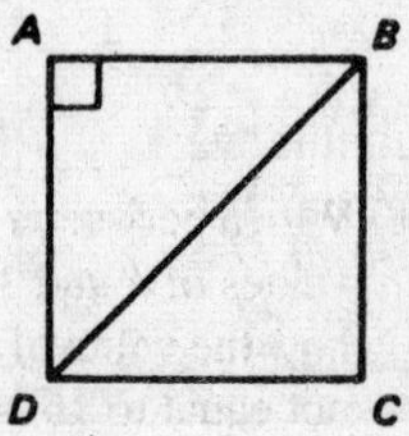

16. C. Area $= \frac{1}{2}(6)(6) = 18$

17. C. $AB = BC$ (given)
Since the measure of angle B equals the measure of angle C, $AB = AC$. Therefore ABC is equilateral and $m\angle A = m\angle B = m\angle C$ and $m\angle B + m\angle C = m\angle B + m\angle A$

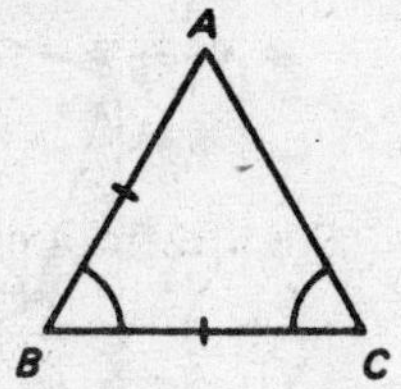

18. A. $36 - 8 = 7x$
$28 = 7x$
$4 = x$
7 is greater than 4.

19. B. Multiply both by 8. Column A $= z + 6$ and column B $= 2z + 6$
$2z > z$, since z is positive.
Therefore $2z + 6 > z + 6$

20. D. We may not assume that ABC is a right triangle. If it were a right triangle, and if we assumed that side AC is the hypotenuse, then the area of ABC $= \frac{1}{2}(5)(8)$ or 20.

21. A. $5x = 2y = AC$ and $2y > \frac{2}{5}y$.

22. A. $3a = 36$ (Cross multiply)
$6a = 72$
$6a > 36$

23. C. Remove parentheses: $x(y + z) = xy + xz$.
Since $z = 0$, $xy + xz = xy$.

24. A. $(x + y)^2 = x^2 + 2xy + y^2$. Since $xy = 9$, $2xy = 18$ and since $x^2 + y^2 = 12$, $(x + y)^2 = 30$ (Column A).

25. C. Area of square = (side)^2. If area = 25 units, side = 5 units. Since perimeter of square = side $\times$ 4, square with perimeter of 20 units, has side = 5 units.

26. B. Solve by factoring: $x^2 - 7x + 12 = 0$
$(x - 4)(x - 3) = 0$
$x = 4,3$

27. D. With a perimeter of 36 units, the sides may have values of 4 and 14, 15 and 3, or 16 and 2. Note how the value of the area would differ. 4×14 is not equal to 15×3 or 16×2.

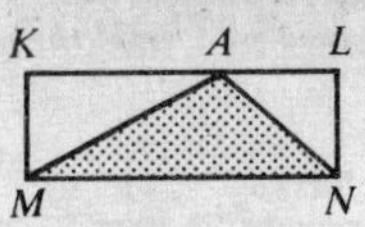

28. B. Since area of $KLNM = 100$
Base $\times$ Altitude $= 100$
$20 \times$ Altitude $= 100$
Altitude $= 5$
Altitude of rectangle equals altitude of triangle AMN
Area of triangle =
$\frac{1}{2}$(base)(altitude)
Area of $AMN = \frac{1}{2}(20)(5)$ or 50

29. A. Average $\times$ Number of cases = Sum
$\left(\frac{1}{6}\right)(3) = \frac{1}{2}$
Sum of $\frac{1}{2} + \frac{1}{3} = \frac{5}{6}$
Let x = fraction to be subtracted from $\frac{5}{6}$ to yield $\frac{1}{2}$
$\frac{5}{6} - x = \frac{1}{2}$
$5 - 6x = 3$ (multiply by 6)
$-6x = -2$
$6x = 2$
$x = \frac{1}{3}$
The alert student will see that if $\frac{1}{3}$ is subtracted from $\left(\frac{1}{2} + \frac{1}{3}\right)$ it will yield $\frac{1}{2}$

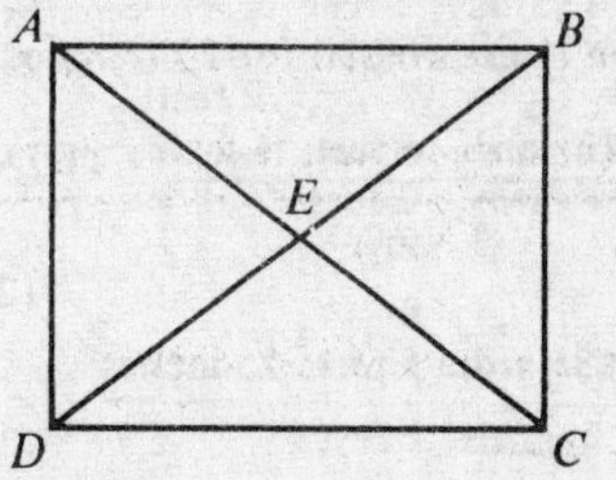

30. B. In right triangle BAD, BD is hypotenuse
$(AB)^2 + (AD)^2 = (BD)^2$
(Pythagorean theorem)
$(16)^2 + (12)^2 = (BD)^2$
$256 + 144 = (BD)^2$
$400 = (BD)^2$
$20 = BD$
$DE = \frac{1}{2}BD$ or 10
(diagonals of a rectangle bisect each other)

31. C. This is a direct proportion
Let x = number of flasks necessary to hold 3.6 liters

$$\frac{\text{Number of flasks}}{\text{Number of liters}} = \frac{1}{0.6} = \frac{x}{3.6}$$

$0.6x = 3.6$ (product of means equals product of extremes)
$6x = 36$ (multiply by 10)
$x = 6$

32. A. $\frac{3}{rs} = \frac{1}{2t}$

$rs = 6t$ (product of means equals product of extremes)

$r = \frac{6t}{s}$ (division by s)

$r = s^2$ (given)

$s^2 = \frac{6t}{s}$ (things equal to the same thing are equal to each other)

$s^3 = 6t$ (product of means equals product of extremes)

$s = \sqrt[3]{6t}$ (extract cube root of both sides of the equation)

33. C.

```
       1 yard
3 ) 13 yards  5 feet  1 inch
    4 yards
```
(13 yards divided by 3 equals 4 yards and 1 yard remaining)

```
               8
3 ) 13 yards  5̸ feet  1 inch
    4 yards
```
(1 yard equals 3 feet)

```
               8
3 ) 13 yards  5̸ feet  1 inch
    4 yards   2 feet
```
(8 feet divided by 3 equals 2 feet and 2 feet remaining)

```
               8       2 feet
3 ) 13 yards  5̸ feet  1 inch
    4 yards   2 feet
```

```
               8
3 ) 13 yards  5̸ feet  25 inches
    4 yards   2 feet
```
(2 feet equals 24 inches)

```
               8
3 ) 13 yards  5̸ feet  25 inches
    4 yards   2 feet  8 1/3 inches
```

34. B. $KM = \frac{1}{2}LK$ and $AC = \frac{1}{2}AB$. Since $KM > AC$ then $KL > AB$ since doubles, triples... etc. of unequal quantities are unequal in the same order.

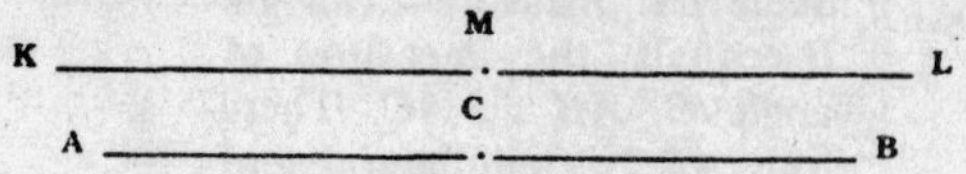

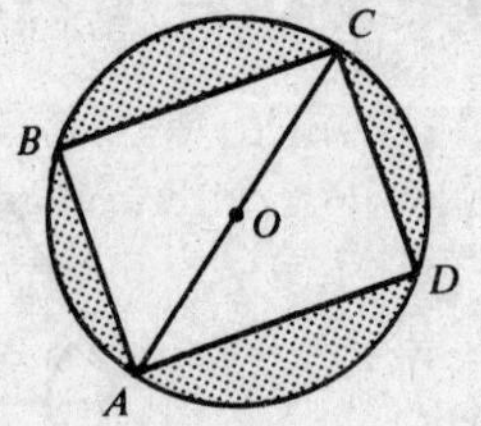

35. A. Angle B is a right angle (an angle inscribed in a semicircle is a right angle)
Diameter $AC = 10$
$(AC)^2 = (BC)^2 + (AB)^2$
$(10)^2 = (8)^2 + (AB)^2$
$100 = 64 + (AB)^2$
$36 = (AB)^2$
$AB = 6$
$CB = DA$
$CB = 8$
$DA = 8$

$\frac{AB}{AD} = \frac{6}{8}$ or $\frac{3}{4}$

SECTION 2

1. A. The opposite of *benediction* (blessing) is *curse.*

2. A. The opposite of *vacillating* (wavering) is *firm.*

3. D. The opposite of *heinous* (atrocious) is *noble.*

4. D. The opposite of *pugnacious* (belligerent) is *conciliatory.*

5. D. The opposite of *perturbed* (disturbed) is *soothed.*

6. C. The opposite of *scanty* (meager) is *profuse* (abundant).

7. D. The opposite of *gauche* (clumsy) is *adroit* (skillful).

8. A. The opposite of *enlighten* (inform; make clear to) is *obscure* (becloud; confuse).

9. B. The opposite of *contaminate* (taint) is *make pure.*

10. D. The opposite of *combustible* (capable of burning) is *flameproof.*

11. C. By definition, an *idiosyncrasy* is a personal *peculiarity.*

12. B. *Levity* (frivolity) is inappropriate during serious moments.

13. D. *Sophisticated* (worldly-wise) listeners would find the *flamboyant* (ornate, bombastic) remarks amusing.

14. B. *Esoteric* (private, confidential) rites would be most interesting to an explorer.

15. E. While all five choices are acceptable, *larcenous* (pertaining to stealing) is best because it fits in with the thought of the sentence.

16. E. *Conscience* keeps man from *sin; indolence* (laziness) keeps man from *work.*

17. C. *Sandals* and *moccasins* are worn on the feet; *sombreros* and *caps* are worn on the head.

18. D. A *dog* is a *mammal;* a *crab,* a *crustacean.*

19. A. *Corn* is stored in a *silo; valuables,* in a *vault.*

20. D. *Necromancy* (black magic) is associated with dealings with *demons* or the devil; *sorcery* (witchcraft) is associated with evil *spirits.*

21. B. A *visionary* (dreamer) is not *practical*; a *braggart* (boaster) is not *modest.*

22. C. One puts *liniment* on an *ache* to promote healing, just as one puts *salve* on a *sore.*

23. E. *Insubordination* (disobedience) may lead to *punishment; diligence* (industry) may lead to *promotion.*

24. B. A *mayfly* is known to be *ephemeral* (short-lived); a *gazelle*, to be *graceful.*

25. A. A *tumbler* is a container for *beverages*; a *quiver*, a container for *arrows.*

26. A. The passage discusses the possibility of more or less snow in future years and whether a trend is being established.

27. A. The fourth sentence supports Choice A.

28. D. The fifth sentence supports Choice D.

29. C. See description of Bosola (lines 36–57 of the passage). Lines 48–51 support Choice C.

30. C. The reference to "an El Greco cardinal" (lines 2 and 3) indicate that the author believes that the reader is acquainted with the work of El Greco, famous Spanish painter.

31. D. Lines 51–52 support Choice D.

32. D. Lines 2–5 inform us that El Greco's characters can be identified by their elongated features.

33. E. Line 51 supports Choice E.

34. E. The statement in the next-to-last sentence of the passage that Bosola must play a "lowly and despicable" role supports Choice E.

35. A. The last sentence supports Choice A.

36. B. Lines 6–13 support Choice B.

37. B. Lines 19–23 support Choice B.

38. D. Lines 13–16 inform us that there is more dust in the atmosphere at sunset.

39. D. In lines 10–11 we are told that the shorter waves are composed of the "violet end of the spectrum." We may infer that the other end of the spectrum (the red) is composed of longer waves.

40. B. Lines 19–23 support Choice B.

SECTION 3

1. B. $1\frac{1}{4}x = \frac{1}{2}$

$\frac{5}{4}x = \frac{1}{2}$

$5x = 2$ **(multiply by 4)**

$x = \frac{2}{5}$ **(divide by 5)**

2. C. Since there are 5 nickels in one quarter, there are $5q$ nickels in q quarters.

3. D. $\frac{\text{yards}}{\text{minutes}} = \frac{y}{m} = \frac{x}{60}$

$mx = 60y$

$x = \frac{60y}{m}$ (divide by m)

4. A. $\frac{1}{2} + \frac{3}{4} \div \left(\frac{5}{6} \times \frac{7}{8}\right) - \frac{9}{10}$

$\frac{1}{2} + \frac{3}{4} \div \left(\frac{35}{48}\right) - \frac{9}{10}$

$\frac{1}{2} + \frac{3}{4} \times \frac{48}{35} - \frac{9}{10}$

$\frac{1}{2} + \frac{3}{\not 4} \times \frac{\not{48}^{12}}{35} - \frac{9}{10}$

$\frac{1}{2} + \frac{36}{35} - \frac{9}{10}$

$\frac{1}{2} + \frac{36}{35} - \frac{9}{10}$ (70 is L.C.D.)

$\frac{35 + 72 - 63}{70}$ or $\frac{44}{70} = \frac{22}{35}$

5. E. Maximum weight of 4 eggs = (25 ounces)(4) or 100 ounces
Maximum weight of the remaining 6 eggs = (25 ounces)(6) or 150 ounces
Combined maximum weight = 250 ounces

6. C. Let x = amount of celery needed for 8 cups of tuna fish

$\frac{\text{Cups of tuna fish}}{\text{Cups of chopped celery}} = \frac{2}{\frac{1}{8}} = \frac{8}{x}$

$2x = 1$

$x = \frac{1}{2}$

7. E. $\sqrt{0.09} = 0.3$

$x\sqrt{0.09} = 3$

$(x)(0.3) = 3$

$0.3x = 3$

$3x = 30$

$x = 10$

8. B. When the clock loses 12 hours or 720 minutes, it will reach a point where it will indicate the correct time.
Let x = number of days it will take for the clock to lose 12 hours or 720 minutes

$\frac{\text{Minutes lost}}{\text{Time in days}} = \frac{10}{1} = \frac{720}{x}$

$10x = 720$

$x = 72$

9. D. $\frac{\text{Amount spent}}{\text{Cost per stamp}}$ = Number of stamps purchased

$\frac{c \text{ cents}}{2 \text{ cents}} = \frac{c}{2}$

10. E. $\frac{3y^2 - x^2}{\frac{1}{2}a^3}$

$\frac{3(3)(3) - (-2)(-2)}{\frac{1}{2}(-1)(-1)(-1)}$

$\frac{27 - 4}{-\frac{1}{2}}$

$\frac{23}{-\frac{1}{2}}$

$23 \cdot -\frac{2}{1} = -46$

11. A. $abc = dbc + e$

$abc - dbc = e$ (subtract dbc)

$bc(a - d) = e$ (factoring)

$\frac{bc(a-d)}{(a-d)} = \frac{e}{a-d}$ (division by $a - d$)

$bc = \frac{e}{a-d}$

12. E. The man earns $p + w$ dollars
Since he works d days, his average earnings per day are $\frac{p+w}{d}$

13. D. The time spent is 8 hours

$\dfrac{\text{Distance}}{\text{Time}} = \text{Average rate}$

$\dfrac{600 \text{ miles}}{8 \text{ hours}} = 75 \text{ miles per hour}$

14. B. The former price is 80 cents each. The new price is \$9.00 per dozen or 75 cents each

$\dfrac{\text{Old price}}{\text{New price}} = \dfrac{80 \text{ cents}}{75 \text{ cents}} = \dfrac{16}{15}$ or $16:15$

15. C. Draw AC

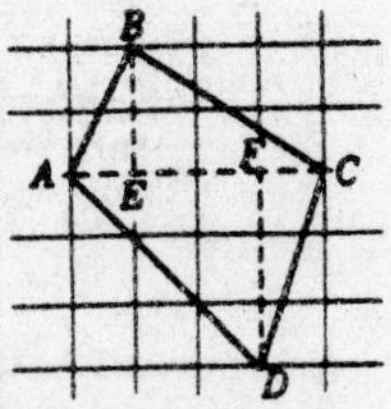

Area of triangle ABC equals $\frac{1}{2}$ base AC (4 units) × altitude BE (2 units) or $\frac{1}{2}(4)(2)$ or 4 units.

Area of triangle DAC equals $\frac{1}{2}$ base AC (4 units) × altitude DF (3 units or $\frac{1}{2}(4)(3)$ or 6 units.

$ABCD$ equals triangle ABC + triangle DAC

Area of $ABCD$ equals 4 + 6 or 10

16. E. Radius $OA = 50'$

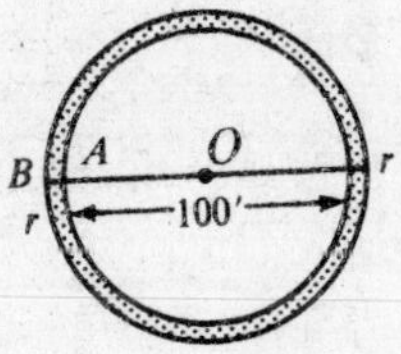

Area of Circle $= \pi r^2$

Area of Circle with radius $OA = \pi\,(50)^2$ or $2500\,\pi$ sq. ft.

Radius $OB = 52'$

Area of Circle with radius $OB = \pi(52)^2$ or 2704π sq. ft.

Difference between area of the two circles equals area of circular grass walk

$2704\pi - 2500\pi = 204\pi$ sq. ft.

17. E. Average × Number of Test Marks = Sum of all test marks

$80 \times 6 = 480$

Sum of tests already taken = 385

Mark necessary on next test = $480 - 385$ or 95%

18. C.

$\sqrt{x^2y^2 + x^3y^4} = 3xy$

$\sqrt{x^2y^2(1 + xy^2)} = 3xy$ (factor)

$xy\sqrt{1 + xy^2} = 3xy$ (extract square root)

$\sqrt{1 + xy^2} = \dfrac{3xy}{xy}$ (divide by xy)

$\sqrt{1 + xy^2} = 3$

$(\sqrt{1 + xy^2})^2 = (3)^2$

$1 + xy^2 = 9$

$xy^2 = 8$ (subtract 1)

19. C. If the cashier had given the man 4 quarters, he would not have to give him any dimes. If the cashier had given the man 3 quarters he would have to give him a nickel in addition to 2 dimes. If the cashier had given the man 1 quarter he would have to give him 7 dimes and 1 nickel. This is contrary to the given statement since the change consisted of dimes and quarters. If he had given him 2 quarters he would then also give him 5 dimes. Therefore the change consisted of 2 + 5 or 7 coins.

20. B. Since $GC = 8$, $EB = 8$

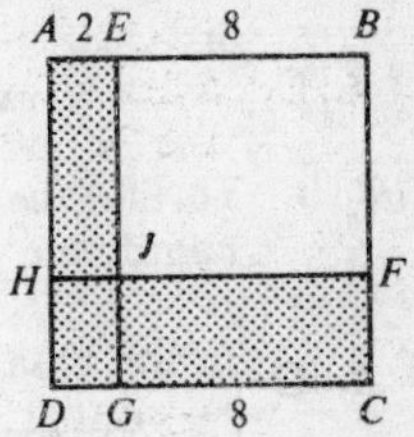

$AB = AE + EB$

$AB = 2 + 8$ or 10

Area of square = $(\text{side})^2$

Area of square $ABCD = (10)^2$ or 100

Area of $FBEJ$ = Area of Square $ABCD$ − Area of shaded portion

Area of shaded portion = 44

Area of $FBEJ = 100 - 44$ or 56

21. D. The sum of the angles of a triangle equals 180°

$(x + 24) + (4x - 12) + \left(\dfrac{3x}{2} + 12\right) = 180°$

$x + 24 + 4x - 12 + \dfrac{3x}{2} + 12 = 180$

$2x + 48 + 8x - 24 + 3x + 24 = 360$ (multiply by 2)

$13x + 48 = 360$

$13x = 312$

$x = 24$

One angle $= (x + 24)$ or 48°

Another angle $= (4x - 12)$ or 84°

Another angle $= \left(\dfrac{3x}{2} + 12\right)$ or 48°

Angle with 84° must be the vertex angle since the base angles of an isosceles triangle are equal.

22. A. $\dfrac{\text{Distance}}{\text{Time}} = \text{Rate}$

$\dfrac{70 \text{ miles}}{2\frac{1}{2} \text{ hours}} = 28 \text{ miles per hour}$

Desired time is $2\frac{1}{2}$ hours − $\frac{3}{4}$ hours or $1\frac{3}{4}$ hours

Desired rate equals

$\dfrac{\text{Distance}}{\text{Time}}$ or $\dfrac{70 \text{ miles}}{1\frac{3}{4} \text{hours}}$ or 40 miles per hour

Since his rate was 28 miles per hour, he should travel 12 miles per hour faster to achieve a rate of 40 miles per hour.

23. D. The locus of points which are at a fixed distance from a given point is a circle whose radius is the fixed distance and whose center is the fixed point.

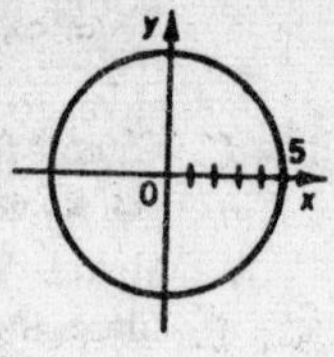

An equation of a circle is of the form $x^2+y^2=r^2$, where r is the radius of the circle.
In this case, $r = 5$.
Therefore, an equation of the circle is

$$x^2 + y^2 = (5)^2$$

or

$$x^2 + y^2 = 25.$$

24. B. To find the distance between two points in the coordinate plane, we use the distance formula

$$d = \sqrt{(x_1 - x_2)^2 + (y_1 + y_2)^2}$$

In this case,

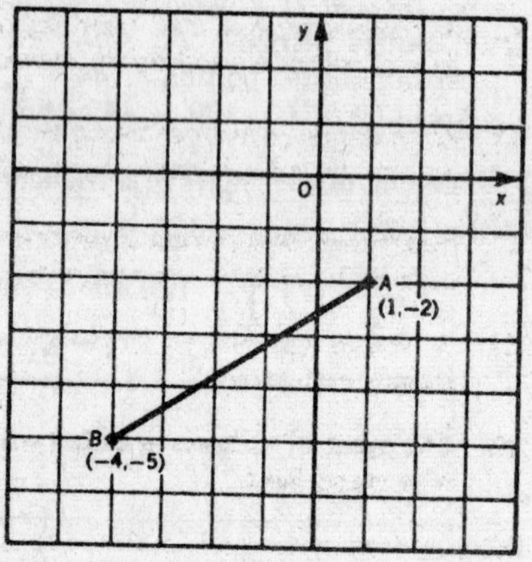

$x_1 = 1, \quad x_2 = -4$
$y_1 = -2, \quad y_2 = -5$

$$d = \sqrt{[1-(-4)]^2 + [-2-(-5)]^2}$$
$$d = \sqrt{(1+4)^2 + (-2+5)^2}$$
$$d = \sqrt{(5)^2 + (3)^2}$$
$$d = \sqrt{25+9}$$
$$d = \sqrt{34}$$

Thus, the length of $\overline{AB}$ is $\sqrt{34}$.

25. B. The locus of points in a plane at a given distance (d) from the given line $\overleftrightarrow{AB}$ is two lines each parallel to the given line, as shown in the diagram.

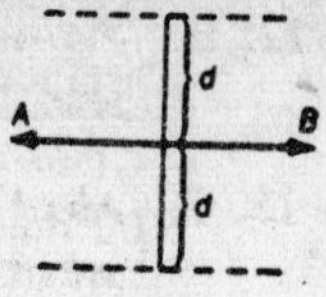

SECTION 4

1. D. The opposite of *taut* (drawn tight) is *loose.*

2. E. The opposite of *prone* (inclined) is *disinclined.*

3. B. The opposite of *segregate* (set apart) is *unite.*

4. B. The opposite of *circumspect* (cautious) is *rash* (reckless).

5. D. The opposite of *nadir* (lowest point) is *peak.*

6. A. The opposite of *paragon* (model of excellence) is *horrible example.*

7. C. The opposite of *wonted* (accustomed) is *unaccustomed.*

8. A. The opposite of *callow* (inexperienced) is *experienced.*

9. D. The opposite of *encomium* (praise) is *opprobrium* (shame, denunciation).

10. B. A *jaundiced* view is an envious view; its opposite would be a *tolerant* view.

11. B. *Invidious* (inciting ill will) is the opposite of *creating good will.*

12. E. *Proximity* (closeness) and *distance* are opposites.

13. C. *Aloof* (apart) and *gregarious* (fond of company) are opposites.

14. A. *Vivacious* (animated) and *lethargic* (sluggish) are opposites.

15. A. *Collaborate* (work together) and *work alone* are opposites.

16. C. *Commiserate* (to express feelings of sympathy) would be appropriate.

17. D. *Sabotage* (intentional damage) may be used by the enemy.

18. A. Without reinforcements, the attack would be difficult: the colonel would probably *countermand* (revoke) the order.

19. E. *Galvanize* means rouse by shock.

20. A. *Chicanery* means trickery and underhand dealing.

21. A. The passage deals with the chemical improvement of aviation fuel.

22. D. In the last sentence we are told that the aviation engine delivers 100% more power than the engine of 1918.

23. E. The next-to-last sentence supports Choice E.

24. B. The opening paragraph suggests that bombers function as long range guns.

25. E. The passage is concerned with tests about the causes of deterioration of coffee.

26. A. The second and third sentences support Choice A.

27. B. The last sentence supports Choice B.

28. A. Of the 70 years of life expectancy (line 5), "twenty will not come again." This indicates that he has already lived 20 of his 70 years.

29. A. "Snow" is used as a metaphor. The tree is covered with white blossoms which resemble snow.

30. A. The poet mentions his pleasure in viewing the loveliness of the scene.

31. C. The 18th-century English poets were interested in teaching; they were *didactic*.

32. C. *Nostalgia* means home-sickness.

33. E. *Inveigling* (enticing, seducing) is a more specific word than *influencing* as used in this sentence.

34. B. *Fortitude* means courage.

35. B. *Gullible* (credulous) people are most easily fooled or *misled* by propaganda.

36. E. A *typewriter* is a tool used by a *journalist;* a pair of *pliers* is used by an *electrician.*

37. D. An *eclogue* (short pastoral poem) is written by a *poet;* a *gown* is made by a *seamstress.*

38. C. *Portentous* and *ominous* are synonyms; *significant* and *pertinent* are synonyms.

39. D. A *mural* (painting) is placed on a *wall;* an *etching,* on *paper.*

40. D. The meat of a *sheep* is called *mutton;* the meat of a *steer, beef.*

41. E. To restrict a *horse,* a *tether* is used; to restrict a *prisoner, manacles* are used.

42. B. A *libretto* (the words of an opera or musical play) is written by an *author;* the *score* (musical arrangement), by a *composer.*

43. C. A *revelation* is a disclosure made by a *prophet;* a *bust* (figure of head, shoulders and chest) is made by a *sculptor.*

44. D. An *entry* is one day's record that is part of a *diary*; an *episode* is one separate performance that is part of a *serial*.

45. A. A *virtuoso* is a gifted performer and therefore *experienced*; a *tyro* is a beginner and therefore *untried*.

SECTION 5

1. B. Let x = number of thirds in $\frac{5}{8}$

$$\frac{x}{3} = \frac{5}{8}$$
$$8x = 15$$
$$x = \frac{15}{8}$$

2. E. $3 + \frac{3}{0.3}$

$$3 + \frac{30}{3}$$
$$3 + 10 = 13$$

3. B. $\frac{(18)(24)}{(12)(16)} \div \frac{18}{16}$

$$\frac{(18)(24)}{(12)(16)} \cdot \frac{16}{18}$$

$$\frac{\cancel{(18)}\overset{2}{\cancel{(24)}}}{\cancel{(12)}\cancel{(16)}} \cdot \frac{\cancel{16}}{\cancel{18}} = 2$$

4. B. Pupils who have memorized fraction–per cent equivalent tables recall that

$$\frac{5}{8} = 62\frac{1}{2}\% \text{ or } .625$$

$$\frac{5}{8} = \frac{?}{32} = \frac{20}{32}$$

or

$$\frac{x}{32} = .625$$
$$x = (32)(.625)$$
$$x = 20$$

5. B. $\frac{1}{1-p} \div \frac{1}{p-1}$

$$\frac{1}{1-p} \cdot \frac{p-1}{1}$$

$$\frac{1}{-p+1} \cdot \frac{p-1}{1}$$

$$\frac{-1}{p-1} \cdot \left(p-1\right)$$ (multiply numerator and denominator by −1)

$$\frac{-1}{p-1} \left(p-1\right)$$

$$\frac{-1}{\cancel{p-1}} \cdot \left(\cancel{p-1}\right) = -1$$

6. E. $\frac{2.6z}{6} = 65$

$2.6z = (65)(6)$ (multiply by 6)
$2.6x = 390$
$26z = 3900$ (multiply by 10)
$z = 150$ (divide by 26)

7. E. $AP = AC$ since $\angle 1 = \angle 2$. If $AB > AC$ then also $AB > AP$ (or $AP < AB$). A quantity may be substituted for its equal any place it occurs.

8. B. $$\frac{\frac{1}{4} - \frac{3}{16}}{\frac{1}{8}} = \frac{\frac{4}{16} - \frac{3}{16}}{\frac{1}{8}} = \frac{\frac{1}{16}}{\frac{1}{8}} = \frac{1}{\underset{2}{\cancel{16}}} \cdot \frac{\cancel{8}}{1} = \frac{1}{2}$$

9. A. $\frac{\text{3 yards, 1 foot, 3 inches}}{3}$ = 1 yard, 5 inches or 41 inches.

10. D. If n = an even whole number, then $x = \pm 1$.
If n = an odd whole number, then $x = -1$.

11. D. $a^6 = (a)(a)(a)(a)(a)(a)$
$6a^5 = (6)(a)(a)(a)(a)(a)$
The quantity in column A would be equal to the quantity in column B only if the value of a were equal to 6.

12. D. The value of x could be 40 or 80.

13. C. If $y = 50$, then angle $DCB \stackrel{\circ}{=} 100$, and angle $ABC \stackrel{\circ}{=} 80$, and $x = 40$. Therefore $x + y = 90$.

14. B. The information given tells us that the measure of angle $A >$ the measure of angle B. Since $A + B = 120$, the measure (in degrees) of angle A is greater than 60, and angle B has a measure of less than 60. Side AC lies opposite the smallest angle of the triangle.

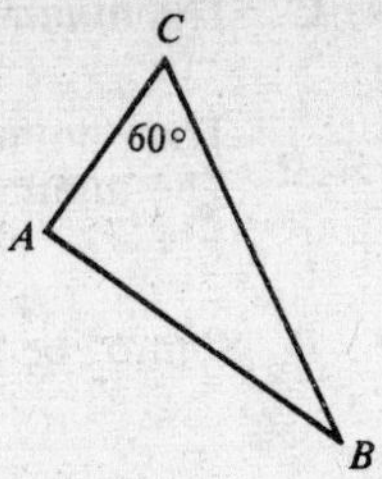

15. C. The sum of the lengths of 2 adjacent sides of a parallelogram equals one-half the perimeter.

16. D. We cannot correctly answer the question because we may not assume that this figure is equilateral.

17. D. The acute angles of a right triangle are complementary. The angles y and z are not acute angles of the same right triangle.

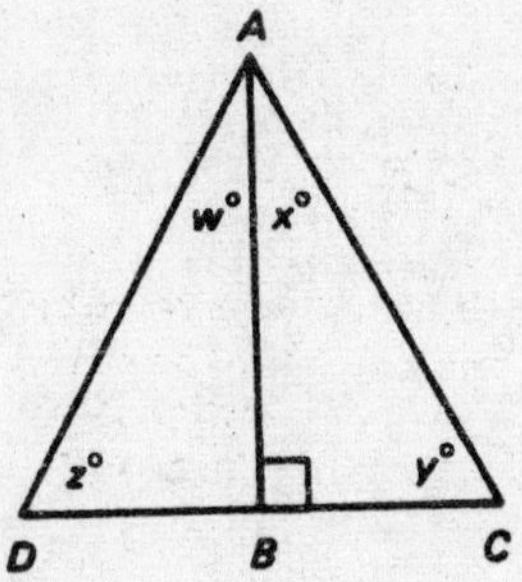

18. C. Since $AB = BC$, $x = y$.

19. C. See #17.

20. D. $w + z = 90$ but we do not know how DB compares with AB.

21. D. We may not assume that BC passes through the center of the circle. We may not assume that $AB = AC$. We may only find the value of BC from the data furnished.

22. A. The sum of 2 sides of a triangle is greater than the length of the third side. A straight line is the shortest distance between 2 points.

23. B. Since angle DOC is a right angle and OD and OC are radii, DOC is an isosceles right triangle. Area of $DOC = \frac{1}{2}(OD)(OC)$ or 8. Therefore $OD = OC = 4$. $(DC)^2 = (4)^2 + (4)^2$ and $DC = \sqrt{32}$ or $4\sqrt{2}$. Perimeter of $ABCD = (4)(4\sqrt{2})$ or $16\sqrt{2}$ or $(16)(1.4)$ or 22.4.

24. C. Area of shaded portion = area of circle (16π) minus the area of the square $(4\sqrt{2})^2$ or 32. Area of shaded portion $= 16\pi - 32$.

25. A. $\left(\frac{X}{Z}\right)\left(\frac{Z}{Y}\right) = \frac{X}{Y}$

X and Y are opposite equal angles and therefore $X = Y$ and $\frac{X}{Y} = 1$

26. B. Since $x = 20$, $\angle FCD \overset{\circ}{=} 40$

$\angle FCB \overset{\circ}{=} 140$ (supplement)

$\angle FAB \overset{\circ}{=} \angle FCB$ (opposite angles of a parallelogram)

Therefore $y = 140$ and $y > 6x$

27. A. Radius of $I = 5$

Radius of $II = 4$

Radius of $III = 3$

$AB = 5 + 3 = 8$

$BC = 3 + 4 = 7$

$AC = 5 + 4 = 9$

Perimeter of $ABC = 24$

28. C. Since he loses 350 eggs, he sells 2750 − 350 or 2400 eggs.

2400 eggs equals 200 dozen.

If he sells these at 70¢ per dozen he receives $140.

Selling Price − Cost = Profit

$140 − $100 = $40

$$\frac{\text{Profit}}{\text{Original Investment}} \times 100 = \text{Per cent profit of original investment}$$

$$\frac{\$40}{\$100} \times 100 = 40$$

29. B. (Average distance covered by one jump) × (Number of jumps) = Total distance

$$\frac{\text{Total distance covered}}{\text{Average distance covered by one jump}} = \text{Number of jumps}$$

$$\frac{3y \text{ feet}}{8 \text{ feet}} = \text{number of jumps}$$ (convert to similar units)

$$\frac{3y}{8} = \text{number of jumps}$$

30. A. $\frac{1}{10} + \frac{1}{3} + \frac{1}{5} =$ Part of salary spent

$\frac{1}{10} + \frac{1}{3} + \frac{1}{5}$ (L.C.D. is 30)

$\frac{3 + 10 + 6}{30}$ or $\frac{19}{30}$ is part of salary spent

Therefore $\frac{11}{30}$ is left for other expenditures and savings.

$\frac{11}{30} = .36\frac{2}{3}$ or $36\frac{2}{3}\%$

31. A. The basic principle involved is similar to that of a work problem. Apply formula

$$\frac{\text{Time actually worked}}{\text{Time required to complete the task}} = \text{Part of task done}$$

$$\frac{1 \text{ hour}}{h \text{ hours}} = \frac{1}{h}$$

32. C. Sum of height of 3 boys = $x+y+y$ or $x+2y$ inches.

$$\text{Average} = \frac{\text{Sum}}{\text{Number of cases}} \text{ or } \frac{x+2y}{3}$$

33. C. Let $x = BC$; then $AB = 2x$

Area of triangle ABC =

$\frac{1}{2}(b)(h)$ or

$(\frac{1}{2})(x)(2x)$ or x^2

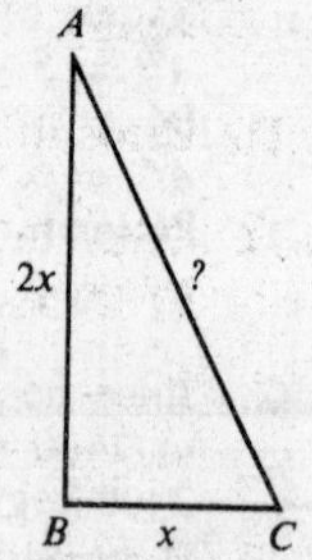

Area is given equal to 64 square feet

$x^2 = 64$

$x = 8$

$BC = 8$; $AB = 16$

$(8)^2 + (16)^2 = (AC)^2$ (Pythagorean theorem)

$64 + 256 = (AC)^2$

$(AC)^2 = 320$

$AC = \sqrt{320}$ or approximately 18 feet

34. C. The minimum weight of one dozen eggs = 24 ounces

The minimum weight of one egg = 2 ounces

The minimum weight of 69 eggs = 138 ounces

35. D Sum of heights equals

6′3″ + 2 (6′) + 5′10″ + 5′11″ or 30 feet

$$\frac{\text{Sum}}{\text{Number of cases}} = \text{Average}$$

$$\frac{30 \text{ feet}}{5 \text{ players}} = \text{Average of 6 feet}$$

SECTION 6

1. C. Lack of parallel structure. Change *to write* to *writing*.

2. D. Misplaced modifier. The phrase *in good condition* should come after the word *piano*.

3. C. Lack of agreement. *School* is singular and should be followed by *was* (singular).

4. A. Dangling participle. Change to a clause: *While we were transacting*.

5. B. Incomplete sentence. By changing *and* to *was* or *is*, we correct the error.

6. D. Unnecessary word. Eliminate *so*.

7. B. Error in case. Change *I* to *me* because the pronoun is the object of the preposition *among*.

8. C. Lack of agreement. The verb should agree with *editor* (singular). Change *were* to *was*.

9. B. Error in case. The pronoun should be *whom* because it is the object of the verb *see*.

10. C. Lack of parallel structure. Change *it presented* to *of its presentation of*.

11. E. Sentence is correct.

12. D. Lack of agreement. The subject is *quantity* (singular) and requires a singular verb *was missing*.

13. A. Misplaced modifier. *I bought only* is preferable.

14. E. Sentence is correct.

15. A. Error in diction. Change *had ought* to *ought*.

16. B. Error in diction. Change *infer* to *imply*.

17. C. Error in tense. Change *did* to *has done*.

18. B. Lack of parallel structure. Change clause to a phrase in order to parallel the preceeding phrase. Change *it has brought about* to *of its*.

19. E. Sentence is correct.

20. D. Lack of agreement. The antecedent of *who* is *I*. *Who*, therefore, should be followed by *am*.

21. C. Error in diction. Delete the article *a*.

22. C. Error in diction. Use *likely* instead of *liable*.

23. C. Lack of agreement. The subject of the verb is *ideal* (singular). Change *were* to *was*.

24. C. Error in case. The subject of *should have* is *who*, not *whom*.

25. E. Sentence is correct.

26. D. This corrects the two errors in the sentence—the idiom error (*to be graduated*) and the error in capitalization.

27. C. This corrects the two errors in the sentence—the capitalization of *Makes* and the placement of the question mark.

28. C. This corrects the two errors in this sentence—the error in case (*me* for *I*) and the error in tense (*had finished* for *finished*).

29. D. *Despite* should be used as a preposition.

30. C. This corrects the lack of parallel structure.

31. C. Unnecessary shift of pronoun. Do not shift from *you* to *one*.

32. C. *From* is a preposition and requires a pronoun in the objective case—*from those* (*people*).

33. D. Choice D corrects the error in diction and the error in parallel structure.

34. E. Misuse of the word *too*.

35. B. Choice B illustrates the proper use of quotation marks in a quotation consisting of two sentences.

36. D. The addition of the conjunction *when* corrects the run-on sentence and shows the relationship between the two clauses.

37. A. The inverted word order used with the subjunctive (*had it been*) is correct.

38. C. As the subject of a sentence *The number* generally is considered a singular and therefore requires a singular verb (*is given*).

39. E. Changing *made* to *make* corrects the sequence of tenses.

40. C. The addition of the conjunction *though*corrects the run-on sentence.

41. A. Double negative. Change *can't hardly* to *can hardly*.

42. D. Error in diction. Change *alright* to *all right*.

43. D. Error in diction. *Different* should be followed by *from*.

44. B. Error in diction. Use *number* instead of *amount*.

45. E. Sentence is correct.

46. B. Error in tense. The past perfect tense of *sink* is *had sunk*.

47. D. Error in diction. Use *uninterested* instead of *disinterested*.

48. B. Error in diction. Use *angry* instead of *mad*.

49. E. Sentence is correct.

50. E. Sentence is correct.

ANSWER SHEET—TEST 5

SECTION 1

1. Ⓐ Ⓑ Ⓒ Ⓓ Ⓔ	11. Ⓐ Ⓑ Ⓒ Ⓓ Ⓔ	21. Ⓐ Ⓑ Ⓒ Ⓓ Ⓔ	31. Ⓐ Ⓑ Ⓒ Ⓓ Ⓔ	41. Ⓐ Ⓑ Ⓒ Ⓓ Ⓔ
2. Ⓐ Ⓑ Ⓒ Ⓓ Ⓔ	12. Ⓐ Ⓑ Ⓒ Ⓓ Ⓔ	22. Ⓐ Ⓑ Ⓒ Ⓓ Ⓔ	32. Ⓐ Ⓑ Ⓒ Ⓓ Ⓔ	42. Ⓐ Ⓑ Ⓒ Ⓓ Ⓔ
3. Ⓐ Ⓑ Ⓒ Ⓓ Ⓔ	13. Ⓐ Ⓑ Ⓒ Ⓓ Ⓔ	23. Ⓐ Ⓑ Ⓒ Ⓓ Ⓔ	33. Ⓐ Ⓑ Ⓒ Ⓓ Ⓔ	43. Ⓐ Ⓑ Ⓒ Ⓓ Ⓔ
4. Ⓐ Ⓑ Ⓒ Ⓓ Ⓔ	14. Ⓐ Ⓑ Ⓒ Ⓓ Ⓔ	24. Ⓐ Ⓑ Ⓒ Ⓓ Ⓔ	34. Ⓐ Ⓑ Ⓒ Ⓓ Ⓔ	44. Ⓐ Ⓑ Ⓒ Ⓓ Ⓔ
5. Ⓐ Ⓑ Ⓒ Ⓓ Ⓔ	15. Ⓐ Ⓑ Ⓒ Ⓓ Ⓔ	25. Ⓐ Ⓑ Ⓒ Ⓓ Ⓔ	35. Ⓐ Ⓑ Ⓒ Ⓓ Ⓔ	45. Ⓐ Ⓑ Ⓒ Ⓓ Ⓔ
6. Ⓐ Ⓑ Ⓒ Ⓓ Ⓔ	16. Ⓐ Ⓑ Ⓒ Ⓓ Ⓔ	26. Ⓐ Ⓑ Ⓒ Ⓓ Ⓔ	36. Ⓐ Ⓑ Ⓒ Ⓓ Ⓔ	46. Ⓐ Ⓑ Ⓒ Ⓓ Ⓔ
7. Ⓐ Ⓑ Ⓒ Ⓓ Ⓔ	17. Ⓐ Ⓑ Ⓒ Ⓓ Ⓔ	27. Ⓐ Ⓑ Ⓒ Ⓓ Ⓔ	37. Ⓐ Ⓑ Ⓒ Ⓓ Ⓔ	47. Ⓐ Ⓑ Ⓒ Ⓓ Ⓔ
8. Ⓐ Ⓑ Ⓒ Ⓓ Ⓔ	18. Ⓐ Ⓑ Ⓒ Ⓓ Ⓔ	28. Ⓐ Ⓑ Ⓒ Ⓓ Ⓔ	38. Ⓐ Ⓑ Ⓒ Ⓓ Ⓔ	48. Ⓐ Ⓑ Ⓒ Ⓓ Ⓔ
9. Ⓐ Ⓑ Ⓒ Ⓓ Ⓔ	19. Ⓐ Ⓑ Ⓒ Ⓓ Ⓔ	29. Ⓐ Ⓑ Ⓒ Ⓓ Ⓔ	39. Ⓐ Ⓑ Ⓒ Ⓓ Ⓔ	49. Ⓐ Ⓑ Ⓒ Ⓓ Ⓔ
10. Ⓐ Ⓑ Ⓒ Ⓓ Ⓔ	20. Ⓐ Ⓑ Ⓒ Ⓓ Ⓔ	30. Ⓐ Ⓑ Ⓒ Ⓓ Ⓔ	40. Ⓐ Ⓑ Ⓒ Ⓓ Ⓔ	50. Ⓐ Ⓑ Ⓒ Ⓓ Ⓔ

SECTION 2

1. Ⓐ Ⓑ Ⓒ Ⓓ Ⓔ	11. Ⓐ Ⓑ Ⓒ Ⓓ Ⓔ	21. Ⓐ Ⓑ Ⓒ Ⓓ Ⓔ	31. Ⓐ Ⓑ Ⓒ Ⓓ Ⓔ	41. Ⓐ Ⓑ Ⓒ Ⓓ Ⓔ
2. Ⓐ Ⓑ Ⓒ Ⓓ Ⓔ	12. Ⓐ Ⓑ Ⓒ Ⓓ Ⓔ	22. Ⓐ Ⓑ Ⓒ Ⓓ Ⓔ	32. Ⓐ Ⓑ Ⓒ Ⓓ Ⓔ	42. Ⓐ Ⓑ Ⓒ Ⓓ Ⓔ
3. Ⓐ Ⓑ Ⓒ Ⓓ Ⓔ	13. Ⓐ Ⓑ Ⓒ Ⓓ Ⓔ	23. Ⓐ Ⓑ Ⓒ Ⓓ Ⓔ	33. Ⓐ Ⓑ Ⓒ Ⓓ Ⓔ	43. Ⓐ Ⓑ Ⓒ Ⓓ Ⓔ
4. Ⓐ Ⓑ Ⓒ Ⓓ Ⓔ	14. Ⓐ Ⓑ Ⓒ Ⓓ Ⓔ	24. Ⓐ Ⓑ Ⓒ Ⓓ Ⓔ	34. Ⓐ Ⓑ Ⓒ Ⓓ Ⓔ	44. Ⓐ Ⓓ Ⓒ Ⓓ Ⓔ
5. Ⓐ Ⓑ Ⓒ Ⓓ Ⓔ	15. Ⓐ Ⓑ Ⓒ Ⓓ Ⓔ	25. Ⓐ Ⓑ Ⓒ Ⓓ Ⓔ	35. Ⓐ Ⓑ Ⓒ Ⓓ Ⓔ	45. Ⓐ Ⓑ Ⓒ Ⓓ Ⓔ
6. Ⓐ Ⓑ Ⓒ Ⓓ Ⓔ	16. Ⓐ Ⓑ Ⓒ Ⓓ Ⓔ	26. Ⓐ Ⓑ Ⓒ Ⓓ Ⓔ	36. Ⓐ Ⓑ Ⓒ Ⓓ Ⓔ	46. Ⓐ Ⓑ Ⓒ Ⓓ Ⓔ
7. Ⓐ Ⓑ Ⓒ Ⓓ Ⓔ	17. Ⓐ Ⓑ Ⓒ Ⓓ Ⓔ	27. Ⓐ Ⓑ Ⓒ Ⓓ Ⓔ	37. Ⓐ Ⓑ Ⓒ Ⓓ Ⓔ	47. Ⓐ Ⓑ Ⓒ Ⓓ Ⓔ
8. Ⓐ Ⓑ Ⓒ Ⓓ Ⓔ	18. Ⓐ Ⓑ Ⓒ Ⓓ Ⓔ	28. Ⓐ Ⓑ Ⓒ Ⓓ Ⓔ	38. Ⓐ Ⓑ Ⓒ Ⓓ Ⓔ	48. Ⓐ Ⓑ Ⓒ Ⓓ Ⓔ
9. Ⓐ Ⓑ Ⓒ Ⓓ Ⓔ	19. Ⓐ Ⓑ Ⓒ Ⓓ Ⓔ	29. Ⓐ Ⓑ Ⓒ Ⓓ Ⓔ	39. Ⓐ Ⓑ Ⓒ Ⓓ Ⓔ	49. Ⓐ Ⓑ Ⓒ Ⓓ Ⓔ
10. Ⓐ Ⓑ Ⓒ Ⓓ Ⓔ	20. Ⓐ Ⓑ Ⓒ Ⓓ Ⓔ	30. Ⓐ Ⓑ Ⓒ Ⓓ Ⓔ	40. Ⓐ Ⓑ Ⓒ Ⓓ Ⓔ	50. Ⓐ Ⓑ Ⓒ Ⓓ Ⓔ

SECTION 3

1. Ⓐ Ⓑ Ⓒ Ⓓ Ⓔ	11. Ⓐ Ⓑ Ⓒ Ⓓ Ⓔ	21. Ⓐ Ⓑ Ⓒ Ⓓ Ⓔ	31. Ⓐ Ⓑ Ⓒ Ⓓ Ⓔ	41. Ⓐ Ⓑ Ⓒ Ⓓ Ⓔ
2. Ⓐ Ⓑ Ⓒ Ⓓ Ⓔ	12. Ⓐ Ⓑ Ⓒ Ⓓ Ⓔ	22. Ⓐ Ⓑ Ⓒ Ⓓ Ⓔ	32. Ⓐ Ⓑ Ⓒ Ⓓ Ⓔ	42. Ⓐ Ⓑ Ⓒ Ⓓ Ⓔ
3. Ⓐ Ⓑ Ⓒ Ⓓ Ⓔ	13. Ⓐ Ⓑ Ⓒ Ⓓ Ⓔ	23. Ⓐ Ⓑ Ⓒ Ⓓ Ⓔ	33. Ⓐ Ⓑ Ⓒ Ⓓ Ⓔ	43. Ⓐ Ⓑ Ⓒ Ⓓ Ⓔ
4. Ⓐ Ⓑ Ⓒ Ⓓ Ⓔ	14. Ⓐ Ⓑ Ⓒ Ⓓ Ⓔ	24. Ⓐ Ⓑ Ⓒ Ⓓ Ⓔ	34. Ⓐ Ⓑ Ⓒ Ⓓ Ⓔ	44. Ⓐ Ⓑ Ⓒ Ⓓ Ⓔ
5. Ⓐ Ⓑ Ⓒ Ⓓ Ⓔ	15. Ⓐ Ⓑ Ⓒ Ⓓ Ⓔ	25. Ⓐ Ⓑ Ⓒ Ⓓ Ⓔ	35. Ⓐ Ⓑ Ⓒ Ⓓ Ⓔ	45. Ⓐ Ⓑ Ⓒ Ⓓ Ⓔ
6. Ⓐ Ⓑ Ⓒ Ⓓ Ⓔ	16. Ⓐ Ⓑ Ⓒ Ⓓ Ⓔ	26. Ⓐ Ⓑ Ⓒ Ⓓ Ⓔ	36. Ⓐ Ⓑ Ⓒ Ⓓ Ⓔ	46. Ⓐ Ⓑ Ⓒ Ⓓ Ⓔ
7. Ⓐ Ⓑ Ⓒ Ⓓ Ⓔ	17. Ⓐ Ⓑ Ⓒ Ⓓ Ⓔ	27. Ⓐ Ⓑ Ⓒ Ⓓ Ⓔ	37. Ⓐ Ⓑ Ⓒ Ⓓ Ⓔ	47. Ⓐ Ⓑ Ⓒ Ⓓ Ⓔ
8. Ⓐ Ⓑ Ⓒ Ⓓ Ⓔ	18. Ⓐ Ⓑ Ⓒ Ⓓ Ⓔ	28. Ⓐ Ⓑ Ⓒ Ⓓ Ⓔ	38. Ⓐ Ⓑ Ⓒ Ⓓ Ⓔ	48. Ⓐ Ⓑ Ⓒ Ⓓ Ⓔ
9. Ⓐ Ⓑ Ⓒ Ⓓ Ⓔ	19. Ⓐ Ⓑ Ⓒ Ⓓ Ⓔ	29. Ⓐ Ⓑ Ⓒ Ⓓ Ⓔ	39. Ⓐ Ⓑ Ⓒ Ⓓ Ⓔ	49. Ⓐ Ⓑ Ⓒ Ⓓ Ⓔ
10. Ⓐ Ⓑ Ⓒ Ⓓ Ⓔ	20. Ⓐ Ⓑ Ⓒ Ⓓ Ⓔ	30. Ⓐ Ⓑ Ⓒ Ⓓ Ⓔ	40. Ⓐ Ⓑ Ⓒ Ⓓ Ⓔ	50. Ⓐ Ⓑ Ⓒ Ⓓ Ⓔ

SECTION 4

1. Ⓐ Ⓑ Ⓒ Ⓓ Ⓔ
2. Ⓐ Ⓑ Ⓒ Ⓓ Ⓔ
3. Ⓐ Ⓑ Ⓒ Ⓓ Ⓔ
4. Ⓐ Ⓑ Ⓒ Ⓓ Ⓔ
5. Ⓐ Ⓑ Ⓒ Ⓓ Ⓔ
6. Ⓐ Ⓑ Ⓒ Ⓓ Ⓔ
7. Ⓐ Ⓑ Ⓒ Ⓓ Ⓔ
8. Ⓐ Ⓑ Ⓒ Ⓓ Ⓔ
9. Ⓐ Ⓑ Ⓒ Ⓓ Ⓔ
10. Ⓐ Ⓑ Ⓒ Ⓓ Ⓔ
11. Ⓐ Ⓑ Ⓒ Ⓓ Ⓔ
12. Ⓐ Ⓑ Ⓒ Ⓓ Ⓔ
13. Ⓐ Ⓑ Ⓒ Ⓓ Ⓔ
14. Ⓐ Ⓑ Ⓒ Ⓓ Ⓔ
15. Ⓐ Ⓑ Ⓒ Ⓓ Ⓔ
16. Ⓐ Ⓑ Ⓒ Ⓓ Ⓔ
17. Ⓐ Ⓑ Ⓒ Ⓓ Ⓔ
18. Ⓐ Ⓑ Ⓒ Ⓓ Ⓔ
19. Ⓐ Ⓑ Ⓒ Ⓓ Ⓔ
20. Ⓐ Ⓑ Ⓒ Ⓓ Ⓔ
21. Ⓐ Ⓑ Ⓒ Ⓓ Ⓔ
22. Ⓐ Ⓑ Ⓒ Ⓓ Ⓔ
23. Ⓐ Ⓑ Ⓒ Ⓓ Ⓔ
24. Ⓐ Ⓑ Ⓒ Ⓓ Ⓔ
25. Ⓐ Ⓑ Ⓒ Ⓓ Ⓔ
26. Ⓐ Ⓑ Ⓒ Ⓓ Ⓔ
27. Ⓐ Ⓑ Ⓒ Ⓓ Ⓔ
28. Ⓐ Ⓑ Ⓒ Ⓓ Ⓔ
29. Ⓐ Ⓑ Ⓒ Ⓓ Ⓔ
30. Ⓐ Ⓑ Ⓒ Ⓓ Ⓔ
31. Ⓐ Ⓑ Ⓒ Ⓓ Ⓔ
32. Ⓐ Ⓑ Ⓒ Ⓓ Ⓔ
33. Ⓐ Ⓑ Ⓒ Ⓓ Ⓔ
34. Ⓐ Ⓑ Ⓒ Ⓓ Ⓔ
35. Ⓐ Ⓑ Ⓒ Ⓓ Ⓔ
36. Ⓐ Ⓑ Ⓒ Ⓓ Ⓔ
37. Ⓐ Ⓑ Ⓒ Ⓓ Ⓔ
38. Ⓐ Ⓑ Ⓒ Ⓓ Ⓔ
39. Ⓐ Ⓑ Ⓒ Ⓓ Ⓔ
40. Ⓐ Ⓑ Ⓒ Ⓓ Ⓔ
41. Ⓐ Ⓑ Ⓒ Ⓓ Ⓔ
42. Ⓐ Ⓑ Ⓒ Ⓓ Ⓔ
43. Ⓐ Ⓑ Ⓒ Ⓓ Ⓔ
44. Ⓐ Ⓑ Ⓒ Ⓓ Ⓔ
45. Ⓐ Ⓑ Ⓒ Ⓓ Ⓔ
46. Ⓐ Ⓑ Ⓒ Ⓓ Ⓔ
47. Ⓐ Ⓑ Ⓒ Ⓓ Ⓔ
48. Ⓐ Ⓑ Ⓒ Ⓓ Ⓔ
49. Ⓐ Ⓑ Ⓒ Ⓓ Ⓔ
50. Ⓐ Ⓑ Ⓒ Ⓓ Ⓔ

SECTION 5

1. Ⓐ Ⓑ Ⓒ Ⓓ Ⓔ
2. Ⓐ Ⓑ Ⓒ Ⓓ Ⓔ
3. Ⓐ Ⓑ Ⓒ Ⓓ Ⓔ
4. Ⓐ Ⓑ Ⓒ Ⓓ Ⓔ
5. Ⓐ Ⓑ Ⓒ Ⓓ Ⓔ
6. Ⓐ Ⓑ Ⓒ Ⓓ Ⓔ
7. Ⓐ Ⓑ Ⓒ Ⓓ Ⓔ
8. Ⓐ Ⓑ Ⓒ Ⓓ Ⓔ
9. Ⓐ Ⓑ Ⓒ Ⓓ Ⓔ
10. Ⓐ Ⓑ Ⓒ Ⓓ Ⓔ
11. Ⓐ Ⓑ Ⓒ Ⓓ Ⓔ
12. Ⓐ Ⓑ Ⓒ Ⓓ Ⓔ
13. Ⓐ Ⓑ Ⓒ Ⓓ Ⓔ
14. Ⓐ Ⓑ Ⓒ Ⓓ Ⓔ
15. Ⓐ Ⓑ Ⓒ Ⓓ Ⓔ
16. Ⓐ Ⓑ Ⓒ Ⓓ Ⓔ
17. Ⓐ Ⓑ Ⓒ Ⓓ Ⓔ
18. Ⓐ Ⓑ Ⓒ Ⓓ Ⓔ
19. Ⓐ Ⓑ Ⓒ Ⓓ Ⓔ
20. Ⓐ Ⓑ Ⓒ Ⓓ Ⓔ
21. Ⓐ Ⓑ Ⓒ Ⓓ Ⓔ
22. Ⓐ Ⓑ Ⓒ Ⓓ Ⓔ
23. Ⓐ Ⓑ Ⓒ Ⓓ Ⓔ
24. Ⓐ Ⓑ Ⓒ Ⓓ Ⓔ
25. Ⓐ Ⓑ Ⓒ Ⓓ Ⓔ
26. Ⓐ Ⓑ Ⓒ Ⓓ Ⓔ
27. Ⓐ Ⓑ Ⓒ Ⓓ Ⓔ
28. Ⓐ Ⓑ Ⓒ Ⓓ Ⓔ
29. Ⓐ Ⓑ Ⓒ Ⓓ Ⓔ
30. Ⓐ Ⓑ Ⓒ Ⓓ Ⓔ
31. Ⓐ Ⓑ Ⓒ Ⓓ Ⓔ
32. Ⓐ Ⓑ Ⓒ Ⓓ Ⓔ
33. Ⓐ Ⓑ Ⓒ Ⓓ Ⓔ
34. Ⓐ Ⓑ Ⓒ Ⓓ Ⓔ
35. Ⓐ Ⓑ Ⓒ Ⓓ Ⓔ
36. Ⓐ Ⓑ Ⓒ Ⓓ Ⓔ
37. Ⓐ Ⓑ Ⓒ Ⓓ Ⓔ
38. Ⓐ Ⓑ Ⓒ Ⓓ Ⓔ
39. Ⓐ Ⓑ Ⓒ Ⓓ Ⓔ
40. Ⓐ Ⓑ Ⓒ Ⓓ Ⓔ
41. Ⓐ Ⓑ Ⓒ Ⓓ Ⓔ
42. Ⓐ Ⓑ Ⓒ Ⓓ Ⓔ
43. Ⓐ Ⓑ Ⓒ Ⓓ Ⓔ
44. Ⓐ Ⓑ Ⓒ Ⓓ Ⓔ
45. Ⓐ Ⓑ Ⓒ Ⓓ Ⓔ
46. Ⓐ Ⓑ Ⓒ Ⓓ Ⓔ
47. Ⓐ Ⓑ Ⓒ Ⓓ Ⓔ
48. Ⓐ Ⓑ Ⓒ Ⓓ Ⓔ
49. Ⓐ Ⓑ Ⓒ Ⓓ Ⓔ
50. Ⓐ Ⓑ Ⓒ Ⓓ Ⓔ

SECTION 6

1. Ⓐ Ⓑ Ⓒ Ⓓ Ⓔ
2. Ⓐ Ⓑ Ⓒ Ⓓ Ⓔ
3. Ⓐ Ⓑ Ⓒ Ⓓ Ⓔ
4. Ⓐ Ⓑ Ⓒ Ⓓ Ⓔ
5. Ⓐ Ⓑ Ⓒ Ⓓ Ⓔ
6. Ⓐ Ⓑ Ⓒ Ⓓ Ⓔ
7. Ⓐ Ⓑ Ⓒ Ⓓ Ⓔ
8. Ⓐ Ⓑ Ⓒ Ⓓ Ⓔ
9. Ⓐ Ⓑ Ⓒ Ⓓ Ⓔ
10. Ⓐ Ⓑ Ⓒ Ⓓ Ⓔ
11. Ⓐ Ⓑ Ⓒ Ⓓ Ⓔ
12. Ⓐ Ⓑ Ⓒ Ⓓ Ⓔ
13. Ⓐ Ⓑ Ⓒ Ⓓ Ⓔ
14. Ⓐ Ⓑ Ⓒ Ⓓ Ⓔ
15. Ⓐ Ⓑ Ⓒ Ⓓ Ⓔ
16. Ⓐ Ⓑ Ⓒ Ⓓ Ⓔ
17. Ⓐ Ⓑ Ⓒ Ⓓ Ⓔ
18. Ⓐ Ⓑ Ⓒ Ⓓ Ⓔ
19. Ⓐ Ⓑ Ⓒ Ⓓ Ⓔ
20. Ⓐ Ⓑ Ⓒ Ⓓ Ⓔ
21. Ⓐ Ⓑ Ⓒ Ⓓ Ⓔ
22. Ⓐ Ⓑ Ⓒ Ⓓ Ⓔ
23. Ⓐ Ⓑ Ⓒ Ⓓ Ⓔ
24. Ⓐ Ⓑ Ⓒ Ⓓ Ⓔ
25. Ⓐ Ⓑ Ⓒ Ⓓ Ⓔ
26. Ⓐ Ⓑ Ⓒ Ⓓ Ⓔ
27. Ⓐ Ⓑ Ⓒ Ⓓ Ⓔ
28. Ⓐ Ⓑ Ⓒ Ⓓ Ⓔ
29. Ⓐ Ⓑ Ⓒ Ⓓ Ⓔ
30. Ⓐ Ⓑ Ⓒ Ⓓ Ⓔ
31. Ⓐ Ⓑ Ⓒ Ⓓ Ⓔ
32. Ⓐ Ⓑ Ⓒ Ⓓ Ⓔ
33. Ⓐ Ⓑ Ⓒ Ⓓ Ⓔ
34. Ⓐ Ⓑ Ⓒ Ⓓ Ⓔ
35. Ⓐ Ⓑ Ⓒ Ⓓ Ⓔ
36. Ⓐ Ⓑ Ⓒ Ⓓ Ⓔ
37. Ⓐ Ⓑ Ⓒ Ⓓ Ⓔ
38. Ⓐ Ⓑ Ⓒ Ⓓ Ⓔ
39. Ⓐ Ⓑ Ⓒ Ⓓ Ⓔ
40. Ⓐ Ⓑ Ⓒ Ⓓ Ⓔ
41. Ⓐ Ⓑ Ⓒ Ⓓ Ⓔ
42. Ⓐ Ⓑ Ⓒ Ⓓ Ⓔ
43. Ⓐ Ⓑ Ⓒ Ⓓ Ⓔ
44. Ⓐ Ⓑ Ⓒ Ⓓ Ⓔ
45. Ⓐ Ⓑ Ⓒ Ⓓ Ⓔ
46. Ⓐ Ⓑ Ⓒ Ⓓ Ⓔ
47. Ⓐ Ⓑ Ⓒ Ⓓ Ⓔ
48. Ⓐ Ⓑ Ⓒ Ⓓ Ⓔ
49. Ⓐ Ⓑ Ⓒ Ⓓ Ⓔ
50. Ⓐ Ⓑ Ⓒ Ⓓ Ⓔ

MODEL SAT TEST 5

SECTION 1 VERBAL ABILITY

40 QUESTIONS - 30 MINUTES

For each question in this section, choose the best answer and blacken the corresponding space on the answer sheet.

Each question below consists of a word in capital letters, followed by five lettered words or phrases. Choose the word or phrase that is most nearly <u>opposite</u> in meaning to the word in capital letters. Since some of the questions require you to distinguish fine shades of meaning, consider all the choices before deciding which is best.

Example:

GOOD: (A) sour (B) bad (C) red (D) hot (E) ugly

Ⓐ ● Ⓒ Ⓓ Ⓔ

1. INVIOLATE:
   (A) enforceable
   (B) indifferent
   (C) desirable
   (D) demonstrable
   (E) desecrated

2. TYRO:
   (A) failure
   (B) prophet
   (C) native
   (D) expert
   (E) benefactor

3. IMMACULATE:
   (A) thin
   (B) extravagant
   (C) indifferent
   (D) anxious
   (E) spotted

4. CULPABLE:
   (A) unable
   (B) innocent
   (C) contradictory
   (D) allusive
   (E) marred

5. EQUANIMITY:
   (A) injustice
   (B) prestige
   (C) antagonism
   (D) agitation
   (E) ability

6. SQUANDER:
   (A) hoard
   (B) create
   (C) study
   (D) stand erect
   (E) remain in place

7. PROFUSION:
   (A) division
   (B) scarcity
   (C) sanction
   (D) confusion
   (E) acceptance

8. DAWDLE:
   (A) alter
   (B) lift
   (C) loosen
   (D) hasten
   (E) locate

9. EMBELLISH:
   (A) refuse
   (B) make holy
   (C) make peaceful
   (D) disfigure
   (E) exhort

10. OBDURATE:
   (A) acute
   (B) yielding
   (C) irregular
   (D) unavoidable
   (E) mortal

> Each sentence below has one or two blanks, each blank indicating that something has been omitted. Beneath the sentence are five lettered words or sets of words. Choose the word or set of words that best fits the meaning of the sentence as a whole.
>
> Example:
>
> Although its publicity has been ----, the film itself is intelligent, well-acted, handsomely produced, and altogether ----.
>
> (A) tasteless..respectable (B) extensive..moderate (C) sophisticated..amateur (D) risqué..crude (E) perfect..spectacular
>
> ● Ⓑ Ⓒ Ⓓ Ⓔ

11. _______ merciful by nature, he was _______ towards the murderer.
   (A) While—unjust
   (B) Albeit—implacable
   (C) Although—unmoving
   (D) Truly–vindictive
   (E) Though—understanding

12. He felt that the office routine was too _______ for a man of his dreams.
   (A) enervating
   (B) exacting
   (C) rigorous
   (D) stimulating
   (E) prosaic

13. A university training enables a man to see things as they are, to go right to the point, to disentangle a _______ of thought.
   (A) line
   (B) web
   (C) mass
   (D) plethora
   (E) skein

14. As long as the acquisition of knowledge is rendered habitually _______, so long will there be a prevailing tendency to discontinue it when free from the coercion of parents and masters.
   (A) repugnant
   (B) irrelevant
   (C) gratifying
   (D) honorable
   (E) disgraceful

15. How soon hath Time, the subtle _______ of youth Stolen on his wing my three-and-twentieth year!
   (A) friend
   (B) foe
   (C) shade
   (D) thief
   (E) bird

> Each question below consists of a related pair of words or phrases, followed by five lettered pairs of words or phrases. Select the lettered pair that best expresses a relationship similar to that expressed in the original pair.
>
> Example:
>
> YAWN : BOREDOM :: (A) dream : sleep (B) anger : madness (C) smile : amusement (D) face : expression (E) impatience : rebellion
>
> Ⓐ Ⓑ ● Ⓓ Ⓔ

16. CONGENIAL : ANIMOSITY ::
   (A) friendly : opposition
   (B) hostile : arrogance
   (C) courteous : bias
   (D) amicable : affability
   (E) brotherly : hatred

17. ANIMATE : TEDIOUS ::
   (A) enliven : entertain
   (B) vitalize : boring
   (C) invigorate : quiet
   (D) live : tiring
   (E) dead : dull

18. CURRY : MANE ::
   (A) spice : food
   (B) bridle : horse
   (C) card : wool
   (D) polish : cloth
   (E) dye : hair

19. BRASH : RETICENCE ::
   (A) crude : reserve
   (B) bold : cowardice
   (C) brazen : shyness
   (D) secret : restraint
   (E) cunning : wisdom

20. CONDENSATION : ABRIDGMENT ::
(A) beauty : originality
(B) appreciation : elongation
(C) attitude : pose
(D) habits : instincts
(E) liability : asset

21. ENTREPRENEUR : PROFITS ::
(A) philanthropist : charity
(B) organizer : union
(C) charlatan : converts
(D) priest : confession
(E) scholar : knowledge

22. AGGRESSOR : VICTIM ::
(A) dictator : foe
(B) accuser : accused
(C) attacker : plaintiff
(D) foe : ally
(E) dictator : despot

23. TROUGH : WAVE ::
(A) basin : water
(B) basement : house
(C) apex : triangle
(D) shore : reef
(E) desert : oasis

24. ASCETIC : PHILANDERING ::
(A) continent : wandering
(B) continent : immoral
(C) sour : dissipated
(D) monkish : noble
(E) monastery : castle

25. UNATTRACTIVE : HIDEOUS ::
(A) complex : confused
(B) dormant : sleeping
(C) marred : disfigured
(D) thrifty : parsimonious
(E) profane : sacred

Each passage below is followed by questions based on its content. Answer all questions following a passage on the basis of what is stated or implied in that passage.

Since 1750, about the beginning of the Age of Steam, the earth's population has more than tripled. This increase has not been an evolutionary phenomenon with biological causes. Yet there was an evolution—it took place in the world's economic organization. Thus 1,500,000,000 more human beings can now remain alive on the earth's surface, can support themselves by working for others who in turn work for them. This extraordinary tripling of human population in six short generations is explained by the speeded-up economic unification which took place during the same period. Thus most of us are now kept alive by this vast cooperative unified world society. Goods are now the great travelers over the earth's surface, far more than human beings. Endless streams of goods crisscross, as on Martian canals, with hardly an inhabited spot on the globe unvisited.

26. The title that best expresses the ideas of this passage is
(A) Modern phenomena
(B) The Age of Steam
(C) Increasing population
(D) Our greatest travelers
(E) Our economic interdependence

27. A generation is considered to be
(A) 20 years
(B) 25 years
(C) 35 years
(D) 50 years
(E) dependent on the average age at marriage

28. The writer considers trade necessary for
(A) travel
(B) democracy
(C) political unity
(D) self preservation
(E) the theory of evolution

29. The basic change which led to the greatly increased population concerns
(A) a revolution
(B) economic factors
(C) biological factors
(D) an increase in travel
(E) the growth of world government

The opposite of adaptive divergence is an interesting and fairly common expression of evolution. Whereas related groups of organisms take on widely different characters in becoming adapted to unlike environments in the case of adaptive divergence, we find that unrelated groups of organisms exhibit adaptive convergence when they adopt similar modes of life or become suited for special sorts of environments. For example, invertebrate marine animals living firmly attached to the sea bottom or to some foreign object tend to develop a subcylindrical or conical form. This is illustrated by coral individuals, by many sponges, and even by the diminutive tubes of bryozoans. Adaptive convergence in taking this coral-like form is shown by some brachiopods and pelecypods that grew in fixed position. More readily appreciated is the streamlined fitness of most fishes for moving swiftly through water; they have no neck, the contour of the body is smoothly curved so as to give minimum resistance, and the chief propelling organ is a powerful tail fin. The fact that some fossil reptiles (Ichthyosaurs) and modern mammals (whales, dolphins) are wholly fishlike in form is an expression of adaptive convergence, for these air breathing reptiles and mammals, which are highly efficient swimmers, are not closely related to fishes. Unrelated or distantly related organisms that develop similarity of form are sometimes designated as homeomorphs (having same form).

30. Organisms that could be classified as homeomorphs are
(A) whale and dolphin
(B) halibut and whale
(C) Ichthyosaurs and dolphins
(D) invertebrate marine animals and vertebrate marine animals
(E) examples of adaptive divergence

31. Adaptive convergence and adaptive divergence are
(A) manifestations of evolution
(B) biological phenomena
(C) ways in which plants and animals adjust to a common environment
(D) demonstrated by brachiopods and pelecypods
(E) ways in which plants and animals adjust to an unlike environment

32. Ichthyosaurs
(A) are mammals that live in the sea
(B) are closely related to fishes
(C) are fossil reptiles
(D) are air breathing animals
(E) are designated as homeomorphs

33. It can be inferred that in the paragraph immediately preceding this passage the author discussed
(A) marine intelligence
(B) adaptive divergence
(C) air breathing reptiles
(D) environmental impacts
(E) organisms with similar forms

There is no question but that the $72 billion budget came as a considerable shock. For one thing, it strengthened fears of a chronically eroding dollar and even tighter money markets, and aroused apprehensions that the next step might be to set up bureaucracies to dictate prices and wages and ration credit. For another, it destroyed the hope that tax reliefs could be enacted for 1958 if not for 1957, and even raised the spectre of still higher taxes. Finally, thanks to the candor of Secretary Humphrey, it gave thinking people pause to wonder to what shape of fiscal crisis the rising curve of government expenditures is leading.

People were ill-prepared for the scheduled increase in federal expenditures, particularly against the background of the State of the Union message which, issued a week earlier, had so sharply focused attention on the dangers and inequities of inflation. Throughout history, high and rising government expenditures have been the most common cause of price inflation.

The President's message took satisfaction in the fact that the budget is balanced with a modest margin for debt retirement. But, from the behavior of prices, it is apparent that this is not enough. As Chairman Martin of the Federal Reserve Board pointed out to the Congressional Joint Economic Committee February 6, both the restraint on credit expansion and the federal surplus have been a "little bit deficient." Raymond J. Saulnie Jr., new Chairman of the President's Council of Economic Advisers, also testified to the desirability of a larger surplus.

34. To halt inflation, it will be necessary to
(A) balance the budget
(B) reduce taxes
(C) create bureaucracies to dictate prices and wages
(D) call attention to the dangers of inflation
(E) reduce government expenditures

35. The $72 billion budget came as a shock because
(A) it balanced the budget too little
(B) it revived hopes for tax reduction
(C) it leads to inflation
(D) the State of the Union message had given no hint of its size
(E) it indicates a fiscal crisis

36. The President has provided
(A) a dwindling money standard
(B) for reduction of public debt
(C) for control agencies
(D) Secretary Humphrey's candor
(E) tighter money markets

Certitude is not the test of certainty. We have been cocksure of many things that were not so. If I may quote myself again, property, friendship, and truth have a common root in time. One cannot be wrenched from the rocky crevices into which one has grown for many years without feeling that one is attacked in one's life. What we most love and revere generally is determined by early associations. I love granite rocks and barberry bushes, no doubt because with them were my earliest joys that reach back through the past eternity of my life. But while one's experience thus makes certain preferences dogmatic for oneself, recognition of how they came to be so leaves one able to see that others, poor souls, may be equally dogmatic about something else. And this again means scepticism. Not that one's belief or love does not remain. Not that we would not fight and die for it if important — we all, whether we know it or not, are fighting to make the kind of world that we should like — but that we have learned to recognize that others will fight and die to make a different world, with equal sincerity of belief. Deep-seated preferences cannot be argued about — you cannot argue a man into liking a glass of beer — and therefore, when differences are sufficiently far-reaching, we try to kill the other man rather than let him have his way. But that is perfectly consistent with admitting that, so far as appears, his grounds are just as good as ours.

37. Knowing why we have certain preferences
(A) helps us understand ourselves
(B) helps us to understand others who disagree with us
(C) makes us want to die for them
(D) makes us certain
(E) makes us sceptical

38. When there are differences of opinion, we
(A) try to kill our opponents
(B) argue with them
(C) revert to our childhood scenes
(D) must respect the sources of his beliefs
(E) drink beer

What is prudence in the conduct of every private family, can scarce be folly in that of a great kingdom. If a foreign country can supply us with a commodity cheaper than we ourselves can make it, better buy it of them with some part of the produce of our own industry, employed in a way in which we have some advantage. The general industry of the country, being always in proportion to the capital which employs it, will not thereby be diminished, no more than that of the above-mentioned artificers; but only left to find out the way in which it can be employed with the greatest advantage. It is certainly not employed to the greatest advantage, when it is thus directed towards an object which it can buy cheaper than it can make. The value of its annual produce is certainly more or less diminished, when it is thus turned away from producing commodities evidently of more value than the commodity which it is directed to produce. According to the supposition, that commodity could be purchased from foreign countries cheaper than it can be made at home. It could, therefore, have been purchased with a part only of the commodities, or, what is the same thing, with a part only of the price of the commodities, which the industry employed by an equal capital would have produced at home, had it been left to follow its natural course. The industry of the country, therefore, is thus turned away from a more, to a less advantageous employment, and the exchangeable value of its annual produce, instead of being increased, according to the intention of the lawgiver, must necessarily be diminished by every such regulation.

39. The writer of the passage would favor
(A) high protective tariffs
(B) running a country like a family
(C) free trade
(D) government regulation of purchases
(E) a barter system

40. Countries should produce
(A) all commodities necessary for existence
(B) only those commodities which it can produce economically
(C) commodities which can be made more cheaply at home
(D) exclusive commodities which provide an advantage
(E) what the lawgivers decide

S T O P

IF YOU FINISH BEFORE TIME IS CALLED, YOU MAY CHECK YOUR WORK ON THIS SECTION ONLY. DO NOT WORK ON ANY OTHER SECTION IN THE TEST.

SECTION 2 MATH ABILITY

25 QUESTIONS - 30 MINUTES

In this section solve each problem, using any available space on the page for scratchwork. Then decide which is the best of the choices given and blacken the corresponding space on the answer sheet.

The following information is for your reference in solving some of the problems.

Circle of radius r: Area $= \pi r^2$; Circumference $= 2\pi r$
The number of degrees of arc in a circle is 360.
The measure in degrees of a straight angle is 180.

Definitions of symbols:

$=$ is equal to	$\leq$ is less than or equal to
$\neq$ is unequal to	$\geq$ is greater than or equal to
$<$ is less than	$\parallel$ is parallel to
$>$ is greater than	$\perp$ is perpendicular to

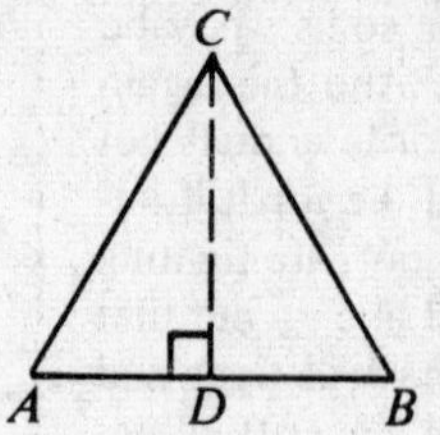

Triangle: The sum of the measures in degrees of the angles of a triangle is 180.
If $\angle CDA$ is a right angle, then

(1) area of $\triangle ABC = \frac{AB \times CD}{2}$

(2) $AC^2 = AD^2 + DC^2$

Note: Figures that accompany problems in this test are intended to provide information useful in solving the problems. They are drawn as accurately as possible EXCEPT when it is stated in a specific problem that its figure is not drawn to scale. All figures lie in a plane unless otherwise indicated. All numbers used are real numbers.

1. 0.3% of ? = 2163
(A) 721
(B) 7210
(C) 72,100
(D) 721,000
(E) 7,210,000

2. How many cents are there in $(x + 2)$ dimes?
(A) 10
(B) 12
(C) 20
(D) $x + 20$
(E) $10x + 20$

3. Which of the following fractions is closest in value to ⅔?
(A) $\frac{11}{19}$
(B) $\frac{13}{19}$
(C) $\frac{14}{19}$
(D) $\frac{15}{19}$
(E) $\frac{16}{19}$

4. What part of a yard is 6 inches?
(A) $\frac{1}{12}$
(B) $\frac{1}{4}$
(C) $\frac{1}{3}$
(D) $\frac{1}{6}$
(E) $\frac{1}{2}$

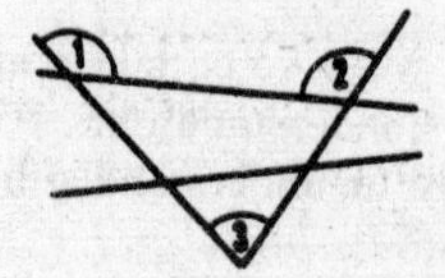

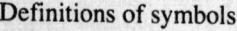

5. In the figure, $\angle 1 \overset{\circ}{=} 145$, $\angle 2 \overset{\circ}{=} 125$, $\angle 3 \overset{\circ}{=} (?)$
(A) 35
(B) 50
(C) 65
(D) 90
(E) 135

6. The perimeter of a square is p inches. What is the area of this square in terms of p?
(A) $\frac{p^2}{16}$
(B) $\frac{p^2}{4}$
(C) $\frac{p^2}{2}$
(D) p^2
(E) $2p^2$

7. $7x - 5y = 13$
$2x - 7y = 26$
$9x - 12y = ?$
(A) 13
(B) 26
(C) 39
(D) 40
(E) 52

8. A motorist leaves at 9:00 A.M. and stops for repairs at 9:20 A.M. If the distance covered was 18 miles, what was the average velocity for this part of the trip?
(A) 5.4
(B) 6
(C) 54
(D) 36
(E) 60

9. One cup of cornstarch weighs $\frac{1}{4}$ pound. Four cups of flour weigh 1 pound. What is the weight of a cup of a mixture of equal parts of flour and cornstarch?
(A) $\frac{1}{4}$
(B) $\frac{1}{2}$
(C) 1
(D) 2
(E) 4

10. A man 5′8″ casts a shadow of 8 feet. What is the height (in feet) of a pole which casts a shadow of 96 feet at the same time?
(A) $4\frac{1}{4}$
(B) 13
(C) 39
(D) 68
(E) 132

11. 1 Angstrom unit = 0.0001 micron
How many Angstrom units are there in 0.01 micron?
(A) 0.001
(B) 0.01
(C) 1
(D) 100
(E) 1000

12. A fertilizer contains 32% nitrate and 10% of the nitrate is pure nitrogen. What per cent of the fertilizer is pure nitrogen?
(A) 0.32
(B) 3.2
(C) 22
(D) 32
(E) 42

13. A family travels 30 miles during the first hour of their motor trip. They cover 40 miles during the second hour. What is the average speed (in miles per hour) for the first two hours of their trip?
(A) 30
(B) 35
(C) 40
(D) 60
(E) 70

14. A man has 85 cents in nickels and dimes, 12 coins in all; how many coins are nickels?
(A) 5
(B) 6
(C) 7
(D) 8
(E) 9

15. A baseball team has won 15 games and lost 9. If these games represent $16\frac{2}{3}\%$ of the games to be played, how many more games must the team win to average 0.750 for the season?
(A) 28
(B) 75
(C) 80
(D) 87
(E) 93

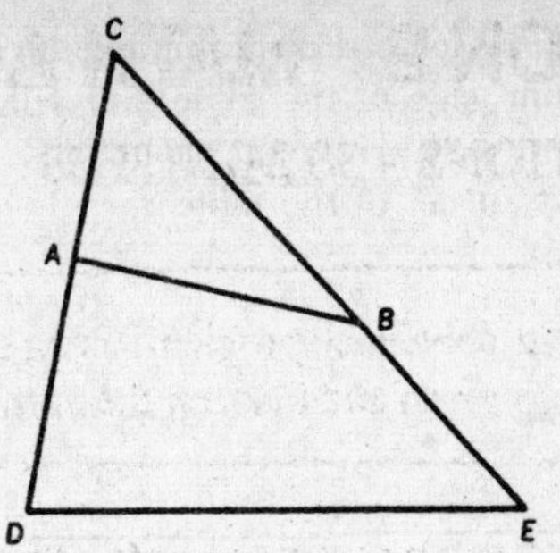

16. In triangle CDE above, $AD = BE$ and $CD < CE$. Which of the following is true?
(A) $CA > CB$
(B) $CA < CB$
(C) $CB > CE$
(D) $CD < CA$
(E) $AB \parallel DE$

17. If a man walks W miles in H hours, and then rides R miles in the same length of time, what is his average rate for the entire trip?
(A) $\frac{R + W}{H}$
(B) $\frac{2(R + W)}{H}$
(C) $\frac{R + W}{2H}$
(D) $\frac{H}{R - W}$
(E) $\frac{RW - H}{2}$

18. Eight telephone poles are each 15 feet apart. What is the distance (in feet) from the first to last pole?
(A) 30
(B) 60
(C) 85
(D) 105
(E) 120

19. $2a = \frac{b}{2}\sqrt{2} = \frac{c}{2.5}\sqrt{2}$
Arrange a, b and c in descending order of value.
(A) a, b, c
(B) b, c, a
(C) a, c, b
(D) c, b, a
(E) c, a, b

20. The area of one circle is 144π. The area of another circle is 196π. The ratio of the diameter of the smaller circle to the larger circle is
(A) $\frac{2}{3}$
(B) $\frac{3}{7}$
(C) $\frac{4}{7}$
(D) $\frac{3}{14}$
(E) $\frac{6}{7}$

21. A checker is placed on a rectangular table 3 inches from one side of the table and 4 inches from the adjacent side. How far (in inches) is it from the nearest corner of the table?
(A) $\sqrt{3}$
(B) $3\frac{1}{2}$
(C) $\sqrt{5}$
(D) $\sqrt{7}$
(E) 5

22. If x is increased by 25% then x^2 is increased by (?)%
(A) $6\frac{1}{4}$
(B) 25
(C) 50
(D) 56
(E) 156

23. Which of the following is the equation of the locus of points whose ordinates are equal to -3?
(A) $x = 3$
(B) $x = -3$
(C) $y = 3$
(D) $y = -3$
(E) $y = \pm 3$

24. Which point lies at the greatest distance from the origin?
(A) $(0, -9)$
(B) $(-2, 9)$
(C) $(-7, -6)$
(D) $(8, 5)$
(E) $(0, 0)$

25. What are the coordinates of the midpoint of the line segment joining the points whose coordinates are $(-2, 3)$ and $(4, -3)$?
(A) $(1, 0)$
(B) $(2, 0)$
(C) $(0, 1)$
(D) $(3, 1)$
(E) $(0, 2)$

S T O P

IF YOU FINISH BEFORE TIME IS CALLED, YOU MAY CHECK YOUR WORK ON THIS SECTION ONLY. DO NOT WORK ON ANY OTHER SECTION IN THE TEST.

SECTION 3 VERBAL ABILITY

45 QUESTIONS - 30 MINUTES

For each question in this section, choose the best answer and blacken the corresponding space on the answer sheet.

Each question below consists of a word in capital letters, followed by five lettered words or phrases. Choose the word or phrase that is most nearly opposite in meaning to the word in capital letters. Since some of the questions require you to distinguish fine shades of meaning, consider all the choices before deciding which is best.

Example:

GOOD: (A) sour (B) bad (C) red (D) hot (E) ugly Ⓐ ● Ⓒ Ⓓ Ⓔ

1. CANDID:
(A) frantic
(B) incapable
(C) urgent
(D) reserved
(E) developed

2. LAVISH:
(A) sparing
(B) unwashed
(C) vexed
(D) nervous
(E) unfriendly

3. CRYPTIC:
(A) ghastly
(B) lawful
(C) perceptive
(D) identical
(E) unconcealed

4. ALIENATE:
(A) renovate
(B) conciliate
(C) deviate
(D) correct
(E) reduce

5. RAUCOUS:
(A) indecisive
(B) bloody
(C) gentle
(D) defiant
(E) active

6. TACITURN:
(A) prolix
(B) tactless
(C) ironic
(D) obvious
(E) futile

7. PROVOKE:
(A) shout
(B) regret
(C) mollify
(D) deny
(E) intensify

8. IGNORANT:
(A) erudite
(B) omniscient
(C) ingenuous
(D) scholastic
(E) callow

9. LOATH:
(A) despicable
(B) adoring
(C) early
(D) choleric
(E) avid

10. FAVORITE:
(A) pariah
(B) supplicant
(C) nepotism
(D) approval
(E) enmity

11. AMENABLE:
(A) inactive
(B) disgruntled
(C) futile
(D) contentious
(E) embarrassed

12. INCIPIENT:
(A) chronic
(B) terminal
(C) obdurate
(D) delinquent
(E) excellent

13. CORRUPTIBILITY:
(A) unity
(B) probity
(C) solvency
(D) futility
(E) duplicity

14. PROFOUND:
(A) lost
(B) admired
(C) stubborn
(D) superficial
(E) supercilious

15. OVERT:
(A) incipient
(B) hateful
(C) omnipresent
(D) omnipotent
(E) clandestine

Each sentence below has one or two blanks, each blank indicating that something has been omitted. Beneath the sentence are five lettered words or sets of words. Choose the word or set of words that best fits the meaning of the sentence as a whole.

Example:

Although its publicity has been ----, the film itself is intelligent, well-acted, handsomely produced, and altogether ----.

(A) tasteless..respectable (B) extensive..moderate
(C) sophisticated..amateur (D) risqué..crude
(E) perfect..spectacular

● Ⓑ Ⓒ Ⓓ Ⓔ

16. His _______ is always a source of irritation; he never uses a single word when he can use a long clause or sentence.
(A) style
(B) prolixity
(C) abandon
(D) rhetoric
(E) eloquence

17. His lugubrious evaluation of the situation convinced all of us that he was _______.
(A) hypocritical
(B) sanguine
(C) an exaggerator
(D) optimistic
(E) a pessimist

18. I listened carefully to the candidate's speech; I was appalled by his empty promises, _______, and clichés.
(A) ingenuousness
(B) vagaries
(C) vapidities
(D) candor
(E) energy

19. To be _______ is to be _______.
(A) reticent—verbose
(B) craven—cowardly
(C) niggardly—benevolent
(D) benign—malignant
(E) bold—daunted

20. He sold a _______ which he claimed was good for _______ stomach distress, headaches, fever, muscular disorders, and seasickness.
(A) remedy—expediting
(B) remedy—relieving
(C) panacea—alleviating
(D) concoction—eradicating
(E) vial—dissolving

Each passage below is followed by questions based on its content. Answer all questions following a passage on the basis of what is stated or implied in that passage.

Mr. Speaker, ours is an open society. It is a pluralistic society. Its strength lies in its institutions. Those institutions remain viable only as long as the majority of our citizens retain a meaningful belief in them. As long as Americans feel that their institutions are responsive to the wishes of the people, we shall endure and prevail.

Everyone will admit freely that today there is a crisis in our institutions and the faith people have in them. No institution is more basic than the Congress—in this case the House of Representatives, which we have the privilege of being a part of.

Over the past year or so, the Nation has been awakened to the fact that the House—this House—our institution—has been less than responsive to the requirements of modern times. The Nation has read one article after the other on how this institution is lacking. One of the most pertinent and irrefutable accusations has to do with the fact that the House operates with too great an emphasis on secrecy, with too great an imbalance of power and too little attention paid to the wishes of the majority of its Members. In effect, this House of the people has been operating all too often in an undemocratic manner.

We cannot pretend to stand for pluralistic democracy for the Nation if we daily deny the democratic process in our deliberations and procedures. This is what is going on each day, nonetheless. It is folly to deny the need for reform. We only add fuel to the fires already being set by reactionaries of every stripe who have a vested interest in the failure of democracy. They anticipate reaction, claiming our lack of response as reason enough for seeking the overthrow of the society we are all a part of. Reform on our part in response to a proven need is to cut short the fuse of rebellion, to cut short those who seek the defeat of democracy.

Such reform can only be accomplished through existing institutions; it can only be accomplished through reform of them, beginning with the rules and procedures of the House of Representatives. We must let the people and their news media see what is transpiring here in their name, rather than shut them out in the name of fear and breach of security. This is their House, and they have a right to know what is happening here.

I believe that every vote that is meaningful must be recorded so the people will know how their elected representatives voted. Recorded teller votes are an essential reform. There is no excuse in the world why any Member of this body should be afraid of allowing his constituents to know how he voted. I favor the recorded teller vote.

The 3-day conference report layover is another essential reform. Often the conference between House and Senate results in a measure that is considerably different from the version we pass. Often the conferees disregard their instructions, even refusing by their makeup or decisions to reflect the wishes of the majority of this body. It is imperative that this body have a chance to study conference reports rather than be required to vote on them immediately.

Open committee sessions are not even negotiable as far as I am concerned. More than 40 percent of all committee sessions of the House are now closed to the public. It is also true that this trend is accelerating . . . fewer sessions of committees, where the really meaningful business of the Congress is transacted, are open to the public. This is, in effect, a denial of the democratic process, rather than an affirmation.

Disclosure of record votes in committees is another laudable effort to let the people know what is going on in their name within the committee structure. Often the people at large have no knowledge of what is happening. When other Members of this body return home, they are asked how such a thing could have occurred . . . how such a bill passed. We are often at a loss as to a reply. It is imperative that other Members of this body be informed of what committees decide and how they arrive at these decisions. For these reasons alone, disclosure of record votes within the confines of committees is essential.

This House is often a cumbersome thing. Its size does not allow for too many lengthy debates. It is often necessary for us to pass legislation swiftly in the interests of time. Nevertheless, there must be greater time for debate on motions to recommit. Too many times the wishes of the majority of Members and the people they represent have been closed off because of the limit on debate in such cases.

The last reform is elementary participatory democracy . . . guaranteed debate time on amendments. To close off debate is to negate the entire democratic process. To close off bills from amendment and discussion, as often has been the case in this body, is to deliberately enrage significant segments of the public. There is often good reason for the cries of outrage vented by many American citizens. When we do not reflect their wishes . . . even in the discussion and amending process . . . we are courting destructive dissent rather than constructive amendment and compromise.

Mr. Speaker, this House really should have little to hide from the people. The national security argument has been worked to death. Recently, an article in the Wall Street Journal by Dr. Edward Teller, no raving liberal, attacks secrecy for its own sake. We defeat our own purposes by being overly secretive.

By closing the House of the people to those very same people, we only alienate growing segments of society, stifle the democratic process and undermine the foundations of the institution and Nation we all love so deeply. If we do not take the initiative in instituting reform, we merely reaffirm the worst that has been stated about the lack of progressivism in the Congress. We add strength to the arguments of the radical revolutionaries among us. We contribute to the erosion of this House and its role.

History's pendulum swings in inexorable, wide arcs. Power swings away from the legislative branch to the executive, and then back again. Strong Presidents take power to themselves at the expense of the Congress. Weak ones lose it back to assertive Congresses.

In recent years, the legislative branch, particularly the House, has been watching helplessly as its power has drained away to the executive branch. However by concentrating power in the House, we take it away from the broad number of Members. In effect, the mass of the House becomes less responsive because of the inner concentration of ability to act and respond.

We end up by becoming weaker as a body—as a branch of Government. We become less able to counterbalance the executive branch because we make ourselves weaker. Only by willing, internal reform can we reverse the trend—make the House stronger through greater diffusion of power to individual Members. If we make each Member stronger through fair distribution of initiatives, we allow Members to reflect the wishes of their constituents. There is a great spread of pressure upon the House and a broader expression of the wishes of the people of this country.

21. The author's purpose in writing this message is to
- (A) encourage Congress to limit the powers of the President
- (B) make Congress more responsive by lifting the secrecy which prevails
- (C) improve Democracy
- (D) answer the radicals who want to overthrow the government
- (E) limit the powers of Congressional committees

22. Which of the following does the author not propose in this passage?
- (A) Recording of votes
- (B) Open committee hearings
- (C) The 3-day conference report layover
- (D) Unlimited debate
- (E) Disclosure of committee votes

23. A strong President
- (A) always wins over Congress
- (B) never gets along with Congress
- (C) can work harmoniously with Congress
- (D) cannot work harmoniously with Congress
- (E) limits the power of Congress

24. The author states that the 3-day conference layover is necessary
- (A) to insure that the House's wishes are respected
- (B) because the conferees ignore the wishes of the members
- (C) to protect the House from the Senate
- (D) to assert Congress's rights against the President
- (E) to delay needed legislation

25. The author regards as a denial of the democratic process the
- (A) failure to keep teller records of votes
- (B) hasty action on conference reports
- (C) closed committee hearings
- (D) limited debate
- (E) a strong President

26. According to the author, in recent years, we have had
- (A) a series of strong Presidents
- (B) a series of weak Presidents
- (C) some weak and some strong Presidents
- (D) a clash between Congress and the Executive Branch
- (E) harmony between Congress and the Executive Branch

27. The author strongly advocates
- (A) guaranteed time to debate amendments
- (B) closed hearings on matters of national security
- (C) speedy action
- (D) the democratic process
- (E) the controlling of subversives in our society

28. The author implies that opponents of our society
- (A) favor the suggestions he is making
- (B) disapprove of the suggestions
- (C) prefer a strong President
- (D) are working for their own selfish ends
- (E) are not concerned with the suggestions being made

Of the poetry of the United States different opinions have been entertained, and prejudice on the one side, and partiality on the other, have equally prevented a just and rational estimate of its merits. Abroad, our literature has fallen under unmerited contumely from those who were but slenderly acquainted with the subject on which they professed to decide; and at home, it must be confessed that the swaggering and pompous pretensions of many have done not a little to provoke and excuse the ridicule of foreigners. Either of these extremes exerts an injurious influence on the cause of letters in our country. To encourage exertion and embolden merit to come forward, it is necessary that they should be acknowledged and rewarded—few will have the confidence to solicit what has been withheld from claims as strong as theirs, or the courage to tread a path which presents no prospect but the melancholy wrecks who have gone before them. National gratitude — national pride — every high and generous feeling that attaches us to the land of our birth, or that exalts our characters as individuals, ask of us that we should foster the infant literature of our country, and that genius and industry, employing their efforts to hasten its perfection, should receive from our hands, that celebrity which reflects as much honor on the nation which confers it as on those to whom it is extended. On the other hand, it is not necessary for these purposes, it is even detrimental to bestow on mediocrity the praise due to excellence, and still more so is the attempt to persuade ourselves and others into an admiration of the faults of favorite writers. We make but a contemptible figure in the eyes of the world, and set ourselves up as objects of pity to our posterity, when we affect to rank the poets of our own country with those mighty masters of song who have flourished in Greece, Italy and Britain.

29. The author's main purpose in writing this passage is to
(A) assert the greatness of our poetry
(B) answer foreign critics who sneer at American literature
(C) deplore the lack of good writing in this country
(D) discuss the need for encouraging our writers
(E) deplore the extravagant claims made on behalf of American authors

30. "Contumely" (line 3) means
(A) praise
(B) evaluation
(C) insulting language
(D) disregard
(E) reading

Select the word or set of words that best completes each of the following sentences.

31. This book is the most inane and _______ work I have read this year.
(A) fascinating
(B) fatuous
(C) factual
(D) fantastic
(E) flagrant

32. A person who is _______ cannot be accused of being _______.
(A) malingering—diligent
(B) assiduous—derogatory
(C) plausible—logical
(D) glib—raucous
(E) miserly—magnanimous

33. The atomic reactor, people have begun to realize, may be a _______ to our energy problem, but it also constitutes a _______ which must be taken into consideration.
(A) panacea—complication
(B) hazard—danger
(C) solution—hazard
(D) solution—complication
(E) catastrophe—hazard

34. This essay lacks originality and freshness; in fact, it is quite _______.
(A) banal
(B) intriguing
(C) boring
(D) enervating
(E) novel

35. When you accuse him of being a chauvinist, you fail to _______ that he _______ this country's militant foreign policy.
(A) recall—supported
(B) think—disregarded
(C) consider—vindicated
(D) mention—supported
(E) consider—opposed

Each question below consists of a related pair of words or phrases, followed by five lettered pairs of words or phrases. Select the lettered pair that best expresses a relationship similar to that expressed in the original pair.

Example:

YAWN : BOREDOM :: (A) dream : sleep
(B) anger : madness (C) smile : amusement
(D) face : expression (E) impatience : rebellion

Ⓐ Ⓑ ● Ⓓ Ⓔ

36. PAIN : SEDATIVE ::
(A) comfort : stimulant
(B) grief : consolation
(C) trance : narcotic
(D) ache : extraction
(E) arrest : warrant

37. PORK : PIG ::
(A) beef : cow
(B) rooster : chicken
(C) mutton : sheep
(D) steer : beef
(E) lobster : crustacean

38. MAXIM : PITHY ::
(A) epitaph : verbose
(B) adage : elegiac
(C) proverb : satiric
(D) proverb : innovative
(E) epigram : terse

39. VIRUS : COLD ::
(A) serum : measles
(B) infection : gangrene
(C) microbe : incision
(D) microbe : germ
(E) virus : tuberculosis

40. CHOLERIC : IRASCIBLE ::
(A) wearisome : refreshing
(B) angry : calm
(C) bellicose : pacific
(D) tiring : enervating
(E) martial : marital

41. FILTER : WATER ::
(A) curtail : activity
(B) expurgate : book
(C) edit : text
(D) condense : novel
(E) review : play

42. MUNDANE : SPIRITUAL ::
(A) common : ghostly
(B) worldly : unworldly
(C) routine : novel
(D) secular : clerical
(E) everlasting : evanescent

43. INDIGENT : WEALTHY ::
(A) angry : rich
(B) native : affluent
(C) gauche : graceful
(D) scholarly : erudite
(E) penurious : affluent

44. THRUST : SPEAR ::
(A) mangle : iron
(B) scabbard : sword
(C) bow : arrow
(D) fence : epee
(E) shoot : discus

45. WAN : COLOR ::
(A) altruistic : unselfishness
(B) corpulent : weight
(C) insipid : flavor
(D) pallid : complexion
(E) enigmatic : puzzle

S T O P

IF YOU FINISH BEFORE TIME IS CALLED, YOU MAY CHECK YOUR WORK ON THIS SECTION ONLY. DO NOT WORK ON ANY OTHER SECTION IN THE TEST.

SECTION 4 TEST OF STANDARD WRITTEN ENGLISH

50 QUESTIONS - 30 MINUTES

The questions in this section measure skills that are important to writing well. In particular, they test your ability to recognize and use language that is clear, effective, and correct according to the requirements of standard written English, the kind of English found in most college textbooks.

Directions: The following sentences contain problems in grammar, usage, diction (choice of words), and idiom.
Some sentences are correct.
No sentence contains more than one error.

You will find that the error, if there is one, is underlined and lettered. Assume that elements of the sentence that are not underlined are correct and cannot be changed. In choosing answers, follow the requirements of standard written English.

If there is an error, select the one underlined part that must be changed to make the sentence correct and blacken the corresponding space on your answer sheet.

If there is no error, blacken answer space Ⓔ.

EXAMPLE:

The region has a climate so severe that plants
A
growing there rarely had been more than twelve
B C
inches high. No error
D E

SAMPLE ANSWER
Ⓐ Ⓑ ● Ⓓ Ⓔ

1. The radio in the child's room was blaring rock and
A
roll music at full volume, which made her mother
B C
very angry. No error
D E

2. Notice the immediate affect this drug has on the
A B C
behavior of the rats in the cage. No error
D E

3. Having read for more than four hours without a
A B C
rest, the book fell from his hands. No error
D E

4. Provided that you pay attention, I shall explain the
A B C D
assignment. No error
E

5. Please do not be aggravated by his bad manners; he
A B C
is merely trying to attract attention. No error
D E

6. Are you going to lie there all day and refuse to see
A B C D
your friends? No error
E

7. Neither the teacher nor her pupils were enthused
A B C
about going on the field trip. No error
D E

8. Because of the gasoline shortage, less tourists have
A B
visited our park this year than in any previous year.
C D
No error
E

9. The general along with the members of his general
A B
staff seem to favor immediate retaliation at this
C D
time. No error
E

10. The audience became restless and noisy before the
A B C
singer appeared on the stage. No error
D E

11. I was kept awake by the baby's continuous crying
A B C
during the night. No error
D E

12. I will have gone before you have come to the
A B C D
party. No error
E

13. To me who am your friend, this accusation comes
A B C
as a shock. No error
D E

14. This scholarship should be awarded to whoever
A B C
best meets the requirements. No error
D E

15. We resented him coming to our meeting and
A B
criticizing our efforts because he had ignored our
C D
requests for assistance up to that time.
No error
E

16. Entering quietly into the ward in order not to
A B C
disturb the sleeping patients, the door was
D
carefully shut. No error
E

17. I must apologize for my late arrival although it was
A B C
not my fault. Because there was a traffic delay.
D
No error
E

18. I fail to understand why you are seeking my
A B
council after the way you ignored my advice last
C D
week. No error
E

19. Who shall I give this package to? No error
A B C D E

20. Sinking slowly into the sea, the sun was a huge ball
A B C
of fire. No error
D E

21. I wish I was the teacher for five minutes: I'd tell
A B C
the class what I think of its behavior. No error
D E

22. To the artist's dismay, the picture was hung upside
A B
down; to his embarrassment, no one noticed the
C D
error. No error
E

23. John usually eats a quick lunch, ignoring the
A B
question whether what he eats is healthy or not.
C D
No error
E

24. We lived in this house for ten years and hope
A B C
to live there for ten more years. No error
D E

25. His story about the strange beings in a space ship
A
was so incredulous that no one believed him.
B C D
No error
E

Directions: In each of the following sentences, some part or all of the sentence is underlined. Below each sentence you will find five ways of phrasing the underlined part. Select the answer that produces the most effective sentence, one that is clear and exact, without awkwardness or ambiguity, and blacken the corresponding space on your answer sheet. In choosing answers, follow the requirements of standard written English. Choose the answer that best expresses the meaning of the original sentence.

Answer (A) is always the same as the underlined part. Choose answer (A) if you think the original sentence needs no revision.

EXAMPLE:

Laura Ingalls Wilder published her first book and she was sixty-five years old then.

(A) and she was sixty-five years old then
(B) when she was sixty-five years old
(C) at age sixty-five years old
(D) upon reaching sixty-five years
(E) at the time when she was sixty-five

SAMPLE ANSWER

Ⓐ ● Ⓒ Ⓓ Ⓔ

26. After conducting the orchestra for six concerts, Beethoven's *Ninth Symphony* was scheduled.
(A) After conducting
(B) After he conducted
(C) Because he had conducted
(D) Although he conducted
(E) After he had conducted

27. I had ought to do my homework before going to the birthday party.
(A) had ought
(B) should
(C) should of
(D) must
(E) ought

28. If you have enjoyed these kind of programs, write to your local public television station and ask for more.
(A) these kind of programs
(B) those kind of programs
(C) these kinds of programs
(D) these kind of a program
(E) this kind of a program

29. In her critique of the newly opened restaurant, the reviewer discussed the elaborate menu, the impressive wine list, and how the waiters functioned.
(A) list, and how the waiters functioned
(B) list and how the waiters functioned
(C) list, and the excellent service
(D) list and even the excellent service
(E) list, and how the waiters' functioned

30. The police officer refused to permit us to enter the apartment, saying that he had orders to stop him going into the building.
(A) stop him going
(B) prevent him going
(C) stop his going
(D) stop us going
(E) stop our going

31. Your complaint is no different from the last customer who expected a refund.
(A) Your complaint is no different from the last customer
(B) Your complaint is no different from that of the last customer
(C) You're complaint is no different than the last customer
(D) You're complaint is no different from that of the last customer
(E) Your complaint is the same as the last customer

32. Sitting in the Coliseum, the music couldn't hardly be heard because of the cheering and yelling of the spectators.
(A) the music couldn't hardly be heard because of
(B) the music couldn't hardly be heard due to
(C) the music could hardly be heard due to
(D) we could hardly hear the music due to
(E) we could hardly hear the music because of

33. If I would have known about the traffic jam at the bridge, I would have taken an alternate route.
(A) If I would have known about
(B) If I could of known about
(C) If I would of known about
(D) If I was aware of
(E) Had I known about

34. Confident about the outcome, President Reagan along with his staff are traveling to the conference.
(A) Confident about the outcome, President Reagan along with his staff are traveling
(B) Confident about the outcome, President Reagan's party are traveling
(C) Confident about the outcome, President Reagan along with his staff is traveling
(D) With confidence about the outcome, President Reagan along with his staff are traveling
(E) President Reagan along with his staff is traveling confidently about the outcome

35. By the time he was apprehended by the police, he had already decided to surrender.
(A) had already decided
(B) had all ready decided
(C) already decided
(D) all ready decided
(E) will have already decided

36. According to the review board, many laboratory tests were ordered by the staff of the hospital that had no medical justification.
(A) many laboratory tests were ordered by the staff of the hospital that
(B) many laboratory tests were ordered by the staff of the hospital who
(C) the staff of the hospital ordered many laboratory tests that
(D) the staff of the hospital, who ordered many laboratory tests that
(E) the ordering of many laboratory tests by the staff of the hospital which

37. Contemporary poets are not abandoning rhyme, but some avoiding it.
(A) but some avoiding it.
(B) but it is avoided by some of them.
(C) but it is being avoided.
(D) but some are avoiding it.
(E) but it has been being avoided by some.

38. Helen Keller was blind and deaf from infancy and she learned to communicate using both sign language and speech.
(A) Helen Keller was blind and deaf from infancy and she
(B) Although blind and deaf from infancy, Helen Keller
(C) Although being blind and deaf from the time she was an infant, Helen Keller
(D) Being blind and deaf from infancy, Helen Keller
(E) Helen Keller, being blind and deaf from infancy, she

39. Standing alone beside her husband's grave, grief overwhelmed the widow and she wept inconsolably.
(A) grief overwhelmed the widow and she wept inconsolably.
(B) grief overwhelmed the widow, who wept inconsolably.
(C) grief overwhelmed the widow that wept inconsolably.
(D) the widow was overwhelmed by grief and wept inconsolably.
(E) the widow was overwhelmed by grief, she wept inconsolably.

40. The difference between Liebniz and Schopenhauer is that the former is optimistic; the latter, pessimistic.
(A) the former is optimistic; the latter, pessimistic.
(B) the former is optimistic, the latter, pessimistic.
(C) while the former is optimistic; the latter, pessimistic.
(D) the former one is optimistic; the latter one is a pessimist.
(E) the former is optimistic; the latter being pessimistic.

Note: The remaining questions are like those at the beginning of the section.

Directions: For each sentence in which you find an error, select the one underlined part that must be changed to make the sentence correct and blacken the corresonding space on your answer sheet.
If there is no error, blacken answer space Ⓔ.

EXAMPLE:

The region has a climate **so severe that** (A) plants **growing there** (B) rarely **had been** (C) more than twelve inches **high**. (D) **No error** (E)

SAMPLE ANSWER

Ⓐ Ⓑ ● Ⓓ Ⓔ

41. The **articles** (A) on sale at the **bazaar** (B) were **so** (C) cheap that I **almost** (D) bought two dresses. **No error** (E)

42. I **should like** (A) to **purchase** (B) a **couple** (C) of soft **rolls;** (D) please let me have four of them. **No error** (E)

43. More than fifty **percent** (A) of this work load still **has** (B) to be completed: I **am afraid** (C) that we shall have to work **overtime** (D) tonight. **No error** (E)

44. **If** (A) you continue to drive **so** (B) recklessly, you **are likely** (C) to have a serious accident in the **very** (D) near future. **No error** (E)

45. **Our's** (A) is a critical period; we **are confronted with** (B) **grave** (C) problems which must be solved if we **are** (D) to avert a tragedy. **No error** (E)

46. **Shakespeare's** (A) line "**Like** (B) Niobe, all **tears**" (C) contains a literary **illusion.** (D) **No error** (E)

47. In **all my years** (A) as a teacher, I **have never encountered** (B) an individual such as **he;** (C) he definitely is **most unique.** (D) **No error** (E)

48. **Due to** (A) the **President's** (B) unpopularity, many candidates feared that **executive** (C) difficulties **would affect** (D) legislative selections. **No error** (E)

49. **Applying** (A) knowledge **intelligently,** (B) education **provides** (C) mankind with the **tools** (D) to control his environment. **No error** (E)

50. Iron rusts **from** (A) disuse; stagnant water loses its purity and in cold weather becomes **frozen;** (B) even so the vigor of the mind **is sapped** (C) by **inactivity.** (D) **No error** (E)

S T O P

IF YOU FINISH BEFORE TIME IS CALLED, YOU MAY CHECK YOUR WORK ON THIS SECTION ONLY.
DO NOT WORK ON ANY OTHER SECTION IN THE TEST.

SECTION 5 MATH ABILITY

35 QUESTIONS - 30 MINUTES

In this section, solve each problem, using any available space on the page for scratchwork. Then decide which is the best of the choices given and blacken the corresponding space on the answer sheet.

The following information is for your reference in solving some of the problems.

Circle of radius r: Area $= \pi r^2$; Circumference $= 2\pi r$

The number of degrees of arc in a circle is 360.

The measure in degrees of a straight angle is 180.

Definitions of symbols:

$=$ is equal to
$\neq$ is unequal to
$<$ is less than
$>$ is greater than
$\leq$ is less than or equal to
$\geq$ is greater than or equal to
$\parallel$ is parallel to
$\perp$ is perpendicular to

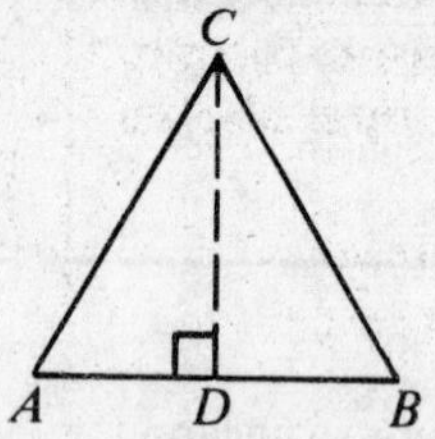

Triangle: The sum of the measures in degrees of the angles of a triangle is 180.

If $\angle CDA$ is a right angle, then

(1) area of $\triangle ABC = \frac{AB \times CD}{2}$

(2) $AC^2 = AD^2 + DC^2$

Note: Figures that accompany problems in this test are intended to provide information useful in solving the problems. They are drawn as accurately as possible EXCEPT when it is stated in a specific problem that its figure is not drawn to scale. All figures lie in a plane unless otherwise indicated. All numbers used are real numbers.

1. What number divided by 50 gives 3.6%?
(A) 1.8
(B) 3.6
(C) 7.2
(D) 18
(E) 36

2. An article sells for $65.00. This price gives the retailer a profit of 30% on his costs. What will be the new retail price if he cuts his profit to 10% of costs?
(A) $42
(B) $45.50
(C) $50
(D) $50.05
(E) $55

3. A picture is 36 inches long and 16 inches wide. If its frame is one inch wide, what is the area of the frame?
(A) 100
(B) 108
(C) 476
(D) 576
(E) 684

4. A graduating class of 356 votes to choose a president. With 5 candidates seeking office, what is the least number of votes a successful candidate could receive and yet have more votes than any other candidate?
(A) 71
(B) 72
(C) 89
(D) 178
(E) 179

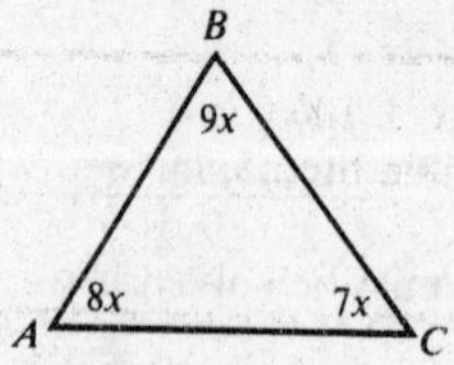

5. In the figure above, $\angle A \stackrel{\circ}{=}$ (?)
(A) 15
(B) 45
(C) 60
(D) 80
(E) 120

6. A home owner uses half of his available oil to heat his home during one week of extreme cold weather. If the tank was $\frac{3}{4}$ full at the beginning of the week, what part of the full capacity did he use this week?

(A) $\frac{3}{16}$
(B) $\frac{1}{4}$
(C) $\frac{3}{8}$
(D) $\frac{5}{8}$
(E) $\frac{2}{3}$

7. A man works 5 days a week and binds 35 sets of books each week. If there are 7 books in a set, what is the number of books he binds each day?

(A) 1
(B) 7
(C) 25
(D) 35
(E) 49

Questions 8–27 each consist of two quantities, one in Column A and one in Column B. You are to compare the two quantities and on the answer sheet blacken space

- A if the quantity in Column A is greater;
- B if the quantity in Column B is greater;
- C if the two quantities are equal;
- D If the relationship cannot be determined from the information given.

AN E RESPONSE WILL NOT BE SCORED.

EXAMPLES

	Column A	Column B	Answers
E1.	2×6	$2 + 6$	● Ⓑ Ⓒ Ⓓ Ⓔ
	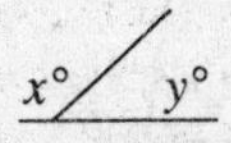		
E2.	$180 - x$	y	Ⓐ Ⓑ ● Ⓓ Ⓔ
E3.	$p - q$	$q - p$	Ⓐ Ⓑ Ⓒ ● Ⓔ

Notes:

1. In certain questions, information concerning one or both of the quantities to be compared is centered above the two columns.
2. In a given question, a symbol that appears in both columns represents the same thing in Column A as it does in Column B.
3. Letters such as x, n, and k stand for real numbers.

	Column A	Column B
8.	$\frac{7 + 7 + 7}{-7 - 7 - 7}$	1

9. $0 < x < 100$
x is divisible by 2,3,5

	Column A	Column B
	30	x
10.	109 inches	3 yards, 1 inch

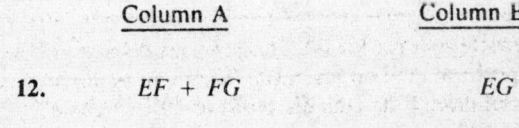

In parallelogram $EFGH$,
$EF + EH = 20$
This concerns #11 and #12

	Column A	Column B
11.	Length of HG	Length of EF
12.	$EF + FG$	EG

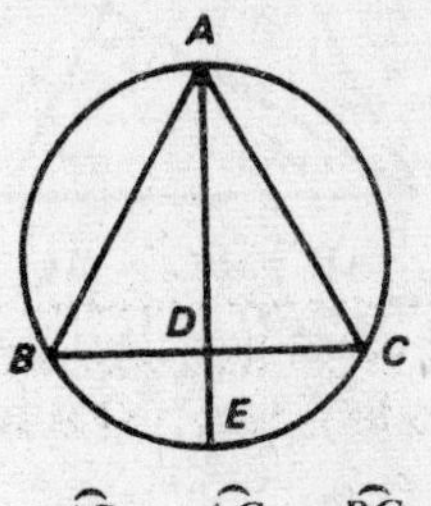

$\widehat{AB} = \widehat{AC} = \widehat{BC}$
$BD = DC$

	Column A	Column B
13.	$\frac{AC}{DC}$	2

Column A	Column B

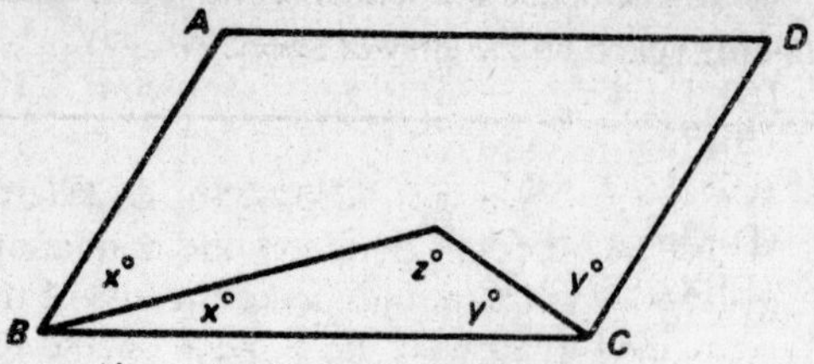

$AB \parallel DC$, and $AD \parallel BC$
$y = 50$

	Column A	Column B
14.	z	90

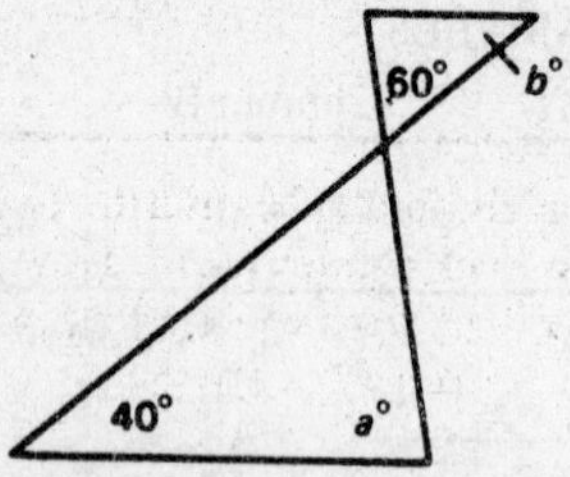

	Column A	Column B
15.	a	b

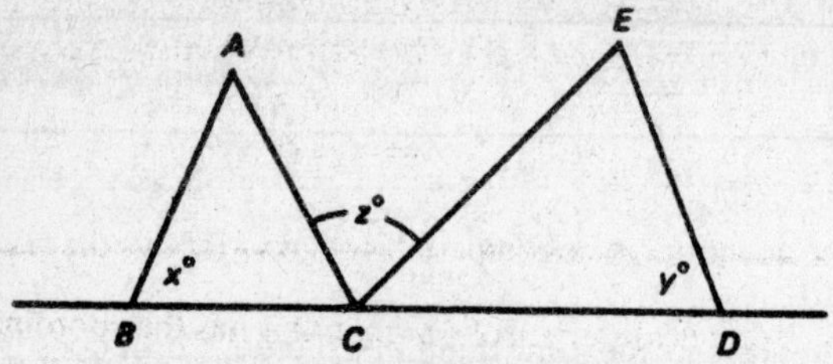

$AB = AC$ and $EC = ED$
$x = 40$ and $y = 80$
This concerns #16 and #17

	Column A	Column B
16.	$3x$	$2z$
17.	y	z

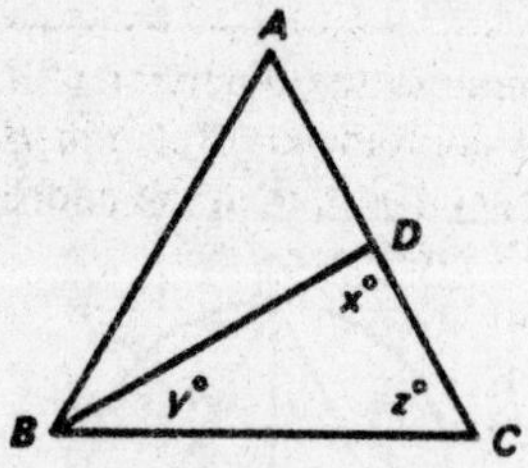

$AB = BC = AC$
$BD \perp AC$

	Column A	Column B
18.	$\frac{x}{y}$	3

Column A	Column B

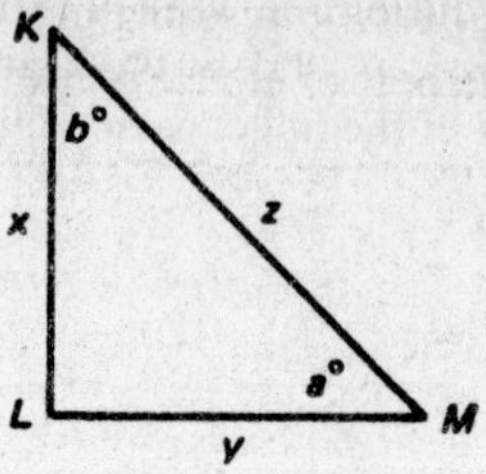

$KL \perp LM$
This concerns #19–#22

	Column A	Column B
19.	x	y
20.	$x + y$	z
21.	a	b
22.	$a + b$	90

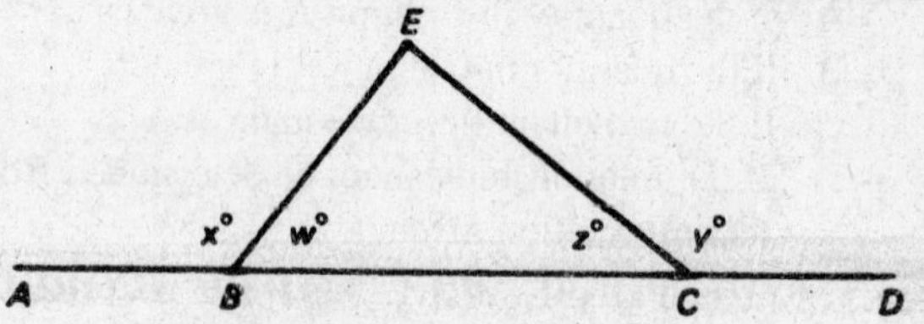

$ABCD$ is a line segment and $BE \perp CE$
This concerns #23–#26

	Column A	Column B
23.	$x + y$	90
24.	x	$z + 90$
25.	$90 - z$	w
26.	w	z

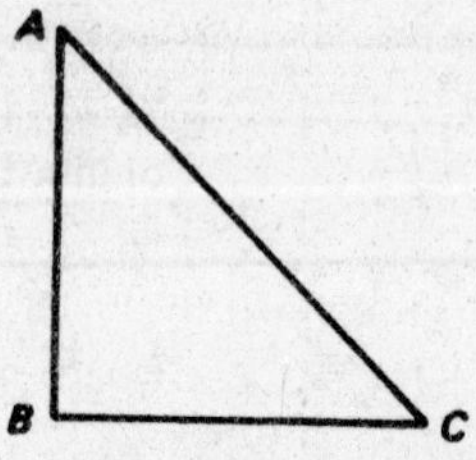

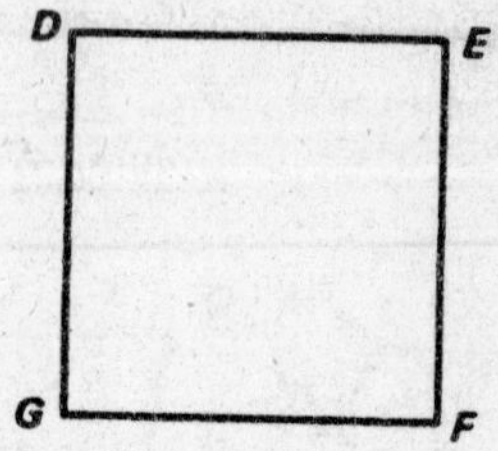

$AB = BC$, and $DE = EF = FG = DG$
Area of right triangle ABC
equals area of square $DEFG$

	Column A	Column B
27.	$\frac{AB}{DG}$	$\sqrt{2}$

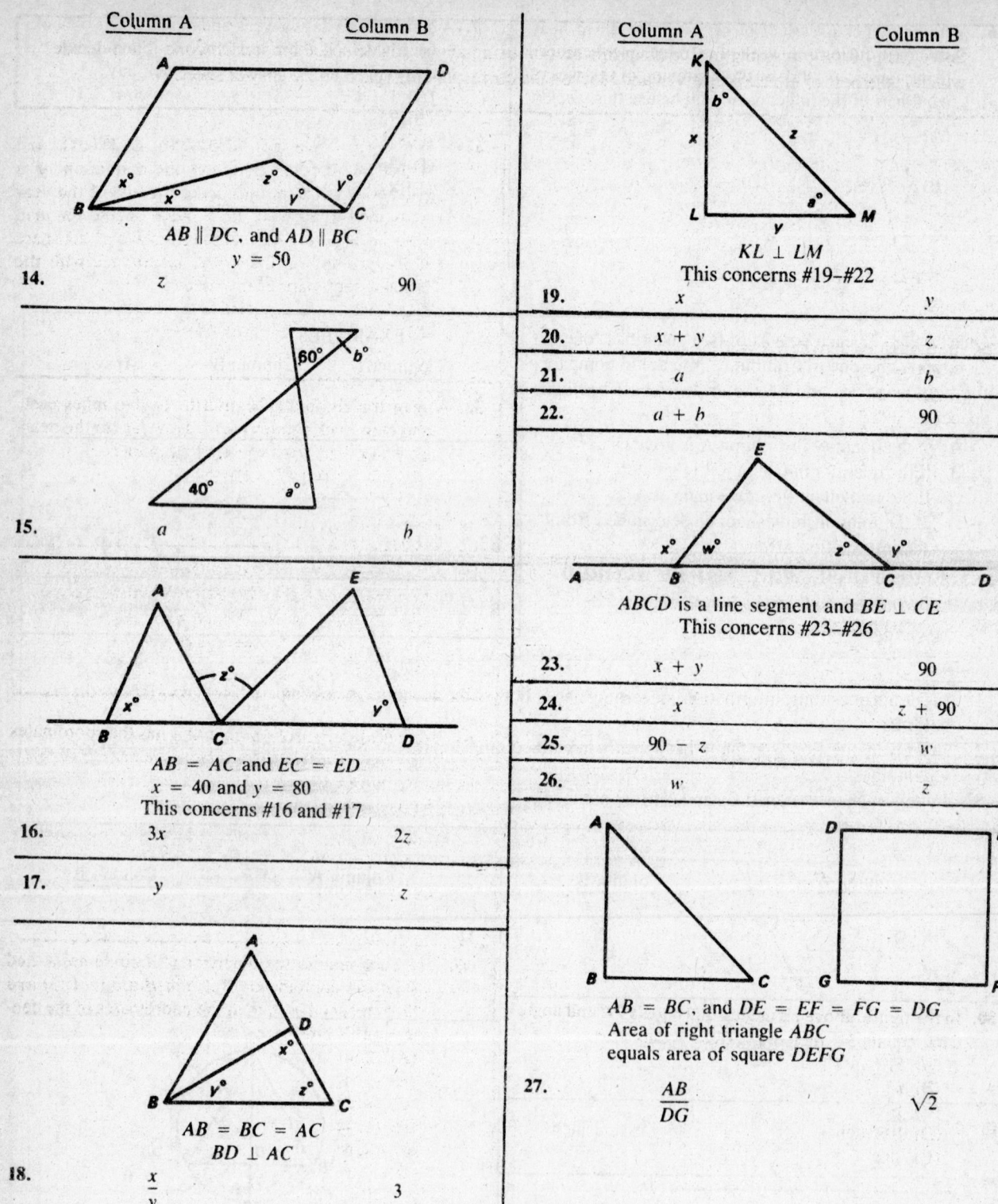

Solve each of the remaining problems in this section using any available space for scratchwork. Then decide which is the best of the choices given and blacken the corresponding space on the answer sheet.

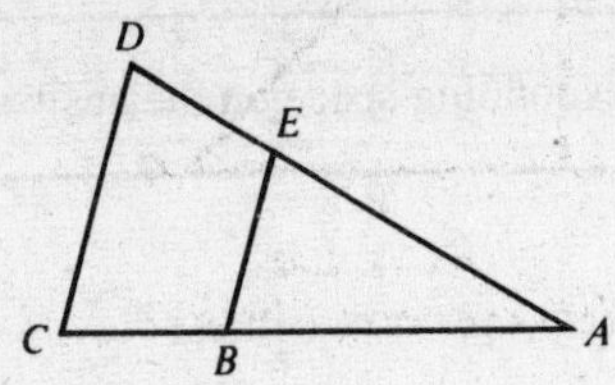

28. In the figure above, $BA = 2BC$
$EA = 2DE$
$BE = 14$
$DC = ?$
(A) 7
(B) 18
(C) 21
(D) 24
(E) 28

29. If $xy = k$, k a constant, and if $y = 5$ when $x = 7$, what is the value of x when $y = 32$?
(A) $\frac{35}{32}$
(B) $22\frac{6}{7}$
(C) 23
(D) 25
(E) $44\frac{4}{5}$

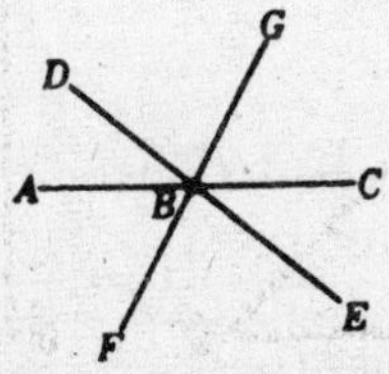

30. In the figure above, if angle DBG equals 79° and angle CBE equals 39° then angle GBE equals
(A) 51°
(B) 62°
(C) 101°
(D) 108°
(E) 202°

31. Three men invested \$2,000.00, \$3,000.00 and \$5,000.00 respectively upon the formation of a partnership. The net profits at the end of the year amounted to \$960.00. How much should the man who invested the least money receive as his share if the profits are divided in accordance with the amount each partner invested?
(A) \$192
(B) \$220
(C) \$240
(D) \$384
(E) \$480

32. A man travels four miles north, twelve miles east, and then twelve miles north. How far (to the nearest mile) is he from the starting point?
(A) 17
(B) 20
(C) 21
(D) 24
(E) 28

33. If the coordinates of A and B are (6, 1) and (−2, 7) then the coordinates of the midpoint of AB are
(A) (2, −4)
(B) (−2, 4)
(C) (2, 4)
(D) (4, 8)
(E) −2, −4)

34. What is the length of AB if point A has the coordinates (2, −1) and point B has the coordinates (10, 3)?
(A) $4\sqrt{3}$
(B) $2\sqrt{17}$
(C) $4\sqrt{5}$
(D) $2\sqrt{37}$
(E) 80

35. The endpoints of the diameter of a circle are A and B. If the coordinates of A and B are (−1, 3) and (5, 5) respectively, then the coordinates of the center of this circle are
(A) (2, 4)
(B) (3, 4)
(C) (4, 8)
(D) (4, 4)
(E) (0, 0)

S T O P

IF YOU FINISH BEFORE TIME IS CALLED, YOU MAY CHECK YOUR WORK ON THIS SECTION ONLY. DO NOT WORK ON ANY OTHER SECTION IN THE TEST.

SECTION 6 VERBAL ABILITY

45 QUESTIONS - 30 MINUTES

For each question in this section, choose the best answer and blacken the corresponding space on the answer sheet.

Each question below consists of a word in capital letters, followed by five lettered words or phrases. Choose the word or phrase that is most nearly opposite in meaning to the word in capital letters. Since some of the questions require you to distinguish fine shades of meaning, consider all the choices before deciding which is best.

Example:

GOOD: (A) sour (B) bad (C) red
(D) hot (E) ugly

Ⓐ ● Ⓒ Ⓓ Ⓔ

1. PUNCTUAL:
   (A) dilatory
   (B) digressive
   (C) deliquescent
   (D) remote
   (E) efficacious

2. DOWDY:
   (A) gifted
   (B) garish
   (C) boring
   (D) pining
   (E) chic

3. OSTENTATIOUS:
   (A) unobservant
   (B) vigorous
   (C) unpretentious
   (D) unmitigated
   (E) unpleasant

4. DULCET:
   (A) cacophonous
   (B) iridescent
   (C) evanescent
   (D) incomprehensible
   (E) ineffectual

5. WAX:
   (A) shine
   (B) polish
   (C) wane
   (D) heat
   (E) chill

6. CUPIDITY:
   (A) love
   (B) altruism
   (C) malice
   (D) roundness
   (E) simplicity

7. NEFARIOUS:
   (A) negative
   (B) wicked
   (C) slanderous
   (D) black
   (E) honorable

8. DOGMATIC:
   (A) feline
   (B) experienced
   (C) reasonable
   (D) religious
   (E) heretic

9. EXTRANEOUS:
   (A) intrinsic
   (B) episodic
   (C) analytic
   (D) muted
   (E) massive

10. COSMOPOLITAN:
    (A) garish
    (B) unlettered
    (C) unrestrained
    (D) provincial
    (E) intellectual

11. CHAOTIC:
    (A) chaste
    (B) chastened
    (C) beaten
    (D) novel
    (E) orderly

12. PALATABLE:
    (A) partial
    (B) plentiful
    (C) scarce
    (D) distasteful
    (E) harmless

13. DESICCATE:
(A) saturate
(B) sate
(C) castigate
(D) destroy
(E) upbuild

14. WANTON:
(A) moral
(B) futile
(C) oriental
(D) wasted
(E) watery

15. GUILELESS:
(A) silvery
(B) crucified
(C) sunless
(D) deceitful
(E) sizable

Each sentence below has one or two blanks, each blank indicating that something has been omitted. Beneath the sentence are five lettered words or sets of words. Choose the word or set of words that <u>best</u> fits the meaning of the sentence as a whole.

Example:

Although its publicity has been ----, the film itself is intelligent, well-acted, handsomely produced, and altogether ----.

(A) tasteless..respectable (B) extensive..moderate
(C) sophisticated..amateur (D) risqué..crude
(E) perfect..spectacular

● Ⓑ Ⓒ Ⓓ Ⓔ

16. The Marines attacked the south beach at daybreak; _______, as a diversionary maneuver, a company landed on the north side of the island.
(A) previously
(B) later
(C) simultaneously
(D) at noon
(E) subsequently

17. Although the members of Congress wanted to go home, no hope for an early _______ could be entertained.
(A) postponement
(B) compromise
(C) adjustment
(D) adjournment
(E) trip

18. One characteristic of the _______ is his ability to use _______ in his work.
(A) charlatan—medicine
(B) mechanic—motors
(C) sailor—knots
(D) scholar—books
(E) mathematician—semantics

19. Her critics maintained that you could tell she was an actress by her _______ manner of speech.
(A) affectionate
(B) romantic
(C) affected
(D) dramatic
(E) cultivated

20. As far as our professional _______ is concerned, each man is out for his own personal _______.
(A) pessimist—happiness
(B) pessimist—gain
(C) optimist—loss
(D) cynic—aggrandizement
(E) cynic—agnosticism

Each passage below is followed by questions based on its content. Answer all questions following a passage on the basis of what is <u>stated</u> or <u>implied</u> in that passage.

Yet the fact remains that as enthusiasm for Shakespearean drama has increased, the tendency has been steadily away from realism and spectacle and steadily toward a rediscovery of the Shakespearean play in conditions resembling its first staging. It has, for instance, been realized that the alternation of scenes—swift scenes following the major crises, gay scenes switching the mood from sadness, comedy breaking in on dire tragedy—enormously enhances the emotional effect of the whole play. Shakespeare wrote his plays to be acted as a single stretch. The alternation of scene and mood is like the orchestration of a symphony, the climaxes carefully prepared in subsidiary themes, the tension heightened or relaxed, the movement quickened or slowed to suit the general rhythm of the drama. It follows that Shakespeare cannot be successfully confined on a stage within a picture-frame set statically fixed throughout the three-quarters of an hour allotted to each act. The stage must be one on which the quick succession of scenes and rapid alternation of moods is technically possible.

21. The title that best expresses the ideas of this passage is
(A) Shortening Shakespeare's plays
(B) Modern trends in stage design
(C) Decline of the picture-frame set
(D) Appropriate Shakespearean staging
(E) Revival of interest in Shakespeare

22. The emotional effect in Shakespeare's plays results from
(A) tension
(B) realism
(C) contrasts
(D) mood music
(E) elaborate spectacles

23. Certain scenes in a Shakespearean play are written to
(A) provide a musical theme
(B) decrease production costs
(C) provide relief for the actors
(D) contribute to a desired effect
(E) show Shakespeare's versatility

Next to Sir Andrew in the club-room sits Captain Sentry, a gentleman of great courage, good understanding, but invincible modesty. He is one of those that deserve very well, but are very awkward at putting their talents within the observation of such as should take notice of them. He was some years a captain, and behaved himself with great gallantry in several engagements, and at several sieges; but having a small estate of his own, and being next heir to Sir Roger, he has quitted a way of life in which no man can rise suitably to his merit, who is not something of a courtier as well as a soldier. I have heard him often lament that in a profession where merit is placed in so conspicuous a view, impudence should get the better of modesty. When he had talked to this purpose, I never heard him make a sour expression, but frankly confess that he left the world because he was not fit for it. A strict honesty, and an even regular behaviour, are in themselves obstacles to him that must press through crowds, who endeavour at the same end with himself, the favour of a commander. He will, however, in his way of talk excuse generals for not disposing according to men's dessert, or inquiring into it; for, says he, that great man who has a mind to help me, has as many to break through to come at me, as I have to come at him: therefore he will conclude that the man who would make a figure, especially in a military way, must get over all false modesty, and assist his patron against the importunity of other pretenders, by a proper assurance in his own vindication. He says it is a civil cowardice to be backward in asserting what you ought to expect, as it is a military fear to be slow in attacking when it is your duty. With this candour does the gentleman speak of himself and others. The same frankness runs through all his conversation. The military part of his life has furnished him with many adventures, in the relation of which he is very agreeable to the company; for he is never overbearing, though accustomed to command men in the utmost degree below him; nor ever too obsequious, from a habit of obeying men highly above him.

24. Captain Sentry, in this passage, demonstrates that he is noteworthy because of his
(A) domineering
(B) conversation
(C) modesty
(D) honesty
(E) frankness

25. Advancement in the army is often given to the person who
(A) calls attention to himself
(B) performs valiantly on the battlefield
(C) is obsequious
(D) is a civil coward
(E) is adventurous

26. Captain Sentry retired to the country because
(A) he was bitter about his rank
(B) he was a hermit
(C) he was Sir Roger's heir
(D) he was too modest to be noticed by his superiors
(E) he was accustomed to obeying people above him

27. "Candour" means
(A) frankness
(B) bias
(C) irritation
(D) optimism
(E) sarcasm

28. Which one of the following traits does Captain Sentry NOT demonstrate?
(A) gallantry
(B) modesty
(C) humility
(D) authority
(E) sycophancy

29. Captain Sentry is a popular member of the club because
(A) he is obsequious
(B) he often talks of his military adventures
(C) he has left the army
(D) he respects people in authority
(E) he will inherit Sir Roger's estate

30. In describing Captain Sentry's failure to advance, the author is
(A) factual
(B) observant
(C) obsequious
(D) sarcastic
(E) gallant

Select the word or set of words that best completes each of the following sentences.

31. I can think of nothing more ______ than arriving at the theater and discovering that I had left the tickets at home.
(A) vicious
(B) tantalizing
(C) vexatious
(D) vitiating
(E) banal

32. He promised immunity to the ______ of the crime if they returned the papers which had been stolen.
(A) actors
(B) victims
(C) plotters
(D) organizers
(E) perpetrators

33. The townspeople immediately suspected an ______ worker of the theft of the Mayor's car.
(A) itinerant
(B) enterprising
(C) indolent
(D) articulate
(E) embarrassed

34. He tried to ______ the issue by bringing up ______ factors.
(A) clarify—ambiguous
(B) becloud—irrelevant
(C) hasten—new
(D) aggravate—irritating
(E) solve—enigmatic

35. When he was accused of being a ______, he retorted that he was not a ______.
(A) traitor—libertine
(B) spy—minion
(C) charlatan—quack
(D) plagiarist—victim
(E) prodigy—star

Each question below consists of a related pair of words or phrases, followed by five lettered pairs of words or phrases. Select the lettered pair that best expresses a relationship similar to that expressed in the original pair.

Example:

YAWN : BOREDOM :: (A) dream : sleep
(B) anger : madness (C) smile : amusement
(D) face : expression (E) impatience : rebellion

Ⓐ Ⓑ ● Ⓓ Ⓔ

36. PISTON : CYLINDER ::
(A) elevator : shaft
(B) rifle : revolver
(C) bullet : revolver
(D) elevator : escalator
(E) water : bridge

37. GAUCHE : DEFT ::
(A) left : apt
(B) rough : smooth
(C) meager : appropriate
(D) awkward : clumsy
(E) cowboy : active

38. SAVORLESS : PIQUANT ::
(A) tasty : provocative
(B) stupid : dull
(C) silly : sweet
(D) flat : spicy
(E) boorish : sticky

39. JOG : SPRINT ::
(A) run : jump
(B) trot : gallop
(C) stride : amble
(D) veer : stampede
(E) hurdle : race

40. TIMOROUS : FEAR ::
(A) apprehensive : grasp
(B) loquacious : listen
(C) condoning : forgive
(D) efficient : condemn
(E) pugnacious : resign

41. SCALPEL : SURGEON ::
(A) stethoscope : physician
(B) cleaver : butcher
(C) awl : cobbler
(D) palette : painter
(E) handcuffs : detective

42. VIRTUE : INTEGRITY ::
(A) vice : sloth
(B) wicked : greedy
(C) goodness : honesty
(D) pleasure : pain
(E) greed : evil

43. CAUTION : ACCIDENT ::
(A) carelessness : pain
(B) worry : harm
(C) sanitation : health
(D) policeman : criminal
(E) radar : collision

44. BUILDING : STORY ::
(A) edifice : tale
(B) ladder : rung
(C) emotion : feeling
(D) character : reputation
(E) construction : design

45. PREJUDICE : INTOLERANT ::
(A) altruism : selfish
(B) benevolence : greedy
(C) magnanimity : bigoted
(D) misery : company
(E) avarice : rapacious

S T O P

IF YOU FINISH BEFORE TIME IS CALLED, YOU MAY CHECK YOUR WORK ON THIS SECTION ONLY. DO NOT WORK ON ANY OTHER SECTION IN THE TEST.

ANSWER KEY

Note: The answers to the math sections are keyed to the corresponding review areas in Chapter 11. The numbers in parentheses after each answer refer to topics as listed below. (Note that to review for number 16, Quantitative Comparison, study Chapter 10.)

1. Fundamental Operations	10. Motion
2. Algebraic Operations	11. Ratio and Proportion
3. Using Algebra	12. Mixtures and Solutions
4. Roots and Radicals	13. Work
5. Inequalities	14. Coordinate Geometry
6. Fractions	15. Geometry
7. Decimals	16. Quantitative Comparison
8. Percent	17. Data Interpretation
9. Averages	

SECTION 1 VERBAL

1. **E**	9. **D**	17. **B**	25. **D**	33. **B**
2. **D**	10. **B**	18. **C**	26. **E**	34. **E**
3. **E**	11. **B**	19. **C**	27. **C**	35. **D**
4. **B**	12. **E**	20. **C**	28. **D**	36. **B**
5. **D**	13. **E**	21. **E**	29. **B**	37. **B**
6. **A**	14. **A**	22. **C**	30. **B**	38. **D**
7. **B**	15. **D**	23. **B**	31. **A**	39. **C**
8. **D**	16. **E**	24. **B**	32. **C**	40. **C**

SECTION 2 MATH

1. **D (8)**	6. **A (15)**	11. **D (11)**	16. **B (15)**	21. **E (15)**
2. **E (3)**	7. **C (2)**	12. **B (8)**	17. **C (10)**	22. **D (4,8)**
3. **B (6)**	8. **C (10)**	13. **B (10)**	18. **D (1)**	23. **D (14)**
4. **D (6)**	9. **A (12)**	14. **C (3)**	19. **D (2,4)**	24. **D (14)**
5. **D (15)**	10. **D (11)**	15. **E (8)**	20. **E (11,15)**	25. **A (14)**

SECTION 3 VERBAL

1. **D**	10. **A**	19. **B**	28. **B**	37. **C**
2. **A**	11. **D**	20. **C**	29. **D**	38. **E**
3. **E**	12. **B**	21. **B**	30. **C**	39. **B**
4. **B**	13. **B**	22. **D**	31. **B**	40. **D**
5. **C**	14. **D**	23. **E**	32. **A**	41. **B**
6. **A**	15. **E**	24. **A**	33. **C**	42. **D**
7. **C**	16. **B**	25. **C**	34. **A**	43. **C**
8. **B**	17. **E**	26. **A**	35. **E**	44. **D**
9. **E**	18. **C**	27. **A**	36. **B**	45. **C**

SECTION 4 TEST OF STANDARD WRITTEN ENGLISH

1. **C**	11. **C**	21. **A**	31. **B**	41. **E**
2. **B**	12. **D**	22. **E**	32. **E**	42. **C**
3. **A**	13. **E**	23. **D**	33. **E**	43. **E**
4. **E**	14. **E**	24. **A**	34. **C**	44. **E**
5. **A**	15. **A**	25. **C**	35. **A**	45. **A**
6. **E**	16. **A**	26. **E**	36. **C**	46. **D**
7. **C**	17. **D**	27. **E**	37. **D**	47. **D**
8. **B**	18. **C**	28. **C**	38. **B**	48. **A**
9. **C**	19. **A**	29. **C**	39. **D**	49. **A**
10. **A**	20. **E**	30. **E**	40. **A**	50. **C**

SECTION 5 MATH

1. A (8)	8. B (6,16)	15. D (15,16)	22. C (15,16)	29. A (11)
2. E (8)	9. D (1,16)	16. C (15,16)	23. A (15,16)	30. C (15)
3. B (15)	10. C (1,16)	17. A (15,16)	24. C (15,16)	31. A (11)
4. B (1)	11. C (15,16)	18. C (15,16)	25. C (15,16)	32. B (15)
5. C (15)	12. A (15,16)	19. D (15,16)	26. D (15,16)	33. C (14)
6. C (6)	13. C (15,16)	20. A (15,16)	27. C (15,16)	34. C (14)
7. E (1)	14. C (15,16)	21. D (15,16)	28. C (15)	35. A (14)

SECTION 6 VERBAL

1. A	10. D	19. C	28. E	37. B
2. E	11. E	20. D	29. B	38. D
3. C	12. D	21. D	30. D	39. B
4. A	13. A	22. C	31. C	40. C
5. C	14. A	23. D	32. E	41. B
6. B	15. D	24. E	33. A	42. A
7. E	16. C	25. A	34. B	43. E
8. C	17. D	26. D	35. C	44. B
9. A	18. D	27. A	36. A	45. E

SELF-EVALUATION

The model SAT test you have just completed has the same format as the actual SAT. As you take more of the model tests in this chapter, you will lose any SAT "stage fright" you might have.

Use the steps that follow to evaluate your performance on Model SAT Test 5. (Note: You'll find the charts referred to in steps 1–5 on the next three pages.)

STEP 1 Use the Answer Key to check your answers for each section.

STEP 2 For each section, count the number of correct and incorrect answers (remember that you don't count omitted answers), and enter the numbers on the appropriate lines of the chart "Obtaining Your Raw Score." Then do the indicated calculations to get your Raw Verbal Score, your Raw TSWE Score, and your Raw Math Score.

STEP 3 Consult the chart "Evaluate Your Performance" to see how well you did.

STEP 4 To pinpoint the specific areas in which you need to improve, circle the numbers of the questions that you either left blank or got wrong on the "Identify Your Weaknesses" charts. This will tell you where to concentrate your efforts to get the most out of your study time. The chart for the math sections gives you page references for review and practice by skill areas. The charts for the verbal and TSWE sections refer you to the appropriate chapters to study for each question type.

STEP 5 Do the review and practice indicated on the charts wherever you had a concentration of circles.

Remember that in addition to evaluating your scores, you should read all of the answer explanations for questions you answered incorrectly, questions you omitted, and questions you answered correctly but found difficult. Reviewing the answer explanations will help you understand concepts and strategies, and may point out shortcuts.

OBTAINING YOUR RAW SCORE

Verbal

Section 1 ______ (number correct) – 1/4 (______) (number incorrect) = ______ (A)

Section 3 ______ (number correct) – 1/4 (______) (number incorrect) = ______ (B)

Section 6 ______ (number correct) – 1/4 (______) (number incorrect) = ______ (C)

Raw Verbal Score = (A) + (B) + (C) = ______

TSWE

Section 4 ______ (number correct) – 1/4 (______) (number incorrect) = Raw TSWE Score = ______

Math

Section 2 ______ (number correct) – 1/4 (______) (number incorrect) = ______ (D)

Section 5 (1-7, 28-35) ______ (number correct) – 1/4 (______) (number incorrect) = ______ (E)

Section 5 (8-27) ______ (number correct) – 1/3 (______) (number incorrect) = ______ (F)

Raw Math Score = (D) + (E) + (F) = ______

EVALUATE YOUR PERFORMANCE

	Verbal	TSWE	Math
Excellent	111-130	45-50	52-60
Very Good	91-110	39-44	45-51
Good	81-90	34-38	36-44
Average	61-80	25-33	30-35
Below Average	40-60	15-24	25-29
Unsatisfactory	below 40	below 15	below 25

IDENTIFY YOUR WEAKNESSES
Verbal

Question Type	Question Numbers			Chapter to Study
	Section 1	Section 3	Section 6	
Antonym	1, 2, 3, 4, 5, 6, 7, 8, 9, 10	1, 2, 3, 4, 5, 6, 7, 8, 9, 10, 11, 12, 13, 14, 15	1, 2, 3, 4, 5, 6, 7, 8, 9, 10, 11, 12, 13, 14, 15	Chapter 4
Analogy	16, 17, 18, 19, 20, 21, 22, 23, 24, 25	36, 37, 38, 39, 40, 41, 42, 43, 44, 45	36, 37, 38, 39, 40, 41, 42, 43, 44, 45	Chapter 5
Sentence Completion	11, 12, 13, 14, 15	16, 17, 18, 19, 20, 31, 32, 33, 34, 35	16, 17, 18, 19, 20, 31, 32, 33, 34, 35	Chapter 6
Reading Comprehension	26, 27, 28, 29, 30, 31, 32, 33, 34, 35, 36, 37, 38, 39, 40	21, 22, 23, 24, 25, 26, 27, 28, 29, 30	21, 22, 23, 24, 25, 26, 27, 28, 29, 30, 31	Chapter 7

TSWE

Question Type	Question Numbers	Chapter to Study
Usage	1, 2, 3, 4, 5, 6, 7, 8, 9, 10, 11, 12, 13, 14, 15, 16, 17, 18, 19, 20, 21, 22, 23, 24, 25, 41, 42, 43, 44, 45, 46, 47, 48, 49, 50	Chapter 12
Sentence Correction	26, 27, 28, 29, 30, 31, 32, 33, 34, 35, 36, 37, 38, 39, 40	Chapter 12

Math

Skill Area	Question Numbers		Pages to Study
	Section 2	Section 5	
Fundamental Operations	18	4, 7, 9	300–302
Algebraic Operations	7, 19		302–308
Using Algebra	2, 14		308–316
Fractions	3, 4	6, 8	316–329
Decimals and Percents	1, 12, 15, 22	1, 2	329–334
Verbal Problems	8, 9, 13, 17		335–352
Ratio and Proportion	10, 11, 20	29, 31	340–346
Geometry	5, 6, 16, 20, 21	3, 5, 11, 12, 13, 14, 15, 16, 17, 18, 19, 20, 21, 22, 23, 24, 25, 26, 27, 28, 30, 32	355–368
Coordinate Geometry	23, 24, 25	33, 34, 35	352–355
Quantitative Comparison		8, 9, 10, 11, 12, 13, 14, 15, 16, 17, 18, 19, 20, 21, 22, 23, 24, 25, 26, 27	279–299
Roots and Radicals	19, 22		306–307; 312–313

ANSWER EXPLANATIONS

SECTION 1

1. E. The opposite of *inviolate* (not desecrated) is *desecrated.*

2. D. Because a *tyro* is a beginner, he is unskilled. He is not *expert.*

3. E. The opposite of *immaculate* (spotless) is *spotted.*

4. B. The opposite of *culpable* (blameworthy) is *innocent.*

5. D. The opposite of *equanimity* (composure) is *agitation.*

6. A. The opposite of *squander* (waste) is *hoard* (store up; accumulate).

7. B. The opposite of *profusion* (unrestrained abundance) is *scarcity.*

8. D. The opposite of *dawdle* (loiter; waste time) is *hasten.*

9. D. The opposite of *embellish* (adorn) is *disfigure.*

10. B. The opposite of *obdurate* (hard; unyielding) is *yielding.*

11. B. *Albeit* means although. The use of *albeit* calls for a contrast to his normal merciful nature. *Implacable* -(stern) provides this contrast.

12. E. *Prosaic* means dull. Routine is dull to an imaginative person.

13. E. *Skein* (bundle of yarn) is something we would have to *disentangle.*

14. A. *Repugnant* means distasteful.

15. D. The use of the word *stolen* calls for *thief.*

16. E. A *congenial* person lacks *animosity*; a *brotherly* person lacks *hatred.*

17. B. *Animate* and *vitalize* are synonyms; *tedious* and *boring* are synonyms.

18. C. We *curry* a horse's *mane* to disentangle or comb it; we *card wool* to disentangle it.

19. C. A *brash* person lacks *reticence* (reserve); a *brazen* person, *shyness.*

20. C. *Condensation* and *abridgment* are synonyms; *attitude* and *pose* are synonyms.

21. E. An *entrepreneur* (person who starts and conducts a business) seeks *profits*; a *scholar* seeks *knowledge.*

22. C. In a law suit involving an *aggressor* or *attacker*, the *victim* would be the *plaintiff* (one prosecuting the case).

23. B. The *trough* is the lowest part of a *wave*; the *basement* is the lowest part of a *house.*

24. B. An *ascetic* (severely abstinent) man is *continent* (moral); a *philandering* person is *immoral.*

25. D. Someone *hideous* is extremely *unattractive*; someone *parsimonious* is *thrifty* to an extreme.

26. E. The passage points out that the great changes that occurred during the past 200 years are due to the "economic unification" of the time. Choice E is best.

27. C. In the fifth sentence, we are informed that "six short generations" have taken place since 1750. If we divide 236 by 6, we get 39.3 as an answer. This answer is closest to Choice C.

28. D. The sixth sentence supports Choice D.

29. B. The third sentence supports Choice B.

30. B. In the last sentence, we are told that homeomorphs are "unrelated organisms that develop similarity of form." Halibut, a fish, and whale, a mammal, have similar forms.

31. A. The first sentence supports Choice A.

32. C. Line 20 supports Choice C.

33. B. Since this passage deals with the topic of adaptive convergence, the *opposite* of adaptive divergence (sentence 1), we may infer that earlier passages discussed the topic of adaptive divergence.

34. E. The last sentence of the second paragraph supports Choice E.

35. D. The first sentence of the second paragraph supports Choice D.

36. B. The opening sentence of the third paragraph states that the budget includes "a modest margin for debt retirement." This supports Choice B.

37. B. The seventh sentence (lines 11–15) supports Choice B.

38. D. The closing statement that "his grounds are just as good as ours" supports the selection of Choice D.

39. C. The passage discusses the folly of not purchasing commodities abroad when they can be produced more cheaply there. He, thus, is supporting free trade (Choice C).

40. C. The author maintains that it is foolish for a country to produce commodities at home which can be purchased more cheaply abroad. Therefore, countries should concentrate on the production of things which they can make more cheaply than other countries.

SECTION 2

1. D. $0.3\%x = 2163$

$$\frac{0.3}{100}x = 2163$$

$$\frac{3}{1000}x = 2163$$

$$3x = 2,163,000$$

$$x = 721,000$$

2. E. Since there are 10 cents in one dime, in $(x + 2)$ dimes there are $10(x + 2)$ or $10x + 20$ cents.

3. B. Let x = number of nineteenths equal to exactly $\frac{2}{3}$

$$\frac{x}{19} = \frac{2}{3}$$

$$3x = 38$$

$$x = 12\frac{2}{3}$$

Therefore $\dfrac{12\frac{2}{3}}{19} = \dfrac{2}{3}$

$\frac{13}{19}$ is the fraction with closest value to $\frac{2}{3}$

4. D. $\dfrac{6 \text{ inches}}{1 \text{ yard}}$ or $\dfrac{6 \text{ inches}}{3 \text{ feet}}$ or $\dfrac{6 \text{ inches}}{36 \text{ inches}}$ or $\dfrac{6}{36}$ or $\dfrac{1}{6}$

5. D. Angle 1 + angle 4 = 180°

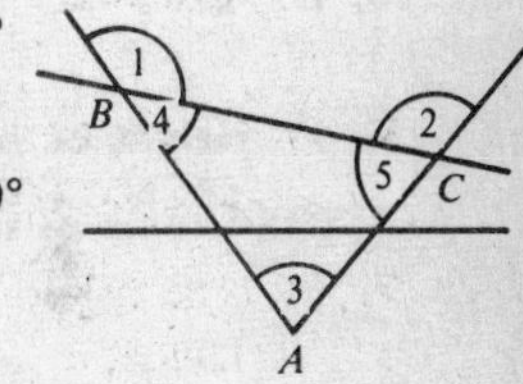

145° + angle 4 = 180°
Angle 4 = 35°
Angle 2 + angle 5 = 180°
125° + angle 5 = 180°
Angle 5 = 55°
Angle 4 + angle 5 + angle 3 = 180°
(the sum of the angle measures of a triangle equals 180°)
35° + 55° + angle 3 = 180°
Angle 3 = 90°

6. A. Since the sides of a square are equal, each side equals $\frac{1}{4}$ of the perimeter. Since the perimeter equals p inches, each side equals $\frac{p}{4}$

Area of square = $(\text{side})^2$

Area of square = $\left(\frac{p}{4}\right)^2$ or $\frac{p^2}{16}$

7. C.

$$7x - 5y = 13$$
$$2x - 7y = 26$$
$$9x - 12y = 39$$

(if equals are added to equals the results are equal)

8. C. Time spent = 20 minutes or $\frac{1}{3}$ of hour

Distance covered = 18 miles

$$\frac{\text{Distance}}{\text{Time}} = \text{Average velocity}$$

$$\frac{18}{\frac{1}{3}} \text{ or } 18 \div \frac{1}{3} \text{ or } 18 \cdot \frac{3}{1} = 54 \text{ miles per hour}$$

9. A. Since the cup contains equal parts of flour and cornstarch the mixture contains $\frac{1}{2}$ cup of flour and $\frac{1}{2}$ cup of cornstarch. Since 1 cup of cornstarch weighs $\frac{1}{4}$ pound, $\frac{1}{2}$ cup of cornstarch weighs $\frac{1}{8}$ pound. Since 4 cups of flour weigh 1 pound, 1 cup weighs $\frac{1}{4}$ pound and $\frac{1}{2}$ cup weighs $\frac{1}{8}$ pound. The weight of flour and cornstarch equals $\frac{1}{8} + \frac{1}{8}$ or $\frac{1}{4}$ pound.

10. D. Let x = height of pole (in feet)

$$\frac{\text{Height of object (feet)}}{\text{Length of shadow (feet)}} = \frac{5\frac{2}{3}}{8} = \frac{x}{96}$$

$(5'8'' = 5\frac{2}{3}')$

$8x = (5\frac{2}{3})(96)$ (the product of the means equals the product of the extremes)

$8x = 544$

$x = 68$ feet

11. D. Let x = the number of Angstrom units

$$\frac{\text{Angstrom units}}{\text{micron}} = \frac{1}{0.0001} = \frac{x}{0.01}$$

$0.0001x = 0.01$

$x = 100$ (multiply by 10,000)

12. B. 10% of 32% or $\frac{1}{10}$ of 32% equals 3.2%

13. B. Distance covered equals 30 miles + 40 miles or 70 miles. Time spent traveling equals 2 hours.

$$\frac{\text{Distance}}{\text{Time}} = \text{Average speed}$$

$$\frac{70}{2} = 35 \text{ miles per hour}$$

14. C. Let n = number of nickels
Since there are 12 coins in all, $12 - n$ = number of dimes
Value of all nickels = $5n$ cents
Value of all dimes = $10(12 - n)$ or $120 - 10n$ cents
Value of all coins = $5n + 120 - 10n$ cents

$5n + 120 - 10n = 85$

$-5n = -35$

$5n = 35$

$n = 7$

15. E. The team has played 24 games. If 24 games represents $16\frac{2}{3}\%$ or $\frac{1}{6}$ of the games, then 100% (total games played) equals (24) (6) or 144 games. To finish the season with a record of 0.750 the team must win a total of (0.750) (144) or 108 games. Since the team has already won 15 games, it must win 93 additional games.

16. B. Since $CD < CE$ and $AD = BE$ then $CA < CB$ because if equal quantities are subtracted from unequal quantities, the remainders are unequal in the same order.

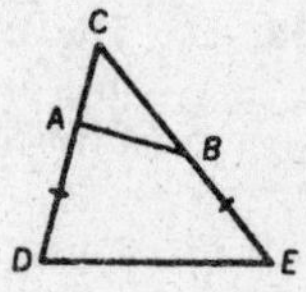

17. C. Distance covered = R miles + W miles

$$\frac{\text{Distance}}{\text{Time}} = \text{Average rate}$$

$$\frac{R + W}{2H}$$

18. D. Distance between first pole and second pole = 15 feet
Distance between first pole and third pole = 30 feet etc. . . .
Distance between first pole and eighth pole = 105 feet

19. D. To eliminate square roots, square each term

$$4a^2 = \frac{2b^2}{4} = \frac{2c^2}{6.25}$$

$$\text{Or, } 4a^2 = \frac{b^2}{2} = \frac{c^2}{3.125}$$

Since the terms are equal, the letter with the smallest coefficient will be the greatest. Therefore c is the greatest and a is the least. In descending order they are c, b, a.

20. E. Area of circle = $\pi(\text{radius})^2$

$144\pi = \pi r^2$

$144 = r^2$ (divide by π)

$r = 12$

diameter = 24

Area of the other circle = 196π

$196\pi = \pi r^2$

$196 = r^2$ (divide by π)

$r = 14$

diameter = 28

$$\frac{\text{Diameter of smaller circle}}{\text{Diameter of larger circle}} = \frac{24}{28} \text{ or } \frac{6}{7} \text{ or } 6:7$$

21. E. Let A be the location of checker, then AD is distance from nearest corner. $DC = AB = 3''$. In right triangle ADC, leg $AC = 4''$ and leg $DC = 3''$.

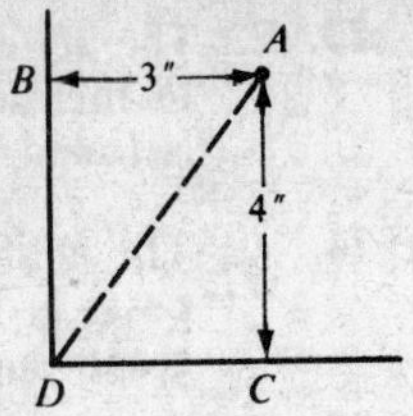

$(AD)^2 = (AC)^2 + (DC)^2$
$(AD)^2 = (4)^2 + (3)^2$
$(AD)^2 = 16 + 9$
$(AD)^2 = 25$
$AD = 5$

22. D. $\left(x + 25\%x\right)^2 = \left(x + \frac{1}{4}x\right)^2 =$

$\left(1\frac{1}{4}x\right)^2 = \left(\frac{5}{4}x\right)^2 = \frac{25}{16}x^2 = 1.56x^2$

$(1x)^2 = 100\%x^2$

Difference between $(x + 25\%x)^2$ and $(x)^2$ is $(156\%x^2 - 100\%x^2)$ or $56\%x^2$ or an increase of 56%

23. D. Ordinate refers to y-value of a point. Ordinates are equal to −3 means

$$\underset{y}{\downarrow} \quad \underset{=}{\downarrow} \quad \underset{-3}{\downarrow}$$

The equation is $y = -3$.

24. D. Distance $OA = 9$.

Distance $OB = \sqrt{(-2-0)^2 + (9-0)^2}$
$= \sqrt{4 + 81} = \sqrt{85}$.

Distance $OC = \sqrt{(-7-.0)^2 + (-6-0)^2}$
$= \sqrt{49 + 36} = \sqrt{85}$.

Distance $OD = \sqrt{(8-0)^2 + (5-0)^2}$
$= \sqrt{64+25} = \sqrt{89}$.

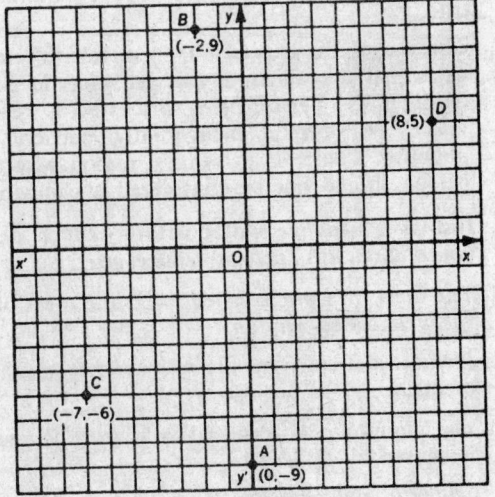

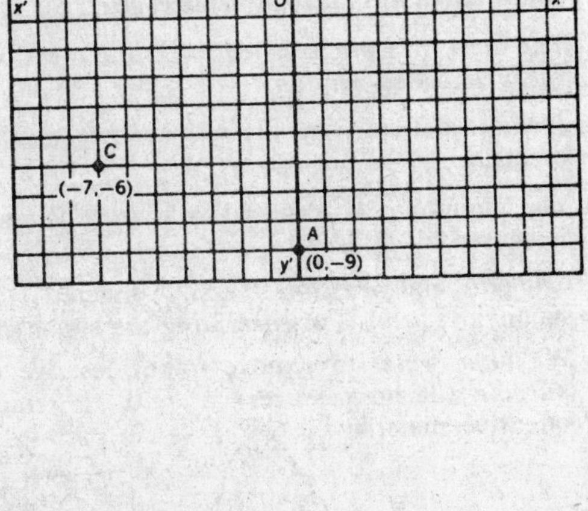

To compare these distances we note that distance $OA = 9 = \sqrt{81}$.

Thus, distance OD is the greatest of the four distances.

Point O, O lies on the origin.

25. A. Let M be the midpoint of AB.

$$x\text{-midpoint} = \frac{x_1 + x_2}{2}$$

$$y\text{-midpoint} = \frac{y_1 + y_2}{2}$$

$$x_m = \frac{-2 + 4}{2} = \frac{2}{2} = 1$$

$$x_m = \frac{3 + (-3)}{2} = \frac{0}{2} = 0$$

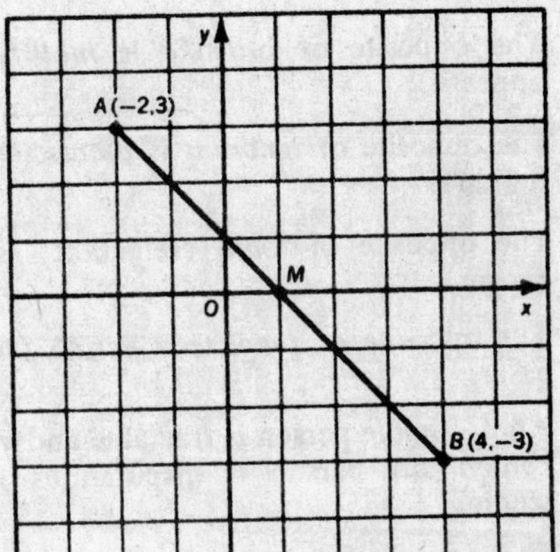

SECTION 3

1. D. The opposite of *candid* (frank) is *reserved.*

2. A. The opposite of *lavish* (liberal; wasteful) is *sparing.*

3. E. The opposite of *cryptic* (mysterious; hidden) is *unconcealed.*

4. B. The opposite of *alienate* (estrange; make hostile) is *conciliate* (pacify; win over).

5. C. The opposite of *raucous* (harsh and shrill) is *gentle.*

6. A. The opposite of *taciturn* (talking little) is *prolix* (verbose).

7. C. The opposite of *provoke* is *mollify* (soothe, appease).

8. B. The opposite of *ignorant* is *omniscient* (knowing all).

9. E. The opposite of *loath* (reluctant) is *avid* (eager).

10. A. The opposite of *favorite* is *pariah* (social outcast).

11. D. An *amenable* person is tractable and yielding; a *contentious* person is disputatious and contending.

12. B. The opposite of *incipient* (beginning) is *terminal* (ending).

13. B. The opposite of *corruptibility* (state of being easily bribed, etc.) is *probity* (integrity).

14. D. The opposite of *profound* (deep, fundamental) is *superficial* (trivial).

15. E. The opposite of *overt* (open, obvious) is *clandestine* (secret).

16. B. A person who is excessively wordy is *prolix.*

17. E. A *pessimist* would present a *lugubrious* (doleful) account.

18. C. *Vapidities* (empty remarks) would be distressing and parallels *empty promises* and *cliches.*

19. B. *Craven* and *cowardly* are synonyms.

20. C. *Panacea* (a cure-all) best describes the concoction he was selling.

21. B. Throughout the passage, the author stresses the need to remove the secrecy which shrouds some Congressional procedures. In Paragraph 3 we read that "the House operates with too great an emphasis on secrecy." This thought is repeated in Paragraphs 5, 7, 8, and 10.

22. D. In Paragraph 9, the author states that the size of the House of Representatives "does not allow for many lengthy debates."

23. E. The statement, "Strong Presidents take power to themselves at the expense of the Congress" is found in the next-to-last paragraph.

24. A. The author discusses the 3-day layover proposal in Paragraph 7. Sentence 3 of this paragraph supports Choice A.

25. C. The last sentence of Paragraph 8 supports Choice C.

26. A. The last two paragraphs discuss the loss of power from the legislative branch to the executive. This occurs when we have a series of "strong Presidents."

27. A. In Paragraph 11, the author emphasizes the need for guaranteed debate time on amendments.

28. B. The entire passage concentrates on methods of making the House of Representatives more democratic. We can infer that opponents of democracy would "disapprove of the suggestions."

29. D. The author wishes to "encourage our writers" by removing the prejudices and biases which only serve to handicap them. In lines 11 - 20, the author gives reasons for the need to encourage our writers.

30. C. In the second sentence, the author mentions "contumely" and the "ridicule of foreigners." This supports Choice C.

31. B. *Inane* and *fatuous* are synonyms.

32. A. Since to *malinger* means to pretend illness to avoid duty, the *malingering* individual is not *diligent* (devoting unremitting application to work).

33. C. The conflict between those who wish to develop atomic energy as a source of electricity and those who wish to preserve the environment is stated in Choice C (*solution -hazard*).

34. A. A work which lacks originality is *banal* and trite.

35. E. The use of the expression, "you fail to," indicates that the writer of this sentence does not consider the person being discussed a "chauvinist," (a person belligerently patriotic, a jingoist). Choice E presents a reason why this person should not be considered a chauvinist.

36. B. Just as a *sedative* will quiet or reduce *pain, consolation* will quiet or reduce *grief.*

37. C. The meat of a *pig* is called *pork;* the meat of a *sheep* is called *mutton.*

38. E. *Maxims* and *epigrams* are *pithy* and *terse* statements.

39. B. The common *cold* is caused by a *virus; gangrene* is caused by *infection.*

40. D. *Choleric* and *irascible* (easily angered) are synonyms; *tiring* and *enervating* are synonyms.

41. B. We *filter water* to remove impurities; we *expurgate* (delete passages) a *book* to remove offensive material.

42. D. *Clerical* and *spiritual* describe things concerned with religion; *mundane* and *secular* refer to worldy and non-religious matters.

43. C. *Indigent* (poor) people are not *wealthy; gauche* (awkward) people are not *graceful.*

44. D. A *spear* is a weapon which people *thrust;* an *epee* is a weapon which people use to *fence* (engage in sword-play).

45. C. That which is *wan* lacks *color;* that which is *insipid* (flat) lacks *flavor.*

SECTION 4

1. C. *Which* should not refer to a clause. Change to *full volume; this.*

2. B. Error in diction. *Affect* is a verb and should not be used in place of *effect.*

3. A. Dangling participle. Change to *After he had read for more.*

4. E. Sentence is correct.

5. A. Error in diction. Use *irritated* instead of *aggravated.*

6. E. Sentence is correct.

7. C. Error in diction. There is no such verb as *enthuse.* Change *enthused* to *enthusiastic.*

8. B. Error in diction. Use *fewer* instead of *less.*

9. C. Error in agreement. The subject, *general,* is singular; the verb should be singular—*seems.*

10. A. Improper sequence of tenses. Change *became* to *had become.*

11. C. Error in diction. Change *continuous* to *continual.*

12. D. Improper sequence of tenses. Omit *have.*

13. E. Sentence is correct.

14. E. Sentence is correct.

15. A. Error in case. The possessive pronoun precedes a gerund. Change *him* to *his.*

16. A. Dangling participle. Change *Entering* to *When she entered.*

17. D. The words *Because there was a traffic delay* form an incomplete sentence. One way of correcting this error is to delete *Because.*

18. C. Error in diction. Change *council* to *counsel.*

19. A. Error in case. Change *Who* to *Whom.* The pronoun is the object of the preposition *to.*

20. E. Sentence is correct.

21. A. Wrong mood. Change *was* to *were* (subjunctive).

22. E. Sentence is correct.

23. D. Error in diction. Change *healthy* to *healthful.*

24. A. Error in tense. Change *lived* to *have lived.*

25. C. Error in diction. Change *incredulous* to *incredible.*

26. E. The dangling modifier is best corrected in Choice E. Choices B and D introduce an error in tense. Choice C changes the meaning of the sentence.

27. E. *Ought* is used correctly in Choice E.

28. C. *Kind* should be modified by *this* or *that; kinds,* by *these* or *those.*

29. C. Parallel structure is retained in Choice C.

30. E. The noun or pronoun preceding a gerund *(going)* should be in the possessive case.

31. B. The faulty comparison is corrected in Choice B.

32. E. The dangling modifier and the double negative are corrected in Choice E.

33. E. The correct use of the subjunctive mood to indicate a condition contrary to fact is found in Choice E.

34. C. The phrase *along with his staff* is not part of the subject of the sentence. The subject is *President Reagan* (singular); the verb should be *is traveling* (singular).

35. A. The correct sequence of tenses (past-perfect) is found in Choice A. *All ready,* as used in Choices B and D, is incorrect.

36. C. Choice C corrects the misplaced modifier and eliminates the unnecessary use of the passive voice.

37. D. This corrects the sentence fragment.

38. B. The use of the subordinating conjunction *Although* and the deletion of unnecessary words strengthen this sentence.

39. D. Choices A, B, and C have dangling modifiers; Choice E creates a run-on sentence.

40. A. The use of the semicolon to separate the pair of clauses is correct.

41. E. Sentence is correct.

42. C. Error in diction. Change *a couple of* to *several*

43. E. Sentence is correct.

44. E. Sentence is correct.

45. A. Error in diction. Change *Our's* to *Our*.

46. D. Error in diction. Change *illusion* to *allusion*.

47. D. Incorrect use of superlative form of adjective. *Unique* does not need *more* or *most*. Delete *most*.

48. A. Confusion of adjective and conjunction. Change *Due to* to *Because of*.

49. A. Dangling participle. Change *Applying* to *When we apply*.

50. C. Unnecessary shift from active to passive voice. The sentence is better as *frozen; even so inactivity saps the vigor of the mind.*

SECTION 5

1. A. $\frac{x}{50} = 3.6\%$

$\frac{x}{50} = \frac{3.6}{100}$

$100x = 180$

$x = 1.8$

2. E. Let x = cost of article

Cost + Profit = Selling Price

$x + (30\%)(x) = \$65$

$x + .3x = 65$

$10x + 3x = 650$ (multiply by 10)

$13x = 650$

$x = \$50$ (cost)

Cost + Profit = Selling Price

$\$50 + (10\%)(\$50)$ = Selling Price

$\$50 + \$5 = \$55$

3. B. Area of frame equals area of outside rectangle minus area of picture. Area of outside rectangle equals (38)(18) or 684 square inches. Area of picture equals (36)(16) or 576 square inches. Area of frame = 684 − 576 or 108 square inches.

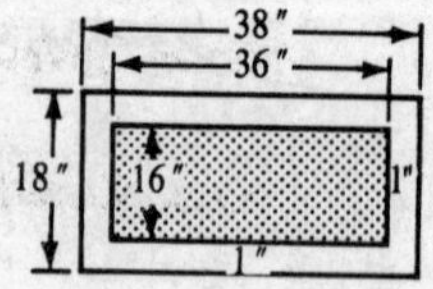

4. B. Let x = the least number of votes received by the successful candidate

$x - 1$ = the maximum number of votes a defeated candidate can receive

$4(x - 1)$ or $4x - 4$ = maximum number of votes all defeated candidates can receive

$x + 4x - 4 = 356$ (total number of votes cast)

$5x = 360$

$x = 72$

5. C. Since the sum of the angles of a triangle equals 180°,

$9x + 8x + 7x = 180$

$24x = 180$

$x = 7.5$ degrees

Angle A or $8x = 8(7.5)$ or 60 degrees

6. C. The home owner used $\frac{1}{2}$ of his $\frac{3}{4}$ of available oil

$\frac{1}{2} \cdot \frac{3}{4}$ equals $\frac{3}{8}$

7. E. Since the man binds 35 sets in 5 days, he binds 7 sets each day. Since there are 7 books in each set, he binds 49 books each day.

8. B. $\frac{7 + 7 + 7}{-7 - 7 - 7} = \frac{21}{-21} = -1$

$1 > -1$

9. D. x may be 30 or 60 or 90

10. C. 3 yards 1 inch = 109 inches

11. C. Opposite sides of a parallelogram are congruent.

12. A. A straight line is the shortest distance between two points.

13. C. Because the arcs are equal, *ABC* is an equilateral triangle. *AE* bisects *BC* (given) therefore *DC* is ½ any of the sides of *ABC*.

14. C. Since $y = 50$, the measure of angle $DCB = 100°$. Since this is a parallelogram the measure of angle $ABC = 80°$ and $x = 40$. In the triangle formed, since $x + y = 90$, the measure of z, the vertex angle, is 90 because the sum of all the angles is a straight angle.

15. D. We may conclude that $a = 80$ but we have no information to determine the value of b, since we may not assume that any lines are parallel.

16. C

$$x + y + z = 180$$
$$40 + 80 + z = 180$$
$$z = 60$$
$$3x = 120$$
$$2z = 120$$

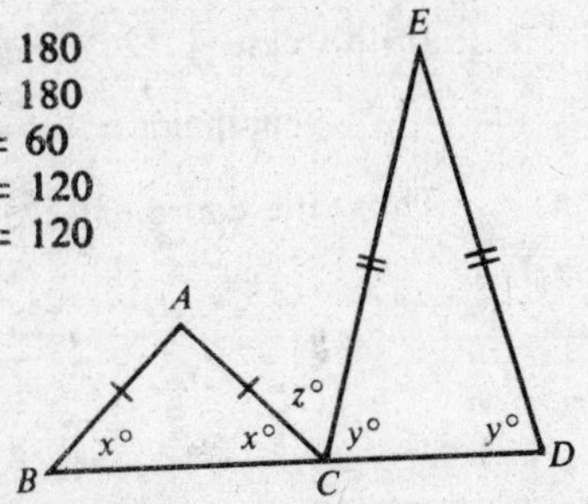

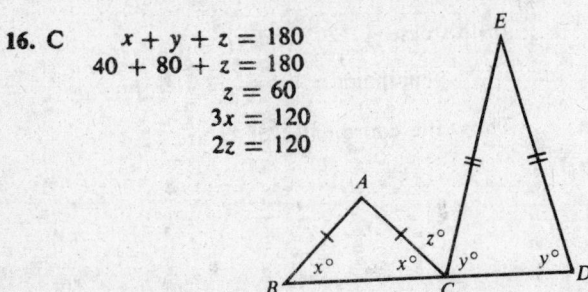

17. A. $y = 80$ (given)
$z = 60$ (see #16)

18. C. Since $BD \perp AC$, $x = 90$
Since ABC is equilateral, $z = 60$
Therefore $y = 30$

$$\frac{x}{y} = \frac{90}{30} = 3$$

19. D. We may not assume any relationship between the lengths of the legs of the triangle.

20. A. The sum of the lengths of 2 sides of a triangle is greater than the third side.

21. D. $a + b = 90$, but we have no information regarding the relationship of the legs of the triangle.

22. C. The acute angles of a right triangle are complementary.

23. A. Angle BEC is a right angle. Therefore $w + z = 90$. Since $w + x + z + y = 360$ and $w + z = 90$, then $x + y = 270$.

24. C. The measure of exterior angle $(x) = z +$ measure of angle BEC.

25. C. Since $w + z = 90$
$90 - z = w$ (by subtraction)

26. D. $w + z = 90$, but we have no data concerning their ratio.

27. C. Let $s =$ side of square
then, area of square $= s^2$
$s^2 =$ area of triangle ABC (given)
Therefore, $AB = BC = s\sqrt{2}$ for $s^2 = \dfrac{(s\sqrt{2})(s\sqrt{2})}{2}$

Therefore $\dfrac{AB}{DG} = \dfrac{s\sqrt{2}}{s}$ or $\sqrt{2}$

28. C. Let $x = CB$
Then $BA = 2x$ and
$CA = 3x$
Let $y = DE$
Then $EA = 2y$ and
$DA = 3y$

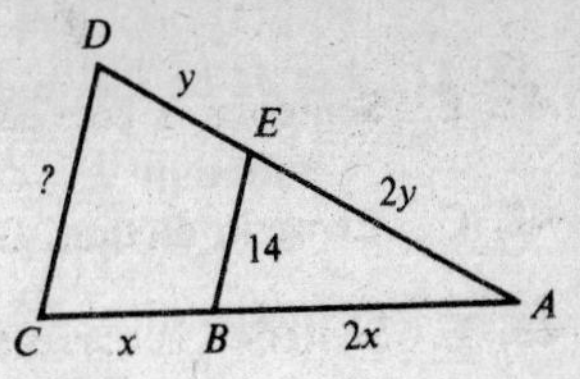

Triangle ABE is similar to triangle ADC since they both have the common angle A and the including sides are in proportion as:

$$\frac{AE}{AD} = \frac{AB}{AC} = \frac{2}{3}$$

Also, $\dfrac{BE}{DC} = \dfrac{2}{3}$ or $\dfrac{2}{3} = \dfrac{14}{DC}$ or $\dfrac{2}{3} = \dfrac{14}{21}$

$DC = 21$

29. A.

$$xy = k$$
$$(7)(5) = k \quad \text{(substitution)}$$
$$35 = k$$
$$(x)(32) = k$$
$$(x)(32) = 35$$
$$32x = 35$$
$$x = \frac{35}{32} \quad \text{(division by 32)}$$

30. C. Angle $DBE = 180°$
(a straight angle)
Angle $GBC =$
$180° - (79° + 39°)$
Angle $GBC =$
$180° - 118°$
Angle $GBC = 62°$
Angle $GBE =$
Angle GBC + Angle CBE
Angle $GBE = 62° + 39°$ or $101°$

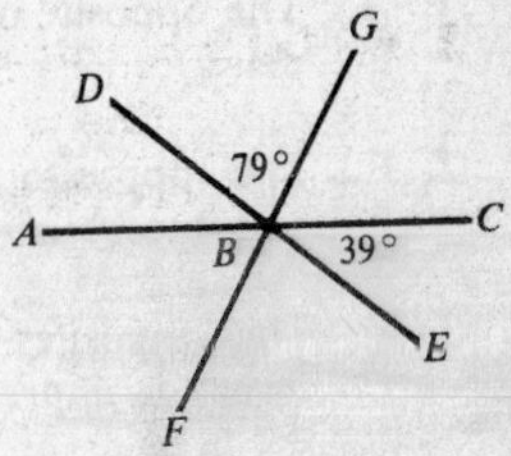

31. A. The total amount of money invested is $10,000. The man who invested the least amount of money invested $\dfrac{\$2000}{\$10.000}$ or $\dfrac{1}{5}$ of the investment. Since he is entitled to $\dfrac{1}{5}$ of the profit. his profit will be $\dfrac{1}{5}$ of $960 or $192.

32. B. Draw AF parallel to BC
Extend DC to F forming rectangle $CFAB$
$FA = CB = 12$
$CF = BA = 4$
In right triangle DFA
$DF = 16$
$FA = 12$
DA (the hypotenuse) $= 20$

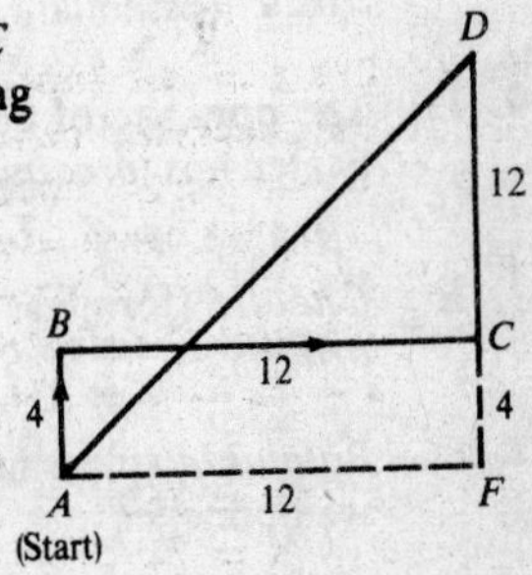

33. C. Let M be the midpoint of $\overline{AB}$.

$$x\text{-midpoint} = \frac{x_1 + x_2}{2}$$

$$y\text{-midpoint} = \frac{y_1 + y_2}{2}$$

$$x_{mid} = \frac{-2 + 6}{2} = \frac{4}{2} = 2$$

$$y_{mid} = \frac{7 + 1}{2} = \frac{8}{2} = 4$$

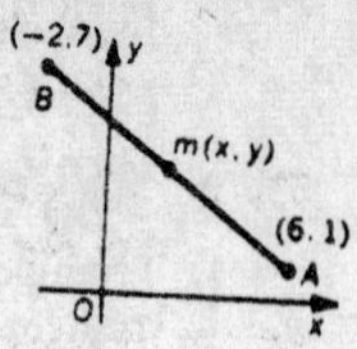

The coordinates of the midpoint are (2, 4).

34. C. Use the distance formula.

$d = \sqrt{(x_1 - x_2)^2 + (y_1 - y_2)^2}$

In this case, $x_1 = 2$, $x_2 = 10$.

$y_1 = -1$, $y_2 = 3$.

$d = \sqrt{(2 - 10)^2 + (-1 - 3)^2}$

$d = \sqrt{(-8)^2 + (-4)^2}$

$d = \sqrt{64 + 16}$

$d = \sqrt{80}$

$\sqrt{80} = \sqrt{5} \cdot \sqrt{16} = \sqrt{5} \cdot 4$,

or $4\sqrt{5}$.

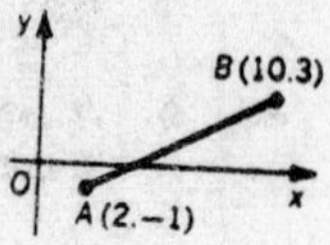

35. A. Use the formula

$$x\text{-midpoint} = \frac{x_1 + x_2}{2}$$

In this case, $x_1 = -1$ and $x_2 = 5$

$$x\text{-midpoint} = \frac{-1 + 5}{2} = \frac{4}{2} = 2$$

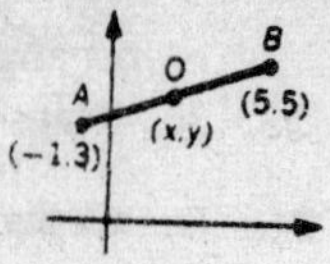

To find the y-coordinate of O use the formula

$$y\text{-midpoint} = \frac{y_1 + y_2}{2}$$

In this case, $y_1 = 3$ and $y_2 = 5$

$$y\text{-midpoint} = \frac{3 + 5}{2} = \frac{8}{2} = 4$$

Thus, the coordinates of O are (2,4).

SECTION 6

1. A. The opposite of *punctual* is *dilatory* (tending to delay).

2. E. The opposite of *dowdy* (lacking style and smartness) is *chic* (stylish).

3. C. The opposite of *ostentatious* (showy, pretentious) is *unpretentious*.

4. A. The opposite of *dulcet* (sweet-sounding) is *cacophonous* (discordant).

5. C. The opposite of *wax* (increase) is *wane* (decrease).

6. B. The opposite of *cupidity* (greed) is *altruism* (unselfishness).

7. E. The opposite of *nefarious* (wicked) is *honorable*.

8. C. The opposite of *dogmatic* (arrogant) is *reasonable*.

9. A. The opposite of *extraneous* (unrelated) is *intrinsic* (essential).

10. D. The opposite of *cosmopolitan* (worldly, sophisticated) is *provincial* (narrow, limited).

11. E. *Chaotic* (formless, confused) is the opposite of *orderly*.

12. D. *Palatable* (pleasant to the taste) and *distasteful* are opposites.

13. A. *Desiccate* (dry up, deprive of moisture) is the opposite of *saturate* (soak thoroughly).

14. A. *Wanton* (immoral) and *moral* are opposites.

15. D. *Guileless* (without treachery or deceit) is the opposite of *deceitful*.

16. C. It is most likely that a diversionary maneuver would occur at the same time as the major attack. *Simultaneously* conveys this thought.

17. D. Congressmen can go home during an *adjournment*.

18. D. A *scholar* must use *books* in the course of his work.

19. C. *Affected* suggests a studied display that could be assumed by an actress.

20. D. A *cynic* (skeptic) would not support the idea that man is altruistic; he, more likely, would state that man is out for his own selfish gain or *aggrandizement*.

21. D. The passage discusses the best way of staging Shakespeare's plays.

22. C. The second sentence discusses Shakespeare's use of contrast.

23. D. According to the author, each scene in a Shakespearean play is planned to contribute to the development of a desired mood.

24. E. The use of the word "frankly" (line 15) and "candour" (line 31) supports Choice E.

25. A. Lines 16–20 support Choice A.

26. D. Captain Sentry was not advanced because he was too modest to force himself upon the attention of his superiors.

27. A. *Candour* means frankness, openness.

28. E. *Sycophancy* means fawning upon one's superiors. This Captain Sentry did not do.

29. B. The last sentence supports Choice B.

30. D. Since the author states that men advance by means of talents other than merit, we may regard the statement as sarcastic.

31. C. *Vexatious* means annoying.

32. E. People who commit crimes are called *perpetrators.*

33. A. People are more likely to suspect an *itinerant* (wandering) person because they are more suspicious of strangers.

34. B. If unrelated or *irrelevant* items are introduced, the issue will become unclear or *beclouded.*

35. C. *Charlatan* and *quack* are synonyms.

36. A. The *piston* of an automobile engine moves up and down in a *cylinder;* an *elevator* moves up and down in a *shaft.*

37. B. *Gauche* (clumsy) is the opposite of *deft; rough* is the opposite of *smooth.*

38. D. *Savorless* (tasteless) and *flat* are synonyms; *piquant* (stimulating) and *spicy* are synonyms.

39. B. To *jog* is less speedy than to *sprint;* to *trot* is less speedy than to *gallop.*

40. C. *Timorous* individuals *fear; condoning* individuals *forgive.*

41. B. A *surgeon* uses a *scalpel* to cut; a *butcher* uses a *cleaver* to cut.

42. A. *Integrity* is regarded as a *virtue; sloth* (laziness) as a *vice.*

43. E. *Caution* will prevent an *accident; radar* is a specific kind of precaution designed to prevent *collisions.*

44. B. A *building* consists of several *stories;* a *ladder,* of several *rungs.*

45. E. *Intolerant* people display *prejudice; rapacious* (extortionate) people display *avarice* (greed).

ANSWER SHEET—TEST 6

SECTION 1

1. A B C D E	11. A B C D E	21. A B C D E	31. A B C D E	41. A B C D E
2. A B C D E	12. A B C D E	22. A B C D E	32. A B C D E	42. A B C D E
3. A B C D E	13. A B C D E	23. A B C D E	33. A B C D E	43. A B C D E
4. A B C D E	14. A B C D E	24. A B C D E	34. A B C D E	44. A B C D E
5. A B C D E	15. A B C D E	25. A B C D E	35. A B C D E	45. A B C D E
6. A B C D E	16. A B C D E	26. A B C D E	36. A B C D E	46. A B C D E
7. A B C D E	17. A B C D E	27. A B C D E	37. A B C D E	47. A B C D E
8. A B C D E	18. A B C D E	28. A B C D E	38. A B C D E	48. A B C D E
9. A B C D E	19. A B C D E	29. A B C D E	39. A B C D E	49. A B C D E
10. A B C D E	20. A B C D E	30. A B C D E	40. A B C D E	50. A B C D E

SECTION 2

1. A B C D E	11. A B C D E	21. A B C D E	31. A B C D E	41. A B C D E
2. A B C D E	12. A B C D E	22. A B C D E	32. A B C D E	42. A B C D E
3. A B C D E	13. A B C D E	23. A B C D E	33. A B C D E	43. A B C D E
4. A B C D E	14. A B C D E	24. A B C D E	34. A B C D E	44. A B C D E
5. A B C D E	15. A B C D E	25. A B C D E	35. A B C D E	45. A B C D E
6. A B C D E	16. A B C D E	26. A B C D E	36. A B C D E	46. A B C D E
7. A B C D E	17. A B C D E	27. A B C D E	37. A B C D E	47. A B C D E
8. A B C D E	18. A B C D E	28. A B C D E	38. A B C D E	48. A B C D E
9. A B C D E	19. A B C D E	29. A B C D E	39. A B C D E	49. A B C D E
10. A B C D E	20. A B C D E	30. A B C D E	40. A B C D E	50. A B C D E

SECTION 3

1. A B C D E	11. A B C D E	21. A B C D E	31. A B C D E	41. A B C D E
2. A B C D E	12. A B C D E	22. A B C D E	32. A B C D E	42. A B C D E
3. A B C D E	13. A B C D E	23. A B C D E	33. A B C D E	43. A B C D E
4. A B C D E	14. A B C D E	24. A B C D E	34. A B C D E	44. A B C D E
5. A B C D E	15. A B C D E	25. A B C D E	35. A B C D E	45. A B C D E
6. A B C D E	16. A B C D E	26. A B C D E	36. A B C D E	46. A B C D E
7. A B C D E	17. A B C D E	27. A B C D E	37. A B C D E	47. A B C D E
8. A B C D E	18. A B C D E	28. A B C D E	38. A B C D E	48. A B C D E
9. A B C D E	19. A B C D E	29. A B C D E	39. A B C D E	49. A B C D E
10. A B C D E	20. A B C D E	30. A B C D E	40. A B C D E	50. A B C D E

Remove answer sheet by cutting on dotted line

SECTION 4

1. Ⓐ Ⓑ Ⓒ Ⓓ Ⓔ	11. Ⓐ Ⓑ Ⓒ Ⓓ Ⓔ	21. Ⓐ Ⓑ Ⓒ Ⓓ Ⓔ	31. Ⓐ Ⓑ Ⓒ Ⓓ Ⓔ	41. Ⓐ Ⓑ Ⓒ Ⓓ Ⓔ
2. Ⓐ Ⓑ Ⓒ Ⓓ Ⓔ	12. Ⓐ Ⓑ Ⓒ Ⓓ Ⓔ	22. Ⓐ Ⓑ Ⓒ Ⓓ Ⓔ	32. Ⓐ Ⓑ Ⓒ Ⓓ Ⓔ	42. Ⓐ Ⓑ Ⓒ Ⓓ Ⓔ
3. Ⓐ Ⓑ Ⓒ Ⓓ Ⓔ	13. Ⓐ Ⓑ Ⓒ Ⓓ Ⓔ	23. Ⓐ Ⓑ Ⓒ Ⓓ Ⓔ	33. Ⓐ Ⓑ Ⓒ Ⓓ Ⓔ	43. Ⓐ Ⓑ Ⓒ Ⓓ Ⓔ
4. Ⓐ Ⓑ Ⓒ Ⓓ Ⓔ	14. Ⓐ Ⓑ Ⓒ Ⓓ Ⓔ	24. Ⓐ Ⓑ Ⓒ Ⓓ Ⓔ	34. Ⓐ Ⓑ Ⓒ Ⓓ Ⓔ	44. Ⓐ Ⓑ Ⓒ Ⓓ Ⓔ
5. Ⓐ Ⓑ Ⓒ Ⓓ Ⓔ	15. Ⓐ Ⓑ Ⓒ Ⓓ Ⓔ	25. Ⓐ Ⓑ Ⓒ Ⓓ Ⓔ	35. Ⓐ Ⓑ Ⓒ Ⓓ Ⓔ	45. Ⓐ Ⓑ Ⓒ Ⓓ Ⓔ
6. Ⓐ Ⓑ Ⓒ Ⓓ Ⓔ	16. Ⓐ Ⓑ Ⓒ Ⓓ Ⓔ	26. Ⓐ Ⓑ Ⓒ Ⓓ Ⓔ	36. Ⓐ Ⓑ Ⓒ Ⓓ Ⓔ	46. Ⓐ Ⓑ Ⓒ Ⓓ Ⓔ
7. Ⓐ Ⓑ Ⓒ Ⓓ Ⓔ	17. Ⓐ Ⓑ Ⓒ Ⓓ Ⓔ	27. Ⓐ Ⓑ Ⓒ Ⓓ Ⓔ	37. Ⓐ Ⓑ Ⓒ Ⓓ Ⓔ	47. Ⓐ Ⓑ Ⓒ Ⓓ Ⓔ
8. Ⓐ Ⓑ Ⓒ Ⓓ Ⓔ	18. Ⓐ Ⓑ Ⓒ Ⓓ Ⓔ	28. Ⓐ Ⓑ Ⓒ Ⓓ Ⓔ	38. Ⓐ Ⓑ Ⓒ Ⓓ Ⓔ	48. Ⓐ Ⓑ Ⓒ Ⓓ Ⓔ
9. Ⓐ Ⓑ Ⓒ Ⓓ Ⓔ	19. Ⓐ Ⓑ Ⓒ Ⓓ Ⓔ	29. Ⓐ Ⓑ Ⓒ Ⓓ Ⓔ	39. Ⓐ Ⓑ Ⓒ Ⓓ Ⓔ	49. Ⓐ Ⓑ Ⓒ Ⓓ Ⓔ
10. Ⓐ Ⓑ Ⓒ Ⓓ Ⓔ	20. Ⓐ Ⓑ Ⓒ Ⓓ Ⓔ	30. Ⓐ Ⓑ Ⓒ Ⓓ Ⓔ	40. Ⓐ Ⓑ Ⓒ Ⓓ Ⓔ	50. Ⓐ Ⓑ Ⓒ Ⓓ Ⓔ

SECTION 5

1. Ⓐ Ⓑ Ⓒ Ⓓ Ⓔ	11. Ⓐ Ⓑ Ⓒ Ⓓ Ⓔ	21. Ⓐ Ⓑ Ⓒ Ⓓ Ⓔ	31. Ⓐ Ⓑ Ⓒ Ⓓ Ⓔ	41. Ⓐ Ⓑ Ⓒ Ⓓ Ⓔ
2. Ⓐ Ⓑ Ⓒ Ⓓ Ⓔ	12. Ⓐ Ⓑ Ⓒ Ⓓ Ⓔ	22. Ⓐ Ⓑ Ⓒ Ⓓ Ⓔ	32. Ⓐ Ⓑ Ⓒ Ⓓ Ⓔ	42. Ⓐ Ⓑ Ⓒ Ⓓ Ⓔ
3. Ⓐ Ⓑ Ⓒ Ⓓ Ⓔ	13. Ⓐ Ⓑ Ⓒ Ⓓ Ⓔ	23. Ⓐ Ⓑ Ⓒ Ⓓ Ⓔ	33. Ⓐ Ⓑ Ⓒ Ⓓ Ⓔ	43. Ⓐ Ⓑ Ⓒ Ⓓ Ⓔ
4. Ⓐ Ⓑ Ⓒ Ⓓ Ⓔ	14. Ⓐ Ⓑ Ⓒ Ⓓ Ⓔ	24. Ⓐ Ⓑ Ⓒ Ⓓ Ⓔ	34. Ⓐ Ⓑ Ⓒ Ⓓ Ⓔ	44. Ⓐ Ⓑ Ⓒ Ⓓ Ⓔ
5. Ⓐ Ⓑ Ⓒ Ⓓ Ⓔ	15. Ⓐ Ⓑ Ⓒ Ⓓ Ⓔ	25. Ⓐ Ⓑ Ⓒ Ⓓ Ⓔ	35. Ⓐ Ⓑ Ⓒ Ⓓ Ⓔ	45. Ⓐ Ⓑ Ⓒ Ⓓ Ⓔ
6. Ⓐ Ⓑ Ⓒ Ⓓ Ⓔ	16. Ⓐ Ⓑ Ⓒ Ⓓ Ⓔ	26. Ⓐ Ⓑ Ⓒ Ⓓ Ⓔ	36. Ⓐ Ⓑ Ⓒ Ⓓ Ⓔ	46. Ⓐ Ⓑ Ⓒ Ⓓ Ⓔ
7. Ⓐ Ⓑ Ⓒ Ⓓ Ⓔ	17. Ⓐ Ⓑ Ⓒ Ⓓ Ⓔ	27. Ⓐ Ⓑ Ⓒ Ⓓ Ⓔ	37. Ⓐ Ⓑ Ⓒ Ⓓ Ⓔ	47. Ⓐ Ⓑ Ⓒ Ⓓ Ⓔ
8. Ⓐ Ⓑ Ⓒ Ⓓ Ⓔ	18. Ⓐ Ⓑ Ⓒ Ⓓ Ⓔ	28. Ⓐ Ⓑ Ⓒ Ⓓ Ⓔ	38. Ⓐ Ⓑ Ⓒ Ⓓ Ⓔ	48. Ⓐ Ⓑ Ⓒ Ⓓ Ⓔ
9. Ⓐ Ⓑ Ⓒ Ⓓ Ⓔ	19. Ⓐ Ⓑ Ⓒ Ⓓ Ⓔ	29. Ⓐ Ⓑ Ⓒ Ⓓ Ⓔ	39. Ⓐ Ⓑ Ⓒ Ⓓ Ⓔ	49. Ⓐ Ⓑ Ⓒ Ⓓ Ⓔ
10. Ⓐ Ⓑ Ⓒ Ⓓ Ⓔ	20. Ⓐ Ⓑ Ⓒ Ⓓ Ⓔ	30. Ⓐ Ⓑ Ⓒ Ⓓ Ⓔ	40. Ⓐ Ⓑ Ⓒ Ⓓ Ⓔ	50. Ⓐ Ⓑ Ⓒ Ⓓ Ⓔ

SECTION 6

1. Ⓐ Ⓑ Ⓒ Ⓓ Ⓔ	11. Ⓐ Ⓑ Ⓒ Ⓓ Ⓔ	21. Ⓐ Ⓑ Ⓒ Ⓓ Ⓔ	31. Ⓐ Ⓑ Ⓒ Ⓓ Ⓔ	41. Ⓐ Ⓑ Ⓒ Ⓓ Ⓔ
2. Ⓐ Ⓑ Ⓒ Ⓓ Ⓔ	12. Ⓐ Ⓑ Ⓒ Ⓓ Ⓔ	22. Ⓐ Ⓑ Ⓒ Ⓓ Ⓔ	32. Ⓐ Ⓑ Ⓒ Ⓓ Ⓔ	42. Ⓐ Ⓑ Ⓒ Ⓓ Ⓔ
3. Ⓐ Ⓑ Ⓒ Ⓓ Ⓔ	13. Ⓐ Ⓑ Ⓒ Ⓓ Ⓔ	23. Ⓐ Ⓑ Ⓒ Ⓓ Ⓔ	33. Ⓐ Ⓑ Ⓒ Ⓓ Ⓔ	43. Ⓐ Ⓑ Ⓒ Ⓓ Ⓔ
4. Ⓐ Ⓑ Ⓒ Ⓓ Ⓔ	14. Ⓐ Ⓑ Ⓒ Ⓓ Ⓔ	24. Ⓐ Ⓑ Ⓒ Ⓓ Ⓔ	34. Ⓐ Ⓑ Ⓒ Ⓓ Ⓔ	44. Ⓐ Ⓑ Ⓒ Ⓓ Ⓔ
5. Ⓐ Ⓑ Ⓒ Ⓓ Ⓔ	15. Ⓐ Ⓑ Ⓒ Ⓓ Ⓔ	25. Ⓐ Ⓑ Ⓒ Ⓓ Ⓔ	35. Ⓐ Ⓑ Ⓒ Ⓓ Ⓔ	45. Ⓐ Ⓑ Ⓒ Ⓓ Ⓔ
6. Ⓐ Ⓑ Ⓒ Ⓓ Ⓔ	16. Ⓐ Ⓑ Ⓒ Ⓓ Ⓔ	26. Ⓐ Ⓑ Ⓒ Ⓓ Ⓔ	36. Ⓐ Ⓑ Ⓒ Ⓓ Ⓔ	46. Ⓐ Ⓑ Ⓒ Ⓓ Ⓔ
7. Ⓐ Ⓑ Ⓒ Ⓓ Ⓔ	17. Ⓐ Ⓑ Ⓒ Ⓓ Ⓔ	27. Ⓐ Ⓑ Ⓒ Ⓓ Ⓔ	37. Ⓐ Ⓑ Ⓒ Ⓓ Ⓔ	47. Ⓐ Ⓑ Ⓒ Ⓓ Ⓔ
8. Ⓐ Ⓑ Ⓒ Ⓓ Ⓔ	18. Ⓐ Ⓑ Ⓒ Ⓓ Ⓔ	28. Ⓐ Ⓑ Ⓒ Ⓓ Ⓔ	38. Ⓐ Ⓑ Ⓒ Ⓓ Ⓔ	48. Ⓐ Ⓑ Ⓒ Ⓓ Ⓔ
9. Ⓐ Ⓑ Ⓒ Ⓓ Ⓔ	19. Ⓐ Ⓑ Ⓒ Ⓓ Ⓔ	29. Ⓐ Ⓑ Ⓒ Ⓓ Ⓔ	39. Ⓐ Ⓑ Ⓒ Ⓓ Ⓔ	49. Ⓐ Ⓑ Ⓒ Ⓓ Ⓔ
10. Ⓐ Ⓑ Ⓒ Ⓓ Ⓔ	20. Ⓐ Ⓑ Ⓒ Ⓓ Ⓔ	30. Ⓐ Ⓑ Ⓒ Ⓓ Ⓔ	40. Ⓐ Ⓑ Ⓒ Ⓓ Ⓔ	50. Ⓐ Ⓑ Ⓒ Ⓓ Ⓔ

Remove answer sheet by cutting on dotted line

MODEL SAT TEST 6

SECTION 1 MATH ABILITY

25 QUESTIONS - 30 MINUTES

In this section solve each problem, using any available space on the page for scratchwork. Then decide which is the best of the choices given and blacken the corresponding space on the answer sheet.

The following information is for your reference in solving some of the problems.

Circle of radius r: Area $= \pi r^2$; Circumference $= 2\pi r$

The number of degrees of arc in a circle is 360.

The measure in degrees of a straight angle is 180.

Definitions of symbols:

$=$ is equal to
$\neq$ is unequal to
$<$ is less than
$>$ is greater than
$\leqq$ is less than or equal to
$\geqq$ is greater than or equal to
$\parallel$ is parallel to
$\perp$ is perpendicular to

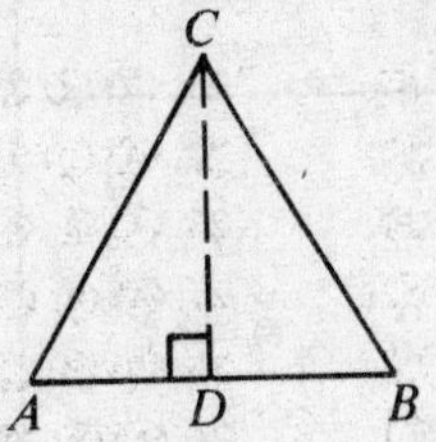

Triangle: The sum of the measures in degrees of the angles of a triangle is 180.

If $\angle CDA$ is a right angle, then

(1) area of $\triangle ABC = \frac{AB \times CD}{2}$

(2) $AC^2 = AD^2 + DC^2$

Note: Figures that accompany problems in this test are intended to provide information useful in solving the problems. They are drawn as accurately as possible EXCEPT when it is stated in a specific problem that its figure is not drawn to scale. All figures lie in a plane unless otherwise indicated. All numbers used are real numbers.

1. $\frac{1}{4}$ % of 2 = ?

(A) $\frac{1}{800}$
(B) $\frac{1}{200}$
(C) $\frac{8}{100}$
(D) $\frac{2}{25}$
(E) $\frac{1}{8}$

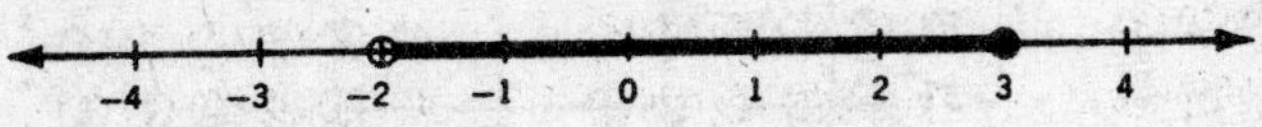

2. Which inequality is represented by the graph above?

(A) $-2 < x \leqq 3$
(B) $2 < x < 3$
(C) $2 < x = 3$
(D) $2 > x > 3$
(E) $-2 > x \leqq 3$

3. The average of two numbers is K. If one number is equal to M, the other number is equal to

(A) $2M - K$
(B) $\frac{-2M + K}{2}$
(C) $\frac{2M - K}{2}$
(D) $\frac{M + K}{2}$
(E) $2K - M$

4. A woman purchases 4 lbs. of steak priced at 80¢ per lb. What change does she receive from a ten-dollar bill?

(A) \$3.20
(B) \$7.20
(C) \$7.80
(D) \$6.80
(E) \$9.20

5. $z + \frac{1}{z} = 2; z = ?$
(A) $\frac{1}{2}$
(B) 1
(C) $1\frac{1}{2}$
(D) 2
(E) $2\frac{1}{2}$

6. What fraction must be added to the following to give an average of exactly $\frac{3}{10}$? $\frac{3}{5}, \frac{1}{4}, \frac{1}{10}, \frac{1}{2}$
(A) $\frac{1}{20}$
(B) $\frac{2}{3}$
(C) $\frac{6}{5}$
(D) $\frac{29}{20}$
(E) $\frac{3}{2}$

7. What is $a\%$ of b divided by $b\%$ of a?
(A) a
(B) b
(C) 1
(D) 10
(E) 100

8. The wey of Scotland is equivalent to 40 bushels. How many weys are there in 4 bushels?
(A) $\frac{1}{10}$
(B) 1
(C) 10
(D) 44
(E) 160

9. How many inches are there in y yards, f feet and i inches?
(A) $y + f + i$
(B) $36y + 12f + i$
(C) $36i + 12f + y$
(D) $\frac{y}{36} + \frac{f}{12} + i$
(E) $36(y + f + i)$

10. A man earns d dollars each week and spends s dollars a week. In how many weeks will he have Q dollars?
(A) $d - s$
(B) $\frac{Q}{d - s}$
(C) $d - Q$
(D) $\frac{d - s}{Q}$
(E) $\frac{d - Q}{s}$

11. $\sqrt{\frac{1}{4}} \cdot \sqrt{\frac{16}{36}} = ?$
(A) $\frac{2}{9}$
(B) $\frac{1}{3}$
(C) $\frac{\sqrt{3}}{3}$
(D) $\frac{5}{6}$
(E) 3

12. The cost of purchasing and mailing party invitations is \$2.09. If the cards are purchased at 3 for 10¢ and each requires a 3¢ stamp, how many cards were purchased?
(A) 11
(B) 22
(C) 33
(D) 66
(E) 99

13. $\frac{x^2 + 4x + 6}{x^2 + 3x + 7} = 1$
$x = ?$
(A) 0
(B) -1
(C) 1
(D) $\frac{7}{6}$
(E) 6

14. A manufacturer finds that 0.4% of his production is defective and not suitable for marketing. How many articles of each 1000 produced will be rejected?
(A) 4
(B) 14
(C) 40
(D) 140
(E) 400

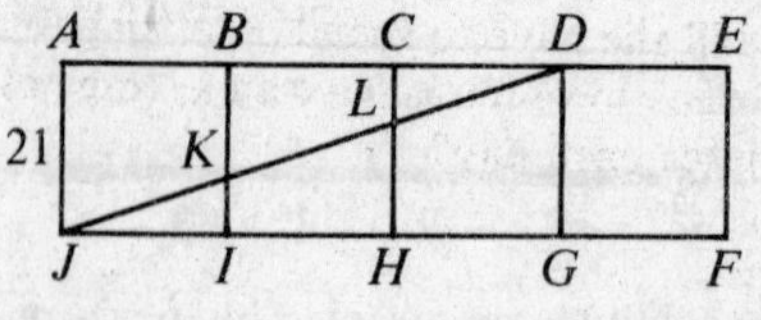

15. In the figure above, $ABIJ$, $BCHI$, $CDGH$, and $DEFG$ are congruent rectangles.
$AJ = 21$
$KI = ?$
(A) 3
(B) 5.25
(C) 7
(D) 10.5
(E) 14

16. If the product xy is constant and if $x = 4$ when $y = 7$, find the value of x when $y = 17\frac{1}{2}$.
(A) 1.6
(B) 2.8
(C) 4.8
(D) 10
(E) 16

17. An automobile travels at the rate of 50 miles per hour on the Pennsylvania Turnpike. How many minutes will it take to travel $\frac{2}{5}$ of a mile at this rate?
(A) 0.2
(B) 0.48
(C) 2.2
(D) 13.5
(E) 22

18. A trailer carries 3, 4, or 5 crates on a trip. Each crate weighs no less than 125 lbs. and no more than 250 lbs. What is the minimum weight (in lbs.) of the crates on a single trip?
(A) 375
(B) 600
(C) 625
(D) 750
(E) 1250

19. The area of a circle with radius r is equal to the area of a rectangle with base b. Find the altitude of the rectangle in terms of π, r, and b.
(A) $\sqrt{\pi r}$
(B) $\frac{2\pi r}{b}$
(C) $\pi r^2 b$
(D) $\frac{\pi r^2}{b}$
(E) $\frac{\pi r^2}{b^2}$

20. A girl keeps a record of time she spends practicing her music. On Monday she spends $1\frac{1}{4}$ hours; on Tuesday and Wednesday she spends 2 hours each day; on Thursday she spends $1\frac{3}{4}$ hours. How many hours will she have to spend practicing for the rest of the week in order to have an average of exactly 90 minutes each day?
(A) $1\frac{1}{2}$
(B) 2
(C) $2\frac{1}{2}$
(D) $3\frac{1}{2}$
(E) 4

21. To raise $500 for a charitable organization a school plans a musical festival with expenses of $250. What is the minimum number of tickets at 75 cents each that will have to be sold to reach this goal?
(A) 100
(B) 300
(C) 334
(D) 1000
(E) 1500

22. If the side of a square is increased by 150%, by what % is the area increased?
(A) 125
(B) 225
(C) 300
(D) 525
(E) 625

23. A circle whose center is the point (−2, 6) is tangent to the x-axis. The coordinates of the point of tangency are
(A) (0, 6)
(B) (−2, 0)
(C) (0, −2)
(D) (6, 0)
(E) (−2, −2)

24. What are the coordinates of the midpoint of the line segment joining point A (−5, −4) and point B (3, −2)?
(A) (−1, −3)
(B) (1, 3)
(C) (−2, −6)
(D) (1, −6)
(E) (−2, −3)

25. The length of the line segment joining the points whose coordinates are (−4, 3) and (2, −5) is
(A) 4
(B) 5
(C) 7
(D) 10
(E) 20

S T O P

IF YOU FINISH BEFORE TIME IS CALLED, YOU MAY CHECK YOUR WORK ON THIS SECTION ONLY. DO NOT WORK ON ANY OTHER SECTION IN THE TEST.

SECTION 2 TEST OF STANDARD WRITTEN ENGLISH

50 QUESTIONS - 30 MINUTES

The questions in this section measure skills that are important to writing well. In particular, they test your ability to recognize and use language that is clear, effective, and correct according to the requirements of standard written English, the kind of English found in most college textbooks.

Directions: The following sentences contain problems in grammar, usage, diction (choice of words), and idiom.

Some sentences are correct.

No sentence contains more than one error.

You will find that the error, if there is one, is underlined and lettered. Assume that elements of the sentence that are not underlined are correct and cannot be changed. In choosing answers, follow the requirements of standard written English.

If there is an error, select the one underlined part that must be changed to make the sentence correct and blacken the corresponding space on your answer sheet.

If there is no error, blacken answer space Ⓔ.

EXAMPLE:

The region has a climate so severe that (A) plants growing there (B) rarely had been (C) more than twelve inches high (D). No error (E)

SAMPLE ANSWER

Ⓐ Ⓑ ● Ⓓ Ⓔ

1. The Joneses (A) moved to Arizona because (B) they (C) thought the climate in that state was very healthful (D). No error (E)

2. Had (A) the teacher been (B) in the room, the students would not of (C) created such (D) a commotion. No error (E)

3. Neither the class officers nor (A) the faculty advisor were (B) in the office at the time of (C) the dean's (D) arrival. No error (E)

4. Some (A) television commercials make me (B) mad (C); they (D) are banal and often stupid. No error (E)

5. Its (A) a magnificent offer but (B) I cannot afford to take (C) advantage of it (D) at this time. No error (E)

6. We must come (A) to the realization that it is our obligation to look (B) after the poorer nations by providing medical care, establishing hospitals and schools, and to insure (C) adequate food supplies for all (D). No error (E)

7. As (A) he sung (B) the school song, the students rose and listened with obvious (C) appreciation (D). No error (E)

8. Because (A) he thought that he was failing in his school work, he felt (B) sadly (C) and tried to work more diligently (D). No error (E)

9. He dashed into (A) the burning building, irregardless of (B) the risk involved (C), to warn the sleeping (D) occupants. No error (E)

10. "Do you know," John asked, "at what time we are
A B C
due at the party?" No error
D E

11. He irritated many of his admirers when he
A B C
abandoned his party. No error
D E

12. There has been and I suppose always will be
A B C
dissident members in our community. No error
D E

13. Because I was late ten times this month was the
A B
reason for my suspension from school for two days.
C D
No error
E

14. If I was the President for a week, I would try to
A B C
eliminate the causes of poverty in this country.
D
No error
E

15. I should like you and he to come to my birthday party
A B C
at 8 p.m. on Friday of this week. No error
D E

16. I am not unmindful of the fact that we owe a vote of
A B
thanks to whoever made this news public.
C D
No error
E

17. He worked very hard in order to provide for his
A
family's comfort and that his children receive a
B C
good education. No error
D E

18. No one can predict what the affect of the Watergate
A B C
disclosures will be on American politics in the near
D
future. No error
E

19. Snowing heavily for six hours, road conditions were
A B
very hazardous and traffic was snarled on most
C D
roads. No error
E

20. I do not know to whom I should mail this complaint
A B C
to. No error
D E

21. He lay down his book and tried to rest his weary
A B
eyes; reading in the dim light was very tiring.
C D
No error
E

22. The renter of the car initialed the clause in the con-
A
tract to show that he was aware of the fact that he
B
was liable for the first fifty dollars of any damages
C D
to the automobile. No error
E

23. Bacon and eggs is not his favorite breakfast food; he
A B
thinks they are less filling than warm cereal.
C D
No error
E

24. Neither the Republican members of the committee
A
who supported the proposed legislation or the
B C
Democratic members who opposed it controlled a
clear majority; the votes of the independents
were crucial. No error
D E

25. All but Henry and I agreed that the proposal was a
A B
satisfactory one; we two opposed it. No error
C D E

Directions: In each of the following sentences, some part or all of the sentence is underlined. Below each sentence you will find five ways of phrasing the underlined part. Select the answer that produces the most effective sentence, one that is clear and exact, without awkwardness or ambiguity, and blacken the corresponding space on your answer sheet. In choosing answers, follow the requirements of standard written English. Choose the answer that best expresses the meaning of the original sentence.

Answer (A) is always the same as the underlined part. Choose answer (A) if you think the original sentence needs no revision.

EXAMPLE:

Laura Ingalls Wilder published her first book and she was sixty-five years old then.

(A) and she was sixty-five years old then
(B) when she was sixty-five years old
(C) at age sixty-five years old
(D) upon reaching sixty-five years
(E) at the time when she was sixty-five

SAMPLE ANSWER

Ⓐ ● Ⓒ Ⓓ Ⓔ

26. During the first year that he and I were neighbors, our conversations turned frequently on the two cardinal points of poetry: the power of exciting the sympathy of the reader by a faithful adherence to the truth of nature and the power to give the interest of novelty by the modifying colors of imagination.
(A) power to give
(B) ability to give
(C) power to bestow
(D) ability to bestow
(E) power of giving

27. If I would have realized the danger involved in this assignment, I would not have asked you to undertake it.
(A) If I would have realized
(B) If I should have realized
(C) If I had realized
(D) When I realized
(E) Because I did not realize

28. Having the best record for attendance, the school awarded him a medal at graduation.
(A) the school awarded him a medal
(B) the school awarded a medal to him
(C) he was awarded a medal by the school
(D) a medal was awarded to him by the school
(E) a school medal was awarded to him

29. Our company's keeping it's promises to the customers is of paramount importance to the stockholders.
(A) Our company's keeping it's promises
(B) Our company keeping it's promises
(C) Our company's keeping its promises
(D) Our company keeping its promises
(E) Our companys keeping their promises

30. The principal along with the teachers and parents demand that the traffic department install a traffic light at the street crossing.
(A) demand
(B) demands
(C) are demanding
(D) were demanding
(E) have demanded

31. Most of the students like to read these kind of detective stories for their supplementary reading.
(A) these kind of detective stories
(B) these kind of detective story
(C) this kind of detective stories
(D) this kinds of detective story
(E) those kind of detective story

32. Because of his throat ailment, the tenor has not and apparently never will sing again.
(A) has not and apparently never will sing
(B) has not sung and apparently never will
(C) has not and apparently never would sing
(D) has not sung and apparently never will sing
(E) had not and apparently never will sing

33. "What do you wish," he asked, "may I help you'
(A) wish," he asked, "may
(B) wish," he asked? "May
(C) wish?" he asked, "may
(D) wish?" he asked. "May
(E) wish?" he asked? "May

34. According to your report card, you are not as clever as he.
(A) not as clever as he.
(B) not so clever as him.
(C) not so clever as he.
(D) not so clever like he.
(E) not as clever like he.

35. The imminent historian stood in bed, recuperating from a viral infection, while his paper was being read at the convention.
(A) imminent historian stood
(B) imminent historian remained
(C) eminent historian stayed
(D) eminent historian stood
(E) eminent historian had remained

36. At the zoo, the brightly-plumaged birds that fluttered overhead like tropical flowers in a breeze.
(A) birds that fluttered
(B) birds fluttering
(C) birds which fluttered
(D) birds fluttered
(E) birds aflutter

37. In India, Mahatma Gandhi was more than a political leader he was the enlightened one embodying the soul of the nation.
(A) political leader he was
(B) political leader; he was
(C) political leader, he was
(D) political leader which was
(E) political leader, although he was

38. The difference between the candidates is that one is radical; the other, conservative.
(A) one is radical; the other, conservative
(B) one is radical; the other being conservative
(C) while one is radical; the other, conservative
(D) one is radical, the other, conservative
(E) one is radical, although the other is more conservative

39. Because he spoke out against Hitler's policies was why Dietrich Bonhoeffer, a Lutheran pastor in Nazi Germany, was arrested and eventually hanged by the Gestapo.
(A) Because he spoke out against Hitler's policies was why Dietrich Bonhoeffer, a Lutheran pastor in Nazi Germany, was arrested and eventually hanged by the Gestapo.
(B) Dietrich Bonhoeffer, a Lutheran pastor in Nazi Germany, was arrested and eventually hanged by the Gestapo because he spoke out against Hitler's policies.
(C) Because he spoke out against Hitler's policies, Dietrich Bonhoeffer, a Lutheran pastor in Nazi Germany, was arrested and eventually hung by the Gestapo.
(D) Dietrich Bonhoeffer, a Lutheran pastor in Nazi Germany, being arrested and eventually hung because he spoke out against Hitler's policies.
(E) A Lutheran pastor in Nazi Germany, Dietrich Bonhoeffer spoke out against Hitler's policies so that he was arrested and eventually hung.

40. Several regulations were proposed by the president of the university that had a sexist bias, according to women students.
(A) Several regulations were proposed by the president of the university that
(B) Several regulations were proposed by the president of the university who
(C) The proposal of several regulations by the president of the university which
(D) The president of the university, who proposed several regulations that
(E) The president of the university proposed several regulations that

Note: The remaining questions are like those at the beginning of the section.

Directions: For each sentence in which you find an error, select the one underlined part that must be changed to make the sentence correct and blacken the coresonding space on your answer sheet.
If there is no error, blacken answer space Ⓔ.

EXAMPLE:
The region has a climate so severe that plants (A: so severe that) growing there (B: growing there) rarely had been (C: had been) more than twelve inches high (D: high). No error (E)

SAMPLE ANSWER
Ⓐ Ⓑ ● Ⓓ Ⓔ

41. We do not have enough (A) money for (B) this purchase between (C) the four of us. (D) No error (E)

42. While (A) in San Francisco, we should try (B) and (C) see as many of the famous places as possible. (D) No error (E)

43. Whenever (A) I travel (B) on a plane, I talk to whoever (C) sits next (D) to me. No error (E)

44. Had (A) I been there, (B) I would have (C) protested. (D) No error (E)

45. I advise (A) you to try to become his friend because he may be (B) very helpful and because of his (C) position on the committee that will decide (D) this case. No error (E)

46. I was irritated (A) by (B) you (C) coming into the room as you did — shouting (D) and screaming. No error (E)

47. We do not ought (A) to go into (B) that abandoned building because (C) we may get hurt. (D) No error (E)

48. I only (A) drank (B) one glass of wine; all (C) the others had two (D) or more. No error (E)

49. That kind of a (A) compromise is repugnant (B) to (C) me because it violates the basic principles (D) of our party. No error (E)

50. The legislator stated that he had voted (A) against (B) the proposed tax not only because it (C) was regressive but because it was also (D) unnecessary. No error (E)

S T O P

IF YOU FINISH BEFORE TIME IS CALLED, YOU MAY CHECK YOUR WORK ON THIS SECTION ONLY. DO NOT WORK ON ANY OTHER SECTION IN THE TEST.

SECTION 3 VERBAL ABILITY

45 QUESTIONS - 30 MINUTES

For each question in this section, choose the best answer and blacken the corresponding space on the answer sheet.

Each question below consists of a word in capital letters, followed by five lettered words or phrases. Choose the word or phrase that is most nearly opposite in meaning to the word in capital letters. Since some of the questions require you to distinguish fine shades of meaning, consider all the choices before deciding which is best.

Example:

GOOD: (A) sour (B) bad (C) red (D) hot (E) ugly Ⓐ ● Ⓒ Ⓓ Ⓔ

1. COMMODIOUS :
   (A) serious
   (B) irregular
   (C) major
   (D) limited
   (E) incompetent

2. NEGLIGENT :
   (A) painstaking
   (B) immaterial
   (C) deleterious
   (D) damaging
   (E) emphatic

3. COVERT :
   (A) open
   (B) enormous
   (C) greedy
   (D) detrimental
   (E) fascinating

4. PITHY :
   (A) tactless
   (B) eliminating
   (C) tacit
   (D) inevitable
   (E) wordy

5. INGENUOUS :
   (A) stupid
   (B) incoherent
   (C) sophisticated
   (D) maturated
   (E) intelligent

6. IMPECUNIOUS :
   (A) affluent
   (B) extravagant
   (C) hysterical
   (D) harmful
   (E) benevolent

7. SANGUINE :
   (A) bloody
   (B) peaceful
   (C) young
   (D) preparing
   (E) pessimistic

8. NEFARIOUS :
   (A) praiseworthy
   (B) criminal
   (C) avuncular
   (D) frequent
   (E) white

9. CHOLERIC :
   (A) indisposed
   (B) healthy
   (C) prominent
   (D) apathetic
   (E) loose

10. VERBOSE :
    (A) gullible
    (B) magnificent
    (C) grandiloquent
    (D) concise
    (E) calculating

11. CALUMNIATE :
    (A) decorate
    (B) level
    (C) whiten
    (D) laud
    (E) avoid

12. VACUOUS :
    (A) bankrupt
    (B) loose
    (C) livid
    (D) superficial
    (E) profound

13. EXPUNGE :
(A) distract
(B) strike
(C) append
(D) delay
(E) admire

14. HEDONISM :
(A) deism
(B) pragmatism
(C) surrealism
(D) dogmatism
(E) asceticism

15. MALIGNANT :
(A) massive
(B) evasive
(C) benign
(D) affluent
(E) overt

Each sentence below has one or two blanks, each blank indicating that something has been omitted. Beneath the sentence are five lettered words or sets of words. Choose the word or set of words that best fits the meaning of the sentence as a whole.

Example:

Although its publicity has been ----, the film itself is intelligent, well-acted, handsomely produced, and altogether ----.

(A) tasteless..respectable (B) extensive..moderate (C) sophisticated..amateur (D) risqué..crude (E) perfect..spectacular

● Ⓑ Ⓒ Ⓓ Ⓔ

16. His critical reviews were enjoyed by many of his audience, but the subjects of his analysis dreaded his comments; he was vitriolic, devastating, irritating and never _______.
(A) analytical
(B) personal
(C) constructive
(D) dynamic
(E) brief

17. For many years, we have interpreted that country's activities in the area as minor irritations; however, the latest episode is an _______ act of war and requires _______ measures.
(A) integral — conciliatory
(B) overt — pacific
(C) overt — retaliatory
(D) unforeseen — remedial
(E) effective — recriminatory

18. Our military defenses have been so carefully designed that we have less to fear from direct attack than from _______.
(A) sabotage
(B) dictatorship
(C) indifference
(D) obsolescence
(E) optimism

19. The claims made by the manufacturers of this product are so extravagant that it is hard to believe that not only the _______ accept them.
(A) cynical
(B) gullible
(C) callow
(D) credible
(E) indifferent

20. He found the hot and humid weather in the city so _______ that he could do very little work even with the aid of air conditioning.
(A) enervating
(B) limiting
(C) exasperating
(D) horrendous
(E) blatant

Each passage below is followed by questions based on its content. Answer all questions following a passage on the basis of what is stated or implied in that passage.

The relentless and merciless pounding of a bear market is a frightening experience. Even those of us who have lived through similar episodes in the past are shocked by the havoc. The younger people who know about bear markets only through the reading of economic history books are aghast at the rapid demolition of "values." For some of the new money managers, this is the first time that they see the world in which they prospered virtually fall apart. What looked like a fabulous growth stock with unlimited potentialities has become unsaleable merchandise overnight.

The stock market is a severe taskmaster: you pay dearly for mistakes. If you think what happened on the New York Stock Exchange is bad, take a look at the American Stock Exchange, not to mention the over-the-counter market. When there is congestion at the exit, there is danger of panic and being trampled to death. That is what is happening when too many people are trying to sell stocks of limited marketability at the same time. The more difficult it is to dispose of them, the more urgent becomes the desire to dump them — at any price. The follow-the-leader investment policy that produced such spectacular gains in a rising market now works in reverse.

The danger of any bear market is demoralization. It conjures up memories of past debacles that wiped out fortunes and led to depressions, but the extreme pessimism that is now rampant in financial circles seems unwarranted, or at least greatly exaggerated. A repetition of the 1929 catastrophe is highly improbable, notwithstanding the rumors of serious problems in Wall Street and within a major European financial empire.

21. A "bear market"
   (A) is a manifestation of panic
   (B) is unprecedented
   (C) involves unsaleable merchandise
   (D) is unwarranted
   (E) is marked by devaluation of values

22. During a "bear market," chaos is created because
   (A) the new money managers are inexperienced
   (B) the stock market is a serious taskmaster
   (C) people rush to sell their stocks
   (D) depression results
   (E) people are trampled to death

23. The author is refuting the idea that
   (A) money managers do not know how to handle the current situation
   (B) a repetition of the 1929 depression is imminent
   (C) there is serious trouble in Wall Street
   (D) a rising market and a falling market are similar
   (E) a growth stock is bound to fall in a "bear market"

24. A factor leading to the current financial situation not mentioned by the author is
   (A) the controls on inflation established by the government
   (B) panic selling
   (C) optimism of money managers
   (D) the financial difficulties of a major European financial house
   (E) the fear of a depression

Flames shot high above a blazing Bank of America branch in Santa Barbara, Calif. one night at the end of February, and big business became the physical victim of the current antiestablishment mood among large segments of youth. The Bank of America hadn't done anything to anybody; it was merely a handy symbol to a young and unruly mob.

Some of the demonstrators claimed they set fire to the bank to protest Judge Julius Hoffman's merciless sentencing of the Chicago Seven. It didn't really matter, though. What did was that a big corporation rather than the police, the draft board or a classroom had been attacked.

It was, however you looked at it, a dramatic demonstration of how business is becoming daily more involved in the social issues that are changing and frequently disrupting American society. It is going to cost billions to even make a dent in such problems as pollution, hardcore unemployment, drug addiction, housing, education, and transportation bottlenecks, which will consume much — if not most — of the top executive time in the next few years. Some of the money must come from big business, which must also contend with fast-changing moods that will have incalculable effects on the markets of the future.

Some American companies already reflect these social changes in their profit-and-loss statements: The growing antimilitary mood, inevitably reflected by Congress, has played havoc with the defense companies. Demands to curb inflation, reflected in a tough federal money policy, have flattened the home-building industry.

25. The fire at Santa Barbara, California
(A) is proof that banks are vulnerable
(B) was set because the bank was handy
(C) is symptomatic of young people's dissatisfaction
(D) attacked an innocent victim
(E) was set because business had not contributed to worthwhile causes

26. The least likely victim of an attack by a youthful mob, according to the author, is
(A) the army
(B) the security forces
(C) financial institutions
(D) Selective Service headquarters
(E) a college office

27. The home-building industry
(A) has been hurt by lack of money
(B) has demanded that inflation be curbed
(C) reflects the tough federal monetary policy
(D) is supported by Congress
(E) is part of the nation's industries' profit and loss statement

28. An alleged reason for setting fire to the bank is
(A) unhappiness with the draft
(B) dissatisfaction with the Vietnam War
(C) college policy
(D) the Chicago trial
(E) the defense companies' profits

29. One problem facing us at this time not mentioned by the author is
(A) the spoiling of our environment
(B) heroin
(C) slums
(D) automobile congestion on the highways
(E) welfare

30. According to the author, business must
(A) concern itself with social problems
(B) settle the antimilitary mood among the young
(C) cope with inflation
(D) seek an understanding of youthful problems
(E) settle such problems as drug addiction, housing, etc.

Select the word or set of words that best completes each of the following sentences.

31. A ______ is a ______ saying.
(A) paradox — startling
(B) cliché — trite
(C) metaphor — pithy
(D) maxim — turgid
(E) solecism — profound

32. We had listened to the bombastic orator previously and were not surprised by the ______ of his oratory.
(A) speciousness
(B) exigencies
(C) brevity
(D) incisiveness
(E) flamboyance

33. We were shocked by his ______ at such a serious moment in our conference.
(A) reticence
(B) levity
(C) ingenuousness
(D) ineptitude
(E) affability

34. The economic leaders of the country attempted to curb the inflationary tendencies by ______ the supply of money available.
(A) curbing
(B) increasing
(C) removing
(D) determining
(E) exacerbating

35. To be ______ is to be ______.
(A) supercilious — condescending
(B) magnanimous — veritable
(C) venerable — outdated
(D) despotic — regal
(E) autocratic — dynamic

Each question below consists of a related pair of words or phrases, followed by five lettered pairs of words or phrases. Select the lettered pair that <u>best</u> expresses a relationship similar to that expressed in the original pair.

Example:

YAWN : BOREDOM :: (A) dream : sleep (B) anger : madness (C) smile : amusement (D) face : expression (E) impatience : rebellion

Ⓐ Ⓑ ● Ⓓ Ⓔ

36. SPICE : FOOD ::
(A) salt : pepper
(B) condiment : salt
(C) wit : conversation
(D) intelligence : integrity
(E) fame : fortune

37. BASS : SOPRANO ::
(A) nadir : perigee
(B) cellar : roof
(C) male : female
(D) astronomy : geology
(E) slow : fast

38. RUNG : LADDER ::
(A) banister : staircase
(B) spring : watch
(C) events : history
(D) knots : rope
(E) fame : notoriety

39. LABORER : WAGES ::
(A) general : results
(B) entrepreneur : profits
(C) farmer : harvest
(D) father : children
(E) water : level

40. BENEVOLENCE : CHARITABLE ::
(A) congenial : animosity
(B) vindictiveness : revengeful
(C) taste : culture
(D) virtue : demure
(E) isolation : loneliness

41. TACITURN : LACONIC ::
(A) early : late
(B) voluble : alert
(C) major : minor
(D) garrulous : loquacious
(E) soft : subdued

42. HAUGHTY : ARROGANT ::
(A) heinous : egregious
(B) snob : sophisticate
(C) general : colonel
(D) sycophant : obsequious
(E) proud : humble

43. MELANCHOLY : EXUBERANT ::
(A) stingy : prosaic
(B) tall : small
(C) sad : gay
(D) sad : lugubrious
(E) lugubrious : morbid

44. SHIP : FOUNDER ::
(A) government : succeed
(B) union : strike
(C) business : reorganize
(D) building : collapse
(E) army : muster

45. ISLAND : ARCHIPELAGO ::
(A) team : player
(B) orchestra : violinist
(C) star : galaxy
(D) multitude : horde
(E) Manhattan : New York

S T O P

IF YOU FINISH BEFORE TIME IS CALLED, YOU MAY CHECK YOUR WORK ON THIS SECTION ONLY. DO NOT WORK ON ANY OTHER SECTION IN THE TEST.

SECTION 4 VERBAL ABILITY

40 QUESTIONS - 30 MINUTES

For each question in this section, choose the best answer and blacken the corresponding space on the answer sheet.

Each question below consists of a word in capital letters, followed by five lettered words or phrases. Choose the word or phrase that is most nearly opposite in meaning to the word in capital letters. Since some of the questions require you to distinguish fine shades of meaning, consider all the choices before deciding which is best.

Example:

GOOD: (A) sour (B) bad (C) red (D) hot (E) ugly

Ⓐ ● Ⓒ Ⓓ Ⓔ

1. PRODIGAL :
   (A) wandering
   (B) thrifty
   (C) infantile
   (D) mature
   (E) energetic

2. INDIGENOUS :
   (A) foreign
   (B) unpatriotic
   (C) exhausted
   (D) impudent
   (E) magnificent

3. EUPHONIOUS :
   (A) healthy
   (B) discordant
   (C) dishonest
   (D) honest
   (E) embarrassing

4. SPORADIC :
   (A) germinal
   (B) antiseptic
   (C) incessant
   (D) summery
   (E) wintry

5. PUSILLANIMOUS :
   (A) small
   (B) immense
   (C) courageous
   (D) knavish
   (E) calm

6. GULLIBLE :
   (A) horrible
   (B) credible
   (C) stingy
   (D) incredulous
   (E) unfriendly

7. PROFANE :
   (A) act impolite
   (B) scare away
   (C) sanctify
   (D) define
   (E) take apart

8. DEARTH :
   (A) abundance
   (B) life
   (C) luck
   (D) mirth
   (E) enormity

9. AUGMENT :
   (A) curse
   (B) deplete
   (C) soothe
   (D) purchase
   (E) save

10. AUSPICIOUS :
    (A) trusting
    (B) indifferent
    (C) irreligious
    (D) unfavorable
    (E) nearby

Each sentence below has one or two blanks, each blank indicating that something has been omitted. Beneath the sentence are five lettered words or sets of words. Choose the word or set of words that best fits the meaning of the sentence as a whole.

Example:

Although its publicity has been ----, the film itself is intelligent, well-acted, handsomely produced, and altogether ----.

(A) tasteless..respectable (B) extensive..moderate (C) sophisticated..amateur (D) risqué..crude (E) perfect..spectacular

● Ⓑ Ⓒ Ⓓ Ⓔ

11. Critics of our society maintain that manufacturers insist that their products have a built-in _______ in order to maintain sales.
(A) esthetic quality
(B) practicability
(C) obsolescence
(D) excellence
(E) advertising appeal

12. He was so docile and _______ that his friends could not understand his sudden outburst against his employers.
(A) complacent
(B) incorrigible
(C) truculent
(D) choleric
(E) frenetic

13. At a time of unprecedented prosperity such as we enjoy today, it is inconceivable that we can tolerate the _______ and suffering in some of our slum areas.
(A) penury
(B) magnitude
(C) violence
(D) ignorance
(E) affluence

14. Among his many contributions to medical science, we must rate highly his discoveries of the _______ ailments found in the lungs of animals and human beings.
(A) malignant
(B) benign
(C) pulmonary
(D) chronic
(E) major

15. Because both sides in the labor dispute were so obviously _______, the mediator announced that an early settlement could not be reached.
(A) inordinate
(B) conciliatory
(C) lackadaisical
(D) opportunistic
(E) obdurate

Each question below consists of a related pair of words or phrases, followed by five lettered pairs of words or phrases. Select the lettered pair that best expresses a relationship similar to that expressed in the original pair.

Example:

YAWN : BOREDOM :: (A) dream : sleep (B) anger : madness (C) smile : amusement (D) face : expression (E) impatience : rebellion

Ⓐ Ⓑ ● Ⓓ Ⓔ

16. THEATER : HISTRIONIC ::
(A) forensic : court
(B) kitchen : culinary
(C) poetry : terpischorean
(D) tragedy : culinary
(E) poetry : muse

17. LEXICOGRAPHER : CARTOGRAPHER ::
(A) words : maps
(B) laws : maps
(C) laws : handwriting
(D) dictionary : appendix
(E) laws : cards

18. PINT : LITER ::
(A) liquid : metric
(B) quart : gallon
(C) yard : meter
(D) liquid : solid
(E) volume : length

19. FORGIVE : OFFENSE ::
(A) condone : crime
(B) pardon : excuse
(C) condone : excuse
(D) pardon : offense
(E) revenge : rebuff

20. LOBSTER : CRUSTACEAN ::
(A) crab : crawling
(B) lizard : crawling
(C) man : humane
(D) whale : aquatic
(E) lizard : reptilian

21. DAWN : DUSK ::
(A) infancy : mortality
(B) infancy : adolescence
(C) infancy : senility
(D) infancy : maturity
(E) birth : death

22. INTEREST : USURY ::
(A) concern : disregard
(B) frugality : prodigality
(C) parsimony : frugality
(D) frugality : parsimony
(E) fortune : misfortune

23. CACOPHONY : EAR ::
(A) calligraphy : eye
(B) piquancy : taste
(C) stench : nose
(D) tracheotomy : throat
(E) retina : eye

24. MOLLIFY : INCITE ::
(A) allay : arouse
(B) irritate : annoy
(C) appease : requite
(D) allay : placate
(E) enjoy : refrain

25. EULOGY : PRAISE ::
(A) elegy : death
(B) slander : vilification
(C) panegyric : abuse
(D) libel : slander
(E) song : laud

Each passage below is followed by questions based on its content. Answer all questions following a passage on the basis of what is stated or implied in that passage.

It is a general law in politics, that the power most to be distrusted, is that which, possessing the greatest force, is the least responsible. Under the constitutional monarchies of Europe, (as they exist in theory at least), the king, besides uniting in his single person all the authority of the executive, which includes a power to make war, create peers, and unconditionally to name to all employments, has an equal influence in enacting laws, his veto being absolute; but in America, the executive, besides being elective, is stripped of most of these high sources of influence, and is obliged to keep constantly in view the justice and legality of his acts, both on account of his direct responsibilities, and on account of the force of public opinion.

In this country, there is far more to apprehend from Congress, than from the executive, as is seen in the following reasons: — Congress is composed of many, while the executive is one, bodies of men notoriously acting with less personal responsibilities than individuals; Congress has power to enact laws, which it becomes the duty of the executive to see enforced, and the really legislative authority of a country is always its greatest authority; from the decisions and constructions of the executive, the citizen can always appeal to the courts for protection, but no appeal can lie from the acts of Congress, except on the grounds of unconstitutionality; the executive has direct personal responsibilities under the laws of the land, for any abuses of his authority, but the member of Congress unless guilty of open corruption, is almost beyond personal liabilities.

It follows that the legislature of this country, by the intention of the constitution, wields the highest authority under the least responsibility, and that it is the power most to be distrusted. Still, all who possess trusts, are to be diligently watched, for there is no protection against abuses without responsibility, nor any real responsibility, without vigilance.

Political partisans, who are too apt to mistake the impulses of their own hostilities and friendships for truths, have laid down many false principles on the subject of the duties of the executive. When a law is passed, it goes to the executive for execution, through the executive agents, and, at need to the courts for interpretation. It would seem that there is no discretion vested in the executive concerning the constitutionality of a law. If he distrusts the constitutionality of any law, he can set forth his objections by resorting to the veto; but it is clearly the intention of the system that the whole legislative power, in the last resort, shall abide in Congress, while it is necessary to the regular action of the government, that none of its agents, but those who are especially appointed for that purpose, shall pretend to interpret the constitution, in practice. The citizen is differently situated. If he conceives himself oppressed by an unconstitutional law, it is his inalienable privilege to raise the question before the courts, where a final interpretation can be had. By this interpretation the executive and all his agents are equally bound to abide. This obligation arises from the necessity of things, as well as from the nature of the institutions. There must be somewhere a power to decide on the constitutionality of laws, and this power is vested in the supreme court of the United States, on final appeal.

26. The author's purpose in writing this passage is to indicate
- (A) the difference between kings and presidents
- (B) the power of the Supreme Court
- (C) the need for vigilance
- (D) the limitations of the presidency
- (E) the irresponsibility of Congress

27. According to the author, the president differs from a constitutional monarch in that he
- (A) has absolute power
- (B) is responsive to public opinion
- (C) lacks an absolute veto
- (D) distrusts Congress
- (E) is almost beyond personal liability

28. According to the author, it is not the president's responsibility to
- (A) veto laws
- (B) question the constitutionality of a law
- (C) have an equal status with Congress
- (D) enforce the laws passed by Congress
- (E) name his assistants

29. The strength of Congress lies in its numbers because
- (A) in numbers, there is strength
- (B) it can override a presidential veto
- (C) it controls the budget
- (D) it does not have to concern itself with the constitutionality of the laws it enacts
- (E) no member can be held individually accountable for its actions

30. One difference between a constitutional monarch and the president not mentioned by the author is that the
- (A) monarch is non-elective
- (B) monarch has unlimited tenure
- (C) president has a limited veto
- (D) president is limited by the constitution
- (E) monarch may appoint his assistants without conditions

31. In this country, it is necessary to have a Supreme Court
- (A) to settle disputes between the president and Congress
- (B) because Congress needs some body to determine the constitutionality of laws
- (C) to protect the individual from the abuses of an unconstitutional law
- (D) because the president has limited ability to determine the constitutionality of a law enacted by Congress
- (E) to dismiss members of Congress

Some very learned and thoughtful people see the computer as facilitating a radical alignment of knowledge, and therefore of power. This they regard as a very dangerous possibility, and so do I. But I don't regard it as inevitable.

What can be done — what must be done — to avoid that sort of perversion of computer technology?

There is a natural human dislike of becoming a statistic — particularly when the statistics grow into a lengthy dossier providing more or less intimate details about one's person and one's daily living habits. Even more particularly when that dossier is secreted within a vast, impersonal electronic information system, to which any number of unknown people may have access.

Privacy is one of our most precious human rights, and in today's crowded and disorganized environment it may be one of the hardest to maintain.

The computer does not of itself create any invasion of privacy. The threat of privacy posed by surveillance and record-keeping has been a fact of life for centuries. The new element introduced by the computer is fantastic efficiency. That is what people fear, and that is the problem that must be faced.

We have too many examples around us today of how technology failed to look ahead at problems it might accelerate, even if it did not create them. Pollution of our environment is one, and now we must reckon with pollution of privacy.

We can build safeguards into system design. We can limit those who are allowed to put information into a system. We can even have the machine check data against a set of values and reject questionable information. There can be ingenious safeguards in the delivery of information. The computer could require a password; it could limit access to a specific type of information; it could record each request, so as to pinpoint blame later if information were misused.

There are many more possible examples of technical security systems; but really determined men, unfortunately, can find ways to get around the best security systems. So we must consider more than physical safety.

The trustworthiness of the operating personnel is an important factor. The question needs to be asked more often: "Is this information really necessary?" Do employers really need to know all about the emotions, personal habits, attitudes and beliefs of their employees?

The burden of answering questions from all sides is growing for the average man. All of us are leaving longer trails behind us of information gained by birth records, employment records, Social Security, the police, hospitals, credit bureaus, the Internal Revenue Service, the census. If we cannot stop this relentless flow of information about ourselves into central files, we can control it. A time limit on all personal data might be a good idea: so that a youthful indiscretion wouldn't haunt a man the rest of his life.

Our old legal framework may not be adequate to defend our privacy against new techniques of data collection and record-keeping. Perhaps the most important new safeguard would provide a citizen with the ability to challenge in court the release of private data about him without his consent.

32. The best title for this passage is
(A) The Computer and Vital Statistics
(B) Invasion of Privacy
(C) Preservation of Privacy
(D) Limiting Records
(E) Statistics and Human Nature

33. The author mentions as sources of information about people all of the following except
(A) social security records
(B) marriage licenses
(C) income tax returns
(D) history of employment
(E) F.B.I. files

34. According to the author, the best way to protect the individual from unnecessary invasion of his privacy is to
(A) limit the number of people who have access to the files
(B) build safeguards into the machine
(C) enable the individual to use the courts as a protection
(D) have the computer require a password
(E) prevent the Internal Revenue Service from using the computer

35. Modern technology is responsible for many of our present-day evils because
(A) it created pollution of our environment
(B) it developed the computer
(C) of its tremendous accuracy
(D) of its tremendous efficiency
(E) it did not anticipate the problems it was encouraging

Out in the Atlantic the other day, in about 3,000 feet of water and about 120 miles east of Charleston, S.C., a converted cargo vessel dropped a string of nine-inch-diameter steel pipe to the ocean floor. Operating somewhat like a vacuum cleaner, it began to suck into the ship a thundering stream of air, water, and nodules — smooth, apple-sized lumps — of rich metallic ore.

From the Research Vessel Deepsea Miner, a jubilant crew of scientists, engineers and sailors flashed the word back to the headquarters of Deepsea Ventures, Inc., "it works," they reported. "Beyond expectations."

This successful first test of a revolutionary technique for mining an untapped source of four important metals was only a single step in a long march, much of which still lies ahead of Deepsea Ventures. The test, however, was one of the biggest strides so far in a program that has absorbed about eight years and $15-million.

Company officials indicated here last week that the success probably had answered favorably the major questions about the mining techniques involved. Questions that still remain concern the international legal status of the widespread ocean-bed deposits, the processing and refining of the unique type of ore they contain and the economics of marketing the manganese, nickel, cobalt and copper that would be produced.

To operate commercially, a consortium would have to begin in the Pacific with a specially built, full-scale mining ship, capable of recovering nodules at depths of 15,000 or 18,000 feet. Pacific deposits are richer and more likely to prove economically feasible than the Atlantic ore that was recovered in the recent exercise, designed strictly to test the recovery technique.

Also, the mining ship would probably have to be served by transports which would take the ore to a refinery ashore. This refinery, moreover, would have to be a pioneering project because conventional processing techniques would not work on manganese nodules.

The origin of the ocean-floor deposits is uncertain, but they were probably formed 10 million to 30 million years ago through a natural process somewhat like the electrochemical technique used to manufacture nickel or copper cathodes. They always have a nucleus, such as a pebble, a shark's tooth or a whale's ear bone.

Thus in broad terms, the atomically bonded elements can only be recovered by reversing the electro-chemical process, which Deepsea Ventures already is doing in a limited scale in a small pilot plant. A bigger pilot plant — to use the same jealously guarded techniques — is under construction a few yards away.

36. The best title for this passage is
(A) A Costly Experiment
(B) Ocean Nodules
(C) Success in the Ocean
(D) Scraping the Ocean Bottom
(E) New Sources of Ore

37. The pilot ship proved that the experiment was feasible; however, it did not duplicate the
(A) depths at which actual mining would take place
(B) principle of a huge vacuum cleaner
(C) method by which the nodules were produced
(D) techniques of refining the ore
(E) kind of ship that would ultimately be needed

38. Questions that still have to be answered about this new mining venture
(A) include problems about procedures for obtaining the ore
(B) involve estimates of the probable cost
(C) may have to be referred to the United Nations
(D) concern techniques for refining the ore
(E) include questions about the profitability of the venture

39. It can be inferred from the description of how nodules are formed that the most likely nucleus for a nodule of ore would be
(A) a copper cathode
(B) a nickel
(C) the core of an apple
(D) a steel pipe
(E) a fragment of a seashell

40. Of the following, which has not as yet started?
(A) Exploring the ocean bottom
(B) Building a large-scale refinery
(C) Constructing a full-scale mining ship
(D) Developing methods of refining manganese
(E) Financing the venture

S T O P

IF YOU FINISH BEFORE TIME IS CALLED, YOU MAY CHECK YOUR WORK ON THIS SECTION ONLY. DO NOT WORK ON ANY OTHER SECTION IN THE TEST.

SECTION 5 MATH ABILITY

35 QUESTIONS - 30 MINUTES

In this section solve each problem, using any available space on the page for scratchwork. Then decide which is the best of the choices given and blacken the corresponding space on the answer sheet.

The following information is for your reference in solving some of the problems.

Circle of radius r: Area $= \pi r^2$; Circumference $= 2\pi r$

The number of degrees of arc in a circle is 360.

The measure in degrees of a straight angle is 180.

Definitions of symbols:

$=$ is equal to | $\leq$ is less than or equal to
$\neq$ is unequal to | $\geq$ is greater than or equal to
$<$ is less than | $\parallel$ is parallel to
$>$ is greater than | $\perp$ is perpendicular to

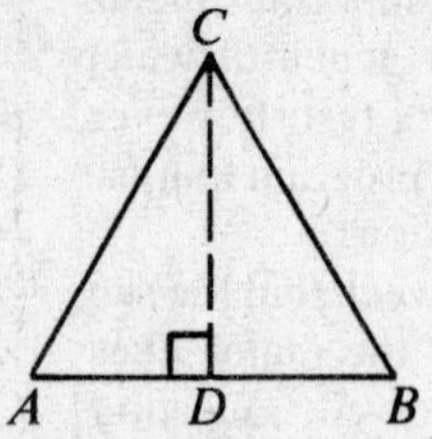

Triangle: The sum of the measures in degrees of the angles of a triangle is 180.

If $\angle CDA$ is a right angle, then

(1) area of $\triangle ABC = \frac{AB \times CD}{2}$

(2) $AC^2 = AD^2 + DC^2$

Note: Figures that accompany problems in this test are intended to provide information useful in solving the problems. They are drawn as accurately as possible EXCEPT when it is stated in a specific problem that its figure is not drawn to scale. All figures lie in a plane unless otherwise indicated. All numbers used are real numbers.

1. An architect uses a scale of $\frac{1}{4}$ inch to a foot. If the dimensions of a room as represented on the plans of a house are $4\frac{1}{4}$ inches by $3\frac{3}{4}$ inches, the actual dimensions in feet are

(A) $8\frac{1}{2} \times 9\frac{1}{2}$
(B) 17×15
(C) 34×30
(D) 51×45
(E) 68×60

2. What was the grade a student received on his first examination, if the grades on his other examinations were 50%, 70% and 90%, and his average on the four was 75%?

(A) 60
(B) 65
(C) 75
(D) 80
(E) 90

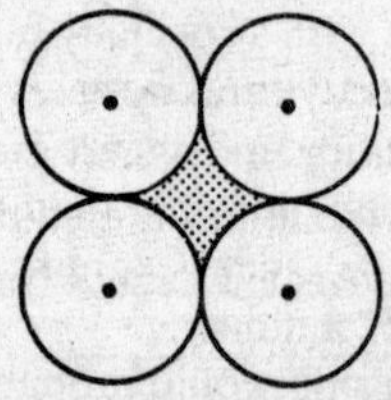

3. Four equal circles of diameter one foot touch at four points as shown in the figure above. What is the area of the shaded portion (in feet)?

(A) $1 - \frac{\pi}{4}$
(B) $1 - \pi$
(C) $1 - 4\pi$
(D) π
(E) $\frac{\pi}{4}$

4. $4y - x - 10 = 0$
$3x = 2y$
$xy = ?$

(A) $\frac{2}{3}$
(B) 1
(C) $1\frac{1}{3}$
(D) 5
(E) 6

5. How much change should one receive from \$1.00 after the purchase of $(30 - a)$ three-cent stamps?
(A) $70 + a$
(B) $70 - a$
(C) $10 - a$
(D) $10 + 3a$
(E) $10 - 3a$

6. A man works a times as fast as any one of his helpers. If the man does a job in h hours, how many hours are required for w helpers to do the job?
(A) $\frac{ah}{w}$
(B) $\frac{aw}{h}$
(C) $\frac{w}{ah}$
(D) awh
(E) $\frac{a}{wh}$

7. A monkey climbs 30 feet at the beginning of each hour and falls back 20 feet during each hourly period. If he begins his ascent at 8:00 A.M., at what time will he first make contact with a point 120 feet distant from the ground?
(A) 4 P.M.
(B) 5 P.M.
(C) 6 P.M.
(D) 7 P.M.
(E) 8 P.M.

Questions 8–27 each consist of two quantities, one in Column A and one in Column B. You are to compare the two quantities and on the answer sheet blacken space

A if the quantity in Column A is greater;
B if the quantity in Column B is greater;
C if the two quantities are equal;
D If the relationship cannot be determined from the information given.

AN E RESPONSE WILL NOT BE SCORED.

EXAMPLES

	Column A	Column B	Answers
E1.	2×6	$2 + 6$	● Ⓑ Ⓒ Ⓓ Ⓔ
	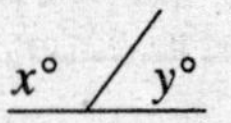		
E2.	$180 - x$	y	Ⓐ Ⓑ ● Ⓓ Ⓔ
E3.	$p - q$	$q - p$	Ⓐ Ⓑ Ⓒ ● Ⓔ

Notes:
1. In certain questions, information concerning one or both of the quantities to be compared is centered above the two columns.
2. In a given question, a symbol that appears in both columns represents the same thing in Column A as it does in Column B.
3. Letters such as x, n, and k stand for real numbers.

	Column A	Column B
8.	105% of 25	26
	$\frac{48}{x} = 4$	
9.	$16\frac{2}{3}$% of 72	x
10.	$\frac{1}{2}$	$\sqrt{\frac{1}{4}}$
11.	$\sqrt{\frac{1}{25}}$	20%
12.	$\sqrt{14.4}$	4
13.	The time required to cover $\frac{1}{2}$ mile traveling at 20 miles per hour	The time required to cover $\frac{1}{3}$ mile traveling at 30 miles per hour
14.	The number of revolutions made by the wheel of a bicycle (diameter of $\frac{7}{\pi}$ feet) covering a distance of 70 feet	The number of revolutions made by the wheel of a motorcycle (diameter of $\frac{10}{\pi}$ feet) covering a distance of 100 feet

Column A		Column B
	$X + Y + Z = 350$ $X + Y = 100$	
15. Z		X
	Distance from X to Y = 3 miles Distance from Y to Z = 2 miles	
16. Distance from X to Z		Distance from X to Y
	$9x^2 = y$	
17. x		y

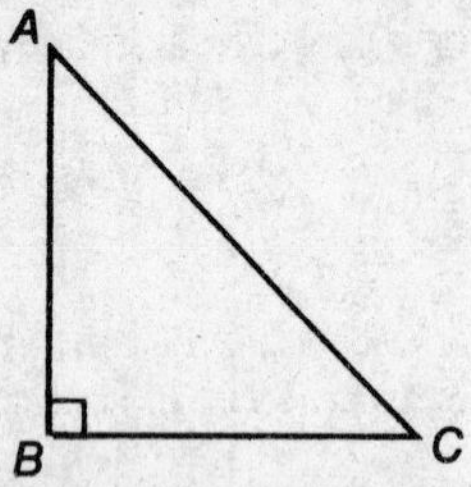

Column A		Column B
	Area of $ABC = 18$	
18. AB		BC

Column A		Column B
	$ABCD$ is a parallelogram	
19. $AD + BC$		$AB + DC$

Column A		Column B

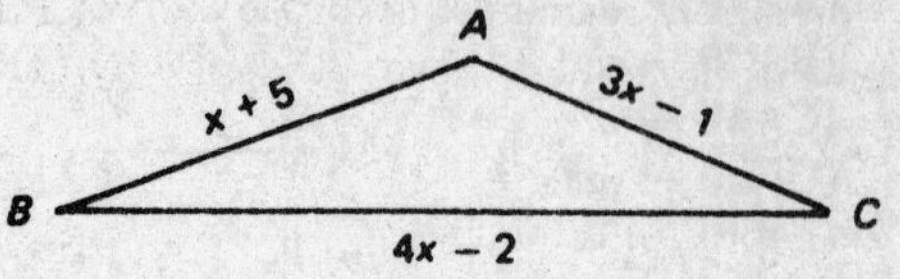

Column A		Column B
	perimeter of $ABC = 34$ This concerns #20–#22	
20. x		4
21. Length of AC		Length of BC
22. The measure of angle BAC		The measure of angle ABC
	In rectangle $ABCD$, $AD = 40$ and area of $ABCD = 1200$ This concerns #23 and #24	
23. Length of BC		Length of AC
24. $AD + BC$		$DC + AB$

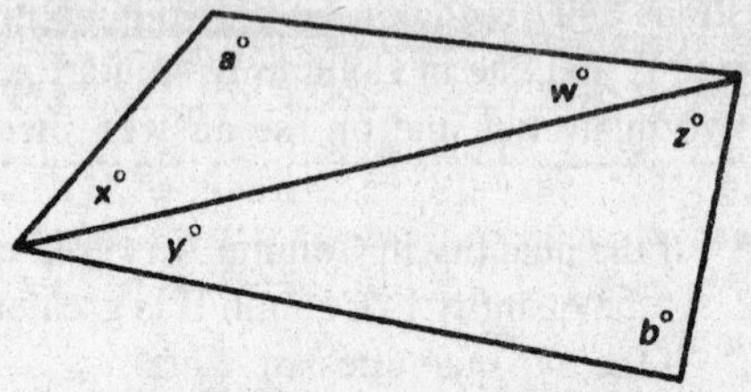

Column A		Column B
	$a = b = 90$ This concerns #25–#27	
25. $w + x + y + z$		360
26. $y + z$		a
27. w		z

Solve each of the remaining problems in this section using any available space for scratchwork. Then decide which is the best of the choices given and blacken the corresponding space on the answer sheet.

28. How many 5-gallon cans of milk will be needed to fill 120 pint bottles?
(A) 3
(B) 6
(C) 9
(D) 12
(E) 24

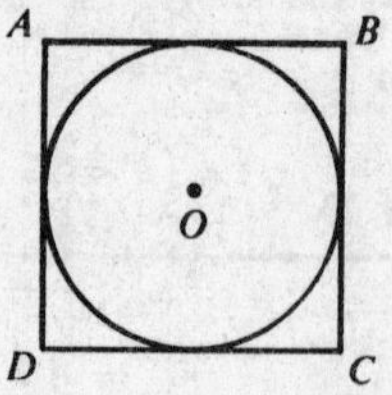

29. In the figure above, the area of circle $O = 9\pi$. What is the area of $ABCD$?
(A) 24
(B) 30
(C) 35
(D) 36
(E) 48

30. Mr. Walker covered a distance of 55 miles in 4 hours by driving his car at 40 M.P.H. part of the way and walking the remainder of the way at 5 M.P.H. What part of the total distance did he go by car?

(A) $\frac{3}{11}$
(B) $\frac{8}{11}$
(C) $\frac{1}{8}$
(D) $\frac{3}{8}$
(E) $\frac{1}{3}$

---

31. At a masquerade party the judges eliminate $\frac{1}{4}$ of the eligible contestants after each half hour. If 256 contestants were present at the party, how many would still be eligible for a prize after two hours?

(A) 0
(B) 16
(C) 32
(D) 64
(E) 81

---

32. A man owned $\frac{5}{8}$ of an interest in a house. He sold $\frac{1}{5}$ of his interest, at cost, for $1000. What is the total value of the house?

(A) $3000
(B) $5000
(C) $6000
(D) $8000
(E) $9000

---

33. A salesman sold a book at 105% of the marked price instead of discounting the marked price by 5%. If he sold the book for $4.20, what was the price for which he should have sold the book?

(A) $3.40
(B) $3.80
(C) $4.20
(D) $4.40
(E) $4.60

---

34. After several tryouts 20% of a football squad was discharged. The coach then had 32 players. How many players were on the squad at first?

(A) 24
(B) 26
(C) 39
(D) 40
(E) 80

---

35. If the sum of a set of odd integers is exactly zero, which of the following would always be true?

1. The product of integers in the set is zero.
2. The average of the set is zero.
3. The number of integers in the set is an even number.

(A) only 1
(B) only 2
(C) 1 and 2
(D) 2 and 3
(E) 1, 2, and 3

S T O P

IF YOU FINISH BEFORE TIME IS CALLED, YOU MAY CHECK YOUR WORK ON THIS SECTION ONLY. DO NOT WORK ON ANY OTHER SECTION IN THE TEST.

SECTION 6 MATH ABILITY

25 QUESTIONS - 30 MINUTES

In this section solve each problem, using any available space on the page for scratchwork. Then decide which is the best of the choices given and blacken the corresponding space on the answer sheet.

The following information is for your reference in solving some of the problems.

Circle of radius r: Area $= \pi r^2$; Circumference $= 2\pi r$
The number of degrees of arc in a circle is 360.
The measure in degrees of a straight angle is 180.

Definitions of symbols:

$=$ is equal to
$\neq$ is unequal to
$<$ is less than
$>$ is greater than
$\leqq$ is less than or equal to
$\geqq$ is greater than or equal to
$\|$ is parallel to
$\perp$ is perpendicular to

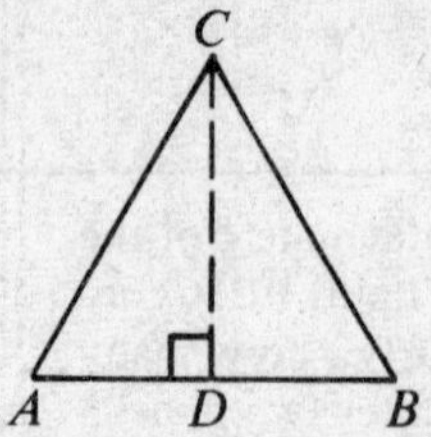

Triangle: The sum of the measures in degrees of the angles of a triangle is 180.

If $\angle CDA$ is a right angle, then

(1) area of $\triangle ABC = \dfrac{AB \times CD}{2}$

(2) $AC^2 = AD^2 + DC^2$

Note: Figures that accompany problems in this test are intended to provide information useful in solving the problems. They are drawn as accurately as possible EXCEPT when it is stated in a specific problem that its figure is not drawn to scale. All figures lie in a plane unless otherwise indicated. All numbers used are real numbers.

1. Of 25 tulip bulbs that are planted each year, from 20 to 22 produce flowers each year. What is the maximum percentage of flowers produced in any one year?
(A) 12
(B) 20
(C) 22
(D) 80
(E) 88

2. $\dfrac{a}{b} = c$; $b = c$; $b = ?$
(A) $\dfrac{a}{2}$
(B) $\sqrt{a}$
(C) a
(D) $2a$
(E) a^2

3. John and James painted a barn for \$100. If John worked 8 days and James worked 12 days, how much should James receive for his work?
(A) \$32
(B) \$40
(C) \$60
(D) \$75
(E) \$80

4. If each of a man's three sons works one eighth as fast as he does, and the man does a job in three hours, how many hours does it take his sons working together to do the job?
(A) 5
(B) 6
(C) 7
(D) 8
(E) 9

5. A chicken farmer has 750 eggs. Four percent of the eggs are cracked and 5% of the remainder are found to be defective after candling. How many eggs can he sell on the market?
(A) 300
(B) 450
(C) 675
(D) 684
(E) 720

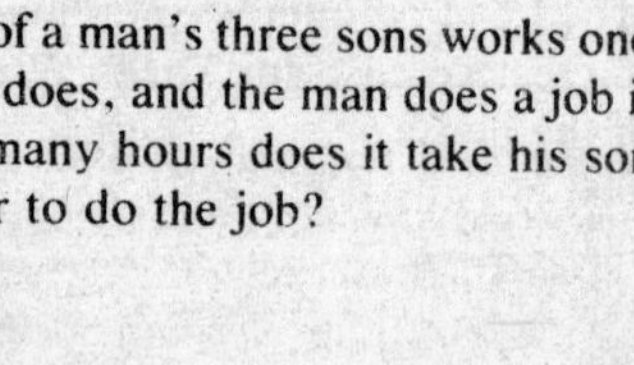

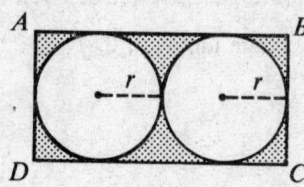

6. The area of the shaded portion above is
(A) $2r^2(4 - \pi)$
(B) $2r^2(2 - 2\pi)$
(C) $2r^2(\pi - 4)$
(D) $2r^2(\pi - 2)$
(E) $r^2(2 - \pi)$

7. A department store offers a typewriter for $72 instead of the list price of $90. What is the rate of discount for this item?
(A) 2%
(B) 5%
(C) 18%
(D) 20%
(E) 25%

8. A man left $5,000.00 to his three sons. For every dollar Abraham received, Benjamin received $1.50 and Charles received $2.50. How much money was left to Benjamin?
(A) $750
(B) $1000
(C) $1100
(D) $1500
(E) $3000

9. The El Capitan of the Santa Fe travels a distance of 152.5 miles from La Junta to Garden City in two hours. What is the average speed in M.P.H.?
(A) 15.25
(B) 31.5
(C) 30.5
(D) 71
(E) 76.3

10. A man travels for 5 hours at an average rate of 40 M.P.H. He develops some motor trouble and returns to his original starting point in 10 hours. What was his average rate, in miles per hour, on the return trip?
(A) 10
(B) 15
(C) 20
(D) 26.6
(E) 40

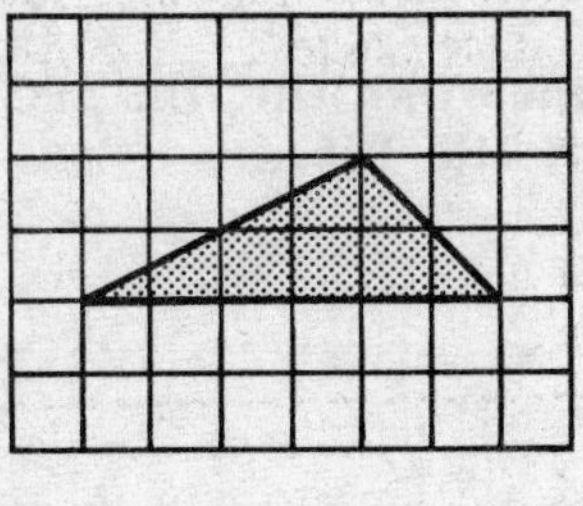

11. How many square units are there in the shaded triangle above?
(A) 4
(B) 6
(C) 8
(D) 9
(E) 12

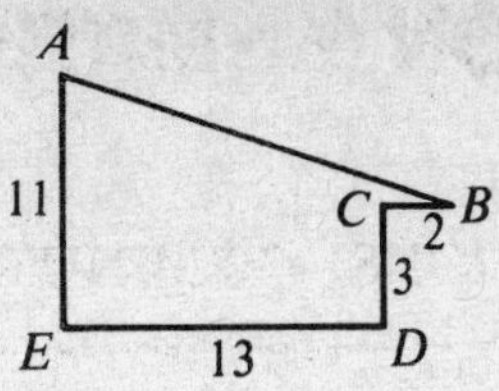

12. $AE \perp ED$ $\quad ED = 13$
$CD \perp ED$ $\quad CD = 3$
$DC \perp CB$ $\quad CB = 2$
$AB = ?$ $\quad AE = 11$
(A) 8
(B) 13
(C) 14
(D) 15
(E) 17

13. If a carload contains from 12 to 18 crates, what is the least number of crates contained in 4 carloads?
(A) 24
(B) 36
(C) 48
(D) 60
(E) 72

14. Of the values 45.9, 49.5, 59.4, and x (where x is more than 45), which of the following *CANNOT* possibly be the average?
(A) 45
(B) 55
(C) 56
(D) 550
(E) 555

15. What is the length of the line segment joining the points whose coordinates are $(-2, -7)$ and $(6, 8)$?
(A) 4
(B) 5
(C) $7\frac{1}{2}$
(D) $8\frac{1}{2}$
(E) 17

16. A line segment has one endpoint at $(3, -2)$, and its midpoint at $(2, -5)$. The coordinates of the other endpoint of the line segment are
(A) $(1, -8)$
(B) $(5, -7)$
(C) $(1, -3)$
(D) $(1, 8)$
(E) $(-1, 8)$

17. The locus of points 2 inches from a given line and 3 inches from a point on that line is exactly
(A) 1 point
(B) 2 points
(C) 3 points
(D) 4 points
(E) 5 points

18. Which of the following is greater than $\frac{1}{4}$?
(A) 0.04
(B) $\left(\frac{1}{4}\right)^2$
(C) $\frac{1}{0.04}$
(D) $(0.04)^2$
(E) none of these

19. $6 + ? \times 2 = 14$
(A) $1\frac{1}{6}$
(B) 4
(C) 6
(D) 9
(E) 10

20. $\frac{3}{4} + \frac{5}{n} = \frac{19}{12}$
$n = ?$
(A) 4
(B) 6
(C) 8
(D) 10
(E) 12

21. $2.4\sqrt{\frac{x^4y^2}{16} + \frac{y^2x^4}{9}} = ?$
(A) xy
(B) xy^2
(C) x^2y
(D) $x\sqrt{y}$
(E) $y\sqrt{x}$

22. How long is the shadow of a 35-foot tree, if a 98-foot tree casts a 42-foot shadow at the same time?
(A) 8
(B) 9
(C) 12
(D) 13
(E) 15

23. If books bought at prices ranging from \$2.00 to \$3.50 are sold at prices ranging from \$3.00 to \$4.25, what is the greatest possible profit that might be made in selling 8 books.
(A) \$2.50
(B) \$4.00
(C) \$6.00
(D) \$9.00
(E) \$18.00

24. Which two of the following are equal?
(A) $1 + \frac{x}{y}$
(B) y
(C) $\frac{y^2 + 2xy}{xy}$
(D) $\frac{y}{x}$
(E) $\frac{2x + y}{x}$

(A) A and C
(B) A and D
(C) A and E
(D) C and E
(E) B and E

25. A salesman reports an increase in sales by 20%. What is the ratio of the increased sales to the original?
(A) 1:5
(B) 4:5
(C) 6:5
(D) 5:4
(E) 5:1

S T O P

IF YOU FINISH BEFORE TIME IS CALLED, YOU MAY CHECK YOUR WORK ON THIS SECTION ONLY. DO NOT WORK ON ANY OTHER SECTION IN THE TEST.

ANSWER KEY

Note: The answers to the math sections are keyed to the corresponding review areas in Chapter 11. The numbers in parentheses after each answer refer to topics as listed below. (Note that to review for number 16, Quantitative Comparison, study Chapter 10.)

1. Fundamental Operations
2. Algebraic Operations
3. Using Algebra
4. Roots and Radicals
5. Inequalities
6. Fractions
7. Decimals
8. Percent
9. Averages
10. Motion
11. Ratio and Proportion
12. Mixtures and Solutions
13. Work
14. Coordinate Geometry
15. Geometry
16. Quantitative Comparison
17. Data Interpretation

SECTION 1 MATH

1. **B (8)**	6. **A (9)**	11. **B (4)**	16. **A (11)**	21. **D (1)**
2. **A (5)**	7. **C (8)**	12. **C (1)**	17. **B (10)**	22. **D (8,15)**
3. **E (9)**	8. **A (11)**	13. **C (2)**	18. **A (1)**	23. **B (14)**
4. **D (1)**	9. **B (1)**	14. **A (8)**	19. **D (15)**	24. **A (14)**
5. **B (2)**	10. **B (2)**	15. **C (15)**	20. **D (9)**	25. **D (14)**

SECTION 2 TEST OF STANDARD WRITTEN ENGLISH

1. **E**	11. **E**	21. **A**	31. **C**	41. **C**
2. **C**	12. **A**	22. **E**	32. **D**	42. **C**
3. **B**	13. **A**	23. **C**	33. **D**	43. **E**
4. **C**	14. **B**	24. **C**	34. **A**	44. **E**
5. **A**	15. **C**	25. **B**	35. **C**	45. **C**
6. **C**	16. **E**	26. **E**	36. **D**	46. **C**
7. **B**	17. **C**	27. **C**	37. **B**	47. **A**
8. **C**	18. **C**	28. **C**	38. **A**	48. **A**
9. **B**	19. **A**	29. **C**	39. **B**	49. **A**
10. **E**	20. **D**	30. **B**	40. **E**	50. **D**

SECTION 3 VERBAL

1. **D**	10. **D**	19. **B**	28. **D**	37. **B**
2. **A**	11. **D**	20. **A**	29. **E**	38. **C**
3. **A**	12. **E**	21. **E**	30. **A**	39. **B**
4. **E**	13. **C**	22. **C**	31. **B**	40. **B**
5. **C**	14. **E**	23. **B**	32. **E**	41. **D**
6. **A**	15. **C**	24. **A**	33. **B**	42. **A**
7. **E**	16. **C**	25. **C**	34. **A**	43. **C**
8. **A**	17. **C**	26. **C**	35. **A**	44. **D**
9. **D**	18. **A**	27. **A**	36. **C**	45. **C**

SECTION 4 VERBAL

1. **B**	9. **B**	17. **A**	25. **B**	33. **B**
2. **A**	10. **D**	18. **C**	26. **E**	34. **C**
3. **B**	11. **C**	19. **A**	27. **C**	35. **E**
4. **C**	12. **A**	20. **E**	28. **B**	36. **E**
5. **C**	13. **A**	21. **C**	29. **E**	37. **A**
6. **D**	14. **C**	22. **D**	30. **B**	38. **C**
7. **C**	15. **E**	23. **C**	31. **C**	39. **E**
8. **A**	16. **B**	24. **A**	32. **C**	40. **C**

SECTION 5 MATH

1. B (11,15)	8. A (8,16)	15. D (2,16)	22. A (15,16)	29. D (15)
2. E (9)	9. C (2,8,16)	16. D (15,16)	23. B (15,16)	30. B (10)
3. A (15)	10. C (4,16)	17. D (2,16)	24. A (15,16)	31. E (6)
4. E (2)	11. C (4,8,16)	18. D (15,16)	25. B (15,16)	32. D (6)
5. D (1,2)	12. B (10,16)	19. D (15,16)	26. C (15,16)	33. B (8)
6. A (13)	13. A (15,16)	20. C (15,16)	27. D (15,16)	34. D (8)
7. B (1)	14. C (2,16)	21. B (15,16)	28. A (1)	35. D (1)

SECTION 6 MATH

1. E (8)	6. A (15)	11. B (15)	16. A (14)	21. C (4)
2. B (2)	7. D (8)	12. E (15)	17. D (14)	22. E (11)
3. C (1,6)	8. D (6,11)	13. C (1)	18. C (6)	23. E (8)
4. D (13)	9. E (10)	14. A (9)	19. B (1)	24. D (6)
5. D (3,8)	10. C (10)	15. E (14)	20. B (2)	25. C (8,11)

SELF-EVALUATION

If you have been doing the model tests in order, you have just completed the last model test. By now you should be totally familiar with the types of questions you will find on the SAT and with the format of the exam.

Do the self-evaluation procedures for this test just as you did for the five model tests you've already taken. Here are the step-by-step procedures that you should follow.

STEP 1 Use the Answer Key to check your answers for each section.

STEP 2 For each section, count the number of correct and incorrect answers (remember that you don't count omitted answers), and enter the numbers on the appropriate lines of the chart "Obtaining Your Raw Score." Then do the indicated calculations to get your Raw Verbal Score, your Raw TSWE Score, and your Raw Math Score.

STEP 3 Consult the chart "Evaluate Your Performance" to see how well you did.

STEP 4 To pinpoint the specific areas in which you need to improve, circle the numbers of the questions that you either left blank or got wrong on the "Identify Your Weaknesses" charts. This will tell you where to concentrate your efforts to get the most out of your study time. The chart for the math sections gives you page references for review and practice by skill areas. The charts for the verbal and TSWE sections refer you to the appropriate chapters to study for each question type.

STEP 5 Do the review and practice indicated on the charts wherever you had a concentration of circles.

Remember that in addition to evaluating your scores, you should read all of the answer explanations for questions you answered incorrectly, questions you omitted, and questions you answered correctly but found difficult. Reviewing the answer explanations will help you understand concepts and strategies, and may point out shortcuts.

OBTAINING YOUR RAW SCORE

Verbal

Section 3 ______________ – 1/4 (______________) = ______________ (A)
number correct number incorrect

Section 4 ______________ – 1/4 (______________) = ______________ (B)
number correct number incorrect

Raw Verbal Score = (A) + (B) = ______________

TSWE

Section 2 ______________ – 1/4 (______________) = Raw TSWE Score = ______________
number correct number incorrect

Math

Section 1 ______________ – 1/4 (______________) = ______________ (C)
number correct number incorrect

Section 5 (1-7, 28-35) ______________ – 1/4 (______________) = ______________ (D)
number correct number incorrect

Section 5 (8-27) ______________ – 1/3 (______________) = ______________ (E)
number correct number incorrect

Section 6 ______________ – 1/4 (______________) = ______________ (F)
number correct number incorrect

Raw Math Score = (C) + (D) + (E) + (F) = ______________

EVALUATE YOUR PERFORMANCE

	Verbal	TSWE	Math
Excellent	75-85	45-50	70-85
Very Good	65-74	39-44	60-69
Good	50-64	34-38	50-59
Average	40-49	25-33	40-49
Below Average	28-39	15-24	30-39
Unsatisfactory	below 28	below 15	below 30

IDENTIFY YOUR WEAKNESSES
Verbal

Question Type	Question Numbers		Chapter to Study
	Section 3	Section 4	
Antonym	1, 2, 3, 4, 5, 6, 7, 8, 9, 10, 11, 12, 13, 14, 15	1, 2, 3, 4, 5, 6, 7, 8, 9, 10	Chapter 4
Analogy	36, 37, 38, 39, 40, 41, 42, 43, 44, 45	16, 17, 18, 19, 20, 21, 22, 23, 24, 25	Chapter 5
Sentence Completion	16, 17, 18, 19, 20, 31, 32, 33, 34, 35	11, 12, 13, 14, 15	Chapter 6
Reading Comprehension	21, 22, 23, 24, 25, 26, 27, 28, 29, 30	26, 27, 28, 29, 30, 31, 32, 33, 34, 35, 36, 37, 38, 39, 40	Chapter 7

TSWE

Question Type	Question Numbers	Chapter to Study
Usage	1, 2, 3, 4, 5, 6, 7, 8, 9, 10, 11, 12, 13, 14, 15, 16, 17, 18, 19, 20, 21, 22, 23, 24, 25, 41, 42, 43, 44, 45, 46, 47, 48, 49, 50	Chapter 12
Sentence Correction	26, 27, 28, 29, 30, 31, 32, 33, 34, 35, 36, 37, 38, 39, 40	Chapter 12

Math

Skill Area	Question Numbers			Pages to Study
	Section 1	Section 5	Section 6	
Fundamental Operations	4, 9, 12, 18, 21	5, 7, 28, 35	1, 3, 19	300–302
Algebraic Operations	5, 10, 13	4, 5, 9, 14, 15, 17	2, 5, 20, 24	302–308
Fractions		31, 32	3, 8, 18, 24	316–329
Decimals and Percents	1, 7, 14, 22	8, 9, 11, 33, 34	1, 5, 7, 18, 23, 25	329–334
Verbal Problems	2, 3, 6, 17, 20	2, 6, 12, 13, 30	4, 9, 10	335–352
Ratio and Proportion	8, 16	1	8, 22, 25	340–346
Geometry	15, 19, 22	1, 3, 16, 18, 19, 20, 21, 22, 23, 24, 25, 26, 27, 29	6, 11, 12	355–368
Coordinate Geometry	8, 23, 24, 25		15, 16, 17	352–355
Inequalities	2			309–311; 315–316
Quantitative Comparison		8, 9, 10, 11, 12, 13, 14, 15, 16, 17, 18, 19, 20, 21, 22, 23, 24, 25, 26, 27		279–299
Roots and Radicals	11	10, 11	2, 21	306–307; 312–313

ANSWER EXPLANATIONS

SECTION 1

1. B. $\frac{1}{4}\% = \frac{\frac{1}{4}}{100}$ or $\frac{1}{4} \div 100$ or $\frac{1}{4} \cdot \frac{1}{100} = \frac{1}{400}$

$\frac{1}{400}$ of 2 or $\frac{1}{400} \cdot \frac{2}{1} = \frac{1}{200}$

2. A. The thickened line between -2 and 3 represents all the numbers whose points (coordinates) are on that line. The open circle at -2 indicates that -2 is not part of the set while the solid circle indicates that 3 is a member of the set. Thus, the inequality shown is all numbers more than -2 and less than or equal to 3.

3. E. Since the average is K the sum of the two numbers is $2K$
Since one number is M the other number is $2K - M$

4. D. At 80¢ per lb. the cost of 4 lbs. is \$3.20. The change is \$10.00 − \$3.20 or \$6.80.

5. B.
$$z + \frac{1}{z} = 2$$
$$z^2 + 1 = 2z \quad \text{(multiply by } z)$$
$$z^2 - 2z + 1 = 0 \quad \text{(subtract } 2z)$$
$$(z-1)(z-1) = 0 \quad \text{(factor)}$$
$$z = 1$$
or you could have checked through the answers to discover the right one.

6. A. To attain an average of $\frac{3}{10}$, the sum of the five fractions must be $5(\frac{3}{10})$ or $\frac{15}{10}$

$$\frac{3}{5} + \frac{1}{4} + \frac{1}{10} + \frac{1}{2}$$
$$\frac{12}{20} + \frac{5}{20} + \frac{2}{20} + \frac{10}{20} = \frac{29}{20}$$

The sum of the four fractions $= \frac{29}{20}$

The fraction to be added must be $\frac{15}{10} - \frac{29}{20}$

or, $\frac{30}{20} - \frac{29}{20} = \frac{1}{20}$

7. C. $a\% = \frac{a}{100}$ $\quad b\% = \frac{b}{100}$

$$\left(\frac{a}{100} \cdot b\right) \div \left(\frac{b}{100} \cdot a\right)$$
$$\frac{ab}{100} \div \frac{ab}{100}$$
$$\frac{\overset{1}{\cancel{ab}}}{\underset{1}{\cancel{100}}} \cdot \frac{\overset{1}{\cancel{100}}}{\underset{1}{\cancel{ab}}} = 1$$

8. A. This is a direct proportion.
Let x = number of weys in 4 bushels

$$\frac{\text{Wey}}{\text{Bushel}} = \frac{1}{40} = \frac{x}{4}$$
$$40x = 4$$
$$x = \frac{4}{40} \text{ or } \frac{1}{10}$$

9. B. Since there are 36 inches in 1 yard there are $36y$ inches in y yards. Since there are 12 inches in 1 foot there are $12f$ inches in f feet.
Total number of inches $= 36y + 12f + i$

10. B. In one week the man saves $(d - s)$ dollars.
To save Q dollars it will take $\frac{Q}{d - s}$ weeks.

11. B. $\sqrt{\frac{1}{4}} \cdot \sqrt{\frac{16}{36}}$

$$\frac{1}{2} \cdot \frac{4}{6}$$
$$\frac{1}{\cancel{2}} \cdot \frac{\overset{2}{\cancel{4}}}{6} = \frac{1}{3}$$

12. C. The cost of 3 cards is 10¢
The postage for 3 cards is 9¢
The total cost of purchasing and mailing 3 cards is 19¢
To find the number of cards purchased and mailed for \$2.09 we have a direct proportion

$$\frac{\text{number of cards}}{\text{cost}} \quad \frac{3}{\$0.19} = \frac{x}{\$2.09}$$
$$0.19x = 3(2.09)$$
$$0.19x = 6.27$$
$$19x = 627$$
$$x = 33 \text{ cards}$$

13. C. $x^2 + 4x + 6 = x^2 + 3x + 7$
$$4x + 6 = 3x + 7 \quad \text{(subtract } x^2)$$
$$x + 6 = 7 \quad \text{(subtract } 3x)$$
$$x = 1 \quad \text{(subtract 6)}$$

14. A. 0.4% of 1000 will be rejected

$$0.4\% = \frac{0.4}{100} = \frac{4}{1000}$$

$$\frac{4}{1000} \cdot \frac{1000}{1} = 4$$

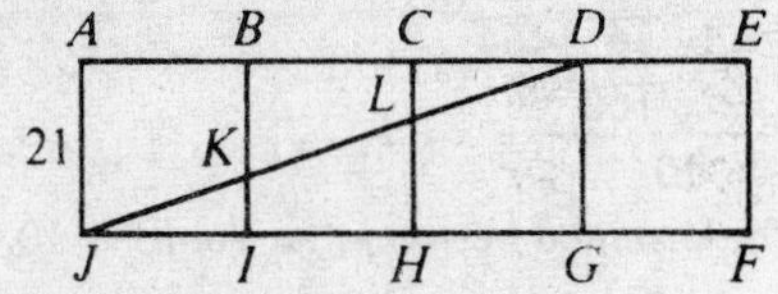

15. C. In triangle DJG, KI is parallel to LH is parallel to DG cutting off equal segments JI, IH, HG. Triangle JKI is similar to triangle DJG.

$$\frac{(KI)}{(DG)} = \frac{(JI)}{(JG)}$$

$\frac{(KI)}{21} = \frac{1}{3}$ (since $JI = IH = HG$ and $AJ = DG = 21$)

$3(KI) = 21$ (product of means equals product of extremes)

$KI = 7$ (divide by 3)

16. A.

$xy = k$
$(4)(7) = k$
$28 = k$
$xy = k$
$(x)(17.5) = 28$

$x = \frac{28}{17.5}$ or 1.6

17. B. This is a direct proportion.
Let x = number of minutes required to travel $\frac{2}{5}$ of a mile

$$\frac{\text{Distance (miles)}}{\text{Time (minutes)}} = \frac{50}{60} = \frac{\frac{2}{5}}{x}$$

$50x = (\frac{2}{5})(60)$ (product of means equals product of extremes)

$50x = 24$

$x = \frac{24}{50}$ or 0.48

18. A. The minimum number of crates on a trip = 3
The minimum weight of a crate = 125 lbs.
Minimum weight of crates on a trip = 375 lbs.

19. D. Area of circle $= \pi(\text{radius})^2$
Area of circle $= \pi r^2$
Area of rectangle $= \pi r^2$ (given)
Area of rectangle = (base)(altitude)
Area of rectangle = (b)(altitude)
$\pi r^2 = (b)$(altitude)
$\frac{\pi r^2}{b}$ = altitude (division by b)

20. D. To have an average of 90 minutes (or $1\frac{1}{2}$ hours) per day, the total time spent practicing for the week must equal $(7)(1\frac{1}{2})$ or $10\frac{1}{2}$ hours. From Monday to Thursday the girl has practiced $1\frac{1}{4} + 2 + 2 + 1\frac{3}{4}$ or 7 hours. She must therefore spend $3\frac{1}{2}$ additional hours practicing for the rest of the week.

21. D. To raise \$500 in addition to the expenses of \$250 the school must receive \$750 for tickets.

At 75 cents per ticket they must sell $\frac{\$750}{\$0.75}$ or 1000 tickets.

22. D. Let s = side of original square
$s + 150\%s$ or $s + 1\frac{1}{2}s$ or $2\frac{1}{2}s$ or $\frac{5}{2}s$ = side of new square
Area of square $= (\text{side})^2$
Area of original square $= (s)^2$ or s^2
Area of new square $= \left(\frac{5s}{2}\right)^2$ or $\frac{25s^2}{4}$ or $6\frac{1}{4}s^2$

Area of new square is $6\frac{1}{4}s^2$ (or $625\%s^2$)
Area of original square is $1s^2$ (or $100\%s^2$)
Increase = 525% of s^2

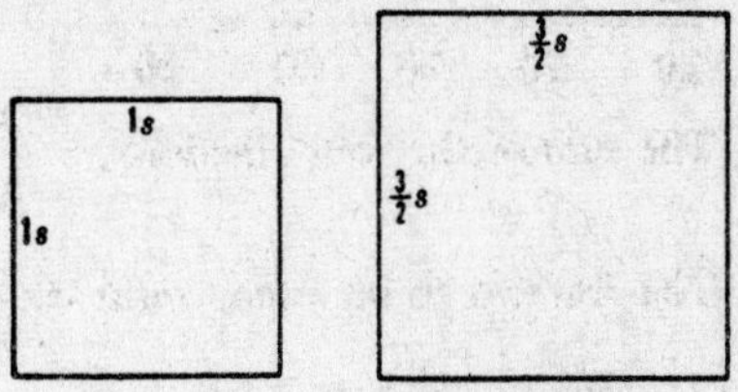

23. B. Observe that the point of tangency is at $(-2, 0)$.

Radius OT is $\perp$ to the x-axis since a radius is $\perp$ to a tangent at the point of contact. Thus OT is parallel to the y-axis and point T, like point O, is two units to the left of the y-axis. Thus $x = -2$. Since the point T lies on the x-axis, $y = 0$. The coordinates of the point of tangency, point T, are $(-2, 0)$.

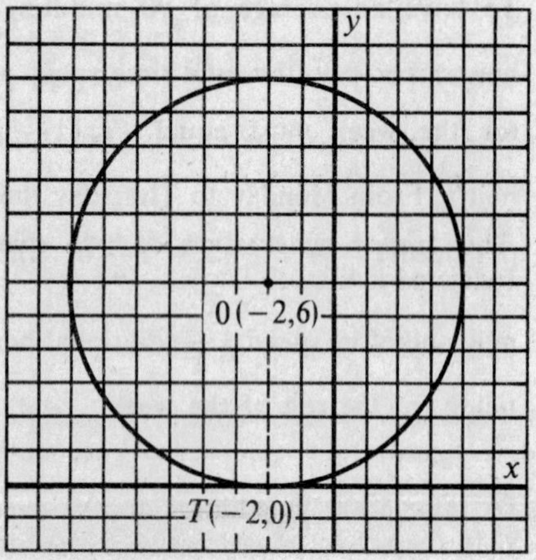

24. A. Let M be the midpoint of $\overline{AB}$

$$x\text{-midpoint} = \frac{x_1 + x_2}{2}$$

$$x_m = \frac{-5 + 3}{2} = \frac{-2}{2}$$

$$= -1$$

$$y\text{-midpoint} = \frac{y_1 + y_2}{2}$$

$$y_m = \frac{-4 - 2}{2} = \frac{-6}{2}$$

$$= -3$$

25. D. Use the distance formula

$$d = \sqrt{(x_1 - x_2)^2 + (y_1 - y_2)^2}$$

In this case, $x_1 = -4$, $x_2 = 2$,

$y_1 = 3$, $y_2 = -5$

$$d = \sqrt{(-4 - 2)^2 + [3 - (-5)]^2}$$

$$d = \sqrt{(-6)^2 + (3 + 5)^2}$$

$$d = \sqrt{(-6)^2 + (8)^2}$$

$$d = \sqrt{36 + 64}$$

$$d = \sqrt{100}$$

$$d = 10$$

The distance between the points is 10.

SECTION 2

1. E. Sentence is correct

2. C. Change *of* to *have.*

3. B. Error in agreement. Change *were* to *was.*

4. C. Error in diction. *Mad* is a slang substitute for *angry.*

5. A. Wrong word. Change *Its* to *It's.*

6. C. Error in parallel structure. Change *to insure* to *insuring.*

7. B. Error in tense. The past tense of *sing* is *sang.*

8. C. Misuse of adverb for adjective. The verb *to feel* should be followed by an adjective—*sad.*

9. B. Error in diction. Change *irregardless* to *regardless.*

10. E. Punctuation of quotation is correct.

11. E. Sentence is correct.

12. A. Error in agreement. Change *has been* to *have been.*

13. A. Error in providing proper subject for verb. Change *Because* to *That.*

14. B. Wrong mood. A condition contrary to fact calls for the subjunctive mood. Change *was* to *were.*

15. C. Error in case. Change *he* to *him.*

16. E. Sentence is correct.

17. C. Lack of parallel structure. Change the *that* clause to an infinitive phrase for parallelism. "To provide for his family's comfort and his children's education" is better.

18. C. Error in diction. Change *affect* to *effect.*

19. A. Dangling participle. Change *Snowing* to *Because it had snowed.*

20. D. Unnecessary repetition. Eliminate *to.*

21. A. Error in diction. Change *lay* to *laid.*

22. E. Sentence is correct.

23. C. Error in agreement. Change *they are* to *it is.*

24. C. Error in diction. Change *or* to *nor.*

25. B. Error in case. Change *I* to *me.*

26. E. This preserves the parallel structure in the sentence.

27. C. The past perfect tense is required in an "if" clause.

28. C. The dangling participle construction is corrected in C.

29. C. *Company's* and *its* are the correct possessive case forms.

30. B. The verb should agree with its subject (*principal*) in number.

31. C. Use *this kind* or *these kinds.*

32. D. The omission of the correct verb form is corrected in Choice D.

33. D. The proper punctuation of two questions is indicated in Choice D.

34. A. Sentence is correct as given.

35. C. The two errors in diction (*imminent* for *eminent* and *stood* for *stayed*) are corrected in Choice C.

36. D. This corrects the sentence fragment.

37. B. Choice B corrects the run-on sentence.

38. A. The use of the semicolon to separate the pair of clauses is correct.

39. B. Choice B eliminates the excessive wordiness of the original sentence without introducing any errors in diction.

40. E. Choice E corrects the misplaced modifier and eliminates the unnecessary use of the passive voice.

41. C. Error in diction. Change *between* to *among.*

42. C. Error in diction. Change *and* to *to.*

43. E. Sentence is correct.

44. E. Sentence is correct.

45. C. Lack of parallel structure. Change *of his* to *he has a.*

46. C. Error in case. Change *you* to *your.*

47. A. Error in diction. Change *do not ought* to *ought not.*

48. A. Misplaced modifier. *Only* should follow *drank.*

49. A. Error in diction. Omit *a.*

50. D. Lack of parallel structure. Change to *but also because it was unnecessary.*

SECTION 3

1. D. The opposite of *commodious* (roomy) is *limited.*

2. A. The opposite of *negligent* (careless) is *painstaking.*

3. A. The opposite of *covert* (hidden, secret) is *open.*

4. E. The opposite of *pithy* (compact, epigrammatic) is *wordy.*

5. C. The opposite of *ingenuous* (naive, unsophisticated) is *sophisticated.*

6. A. The opposite of *impecunious* (penniless) is *affluent* (well-to-do).

7. E. The opposite of *sanguine* (hopeful) is *pessimistic.*

8. A. The opposite of *nefarious* (wicked) is *praiseworthy.*

9. D. The opposite of *choleric* (irascible) is *apathetic* (indifferent).

10. D. The opposite of *verbose* (overly wordy) is *concise* (brief).

11. D. *Calumniate* (slander) and *laud* (praise) are opposites.

12. E. *Vacuous* (lacking in ideas) and *profound* (demanding much thought) are opposites.

13. C. *Expunge* (remove) and *append* (add to) are opposites.

14. E. *Hedonism* (belief that pleasure is the chief good) and *asceticism* (practice of extreme self-denial) are opposites.

15. C. A *malignant* tumor is cancerous; a *benign* tumor is not.

16. C. A *constructive* critic offers advice and does not abuse the subject of his criticism.

17. C. An *overt* (obvious) act of war calls for *retaliation.*

18. A. *Sabotage* implies internal damage by workmen, etc.

19. B. *Gullible* (credulous) people would, of course, be likely to accept any kind of statement.

20. A. *Enervating* means depriving of energy, exhausting.

21. E. Sentence 3 discusses the "demolition" or devaluation of values.

22. C. Sentences 3 and 4 of the second paragraph discuss the rush of people to dump or sell their stocks.

23. B. The last sentence refutes the idea that a repetition of 1929 is about to occur.

24. A. Choice B is referred to in lines 16–18. Choice C (the optimism of money managers) is referred to in lines 7 and 8. Choice D is mentioned in the last sentence. Choice E is mentioned in lines 23–25. Choice A is not mentioned.

25. C. The opening sentence supports Choice C.

26. C. The statement that "the Bank of America hadn't done anything to anybody" indicates that financial institutions are normally not targets for demonstrations.

27. A. The last sentence supports Choice A.

28. D. The second paragraph supports Choice D.

29. E. Choices A, B, C, and D are mentioned in the third paragraph (the spoiling of our environment by the word "pollution," heroin by the reference to drug addiction, slums by the reference to housing, and automobile congestion by the reference to transportation bottlenecks). Choice E is not mentioned.

30. A. Choice A is supported by the last sentence in paragraph 3.

31. B. By definition, a *cliché* is a *trite* (banal, overworked) saying.

32. E. A *bombastic* orator's speech would be filled with highly inflated talk and *flamboyant* (flowery and ornate).

33. B. *Levity* (frivolity) is inappropriate during serious moments.

34. A. One method of reducing inflationary tendencies is to limit or *curb* the supply of money.

35. A. A *supercilious* (haughty, arrogant) individual is *condescending.*

36. C. Just as *spice* adds flavor to *food, wit* adds flavor to *conversation.*

37. B. A *bass* has a low register and a *soprano* a high register. The *cellar* is the low part of a house and the *roof* the high or top part.

38. C. A *ladder* consists of a series of *rungs; history* consists of a series of *events.*

39. B. A *laborer* works for *wages;* an *entrepreneur* (business man), for *profits.*

40. B. A person filled with *benevolence* (kindliness) is *charitable;* a person filled with *vindictiveness* is *revengeful.*

41. D. *Taciturn* and *laconic* are synonyms and mean speaking very little; *garrulous* and *loquacious* are synonyms meaning very talkative.

42. A. *Haughty* and *arrogant* are synonyms; *heinous* (atrocious) and *egregious* (outstandingly bad) are synonyms.

43. C. *Melancholy* and *exuberant* are opposites; *sad* and *gay* are also opposites.

44. D. When a *ship founders,* it sinks. The same idea of disaster is found when a *building collapses.*

45. C. An *island* is part of an *archipelago;* a *star,* part of a *galaxy.*

SECTION 4

1. B. The opposite of *prodigal* (extravagant) is *thrifty.*

2. A. The opposite of *indigenous* (native) is *foreign.*

3. B. The opposite of *euphonious* (pleasant sounding) is *discordant.*

4. C. The opposite of *sporadic* (occurring casually or infrequently) is *incessant* (constant).

5. C. The opposite of *pusillanimous* (lacking courage) is *courageous.*

6. D. The opposite of *gullible* (easily deceived) is *incredulous* (skeptical).

7. C. The opposite of *profane* (desecrate) is *sanctify.*

8. A. The opposite of *dearth* (scarcity) is *abundance.*

9. B. The opposite of *augment* (increase) is *deplete.*

10. D. The opposite of *auspicious* (favorable) is *unfavorable.*

11. C. We may criticize manufacturers who make sure that the goods they sell will wear out after a period of time. If the *obsolescence* is planned criticism is justified.

12. A. A *complacent* or satisfied person would not normally burst into a rage.

13. A. *Penury* means destitution, poverty.

14. C. *Pulmonary* pertains to the lungs.

15. E. *Obdurate* means stubborn, hardened.

16. B. *Histrionic* (pertaining to acting) skills are displayed in a *theater; culinary* (pertaining to cooking) skills, in a *kitchen.*

17. A. A *lexicographer* (writer of dictionaries) is interested in *words;* a *cartographer* (mapmaker) is interested in *maps.*

18. C. *Pint* and *yard* are units in the English system of measurements; *liter* and *meter* are units in the Metric system.

19. A. We *forgive* an *offense* and *condone* (treat as non-existent) a *crime.*

20. E. A *lobster* is a *crustaceous* animal; a *lizard,* a *reptilian* animal.

21. C. *Dawn* and *dusk* occur at the beginning and end of day respectively. *Infancy* occurs at the beginning of life and *senility* usually occurs in old age (the end of life).

22. D. *Usury* is excessive or illegal *interest; parsimony* (stinginess) is excessive *frugality* (thrift).

23. C. Cacophony (harsh sounds; discord) offends the *ear*; a *stench* (bad smell) offends the *nose*.

24. A. *Mollify* (lessen feelings of anger) and *allay* (lessen pain) may be regarded as synonyms; *incite* and *arouse* are synonyms.

25. B. A *eulogy* consists of *praise; slander,* of *vilification* (speaking ill of).

26. E. Although the author mentions all 5 choices in his article, he is calling attention to the checks on the executive branch to emphasize the lack of control over Congress and the need to exercise a diligent watch against its irresponsibility.

27. C. A king has an absolute veto (line 5); a president does not have such a veto.

28. B. The third sentence of the last paragraph supports Choice B.

29. E. The first sentence of the second paragraph supports Choice E.

30. B. The author does not mention the fact that a monarch rules for life while a President holds office for four years.

31. C. The last five sentences of the passage indicate that the only defense a citizen has against an oppressive and unconstitutional law is an appeal to the Supreme Court.

32. C. The author states that he is alarmed by the ease with which our privacy may be invaded by the use of the computer and spends most of his discussion on the ways the individual can preserve that privacy.

33. B. In the second sentence of the last paragraph, the author mentions all the items listed except marriage licenses.

34. C. The last sentence of the passage mentions the courts as the "most important safeguard."

35. E. The sixth paragraph of the passage supports Choice E.

36. E. The author emphasizes throughout the passage that the experiment being conducted on the ocean bottoms is intended to discover new sources of ore.

37. A. We are told that the "pilot ship" worked in about 3000 feet of water and that mining would have to take place at depths of 15,000 to 18,000 feet.

38. C. In the fourth paragraph, the international legal status of the mining is questioned. Such a problem could be settled by an international body such as the United Nations or the World Court.

39. E. In the next-to-last paragraph we learn that nodules of ore take shape around hard natural objects normally found in the sea—whale ear bones, pebbles, and the like. A seashell fragment is such an object.

40. C. The fifth paragraph discusses the need for a full-scale mining ship.

SECTION 5

1. B. Let x = actual length of the room

$$\frac{\text{Dimensions on drawing (inches)}}{\text{Actual dimensions (feet)}} = \frac{\frac{1}{4}}{1} = \frac{4\frac{1}{4}}{x}$$

$$\frac{1}{4}x = 4\frac{1}{4}$$

$$\frac{1}{4}x = \frac{17}{4}$$

$x = 17$ (multiply by 4)

Let y = actual width of the room

Using ratio above

$$\frac{\frac{1}{4}}{1} = \frac{3\frac{3}{4}}{y}$$

$$\frac{1}{4}y = 3\frac{3}{4}$$

$$\frac{1}{4}y = \frac{15}{4}$$

$y = 15$ (multiply by 4)

Actual dimensions 17′ × 15′

2. E. If average of four examinations was 75%, the sum of all examination marks was (75%) (4) or 300%

Sum of three examinations is 50 + 70 + 90 or 210%

Therefore the first examination grade was 90%

3. A. Draw *ABCD*. Area of shaded portion equals area of square *ABCD* minus the 4 equal sectors. Each sector equals $\frac{1}{4}$ of the circle. The sum of the 4 sectors equals 1 circle. Therefore the area of the shaded portion equals the area of square *ABCD* minus the area of one circle.

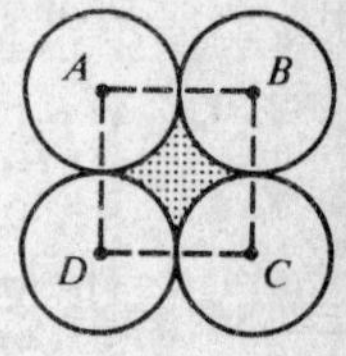

AB = 2 radii = 1 foot

Area of square = $(AB)^2 = (1)^2 = 1$ square foot

Area of circle = πr^2

Diameter = 1 foot; Radius = $\frac{1}{2}$ foot

Area of circle = $\pi\left(\frac{1}{2}\right)^2 = \frac{1}{4}\pi$

Area of shaded portion = $1 - \frac{1}{4}\pi$ or $1 - \frac{\pi}{4}$

4. E.

$4y - x - 10 = 0$	
$4y = x + 10$	
$2y = 3x$	(given)
$4y = 6x$	(multiply by 2)
$6x = x + 10$	(things equal to the same thing are equal to each other)
$5x = 10$	(subtract x)
$x = 2$	(divide by 5)
$3x = 2y$	(given)
$6 = 2y$	(substitute value of x)
$y = 3$	(divide by 2)
$xy = 6$	(substitute values of x and y)

5. D. Cost of $(30 - a)$ three-cent stamps $= 3(30 - a)$ cents or $90 - 3a$ cents
($1.00) or 100 cents $- (90 - 3a) =$ change
$100 - 90 + 3a =$ change
$10 + 3a =$ change

6. A. If the man can do the job in h hours each of the helpers will take ah hours to do the job. Let x = number of hours required by w helpers to do the job. This is an inverse proportion.

$$\frac{1 \text{ helper}}{w \text{ helpers}} = \frac{x \text{ hours}}{ah \text{ hours}}$$

$wx = ah$ (product of means equals product of extremes)

$x = \frac{ah}{w}$ (divide by w)

7. C. At the very beginning of each hour the monkey ascends 30 feet and during the hour falls back 20 feet. Thus, the monkey gains $(30 - 20)$ or 10 feet by the end of each hour. In 9 hours (from 8 A.M. to 5 P.M.) he will have gained 90 feet. At 5 P.M., which is the *beginning* of the tenth hour, he ascends 30 feet to reach a point 120 feet above the ground.

8. A. 100% of 25 = 25; 5% of 25 = 1.25
105% of 25 = 26.25

9. C. $4x = 48$; $x = 12$

$16\frac{2}{3}\% = \frac{1}{6}$; $\frac{1}{6}$ of $72 = 12$

10. C. $\sqrt{\frac{1}{4}} = \frac{1}{2}$

11. C. $\sqrt{\frac{1}{25}} = \frac{1}{5} = 20\%$

12. B. $\sqrt{14.4} = 3.79$ or $3+$
$3.79 < 4$

13. A. $\text{Time} = \frac{\text{Distance}}{\text{Rate}}$

$$\text{Time} = \frac{\frac{1}{2} \text{ mile}}{20 \text{ miles per hour}} = \frac{1}{40} \text{ hour}$$

$$\text{Time} = \frac{\frac{1}{3} \text{ mile}}{30 \text{ miles per hour}} = \frac{1}{90} \text{ hour}$$

14. C. $\frac{\text{Distance}}{\text{Circumference}} =$ number of revolutions

Circumference $= \pi D$

Circumference $= (\pi) \cdot \frac{7}{(\pi)} = 7$

Circumference $= (\pi) \cdot \frac{10}{(\pi)} = 10$

$\frac{70 \text{ feet}}{7 \text{ feet}} = 10$ revolutions (Column A)

$\frac{100 \text{ feet}}{10 \text{ feet}} = 10$ revolutions (Column B)

15. D. If $X + Y = 100$; then $100 + Z = 350$ and $Z = 250$
However since Y could be either positive or negative, X could be either greater than or less than 250.

16. D. If Y is at the center of both circles, then Z could be anywhere on the circumference of the circle with radius = 2 and X could be at any point on the circumference with radius = 3. There are many possibilities for the location of X in respect to the location of Z.

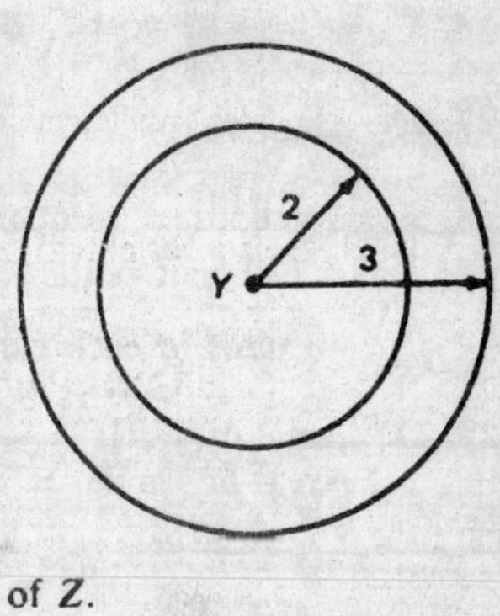

17. D. If x is > 1, x^2 will be greater than 1, and y will be greater than x since $y = 9x^2$. However, if x is a small positive number, say $x = .01$, x^2 will equal .0001 and y will be .0009 and therefore less than x.

18. D. From the information given, we can only deduce that ½ the product of these two values equals 18.

19. D. We may conclude only that $AD = BC$ and $AB = DC$

20. C. $x + 5 + 3x - 1 + 4x - 2 = 34$ (given)
$8x + 2 = 34$
$8x = 32$
$x = 4$

21. B. Since $x = 4$ (see #20)
$AC = 3x - 1$ or 11
$BC = 4x - 2$ or 14

22. A. Since $AC = 11$
and $BC = 14$ (see #21)
the measure of angle $BAC >$ the measure of angle ABC

23. B. Since $AD = 40$, BC also equals 40. Since the area of $ABCD = 1200$, then $AB = 30$. ABC is a right triangle. Since the legs are 40 and 30, the hypotenuse (AC) must be 50, and $AC > BC$.

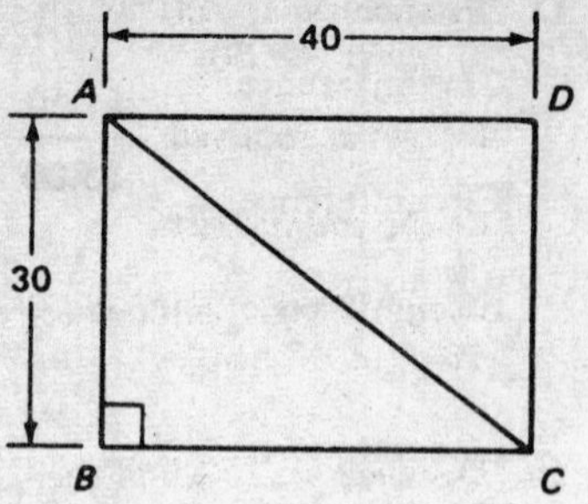

24. A. $AD + BC = 80$ (see #23)
$DC + AB = 60$

25. B. Since $a = 90$, then $x + w = 90$

Since $b = 90$, then $y + z = 90$

$w + x + y + z = 180$

26. C. $y + z = 90$ (see #25)

27. D. No data given to determine the relative sizes.

28. A. 5 gallons = 20 quarts = 40 pints

$$\frac{\text{120 pint bottles}}{\text{40 pints in each can}} = 3 \text{ cans}$$

29. D. Area of circle $= \pi r^2$
Area of circle $= 9\pi$
$\pi r^2 = 9\pi$
$r^2 = 9$ (divide by π)
$r = 3$
AB (side of square) $= 2r$ or 6
Area of square $= (\text{side})^2$ or $(6)^2$ or 36

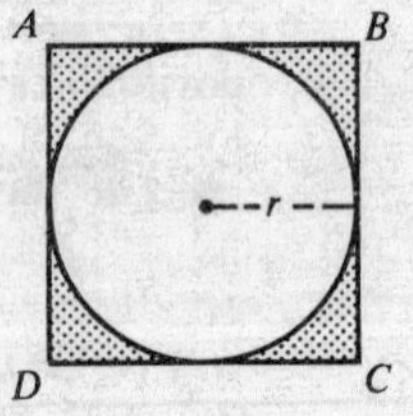

30. B. Let x = distance covered by driving car
$55 - x$ = distance covered by walking
Rate riding = 40 M.P.H.
Rate walking = 5 M.P.H.

$$\frac{\text{Distance}}{\text{Rate}} = \text{Time}$$

Time driving car $= \frac{x}{40}$

Time walking $= \frac{55 - x}{5}$

Total time = 4 hours (given)

$$\frac{x}{40} + \frac{55 - x}{5} = 4$$

$x + 8(55 - x) = 160$ (multiply by 40)
$x + 440 - 8x = 160$
$-7x = -280$
$7x = 280$
$x = 40$ (distance covered by driving car)

$$\frac{\text{Distance covered bv driving car}}{\text{Total distance}} = \frac{40}{55} = \frac{8}{11}$$

31. E. At the end of the first half hour $\frac{1}{4}$ of 256 or 64 contestants are eliminated and 192 remain eligible. At the end of the first hour $\frac{1}{4}$ of 192 or 48 contestants are eliminated and 144 remain eligible. After one and one-half hours $\frac{1}{4}$ of 144 or 36 contestants are eliminated and 108 remain eligible. After two hours $\frac{1}{4}$ of 108 or 27 contestants are eliminated and 81 contestants remain eligible.

32. D. The man sold $\frac{1}{5}$ of $\frac{5}{8}$ or $\frac{1}{8}$ of the property.

Since this represents $1000, then $\frac{8}{8}$ (the whole) has a value of $8000.

33. B. Let x = Marked Price

$\frac{105x}{100} = \$4.20$
$105x = 420$ (product of means equals product of the extremes)
$x = \$4.00$ (division by 105)
$4.00 less 5% discount = $3.80

34. D. Let x = number of players who were on the squad at first
$x - 20\%$ of $x = 32$
$x - .2x = 32$
$10x - 2x = 320$ (multiply by 10)
$8x = 320$
$x = 40$

35. D. (1) Since no integer is zero (all are odd) the product of these integers cannot be zero.
(2) Since the sum is zero, the average must be zero.
(3) The sum of all the negative integers must be the negative of the sum of all the positive integers in order for the total sum to be zero. If there is an even number of positive (odd) integers, their sum will be even and there will also have to be an even number of negative (odd) integers to balance this sum. If there is an odd number of positive (odd) integers, their sum will be odd and there will also have to be an odd number of negative (odd) integers to balance this sum. In either case the total number of positive and negative integers will be even.

SECTION 6

1. E. The maximum of bulbs that produce flowers $= 22$

$\frac{22}{25} \times 100 =$ Per cent that produce flowers

$\frac{22}{\not{25}} \times \frac{\not{100}^{4}}{1} = 88\%$

2. B. $\frac{a}{b} = c$

$b = c$

$b = \frac{a}{b}$ (things equal to the same thing are equal to each other)

$b^2 = a$ (multiply by b)
$b = \sqrt{a}$ (extract square root)

3. C. The total number of days required to paint the barn was 20 days

James worked $\frac{12}{20}$ or $\frac{3}{5}$ of the total days

He should receive $\frac{3}{5}$ of \$100 or \$60

4. D. Each son takes 8 times as much time as the father (or 24 hours each). With the three sons working it would take $\frac{1}{3}$ the time or $\frac{1}{3}$ of 24 $= 8$ hours.

5. D. 4% of 750 or (0.04) (750) or 30 eggs cracked
$750 - 30 = 720$ eggs remaining
5% of 720 or (0.05) (720) or $36 =$ eggs found defective after candling
$720 - 36$ or 684 eggs that can be sold

6. A. Area of shaded portion equals area of rectangle *ABCD* minus area of the two circles.

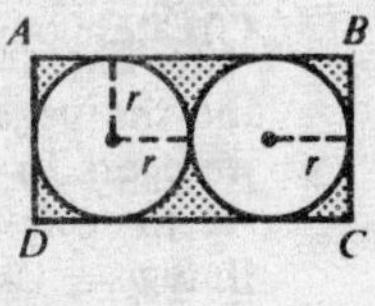

Length of rectangle equals four radii ($4r$)
Width of rectangle equals two radii ($2r$)
Area of rectangle = (base) (altitude)
Area of rectangle $= (4r)(2r)$ or $8r^2$
Area of one circle $= \pi r^2$
Area of two circles $= 2\pi r^2$
Area of shaded portion $= 8r^2 - 2\pi r^2$
Or, $2r^2(4 - \pi)$ (factoring)

7. D. List Price − Discount = Selling Price
\$90 − Discount = \$72
Discount = \$18

$\frac{\text{Discount}}{\text{List Price}} \times 100 =$ Rate of Discount

$\frac{18}{90} \times 100 = 20\%$

8. D. For every \$5 left by the father Benjamin received \$1.50

Benjamin received $\frac{\$1.50}{\$5.00}$ or $\frac{3}{10}$ of the money left

$\frac{3}{10}$ of \$5000 (amount left by father) $=$ \$1500

9. E. Distance $= 152.5$ miles
Time $= 2$ hours

$\frac{\text{Distance}}{\text{Time}} =$ Average speed

$\frac{152.5}{2} = 76.25$ or 76.3 miles per hour

10. C. Distance = (Rate) (Time)
Distance = (40 M.P.H.) (5 hours)
Distance (one way) = 200 miles

Average rate for return trip $= \frac{\text{Distance}}{\text{Time}}$

Average rate for return trip $= \frac{200 \text{ miles}}{10 \text{ hours}}$

or 20 miles per hour

11. B. Area of triangle $= \frac{1}{2}$(base) (altitude)

Area of triangle $= \frac{1}{2}$(6 units) (2 units)

Area of triangle = 6 square units

12. E. Draw *CF* parallel to *DE* forming rectangle *FEDC*

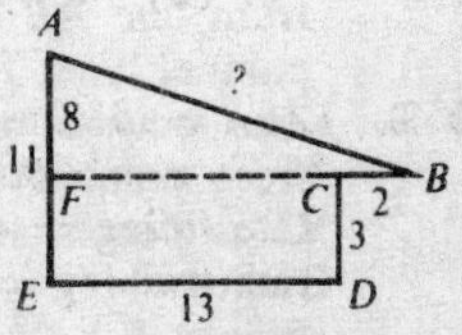

$FC = ED = 13$
$FB = FC + CB$
$FB = 13 + 2$ or 15
$FE = CD = 3$
$AF = AE - FE$
$AF = 11 - 3$ or 8
In right triangle *AFB*,
$(AB)^2 = (AF)^2 + (FB)^2$ (Pythagorean theorem)

$(AB)^2 = (8)^2 + (15)^2$
$(AB)^2 = 64 + 225$
$(AB)^2 = 289$
$AB = 17$ (extract square root)

13. C. The least number of crates in a carload is 12. The least number in 4 carloads is (4) (12) or 48.

14. A. Since x equals more than 45, each of the four values is more than 45 and the average of the numbers cannot possibly be 45.

15. E. We are given the points whose coordinates are $(-2, -7)$ and $(6, 8)$. We are required to find the distance between these points.

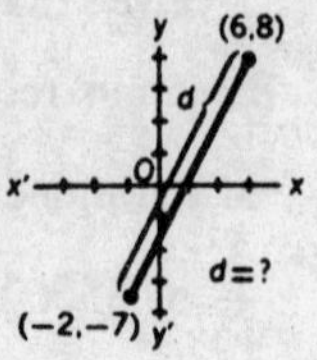

We use the distance formula:

$d = \sqrt{(x_1-x_2)^2+(y_1-y_2)^2}$

In this case, $x_1 = -2$, $x_2 = 6$,

$y_1 = -7$, $y_2 = 8$

$d = \sqrt{(-2-6)^2 + (-7-8)^2}$

$d = \sqrt{(-8)^2 + (-15)^2}$

$d = \sqrt{64 + 225}$

$d = \sqrt{289}$

$d = 17$

16. A. Let the coordinates of the other end-point of the line segment be (a, b).

$$x_m = \frac{x_1 + x_2}{2}$$

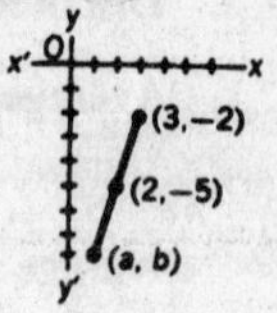

In this case, $x_m = 2$, $x_1 = 3$, and $x_2 = a$.

$$2 = \frac{3 + a}{2}$$

$4 = 3 + a$, $a = 4 - 3$

$a = 1$

$$y_m = \frac{y_1 + y_2}{2}$$

In this case, $y_m = -5$, $y_1 = -2$, and $y_2 = b$.

$$-5 = \frac{-2+b}{2}$$

$-10 = -2 + b$, $b = -10 + 2$

$b = -8$

17. D. The locus of points 2 inches from line AB consists of two parallel lines, P_1P_2 *and* P_3P_4. The locus of points 3 inches from point C is a circle with C as center and 3 inches as radius.

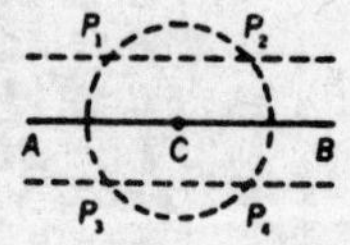

Points P_1, P_2, P_3, P_4 are both 2 inches from AB and 3 inches from C.

18. C. $0.04 = 4\%$

$\left(\frac{1}{4}\right)^2 = \frac{1}{16} = 6\frac{1}{4}\%$

$\frac{1}{0.04} = \frac{100}{4} = 25 = 2500\%$

$(0.04)^2 = 0.0016 = 0.16\%$

Answer $= \frac{1}{0.04}$

19. B. $6 + x(2) = 14$

$2x = 8$

$x = 4$

20. B. $\frac{3}{4} + \frac{5}{n} = \frac{19}{12}$

$\frac{3}{4} + \frac{5}{n} = \frac{19}{12}$ (multiply by $12n$)

$9n + 60 = 19n$

$-10n = -60$

$10n = 60$

$n = 6$

21. C. $2.4\sqrt{\frac{x^4y^2}{16} + \frac{y^2x^4}{9}}$

$2.4\sqrt{\frac{9x^4y^2 + 16y^2x^4}{144}}$ (144 is L.C.D.)

$2.4\sqrt{\frac{25x^4y^2}{144}}$ (combine fractions)

$2.4\left(\frac{5x^2y}{12}\right)$ (extract square root)

$\frac{12x^2y}{12}$ (multiply)

x^2y (cancellation)

22. E. Let x = length of shadow of 35 foot tree

$$\frac{\text{Length of object (feet)}}{\text{Length of shadow (feet)}} = \frac{35}{x} = \frac{98}{42}$$

$98x = (35)(42)$ (product of means equals product of extremes)

$98x = 1470$

$x = 15$ (division by 98)

23. E. To ascertain the greatest profit we must assume the maximum selling price for 8 books.

Minimum cost of 8 books at \$2.00 per book = \$16.00

Maximum selling price of 8 books at \$4.25 per book = \$34.00

Greatest possible profit = \$18.00

24. D. A. $1 + \frac{x}{y} = \frac{y + x}{y}$

B. y

C. $\frac{y^2 + 2xy}{xy} = \frac{y(y + 2x)}{xy} = \frac{y + 2x}{x}$

D. $\frac{y}{x}$

E. $\frac{2x + y}{x}$ or $\frac{y + 2x}{x}$

C and E are equal

25. C. If 100% represents his original sales 120% represents his increased sales

$$\frac{\text{Increased sales}}{\text{Original sales}} = \frac{120\%}{100\%} = \frac{120}{100} = \frac{6}{5} \text{ or } 6:5$$

PART FIVE

ORGANIZE YOUR ADMISSIONS GAME PLAN

GETTING INTO COLLEGE

14

- **Choosing a College**
- **From Application to Acceptance**
- **Meeting the Cost**

CHOOSING A COLLEGE

Not long ago colleges had to turn away some well-qualified applicants because of the great number of college-bound high school seniors and the limited space for the entering freshman class. But what is the case today? Since 1977 there has been a steady decline in the number of high school graduates. From almost 3.2 million in 1977, it is estimated that the number will be reduced to 2.3 million by 1992, a decline of almost one quarter. Many colleges are therefore facing difficulties. To avoid closing, some colleges have merged. A number of women's institutions have become coeducational. Schools may not have lowered their standards, but many schools with very high standards are now seeking students in ways they haven't before. In other words, it is now a buyer's market: qualified applicants can usually count on acceptance by one or more of their first-choice colleges.

Gathering Information

College Directories

There are a number of guides available. *Profiles of American Colleges* (Barron's Educational Series, Inc., Woodbury, N.Y. 11797) is a comprehensive directory. It has complete, succinct descriptions of 1500 four-year colleges including such items as admission standards, costs, student life, and courses of study. Colleges are indexed alphabetically and by admissions competitive rating. Two charts present at-a-glance data about the colleges regarding costs, enrollments, and standardized entrance examination scores, and career pursuits related to major fields of study. Other valuable information regarding applying to college, financial aid, selecting a major, and information for international students is also included. Another Barron's book, *Index of College Majors*, offers a systematic approach to college selection by means of an index of major programs of study available at these 1500 colleges. For instance, if you are interested in attending a four-year college that offers a major in Urban Studies, you will find it easy to identify these colleges in your area or other geographical areas.

The College Catalog

Consult college catalogs in your school or public library and write for those in which you seem to have a genuine interest. Observe the number of courses offered. Look for the strength of the faculty in the subject areas that are of most interest to you. Remember that a fantastic physics department is of no use to you if you never plan to enter a science laboratory. A magnificent music department will not help you if you are tone deaf. Examine descriptions of the library, science laboratories, and other facilities in areas of interest to you. Information in a catalog may save you a time-consuming, expensive visit to a campus that is not a college for you.

Exploring the Campus

Planning Your Visit to a College Campus

If the college you are visiting is near your home, you should walk on the college grounds often and engage students in conversations about the college. You should familiarize yourself with the buildings, visit the library, and ask permission to enter laboratories, classrooms, and dormitories. If practical, you should inquire whether you may receive a guided tour.

In most cases, however, the college of interest to you may be far from home. This involves expense and special preparation. From a practical point of view, these visits should be confined to those colleges in which you have a sincere interest. Be alert to advertisements on your school bulletin boards and in local papers of group tours to several campuses during a school holiday period. These relatively inexpensive trips are generally organized by bus companies or travel agents.

There are at least two schemes for making visits to colleges:

1. The visit planned through the admissions office, complete with a formal interview and guided campus tour.
2. The visit informally arranged with some student of your acquaintance who already attends the school. In this case, a casual weekend visit should be planned during which time you can ask questions and examine all the interesting places and facilities on campus. Ideally, if time and money permit, you should plan both types of visits to the two or three schools you are most seriously considering.

If you are taking the trip on your own, you should make certain arrangements ahead of time. If you are planning a formal visit, you should write to the admissions office telling them of your contemplated trip. Perhaps you should give them an alternate date to suit the convenience of the busy office. In many cases a member of the staff will chat with you, perhaps take notes of impressions made by you, and you may leave with a feeling of encouragement to file an application.

To save time and money, try to include colleges in the same geographic area on the same trip. It is foolish to attempt to visit more than two colleges in one day; in fact, it is advisable to devote at least a full day to exploring each of those universities you are seriously considering. If an overnight stay is involved, be sure to make reservations considerably in advance. Some colleges are in a position to recommend accommodations in their areas. If the opportunity exists, ask to spend the night in a typical dormitory with the students themselves.

If possible, your parents should accompany you. Most colleges are interested in seeing parents, though they may want some time alone with the prospective student. The wise parent and prospective student will withhold judgment of a college until they get back home and an objective judgment can be made concerning the entire excursion. Relax throughout the entire visit. Don't make it a hasty, pressure-filled shopping trip. Regard it as an inspection, an educational experience, where you are learning first hand about institutions you have heard about. In addition, the trip will tell you more about the college you really want and what colleges expect of you.

Some Special Hints on How to Visit a College

Just before you make the trip, re-read the catalog. Make notes on specific things you would like to see, such as a particular arts center or a language laboratory. Make notes on specific questions you have. When you speak to a college official, do not hesitate to discuss finances, scholarships and work opportunities as well as your high school record. After all, if you decide to apply to this college, its officials are going to learn of your financial situation eventually. Tactfully, you may ask for some estimate of your chances for admission. Most probably you will not get any firm commitment, but a word of encouragement may be sufficient at this time.

What You Should Look for on the Campus Tour

Devote a good deal of time to an examination of the college library. Get an idea of the size of its collections, its study facilities, and other special features such as listening rooms. Make time in your visit to attend several classes, possibly choosing those that are of special interest to you. Be sure to visit a typical dormitory room, dining hall, student lounge, the college's athletic and recreational facilities, and, if you so desire, fraternity or sorority houses. If a student guide accompanies you on your tour, feel free to ask about any aspect of college life. The guide will welcome some clue about your interests—sports, dramatics, debate, and so forth—and may include a visit to the headquarters for such activities if time permits. But it's up to you to see what interests you—the responsibility is not the guide's.

Whether you are touring the campus alone or with your parents, make it your business to talk to students. Tell them who you are. Very often they will tell you that they were in your position a few years ago. Observe their patterns of speech, their dress, and ask yourself if you belong there. Feel free to ask them about gripes; more than likely, they'll unburden their likes and dislikes without being asked.

Obtain a copy of the college newspaper. What problems seem to face the students? Does the newspaper seem to reflect the atmosphere of the campus? What is the general tone, morale, and quality of the paper?

After the visit, make some notes on your reactions to the college; they'll be useful later on when you're trying to evaluate various institutions, and they may suggest some additional points for discussion with your guidance counselors and parents.

How the College Board Can Help You Select a College

The Admissions Testing Program (ATP) of the College Board can help you select a college that will satisfy your educational goals through its Student Search Service, which is free. The Student Search Service helps colleges find students with characteristics they are seeking. To take advantage of this service, you must fill out a participation form with your formal application for the SAT and/or the Achievement Tests.

FROM APPLICATION TO ACCEPTANCE

Applying for Admission

The first step in the application procedure is to obtain applications from the colleges you're planning to apply to.

You do this by writing (a postcard is quite acceptable) or calling the admissions office of each school and asking them to mail you an application.

When you receive the application forms, you will be asked to deliver certain parts to your high school authorities so that they may fill out the data in connection with the evaluation of your school record. Your parents may be asked to fill out one section with information regarding your personal health. Another part of the application will delve into your family background, your past history, and your interests and hobbies, as well as your plans for the future. You will be asked to fill out certain parts in your own handwriting. Don't worry about your handwriting. It is too late to change it now, but do be careful about neatness.

Filling Out the Application

Neatness counts. Read the entire application before you start to write, and then put it away in a safe place. Writing for a second application may not count in your favor. When you are ready to answer the questions, jot down the facts you must collect. Collect all your data on scrap paper and have some reliable person such as a teacher or guidance counselor review the answers and make suggestions for the necessary mechanical corrections. Some colleges require that all parts of the application be completed in the handwriting of the applicant. In such cases, write out the corrected answers very carefully. If permitted, type or print the answers on the application form.

If a photograph is requested, choose one that is simple and does you justice. Do not use a snapshot with extraneous background. It is not wise to use a photograph that shows you in unusual dress or attire.

Many applications require you to write an essay. This is an interesting, decisive, and revealing part of the application. A superb, original, thoughtful, literate, and mature life story can tip the scales in your favor, if all the phases of the application are satisfactory. A poor essay, on the other hand, might provide sufficient reason for rejection. This does not mean that you should hire a "ghost writer." Members of an admissions board are quick to detect "masterpieces" written by well-meaning parents or friends of the family.

The college is as interested in getting to know you better through your own picture of yourself as it is in seeing how you handle this task. Besides an immediate view of your writing, grammar, sentence structure, style, and spelling, the admissions committee gets an insight into your resourcefulness, creative abilities, and imagination, as well as the personal experiences and factors that have shaped your mind, attitudes, and character.

Sometimes a choice of topics is permitted. The following are typical:

High School Subjects Which Interested You Most
High School Subjects Which Interested You Least
Your School Activities
Your Autobiography
Camping Experience
Community Activities
Travel Experience
Summer Work
Books Read Outside of School Assignments
Reasons for Going to College
Reasons for Going to *This* College
Student Government on the College Campus
What Do You Hope to be Like ____ Years From Now?

If you are not given a topic for your essay, you may need some suggestions as to how to get started. Make a list of the features of your life, then put these in appropriate categories. Perhaps some are educational, while others are social or personal. At first you will feel that your life and family background are no different from anyone else's, but consider the following possibilities:

1. Do you take any special instruction in art, music, or religion?
2. Have you traveled extensively?
3. How many languages do you speak fluently?
4. Have you held any special jobs?
5. Have you assumed any special responsibilities?
6. Have you overcome any special handicaps?
7. How did you solve a family tragedy or misfortune?
8. Do you have an unusual hobby?
9. What are your reading habits?
10. How do you spend your vacation?

Evaluation of Your School Record

This is by far the most significant part of the application. Officers of admissions committees were not at all surprised at a recent study that showed that about half of the first year dropouts left school for academic reasons, which included poor grades in college and poor high school preparation.

Some colleges communicate with your high school as soon as your application is filed. Others ask you to deliver a special form to your principal, headmaster, or guidance counselor. The college will want to know if you have met or will meet the entrance requirements. They will therefore request a transcript of your high school record.

In examining this record, the committee looks for grades and the subjects completed. They look for subjects that gave the applicant difficulty and take into account such extenuating circumstances as temporary illness, or lack of interest in certain (but not all) subjects. They attempt to determine whether the student elected challenging courses, and are on the lookout for students who took easy courses in order to raise their averages.

Your standing in the class is quite significant. This is a direct way of comparing you with the other students in your graduating class. If you have high grades, but a low rank in your class, it is usually a sign that the marking system in your school suffers from inflation. If you attend a specialized school for selected or gifted pupils, then class standing needs special consideration, for you are being compared with special students. Finally, if you attend a very small school, your achievement involves small numbers and therefore carries less significance.

Extracurricular Activities

Activities outside the classroom, both in school and in the community, are important. They afford the opportunity to develop personal talents, to pursue special interests, and to stimulate qualities of initiative and leadership. However, admissions officers are not impressed with a long list of rather insignificant activities, most of which merely involved occasional passive attendance at meetings. These make an attractive listing in a high school yearbook but do not impress the scrutinizing eye of a college admissions officer, who is more concerned with any elected and appointed offices you might have held, and those activities you might have engaged in which suggest definite signs of leadership in your character, and who is also very interested in your ability to play an unusual musical instrument, paint a canvas, or write a line of poetry.

Certainly no good college will entirely put aside its other standards for admission for a good extracurricular record. However, all other things being equal, in choosing one of two applicants, the admissions office will generally choose the student who participated in out-of-class activities.

Letters of Reference

Many colleges will ask you to submit the names and addresses of people who will furnish information regarding your character. Of course, common courtesy requires that you first ask the individual for permission to use his or her name. In choosing these individuals, it is well to bear in mind that they will be requested to give answers to such questions as:

1. Are you related to the applicant?
2. How long have you known the applicant?
3. In what capacity have you been in contact with the applicant?
4. Give any evidences of good moral character, leadership, maturity, and consideration for others that you have had opportunity to observe in the applicant.

Some colleges send you forms to be given to people who can furnish information about your character. It is courteous to supply each of these people with a stamped envelope addressed to the office of admissions. The people you might ask for recommendations include:

1. teacher of the subject in which you excel
2. instructor, teacher or coach of a creative activity in which you excel (e.g., art, music, drama)
3. advisor of a club or service activity in which you participated
4. coach of a team on which you served
5. scout leader
6. sponsor of a youth group
7. clergyman
8. professional or business person active in your community
9. camp counselor or director
10. employer of your part-time or summer position
11. public official

Keep in mind that college personnel are not likely to be swayed by letters containing empty platitudes and sweeping praise. They read scores of these letters every day. Certainly they want to know your accomplishments and strong points, those things which make you different from the other applicants; but at the same time they are anxious to learn about a flesh and blood person, *not* the subject of some glorious ode. The typically general, impersonal recommendation of some well-known personality will have less impact on admissions officers than a warm, sensitive letter from a less well-known individual who intimately knows you and is therefore in a better position to appraise your particular qualities.

Avoid suggesting as references individuals who will not answer the college questionnaire promptly. Likewise, do not use individuals who might not show good judgment, neatness, or taste in corresponding with the admissions office of the college.

The Personal Interview

There is no uniformity among the schools as to the time for holding the interview. It may occur after all other factors determining admission have been inspected and tentatively approved, or it may occur before the secondary school records and test scores have been received. In addition, some schools require an interview, and others consider the interview only a way to give you more information about the school.

If an interview is required, you should write early in the school year for an appointment. If the interview is optional but you can arrange for one, you should also make an appointment. (Where distance makes a visit impractical, a local alumnus may be assigned to talk with you.) Plan your trip to the college so that you arrive punctually. Your appearance and dress should be in good taste. Remember you are not going to a formal dance, nor to a sporting event. Make certain that your shoes are shined, your hair is combed, and your fingernails are clean. Dress conservatively. Be careful about odors of perfumes, tobacco, or foods. This is the day when you should start breaking the habit of chewing gum.

As far as the interview itself is concerned, the best advice is to *be yourself*. Since this is not an interview for a role as actor or actress, you should relax and answer all questions with frankness and honesty. If you do not possess a particular characteristic for which they are looking, you may not be happy at this school. The interviewer may give you some valuable counsel and send you off to the school where you really belong.

If you haven't ever experienced such an interview you will be wondering about the topics of conversation and the general tone of this event. It will be informal, and it is safe to say that it will be conducted on a most pleasant level. You will perhaps discuss people and things you like or dislike. Again, be honest. Perhaps the official interviewing you likes jazz music himself. Even if he doesn't, he won't hold it against you if you do. Don't hide your distastes or weaknesses. Some of our poor high school mathematics students have gone on to become college professors in other fields.

You may be asked about your career plans. If you are not certain about your future, state that as a fact. It is not a sign of weakness. Most students enter college with only vague ideas about what they want to do after graduation. If you have applied to other colleges, don't hesitate to mention them if that question comes up.

Toward the close of the interview you may be given an opportunity to ask questions about the college. Don't feel that you have to ask a question and then hastily compose a question which may show your unfamiliarity with data furnished in the catalog. It may be wiser to say that you have no questions to ask about the school.

Your College Board Scores

Colleges use standardized scores to enable them to compare students from different schools. A high school record alone cannot be a yardstick of academic promise. Grading standards differ among high schools. Class standing in a small high school is not as significant as it is in a large city school. The standing in a specialized school is of little significance except for those at the very top. Entrance examinations afford equal opportunity to each college-bound student.

Do not, however, feel that you are a failure because you fell short of an 800 on your SAT. Bear in mind that the average SAT scores on a national basis are somewhere between 400 and 500 reported on a scale of 200 to 800. Even highly competitive schools admit students with a wide range of scores.

A college that reported a median score of 610 in the verbal part of the SAT for its freshman class indicated that 25% of freshmen scored between 550 and 559, 14% received 500 to 549, and 6% had scores between 400 and 450. For the mathematics part of the SAT the same school reported a median score of 700, but 20% of the admitted students received scores between 500 and 599.

Another school, reporting an average of 669 in the verbal part of the SAT for the 500 accepted applicants, indicated that 33 of them scored between 550 and 599, and 10 scored below 550. It is interesting to note that this school failed to accept 15 applicants with SAT verbal scores of 700 to 749 and one applicant with a score above 750.

Thus we see that College Board scores are important, but additional criteria are used. It is well to repeat that SAT scores are used to *supplement* such factors as high school grades, class rank, and personal qualities. Another factor that admissions officers are reporting is that they are giving special consideration to applicants with low SAT scores from deprived areas or to applicants for whom English is not the native language. Of course, these college-bound students must present evidence of academic promise.

To Sum it Up

You will gain admission to college on the basis of your school record, your personality, your extracurricular activities, the impressions you made on others, and your performance on college entrance examinations. Your acceptance is an indication that the college has faith in your ability to succeed in that school.

MEETING THE COST

Types of Financial Aid

The main types of financial aid are grants and scholarships, loans, and student employment. Grants are awarded on the basis of need and do not have to be repaid. These may come from government agencies, college funds, or special programs. Scholarships are similar to grants but usually are awarded on the basis of academic achievement and/or financial need. College employment offices often furnish on- or off-campus jobs to help supplement other forms of aid. Finally, low-interest loans that do not have to be repaid until after graduation can help pay for college.

Chief Sources of Financial Aid

There are four main sources of financial aid: the federal government, state governments, private sources, and the colleges themselves.

Federal Government

The federal government has five different student aid programs: the Pell Grant Program, the Supplemental Educational Opportunity Grant (SEOG), the College Work-Study Program (CWS), National Defense Student Loans (NDSL), and Guaranteed Student Loans (GSL).

The Pell Grant Program, the largest of the federal student aid programs, and SEOG are the two federal grant programs. They are both based on need, and they do not have to be repaid. College Work-Study is a student employment program that provides on- and off-campus jobs for students who demonstrate need. NDSL and GSL are both low-interest loan programs, also based on demonstrated need. Monies borrowed through these loan programs do not have to be repaid until after graduation.

In addition to the federal student aid programs already mentioned, the Veterans Administration provides two types of funds—G.I. Bill benefits and War Orphan benefits—to veterans of all wars and to the children of deceased or entirely disabled veterans whose disability or death was service-related. Contact a local office of the Veterans Administration for details on eligibility.

State Governments

Most states have some type of scholarship or grant program for residents. These are usually based on achievement in high school and scores on college entrance examinations, but need is often also a determining factor. Often the scholarship or grant applies only if the student attends a college in that state. Some states also have loan programs and student employment programs.

Private Sources

Many individual scholarships are available from labor unions, benevolent societies, patriotic organizations, and business. Look in your high school guidance office and in your local library for information on private scholarships such as these as well as local scholarships available in your community. Awards made available by local fraternal societies, women's clubs, civic and businessmen's organizations, ethnic and religious groups, alumni, and PTAs are numerous but usually modest in dollars and cents value. Your parents' employer or labor union may turn out to be another source of aid.

The largest independently funded scholarship program in the United States is administered by the National Merit Scholarship Corporation and is funded by company foundations and colleges and universities. Scholarship recipients are selected on the basis of their score on the Preliminary Scholastic Aptitude Test/National Merit Scholarship Qualifying Test (PSAT/NMSQT), other academic factors, and their character. For further information, write to the National Merit Scholarship Corporation, One American Plaza, Evanston, Illinois 60201, and ask for the PSAT/NMSQT Student Bulletin.

Colleges

Nearly every college offers a number of scholarships and grants that range from partial payment of tuition to complete payment of all expenses. These grants are awarded in recognition of academic achievement and/or financial need. Special scholarships may be given to attract outstanding athletes or students with special talents in such areas as music, drama, or journalism.

In addition to their own scholarship and grant funds, colleges often act as agents of distribution for federal and state programs.

Since each college has different scholarships, grants, loans, and student-employment opportunities to offer, and since there is an often enormous difference in the amount of money available for student aid from one college to another, it is important that you get your information about student aid directly from the financial aid office of each college you are thinking of applying to.

How to Apply for Financial Aid

Most financial aid programs, whether they are government programs, private programs, or individual college programs, require applicants to file either the Financial Aid Form (FAF) of the College Scholarship Service or the Family Financial Statement (FFS) of the American College Testing Program to apply for the various types of aid available. Both financial aid forms ask the applicant to itemize all family information and financial data pertinent to the candidate's application for aid.

It is important to find out which form or forms the colleges you are applying to require. Some schools will want their own aid application filed in addition to either the FAF or the FFS. And some government and private programs request additional forms as well; they use the FAF or FFS as an initial qualifying form but then require a separate application for their program.

Both FAF and FFS forms are available from your high school guidance counselor or local college financial aid offices.

We've left the two most important facts about applying for financial aid for last: (1) you must apply for financial aid, you are not automatically considered for aid when you apply to a college; and (2) apply as early as possible so that you have the best possible chance at a share of the available funds before they are used up on applicants who applied for aid earlier. There is no getting away from the fact that you'll have to do some research, and that you and your parents will have to spend some time filling out some rather detailed forms, but there is no way to get around this paperwork when you're applying for any kind of financial aid. So be patient and be thorough; hopefully, your efforts will pay off.

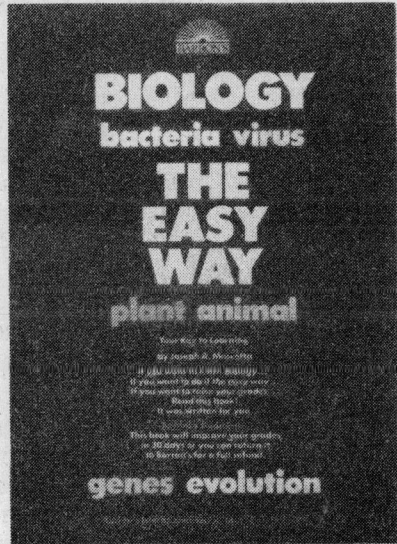